THE GOOD
CD
1993
GUIDE

THE GOOD
C D
1993
GUIDE

Published by

General Gramophone

Publications Ltd

177-179 Kenton Road

Harrow Middlesex HA3 0HA

Great Britain

in association with

Quad Electroacoustics Ltd

In a similar way to Gramophone
magazine, which has been
published monthly since 1923,
Quad is practically an institution.
Most audio-aware readers will know
that Quad Electroacoustics Ltd
(known worldwide simply as Quad,
the name of their first amplifier),
has always been the epitome of
quality and of innovative, practical
design. The publishers gratefully
acknowledge their help with this
publication which, for the fifth year
in succession, benefits from their
involvement.

Editorial Director	Christopher Pollard
Editor	Máire Taylor
Consulting Editors	Nicholas Anderson, Alan Blyth, Michael Stewart, Jonathan Swain
Production Editors	Dermot Jones, Ivor Humphreys, Christine Narain
Contributors	Andrew Achenbach, Nicholas Anderson, Mary Berry, Alan Blyth, Kate Bolton, Joan Chissell, Peter Dickinson, John Duarte, Jessica Duchen, Michael Emery, David Fallows, David J. Fanning, Edward Greenfield, David Gutman, Douglas Hammond, Christopher Headington, Michael Jameson, Stephen Johnson, James Jolly, Lindsay Kemp, Robert Kenchington, Michael Kennedy, Andrew Lamb, Robert Layton, Ivan March, John Milsom, Michael Oliver, David Patmore, Marc Rochester, Julie-Anne Sadie, Stanley Sadie, Lionel Salter, Alan Sanders, Edward Seckerson, Harriet Smith, John B. Steane, Michael Stewart, Jonathan Swain, Arnold Whittall, Mark Wiggins and Richard Wigmore.

© General Gramophone Publications Ltd 1992
ISBN 0-902470-38-8

Recording companies reserve the right to withdraw any Compact Disc without giving previous notice, and although every effort is made to obtain the latest information for inclusion in this book, no guarantee can be given that all the discs listed are immediately available. Any difficulties should be referred to the issuing company concerned. When ordering, purchasers are advised to quote all the relevant information in addition to the disc numbers. The publishers cannot accept responsibility for the consequences of any error.

Typeset on Acorn Archimedes computers using Impression II by Computer Concepts Ltd., Gaddesden Place, Hemel Hempstead, Hertfordshire HP2 6EX.

Printed in Great Britain by William Clowes Ltd, Beccles, Suffolk, NR34 9QE.

Contents

Introduction

If ever one imagined that the synergy of interests between the manufacturers of music reproduction systems and the record companies might make close communication a prerequisite one would, sadly, be wrong. Less optimistically, one might expect that companies such as Philips and Sony which actually operate in both sectors really would plan, execute and communicate their activities in some reasonably co-operative and complementary way; once again one would be wrong.

Judging by the media coverage of the conflicting launches of DCC (Digital Compact Cassette — a digital hybrid of the old musicassette from Philips) and MD (Mini Disc — a recordable cross between a compact disc and computer floppy disc from Sony) the CD is on its way out, swept away by newer technologies. This, almost certainly, is the conclusion which many interested consumers have reached.

In fact, they also would be wrong. Impending announcements are due to confirm CD's position as the top-line, top-quality music carrier for the foreseeable future — DCC and MD to be (hopefully) lower-priced, recordable media aimed at the market for music on the move (in-car, Walkman and so on).

It's a shame that this grand strategy couldn't have been revealed a little earlier — ideally at the same time that the new technologies were first announced. In its absence the consumer may, quite reasonably, have concluded that CD had had its day and the time had come to move on to the next carrier, hardly a thought process likely to encourage the ongoing purchase of CDs.

It is a fundamental truth that when the consumer is confused he or she suspends purchasing activity. An example of this occurred during CD's early and lusty sales progress; out of the blue *The Sunday Times* carried a report that a new Japanese invention, Digital Audio Tape (DAT), would shortly supersede the CD. Sales of CD were instantly affected. Ultimately DAT didn't happen and the CD continued on its happy way as, apparently, it is destined to do now.

What is so unfortunate about the current situation is that it could have been avoided. At the very least the marketing and public relations sides of Philips and PolyGram (its record company subsidiary) could have unveiled a thoroughly thought-out scenario for DCC — its relationship to CD, the extent of software availability, its price — and the relevant parts of Sony could have shown the same for MD. Happily, CD owners can go on buying CDs on the basis that the technology is not due for imminent replacement and that software availability is not likely to be a problem for many years to come.

But what software availability it is .... the CD catalogue is the most extra-ordinary treasure chest containing just about everything that the collector could dream of — the great recordings of the past, spruced up for the digital age, and the unbelievable range of repertoire and performance offered by today's record producers. The only slight drawback is the range; it is vast and, to many, not a little daunting. Hence this book, a gathering together of the jewels of the catalogue. The point is though that even the cheapest of these jewels is not made from paste!

How to use the Guide

Details are given of composer(s), work(s), instrument(s), voice range(s), record company or label (see Index of Labels/Manufacturers and Distributors), disc number (and previous number when the newcomer is a reissue) and review date(s) in *Gramophone*. Addresses of distributing companies are provided at the rear of this book.

On the musical staves following a heading, information is provided by a system of symbols as follows:

The symbols

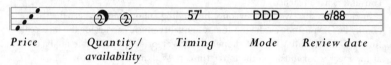

Price	Quantity/ availability	Timing	Mode	Review date

Price

••• Full price: £10·00 and over   •• Medium price: £7·00–£9·99

•• Ü Budget price: £5·00–£6·99   • Super-budget price: below £4·99

Quantity/availability
If there is more than one disc, the number involved is shown here. The first type of circle indicates sets in which the individual discs are not available separately. The second type indicates that the discs are *only* available separately.

Timing
Calculated to the nearest minute.

Mode
This three-letter code is now used by almost all manufacturers to indicate the type of processing employed during manufacture. The letters A or D are used to denote Analogue or Digital and the letter sequence represents chronological steps in the chain: the recording session itself; the editing and/or mixing routines; and finally the mastering or transcription used in preparation of the master tape which is sent to the factory.

Review date
The month and year in which the recording was reviewed in *Gramophone*.

Bargains	Quality of sound	Discs worth exploring	Caveat emptor
£ Quality of performance	P Basic Library	? Period performance	▲

Bargains
Sometimes it is more than price alone which makes for a true bargain. A disc which involves some of the finest artists in a superlative performance and recording, for example, or possibly the sheer length in terms of playing time, will occasionally emerge at mid or bargain price. This symbol is the key to these special releases.

Quality of performance
Recordings which really brook no argument—'musts' for the keen collector. Often the older recordings among these might well have won a *Gramophone* Award had the Awards existed when they first appeared.

Quality of sound
Those recordings which truly merit the epithet 'demonstration quality'.

Basic library
Recordings with which to begin building your CD collection.

Discs worth exploring
For the adventurous! Recordings which might easily be overlooked since they are not among the best-known works or by the better-known composers. But they could well provide some interesting surprises.

Period performance
Recordings in which some attempt is made at historical authenticity. Typically these involve the use of period instruments and/or original manuscript sources.

Caveat emptor
Performances which have stood the test of time but where the recording quality may not be up to the highest standards. This generally applies to pre-1960 recordings.

Two further symbols are used in the reviews:

Gramophone Award winners
The classical music world's most coveted accolades for recordings, these are awarded each year by *Gramophone* in categories ranging from Orchestral to Operatic, Baroque to Contemporary. One recording is also chosen from the overall list to be given the Award of Record of the Year.

Artists of the Year
Four artists whose qualities of musicianship and overall interpretation have consistently brought them to our attention.
See also the artist profiles beginning on page 22.

Introduction

On pourrait imaginer qu'une étroite liaison entre les fabricants de systèmes de reproduction musicale et les maisons de disques est une condition sine qua non étant donnée la synergie de leurs intérêts. Ce serait, hélas, faire erreur! Sans être aussi optimiste, on pourrait toutefois s'attendre de las part de Philips et de Sony, sociétés présentes dans ces deux secteurs, à une certaine coopération et à un certain souci de complémentarité dans la planification, l'exécution et la communication de leurs activités: là encore, erreur!

A en juger par la couverture médiatique des lancements rivaux de la cassette compacte numérique (DCC) Philips (un hybride, issu de l'application de la technilogie numérique à la bonne vieille cassette) et du mini-disque (MD) Sony (un support d'enregistrement qui procède du croisement entre le disque compact et la disquette d'ordinateur), c'en est fini du disque compact, balayé par la vague des technologies plus récentes. C'est là, à n'en pas douter, la conclusion à laquelle seront arrivés de nombreux consommateurs intéressés.

Erreur, toujours! Des announces devraient bientôt le confirmer, le disque compact demeure pour les années à venir le support musical de haut de gamme et de haute qualité. La cassette compacte numérique et le mini-disque seront eux des supports d'enregistrement moins onéreux (du moins l'espère-t-on) plus particulièrement destinés à être écoutés en voiture, sur un Walkman etc.

On déplore que la révélation de cette stratégie géniale se soit un peu fait attendre; elle aurait en effet idéalement coïncidé avec l'annonce de l'avènement de ces nouvelles technologies. Sans cet éclaircissement, le concommateur aurait fort bien pu en conclure que le disque compact avait fait son temps et allait maintenant faire place à un nouveau support, ce qui n'aurait pas constitué une incitation à continuer à acheter des disques compacts.

Plongé dans la perplexité, le consommateur cesse d'acheter. C'est là une loi fondamentale que l'on a pu vérifier lorsque le disque compact connaissait la première vigoureuse poussée de ses ventes, et que, sans crier gare, *The Sunday Times* a announcé qu'une nouvelle invention nipponne, la bande sonore numérique (DAT), viendrait bientôt le remplacer. Les ventes de disques compacts ont immédiatement accusé le coup. Mais la bande sonore numérique n'ayant pas eu le succès escompté, le disque compact a poursuivi son essor, et c'est sans doute là ce qui va se reproduire maintenant.

La situation actuelle est regrettable dans la mesure où elle aurait pu être évitée. Pourquoi les services de marketing et de relations publiques de Philips et de sa filiale, la maison de disques PolyGram, n'ont-ils pas songé à dévoiler un seénario bien pensé pour la cassette compacte numérique, mettant en lumière sa relation par rapport au disque compact, la disponibilité du logiciel, son prix, et purquoi leurs homologues de chez Sony n'en ont-ils pas fait de même pour le mini-disques? Mais tout est bien qui finit bien et les possesseurs de disques compacts peuvent continuer à agrandir leur collection, un remplacement de cette technologie n'étant pas pour demain et la disponibilité du logiciel ne risquant pas de poser de problèmes pendant de nombreuses années.

Et quelle disponibilité … la gamme de disques compacts, telle un extraordinaire coffre débordant de trésors, s'ouvre pour vous révéler presque tout ce dont le collectionneur pourrait rêver — les grands enregistrements d'antan auxquels l'ère du numérique fait l'effet d'une cure de jouvence, et l'incroyable diversité de répertoires et d'interprétations offerts par les producteurs d'aujourd'hui. Un seul petit problème: cette gamme est vaste et, de l'avis de beaucoup, pour le moins intimidante. D'où l'idée de cet ouvrage, une sélection des bijoux proposés, parmi lesquels vous pourrez même dénicher des affaires en or.

Comment utiliser ce guide?

Compositeur(s), oeuvre(s), instrument(s), registre(s) de voix, maison de disques ou label (reportez-vous à l'index des labels/fabricants et sociétés de distribution), numéro de disque (et le numéro précédent lorsque le disque est ressorti) et date(s) de critique(s) dans *Gramophone* sont indiqués.

Les portées à la suite des titres vous fournissent des informations grâce au système de symboles suivant.

Les symboles

| Prix | Quantité/ disponibilité | Durée | Mode | Date de la critique |

Prix

Prix normal   **Prix moyen**

Prix modique   **Prix très modique**

Quantité/disponiblité
S'il y a plus d'un disque, le nombre est indiqué ici. Le premier type de cercle indique des séries dont les disques ne sont pas vendus séparément. Le second type indique que les disques ne sont disponibles *que* séparément.

Durée
Calculée à la minute près.

Mode
Ce code de trois lettres est maintenant utilisé par presque tous les fabricants pour indiquer le procédé utilisé lors de la fabrication. Les lettres A ou D signifient 'analogique' ou 'numérique' et l'ordre des lettres correspond aux étapes, par ordre chronologique, dans la chaîne: la séance d'enregistrement à proprement parler, le mixage et/ou le montage, et enfin la gravure pour la préparation de la bande maîtresse envoyée à l'usine.

Date de la critique
Le mois et l'année de publication de la critique de l'enregistrement dans *Gramophone*.

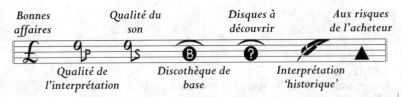

| Bonnes affaires | Qualité du son | Disques à découvrir | Aux risques de l'acheteur |

| Qualité de l'interprétation | Discothèque de base | Interprétation 'historique' |

Bonnes affaires

Parfois, ce n'est pas le prix seul qui fait la bonne affaire. Un disque regroupant certains des meilleurs artistes dans une interprétation et un enregistrement excellents par exemple, ou peut-être même un enregistrement particulièrement long, est parfois vendu à un prix moyen ou très modique. Ce symbole indique ces disques spéciaux.

Qualité de l'interprétation

Des enregistrements dont la qualité est indiscutable—des 'musts' pour le collectionneur passionné. Les plus anciens parmi ceux-ci auraient souvent remporté le prix du disque *Gramophone* s'il avait existé à leur sortie.

Qualité du son

Des enregistrements dont on peut vraiment dire qu'ils sont de 'qualité démonstration'.

Discothèque de base

Des enregistrements qui constitueront les fondements de votre collection de disques compacts.

Disques à découvrir

Pour les touche-à-tout de la musique! Des enregistrements à côté desquels on aurait tendance à passer parce qu'on ne les doit pas aux compositeurs les plus célèbres, mais qui peuvent réserver de bien agréables surprises.

Interprétation 'historique'

Des enregistrements empreints de tentatives d'authenticité historique, généralement grâce à l'utilisation d'instruments d'époque et/ou de manuscrits d'origine.

Aux risques de l'acheteur

Des interprétations qui ont "bien vieilli", mais dont l'enregistrement n'est peut-être pas de la plus haute qualité. C'est généralement le cas des enregistrements datant d'avant 1960.

Deux autres symboles sont utilisés dans les critiques:

Lauréats du prix Gramophone

La distinction la plus convoitée dans le monde de la musique classique, décernée chaque année par le magazine dont nous sommes issus, par catégories allant d'Orchestral à Opéra en passant par Baroque et Contemporain. Un enregistrement est également sélectionné sur toute la liste pour le prix du disque de l'année.

Artistes de l'année

Quatre artistes qui se sont distingués par leurs qualités de musiciens et d'interprètes. Voir aussi les profils page 22 et suivantes.

Einleitung

Man könnte sich vorstellen, daß eine enge Zusammenarbeit zwischen den Herstellern von Musik-Wiedergabesystemen und Plattenfirmen aufgrund ihrer Interessensynergie unerläßlich ist; doch dies ist traurigerweise nicht der Fall. Mit etwas geringerem Optimismus sollte man dennoch erwarten, daß Unternehmen wie Philips und Sony, die in beiden Bereichen tätig sind, bei Planung, Ausführung und Kommunikation ihrer Aktivitäten vernünftigerweise Kooperation beweisen und sich gegenseitig ergänzen würden; doch auch hier liegt man falsch.

Angesichts des Medienrummels um die miteinander revalisierenden Lacierungen von DCC (Digital Compact Cassette einem digitalen Ableger der alten MusiCassette von Philips) und MD (Mini Disc einer aufnahmefähigen Kreuzung zwischen Compact Disc und Computerdiskette von Sony) sollte man annehmen, daß die Tage der CD gezählt sind, hinweggefegt von neueren Technologien. Dies, so läßt sich fast mit Sicherheit annehmen, ist der Schluß, zu dem viele interessierte Verbraucher gelangt sind.

Doch auch dies ist ein Irrtum. In bevorstehenden Ankündigungen wird die Spitzenstellung der CD als Qualitäts-Aufnahmeträger für die vorhersehbare Zukunft bestätigt, wobei DCC und MD als (hoffentlich) preisgünstigere, aufnahmefähige Medien klassifiziert werden, die auf den "beweglichen" Markt abzielen (Autosterio, Walkman usw.).

Schade, daß diese phantastische Strategie nicht etwas früher enthüllt werden konnte, am besten zu der Zeit, als die neuen Technologien erstmals angekündigt wurden. Da dies nicht geschah, konnte der Verbraucher durchaus vernünftigerweise zu dem Schluß gelangen, daß die CD auf dem absteigenden Ast und die Zeit für das nächste Trägermedium gekommen sei; dieser Gedanke wird sich kaum förderlich auf das aktuelle Kaufinteresse an CDs ausgewirkt haben.

Es ist eine Grunderkenntnis, daß der Verbraucher seine Kaufaktivitäten einstellt, wenn er verwirrt ist. Ein Beispiel hierfür gab es bei den rapide ansteigenden Verkäufen in der Frühzeit der CD. Aus heiterem Himmel prophezeite ein Artikel der *Sunday Times*, daß eine neue japanische Erfindung, Digital Audio Tap (DAT) die CD schon bald ersetzen würde. Der Effekt auf CD-Verkäufe war sofort spürbar. Schließlich wurde aus DAT nichts, und der Siegeszug der CD ging unbeirrt weiter und wird sich anscheinend auch in Zukunft fortsetzen.

Die derzeitige Situation ist deshalb so bedauerlich, weil sie hätte vermieden werden können. Zumindest hätten die Marketing- und PR-Abteilungen von Philips und PolyGram (ihrer Plattenfirma und Tochtergesellschaft) ein gründlich durchdachtes Szenario für DCC vorlegen sollen — Beziehung zur CD, Grad der Software-Verfügbarkeit, Preisgestaltung — und die Verantworlichen von Sony hätten mit Bezug auf MD ebenso verfahren können. Besitzer von CD-Spielern können unbesorgt weiterhin CDs kaufen, da sie nun wissen, daß ein unmittelbarer Ersatz der Technologie nicht zu erwarten ist und die Software-Verkügbarkeit über viele Jahre hinaus kein Problem sein dürfte.

Und die Auswahl an Software ist wahrhaft beeindruckend ... Das CD-Sortiment ist eine wahre Schatzkiste, die praktisch alles enthält, wovon der Sammler träumen könnte — die großen Aufnahmen der Vergangenheit, für das digitale Zeitalter auf Vordermann gebracht, und daneben das unglaublich vielfältige Spektrum an Darbietungen, das die Plattenproduzenten von heute in ihrem Angebot haben. Der einzige leichte Nachteil ist die Fülle dieses Angebots; es ist riesig und wirkt für viele recht überwältigend. Daher dieses Buch, eine Sammlung der Schmuckstücke des Sortiments. Zu beachten ist dabei, daß auch die billigsten dieser Schmuckstücke keineswegs Imitationen sind!

Benutzungshinweise

Die angegebenen Einzelheiten betreffen Komponist(en), Werk(e), Instrument(e), Stimmumfang, Plattenfirma oder Label (siehe das Verzeichnis von Labels/Herstellern und Händlern), CD-Nummer (plus alter Nummer, falls es sich um eine Wiederveröffentlichung handelt) und Besprechungsdatum in *Gramophone*. Auf den Notenlinien unter einer Überschrift werden folgende Informationen durch Symbole wiedergegeben:

Symbole

| Preis | Anzahl/ Verfügbarkeit | Dauer | Modus | Besprechungs- datum |

Preis

.·* Normalpreis   •·* Mittlere Preislage

•·* Sparpreis   • Super-Sparpreis

Anzahl/Verfügbarkeit
Falls es sich um mehr als eine CD handelt, wird die entsprechende Zahl hier angegeben. Der erste Kreistyp zeigt Sets an, bei denen individuelle CDs nicht separat verfügbar sind. Der zweite Kreistyp zeigt an, daß die CDs *nur* separat verfügbar sind.

Dauer
Auf volle Minuten ab-oder aufgerundet.

Modus
Dieser Code aus drei Buchstaben wird heute von fast allen Herstellern verwendet, um Verfahren bei Aufnahme, Schnitt und Abmischung zu kennzeichnen. Die Buchstaben A und D stehen für Analog bzw Digital, und die Buchstabenfolge bezeichnet die chronologischen Schritte der Produktionskette: die Aufnahme selbst; das Schnitt- und/oder Abmischverfahren; und schließlich die Art der Überspielung oder Transkription, die zur Vorbereitung des Originalbandes verwendet wird, welches dann die Vorlage für die Pressung bildet.

Besprechungsdatum
Monat und Jahr, in dem die Aufnahme in *Gramophone* besprochen wurde.

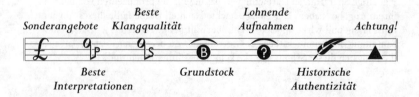

| Sonderangebote | Beste Klangqualität | | Lohnende Aufnahmen | | Achtung! |
| Beste Interpretationen | | Grundstock | | Historische Authentizität | |

Sonderangebote
Manchmal ist es nicht der Preis allein, der ein wahres Sonderangebot ausmacht.
Eine CD, die die besten Künstler zu einer unübertrefflichen Aufnahme bei bester
Aufnahmetechnik vereint, oder die sich vielleicht einfach durch die
außergewöhnliche Länge der Spielzeit auszeichnet, wird gelegentlich in der
mittleren oder Sonderpreislage auftauchen. Dieses Symbol ist der Schlüssel zu
diesen speziellen Veröffentlichungen.

Beste Interpretationen
Aufnahmen, die über jede Kritik erhaben sind—ein 'Muß' für jeden Sammler.
Viele der älteren Aufnahmen hätten *Gramophone*-Preise gewonnen, hätte es diese
Auszeichnung bei ihrem ersten Erscheinen bereits gegeben.

Beste Klangqualität
Aufnahmen, die wirklich die Bezeichnung "Vorspielqualität" verdienen.

Grundstock
Aufnahmen, die die Basis für Ihre CD-Sammlung bilden sollten.

Lohnende Aufnahmen
Nur für musikalisch Vielseitige! Diese Aufnahmen könnten leicht übersehen
werden, da sie von weniger bekannten Komponisten stammen, sind jedoch oft
für eine angenehme Überraschung gut.

Historische Authentizität
Aufnahmen, bei denen der Versuch historischer Authentizität unternommen
wurde, etwa durch Verwendung von zeitgenössischen Instrumenten und/oder
Originalmanuskripten.

Achtung!
Interpretationen, die die Zeiten überdauert haben, deren Aufnahmequalität jedoch
eventuell nicht dem höchsten Standard entspricht. Dies betrifft im allgemeinen
Aufnahmen von vor 1960.

Zwei weitere Symbole werden in Besprechungen verwendet:

Gramophone-Preisträger
Die begehrtesten Auszeichnungen für Aufnahmen im Bereich der klassischen
Musik. Sie werden jedes Jahr von unserer Mutterzeitschrift in verschiedenen
Kategorien verliehen, die von Orchestermusik bis Oper, von Barock- bis zu
zeitgenössischer Musik reichen. Aus dieser Liste wird ebenfalls eine Aufnahme
ausgewählt, die den Titel Platte des Jahres erhält.

Musiker des Jahres
Vier Künstler, die uns regelmäßig aufgrund ihrer Fähigkeiten als Musiker und
Interpreten aufgefallen sind. Siehe auch die Künstlerprofile auf Seite 22.

Introducción

Si uno imagina que la sinergía de intereses intre los fabricantes de sistemas de reproducción musical y las compañías discográficas exige como condición previa una estrecha comunicación entre ambas partes, se está en un grave error. Sin ser tan optimista, uno podría suponer que compañías tales como Philips y Sony (que operan en ambos sectores), planean, ejecutan y hacen públicas sus actividades de manera m-als o menos conjenta y complementaria; de nuevo se estaría en un error.

A juzgar por la cobertura periodística a propósito del lanzamiento del DCC (Cassette Compacto Digital — un híbrido digital del antiguo musicassette de Philips) y su rival, el MD (Mini Disc un aparato con grabadora resultado del cruce entre un disco compacto y un diskette de Sony), el CD está en vías de desaparecer, arrastrado por las nuevas tecnologías. Esta es, casi con toda seguridad, la condlusión a la que han llegado nuchos consumidores interesados.

En realidad, también ellos están en un error. Según informes de inminente aparición, el CD mantendrá por mucho tiempo su posición como el reproductor musical de mejor calidad. El DDC y el MD serán productos más baratos (esperomos), debido a que los aparatos con grabadora serán orientados al mercado de los equipos musicales portátiles (los del coche, los Walkman, etc). !Qué pena que tan magnífica estrategia no haya sido revelada un poco antes! Lo ideal habría sido hacerlo a la vez que se anunciaban las nuevas tecnologías. En su defecto, el consumidor puede haber llegado a la conclusión, aparentomente razonable, que los días del CD estaban contados y que había llegado el momento de pasarse al nuevo reproductor, una línea de pensamiento poco propicia a estimular las actuales ventas de CDs.

Está comprobado que cuando el consumidor se siente confundido, éste o ésta suspende las compras. Un ejemplo de esto ocurrió en los primeros momentos del vigoroso progreso de ventas de los CDs. Un buen día, *The Sunday Times* publicó un reportaje sobre un nuevo invento japonés, la Cinta Audio Digital (DAT), que muy pronto iba a reemplazar al CD. Las ventas de CDs quedaron efectadas al enstante. Al final el DAT no vio la luz y el CD continuó felizmente su camino hacia adelante como, al parecer, está llamado a hacer ahora.

Lo más triste de la situación actual es que podía haberse evitado. Como mínimo, los departamentos de marketing y de relaciones públicas de Philips y PolyGram (su compañía discográfica filial) podrían haber montado una campaña de presentación perfectamente diseñada para el DCC — su relación con el CD, la disponibilidad del software, su precio — y Sony podría haber hecho otro tanto con el MD. Afortunadamente, los propietarios de CDs pueden seguir comprándolos al saber que éstos no serán reemplazados por otros inventos a corto plazo y que el software estará disponible por muchos años.

!Y qué amplia disponibilidad! El catálago de CD es un verdadero tesoro que contiene todo cuanto el coleccionista pueda soñar — las grandes grabaciones del pasado, arregladas para la era digital, y la increíble gama de repertorios e interpretaciones que ofrecen los productores de discos actuales. El único pequeño inconveniente es la gama; es extensísima y, para muchos, hasta imponente. De ahí este libro, una recopilación de las joyas del catálogo. Pero lo importante es que ni la más barata de estas joyas es de imitación.

Cómo valerse de esta Guía

Se ofrecen detalles de los compositores, obras, instrumentos, escala vocal, compañía o etiqueta productora de los discos (véase el índice de Etiquetas/Fabricantes y Distribuidores), número de disco (y número anterior cuando el nuevo es una reedición), así como la fecha o fechas de la revisión en *Gramophone*. En los pentagramas musicales que siguen el título se facilita un índice informativo con el sistema de símbolos siguiente:

Los símbolos

Precio	Cantidad/disponibilidad	Duración	Proceso	Fecha revisión
	② ②	57'	DDD	6/88

Precio

Precio completo	Precio intermedio
Precio asequible	Precio módico

Cantidad/Disponibilidad

Si hubiese más de un disco, el número de que se trate se mostrará aquí. El primer tipo de círculo indica los álbumes en que no están disponibles los discos por separado. El segundo tipo indica que los discos *solamente* están disponibles por separado.

Duración

Cálculo redondeado hasta el minuto más próximo.

Proceso

Este es un código formado por tres letras, que usan en la actualidad casi todos los fabricantes para indicar el tipo de proceso empleado en la manufactura. Las letras A ó D se emplean como denotadoras de Análogo o Digital, y la secuencia de las letras representa los pasos cronológicos en la cadena: la misma sesión de grabación, los procesos de edición y/o mezcla y, por último, la preparación del disco maestro de la transcripción, según el método de preparación de la cinta maestra que se envía a la fábrica.

Fecha de revisión

El mes y el año en qué se revisó la grabación en *Gramophone*.

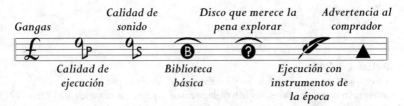

Gangas	Calidad de sonido		Disco que merece la pena explorar			Advertencia al comprador
	Calidad de ejecución	Biblioteca básica		Ejecución con instrumentos de la época		

Gangas

A veces, hay otros elementos, aparte del precio, que hacen del disco una verdadera ganga. Un disco grabado por buenas artistas en una ejecución excepcional con una magnífica grabación, por ejemplo, o quizá la gran duración de la grabación, pueden a veces venderse a precios de ganga o intermedios. Este símbolo es el que denota tales ediciones.

Calidad de la Ejecución

Grabaciones·indiscutibles—'obligatorias' para el buen coleccionista. A veces, las ediciones más antiguas hubieran merecido un Premio al Disco de *Gramophone* si dicho Premio hubiese existido cuando aparecieron.

Calidad de Sonido

Estas grabaciones merecen verdaderamente el epíteto de 'parangones de buena calidad'.

Colección Fundamental

Grabaciones con que comenzar a coleccionar discos compactos.

Discos que merece la pena explorar

¡Para el musicalmente promiscuo! Grabaciones que podrían pasarse por alto con facilidad puesto que no pertenecen a los compositores más conocidos. Pero quizá encierran agradables sorpresas.

Ejecución con instrumentos de la época

Grabaciones en que se ha intentado una autenticidad histórica. Habitualmente se han ejecutado con instrumentos de la época y/o empleando los manuscritos originales.

Advertencia al comprador

Interpretaciones que han resistido al paso del tiempo, pero en las que la calidad de la grabación puede no ser del más alto nivel. Esto generalmente se aplica a las grabaciones anteriores a 1960.

Dos símbolos más que se emplean en estas revisiones:

Ganadores de Premios Gramophone

Los más ambicionados en el mundo de la música clásica; se conceden todos los años por nuestra revista matriz en categorías desde Orquestal hasta Opera, Barroco y Contemporánea. Una grabación se escoge también en la lista general para recibir el Premio al Disco del Año.

Artistas del Año

Cuatro artistas, cuyas cualidades y maestría musical, junto con sus interpretaciones generales, les han dado, a nuestro juicio, la notoriedad. Véanse también las reseñas de los mismos, que comienzan en la página 22.

Abbreviations

alto	counter-tenor	*ob*	oboe
anon	anonymous	*Op*	opus
arr	arranged	*orig*	original
attrib	attributed	*org*	organ
bar	baritone	*perc*	percussion
bass-bar	bass-baritone	*pf*	piano
bn	bassoon	*picc*	piccolo
c.	circa (about)	*pub*	publisher/published
cl	clarinet	*rec*	recorder
clav	clavichord	*rev*	revised
cont	continuo	*sax*	saxophone
contr	contralto	*sngr*	singer
cor ang	cor anglais	*sop*	soprano
cpte(d)	complete(d)	*spkr*	speaker
db	double-bass	*stg*	string
dig pf	digital piano	*synth*	synthesizer
dir	director	*tbn*	trombone
ed	edited (by)/edition	*ten*	tenor
exc	excerpt	*timp*	timpani
fl	flute	*tpt*	trumpet
fp	fortepiano	*trad*	traditional
gtr	guitar	*trans*	transcribed
harm	harmonium	*treb*	treble
hn	horn	*va*	viola
hp	harp	*va da gamba*	viola da gamba
hpd	harpsichord	*vars*	variations
keybd	keyboard	*vc*	cello
lte	lute	*vib*	vibraphone
mez	mezzo-soprano	*vn*	violin
mndl	mandolin	*voc*	vocal/vocalist
narr	narrator	*wds*	words

Chamber Music Forms

string trio	violin, viola, cello
piano trio	violin, cello, piano
horn trio	horn, piano, violin
clarinet trio	clarinet, piano, cello
wind trio	oboe, clarinet, basssoon
baryton trio	baryton, viola, bass instrument
string quartet	2 violins, viola, cello
piano quartet	piano, string trio
wind quartet	flute, clarinet, horn, bassoon
string quintet	2 violins, 2 violas, cello
piano quintet	piano, string quartet
clarinet quintet	clarinet, string quartet
flute quartet	flute, string quartet
wind quintet	flute, oboe, clarinet, basson, horn
string sextet	piano, violin, 2 violas, cello, double bass

Articles

Artists of the Year

Dame Kiri Te Kanawa

The front cover of *Gramophone* invariably these days carries the photograph of a distinguished artist. The face itself may be distinguished too, sometimes by white hairs (or none), sometimes by brows bent as in concentration on a problematic masterpiece, or, rather rarely, it has to be admitted, by a beauty of feature so striking that the observer pauses to make some poetic observation, such as "Stunning!". September 1991 must have brought many occasions for the appreciative pause. There on the cover of *Gramophone*, against a cyclorama of evening sky, clad in a gown of purple satin, her tresses adorned with star-like jewels, stood a woman of lustrous beauty and noble bearing. It was of course Dame Kiri, and September 1991 was very much her month. Those who looked again at the photograph and in a mood of more detailed enquiry might have observed the finely-wrought batlike mask in her hand: here no doubt she is Rosalinde in *Die Fledermaus*. Edward Greenfield's review of the recording under André Previn noted that she was for the second time that month proving herself a very positive Straussian heroine, only this time it was for Johann rather than Richard. Her thoughtful performance as the Marschallin in *Der Rosenkavalier* had also appeared, with Haitink conducting and a glorious climax reached in the trio, Te Kanawa's "Hab mirs gelobt" arching with all the grace and power of a lovely voice in its prime. There was more Richard Strauss too with her second recording of the *Four Last Songs*, now under Solti who also played her piano accompaniments in 13 of the best-known Strauss Lieder. Alan Blyth, reviewing, found "a delightful spontaneity" in the lighter songs, while the uninhibited ecstasy of "Cacilie" provoked memories of Lotte Lehmann. The collaboration with Solti continued in the November release of one of the year's most eagerly awaited recordings, the *Otello* in which Pavarotti sang the title-role. Desdemona has long been among Te Kanawa's loveliest portrayals, yet this was her first recording of it. A listener who could go back in mind to her early days (*Otello* was the opera of her début at the Metropolitan in 1974, followed almost immediately by some unforgettable performances at Covent Garden) would marvel at the preservation of her voice over those years. Similarly with *Le nozze di Figaro*, another of the September releases: under James Levine, she sings the part of the Countess with the beauty that brought such an extraordinary demonstration from the audience after her "Dove sono" at Covent Garden in 1971. "Kiri sings Mozart" is the title of a video, also among this year's issues, of a concert at Cardiff in 1990; and this of course brings both the voice heard on record and the physical beauty caught in the cover-photograph, potent when experienced singly, overwhelming in combination.

[photo: Teldec / Katz / Richmond]

Nikolaus Harnoncourt

When he walks onto the stage one could be forgiven for thinking that Nikolaus Harnoncourt was making his début. He proceeds stiffly, even apprehensively, and takes his bow before the public. Then all changes: his eyes fix on the orchestra, his arms tense and with a characteristic deep inhalation of breath, the music begins. "I cannot do or be anything without the music. I feel myself to be a medium between the composer and the public but that doesn't mean that my interpretations are the last word. In another 50 years musicians will view the same music differently." Thus spoke Harnoncourt in a recent interview.

Born in Berlin in 1929 but brought up in Graz in southern Austria, Harnoncourt never intended to become a full-time musician. After he left school Paul Grümmer (of Busch Quartet fame) heard him play and was so impressed that he gave cello lessons free of charge to the young Harnoncourt. He joined the Vienna Symphony Orchestra where he stayed for 17 years. Then in 1953 he founded the Vienna Concentus Musicus with his wife, the violinist Alice Harnoncourt. The VCM specialize in early and baroque music on original instruments though nowadays they also play music written at the turn of the nineteenth century. A characteristic of Harnoncourt's performance with this group is the intense vitality and drama he brings to baroque music which he feels is "some of the most amazing in all musical history". Having studied the music of this period Harnoncourt could not understand why such vital and energetic music was performed in such a dull style. His revolutionary approach caused uproar in the late 1950s and early 1960s but ushered in a new era in performing practice and style.

He first recorded for Teldec in 1963, beginning an association which is now in its thirtieth year. Some of his most outstanding achievements have been his recordings of Monteverdi operas, Handel oratorios, Haydn's *Die Schöpfung* and *Die Jahreszeiten* and the award-winning Requiem by Mozart. In the early 1980s Harnoncourt started recording the Mozart symphonies with the Royal Concertgebouw Orchestra; recordings which caused shock waves to ripple through the classical music world in Europe. He was accused of distorting the 'classical style', and of opening up great rifts in Mozart's music. Ten years later these same performances are considered to be some of the most illuminating and dramatic he ever committed to disc and Harnoncourt's influence can be heard on recordings of the same works by other period performance specialists such as Frans Brüggen and Gustav Leonhardt.

Working closely with his own VCM, the Royal Concertgebouw Orchestra and, more recently, the Chamber Orchestra of Europe, Harnoncourt continues his foray into the nineteenth century. Recordings of Haydn's symphonies (the earlier ones with the VCM, the later ones with the Concertgebouw) have been issued and more are planned, as are recordings of Mozart's church music. His complete cycle of Beethoven symphonies, recorded with the Chamber Orchestra of Europe, received wide acclaim and he continues to record with this orchestra — Mendelssohn's *Midsummer Night's Dream* and *Die erste Walpurgisnacht* will be issued in 1993. We will also see his studio recordings of the complete Schubert symphonies with the Concertgebouw in 1993. As if this were not enough, a new recording of Mozart's *La finta gardineira* with Edita Gruberová is expected to be released soon and plans are under way for a new *Figaro*. He has come a long way from the days when he embarked, with Gustav Leonhardt, on their *Gramophone* Award-winning recordings of the complete Bach cantatas. He made his Salzburg début in February 1992 with the *Missa solemnis* and will conduct Weber's *Der Freischütz* in February 1993 at the Zurich Opera — two more to be committed to disc in the near future perhaps?

Thomas Hampson

Thomas Hampson has, in a relatively brief period, propelled himself to the forefront of the recording scene by virtue of his attributes as an opera singer and an interpreter of song. Last April, in one fell swoop, he was showered with plaudits by *Gramophone* reviewers for his authoritative readings of three very different idioms, all of them comparatively neglected — the songs of Rossini and Meyerbeer, the Lieder of three American composers (Ives, Griffes and MacDowell) and the lesser-known Lieder of Schubert. The achievement was all the more remarkable in that the discs were made by three different companies, all thirsting for Hampson's services. Then there has been his ongoing contribution to the Mahler discography — his championing, in particular, of the piano versions of the songs, lately brought to fruition in a critical edition of *Des Knaben Wunderhorn*. That nature should have given such an inquiring and positive musician a handsome presence seems almost an embarrassment of riches. Indeed he has been described as "indecently gifted". Of course his achievement is not confined to the recording studio. In 1990 and 1991 he was part of the much-admired ensemble in *Così fan tutte* at the Salzburg Festival under Riccardo Muti, and anyone who heard the Rossini bicentenary relay of *Il barbiere di Siviglia* from the Metropolitan will have no doubts that he is the Figaro of the day with his high-ranging voice and effortless technique. Indeed it is in that role that he will finally make his Covent Garden début in the 1992-93 season. His Don Giovanni has already won praise on the stage and on disc. And if even that wasn't enough, Hampson has been prominent in the current revival of

[photo: EMI/Leighton]

the American musical in concert and on disc — taking part most recently in DG's recording of *On the Town* under Michael Tilson Thomas. All this has been achieved by a singer who is still only 37. After appearances in Europe he made his significant Metropolitan début in 1986 as Count Almaviva. Very swiftly first appearances at the Vienna State Opera, the Bavarian State Opera in Munich and the Salzburg Festival followed. His London recital at the Wigmore Hall in 1986 was an outstanding success. Since that auspicious beginning he has progressed steadily to the front rank of the musical scene, but has not lost the eager spontaneity allied to discerning intelligence that has proved such a potent combination, not forgetting a mellow, supple, firmly sustained baritone. With that prodigious talent, his future looks as bright and rewarding (for us as much as for him) as his present.

Sir Georg Solti

Sir Georg Solti, as he enters his eighty-first year, as inimitable and seemingly indestructible as ever, maintains a workload that would fell many half his age. Generally regarded as one of the great conductors of the twentieth century, Solti's performances have been extensively preserved on LP, CD and latterly on video. Whether conducting expensively assembled operas by Richard Strauss, Verdi or Wagner with the greatest orchestras in the world, or firing the youthful Chamber Orchestra of Europe with enthusiasm, or simply busking at the piano with Dudley Moore, Sir Georg seems perfectly at ease and — like Leonard Bernstein — brilliantly caters for the serious collector as well as the casual enthusiast.

Solti has become something of a Grand Old Man of classical music and, after 22 hugely successful years conducting the Chicago Symphony Orchestra, has chosen to devote much of his time to music-making in Austria, invariably at the helm of the Vienna Philharmonic. Despite a more overtly lyrical aspect in his recent interpretations (his *Magic Flute* positively exudes charm), Solti's characteristic incisiveness remains, with urgent tempos, keen rhythmic attack and a brilliant orchestral palette. Anyone who saw the televised performance of Mozart's Requiem on the 200th anniversary of the composer's death or his homage to Bartók, recorded in Budapest, will recognize that his fiery, frenetic podium manner with its dramatic gestures and sense of occasion, has remained unaltered.

It is fair to say that Solti's career, initially hampered by the Nazis and the deprivations of war, was made by records. Sought out by Decca in the early 1950s, Solti began a unique association with the company which remains unbroken to this day. This continuity is matched by Solti's love of opera. His most famous operatic project was the first complete studio recording of Wagner's *Ring* cycle, whose blazing, cinematic sound surged through people's stereo systems whilst Solti was galvanizing Covent Garden in the 1960s. Despite operatic success in London, most of Solti's opera recordings have been made with the Vienna Philharmonic, from his barnstorming *Tristan und Isolde* with Birgit Nilsson to the recent and lavish *Die Frau ohne Schatten*, a lifelong ambition of his to commit to disc. Solti's taking up of Karajan's mantle at the Salzburg Festival is a further guarantee of his continued work in opera.

Orchestrally, Solti's greatest achievement has been with the Chicago Symphony Orchestra. During the 1970s and 1980s Solti and the Chicago orchestra became synonymous as this Hungarian dynamo turned Jean Martinon's ensemble into one of the world's great orchestras; Grammy Award-winning recordings of the Beethoven, Brahms and Mahler symphonies have focused attention on this powerful combination and attracted large audiences to their whistle-stop world-wide tours. Hopefully when he returns to Chicago as Conductor Emeritus he will conjure up once again the old magic. As he does when he returns to another of his old orchestras, the London Philharmonic, whose Music Director he was during the early 1980s. Together they made many fine recordings, not least of which were the Elgar symphonies in full-blooded vigorous accounts. His Haydn symphonies, too, were perhaps the crispest, wittiest readings since Beecham's, and his *Nozze di Figaro*, with a cast of dreams, remains one of the finest.

Amidst these numerous engagements Solti has found time to guest-conduct ensembles like the Royal Concertgebouw (more recordings from Amsterdam are scheduled), the Bavarian Radio Symphony Orchestra, the Berlin Philharmonic (1993 promises a new Verdi *Falstaff*) and the Chamber Orchestra of Europe. And as if that isn't enough, Solti has retained his early skills as a pianist. Recent recordings include his sparkling collaboration with Daniel Barenboim and András Schiff in Mozart's concertos for two and three pianos. With 29 Grammys, 15 Grand Prix du Disque awards and numerous University Doctorates to his credit, this remarkable musician can add *Gramophone*'s Lifetime Achievement Award 1992 to his roster of well-earned honours.

The Vienna Philharmonic Orchestra at 150

by Christopher Headington

See to their desks Apollo's sons repair,
Swift rides the rosin o'er the horse's hair!
In unison their various tones to tune
Murmurs the hautboy, growls the hoarse bassoon.

So wrote the British humorists Horatio and James Smith in 1812, which must have been a good year for sounds (cannons included) if Tchaikovsky's famous overture is anything to go by.

Thirty years later, the Vienna Philharmonic Orchestra was founded, not by the city council or any other institution but by the musicians themselves, mostly from opera house orchestras, who got together and through youthful enthusiasm made it all happen. Franz Lachner, a conductor friend of Schubert, had already put together a Künstlerverein (artists' society) of players nine years before who put on concerts to play Beethoven's symphonies, and after regular convivial meetings in the happily named inn, Zum Amor (Cupid's Place), they eventually established a permanent Vienna Philharmonic Orchestra. One of these musicians was the composer, Otto Nicolai, then aged 31, and at noon on March 28th, 1842 he lifted his baton to conduct the new 'Philharmonic Academy' in the Grosse Redoutensaal in the first of a series of concerts, each of which had a major classical symphony on the programme.

Nicolai conducted 11 concerts in all before leaving Vienna in 1847, but then came a dozen years of relative stagnation in which the players promoted just ten more concerts. However, on January 15th, 1860 Carl Eckert conducted the first of four subscription concerts and soon the Vienna Philharmonic established a pattern of eight concerts per season. In 1870 the orchestra left the Kärntnertortheater and moved into its permanent home of the Grosser Musikvereinssaal, in other words the Great Hall of the Society of Music.

Arturo Toscanini

Thereafter the story of the Vienna Philharmonic is continuous, and closely tied in with some of the great names of music. Brahms played his First Piano Concerto with them in 1871 and conducted them two years later in his *St Antoni Variations*. Mahler was among their chief conductors, and the orchestra made its overseas début under him at the Paris Exhibition in 1900. Weingartner, Furtwängler, Clemens Krauss and Toscanini (who directed 46 concerts between 1934 and 1937) were other major conductors during the next decades.

But then came Hitler's annexation of Austria (the Anschluss) in March 1938. The Nazis actually dissolved the orchestra, and though Furtwängler managed to get the decree rescinded, they insisted on the dismissal of all Jewish players and six of them later died in concentration camps. Though Furtwängler was German rather than Austrian, he was really the principal conductor of the VPO from 1927 until his death in 1954, appearing with them in over 500 concerts. Richard Strauss was another stalwart German supporter of the orchestra who conducted them on 85 occasions throughout the period 1906-44 and doubtless also helped them to survive the war years. In turn the orchestra's staying power and indomitable musical courage in those tough times must have helped its fellow Viennese: listening to its performance under Krauss of Johann Strauss's polka, *Vergnügungszug* (literally "The Pleasure Train"), at its New Year Concert on December 30th, 1944 (not that long before Germany's surrender in May 1945), makes one realize that the life-affirming spirit of such music is as indestructible as Richard Strauss's *Till Eulenspiegel*.

That performance, which still sounds surprisingly well, comes on a two-disc set from Deutsche Grammophon which was issued in 1992 to mark the VPO's 150th anniversary. It is called "The Vienna Philharmonic play Johann and Josef Strauss 1929-1990" and comes at mid-price (435 335-2GWP2). It features no less than 13 conductors from Mahler's disciple Bruno Walter to younger figures like Claudio Abbado and Zubin Mehta with the giants Furtwängler and Karajan coming in between. Incidentally, one unusual thing about it is that it gives us no less than three versions of the younger Johann Strauss's *Emperor* Waltz, which are Walter's from 1937, Furtwängler's from 1950 and Karajan's from 1987 — all, of course, recorded in the same Grosser Musikvereinsaal. Each sounds authentically Viennese, but Walter's performance has a special elegance, Furtwängler's is crisply minted and Karajan's is more richly tender as well as being longer than either by some two minutes — maybe he and the orchestra guessed that it might be his farewell to them, for he was then 79 and died two years later.

What marvellous music this is, and how right it is that these great conductors performed it so lovingly! It reminds me of the saying that went around early in the nineteenth century, when the waltz was new, that "all Vienna danced". Strauss himself, violin in hand, conducted this orchestra in his waltz *Vienna Blood* on April 22nd, 1873, for Vienna has no snobbery about playing 'light music', whatever that is, and Brahms was another Strauss fan.

All this means, of course, that the *echt-wienerisch* Vienna Philharmonic Orchestra understand and convey, more than most, the disturbing undercurrents that run through Mozart, Schubert and to a lesser extent Beethoven. They're powerful, too, in Mahler, who lived in Vienna but was often unhappy there. They seem rather less at home with that un-Viennese Austrian Haydn. Yet they get to the heart of another such composer, Bruckner: though like Mahler he died in the city, he remained a devout peasant at heart and the grand simplicity of his symphonies (as well as their darker and wilder side) comes over strongly in the VPO's recordings of them under various conductors.

Two Bruckner symphonies come on a 12-disc Vienna Philharmonic set which Deutsche Grammophon also issued in 1992. These are No. 5 under Carl Schuricht, recorded in 1963 ("rarely has a conductor brought out so well Bruckner's spiritual innocence", thought Richard Osborne in *Gramophone*), and a truly thrilling No. 9 under Karajan that was recorded in Salzburg in 1976. This set provides a valuable overview of the VPO playing its central repertory over a number of years, and most of the performances are rather special. However, I must be honest and add that listening to Leonard Bernstein playing and directing the Ravel Piano Concerto in 1971 and Krauss conducting Stravinsky's *Pulcinella* in 1952 suggests that the orchestra had its limits stylistically.

It's worth noting that with the exceptions of those conducted by Richard Strauss (see below) all the performances on this DG set were recorded in concert (most are new to the record catalogue), so that there's the usual degree of audience noise and no editorial tidying-up has been possible, though people who especially like the freshness of a recorded real occasion will feel that the price for immediacy is worth paying. Richard Strauss's performances of his own *Sinfonia domestica* and *Till Eulenspiegel* were recorded without rehearsal on June 15th, 1944 in an empty hall to celebrate his eightieth birthday four days earlier, but his performance of Wagner's *Meistersinger* Prelude belongs to a live concert in the same year.

While the sound of these historical recordings (many coming from Austrian Radio tapes) is often surprisingly good, elsewhere it takes some putting up with. The Strauss symphonic poems are pretty rough soundwise, not least in the elaborate tuttis, though there are major compensations in the perky woodwind playing that is a hallmark of this orchestra in such music and it is, of course, marvellous to hear these two works under the composer's own baton. Note, however, that the first horn manages to get his second note wrong in the famous opening solo of *Till Eulenspiegel*. Similarly, someone has likened Krauss's noble account of Beethoven's *Missa solemnis*, recorded at a concert on 5th November 1940, to an oil painting that has been sand-blasted. Still, if you want a potted history of the Vienna Philharmonic's concert performances with conductors from Richard Strauss to Klemperer, Böhm and Bernstein you will find this a convenient package, although you will have to dig fairly deep into your pocket for a dozen mid-price discs (DG 435 321-2GWP12) and you may prefer to choose from among them — in which case, you could well start with that exciting and monumental Karajan Bruckner Ninth (DG 435 326-2GWP).

The same kind of advice goes for a similar set of 12 mid-price discs from Decca (433 330-2DM12); it's intended to be sold complete, and though perhaps some dealers will allow individual discs to be sold, in that case who gets the substantial booklet? This covers some similar repertory and offers performances by some of the same conductors. But there are also others: they include Monteux in two Haydn symphonies, Reiner and Maazel respectively in Strauss's *Tod und Verklärung* and *Don Quixote*, Szell in a Beethoven programme that includes the incidental music to *Egmont*, Solti in Schubert's *Great* C major Symphony, Mehta in Schumann's *Spring* Symphony, Abbado in Beethoven's No. 8 and Bruckner's No. 1, and Boskovsky in Johann Strauss. However, unlike the performances on the DG set, these Decca ones are from discs issued between 1951 and 1983 and they therefore don't have the same special 'live' quality. EMI also announced a five-disc VPO set for 1992 covering the period when they recorded the orchestra, between 1928 and 1949, but it had not yet appeared at the time of my writing this article.

It goes without saying that every conductor named above brought something personal to his performances, and it can be argued that an orchestra, even a great one like the Vienna Philharmonic, is really just a kind of many-handed instrument that the conductor plays. All the same, this particular orchestra has its own personality as a self-governing body of individual musicians (as a matter of fact, it was the first such body in Europe), and any conductor who wants it to play at its best knows that he must allow that personality to emerge along with his own. The result is that all these performances have a recognizable VPO sound and style that has something to do with the players and their actual instruments (the Viennese oboe sound is a case in point and so is the intense-sounding brass) as well as things like the tonal warmth of the string section and the articulation that its members achieve by a special way of bowing.

All this makes for both a strength and a weakness. Playing the music which suits it best under a sympathetic conductor, the Vienna Philharmonic has no equal.

Claudio Abbado   *[photo: DG/Fayer*

Herbert von Karajan　　　　*[photo: DG*

On the other hand, its repertory is limited and when it goes outside it it can be less at ease and less convincing, as the Ravel and Stravinsky works on the big DG set show. The range of music on this and the Decca set also excludes a lot more of the symphonic repertory than it contains — it's remarkable, when you think about it, that there's no Berlioz, Lizst, Tchaikovsky, Dvořák, Sibelius, Debussy, Bartók or Shostakovich, and no note of British, American, Scandinavian, Italian or Spanish music. There's nothing earlier than Haydn and nothing more contemporary in style than the Ravel and Stravinsky mentioned above plus Schoenberg's *Pelleas und Melisande* under Karl Böhm. Even the Viennese-born Berg and Webern are conspicuous by their absence, suggesting that this orchestra has no liking for the Second Viennese School.

The DG and Decca sets also offer only one work each by Mahler, both conducted by Walter (the Fourth Symphony on DG and the famous account of *Das Lied von der Erde* with Ferrier and Patzak on Decca), although Mahler was the orchestra's chief conductor for a time, and I wonder if this reflects memories of the uneasy relationship between the players and this great but dictatorial director. More surprisingly, there's not much Mozart either, just the *Prague* Symphony under Walter on DG and Bernstein doing the Piano Concerto No. 15 and *Linz* Symphony on Decca, while another great Viennese resident, Brahms, is represented by only two works, the Second Symphony under Furtwängler on DG and the Third under Karajan on Decca.

So don't look for a full representation here of the symphonic repertory or even of Viennese music. But there it is, this is an orchestra that is one of a kind, to be taken as it is. And it has another controversial feature that I've not yet mentioned: you don't have to be a feminist to regret that every musician playing here is by tradition male, like the composers and conductors.

But if you want to celebrate the Vienna Philharmonic Orchestra's 150th anniversary, and it seems to me a good idea, you can certainly acquire some fine recordings with a historical perspective from the issues discussed above. Alternatively, your interest may be still better served by acquiring existing separate recordings; for example, enthusiasts for British music could investigate Karajan's vivid VPO account of Holst's *The Planets* (DG 417 709-2DM), though it dates from 1961 and there's some edge to the sound. In any case, why not turn to the orchestra's entry in the Index to Artists at the end of this book? You're presented there with plenty of excellent choices!

Gioachino Rossini

**John B. Steane looks at his life and
works ... and his centenaries**

[photo: Mary Evans Picture Library

"As far as we are aware, no special or prominent notice was accorded to
it in this country, which has forgotten all it ever learned about Rossini's
operas, and knows the 'swan of Pesaro' only as the composer of a *Stabat
Mater*".

That was the *Musical Times*'s comment on the first Rossini centenary, in
1892. There is clearly a marked contrast between the more recent
celebrations and those, such as they were, of a hundred years ago. The
Musical Times recalled the then-recent Mozart centenary, which had been
commemorated in a way that did fitting honour to a genius with an
acknowledged place among the immortals. Not, they believed, that any
useful purpose could be served by comparing Rossini with Mozart: "As
well might we compare the capital of a Corinthian column with the
acanthus whose leaves it artistically reproduces, or a well-ordered
landscape garden with some bosky dell where nature does as she pleases".
If it takes a moment for the modern reader to be sure which composer is
the column and which the acanthus, all is made clear when Rossini is
described as "warbling his native woodnotes wild". So Mozart is the
landscape garden, 'classical' and with everything laid out according to
rule, while Rossini is the anarchic bosky dell. Rossini, moreover, was
Italian: "an Italian composer, *pur et simple*, during that part of his career

which made his name and fame". That apparently explained everything, for Italians were well-known for doing what they wanted when they wanted, and taking early retirement.

This may seem to us a strange way of conducting Rossini's defence, for that is what the article purported to be doing. He was, it held, essentially a melodist, "like the happy child in Sydney's *Arcadia* who made melody as though he would never grow old". He "must be judged by the standard of his day in the country for which he wrote" and must also be seen "to stand first among those in whom Melody, the 'soul of music', has enriched itself". This, the writer considered, was Rossini's great gift, and in it lay the value of his music to modern times "when the art is becoming artificial". It had been useful, even in Beethoven's time, to assert "the might of simple melody", and "it is, in sooth, much more necessary to do it now".

Heaven knows what the writer would have had to say ('in sooth') if he could have witnessed the fate of "simple melody" a hundred years later. Still, even though we today may not be very good at producing melody, at least we appreciate it, and, ironically, one of the attributes most valued in the 'classical' Mozart is his apparently inexhaustible melodic gift, whereas with Rossini it is rather different. In the catalogue of "Your hundred best tunes" he, no doubt, has a place: we might find ourselves whistling tunes from the overtures, or perhaps "Cujus animam" from that *Stabat mater* beloved of our great-grandparents, or perhaps it might be something from one of the operas, the finale to Act I of *Il barbiere di Siviglia* for instance. Yet on the whole, the name of Rossini does not nowadays stand, first and foremost, for melody.

Take that finale, for example ("Mi par d'esser colla testa"). It *is* a good tune, but mostly by courtesy of its rhythm. Subtract the dots from the notes, also the contrast of long and short, and the melodic phrases would be exposed as commonplace arpeggio and scale sequences. Much more that is characteristic lies in the way of using them to generate excitement. I remember this as the great flavour in my own first taste of Rossini. At a Robert Mayer concert for children, Dr Sargent (as he was then) told us that here was a composer who loved excitement; and I think he went on to say something about the 'build-up' of sound and perhaps even to use the élitist word 'crescendo'. Reverting to that finale, we may begin with melody, but even from that start some kind of rhythmic movement is stirring the pot, helping to bring it to the boil; and certainly what takes over and places this ensemble as 'essential Rossini' is something that, in its mêlée of instruments, voices, rhythms and counterpoint, almost amounts to the annihilation of melody.

It is, then, a more sophisticated Rossini that we call to mind when we use his name nowadays. Curiously, the particular example chosen, the great 'confusion' ensemble in *Il barbiere*, might seem of itself to contradict such a notion: it is about as sophisticated, you might say, as a war-dance. There is something peculiarly primitive about it, for while the upper voices engage in a delirium of chatter the basses have a rhythmic ostinato as of the native warming up for battle in *Sanders of the River*. But of course there *is* sophistication here, too, and it takes two forms: ingenuity of means, and witty ends. Civilized bourgeois Seville, with the home of a highly 'correct' doctor as its representative centre, is turned into a bedlam, where anarchy reigns and the natives run amok.

This is the sophistication of gaiety. Rossini's great admirer and chronicler, Stendhal, reverts several times to this concept. It is a gaiety which he thinks Mozart allowed himself only twice (in Leporello's invitation to the statue and in *Così fan tutte*), and which the very climate of Italy, its traditions and even its government ("the bane and blight of Italy") helped to nourish in Rossini. Born in a more sophisticated country, Rossini might not have needed to cultivate the comic pugnacity which gave him the reputation of an eccentric, yet the gaiety that is Rossini's great quality is not to be found in the Germans, for all their prosperous orderliness and thorough tuition. Only someone from Rossini's background could have had the free spirit to move from *opera buffa* to *opera seria* and back again, infusing farce with discipline and high-seriousness with gaiety: this too showed Rossini's sophistication at work.

Stendhal was no doubt right in assuming that orderliness and thorough tuition were not prominent features of Rossini's upbringing. Born on February 29th,1792, he came into the world five months after his parents' marriage, and quickly found it an excitingly rough place where there were noble causes and patriotic victories to be cheered and reversals to be lamented. On one of the latter occasions his Republican papa was put in prison, to be released only when the Austrians were defeated at Marengo. At the age of six, young Gioachino is said to have played in the percussion section of Pesaro's Civil Guard band, and during his father's term of imprisonment he travelled with his mother who sang in the opera houses of Trieste, Imola and Ravenna. He gained an education of sorts, and took music lessons from a number of teachers including his father. By

the age of 12 he had several compositions to his name, among them a set of six sonatas for string quartet. In 1805 he made his operatic début as a singer at Bologna, and the following year joined the town's school of music, studying harmony, counterpoint and the works of the masters he most admired, Haydn and Mozart. Much has been made of his rebellion against the unreasoning conservatism of the Academy yet he stayed there until 1810 and during his time wrote a prize-winning cantata. Throughout these years he was enriching his acquaintance with music and musicians, and when opportunities to start his professional life opened in Venice he was not at all badly equipped.

He now began writing in earnest, and to these apprentice years belong *La cambiale di matrimonio* (1610), *L'equivoco*

Rossini.

stravagante (1811), *L'Inganno felice, La scala di seta* and *L'occasione fa il ladro*, all written in 1812 for Venice, while the same year also brought *Ciro in Babilonia* for Ferrara and *La pietra di paragone* for Milan. Then came the *annus mirabilis*, 1813. It opened with the delightful *Il Signor Bruschino*, and went on to a triumph in the two main departments of an operatic composer's business, 'serious' opera with *Tancredi* and comic with *L'italiana in Algeri*. Not that all had been plain sailing up to this happy point. Piqued by the theatre manager's slighting behaviour towards him, and having the security of a commission for Milan in his pocket, Rossini had completed *La scala di seta* on time but, as Stendhal relates, had also introduced "for this same insolent impresario every freak, extravagance and musical oddity which he could manage to hatch out of his fertile and unquestionably eccentric imagination". In the overture, it appears, the violins were repeatedly to tap with their bows on the music-stands. It drove the audience mad, and they started to whistle, at which Rossini made himself scarce and left the impresario to sort it out. His popularity and fame had nevertheless grown sufficiently for him to be soon forgiven and re-engaged.

The success of *Tancredi* was not merely local or a thing of the moment. No doubt its patriotism appealed, and the tunefulness of its most admired aria, "Di tanti palpiti", with the legend of its having been written as a substitute-aria in the four or five minutes it took while the rice was being prepared for his evening meal. But it had more to it than that: principally the recognition of something fresh in the writing, and not least in the orchestration. During the next ten years it travelled all over Europe, and by 1825 had reached New York. Similarly *L'italiana in Algeri* spread like wildfire: 1814 La Scala, 1815 Naples and Barcelona, 1816 Munich, 1817 Paris and Vienna. It also enhanced Rossini's reputation as a fast worker: the music had had to be written in three weeks, and, since nothing acts as a better stimulant than a recent taste of success and the expectation of more in the near future, Rossini was able to deliver promptly and enjoy the "deafening, continuous general applause" which greeted its première. "Pensa alla patria" proved a worthy successor to Tancredi's "Di tanti palpitti", the "Pappataci" ceremony was found richly comical, and more serious musicians could discern throughout the score those special touches which proclaim the inspiration of genius.

Sequels rarely enjoy as much success as the original, and while the modern listener probably finds *Il turco in Italia* quite as enjoyable as *L'italiana* it was at first seen as too predictable an inversion of the familiar theme. *Aureliano in Palmira* (1913), *Egre ed Irene* and *Sigismondo* (1914), *Elisabetta* and *Torvaldo e Dorliska* (1815) intervened before the celebrated première of *Il barbiere di Siviglia* (originally called *Almaviva*) in Rome in the February of 1816; and this was another turning-point in Rossini's career. Stories of the fiasco are sometimes said to have been exaggerated, and it is true that the second performance was a success. But there is no doubt that it was a pretty wild night, with supporters of Paisiello, the still-living composer of a previous opera on the subject, out in force, and a number of nightmarish disasters occurring on stage. When Rossini heard the jubilant sound of the second audience making in the direction of his hotel, he supposed they were coming to lynch him and spent a cold night with the bedroom windows broken by admirers clamouring for his appearance.

He was then not quite 24 years old. Already one of the most famous men in Italy, he would soon be one of the most famous, and one of the busiest, in Europe. Over the next decade a Rossini-craze infected the continent. He himself travelled widely: to Vienna in 1822, London and Paris the following year. He met whoever he wanted to, from Beethoven to George IV. The aristocracy, though surprised to find he looked so little like their idea of an Italian genius and so much like a well-fed English shopkeeper, lionized and fêted him none the less. In 1822 he married his prima donna, Isabella Colbran, and between them they made what would then have been termed a pretty penny. His life-style, which involved eating and drinking on a grand scale, exacted its penalties, and for part of 1818 he was a sick man. But still the operas got written: *Otello* as well as *Barbiere* in 1816, *La cenerentola*, *La gazza ladra*, *Armida* and *Adelaide di Borgogna* all in 1817, *Mosè in Egitto* and *Ricciardo e Zoraide* in 1818, the year of his illness, *Omaggio umiliato*, *Ermione*, *Eduardo e Cristina*, *La donna del Lago* and *Bianca e Falliera*, a total of five in 1819; and this was the man musical mythology has dubbed lazy.

In 1820, it is true, the rate of his output began to decline. *Maometto Secondo* was the only new opera that year, though there was also a choral work, the *Messa di Gloria*. *Matilde di Shabran* (1821), *Zelmira* (1822) and *Semiramide* (1823) brought to an end the long line of Italian operas, and thereafter, though much was done, including major revisions (*Maometto* into *Le siège di Corinthe*, *Mosè in Egitto* into *Moïse et Pharaon*), a new opera became an increasingly rare event. *Il viaggio a Reims*, a brilliant entertainment for the coronation of Charles X (1825), was followed by *Le Comte Ory* in 1828. Finally *Guillaume Tell*, produced in Paris in August 1829, brought his whole creative achievement to a point beyond which he seems to have felt he should not attempt to go. It closes the door on one lifetime's work and points ahead to another. Thirty-seven, he must have felt, was no age at which to start again.

Nor was it an age for retirement, and, despite illness and black bouts of depression, he remained a busy man right to the end, in 1868, when he was 75. He wrote the *Stabat mater* in 1832 (thereby ensuring that something of him should remain in the English memory 60 years later at the time of his centenary). Every so often songs and small occasional pieces would appear, and in his sixties he began to commit to paper the compositions he called sins of old age. For the last ten years of his life his Saturday soirées were a celebrated feature of the artistic scene in Paris. The great, the famous and the inevitable hangers-on were to be found there; the musical programmes often included something new or newly arranged by the host; and there were also jokes, both musical and verbal, Rossini's brand of humour having by this time acquired a flavour which for many was the very essence of Paris in these years of the Second Empire, just before the city's ordeal of 1870, which, thankfully perhaps, this great survivor of wars and revolutions did not live to see.

He has since survived the changes and chance of taste and fashion, emerging in his second centenary year of 1992 looking more healthy and vigorous than at any time since the golden years of the 1820s and 1830s. A hundred years ago, as the *Musical Times* article shows, it seemed unlikely that he would make his way into the musical life of the twentieth century at all. In that year, 1892, even at Covent Garden, the Royal Opera Season had nothing of Rossini in its programme. In 1992 Covent Garden mounted a new production of — of all unlikely things — *Il viaggio a Reims*. Earlier the same year, *Ermione* came out of storage and received its British première in a fine concert performance at the Queen Elizabeth Hall. Rossini had called it "my little *Guillaume Tell* in Italian" and prophesied that it would not see the light of day again in his lifetime. The current edition of *The Classical Catalogue* lists recordings of no less than 29 operas, several of them in more than one version. The *Soirées musicales, Péchés de vieillesse*, and *Petite messe solonnelle* are there too; songs and sonatas also, and of course the *Stabat mater*.

As Richard Osborne says in his book on Rossini for the *Master Musicians* series (Dent, 1986), "the detractors have had their way with Rossini for far too long" and there is now a much clearer recognition that he was not only among the most influential, but also "one of the most industrious and at the same time one of the most emotionally complex of nineteenth century composers".

The Legacy of the Last Romantic

Michael Jameson considers Rachmaninov's music on CD

Today, 50 years after the death of Rachmaninov, the tourist buses file regularly toward Ivanovka, once the composer's summer retreat, just as they throng to the Tchaikovsky museum at Klin. But the very fact that the faithful and the curious alike now flock to pay homage at this latter-day shrine, now complete with its adjacent luxury hotel, surely speaks volumes for the vast influence of one man's artistry upon our collective musical awareness. That 1993 will, in its wake, bring a plethora of new recordings of his works seems inevitable. But at least one crucial question seems likely to remain unanswered; for the fact is that, for one so prodigiously talented, Sergey Vassilievich Rachmaninov died largely unfulfilled. The popular misconception that any Russian artist, be he composer or otherwise, must necessarily lapse into obscurity without the soil of his mother country beneath his feet is confounded by the achievements of Stravinsky, Diaghilev, Marc Chagall, Vladimir Nabakov and Prokofiev, to name but a few. And yet, in Rachmaninov's case, his self-imposed exile from Russia in 1917 became an enduring spiritual tragedy, never to be resolved. It is both poignant, yet nevertheless paradoxical, to reflect upon his constant assertion that it was this very separation from his homeland which often made composition difficult, especially when the music of Chopin, a fellow brother in exile, was never far from the soul, or indeed the fingers of one of the greatest piano virtuosos of all time. But while the long-breathed chain melodies and the rhythmic vitality so typical of the composer elicit the admiration of music lovers the world over, Rachmaninov the man remains as enigmatic a figure as ever.

Rachmaninov's early Ampico piano rolls present tantalizing glimpses of an artist of unusual refinement and conservatism, whilst later accounts of his own works have become major documents in the history of the gramophone. Primitive as they are, Rachmaninov's recordings of his Second and Third Piano Concertos (dating from 1929 and 1940 respectively) preserve the composer's personal insights into his own music, but the heroic urgency and sheer verve of the playing plus, of course, the unique sound of the orchestra he admired above all others, the Philadelphia, make this classic RCA release essential listening. The veteran American pianist Earl Wild recorded these same works with Jascha Horenstein and the RPO in 1965, and his version of the Third Concerto, a model of disciplined, yet often incandescent pianism, is the highlight of a very useful disc from Chandos, in their budget Collect series. Rachmaninov's First Concerto, however, still continues to labour against the universal popularity of the Second, and for all its musical virtues, it requires a pianist of the stature and perception of Vladimir Ashkenazy to convince many of its true worth. His performance, with Bernard Haitink conducting the Royal Concertgebouw Orchestra, remains superlative; but his 1972 recording of the Second Concerto, with Previn and the London Symphony Orchestra, also offers an intrepid, yet unusually searching account of Rachmaninov's final masterpiece for piano and orchestra, the *Rhapsody on a theme of Paganini*. Although this Decca release still sounds thoroughly acceptable, Jenö Jandó's coupling of these works on the super-bargain Naxos label did much to confirm the reputation of this little-known Hungarian pianist as an artist of rare distinction. He receives magnificent support from the Budapest Symphony Orchestra under the late György Lehel, in performances of gripping commitment and integrity, whilst the technical quality of the digital sound is excellent. Turning briefly to the exploratory, even severe language of the fourth Piano Concerto, the composer's 1941 interpretation in the company of Eugene Ormandy and the Philadelphia Orchestra is essential listening for any historically-motivated collector, with Ashkenazy (Decca 414 475-2DH, 4/86) and Earl Wild (Chandos CHAN8521/2, 9/87) leading the field as far as more recent versions are concerned.

If the adulation accorded to the Second Concerto has at times approached incredible proportions, we would do well to remember that the immediate popular success of the work marked a clear turning point in the composer's fortunes, following the catastrophic failure of his First Symphony in 1897. Popular reports of its première, a complete travesty by any standards, suggest that the conductor, Glazunov, was apparently drunk at the time! Yet on hearing this craggy and defiant symphony today, one realizes that the first performance must indeed have been indescribably lamentable, for Rachmaninov abandoned the score (it was considered lost at Ivanovka), and no trace of the work remained until the manuscript orchestral parts came to light in 1945. In reviewing Andrew Litton's outstanding three-disc set of the symphonies with the Royal Philharmonic Orchestra in *Gramophone*, Edward Seckerson had much praise for a performance highlighting the "sombre imperial splendours" of the First Symphony, "wrought with enormous conviction" by the young American conductor. Turning from the keyboard to the podium, Vladimir Ashkenazy brings a familiarly expansive ardour to his complete set of the symphonies for Decca, with the Royal Concertgebouw Orchestra and these memorably incisive performances combine rugged emotional power with an authoritative feeling for Rachmaninov's spacious musical architecture, and this set also includes the 18-year-old composer's aptly named *Youth* Symphony. Semyon Bychkov and the Orchestre de Paris caused a sensation during the 1991 Prom season with their performance

of the Second Symphony, an interpretation which continues to astonish on an excellent Philips CD. The cultivated yet vibrant Paris playing prompted many to resort to superlatives in commenting on Bychkov's account of the work, certainly one of the finest yet recorded, and well deserving of a place in any collection. Rachmaninov's Third Symphony dates from 1935-36, and its originality and comparative economy of scale made it a major milestone in the final flowering of his career. Although the work never faced the damning critical censure engendered by the First Symphony, the lukewarm reception which greeted it perplexed Rachmaninov, who regarded the symphony as one of his finest achievements. The masterly orchestration and epic scale of the earlier symphonies combine with a predictable vein of modernism in the Third, which finds an ideal interpreter in André Previn. His recording dates from the halcyon years of collaboration with the London Symphony Orchestra, and comes on a distinguished mid-priced EMI Studio CD, which also includes a valuable reading of Shostakovich's Sixth Symphony. Previn's performance of the Third Symphony makes for fascinating listening alongside the composer's own recording of the work, now reissued on the Pearl label in a particularly successful CD transfer made from the original masters. The sound remains dated and congested certainly, but the historical significance of this issue cannot be over stated.

Berlioz's *Symphonie fantastique* and Liszt's *Totentanz* introduced the endless possibilities of the archaic and doom-laden "Dies Irae" plainchant to Russian composers, none of whom seized more eagerly than Rachmaninov upon its sinister implications; hardly surprising, in retrospect, for the composer who (in common with Tolstoy, in *Anna Karenina*) had already placed the chilling biblical epigraph "Vengeance is mine, I will repay" at the head of his First Symphony. The fact is that literary and visual stimuli provided inspiration for much of Rachmaninov's music, with the fearsome cliffs of Arnold Böcklin's visionary painting *The isle of the dead* presenting imaginative impulse for the symphonic poem of the same name. Ashkenazy and the Concertgebouw Orchestra never shrink from revealing the full macabre impact of the piece in a black-browed reading of awesome intensity, coupled with an equally imposing account of Rachmaninov's *Symphonic Dances* on Decca. André Previn, however, brought a charismatic authority and flamboyant grandeur to his 1976 EMI recording of the *Symphonic Dances* with the London Symphony Orchestra, in a reading which is hardly less memorable than Eugene Ormandy's definitive Philadelphia version (recorded 30 years ago by CBS but never reissued on CD). The *Dances* were completed in August 1940, and have come to be recognized as the supreme achievement of the composer's final creative period. Speculation continues, though, over the quotation of the vengeful motto theme from the First Symphony, now transformed in character to a submissive and autumnal C major twilight in the coda of the first dance. As if to lay the tragic memories of the First Symphony finally aside, the then 68-year-old Rachmaninov added an exultant "Alliluya" to the score, some 26 bars before the end of the final dance, whether as an expression of thanksgiving at completing his final master-piece, or indeed as a symbol of ultimate triumph over death itself, we do not know. Previn's performance has superb brilliance and drive, with an appropriately resigned nostalgia in the waltz.

The mysterious chantings of Russian Orthodox liturgy are so superbly integrated into much of Rachmaninov's orchestral music that it is all too easy to overlook his uniquely personal setting of the *Vespers*. This all-night vigil was completed in under two weeks during 1915, and Matthew Best's Hyperion recording with the Corydon Singers comes with a typically in-formative booklet note on the work. Edgar Allan Poe's *The Bells* provided Rachmaninov with an ideal basis for a large four-part choral symphony, which has gained increasing acceptance in the concert-hall during recent years. The Scottish National Orchestra and Chorus join forces with three soloists in Neeme Järvi's atmospheric Chandos performance of *The bells* coupled with two Tchaikovsky rarities.

Turning briefly to Rachmaninov's solo piano works, Gordon Fergus-Thompson's titanic and persuasive accounts of the two piano sonatas have been well recorded by Kingdom records, on an authoritative and generously-filled CD. The Second Sonata, incidentally, is played in its original uncut version, and remains enthralling throughout its half-hour duration. For many collectors, Vladimir Ashkenazy's complete recording of the 24 Preludes has acquired classic status, and his two disc set for Decca offers magnificent sound, and a degree of technical mastery which could hardly be surpassed. Throughout his career, Rachmaninov continued to write four- and six-hand piano music, ranging in scope from his *Russian Rhapsody* of 1891, to the piano version of the *Symphonic Dances*, completed almost half a century later. Brigitte Engerer and Oleg Maisenberg make an exploratory excursion into this repertoire on a valuable Harmonia Mundi disc.

Whilst two of the Rachmaninov symphonies and three of the concertos have attained regular repertoire status, one can only hope that much of his remaining output may yet capture public imagination in the same way. Suspicion and unjust criticism undoubtedly prejudiced many misguided commentators against Rachmaninov during his own lifetime, but as has so often been the case, the art of recording alone has brought his music to many who might otherwise never have had the opportunity to experience it for themselves. The irresistible melodic force and potent emotionalism of so much of Rachmaninov's output invites us to confront those individual and personal issues which are the shared burden of humanity, and only rarely have composers probed with such acuity into such areas as Sergey Rachmaninov; the last true romantic.

Refer to the Index to Reviews to guide you to the CDs discussed above.

The Gramophone Awards

by James Jolly

Luciano Pavarotti and Dame Joan Sutherland

Every October record dealers around the country receive the results of the *Gramophone* Awards and with them a sudden demand for the winning discs. Since the Awards were introduced in 1977, their importance, scale and influence has grown to make them the most respected window on the international classical record industry. The list of Award winners reads like a line-up of the great musicians of the day, and the range of music represented is a tribute to the diversity of the recording policies of the companies (with, invariably, the majors providing the artists of real stature and the independents the repertoire of note and enterprise).

The voting procedure has evolved over the years, primarily in response to the sheer volume of recordings released each month. The panel comprises the contributors to *Gramophone* and is subdivided into the various specialist committees who hone the lists into more manageable units. An initial short-list, comprising many hundreds of discs, is drawn up by the editorial team of the magazine in collaboration with a small committee of critics. This is then submitted to the specialist panels who add any discs they feel have been omitted. The list is then voted upon and a second-round group comprising six discs per category is submitted to any *Gramophone* contributor who opts into that particular category. The results are then drawn from these votes. The Record of the Year is then selected from the winning discs in each category and is chosen as the disc that is most highly and most consistently highly voted for. The Records of the Year make impressive reading for they act as yardsticks for the most outstanding efforts of the record industry in any one year.

Although many of the early Award winners have been available on CD for some considerable time (see the list which follows), some are still reappearing in CD format. Take, for instance, The Record of the Year in 1979 which has appeared on CD within the last 12 months: it was the Beaux Arts Trio's survey for Philips of Haydn's piano trios — glorious music, gloriously performed. Other imaginative pioneering ventures have similarly been rewarded.

Sir Charles Mackerras's magnificent Janáček opera series for Decca received the Opera Award in 1977, 1980, 1982/3 and 1984, taking the Record of the Year Award in 1977 and 1980 for *Káta Kabanová* and *From the House of the Dead* respectively. Herbert von Karajan's celebrated reading of *Parsifal* was the Record of the Year in 1981 and his two recordings of Mahler's Ninth Symphony, a work with which he had an extraordinary rapport, both won the Orchestral Award (in 1981 and 1984); the second, live recording being voted Record of the Year. Nigel Kennedy's fine reading of the Elgar Violin Concerto, Simon Rattle's Mahler Second, The Tallis Scholars's disc of Josquin Masses, the Emerson Quartet's Bartók — all these have been judged as the outstanding discs of their respective years.

There have been changes over the years. The advent of the early music revolution has required adjustments: the categories have changed and now embrace Early Music and two Baroque awards. Period performance was acknowledged and then incorporated into the general categories, and the enormous enthusiasm and care lavished upon the great works of the Music Theatre has been recognized — with the indefatigable John McGlinn winning the Award two years in succession when the category was first introduced.

A large number of artists have consistently reappeared in the list of winners over the years, a tribute no doubt to their remarkable musicianship. Alfred Brendel has been honoured for his Haydn and Liszt, Pierre Boulez has received awards both as conductor and composer, Haitink similarly has found favour as symphonic conductor as well as man of the theatre. One musician who has returned to the Awards year after year is John Eliot Gardiner, a conductor whose interpretative prowess has never been limited by narrow stylistic categories. 1991 saw him receive the Record of the Year Award for his Archiv disc of Beethoven's *Missa solemnis*, a work of great symbolic power, recorded at the same time as the Berlin Wall fell and marking the start of Gardiner's recordings of this great composer's music.

But the Awards don't merely celebrate the present. In the two historic categories tribute is paid to the great performers of the past and the zeal of the producers and engineers (not that they often had such titles) who delivered those pioneering readings on to disc. With the advances in transfer techniques that have been made over the years, the restoration of these old recordings have achieved new standards and the results are

literally breathtaking in their freshness and naturalness. The record industry has a long and distinguished tradition, a tradition nearly matched in time by *Gramophone* itself (founded in 1923) which has commentated on new recordings for 70 years.

1991 saw the advent of special awards. For his outstanding role in broadening the public awareness of classical music, Luciano Pavarotti was nominated Artist of the Year with his colleague and long-time stage-partner Dame Joan Sutherland receiving the Award for Lifetime Achievement. The Awards have come a long way since their relatively sheltered beginnings and are set to become more than the classical record event of the year.

John Eliot Gardiner

The Gramophone Awards 1977-1992

Gramophone Award winners since the event's inauguration in 1977 are listed below. Every year, one recording is nominated as The Record of the Year. Although catalogue numbers are given for the issues which are currently available (together with review dates in *Gramophone*, where applicable), in some instances there have been no CD reissues. When this is the case, the original LP number is retained. Also, some items are not available separately as they have been reissued as parts of larger sets.

1977

CHAMBER
Shostakovich. String Quartets Nos. 4 and 12. **Fitzwilliam Quartet**. Decca 433 078-2DM6 (contains Nos.1-15, 6/92).

CHORAL
Elgar. Coronation Ode.
Parry. I was glad.
Traditional (arr. Elgar). The National Anthem. **Soloists; King's College Choir, Cambridge, Cambridge University Musical Society; Band of the Royal Military School of Music, Kneller Hall; New Philharmonia Orchestra/Philip Ledger**. EMI CDZ7 62528-2.

CONCERTO
Mozart. Piano Concerto No. 22. Rondos, K382 and K386. **Alfred Brendel** (pf); **Academy of St Martin in the Fields/Sir Neville Marriner**. Philips 412 856-2PH10 (4/86) (contains 23 Piano Concertos).

CONTEMPORARY
Berio. Concerto for two pianos. Nones. Allelujah II. **Bruno Canino, Antonio Ballista** (pfs); **London Symphony Orchestra, BBC Symphony Orchestra/Pierre Boulez, Luciano Berio**. RCA Red Seal RL11674 (8/77). No longer available.

EARLY MUSIC
Dowland. LUTE WORKS. **Julian Bream**. RCA Red Seal RD89977 (11/87).

HISTORICAL
THE RECORD OF SINGING, Volume 1. Various artists and accompaniments. HMV RLS724 (1/78). No longer available.

INSTRUMENTAL
Beethoven. Piano Sonatas Nos. 27-32. **Maurizio Pollini**. DG 419 199-2GH2 (12/86).

OPERATIC
RECORD OF THE YEAR
Janáček. KATA KABANOVA. **Soloists; Vienna State Opera Chorus; Vienna Philharmonic Orchestra/Sir Charles Mackerras**. Decca 421 852-2DH2 (10/89).

ORCHESTRAL
Elgar. Symphony No. 1. **London Philharmonic Orchestra/Sir Adrian Boult**. EMI CDM7 64013-2.

SOLO VOCAL
Shostakovich. Suite on Verses of Michelangelo, Op. 145. Six Songs to Lyrics by English poets. Six Songs to Poems by Marina Tsvetayeva. **Irina Bogacheva** (mez); **Yevgeny Nesterenko** (bass); **Moscow Radio Symphony Orchestra/Maxim Shostakovich; Moscow Chamber Orchestra/Rudolf Barshai**. HMV Melodiya SLS5078 (5/77). No longer available.

1978

CHAMBER
Bartók. Sonata for two pianos and percussion. *Debussy*. En blanc et noir. *Mozart*. Andante and Variations, K501. **Martha Argerich, Stephen Kovacevich** (pfs); **Willy Goudswaard, Michael de Roo** (perc). Philips 9500 434 (8/78). No longer available.

CHORAL
Handel. Dixit Dominus. Zadok the Priest. **Soloists; Monteverdi Choir and Orchestra/John Eliot Gardiner**. Erato 2292-45136-2.

CONCERTO
Prokofiev. Piano Concerto No. 1. Romeo and Juliet — excerpts. *Ravel*. Piano Concerto in D major for the left hand. Pavane pour une infante défunte. **Andrei Gavrilov** (pf); **London Symphony Orchestra/Simon Rattle**. HMV Melodiya ASD3571 (9/78). No longer available. The Prokofiev Piano Concerto is now available on EMI Studio Plus CDM7 64329-2.

CONTEMPORARY
Webern. COMPLETE WORKS, Volume 1. Various artists and ensembles/**Pierre Boulez**. Sony 45845 (6/91).

EARLY MUSIC
Handel. Acis and Galatea. **Soloists; English Baroque Soloists/John Eliot Gardiner**. Archiv Produktion 423 406-2AH2 (8/88).

HISTORICAL
Gluck. Orfeo ed Euridice. **Kathleen Ferrier** (contr); **Greet Koeman** (sop); **Nel Duval** (sop); **Netherlands Opera Chorus and Orchestra/Charles Bruck**. EMI CDH7 61003-2 (6/88).

INSTRUMENTAL
Liszt. PIANO WORKS. **Alfred Brendel.**
Philips 9500 286 (5/78). No longer available.

OPERATIC
RECORD OF THE YEAR
Puccini. LA FANCIULLA DEL WEST.
**Soloists; Chorus and Orchestra of the
Royal Opera House, Covent Garden/
Zubin Mehta.** DG 419 640-2GH2 (11/87).

ORCHESTRAL
Mozart. Symphonies Nos. 25 and 29. **English
Chamber Orchestra/Benjamin Britten.**
Decca 430 495-2DW0 (10/91).

SOLO VOCAL
Chausson. Poème de l'amour et de la mer.
Duparc. MELODIES. **Dame Janet Baker**
(mez); **London Symphony Orchestra/
André Previn.** HMV ASD3455 (4/78). No
longer available.

1979

CHAMBER
RECORD OF THE YEAR
Haydn. PIANO TRIOS. **Beaux Arts Trio.**
Philips 432 061-2PM9 (7/92)
(contains 43 Piano Trios).

CHORAL
Schoenberg. Gurrelieder. **Soloists; Tanglewood Festival Chorus; Boston Symphony
Orchestra/Seiji Ozawa.** Philips 412 511-
2PH2 (3/85).

CONCERTO
Bartók. Piano Concertos Nos. 1 and 2.
Maurizio Pollini (pf); **Chicago Symphony
Orchestra/Claudio Abbado.** DG 415 371-
2GH (9/86).

CONTEMPORARY
Maxwell Davies. Symphony No. 1.
Philharmonia Orchestra/Simon Rattle.
Decca HEAD21 (11/79). No longer available.

EARLY MUSIC
Mozart. SYMPHONIES, Volume 3 (Salzburg
Period). **Academy of Ancient Music/Jaap
Schröder, Christopher Hogwood.** Decca
417 529-2OH3.

ENGINEERING
Debussy. Images. Prélude à l'après-midi d'un
faune. **London Symphony Orchestra/
André Previn.** EMI CDZ7 62504-2.

HISTORICAL
THE RECORD OF SINGING, Volume 2.
Various artists and accompaniments. HMV
RLS743 (1/80). No longer available.

INSTRUMENTAL
Bach. ORGAN WORKS, Volume 3. **Peter
Hurford.** Argo 414 206-1ZX25 (11/85).
Available on LP only.

OPERATIC
Berg. LULU. **Soloists; Paris Opéra
Orchestra/Pierre Boulez.** DG 415 489-
2GH3 (11/86).

ORCHESTRAL
Debussy. Images. Prélude à l'après-midi d'un
faune. **London Symphony Orchestra/
André Previn.** EMI CDZ7 62504-2.

SOLO VOCAL
Grechaninov. Five Children's Songs, Op. 89.
Mussorgsky. The Nursery.
Prokofiev. The Ugly Duckling, Op. 18.
Elisabeth Söderström (sop); **Vladimir
Ashkenazy** (pf). Decca SXL6900 (7/79). No
longer available.

1980

CHAMBER
Brahms. Piano Quintet. **Maurizio Pollini**
(pf); **Quartetto Italiano.** DG 419 673-2GH
(6/87).

CHORAL
Handel. L'Allegro, il Penseroso ed il Moder-
ato. **Soloists; Monteverdi Choir; English
Baroque Soloists/John Eliot Gardiner.**
Erato 2292-45377-2 (7/85).

CONCERTO
Ravel. Piano Concerto in G major. Piano
Concerto in D major for the left hand. **Jean-
Philippe Collard** (pf); **French National
Orchestra/Lorin Maazel.** HMV ASD3845
(6/80). No longer available.

CONTEMPORARY
Birtwistle. Punch and Judy. **Soloists; London
Sinfonietta/David Atherton.** Etcetera
KTC2014 (12/89).

EARLY MUSIC
C.P.E. Bach. Sinfonias, Wq182. **English
Concert/Trevor Pinnock.** Archiv Produktion
415 300-2AH (5/86).

ENGINEERING
Debussy. Nocturnes. Jeux. **Concertgebouw
Orchestra, Amsterdam/Bernard Haitink.**
Philips 400 023-2PH (6/83).

HISTORICAL — Non-vocal
Bartók. Mikrokosmos — excerpts. Contrasts.
Béla Bartók (pf); **Joseph Szigeti** (vn);
Benny Goodman (cl). CBS Classics 61882
(12/80). No longer available.

HISTORICAL — Vocal
THE GRAMOPHONE COMPANY RECORD-
INGS, 1902-09. **Fernando de Lucia** (ten)
with various accompaniments. Rubini RS305
(3/80). No longer available.

INSTRUMENTAL
Brahms. Piano Sonatas Nos. 1 and 2. **Krystian
Zimerman** (pf). DG 2531 252 (6/80). No
longer available.

OPERATIC
RECORD OF THE YEAR
Janáček. FROM THE HOUSE OF THE
DEAD. **Soloists; Vienna State Opera
Chorus; Vienna Philharmonic Orchestra/
Sir Charles Mackerras.** Decca 430 375-2DH2
(10/91).

ORCHESTRAL
Debussy. Nocturnes. Jeux. **Concertgebouw Orchestra, Amsterdam/Bernard Haitink**. Philips 400 023-2PH (6/83).

SOLO VOCAL
A SHROPSHIRE LAD. MUSICAL SETTINGS OF HOUSMAN. **Graham Trew** (bar); **Roger Vignoles** (pf). Meridian CDE84185 (11/90).

1981

CHAMBER
Bartók. String Quartets Nos. 1-6. **Tokyo Quartet**. DG 2740 235 (4/81). No longer available.

CHORAL
Delius. THE FENBY LEGACY. **Soloists; Royal Philharmonic Orchestra/Eric Fenby**. Unicorn-Kanchana DKPCD9008/9 (12/87).

CONCERTO
Beethoven. Violin Concerto. **Itzhak Perlman** (vn); **Philharmonia Orchestra/Carlo Maria Giulini**. EMI CDC7 47002-2 (2/84).

CONTEMPORARY
Tippett. King Priam. **Soloists; London Sinfonietta and Chorus/David Atherton**. Decca 414 241-2LH2 (1/90).

EARLY MUSIC
GERMAN CHAMBER MUSIC BEFORE BACH. **Cologne Musica Antiqua.** Archiv Produktion 2723 078 (10/81). No longer available.

ENGINEERING
Massenet. WERTHER. **Soloists; Children's Choir; Orchestra of the Royal Opera House, Covent Garden/Sir Colin Davis**. Philips 416 654-2PH2 (2/87).

HISTORICAL — Non-vocal
Brahms. CHAMBER WORKS. **Busch Quartet; Rudolf Serkin** (pf); **Reginald Kell** (cl); **Aubrey Brain** (hn). World Records SHB61 (4/81). No longer available.

HISTORICAL — Vocal
THE HUGO WOLF SOCIETY. LIEDER, Volumes 1-7. Various artists. HMV RLS759 (3/81). No longer available.

INSTRUMENTAL
Liszt. PIANO WORKS. **Alfred Brendel** (pf). Philips 420 837-2PM.

OPERA
RECORD OF THE YEAR
Wagner. PARSIFAL. **Soloists; Chorus of the Deutsche Oper, Berlin; Berlin Philharmonic Orchestra/Herbert von Karajan**. DG 413 347-2GH4 (10/84).

ORCHESTRAL
Mahler. Symphony No 9. **Berlin Philharmonic Orchestra/Herbert von Karajan**. DG 410 726-2GH2 (7/84).

SOLO VOCAL
Liszt. LIEDER. **Dietrich Fischer-Dieskau** (bar); **Daniel Barenboim** (pf). DG 2740 254 (10/81). No longer available.

1982-3

CHAMBER
Borodin. String Quartets Nos. 1 and 2. **Borodin Quartet**. EMI CDC7 47795-2 (5/88).

CHORAL
Bach. Mass in B minor, BWV232. **Soloists; Bach Ensemble/Joshua Rifkin**. Elektra-Nonesuch 7559-79036-2.

CONCERTO
RECORD OF THE YEAR
Tippett. Triple Concerto. **György Pauk** (vn); **Nobuko Imai** (va); **Ralph Kirshbaum** (vc); **London Symphony Orchestra/Sir Colin Davis**. Philips 420 781-2PH (3/89).

CONTEMPORARY
Boulez. Pli selon pli. **Phyllis Bryn-Julson** (sop); **BBC Symphony Orchestra/Pierre Boulez**. Erato 2292-45376-2 (3/89).

EARLY MUSIC — Baroque
Charpentier. ACTEON. **Soloists; Les Arts Florissants Vocal and Instrumental Ensembles/William Christie**. Harmonia Mundi HMA190 1095.

EARLY MUSIC — Medieval and Renaissance
Hildegard of Bingen. SEQUENCES AND HYMNS. **Gothic Voices/Christopher Page**. Hyperion CDA66039 (7/85).

ENGINEERING
Shostakovich. Symphony No. 5. **Concertgebouw Orchestra, Amsterdam/Bernard Haitink**. Decca 410 017-2DH (9/83).

HISTORICAL — Non-vocal
Bartók. AT THE PIANO, 1920-45, Volume 1. Hungaroton HCD12326/31.

HISTORICAL — Vocal
Schubert. HISTORICAL RECORDINGS OF LIEDER (1898-1952). Various artists. HMV RLS766 (9/82). No longer available.

INSTRUMENTAL
Liszt. Piano Sonata in B minor. Légende. La lugubre gondola Nos. 1 and 2. **Alfred Brendel** (pf). Philips 410 040-2PH (10/83).

OPERA
Janáček. THE CUNNING LITTLE VIXEN. **Soloists; Vienna State Opera Chorus; Bratislava Children's Choir; Vienna Philharmonic Orchestra/Sir Charles Mackerras**. Decca 417 129-2DH2 (11/86).

ORCHESTRAL
R. Strauss. Metamorphosen for 23 solo strings. Tod und Verklärung. **Berlin Philharmonic Orchestra/Herbert von Karajan**. DG 410 892-2GH (2/84).

SOLO VOCAL
Brahms. LIEDER. **Jessye Norman** (sop);
Dietrich Fischer-Dieskau (bar); **Daniel
Barenboim** (pf). DG 413 311-2GH (9/87).

SOLO VOCAL
R. Strauss. Four Last Songs. **Jessye Norman**
(sop); **Leipzig Gewandhaus Orchestra/Kurt
Masur**. Philips 411 052-2PH (2/84).

1984

CHAMBER
Beethoven. String Quartets Nos. 12-16. Grosse
Fuge. **Lindsay Quartet**. ASV CDDCS403 (1/89).

CHORAL
Mozart. Requiem, K626. **Soloists; Leipzig
Radio Chorus; Staatskapelle Dresden/
Peter Schreier**. Philips 411 420-2PH (6/84).

CONCERTO
Mozart. Piano Concertos Nos. 15 and 16.
**English Chamber Orchestra/Murray
Perahia** (pf). CBS Masterworks CD37824.

CONTEMPORARY
Carter. String Quartet No. 3.
Ferneyhough. String Quartet No. 2.
Harvey. String Quartet No. 2. **Arditti
Quartet**. RCA Red Seal RS9006 (5/84). No
longer available.

EARLY MUSIC — Baroque
Bach. CHAMBER WORKS. **Cologne Musica
Antiqua/Reinhard Goebel**. Archiv Produk-
tion 2742 007 (1/84). No longer available.

**EARLY MUSIC — Medieval and
Renaissance**
Dunstable. MOTETS. **Hilliard Ensemble/
Paul Hillier**. HMV ASD146703-1 (5/84). No
longer available.

ENGINEERING and PRODUCTION
Bax. Symphony No. 4. Tintagel. **Ulster
Orchestra/Bryden Thomson**. Chandos
CHAN8312 (8/84).

HISTORICAL — Non-vocal
Beethoven. Piano Sonatas Nos. 30-32. **Egon
Petri**. dell'Arte DA9012. No longer available.

HISTORICAL — Vocal
Brahms. Schumann. HISTORICAL RECORD-
INGS OF LIEDER (1901-1952). Various artists.
HMV RLS154700-3 (1/84). No longer available.

INSTRUMENTAL
Beethoven. Piano Sonata No. 29,
"Hammerklavier". **Emil Gilels** (pf). DG 410
527-2GH (2/84).

OPERA
Janáček. JENUFA. **Soloists; Vienna State
Opera Chorus; Vienna Philharmonic
Orchestra/Sir Charles Mackerras**. Decca
414 483-2DH2 (12/85).

ORCHESTRAL
RECORD OF THE YEAR
Mahler. Symphony No. 9. **Berlin Philhar-
monic Orchestra/Herbert von Karajan**.
DG 410 726-2GH2 (7/84).

CHAMBER
Beethoven. String Quartets Nos. 12-16. Grosse
Fuge. **Alban Berg Quartet**. EMI CDS7
47135-8 (8/85).

CHORAL
Fauré. Requiem (ed. Rutter). Cantique de Jean
Racine (orch. Rutter). **Soloists; Cambridge
Singers**; members of the **City of London
Sinfonia/John Rutter**. Collegium
COLCD109 (1/89).

CONCERTO
RECORD OF THE YEAR
Elgar. Violin Concerto. **Nigel Kennedy** (vn);
**London Philharmonic Orchestra/Vernon
Handley**. EMI CDC7 47210-2 (12/85).

CONTEMPORARY
Kurtag. Mesages de feu Demoiselle R. V.
Troussova, Op. 17.
Birtwistle. . . . agm. . . **Adrienne Csengery**
(sop); **Marta Fabian** (cymbalum); **John Alldis
Choir; Ensemble Intercontemporain/
Pierre Boulez**. Erato STU71543 (9/84). No
longer available.

EARLY MUSIC — Baroque
Charpentier. MEDEE. **Soloists; Les Arts
Florissants Chorus and Orchestra/William
Christie**. Harmonia Mundi HMC90 1139/41
(3/85).

**EARLY MUSIC — Medieval and
Renaissance**

Victoria. MASSES AND MOTET. **Westminster Cathedral Choir/David Hill**. Hyperion
CDA66114 (6/86).

ENGINEERING and PRODUCTION
Ravel. Ma mère l'oye. Pavane pour une infante
défunte. Le tombeau de Couperin. Valses nobles
et sentimentales. **Montreal Symphony
Orchestra/Charles Dutoit**. Decca ① 410
254-2DH (11/84).

HISTORICAL — Non-Vocal
Nielsen. Symphonies Nos. 1-6. **Danish Radio
Symphony Orchestra/Erik Tuxen, Thomas
Jensen, Launy Grondahl**. Danacord
DACO121/3 (7/84). No longer available.

HISTORICAL — Vocal
OPERA ARIAS AND SONGS. **Claudia Muzio**
(sop); orchestra/**Lorenzo Molajoli, Licinio
Refice**. EMI Références CDH7 69790-2 (8/89).

INSTRUMENTAL
Liszt. Années de pèlerinage, Première année,
"Suisse". **Jorge Bolet** (pf). Decca ① 410 160-
2DH (12/84).

OPERA
Mozart. DON GIOVANNI. **Soloists; Glyndebourne Festival Chorus; London Philharmonic Orchestra/Bernard Haitink.** EMI ① CDS7 47037-8 (12/84).

ORCHESTRAL
Prokofiev. Symphony No. 6. Waltz Suite, Op. 110 — Nos. 1, 5 and 6. **Scottish National Orchestra/Neeme Järvi.** Chandos CHAN8359 (7/85).

SOLO VOCAL

Sibelius. SONGS. **Elisabeth Söderström** (sop); **Tom Krause** (bar); **Vladimir Ashkenazy, Irwin Gage** (pfs). Argo 411 739-1ZH5 (2/85). No longer available.

1986

CHAMBER
Fauré. Piano Quartets Nos. 1 and 2. **Domus.** Hyperion CDA66166 (10/86).

CHORAL
Janáček. Glagolitic Mass. **Soloists; Czech Philharmonic Chorus and Orchestra/Sir Charles Mackerras.** Supraphon C37-7448 (10/86).

CONCERTO
Beethoven. Piano Concertos Nos. 3 and 4. **Murray Perahia** (pf); **Concertgebouw Orchestra, Amsterdam/Bernard Haitink.** CBS Masterworks CD39814 (10/86).

CONTEMPORARY
Lutoslawski. Symphony No. 3. Les espaces du sommeil. **John Shirley-Quirk** (bar); **Los Angeles Philharmonic Orchestra/Esa-Pekka Salonen.** CBS Masterworks CD42271 (6/87).

EARLY MUSIC — Baroque
Bach. The Art of Fugue, BWV1080. **Davitt Moroney** (hpd). Harmonia Mundi HMC90 1169/70 (5/86).

EARLY MUSIC — Medieval and Renaissance
CHANSONS DE TOILE. Esther Lamandier (sop). AL1011 (5/86).

ENGINEERING and PRODUCTION
Respighi. Belkis, Queen of Sheba — orchestral suite. Metamorphosen modi XII. **Philharmonia Orchestra/Geoffrey Simon.** Chandos CHAN8405 (5/86).

HISTORICAL — Non-vocal
Beethoven. String Quartets Nos. 1, 9, 11-13, 14-16. Violin Sonatas Nos. 3, 5 and 7. **Busch Quartet; Rudolf Serkin** (pf). HMV EX290306-3 (11/85). No longer available.

HISTORICAL — Vocal
THE RECORD OF SINGING. Volume 3. Various artists and accompaniments. HMV EX290169-3 (10/85). No longer available.

INSTRUMENTAL
Mozart. Sonata for two pianos in D major, K448.
Schubert. Fantasia in F minor, D940. **Murray Perahia, Radu Lupu** (pfs). CBS Masterworks CD39511 (10/86).

OPERA
RECORD OF THE YEAR
Rossini. IL VIAGGIO A REIMS. **Soloists; Prague Philharmonic Chorus; Chamber Orchestra of Europe/Claudio Abbado.** DG 415 498-2GH3 (1/86).

ORCHESTRAL
Vaughan Williams. Sinfonia antartica. **Sheila Armstrong** (sop); **London Philharmonic Choir and Orchestra/Bernard Haitink.** EMI CDC7 47516-2 (1/87).

REMASTERED COMPACT DISC
Britten. PETER GRIMES. **Soloists; Chorus and Orchestra of the Royal Opera House, Covent Garden/Benjamin Britten.** Decca 414 577-2DH3 (4/86).

SOLO VOCAL
Schubert. Winterreise. **Peter Schreier** (ten); **Sviatoslav Richter** (pf). Philips 416 289-2PH2 (3/86).

1987

CHAMBER
Chausson. Concert for piano, violin and string quartet. String Quartet. **Jean-Philippe Collard** (pf); **Augustin Dumay** (vn); **Muir Quartet.** EMI CDC7 47548-2. No longer available.

CHORAL
Handel. Athalia. **Soloists; New College Choir, Oxford; Academy of Ancient Music/Christopher Hogwood.** L'Oiseau-Lyre 417 126-2OH2 (2/87).

CONCERTO
Hummel. Piano Concertos — A minor; B minor. **Stephen Hough** (pf); **English Chamber Orchestra/Bryden Thomson.** Chandos CHAN8507 (4/87).

CONTEMPORARY
Tippett. The Mask of Time. **Soloists; BBC Singers; BBC Symphony Chorus and Orchestra/Andrew Davis.** EMI CDS7 47705-8 (10/87).

EARLY MUSIC
RECORD OF THE YEAR
Josquin Desprez. Masses — Pange lingua; La sol fa re mi. **The Tallis Scholars/Peter Phillips.** Gimell CDGIM009 (3/87).

ENGINEERING and PRODUCTION
Holst. The Planets. **Montreal Symphony Orchestra/Charles Dutoit.** Decca 417 553-2DH (4/87).

HISTORICAL — Non-vocal
Schubert. String Quartets D87, D112 and D810. Piano Trio, D929. Fantasia, D934. **Busch Quartet; Rudolf Serkin** (pf). EMI EX290950-3 (10/86). No longer available.

HISTORICAL — Vocal
THE ART OF TITO SCHIPA. **Tito Schipa** (ten) with various artists and accompaniments. EMI Treasury EX290948-2 (4/87). Available on LP only.

INSTRUMENTAL
Haydn. COMPLETE PIANO SONATAS. **Alfred Brendel**. Philips 416 643-2PH4 (3/87).

OPERATIC
Verdi. LA FORZA DEL DESTINO. **Soloists; Ambrosian Opera Chorus; Philharmonia Orchestra/Giuseppe Sinopoli**. DG 419 203-2GH3 (5/87).

ORCHESTRAL
Mahler. Symphony No. 8. **Soloists; Tiffin Boys' School Choir; London Philharmonic Choir and Orchestra/Klaus Tennstedt**. EMI CDS7 47625-8 (5/87).

PERIOD PERFORMANCE
Beethoven. Symphonies Nos. 2 and 8. **London Classical Players/Roger Norrington**. EMI CDC7 47698-2 (3/87).

SOLO VOCAL
Liszt. R. Strauss. LIEDER. **Brigitte Fassbaender** (mez); **Irwin Gage** (pf). DG 419 238-2GH (4/87).

REMASTERED COMPACT DISC
BEECHAM CONDUCTS DELIUS. THE COMPLETE STEREO RECORDINGS. **Royal Philharmonic Orchestra/Sir Thomas Beecham**. EMI CDS7 47509-8 (6/87).

1988

CHAMBER
Mendelssohn. Violin Sonatas in F minor and F major. **Shlomo Mintz** (vn); **Paul Ostrovsky** (pf). DG 419 244-2GH (8/87).

CHORAL
Verdi. Messa da Requiem. OPERA CHORUSES. **Soloists; Atlanta Symphony Orchestra and Chorus/Robert Shaw**. Telarc CD80152 (3/88).

CONCERTO
Tchaikovsky. Piano Concerto No. 2 (original version). **Peter Donohoe** (pf); **Bournemouth Symphony Orchestra/Rudolf Barshai** with **Nigel Kennedy** (vn); **Steven Isserlis** (vc). EMI CDC7 49124-2 (11/87).

CONTEMPORARY
Birtwistle. Carmen Arcadiae Mechanicae Perpetuum. Silbury Air. Secret Theatre. **London Sinfonietta/Elgar Howarth**. Etcetera KTC1052 (4/88).

EARLY MUSIC — Baroque
Leclair. SCYLLA ET GLAUCUS. **Soloists; Monteverdi Choir; English Baroque Soloists/John Eliot Gardiner**. Erato 2292-45277-2 (4/88).

EARLY MUSIC — Medieval and Renaissance
THE SERVICE OF VENUS AND MARS. **Andrew Lawrence-King** (medieval hp); **Gothic Voices/Christopher Page**. Hyperion CDA66238 (11/87).

ENGINEERING and PRODUCTION
RECORD OF THE YEAR
Mahler. Symphony No. 2, "Resurrection". **Soloists; City of Birmingham Symphony Orchestra and Chorus/Simon Rattle**. EMI CDS7 47962-8 (12/87).

HISTORICAL — Non-vocal
Brahms. Violin Concerto.
Sibelius. Violin Concerto. **Ginette Neveu** (vn); **Philharmonia Orchestra/Issay Dobrowen, Walter Susskind**. EMI Références CDH7 61011-2 (3/88).

HISTORICAL — Vocal
FEODOR CHALIAPIN (1873-1938). **Feodor Chaliapin** (bass) with various artists and accompaniments. EMI Treasury EX761065-1 (6/88). No longer available.

INSTRUMENTAL
Poulenc. PIANO WORKS. **Pascal Rogé**. Decca 417 438-2DH (7/87).

OPERATIC
Britten. PAUL BUNYAN. **Soloists; Plymouth Music Series Chorus and Orchestra/Philip Brunelle**. Virgin Classics VCD7 90710-2 (8/88).

ORCHESTRAL
RECORD OF THE YEAR
Mahler. Symphony No. 2, "Resurrection". **Soloists; City of Birmingham Symphony Orchestra and Chorus/Simon Rattle**. EMI CDS7 47962-8 (12/87).

PERIOD PERFORMANCE
Haydn. Mass in D minor, "Nelson". Te Deum in C major. **Soloists; The English Concert and Choir/Trevor Pinnock**. Archiv Produktion 423 097-2AH (2/88).

REMASTERED COMPACT DISC
R. Strauss. DER ROSENKAVALIER. **Soloists; Loughton High School for Girls and Bancroft's School Choirs; Philharmonia Chorus and Orchestra/Herbert von Karajan**. EMI CDS7 49354-8 (1/88).

SOLO VOCAL
Schubert. Die schöne Müllerin. **Olaf Bär** (bar); **Geoffrey Parsons** (pf). EMI CDC7 47947-2 (8/87).

1989

CHAMBER
RECORD OF THE YEAR
Bartók. String Quartets Nos. 1-6. **Emerson Quartet**. DG 423 657-2GH2 (12/88).

CHORAL
Handel. JEPHTHA. **Soloists; Monteverdi Choir; English Baroque Soloists/John Eliot Gardiner.** Philips 422 351-2PH3 (6/89).

CONCERTO
Nielsen. Violin Concerto.
Sibelius. Violin Concerto. **Cho-Liang Lin** (vn); **Swedish Radio Symphony Orchestra, Philharmonia Orchestra/Esa-Pekka Salonen.** CBS Masterworks CD44548 (1/89).

CONTEMPORARY
Simpson. Symphony No. 9. **Bournemouth Symphony Orchestra/Vernon Handley.** Hyperion CDA66299 (12/89).

EARLY MUSIC — Baroque
Corelli. 12 Concerti grossi, Op. 6. **The English Concert/Trevor Pinnock.** Archiv Produktion 423 626-2AH2 (1/89).

EARLY MUSIC — Medieval and Renaissance
A SONG FOR FRANCESCA. **Andrew Lawrence-King** (medieval hp); **Gothic Voices/Christopher Page.** Hyperion CDA66286 (12/88).

ENGINEERING and PRODUCTION
Tubin. Symphonies Nos. 3 and 8. **Swedish Radio Symphony Orchestra/Neeme Järvi.** BIS BIS-CD342 (9/88).

HISTORICAL — Non-vocal
Mahler. Symphony No. 9. **Vienna Philharmonic Orchestra/Bruno Walter.** EMI Références CDH7 63029-2 (8/89).

HISTORICAL — Vocal
RECORD OF SINGING, Volume 4. Various artists. EMI EX76974-1 (4/89).

INSTRUMENTAL
Mozart. COMPLETE PIANO SONATAS. **Mitsuko Uchida.** Philips 422 115-2PH6 (2/89).

MUSIC THEATRE
Kern/Hammerstein. SHOW BOAT. **Soloists; Ambrosian Chorus; London Sinfonietta/John McGlinn.** EMI CDS7 49108-2 (11/88).

OPERATIC
Gershwin. PORGY AND BESS. **Soloists; Glyndebourne Chorus; London Philharmonic Orchestra/Simon Rattle.** EMI CDS7 49568-2 (6/89).

ORCHESTRAL
Schubert. Symphonies Nos. 1-6, 8 and 9. Overtures. **Chamber Orchestra of Europe/Claudio Abbado.** DG 423 651-2GH5 (2/89).

REMASTERED COMPACT DISC
Ravel. L'enfant et les sortilèges. **Soloists; Chorus and Children's Voices of French Radio; French Radio National Orchestra/Lorin Maazel.** DG 423 718-2GH (3/89).

SOLO VOCAL
Schubert. LIEDER, Volume 1. **Dame Janet Baker** (mez); **Graham Johnson** (pf). Hyperion CDJ33001 (10/88).

BAROQUE — Vocal
Bach. St Matthew Passion. **Soloists; London Oratory Junior Choir; Monteverdi Choir; English Baroque Soloists/John Eliot Gardiner.** Archiv Produktion 427 648-2AH3 (10/89).

BAROQUE — Non-vocal
Bach. Orchestral Suites, BWV1066-9. **Amsterdam Baroque Orchestra/Ton Koopman.** Deutsche Harmonia Mundi RD77864 (1/90).

CHAMBER
Respighi. Violin Sonata.
R. Strauss. Violin Sonata. **Kyung-Wha Chung** (vn); **Krystian Zimerman** (pf). DG 427 617-2GH (2/90).

CHORAL
Schumann. Das Paradies und die Peri. **Soloists; Lausanne Pro Arte Choir; Suisse Romande Chamber Choir and Orchestra/Armin Jordan.** Erato 2292-45456-2 (4/90).

CONCERTO
Shostakovich. Violin Concertos Nos. 1 and 2. **Lydia Mordkovitch** (vn); **Scottish National Orchestra/Neeme Järvi.** Chandos CHAN8820 (4/90).

CONTEMPORARY
G. Benjamin. Antara.
Boulez. Dérive. Memoriale.
J. Harvey. Song Offerings. **Penelope Walmsley-Clark** (sop); **Sebastian Bell** (fl); **London Sinfonietta/George Benjamin.** Nimbus NI5167 (10/89).

EARLY MUSIC
G. and *A. Gabrieli.* A VENETIAN CORONATION, 1595. **Gabrieli Consort and Players/Paul McCreesh.** Virgin Classics Veritas VC7 91110-2 (5/90).

ENGINEERING
Britten. THE PRINCE OF THE PAGODAS. **London Sinfonietta/Oliver Knussen.** Virgin Classics VCD7 91103-2 (7/90).

HISTORICAL — Non-vocal
Delius. ORCHESTRAL WORKS. **London Philharmonic Orchestra/Sir Thomas Beecham.** Sir Thomas Beecham Trust BEECHAM 2 (6/89).

HISTORICAL — Vocal
Massenet. WERTHER. **Soloists; Cantoria Children's Choir; Chorus and Orchestra of the Opéra-Comique, Paris/Elie Cohen.** EMI Références CHS7 63195-2 (3/90).

INSTRUMENTAL
Debussy. PIANO WORKS. **Zoltán Kocsis** (pf). Philips 422 404-2PH (2/90).

MUSIC THEATRE
Porter. ANYTHING GOES. **Soloists; Ambrosian Chorus; London Symphony Orchestra/John McGlinn.** EMI CDC7 49848-2 (12/89).

OPERA
RECORD OF THE YEAR
Prokofiev. THE LOVE FOR THREE ORANGES. **Soloists; Chorus and Orchestra of Lyon Opéra/Kent Nagano**. Virgin Classics VCD7 91084-2 (12/89).

ORCHESTRAL
Vaughan Williams. A Sea Symphony. **Soloists; Cantilena; London Philharmonic Choir and Orchestra/Bernard Haitink**. EMI CDC7 49911-2 (1/90).

SOLO VOCAL
Schubert. Schwanengesang. Heine and Seidl Lieder. **Peter Schreier** (ten); **András Schiff** (pf). Decca 425 612-2DH (6/90).

SPECIAL ACHIEVEMENT
Bach. Sacred Cantatas, Vols. 1-45. **Soloists; Choruses; Vienna Concentus Musicus/ Nikolaus Harnoncourt; Leonhardt Consort/Gustav Leonhardt**. Teldec. Various catalogue numbers.

1991

BAROQUE — Vocal
Handel. Susanna. **Soloists; Chamber Chorus of the Universily of California, Berkley; Philharmonia Baroque Orchestra/ Nicholas McGegan**. Harmonia Mundi HMC90 7030/2 (10/90).

BAROQUE — Non-Vocal
Biber. Mystery Sonatas. **John Holloway** (vn); **Davitt Moroney** (org/hpd); **Tragicomedia**. Virgin Classics Veritas VCD7 90838-2 (5/91).

CHAMBER
Brahms. Piano Quartets Nos. 1-3. **Isaac Stern** (vn); **Jaime Laredo** (va); **Yo-Yo Ma** (vc); **Emanuel Ax** (pf). Sony Classical CD45846 (3/91)

CHORAL
RECORD OF THE YEAR
Beethoven. Mass in D major, "Missa solemnis". **Soloists; Monteverdi Choir; English Baroque Soloists/John Eliot Gardiner**. Archiv Produktion 429 779-2AH (3/91).

CONCERTO
Sibelius. Violin Concerto. **Leonidas Kavakos** (vn); **Lahti Symphony Orchestra/Osmo Vänskä**. BIS CD500 (4/91).

CONTEMPORARY
Casken. GOLEM. **Soloists; Music Projects London/Richard Bernas**. Virgin Classics VCD7 91204-2 (8/91).

EARLY MUSIC
Palestrina. Masses and Motets. **The Tallis Scholars/Peter Philips**. Gimell CDGIM020 (9/90).

ENGINEERING
Wordsworth. Symphonies Nos. 2 and 3. **London Philharmonic Orchestra/Nicholas Braithwaite**. Lyrita SRCD207 (11/90).

HISTORICAL — Non-Vocal
Berg: Violin Concerto. Lyric Suite. **Louis Krasner** (vn); **Galimir Quartet; BBC Symphony Orchestra/Anton Webern**. Continuum SBT1004 (6/91).

HISTORICAL — Vocal
Fauré/Chausson. FRENCH SONGS. **Gérard Souzay** (bar); **Jacqueline Bonneau** (pf). Decca 425 975-2DM (7/91).

INSTRUMENTAL
Shostakovich. 24 Preludes and Fugues. **Tatyana Nikolaieva** (pf). Hyperion CDA66441/3 (3/91).

MUSIC THEATRE
Sondheim. INTO THE WOODS. **Original London Cast**. RCA Victor Red Seal RD60752 (9/91).

OPERA
Mozart. IDOMENEO. **Soloists; Monteverdi Choir; English Baroque Soloists/John Eliot Gardiner**. Archiv Produktion 431 674-2AH3 (6/91).

ORCHESTRAL
Nielsen. Symphonies Nos. 2 and 3. **Nancy Wait Fromm** (sop); **Kevin McMillan** (bar); **San Francisco Symphony Orchestra/Herbert Blomstedt**. Decca 430 280-2DH (8/90).

SOLO VOCAL
Schubert. Die schöne Müllerin. **Peter Schreier** (ten); **András Schiff** (pf). Decca 430 414-2DH (5/91).

SPECIAL ACHIEVEMENT AWARD
Mozart. COMPLETE EDITION. Various soloists, orchestras and conductors. Philips 422 501/45-2 (45 volumes: 180 discs).

1992

BAROQUE — Vocal
Handel. GIULIO CESARE. **Soloists; Concerto Cologne/René Jacobs.** Harmonia Mundi HMC90 1385/7 (4/92).

BAROQUE — Non-Vocal
Rameau. HARPSICHORD WORKS. **Christophe Rousset**. L'Oiseau-Lyre 425 886-2OH2 (12/91).

CHAMBER
Szymanowski. String Quartets Nos. 1 and 2. *Webern*. Slow Movement. **Carmina Quartet**. Denon CO-79462 (3/92).

CHORAL
Britten. War Requiem, Op. 66. Sinfonia da Requiem, Op. 20. Ballad of Heroes, Op. 14. **Soloists; St Paul's Cathedral Choir; London Symphony Chorus and Orchestra/ Richard Hickox**. Chandos CHAN8983/4 (11/91).

CONCERTO
Medtner. Piano Concertos Nos. 2 and 3. **Nikolai Demidenko** (pf); **BBC Scottish Symphony Orchestra/Jerzy Maksymiuk**. Hyperion CDA66580 (4/92).

CONTEMPORARY
Tavener. The Protecting Veil. Thrinos
Britten. Solo Cello Suite No. 3, Op. 87.
Steven Isserlis (vc); **London Symphony Orchestra/ Gennadi Rozhdestvensky.**
Virgin Classics VC7 91474-2 (3/92).

EARLY MUSIC
THE ROSE AND THE OSTRICH FEATHER.
Music from the Eton Choirbook, Volume 1.
The Sixteen/Harry Christophers. Collins Classics 1314-2 (4/92).

ENGINEERING
Britten. War Requiem, Op. 66. Sinfonia da Requiem, Op. 20. Ballad of Heroes, Op. 14.
Soloists; St Paul's Cathedral Choir; London Symphony Chorus and Orchestra/ Richard Hickox. Chandos CHAN8983/4 (11/91).

HISTORIC — Non-Vocal
THE ELGAR EDITION, Volume 1. **London Symphony Orchestra/Royal Albert Hall Orchestra/Edward Elgar.** EMI mono CDS7 54560-2 (6/92).

HISTORIC — Vocal
COVENT GARDEN ON RECORD, Volumes 1-4. Singers with various accompaniments. Pearl mono GEMMCDS9923/6 (7/92).

INSTRUMENTAL
Alkan. 25 Préludes dans les tons majeurs et mineur, Op. 31.
Shostakovich. 24 Preludes, Op. 34. **Olli Mustonen** (pf). Decca 433 055-2DH (10/91).

MUSIC THEATRE
Bernstein. CANDIDE. **Soloists; London Symphony Chorus and Orchestra/Leonard Bernstein.** DG 429 734-2GH2 (8/91).

OPERA
R. Strauss. DIE FRAU OHNE SCHATTEN.
Soloists; Vienna Boys' Choir; Vienna State Opera Chorus; Vienna Philharmonic Orchestra/Sir Georg Solti. Decca 436 243-2DH3 (5/92).

ORCHESTRAL
Beethoven. Symphonies Nos. 1-9. **Chamber Orchestra of Europe/Nikolaus Harnoncourt.** Teldec 2292-46452 (11/91).

SOLO VOCAL
Schubert. LIEDER. **Brigitte Fassbaender** (mez); **Aribert Reimann** (pf). DG 429 766-2GH (6/92).

R
e
v
i
e
w
s

Adolphe Adam

Adam. Giselle (abridged). **Vienna Philharmonic Orchestra/Herbert von Karajan.** Decca Ovation 417 738-2DM. From SXL6002 (11/62).

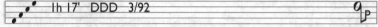

£ 9 P
lh ADD

NEW REVIEW

Adam. Giselle (abridged). **London Symphony Orchestra/Michael Tilson Thomas.** Sony Classical CD42450.

lh 17' DDD 3/92 9 P

Adam's ballet *Giselle* is a typically romantic work and tells of the Wilis, affianced maidens who die before their wedding. Unable to rest they rise from their graves at night and enjoy the dancing that they were unable to indulge in whilst living. Anyone who comes across them as they dance is forced to join them until he drops dead. Set into this framework is the love between Giselle and Prince Albrecht. The music is lively, tuneful and evocative — in other words, excellent ballet music. Given a performance as recorded by Decca which unites a top-class conductor, an outstanding orchestra and a superb recording (totally belying its years) *Giselle* could wish for nothing more.

Like the Karajan recording that has for 30 years been the best single-disc version, Tilson Thomas gives an abridged version of the score, but the cuts in transitions and repeats are just that bit less severe, thereby giving us an extra quarter of an hour or so of music. Nobody wanting a single-CD version of *Giselle* should imagine that he or she will be losing anything of major value. On any count this new version is a very good one indeed. Above all, Tilson Thomas resists any temptation to force upon the music an intensity that is alien to it. His feel for characterization and atmosphere is readily apparent. Where Karajan is perhaps more magical in one place, Tilson Thomas is that bit more elegant in another. The recorded sound is obviously that bit more vivid than the Karajan — good though the latter still sounds. For all but the specialist ballet collector who insists on *Giselle* absolutely complete, this new version is the clear first choice among modern recordings.

John Adams

Adams. ORCHESTRAL WORKS. **San Francisco Symphony Orchestra/ Edo de Waart.** Elektra-Nonesuch 7559-79144-2.
The Chairman Dances — foxtrot for orchestra (1985). Christian Zeal and Activity (1973). Two Fanfares for Orchestra — Tromba Iontana (1986); Short Ride in a Fast Machine (1986). Common Tones in Simple Time (1980).

52' DDD 8/88

John Adams   [photo: O'Grady]

There is no better way of sampling the music of John Adams than through this attractive compilation. His descriptive scores combine pastiche or parody with glossy orchestration and also set out to shrewdly scrutinize his own nationality. Thus the earliest piece, *Christian Zeal and Activity*, is a variation on *Onward, Christian Soldiers*, not sung with upstanding confidence but rather played *pianissimo* by a small body of strings, naked and vulnerable. In similar but more flamboyant vein, *The Chairman Dances* enters the world of American politics, drawing on the same events as Adams's opera *Nixon in China*. It's a Hollywood-like fantasy, part slick, part sleazy, that evokes a bygone age of glamour and style. Even the works that have no obvious story to tell have a sensuality that makes them instantly alluring. Both orchestra and conductor have long-standing connections with Adams, and the performances are as full of life as they are authoritative.

Adams. The Wound-dresser[a]. Fearful symmetries. [a]**Sanford Sylvan** (bar); **St Luke's Orchestra/John Adams.** Elektra-Nonesuch 979 218-2. Text included.

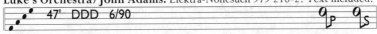

This disc displays particularly well the two "opposing polarities" (the composer's words) of Adam's creativity. *The Wound-dresser* is a setting of Walt Whitman's poem of the same name, recounting Whitman's own experience of nursing the wounded and dying soldiers during the American Civil War. Though the poem is graphic in its description of the atrocities of war, it is also a profoundly moving testament of compassion and humanity. Adams's elegiac and atmospheric setting is one of his most accessible and luminously scored pieces — its strong triadic harmonies and lyrical, melodic beauty underpinning and elevating the compassionate overtones of the text. *Fearful symmetries* on the other hand is an example of what Adams calls his "trickster" pieces — irreverent and hugely entertaining. More overtly minimalist in its language, its relatively slender material sometimes comes close to outstaying it welcome. But the work's propulsive energy and its almost diabolic moto-perpetuam (one is reminded of the complex and comical inventions of Heath Robinson or even the paintings of Hieronymus Bosch) seem to keep the listener riveted and fascinated until the very last note. Performances and recording are excellent.

Adams. NIXON IN CHINA. **Sanford Sylvan** (bar) Chou en-Lai; **James Maddalena** (bar) Richard Nixon; **Thomas Hammons** (bar) Henry Kissinger; **Mari Opatz** (mez) Nancy T'ang (First Secretary to Mao); **Stephanie Friedman** (mez) Second Secretary to Mao; **Marion Dry** (mez) Third Secretary to Mao; **John Duykers** (ten) Mao Tse-Tung; **Carolann Page** (sop) Pat Nixon; **Trudy Ellen Craney** (sop) Chiang Ch'ing; **St Luke's Chorus and Orchestra/Edo de Waart.** Elektra-Nonesuch 7559-79177-2. Notes and text included.

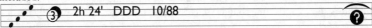

If few operas deal with current affairs and even fewer address political issues, then *Nixon in China* takes the unusual risk of bordering on the documentary. But it is also a study in the psychology of its principal characters, and by peering into the personalities it goes well beyond fact alone, revealing instead a truly human drama. Alice Goodman's libretto is structured around the American presidential visit to Beijing in February 1972. At first all is a whirl of formalities, functions and fervent debate, but as the energy begins to flag so human vulnerabilities show through, and the opera ends in a state of lassitude, a strange superimposition of bedroom scenes in which the protagonists share with one another their various reminiscences and dreams. Adams's score is particularly strong when the action is fast-moving: he is a master of energetic, sonorous music, and his minimalist leanings serve him well in those parts of the story that require movement or depend upon quick-fire exchanges. Less dynamic moments — and Goodman's libretto is rich in poetical soliloquies and dialogues — he perhaps handles less elegantly, though in the long final act the mood of intimacy and soul-searching is cleverly caught. Best of all, however, is the music that captures the mood of the public scenes. Adams revels in evoking tawdry glamour, and a hint of fox-trot often hangs deliciously in the air. The cast is a strong one; James Maddalena in particular faces us with a life-like Richard Nixon, and Trudy Ellen

Craney is memorable in Adams's most exaggerated character, the coloratura Madame Mao. So familiar are the faces behind the names that *Nixon in China* cannot be an easy work to watch on stage. On disc, with a few photographs provided in the insert booklet to jog the memory, it's perhaps easier to reconcile historical truth with the fantasy-world of this curious opera.

Richard Addinsell *Refer to Index* *British 1904-1977*

Jehan Alain *French 1911-1940*

Alain. ORGAN WORKS. **Thomas Trotter.** Argo 430 838-2ZH. Played on the Het Van den Heuvel organ, Nieuwe Kerk te Katwijk aan Zee, Holland.
Trois danses (1937-9). Fantasmagorie (1935). Première fantasie (1934).
Deuxième fantasie (1936). Suite (1934-6). Deux danses à Agni Yavishta (1934).
Trois pièces (1934-7).

1h 16' DDD 7/91

No doubt Jehan Alain would have become one of the most significant composers of his generation had he not been killed in action during World War II. As it is, though, he left sufficient music of considerable genius and originality to earn him a lasting place among this century's major French composers of organ music. A strong impression left after listening through this generously-filled disc is of electrifying rhythmic intensity reaching a climax, as it were, with his most enduringly popular piece, "Litanies". The *Trois danses* and the two dances to the Hindu God of fire, Agni Yavishta, have an equally hypnotic effect which Thomas Trotter's compelling playing underlines superbly. This splendid Dutch organ helps matters immeasurably as does Argo's close recording. Particularly successful is the delightful set of ornate variations Alain based on a charming melody attributed to the sixteenth-century composer, Clément Jannequin. Perhaps in the few more reflective moments which this programme offers (such as the evocation of the Hanging Gardens of Babylon, "Le Jardin Suspendu") the very directness of the organ sound, not to mention some rather obvious action noise detracts from the atmosphere. But against this the organ possesses some magical colours and produces some captivating sounds which suit this somewhat other-worldly music.

Isaac Albéniz *Spanish 1860-1909*

Albéniz (orch. Halffter). Rapsodia española, Op. 70.
Falla. Nights in the gardens of Spain (1915).
Turina. Rapsodia sinfónica, Op. 66. **Alicia de Larrocha** (pf); **London Philharmonic Orchestra/Rafael Frühbeck de Burgos.** Decca 410 289-2DH. From 410 289-1DH (6/84).

52' DDD 10/84

The three magically beautiful nocturnes which make up Falla's *Nights in the gardens of Spain* express the feelings and emotions evoked by contrasted surroundings, whilst Albéniz's enjoyably colourful *Rapsodia española* is a loosely assembled sequence of Spanish dances such as the *jota* and the *malagueña*. Like Falla's *Nights* the work was conceived as a piano solo, but this disc contains a version with orchestra arranged by Cristobal Halffter. The disc is completed by Turina's short, two-part work for piano and strings. All three pieces are excellently performed, but it is the Falla work which brings out the quality of Larrocha's artistry; her ability to evoke the colour of the Spanish atmosphere is remarkable. Frühbeck de Burgos supports her magnificently and persuades the LPO to some very Latin-sounding playing. The recording is suitably atmospheric.

NEW REVIEW

Albéniz. Iberia[a] (arr. Gray) — El Albaicín; Triana; Rondeña.
Granados. Seven Valses poéticos (trans. Williams).
Rodrigo. Invocación y Danza. En los trigales. **John Williams** (gtr); [a]**London Symphony Orchestra/Paul Daniels.** Sony Classical CD45759.
Anonymous (arr. Llobet): Ten Catalan Folk-songs — Cançó del lladre; El testament d'Amelia; La filadora; El mestre; La nit de Nadal; L'hereu Riera; Lo fill del Ré; La Pastoreta; El Noi de la Mare.

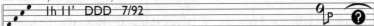

The amalgam of technical guitaristic perfection in the face of daunting demands, fluid musicality and exemplary tone-production, caught in this exceptionally lifelife recording, represents a landmark in the instrument's march towards true parity with other instruments. Granados's *Valses* are unabridged, Rodrigo's moody *Invocación y Danza* comes in its original and more effective form, and two of the charming settings of Catalan folk-songs arranged by Llobet have no other recording. Nothing in Albéniz's virtuosic *Iberia* is accessible to the solo guitar, but with the aid of the London Symphony Orchestra and Gray's enchantingly evocative arrangements, Williams shows three of its movements in a new and colourful light. To anyone with the slightest interest in the guitar or Spanish romantic music this disc is a required purchase.

Albéniz. Suite Iberia. Navarra (compl. de Séverac). Suite española, Op. 47.
Alicia de Larrocha (pf). Decca 417 887-2DH2.

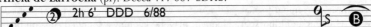

The *Iberia* suite is the greatest piano work in all Spanish musical literature and when played by Spain's leading pianist and recorded with warm but superlatively clean sound-quality is pure joy. A Catalan like Albéniz himself, Larrocha revels in the colour of these 12 highly picturesque and mostly Andalusian impressions, such as the quiet reverie of "Evocación", the lively bustle of "El puerto", the tense religious fervour of "El Corpus Christi en Sevilla", the swirling gaiety of "Triana", the brooding melancholy of "El Albaicín" and the exuberant bravura of *Navarra*. The Albéniz of 20 years earlier is illustrated by the 1886 *Suite española*, which Larrocha presents with winningly natural ease and charm.

Tomaso Albinoni
Italian 1671-1750

Albinoni. WIND CONCERTOS.
Vivaldi. WIND CONCERTOS. **Paul Goodwin** (ob); **King's Consort/ Robert King.** Hyperion CDA66383.
Albinoni: Concertos, Op. 9 — No. 2 in D minor; No. 6 in G major; No. 9 in C major. Concerto in C major. **Vivaldi:** Concertos — C major, RV560; F major, RV457; C major, RV559.

Few lovers of baroque concertos will be disappointed by this anthology. For the most part the programme has been well chosen both for the quality of the music and for the variety of instrumental colour which it affords. One piece, though, for trumpet, three oboes and a bassoon, for whom Albinoni's authorship is claimed is spurious and musically of a lower order than the remainder of the concertos. Albinoni was, if not the first, one of the first to write concertos for one and two solo oboes. They are without exception appealing for their warm colours and alluring conviviality. Happily, the disc includes one of Albinoni's most impressive compositions, the Oboe Concerto in D minor (Op. 9 No. 2) with its lyrical, aria-like *Adagio*; thankfully, not *the Adagio* but a genuine product from the composer's pen and an incomparably superior creation. The Vivaldi concertos are immediately engaging for their rhythmic energy and their varied colours. Two of the works are for pairs of oboes and clarinets, the latter very much in their infancy; the third is a piece for oboe and strings which the composer adapted from an earlier bassoon concerto. It has an especially effective opening movement, sensitively played by Paul Goodwin.

Albinoni. Concerti a cinque, Op. 7. **Heinz Holliger,** [a]**Hans Elhorst** (obs); **Berne Camerata.** Archiv Produktion Galleria 427 111-2AGA. From 2533 404 (11/79).
No. 2 in C major[a]; No. 3 in B flat major; No. 5 in C major[a]; No. 6 in D major; No. 8 in D major[a]; No. 9 in F major; No. 11 in C major[a]; No. 12 in C major.

♪ 57' ADD 4/89

Tomaso Albinoni, thanks to family money, was able to pursue his art without worrying overly about where the next ducat was coming from. He also had musical talent in abundance, writing 53 operas and over 150 instrumental works including the 12 *Concerti a cinque*, published in 1715. At that time concertos were customarily works for strings only, but those of Albinoni's Op. 7 were among the first (and his own first) to include wind instruments such as the oboe, and his use of the instrument displays the composer's remarkable gift of melody. It was however not only in their inclusion of wind instruments that these works were significant: in them Albinoni moved away from Corelli, in adopting a fast-slow-fast, three-movement format, and towards Vivaldi in sowing the seeds of *ritornello* form. Holliger and Elhorst are eloquent players, keeping a rounded edge on their sounds and they receive the most spruce and spirited of support from Berne Camerata. The recorded sound, acoustic and balance could hardly be bettered.

Hugo Alfvén
Swedish 1872-1960

NEW REVIEW

Alfvén. Symphony No. 2 in D major, R28. Midsummer Vigil — Swedish Rhapsody No. 1, R45. **Stockholm Philharmonic Orchestra/Neeme Järvi.** BIS CD385.

♪ 1h 8' DDD 7/88 ❓

Hugo Alfvén was one of Sweden's major symphonists, but also wrote several melodies that are popular the world over. Best known of all is the dance theme of *Midsummer Vigil*, the first of three Swedish Rhapsodies and the one that is generally known as *the* Swedish Rhapsody. The piece as a whole is a charming tone poem depicting youthful, high-spirited revelry during a midsummer Scandinavian night. Of Alfvén's four symphonies, the Second is the one that put him on the map in 1899. Its idiom is rooted in the music of Dvořák, with a touch of the freshness of Svendsen. Perhaps the best music is to be found in the first three movements, which Alfvén said were sketched beside the sea. The first (*moderato*) is bubbling over with freshness and melody, and is followed by sounds of grim foreboding from the lower brass in the *andante* second movement. The *scherzo* is followed by a final movement in the form of a prelude and fugue. Neeme Järvi brings to the works his feel for Scandinavian music, and the recording lives up to BIS's regular high standards.

Charles-Valentin Alkan

French 1813-1888

NEW REVIEW

Alkan. 25 Préludes dans les tons majeurs et mineur, Op. 31.
Shostakovich. 24 Preludes, Op. 34. **Olli Mustonen** (pf). Decca 433 055-2DH.

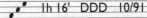 1h 16' DDD 10/91

It was brave of Decca to launch the career of their latest star pianist with a disc of miniatures few people actually know. Despite the sterling efforts of Ronald Smith, the *oeuvre* of Charles-Valentin Alkan is usually confined to specialist labels and second-rate executants. The 25 Preludes are a reasonably benign introduction to Alkan's idiosyncratic world — elusive and quirky to be sure but less ruthlessly barnstorming than much of his output. They are by no means easy pieces to bring off, but you wouldn't

Olli Mustonen   [*photo: Decca*]

know it from Mustonen's exceptionally assured, brilliantly poised readings. Where rival versions are content to offer the 25 Preludes without coupling, Mustonen adds deft and sparkling performances of Shostakovich's not exactly insubstantial Op. 34 Preludes. Exceptional pianism, excellent, bright recording and helpful notes.

Gregorio Allegri

Italian c.1582-1652

Allegri. Miserere[a].
W. Mundy. Vox patris caelestis.
Palestrina. Missa Papae Marcelli. [a]**Alison Stamp** (sop); **The Tallis Scholars/Peter Phillips.** Gimell CDGIM339. From Classics for Pleasure CFP40339 (10/80).

 1h 9' ADD 7/86   **Ⓑ**

This is a favourite recording of Allegri's *Miserere*. Peter Phillips has used the natural acoustics of Merton College Chapel, adding a note of variety which relieves the repetitive nature of the long penitential psalm: what a simple idea it was to space the singers so that those with the low-lying verses were near the microphone and the others half-way down the chapel, with Alison Stamp's high C rising pure and clear above distant hushed voices! *Vox patris caelestis* is an imaginative and cleverly-designed motet for the Assumption of the Virgin, dating from the mid-sixteenth century-Catholic revival and based on texts from the *Song of Songs*. The music rises to an ecstatic climax at the words "Veni, veni ...", with two high trebles at the top of their range crowning the rich harmonies of the lower voices. In marked contrast to such exuberance, Palestrina's *Missa Papae*

Marcelli, dating from the same period, represents a sober, lapidary style. The declamatory speech-rhythms are admirably rendered and the performance is not lacking in its moments of intense, if restrained, emotion. Highly recommended.

Hans Erich Apostel

Austrian 1901-1972

NEW REVIEW

Apostel. String Quartet No. 1, Op. 7[a].
Zemlinsky. String Quartets — No. 1 in A major, Op. 4[a]; No. 2, Op. 15[b]; No. 3, Op. 19[a]; No. 4, Op. 25[a]. **LaSalle Quartet** (Walter Levin, Henry Meyer, vns; Peter Kamnitzer, va; Lee Fiser, vc). DG 427 421-2GC2. Items marked [a] from 2741 016 (2/84), [b] 2530 082 (4/79).

② 2h 18' DDD/ADD 8/89

When the LaSalle Quartet's pioneering recording of Zemlinsky's Second Quartet was first issued, the composer — the *Lyric Symphony* apart — was still a relatively unknown quantity. Today his strengths and weaknesses (especially in opera) can be more completely and realistically evaluated, and alternative performances of various works have begun to appear. Just occasionally the LaSalle Quartet may seem to press the music too hard, and the sound to lack that last degree of bloom and warmth which present-day techniques can ensure. But these are minor quibbles compared with the confidence and conviction of the enterprise as a whole. The second quartet remains the jewel in the crown, a powerful, large-scale conception far from dwarfed by comparison with the Schoenberg First Quartet that was its evident model. From the Brahmsian late-romanticism of No. 1 to the well-balanced tensions of the later pieces, the LaSalle players are persuasive advocates. With the bonus of a well-crafted, pithily-argued piece by the Schoenberg pupil, Hans Erich Apostel, this medium-priced issue is highly attractive.

Anton Arensky   *Refer to Index*

Russian 1861-1906

Thomas Arne

British 1710-1778

Arne. INSTRUMENTAL WORKS. **Le Nouveau Quatuor** (Utako Ikeda, fl; Catherine Weiss, vn; Mark Caudle, vc; [a]Paul Nicholson, hpd). Amon Ra CDSAR-42.
Favourite Concertos — No. 1 in C major (solo hpd version)[a]. Keyboard Sonatas (1756) — No. 1 in F major[a]. Trio Sonatas (1757) — No. 2 in G major; No. 5; No. 6 in B minor; No. 7 in E minor.

58' DDD 5/90

If the music history books offer little more than a passing reference to the slim repertoire of enchanting chamber music by Thomas Arne, the ordinary man in the street, who can at least whistle *Rule Britannia*, is unlikely even to have heard that any exists. This disc comes therefore as something of a revelation. The members of the Nouveau Quatuor perform on instruments dating from the composer's lifetime, tuned down a semitone. The trio sonatas, originally published for two violins and continuo, are played here by a mixed quartet: flute, violin, cello and harpsichord, which is believed to have been what the composer really intended. The introduction of the flute adds colour, brightness and definition to these charming pieces and gives the listener a chance to savour the admirable tone and phrasing of the flautist, Utako Ikeda. Paul Nicholson's harpsichord solos are distinguished as much by their elegance as by their extraordinary power and brilliance. A word, finally, in praise of Peter Holman's excellent sleeve-notes: they are both scholarly and extremely readable.

Malcolm Arnold

British 1921-

Arnold. CONCERTOS. [a]**Karen Jones** (fl); [b]**Michael Collins** (cl); [c]**Richard Watkins** (hn); [d]**Kenneth Sillito**, [d]**Lyn Fletcher** (vns); **London Musici/ Mark Stephenson.** Conifer CDCF172.
Concerto for two violins and orchestra, Op. 77[d]. Concerto No. 1 for clarinet and strings, Op. 20[b]. Concerto No. 1 for flute and strings, Op. 45[a]. Concerto No. 2 for horn and strings, Op. 58[c].

 56' DDD 8/89

The four concertos presented on this disc provide an excellent opportunity to sample Arnold's wonderful gift for concertante writing. Each was written for or commissioned by an outstanding British virtuoso, which in turn reflects the admiration and respect with which Arnold is held by his musical colleagues. Listening to these concertos it's easy to see why he is so frequently commissioned by soloists for new works, as his ability to bring out the natural characteristics of each instrument as well as capture something of the style and personality for whom he writes is quite extraordinary. The Clarinet Concerto dates from 1948 and is a work full of contrast and contradictions, sometimes introspective and serious (slow movement), sometimes humorous and light-hearted, but always extremely approachable and lyrical. The exuberant and extrovert outer movements of the Flute Concerto capture the mercurial qualities of the instrument very well, and these are contrasted by a slow movement of great beauty and simplicity. Not surprisingly the Horn Concerto reflects the considerable virtuosity of its dedicatee, Dennis Brain, who died so tragically only a few weeks after its first performance in 1957. The Double Violin Concerto of 1964 surprisingly finds its way on to disc for the first time, and a most welcome addition to the catalogue it is too. Though it has a rather more serious, neo-classical approach than the other concertos its immediacy and charm are evident from the very beginning, and one is left wondering why this work is not heard or recorded more frequently. The superb performances from all concerned, not least the beautifully rich string tone of the London Musici, make this a highly recommendable introduction to Arnold's music.

NEW REVIEW

Arnold. ORCHESTRAL WORKS. [a]**Phyllis Sellick**, [a]**Cyril Smith** (pfs); [b]**Bournemouth Symphony Orchestra**, [c]**City of Birmingham Symphony Orchestra**, [d]**Phiharmonia Orchestra/Malcolm Arnold.** EMI British Composers [abc]stereo/[d]mono CDM7 64044-2.
Concerto for two pianos (three hands), Op. 104[ac] (from HMV ASD2612, 10/70). Symphony No. 1, Op. 22[b]. Solitaire[b] — Sarabande; Polka (all from ASD3823, 6/80). Tam O'Shanter — Overture, Op. 51[d]. English Dances[d] — No. 3, Op. 27 No. 3; No. 5, Op. 33 No. 1 (Columbia SED5529, 2/56).

 1h 16' ADD 10/91

When Malcolm Arnold celebrated his seventieth birthday in 1991, many people realized how badly he had been neglected by the stiff British establishment as too tuneful, uninhibited and (worst of all!) communicative to be 'serious'. These recordings under his own baton were ripe for this mid-price reissue, for although the sound is not new — the *Tam O'Shanter* Overture and *English Dances* are in mono and date from 1955 — it is surprisingly good. Newcomers to Arnold's music (or who think they are, for they've probably heard it in several famous British films) could well start with *Tam O'Shanter*, which was inspired by a Robert Burns poem about a Scotsman's wild night ride with the devil in pursuit. The boisterous and brilliant scoring here is a delight, as is the marvellous sense of atmosphere. The Two Piano Concerto was commissioned for the 1969 Proms and the duo of Phyllis Sellick and Cyril Smith, the "three hands" being because Smith had lost the use of his left hand after a stroke a decade before. Such is Arnold's skill that one's not conscious of a limitation, although his keyboard writing is more as if laid out for one three-handed pianist than for two players of whom one is at a disadvantage. As usual with him, there are contrasts of noisy high spirits and gentle lyricism, and no shortage of tunes, as in the cool, slow movement in slow waltz time. This concerto makes us realize that Arnold is the nearest British equivalent to Poulenc. But like Poulenc, he also had a darker and tougher side, and it comes across in the First Symphony which, for all its vigour, contains real bitterness too. One sometimes thinks of Sibelius and Nielsen as it unfolds, but the voice is still Arnold's and this is fine music if not by any means cosy listening (the end of the finale reaches unmistakable tragedy). The other, lighter pieces make up a valuable issue, with unfailingly strong, authentic-sounding performances.

Arnold. ORCHESTRAL WORKS. **London Philharmonic Orchestra/Malcolm Arnold.** Lyrita SRCD201. Item marked [a] from SRCS109 (3/79).
Four Cornish Dances, Op. 91[a]. English Dances, Op. 27; Op. 33[a]. Irish Dances, Op. 126. Four Scottish Dances, Op. 59[a]. Solitaire — Sarabande; Polka.

Ih I' ADD/DDD 12/90

The arrival of Malcolm Arnold as a composer in the 1940s blew a gust of fresh air through English music, as William Walton's had some decades earlier. His training was as a composer and a trumpet player, in which latter capacity he first achieved prominence; his experience as a "rude mechanical" both gave him the insight that contributed to his remarkable skill in orchestration, and helped him to keep his aesthetic feet on the ground. Arnold has never lost faith in tonality, has never hesitated to write tunes that, despite their subtle craftsmanship, sound 'popular', and has not remained aloof from the influences of jazz and rock; he is in the best sense 'Everyman's composer'. The regional characters of his dances (1950-86) are as he perceives them to be, for he makes no use of folk material, and they are reinforced by the versatility of his orchestration. This is music that speaks directly, but does not talk down to the common man, and here it has the benefit of joyous performances conducted by the composer himself, and recorded sound that is as clear as Arnold's orchestral textures. One might describe it as 'Music for Pleasure'.

Arnold. Guitar Concerto, Op. 67.
Brouwer. Retrats Catalans.
Chappell. Guitar Concerto No. 1, "Caribbean Concerto". **Eduardo Fernández** (gtr); **English Chamber Orchestra/Barry Wordsworth.** Decca 430 233-2DH.

Ih DDD 4/91

In a world swamped by Rodrigo's *Concierto de Aranjuez*, Malcolm Arnold's Guitar Concerto has been heard much less often than it deserves. His musical roots spread in many directions, here toward lighter soil; the first movement's second subject might make a very popular song (if someone provided it with lyrics), the second movement, a lament for Django Reinhardt, breathes the late-night air of a jazz club, and the one-octave glissando that ends the third is the last of the many demands placed on the soloist in this joyous romp. Brouwer's *Retrats* (portraits) are of Federico Mompou and Antoni Gaudi, painted in fresh colours to which the guitar (and, unusually, the piano) contributes; the guitar here acts as an orchestral 'voice', rather than a concerto-status soloist, and, like Arnold, Brouwer is a master of the orchestral medium. Herbert Chappell, avoiding the cliché of 'Spanishry', enters the guitarist's domain via the Caribbean door; his Concerto is a stunning *tour de force*, a kaleidoscope of colour and movement, and no less a vehicle for the virtuosity of anyone bold enough to approach it. If *Aranjuez* is to have a successor, this could well be it; if so, this recording will long remain a touchstone. Fernández plays brilliantly — and stimulates the ECO to do likewise.

NEW REVIEW

Arnold. OVERTURES. **London Philharmonic Orchestra/Malcolm Arnold.** Reference Recordings RR48CD.
A Sussex Overture, Op. 31. Beckus the Dandipratt, Op. 5. The Smoke, Op. 21. The Fair Field, Op. 110. Commonwealth Christmas Overture, Op. 64.

1h 3' DDD 6/92

Malcolm Arnold's seventieth birthday in 1991 reminded us, and none too soon, that he is a gifted composer who, unlike some of his contemporaries, writes music that is actually enjoyable! For this dreadful sin he was cold-shouldered by the British music establishment for over 20 years of his career, and we must be thankful that he survived this rejection, continued to write fine new music and is now recognized as a master. Four of the overtures here are early pieces composed before 1960, while *The Fair Field* (written for the Fairfield Halls in Croydon, Surrey) dates from 1972. All have recognizably and affectionately British origins, and their brilliant colour reminds us of Arnold's many outstanding film scores. The earliest piece is *Beckus the Dandipratt* — a dandipratt was an Elizabethan coin, but the word was also used for a cheeky small boy — and was inspired by a youngster that the composer and his wife befriended on a wartime Cornish holiday. *The Smoke* (a Cockney term for London) has raucous jazz elements, while the *Commonwealth Christmas Overture* places cosy English chimes alongside the more urgent Christmas music of a Caribbean pop group. Though much of this music is cheerfully extrovert, by no means all of it is, and for all its tunefulness it is not easy-listening music in the usual sense. Under the composer, the London Philharmonic play it brilliantly and lovingly, and the recording is rich and detailed. The booklet note by the producer, Christopher Palmer, is a model of information, enthusiasm and style and complements a splendid issue.

Arnold. Symphonies — No. 7, Op. 113; No. 8, Op. 124. **Royal Philharmonic Orchestra/Vernon Handley.** Conifer CDCF177.

1h 4' DDD 3/91

When we consider the music of Malcolm Arnold we generally conjure up his marvellously ebullient and good humoured works such as his Suites of English and Scottish Dances, his Overtures *Tam o'Shanter* and *Beckus the Dandipratt* or one of his many brilliant and lyrical concertos. But there is a darker, more serious side too, to this versatile and much misunderstood composer. Here we are presented with two of his most fierce and dissonant works — the Seventh and Eighth Symphonies. The Seventh was written in 1973 and is one of his longest and darkest symphonic utterances. The Symphony is dedicated to Arnold's three children — Katherine, Robert and Edward, and the composer explains that each are loosely portrayed in one of the three movements. Quite why they should be linked with such bleak and ferocious music remains something of an enigma. However, what we do have is a fascinating and compelling work that gives us a deeper insight into Arnold's creative personality. The dissonance and savagery of the first movement is heightened by the movement's disturbing and restless spirit and builds to an impressive, well-calculated climax. The second movement is a dark and melancholy landscape that, as the sleeve-notes point out, is conceivably an evocation of the world of Arnold's autistic Edward. The last movement returns to the unsettled, restless nature of the first, and includes a folksy Irish episode that imitates the style of the Irish folk band, The Chieftains — a

particular favourite of Arnold's son Robert. The Eighth Symphony shares with the Seventh a quixotic and dissonant nature, if perhaps somewhat less pessimistic in its overall mood. Arnold's fondness for Irish whimsy makes another appearance with the inclusion in the first movement of a marching tune first used in his score to the film *The Reckoning*. The final movement recalls the high spirits of Arnold's earlier symphonies, though one is constantly aware of sobering and more dramatic undercurrents at work. Vernon Handley's affection for and commitment to these symphonies is evident from these powerful and persuasive performances. Recordings are first-class. Well worth investigating.

Malcolm Arnold   *[photo: Reference Recordings/Rowland*

Carl Philipp Emanuel Bach   *German 1714-1788*

C.P.E. Bach. Cello Concertos — A major, Wq172; A minor, Wq170; B flat major, Wq171. **Anner Bylsma** (vc); **Orchestra of the Age of Enlightenment/Gustav Leonhardt.** Virgin Classics Veritas VC7 90800-2.

1h 10' DDD 2/90

During his many years at the court of Frederick the Great, C.P.E. Bach composed these three cello concertos. The fact that they also exist in his transcriptions for harpsichord and flute hardly suggests very idiomatic writing for the cello and in a way the implied comment is true; nevertheless, they go very well on the tenor instrument and Anner Bylsma brings out their quirky charm (a quality never in short supply with this composer) while coping adequately with some tricky figuration in the quicker movements; he's also eloquent in the highly expressive slower ones that are especially characteristic of this Bach. This is perhaps not a CD for a basic collection, even of cello music, but it should give the pleasure which is itself audible in the music-making by players completely at home in the idiom. The recording was made in the well-tried location of All Saints' Church in Petersham in the UK; it places the cello rather far back, but convincingly, and has an agreeably warm sound. The period pitch is about a quarter of a tone lower than a modern one and the booklet gives the date and maker's name of the orchestra's 23 instruments, though, oddly, not those of the soloist's baroque cello.

C.P.E. Bach. Harpsichord Concertos — D minor, Wq23; C minor, Wq31; F major, Wq33. **Miklós Spányi** (hpd); **Budapest Concerto Armonico.** Hungaroton Antiqua HCD31159.

· 1h 12' DDD 10/90

C.P.E. Bach, in keeping with family tradition, was both original composer and skilful keyboard player. His legacy of music for harpsichord and clavichord is large and varied and includes some 50 harpsichord concertos. This disc contains three of them, well-chosen for their contrasting features, imaginatively played and vividly recorded. These and indeed the majority of the others date from Bach's long period of employment as court harpsichordist to Frederick the Great. Each contains qualities which reflect the north German *empfindsamer Stil* or 'sensitive style' of which this member of the Bach family was a noted exponent. Emotions are projected in a powerful musical language whose idiom resists definition but has recognizable features; among these are short-winded phrases, strong dynamic contrasts, abrupt rhythmic disturbances and an abstracted intimacy. In short, temperamental unpredictability is of the essence. Miklós Spányi and the period-instrument ensemble enter wholeheartedly into this world of turbulent emotions and passionate gestures with vigour, insight and, especially where slow movements are concerned, affecting sensibility. These are vivid accounts of three strong compositions and should make an impact on any listener.

C.P.E. Bach. Oboe Concerto in E flat major, H468.
Lebrun. Oboe Concerto No. 1 in D minor.
Mozart. Oboe Concerto in C major, K314/285*d*. **Paul Goodwin** (ob); **The English Concert/Trevor Pinnock.** Archiv Produktion 431 821-2AH.

· 1h 2' DDD 7/91

The oboe is supposed to have been Handel's favourite instrument, and with the move away from baroque to classical styles in the later eighteenth century, it still continued to attract composers, not least because there were fine players to inspire them. Of the three concertos here, Mozart's is the most familiar and arguably the finest, but the others are also well worth getting to know. Mozart himself admired C.P.E. Bach for his originality and expressive force, and his individuality comes out at once here: the vigorous first movement of his concerto has an unusual opening theme with repeated notes, and the *Adagio* a depth of feeling that looks forward to Beethoven, while a bouncily *galant* finale in triple time rounds things off well. Paul Goodwin's cadenzas are imaginative and appropriate, and the tone of his two-keyed modern replica of an old instrument is entirely convincing as well as pleasingly rounded. Lebrun is an almost forgotten figure today, but on the evidence of this piece this oboist-composer had plenty to say and his Concerto in D minor has an urgently dramatic first movement with trumpets and timpani often to the fore; in fact, there seems to be an operatic influence here and the slow movement is like a graceful aria. A finely textured recording complements the skilful playing of the soloist and Trevor Pinnock's orchestra.

C.P.E. Bach. Symphonies, Wq 182. **The English Concert/Trevor Pinnock.** Archiv Produktion 415 300-2AH. From 2533 499 (10/80).
No. 1 in G major; No. 2 in B flat major; No. 3 in C major; No. 4 in A major; No. 5 in B minor; No. 6 in E major.

· 1h 5' ADD 5/86

Carl Philipp Emanuel worked for 28 years at the Potsdam Court of Frederick the Great and although the post provided secure employment, Frederick's dictatorial attitude did nothing to encourage Bach's aspirations to break new ground. His 'imprisonment' ended when Frederick reluctantly released him to succeed Telemann, his godfather, as Music Director at Hamburg. Now he was able to give free rein to his imagination and the Symphonies are as remarkable as they are stimulating, with abrupt, even wild changes of mood, dynamics and key. They are required listening, not least when they are played with so much vitality and vivid response to their wayward changeability as they are here by The English Concert, using period instruments. The engineers use theirs, of a much later period, in securing the cleanest of recordings.

C.P.E. Bach. SINFONIAS, Wq183. **Orchestra of the Age of Enlightenment/Gustav Leonhardt.** Virgin Classics Veritas VC7 90806-2.
No. 1 in D major; No. 2 in E flat major; No. 3 in F major; No. 4 in G major. Wq182 — No. 5 in B minor.

54' DDD 8/90

C.P.E. Bach. SINFONIAS, Wq183. **Amsterdam Baroque Orchestra/Ton Koopman.** Erato 2292-45361-2.
No. 1 in D major; No. 2 in E flat major; No. 3 in F major; No. 4 in G major.

43' DDD 8/89

Ton Koopman   [photo: Erato/Sarrat]

C.P.E. Bach wrote two sets of symphonies during his period as Hamburg city's Music Director. The Virgin disc contains all four works from the second set (*c.*1776) and one from the earlier collection (1773). At least in terms of orchestration the later set, with its parts for horns, flutes, oboes, bassoon and strings, is more ambitious than the other providing an excellent showcase for the wind players of the Orchestra of the Age of Enlightenment. Gustav Leonhardt enjoys a warm rapport both with the Orchestra and the repertory and his interpretation of these symphonies is perceptive and spirited. Rhythms are taut yet with an effective elasticity well-suited to Bach's individual, sometimes quirky temperament. Leonhardt prefers a somewhat larger band than some of his competitors and this too, has positive advantages in as much as it allows for more telling contrasts between strings and wind; it is recorded that Emanuel Bach himself fielded an ensemble of 40 instrumentalists, no less. For good measure, Leonhardt gives us an additional symphony from Bach's earlier Hamburg set of six, Wq182 (1773). Perhaps the performance of this does not quite match the others in vigour and finesse, but its phrases are beautifully shaped and well articulated. The recorded sound is bright, clear and ideally resonant.

Ton Koopman's Amsterdam Baroque Orchestra consists of rather less than half the number of players that would have performed these pieces originally, but this is of benefit rather than hindrance to the music's colourful textures. Each symphony is scored for pairs of horns, flutes and oboes, with bassoon, violins, viola, cello, bass and continuo. Emanuel Bach himself described these works as the most substantial works of the kind that he had written; "modesty forbids me to say more", he added. Certainly they are strikingly original if not, in the end, *entirely* satisfying. Wind instruments are freed from their hitherto supporting role and given a greater degree of independence, yet the music remains anchored to the basso continuo. Bach's strongly personal idiom, darkly reflective at one moment, intense and agitated at another, is vividly captured in Koopman's lively performances and the orchestral playing maintains a high standard throughout. Flutes, oboes and horns emerge clearly from the full texture and careful thought has been given to sonority and internal balance. The recording is spacious yet allowing for detail and the character of period instruments is again pleasingly captured.

NEW REVIEW

C.P.E. Bach. Viola da gamba Sonatas — G minor, Wq88; C major, Wq136; D major, Wq137. **Paolo Pandolfo** (va da gamba); **Rinaldo Alessandrini** (hpd). Tactus TC71020501.

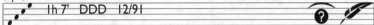

1h 7' DDD 12/91

C.P.E. Bach's two sonatas for viola da gamba with continuo (Wq136 and 137) and the sonata for gamba with obbligato harpsichord (Wq88) are among the last solo pieces written outside France for an instrument which had been largely supplanted by the cello. The two continuo works date from the 1740s while the other was written some ten years later. Bearing in mind Emanuel Bach's family background it is hardly surprising to find him writing in a virtuoso manner for the viola da gamba, exploring its full technical and expressive range. In these accomplished performances Paolo Pandolfo not only draws a beautiful and sonorous tone from his instrument but proves himself to be a musician of sensibility and interpretative discernment. It is no easy matter to establish a close rapport with Bach's melancholic expression yet Pandolfo succeeds in doing this and is ably supported and partnered by his harpsichordist, Rinaldo Alessandrini. Phrases eloquently spoken and a feeling for Bach's distinctive idiom are constant pleasures in these performances; indeed, readers as yet unfamiliar with these at times almost startlingly expressive pieces will find much to delight them. The disc is effectively recorded and an accompanying note by Pandolfo himself makes interesting reading.

Johann Christian Bach
German 1735-1782

J.C. Bach. CHAMBER WORKS. **The English Concert** (Lisa Beznosiuk, fl; David Reichenberg, ob; Anthony Halstead, David Cox, hns; Simon Standage, vn; Trevor Jones, va; Anthony Pleeth, vc; Trevor Pinnock, hpd, fp, square pf). Archiv Produktion 423 385-2AH.
Quintet in D major for flute, oboe, violin, cello and keyboard, Op. 22 No. 1. Sextet in C major for oboe, two horns, violin, cello and keyboard. Quintets for flute, oboe, violin, viola and continuo, Op. 11 — No. 1 in C major; No. 6 in D major.

1h 9' DDD 5/88

Johann Christian Bach was the youngest of J.S. Bach's sons and the most widely travelled of them. After studying with his father and with his half-brother C.P.E. Bach, Johann Christian worked in Italy and in England where he settled in 1762. For the remaining 20 years of his life J.C. Bach played a central role in London musical circles composing, playing and teaching. As well as operas, sacred music, symphonies and concertos the "London Bach" as he became affectionately known, composed various types of chamber music. Among the most engaging of these are the six Quintets, Op. 11, those of Op. 22 and the Sextet in C major once thought to be the work of his elder brother J.C.F. Bach. Trevor Pinnock and members of The English Concert give sparkling performances of music conspicuous for its abundance of captivating melodies, transparent textures and fine craftsmanship. Slow movements are especially beguiling and the subtly shaded dynamics, delicately contrived instrumental sonorities and informed sense of style with which these artists bring the music to life give the performances a rare delicacy and refinement. Pinnock himself plays a variety of keyboard instruments whose contrasting sound adds another pleasing dimension to the interpretations. Each of the artists makes a strong contribution but special praise, perhaps, should be given to the artistry of the late David Reichenberg, an oboist with outstanding lyrical gifts. Good recorded sound.

Johann Sebastian Bach *German 1685-1750*

Bach. Violin Concertos — No. 1 in A minor, BWV1041; No. 2 in E major, BWV1042. Double Violin Concerto in D minor, BWV1043[a]. **Simon Standage, [a]Elizabeth Wilcock** (vns); **The English Concert/Trevor Pinnock** (hpd). Archiv Produktion 410 646-2AH. From 410 646-1AH (10/83).

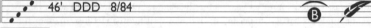
46' DDD 8/84

NEW REVIEW

Bach. Violin Concertos — No. 1 in A minor, BWV1041; No. 2 in E major, BWV1042. Double Violin Concerto in D minor, BWV1043[a]. Violin and Oboe Concerto in C minor, BWV1060[b]. [a]**José-Luis Garcia** (vn); [b]**Neil Black** (ob); **English Chamber Orchestra/Dimitri Sitkovetsky** (vn). Novalis 150 017-2.

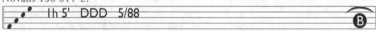
1h 5' DDD 5/88

Archiv gives us bright, fresh-faced playing of these three baroque concertos that brings out all their tireless energy, crispness and intellectual force. They are a model of baroque instrumental utterance: quintessentially Bachian in their superlative craft and strength of purpose. The soloist Simon Standage is particularly good and sounds wholly authentic in appearing to be a first among equals in an ensemble instead of an artistically separate being. If the studied authenticity of the skilled English Concert may, for some collectors, leave an impression of impersonality and inflexibility, for those who like their Bach vigorous and without frills their performances can be recommended as a safe choice.

There are still some who prefer the sounds of modern instruments to the leaner ones of their period equivalents, and providing that their players are respectful of the style and essential character of the music there is no compelling reason why they should be condemned for doing so.

Dimitri Sitkovetsky   *[photo: Virgin Classics/Maeder*

In the performances by Sitkovetsky and the English Chamber Orchestra the
energy comes from within and does not depend on fast tempos for its projection,
and the warmth of expression never turns to anachronistic sentimentality.
Sitkovetsky's range of volume is impressive, with whispered sounds at its lower
end, and in the quicker movements his tone has a slight 'authentic' cutting edge.
Garcia, his partner in the Double Concerto, produces a slightly warmer sound
that, whilst complementing Sitkovetsky's, helps the ear to keep the two
protagonists separated, and as a player of baroque music (here BWV1060) on the
modern oboe Neil Black has few peers. The English Chamber Orchestra give
their wholehearted and attentive support and, with the harpsichord neither
inaudible nor obtrusive, are excellently balanced with the soloists. At the time of
this *Guide*'s publication, there is no better 'middle of the road' recording of these
essential works.

Bach. BRANDENBURG CONCERTOS[a]. Orchestral Suites, BWV1066-9[b]. **The
English Concert/Trevor Pinnock.** Archiv Produktion 423 492-2AX3. Items
marked [a] from 2742 003 (2/83), [b] 2533 410/1 (5/79).
No. 1 in F major, BWV1046; No. 2 in F major, BWV1047; No. 3 in G major,
BWV1048; No. 4 in G major, BWV1049; No. 5 in D major, BWV1050; No. 6
in B flat major, BWV1051.

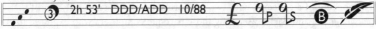

Bach. BRANDENBURG CONCERTOS. **English Chamber Orchestra/
Raymond Leppard** (hpd). Philips Silver Line 420 345/6-2PM. From 6747 166
(4/75).
420 345-2PM — No. 1 in F major, BWV1046; No. 2 in F major, BWV1047;
No. 3 in G major, BWV1048. *420 346-2PM* — No. 4 in G major, BWV1049;
No. 5 in D major, BWV1050; No. 6 in B flat major, BWV1051.

These concertos, written in 1721, were Bach's response to a request from the
Margrave of Brandenburg, whose name they now bear, but despite the dedication
we do not know whether the Margrave acknowledged their receipt or ever heard
them. Two, Concertos Nos. 3 and 6, are written for strings only, the latter
without violins, but the others call for different combinations of other instrumental soloists. The music itself displays an amazing variety of form and use of
instrumental colour, and since The English Concert use period instruments their
performances must closely approach those which Bach may have heard, in both
colour and balance — but he is unlikely to have heard them to greater advantage
than we can through these excellent recordings.

As a modern instrument alternative to Pinnock's spirited readings, Raymond
Leppard's 1974 recordings offer vigorous, rhythmically stylish performances with
some fine individual contributions from the accomplished soloists. Leppard's alert
harpsichord continuo lays the foundations for performances where the colour and
energy of the music are finely observed. Particular joys are the late David Munrow's recorder, John Wilbraham's trumpet and Leppard's harpsichord playing.
The recording is well focused and warm.

Bach. Keyboard Concertos, BWV1052-58. **Chamber Orchestra of Europe/
András Schiff** (pf). Decca 425 676-2DH2.

Although Bach's duties in Leipzig centred on the church he also wrote secular
music for a series of coffee-house concerts, at which his keyboard concertos were
probably first performed. The *Brandenburgs* were *concerti grossi*, in which the
keyboard shares the limelight with other instruments; BWV1052-58 were the

first-ever true keyboard concertos, a genre of which Bach was the 'father'. Practically all the music of the concertos was adapted from existing works of various kinds — cantatas and concertos (mostly for the violin) and the Fourth *Brandenburg* Concerto, a time-saving expedient for a hard-pressed composer. The instrument for which they were written was of course the harpsichord, but only the most rabid purist would now object to their presentation on the piano — providing that it embodies no stylistic anachronism. Schiff, with the attentive support of both the COE and the recording engineers, comes the closest yet to achieving that elusive goal.

Bach. DOUBLE CONCERTOS. [a]**Jaap Schröder**, [a]**Christopher Hirons**, [b]**Catherine Mackintosh** (vns); [b]**Stephen Hammer** (ob); [c]**Christophe Rousset** (hpd); **Academy of Ancient Music/Christopher Hogwood** ([c]hpd). L'Oiseau-Lyre Florilegium 421 500-2OH. Item marked [a] from DSDL702 (8/82), [b] and [c] new to UK.
D minor for two violins, BWV1043[a]; C minor for violin and oboe, BWV1060[b]; C minor for two harpsichords, BWV1060[c]; C minor for two harpsichords, BWV1062[c].

58' DDD 9/89

The concept of a concerto with two or more soloists grew naturally out of the *concerto grosso*, and Bach was among those baroque composers who explored its possibilities. The Concerto in D minor, BWV1043, for two violins is perhaps the best known of his works in the *genre*, which Bach himself reworked as a Concerto for two harpsichords, BWV1062, in the key of C minor. No alternative version has survived in the case of the two-harpsichord Concerto BWV1060, also in C minor, but musicological evidence suggests that it was originally intended for two single-line instruments — two violins or one violin and an oboe. The work has thus been notionally reconstructed in the latter form and, unlike the other three concertos in this recording, it has at present no other version on CD; neither are these two revealing comparisons available on any other single disc. Baroque music never sounds better than when it is played on period instruments, in proper style, and by performers of the quality of those in this recording, not least the well matched soloists. The famous slow movement of BWV1043 is taken a little faster than usual, convincingly stripped of the specious senti-mentality with which it is often invested. The recording is of suitably high quality.

Bach. OBOE CONCERTOS — F major, BWV1053; D minor, BWV1059; A major, BWV1055. **Chamber Orchestra of Europe/Douglas Boyd** (ob, ob d'amore). DG 429 225-2GH.

46' DDD 4/90

Although Bach is not known to have written any concerto for the oboe he did entrust it with some beautiful *obbligato* parts, so he clearly did not underrate its expressive capacities. He did however rearrange many of his works for different instrumental media and there is musicological evidence that original oboe concertos were the (lost) sources from which other works were derived. The Harpsichord Concerto in A major, BWV1055, is believed originally to have been written for the oboe d'amore, whilst the other two Oboe Concertos have been reassembled from movements found in various cantatas. Whatever the validity of the academic reasoning, the results sound very convincing. Douglas Boyd is a superb oboist, with a clear sound that is free from stridency, and a fluency that belies the instrument's technical difficulty. He plays the faster, outer movements with winsome lightness of tongue and spirit, and with alertness to dynamic nuance; the slow ones, the hearts of these works, are given with sensitivity but without sentimentality — which can easily invade that of BWV1059, taken from Cantata No. 156, *Ich steh mit einem Fuss im Grabe*. The Chamber Orchestra of Europe partners him to perfection in this crisp recording.

Bach. ORCHESTRAL SUITES Nos. 1-4, BWV1066-69. **Amsterdam Baroque Orchestra/Ton Koopman.** Deutsche Harmonia Mundi RD77864. No. 1 in C major; No. 2 in B minor (with Wilbert Hazelzet, fl); No. 3 in D major; No. 4 in D major.

② 1h 19' DDD 1/90   P Ⓑ

There is no shortage of stylish performances on disc of Bach's four Orchestral Suites but the prospective buyer can be pointed towards this set with confidence. Ton Koopman and his Amsterdam Baroque Orchestra capture variously the ebullience, the courtly elegance and the subtle inflections of the music with unfailing charm. There are strongly contrasting colours in Bach's instrumentation and these are realized sensitively and with a degree of technical skill barely rivalled by other period instrument competitors. Oboes and bassoon play with assurance in the Suite No. 1 while in Suites Nos. 3 and 4, trumpets and drums make a thrilling contribution. The Suite No. 2 is a work of an altogether different character and here the solo flute playing of Wilbert Hazelzet deserves high praise. He is an artist of rare sensibility who reveals both a deep understanding of and warmth of affection towards music sometimes more elusive in character than that of the other three works. In short, there is little to disappoint the listener in playing that is stylistically informed, technically accomplished and altogether musicianly. Fine recorded sound.

Bach. The Art of Fugue, BWV1080[a]. A Musical Offering, BWV1079[b]. Canons, BWV1072-8; 1086-7[a]. **Cologne Musica Antiqua/Reinhard Goebel.** Archiv Produktion 413 642-2AH3. Booklet included. Items marked [a] from 413 728-1AH2 (4/85); [b] 2533 422 (11/79).

③ 2h 20' ADD 4/85

The great compilation of fugues, canons and a trio sonata which Bach dedicated to King Frederick the Great is one of the monuments of baroque instrumental music. Every contrapuntal device of canon at various intervals, augmentation, inversion, retrograde motion and so on is displayed here, and the performances are splendidly alive and authentic-sounding. It goes without saying that period instruments or modern replicas are used. The intellectually staggering *Art of Fugue* is a kind of testament to Bach's art and for this recording the instrumentation, unspecified by the composer, has been well chosen. The 14 miniature Canons which close this issue are for the most part a recent discovery and were written on a page of Bach's own copy of the *Goldberg Variations*; of curiosity value certainly but not much more than that. Excellent recording for these performances which have great authority.

NEW REVIEW

Bach. THE WORLD OF BACH. **Various artists**. Decca 430 499-2DWO. Suite No. 3 in D major, BWV1068 — Air (Academy of St Martin in the Fields/ Sir Neville Marriner). Cantata No. 147, Herz und Mund und Tat und Leben (Peter White, org; St John's College Choir, Cambridge/George Guest). Toccata and Fugue in D minor, BWV565 (Peter Hurford, org). Brandenburg Concerto No. 2 in F major, BWV1047 (Stuttgart Chamber Orchestra — Bernard Gabel, tpt; Aurèle Nicolet, fl; Helmut Winschermann, ob/Karl Münchinger). Cantata No. 140, Wachet auf! ruft uns die Stimme (Hurford, org). Suite No. 2 in B minor, BWV1067 — Menuet and Badinerie (Academy of St Martin in the

Fields/Marriner). Christmas Oratorio, BWV248 — Jauchzet, frohlocket! (Lübecker Kantorei; Stuttgart CO/Münchinger). Cantata No. 12, Weinen, Klagen, Sorgen, Zagen — Sinfonia (Roger Reversy, ob; Suisse Romande Orchestra/Ernest Ansermet). Mass in B minor, BWV232 — Agnus Dei (Kathleen Ferrier, contr; London Philharmonic Orchestra/Sir Adrian Boult). St Matthew Passion, BWV244 — Wir setzen uns mit Tränen nieder (Hymnus-Chorknaben Stuttgart; Stuttgart CO/Münchinger).

Ih 9' ADD 10/91 £ Ⓑ

Collections of this kind have had a tendency to be somewhat hotch-potch affairs. At best they provide the casual listener with a kind of mini-jukebox of 'classical hits' (presumably the more palatable offerings of the said composer), at worst a selection of badly edited out-takes of amputated chunks from great classics. Decca's "World of ..." series, however, has an excellent pedigree, nicely balancing the familiar with the not-so-familiar as well as preserving the artistic integrity of the original recordings from which they are taken. The familiar items on this disc need hardly any introduction: from the *Air on the G string* (made famous by a certain TV commercial advertising cigars), and the chorale *Jesu Joy of Man's Desiring* (a seemingly mandatory inclusion to any wedding service) through to the ubiquitous Toccata and Fugue in D minor. Less familiar perhaps (but no less ear catching) will be the opening chorus, "Jauchzet, frohlocket!" from the *Christmas Oratorio* and the Sinfonia from Cantata No. 12, *Weinen, Klagen, Sorgen, Zagen*. Other notable items include a very moving performance of the *Agnus Dei* from the Mass in B minor sung by Kathleen Ferrier (one of her finest recordings) and an equally moving account of the final chorus from *St Matthew Passion*. Fine performances, good recordings and a definite bargain.

Bach. VIOLIN SONATAS. **Monica Huggett** (vn); **Ton Koopman** (hpd). Philips 410 401-2PH2. From 410 401-1PH2 (8/84).
B minor, BWV1014; A major, BWV1015; E major, BWV1016; C minor, BWV1017; F minor, BWV1018; G major, BWV1019. Cantabile, ma un poco adagio, BWV1019*a*/1. Adagio, BWV1019*a*/2.

Ⓢ Ih 41' DDD 3/86

These six Sonatas were preserved only in the form of copies made by Bach's pupils and the date of their composition is unknown. Fortunately several copies were made and except in the case of the Sixth Sonata all the versions correspond. The works are of great importance in the historical development of the violin sonata. For the first time the keyboard instrument has a fully written out part and is treated as an equal and not merely as an obbligato instrument — indeed it is in many ways the senior partner. Huggett and Koopman have worked together for several years, and this is apparent in their confident and secure performances. Sometimes Huggett inclines towards blandness of expression, and Koopman seems the livelier musical personality, but these two discs will give great pleasure to those who like Bach played on period instruments. The recording leaves nothing to be desired.

Bach. FLUTE SONATAS. **Stephen Preston** (fl); [a]**Trevor Pinnock** (hpd); [b]**Jordi Savall** (va da gamba). CRD CRD3314/15. From CRD1014/15 (8/75).
Sonatas — B minor, BWV1030[a]; E flat major, BWV1031[a]; A major, BWV1032[a]; C major, BWV1033[ab]; E minor, BWV1034[ab]; E major, BWV1035[ab]. Partita in A minor, BWV1013.

Ⓢ Ih 38' ADD 1/90

Eight Flute Sonatas have at various times been attributed to Bach. Five of these are certainly from his hand: BWV1030, 1032, 1034-5 and 1013. The first two are for flute and 'concertate' harpsichord (true duos in which the keyboard part is fully notated), the second are for flute and continuo (the keyboard player is left to fill out his part from the figured bass), and the last, a Partita, is for flute alone. The authenticity of two, BWV1031 and 1033 (both for flute and continuo), is questioned but their musical quality is sufficient to make the doubts almost irrelevant; the remaining Sonata, BWV1020, omitted from this recording, is now recognized to have been misattributed. These were not the earliest works of their kind but they are by far the most adventurous and substantial of their time, and the best of them have rightly been described as masterpieces; BWV1013 is a *tour de force* in which the single-line instrument clothes its melody with implied harmony — and even counterpoint. The baroque flute is a gentle instrument that caresses the sound and pitch of its notes, an art of which Preston is a master. Pinnock is the perfect partner, as also is Savall in the 'with-continuo' items, and the recording captures the warm intimacy of these wonderful works.

Bach. Sonatas and Partitas for Solo Violin, BWV1001-06. **Oscar Shumsky** (vn). ASV CDDCD454.
Sonatas: No. 1 in G minor, BWV1001; No. 2 in A minor, BWV1003; No. 3 in C major, BWV1005. *Partitas:* No. 1 in B minor, BWV1002; No. 2 in D minor, BWV1004; No. 3 in E major, BWV1006.

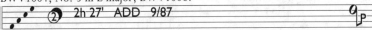

2h 27' ADD 9/87

NEW REVIEW

Bach. Sonatas and Partitas for Solo Violin, BWV1001-06. **Henryk Szeryng** (vn). CBS Masterworks Portrait mono CD46721. Recorded in 1956, new to UK.
Sonatas: No. 1 in G minor, BWV1001; No. 2 in A minor, BWV1003; No. 3 in C major, BWV1005. *Partitas:* No. 1 in B minor, BWV1002; No. 2 in D minor, BWV1004; No. 3 in E major, BWV1006.

2h 8' ADD 12/91

It was during his employment at the Court of Prince Leopold of Cöthen that Bach was able to devote himself to writing secular music. His six innovatory Suites for the cello and the six works for solo violin date from this period (*c.*1720) and could have been written only by someone with an intimate practical knowledge of the instrument. As the small fingerboard of the violin enables the player's left hand to encompass complex textures, Bach took full advantage of this. It remains difficult, even in the hi-tech state of today's violinistic art, simply to produce the notes with accurate intonation and without making heavy weather of the three- and four-note chords, but that is only the beginning. The player still has to realize the part-writing and to absorb and project the style and spirit of the immensely varied movements. All these parameters, and more, are admirably met by Oscar Shumsky; with his excellent recording one is able to fully appreciate the richness of the music, with little consciousness of the immense technical skill that makes the performances possible.

Excellent as Shumsky is, CBS offers us a mid-price alternative with their reissue demonstrating the extraordinary combination of virtuosity and musical insight displayed by the Polish violinist Henryk Szeryng. More widely known for his performances of the romantic rather than the baroque repertoire, in this recording Szeryng's immaculate technique is placed entirely at the service of some of Bach's most beautiful music. His sureness of intonation and mastery of phrasing and tempo result in readings which reach to the core of these great works. CBS's rich and atmospheric acoustic creates exactly the right sense of distance between player and listener. This reissue, by any standards an outstanding recording of violin playing, should do much both to enhance and revive Szeryng's posthumous reputation, and to communicate Bach's genius as a composer.

Bach. Solo Cello Suites, BWV1007-12. **Pierre Fournier.** DG 419 359-2GCM2. Items marked [a] from Archiv Produktion SAPM198 186 (11/62), [b] SAPM198 187 (3/63), [c] SAPM198 188 (6/63).
No. 1 in G major[a]; No. 2 in D minor[a]; No. 3 in C major[b]; No. 4 in E flat major[b]; No. 5 in C minor[c]; No. 6 in D major[c].

② 2h 19' ADD 3/89 £

Pierre Fournier made this fine recording during the early 1960s. His sense of style, unerring rhythmic intuition, polished technique and noble poise have lost none of their charm or potency during the intervening years. Fournier is out-standingly perceptive in his treatment of the Preludes with their improvisatory character. In his hands they unfold with a majestic grace whose grand gestures are nevertheless light of tread. Sarabandes are declaimed with a profound aware-ness of their poetic content while Allemandes, Courantes and the little 'galan-teries' are full of nimble, dance-like gestures. Above all, Fournier's playing is richly endowed with eloquence and lyricism matched by a warm, resonant tone. He belonged to a generation which generally did not make concessions towards 'authenticity' where tuning and choice of instruments are concerned. Thus in the Fifth and Sixth Suites Fournier remains content with his standard cello with its conventional tuning and four strings. No matter, for in these works he is bril-liantly communicative, placing an unsurpassed technique at the service of two of the most challenging works in the solo cello repertory. The recorded sound is excellent.

Bach. KEYBOARD WORKS. **Maggie Cole** (hpd). Virgin Classics Veritas VC7 90712-2.
Chromatic Fantasia and Fugue in D minor, BWV903. Partita No. 1 in B flat major, BWV825. Toccata, Adagio and Fugue in G major, BWV916. Prelude, Fugue and Allegro in E flat major, BWV998. Italian Concerto in F major, BWV971.

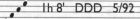
1h 2' DDD 1/89

NEW REVIEW

Bach. KEYBOARD WORKS. **Christophe Rousset** (hpd). L'Oiseau-Lyre 433 054-2OH.
Italian Concerto in F major, BWV971. Overture in the French style in B minor, BWV831. Duettos, BWV802-05. Chromatic Fantasia and Fugue in D minor, BWV903.

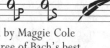
1h 8' DDD 5/92

Christophe Rousset   [photo: Decca/Masclet]

The recital by Maggie Cole includes three of Bach's best known solo harpsichord pieces: the *Italian Concerto*, the *Chromatic Fantasia and Fugue* in D minor, and the *Partita No. 1 in B flat*. The other works will perhaps be less familiar, but together these pieces provide a fascinating example of the wide range of forms, disciplines and national traits which Bach assimi-lated into his keyboard writing. Cole's performances are carefully thought out and meticulously executed, with a nice sense of poise and easy gracefulness in her playing. There is no empty rhetoric here but rather a lucid exposition of the music which is almost always coherent in its articulation, elegant in its phrasing and unhurried in its measure. The instrument itself is a beauty — a Dutch harpsichord of 1612 by Ruckers — and the fine recording was made in the National Trust's Fenton House, Hampstead in north London. Helpful, informed presentation furthermore sets the seal on a splendid issue.

The French harpsichordist, Christophe Rousset brings a comparable lucidity to Bach's music in his recital where, like Cole, he shows concern for eloquent phrasing and refinement of detail. Rousset's *Italian Concerto* is free from intrusive affectation and interpreted with commendably modest virtuosity while in the *Chromatic Fantasia and Fugue* he illuminates for the listener Bach's harmonically bold and broad concept. The other major work in his recital is the Overture in B minor from the second part of Bach's *Clavier-Übung*. Here the composer translates a French-style orchestral suite to the medium of a two-manual harpsichord. Rousset effectively conveys the occasional character of the overture itself, as well as bringing out the varied character of the subsequent dance movements. Four Duettos, which closely correspond with Bach's better-known *Two-Part Inventions* but which do not specifically belong to the harpsichord repertory, round off an impressive recital. The mid-eighteenth century instrument by Henri Hemsch is very well recorded.

Bach. The Well-tempered Clavier, Book 2, BWV870-93. **András Schiff** (pf). Decca 417 236-2DH2.

2h 24' DDD 3/87

NEW REVIEW

Bach. The Well-tempered Clavier, Books 1 and 2, BWV846-93. **Davitt Moroney** (hpd). Harmonia Mundi HMC90 1285/8.

4h 32' DDD 4/89

NEW REVIEW

Bach. The Well-tempered Clavier, Books 1 and 2, BWV846-93. **Edwin Fischer** (pf). EMI Références mono CHS7 63188-2. From HMV DB2079/85 (recorded 1933), DB2292/8 (12/34), DB2532/8 (1935), DB2944/50 (2/37) and DB3236/9 (9/37).

3h 57' ADD 3/90 ▲

There are currently several versions in the catalogue which shed light in a variety of different ways on this orderly yet entertaining anthology. András Schiff, playing Book 2, shows that he possesses the technical assurance and exceptional mental clarity needed to play Bach's *48* well. He produces lucid textures, keeping contrapuntal strands alive and particularly interesting is the way he varies phrasing or balance in the repeats of Prelude sections. Sensibly, he uses the piano as a piano and not an imitation harpsichord, managing to steer a middle course between coldly mechanical and overly romantic treatments. For the most part his rhythmic control is admirable; and after the excesses of some other noted Bach pianists his freedom from eccentricities is particularly welcome. The recorded quality is excellent, and to have satisfactorily contained 144 minutes of music on two discs is altogether admirable.

For those wanting both books of the *48*, the choice is wide. With some 16 or more versions currently available on CD the listener is confronted by a daunting process of selection. Davitt Moroney is a gifted and serious-minded artist whose performances are technically secure, stylistically informed and thoughtful. Empty rhetoric, uncalled-for flamboyance or superfluous gesture are not for him; indeed, on occasion listeners might feel that a degree of spontaneity is lacking. Yet where this playing is constantly impressive is in the successful marriage of virtuosity with the poetic content of the music. In short Moroney makes the music sing with carefully shaped phrases, admirable rhythmic suppleness and well-defined articulation. No listener will find all he wants from any one performance of these masterpieces since different registrations, tempos and indeed instruments bring out different colours and induce in us different responses. Moroney highlights many of the almost infinite contrasts which exist in the music with sensibility and affection. The instrument is effectively balanced, if a shade too closely, allowing listeners to discern subtle details in Bach's writing.

Edwin Fischer's recording was made in the early- to mid-1930s and possesses a quality recently described by Alfred Brendel in a letter to *Gramophone* as utterly timeless, thoroughly unmannered and deeply moving. Fischer was seldom at ease in the recording studio and prospective investors in this set may as well accept from the start that he probably plays more wrong notes than any of his competitors in the same field. But his interpretations are so full of insight, his sensibility so acute and his feeling for poetry often so intense that fluffs and stumbles which would bring down any artist with less to say pale into relative insignificance. Notwithstanding notational errors, Fischer's technique is well able to convey shades of expressive nuance and it is this rare quality, more than any other, which serves to underline the poetic element in Bach's music. Nowadays, we may consider his approach "romantic", but "expressive" would be a more appropriate term. The direct, unpretentious, uncluttered line Fischer maintains between the music and the listener is one of many delights contained in this historic recording. The transfer from the original 78s is as clear and sympathetic as one could realistically hope for.

Bach. French Suites, BWV812-7. Suite in A minor, BWV818*a*. Suite in E flat major, BWV819*a*. **Davitt Moroney** (hpd). Virgin Classics Veritas VCD7 91201-2.

2h 24'　DDD　4/91

Bach. French Suites, BWV812-17. **Gustav Leonhardt** (hpd). RCA Victor Seon GD71963. From Philips 6709 500 (10/77).

1h 18'　ADD　5/90

Bach compiled his *French Suites*, so-called — the composer himself did not give them this title — towards the end of his Cöthen period and at the beginning of his final appointment at Leipzig. As well as performing the customary six suites, five of which have survived in Bach's own hand, Davitt Moroney includes two further suites prepared by Bach's pupil, Heinrich Nikolaus Gerber, in 1725. These and extra movements to the well-known six suites belong to various surviving sources and though we can be sure that Bach himself had good reason to discard them from his final thoughts, so-to-speak, their presence in this album is nonetheless welcome. Moroney has given careful thought and preparation to the project and the results are often illuminating. His interpretations are relaxed, articulate and show a lively awareness of the music's poetic content. There is a clarity in these performances which stems from lucid punctuation highlighting the significance of every phrase. Shorter dance movements have poise and are allowed to breathe while longer ones, notably *allemandes,* have a taut rhythmic elasticity which enable the listener to savour their eloquent often pensive inflexions. Perhaps *sarabandes* are sometimes a little too weighty, but this is to some extent a matter of taste and few will be disappointed by Moroney's stylistically informed and technically fluent playing. The recording is excellent.

Over a period of some 25 years Gustav Leonhardt has recorded all the major Bach harpsichord repertory. Many of the releases have established themselves at the forefront of Bach interpretation, illuminating audiences and an inspiration to a younger generation of harpsichord players. One aspect of more recent recordings by Leonhardt which must disappoint listeners is his disdain for the conventional double-bar repeat. In this respect the French Suites fare better since many, though not all, repeats are observed. Allemandes and Gigues generally are not afforded repeats while Courantes, Sarabandes and the simpler galanteries such as Menuets, Gavottes and Bourrées usually qualify for some or all of them. The most beguiling features of Leonhardt's interpretation, however, lies in rhythmic suppleness, a graceful feeling for gesture, eloquence of phrase, clarity of articulation and a sure understanding of Bach's infinitely varied melodic patterns. These are performances full of energy yet retaining a courtly elegance which complements the spirit of the stylized dance. The character of the harpsichord, a Taskin copy, is faithfully conveyed, though the recorded sound may strike listeners as a shade too reverberant

NEW REVIEW

Bach. Goldberg Variations, BWV988. **Huguette Dreyfus** (hpd). Denon CO-73677.

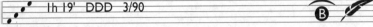

NEW REVIEW

Bach. Goldberg Variations, BWV988. KEYBOARD WORKS. **Virginia Black** (hpd). Collins Classics 7003-2.
Prelude in G major, BWV902/1. Fantasia in C minor, BWV906/1. Adagio in G major, BWV968. Chromatic Fantasia and Fugue in D minor, BWV903.

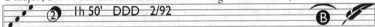

Bach. Goldberg Variations, BWV988. **András Schiff** (pf). Decca 417 116-2DH. From D275D2 (1/84).

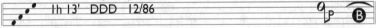

Insomniac Count Hermann Carl von Kayserling, so that his harpsichordist might relieve the monotony of his sleepless hours, commissioned Bach to write some quiet and cheerful music for which he rewarded him with a golden goblet containing 100 Louis d'or, probably the largest single fee he ever received. The *Variations*, a virtual compendium of contemporary keyboard techniques, become more difficult as the work progresses, but all the above players meet their demands brilliantly. The theme itself and each variation is in two sections, each marked to be repeated, and every performer has his/her own view on their appropriate speeds; only those chosen by Schiff have allowed the work to be confined to one disc, whilst still giving each repeat. A performance of this quality is a *tour de force* (the *Variations* are much harder to play on the single keyboard of a piano) and will satisfy anyone who prefers a piano to a harpsichord. Huguette Dreyfus gives a fine account of the work on one disc, but has to sacrifice the repeats in the *da capo Aria*. Virginia Black, with some beneficially slower tempos, omits nothing and thus overflows onto a second disc, which she fills with other solid fare. If you are content with a loaf that has a bit chopped off one end, and want no further sustenance, Dreyfus will give every satisfaction; if not, Black's two-disc set is clearly the first choice. All three versions, though different in some of their approaches, are of such quality that your choice will depend on the other factors mentioned above.

NEW REVIEW

Bach. Orgelbüchlein, BWV599-644. **Simon Preston** (org). DG 431 816-2GH. Played on the Lorentz organ of Sorø Abbey, Denmark.

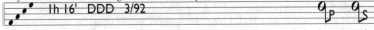

Bach's *Orgelbüchlein* ("Little Organ Book") contains 46 short preludes based on the chorale melodies used in the Lutheran church. It is arranged to follow the course of the church's year, beginning in Advent, passing through Christmas, Lent,

Easter, Ascension, Pentecost and Trinity and ending with those miscellaneous areas classified in most hymn-books as "General". But Bach was not merely providing the church organist with something useful (although its enduring usefulness is still evident today — walk into almost any church and at some point you are likely to find the organist delving into a copy of Bach's *Orgelbüchlein*), he also intended these as teaching pieces. The title page describes them as offering "instruction in the various ways of working out a chorale, and also practice in the use of the pedals". What wonderful teaching pieces these are for any organ student — training exercises of this calibre would surely be enough to tempt anyone into learning how to play the organ! Here with that accomplished organist, Simon Preston, playing a ravishing Danish instrument sumptuously recorded by DG, the full genius of Bach is revealed. At just over an hour and a quarter, this CD represents astonishing value not just in playing time, but also in the quality of the playing, the magnificent recorded sound and, above all, the wealth of truly great music.

Bach. ORGAN PARTITAS. **Simon Preston.** DG 429 775-2GH. Played on the Lorentz organ of Sorø Abbey, Denmark.
Christ, der du bist der helle Tag, BWV766; O Gott, du frommer Gott, BWV767; Sei gegrüsset, Jesu gütig, BWV768; Ach, was soll ich Sünder machen?, BWV770.

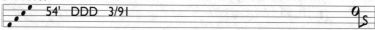

At the last count the number of chorale preludes for organ believed to be by Bach was 239. In addition there are six Chorale Preludes — more extended sets of variations on the Lutheran chorales. These continue a tradition some of the greatest masters of which were Bach's immediate predecessors Böhm, Buxtehude and Pachelbel. While Bach's magnificent set on *Vom Himmel hoch, da komm ich her* (not included on this disc) is generally regarded as the pinnacle of the genre, the other partitas are all early works and with the exception of that based on *Sei gegrüsset* do not call for pedals. It seems that these pieces could just as easily have been intended for domestic consumption by harpsichordists as for church use by organists. As such, they have perhaps been somewhat overlooked by present-day organists, yet as this captivating disc shows most convincingly, the music contains an abundant wealth of variety, interest and charm. Simon Preston is on excellent form, showing his customary formidable technical mastery. His performances bring this music vividly to life and he unearths an astonishing variety of tone colours from a famous and historic organ. All of this is recorded with outstanding clarity and the overall sound is simply delicious.

Bach. ORGAN WORKS. **Christopher Herrick.** Hyperion CDA66434. Played on the Metzler organ of the Stadtkirche, Zofingen, Switzerland.
Toccatas and Fugues — D minor, BWV565; F major, BWV540; D minor, BWV538, "Dorian". Toccata, Adagio and Fugue in C major, BWV564. Passacaglia and Fugue in C minor, BWV582.

If you only have one disc of organ music in your collection, this must be it. It more than fulfils all the basic criteria which combine to make a 'Good CD'. First the music. Here are the five most important and impressive organ works by the indisputable king of organ music. Everyone knows Bach's *Toccata and Fugue* in D minor and such is its popularity that it is currently the most widely available piece of organ music on CD. Of the others, many would consider the *Passacaglia and Fugue* as the finest piece of organ music ever written while the *Adagio* from the *Toccata, Adagio and Fugue* is as beautiful a melody as can ever have been composed for the instrument. Second the performances. Christopher Herrick's playing is simply outstanding. He has just the right blend of dramatic flair, technical virtuosity and musical sensitivity. He avoids personal idiosyncrasies (rare indeed in such an old war-horse as the D minor) and maintains a bright, lively approach throughout the entire programme, giving it all a wonderful lift. Finally the recording. Hyperion have found the ideal organ set in the most magnificent of acoustics. Their recording has caught the finest detail with total clarity while the overall opulence of sound is a sheer aural delight.

Bach. ORGAN WORKS. Volume 3. **Peter Hurford.** Decca Ovation 421 617-2DM3. From Argo D150D3 (7/79).
Chorale Variations and Partitas, BWV766-71. The Schübler Chorale Preludes, BWV645-50. Chorale Preludes — Herr Jesu Christ, dich zu uns wend', BWV726; Herzlich tut mich verlangen, BWV727; Jesus, meine Zuversicht, BWV728; In dulci jubilo, BWV729; Liebster Jesu, wir sind hier, BWV730; Liebster Jesu, wir sind hier, BWV731; Lobt Gott, ihr Christen, allzugleich, BWV732; Meine Seele erhebt den Herrn, BWV733; Nun freut euch, lieben Christen g'mein, BWV734; Valet will ich dir geben, BWV735; Valet will ich dir geben, BWV736; Vater unser im Himmelreich, BWV737; Vom Himmel hoch, da komm'ich her, BWV738; Wie schön leuchtet der Morgenstern, BWV739; Wir glauben all' an einen Gott, BWV740. Concertos — No. 1 in G major, BWV592; No. 2 in A minor, BWV593; No. 3 in C major, BWV594; No. 4 in C major, BWV595; No. 5 in D minor, BWV596; No. 6 in E flat, BWV597.

③ 3h 31' ADD 6/90

Peter Hurford   *[photo: Decca/Holt*

Most record collectors will be familiar with Bach's great organ works; not least the ubiquitous *Toccata and Fugue* in D minor. While these are undeniably essential ingredients in any CD collection they represent only a tiny fraction of Bach's enormous output for the instrument. The majority of his organ music was based on Lutheran chorales: the equivalent of today's hymn-tune. Generally these are what are known as chorale preludes; miniature pieces reflecting both the chorale's melody and the character of its words. Here are some of Bach's most ingenious and personal creations. In more extended form are the six Chorale Partitas which provide variations for each of the verses of the original chorale. Unique among his organ works are the secular concertos, transcriptions of string concertos by Vivaldi and Ernst. While Bach made few changes to the original, his unique genius has turned typically Italianate violin writing (in the third even the violin cadenzas have been retained) into something utterly at ease on the organ. Here is some of the most charming and effervescent music in the entire repertoire. Peter Hurford's playing, Decca's superlative recordings and a selection of top-rate organs from around the world provide the best realization imaginable of these works. If a three-disc set of lesser-known Bach organ works (even at mid-price) seems a tall order, rest assured you are buying some of the finest organ music, organ playing and organ recordings available. Here is a recording to be dipped into time and time again; it never loses its freshness or ability to captivate.

Bach. ORGAN WORKS. Volume 4. **Peter Hurford.** Decca Ovation 421 621-2DM3.

Chorales from the Neumeister Collection Nos. 1-35. Chorale Preludes, BWV651-668, The "Eighteen". Chorale Preludes — O Lamm Gottes unschuldig, NBA; Ach Gott und Herr, BWV714; Allein Gott in der Höh' sei Ehr', BWV715; Allein Gott in der Höh' sei Ehr', BWV716; Allein Gott in der Höh', BWV717; Christ lag in Todesbanden, BWV718; Der Tag, der ist so freudenrich, BWV719; Ein' feste Burg ist unser Gott, BWV720; Erbarm' dich mein, o Herre Gott, BWV721; Gelobet seist du, Jesu Christ, BWV722; Gelobet seist du, Jesu Christ, BWV723; Gottes Sohn ist kommen, BWV724; Herr Gott, dich loben wir, BWV725.

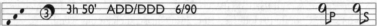
③ 3h 50' ADD/DDD 6/90

It's tantalizing to think that there is still music written by the great composers lying untouched and unrecognized by past generations just waiting to be discovered. That such major finds are still cropping up was evidenced in 1984, fortuitously timed for the tercentenary celebration of Bach's birth, when two scholars working independently in Yale University library came across a substantial manuscript put together in the early nineteenth century by J.G. Neumeister. Here they unearthed no less than 38 chorales for organ by Bach, most of which were not previously known to exist. Most experts accept them as genuine, although some doubts still exist. But for the CD collector such doubts should be irrelevant, for regardless of the music's origins, here is the fourth (and final) boxed set of Peter Hurford's landmark recordings of Bach's complete organ music; recordings no serious collector should be without. The music is wonderful; included here are, in addition to the 'Neumeister' chorales, some of Bach's greatest chorale-based organ works. Hurford's playing is a delight to behold. Every piece, no matter how small or simple, is treated as the gem it is; with loving care and an unerring sensitivity towards the finest detail. As with the other discs in the series, Decca have taken their microphones quite literally around the world to find the best instruments for the music — here organs from England, Germany, Austria, America and Australia are featured. The results from both a musical and technical point of view are superlative. Discs two and three were originally issued on LP and it goes almost without saying, given the emphasis on excellence with this entire venture, that the transfers to CD are magnificent.

Bach. ORGAN WORKS. Volume 3. **Ton Koopman.** Novalis 150036-2.
Played on the organ of the Great Church, Leeuwarden, Holland.
"Dorian" Toccata and Fugue in D minor, BWV538. Partita on "Sei gegrüsset, Jesu gutig", BWV768. Fantasia in G major, BWV572. Trio Sonata No. 6 in G major, BWV530. Chorale Preludes — "Vater Unser im Himmelreich", BWV682; "Jesu Christus unser Heiland", BWV688. Prelude and Fugue in A minor, BWV543.

1h 10' DDD 8/89

The Young Bach. Michael Murray. Telarc CD80179. Played on the organ of the College of St Thomas, St Paul, Minnesota, USA.
Prelude and Fugues — C major, BWV531; G minor, BWV535; D minor, BWV539. Concerto No. 1 in G major, BWV592. Fantasia in G major, BWV572. Prelude in C major, BWV567. "Little" Fugue in G minor, BWV578. Canzona in D minor, BWV588. Chorale Prelude "In dulci jubilo", BWV751.

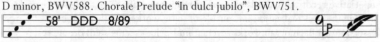
58' DDD 8/89

It is inconceivable that any self-respecting CD collection would not contain at least one disc of Bach's organ music and here are two which constitute 'Good CDs' from any standpoint. The playing is unwavering in its excellence, the instruments are well chosen, the combined programmes present a good cross-section of some of Bach's finest (if not exactly his best-known) organ compositions and the recordings are superlative (indeed Telarc's sound is nothing short of stunning). The one work common to both (the *Fantasia* in G) receives such utterly different interpretations that it is well worth having in both versions. Ton Koopman (playing on an instrument built when Bach was 42) is an acknowledged Bach expert and whilst his performances undoubtedly show scholarship and a keen appreciation of style, they are also exceedingly enjoyable in their own right. In fact, Koopman's playing is so compelling and vivacious that he manages to make accessible works which in lesser hands come across as dull and academic. Michael Murray uses a much more modern instrument. It has a bright, forthright tone which is ideally suited to this joyous and energetic music. Murray, too, plays with an infectious enthusiasm and allows the music to speak for itself, never allowing fussiness of detail or extravagant use of the organ to obscure the sheer ebullience of the writing.

Bach. ORGAN WORKS. **Nicholas Danby.** CBS Digital Masters CD45807. Played on the organ of Lübeck Cathedral, Germany.
Chorale Preludes — Wachet auf, ruft uns die stimme, BWV645; Nun komm' der Heiden Heiland, BWV659; Dies sind die Heil'gen zehn gebot', BWV678; Liebster Jesu, wir sind hier, BWV706; Herr Jesu Christ, dich zu uns wend', BWV709; Erbarm' dich mein, O Herre Gott, BWV721; Herzlich thut mich verlangen, BWV727; Vater unser im Himmelreich, BWV737; Aus der tiefe rufe ich, BWV745. Fantasia in G major, BWV572. Prelude and Fugues — A minor, BWV543; C minor, BWV546. Toccata and Fugue in D minor, BWV565.

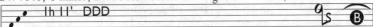

This is an excellent CD on every count. The music is wonderful, Bach at his most varied and interesting. The playing is sympathetic, tasteful, elegant and persuasive, with the organ making a really sumptuous sound. And the recording is exemplary, perfectly realizing the cathedral's warm atmosphere and the organ's splendid array of charms, but without any disturbing background thuds or clatters. Add to all this a generous playing time (forget about the useless accompanying booklet) and here is a disc for everyone's collection. Nicholas Danby has planned his programme with commendable good sense. It begins and ends with quiet reflective Chorale Preludes and passes through the powerful, quasi-orchestral C minor Prelude and Fugue, the exciting A minor Prelude and Fugue, the colourful Fantasia (one of the best performances of all, this) and numerous Chorale Preludes of widely differing moods before launching into everybody's favourite, the Toccata and Fugue in D minor. It makes compelling listening. This is not a disc from which to pick out your favourites; sit down, press 'play' and enjoy an hour and ten minutes' worth of unfettered pleasure.

Bach (arr. Bylsma). Partita in E major, BWV1006. Sonata in A minor, BWV1013 (trans. G minor). Sonata in A minor, BWV1003. **Anner Bylsma** (vc piccolo). Deutsche Harmonia Mundi RD77998.

Anner Bylsma, one of Holland's leading string players, has produced here a recording of sheer delight, revealing with amazing insight, dexterity and musicianship the unexplored potential of the violoncello piccolo — in this instance a genuine child's instrument, tuned down a generous semitone and played with a Dutch Baroque bow. The three unaccompanied works are well calculated to demonstrate the unexpected qualities of the smaller cello, which, according to Bylsma, is the true bass of the violin family. In the *Partita* we are given a first taste of the delicacy, grace and lightness of touch appropriate to such a diminutive bass instrument. In the *Allemande* and the *Sarabande* of the G minor Sonata we experience the full palette of its varied sonorities, so different from those of the larger standard instrument; enjoy the speed and flow of the *Corrente* and the quiet humour of the *Bourrée Anglaise*. The *Grave*, which opens the A minor Sonata, is one of those pieces where composer, performer and instrument are totally at one and it was precisely such a coming together of all the elements that makes the 'rightness' of this unique recital convincing; indeed, it provides a degree of musical enjoyment rarely encountered.

Bach. TOCCATAS. **Bob van Asperen** (hpd). EMI Reflexe CDC7 54081-2. F sharp minor, BWV910; C minor, BWV911; D minor, BWV912; D minor, BWV913; E minor, BWV914; G minor, BWV915; G major, BWV916.

1h 7' DDD 5/91

Bob van Asperen is a fine exponent of Bach's harpsichord music. His interpretations are considered, articulate and technically fluent if on occasion a shade severe. The latter reservation, however, would be entirely misplaced in the context of his recital of Bach's seven harpsichord Toccatas (BWV910-16). The music dates from the composer's Weimar period (1708-17) and its idiom is richly endowed with contrast and variety. A youthful energy infuses these pieces with flourishes, embellishments, exuberant passagework, engaging dance measures and a multitude of expressive gestures. Van Asperen conveys the markedly improvisatory character present in several of the movements with panache while at the same time never sacrificing clarity of thought or a firm rhythmic pulse in the interests of empty virtuosity. This is firmly disciplined playing with an under-lying passion which perhaps might have been allowed to surface more prominently. These are, nevertheless, interpretations which enable us to marvel at Bach's fertile imagination and wide terms of reference; performances which in equal measure stem from intellectual and technical rigour. The recorded sound is ideal.

Bach. The Art of Fugue, BWV1080. **Davitt Moroney** (hpd). Harmonia Mundi HMC90 1169/70.

(2) 1h 39' DDD 5/86

Bach died before the process of engraving his last great work had been completed, thus leaving a number of issues concerning performance in some doubt. However, Davitt Moroney is a performer-scholar who has a mature understanding of the complexity of Bach's work; in a lucid essay in the booklet, he discusses the problems of presenting *The Art of Fugue* whilst at the same time explaining his approach to performing it. Certain aspects of this version will be of particular importance to prospective buyers: Moroney, himself, has completed Contrapunctus 14 but he also plays the same Contrapunctus in its unfinished state as a fugue on three subjects. He omits Bach's own reworkings for two harpsichords of Contrapunctus 13 on the grounds that they do not play a part in the composer's logically-constructed fugue cycle; and he omits the Chorale Prelude in G major (BWV668a) which certainly had nothing to do with Bach's scheme but was added in the edition of 1751 so that the work should not end in an incomplete state. Moroney's performing technique is of a high order, placing emphasis on the beauty of the music which he reveals with passionate conviction. Exemplary presentation and an appropriate recorded sound enhance this fine achievement.

Bach. Cantatas — Nos. 5-8. **Paul Esswood** (alto); **Kurt Equiluz** (ten); **Max van Egmond** (bass); **Vienna Boys' Choir; Chorus Viennensis; Vienna Concentus Musicus/Nikolaus Harnoncourt; Regensburger Domspatzen; King's College Choir, Cambridge; Leonhardt Consort/Gustav Leonhardt.** Teldec 2292-42498-2. Texts and translations included. From Telefunken SKW2 (2/72).

No. 5, Wo soll ich fliehen hin; No. 6, Bleib bei uns, denn ens will Abend werden; No. 7, Christ unser Herr zum Jordan kam; No. 8, Liebster Gott, wann werd' ich sterben.

② 1h 27' ADD 9/85

King's College Choir, Cambridge [photo: EMI/Chlala]

It was during Bach's final period of employment as Cantor at the Leipzig Thomass that he wrote his great series of church cantatas. His powerful Lutheran beliefs here fuse with his musical genius to create a series of beautifully integrated works. *Wo soll ich fliehen hin* follows the typical pattern: opening chorale; bass recitative; tenor aria (with a lovely viola obbligato); alto recitative; bass aria (with a characterful rhythm); soprano recitative; final chorale (in a stately measured gait). The effect is to illustrate with the greatest possible variety the religious measure of the service. This set is an excellent introduction to Bach's cantata writing with four uniformly accomplished and varied works. Harnoncourt and Leonhardt's cantata series is one of the monuments of the recorded age, a magnificent achievement that still continues. The soloists are excellent and the orchestras and choirs perform with imagination.

NEW REVIEW

Bach. Cantatas — No. 56, Ich will den Kreuzstab gerne tragen; No. 82, Ich habe genug; No. 158, Der Friede sei mit dir[a]. [a]**Laurie Monahan** (sop); [a]**Douglas Stevens** (alto); [a]**William Hite** (ten); **Jan Opalach** (bass); **The Bach Ensemble/Joshua Rifkin** (org). L'Oiseau-Lyre 425 822-2OH. Texts and translations included.

51' DDD 9/91 Ⓑ

The three cantatas on this disc are for solo bass voice with an additional concluding four-voice chorale in two of them. *Ich habe genug* and *Ich will den Kreuzstab* are among Bach's best-known cantatas, the former containing the sublime aria "Schlummert ein, ihr matten Augen". Bach penned several versions of this tender lullaby and, in the present one the director Joshua Rifkin opts for that which the composer used for his last known performance in the late 1740s. It includes an oboe de caccia which reinforces the first violin part — an inspired, deeply affecting masterstroke. The bass, Jan Opalach, is a thoughtful singer whose close attention to the texts results in subtly coloured declamation. The performances are not without occasional weak moments felt mainly in ensemble but also occasionally in rhythm. The fine oboe playing of Stephen Hammer — his role is prominent in Cantatas 56 and 82 — provides a rewarding partnership with the voice though he cannot always conceal fatigue induced by the heavy demands made upon him by the music. But all-in-all this is a satisfying disc well recorded and well documented.

Bach. Cantatas — No. 106, Gottes Zeit ist die allerbeste Zeit, "Actus tragicus"; No. 118, O Jesu Christ, meins Lebens Licht; No. 198, Lass, Fürstin, lass noch einen Strahl, "Trauer Ode". **Nancy Argenta** (sop); **Michael Chance** (alto); **Anthony Rolfe Johnson** (ten); **Stephen Varcoe** (bass); **Monteverdi Choir; English Baroque Soloists/John Eliot Gardiner.** Archiv Produktion 429 782-2AH. Texts and translations included.

59' DDD 5/91

The cantatas on this disc illustrate the astonishing range of effects with which Bach, at different periods in his life, treated the subject of death. Cantata No. 106 is one of the very earliest of Bach's surviving sacred cantatas and dates from 1707 when the composer was employed briefly at Mühlhausen. Cantata No. 198, by contrast, is a Leipzig piece written in 1727 and performed at a memorial service for Christiane Eberhardine, Queen of Poland, Electoral Princess of Saxony and wife of Augustus the Strong. The two works could hardly be more different from one another, the earlier with a strong biblical orientation, the later an elegy, an evocation of death by the German Enlightenment poet Gottsched. Gardiner's interpretations have all the technical refinement with which we associate his performances and his soloists by-and-large are first rate. The *Actus tragicus* comes over especially well with unhurried but effectively contrasted tempos; the other is perhaps more variable only intermittently capturing the deep pathos of Bach's music. The disc also includes a beautiful funeral motet, *O Jesu Christ, meins Lebens Licht* (BWV118), performed here in its later version dating from around 1740.

Bach. Cantatas — No. 140, Wachet auf! ruft uns die Stimme; No. 147, Herz und Mund und Tat und Leben. **Vienna Concentus Musicus/Nikolaus Harnoncourt.** Teldec 2292-43109-2.

1h ADD

Nikolaus Harnoncourt   *[photo: Teldec/Katz/Richmond]*

This is another disc drawn from Teldec's pioneering Bach Cantata series shared by Harnoncourt and Leonhardt. Harnoncourt directs both cantatas here with a strong team of soloists, the Tolz Boys' Choir and the Vienna Concentus Musicus. Cantata No. 140 *Wachet auf!*, which includes the famous 'Sleepers wake', is variously charged with excitement, anticipation and tenderness. There are strong contributions from the solo treble, Allan Bergius, Kurt Equiluz, the oboist Jürg Schaeftlein and Alice Harnoncourt who gives a lyrical account of the violino piccolo solo in the first duet. Cantata No. 147 *Herz und Mund und Tat und Leben* includes the much loved chorale verses which conclude the first and second parts of the work, popularly known as "Jesu, joy of man's desiring", with a colourful assembly of instruments underlining the joyful nature of the Feast of the Visitation of Mary the Virgin. The four solo vocalists are impressive and the Vienna Concentus Musicus is on characteristically fine form in these brisk, joyful performances.

NEW REVIEW

Bach. ARIAS AND DUETS. **Thomas Hampson** (bar); [a]**Allan Bergius,**
[b]**Christoph Wegmann,** [a]**Helmut Wittek,** [d]**Stefan Gienger** (trebs); [e]**Kurt
Equiluz** (ten); **Vienna Concentus Musicus/Nikolaus Harnoncourt.**
Teldec 9031-74798-2.
Cantata No. 140 — Wann kommst du, mein Heil?[a]; Mein Freund ist mein![a].
Cantata No. 146 — Wie will ich mich freuen[e] (all from 6 35653, 1/85).
Cantata No. 147 — Ich will von Jesu Wundern singen (6 35654, 7/85). Cantata
No. 152 — Tritt auf die Glaubensbahn; Wie soll ich dich, Liebster der Seelen[b].
Cantata No. 153 — Fürchte dich nicht, ich bin bei dir. Cantata No. 154 —
Wisset ihr nicht (6 35656, 4/86). Cantata No. 185 — Das ist der Christen
Kunst (2292-44179-2, 9/89). Cantata No. 192 — Der ewig reiche Gott[e].
Cantata No. 194 — Was des Höchsten Glanz erfüllt; O wie wohl ist uns
geschehn[d] (2292-44193-2, 5/90). Cantata No. 196 — Der Herr segne euch[e]
(2292-44194-2, 5/90).

55' DDD 4/92

This disc is both an alluring shop window for Teldec's complete series of Bach
cantatas — though in no sense a substitute — and an attractive programme in its
own right. Bach's sacred cantatas are richly endowed with vocal duets and the
present issue offers only a selection from them. The common factor is the
baritone, Thomas Hampson, who is partnered by some of the talented boy
trebles who made such a distinctive contribution to the complete edition,
and by the tenor, Kurt Equiluz. Hampson joined the team when the series
was already two-thirds of the way through, so the earliest cantata to feature
here is No. 140, "Wachet auf, ruft uns die Stimme". That work, however,
provides an auspicious starting-point since it contains two especially fine duets
which are also among the most popular with audiences. Much else, though,
will be comparatively unfamiliar to all but well-seasoned Bach cantata enthusiasts.
In short, a very attractive compilation which, if it draws unsuspecting listeners
into Bach's sacred dramatic wonderland will have more than fulfilled its purpose.
Texts are not included, alas, but an accompanying note provides useful signposts
to travellers in a strange land.

NEW REVIEW

Bach. Cantatas — No. 206, Schleicht, spielende Wellen; No. 207a, Auf,
schmetternde Töne der muntern Trompeten. Ruth Ziesak (sop); Michael Chance
(alto); Christoph Prégardien (ten); Peter Kooy (bass); Stuttgart Chamber Choir;
Cologne Concerto/Frieder Bernius. Sony Classical Vivarte CD46492.

1h 7' DDD 9/91

This disc contains two splendid examples of Bach's secular occasional style.
Auf, schmetternde Töne dates from 1735 when it was performed in honour of
the name day of Elector Frederick Augustus II. Lovers of the Brandenburg
Concertos will be enchanted by two dazzling instances of Bach's art of parody
contained in this colourfully scored work. The other cantata, Schleicht,
spielende Wellen dates from 1736 when it was performed on the birthday
of the selfsame Augustus. Here each of the principal rivers flowing through the
countries united under Augustus's rule competes for the monarch's special
affection. Inconsequential as the text may be, the music certainly is not; as
well as two vigorous choruses there are four beautifully contrasted arias,
pride-of-place to which might understandably be given the robust polonaise. This
is the piece with which the Polish river Vistula (bass) serenades his ruler, and its
rhythm and melody once heard, haunt the memory evermore. The performances
are among the strongest to have emerged in this repertoire in recent years.

Soloists and choir are first-rate and the orchestral playing on period instruments, comparably so. Full texts with translations are included.

Bach. Cantatas — No. 211, Schweigt stille, plaudert nicht, "Coffee"; No. 212, Mer hahn en neue Oberkeet, "Peasant". **Emma Kirkby** (sop); **Rogers Covey-Crump** (ten); **David Thomas** (bass); **Academy of Ancient Music/Christopher Hogwood.** L'Oiseau-Lyre 417 621-2OH.

♪ 52' DDD 10/89

These two most delightful of Bach's secular cantatas here receive sparkling performances fully alive to the humour and invention of the music. The *Coffee* Cantata illustrates a family altercation over a current enthusiasm, the drinking of coffee. A narrator tells the story whilst the soprano and bass soloists confront each other in a series of delightful arias. Thomas brings out the crabby dyspeptic side of Schlendrian's character imaginatively and Kirkby makes a charming minx-like Lieschen. Covey-Crump's sweet light tenor acts as a good foil. The *Peasant* Cantata also takes the form of a dialogue, here between a somewhat dull and simple young man and his sweetheart Mieke, a girl who intends to better herself. Through the 24 short movements Bach conjures up a wonderfully rustic picture with some vivid dance numbers and rumbustious ritornellos. The soloists' nicely rounded characterizations emerge with great humour and Hogwood directs with vitality and sprightly rhythmic control. The recording is excellent.

Bach. CANTATAS, Volumes 44 and 45. [ad]**Helmut Wittek,** [a]**Hans Stricker,** [b]**Stefan Gienger,** [cef]**Jan Patrick O'Farrell** (trebs); [g]**Barbara Bonney** (sop); [cef]**René Jacobs** (alto); [cf]**John Elwes,** [bd]**Kurt Equiluz** (tens); [abd]**Thomas Hampson,** [cef]**Harry van der Kamp** (basses); [abd]**Tölz Boys' Choir;** [cef]**Hanover Boys' Choir;** [cef]**Ghent Collegium Vocale;** [abdg]**Vienna Concentus Musicus/Nikolaus Harnoncourt;** [cef]**Leonhardt Consort/Gustav Leonhardt.** Teldec Das Alte Werk 244 193/4-2.
244 193-2 — No. 192, Nun danket alle Gott[a]; No. 194, Höchsterwünschtes Freudenfest[b]; No. 195, Dem Gerechten muss das Licht immer wieder aufgehen[c].
244 194-2 — No. 196, Der Herr denket an uns[d]; No. 197, Gott ist unser Zuversicht[e]; No. 198, Lass, Fürstin, lass noch einen Strahl[f]; No. 199, Mein Herze schwimmt im Blut[g].

♪ 1h 11' DDD ② 102' DDD 5/90

Almost inevitably, in Teldec's Bach Cantata series, the interpretations and performances have their ups and downs, but their finest qualities serve Bach's music well. In general, Harnoncourt's Vienna Concentus Musicus has the edge over the Leonhardt Consort but Harnoncourt can be stridently idiosyncratic on occasion and his inclination to over-stress strong beats is a feature of his direction which has found few adherents. Volumes 44 and 45 contain strengths and weaknesses characteristic of the series as a whole with strong solo contributions but less convincing choral ones. Much of the instrumental obbligato playing is first-rate and both directors give careful thought to phrasing and articulation. Two works only throughout the series introduce a female voice, Cantata No. 51 (Vol. 14) and Cantata No. 199 with which the project is concluded. Elsewhere, the solo soprano parts are sung by boys and the alto parts by counter-tenors in all but a handful of instances where boys' voices are preferred. Accompanying documentation is informative and translations of the German texts are included. Recorded sound is usually clear and effective in the later volumes of the series but is variable in the earlier ones which have been transferred from LP to CD.

Bach. SECULAR CANTATAS. [a]**Elly Ameling** (sop); [b]**Gerald English** (ten); [c]**Siegmund Nimsgern** (bass); **Collegium Aureum.** Deutsche Harmonia Mundi Editio Classica GD77151. Texts and translations included. From BASF BAC3052/3 (9/74).
No. 202, Weichet nur, betrübte Schatten, "Wedding Cantata"[a]. No. 209, Non sa che sia dolore[a]. No. 211, Schweigt stille, plaudert nicht, "Coffee Cantata"[abc]. No. 212, Mer hahn en neue Oberkeet, "Peasant Cantata"[abc].

② 1h 46' ADD 10/90

Nowadays there is no shortage of recordings of Bach's best known secular cantatas; but the four contained in this double album, though now comparatively elderly — they were first issued on LPs in 1968 — were among the most stylish of their day. Much has happened in the sphere of baroque playing and interpretation since then and not everything here is as polished and assured as listeners will have come to expect from today's finest ensembles. Nevertheless, the performances are anything but dull and much of the singing is first rate. It is the *Coffee* Cantata and the *Peasant* Cantata which come over with the greater conviction with Elly Ameling as a beguiling but wilful Lieschen in the former, and a spirited, coquettish Miecke in Bach's pastoral romp. In these works the two other singers, Gerald English as the narrator and Siegmund Nimsgern as the peppery Schlendrian (BWV211) and the country lad with little on his mind but opening time and a good roll in the hay (BWV212) are excellent. Much of the instrumental playing by members of the Collegium Aureum is enjoyable, too, with stylish harpsichord continuo. Good recorded sound and full texts in German, English and French for each cantata.

Bach. Mass in B minor, BWV232. **Emma Kirkby, Emily Van Evera** (sops); **Panito Iconomou, Christian Immler, Michael Kilian** (altos); **Rogers Covey-Crump** (ten); **David Thomas** (bass); **Taverner Consort; Taverner Players/Andrew Parrott.** EMI Reflexe CDS7 47293-8. Notes, text and translation included. From EX270239-3 (10/85).

② 1h 43' DDD 8/86

The richly contrasting styles and colours of the B minor Mass demonstrates Bach's prowess as a composer as well as his profound Christian faith. In this recording Andrew Parrott pursues a train of thought motivated by the American scholar/performer, Joshua Rifkin, who has argued in favour of one singer to each vocal part, although Parrott prefers to use a ripieno group of voices in addition to his soloists. In this and other respects, he has aimed in his own words "to adopt the conventions of a hypothetical performance by Bach himself at Leipzig, where the work was written". Voices and instrumentalists comprise a strong team and Parrott's direction is lively and

Andrew Parrott   [photo: EMI/Faulks]   authoritative, generating excitement and a vigorous sense of purpose. The recorded sound is clear and effectively resonant and the disc includes a booklet with full texts.

NEW REVIEW

Bach. Magnificat in D major, BWV243[a].
Vivaldi. Ostro picta, RV642[b]. Gloria in D major, RV589[c]. [abc]**Emma Kirkby,**
[ac]**Tessa Banner** (sops); [ac]**Michael Chance** (alto); [a]**John Mark Ainsley** (ten);
[a]**Stephen Varcoe** (bar); **Collegium Musicum 90 Chorus and Orchestra/**
Richard Hickox. Chandos CHAN0518. Texts and translations included.

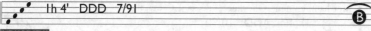

1h 4' DDD 7/91 · Ⓑ

NEW REVIEW

Bach. Magnificat in D major, BWV243[a].
Vivaldi. Gloria in D major, RV589. **Barbara Hendricks** (sop); **Ann**
Murray (mez); [a]**Jean Rigby** (contr); [a]**Uwe Heilmann** (ten); [a]**Jorma**
Hynninen (bass) **Academy of St Martin in the Fields Chorus and**
Orchestra/Sir Neville Marriner. EMI CDC7 54283-2. Texts and translations
included.

56' DDD 3/92 · Ⓑ ✐

The Chandos issue was the first CD release featuring the then newly founded
Collegium Musicum 90 under its directors Richard Hickox and Simon Standage.
The Collegium embraces both choir and orchestra who are joined in this
programme of Bach and Vivaldi by a comparably fine team of soloists. Hickox
sets effective tempos in Bach's *Magnificat* and points up the many striking
contrasts in colour and texture with which the piece abounds. From among the
many successful features of the recording Stephen Varcoe's "Quia fecit mihi
magna" and the "Et misericordia" sung by Michael Chance and John Mark Ainsley
stand out. Vivaldi's *Gloria*, RV589 is the better known of two settings by the
composer in D major. In this programme it is prefaced by an introductory motet
Ostro picta, which may well in fact belong to the *Gloria* and here sung with
warmth and radiance by Emma Kirkby. Hickox's performance of this evergreen
vocal masterpiece comes over with conviction. It is gracefully phrased, sensitively
sung and affectingly paced with an admirable rapport between vocalists and
instrumentalists. Full texts for both works are included and recorded sound is
first-rate.

For his recording of the same works Sir Neville Marriner has chosen a group
of soloists who complement one another stylistically. But the chief merit of this
disc perhaps lies in the fine singing of the Academy Chorus under Laszlo Heltay's
direction. Marriner's tempos are generally well judged though the "Et in terra
pax hominibus" of Vivaldi's *Gloria* is perhaps a shade too slow. Sadly, Marriner
does not include *Ostro picta*, which no lover of Vivaldi's music would wish to be
without, but in most other respects these versions offer attractive alternatives to
Hickox's version for readers who prefer modern instruments to the sounds of the
somewhat lower pitched period instruments.

Bach. St John Passion, BWV245. **Anthony Rolfe Johnson** (ten) Evangelist;
Stephen Varcoe (bass) Jesus; **Nancy Argenta, Ruth Holton** (sops);
Michael Chance (alto); **Neill Archer, Rufus Müller** (tens); **Cornelius**
Hauptmann (bass); **Monteverdi Choir; English Baroque Soloists/John**
Eliot Gardiner. Archiv Produktion 419 324-2AH2. Notes, text and translation
included.

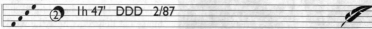

② 1h 47' DDD 2/87 · ✐

Like most other oratorio passions of this period, the *St John Passion* is in two
parts with the biblical text paragraphed by contemplative 'madrigal' numbers.
This is glorious, timeless music and few who encounter numbers like the opening
("Lord, our master") and penultimate ("Lie in peace") choruses or the incompar-
able aria, "It is accomplished", can fail to respond and to be deeply moved.
Gardiner gives a fresh appraisal of the work, with consistently fast tempos which

suit his authentically-scaled forces. Superb solo singers and splendidly fresh and
alert choral singing are features of this interpretation, which stresses above all
else the continuity of the work. The recording is in every way sympathetic to
this approach, with excellent detail and a fine overall balance.

Bach. St Matthew Passion, BWV244. **Anthony Rolfe Johnson** (ten)
Evangelist; **Andreas Schmidt** (bar) Jesus; **Barbara Bonney, Anne Mono-
yios** (sops); **Anne Sofie von Otter** (mez); **Michael Chance** (alto); **Howard
Crook** (ten); **Olaf Bär** (bar); **Cornelius Hauptmann** (bass); **London
Oratory Junior Choir; Monteverdi Choir; English Baroque Soloists/
John Eliot Gardiner.** DG 427 648-2AH3. Notes, text and translation included.

③ 2h 47' DDD 10/89

What makes John Eliot Gardiner's *St Matthew Passion* stand out in the face of stiff
competition is perhaps more than anything his vivid sense of theatre. Bach's score
is, after all, a sacred drama and Gardiner interprets this aspect of the work with
lively and colourful conviction. That in itself, of course, is not sufficient to
ensure a fine performance but here we have a first-rate group of solo voices,
immediately responsive choral groups in the Monteverdi Choir and the London
Oratory Junior Choir — a distinctive element this — and refined obbligato and
orchestral playing from the English Baroque Soloists. Anthony Rolfe Johnson
declaims the Evangelist's role with clarity, authority and the subtle inflexion of an
accomplished story-teller. Ann Monoyios, Howard Crook and Olaf Bär also make
strong contributions but it is Michael Chance's "Erbarme dich", tenderly
accompanied by the violin obbligato which sets the seal of distinction on the
performance. Singing and playing of this calibre deserve to win many friends and
Gardiner's deeply-felt account of Bach's great Passion does the music considerable justice. Clear recorded sound.

NEW REVIEW

Bach. Christmas Oratorio, BWV248. **Theo Altmeyer** (ten) Evangelist and
arias; **Hans Buchhierl** (treb); **Andreas Stein** (boy alto); **Barry McDaniel**
(bar); **Tölz Boys' Choir; Collegium Aureum/Gerhard Schmidt-Gaden.**
Deutsche Harmonia Mundi GD77046. Notes, text and translation included. From
CDS7 49119-8 (4/88).

③ 2h 43'

Although recorded as long ago as 1973 this performance of Bach's *Christmas
Oratorio* possesses a radiance and a spontaneity perhaps unrivalled by more
carefully contrived versions. It is not without its weaknesses, which lie mainly in
passages of insecure instrumental playing; but these are outweighed by its merits
chief among which, perhaps, are the contributions, both solo and choral, of the
Tölz Boys' Choir. All the soprano and alto solos are sung by boys and in the
choruses it is boys rather than countertenors who sing the alto line. Gerhard
Schmidt-Gaden, the chorusmaster and conductor, effectively relaxed tempos
which may at first sound too leisurely to ears accustomed to the frenetic pace
chosen by some rival versions. Occasionally, he is a little too slow as, for
instance, in the opening chorus of Part Four but for the most part he directs a
performance free from intrusive mannerisms which bedevil too many performances of baroque music today. The treble, Hans Buchhierl and the alto, Andreas
Stein, are outstanding, and the tenor Theo Altmeyer and the bass, Barry McDaniel,
are hardly less impressive. With its ingenuousness, its spirit of innocent joy and
in its simple but sensitive response to the music this performance comes closer
than most to the contemplative heart of Bach's Christmas masterpiece.

Simon Bainbridge

British 1952-

Bainbridge. Viola Concerto (1976)[a]. Fantasia for Double Orchestra (1983-4)[b]. Concertante in Moto Perpetuo (1979, rev. 1983)[c]. [a]**Walter Trampler** (va); **London Symphony Orchestra/Michael Tilson Thomas;** [b]**BBC Symphony Orchestra;** [c]**The Composers Ensemble/**[bc]**Simon Bainbridge.** Continuum CCD1020. Item marked [a] from Unicorn RHD400 (2/82), [bc] new to UK.

54' DDD 5/91

Michael Tilson Thomas   [photo: Sony Classical/Friedman

When the recording of Simon Bainbridge's early Viola Concerto was first issued, it was rather over-shadowed by the more outgoing, brightly-coloured music of Oliver Knussen with which it was coupled. Now the more outgoing, brightly-coloured coupling has been provided by Bainbridge himself, and the result is a disc as distinctive as it is distinguished. Bainbridge's music is modern in tone, romantic in temperament, and the most recent work on the disc, the *Fantasia for Double Orchestra*, presents a wide-ranging tapestry of moods and textures with an air of complete and justified confidence. There is a boldness, a directness that enables Bainbridge to evoke the opening of Wagner's *Das Rheingold* at the start without either irony or inappropriateness. His intention is evidently not to parody, but to build his own edifice on archetypically striking and substantial foundations. Structurally, the *Fantasia* works extremely well: expressively, it can be enjoyed even if the structure passes you by. The Viola Concerto is more introspective and more intense, but no less cogent. It may take longer to get the hang of than the *Fantasia*, but the results will be no less rewarding. The brief *Concertante in Moto Perpetuo* is an uncomplicated delight, and the whole disc has excellent sound and first-rate performance.

Mily Balakirev

Russian 1837-1910

Balakirev. Symphony No. 1 in C major[a]. Tamara — symphonic poem[b]. **Royal Philharmonic Orchestra/Sir Thomas Beecham.** EMI Beecham Edition CDM7 63375-2. Item marked [a] from HMV SXLP30002 (6/62), [b] Philips mono ABL3047 (6/55).

1h 1' ADD 7/90

NEW REVIEW

Balakirev. Symphony No. 1 in C major. Russia — symphonic poem. **Philharmonia Orchestra/Evgeni Svetlanov.** Hyperion CDA66493.

1h DDD 12/91

Balakirev was a major figure of Russian nationalism and one of the group of composers called "The Five", and he also gave useful advice and encouragement to Tchaikovsky. In some ways the most intellectual of these artists, he was also highly self-critical and this meant that his output was all too small, though of high quality. The spacious and sombre beginning of the First Symphony tells us at once that this is a work of epic proportions, imbued with the kind of Russianness that is hard to describe but easy to recognize. Sir Thomas Beecham had a real affinity with this music, and his performance is one of power as well as ample colour, with good detail but holding the attention throughout the big structure. Both in this work and *Tamara*, which was inspired by a Lermontov poem depicting a kind of Lorelei figure, a siren whose beauty lures travellers to their doom, the Royal Philharmonic Orchestra plays with fervour and skill. Their stereo recording of the Symphony was made as long ago as December 1955, and that of the symphonic poem *Tamara* in mono early in 1954, but no apology need be made for the sound on the present digital transfers, which is vivid although with less definition than we would expect today; the slight background hiss in quieter passages is not obtrusive.

It is not surprising to find that Evgeni Svetlanov's view of Balakirev's First Symphony is very Russian in its power and whole-hearted commitment. In the first movement his pacing of the introductory *Largo* section is somewhat deliberate, in a manner which creates tension and very much whets the appetite. The main *Allegro vivo* part of the movement is played with a good deal of vigour and wit, and Svetlanov varies the basic pulse to bring out the music's changing moods very effectively. In the second movement he adopts quite a slow tempo and phrases the music with much care and delicacy. The *Andante* is shaped in a very appealing fashion, and in the finale Svetlanov's feather-light, bright-eyed manner is very attractive, though the work's ending is played strongly by the excellent Philharmonic Orchestra. While Beecham's mid-price performance brings out the work's charm Svetlanov digs a little deeper, to find more character, more strength and variety of mood. *Russia*, an attractive, very well-written symphonic poem, is also played in a virile, vivacious fashion. Hyperion's recording has neither optimum clarity nor the greatest degree of atmosphere, but it serves well enough.

Granville Bantock

British 1868-1946

Bantock. Fifine at the Fair[a].
Bax. The Garden of Fand[b].
Berners. The Triumph of Neptune — ballet suites[c]. [ab]**Royal Philharmonic Orchestra,** [c]**London Philharmonic Orchestra/Sir Thomas Beecham.** EMI Beecham Edition mono CDM7 63405-2. Item marked [a] from HMV DB21145/8 (1/51), [b] DB6654/5 (8/48), [c] Columbia LX697/8 (2/38).
The Triumph of Neptune — Schottische; Hornpipe; Polka (with Robert Alva, bar); Harlequinade; Dance of the Fairy Princess; Intermezzo; Apotheosis of Neptune.

Apart from his magnificent legacy of Delius recordings in the 1940s and 1950s Sir Thomas Beecham made relatively few recordings of the contemporary British composers that he so vigorously supported in the concert-hall. Fortunately, three pieces which were very much part of his repertoire were captured for posterity, and these have now been gathered together on this marvellous mid-price CD as part of EMI's Beecham Edition. His recording of Bantock's luxurious tone-poem *Fifine at the Fair* enjoyed several revivals on LP, but only here, in its first ever issue on CD, has the marvellously atmospheric performance and recording been heard to anything like its full potential. The same is true of his evocative account of Bax's Celtic inspired tone-poem *The Garden of Fand*, which was recorded in the presence of the composer in 1947; for the dedicated Bax enthusiast this performance alone is worth the price of this CD. The rather eccentric but jolly ballet suite *The Triumph of Neptune* by Lord Berners was recorded twice by Beecham and although in this, his first recording, he omits two of the suite's numbers ("Cloudland" and "Frozen Forest"), it is nevertheless a highly enjoyable performance which makes a welcome return to the catalogue. The transfer to CD is clear and well-detailed.

Bantock. The Pierrot of the Minute — comedy overture (1908).
Bridge. Suite for strings (1908). Summer (1914). There is a Willow Grows Aslant a Brook (1928).
Butterworth. The Banks of Green Willow (1913). **Bournemouth Sinfonietta/Norman Del Mar.** Chandos CHAN8373. From RCA Red Seal RL25184 (12/79).

58' ADD 8/85

All the works on this disc of English music were composed in the first three decades of this century, yet they inhabit very different sound-worlds. Granville Bantock's sparkling *The Pierrot of the Minute* Overture has its heart in the nineteenth century and has few undercurrents of disquiet. Butterworth's *The Banks of Green Willow,* with its folk-song base, already has signs of nostalgia for the passing of a whole way of life. Bridge's delightful *Suite* still retains the Edwardian glow of his earlier compositional style, with darkness only intruding, appropriately enough, in the third-movement Nocturne; even the shimmering textures of *Summer* intimate little of the cataclysm to come. With *There is a Willow Grows Aslant a Brook*, however, Bridge realized his bleakest misgivings — the security of pre-World War I England was never to be regained and could only be glimpsed fleetingly, in dream-like recollection. The diverse moods of all these works are splendidly captured by Del Mar and his Bournemouth players, and what the Sinfonietta lacks here in terms of solid ensemble and weight of string tone, it more than makes up for in zest and commitment to this music.

Samuel Barber
American 1910-1981

Barber. Cello Concerto, Op. 22.
Britten. Symphony for cello and orchestra, Op. 68. **Yo-Yo Ma** (vc);
Baltimore Symphony Orchestra/David Zinman. CBS Masterworks CD44900.

1h 2' DDD 6/89

This recording is highly recommended. The acoustic is warm, balance ideal and there is sufficient resonance. On this evidence, the Baltimore is a splendid orchestra, responding alertly and intelligently to David Zinman's very positive interpretation. How enterprising, too, to record two works which are not in the main repertoire of cello concertos, excellent though they are. Barber's dates from 1945 and has something of the late-romanticism of the Violin Concerto, but with a more classical approach. It makes large demands on the virtuosity of the soloist, which are met with apparent ease and relish by Yo-Yo Ma. Britten's Cello Symphony is more problematical. Its predominantly dark and brooding mood, with a savage *scherzo* followed by an almost jaunty finale, disconcerts some listeners, but the clue lies in the dedication to Rostropovich, for the music seems also to be an act of homage to the composer's friend Shostakovich and emulates the Russian master's ability to combine the tragic and the bizarre within one framework. Once the listener has penetrated the rather forbidding outer shell of this work, the rewards are great. Ma and Zinman obviously agree on the music's stature, for this is a compelling performance.

Barber. Essays for orchestra — No. 1, Op. 12; No. 2, Op. 17; No. 3, Op. 47.
Ives. Symphony No. 1, kk/V8. **Detroit Symphony Orchestra/Neeme Järvi.** Chandos CHAN9053.

Ih 10'   DDD   3/92

This issue comes with a booklet celebrating Neeme Järvi's 100th disc for Chandos and a remarkable joint achievement by this conductor and company. Järvi's wide-ranging sympathies are proved yet again in the music of these two American composers, but there is a paradox here in that it is the innovator Ives who is the more conventional and the conservative Barber who challenges the ear. The explanation is that Ives's First Symphony is a graduation work from his years at Yale University, representing a compromise between his natural boldness and the discipline that he grudgingly accepted from his teacher Horatio Parker. The result is romantically expansive, often fascinating and occasionally beautiful, with influences including Brahms and Dvořák (there are echoes of the *New World* Symphony in the slow movement) but also a bold homespun element in places suggesting the Ivesian innovations that were yet to come. Samuel Barber seemed

unhappy with the symphony as a form, writing a one-movement First Symphony in 1936 and eventually destroying all but one movement of his wartime Second (1944). Instead he wrote three impressive *Essays for orchestra* that have been called "surrogate symphonies" and of which No. 3 was his final work before his death. Each has a sequence of moods and tempos, the *First Essay* being partly elegiac (recall-ing his *Adagio for Strings*), the Second having some vigorously busy music and the Third being the most enigmatic. While none of these works sound especially American, the performances are convinc-ing and the recording offers rich sound.

Neeme Järvi   *[photo: Chandos/Maeder]*

Barber. Adagio for Strings.
Copland. Appalachian Spring — suite.
Gershwin. Rhapsody in Blue. **Los Angeles Philharmonic Orchestra/ Leonard Bernstein** (pf). DG 431 048-2GBE. Recorded at a performance in Davies Symphony Hall, San Francisco in July 1982.

54'   DDD

This disc shows Bernstein on home ground: American music played by an American orchestra. It captures, too, the most enduring elements of his music-making — the ryhthmic vitality and the sense of poise that he could so winningly embrace in music with a strong melody. This is Bernstein at his most engaging, his piano-playing as impressive as always, his feeling for the ebb and flow of this most elusive music beautifully judged. The 'big-band' version of the piece is used but with such a vital response from soloist and orchestra alike — the sense of real interplay between the musicians is almost palpable. Copland's lyrical *Appalachian Spring* is gloriously unfolded, the tempos are nicely judged and the Los Angeles orchestra clearly revels in the melodic weave of the piece. Similarly, the serene *Adagio* by Barber finds the strings rapt, unhurried and poised, the tempo dangerously slow but carried along by the commitment of the inspirational conductor. The live recordings are well handled, with virtually no evidence of the audience to be heard.

NEW REVIEW

Barber. Symphony No. 1, Op. 9. The School for Scandal Overture, Op. 5.
Beach. Symphony in E minor, Op. 32, "Gaelic". **Detroit Symphony
Orchestra/Neeme Järvi.** Chandos CHAN8958.

> ♪♪ 1h 12' DDD 10/91

NEW REVIEW

Barber. Symphony No. 1, Op. 9[a]. Piano Concerto, Op. 38[b]. Souvenirs,
Op. 28[c]. [bc]**John Browning** (pf); [ab]**St Louis Symphony Orchestra/Leonard
Slatkin** ([c]pf). RCA Victor Red Seal RD60732.

> ♪♪ 1h 10' DDD 11/91

Amy Beach (or Mrs H.H.A. Beach, as she was known professionally in her
lifetime) was born in Henniker, New Hampshire in 1867. By all accounts she
was a prodigiously talented youngster — she could sing 40 tunes by the age of
two, and at four she was composing small pieces for the piano. She made her
'official' début as a pianist at the age of 16 playing Chopin's Rondo in E flat and
Moscheles's G minor Piano Concerto, but after her marriage to a noted Boston
surgeon in 1885 she abandoned her concert career and devoted her time
exclusively to composition. The *Gaelic* Symphony (her only work in the genre)
dates from 1896. Like Dvořák's *New World* Symphony, which had received its
American première just a few years earlier, it draws its inspiration from folk
material; though Beach's sources are drawn not from native America but
rather from her Gaelic forebears. The writing reveals a remarkable degree of
craftsmanship and maturity, and although the music contains perhaps more
imitation than originality (Brahms, Tchaikovsky and Parry spring to mind) there
is nevertheless plenty of enjoyment to be had from this fresh and engaging work.
The music of Samuel Barber needs less introduction, though his First Symphony
makes a welcome return after a protracted absence from the catalogue. This one-
movement, highly compact work deserves to be much better known as it
contains some of Barber's most invigorating and memorable material. Stylistically
it finds allegiance with the post-romanticism of symphonies such as Walton's First
and Howard Hanson's Second (*Romantic*). The disc also includes Barber's equally
engaging Overture to *The School for Scandal*. Committed performances.
  Leonard Slatkin's account of the First Symphony is more satisfactory. His
orchestra seems more comfortable, and the American conductor clearly has an
innate grasp of the music's style. Barber's Piano Concerto was written for John
Browning in 1962. Composer and pianist worked closely together on this big,
virtuoso, neo-romantic work, and thus Browning's performance, brilliantly
played, is as authentic as it could be. Slatkin conducts with perfect sympathy, and
in the light-hearted *Souvenirs* he shows himself to be a good match for Browning
at the keyboard. RCA's recording of the piano duet work is a little shallow in
tone. The Piano Concerto is very well-recorded, though the soloist is rather too
far forward, and the Symphony enjoys very good sound.

NEW REVIEW

Barber. Prayers of Kierkegaard, Op. 30. The lovers, Op. 43. **Sarah Reese**
(sop); **Dale Duesing** (bar); **Chicago Symphony Chorus and Orchestra/
Andrew Schenck.** Koch International 37125-2. Recorded at performances in
Orchestra Hall, Chicago during October 1991.

> ♪♪ 52' DDD 3/92   ❓

Barber never earned the popularity of Copland or Bernstein, nor their status as
great American figures. Yet one of his pieces, the *Adagio for Strings* (originally the
slow movement of a string quartet) has touched people's hearts for half a
century. This disc is one to win him more admirers, and he could not be in
better hands than those of the late Andrew Schenck, a Barber specialist. It also

reminds us that this composer was a trained singer who cared deeply about words and said that when setting them he "let the music flow". *The lovers* is a late work, commissioned in 1971 by a Philadelphia bank whose committee was at first shocked by the eroticism of these poems by Pablo Neruda. Barber's music has personality and sensual power without in any way following the atonal path laid down by the Second Viennese School, and the toughly lyrical baritone soloist Dale Duesing is perfectly suited to these poems of Chilean peasant love and receives excellent support from the chorus and orchestra. *Prayers of Kierkegaard* is earlier (1954) and also comes across strongly, but its passions are of a more spiritual kind and Barber himself called this Danish philosopher "an exciting and enigmatic intellectual force". It begins with a plea for peace that soon rises to a fervent climax, and goes on to maintain considerable emotional force. Both of these works are beautifully laid out for the voices and orchestra. The live Chicago recording could ideally be better balanced, and there is a little audience noise, but it is effective and this issue should not be missed if you care about the music of this fine twentieth-century composer who dared to go his own way.

NEW REVIEW

Barber. Piano Sonata in E flat major, Op. 26. Excursions, Op. 20.
Ives. Piano Sonata No. 1. **Joanna MacGregor** (pf). Collins Classics 1107-2.
Ih 8' DDD 3/92

There are other fine recordings of the Barber Sonata, including Peter Lawson's which is reviewed in the "Collections" section of this book (refer to the Index to Reviews). It is a work which has attracted well-equipped players right from the start. MacGregor stands up well, but the greater attraction is her Ives Sonata No. 1, which ought to sweep the board on both sides of the Atlantic now. The work, which waited 45 years for a first performance, is just as characteristic of Ives as the Second Sonata (refer to the Index to Reviews), and in some ways its mixture of hymn-tunes and ragtime makes a more coherent impact. The ragtime aspects are based on what Ives heard improvised or played that way himself: he went to a lot of trouble to catch the difference between playing the dots and swinging away. This informality is superbly caught by MacGregor, who risks all in truly Ivesian fashion in one or two places. She thoroughly understands the driving rhythms as well as the transcendental calm. By comparison anything by Barber is more polite. But the four *Excursions* come off well and show a different approach to popular idioms — more that of a tourist than an insider. But both composers know how to make use of sonata structure in these two American classics, vividly played and recorded.

Barber. SONGS. **Roberta Alexander** (sop); **Tan Crone** (pf). Etcetera KTC1055.
Three Songs, Op. 2. Three Songs, Op. 10. Four Songs, Op. 13. Two Songs, Op. 18. Nuvoletta, Op. 25. Hermit Songs, Op. 29. Despite and Still, Op. 41.
Ih I' DDD 9/88

If Samuel Barber had not been a composer he could have had a very respectable career as a baritone; he made a beautiful recording of his own *Dover Beach* many years ago. He also confessed to having "sometimes thought that I'd rather write words than music". Good qualifications for writing songs, both of them; so is his individual and discriminating taste in poetry. The average length of the ten *Hermit Songs* (settings of medieval Irish texts) is less than two minutes, but they often distil big images from tiny ones: the ringing of a little bell amid silence evokes a longing for the solitary life and the tranquil solitude of death, the cry of a bird is the starting point for a pitying description of the crucified Christ and his mother, a lazy rocking in the piano serves as metaphor for the simple contentment of an old scholar-monk and the purring of his companionable cat. Simplicity of imagery plus economy of means equals intensity of utterance is often Barber's equation, but there is humour here as well (lines from James Joyce's *Finnegan's Wake* are set as a brilliant, slightly dizzy waltz-song) and suave melodiousness ("Sure on this shining night") and bold, almost operatic declamation ("I hear an army"). There is scarcely a weak song among them. They need a singer with quite a range, and Roberta Alexander has it; her bright, vibrant but precise singing is as sensitive to words as Barber himself, and she never allows her expressiveness to break the poised elegance of his lines. Her pianist is excellent and the recording is clean, though rather close.

NEW REVIEW

Barber. VOCAL WORKS. Various artists. CBS Masterworks Portrait CD46727.
Knoxville: Summer of 1915 (Eleanor Steber, sop; Dumbarton Oaks Orchestra/ William Strickland. New to UK. Recorded 1950). Dover Beach, Op. 3 (Dietrich Fischer-Dieskau, bar; Juilliard Quartet — Robert Mann, Earl Carlyss, vns; Raphael Hillyer, va; Claus Adam vc. From 72687, 11/68). Hermit Songs, Op. 29 (Leontyne Price, sop; Samuel Barber, pf. New to UK. 1954). Andromache's Farewell, Op. 39 (Martina Arroyo, sop; New York Philharmonic Orchestra/Thomas Schippers. New to UK. 1963).
51' AAD 10/91

This is a fascinating collection of Barber performances from the CBS vaults. Eleanor Steber, a familiar figure at New York's Metropolitan Opera, commissioned *Knoxville*, so her authoritative account, made as early as 1950, has special status. Her reading of this enchanting music is fresh and straightforward: *Knoxville* is, after all, supposed to be sung by a child, or rather by a man reliving his childhood so intensely that the child's voice speaks through him. *Dover Beach*, a much earlier work, is no less exquisite. Here, Fischer-Dieskau sings most beautifully, but Matthew Arnold's words are less well-served — and there are no texts provided. The high point of the anthology comes with Leontyne Price's

moving account of the *Hermit Songs*. She premièred the cycle with the composer in 1953, taking time out from the celebrated run of *Porgy and Bess* which made her name. Barber again accompanies, and Price's lovely timbre and faultless diction are well preserved in the 1954 recording. Martina Arroyo is at *her* very best in *Andromache's Farewell*, a highly dramatic scene based on Euripides. Unfortunately, the music is reminiscent of a Hollywood sand and sandal epic, with Thomas Schippers and the New York Philharmonic working themselves up into a rare old sweat. All the same, this is an attractive way of exploring unfamiliar Barber, never less than decently recorded and often quite superbly performed. Robert Cushman's insert-notes are helpful too.

Dietrich Fischer-Dieskau *[photo: DG*

Béla Bartók

Hungarian 1881-1945

Bartók. Piano Concertos — No. 1, Sz83; No. 2, Sz95. **Maurizio Pollini** (pf); **Chicago Symphony Orchestra/Claudio Abbado.** DG 415 371-2GH. From 2530 901 (7/79).

52' ADD 9/86   **B**

Bartók. Piano Concertos — No. 1, Sz83[a]; No. 2, Sz95[b]; No. 3, Sz119[a]. **Stephen Kovacevich** (pf); [a]**London Symphony Orchestra;** [b]**BBC Symphony Orchestra/Sir Colin Davis.** Philips 426 660-2PSL. Items marked [a] from 9500 043 (7/76), [b] SAL3779 (3/70).

1h 17' ADD 5/91   **B**

The First Piano Concerto of 1926 was one of the first fruits of a new-found confidence in Bartók — a totally serious, uncompromisingly aggressive assertion that the future could be faced and shaped by human will-power. It is tough listening, and Bartók admitted as much, promising that the Second Concerto would be easier to play and to take in. Certainly the themes here tend to be a little more folk-like, but in no other respect could Bartók be said to have realized that aim. The pianist has to cope with one of the most fearsome cadenzas in the repertoire on top of an unrelenting complexity of argument which draws the orchestra into its maelstrom. Not surprisingly these concertos can sound dauntingly abstract and nothing more. Pollini's pianistic mastery is so complete, however, that he can find all sorts of shades and perspectives which turn apparently abstract geometry into a three-dimensional experience. Abbado and the Chicago orchestra are the perfect partners for his diamond-edged virtuosity, and the faithful recording provides an admirable vehicle for communication.

Kovacevich is also as intelligent a virtuoso as they come, and both the LSO and the BBC Symphony make first-rate contributions under Sir Colin Davis; together they achieve a winning blend of drive, fantasy and inner intensity. More recent recordings may have captured more orchestral detail, and the interplay between piano and orchestra is not always as clear here as it might be, but this disc is still an admirable mid-price alternative to Pollini's recording.

Bartók. Violin Concertos — No. 1, Sz36[a]; No. 2, Sz112[b]. **Kyung-Wha Chung** (vn); [a]**Chicago Symphony Orchestra;** [b]**London Philharmonic Orchestra/Sir Georg Solti.** Decca Ovation 425 015-2DM. Item marked [a] from 411 804-1DH (10/84), [b] SXL6212 (4/78).

59' ADD/DDD 2/91   **B**

Long gone are the times when Bart²³²³ók was thought of as an arch-modernist incapable of writing a melody and the young Yehudi Menuhin was considered daring in championing his Violin Concerto. Today this work is listed as his second in this form, but four decades ago it stood alone because the composer had suppressed an earlier one dating from 1908, or more precisely reshaped it into another work called *Two Portraits*. When this earlier piece was finally published in its original form some 30 years ago, it became his First Concerto and the more familiar one of 1938 his Second. The First was inspired by a beloved woman friend, but it does not by any means wear its heart on its sleeve, being a complex and edgy work to which Kyung-Wha Chung brings a passionate lyricism. Her conductor Sir Georg Solti is the composer's compatriot and was actually his piano pupil as well, so that he too knows how to make this music breathe and sing. Chung and Solti are equally at home in the more obviously colourful and dramatic Second Concerto, giving it all the range, expressive force and occasional violence, driving momentum and sheer Hungarian charm that one could desire. The London Philharmonic Orchestra play as if inspired and the recordings (in two locations, seven years apart) are subtle yet lit with the right brilliance.

Bartók. ORCHESTRAL WORKS. [bc]**Géza Anda** (pf); **Berlin RIAS Symphony Orchestra/Ferenc Fricsay.** DG Dokumente 427 410-2GDO2. Item marked [a] from DGM18377 (1/58), [b] SLPM138708 (1/62), [c] SLPM138111 (5/61).
Concerto for Orchestra, Sz116[a]. Rhapsody for piano and orchestra, Op. 1[b].
Piano Concertos — No. 1, Sz83[b]; No. 2, Sz95[c]; No. 3, Sz119[c].

② 2h 19' ADD 5/89 £ Ⓑ ▲

This very useful compilation gathers together all of Bartók's *concertante* works for piano and orchestra as well as a simply magnificent account of the *Concerto for Orchestra*. Ferenc Fricsay was a pupil of Bartók in Hungary and the experience clearly gave him some very special insights into the composer's music. He discerns better than the majority of conductors the darker elements of the music, the subtle undertones. He phrases the music with great breadth which is perhaps his secret for capturing and sustaining a sense of atmosphere. Géza Anda, too, brings to the piano works a zest and unsophisticated directness that the music often fails to receive. Like Fricsay, Anda speaks the right language and the performances are the better for it. The Third Concerto, written as an insurance policy for his wife Ditta in the face of his inevitable death, is a very fine reading. The recordings, 30 years old, sound well and the attractive price of these two well-filled discs makes this a set worth exploring.

Bartók. Two Portraits, Sz46[a].
Szymanowski. Symphonies — No. 2 in B flat major, Op. 19[b]; No. 3, Op. 27, "The song of the night"[c]. [c]**Ryszard Karczykowski** (ten); [c]**Kenneth Jewell Chorale; Detroit Symphony Orchestra/Antál Dorati.** Decca Enterprise 425 625-2DM. Text and translation included. Item marked [a] from SXL6897 (10/79), [bc]SXDL7524 (7/81).

1h 10' [a]ADD /DDD 7/90

Szymanowski was the first major Polish composer after Chopin, and is a leading figure of a generation that also includes Bartók and Stravinsky. Although his music is less well known than theirs, it has a strong personality of its own, exotic and ecstatic by turns, with an extraordinary opulence. Though we may not want to hear such richness (and decadence maybe) every day, there are certain aspects of the human spirit that it expresses with an unashamed hedonism for which the nearest parallels are perhaps Scriabin and, in certain moods, Messaien. The opening of the Third Symphony is typical of him, with its mysterious sustained chord, faintly throbbing drums and luscious string melody conveying the mood of the Persian poem celebrating the beauty of night which is here set for tenor and chorus. The performance of this exotically scored music by the Detroit orchestra under Dorati is highly idiomatic, and so is the singing of the Polish soloist and the American choir. The Second, completed six years previously, is less extreme in mood and shows us that the composer had learned much from the music of Richard Strauss; but though more obviously melodious than the Third, it is still sumptuous and sensuous music. Bartók's *Two Pictures* are contemporary with this work, but while they also evoke nature in an impressionistic way they are sharper in feeling and the composer's compatriot Dorati directs them strongly. The recording is rich yet detailed.

Bartók. The wooden prince — ballet, Sz60. Hungarian sketches, Sz97.
Philharmonia Orchestra/Neeme Järvi. Chandos CHAN8895.

```
•ᵈ  1h 6'  DDD  10/91
```

The wooden prince is a sumptuous dance-pantomime with an unlikely story-line: a
Princess finds a Prince's wooden staff more desirable than the Prince himself. In
time the roles are reversed: the Princess changes her mind but now the Prince
resists her, and only when she cuts off her hair does he relent and allow a happy
ending. Neeme Järvi reveals the full beauty of the score — the only complaint a
collector might have is that such rich beauty is not what we expect from Bartók!
But though it starts with a plain chord of C major, the way it grows to a mighty
climax after nearly four minutes is typically Bartókian in its power. Chandos's
recording was made in the London venue of St Jude's Church and has tremendous atmosphere which is as it should be since the score is brimful of colour as
well as being extremely elaborate. The Philharmonia Orchestra rise splendidly to
this challenge and play most idiomatically although the work must have been
unfamiliar as well as difficult. As with most ballets, the score is loosely
constructed, but the music is so imaginative that it holds the attention, especially
since the booklet note gives a detailed synopsis. The "Dance of the Waves" and
the colossal climax near the end of the fourth (and longest) dance of the seven,
where Nature herself bows to the Prince, are just two examples of the sonorous
orchestral writing. The *Hungarian sketches* are Bartók's transcriptions of five short
and fairly simple piano pieces (three of them written for children) which draw on
Hungarian folk style and make flavoursome listening.

Bartók. The miraculous mandarin, Sz73 — ballet[a]. Two portraits, Sz37[b].
Prokofiev. Scythian Suite, Op. 20[c]. [b]**Shlomo Mintz** (vn); [a]**Ambrosian
Singers;** [ab]**London Symphony Orchestra,** [c]**Chicago Symphony
Orchestra/Claudio Abbado.** DG 410 598-2GH. Items marked [a] and [b] from
410 589-1GH (9/83), [c] 2530 967 (11/78).

```
•ᵈ  63'  ADD/DDD  6/87                                    𝄞ᴘ
```

Bartók. The miraculous mandarin, Sz73 — ballet[a].
L. Weiner. Suite on Hungarian Folk-tunes, Op. 18. [a]**London Voices;**
Philharmonia Orchestra/Neeme Järvi. Chandos CHAN9029.

```
•ᵈ  1h 2'  DDD  3/92                                  𝄞ᴘ  𝄞ˢ
```

It is scarcely surprising that *The miraculous mandarin* failed to reach the stage for
some years after it was composed, for the plot concerns three ruffians who force
a girl into luring men from the street up to a shabby garret where they rob
them. Bartók's music matches the savagery of the subject, with wild pounding
rhythms and jagged outbursts: it is a marvellously imaginative and inventive score
which Abbado realizes with enormous energy and knife-edge playing from the
orchestra. No greater contrast could be provided than the first of the *Two
Portraits*, where in the most tender and ethereal fashion Bartók expresses his love
for the young violinist Steffi Geyer. Here Mintz plays most beautifully. The
second *Portrait* is a brief, boisterous, transcription of a piano *Bagatelle*. An
excellent disc is completed by Prokofiev's *Scythian Suite*. Here Prokofiev was very
much influenced by Stravinsky's *Rite of Spring* in a scenario involving an ancient
tribe who worship the sun god. Again it is a score with savage, pungent rhythms
expressed through the medium of a very large orchestra; and again Abbado
conducts with virtuoso control and vehemence. Though the recordings come
from different sources they are all first class.

Järvi may not manage Abbado's precise control in the *Mandarin* (quite as
miraculous as the subject matter itself), but is more flexible in the early scenes.

These are slower and even more characterfully drawn, bringing, at times a welcome touch of humanity to the score. And the benefit of this holding back of tempo is felt immediately the Mandarin's passion explodes and he begins his frenzied pursuit of the girl; not one opportunity is missed to deliver the violence of the succeeding scenes (suffocation, stabbing and electrocution) with a graphic impact that renders the visual element completely unnecessary. Chandos are on hand to supply wide-screened sound that is literally stunning. Weiner's *Suite* comprises four short tone poems which draw on phonographic collections of original Hungarian folk-music. But there the parallels with his contemporary, Bartók, cease. The idiom is most definitely nineteenth rather than twentieth century, and the orchestration has a Respighian richness and colour. On this showing Järvi and the Philharmonia must surely be born, bred and proud Hungarians.

Bartók. Concerto for two pianos and orchestra, Sz115[a]. Sonata for two pianos and percussion, Sz110. **Katia and Marièlle Labèque** (pfs); **Sylvio Gualda, Jean-Pierre Drouet** (perc); [a]**City of Birmingham Symphony Orchestra/ Simon Rattle.** EMI CDC7 47446-2.

52' DDD 9/87

Amongst other things Bartók is famous for having acknowledged the 'true' status of the piano as a percussion instrument and his alliance of the instrument with an array of percussion in the Sonata of 1937 certainly indicates an attitude to the piano that no nineteenth-century composer could have envisaged. In fact it is not an especially violent or even astringent work, for all the calculated rigour of its construction. The three movements are dominated respectively by asymmetrical pulse, nocturnal atmospherics and folk-like exuberance, and the percussion adds colour, punctuation and dialogue, but hardly ever noise or harshness for its own sake. Successful performance depends on close understanding and an especially acute rhythmical sense from all four players. This is precisely what the Labèque sisters and their percussionists supply, plus an irresistible verve and interplay of accent. Recording quality is on the soft-focused side of ideal, and in the Concerto (a modest re-texturing of the same piece) the orchestra is surprisingly remote. Still, there are no finer performances of this exhilarating music currently available, the coupling is convenient (and unique) and minor reservations need not deter the interested listener.

NEW REVIEW

Bartók. Concerto for Orchestra, Sz116. Music for Strings, Percussion and Celesta, Sz106. **Chicago Symphony Orchestra/Fritz Reiner.** RCA GD60175. From VICS1110 (12/65).

1h 5' ADD 1/90　　　　　Ⓑ

These famous performances are by a compatriot of Bartók who was born in 1888, just seven years after the composer himself. Although they come from 1955 and 1958 respectively, the recorded sound has tremendous presence and only the lack of the fullest dynamic range and really soft sound in the *Music for Strings, Percussion and Celesta* betrays its age, along with a certain residual tape hiss. As for the performances, they have long been praised for their superb orchestral playing and above all for the sheer atmosphere that Reiner conjures up. The music itself is of monumental quality, demonstrating Bartók's stature as one of the great composers of the early twentieth century. The *Concerto for Orchestra* is the more obviously approachable work, for here the composer, in response to a commission near the end of his life, displayed a joy in writing a superbly Hungarian-sounding piece for a first-class American orchestra — incidentally, Fritz Reiner was partly responsible for Koussevitzky offering the commission and thus for the existence of the work itself. The other work, however, is no less rewarding and maybe more so, for it shows Bartók's extraordinary aural imagination — no one before or since has dared to write for this particular combination of instruments — and it, too, has a strange yet unforgettable beauty as well as an elemental strength.

NEW REVIEW

Bartók. Music for Strings, Percussion and Celesta, Sz106. Divertimento, Sz113. The miraculous mandarin, Sz73 — suite. **Chicago Symphony Orchestra/Sir Georg Solti.** Decca 430 352-2DH.

Ih 9' DDD 5/91

Two generations ago, Bartók's *Music for Strings, Percussion and Celesta* was considered the height of modernity, and people saw eccentricity in such things as the glacial xylophone tappings on a high note at the start of the slow movement. Nowadays, the work is perfectly approachable (after all, it owes much to folk music) although still boldly imaginative. Solti takes the opening *Andante tranquillo* fast, and the recording is close and brightly lit, but we still feel some of the mystery which is so important in this composer. The conductor comes into his own in the rhythmically exciting *Allegro* that follows and in the marvellously dancelike finale, and he also brings plenty of atmosphere to the *Adagio* with its wondrously strange sounds. The *Divertimento* is gentler, at least by the standards of this composer whose music always shows nervous tension. Though one can imagine Count Dracula approaching in the inexorable slow *crescendo* of the slow movement, much of it bubbles over with melody and, as always, rhythms invigorate. Solti's gusto makes this music irresistible. *The miraculous mandarin* is the earliest and toughest music here, written in 1918-19 for a ballet with an erotic and gruesome story of a Chinese man who is lured into a prostitute's room and attacked by three male accomplices; but although in turn strangled, stabbed and hanged he cannot die until she embraces him. It makes for uncomfortable but compelling listening, not least in this gutsy performance which pulls no punches. A thrilling disc, with sound that leaps out of your speakers.

Bartók. CHAMBER WORKS. [a]**Michael Collins** (cl); **Krysia Osostowicz** (vn); [b]**Susan Tomes** (pf). Hyperion CDA66415.
Contrasts, Sz111[ab]. Rhapsodies — No. 1, Sz86; No. 2, Sz89[b]. Romanian folk-dances, Sz56 (arr. Székely)[b]. Sonata for solo violin, Sz117.

Ih 12' DDD 4/91

Unusually for a composer who wrote so much fine chamber music Bartók was not himself a string player. But he did enjoy close artistic understanding with a succession of prominent violin virtuosos, including the Hungarians Jelly d'Arányi, Joseph Szigeti and Zoltán Székely and, towards the end of his life, Yehudi Menuhin. It was Menuhin who commissioned the Sonata for solo violin, but Bartók died before he could hear him play it — Menuhin was unhappy with the occasional passages in quarter-tones and the composer had reserved judgement on his proposal to omit them. It was Menuhin's edition which was later printed and which has been most often played and recorded; but Krysia Osostowicz returns to the original and, more importantly, plays the whole work with intelligence, imaginative flair and consummate skill. The Sonata is the most substantial work on this disc, but the rest of the programme is no less thoughtfully prepared or idiomatically delivered. There is the additional attraction of an extremely well balanced and natural-sounding recording. As a complement to the string quartets, which are at the very heart of Bartók's output, this is a most recommendable disc.

Bartók. STRING QUARTETS. **Emerson Quartet** (Eugene Drucker, Philip Setzer, vns; Lawrence Dutton, va; David Finckel, vc). DG 423 657-2GH2. No. 1 in A minor; No. 2 in A minor; No. 3 in C sharp minor; No. 4 in C major; No. 5 in B flat major; No. 6 in D major.

② 2h 29' DDD 12/88

It has long been recognized that this series of string quartets written over three decades has been one of the major contributions to Western music. The Emerson Quartet does not play them all the same way, for as its first violinist Eugene Drucker rightly says, "each has its own style". The Quartet has a fine unanimity and is equally good in the tense melodic lines and harmony of slower movements and the infectious rhythmic drive of quicker ones; and it also copes extremely well with Bartók's frequent changes of dynamics, texture and tempo. Here is not only striking virtuosity — to be convinced, listen to the wildly exciting *Allegro molto* finale of No. 4 — and yet great subtlety too. The recording is excellent, with good detail yet without harshness. Where most Bartók cycles take three discs, here 149 minutes are accommodated on two CDs. One readily concurs with the critic who called this "one of the most exciting chamber music recordings of recent years".

NEW REVIEW

Bartók. Violin Sonatas — No. 1, Sz75; No. 2, Sz76. **Gidon Kremer** (vn); **Yuri Smirnov** (pf). Hungaroton HCD11655-2. From SLPX11655 (1/75).

52' ADD 6/87

They don't come tougher than Bartók's two violin sonatas. Even listeners who can take all six of his string quartets in their stride may find themselves struggling here. The sonatas were composed between 1918 and 1923, a period when Bartók was as close as he would ever come to the expressionist world of Schoenberg's atonality. So you can expect free-floating harmonies and structures, a succession of intense ideas, channelled not so much by the conscious will as by the inner demands of the psyche. Yet the influence of folk-music is not to be denied, and both sonatas end with driving, at times barbaric finales. The mixture of styles is as demanding for the players as for the listener and Kremer and Smirnov display formidable intellectual as well as technical grasp. Their performances have not been surpassed in the 18 years since they were recorded, and although the sound quality imparts a certain wiriness to the violin it is more than acceptable.

NEW REVIEW

Bartók. 44 Duos for two violins, Sz98. **Sándor Végh, Albert Lysy** (vns). Astrée E7720. From AS70 (4/82).

50' AAD 3/88

Sándor Végh and Alberto Lysy offer an unquestionably definitive version of Bartók's 44 *Duos* for two violins on this Astrée CD, which originally appeared over 20 years ago when complete performances of this set would have attracted very little interest from the majority of collectors. Today, however, Bartók's ostensibly educational miniatures are recognized as musically significant too, given that he devoted so much of his life to collecting and editing traditional central European folk-music, examples of which figure prominently here. Végh and Lysy do not follow Bartók's original sequence, and add endless variety and interest by juxtaposing differing idioms, but the composer himself sanctioned regrouping for concert performances and on this occasion the ear is constantly stimulated and captivated by the diversity and range of expression drawn from two string voices. Végh knew the composer personally, and so this performance has special historical significance; he and Lysy are ideally matched and their unique account of *Mikrokosmos* for violinists is unlikely to be surpassed as an enriching musical experience. The recorded sound is clear and well balanced, and the players are heard in an ideal acoustic setting.

Bartók. DUKE BLUEBEARD'S CASTLE. **Christa Ludwig** (mez) Judith; **Walter Berry** (bass) Bluebeard. **London Symphony Orchestra/István Kertész.** Decca 414 167-2DH. From SET311 (5/66).

· 1h ADD 1/89

Bartók's lucid but mysterious fable is ideally suited to recording. On CD in particular the mysterious arrival of the music from darkness and silence and its return to shadow at the end are as gripping as (and can be more disturbing than) any stage production. That is certainly true of this performance, which has had many rivals but still stands up well to comparison with the best of them. You will need to hunt out a copy of the libretto and a translation, alas (the opera is sung in Hungarian). Decca provides neither, and although a detailed synopsis is supplied, keyed to cueing bands at crucial points, it would be a pity to miss the detail of Berry's subtle colouring of words, the sense of urgent attack and defence, of fear and concern as Ludwig's Judith unlocks the secrets of Bluebeard's heart and her attempts to let light into his castle draw her inexorably towards endless dark. Kertész is outstandingly imaginative and the orchestral playing is both vivid and rich. The sound has dated little: even some very up-to-date versions have a less satisfying blaze of orchestra-plus-organ major chords when the fifth door opens on Bluebeard's dominions.

Arnold Bax

British 1883-1953

NEW REVIEW

Bax. ORCHESTRAL WORKS. [a]**Lydia Mordkovitch** (vn); **London Philharmonic Orchestra/Bryden Thomson.** Chandos CHAN9003. Violin Concerto. A Legend. Romantic Overture. Golden Eagle — incidental music.

· 1h 15' DDD 4/92

The rehabilitation of Bax's music after long neglect has been largely due to the zeal of the record companies, not least Chandos and the late Bryden Thomson, who brought to it commitment and insight. Now that most of his major works are available on disc, new issues can be bolder in programming and much of the music here will be unfamiliar save to specialists. The Violin Concerto is a substantial work (lasting 35 minutes) with a chequered history. It was written in 1937-38 for Jascha Heifetz, but he did not like it enough to perform and it did not reach the public until the British violinist Eda Kersey played it in 1943. When she died, aged 40, a few months later, the work was largely forgotten. One can see what might have worried Heifetz, for Bax does not always place the soloist

Bryden Thomson   *[photo: Chandos/Ross*

centre stage and virtuosity is in short supply. But there are many lovely things, such as the Celtic-sounding melody in the slower middle part (called "Ballad") of the first movement. Lydia Mordkovitch's playing here is not only beautiful but gives us some idea of how Heifetz himself might have performed the work. Not all the music is equally inspired, but this concerto is a must for Bax enthusiasts. The other pieces are also worth getting to know. The somewhat Sibelian *Legend* (1943) is music intended to evoke "the tales of some northern land"; while the *Romantic Overture* (1926) was written in homage to Delius. The *Golden Eagle* music was devised for a play about Mary, Queen of Scots, by Clifford Bax, the composer's brother, and has a pleasant period flavour. The fine recording copes well with Bax's characteristically dense scoring.

Bax. TONE-POEMS. **Ulster Orchestra/Bryden Thomson.** Chandos CHAN8307. From ABRD1066 (4/83).
November Woods. The Happy Forest. The Garden of Fand. Summer Music.

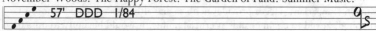

57' DDD 1/84

In a well-balanced programme, here are four of the descriptive pieces Bax composed before turning to symphonic writing. The least well known is *Summer Music*, a short, serene, exquisite tone painting of a hot June midday in the woods of southern England. In *The Happy Forest* a nimble-footed dance-like portrayal of merry-making wood spirits flanks a slow, reflective and passionate middle section, whilst *November Woods* is a darker, more complex evocation of woodland nature. The best known and most sumptuous of the four, however, is *The Garden of Fand*, an opulent piece inspired by the legends and heroes of western Eire. Everywhere the orchestral playing is excellent and the recording has a marvellous presence and depth of tone, so that every strand of Bax's complex orchestration is reproduced clearly and tellingly.

Bax. Symphony No. 3 in C major. Four Orchestral Sketches — Dance of Wild Irravel. Paean. **London Philharmonic Orchestra/Bryden Thomson.** Chandos CHAN8454.

59' DDD 12/86

NEW REVIEW

Bax. Symphony No. 3 in C major[a].
Ireland. These Things Shall Be[b]. The Forgotten Rite[c]. April[d]. [b]**Parry Jones** (ten); [d]**John Ireland** (pf); **Hallé** [b]**Choir and** [abc]**Orchestra/Sir John Barbirolli.** EMI Great Recordings of the Century mono CDH7 63910-2. Text included. Item marked [a] from HMVC3380/85 (2/44), [b] C3826/7 (2/49), [c] C3894 (8/49), [d] HMV DB9651 (10/51).

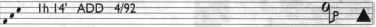

1h 14' ADD 4/92

Bax's Third Symphony has a long and gravely beautiful epilogue, one of the most magical things he ever wrote: a noble processional with a disturbing, motionless glitter at its centre and, just before the very end, a sudden bitter chill. It is pure Bax, and will haunt you for days. We may associate some of the Symphony with the lonely sands and the shining sea of Morar in Inverness-shire (where the work was written), the impassioned string music that rises from that sea in the centre of the slow movement with deep emotion, the war-like dance of the finale with conflict or war and the frequent violent intercuttings of lyricism and darkness with what we know about Bax's temperament. But it is harder to explain in programmatic terms why lyric can become dark or vigour become brooding within startlingly few bars, why that epilogue seems so inevitable, why the

Symphony for all its wild juxtapositions does not sound like a random sequence of vivid memories and passionate exclamations. That it is a real symphony after all, powered by purely musical imperatives, is suggested by the finely paced and tautly controlled performance on the Chandos disc, one of the finest in Thomson's Bax cycle. The enjoyable racket of *Paean* and the glittering colour of *Irravel* respond no less gratefully to the sumptuousness of the recording.

Excellent as the Thomson version is, it has not got quite the atmosphere or insight brought to the work by Barbirolli. This was the first Bax symphony ever to be recorded, and was made under the auspices of the British Council. It was also the first recording made by the Hallé after it had been reorganized by Barbirolli after his return from America. There are some rough edges in the playing, particularly in the horn section, but these slight defects, and the dated recording, matter little in the context of such a satisfying committed performance. Ireland's *Forgotten Rite* is most beautifully realized by Barbirolli and his orchestra, but the choral work *These Things Shall Be* presents some problems in the shape of an embarrassingly fulsome text, whose prophecies of post-war peace have proved to be sadly wide of the mark. Ireland's inspiration here is not at its greatest, either, but the work is performed with great conviction. The final item brings forward Ireland as a pianist, in a delicately poetic performance of his own *April*, the only piece he ever recorded; and it is clearly a matter of great regret that he recorded no other solo piano work. The sound in all the Ireland works is quite acceptable.

Bax. Symphony No. 4. Tintagel — tone-poem. **Ulster Orchestra/Bryden Thomson.** Chandos CHAN8312. From ABRD1091 (1/84).

57' DDD 8/84

Bax's Fourth Symphony is less well regarded than most of his others, yet after several hearings it is still deeply affecting. The opening *Allegro moderato* movement has a dark, brooding eloquence typical of the composer, but it is well-argued and coherent in form. There follows a *Lento* movement, full of sad passion and poetry, and then the mood lightens a little in the last movement with a defiant *Allegro*, sub-titled *Tempo di marcia trionfale*. Thomson directs a performance which is lucid, extremely well played by the orchestra, and objective in style. The more familiar *Tintagel* is from an earlier, more rhapsodic phase of Bax's development. It portrays not only the Cornish seascape but also more intimate feelings arising from a romantic relationship. Here Thomson responds more to the ardent romanticism of the score. Both works are written for a very large orchestra and benefit from an outstanding recording which reproduces the heaviest passages with richness as well as clarity.

Bax. Oboe Quintet.
Bliss. Oboe Quintet.
Britten. Phantasy for oboe quartet, Op. 2. **Pamela Woods** (ob); **Audubon Quartet** (David Ehrlich, David Salness, vns; Doris Lederer, va; Thomas Shaw, vc). Telarc CD80205.

55' DDD 10/89

The wealth of British chamber music composed during the first half of this century is now enjoying a richly-deserved boom, with the release of a number of first-class discs that revitalize pieces neglected for over 60 years. This disc is a prime example, effectively coupling works from the 1920s and early 1930s in deliciously idiomatic performances from these American players. The three-movement Bax Quintet dates from the time of his First Symphony and finds him in fine humour, characteristically infiltrating his rhapsodic style with Irish idioms and ending up with a spirited jig. The Bliss, composed in response to a Coolidge commission, still has much of the flame of adventure and innovation that was a feature of his early music, but which tended to spark less frequently in his later career. The better-known *Phantasy* Quartet of Benjamin Britten, with its satisfying, one-movement arch shape, brilliantly shows a major composer at the outset of his career already displaying those main features of his genius that were to bear such marvellous fruit later. All these works are played with vibrant involvement, the rounded, open sounds of Pamela Wood's timbre set in balanced contrast with the more effulgent warmth of the Audubon Quartet. Only a touch of plumpness in the loudest sections mars an otherwise exemplary recording.

Bax. PIANO WORKS. **Eric Parkin** (pf). Chandos CHAN8732.
Two Russian Tone Pictures — Nocturne, "May Night in the Ukraine"; Gopak, "National Dance". The Maiden with the Daffodil — Idyll. The Princess's Rose Garden — Nocturne. Apple Blossom Time. On a May Evening. O Dame get up and bake your pies — Variations on a North Country Christmas carol. Nereid. Sleepy Head. A romance. Burlesque.

59' DDD 7/90

These are ideal performances of Bax's piano music, recorded by Chandos in the Snape Maltings in very true sound. It is the third volume of Eric Parkin's series and covers mainly the years 1912 to 1916, a crucial period in the composer's life. The works on this disc were inspired by his visit to Russia at the height of a love affair, then the beginning of his long association with the pianist Harriet Cohen, and the Easter Rising in Dublin. *May Night in the Ukraine* is a nocturnal tone-poem, evoking the heat of summer in languorous, shifting harmonies, and is perhaps the finest music in the selection. Bax's first meeting with Harriet Cohen is preserved in *The Maiden with the Daffodil*, a most touching piece. His gift for suggesting a wide

Eric Parkin   *[photo: Chandos/Chlala]*

range of colour on the keyboard rivals that displayed in his scoring for orchestra, while in these shorter forms his tendency to sprawl is curbed. In Parkin he has a sympathetic and persuasive interpreter.

Antonio Bazzini   *Refer to Index*   *Italian 1818-1897*

Amy Beach   · *Refer to Index*   *American 1867-1944*

Ludwig van Beethoven

German 1770-1827

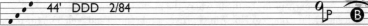

Beethoven. Violin Concerto in D major, Op. 61. **Itzhak Perlman** (vn); **Philharmonia Orchestra/Carlo Maria Giulini.** EMI CDC7 47002-2. From ASD4059 (9/81).

• 44' DDD 2/84

Beethoven. Violin Concerto in D major, Op. 61[a]. Two Romances — No. 1 in G major, Op. 40[b]; No. 2 in F major, Op. 50[b]. [a]**Wolfgang Schneiderhan,** [b]**David Oistrakh** (vns); [a]**Berlin Philharmonic Orchestra/Eugen Jochum;** [b]**Royal Philharmonic Orchestra/Sir Eugene Goossens.** DG Privilege 427 197-2GR. Item marked [a] from SLPM138999 (11/62), [b] SEPL121586 (12/61).

• Ih 3' AAD 10/89

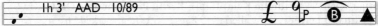

Perlman and Giulini fuse the classical and romantic elements of this work together skilfully. The first movement's opening tutti is beautifully managed by Giulini, for it has a blend of purpose and repose, the tempo unhurried yet with plenty of momentum. Perlman's clear-cut, delicately poised playing then takes the stage: his style is classical, but quietly expressive. He has a beautiful, elegant tone-quality and a rock-like technique, and it is interesting that in Kreisler's excellent but more overtly romantic cadenza his tone becomes a little more ripe. Not often does the shape of the first movement emerge so clearly as here. In the second movement Perlman and Giulini find a good balance of serenity and expressive warmth; the music is never allowed to dawdle or lose its way. The last has a well-defined rhythmic 'lift' at a good, steady tempo and never plods as it sometimes can. The sound-quality is luminous, clear and well balanced. This is one of the most satisfying accounts of a difficult and elusive concerto.

Although the DG recording is perhaps less than ideal compared with today's standards it, too, remains one of the finest accounts of Beethoven's Violin Concerto on disc. Schneiderhan and Jochum work well together, creating a well-structured performance that eschews the often romantic and sentimental approach taken by many performers. This is a performance of innate sensibility, where poetry takes precedence over virtuosity; although Schneiderhan is certainly not lacking in the latter. The slow movement has great serenity and beauty and the finale an infectious joyfulness that makes it hard to resist. It is also worth pointing out that Schneiderhan uses Beethoven's cadenzas for his transcription of the work for piano and orchestra. This disc is made all the more attractive with the inclusion of Oistrakh's outstanding performances of the two *Romances*. At bargain price, this CD is to be strongly recommended.

NEW REVIEW

Beethoven. Triple Concerto in C major, Op. 56[a].
Boccherini. Cello Concerto No. 7 in G major, G480[b]. **Trio Zingara** ([a]Elizabeth Layton, vn; [ab]Felix Schmidt, vc; [a]Annette Cole, pf); **English Chamber Orchestra/Edward Heath.** Pickwick IMP Classics PCD917.

• 56' DDD 6/89

At one time Beethoven's Triple Concerto seemed condemned to languish as a kind of ugly duckling among a group of swans in the shape of his Violin Concerto and the five for piano. Quite apart from the fact that it needs three good soloists who also play well as an ensemble, its expansive first movement has fewer memorable tunes than the other concertos. However, a good performance definitely yields rewards and few collectors acquiring the work regret doing so. This mid-price account of the concerto had the support of a music-loving banker and features a British-based ensemble, while the conductor is none other than the former British Prime Minister Edward Heath — and the performance under his direction is positive as well as sensitive. Thus the first movement, all 17 minutes of it, does not outstay its welcome here, and indeed is heartwarming in its rugged and forthright utterance. The central *Largo* is spacious and eloquent, and the final Polacca (polonaise) bounces along melodiously as well as good-humouredly. The recording is a touch bassy but remains agreeable and clear, and the young soloists of the Trio Zingara are nicely balanced against the orchestra as a whole, save perhaps in the finale where the piano is a touch loud. The Boccherini Cello Concerto No. 7 in G proves a substantial and welcome fill-up and allows us to enjoy Felix Schmidt's artistry as well as the sound of his fine Jansen Stradivarius.

Beethoven. Piano Concertos — No. 1 in C major, Op. 15[a]; No. 2 in B flat major, Op. 19[b]. **Wilhelm Kempff** (pf); **Berlin Philharmonic Orchestra/ Ferdinand Leitner.** DG Galleria 419 856-2GGA. Item marked [a] from SLPM138774 (6/62), [b] SLPM138775 (9/62).

1h 5' ADD 9/88

The Second Piano Concerto was in fact written before the First, and recent research suggests that an initial version of the so-called Second Concerto dates back to Beethoven's teenage years. If the Second Concerto inevitably reflects eighteenth-century classical style, it has Beethoven's familiar drive and energy and a radical use of form and technique. The First Concerto pre-dates the revolution-ary *Eroica* Symphony by some eight years and still shows classical influences, but it is on a larger scale than the Second Concerto, and has greater powers of invention. Kempff's recording of these two works dates from the early 1960s, but the sound quality is pleasingly open and full-bodied, so that the soloist's pearly, immaculate tone quality is heard to good effect. Kempff and Leitner enjoy what is obviously a close rapport and their aristocratic, Olympian but poetic music-making suits both works admirably well.

Beethoven. Piano Concertos — No. 3 in C minor, Op. 37; No. 4 in G major, Op. 58. **Murray Perahia** (pf); **Concertgebouw Orchestra, Amsterdam/ Bernard Haitink.** CBS Masterworks CD39814. From IM39814 (7/86).

1h 10' DDD 10/86   *9* P **Ⓑ**

Beethoven. Piano Concertos — No. 3 in C minor, Op. 37; No. 4 in G major, Op. 58. **Vladimir Ashkenazy** (pf); **Chicago Symphony Orchestra/Sir Georg Solti.** Decca Ovation 417 740-2DM. From SXLG6594/7 (9/73).

1h 11' ADD 5/88   £ *9* P **Ⓑ** ▲

The CBS issue is an outstanding disc, containing two of the finest Beethoven performances to appear in recent years. In both works one feels that there is no conscious striving to interpret the music, rather that Perahia is allowing it simply to flow through him — an illusion, of course, but one which he is able to sustain with almost miraculous consistency. But the honours do not belong solely to Perahia: the contributions of Haitink and the Concertgebouw cannot be praised too highly, and the extraordinary sense of rapport and shared purpose that exist between these two fine musical minds is perhaps the most impressive aspect of the performances. The recordings are unusually sensitive, both to the sound of the piano and to the need for an overall balance that is homogeneous and clearly detailed.

At medium price, Ashkenazy's compelling and brilliantly vital account of these two splendid piano concertos is a bargain, particularly when the length of the CD is over 71 minutes. It does not displace all others, but offers other kinds of truths about these works. Throughout the Third Ashkenazy goes for youthful strength and energy as well as the sense of exaltation that the possession of these qualities inspires, and Solti follows him with orchestral playing of great musical electricity. In the Fourth he offers a different approach which is more relaxed and consciously poetic, bringing a sense of spontaneity to a work which in its lyricism provided a model for the gentler kind of 'romantic' piano concerto. These 1972 recordings do not betray their age in any significant way, although some collectors may feel that their sheer impact demands that one turns both the treble and bass controls down a little from their normal setting: there is still more than enough power after doing so.

Beethoven. Piano Concerto No. 5 in E flat major, Op. 73, "Emperor". **Claudio Arrau** (pf); **Staatskapelle Dresden/Sir Colin Davis.** Philips 416 215-2PH. From 416 215-1PH (4/86).

· 41' DDD 8/86

Beethoven. Piano Concerto No. 5 in E flat major, Op. 73, "Emperor"[a]. Piano Sonata in C minor, Op. 111[b]. **Wilhelm Kempff** (pf); [a]**Berlin Philharmonic Orchestra/Ferdinand Leitner.** DG Galleria 419 468-2GGA. Item marked [a] from SLPM138777 (5/62), [b] SLPM138945 (3/68).

· 1h 3' ADD 12/87

NEW REVIEW

Beethoven. Piano Concerto No. 5 in E flat major, Op. 73, "Emperor"[a]. Triple Concerto in C major, Op. 56[b]. [a]**Leon Fleisher** (pf); [a]**Cleveland Orchestra/ George Szell;** [b]**Eugene Istomin** (pf); [b]**Isaac Stern** (vn); [b]**Leonard Rose** (vc); [b]**Philadelphia Orchestra/Eugene Ormandy.** Sony Essential Classics CD46549. Item marked [b] from SBRG72346 (10/65).

· 1h 14' ADD 8/91

By the time he wrote his Fifth Concerto, Beethoven was too deaf to continue playing in public and though he was still only 39 years old he wrote no more concertos. So the *Emperor* has a particular heroic quality, as if the composer was making a final, defiant contribution to a medium in which he could no longer physically participate. Arrau's is a highly personal and obviously deeply considered reading which appears to have gained in depth and insight over the years. The *Adagio* and *Rondo* come over particularly well: the slow movement sounds very relaxed, but there is actually considerable tension in Arrau's playing, as when he arrives at the astonishing transitional passage from which the finale suddenly erupts; it's as if a store of accumulated energy were suddenly translated into action, though once again there's a wonderful leisurely quality here, for all the purposefulness of the playing. Davis and the orchestra provide firm and dynamic support in a recording whose aural perspective is entirely plausible.

Wilhelm Kempff's recording dates from 1962, but the sound doesn't show its age and the performance takes on board the work's wartime background without descending to the jingoism that hovers dangerously near. Kempff and his sympathetic partners are spacious and dignified yet alert to details and are especially good in the poised central *Adagio*. The Piano Sonata is not an ideal partner for a concerto, but this performance too is a good one. Kempff keeps things in proportion and an evident crisp intelligence is at work; and though the piano sound is unyielding to say the least this reflects his consistent approach to what he himself calls the "rocklike and inflexible" mood of the first subject and the consoling descent "from azure heights" of the second.

Leon Fleisher's account of the *Emperor* is also a commanding one. This American pianist, born in 1928 and thus still young when this recording was made in 1961, has never been a household name like Arrau and Kempff but he plays the work with a well-balanced strength and sweetness as well as youthful zest. With Szell as a skilful partner, this performance comes up with an attractive freshness that in no way deprives the music of its innate power, and the *Adagio*

Sir Colin Davis   *[photo: BMG Classics*

has a poised beauty. Another plus with this issue is that the Triple Concerto offers a far more satisfying and better-value companion piece to the *Emperor* than the sonata on the DG disc, while Arrau's account of it has no fill-up at all. Despite several good recordings, the work itself remains relatively unfamiliar, and is likely to remain so, at least in the concert-hall, since it needs three good soloists who also play well as a trio — and persuasive advocacy, too, in a long first movement which does not have Beethoven's most memorable themes. That is exactly what it gets here, for Isaac Stern often performed chamber music with these two colleagues and the eloquence of the playing by both the soloists and the orchestra under Eugene Ormandy suggest true inspiration as well as the necessary level of skill. The sound in both these concertos is much better than its age of around three decades might suggest. All in all, this is a most desirable disc.

92
NEW REVIEW

Beethoven. SYMPHONIES. [a]**Charlotte Margiono** (sop); [a]**Birgit Remmert** (mez); [a]**Rudolf Schasching** (ten); [a]**Robert Holl** (bass); [a]**Arnold Schönberg Choir; Chamber Orchestra of Europe/Nikolaus Harnoncourt.** Teldec 2292-46452-2.
No. 1 in C major, Op. 21. No. 2 in D major, Op. 36. No. 3 in E flat major, Op. 55, "Eroica". No. 4 in B flat major, Op. 60. No. 5 in C minor, Op. 67. No. 6 in F major, Op. 68, "Pastoral". No. 7 in A major, Op. 92. No. 8 in F major, Op. 93. No. 9 in D minor, Op. 125, "Choral"[a].

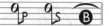

⑤ 5h 58' DDD 11/91   ♀p ♀s Ⓑ

Brimful of intrepid character and interpretative incident, Nikolaus Harnoncourt and the splendid Chamber Orchestra of Europe give us what is surely the most stimulating Beethoven symphony cycle of recent times. As Harnoncourt himself states in a lively interview for the accompanying booklet to this set: "It has always been my conviction that music is not there to soothe people's nerves ... but rather to open their eyes, to give them a good shaking, even to frighten them". So it transpires that there's a re-creative daring about his conducting — in essence an embracement of recent scholarly developments and Harnoncourt's own pungent sense of characterization — which is consistently illuminating, thus leaving the listener with the uncanny sensation that he or she is in fact encountering this great music for the very first time. In all of this Harnoncourt is backed to the hilt by some superbly responsive, miraculously assured playing from the COE: their personable, unforced assimilation of Harnoncourt's specific demands (complete with period-style lean-textured strings and bracingly cutting brass and timpani), allied to this conductor's intimate knowledge of the inner workings of these scores, make for wonderfully fresh, punchy results. In this respect Symphonies Nos. 6-8 in particular prove immensely rewarding, but the *Eroica* and (especially) the Fourth, too, are little short of superb. In sum, it's a cycle which excitingly reaffirms the life-enhancing mastery of Beethoven's vision for the 1990s and into the next century beyond: a more thought-provoking, unimpeachably eloquent achievement one does not expect to encounter for many moons to come.

Beethoven Symphonies — No. 1 in C major, Op. 21[a]; No. 4 in B flat major, Op. 60[b]. Egmont Overture, Op. 84[b]. **Berlin Philharmonic Orchestra/ Herbert von Karajan.** DG Galleria 419 048-2GGA. Item marked [a] from 2740 172 (10/77), [b] 2707 046 (7/71).

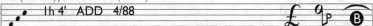

Beethoven. Symphonies — No. 1 in C major, Op. 21; No. 5 in C minor, Op. 67. **Leipzig Gewandhaus Orchestra/Kurt Masur.** Philips 426 782-2PH.

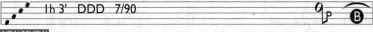

NEW REVIEW

Beethoven. Symphonies — No. 1 in C major, Op. 21; No. 6 in F major, Op. 68, "Pastoral". **Chicago Symphony Orchestra/Fritz Reiner.** RCA GD60002. From SB6500 (10/62).

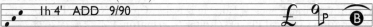

The DG mid-price issue is taken from Karajan's third complete Beethoven symphony cycle made in 1977. Some collectors favoured his earlier DG cycle from the 1960s but there's no denying the sheer beauty and lustre of these performances. Conductor and orchestra give thoroughly committed readings of these two surprisingly rarely played symphonies. The First is light on its toes though the setting is undoubtedly large scale: the Berlin strings play with great crispness and precision. The Fourth Symphony, a work that has always drawn an interesting response from Karajan, is again carefully conceived; the weight and drama of the work are never underplayed but neither is the detail. Karajan always conducted the *Egmont* Overture fully aware of its dramatic intensity and colour. The recordings are good with a nice sense of space around the orchestra whilst detail is never blurred.

So many loud partisan claims are made about Beethoven performances these days that you must use the instruments of the composer's own time, or that it's hopeless trying to equal past giants like Furtwängler, Toscanini or Klemperer — that it's very refreshing indeed to discover a conductor who pursues his own course, and argues for it so convincingly. Kurt Masur always gives the impression of having gone back to the score and thought it all through afresh. He not only adopts the recent innovation of restoring the scherzo-trio repeat in No. 5, he shows deep understanding of how this affects the finale's thunderous self-assertion. And while he avoids the old-fashioned wallowing of a Leonard Bernstein, the *Andantes* of both symphonies show that classicism doesn't mean coldness far from it and the dancing energy of the First Symphony's *Scherzo* and finale make some revered older versions sound stodgy. There is a slight snag: the recording in the Fifth Symphony pushes the trumpets and drums back and the piccolo in the finale isn't the glittering presence it should be, but don't let that put you off buying these refreshing and authoritative Beethoven performances.

If the coupling of the First and Sixth Symphonies suits you, Fritz Reiner's mid-price disc has a lot going for it. It was recorded two-and-a-half years before his death in 1963, but he was still at the height of his powers and had already spent eight years directing the Chicago orchestra which Stravinsky called "the most precise and flexible orchestra in the world". The *Pastoral* comes first here, and the quietly affectionate start is such that one rightly guesses that this will be a warm and gentle view of Beethoven's countryside. The sound is right, too, with a lovely bloom on strings and horns, and altogether this tone-picture is a reassuring one, Nature at her kindest. Even the storm that occurs in the fourth movement, powerful though it is, does not sound really hostile, and one feels that the Austrian peasants whose merrymaking precedes it and who give thanks when it is over are glad to have the downpour that provides water for themselves, their animals and their crops. This 'song of thanksgiving' finale is wonderfully serene. The First Symphony is also thoroughly enjoyable if not quite so inspired an interpretation. When this music was first heard, the opening shocked purists by being in the 'wrong' key (F major), but there is nothing disturbing about it today although we may still simply marvel that Beethoven showed this total command of symphonic form at his first attempt. The recording of these two works has been most successfully remastered, with a strong bass but no hint of heaviness, and few would guess its age.

Beethoven Symphonies — No. 2 in D major, Op. 36; No. 4 in B flat major, Op. 60. **North German Radio Symphony Orchestra/Günter Wand.** RCA Victor Red Seal RD60058.

> 1h 8' DDD 9/89

Beethoven Symphonies — No. 2 in D major, Op. 36; No. 8 in F major, Op. 93. **London Classical Players/Roger Norrington.** EMI CDC7 47698-2.

> 59' DDD 3/87

Seldom has Beethoven's Second Symphony sounded as fresh, dynamic or persuasive as this. The work occupies a transitional place in the symphonic line as begun by Mozart and Haydn; on the one hand it forms the climax of that line, on the other it looks forward to new beginnings. Gunter Wand's stance clearly leans towards those new beginnings, with a reading that is more 'Beethovian' in approach than most, highlighting the fingerprints of his future symphonic style. The Fourth Symphony has always tended to be eclipsed by the towering edifices of the Third and Fifth Symphonies, but the Fourth takes stock, and with the maturity gained in the writing of the Third, looks back once more in an act of hommage to the triumphs of the past. Wand's performances are inspired; he is a conductor who never imposes his own ego and never does anything for the sake of effect, resulting in performances that are honest, direct and unpretentious. His tempos are superbly judged; brisk, but not hurried, allowing the pristine articulation of the strings to come shining through (this needs to be heard to be believed; orchestral playing such as this is rare indeed). The orchestral balance is ideal, with woodwind textures nicely integrated into the orchestral sound, and this is supported by the excellent recorded sound which approaches demonstration quality. A very fine issue indeed.

The thrilling recording with which Roger Norrington launched his period-instrument Beethoven cycle has changed many people's conception of just what to expect from a Beethoven performance. Norrington brings all his experience as a conductor of opera to these two delightful works with outstanding results. His orchestra of 44 make a wonderful sound with crisp articulation the dominant feature. The strings have the bite and dexterity one has come to expect from period instruments, but it is the wind and percussion that are ultimately so thrilling. The 12 years that separate these two works is interestingly illuminated on this disc. The scale is not dissimilar but the individuality and innovation of the later work seem all the more remarkable when so clearly articulated as here. Beethoven on record will never be quite the same again.

Beethoven. Symphony No. 3 in E flat major, Op. 55, "Eroica"[a]. Grosse Fuge, Op. 133[b]. **Philharmonia Orchestra/Otto Klemperer.** EMI Studio CDM7 63356-2. Item marked [a] from CDC7 47186-2 (10/85), [b] ED290171-1 (5/85).

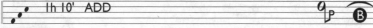

`1h 10' ADD` | P | **B**

NEW REVIEW

Beethoven. Symphony No. 3 in E flat major, Op. 55, "Eroica"[a]. Overture — Leonora No. 3, Op. 72*a*[b]. **North German Radio Symphony Orchestra/ Günter Wand.** RCA Victor RD60755. Recorded at performances in the Musikhalle, Hamburg in [a] December 1989, [b] June 1990.

`1h 5' DDD 10/91` | P | **B**

Günter Wand   *[photo: EMI/Scheels]*

At the time of this Symphony's conception Beethoven was coming face to face with debilitating deafness. In 1802 he wrote the celebrated Heiligenstadt Testament in which he openly contemplates suicide and, in terms which remain awe-inspiring to this day, rejects it. Thus the fierce discords which cry out from the height of the *Eroica*'s first movement development, not to mention the symphony's defiant opening chords or Prometheus-based finale, speak of Beethoven's pain and his resolute response. No single conductor has ever had the symphony's complete measure in a single performance. None the less, Klemperer's 1961 stereo recording still stands out. His Funeral March is certainly awe-inspiring and elsewhere his reading is classical in its formal shaping, romantic in its sensing the huge issues that are being addressed by the composer. The performance is marked out by a certain deliberation of gait, a persistent steadiness of tempo; but it is as satisfying a reading as any before the public and there is a commanding account of the orchestral version of the *Grosse Fuge* with which to round off the disc. The recordings come up very well in the remasterings.

Günter Wand's live performance of the *Eroica* represents a worthy alternative to Klemperer's landmark recording. In many ways Wand stands as a legitimate successor to Klemperer as one of the holders of the great Teutonic tradition of interpreting Beethoven in terms of struggle and triumph. Certainly he launches into the symphony with tremendous vigour and power and he sustains these characteristics throughout. Following an opening movement in which the tension never relaxes at all, Wand leads a reading of the Funeral March which is deeply felt but without self-indulgence. The scherzo and trio provide well-pointed relief prior to an epic reading of the triumphant final movement, which carries all before it. The fill-up, an equally powerful reading of the *Leonora* Overture No. 3, precedes the performance of the *Eroica* and acts as an excellent curtain-raiser and introduction to Wand's interpretative style: genuine and powerful and wholly without self-indulgence. The North German Radio recording is excellent, capturing the involved atmosphere of a live performance without any of the distractions normally encountered. Highly recommended.

Beethoven. Symphony No. 5 in C minor, Op. 67. **Vienna Philharmonic Orchestra/Carlos Kleiber.** DG 415 861-2GH. From 2530 516 (6/75).

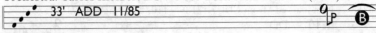

NEW REVIEW

Beethoven. Symphonies[a] — No. 5 in C minor, Op. 67; No. 6 in F major, Op. 68. OVERTURES. [a]**Vienna Philharmonic Orchestra/Karl Böhm.** DG Compact Classics 413 144-2GW2. From 2530 062 (7/71).
Overtures — Egmont, Op. 84[a]. Name-Day, Op. 115; The Consecration of the House, Op. 124 (Orchestre Lamoureux, Paris/Igor Markevitch). The Ruins of Athens, Op. 133 (Bavarian Radio Symphony Orchestra/Eugen Jochum). From SLPM138039 (6/60).

NEW REVIEW

Beethoven. Symphonies — No. 5 in C minor, Op. 67[a]; No. 7 in A major, Op. 92[b]. **Philharmonia Orchestra/Vladimir Ashkenazy.** Decca Ovation 430 701-2DM. Item marked [a] from SXDL7540 (6/82), [b] 411 941-2DH (1/85).

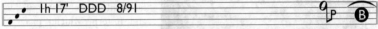

Rarely, if ever, has the spirit of revolutionary turbulence been better expressed in music than in the first movement of the Fifth Symphony; and no musical transformation is more likely to lift the spirits than the transition from scherzo to finale over which Beethoven laboured so hard and pondered so long. Even if our century cannot always share Beethoven's unshakeable sense of optimism, the visionary goal he proposes is one which we abandon at our peril. The trouble with the Fifth Symphony is that it is, for all its apparent familiarity, a brute of a piece to conduct. The opening bars have unseated many a professional conductor, and it must be admitted that even Carlos Kleiber comes perilously close to allowing the famous motto to be played as a fast triplet. Thereafter, Kleiber barely puts a foot wrong. There have been a handful of distinguished interpreters of the symphony before Kleiber, but his reading has an electricity, a sense of urgency and fresh discovery which put it in a class of its own. The DG recording is rather dry and immediate, but the lean texturing is an aspect of Kleiber's radicalism without which the reading would not be the astounding thing it is.

Superb though the Kleiber reading is, collectors who are understandably reluctant to pay full price for a disc with just 33 minutes of music (but see the counter-argument below, about the Kleiber/VPO account of the Seventh), will find DG's budget-price two-disc set — with over four times as much music! — a more attractive proposition. Here are two contrasting symphonies and four overtures, and not only does Karl Böhm yield nothing to Kleiber as a stylist, he conducts the same great orchestra. His account of the Fifth is more spacious and less urgent than Kleiber's, but it is just as strong in its own way and you may well prefer the extra weight of this interpretation. The second movement with its warm melody is a touch slower than usual, and the scherzo has mystery and leads spellbindingly to the mighty and triumphant finale. Böhm's performance of the *Pastoral* Symphony is also very satisfying in its affectionate yet unsentimental depiction of the country scenes much loved by Beethoven himself, who often walked alone in the countryside near Vienna. These recordings from around 1970 have fine rich sound, and though the overtures under Markevitch and Jochum go back another decade these too are acceptable as well as being played with much panache. The DG box is very convenient in being as slim as for a single disc, but in order to open it you need to know that it is hinged on both sides!

Ashkenazy's is a good value coupling of two of Beethoven's most popular symphonies in straightforward and no-nonsense interpretations, with the Philharmonia on fine form. The Fifth is given a powerful, if traditional, performance: Ashkenazy drives the music forward vigorously with a great sense of momentum. In general he concentrates more on overall impact than the finer details of the score. All the work's powerful climaxes stand out strongly and the triumphant finale is suitably rousing. By contrast his reading of the Seventh is more subtle and even more satisfying — recorded in 1984, two years after the Fifth, it is very well considered, with calmer tempos and greater attention to detail. While the rhythmic sweep of the work as a whole is strongly maintained, Ashkenazy takes care to balance this with careful observation of phrasing and dynamics, and he encourages the Philharmonia to play with considerable sensitivity. Decca's sound is very fine indeed: excellently balanced and with plenty of depth. This disc would make an excellent introduction to these two keystone masterworks.

Beethoven. Symphony No. 7 in A major, Op. 92[a]. Die Geschöpfe des Prometheus — Overture, Op. 43[b]. **Philharmonia Orchestra/Otto Klemperer.** EMI Studio CDM7 69183-2. Item marked [a] appears in stereo for the first time, [b] from Columbia SAX2331 (9/60).

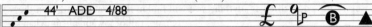

Beethoven. Symphony No. 7 in A major, Op. 92. **Vienna Philharmonic Orchestra/Carlos Kleiber.** DG 415 862-2GH. From 2530 706 (9/76).

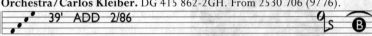

Beethoven. Symphonies — No. 7 in A major, Op. 92; No. 8 in F major, Op. 93. **London Symphony Orchestra/Wyn Morris.** Pickwick IMP Classics PCD918.

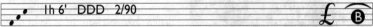

Klemperer may sometimes have been idiosyncratic in his approach, but he nearly always had something original and revelatory to say in his readings and here is probably the best of his recordings of Beethoven's No. 7. His tempos are especially apposite, not fast, but just right to lift the lightness of articulation and phrasing he draws from his players. Insistent melodic and accompaniment figures are always difficult to handle but Klemperer keeps the Philharmonia on its collective toes for the 'Amsterdam' rhythm of the first movement and throughout the following slow movement, with its characteristic rhythmic identity. The *Scherzo* and finale may seem a touch deliberate at first, but so vivacious is the playing and so persuasive the conductor's long-term view of the music, that few will find themselves unmoved. The recording itself has a fascinating history, being the result of a secret stereo taping made simultaneously with the mono recording. It is remarkably fine for its vintage and has been further refined in the digital remastering. The splendid coupled performance of the not-too-often-heard *Prometheus* Overture gives added weight to this recommendation.

DG's 39 minutes may seem short measure, but when the performance is of this revealing quality, the duration of the experience is of relatively little importance. Kleiber's performance fairly bristles with electricity, but at all times one is aware of a tight control which never lets the exuberance get out of hand; moreover, he shows a scrupulous regard for the composer's instructions: all repeats are observed (to thrilling effect in the scherzo and finale) and tempo relationships are carefully calculated. It is Kleiber's feeling for the overall shape of each movement that is most impressive: how else could there be such a powerful sense of cumulative excitement in the finale? The recording is pre-digital, but it hardly seems to matter when given such a high-quality CD transfer.

However, don't be put off by the 'special offer' price of the Pickwick disc or the fact that you may not have heard of the conductor: these are among the finest recordings of these two symphonies to have appeared in a long time. Morris doesn't show any of the tendency to play around with tempo that keeps Furtwängler's Beethoven controversial; he takes Beethoven's markings very seriously (all the repeats are observed — and a good thing too!), but there's nothing rigid about the results. Rarely has Wagner's famous description of the Seventh Symphony, "the apotheosis of the dance", sounded more appropriate. If Morris's Eighth takes a little longer to show its true colours, it soon develops into a performance which, no less than the Seventh, is full of character and delight in movement. Those who don't know the works could have no better introduction; those who know them too well may find these performances the ideal restorative for the jaded palate.

Beethoven. Symphony No. 8 in F major, Op. 93. Overtures — Coriolan; Fidelio; Leonore No. 3. **Berlin Philharmonic Orchestra/Herbert von Karajan.** DG 415 507-2GH.

> 56' DDD 6/86

The Eighth, for all its apparent brevity, lean athleticism and snapping vitality is at times generously expansive. The Trio of the steadily treading scherzo is as leisurely and countrified as anything you will find in the *Pastoral*; and even the

finale, full of joy and abrupt changes of direction and mood, was expanded by Beethoven from material that was too dry, too laconic even for his taste. Following in Toscanini's footsteps, Karajan has always been a gifted exponent of this symphony, treating it as a vibrant and witty successor to the great Seventh rather than a throwback to the style of the First. His 1962 Berlin performance was more careful and keener-eared than this later CD version, but the performance here is a distinguished one still and the overtures are played and recorded with a great deal of power.

Herbert von Karajan   *[photo: DG*

Beethoven. Symphony No. 9 in D minor, Op. 125, "Choral". **Anna Tomowa-Sintow** (sop); **Agnes Baltsa** (mez); **Peter Schreier** (ten); **José van Dam** (bass-bar); **Vienna Singverein; Berlin Philharmonic Orchestra/ Herbert von Karajan.** DG Galleria 415 832-2GGA. Text and translation included. From 2740 172 (10/77).

> 1h 7' ADD 4/87   £ ⁹|ₚ Ⓑ

Beethoven. Symphony No. 9 in D minor, Op. 125, "Choral". **Eileen Farrell** (sop); **Nan Merriman** (mez); **Jan Peerce** (ten); **Norman Scott** (bass); **Robert Shaw Chorale; NBC Symphony Orchestra/Arturo Toscanini.** RCA Gold Seal mono GD60256. From EMI ALP1039/40 (4/53).

> 1h 5' ADD 3/88   ⁹|ₚ Ⓑ ▲

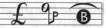

Beethoven. Symphony No. 9 in D minor, Op. 125, "Choral". **Joan Rodgers** (sop); **Della Jones** (mez); **Peter Bronder** (ten); **Bryn Terfel** (bass); **Royal Liverpool Philharmonic Choir and Orchestra/Sir Charles Mackerras.** EMI Eminence CD-EMX2186.

> 1h 1' DDD 12/91   £ ⁹|ₛ Ⓑ

All collections need Beethoven's *Choral* Symphony as one of the works at the very core of the nineteenth-century romantic movement. Within its remarkable span, Beethoven celebrates both the breadth and power of man's conception of his position in relation to the Universe; his sense of spirituality — especially in the great slow movement — and in the finale the essential life-enhancing optimism emerges, which makes human existence philosophically possible against all odds. Karajan lived alongside the Beethoven symphonies throughout his long and very distinguished recording career, and he recorded the Ninth three times in stereo. Sadly the most recent digital version, in spite of glorious playing in the *Adagio*, is flawed, but both analogue versions are very impressive indeed. His 1977 version is the best of the three. The slow movement has great intensity, and the finale brings a surge of incandescent energy and exuberance which is hard to resist. All four soloists are excellent individually and they also make a good team. The reading as a whole has the inevitability of greatness and the recording is vivid, full and clear. At mid-price this is very recommendable indeed.

Toscanini's 1952 performance remains one of the greatest ever committed to record. Seldom, if ever, has the urgency and the blazing conviction of Beethoven's vision been so completely captured in performance, and Toscanini's own drive and intensity of vision has an inspiring effect on his performers. Some feat for an 85-year-old conductor. The recording is a little coarse and confined, and one yearns for such a performance to be liberated from its sonic strait-jacket, but we can hear more than sufficient to appreciate Beethoven's and Toscanini's genius.

And now we have a modern, alternative from which to choose. "The object of this performance," says Sir Charles Mackerras, "is to represent Beethoven's Ninth Symphony rather than Wagner's." He's not the first to attempt such a thing: it looks as though the post-Wagnerian vision of the Ninth has had its day and thus we find him swelling the ranks of conductors who take in the thinking of the 'authentic' movement and apply it to modern instruments. Mackerras's is one of the most inquiring minds on the current musical circuit and here he gives us one of the freshest, most convincingly rethought Ninths to appear in some time. His account of the first movement is cogent and at times, abrupt, while there's a Schubertian grace in the central *Adagio*, taken at a flowing tempo in keeping with Beethoven's original metronome marks. His vision of the "Ode to Joy" finale is anything but solemn, with a bright and breezy chorus and alert, homogeneous soloists. The Royal Liverpool Philharmonic can't muster the weight and richness of tone we associate with their Berlin colleagues, but their crisp enthusiastic playing clarifies the symphony's involved orchestration. All this plus excellent sound, on a mid-price label.

Beethoven. OVERTURES. **Bavarian Radio Symphony Orchestra/Sir Colin Davis.** CBS Masterworks CD44790. From MK42103 (9/86). The Ruins of Athens, Op. 113. Coriolan, Op. 62. Leonore Nos. 1 and 3. The Creatures of Prometheus, Op. 43. Egmont, Op. 84. Fidelio, Op. 72*b*.

1h 3' DDD 9/89

A collection of overtures must offer more than just a series of good performances: the juxtaposition of the works must provide contrast and variety, and the whole should progress so that some sense of climax and finality is reached at the end of the CD. Of course, it is possible for the listener to program the items in any order, but that shouldn't be necessary. Sir Colin Davis has here ordered the overtures in a way that could hardly be bettered, with the programme building through light and shade until the exultant finale of the *Fidelio* Overture is reached. In a full-bodied recording that allows the bloom of the strings to develop their richness, each overture receives a thoughtful, well-prepared reading that might not outrank the best of the competition, but which fits exactly in place in this Beethoven concert. *Coriolan* and *Egmont* make the most substantial individual effect here, Davis obviously warming to their expressive weight and the power with which Beethoven moves inexorably to their dramatic conclusions, yet the lighter works, the *Ruins of Athens* and *Prometheus* for example, are done with no less commitment, and the smoothness of approach adds a new dimension to their interpretation. In all, then, probably the most convincing collection of its kind in the catalogue.

NEW REVIEW

Beethoven. Romance No. 2 in F major, Op. 50. Violin Sonata in D major, Op. 12 No. 1[b].
Mozart. Violin Concerto No. 3 in G major, K216[a]. **David Oistrakh** (vn); [b]**Vladimir Yampolsky** (pf); [a]**Czech Philharmonic Orchestra/Karel Ančerl.** Supraphon Great Artists mono 11 0582-2. From LPV244 (11/57).

49' AAD 12/91 ▲

The sound may be less rich and expansive than in modern recordings but this playing has a wonderful generosity of feeling and purity of spirit, particularly the slow movement of the Mozart concerto, which is even broader than the later (and much better recorded) version he made two years later with the Philharmonia Orchestra (not available on CD). There is playing of the old school and of the greatest eloquence both here and in the F major Beethoven *Romance*. The D major Sonata also serves as a reminder of the excellent rapport he had with Vladimir Yampolsky, his partner in many fine recordings of the 1950s. Wonderfully musical playing which soon makes you forget its undoubted sonic limitations.

Beethoven. Quintet in E flat major for piano and wind, Op. 16.
Mozart. Quintet in E flat major for piano and wind, K452. **Murray Perahia** (pf); members of the **English Chamber Orchestra** (Neil Black, ob; Thea King, cl; Antony Halstead, hn; Graham Sheen, bn). CBS Masterworks CD42099. From IM42099 (8/86).

53' DDD 12/86 P

"I myself consider it to be the finest work I have ever composed", stated Mozart on his Piano Quintet in a letter to his father in April 1784. The Quintet had in fact been composed at great speed but, dating as it does from the beginning of the composer's most impressive creative period, there are no signs of hasty work — indeed, it is written on quite an ambitious scale. Beethoven obviously knew the Mozart work when he came to write a quintet for the same combination of instruments and in the same key of E flat some 12 years later. There is but one difference in style. Mozart wrote the piano part as an

Murray Perahia [photo: Sony Classical

integral part of the ensemble, whereas Beethoven wrote a piano part which was more soloistic. It is a delight to hear such immaculate ensemble and understanding between the players in these recordings. The clean and clear tone of the wind players, particularly that of the oboist Neil Black, is also a source of pleasure, as is Perahia's elegant pianism. Tempos are predominantly expansive and occasionally both works could have benefited from a little more thrust and brio, but the performances are most accomplished. The recording is pure in tone and well balanced.

Beethoven. Septet in E flat major, Op. 20[a].
Mendelssohn. Octet in E flat major, Op. 20[b]. Members of the **Vienna Octet.** Decca 421 093-2DM. Item marked [a] from SXL2157 (3/60), [b] SDD389 (12/73).

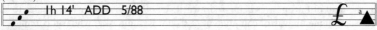

Ih 14' ADD 5/88   £ [a] ▲

NEW REVIEW

Beethoven. Septet in E flat major, Op. 20[a].
Mozart. Horn Quintet in E flat major, K407/386c[b]. **Berlin Soloists** ([a]Karl Leister, cl; [a]Milan Turkovič, bn; Radovan Vlatkovič, hn; Bernt Gellermann, vn; Rainer Moog, [b]Bernhard Hartog, vas; Jörg Baumann, vc; [a]Klaus Stoll, db). Teldec 2292-46467-2.

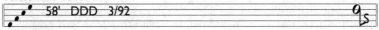

58' DDD 3/92   ⊘ ʃ

Beethoven's Septet is a happy, relaxed divertimento-like work in six movements, scored for string trio with double-bass, clarinet, horn and bassoon. After its highly successful first performance in 1800 the work became very popular, and was arranged for many different instrumental combinations. Mendelssohn's Octet was written when the composer was only 16 years old. Scored for double string quartet, it is his first work to show individuality of expression and mastery of form and its mood is outgoing and high-spirited. Though the Decca recording of the Beethoven work dates from 1959 the sound is warm and attractive, to complement a delightfully unhurried, spontaneous yet relaxed performance which has a good deal of old-fashioned Viennese charm. The Octet performance dates from 1972, and has a less atmospheric, rather clean quality of sound. But the playing has just the right degree of delicacy and buoyancy, with textures very light and clear.

The Berlin Soloists offer a scholarly and spontaneous account of the Septet on the finely-engineered Teldec disc. Collectors seeking a good performance of the work in state-of-the-art digital sound will certainly want to evaluate this performance alongside the classic Decca version and this newer arrival to the catalogue will certainly not disappoint in any way. The lordly demeanour of the opening soon gives way to playing of tremendous verve and vitality in the remainder of the opening movement, where a superb grasp of the line and inclination of the music typifies the performance as a whole. The Berliners phrase the slower movements with affection and dignity, and they find just the right jocular old-world charm in Beethoven's witty minuet. If the Vienna Octet performance captures an extra degree of alluring grace in this work, then it falls to the Berlin Soloists to reveal Beethoven in his most 'unbuttoned' and jovial mood in the *Scherzo*, after the short-lived severity of its introduction, in the ingenious finale of the Septet. The work is coupled here with Mozart's Horn Quintet in E flat major in a thoroughly accomplished performance featuring Radovan Vlatkovič. This fascinating work was composed for the Salzburg virtuoso, Leutgeb, and makes an ideal, albeit rather unusual foil to the Beethoven Septet. An admirable and highly enjoyable disc, well worthy of investigation, even for those who have a special affection for the playing of the Vienna Octet.

Beethoven. String Quartet in F major, Op. 59 No. 1, "Rasumovsky". **Lindsay Quartet** (Peter Cropper, Ronald Birks, vns; Roger Bigley, va; Bernard Gregor-Smith, vc). ASV CDDCA553. From ALHB307 (10/84).

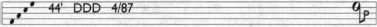

44' DDD 4/87

Beethoven. String Quintet in C major, Op. 29[a]. String Quartet in F major, Op. 59 No. 1, "Rasumovsky". **Medici Quartet** (Paul Robertson, David Matthews, vns; Ivo-Jan van der Werff, va; Anthony Lewis, vc); [a]**Simon Rowland-Jones** (va). Nimbus NI5207.

1h 14' DDD 3/90

In the few years that separate the Op. 18 from the Op. 59 quartets, Beethoven's world was shattered by the oncoming approach of deafness and the threat of growing isolation. The Op. 59 consequently inhabit a totally different plane, one in which the boundaries of sensibility had been extended in much the same way as the map of Europe was being redrawn. Each of the three quartets alludes to a Russian theme by way of compliment to Count Rasumovsky, who had commissioned the set. The immediate impression the F major Quartet conveys is of great space, breadth and vision; this is to the quartet what the *Eroica* is to the symphony. The Lindsays' performance is very impressive indeed, with the tempos sounding so completely right and ideally judged in relation to their overall conception of the work. In each movement the players make all the interpretative points they wish without our feeling hurried. Not only is theirs the most consistently illuminating reading but arguably the most inspired account of this wonderful quartet on record — and they are eminently well served by the engineers.

The neglect of Beethoven's C major Quintet is unaccountable for it is a rewarding and remarkable score, written only a year before the First Symphony. At one time the presto finale earned it the nickname "Der Sturm", doubtless on account of the similarity, or rather anticipation of the storm in the *Pastoral* Symphony. The Medici Quartet with Simon Rowland-Jones give an eminently faithful and musical reading, free from any egocentric posturing. Tempos are sensible and the performance has all the spontaneity of live music-making: nothing is glamorized, yet there is no lack of polish. The first *Rasumovsky*, on the other hand, is not quite as successful: it is well played and there are some felicitous touches of phrasing and colour. Their first movement is on the fast side — not unacceptably so, but the slow movement is far too brisk and this may pose problems for some collectors. All the same the String Quintet alone is worth the price of the disc.

NEW REVIEW

Beethoven. String Quartets — E minor, Op. 59 No. 2, "Rasumovsky"; C major, Op. 59 No. 3, "Rasumovsky". **Lindsay Quartet** (Peter Cropper, Ronald Birks, vns; Roger Bigley, va; Bernard Gregor-Smith, vc). ASV CDDCA554. From ALHB307 (10/84).

1h 11' DDD 1/89

Although the Lindsays may be rivalled (and even surpassed) in some of their insights by the Végh and the Talich, taken by and large, they are second to none and superior to most. In each movement of the E minor they find the *tempo giusto* and all that they do as a result has the ring of complete conviction. The development and reprise of the first movement are repeated as well as the exposition and how imaginatively they play it too! The *pp* markings are scrupulously observed but are not obtrusively pasted on as they are in some sets. The C major is not quite in the same class though the opening has real mystery and awe and some listeners might legitimately feel that the whole movement could do with a little more momentum. On the other hand, they move the second movement on rather too smartly. Yet how splendidly they convey the pent-up torrent of energy unleashed in this fugal onrush. Even if it does not command quite the same elevation of feeling or quality of inspiration that distinguishes their F major and E minor quartets, it is still pretty impressive.

Beethoven. String Quartets — F minor, Op. 95, "Serioso"[a]; A minor, Op. 132[b]. **Végh Quartet** (Sándor Végh, Sándor Zöldy, vns; Georges Janzer, va; Paul Szabó, vc). Auvidis Valois V4406. Item marked [a] from Telefunken EX6 35041 (8/76); [b] EX6 35040 (10/74).

lh 8' ADD 4/88

Beethoven. String Quartets — A minor, Op. 132[a]; F major, Op. 135[b]. **Talich Quartet** (Petr Messiereur, Jan Kvapil, vns; Jan Talich, va; Evžen Rattai, vc). Calliope CAL9639. Item marked [a] from CAL1639, (6/80), [b] CAL1640 (6/80).

lh 8' ADD 12/86

After the expansive canvas of the Op. 59 Quartets and the *Eroica*, Beethoven's F minor Quartet, Op. 95, displays musical thinking of the utmost compression. The first movement is a highly concentrated sonata design, which encompasses in its four minutes almost as much drama as a full-scale opera. With it comes one of the greatest masterpieces of his last years, the A minor, Op. 132. The isolation wrought first by his deafness and secondly, by the change in fashion of which he complained in the early 1820s, forced Beethoven in on himself. Op. 132 with its other-worldly *Heiliger Dankgesang*, written on his recovery from an illness, is music neither of the 1820s nor of Vienna, it belongs to that art which transcends time and place. Though other performances may be technically more perfect, these are interpretations that come closer to the spirit of this great music than any other on CD.

Collectors need have no doubts as to the depth and intelligence of the Talich Quartet's readings for they bring a total dedication to this music: their performances are innocent of artifice and completely selfless. There is no attempt to impress the listener with their own virtuosity or to draw attention to themselves in any way. The recordings are eminently faithful and natural, not 'hi-fi' or overbright but the overall effect is thoroughly pleasing.

Beethoven. EARLY STRING QUARTETS. **Alban Berg Quartet** (Günter Pichler, Gerhard Schulz, vns; Thomas Kakuska, va; Valentin Erben, vc). EMI CDC7 47127/8/9-2. From SLS5217 (1/82).
CDC7 47127-2 — Op. 18: F major, No. 1; G major, No. 2. *CDC7 47128-2* — Op. 18: D major, No. 3; C minor, No. 4. *CDC7 47129-2* — Op. 18: A major, No. 5; B flat major, No. 6.

③ 52' 48' 52' ADD/DDD 1/89

Beethoven was in his late twenties when he started work on the Op. 18 string quartets and he had reached 30 by the time they were complete. Even so, they are far more than a summation of the string quartet as it had developed in the hands of Haydn and Mozart, though they could not have been written without these masters. Beethoven is his own man right from the start and the F major with its Shakespearian inspiration explores depths that seem quite new. The formal symmetry and grace of Haydn can be found in the first movements of the G major and the D major but the sense of scale is different. The dramatic fire of the C minor has clear precedents in Haydn but the strange harmonies that haunt the Adagio opening of the finale of the B flat point to a new era. The Alban Berg Quartet is undoubtedly one of the greatest ensembles now before the public and they offer performances of enormous polish and finesse. The playing is immaculate and the sound has excellent definition, presence and body. Strongly recommended.

Beethoven. STRING QUARTETS. **Végh Quartet** (Sándor Végh, Sándor Zöldy, vns; Georges Janzer, va; Paul Szabó, vc). Auvidis Valois V4405, V4408. Items marked [a] from Telefunken EX6 35041 (8/76), [b] SKA25113T/1-4 (10/74). *V4405* — E flat major, Op. 74, "Harp"[a]; E flat major, Op. 127[b]. *V4408* — C sharp minor, Op. 131[b]; F major, Op. 135[b].

② 1h 11' 1h 6' ADD 6/87 ⑨ℙ

Beethoven stepped both outside and beyond his period nowhere more so than in the late quartets and the last five piano sonatas. The Op. 127 has been called Beethoven's "crowning monument to lyricism", whilst the Op. 131 is more inward-looking. Every ensemble brings a different set of insights to this great music so that it is not possible to hail any single quartet as offering the whole truth — yet these are as near to the whole truth as we are ever likely to come. The Végh give us music-making that has a profundity and spirituality that completely outweigh any tiny blemish of intonation or ensemble. One does not get the feeling of four professional quartet players performing publicly for an audience but four thoughtful musicians sharing their thoughts about this music in the privacy of their home. They bring us closer to this music than do any of their high-powered rivals.

Beethoven. String Quartets — B flat major, Op. 130[a]; E minor, Op. 59 No. 2, "Rasumovsky"[b]. **Talich Quartet** (Petr Messiereur, Jan Kvapil, vns; Jan Talich, va; Evžen Rattai, vc). Calliope CAL9637. Item marked [a] from CAL1637/40, [b] CAL1634/6.

1h 13' ADD 3/87

The Beethoven quartets are one of the greatest musical expressions of the human spirit and they must be represented in any collection. The advantage of this Talich recording is that it couples a masterpiece from Beethoven's middle period, the great E minor Quartet, with one of the greatest of his last years. The B flat was the third of the late quartets to be composed and at its first performance in 1826 its last movement, the *Grosse Fuge*, baffled his contemporaries. Later that same year, he substituted the present finale, publishing the *Grosse Fuge* separately. The Talich Quartet have a no less impressive technical command than other ensembles but theirs are essentially private performances, which one is privileged to overhear rather than the over-projected 'public' accounts we so often hear on record nowadays. At 73 minutes this is marvellous value too.

NEW REVIEW

Beethoven. Clarinet Trio in B flat major, Op. 11.
Brahms. Clarinet Trio in A minor, Op. 114. **Musicfest Trio** (David Campbell, cl; Lionel Handy, vc; Iwan Llewelyn-Jones, pf). Pickwick IMP Classics PCD959.

44' DDD 11/91

With the possible exception of Mozart's *Kegelstatt* Trio, clarinet trios are a rarity in concerts and on collectors' shelves, and not all enthusiasts for Beethoven and Brahms know that these composers wrote one work each for the combination of clarinet, cello and piano. The Brahms was a late work of 1891, written after a year in which he had composed nothing and had confessed to his publisher that he was thinking of retiring — but then, fortunately for us, he heard the clarinettist Richard Mühlfeld and changed his mind. His trio has a quiet beauty which does not reveal itself all at once to the listener but is all the more rewarding for its depth, and this thoughtful performance offers fine tone and shapely phrasing, with each of the three artists playing with affection as well as skill. By contrast, Beethoven's Clarinet Trio is an early work, written in 1797 before his first string quartets. It bubbles over with youthful vigour and invention and has a particularly fetching finale in variation form on a theme by Joseph Weigl, a minor operatic composer of the day. All three instruments are given plenty to do, and the playing generally has a fine freshness with the pianist as well as the clarinettist sharing the melodic honours. The recording, though a touch over-reverberant, is perfectly acceptable. A pity, though, that room wasn't found for another work to go with these agreeable 44 minutes of attractively played music.

Beethoven. Piano Trios — E flat major, Op. 1 No. 1; B flat major, Op. 97, "Archduke". **Trio Zingara** (Elizabeth Layton, vn; Felix Schmidt, vc; Annette Cole, pf). Collins Classics 1057-2.

Ih 13' DDD 5/90

The young Trio Zingara's performance of Beethoven's great *Archduke* Trio is one of the most impressive versions in the current catalogue. It's a performance that flows, sometimes slowly and thoughtfully, sometimes with elegant quickness. Despite a slightly hesitant start, the *Andante* third movement grows steadily in intensity, and its quietly rippling fourth variation is revealed as the heart of the work. Impressive too is the way Trio Zingara manage the transition to the genial finale: all too often this can seem like a let-down — not here. The early E flat Trio makes a fine foil for the *Archduke*, and Zingara wisely don't try to find intimations of later profundity here, but then neither is there any twee 'classicizing' — the tone seems just right throughout. Balancing a grand piano with two solo strings is a nightmare for any recording producer, but the Collins team seem to have got it about right: the strings are clearly audible, the piano doesn't sound over-restrained. One minor word of warning though: the insert note refers to the wrong E flat trio — Op. 70/2, instead of Op. 1/1.

NEW REVIEW

Beethoven. Cello Sonatas, Op. 5 — No. 1 in F major; No. 2 in G minor. 12 Variations in F major on "Ein Mädchen oder Weibchen" from "Die Zauberflöte", Op. 66. Seven Variations in E flat major on Mozart's "Bei Männern, welche Liebe fühlen" from "Die Zauberflöte", WoO46. **Mischa Maisky** (vc); **Martha Argerich** (pf). DG 431 801-2GH.

Ih 6' DDD 2/92

Beethoven wrote five cello sonatas in all, and this disc, which concentrates on his earlier music for the instrument, has Nos. 1 and 2 (which date from 1796) flanked by two melodious sets of variations on themes from Mozart's *Die Zauberflöte* ("The Magic Flute"). This makes for an attractive programme that is on the light and playful side. The playing of Mischa Maisky and Martha Argerich is so vivid that we feel no monotony even though the *Ein Mädchen oder Weib*

Martha Argerich   [photo: DG/Steiner]

chen Variations (which are a bit conventional but make for very pleasant listening) and the First Sonata are in the same key of F major. Above all, it has a freshness that reminds us that we are listening to a young man's music. Maisky's cello tone has plenty of glow and warmth, and Argerich is a sensitive partner, her piano being placed a little backwardly but for that reason never threatening to overpower the cello as might otherwise happen with this gifted and passionate artist. Here, in sum, is impeccable ensemble, agility and wit, together with the broader style of utterance that we require in the slower music of the two sonatas. The special strength of the whole disc is that it conveys an infectious feeling of sheer enjoyment that was undoubtedly felt by Beethoven himself and then communicates in turn to the artists and, finally, ourselves as listeners.

NEW REVIEW

Beethoven. Cello Sonatas — A major, Op. 69; C major, Op. 102 No. 1; D major, Op. 102 No. 2. **Anner Bylsma** (vc); **Malcolm Bilson** (fp). Elektra-Nonesuch 7559-79236-2.

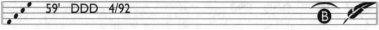
· 59' DDD 4/92   ⓑ

Sandwiched in Beethoven's output by the *Pastoral* Symphony and the *Emperor* Concerto, the A major Cello Sonata is one of the great symphonic works for the instrument — a turning-point in the repertoire. The two Sonatas, Op. 102, on the other hand, stand on the threshold of Beethoven's late period and are more private in feeling, almost experimental at times. Byslma and Bilson are not the first to perform these works on period instruments, but they are probably the first to do so with as much freedom of spirit and natural phrasing as their counterparts on modern instruments. If anything they enjoy greater freedom, thanks to the exquisite blend of the 1690s Goffriller cello with the 1825 Graff fortepiano. The resonant acoustic of the Catholic church in Utrecht is beautifully captured and helps the sound to live and breathe, although the close miking of the cello amplifies the squeaking of fingers on fingerboard.

NEW REVIEW

Beethoven. VARIATIONS.
Schumann. Etudes symphoniques, Op. 13 and posth. **Alfred Brendel** (pf). Philips 432 093-2PH.
Variations — Six in F major on an Original Theme, Op. 34; Five in D major on "Rule Britannia", WoO79; Six in G major on "Nel cor più non mi sento" from Paisiello's "La mollinara", WoO70.

· 59' DDD 3/92

Throughout his life Beethoven was scarcely less drawn to variations than sonata form. Brendel includes the early Paisiello set as an example of the inherited classical tradition, but clearly enjoys himself most in the surprises of the composer's early thirties. "Worked out in quite a new manner" was Beethoven's own description of his Op. 34, in which he changes tempo, time-signature and even key for each successive number. In the *Rule Britannia* set we're not only given a "stylization of the sea in its various ruffles and wind speeds" but also racy humour, for "Beethoven treats the imperial folk-song with a broad wink" as Brendel himself puts it in insert-notes as stimulating and fresh as his own playing. The disc's main interest nevertheless centres in Schumann's *Etudes symphoniques* (or *Etudes en forme de variations* as he renamed his later revision) in a performance including the five posthumously published Eusebius-like variations rejected by the composer from both versions. Admitting to no longer being able to do without them ("since it is their inclusion that makes Schumann's Op. 13 one of his finest compositions") Brendel in fact inserts them so judiciously and imparts so splendid a romantic fervour and continuity to the performance as a whole that all doubts about defiance of Schumann's own wishes are silenced — at least temporarily! Made at The Maltings, Snape, the recording is wholly truthful.

Beethoven. 33 Variations on a Waltz by Diabelli, Op. 120. **Stephen Kovacevich** (pf). Philips Concert Classics 422 969-2PCC. From SAL3676 (1/69).

54' ADD 8/90 £

NEW REVIEW

Beethoven. 33 Variations on a Waltz by Diabelli, Op. 120. 32 Variations on an Original Theme in C minor, WoO80. **Benjamin Frith** (pf). ASV CDDCA715.

1h 1' DDD 11/91

In 1819, when Anton Diabelli asked some 50 composers to contribute a variation on a waltz of his composition, he might have guessed that Beethoven would not take kindly to such a democratic proposal. Diabelli could hardly have dreamed, however, that four years later Beethoven would produce a set of no fewer than 32 variations, the most monumental work in the entire classical keyboard literature. The result is one of those supreme masterpieces for which performer and listener must gird their spiritual loins. It is not only a summing-up of Beethoven's keyboard writing, or a compendium of the resources of the classical style, but also a journey through inner realms — demanding courage and rewarding it with revelation. There have been many fine performances of this mighty work and few recordings of the *Diabelli* Variations fail to present new insights into some hitherto neglected corner of this enduringly fascinating work. Kovacevich does not quite bring off the final climactic build-up of the set, but he does manage to reach the heart of an abnormally high number of these variations; in some, such as Variation 6 with its brilliant, imitative trills and plummeting arpeggios, he is the only pianist on disc to come to grips fully with the implications of the score. A further bonus of this issue is the clarity of the recording — already over 23 years old, it has been shone up like a new pin for CD issue. Detail abounds, and the sheer quality of the bright piano sound is deeply satisfying in itself.

However, no one performance can reveal everything, any more than a single actor can tell us everything about Hamlet, and the ASV disc with a younger artist is most welcome. Benjamin Frith possesses the technique to encompass Beethoven's many and varied demands, not only in dexterity but also in tonal and textural subtlety; and he also knows when to be unfussily plain and when to be more consciously expressive. He balances overall shape with attention to detail in a way that has eluded some bigger names among today's pianists, so that the whole sequence of the theme and 33 variations (with a fugue as the penultimate one) unfolds strongly and naturally, with each of the many moods, textures and tempos leading on to the next. His piano is a fine instrument in good condition and the recording is clear yet atmospheric. The *32 Variations* are also well played and are much more than a mere fill-up, although in later life Beethoven was scornful about this earlier work with its conventional processing of a theme that is really just a C minor chord sequence.

Beethoven. PIANO SONATAS. **Wilhelm Kempff** (pf). DG Galleria 415 834-2GGA. From SKL901/11 (12/66).
C minor, Op. 13, "Pathétique"; C sharp minor, Op. 27 No. 2, "Moonlight"; D major, Op. 28, "Pastoral"; F sharp major, Op. 78.

1h ADD 8/87 Ⓑ

The discography of the Beethoven piano sonatas has been dominated by two pianistic giants, Wilhelm Kempff and Emil Gilels who, alas, did not live to finish his planned complete cycle for DG. If Gilels's recordings are notable for their searching eloquence and intellectual strength, Kempff's performances are hardly less impressive for their combination of classical purity and lyrical individuality. They may at times be less imposing, but they are not less profound. Moreover Kempff had the supreme gift of achieving complete spontaneity, giving the impression to the listener that the music is being re-created for him at that moment. Kempff's timbre was essentially cool and clean, yet there is no lack of warmth or colour, so that the opening of the *Moonlight* Sonata with its serene simplicity and the crisply articulated *Allegretto* make a perfect foil for the stormy finale. The *Adagio* of the *Pathétique* has a disarming direct eloquence, with the urgency of the outer movements in perfect perspective; the *Pastoral* too, again shows Kempff in his element. The two-movement F sharp Sonata makes a fitting bonus for a popular collection that is worthy of any collector's allegiance.

Beethoven. Piano Sonatas — C major, Op. 53, "Waldstein"; F minor, Op. 57, "Appassionata"; E flat major, Op. 81*a*, "Les adieux". **Melvyn Tan** (fp). EMI Reflexe CDC7 49330-2.

| Ih 3' DDD 5/88 |

Here are three of Beethoven's most popular sonatas, played on the kind of instrument the composer himself would have used. Tan is a very brilliant player; the outer movements of the *Waldstein* are dazzlingly done, yet carefully too and with due attention to detail. But both here and in *Les adieux*, where the quick music again abounds in vitality, one sometimes wonders whether Tan is fully in command of the music's structure, for he does not always manage to convey just where it is going. A little more intellectual weight occasionally seems to be needed. It is more in evidence in the *Appassionata*, which is the most successful performance of the three works. Nevertheless, this is an impressive disc, with much brilliance and immediacy making the music seem just a little unnerving, which perhaps is what it should be.

Beethoven. Piano Sonatas — D minor, Op. 31 No. 2, "Tempest"; E flat major, Op. 31 No. 3; E flat major, Op. 81*a*, "Les Adieux". **Murray Perahia** (pf). CBS Masterworks CD42319.

| Ih I' DDD 2/88 |

"I am by no means satisfied with my works hitherto, and I intend to make a fresh start", so Beethoven is reputed to have remarked before embarking on the three sonatas comprising his Op. 31 in 1802. Ominous symptoms of deafness were already overshadowing his private life, as the flanking movements of the D minor Sonata betray even if feeling runs too deep to ruffle the tranquil surface of the central *Adagio*. Perahia's texture is crystalline (with skilful half-pedalling in the problematical recitatives in the opening movement of the D minor work) and even amidst the *con fuoco* of the E flat Sonata's finale rhythm is held on a tautly controlled rein. Whereas these two sonatas were studio recordings, the venue for *Les Adieux* was a warmer, more reverberant concert hall. Here we rightly meet a more impressionably romantic Perahia making every passing innuendo wholly his own in response to Beethoven's overtly expressed sadness, yearning and joy at the departure from — and return to — Vienna at the time of the Napoleonic invasion. Ingratiating in tone throughout a wide dynamic range, perfectly proportioned and finally excitingly brilliant, this performance has with good reason been widely hailed as "one of the most complete realizations of this work that has appeared in recent years".

Beethoven. Piano Sonata No. 29 in B flat major, Op. 106, "Hammerklavier".
Emil Gilels (pf). DG 410 527-2GH. From 410 527-1GH (12/83).

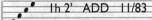 49' DDD 2/84

The great Soviet pianist Emil Gilels died in 1986, not many months before his
70th birthday, and left behind him a major legacy of recorded performances. This
account of the *Hammerklavier* is a fine memorial. The work is very long and
exceedingly taxing technically and the pianist must plumb its often turbulent
emotional depth, not least in the enormous 20-minute slow movement which
requires deep concentration from player and listener alike. After the recording
was made in 1983, the pianist told his producer: "I feel that the weight has been
lifted, but I feel very empty." Gilels manages to give it more tonal beauty and
warmth than most pianists, without any loss of strength or momentum. His is
measured and beautiful playing, and finely recorded too.

Beethoven. LATE PIANO SONATAS. **Maurizio Pollini** (pf). DG 419 199-
2GH2.
A major, Op. 101 (from 2740 166, 1/78); B flat major, Op. 106, "Hammerklavier" (2740 166, 1/78); E major, Op. 109 (2740 166, 1/78); A flat major,
Op. 110 (2530 645, 5/76); C minor, Op. 111 (2530 645, 5/76).

 ② 2h 6' ADD 12/86

If Beethoven's 32 piano sonatas may be likened to a range of foothills and
mountains, then these five sonatas are the last lofty pinnacles, difficult of
access but offering great rewards to both pianist and listener. No library is
complete without them. Pollini made these recordings between 1975-7 and his
playing must be praised for its interpretative mastery as well as its exemplary
keyboard skill. This is a prizewinning issue which has been widely admired, not
least for the magnificent last sonata of all, Op. 111, and the recording hardly
shows its age.

Beethoven. Violin Sonatas — No. 5 in F major, Op. 24, "Spring"[a]; No. 9 in A
major, Op. 47, "Kreutzer"[b]. **Itzhak Perlman** (vn); **Vladimir Ashkenazy** (pf).
Decca 410 554-2DH. Item marked [a] from SXL6736 (7/76), [b] SXL6632 (2/75).

1h 2' ADD 11/83

Under ideal conditions this is music
which can give the listener the feeling that anything is possible, just as
it seemed to be, artistically, for
Beethoven. Perlman and Ashkenazy
come remarkably close to that ideal.
So complete is the identification
between performers and music that
to praise the one is in effect to
praise the other. From the open-
hearted ease of the *Spring* Sonata's
first phrase, Perlman and Ashkenazy
steer a delightful course. In the
Kreutzer they each find remarkable
reserves of strength, never under-
playing the sense of struggle but
always sufficiently in control to
keep longer-term goals in view.
The recording places the listener in

Vladimir Ashkenazy   *[photo: Decca]*

the front row of the stalls, close enough to feel involved in the performance but without artificially jacking up the excitement. Neither Beethoven nor Perlman and Ashkenazy need it.

Beethoven. CHORAL WORKS. **Ambrosian Singers; London Symphony Orchestra/Michael Tilson Thomas.** CBS Masterworks CD76404. Texts and translations included. From 76404 (11/75).
König Stephan — incidental music, Op. 117. Elegischer Gesang, Op. 118.
Opferlied, Op. 121*b* (with Lorna Haywood, sop). Bundeslied, Op. 122.
Meeresstille und glückliche Fahrt, Op. 112.

> 52' ADD 11/88

Astonishing as it may seem, none of the choral works here, with the exception of the imaginative setting of Goethe's *Calm sea and prosperous voyage*, appears to have been recorded before. This disc is therefore warmly to be welcomed because of its first-class orchestral playing (heard on its own in the curious but lively *King Stephan* overture) and splendid choral singing, with a recording quality to match. The tender orchestral introduction to the elegy for the wife of Beethoven's sympathetic landlord Baron Pasqualati is a real gem (and is beautifully played); and two of the other works are of particular interest for their unusual scoring. The light-hearted convivial *Bundeslied* was mulled over in the composer's mind for a quarter of a century before emerging in 1822; and Beethoven was so fascinated by the poem of the *Opferlied* that he made no fewer than three settings of it before this last one.

Beethoven. LIEDER.
Brahms. LIEDER. **Dietrich Fischer-Dieskau** (bar); **Jörg Demus** (pf). DG 415 189-2GH. Notes, text and translations included.
Beethoven: An die ferne Geliebte. Op 98. Adelaide, Op. 46. Zärtliche Liebe, WoO123. L'amante impaziente, Op. 82 Nos. 3 and 4. In questa tomba oscura, WoO133. Maigesang, Op. 52 No. 4. Es war einmal ein König, Op. 75 No. 3 (all from SLPM139216/18, 2/67). **Brahms:** Vier ernste Gesänge, Op. 121[a].
O wüsst' ich doch den Weg zurück, Op. 63 No. 8[b]. Auf dem Kirchhofe, Op. 105 No. 4[b]. Alte Liebe, Op. 72 No. 1[b]. Verzagen, Op. 72 No. 4.[b] Nachklang, Op. 59 No. 4[b]. Feldeinsamkeit, Op. 86 No. 2[b] ([a] from SLPM138644, 10/61; [b] SLPM138011 (5/59).

> 1h 11' ADD 9/85 ▲

Beethoven's small oeuvre of songs is rich and varied. The six songs of *An die ferne Geliebte* follow the unrequited lover's reflections on his beloved, with the piano weaving its way between the individual songs setting the mood and gently assisting the narrative; indeed, it even has the last word. Fischer-Dieskau's intelligent and intense delivery are assisted by his warm tone and easy legato. He adds Beethoven's great song *Adelaide* and, among others, three Italian settings, lightening the tone and raising the spirits for the second half of the programme. Brahms's *Vier ernste Gesänge*, drawn from the image-laden texts of the Old Testament, reflect on man's fate in the great order of life and more particularly on death. The songs have a solemn character and settle in the lower register of the baritone's vocal range, a range that finds a particularly appropriate tone-colour in Fischer-Dieskau's expressive voice. The remainder of the recital draws on similarly severe songs, making for a well-devised programme with a consistent theme. Jörg Demus accompanies sensitively and the elderly recordings sound well.

Beethoven. Mass in D major, Op. 123, "Missa solemnis"[a]. Choral Fantasia in C major, Op. 80[b]. [a]**Elisabeth Söderström** (sop); [a]**Marga Höffgen** (contr); [a]**Waldemar Kmentt** (ten); [a]**Martti Talvela** (bass); [b]**Daniel Barenboim** (pf); [a]**New Philharmonia Chorus;** [b]**John Alldis Choir; New Philharmonia Orchestra/Otto Klemperer.** EMI CMS7 69538-2. Texts and translations included. Item marked [a] from SAN165/6 (7/66), [b] SLS5180 (4/69).

1h 40'　ADD　12/88　ｐ　Ⓑ

Beethoven. Mass in D major, Op. 123, "Missa solemnis". **Charlotte Margiono** (sop); **Catherine Robbin** (mez); **William Kendall** (ten); **Alastair Miles** (bass); **Monteverdi Choir; English Baroque Soloists/John Eliot Gardiner.** Archiv Produktion 429 779-2AH. Text and translation included.

1h 12'　DDD　3/91　ｐ　Ⓑ

"Nothing shakes my conviction that Klemperer comes nearest to the heart of the matter, the grandeur and spiritual intensity of Beethoven's vision". That was Alec Robertson's 1966 view in *The Gramophone* whilst Trevor Harvey, reviewing a version under Solti in 1978, returned to Klemperer in the course of his listening and found, as he said, "unrivalled depth: of exultation, as in the *Gloria*, and of inward feeling as in the many slow and soft sections". These critics, despite their enthusiasm, were certainly not unaware of some shortcomings, especially in the soloists, who are not entirely satisfactory either individually or as a well-integrated quartet. Modern listeners may also find an almost plodding earnestness in the fugues which more recent practice has set free to dance their way to the life to come. But the sense of authority, of power and purpose, is there from the start and throughout the performance, with the New Philharmonia Orchestra playing magnificently; it is their Chorus that provides the special joy. Not only are they on top form but they are recorded so as to sound much more forward in the balance than would be likely nowadays. The choir is the true protagonist here, giving the Mass to the human voice and so coming through to the human heart as its composer in his famous *envoi* said he wished it to.

However, no modern recording goes further than Gardiner's towards catching the immense spirit of the work, and certainly none has been so well served by all the forces involved, including producer and technical staff. With a highly expert choir of 36 singers and the orchestra of 60 playing on period instruments, Gardiner aims in the first place at a "leaner and fitter" sound. There is still plenty of body to it, no feeling of miniaturism, but it does mean that the *allegro*

passages can dance more fleet of foot and with more clarity of movement. A superb example is the "Et vitam venturi" section of the *Credo*: these fugues, so intricate and exhausting for the singers, have a joyful energy and sense of liberation about them. But again this is not achieved at the expense of depth and, at the right moments, stillness. The play of serenity and conflict in the "Dona nobis pacem" achieves exactly the right profundity of expression. The soloists, too, form an unusually homogeneous quartet, all of them doing fine work. They are recorded in due proportion with the choir and orchestra, and that is more exceptional still.

John Eliot Gardiner　　　*[photo: DG*

Beethoven. FIDELIO. **Gundula Janowitz** (sop) Leonore; **René Kollo** (ten) Florestan; **Lucia Popp** (sop) Marzelline; **Manfred Jungwirth** (bass) Rocco; Hans Sotin (bass) Don Pizarro; **Adolf Dallapozza** (ten) Jacquino; **Dietrich Fischer-Dieskau** (bar) Don Fernando; **Karl Terkal** (ten) First Prisoner; **Alfred Sramek** (bar) Second Prisoner; **Vienna State Opera Chorus; Vienna Philharmonic Orchestra/Leonard Bernstein.** DG 419 436-2GH2. Notes, text and translation included. From 2709 082 (10/78).

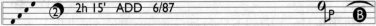

Beethoven. FIDELIO. **Christa Ludwig** (mez) Leonore; **Jon Vickers** (ten) Florestan; **Walter Berry** (bass) Don Pizarro; **Gottlob Frick** (bass) Rocco; **Ingeborg Hallstein** (sop) Marzelline; **Gerhard Unger** (ten) Jacquino; **Franz Crass** (bass) Don Fernando; **Kurt Wehofschitz** (ten) First Prisoner; **Raymond Wolansky** (bar) Second Prisoner; **Philharmonia Chorus and Orchestra/ Otto Klemperer.** EMI CMS7 69324-2. Notes, text and translation included. From Columbia SAX2451/3 (6/62).

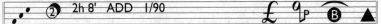

Fidelio teems with emotional overtones and from the arresting nature of the Overture, through the eloquence of the quartet, through the mounting tension of the prison scene to the moment of release when the wrongly imprisoned Florestan is freed, Beethoven unerringly finds the right music for his subject. You can sense this theatrical excitement in Bernstein's ebbing and flowing interpretation, sometimes free with *ritardandos* and other of the conductor's quirks but at all times a reading that catches the listener by the throat. Bernstein obviously inspired Janowitz to give a performance as Leonore that projects all her sorrow and struggle against evil. Kollo is a properly agonized and pained Florestan, Sotin the incarnation of terror as Pizarro. Jungwirth's fatherly Rocco, Popp's charming Marzelline, Dallapozza's fresh Jacquino and Fischer-Dieskau's noble Don Fernando complete the excellent cast.

Klemperer's set has been a classic since it first appeared on LP way back in 1962. The performance draws its strength from Klemperer's conducting: he shapes the whole work with a granite-like strength and a sense of forward movement that is unerring, while paying very deliberate attention to instrumental detail, particularly as regards the contribution of the woodwind. With the authoritative help of producer Walter Legge, the balance between voices and orchestra is faultlessly managed. The cumulative effect of the whole reading is something to wonder at and shows great dedication on all sides. Most remarkable among the singers is the soul and intensity of Christa Ludwig's Leonore. In her dialogue as much as in her singing she conveys the single-minded conviction in her mission of rescuing her beleaguered and much-loved husband. Phrase after phrase is given a frisson that has the ring of truth to it. As her Florestan, Jon Vickers conveys the anguish of his predicament. One or two moments of exaggeration apart this is another memorable assumption. Walter Berry, as Pizarro, suggests a small man given too much power. Gottlob Frick is a warm, touching Rocco, Ingeborg Hallstein a fresh, eager Marzelline, Gerhard Unger a youthful Jacquino, Franz Crass a noble Don Fernando. This is a set that should be in any worthwhile collection of opera.

Vincenzo Bellini

Italian 1801-183

Bellini. OPERATIC ARIAS.
Puccini. OPERATIC ARIAS. **Maria Callas** (sop); [a]**Philharmonia Orchestra;** [b]**Orchestra of La Scala, Milan/Tullio Serafin.** EMI mono CDC7 47966-2. Notes, texts and translations included. Items marked [a] from Columbia mono 33CX1204 (12/54), [b] HMV stereo ASD3535 (8/78).

Puccini: MANON LESCAUT[a] — In quelle trine morbide; Sola, perduta, abbandonata. MADAMA BUTTERFLY[a] — Un bel dì vedremo; Con onor muore. LA BOHEME[a] — Sì, mi chiamano Mimì; Donde lieta uscì. SUOR ANGELICA[a] — Senza mamma. GIANNI SCHICCHI[a] — O mio babbino caro. TURANDOT[a] — Signore, ascolta!; In questa reggia; Tu che di gel sei cinta. **Bellini:** LA SONNAMBULA[b] — Compagne, teneri amici … Come per me sereno; Oh, se una volta sola … Ah, non credea mirarti … Ah, non giunge.

1h 5' ADD 12/87 ▲

This coupling gives a fine insight into Maria Callas's unparalleled interpretative powers. The Puccini arias are all much-loved favourites. As Mimì, the heroine of *La bohème*, Callas softens the voice, seeking out the character's gloriously wide-eyed view of life as well as the vulnerability, whilst as Butterfly she displays a nobility and powerful optimism that holds our attention quite as powerfully as our obvious sympathy for her plight. Those two most beautiful melodies "Senza mamma" and "O mio babbino caro" are gently shaded and masterfully accompanied by Tullio Serafin, one of Callas's most sensitive accompanists. The sound dates from 1954-5 but is clear, well balanced and atmospheric. The two Bellini arias elicit a different response from singer and conductor. The character is carried totally in the voice, the shaping of a line, the shading of a word. The great Sleepwalking scene with which the disc closes is one of Callas's greatest assumptions and shows an insight into the psychology of the opera's central character that has never been equalled.

Bellini. NORMA. **Maria Callas** (sop) Norma; **Ebe Stignani** (mez) Adalgisa; **Mario Filippeschi** (ten) Pollione; **Nicola Rossi-Lemeni** (bass) Orovesco; **Paolo Caroli** (ten) Flavio; **Rina Cavallari** (sop) Clotilde; **Chorus and Orchestra of La Scala, Milan/Tullio Serafin.** EMI mono CDS7 47304-8. Notes, text and translation included. From Columbia mono 33CX1179/80 (11/54).

③ 2h 40' ADD 3/86 ▲

Norma may be considered the most potent of Bellini's operas, both in terms of its subject — the secret love of a Druid priestess for a Roman general — and its musical content. It has some of the most eloquent music ever written for the soprano voice and two duets that show Bellini's gift for liquid melody. The title-role has always been coveted by dramatic sopranos, but there have been few in the history of the opera who have completely fulfilled its considerable vocal and histrionic demands: in recent times the leading exponent has been Maria Callas. The mono recording comes up sounding remarkably forward and immediate on CD, and it captures Callas's commanding and moving assumption of the title part, the vocal line etched with deep feeling, the treatment of the recitative enlivening the text. Stignani is a worthy partner whilst Filippeschi is rough but quite effective. Serafin knew better than anyone since how to mould a Bellinian line to best effect.

Bellini. I PURITANI. **Montserrat Caballé** (sop) Elvira; **Alfredo Kraus** (ten) Arturo; **Matteo Manuguerra** (bar) Riccardo; **Agostino Ferrin** (bass) Giorgio; **Júlia Hamari** (mez) Enrichetta; **Stefan Elenkov** (bass) Gualtiero; **Dennis O'Neill** (ten) Bruno; **Ambrosian Opera Chorus; Philharmonia Orchestra/ Riccardo Muti.** EMI CMS7 69663-2. Notes, text and translation included. From SLS5201 (1/81).

③ 2h 52' ADD 4/89

Bellini's opera of the English Civil War is probably his most readily attractive score, for its moods encompass a gaiety unknown to *Norma* and the writing is

Riccardo Muti   [photo: EMI]

much more robust than *La sonnambula*. As in all of his work, a
great deal depends upon the singers and it is to them that one
normally looks first. Here,
however, Riccardo Muti is in
charge, a conductor with strong
ideas about what may be allowed
the singers by way of traditional
license: on the whole he keeps a
tight rein but compensates by
taking slow speeds so that the
melodies may never pass by with
their beauties unobserved. The
refinement is notable in the
introduction to the bass aria near
the start of Act 2, and there is
no lack of strength and rhythmic
excitement in the surging
melody of the Finale to Act 1.
The performance also benefits
from particularly alert choral
work by the Ambrosians, and from imaginative production. The spotlight is on
the singers even so. As the sorely tried heroine Caballé is ideal as long as nothing
too strenuous arises to put pressure on her exceptionally lovely voice. Her
ethereal tones have a fine effect in the off-stage prayer, and her "Qui la voce" is
deeply felt as well as beautifully sung. Kraus is perhaps the best tenor of recent
times in this repertoire and there is nearly always a personal character about his
singing that gives it distinction. This is a quality somewhat lacking in the
baritone, Matteo Manuguerra; all the same there is some good solid tone and he
makes an honest job of his cadenzas.

Bellini. LA SONNAMBULA. **Maria Callas** (sop) Amina; **Nicola Monti** (ten)
Elvino; **Nicola Zaccaria** (bass) Count Rodolfo; **Fiorenza Cossotto** (Mez)
Teresa; **Eugenia Ratti** (sop) Lisa; **Giuseppe Morresi** (bass) Alessio; **Franco
Ricciardi** (ten) Notary. **Chorus and Orchestra of La Scala, Milan/
Antonino Votto.** EMI mono CDS7 47378-8. Notes text and translation
included. From EX290043-3 (6/86).

② 2h 1' ADD 9/86 ▲

Dramatically this opera is a tepid little mix which might be subtitled *The mistakes
of a night* if that did not suggest something more amusing than what actually takes
place. Musically, the promise of a brilliant finale keeps most people in their seats
until the end, and there are half-a-dozen charming, sometimes exquisite items on
the way. But it is all a little insubstantial, and much depends upon the performance, especially that of the soprano. The name of Maria Callas is sufficient to
guarantee that there will be a particular interest in the work of the heroine. As
usual, her individuality is apparent from the moment of her arrival. Immediately
a character is established, not an insipid little miss but a woman in whom lurks a
potential for tragedy. This is the pattern throughout and much has exceptional
beauty of voice and spirit. Nicola Monti has all the sweetness of the traditional
lyric tenor; the pity is that what might have been a most elegant performance is
marred by the intrusion of unwanted aspirates. Nicola Zaccaria sings the bass aria
gracefully, and carrying off her small role with distinction is Fiorenza Cossotto,
at the start of her career. The orchestral playing is neat, the conducting sensible

and the recording clear.

George Benjamin
British 1960-

G. Benjamin. Antara.
Boulez. Dérive. Memoriale[a].
J. Harvey. Song Offerings[b]. [b]**Penelope Walmsley-Clark** (sop); [a]**Sebastian Bell** (fl); **London Sinfonietta/George Benjamin.** Nimbus NI5167. Text included.

50' DDD 10/89

Well before reaching his thirtieth birthday in 1990 George Benjamin achieved a high reputation as a promising young composer and conductor. This disc sees that promise abundantly fulfilled with a well-balanced, satisfying programme of modern music. Benjamin's own work takes its titles from the Inca word for the panpipe and *Antara*'s scoring includes two synthesizer keyboards, linked to a sophisticated computer system, which enrich and transform the music's fascinating exploration of panpipe sound. Jonathan Harvey's inspiration is Indian rather than South American. In *Song Offerings* he sets a group of mystical love poems by Rabindranath Tagore in English, the music lacking nothing in immediacy of mood and exotic variety of vocal and instrumental colour. The two short pieces by Pierre Boulez are characteristically refined tributes: *Dérive* for Sir William Glock, who brought Boulez to the BBC in the 1960s, *Memoriale* for the French flautist Lawrence Beauregard, who died in 1985. They complete an excellently performed, atmospherically recorded disc: a cross-section of contemporary European music at its best.

Richard Rodney Bennett
Refer to Index *British 1936-*

Alban Berg
Austrian 1885-1935

Berg. Violin Concerto (1935).
Stravinsky. Violin Concerto in D major (1931). **Itzhak Perlman** (vn); **Boston Symphony Orchestra/Seiji Ozawa.** DG 413 725-2GH. From 2531 110 (3/80).

48' ADD 12/84

Berg. Violin Concerto (1935)[a].
Stravinsky. Violin Concerto in D major (1931)[b]. **Arthur Grumiaux** (vn); **Concertgebouw Orchestra, Amsterdam/[a]Igor Markevitch, [b]Ernest Bour.** Philips Legendary Classics 422 136-2PLC. From SAL3650 (4/68).

45' ADD 10/88

NEW REVIEW

Berg. Violin Concerto (1935)[a]. Lyric Suite (1925-6)[b]. [a]**Louis Krasner** (vn); [b]**Galimir Quartet** (Felix Galimir, Adrienne Galimir, vns; Renée Galimir, va; Marguerite Galimir, vc); [a]**BBC Symphony Orchestra/Anton Webern.** Continuum Testament SBT1004. Item marked [a] recorded at a broadcast performance on May 1st, 1936, [b] from Decca-Polydor CA8244/7 (9/36).

57' ADD 6/91

The lifeblood of the nineteenth-century concerto was the self-assertion of the soloist, but since about 1910, with the general collapse of faith in individualism, most concertos have had to replace or redefine these qualities. Stravinsky's Violin

Concerto redefines virtuosity in terms of "circusization" (a buzz-word of the Parisian theatrical circles in which he moved), whereas Berg redefines poetic eloquence in terms of heartbreak and protest. Perlman brings to each concerto his characteristically generous musicianship and clarity of execution. DG have obliged him in his liking for forward placement of the violin, but without serious loss of orchestral detail. Indeed the balance in the final pages of the Berg, where the Bach chorale *Es ist genug* ("It is enough") stands as a poignant symbol of loss, is exceptionally fine, thanks not least to the tonal refinement of the Boston Orchestra. In the Stravinsky the violin is cast in the role of acrobat, or maybe puppet, with the Devil from *The Soldier's Tale* pulling the strings. Meanwhile the orchestra introduces, whips up excitement, spotlights the soloist's tricks, and incites to applause. Perlman and Ozawa are in their element here and once again the recording is clear and lifelike. Arthur Grumiaux's performances have rightly been acclaimed as classics and are also highly recommended. Some may prefer more weight and demonic drive in the Berg, but Grumiaux's relatively restrained interpretation convinces on its own terms, and the Stravinsky is deliciously deft. The sound is never less than clear in detail and balance, and with such playing who could wish for more?

Louis Krasner's recording of the Berg Concerto is of extraordinary documentary interest. Krasner had commissioned the piece and gave the first performance at the 1936 ISCM Festival in Barcelona on the eve of the Spanish Civil War. Berg's death in December 1935 had shocked the musical world though not as much as the death of the 18-year-old Manon Gropius had shaken the composer. What strikes one most of all about this performance is its glowing intensity. There is no sense of the barline or of the music ever being 'moved on'; time seems to stand still and yet there is at the same time a natural sense of musical pace. The audience coughs, moments of distortion and surface noise on this recording made before an invited audience in the Concert-hall of Broadcasting House, London are distracting but the care with which the textures are balanced and the finesse of the wind playing comes across. It has all the anguish and poignancy this music should have. It is obvious that those taking part were well aware that this was no ordinary occasion, and this atmosphere is vividly conveyed. This is only one of two representations of Webern as a conductor in *The Classical Catalogue*. The Galimir Quartet's pioneering account of the *Lyric Suite*, made shortly before the performance of the Violin Concerto, was hampered by a very dry acoustic. All the same every strand in the texture comes across clearly.

Berg. Lyric Suite — arr. string orchestra (1929).
Schoenberg. Pelleas und Melisande, Op. 5. **Berlin Philharmonic Orchestra/Herbert von Karajan.** DG 423 132-2GH. From 2711 014 (3/75).

Ih I' ADD 5/88

If you thought Schoenberg's music was dominated by a singular distrust of harmony and other a-traditional beliefs then his vast tone-poem *Pelleas und Melisande* should restore the balance. Dating from 1903, *Pelleas* employs all the resources of the late-romantic symphony orchestra and the magnificent wash of colour Schoenberg conjures from these forces receives magnificent advocacy from Karajan and his Berliners. The music evocatively delineates the psychological contours of Maeterlinck's mysterious and emotionally-laden plot. Berg's *Lyric Suite* was composed as a six-movement chamber work but in 1927 his publisher suggested a string transcription. Berg chose the second, third and fourth movements as a suite for strings. Sparer and more advanced in sound than *Pelleas* these pieces have a shimmering beauty that is very intoxicating. Karajan obviously has great sympathy with this music and it receives a tender performance from him. The recordings are good if a trifle hazy.

Berg. Lulu Suite (1935)[a]. Three Orchestral Pieces, Op. 6 (rev. 1929).
Altenberg Lieder, Op. 4[a]. [a]**Margaret Price** (sop); **London Symphony
Orchestra/Claudio Abbado.** DG 20th Century Classics 423 238-2GC. Texts
and translations included. From 2530 146 (4/72).

⟶ **1h 7' ADD 8/88**   **Ⓑ**

For all its subtlety and calculation, this is music that constantly spills over into
raw, uninhibited aggressiveness, and Abbado's interpretations convey this quality
magnificently. Berg's destiny as an opera composer is already discernible in the
poised, arching vocal lines of the *Altenberg Lieder*, whose intricate accompaniments
seem extravagantly detailed, given the brevity of the structures. Here, and even
more clearly in the Three Orchestral Pieces, we can hear the sound-world and
thematic characteristics of Mahler's later works carried to a still higher power,
the music veering from frozen calm to frenzy in an instant. Berg's last years were
dominated by his two great operas *Wozzeck* and *Lulu*, complementary studies in
the psychopathology of degradation and despair that work the aesthetic miracle of
drawing sublime music from the most sordid subject-matter. Although *Lulu* can
now be heard complete, there is still a place for this suite of extracts that draws
together some of the opera's most gripping and poignant music. Here, as in the
Altenberg Lieder, the young Margaret Price is ideally flexible and full-toned.
Although the digital remastering has produced an almost harshly immediate sound,
the glare is tameable to a degree and is not inappropriate, given performances
that vividly convey the barely-controlled violence of Berg's emotions.

Berg. Lulu Suite (1935)[a].
Schoenberg. Five Orchestral Pieces, Op. 16.
Webern. Six Pieces, Op. 6. [a]**Arleen Auger** (sop); **City of Birmingham
Symphony Orchestra/Simon Rattle.** EMI CDC7 49857-2.

⟶ **1h 6' DDD 11/89**

Simon Rattle doesn't go to ostentatious lengths to demonstrate the different
sound worlds these three composers inhabit (Schoenberg equals sinewy and
Brahmsian, Berg equals lusciously Mahleresque, Webern equals coolly crystalline,
would be an over-simple set of equations anyway) but he is good at recognizing
each composer's tone of voice and his particular preoccupations; Berg's for a sort
of sumptuous but ordered complexity, for instance, or Schoenberg's for an
urgent forward impulse. All three have a refined lyricism in common, but
Rattle's is a lighter, somewhat cooler lyricism than the polished but rather heavy-
featured manner offered by many conductors in this repertory, and he reaches
subtle or poignant areas of expression with greater ease. With the exception of a
slight recessing of the soloist in the Berg, the recordings are excellent, their
clarity revealing much beautifully moulded playing and precisely calculated
internal balance.

Berg. WOZZECK. **Franz Grundheber** (bar) Wozzeck; **Hildegard Behrens**
(sop) Marie; **Heinz Zednik** (ten) Captain; **Aage Haugland** (bass) Doctor;
Philip Langridge (ten) Andres; **Walter Raffeiner** (ten) Drum-Major; **Anna
Gonda** (mez) Margret; **Alfred Sramek** (bass) First Apprentice; **Alexander
Maly** (bar) Second Apprentice; **Peter Jelosits** (ten) Idiot; **Vienna Boys'
Choir; Vienna State Opera Chorus; Vienna Philharmonic Orchestra/
Claudio Abbado.** DG 423 587-2GH2. Notes, text and translation included.
Recorded at performances at the Vienna State Opera during June 1987.

⟶ ② **1h 29' DDD 2/89**

A live recording, in every sense of the word. The cast is uniformly excellent,
with Grundheber, good both at the wretched pathos of Wozzeck's predicament

and his helpless bitterness, and Behrens as an outstandingly intelligent and involving Marie, even the occasional touch of strain in her voice heightening her characterization. The Vienna Philharmonic respond superbly to Abbado's ferociously close-to-the-edge direction. It is a live recording with a bit of a difference, mark you: the perspectives are those of a theatre, not a recording studio. The orchestra is laid out as it would be in an opera house pit and the movement of singers on stage means that voices are occasionally overwhelmed. The result is effective: the crowded inn-scenes, the arrival and departure of the military band, the sense of characters actually reacting to each other, not to a microphone, makes for a grippingly theatrical experience. Audiences no longer think of *Wozzeck* as a 'difficult' work, but recordings have sometimes treated it as one, with a clinical precision either to the performance or the recorded perspective. This version has a raw urgency, a sense of bitter protest and angry pity that are quite compelling and uncomfortably eloquent.

NEW REVIEW

Berg. WOZZECK[a]. **Dietrich Fischer-Dieskau** (bar) Wozzeck; **Evelyn Lear** (sop) Marie; **Gerhard Stolze** (ten) Captain; **Karl Christian Kohn** (bass) Doctor; **Fritz Wunderlich** (ten) Andres; **Helmut Melchert** (ten) Drum-Major; **Alice Oelke** (contr) Margret; **Kurt Böhme** (bass) First Apprentice; **Robert Koffmane** (bass) Second Apprentice; **Martin Vantin** (ten) Idiot. **Chorus and Orchestra of the Deutsche Oper, Berlin/Karl Böhm.**

NEW REVIEW

Berg. LULU[b] (two-act version). **Evelyn Lear** (sop) Lulu; **Patricia Johnson** (mez) Countess Geschwitz; **Alice Oelke** (mez) Wardrobe Mistress; **Barbara Scherler** (mez) Schoolboy; **Walther Dicks** (bar) Doctor; **Loren Driscoll** (ten) Painter; **Dietrich Fischer-Dieskau** (bar) Dr Schön; **Donald Grobe** (ten) Alwa; **Gerd Feldhoff** (bass) Animal Trainer, Rodrigo, Schigolch; **Karl-Ernst Mercker** (ten) Prince. **Chorus and Orchestra of the Deutsche Oper, Berlin/Karl Böhm.** DG 435 705-2GH3. Notes, texts and translations included. Item marked [a] from SLPM138991-2 (7/68), [b] SLPM139273-5 (12/65).

③ ADD 3h 37'

Acquaintance with the grim, compassionate masterpiece that is *Wozzeck* is a good way to follow Berg into the psychological woods of *Lulu* and get closer to the twelve-note rigour so recently evolved by his master, Schoenberg. One wouldn't claim this is the best possible introduction to Berg's operatic genre; for that you must invest in the full-price *Wozzeck* (reviewed above), which reinforces the terrible beauty of Büchner's tale with a cliff-hanging command of dynamic extremes. However, Böhm's reading remains a most fascinating compendium, testament to the highest standards of orchestral preparation and vocal accuracy. And perhaps even more astonishing than this studio *Wozzeck* is the flawless live Deutsche Oper *Lulu* (a torso, alas, since Friedrich Cerha's finely moulded completion of the third act first only saw the light of day in 1979). A hard taskmaster he may have been, but Böhm casts his emotional net wide enough to embrace silky atmospherics in the more introspective of *Wozzeck*'s interludes, as well as realizing dance and dream for the opera's inn-garden scenes — with no punches pulled for the gut-wrenching précis of the D minor interlude which follows Wozzeck's drowning.

A further unity in this newly-packaged double-bill is imposed by a common team of dedicated singers. Purists may take issue with the amount of speech-song observed by Fischer-Dieskau in both operas — Berg is very precise about all this — though even they could not deny the harrowing success of such deployment in *Wozzeck*'s final scene. Evelyn Lear, mature of tone and masterful of phrase, is not perhaps the Lulu of the playwright Wedekind's dreams and she uses her wisdom to give us a rather aristocratic, *faux-naif* manipulator rather than the instinctive earth-spirit. But she has all the ease for high-lying melismas and as

Lulu waxes expansive to the schoolboy, or welcomes freedom after her jail-sentence, the opulence of the voice becomes indispensable. One tragic loss to the *Lulu* was the death, in 1966, of the great Fritz Wunderlich, in the *Wozzeck* a soldier's friend of ringing normality; he would no doubt have made a warmer Alva than the strong and serviceable Donald Grobe. Other distinguished singers fully immersed in the crazed-comedy spirit of their roles are Gerhard Stolze (the neurasthenic Captain in *Wozzeck*) and Gerd Feldhoff (doubling Animal-tamer and Athlete in *Lulu*): careful casting which does Böhm as much credit as the chamber-music integrity of the Deutsche Oper players. The sound certainly isn't mellow — inevitably, the live recording is the harsher of the two — but it reflects all the sinew of Böhm's immaculate balancing act: a rigorous document indeed.

Luciano Berio

Italian 1925-

Berio. Sinfonia (1969)[a]. Eindrücke (1973-4). [a]**Regis Pasquier** (vn); [a]**New Swingle Singers; French National Orchestra/Pierre Boulez.** Erato 2292-45228-2. From NUM75198 (2/86).

> 45' DDD 7/88

Berio. Formazioni. 11 Folk Songs[a]. Sinfonia[b]. [a]**Jard van Nes** (mez); [b]**Electric Phoenix; Royal Concertgebouw Orchestra/Riccardo Chailly.** Decca 425 832-2DH. Texts and translations included.

> 1h 10' DDD 8/90

It's now far easier to distinguish avant-garde pieces of lasting value from ones that stand rather as historical curiosities and without question the music of Berio lives on, and his audience grows rather than dwindles. It says much for Berio's craftsmanship that his works still have a freshness about them where others today sound impossibly dated. Even *Sinfonia*, with its reference to Lévi-Strauss, Samuel Beckett and the death of Martin Luther King, transcends its original context and challenges us with extraordinary riches. Especially striking is the third movement, a weird collage of quotations from all manner of composers from Bach to Berg and from Beethoven to Boulez, carried out in stream-of-consciousness fashion against the ever-present background of the scherzo from Mahler's second symphony. Nor is it easy to forget the haunting second movement, in which a cloud of isolated floating syllables gradually coalesce into the words "Martin Luther King". Even in the movements that lack such a neat framework, the sheer energy of Berio's sound-world and the logic of his invention is utterly fascinating. This Boulez recording is authoritative and supersedes Berio's own. It is nicely complemented by the short but imposing orchestral score *Eindrücke*.

Riccardo Chailly's performance offers an innovative though still valid perspective of the *Sinfonia*. This is particularly noticeable in the now famous 'Mahler' movement, where Chailly tends to favour a more veiled and recessed balancing of the voices. This may seem rather an odd preference at first but it should be remembered that Berio himself asks for the voices to be only half-heard throughout the orchestral web of sound — an approach that is intended to encourage the listener to re-explore the music on each successive hearing. Chailly's performance certainly reveals more of the orchestral detail, and whereas Boulez brings to the surface the more menacing aspects of the work, in this recording they become submerged into an uneasy, subterranean undercurrent. The inclusion of the splendid *Formazioni* (Formations) of 1987 make this disc all the more desirable. The title reflects Berio's fascination for unusual displacements and groupings of instruments; in this case the dramatic deployment of antiphonal brass sections seated on either side of the orchestra, with strings occupying centre stage (the spatial qualities of this work are particularly effective in this recording). The result is a marvellously compelling and sonically spectacular piece of music which surely ranks as one of his most cogently structured and impressive works. The Decca recording is excellent.

Berio. A-ronne. Cries of London — for eight voices (1975). **Swingle II** (Olive Simpson, Catherine Bott, sops; Carol Hall, Linda Hirst, mez; John Potter, Ward Swingle, tens; John Lubbock, David Beaven, basses)/**Luciano Berio.** Decca Enterprise 425 620-2DM. Texts included. From HEAD15 (1/77).

45' ADD 7/90

Berio's *A-ronne* is considered by many to be one of the finest pieces of avant-garde choral writing to emerge from the seventies. The title is derived from an old Italian dictum "from A to ronne" (the equivalent to our saying "from A to Z"), and Berio calls the composition "a documentary on a poem by Edoardo Sanguinetti" and describes his approach to the text as "a text to be analysed and used as a generator of different vocal situations and expressions" (the poem itself is a collage built out of various sources as diverse as *The Communist Manifesto*, *The Bible* and a verse by Dante). The resulting musical collage is a brilliant *tour de force*, confronting the listener with a tirade of vocal techniques ranging from shouts, groans, sighs and whistling to conventional singing. The effect created is a superb piece of theatre for the imagination. The hauntingly beautiful *Cries of London* is a reworking of a piece originally written for The King's Singers, and its immediate, often humorous charm provides an excellent contrast to the more modernistic sounds of *A-ronne*. The texts are the same as those used by the Elizabethan madrigalists, though the musical techniques used by Berio are closer to those of the medieval composers. Swingle II are extremely persuasive advocates for these challenging and compelling works and the recording is of demonstration quality.

Lennox Berkeley *Refer to Index* *British 1903-1989*

Hector Berlioz *French 1803-1869*

Berlioz. BEATRICE ET BENEDICT — Overture[a].
Franck. Symphony in D minor[b].
d'Indy. Symphonie sur un chant montagnard français (Symphonie cévenole)[c].
[c]**Nicole Henriot-Schweitzer (pf); [ac]Boston Symphony Orchestra/Charles Munch; [b]Chicago Symphony Orchestra/ Pierre Monteux.** RCA Victor Papillon GD86805. Item marked [a] from SB2125 (10/61), [b] SB6631 (10/65), [c] SB2053 (1/60).

1h 12' ADD 3/89

This exceptionally well-filled disc links three French favourites. Munch directs a fine performance of the Berlioz overture, one which truly relishes the long-breathed string writing. The Boston orchestra play superbly. A similar freshness and idiomatic flair is brought to the rarely heard but delightful d'Indy work, in essence a piano concerto of rhapsodic exuberance. Munch conducts with a great deal of vigour and Gallic verve, and orchestra and soloist join in with high spirits and evident pleasure. The piano tone in this 1958 recording is a trifle clangy but not disagreeably so. Pierre Monteux, surely one of the great conductors of the century, reminds us in his fine reading of the Franck Symphony, that he was quite as adept at controlling the long line and regal architecture of a work that has closer ties to the German symphonic tradition than is sometimes granted, as he was as an equalled colourist in the great French tradition. His performance is never lugubrious but has an appropriate weight and scale whilst always being alive to the work's ardent moments. The 1961 recording still sounds remarkably well for its age.

Berlioz. Rêverie et caprice, Op. 8.
Lalo. Symphonie espagnole, Op. 21. **Itzhak Perlman** (vn); **Orchestre de Paris/Daniel Barenboim.** DG 400 032-2GH. From 2532 011 (1/82).

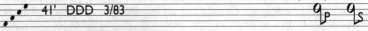

> 41' DDD 3/83 ⓠ ₚ ⓠ ₛ

Daniel Barenboim   [photo: DG

Among the *concertante* works where the solo violin is invited to entertain the listener by alternately seducing and dazzling the ear, Lalo's *Symphonie espagnole* stands out. As well as the bravura excitement there are plenty of good tunes, too, which Perlman plays with freshness and flair, yet without missing its underlying sultry colour. He is greatly helped by the strong character of Barenboim's accompaniment which provides a firm, supple base for the wizardry of the solo fireworks. There has been no more enticing version than this. Berlioz's *Rêverie et caprice* makes an imaginative coupling, a less memorable piece, perhaps, but still ripely enjoyable when presented with such conviction. The DG recording is brilliant and clear and even though the soloist is forwardly balanced the orchestral focus is sharp enough to ensure that no detail is obscured. The effect is undoubtedly exhilarating.

Berlioz. Harold in Italy, Op. 14[a]. Tristia, Op. 18[b]. Les troyens à Carthage — Act 2, Prelude[c]. [a]**Nobuko Imai** (va); [b]**John Alldis Choir; London Symphony Orchestra/Sir Colin Davis.** Philips 416 431-2PH. Texts and translations included. Item marked [a] from 9500 026 (3/76), [b] 9500 944 (6/83), [c] SAL3788 (3/70).

> 1h 10' ADD 12/86

Berlioz was much influenced by the British romantic poet, Byron, and his travels in Italy — where he went in 1831 as the winner of the Prix de Rome — led him to conceive a big orchestral work based on one of Byron's most popular works, *Childe Harold's Pilgrimage*. Like Berlioz's earlier *Symphonie fantastique*, *Harold in Italy* was not only a programme work but brilliantly unconventional and imaginative in its structure and argument. A commission from the great virtuoso, Paganini, led him to conceive a big viola concerto, but the idea of a Byronic symphony got in the way of that. Though there is an important viola solo in the symphony as we know it — richly and warmly played on this recording by Nobuko Imai — it is far from being the vehicle for solo display that Paganini was wanting. Sir Colin Davis's 1975 performance, beautifully transferred to CD, emphasizes the symphonic strength of the writing without losing the bite of the story-telling. The shorter works are also all valuable in illustrating Berlioz's extraordinary imagination. Excellent sound on all the different vintage recordings.

Berlioz. Symphonie fantastique, Op. 14. **London Classical Players/Roger Norrington.** EMI Reflexe CDC7 49541-2.

> 53' DDD 4/89   Ⓑ

The advances by the period instrument movement have often been startling in the way they force us to listen afresh to classic works of the repertoire, but none has been so remarkable as Norrington's recording of the *Symphonie*. For a work that was already advanced in its own time, and one conceived with great attention to colour and its pictorial detail, the 'new' sounds created by period instruments are even more extraordinary. Quite apart from the restoration of the ophicleide to the orchestral texture Norrington's attention to the detail of the score consistently re-awakens our perceptions of this remarkable work. Tempos are re-thought, the March is taken at a steady, menacing pace and the Ball dances at what is surely the perfect speed. The whole recording has an impulsive, trail-blazing quality that comes from the joining of scholarship and imagination and really demands to be heard, even by those sceptical of the period performance movement.

Berlioz. Roméo et Juliette — dramatic symphony, Op. 16. **Patricia Kern** (contr); **Robert Tear** (ten); **John Shirley-Quirk** (bar); **John Alldis Choir; London Symphony Chorus and Orchestra/Sir Colin Davis.** Philips 416 962-2PH2. Notes, text and translation included. From SAL3695/6 (12/68).

> ② 1h 37' ADD 6/88   Ⓟ

Berlioz's 'dramatic symphony' of 1839 is a prime example of early and full-blooded romanticism. The impulsive young composer adored Shakespeare and here he took the English playwright's celebrated love story and set it to music, not as an opera but a symphony with voices, partly because he felt that the language of instrumental music was "richer, more varied and free of limitations and ... incomparably more powerful". This music is, nevertheless, sometimes inspired and sometimes simply naïve, but always spontaneous and Sir Colin Davis, a great Berlioz champion, plays it as if he believed passionately and urgently in every note. He is well supported by his three vocal soloists and the London Symphony Orchestra and Chorus plus the John Alldis Choir, and although the recording is now over 25 years old it does not show its age to any significant extent and indeed may be regarded as a classic Berlioz performance although the total length of 97 minutes for two discs is not generous by CD standards.

Berlioz. Grande messe des morts[a]. Symphonie funèbre et triomphale[b]. [a]**Ronald Dowd** (ten); [b]**Dennis Wick** (tb); [a]**Wandsworth School Boys' Choir;** [b]**John Alldis Choir; London Symphony Chorus**[a] **and Orchestra/Sir Colin Davis.** Philips 416 283-2PH2. Notes, texts and translation included. Item marked [a] from 6700 019 (9/70), [b] SAL3788 (3/70).

> ② 2h 7' 4/86

Berlioz's Requiem is not a liturgical work, any more than the *Symphonie funèbre* is really for the concert hall; but both are pieces of high originality, composed as ceremonials for the fallen, and standing as two of the noblest musical monuments to the French ideal of a *gloire*. The Requiem is most famous for its apocalyptic moment when, after screwing the key up stage by stage, Berlioz's four brass bands blaze forth "at the round earth's imagin'd corners"; this has challenged the engineers of various companies, but the Philips recording for Colin Davis remains as fine as any, not least since Davis directs the bands with such a strong sense of character. He also gives the troubled rhythms of the *Lacrymosa* a stronger, more disturbing emphasis than any other conductor, and time and again finds out the expressive counterpoint, the emphatic rhythm, the telling few notes within the texture, that reveal so much about Berlioz's intentions. The notorious flute and trombone chords of the *Hostias* work admirably. Ronald Dowd is a little strained in the *Sanctus*, but the whole performance continues to stand the test of time and of other competing versions. The same is true of the *Symphonie funèbre et triomphale*, which moves at a magisterial tread and is given a recording that does well by its difficult textures. A fine coupling of two remarkable works.

NEW REVIEW

Berlioz. Béatrice et Bénédict. **Susan Graham** (sop) Béatrice; **Jean-Luc Viala** (ten) Bénédict; **Sylvia McNair** (sop) Héro; **Catherine Robbin** (mez) Ursule; **Gilles Cachemaille** (bar) Claudio; **Gabriel Bacquier** (bar) Somarone; **Vincent Le Texier** (bass) Don Pedro; **Philippe Magnant** (spkr) Léonato; **Lyon Opera Chorus and Orchestra/John Nelson.** Erato MusiFrance 2292-45773-2. Notes, text and translation included.

② 1h 51' DDD 6/92

We have to note that the title is not a French version of *Much Ado about Nothing*, but that it takes the two principal characters of Shakespeare's play and constructs an opera around them. The comedy centres on the trick which is played upon the protagonists by their friends, producing love out of apparent antipathy. Much of the charm lies in the more incidental matters of choruses, dances, the magical "Nocturne" duet for Béatrice and Héro, and the curious addition of the character Somarone, a music-master who rehearses the choir in one of his own compositions. There is also a good deal of spoken dialogue, the present recording having more of it than did its closest rival, a version made in 1977 with Sir Colin Davis conducting and Dame Janet Baker and Robert Tear in the title-roles (Philips 416 952-2PH2). Perhaps surprisingly, the extra dialogue is a point in favour of the new set, for it is done very effectively by good French actors and it makes for a more cohesive, Shakespearian entertainment. John Nelson secures a well-pointed performance of the score, comparing well with Davis's, and with excellent playing by the Lyon Orchestra. Susan Graham and Jean-Luc Viala are attractively vivid and nimble in style, and Sylvia McNair makes a lovely impression in Héro's big solo. The veteran Gabriel Bacquier plays the music-master with genuine panache and without overmuch clownage. There is good work by the supporting cast and the chorus and the recording is finely produced and well recorded.

Berlioz. Les nuits d'été[a]. La mort de Cléopâtre[b]. Les troyens — Act 5, scenes 2 and 3[c]. **Dame Janet Baker** (mez); [c]**Bernadette Greevy** (contr); [c]**Keith Erwen** (ten); [c]**Gwynne Howell** (bass); [c]**Ambrosian Opera Chorus;** [a]**New Philharmonia Orchestra/Sir John Barbirolli;** [bc]**London Symphony Orchestra/Sir Alexander Gibson.** EMI Studio CDM7 69544-2. Item marked [a] from ASD2444 (2/69), [b] and [c] ASD2516 (12/69).

1h 18' ADD 11/88   £ Ⓑ

These performances can be recommended without hesitation, but unfortunately the presentation provides no texts and little information about the music. This is all very well if the listener has access to scores or librettos, but except for the laziest kind of enjoyment there is a real need here to know what the soloist is singing about. The words of *Les nuits d'été* are not too difficult to find, but with the deaths of Cleopatra and Dido you need to have more than a broad knowledge of the general situation. In mitigation it might be said that if any singer can be relied on to convey the sense of the words purely by her expression, and if any composer has a power of communication so vivid that words can almost be dispensed with, these are surely Baker and Berlioz respectively. The yearning and desperation of Cleopatra live in the singer's tone, just as surely as her pulse weirdly beats and then dies in the music. Similarly, Dido's changes of mood, her passionate intensity, her tender farewell to Carthage, are all imaginatively realized and deeply felt. *Les nuits d'été,* too, is wonderfully well caught in the whole range of its moods, with Barbirolli handling the orchestral score with unsurpassed sensitivity and care for detail.

Berlioz. La damnation de Faust. **Nicolai Gedda** (ten) Faust; **Jules Bastin** (bass) Méphistophélès; **Josephine Veasey** (mez) Marguérite; **Richard Van Allan** (bass) Brander; **Gillian Knight** (mez) Celestial Voice; **Wandsworth School Boys' Choir; Ambrosian Singers; London Symphony Chorus and Orchestra/Sir Colin Davis.** Philips 416 395-2PH2. Notes, text and translation included. From 6703 042 (1/74).

② 2h 11' ADD 1/87

Sir Colin Davis's performance of *La damnation* reveals the colour and excitement of a work that has never found a true home in the opera house. No other of Berlioz's scores excels it in the subtle and telling use of detail, from the whole orchestra in full cry to the subtly judged chamber music combinations and to details of instrumental choice (as when the husky viola for Marguérite's touching little song about the bereft King of Thule yields to the mournful cor anglais for her abandonment by Faust). Davis's performance has the grandeur and excitement of Berlioz's vision of romantic man compassing his own damnation by being led to test and reject the consolations maliciously offered by Méphistophélès. No other conductor has made the Hungarian March turn so chillingly from its brave panoply to a menacing emptiness. The sylphs and will-o'-the-wisps flit and hover delicately. The transformation from the raucous boozers in Auerbach's cellar to Faust's dream of love on the banks of the Elbe is beautifully done, as the hurtling pace slows and the textures soften, Méphistophélès's sweet melodic line betrayed by the snarling brass accompaniment. The arrival of CD gave an extra edge to all this vivid and expressive detail. The singers are very much within this fine and faithful concept of the work. Gedda is an incomparably elegant, noble Faust, whose very gentleness is turned against him by the cold, sneering, ironic Méphistophélès of Jules Bastin. Josephine Veasey is a touching Marguérite who is not afraid to be simple; and Richard Van Allan knocks off a jovial Brander. Chorus and orchestra clearly enjoy the whole occasion, and rise to it.

Berlioz. SONGS. [a]**Brigitte Fournier** (sop); [b]**Diana Montague,** [c]**Catherine Robbin** (mezs); [d]**Howard Crook** (ten); [e]**Gilles Cachemaille** (bar); **Lyon Opéra Orchestra/John Eliot Gardiner.** Erato MusiFrance 2292-45517-2. Texts and translations included.
Le jeune pâtre breton, Op. 13 No. 4[d]. La captive, Op. 12[c]. Le chasseur danois, Op. 19 No. 6[e]. Zaïde, Op. 19 No. 1[a]. La belle voyageuse, Op. 2 No. 4[b]. Les nuits d'été, Op. 7 — Villanelle[d]; Le spectre de la rose[c]; Sur les lagunnes[e]; Absence[b]; Au cimetière[d]; L'île inconnue[b]. Aubade[d]. Tristia, Op. 18 — No. 2, La mort d'Ophélie[c].

1h 5' DDD 2/91

Berlioz intended the songs in his cycle *Les nuits d'été* to be assigned to different types of singers. This excellent issue fulfils his wishes, and each of the performers has been carefully chosen to fit his or her particular offering. In turn, Montague, Robbin, Crook and Cachemaille ideally catches the mood and feeling of his or her piece, and each has the kind of tone that seems perfectly suited to Berlioz's idiom. In support, Gardiner finds just the right tempo for each song, never indulging in the over-deliberate speed that can kill the slower songs with kindness. He and his orchestra play Berlioz's wonderfully atmospheric accompaniments with beauty and sensitivity. To add to one's pleasure there is a generous selection of Berlioz's other songs with orchestra, equally well interpreted. Robbin's account of the marvellous *La captive*, the very essence of this composer's brand of romanticism, is a particular joy.

Berlioz. L'enfance du Christ, Op. 25. **Robert Tear** (ten) Narrator; **David Wilson-Johnson** (bar) Herod; **Ann Murray** (mez) Mary; **Thomas Allen** (bar) Joseph; **Matthew Best** (bass) Ishmaelite Father; **Gerald Finley** (bar) Polydorus; **William Kendall** (ten) Centurion; **Choir of King's College, Cambridge; Royal Philharmonic Orchestra/Stephen Cleobury.** EMI CDS7 49935-2. Notes, text and translation included.

(2) 1h 37' DDD 12/90

The Choir of King's College, Cambridge has made this splendid recording of *L'enfance du Christ* with a strong, well-chosen all-English cast. The important role of Narrator falls to Robert Tear, who assumes it with warmth and sympathy and a good sense of the drama as it unfolds. David Wilson-Johnson makes a superb Herod, tortured and anguished in his mind before delivering his half-demented sentence of death upon the Holy Innocents. Ann Murray, as Mary, is tender and gentle, particularly in the quiet, idyllic stable scene. Thomas Allen portrays a convincing Joseph, firm and decisive in his singing, well able to face up to his responsibilities as head of the Holy Family. Matthew Best sings a rich and heart-warming welcome to them on their

arrival in Egypt. The King's Choir, amply assisted by the chapel acoustics, are able to make the choir of angelic voices sound truly other-worldly, their repeated "Hosannas" fading gently upwards and away into the fan-vaulting — like clouds of incense — with magical effect. The acoustics also play an important part at the close of the oratorio, enabling the choir to bring it almost inevitably to its breathtaking conclusion of peace and quiet contemplation. Even if you've never heard any of this music before, except the famous "Shepherds' farewell" chorus, this really is compulsory Christmas listening!

Ann Murray   *[photo: EMI/Hickey*

Berlioz. LES TROYENS. **Jon Vickers** (ten) Aeneas; **Josephine Veasey** (mez) Dido; **Berit Lindholm** (sop) Cassandra; **Peter Glossop** (bar) Corebus, Ghost of Corebus; **Heather Begg** (sop) Anna; **Roger Soyer** (bar) Narbal, Spirit of Hector; **Anne Howells** (mez) Ascanius; **Anthony Raffell** (bass) Panthus; **Ian Partridge** (ten) Iopas; **Pierre Thau** (bass) Priam, Mercury, a Trojan soldier; **Elizabeth Bainbridge** (mez) Hecuba, Ghost of Cassandra; **Ryland Davies** (ten) Hylas; **David Lennox** (ten) Helenus; **Raimund Herincx** (bass) Ghost of Priam, First Sentry; **Dennis Wicks** (bar) Ghost of Hector, Second Sentry, Greek Chieftain; **Wandsworth School Boys' Choir; Royal Opera House, Covent Garden Chorus and Orchestra/Sir Colin Davis.** Philips 416 432-2PH4. Notes, text and translation included. From 6709 002 (5/70).

(4) 4h 1' ADD 12/86

One of the largest canvases in the whole genre of opera, *Les troyens* was for long considered unperformable. Yet it is no longer than some of Wagner's scores and certainly no more difficult to encompass in one evening. That has been proved conclusively in a succession of productions at Covent Garden, this one recorded not actually 'live' but immediately after stage performances. Sir Colin Davis, the leading Berlioz conductor of the day, fired his forces to give the kind of reading that could only have emerged from experience of the work in the opera house. He is fully aware of the epic quality of the story and no one else has quite so successfully conveyed the score's dramatic stature, its nobility and its tragic consequences. There are many splendid performances on this set, but in the end it is the sense of a team effort, of a cast, chorus and orchestra utterly devoted to the task in hand that is so boldly declared. The recording matches the quality of the music-making.

Lord Alfred Berners
British 1883-1950

Leonard Bernstein
American 1918-1990

Bernstein. ORCHESTRAL WORKS. **New York Philharmonic Orchestra/ Leonard Bernstein.** CBS Maestro CD44773. Items marked [a] from 72405 (5/66), [b] Philips SBBL652 (2/62).
Candide — Overture[a]. West Side Story — Symphonic dances[b]. On the Town — Three dance episodes[a]. On the Waterfront — Symphonic suite[b].

55' ADD 2/91

Broadway and Hollywood form a backcloth to all the music on this disc. A maniacally driven Overture to Bernstein's third Broadway musical, *Candide*, sets the style from the outset with the conductor intent on squeezing every last ounce from both his music and players. The orchestra can sound hard-pressed at times and details get smudged, especially so in the cavernous acoustic, but the dazzling zest of this approach is totally winning and, when the music does relax into more tender moments, the pathos is overwhelming. In the Symphonic dances from *West Side Story*, few orchestras could better the NYPO's intuitive feel for the dance rhythms and cross accents, the rampaging Latin percussion barrage, the screaming trumpet writing, or the theatre-pit instrumental balance. The Three Dance Episodes from Bernstein's first musical, *On the Town*, are more overtly eclectic, with hints of Gershwin alongside allusions to Stravinsky, whilst the magnificent score for the film, *On the Waterfront*, finds Bernstein inventively complementing the highlights and deep shadows of Elia Kazan's visual style, and the savagery of the plot. As his own best interpreter, Bernstein goes straight for the key features of all these scores and inspires his orchestra to produce its best.

NEW REVIEW

Bernstein. Concerto for Orchestra, "Jubilee Games" (1986-9)[a].
Del Tredici. Tattoo (1986)[b].
Rorem. Violin Concerto (1984)[bc]. [c]**Gidon Kremer** (vn); [a]**José Eduardo Chama** (bar); [a]**Israel Philharmonic Orchestra,** [b]**New York Philharmonic Orchestra/Leonard Bernstein.** DG 429 231-2GH. Recorded at performances in [a]Frederic R. Mann Auditorium, Tel Aviv during June 1988 and April 1989, [b] and [c] Avery Fisher Hall, New York during November 1988.

1h 12' DDD 1/92

Leonard Bernstein was an ardent advocate of American music and this generous programme of live recordings show him exploring new repertoire at an age when most conductors are content to recycle their old favourites. David Del Tredici will be familiar to some record-buyers as the composer of an extraordinary sequence of large-scale, lushly romantic works based on *Alice in Wonderland* (refer to the Index to Reviews at the end of this book). "*Tatoo* is not *Alice*", the composer warns in the excellent booklet; and yet it's hard to take the proceedings too seriously as Mahler, Varèse, Paganini *et al* battle for allusive supremacy in a noisy postmodernist extravaganza. The music of Ned Rorem is barely known in the UK, but his elegiac lyrical invention should hold no terrors for admirers of Samuel Barber or Virgil Thomson. Under an enthusiastic Bernstein (who sings along in the most passionate sections) Gidon Kremer and the New York Philharmonic have you convinced that, in its unpretentious way — more suite than conventional concerto the work is a small masterpiece. Bernstein's own *Concerto for Orchestra* is a characteristically uneven piece, aping Lutoslawski and even Bartók before settling into that familiar *West Side Story* vein for some infectious "Diaspora Dances". The closing "Benediction" goes deeper and Bernstein's final plea for peace is beautifully intoned by baritone José Eduarda Chama. The Israel Philharmonic play less well than their American rivals but there are few major disasters and the sound throughout, though necessarily close-miked, gives the music plenty of room to breathe.

NEW REVIEW

Bernstein. Candide — Overture. Symphony No. 2, "The Age of Anxiety"[a]. Fancy Free — ballet[b]. [b]**Billie Holiday** (sngr); [a]**Jeffrey Kahane** (pf); **Bournemouth Symphony Orchestra/Andrew Litton.** Virgin Classics VC7 91433-2.

1h 7' DDD 9/91

Stunning performances of three of Bernstein's most popular orchestral works. *The Age of Anxiety* (the second of his three symphonies) takes its inspiration from a W.H. Auden poem concerning four lonely characters on a journey of self-discovery, whose collective consciousness is represented in the symphony by a solo piano. Bernstein identified strongly with the theme of the poem, though on hearing it Auden is said to have disliked his treatment of it. It has, however, won many admirers and is by far the most frequently performed of Bernstein's symphonies. On a purely musical level it is a fascinating blend of Brahmsian romanticism, quasi-serial writing and jazz. The Overture to *Candide* hardly needs any introduction — a case of once heard never forgotten. Litton's performance is a real *tour de force* (by far the fastest on disc) with plenty of explosive vitality and an astonishing attention to minor detail. The ballet *Fancy Free* is another firm favourite, and here again Litton and the Bournemouth Symphony Orchestra pull out all the stops out in a suitably brash and raunchy performance — the inclusion of Billie Holiday's original recording of *Big Stuff* at the opening is inspired. Excellent sound, though an extra touch of volume is required for maximum enjoyment.

Bernstein. Songfest[a]. Chichester Psalms[b]. [a]**Clamma Dale** (sop); [a]**Rosalind Elias**, [a]**Nancy Williams** (mezs); [a]**Neil Rosenshein** (ten); [a]**John Reardon** (bar); [a]**Donald Gramm** (bass); [b]soloist from the **Vienna Boys' Choir;** [b]**Vienna Jeunesse Choir;** [a]**National Symphony Orchestra of Washington,** [b]**Israel Philharmonic Orchestra/Leonard Bernstein.** DG 415 965-2GH. Texts and, where appropriate, translations included. Item marked [a] from 2531 044 (11/78), [b] 2709 077 (9/78) which was recorded at a performance in the Philharmonie, Berlin during August 1977.

1h 2' ADD 5/86

"I, too, am America", is the message of Leonard Bernstein's orchestral song-cycle *Songfest*. The subject of the work is the American artist's emotional, spiritual and intellectual response to life in an essentially Puritan society, and, more specifically, to the eclecticism of American society and its many problems of social integration (blacks, women, homosexuals and expatriates). As expected from a composer/conductor equally at home on Broadway or in Vienna's Musikverein, the styles range widely. The scoring is colourful, occasionally pungent, always tuneful. Bernstein's soloists are well chosen and sing with feeling. This vivid live recording of the *Chichester Psalms* offers the full orchestral version and the performers all give their utmost.

Bernstein. SONGS AND DUETS. **Judy Kaye** (sop); **William Sharp** (bar); [a]**Sara Sant'Ambrogio** (vc); **Michael Barrett, Steven Blier** (pfs). Koch International Classics 37000-2. Texts included.
Arias and Barcarolles. ON THE TOWN — Some other time; Lonely town; Carried away; I can cook. WONDERFUL TOWN — A little bit in love. PETER PAN — Dream with me[a]. Songfest — Storyette, H.M.; To what you said[a].

59' DDD 6/90

One of Bernstein's last compositions was the song-cycle *Arias and Barcarolles*, a work that gets its title from a remark made by President Eisenhower after hearing the composer play Mozart and Gershwin at the White House in 1960. "You know, I liked that last piece — it's got a *theme*. I like music with a theme, not all them arias and barcarolles." Well, Bernstein may have enjoyed a reputation as a conductor quite at home amongst the 'arias and barcarolles' of the repertoire, but as a composer his language would have surely spoken directly to Eisenhower. Tunes were his meat and drink, and he certainly knew how to write them. *Arias and Barcarolles* is about irony, capturing head-on clashes of emotion experienced in childhood, growing-up and everyday life. Bernstein draws on his own experiences — Jewish weddings, boyhood, bringing up children and so on. The two soloists interweave with different levels of consciousness and different outlooks. Initially difficult to grasp, these little vignettes, skilfully developed and harnessing the quintessential Bernstein, repay acquaintance. The remainder of the disc speaks directly to the heart and senses; here are a stream of Bernstein's most delicious melodies performed with style, wit and a great deal of elegance. This is the part of the record that speaks directly to the senses. Judy Kaye and William Sharp are nicely matched, and the piano duo team supply ideal accompaniments. It is no wonder that this enchanting record has garnered so many plaudits.

Bernstein. WEST SIDE STORY. **Dame Kiri Te Kanawa** (sop) Maria (Nina Bernstein); **José Carreras** (ten) Tony (Alexander Bernstein); **Tatiana Troyanos** (mez) Anita; **Kurt Ollmann** (bar) Riff; composite chorus and orchestra from 'on and off' Broadway/**Leonard Bernstein** with **Marilyn Horne** (mez). DG 415 253-2GH2. Including "On the Waterfront" — Israel Philharmonic Orchestra/Bernstein. From 2532 051 (7/82) and recorded live in May 1981. Notes and text included.

② 1h 38' DDD 4/85

A complete recording of a full-blooded musical with five leading operatic stars? Here's 'crossover' with a vengeance! Before this recording Bernstein had not conducted the original full-length score. To have his presence at the sessions was clearly an enormous benefit — not only in his authoritative conducting but in his influence over the starry cast, all of whom respond with zest to his direction. The recording quality is dry and immediate, to enhance the dramatic impact of the score, but there is plenty of bloom on the voices. The suite from Bernstein's music for the 1954 film *On the Waterfront* is terse and powerful and provides an appropriate make-weight.

Bernstein. CANDIDE. **Jerry Hadley** (ten) Candide; **June Anderson** (sop) Cunegonde; **Adolph Green** (ten) Dr Pangloss, Martin; **Christa Ludwig** (mez) Old lady; **Nicolai Gedda** (ten) Governor, Vanderdendur, Ragotski; **Della Jones** (mez) Paquette; **Kurt Ollmann** (bar) Maximilian, Captain, Jesuit father; **Neil Jenkins** (ten) Merchant, Inquisitor, Prince Charles Edward; **Richard Suart** (bass) Junkman, Inquisitor, King Hermann Augustus; **John Treleaven** (ten) Alchemist, Inquisitor, Sultan Achmet, Crook; **Lindsay Benson** (bar) Doctor, Inquisitor, King Stanislaus; **Clive Bayley** (bar) Bear-Keeper, Inquisitor, Tsar Ivan; **London Symphony Chorus and Orchestra/Leonard Bernstein.** DG 429 734-2GH2. Notes and text included.

② 1h 52' DDD 8/91

Leonard Bernstein   *[photo: DG/Bayat]*

And it came to pass that Leonard Bernstein's prodigal son finally found immortality. *Candide*'s chequered history, its many trials and tribulations, can almost rival that of its hapless hero. But here it is — all of it, at last — musical comedy, grand opera, operetta, satire, melodrama, all rolled into one. We can thank John Mauceri for much of the restoration work: his 1988 Scottish Opera production was the spur for this long-awaited recording and prompted exhaustive reappraisal. Numbers like "We Are Women", "Martin's Laughing Song" and "Nothing More Than This" have rarely been heard, if at all. The last mentioned, Candide's 'aria of disillusionment', is one of the enduring glories of the score, reinstated where Bernstein always wanted it (but where no producer would have it), near the very end of the show. Bernstein called it his "Puccini aria", and that it is — bitter-sweet, long-breathed, supported, enriched and ennobled by its inspiring string counterpoint. And this is but one of many forgotten gems.

Who but a Bernstein could have seen Voltaire's irreverent satire in terms of central-European operetta traditions? The horrors of the Spanish Inquisition ("Oh what a day for an auto-da-fe!") turned Gilbert and Sullivanesque romp laced with cheap flamenco; Cunegonde's hypocrisy brilliantly encapsulated in the mad mocking coloratura of "Glitter and Be Gay" (Gounod was never this much fun); everywhere whiffs of Lehár and Johann Strauss waltzes, Offenbach galops; and of course Bernstein's own sweeter than sweet lyricism — ultimately the heart of the matter in such numbers as "It Must Be So", "The Ballad of Eldorado" (Bernstein's favourite), the aforementioned "Nothing More Than This" and the great choral finale "Make Our Garden Grow". Of course, the style of the show lends itself to the kind of high-level 'operatic' casting that was to prove something of an problem in the composer's own *West Side Story* recording. No such embarrassment here. Indeed, it was an inspiration on someone's part (probably Bernstein's) to persuade the great and versatile Christa Ludwig (so "Easily Assimilated") and Nicolai Gedda (in his sixties and still hurling out the top Bs) to fill the principal character roles. To say they do so ripely is to do them scant justice. Bernstein's old sparring partner Adolph Green braves the tongue-twisting and many-hatted Dr Pangloss with his own highly individual form of *sprechstimme*, Jerry Hadley sings the title role most beautifully, *con amore*, and June Anderson has all the notes, and more, for the faithless, air-headed Cunegonde. It is just a pity that someone didn't tell her that discretion is the better part of comedy. "Glitter and Be Gay" is much funnier for being played straighter, odd as it may sound. Otherwise, the supporting roles are all well taken and the LSO Chorus have a field-day in each of their collective guises.

Having waited so long to commit every last note (or thereabouts) of his cherished score to disc, there are moments here where Bernstein seems almost reluctant to move on. His tempos are measured, to say the least, the score fleshier now in every respect: even that raciest of Overtures has now acquired a more deliberate gait, a more opulent tone. But Bernstein would be Bernstein, and there are moments where one is more than grateful for his indulgence: the grandiose chorales, the panoramic orchestrascapes (sumptuously recorded), and of course, that thrilling finale — the best of all possible Bernstein anthems at the slowest of all possible speeds — and why not (prepare to hold your breath at the choral *a capella*). It's true, perhaps, that somewhere in the midst of this glossy package there is a more modest show trying to get out, but let's not look gift horses in the mouth.

Franz Adolf Berwald *Swedish 1796-1868*

Berwald. SYMPHONIES. **Gothenburg Symphony Orchestra/Neeme Järvi.** DG 415 502-2GH2.
No. 1 in G minor, "Sérieuse"; No. 2 in D major, "Capricieuse"; No. 3 in C major, "Singulière"; No. 4 in E flat major.

② 1h 51' DDD 12/85

Franz Berwald is certainly not an everyday name, but his almost total exclusion from concert programmes is inexcusable. The opening of the *Sinfonie singulière* is simple in technique but provides a rich germ for development. The *Sinfonie capricieuse* has momentary whiffs of Mendelssohn but as with all of Berwald's music parallels are not made easily. The smiling world of the last symphony, the E flat, finds Berwald in light-hearted mood proffering a particularly charming and classical *Scherzo*. Paired on the second disc with the earlier *Sinfonie sérieuse* the darker hues of that work seem to glow more impressively. Järvi's advocacy of these works is totally committed and the Gothenburg Symphony Orchestra play splendidly with some fine wind articulation. The recording is well-detailed and crisp.

Heinrich Biber *Bohemian 1644-1704*

Biber. Mensa sonora. Sonata violino solo representativa in A major[a]. **Cologne Musica Antiqua/Reinhard Goebel** ([a]vn). Archiv Produktion 423 701-2AH.

1h 2' DDD 11/89

Biber was one of the greatest German composers of his generation, furthermore enjoying a reputation as a virtuoso violinist of the first rank. This invigorating and stylish disc embraces both aspects of Biber's talent. *Mēnsa sonora* is a six-part anthology of music which occupies territory belonging to the chamber sonata and the suite. This is delightful music, strongly dance-orientated and with a marked feeling for gesture. These qualities, and others too, are affectingly realized by Reinhard Goebel and his impeccably drilled ensemble in such a way that a listener might be excused for leaving the comfort of an armchair and taking to the floor. By way of an entr'acte between the first three and the last three parts of the anthology, Goebel gives a virtuoso performance of Biber's *Sonata violino solo representativa* in which a nightingale, cuckoo, cockerel, frog, and other creatures make themselves heard; a cat wreaks havoc with them but is in turn sent packing by a musketeer. Many tricks of the violinist's trade are on display and Goebel revels in them all. A splendid achievement by all concerned.

NEW REVIEW

Biber. TRUMPET MUSIC.
Schmelzer. TRUMPET MUSIC. **New London Consort/Philip Pickett.**
L'Oiseau-Lyre 425 834-2OH.
Biber: Sonata à 7. Sonata pro tabula. Sonata VII à 5. Sonata à 3. Sonata à 6.
Sonata I à 8. Sonata Sancti Polycarpi à 9. **Schmelzer:** Sonata con arie zu der kaiserlichen Serenada. Sonata à 7 flauti. Balletto di spiritelli. Sonata I à 8. Balletto di centauri, ninfe e salvatici.

Ih 7' DDD 9/91

Philip Pickett and his New London Consort perform a varied programme of pieces by two gifted composers of the German baroque, Austrian Schmelzer and Bohemian Biber. The pieces are drawn from various collections and publications and reflect an assortment of stylistic influences, sonorities and instrumental colours. Not all the music is even in quality but the finest pieces here illustrate the skill with which both composers were able to deploy contrasting groups of instruments to striking effect. Among the greatest delights are Schmelzer's Serenade in honour of his musical employer, the Emperor Leopold I, an eight-part Sonata from the composer's Sacro-Profanus Concentus Musicus, Biber's resonant Sonata for six trumpets and timpani, a more delicately wrought *Sonata pro tabula* and the impressive nine-part *Sonata Sancti Polycarpi*. This is a programme to be dipped into rather than listened to without interruption but the performances are stylish, technically secure and effectively recorded.

Biber. Mystery Sonatas. **John Holloway** (vn); **Davitt Moroney** (org/hpd); **Tragicomedia** (Stephen Stubbs, lte/chitarrone; Erin Headley, va da gamba/lirone; Andrew Lawrence-King, hp/regal). Virgin Classics Veritas VCD7 90838-2.

② 2h II' DDD 5/91

Biber was among the most talented musicians of the late seventeenth century. He was a renowned violinist and his compositions, above all for the violin, are technically advanced and strikingly individual. The 15 *Mystery Sonatas* with their additional *Passacaglia* for unaccompanied violin were written in about 1678 and dedicated to Biber's employer, the Archbishop of Salzburg. Each Sonata is inspired by a section of the Rosary devotion of the Catholic Church which offered a system of meditation on 15 Mysteries from the lives of Jesus and His mother. The music is not, strictly speaking, programmatic though often vividly illustrative of events which took place in the life of Christ. All but two of the 16 pieces require *scordatura* or retuning of the violin strings; in this way Biber not only facilitated some of the fingerings but also achieved sounds otherwise unavailable to him. The Sonatas are disposed into three groups of five: Joyful, Sorrowful and Glorious Mysteries whose contrasting states are affectingly evoked in music ranging from a spirit reflecting South German baroque exuberance to one of profound contemplation. John Holloway plays with imaginative sensibility and he is supported by a first-rate continuo group whose instruments include baroque lute, chitarrone, viola da gamba, a 15-string lirone, double harp and regal.

Sir Harrison Birtwistle

Birtwistle. Carmen Arcadiae Mechanicae Perpetuum (1978). Silbury Air (1977). Secret Theatre (1984). **London Sinfonietta/Elgar Howarth.** Etcetera KTC1052.

58'   DDD   4/88

Birtwistle is only 'difficult' if you are convinced in advance that he is going to be, or if you have read somewhere about the obscure numerical techniques that he uses to help him compose. Forget them: they're his concern, not the listener's; you don't get to understand Bach by reading textbooks on counterpoint. Jump straight in, with ears and mind open, and the sheer exhilaration of his music, its alluringly strange patterns and textures, its suggestions of mysterious ritual, above all the unmistakable sense of a composer in total control of a rich and resourceful language, will soon draw you in. The fact that it cannot be wholly comprehended at a single hearing is no drawback, but a positive bonus: this is music that changes each time you hear it, as a landscape changes when you explore different paths through it. The performances throughout are vividly virtuosic and the recording has tremendous impact.

Birtwistle. Endless Parade[a].
Blake Watkins. Trumpet Concerto.
Maxwell Davies. Trumpet Concerto. **Håkan Hardenberger** (tpt); [a]**Paul Patrick** (vib); **BBC Philharmonic Orchestra/Elgar Howarth.** Philips 432 075-2PH.

1h 19'   DDD   6/91

This is very much Håkan Hardenberger's record. The balance places him firmly in front of the orchestra, and his style of playing — bright in tone, often with a strong vibrato — underlines his dominance. Fortunately he has the technical skill and expressive flexibility to stand up to the spotlight, and the result (which also owes much to the unobtrusive excellence of Elgar Howarth and the BBC Philharmonic) is imposing and enthralling. You are left in no doubt that contemporary trumpet writing has much more to offer than varieties of fanfare at one extreme and sentimental brass-band melody at the other. Sir Peter Maxwell Davies and Michael Blake Watkins each in their very different ways devise large-scale symphonic structures in order to

  Håken Hardenberger   *[photo: Philips/Van Teylingen*

give the soloist the widest perspectives within which to place his often dazzlingly florid thematic lines. The trumpet virtuoso today needs to be able to shape and project phrases which might tax a flautist or a clarinettist, and Hardenberger does so with staggering consistency. Sir Harrison Birtwistle's *Endless Parade* is perhaps the most exhilarating of all, less lyric in style than the two concertos but supremely assured as drama, now abrasively comic, now sinisterly serious. It crowns a disc that would be memorable without it.

Birtwistle. PUNCH AND JUDY. **Stephen Roberts** (bar) Punch; **Jan DeGaetani** (mez) Judy, Fortune-teller; **Phyllis Bryn-Julson** (sop) Pretty Polly, Witch; **Philip Langridge** (ten) Lawyer; **David Wilson-Johnson** (bar) Choregos, Jack Ketch; **John Tomlinson** (bass) Doctor; **London Sinfonietta/David Atherton.** Etcetera KTC2014. Notes and text included. From Decca Headline HEAD24/5 (9/80).

② 1h 43' ADD 12/89

In *Punch and Judy* Sir Harrison Birtwistle and his inspired librettist Stephen Pruslin succeeded in giving characters normally presented as simple caricatures an almost mythic power and substance. As opera *Punch and Judy* may owe more to such Stravinskian fables as *Renard* than to the great lyric tragedies of the Monteverdi/Wagner tradition, yet even in *Punch and Judy* the music is most memorable in moments of reflection — sinister, poignant, or both. Though different performers have presented the work brilliantly in the theatre since this recording was made, it is hard to imagine a more effective account of the opera on disc. The singers are expert and well contrasted, with none of the ranting and approximation that this kind of expressionistic vocal writing often elicits. Moreover, the London Sinfonietta are at their most responsive, as well they might be given the outstandingly musical direction of David Atherton, who conducted the opera's première at Aldeburgh in 1968. The analogue recording may sound a trifle shallow by the latest standards, but it leaves you in no doubt as to the brilliance and resourcefulness of Birtwistle's vocal and instrumental design.

Georges Bizet

French 1838-1875

Bizet. Symphony in C major[a]. L'Arlésienne — Suite No. 1[b]; Suite No. 2 (arr. Guiraud)[b]. [a]**French Radio National Symphony Orchestra,** [b]**Royal Philharmonic Orchestra/Sir Thomas Beecham.** EMI CDC7 47794-2. Item marked [a] from ASD388 (4/61), [b] ASD252 (2/59).

1h 5' ADD 11/87

Bizet's only symphony was written within the space of a month just after his seventeenth birthday. It is an easy piece to listen to, fairly light-weight and with a hint of the mature composer-to-be in a long and beautiful oboe solo. But it has many conventional, immature features too, and needs special advocacy in performance. Beecham had a genius for making second-rate works seem masterpieces and his recording has tremendous flair, imagination and affection. From the incidental music for *L'Arlésienne* Bizet salvaged four pieces and re-orchestrated them for full orchestra in the form of what we know now as Suite No. 1. After his death Bizet's friend Ernest Guiraud re-scored four more numbers to make up Suite No. 2. The music has a marvellous sense of colour and atmosphere and Bizet's inspired invention reaches great heights of expression. It is difficult to imagine a more inspired, more sympathetic and beautifully played performance, for Beecham makes the music live and breathe in a way that is head and shoulders above any other conductor. The recordings were made in 1959 and 1956 respectively but both sound rich and clear.

Bizet (ed. Riffaud). L'Arlésienne — complete incidental music. **Orfeon Donostiarra; Toulouse Capitole Orchestra/Michel Plasson.** EMI CDC7 47460-2.

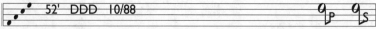

Bizet. L'Arlésienne — Suites Nos. 1 and 2. Carmen — Suites Nos. 1 and 2. **Montreal Symphony Orchestra/Charles Dutoit.** Decca 417 839-2DH.

Incidental music written for a play is usually rather bitty, and while a selection may often be made into a well-balanced suite it is rarely that we can assemble it complete and still make a satisfying musical shape. However, Bizet's music triumphantly passes the test, and we have it in its fullest form, including the choral element that is absent from the more familiar orchestral suites (see below). The play itself, set in the Camargue, is brimful of Latin passion and in some ways resembles *Carmen*, for here too the hero is obsessed with a girl (L'Arlésienne of the title) and finally dies rather than live without her. But though this story of star-crossed love is a tough one it is also highly colourful and the young farmer Frédéric's suicide by throwing himself from a window takes place while peasants are dancing a farandole. First heard in 1872, Bizet's music was originally written for an orchestra of 26 players including a piccolo and harmonium, and the original scoring has now been restored by Dominique Riffaud. The result is a revelation of colours and textures entirely appropriate to the luminous landscape of Southern France, and the performance by the Toulouse Capitole Orchestra under their director Michel Plasson is highly idiomatic in its vivacity and warmth with a recording to match. There is a small but valuable contribution from the Orfeo Donostiarra Chorus trained by Antxon Ayestaran, whose very name suggests regions that are remote from sophisticated urban France.

The four suites on the Decca disc need qualities of subtlety and delicacy as well as an earthy vitality, which they receive here in full measure. The playing of the Montreal Symphony Orchestra under Charles Dutoit is consistently satisfying and there are some impressive contributions from the solo flautists. The recording is vivid and rich yet natural-sounding; only in a few places might one feel that big tuttis with percussion are too resonant. At 73 minutes this CD is generous in quantity as well as quality, and is distinctly impressive as music, performance and sheer sound.

Bizet. Jeux d'enfants.
Ravel. Ma mère l'oye — ballet.
Saint-Saëns. Le carnaval des animaux[a]. [a]**Julian Jacobson,** [a]**Nigel Hutchinson** (pfs); members of **London Symphony Orchestra/Barry Wordsworth.** Pickwick IMP Classics PCD932.

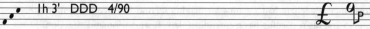

These three works make a very attractive programme and as a mid-price issue this CD is desirable indeed. No attempt is made to sensationalize the *Carnival of the Animals*, which is played with just ten instrumentalists as the composer intended, but there is plenty of wit and brilliance from the pianists Julian Jacobson and Nigel Hutchinson, not only in their charmingly droll own number (No. 11) which relegates them firmly to the animal kingdom but also in the work as a whole. The violinists' donkeys (No. 8) are no less amusing, and the cello 'swan' in No. 13 is serenely touching, but all the players are good and the finale is rightly uproarious. Barry Wordsworth's sense of style in this French repertory is no less evident in the Bizet *Children's Games* and Ravel's *Mother Goose*, which in the latter case is the entire score of the ballet and not just the more familiar suite taken from it. We may single out such pleasures as the gently stated and lovingly shaped "Berceuse" and "Petit mari, petite femme" in the Bizet, but all is charmingly done and then in the Ravel we are transported at once into a child's fairyland of infinite delicacy, wit and tenderness which is crowned unforgettably by the inspired final number, *The Fairy Garden*. A special word of praise to the LSO's oboists, so important in Ravel's score. EMI's Studio No. 1 in Abbey Road provides a beautifully atmospheric recording, close but not glaring.

Bizet. CARMEN. **Julia Migenes** (mez) Carmen; **Plácido Domingo** (ten) Don José; **Faith Esham** (sop) Micaëla; **Ruggero Raimondi** (bass) Escamillo; **Lilian Watson** (sop) Frasquita; **Susan Daniel** (mez) Mercédès; **Jean-Philippe Lafont** (bar) Dancairo; **Gérard Garino** (ten) Remendado; **François Le Roux** (bar) Moralès; **John Paul Bogart** (bass) Zuniga; **French Radio Chorus; French Radio Children's Chorus; French National Orchestra/Lorin Maazel.** Erato 2292-45207-2. Notes, text and translation included. From NUM75113 (3/84).

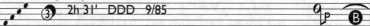

③ 2h 31' DDD 9/85

Bizet. CARMEN. **Victoria de los Angeles** (sop) Carmen; **Nicolai Gedda** (ten) Don José; **Janine Micheau** (sop) Micaëla; **Ernest Blanc** (bar) Escamillo; **Denise Monteil** (sop) Frasquita; **Marcelle Croisier, Monique Linval** (sops) Mercédès; **Jean-Christophe Benoit** (bar) Dancairo; **Michel Hamel** (ten) Remendado; **Bernard Plantey** (bar) Moralès; **Xavier Depraz** (bass) Zuniga; **Les Petits Chanteurs de Versailles; French National Radio Chorus and Orchestra/Sir Thomas Beecham.** EMI CDS7 49240-2. Notes, text and translation included. From ASD331/3 (5/60).

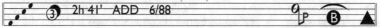

③ 2h 41' ADD 6/88

With some justification, *Carmen* is reckoned to be the world's most popular opera. Its score is irresistible, its dramatic realism riveting, its sense of *milieu* unerring, though it has to be remembered that the work was not an immediate triumph. Too many recordings have blown up the work to proportions beyond its author's intentions but here Maazel adopts a brisk, lightweight approach that seems to come close to what Bizet wanted. Similarly Julia Migenes approaches the title part in an immediate, vivid way, exuding the gipsy's allure in a performance that suggests Carmen's fierce temper and smouldering eroticism, and she develops the character intelligently into the fatalistic person of the card scene and finale. Her singing isn't conventionally smooth but it is compelling from start to finish. Plácido Domingo has made the part of Don José very much his own, and here he sings with unstinting involvement and a good deal of finesse. Ruggero Raimondi is a macho Toreador though Faith Esham is a somewhat pallid Micaëla.

While the Maazel set remains a strong recommendation, Beecham's remains supreme in many respects. It has a peculiar individuality and style all its own and a degree of elegance in the conducting that seems a lost quality today. Beecham's feeling for the wit and charm of Bizet's miraculous score doesn't preclude his understanding of the tragic passion of the last two acts. If De Los Angeles is not quite as immediately alluring or earthy as Migenes, she manages to capture almost every facet of the complex and difficult role. Gedda turned in one of his most persuasive and musical performances as José, one full of good singing wanting only Domingo's dark, doomed intensity. Blanc is an idiomatic, powerful

Escamillo, Micheau a stylish if somewhat dry-toned Micaëla. The supporting cast, chorus and orchestra are all authentically French. The recording is a bit restricted in range by modern standards, but has a perfect balance between voice and orchestra.

Bizet. LES PECHEURS DE PERLES. **Barbara Hendricks** (sop) Leïla; **John Aler** (ten) Nadir; **Gino Quilico** (bar) Zurga; **Jean-Philippe Courtis** (bass) Nourabad; **Chorus and Orchestra of the Capitole, Toulouse/Michel Plasson.** EMI CDS7 49837-2. Notes, text and translation included.

② 2h 7' DDD 1/90

NEW REVIEW

Bizet. LES PECHEURS DE PERLES. **Ileana Cotrubas** (sop) Leïla; **Alain Vanzo** (ten) Nadir; **Guillermo Sarabia** (bar) Zurga; **Roger Soyer** (bass) Nourabad; **Paris Opéra Chorus and Orchestra/Georges Prêtre.** Classics for Pleasure CD-CFPD4721. From HMV SLS5113 (5/78).

② 1h 44' ADD 10/91 £

Let a tenor and a baritone signify that they are willing to oblige with a duet, and the cry will go up for *The Pearl Fishers*. It's highly unlikely that many of the company present will know what the duet is about — it recalls the past, proclaims eternal friendship and nearly ends up in a quarrel — but the melody and the sound of two fine voices blending in its harmonies will be quite sufficient. In fact there is much more to the opera than the duet, or even than the three or four solos which are sometimes sung in isolation; and the EMI recording goes further than previous versions in giving a complete account of a score remarkable for its unity as well as for the attractiveness of individual numbers. It is a lyrical opera, and the voices need to be young and graceful. Barbara Hendricks and John Aler certainly fulfil those requirements, she with a light, silvery timbre, he with a high tenor admirably suited to the tessitura of his solos. The third main character, the baritone whose role is central to the drama, assumes his rightful place here: Gino Quilico brings genuine distinction to the part, and his aria in Act 3 is one of the highlights. Though Plasson's direction at first is rather square, the performance grows in responsiveness act by act. It is a pity that the accompanying notes are not stronger in textual detail, for the full score given here stimulates interest in its history. One of the changes made in

the original score of 1863 concerns the celebrated duet itself, the first version of which is given in an appendix. It ends in a style that one would swear owed much to the 'friendship' duet in Verdi's *Don Carlos* — except that Bizet came first.

The reissued Prêtre version also uses the 1863 score and was the first recording to do so. It is a businesslike performance, not particularly imaginative or idiomatic despite the fact that most of the singers are French and the orchestra and chorus must be steeped in this opera which came to be so loved after the composer's death,

Barbara Hendricks *[photo: EMI/Fabian/Sygma]*

having been so neglected in his lifetime. Prêtre conducts without apparent affection, though at least he ensures cohesion and the avoidance of sentimentality. The bass and baritone are undistinguished, which cannot be said of the tenor who was much the best of his generation to be heard regularly in Paris. Cotrubas sings with lovely tone and acute sensitivity: she does much to make this an attractive proposition at a bargain price and with good recorded sound.

Michael Blake Watkins   *Refer to Index*   *British 1948-*

Arthur Bliss   *British 1891-1975*

Bliss. Piano Concerto, Op. 58ª. March, Op. 99, "Homage to a Great Man". ª**Philip Fowke** (pf); **Royal Liverpool Philharmonic Orchestra/David Atherton.** Unicorn-Kanchana Souvenir UKCD2029. From DKP9006 (9/81).

`44' DDD 8/90`

Bliss's Piano Concerto, written for the New York World Fair in 1939, is a deliberate essay in the grand manner, full of big, rhetorical gestures and opulent Rachmaninovian melodies. This performance does it full justice in a recording that has transferred well from LP, though some may find the sound rather unreverberant in places. Bliss was half-American and the music seems to reflect also the exuberance of the United States. It is romantic music in the best sense, not only in its richness of orchestration and the Lisztian virtuosity of the solo part, commandingly played by Philip Fowke — listen to the double octaves at the start — but in the sheer beauty of the meditative quieter passages, as when flute and oboe accompany the soloist's musings in the recapitulation section of the first movement. The *March of Homage* is a reminder of how splendidly Bliss fulfilled the role of Master of the Queen's Music. The homage is to Churchill and the work was broadcast just before the great man's funeral in 1965. In a short time, it goes to the heart of the matter. David Atherton and the RLPO are completely at home in these two fine works.

NEW REVIEW

Bliss. Morning Heroes. **John Westbrook** (narr); **Liverpool Philharmonic Choir; Royal Liverpool Philharmonic Orchestra/Sir Charles Groves.** EMI British Composers CDM7 63906-2. Text included. From HMV SAN365 (3/75).

`1h ADD 10/91`

Morning Heroes stands as a monument to those who lost their lives in the First World War. Among these were Sir Arthur Bliss's elder brother Kennard, and the writing of this symphony was a necessary expression of Bliss's sense of loss and bereavement. Premièred in 1930, the work has an unusual form: five movements describe the various stage of war, from farewell, excitement, presentiment, to battle and finally loss. Each movement is set around an evocative selection of verse which is either declaimed by a narrator (here the excellent John Westbrook) or sung by the chorus. Bliss's style is easily accessible and in this, one of the most important works in his whole output, he rises above the usual to create a powerful evocation of war and the various emotions which it necessarily triggers. In many ways *Morning Heroes* is more complete a depiction of war than other, equally personal, views such as Britten's *War Requiem* and Delius's

Requiem, in that it captures both the public feel of anticipation and the private sense of loss. Sir Charles Groves was a natural champion for English music and his 1974 recording does this work full justice. He has complete command of Bliss's idiom and draws impassioned as well as sensitive performances from both the Royal Liverpool Philharmonic Orchestra and Choir. The recorded sound is excellent, with the tricky balance between narrator and orchestra being articularly well handled. In sum, a magnificent reading of a great, if neglected, British work of the inter-war years.

Bliss. Checkmate — suite.
Lambert. Horoscope — suite.
Walton. Façade — Suites Nos. 1 and 2. **English Northern Philharmonia/ David Lloyd-Jones.** Hyperion CDA66436.

$\quad$ 1h 14' DDD 3/91

A programme devoted to British ballet music may raise eyebrows — is there any? Yes, not least because ballet played an important part in the London theatre in the first half of this century: Beecham and Boult conducted in London for Diaghilev's *Ballets Russes*, while Lambert was for many years the Musical Director of the Vic-Wells Ballet, one of several fine native companies. Not surprisingly, the three works represented here all owe something to the example of Stravinsky, not least in their rhythmic verve and colourful instrumentation, but each has individuality too and it is good to have the fine ballet scores by Bliss and Lambert, for these composers are too neglected. Of course, Walton's splendidly witty *Façade* was not written as a ballet, but it works admirably as such. It was Lambert who conducted the première in 1931 of Frederick Ashton's stage version; and seven years later, with the same choreographer, came that of his own *Horoscope*, a love story in which the female lead was created by Margot Fonteyn. This is music that bubbles over with vivacity, good tunes and in places (such as the finale) real romantic warmth. Bliss's *Checkmate* was inspired by the game of chess and turns the stage into a chessboard (thus anticipating Tim Rice's musical), but here, too, one of the characters represents Love and the music, though forceful, also has a romantic element. All three of these scores are played with real flair by a conductor and orchestra that have specialized in British music, and the recording has clarity and atmosphere. The booklet essay by Christopher Palmer is both informative and stylish.

Ernest Bloch
Swiss/American 1880-1959

NEW REVIEW

Bloch. Schelomo.
Bruch. Kol Nidrei, Op. 47. Canzone, Op. 55. Adagio on Celtic Themes, Op. 56. Ave Maria, Op. 61. **Ofra Harnoy** (vc); **London Philharmonic Orchestra/Sir Charles Mackerras.** RCA Victor Red Seal RD60757.

$\quad$ 58' DDD 12/91

NEW REVIEW

Bloch. Schelomo. Concerti grossi — No. 1; No. 2. **Georges Miquelle** (vc); **Eastman Rochester Orchestra/Howard Hanson.** Mercury 432 718-2MM.

$\quad$ 1h 3' ADD 11/91

If *Schelomo* is your primary concern here — and well it might be, for Bloch's passionate, improvisatory rhapsody, with its hebraic intensity, certainly makes a

powerful impression — then Harnoy's outstanding performance is probably the
one to go for. Mackerras matches her imaginative intensity with a central climax
of great fervour, and throughout the changing moods and colours are imaginatively caught by soloist and orchestra alike. Bruch's *Kol Nidrei* also has a noble,
Hebrew theme (though Bruch was not Jewish) and its sombre, ruminative
character brings an equally sympathetic response from both soloist and orchestra.
The mood lightens in the *Adagio on Celtic Themes*, a work as tuneful as it is
charming, yet Mackerras's strong introduction again emphasizes his commitment
to what proves a real musical partnership. Bruch's *Ave Maria* is less simply
melismatic than more familiar settings, and there is finespun embroidery from the
soloist before the tender reprise of the tune. Very good, expansive recording,
with the acoustics providing spaciousness and breadth for these warm yet often
poignant melodies.

On the alternative Mercury CD the cellist, Georges Miquelle, also responds
sensitively to Bloch's Hebrew soliloquy, but his image, as recorded, is relatively
small and he tends to be slightly dwarfed by Hanson's passionate orchestral
backcloth. Yet this is still a lyrically appealing performance, and providing one
gets the volume level set right, the balance can be made real, for it is not
artificially aided. What makes this CD particularly enticing is the inclusion of the
two neo-classical *Concerti grossi*, very persuasively presented by Hanson and his
excellent Eastman Rochester group. Bloch has the courage of his twentieth-
century convictions, and although this pair of works is essentially baroque in style
and feeling, the continuo in No. 1 is a piano rather than a harpsichord, and very
effective it is too. The second, for strings alone is slightly less genial, more
intense, yet the "Dirge" and "Pastoral" of the First have a real depth of expressive
feeling to contrast with the dancing *allegros*. This music is most rewarding and
the bright, slightly astringent Mercury sound balance with plenty of bite on the
violins suits its character.

John Blow
British bapt. 1649-1708

Blow. VENUS AND ADONIS. **Nancy Argenta** (sop) Cupid; **Lynne Dawson**
(sop) Venus; **Stephen Varcoe** (bar) Adonis; **Emily Van Evera** (sop)
Shepherdess; **John Mark Ainsley, Charles Daniel** (tens), **Gordon Jones**
(bass) Shepherds; **Rogers Covey-Crump** (ten) Huntsman; **Chorus; London
Baroque/Charles Medlam.** Harmonia Mundi HMA190 1276. Notes and text
included.

50' DDD 9/88

This is seventeenth-century court entertainment with nothing lacking in its
charm and elegance. We know that Blow's mini opera was first performed in
Oxford in 1681, with Moll Davies, the mistress of Charles II in the role of
Venus. Her nine-year-old daughter, Lady Mary Tudor, must have been a
particularly gifted child to have been able to sing and act the part of Cupid,
and we can well imagine the delight of the court at such scenes as the spelling
lesson with the infant Cupids. As for us, we can enjoy the accomplished
performance of an expert cast, with the sprightliness of Nancy Argenta as Cupid
matched only by the gently dramatic flexibility of Lynne Dawson and Stephen
Varcoe in the title roles. Even the members of the chorus and those with lesser
parts have all been hand-picked, and London Baroque are in their element. Yet
nothing is exaggerated or overdone. What is outstanding in this performance is
the fact that although we have sound alone, it is so cleverly recorded that we
have the delightful illusion that the opera is actually taking place before our very
eyes.

Luigi Boccherini

Boccherini. Symphonies — D minor, Op. 12 No. 4, G506, "La casa del Diavolo"; A major, Op. 12 No. 6, G508; A major, Op. 21 No. 6, G498. **London Festival Orchestra/Ross Pople.** Hyperion CDA66236.

54' DDD 9/87

Boccherini may not have been the most purposeful of composers of his time, but he was certainly one of the most endearing. Not for him the sturdy, strongly argued symphonic structures of a Haydn, in which each note has its place and its meaning, but rather pieces, coloured by the relaxed and sunny south, that indulge in graceful lines and tellingly manipulated detail. Boccherini loved playing with textures and producing sounds that are pleasurable in themselves; he also liked experimenting with musical forms, and one of the three symphonies here has as its finale just a slow introduction followed by a replay of part of the first movement. The symphony here from Op. 21 is a slight piece, with playful themes in its first movement, a refined little *Andantino* to follow and a cheerful minuet. The other two are on a larger scale, with quite expansive opening movements and in one case a wistful minor-key *Larghetto*, the other a charming minor-key gavotte, to follow. The D minor symphony ends with a reworking of the movement we know as the "Dance of the Furies" from Gluck's *Orphée*. The spirit of the music is happily captured in these performances even though modern instruments are used. The articulation is delightfully clear, light and rhythmic, and the tempos are lively; clearly Ross Pople has a sympathetic feeling for Boccherini.

Boccherini. CELLO CONCERTOS. **David Geringas** (vc); **Orchestra da Camera di Padova e del Veneto/Bruno Giuranna.** Claves CD50-8814/16. No. 1 in E flat major, G474; No. 2 in A major, G475; No. 3 in D major, G476; No. 4 in C major, G477; No. 5 in D major, G478; No. 6 in D major, G479; No. 7 in G major, G480; No. 8 in C major, G481; No. 9 in B flat major; No. 10 in D major, G483; No. 11 in G major, G573; No. 12 in E flat major.

③ 3h 24' DDD 7/89

"Boccherini: 12 Concerti per il Violoncello" proclaims the cover, a little ambitiously, perhaps — for Boccherini probably didn't compose that many. David Geringas has had to exercise a little ingenuity to reach this figure (two of the concertos are almost certainly spurious), but it was probably worth the effort, and the set is a thoroughly enjoyable one in its undemanding way. His intonation is virtually perfect, even high up on the A string, his passage-work is clean, his rhythms are crisp, and he produces (not using a period instrument) a light but pleasingly resonant tone. Listen in particular to the slow movements (such as those of G477 or G483) for eloquence and neatly timed detail. Geringas provides his own cadenzas, including one that quotes Mozart. A very pleasing release. The recording quality and balance are exemplary.

Boccherini. Guitar Quintets — No. 3 in B flat, G447; No. 9 in C major, G453, "La ritirata di Madrid". **Pepe Romero** (gtr); **Academy of St Martin in the Fields Chamber Ensemble** (Iona Brown, Malcolm Latchem, vns; Stephen Shingles, va; Denis Vigay, vc). Philips Musica da Camera 426 092-2PC. From 9500 789 (10/81).

51' ADD 6/90

Boccherini was asked by his friend and patron, the Marquis of Benavente, for some chamber music in which he, a guitarist of now-unknown ability — as was

Boccherini, might take part. He responded by adapting a number of his existing works (mostly piano quintets) as guitar quintets, of which eight are known; in his catalogue of Boccherini's works Gérard assigns the numbers G445-53 to these works, but G452 represents four 'lost' quintets — which explains why one of

eight is labelled No. 9. The Quintet G447 is based on the Piano Quintet, Op. 57/2, but G453 is of mixed parentage: the first three movements are derived from the Piano Quintet, Op. 56/3, but the fourth is adapted from a String Quintet (Op. 30/6), *La musica notturna delle strade di Madrid*. In this last, a military parade (in the form of a theme and 12 variations) approaches, passes and disappears into the distance via dynamic 'hairpins'. The original forms of these works, long on charm, grace and refined craftsmanship, are now rarely heard, but their survival as guitar quintets is fully justified in superb (and superbly recorded) performances such as those in this recording.

Pepe Romero   *[photo: Philips*

NEW REVIEW

Boccherini. Guitar Quintets — No. 4 in D major, G448; No. 6 in G major, G450.
Castelnuovo-Tedesco. Guitar Quintet, Op. 143. **Kazuhito Yamashita** (gtr); **Tokyo Quartet** (Peter Oundjian, Kikuei Ikeda, vns; Kazuhide Isomura, va; Sadao Harada, vc). RCA Victor Red Seal RD60421.

Ih I' DDD 1/92

As explained above, Boccherini's Guitar Quintets are mostly revampings of movements from pre-existing chamber works, an exercise in which the French guitarist François de Fossa lent a helping hand that is seldom acknowledged. Castelnuovo-Tedesco was never stuck for a winsome tune, nor did he ever waver in his loyalty to traditional musical forms; written specifically as a with-guitar work and at a much later time, when guitar techniques had advanced beyond the bounds of Boccherini's day, his Quintet makes much more telling use of the instrument and elevates it to *concertante* status. Neither he nor Boccherini presents the listener with any problem, intellectual or emotional, but both provide exceptionally skilfully written and immediately appealing music. Yamashita, long associated with smash-and-grab displays of hard dexterity, plays with the utmost sensitivity and respect for good sound, as befits the company he keeps here, and the recording is managed with equal fidelity.

NEW REVIEW

Boccherini. String Quintets — F minor, G274 (Op. 11 No. 4); E major, G275 (Op. 11 No. 5); D major, G276 (Op. 11 No. 6). **Smithsonian Chamber Players** (Marilyn MacDonald, Jorie Garrigue, vns; Anthony Martin, va; Anner Bylsma, Kenneth Slowik, vcs). Deutsche Harmonia Mundi RD77159.

Ih 7' DDD 4/92

Boccherini was a virtuoso cellist and often played together with a family string quartet in Madrid and the experience was obviously a very pleasant one, for he wrote 100 quintets for two violins, viola and two cellos. He was never at a loss for ideas: the quintets are richly varied in form and texture, the latter enhanced by Boccherini's intimate knowledge of the techniques and sound-qualities of the bowed-string instruments. Many of us know the famous Minuet — but how many are familiar with the work from which it comes? The Quintet in E, the fifth of the six Quintets of his Op. 11 (1775), of which it is the third movement, is one of those in this recording. The bucolic Quintet in D, *dello l'ucceleria*, ("The aviary") is a cyclic work with bird-song, shepherd's pipes and hunting sounds. If Boccherini was, as Giuseppe Pupo described him, "the wife of Haydn", his music has the charm, grace and poise of the best wives, and there is nothing wrong with that"! The Smithsonian Players, using original Stradivarius instruments (1688-1787), play like good Italians, which none of them is, and are superbly recorded in this irresistibly attractive album.

Alexander Borodin   *Russian 1833-1887*

NEW REVIEW

Borodin. Symphonies — No. 1 in E flat major; No. 2 in B minor; No. 3 in A minor (compl. Glazunov). **CSR Symphony Orchestra, Bratislava/ Stephen Gunzenhauser.** Naxos 8 550238.

Ih 16'   DDD   8/91   £

A veritable bargain if ever there was — all three of Borodin's symphonies for less than half the price of two! Don't let the bargain price fool you into expecting inferior performances either — these accounts are vigorous, energetic and full of Slavonic sparkle and colour. Stephen Gunzenhauser positively revels in Borodin's rich melodic invention, and although the CSR Symphony Orchestra may at times sound a little under-powered alongside the likes of better-known orchestras, they more than compensate with affectionate, spirited and persuasive performances. Also, for those who are only familiar with the more popular Second Symphony here's an excellent opportunity to explore the less frequently heard though equally enjoyable and memorable companions; the First Symphony took Borodin five years to complete (his composing time was limited due to his parallel career as a professor of chemistry) though its freshness of invention gives the impression of a swiftly composed work, whilst the Third Symphony remained unfinished at the time of his death and consists of only two movements which were completed by Glazunov.

Borodin. Symphony No. 2 in B minor. In the Steppes of Central Asia. Prince Igor — Overture; March; Dance of the Polovtsian Maidens; Polovtsian Dances. **John Alldis Choir; National Philharmonic Orchestra/Louis Tjekna-vorian.** RCA Victor Silver Seal VD60535. From RL25098 (8/77).

Ih 4'   ADD   8/77

A nicely turned, sumptuously recorded concert comprising Borodin's most popular symphony in harness with the familiar orchestral items from his only opera, *Prince Igor*. Tjeknavorian revels in the Symphony's frequent dramatic outburst and opulent tunes (sampling the first movement should convince anyone), while the hand-picked National Philharmonic — well known for their virtuoso performances of classic film scores under this disc's producer, Charles Gerhardt — is enthusiastically assisted by the John Alldis Choir in the March and Dances from *Prince Igor*. Add a warmly played account of the appealing *In the Steppes of Central Asia* and you have a most attractive selection, expertly transferred from fine-sounding tapes. One hopes that it will soon be joined by the remaining two symphonies in Tjeknavorian's Borodin cycle.

Borodin. String Quartets — No. 1 in A major; No. 2 in D major. **Borodin Quartet** (Mikhail Kopelman, Andrei Abramenkov, vns; Dmitri Shebalin, va; Valentin Berlinsky, vc). EMI CDC7 47795-2. From EMI Melodiya ASD4100 (3/82).

 1h 6' DDD 5/88

These quartets are delightful music, and they are played here by the aptly-named Borodin Quartet with a conviction and authority that in no way inhibits panache, spontaneity and sheer charm. Doubtless the most popular music of Borodin and the other members of the Russian 'Five' will always be their colourful orchestral and stage music, but no CD collector should ignore these chamber works. Their style derives from a mid-nineteenth-century Russian tradition of spending happy hours in music-making at home and also from the refreshing musical springs of folk-song. This performance offers not only first-rate playing from artists who 'have the music in their blood' but also a warm and convincing recorded sound.

Borodin. String Quartet No. 2 in D major[a].
Shostakovich. String Quartet No. 8 in C minor, Op. 110[a].
Tchaikovsky. String Quartet No. 1 in D major, Op.11[b]. [a]**Borodin Quartet** (Rostislav Dubinsky, Jaroslav Alexandrov, vns; Dmitri Shebalin, va; Valentin Berlinsky, vc); [b]**Gabrieli Quartet** (Kenneth Sillito, Brendan O'Reilly, vns; Ian Jewel, va; Keith Harvey, vc). Decca 425 541-2DM. Items marked [a] from SXL6036 (2/63), [b] SDD524/5 (10/77).

1h 16' ADD 5/90

The programme adopted here deserves wide emulation: take the contents of a highly reissue-worthy LP and hunt for something appropriate to supplement it. The Borodin Quartet's affection for the composer after whom they named themselves was evidently still warmly fresh when this performance was recorded. The quiet charm of the piece (it was fondly dedicated to Borodin's wife) comes over beautifully. They are Shostakovich specialists, too, and their account of his most famous quartet is one of the noblest and most vehement it has ever received: superbly virtuoso and hair-raisingly expressive. But what should preface these two performances? An English quartet in Tchaikovsky might not seem the obvious choice, but it works very well, with the Gabrieli showing a fine responsiveness to the work's singing qualities and its refined colour, even in passages which can seem as though Tchaikovsky would just as soon have been writing for string orchestra. They (recorded in 1976) receive a rather closer recorded sound than the Borodin (whose performances date from 1962) but all three still sound very well.

Borodin. PRINCE IGOR. **Boris Martinovich** (bar) Igor; **Nicolai Ghiuselev** (bass) Galitsky; **Nicolai Ghiaurov** (bass) Konchak; **Kaludi Kaludov** (ten) Vladimir; **Angel Petkov** (ten) Eroshka; **Stoil Georgiev** (bass) Skula; **Mincho Popov** (ten) Ovlur; **Stefka Evstatiev** (sop) Yaroslavna; **Alexandrina Milcheva** (contr) Konchakovna; **Elena Stoyanova** (sop) Nurse, Polovtsian Girl; **Sofia National Opera Chorus; Sofia Festival Orchestra/Emil Tchakarov.** Sony Classical CD44878. Notes, text and translation included.

③ 3h 30' DDD 6/90

Borodin's limited time to devote to composition meant that many of his works often took years to complete. *Prince Igor* was no exception; even after 18 years of work it remained unfinished at his death in 1887, and it was finally completed by Rimsky-Korsakov and Glazunov. Borodin's main problem with *Prince Igor* was the daunting task of turning what was principally an undramatic subject into a convincing stage work. In many ways he never really succeeded in this and the end result comes over more as a series of epic scenes rather than a musical drama. Despite this, however, one is nevertheless left with an impression of a rounded whole, and it contains some of Borodin's most poignant and moving music, rich in oriental imagery and full of vitality. Tchakarov conducts a performance that is both vigorous and refined, and there are some excellent performances from the principal singers too — Boris Martinovich makes a particularly strong Igor and Nicolai Ghiuselev and Nicolai Ghiaurov in the roles of Prince Galitsky and the Polovtsian Khan Konchak deserve special mention also. This Sony issue is a particularly welcome addition to the catalogue as it represents the only *complete* version of the opera on disc.

Pierre Boulez

French 1925-

NEW REVIEW

Boulez. MISCELLANEOUS WORKS. [ad]**Sophie Cherrier** (fl); [e]**Alain Damiens** (cl); [ab]**Pierre-Laurent Aimard** (pf); [e]**Andrew Gerzo** (musical assistant); [f]**BBC Singers**; [cdf]**Ensemble Intercontemporain/Pierre Boulez.** Erato 2292-45648-2.
Flute Sonatine[a]. Piano Sonata No. 1[b]. Dérive[c]. Mémoriale (... explosante-fixe ... originel)[d]. Dialogue de l'ombre double[e]. Cummings ist der Dichter[f].

1h 3' DDD 2/92

The conjunction of early and relatively recent Boulez on this valuable disc is likely to inspire mixed feelings: admiration for his integrity, and regret at his reluctance to complete certain works and compose more new ones. The early sonatas (for the Flute Sonatine is as much a fully-fledged, substantial composition as the Piano Sonata No. 1) have confidence in their handling of form and a control of the way the thematic ideas evolve that seem both supremely cogent and remarkably spontaneous. Alongside the sonatas, short essays in expanding sonority like *Dérive* and *Mémoriale*, for all their refinement of tone colour, may seem almost wilfully unpretentious, while the reworked version of *Cummings ist der Dichter*, fascinating and convincing though it is on its own terms, is fussier than the original — less direct rather than more intense. What is beyond doubt is that in *Dialogue de l'ombre double* (1985) Boulez proves that he is still a master, not just of the memorable single line (a solo clarinet) but of the polyphony that results when that line is combined with a subtly varied electronic 'shadow' of itself. The quality of invention here is well-matched by Alain Damiens's superb performance, though all the playing is excellent, and the recordings are generally very good.

Boulez. Rituel (1974-75). Messagesquisse (1976). Notations 1-4 (1978). **Orchestre de Paris/Daniel Barenboim.** Erato 2292-45493-2.

41' DDD 10/90

Obviously enough, this disc wins no prizes for length. It is nevertheless important in several significant respects. Only rarely do we have the chance to hear Boulez's music, not only under a conductor other than the composer, but a conductor whose whole artistic background is so different to Boulez's own. Barenboim clearly has his own point of view, and the technical skill to realize it convincingly with a first-class French orchestra. Boulez himself now tends to underline the public ceremonial of *Rituel* (a tribute to the Italian composer and conductor Bruno Maderna), whereas Barenboim, restraining the cumulative clangour of the music's dialogues between the implacable reiterations of gongs and tamtams and the seven other instrumental groups, preserves more of the intimacy of personal regret and loss. *Rituel* is unusual for Boulez in the clear-cut logic of its gradually evolving form, and Barenboim does well to convey that logic without making the whole design seem too predictable for its own good. He is equally attentive to the need to balance striking details with a feeling for overall shape in the shorter but no less personal structures of *Notations* and *Messagesquisse*. The recording is outstanding in its spaciousness and tonal range.

Boulez. Pli selon pli. **Phyllis Bryn-Julson** (sop); **BBC Symphony Orchestra/Pierre Boulez.** Erato 2292-45376-2. From NUM75050 (5/83).

· 1h 8' DDD 3/89

Pli selon pli (1957-62) is one of the great pillars of post-war musical modernism. If that proclamation merely makes it sound forbidding, then it could scarcely be less appropriate. 'Pillar' it may be, but as exciting in its moment-to-moment shifts of colour and contour, and as compelling in its command of large-scale dramatic design as anything composed since the great years of Schoenberg and Stravinsky. Easy, no: enthralling and rewarding — yes. This is no grand, single-minded work in the great Germanic symphonic tradition, but a sequence of distinct yet balanced responses to aspects of the great symbolist poet Mallarmé. In this his second recording of the piece Boulez is prepared to let the music expand and resonate, the two large orchestral tapestries enclosing three "Improvisations", smaller-scale vocal movements in which the authority and expressiveness of Phyllis Bryn-Julson is heard to great advantage. The sound is brilliantly wide-ranging and well-balanced, and while the contrast between delicacy and almost delirious density embodied in *Pli selon pli* does take some getting used to, to miss it is to miss one of modern music's most original masterworks.

NEW REVIEW

Boulez. Le visage nuptial[a]. Le soleil des eaux[b]. Figures, Doubles, Prismes. [ab]**Phyllis Bryn-Julson** (sop); [a]**Elizabeth Laurence** (mez); [ab]**BBC Singers; BBC Symphony Orchestra/Pierre Boulez.** Erato 2292-45494-2. Texts and translations included.

· 1h 2' DDD 12/90

Pierre Boulez   *[photo: Erato/Sarrat*

Anyone approaching Boulez the composer for the first time would do well to start with his short cantata *Le soleil des eaux* which, like everything on this disc, is expertly performed and effectively recorded. Here is lyricism and drama, refinement and prodigious energy, in a style that acknowledges a Debussian delicacy as well as a complementary expressionist vehemence. It is certainly rare to find Boulez choosing a text which celebrates the natural world so directly. In *Le visage nuptial* it is human love and loss to which René Char's complex, surrealist word-patterns allude, and the music (begun in the mid-1940s but revised as recently as the late 1980s) is imposingly resourceful in its response. Even if you conclude that in this case the mixture simply doesn't work, the confrontation of poet and composer, which reached its fullest expression in *Le marteau sans maitre*, is endlessly absorbing. *Figures, Doubles, Prismes* is a characteristic Boulez title suggesting a subtle process of reflection and variation. Variety is abundant in this purely orchestral score, yet a sense of the larger span also comes through — so much so that the forceful ending can seem like a disconcerting contradiction. If so, it is all the more authentically Boulezian for that.

NEW REVIEW

Boulez. Le soleil des eaux[a].
Koechlin. Les Bandar-Log, Op. 176[b].
Messiaen. Chronochromie[c]. Et exspecto resurrectionem mortuorum[d].
[a]**Josephine Nendick** (sop); [a]**Barry McDaniel** (ten); [a]**Louis Devos** (bass); [a]**BBC Chorus**; [abc]**BBC Symphony Orchestra/Pierre Boulez**, [bc]**Antal Dorati**; [d]**Paris Orchestra/Serge Baudo.** EMI CDM7 63948-2. From [abc]ASD639 (7/65), [d] ASD2467 (12/69).

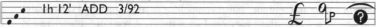

Koechlin's symphonic poem *Les Bandar-Log*, written in 1940, is part of a monumental work, *Livre de la Jungle*, which he had started over 40 years before. In the work played here he evokes the behaviour of monkey tribes and equates them satirically with musicians who wish to be in fashion but who are merely imitators of trends. Caricatures of various styles are woven into Koechlin's own highly individual and expressive style, which after over half a century still sounds very modern. Boulez has produced four versions of *Le soleil des eaux*, and the third is performed here. This short work is in two contrasted sections, which are based on two poems by René Char, *Lament of the Love-Sick Lizard* and *Night-time*. Though Boulez's writing is highly complex, there is still a very French preoccupation with beauty of sound, and the result is an attractive composition. The two Messiaen works explore subjects which have continually exercised the composer. In *Chronochromie* we are taken into the world of nature, and birdsong in particular. *Et exspecto resurrectionem mortuorem* is inspired by meditation on the resurrection of Christ and the prospect of life everlasting. In this last work the Paris Orchestra acquits itself well under Baudo (the composer was also present at the sessions), and the sound is very good. The BBC Symphony Orchestra performances were recorded at a time when Dorati was its chief conductor, and when Boulez was just commencing his relationship with the orchestra. Their performances are strikingly brilliant, and the recordings have amazing presence for the mid-1960s.

William Boyce

British 1711-1779

Boyce. SYMPHONIES. **The English Concert/Trevor Pinnock** (hpd). Archiv Produktion 419 631-2AH.
No. 1 in B flat major; No. 2 in A major; No. 3 in C major; No. 4 in F major; No. 5 in D major; No. 6 in F major; No. 7 in B flat major; No. 8 in D minor.

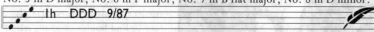

Boyce's *Eight Symphonys* (to follow his own spelling) were written over a period of some 20 years, as overtures for court odes and theatre pieces; later he collected them for publication and use as concert music. They are typically English, in a variety of ways: their tunefulness, their eccentricities of melody and rhythm, their refusal to obey any of the rules about style. And if you think, on hearing the trumpets and drums of No. 5, that Boyce is giving way to Handel's influence (it's very like the *Fireworks Music*), pause a moment: this piece dates from 1739, ten years earlier than the Handel work. The freshness and the vivacity of Boyce's invention are beautifully caught in these performances by Trevor Pinnock and The English Concert, with their sure feeling for tempo, their sprightly dance rhythms, and indeed their understanding of the gentle vein of melancholy.

Boyce. Solomon — a serenata. **Bronwen Mills** (sop) She; **Howard Crook** (ten) He; **The Parley of Instruments/Roy Goodman.** Hyperion CDA66378. Text included.

1h 16' DDD 11/90

Boyce's *Solomon* is not a biblical oratorio, like Handel's, but an extremely secular serenata based on *The Song of Solomon* — in short, a celebration of nature and of erotic love. It has just two 'characters', He and She, and most of their music is amorous — all of it gracefully written, some of it unsophisticatedly jolly, some markedly sensual. The most famous number is "Softly arise, O southern breeze!", for tenor with an eloquent bassoon obbligato and throbbing strings. For the most part the listener will be reminded of Handel's *Acis and Galatea*, with its typically pastoral features such as nature imitations (there are trilling birds and Purcellian frosty shivers); no one could fail to be charmed by this appealing, very English work. The singers here, Bronwen Mills and Howard Crook, are both of them good stylists, not perhaps as naturally sensuous in tone or phrasing as they might be but natural and fluent and showing an instinctive feeling for the shape of Boyce's lines, and they give due weight to the words. Roy Goodman conducts expertly with a period-instrument band, and the result is a gently beguiling performance.

Johannes Brahms

German 1833-1897

Brahms. Piano Concerto No. 1 in D minor, Op. 15[a]. Intermezzos[b] — E flat major, Op. 117 No. 1; C major, Op. 119 No. 3. **Sir Clifford Curzon** (pf); [a]**London Symphony Orchestra/George Szell.** Decca 417 641-2DH. Item marked [a] from SXL6023 (12/62), [b] SXL6041 (5/63).

57' ADD 10/87

This is a classic recording of the concerto, one which teamed a supremely civilized pianist with a conductor renowned for ruling with a rod of iron when directing his own orchestra, the Cleveland. In London, the results were quite magical; Szell's approach, while never less than totally authoritative has a warmth and smile to it that was often lacking in the States. Curzon is, quite simply, peerless. With a work like the Brahms First Piano Concerto a total rapport between piano and orchestra is vital simply because there are passages when the soloist must accompany the orchestra quite as much as vice versa. The two solo works are carried off with a beautiful sense of poetry and poise and all in all this is a magnificent achievement, well worth having.

Brahms. Piano Concertos[a] — Nos. 1 and 2. Fantasias, Op. 116[b]. **Emil Gilels** (pf); [a]**Berlin Philharmonic Orchestra/Eugen Jochum.** DG 419 158-2GH2. Items marked [a] from 2707 064 (12/72), [b]2530 655 (7/76).

2h 6' ADD 9/86

Emil Gilels was an ideal Brahms interpreter and his account of the two concertos with Eugen Jochum, another great Brahmsian, is one of the inspired classics of the gramophone. The youthful, leonine First Concerto and the expansive, lyrical Second were both played for the first time by Brahms himself, and it would be difficult to imagine any performances coming closer to the spirit of his music than these. They should not be missed and their value is further enhanced by the addition of the autumnal Fantasias, Op. 116. The recording, too, is natural and has plenty of concert hall ambience and an ideal balance between soloist and orchestra. This set cannot be too strongly recommended.

Brahms. Violin Concerto in D major, Op. 77. **Itzhak Perlman** (vn); **Chicago Symphony Orchestra/Carlo Maria Giulini.** EMI CDC7 47166-2. From ASD3385 (11/77).

> 43' ADD 1/87   **B**

Brahms. Violin Concerto in D major, Op. 77. **David Oistrakh** (vn); **French Radio National Orchestra/Otto Klemperer.** EMI Studio CDM7 69034-2. From Columbia SAX2411 (11/61).

> 41' ADD 12/89   *p* **B** ▲

Brahms. Violin Concerto in D major, Op. 77.
Mendelssohn. Violin Concerto in E minor, Op. 64. **Xue-Wei** (vn); **London Philharmonic Orchestra/Ivor Bolton.** ASV CDDCA748.

> 1h 7' DDD 4/91   **B**

Carlo Maria Giulini   [*photo: Sony Classical/Dominique*]

Giulini conducts the opening of this work in a strong and serious fashion, and at a moderate tempo. The unhurried pace indeed seems dangerously slow for the soloist, but then Perlman enters the scene and all is found to be well. His magisterial playing, ardent, powerful, and with magnificent breadth of phrase and tone makes for a very satisfying first movement. The *Adagio* has a good solo oboe from Ray Still; here Perlman's playing is reflective at first and then it becomes more overtly passionate as the movement develops. The last movement's 'gipsy' rondo finale makes an effective contrast, with plenty of sharp attack and rhythmic bite. The late 1970s recording is of good tonal quality and well balanced.

When the earlier EMI recording was made, it was not possible to bring Oistrakh and Klemperer together in London, so the veteran conductor travelled to Paris, and to an unfamiliar orchestra. We are told that the sessions were not without incident and provided a headache or two for the producer Walter Legge. But there is no hint of this in one of the finest versions of the concerto ever recorded for conductor and soloist seem in perfect artistic accord. Oistrakh's account of the first movement is richly communicative and deeply affecting, and in the slow movement his glorious tone quality and eloquent, soaring lyricism suit the music perfectly. The finale is executed in a strong, ruggedly good-humoured fashion and throughout the work the excellent French orchestra play with magnificent strength and commitment under Klemperer's magisterial direction. The recording is attractively spacious and has plenty of tonal lustre.

Congratulations to ASV for finding a much more appropriate coupling for the Mendelssohn than the amiable but decidedly second-rate Bruch G minor Concerto. But the outstanding advantage of this recording is the quality and exceptional freshness of Xue-Wei's playing. His Mendelssohn is that rare kind of performance that makes one hear a very familiar work as though for the first time, and there's a similar sense of discovery in the Brahms. There may be a few rough edges here and there — and the way he pushes forward in the great *Andante* melody of the Mendelssohn might not be to everyone's taste — but in both works what Xue-Wei turns out has the immediacy, urgency and sweep of a live performance. This is very much a young man's performance, and like a lot of young players Xue-Wei can be expansive, but he never loses his feel for the long phrase, and the central climax in the first movement of the Brahms is pulse-quickening stuff. Recommended to enthusiasts and jaded palates alike.

Brahms. Double Concerto in A minor, Op. 102[a]. Piano Quartet No. 3 in C minor, Op. 60[b]. **Isaac Stern** (vn); [b]**Jaime Laredo** (va); **Yo-Yo Ma** (vc); [b]**Emmanuel Ax** (pf); [a]**Chicago Symphony Orchestra/Claudio Abbado.** CBS Masterworks CD42387.

Ih 8' DDD 6/88

The grave, declamatory utterances at the beginning of the Double Concerto tell us much about the nature of what will follow. They can also reveal a great deal about the two soloists who enter in turn with solo cadenzas separated by thematic orchestral material. Perhaps surprisingly it is the much younger man, Yo-Yo Ma, who brings out most strongly the noble gravity of the composer's inspiration, while the relatively veteran Isaac Stern is more melodious and spontaneous-sounding. The music's steady but unhurried paragraphs are very well handled by Claudio Abbado and the excellent Chicago Symphony Orchestra is responsive and pretty faithfully balanced with the soloists. This is a performance to satisfy rather than to thrill, perhaps, but satisfy it does. The recording is rich and rather reverberant, notably in orchestral tuttis. The powerful C minor Piano Quartet is also well played and provides a substantial partner to the concerto. Apparently Brahms once said that it had the mood of a man thinking of suicide, but one hastens to say that it is nothing like as gloomy as that would suggest.

Brahms. Serenades — No. 1 in D major, Op. 11; No. 2 in A major, Op. 16. **Vienna Symphony Orchestra/Gary Bertini.** Orfeo C008101A.

Ih 16' ADD 6/90

Brahms's two serenades were his first published works for orchestra alone. He composed his First Serenade as a nonet for flute, two clarinets, horn, bassoon and strings but later rescored it for larger forces as well as expanding it structurally. It has many features which look forward to his mature symphonic works but at the same time it has a lightness of touch reminiscent of the classical serenades of Mozart and Haydn. The Second Serenade uses a much smaller orchestra than the First, and texturally it differs in not using violins at all. The atmosphere is serene, bucolic even, and one is constantly reminded of folk-dances. The main impression one has from these performances is of mellow warmth, a cosy German humour and a feeling for the dance, for Gary Bertini takes a pleasantly flexible view of the music and the Vienna Symphony Orchestra follow him well with some particularly attractive woodwind playing. It is good to have both these longish works together on a single disc. The recording is pleasingly rich, though with a touch of edge to the woodwind in the treble register.

Brahms. Hungarian Dances Nos. 1-21 — orchestrations. **Vienna Philhar-monic Orchestra/Claudio Abbado**. DG 410 615-2GH. From 2560 100 (3/83).
Brahms: Nos. 1, 3 and 10. **Hallén:** No. 2. **Juon:** No. 4. **Schmeling:** Nos. 5 and 6. **Gál:** Nos. 7, 8 and 9. **Parlow:** Nos. 11-16. **Dvořák:** Nos. 17-21.

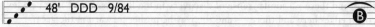

・・ 48' DDD 9/84   Ⓑ

To play the 21 *Hungarian Dances* through at one sitting is not recommended: far better for the CD user to choose a group of four or five and then just sit back and enjoy some charming and vivacious music, full of good tunes. High spirits predominate in the first set; in the second set there is more a mixture of liveliness and minor key 'gipsy' melancholy, though the introspection never becomes more than skin-deep. Abbado persuades the VPO to play with much brilliance and an engaging rhythmic lift and lightness of touch. These are highly enjoyable performances and the sound-quality emphasizes the nature of the playing, clear and brilliant, if a little lacking in warmth.

NEW REVIEW

Brahms. Symphony No. 1 in C minor, Op. 68[a]. Tragic Overture, Op. 81[b]. Academic Festival Overture, Op. 80[c]. **Philharmonia Orchestra/Otto Klemperer.** EMI Studio CDM7 69651-2. Items marked [a] from SAX2262 (10/59), [b] SAX2362, [c] SAX2351.

・・ 1h 7' ADD 1/90   ᎲⱣ Ⓑ

Otto Klemperer's recording of Brahms's First Symphony, made between 1955 and 1957, is one of the towering monuments of the gramophone. It is indicative of its quality that it still sounds as good now as when first issued over 30 years ago. Klemperer adopts conservative tempos for each movement, but drives the music forward with a relentless, cumulative power that results in a massive sense of architecture, and a series of very powerful climaxes. However, where required, such as in the tranquil third movement, Klemperer is capable of the requisite lightness of touch, and in the lyrical second movement he is expansive without being self-indulgent. When combined with the vintage playing of the Philharmonic Orchestra and a superbly clear recording the result is a perfor-mance of colossal stature. No other conductor since Klemperer has been able to combine the key elements of this master-work — objective grandeur and heroic passion — with such perfect balance. At mid price and with the added bonus of vintage performances of the *Academic Festival* and *Tragic* Overtures, this CD is self-selecting as one of the essential elements in any collection of classical performances.

NEW REVIEW

Brahms. Symphony No. 2 in D major, Op. 73. Alto Rhapsody, Op. 53[a]. [a]**Marjana Lipovšek** (contr); [a]**Ernst Senff Choir; Berlin Philharmonic Orchestra/Claudio Abbado.** DG 427 643-2GH.

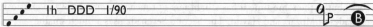

・・ 1h DDD 1/90   ᎲⱣ Ⓑ

This disc opens with a tense, grandly operatic *Alto Rhapsody*; the lower Berlin strings (and DG's recording of them) immediately gripping with their rich, dark sonority, a quality matched in full measure by Lipovšek's contralto. There have been more intimate, expressive accounts of the Rhapsody, but few as powerfully dramatic. In the Symphony Abbado draws out and movingly shapes the darker colourings; the solemnity and anxiety that give life and meaning to its predomi-nantly sunny discourse. Brahms's use of trombones was nowhere more imaginative and resourceful than in this work, as witness their chilling moans here in the slow movement (around the five minute mark), and it is a more troubled journey than usual to their sustained blast of triumph over the finale's concluding chords; one which offers profound satisfaction, possibly at the expense of a little physical elation in the finale.

Brahms. Symphony No. 3 in F major, Op. 90. Tragic Overture, Op. 81. Schicksalslied, Op. 54[a]. [a]**Ernst-Senff Choir; Berlin Philharmonic Orchestra/Claudio Abbado.** DG 429 765-2GH.

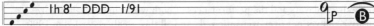

Brahms. Symphony No. 3 in F major, Op. 90[a]. Variations on a Theme by Haydn, "St Antoni"[b]. **Columbia Symphony Orchestra/Bruno Walter.** CBS Masterworks CD42531. From CD42022 (9/86). Item marked [a] from M3P 39631 (7/85), [b] Philips SABL185 (2/61).

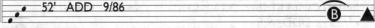

NEW REVIEW

Brahms. Symphony No. 3 in F major, Op. 90. Serenade No. 1 in D major, Op. 11. **Belgian Radio and Television Philharmonic Orchestra, Brussels/Alexander Rahbari.** Naxos 8 550280.

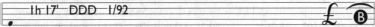

The DG disc is gloriously programmed for straight-through listening. Abbado gets off to a cracking start with an urgently impassioned *Tragic Overture* in which the credentials of the Berlin Philharmonic to make a richly idiomatic, Brahmsian sound — already well accepted — are substantially reaffirmed. A wide-eyed, breathtaking account of the *Schicksalslied* ("Song of Destiny") follows to provide sound contrast before the wonders of the Third Symphony are freshly explored. This is a reading of the Symphony to be savoured; it is underpinned throughout by a rhythmic vitality which binds the four movements together with a forward thrust, making the end inevitable right from the opening bars. Even in the moments of repose and, especially, the warmly-felt *Andante*, Abbado never lets the music forget its ultimate goal. Despite this, there are many moments of wonderful solo and orchestral playing along the way in which there is time to delight, and Abbado seems to bring out that affable, Bohemian-woods, Dvořák-like element in Brahms's music to a peculiar degree in this performance. The Symphony is recorded with a particular richness and some may find the heady waltz of the third movement done too lushly, emphasized by Abbado's lingering tempo. Nevertheless, this is splendid stuff, and not to be missed.

The engineers have done a grand job in revitalizing Walter's 1960 recordings, but even they cannot totally disguise moments of overloading and touches of thin stridency. Forget the sound, then, and listen to the performances and it soon becomes apparent why this disc can still be recommended. Bruno Walter, just a couple of years before his death, still exuded more energy and vitality than most conductors many years his junior, and he had all that wealth of experience behind him. The Brahms symphonies were old friends and the warmth of that relationship effuses from every note of this performance. There are only a few performances that really seem to get to grips with the Third Symphony's meaning and this is one of them. There is control here, yet above all the orchestra sounds as though it has been allowed its head — it can rely on Walter to shape the larger paragraphs but, given a luscious melody or fruity harmonies, it need not fear restraint. The *Variations* are kept more under rein, yet even here the result is still remarkably vital. This disc is a testament to a great conductor.

Noticing that the two works on the Naxos disc last not far short of 80 minutes, one sees also that it is not the symphony but the serenade which is the longer, and by some way too at around 44 minutes. Whilst it is symphonic in proportion it also resembles a classical serenade such as Mozart's *Haffner* Serenade in the same key, being in more movements than a symphony and having a smiling character. There are six movements including two scherzos and an *Adagio non troppo* (the third) which is also the longest. This is Brahms in his warmest vein, providing abundant lilting melody while also using his big orchestra with strength, while here and there (as at the start, in the *Adagio* and in the bucolic minuet) the mood is delightfully pastoral. The Third Symphony is also an essentially genial piece with a motto theme consisting of the notes F, A, F that the composer said stood for his own state of mind, "Frei, aber froh" ("free but happy"). This Brussels orchestra is not as widely known as the others, but it is a fine body of players and the performances of both works under Rahbari are sensitive and yet not over-romanticized. And all this, richly recorded in 1990, comes at super-budget price!

Brahms. Symphony No. 4 in E minor, Op. 98. **Vienna Philharmonic Orchestra/Carlos Kleiber.** DG 400 037-2GH. From 2532 003 (4/81).

39' DDD 9/85   Ⓑ

Carlos Kleiber's reading of Brahms's Fourth Symphony is highly individual and thought-provoking but those listeners who know Kleiber from his thrilling recordings of Beethoven's Fifth and Seventh Symphonies and are expecting similarly uncompromising, high-tension performances with enormous muscular energy are in for a surprise! His reading certainly has plenty of muscle, but he shows considerable patience and generosity in his handling of Brahms's long, constantly developing melodic lines. Sound is generally good, though the bass may need assistance on some equipment.

NEW REVIEW

Brahms. ORCHESTRAL AND VOCAL WORKS. **NBC Symphony Orchestra/Arturo Toscanini.** RCA Gold Seal mono GD60325. Texts and translations included.
Symphonies — No. 1 in C minor, Op. 68 (from HMV ALP1012, 11/52); No. 2 in D major, Op. 73 (ALP1013, 11/52); No. 3 in F major, Op. 90 (ALP1166, 10/54); No. 4 in E minor, Op. 98 (ALP1029, 6/53). Double Concerto in A minor, Op. 102 (with Mischa Mischakoff, vn; Frank Miller, vc. RB16066, 7/58). Variations on a Theme by Haydn, Op. 56a (ALP1204, 12/54). Tragic Overture, Op. 81 (VCM3, 4/67). Academic Festival Overture, Op. 80 (VCM3, 4/67). Hungarian Dances — No. 1 in G minor; No. 17 in F sharp minor; No. 20 in E minor; No. 21 in E minor (ALP1235, 5/55). Gesang der Parzen, Op. 89 (Robert Shaw Chorale. AT125, 4/74). Liebeslieder-Walzer, Op. 52 (Chorus; Artur Balsam, Joseph Kahn, pfs. Recorded in 1948. New to UK).

④ 4h 27' ADD 5/90   ▲

Arturo Toscanini

Despite many reissues, technical tinkerings, and critical re-evaluations, the recordings of the great Italian maestro Arturo Toscanini still stand head and shoulders above those which have the unenviable task of rivalling his genius as conductor and interpreter. This generous Brahms set is an excellent example of why Toscanini's recordings are still essential. The readings of the four symphonies must stand as benchmarks against which others are compared, and generally are found wanting. Toscanini's command of this music is total: his sense of architecture is unfailing, his control of tempos and rubato are masterly, and his ability to persuade the NBC Symphony Orchestra to play with extraordinary dynamic variety and tonal beauty is proof of his genius. In addition to the symphonies the set contains a fiery performance of the Double Concerto with the orchestra's principals as eloquent, if occasionally overshadowed, soloists and excellent readings of the essential shorter works of Brahms: the *Haydn Variations, Academic* and *Tragic* Overtures and *Hungarian Dances*. And to round off the set there are good, if not perfect, performances of two choral works, the rarely performed *Song of the Fates* and the *Liebeslieder Waltzes*, Op. 52. The transfer to CD of the original tapes has been handled particularly well: the worst tonal excesses have been successfully tamed, and there is a fine sense of balance throughout (the recordings range from 1948 to 1963). With such a giant as Toscanini recommendation really becomes superfluous. Suffice it to say that these recordings are testimony to the genius of one of the greatest conductors this century has ever known.

Brahms. String Sextets — No. 1 in B flat major, Op. 18; No. 2 in G major, Op. 36. **Raphael Ensemble** (James Clarke, Elizabeth Wexler, vns; Sally Beamish, Roger Tapping, vas; Andrea Hess, Rhydian Shaxson, vcs). Hyperion CDA66276.

Ih 14' DDD 1/89

Completed after the First Piano Concerto, but still comparatively early works, the Sextets are typified by lush textures, ardent emotion, and wonderfully memorable melodic lines. The first is the warmer, more heart-on-the-sleeve piece, balancing with complete naturalness a splendidly lyrical first movement, an urgent, dark set of intricate variations, a lively rustic dance of a *Scherzo*, and a placidly flowing finale. The Second Sextet inhabits at first a more mysterious world of half-shadows, occasionally rent by glorious moments of sunlight. The finale, however, casts off doubt and ends with affirmation. Both works are very susceptible to differing modes of interpretation, and the Raphael Ensemble has established very distinctive views of each, allowing the richness of the texture its head without obscuring the lines, and selecting characteristically distinct tone qualities to typify the two works. The recording is clear and analytic without robbing the sound of its warmth and depth. Altogether an impressive recording début for this ensemble.

Brahms. Clarinet Quintet in B minor, Op. 115[a].
Mozart. Clarinet Quintet in A major, K581[b]. **Gervase de Peyer** (cl); Members of the **Melos Ensemble** (Emanuel Hurwitz, Ivor McMahon, vns; Cecil Aronowitz, va; Terence Weill, vc). EMI CDM7 63116-2. Item marked [a] from ASD620 (3/65), [b] ASD605 (9/64).

Ih 5' ADD 11/89

There can be few who hear the opening to Brahms's Clarinet Quintet who fail to succumb to the main subject's tender and haunting melancholy — surely one of Brahms's most poignant utterances and certainly one guaranteed to send tingles down the spine. Gervase de Peyer's warm, full-bodied tone and liquid playing is a delight to the ear, and the autumnal beauty of the work is captured particularly well in this affectionate and thoughtful performance. Unlike the Mozart Quintet, which treats the clarinet very much as a concertante instrument, Brahms integrates the clarinet into the overall texture, skilfully blending and juxtaposing the characteristic timbre with that of the strings into an homogeneous whole, a quality that comes over exceptionally well in this performance. The Mozart

Quintet makes an ideal contrast to the autumnal glow of the Brahms, and receives an equally fine and engaging performance, if perhaps lacking just that extra bit of magic that makes the Brahms so irresistible. The Melos Ensemble convey the work's geniality and freshness from beginning to end, and the slow movement is imbued with great serenity and beauty. The 1964 recordings have retained a remarkable freshness, and are both naturally balanced and beautifully clear. At mid-price this reissue should not be missed.

80

Brahms. Piano Quintet in F minor, Op. 34. **Maurizio Pollini** (pf); **Quartetto Italiano** (Paolo Borciani, Elisa Pegreffi, vns; Dino Asciolla, va; Franco Rossi, vc). DG 419 673-2GH. From 2531 197 (9/80).

43' AAD 6/87

Brahms. Piano Quintet in F minor, Op. 34. **André Previn** (pf); **Musikverein Quartet** (Rainer Küchl, Eckhard Seifert, vns; Peter Götzel, va; Franz Bartolomey, vc). Philips 412 608-2PH. From 412 608-1PH (11/85).

41' DDD 1/86

Brahms. Piano Quintet in F minor, Op. 34.
Schumann. Piano Quintet in E flat major, Op. 44. **Jenö Jandó** (pf); **Kodály Quartet** (Attila Falvay, Tamás Szabo, vns; Gábor Fias, va; János Devich, vc). Naxos 8 550406.

1h 7' DDD 2/91

This work was originally composed as a string quintet with two cellos. Brahms's influential friend Joseph Joachim then subjected the composition to a good deal of criticism, and Brahms took this to heart so much that he converted the quintet into a sonata for two pianos. As this version also was not well received Brahms turned to another friend, Clara Schumann, and as a result of her advice the work emerged in a third form, for piano quintet. This powerfully argued work gives little indication of its varied origins. The long first movement has a particularly strong yet highly romantic vein of expression, and in their performance Pollini and his colleagues bring out particularly well its stormy, dramatic nature. In the slow movement the performers bring a certain restless, questing quality to Brahms's rich lyricism and the *Scherzo*, perhaps the most inventive movement, is quickly and urgently expressed. The rondo-finale is a very substantial movement in its own right and is given its full weight by the five excellent players. The recording is clear and very immediate. Previn's high regard for the work is evident in the cogency and eloquence of his playing, and he listens and responds well to the Musikverein Quartet, who match his vision with playing of high concentration. This is chamber music-making of very satisfying quality. Happily the sound and recorded balance is excellent.

Maybe the Hungarian players on the Naxos disc don't have the refinement of the finest ensembles, and in the second main theme in the first movement of the Schumann the cellist sounds an honest player rather than a Rostropovich, but the feeling is right. The Brahms Quintet, which is the later and bigger work, is also most enjoyable, with the right blend of passion and mystery, and although we may look for a more Schubertian warmth in the slow movement, generally the feeling is right and perhaps only purists will regret that unlike some other ensembles the Hungarians omit the exposition repeat in the first movement, for even so it is still the longest at over 11 minutes although their tempo in no way drags and indeed has the right urgency. The recording is not quite as good as the playing, being a little plummy and reverberant, but it is perfectly serviceable and at this bargain price no collector wanting this coupling need hesitate.

Brahms. Piano Quartets — No. 1 in G minor, Op. 25; No. 2 in A major, Op. 26; No. 3 in C minor, Op. 60. **Isaac Stern** (vn); **Jaime Laredo** (va); **Yo-Yo Ma** (vc); **Emanuel Ax** (pf). Sony Classical CD45846.

② 2h 8' DDD 3/91

These three piano quartets belong to the middle of Brahms's life. They have all the power and lyricism that we associate with his music, as well as the fine craftsmanship that he acquired when young and, with the high standards he set himself, demonstrated in every work thereafter. The mood of the music is again Brahmsian in that alongside a wealth of melodic and harmonic invention there are some shadows: all we know of Brahms's life suggests that he was never a happy man. But if this is reflected in the music, and especially the C minor Quartet, we can recognize the strength of intellect and will that keeps all in proportion so that there is no overt soul-bearing. These quartets are big pieces which often employ a grand manner, though less so in No. 2 than the others. For this reason, the present performances with their exuberant sweep are particularly telling, and although no detail is missed the players offer an overall strength. Top soloists in their own right, they combine their individual gifts with the ability to play as a well integrated team. The recording is close but not overwhelmingly so. Only the booklet, with notes in four languages, mars at least some copies of this issue, for it has some blank pages and details of the movements are missing, as are parts of the English and Italian notes.

Brahms. String Quartets — C minor, Op. 51 No. 1; A minor, Op. 51 No. 2. **Takács Quartet** (Gábor Takács-Nagy, Károly Schranz, vns; Gábor Ormai, va; András Fejer, vc). Decca 425 526-2DH.

1h 6' DDD 9/90

Brahms. String Quartets — A minor, Op. 51 No. 2; B flat major, Op. 67. **Orlando Quartet** (John Harding, Heinz Oberdorfer, vns; Ferdinand Erblich, va; Stefan Metz, vc). Ottavo OTRC68819.

1h 15' DDD 6/90

Few composers have ever been more self-critical than Brahms. He is said to have suppressed some 20 string quartets before writing one he deemed worthy of publication, and by then he was 40 years old. The C minor work was quickly followed by a second in A minor in the same year of 1873, and just two years later he produced his third and last in the major key of B flat. As yet, Hungary's Takács Quartet has only recorded the first two. But on the strength of such vivid playing and vibrant reproduction, few collectors are likely to be content until given the third. Though these four artists have now been together long enough to play as one, they are in fact still young enough to bring up every phrase with the immediacy of a new discovery. The two powerfully challenging flanking movements of the C minor work are sustained with splendid strength and drive. Yet how sensitively and subtly they convey the vulnerable heart concealed behind the classical façade in the second subject of the opening *Allegro*, for instance, and again, of course, in the work's two gentler central movements. They at once enter the more lyrical world of the first two movements of the A minor work, with its reminders of the motto themes adopted by both the composer himself and his great friend, the half-Hungarian violinist, Joachim. And how they relish the zest of the Hungarian-spiced finale.

The Orlando Quartet perform the last two quartets with affecting empathy for the music's beauty and radiance, its dramatic power and tender delicacy. These are warm, generous performances which clearly look forward to the autumnal shadows that were later to cross Brahms's music. The out-of-doors vigour of the first movement of Op. 67 may seem tamed because of this but, in the long term, this unusual interpretation makes a convincing case for itself by subduing the contrast between the movements and consequently making the whole work more coherent. In Op. 51 No. 2, one is immediately struck by how well the Orlando's rather slowish speed for the opening *Allegro non troppo* works, providing time for its intricacies to register and its heart-on-the-sleeve emotions to establish themselves. The characterful acoustic of Old-Catholic Church in Delft allows the music to breathe and the work's romantic centre to expand. Altogether, then, the Ottavo disc also substantially pushes forward the cause of these often misunderstood masterworks.

Brahms. PIANO TRIOS. **Beaux Arts Trio** (Isidore Cohen, vn; Bernard Greenhouse, vc; Menahem Pressler, pf). Philips 416 838-2PH2.
No. 1 in B major, Op. 8; No. 2 in C major, Op. 87; No. 3 in C minor, Op. 101; A major, Op. posth. (attrib. Brahms).

② 1h 59' DDD 1/88

Brahms. Piano Trio No. 1 in B major, Op. 8.
Ives. Piano Trio. **Trio Fontenay** (Michael Mücke, vn; Niklas Schmidt, vc; Wolf Harden, pf). Teldec 2292-44924-2.

57' DDD 4/90

NEW REVIEW

Brahms. Piano Trio in A major, Op. posth (attrib. Brahms).
Schumann. Piano Trio No. 1 in D minor, Op. 63. **Trio Fontenay** (Michael Mücke, vn; Niklas Schmidt, vc; Wolf Harden, pf). Teldec 2292-44927-2.

1h 5' DDD 3/92

The joy of the Beaux Arts performances of all these works is their obvious sense of delight in just that relaxed, intimate sort of music-making which takes time and space enough to sing through the broad river-flow of both opening movements, and to get dug into the contrasting developmental material with great gusto. Their C major Trio shows them getting down to business: they give a real sense of clambering, of the traversal of time in their ebullient working-through of rhythm and key. There are times when they can sound over-busy; but the Trio offer here the affectionate, fallible, but ever-generous powers of communication, recorded in a warm, close acoustic.

The first Teldec disc is certainly a very curious coupling, but anybody who is interested in both works need not hesitate, for performances are first-rate. Ives's Piano Trio was written in 1904-05 and revised in 1911. If what we hear is the final 1911 version without any later changes then the work is remarkably forward-looking for its day. The first *moderato* movement has some intriguing patterns and sonorities and is followed by "TSIAJ" (This Scherzo Is A Joke). Then comes a more substantial finale, where Ives's writing becomes more expressive, almost romantic. The Fontenay Trio play the work with obvious dedi-

Trio Fontenay   *[photo: Teldec/Thumser*

cation, great understanding and high expertise. Their account of the B major Brahms Trio is also very distinguished. The Fontenays play the first movement with a good deal of strength, but in a generous-spirited fashion, with considerable flexibility of phrase. Their account of the Scherzo has great conviction and they maintain tension and pulse throughout the *Adagio*. They round off the work with a majestically delivered finale. This outstanding disc is superbly recorded.

The special interest of the second Teldec disc, like that of the Philips, is the A major Piano Trio attributed to the young Brahms. Not discovered until 1924, the manuscript (published 14 years later) is unfortunately not in the composer's own hand, only that of some unidentified copyist. But in correspondence with Schumann soon after their momentous meeting in the autumn of 1853 Brahms did in fact mention two trios that he himself, intensely self-critical even at 20, deemed unworthy of publication, and who is to say that this work is not one of them? Though not without its naïveties, there are certainly enough boldly-glowing pre-echoes of the Brahms-to-come to silence most doubting Thomases. It is good to have it, at long last, on a single CD, especially when played with the exhilarating youthful enthusiasm and freshness of the Fontenay team. Schumann's own First Piano Trio of 1847 makes a particularly apt coupling. Both works are brought up as if newly minted even if adherence to Schumann's fastish metronome markings slightly reduces the ghostliness of the *sul ponticello* episode in the first movement's development, and perhaps, even, just a little of the intimacy of the slow movement's Innigkeit. The recording itself is splendidly vivid and true.

Brahms. Piano Trio No. 2 in C major, Op. 87.
Dvořák. Piano Trio No. 1 in B flat major, B51. **Trio Fontenay** (Michael Mücke, vn; Niklas Schmidt, vc; Wolf Harden, pf). Teldec 2292-44177-2

1h 4' DDD 2/90	9p	9s

These two works were written within a few years of each other. In 1875, when Dvořák wrote his Piano Trio No. 1 (he revised it a little later), he was still an emerging talent. Brahms, the older composer by eight years, was very much an established figure when he completed his Second Piano Trio in 1882. The Dvořák work still has a spirit of youthfulness, which is reflected faithfully in the Fontenay Trio's spontaneous-seeming, beautifully poised and generously phrased performance. There is an unhurried, affectionate quality in their playing which is highly attractive and they seem to be enjoying the recording process greatly. In the mature, masterful Brahms work the Fontenay's playing has similar virtues. They project the music with great understanding and a superb sense of style. The tonal quality of the two string players is warm and sonorous and all three artists are technically immaculate. Teldec have crowned this disc with an excellent recording which clearly has taken place in an appropriately small chamber, but one which possesses plenty of resonance.

Brahms. Horn Trio in E flat major, Op. 40[a].
Franck. Violin Sonata in A major. **Itzhak Perlman** (vn); [a]**Barry Tuckwell** (hn); **Vladimir Ashkenazy** (pf). Decca 414 128-2DH. From SXL6408 (5/69).

56' AAD 4/85	9p

Anyone who thinks of chamber music as predominantly an intellectual medium should easily be persuaded otherwise by these two mellow works of the late nineteenth century. Brahms is the more classically shaped of the two, while the third movement of the Franck Sonata is a "recitative-fantasia" whose quiet eloquence seems more than a little to foreshadow Debussy. Here, as in the strictly

canonic theme of the finale, Franck shows us that even baroque techniques can
be turned with no apparent effort to romantic ends. In the Brahms Horn Trio,
Perlman and Ashkenazy are joined by another virtuoso in the person of Barry
Tuckwell; but it is not their dazzling technical command that we notice so much
as their musicianly subtlety. In the rich textures of this work we are reminded of
the composer's inspiration by the beauty of the Black Forest and also of his grief
at the recent loss of his beloved mother. The combination of these three
instruments is rare to say the least, but the engineer has balanced them
satisfactorily.

Brahms. Clarinet Sonatas, Op. 120 — No. 1 in F minor; No. 2 in E flat major.
Weber. Grand duo concertant, J204. **Paul Meyer** (cl); **François-René
Duchable** (pf). Erato 2292-45480-2.

 · 1h 6' DDD 9/90

It was the clarinettist Richard Mühlfeld who inspired Brahms to write his clarinet
music, a Quintet with strings and these two sonatas, and as in the similar case of
Anton Stadler and Mozart, it happened towards the end of his life. Again like
Mozart, Brahms displays the richly lyrical aspect of the instrument as well as its
force, agility and big compass ranging from tenor to high soprano. Perhaps the
generally mellow nature of the writing owes something also to the composer's
recognition that he was in the autumn of his life. Paul Meyer and François-René
Duchable treat these sonatas lovingly and unhurriedly, and in the first movement
of the E flat major they give us all the warmth implied by the composer's
marking *amabile*. Although it is the second sonata, this work is played first; but in
any case both were written in the same year and the rather more urgent and
passionate F minor Sonata follows on naturally. Even here, the two artists take a
broad and graceful view of the music, and its essential seriousness and occasional
melancholy come across, not least in the eloquent sad tread of the slow movement. Weber's *Grand duo concertant* is quite different, being a melodious and
vivacious piece with a strong element of wit and even the theatre about it, and
there is a pleasing Gallic panache and elegance to this performance as well as
dexterity and fine ensemble. The recording is admirably clear as well as being
faithful to both instruments.

Brahms. Cello Sonatas — No. 1 in E minor, Op. 38; No. 2 in F major, Op.
99. **Steven Isserlis** (vc); **Peter Evans** (pf). Hyperion CDA66159. From
A66159 (10/85).

 · 50' DDD 4/86

Brahms worked on his Cello Sonata No. 1 over a period of three years, from
1862 to 1865. Originally the work included an *Adagio*, but this was destroyed by
the composer before publication, and as a result we have a three-movement
sonata consisting of a somewhat dark-hued, questing *Allegro non troppo*, a central
Allegretto quasi menuetto, which has a slight eighteenth-century pastiche flavour,
and a bold, tautly argued *Allegro* finale. The F major Sonata of 1886 is a bigger
work in every way. It was one of three chamber works written during a summer
stay in Switzerland, and the glorious scenery stimulated Brahms to compose in a
warm, open-hearted fashion. Steven Isserlis plays throughout both works with an
impressive tone-quality and an immaculate technique. Though his sympathy for
the music is everywhere evident, he does lack the last ounce of interpretative
insight. But with fine playing from the pianist Peter Evans, and a very good,
natural sounding recording, this is a disc which will give much pleasure.

NEW REVIEW

Brahms. Piano Sonata No. 1 in C major, Op. 1.
Liszt. PIANO WORKS. **Sviatoslav Richter.** RCA Victor Red Seal RD60859.
Recorded at performances in the Schleswig-Holstein Festival in July 1988.
Consolation S172 No. 6. Hungarian Rhapsody in D minor, S244 No. 17. Scherzo
and March, S177. Etudes d'exécution transcendante, S139 — No. 11, Harmonies
du soir.

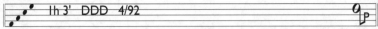

Ih 3' DDD 4/92

Sviatoslav Richter was born in 1915 and has been a part of the pianistic scene for
as long as most people can remember. Even so, it is difficult to believe that this
Russian pianist who gave the première of Prokofiev's Sixth Sonata in 1942 is still
very much with us and, as this disc demonstrates, still a master of his instrument. The septuagenarian pianist plays a Brahms sonata written when the
composer was 20, but the finest art knows no generation gaps and he brings
great authority to a work which in lesser hands can seem naïve with its
youthfully grandiloquent gestures. The first movement has an unforced strength,
but essentially Richter's is a thoughtful reading rather than a virtuoso one, and
there are delicate textures to admire along with the necessary dexterity. The
Liszt pieces include two rarities that are well worth hearing (the second and third
of the four listed above) flanked by the popular Sixth Consolation and the
celebrated *Harmonies du soir*: the last of these is a magnificent example of pre-
Debussian impressionism to which Richter brings both passion and nobility. The
live recording could be richer and has a few creaks and clatterings, but not
enough to disturb.

Brahms. Piano Sonata No. 3 in F minor, Op. 5. **Zoltán Kocsis.** Hungaroton
HCD12601.

40' DDD 1/85

NEW REVIEW

Brahms. PIANO WORKS. **Murray Perahia.** Sony Classical CD47181.
Piano Sonata No. 3 in F minor, Op. 5. Capriccio in B minor, Op. 76 No. 2.
Intermezzo in E flat minor, Op. 118 No. 6. Rhapsodies — B minor, Op. 79
No. 1; E flat major, Op. 119 No. 4.

Ih DDD 10/91

Brahms composed his three piano sonatas early in life, completing the Third
during his important friendship with Robert Schumann. It is a work of colossal
scale and dimension, possessing a grandeur that seems to cry out for comparison
with Beethoven's last compositions. The listener's attention is seized right at the
outset by the massive opening theme that sweeps through the movement and
there follows a meditative *Andante*, a gipsy-like *Scherzo* and an almost funereal
Intermezzo. The final movement brings this huge structure to a resounding close.
Zoltán Kocsis brings youthful ardour to this vivid work, relishing its moments of
rapt intensity as well as its torrential verve. The recording is full and rich.

The more recent recording of the sonata by Murray Perahia provides a superb
complement to Kocsis's disc and should give great satisfaction to collectors who
savour different approaches to a masterwork. Perahia's playing is riper and less
youthfully impetuous and ardent, yet this too yields its rewards and makes him
all the more capable of encompassing the many changes from virtuoso vigour to
quiet lyricism in the first movement. He reminds us that Brahms was naturally
introspective even when he was 20 and writing a virtuoso, leonine work such as
this one — yet such is his pianistic intelligence and sensitivity that he does so
without sacrificing vigour and forward movement, essential qualities in this big
five-movement work. Needless to say, he is in his element in the songful twilight
musings of the *Andante* and Intermezzo, but the big *Scherzo* and fleet finale (with

a whirling, triumphant coda) are just as effective. The other four pieces are also satisfying, with tremendous vigour in the Rhapsody and all the brooding drama one could wish for in the tragic E flat minor Intermezzo. The recorded sound is faithful and enjoyable in all sound levels and textures — and that last word reminds me to praise his finely judged use of the sustaining pedal, so important in this composer.

Brahms. Violin Sonatas — No. 1 in G major, Op. 78; No. 2 in A major, Op. 100; No. 3 in D minor, Op. 108. **Josef Suk** (vn); **Julius Katchen** (pf). Decca Ovation 421 092-2DM. From SXL6321 (1/68).

Ih 8' ADD 5/88

Brahms was 45 when he began to work on the first of these Sonatas and he completed the final one some ten years later. These products of his mature genius are certainly the greatest works written in this form since Beethoven's. Though they are lovingly crafted and have a predominant air of lyricism, there is great variety of melody and of mood. The invention always sounds spontaneously conceived and they fit the CD format like a kid glove. Suk's control over nuance is magical whilst Katchen has a complete understanding of the style. In every way these are performances that truly deserve to be labelled as classics and the naturally vivid recorded sound brings them to life with magnificent immediacy.

Brahms. Four Ballades, Op. 10.
Weber. Piano Sonata No. 2 in A flat major, J199. **Alfred Brendel** (pf). Philips 426 439-2PH.

53' DDD 6/91

Alfred Brendel   [photo: Philips

It is hard to imagine piano music by German romantic composers more different than these works by Weber and Brahms, the former being full of fluent expressiveness and the latter of introspection. Part of the reason is that Weber was one of the earliest romantics and Brahms a late one, and their dates do not even overlap; but besides this, in character they were unalike, Weber being a brilliant, nervous man of the theatre and Brahms a shy, dour Northerner. Setting aside the chronological order that he follows in his valuable booklet essay, Alfred Brendel plays the Brahms *Ballades* first, and does so with force and momentum, not least in No. 1 with its evocation of the grim Scottish ballad about a patricide that is quoted in the score. Considering that the composer was only 21 when he wrote these pieces, they are surprisingly sombre, and although No. 3 is a kind of scherzo (which Schumann called demonic) all are in a minor key. This music is hardly easy listening, but the authority of the playing is compelling. The Weber "Grand Sonata" in A flat major is a four-movement work, lasting over half an hour, which was once better known than it is now: the elegant writing sometimes reminds us of his *Invitation to the Dance*, and we can also see why Liszt and Chopin admired him and learned from him. Though the music is discursive, as Liszt and Chopin are not, it is in excellent hands here and Brendel holds things together in a way that would elude lesser artists. There are awkwardnesses and naïveties here, but the work is still one of great interest and the playing most persuasive. Fine, faithful piano sound.

Brahms. Rhapsodies, Op. 79 — No. 1 in B minor; No. 2 in G minor. 16 Waltzes, Op. 39. Six Piano Pieces, Op. 118. **Stephen Kovacevich** (pf). Philips 420 750-2PH. From 6514 229 (4/83).

> 53' DDD 4/88

The Op. 79 Rhapsodies have been described as the "most temperamental" of all Brahms's later keyboard works. It would certainly be hard to imagine more vehement performances than those given by Kovacevich, thanks to his robust tone, trenchant attack and urgent tempos — perhaps even a shade too fast for the *Molto passionato, ma non troppo allegro* of the second. But the pleading second subject of No. 1 in B minor brings all the requisite lyrical contrast. The Waltzes, too, have their tenderer moments of *Ländler*-like sentiment and charm. However, they emerge faster and more excitable than usual, as if Kovacevich were trying to remind us of Brahms's old love of Hungary no less than his new love of Vienna. "It is wonderful how he combines passion and tenderness in the smallest of spaces" was Clara Schumann's comment on the miniatures and the phrase fits Kovacevich's warmly responsive account of the Op. 118 set just as well. The piano is faithfully and fearlessly reproduced in what sounds like a ripely reverberant venue.

Brahms. Variations and Fugue on a Theme by Handel, Op. 24.
Reger. Variations and Fugue on a Theme by Telemann, Op. 134. **Jorge Bolet** (pf). Decca Ovation 417 791-2DM. From SXL6969 (11/81).

> 59' ADD 2/90 £ P

Brahms. Variations and Fugue on a Theme by Handel, Op. 24. Four Ballades, Op. 10. Variations on a Theme by Schumann, Op. 9. **Jorge Federico Osorio** (pf). ASV CDDCA616.

> 1h 8' DDD 11/88 S

The Decca issue is one of Bolet's finest studio recordings. Although his playing was very much founded on the great virtuoso tradition there is never a sense of mere virtuosity for its own sake, though his technical command and imposing virtuosity (as these recordings bear witness) are never in doubt. The Brahms *Variations and Fugue on a Theme by Handel* is one of the great masterpieces of variation form and has always maintained a high place in the piano repertoire. The theme (taken from Handel's three "Lessons for Harpsichord") is simplicity itself, though around the simplicity Brahms weaves an imaginative profusion of ideas. His love of Bach can be detected in the highly contrapuntal textures and which find their ultimate *coup de grâce* in the enormously effective concluding fugue. Reger's magnificent set of variations date from 1914 and was his last major work for the solo piano. It shares with the Brahms a remarkable mastery of counterpoint, and its Herculean technical demands place it out of bounds to all but the most accomplished of pianists. Under Bolet's hands all musical and technical difficulties are quashed, and both here and in the Brahms his clarity of texture and balance of parts is most impressive. The recording is vivid and naturally balanced.

Jorge Federico Osorio is a Mexican-born pianist whose teachers included Wilhelm Kempff, and he brings to this music a real feel for its style as well as fine technical resource; tempos are well judged and textures no less so, and altogether the playing is most compelling. The recording of the piano is unusually good even by today's high standards, with a resonant bass and a spacious acoustic, and it encompasses Brahms's biggest climaxes remarkably well, with the vigorous Third Ballade being specially striking here. This piano music is not the easiest to play and interpret, but this CD brings us fine performances from an artist who fully understands the music, and the playing of the *Schumann Variations* should help to re-establish this rather neglected work in the piano repertory.

Brahms. PIANO WORKS. **Julius Katchen** (pf). Decca 430 053-2DM6. Variations on a Theme by Paganini, Op. 35. Variations and Fugue on a Theme by Handel, Op. 24 (both from SXL6218, 4/66). Four Ballades, Op. 10 (SXL6160, 5/56). Variations on a Theme by Schumann, Op. 9. Variations on an Original Theme, Op. 21 No. 1. Variations on a Hungarian Song, Op. 21 No. 2 (all from SXL6219, 3/66). Waltzes, Op. 39. Two Rhapsodies, Op. 79 (both from SXL6160, 5/65). Piano Sonatas — No. 1 in C major, Op. 1; No. 2 in F sharp minor, Op. 2 (both from SXL6129, 12/64); No. 3 in F minor, Op. 5. Scherzo in E flat minor (both from SXL6228, 6/66). Piano Pieces — Op. 76. Fantasias, Op. 116 (both from SXL6118, 9/64); Op. 118; Op. 119. Three Intermezzos, Op. 117 (all from SXL6105, 5/64). Hungarian Dances (with Jean-Pierre Marty, pf. SXL6217, 12/65).

⑥ 6h 28' ADD 2/91 ▲

The American pianist Julius Katchen, who died in 1969 at the age of 42, was a virtuoso much in demand for his performance of such works as the Rachmaninov Second Concerto, but he was also a philosophy graduate who brought intellectual force and subtlety to his playing. Brahms was a special favourite of his, and these performances recorded in the 1950s and 1960s have real distinction, for he is at home in all the areas of the composer's world, ranging from the youthful ardour of the sonatas and *Paganini* Variations to the autumnal musings of the later pieces such as the intermezzos and fantasias, which are shorter but say much in little and sometimes show a wistful sunset glow. The immensely difficult *Paganini* Variations, based on a theme used by several other composers, show the leonine side both of Brahms and the pianist: this is an outstandingly athletic performance, powerful and yet sometimes more delicate too, and if there's a touch of hardness to the piano tone, that is not out of place. The *Handel* Variations are more varied in mood and texture and link up more with the world of the Two Rhapsodies in which storm and lyricism are finely balanced here, while the humour, tenderness, twilight mystery and sadness of the late pieces are perfectly realized, as are the lilt of the Waltzes and the gipsy bravura of the Hungarian Dances, in 11 of which Katchen plays as a duettist with Jean-Pierre Marty.

Brahms. PIANO WORKS. **Radu Lupu.** Decca 417 599-2DH. Items marked [a] from SXL6504 (5/71), [b] SXL6831 (11/78). Rhapsodies, Op. 79 — No. 1 in B minor[a]; No. 2 in G minor[b]. Three Intermezzos, Op. 117[a]. Six Piano Pieces, Op. 118[b]. Four Piano Pieces, Op. 119[b].

1h 11' ADD 8/87 P Ⓑ

Brahms. PIANO WORKS. **François-René Duchable.** Erato 2292-45477-2. Theme and Variations in D minor. Three Intermezzos, Op. 117. Two Rhapsodies, Op. 79. Variations on a Theme by Paganini, Op. 35.

1h 3' DDD 3/91 Ⓑ

Brahms's late piano music inhabits a very special world, equally appealing to the sentimental as to the intellectually inclined listener. A poignant sense of resignation, of autumnal wistfulness, is allied to consummate mystery of compositional technique, and these elements are mutually transformed, producing an effect impossible to capture in words. Radu Lupu's playing captures it, though. Listen to the quiet rapture as he sleepwalks into the last section of Op. 117 No. 3 or the revelation in Op. 118 No. 2 that the inversion of the theme is even more beautiful than its original statement. One senses a complete identity with the composer's thoughts, and it is to be doubted whether any finer recording of these works has ever been made.

Nevertheless, François-René Duchable is an extremely gifted pianist who has the technique to do justice to Brahms's dauntingly challenging *Paganini* Variations and does so to notable effect in his 1989 recording made in a well chosen Swiss location. Technique here means more than the necessary dexterity, of course, and he also gives us poise and poetry. This is aristocratic playing of a work which has the average concert pianist struggling to achieve accuracy at an acceptable pace (wise amateurs do not even attempt it) and it gives much pleasure, not least because Duchable also keeps the momentum going from one variation to the next and so avoids the sectional effect that we hear from some other artists in this music, even good ones. The other pieces are finely done, too. The Op. 117 Intermezzos have a quiet persuasiveness, and the two passionate Rhapsodies are exciting in keyboard terms yet always lyrical as well. We also have a rarity in the D minor Theme and Variations which is a transcription of a famous slow movement in the String Sextet, Op. 18. The recording is a good one, and the trace of hardness in the piano's treble register that one notices in the *Paganini* Variations is not out of place.

Brahms. CHORAL WORKS. [a]**Jard van Nes** (mez); **San Francisco Symphony Chorus and Orchestra/Herbert Blomstedt.** Decca 430 281-2DH. Texts and translations included.
Gesang der Parzen, Op. 89. Nänie, Op. 82. Schicksalslied, Op. 54. Begräbnisgesang, Op. 13. Alto Rhapsody, Op. 53[a].

1h 3' DDD 8/90

Herbert Blomstedt   *[photo: Decca/Stoddard*

Brahms is such a familiar figure that it is salutary to be reminded that one area of his work, choral music, remains mostly unknown to collectors save for the *German Requiem* and *Alto Rhapsody*. This is a pity, for this composer who was also a distinguished choral conductor drew some of his finest inspiration from this medium. This issue includes the *Rhapsody*, warmly and movingly sung by Jard van Nes, but its importance lies in the fact that it also does much to give us a better knowledge of other big pieces too. Don't be put off by the sombre subject mater — including *Begräbnisgesang,* "A Song of the Fates" (a tremendous piece), another work about fate itself and not one but two funeral hymns! — but listen instead to thrilling choral singing and orchestral playing under the direction of a conductor who believes passionately in the music. "Plenty of strength, light and drama" is what *Gramophone*'s critic found in this programme when it first came out, and to that one would add that the San Francisco Symphony Chorus sing the German texts with complete conviction. If this music makes us regret that Brahms wrote no opera, we may at least feel that here is something not far short of it even though it was not intended for the stage; to see this, listen only to the *Schicksalslied* which is the first work performed. A good recording complements the quality of performance, though ideally the choral textures could be clearer.

Brahms. MOTETS. **Trinity College Choir, Cambridge/Richard Marlow.** Conifer CDCF178. Texts and translations included.
Op. 29 — Es ist das Heil uns kommen her; Schaffe in mir, Gott. Psalm 13, Op. 27 (with Richard Pearce, org). Op. 110 — Ich aber bin elend; Ach, arme Welt, du trügest mich; Wenn wir in höchsten Nöten sein. Ave Maria, Op. 12 (Pearce). Op. 109 — Unsere Väter; Wenn ein starker Gewappneter; Wo ist ein so herrlich Volk. Geistliches Lied, Op. 30 (James Morgan, org). Op. 37 — O bone Jesu; Adoramus te Christe; Regina coeli, Op. 74 — Warum ist das licht gegeben dem Mühseligen?; O Heiland, reiss die Himmel auf.

Ih 5' DDD 2/90

The Choir of Trinity College, Cambridge have the remarkable gift of making music heavily overladen with contrapuntal wizardry sound, not only inevitable, but extraordinarily lovely. This recording of the complete set of Brahms's motets may be recommended unreservedly. The singing is of a high quality and the acoustic of the chapel serve to enhance both the clarity and the blend. The motets range from a fairly straightforward chorale style of writing to some very ,substantial double-choir composition. A few pieces are written for female voices only — not for nothing was Brahms conductor of the Hamburg Frauenchor and thus well-acquainted with that medium — the performance of these pieces by the high voices of the Trinity Choir is a model of lightness, lucidity and skill. The ingenious *Regina coeli* comes across with something of the sprightliness of an Elizabethan ballet (albeit with alleluias instead of Fa-la-la-ing!). This is a disc calculated to delight both the Brahms specialist and all music lovers.

Brahms. LIEDER. **Thomas Allen** (bar); **Geoffrey Parsons** (pf). Virgin Classics VC7 91130-2. Texts and translations included.
Wir wandelten, Op. 96 No. 2. Der Gang zum Liebchen, Op. 48 No. 1. Komm bald, Op. 97 No. 5. Salamander, Op. 107 No. 2. Nachtigall, Op. 97 No. 1. Serenade, Op. 70 No. 3. Geheimnis, Op. 71 No. 3. Von waldbekränzter Höhe, Op. 57 No. 1. Dein blaues Auge hält so still, Op. 59 No. 8. Wie bist du, meine Königin, Op. 32 No. 9. Meine Liebe ist grün, Op. 63 No. 5. Die Kränze, Op. 46 No. 1. Sah dem edlen Bildnis, Op. 46 No. 2. An die Nachtigall, Op. 46 No. 4. Die Schale der Vergessenheit, Op. 46 No. 3. In Waldeseinsamkeit, Op. 85 No. 6. Wiegenlied, Op. 49 No. 4. Sonntag, Op. 47 No. 3. O wüsst ich doch den Weg zurück, Op. 63 No. 8. Minnelied, Op. 71 No. 5. Feldeinsamkeit, Op. 86 No. 2. Ständchen, Op. 106 No. 1. Von ewiger Liebe, Op. 43 No. 1. Die Mainacht, Op. 43 No. 2. Botschaft, Op. 47 No. 1.

Ih 2' DDD 9/90

Brahms's songs are, on the whole, intimate, one-to-one statements. They rarely approach the nature of public announcements and thus only occasionally explore extreme loudness: they are ideally suited to home listening. The darkening timbre of Thomas Allen's voice makes it increasingly suited to Brahms, and his characteristic, though far from common, qualities of heroic breath control and vital, lissom phrasing compound his affinity with this music. The songs make best use of the distinctive parts of his range and this, wedded to Allen's innate musicianship, sets a solid foundation for an engrossing recital. Geoffrey Parsons picks up these features and mirrors them in the searching piano parts, bringing light and shade, clarity and mist to support the voice. The recital as a whole is well thought out: the songs have clear, unifying links in terms of mood and gesture, but there is enough variety here to retain interest throughout. A pleasantly close recording of the voice emphasizes subtleties of tonal shading, and the more subdued setting of the piano allows it to make its effect without overpowering the singer. A disc to delight both novice and seasoned listener alike, then.

Brahms. LIEDER. **Anne Sofie von Otter** (mez); **Bengt Forsberg** (pf). DG 429 727-2GH. Texts and translations included.
Zigeunerlieder, Op. 103 — No. 1-7 and 11. Dort in den Weiden, Op. 97 No. 4. Vergebliches Ständchen, Op. 84 No. 4. Die Mainacht, Op. 43 No. 2. Ach, wende diesen Blick, Op. 57 No. 4. O kühler Wald, Op. 72 No. 3. Von ewiger Liebe, Op. 43 No. 1. Junge Lieder I, Op. 63 No. 5. Wie rafft' ich mich auf in der Nacht, Op. 32 No. 1. Unbewegte laue Luft, Op. 57 No. 8. Heimweh II, Op. 63 No. 8. Mädchenlied, Op. 107 No. 5. Ständchen, Op. 106 No. 1. Sonntag, Op. 47 No. 3. Wiegenlied, Op. 49 No. 4. Zwei Gesänge, Op. 91 (with Nils-Erik Sparf, va).

· 1h 1' DDD 4/91

Many of the lieder here are but meagrely represented in current catalogues, so that this recital is all the more welcome, particularly in view of the perceptive musicality of both singer and pianist. They show a fine free (but unanimous!) flexibility in the *Zigeunerlieder*, with a dashing "Brauner Bursche" and "Röslein dreie" and a passionate "Rote Abendwolken"; but there is also lightness, happy in "Wisst ihr, wann mein Kindchen", troubled in "Lieber Gott, du weisst"; and Otter's coolly tender tone in "Kommt dir manchmal in den Sinn" touches the heart. Also deeply moving are the profound yearning and the loving but anxious lullaby in the two songs with viola obbligato (most sensitively played). Elsewhere, connoisseurs of vocal technique will admire Otter's command of colour and legato line in the gravity of *O kühler Wald*, the stillness of *Die Mainacht* and the intensity of *Von ewiger Liebe*, and her lovely *mezza voce* in the *Wiegenlied* and the partly repressed fervour of *Unbewegte laue Luft*; but to any listener her remarkable control, her responsiveness to words and, not least, the sheer beauty of her voice make this a most rewarding disc, aided as she is by Forsberg's characterful playing.

Brahms. Ein deutsches Requiem, Op. 45. **Elisabeth Schwarzkopf** (sop); **Dietrich Fischer-Dieskau** (bar); **Philharmonia Chorus and Orchestra/ Otto Klemperer.** EMI CDC7 47238-2. Notes, text and translation included. From Columbia SAX2430/31 (2/62).

· 1h 9' ADD 6/87

Brahms. Ein deutsches Requiem, Op. 45. **Charlotte Margiono** (sop); **Rodney Gilfry** (bar); **Monteverdi Choir; Orchestre Révolutionnaire et Romantique/John Eliot Gardiner.** Philips 432 140-2PH. Text and translation included.

· 1h 6' DDD 4/91

Brahms's *German Requiem*, a work of great concentration and spiritual intensity, is, rather surprisingly, the creation of a man barely 30 years old. He turned for his text not to the liturgical Mass but to the German translations of the Old Testament. It is decidedly *not* a Requiem of 'fire and brimstone' overshadowed by the Day of Wrath; instead it is a work for those who mourn, those who remain in sorrow ("As one whom his mother comforteth, so I will comfort you", sings the soprano in a soaring hymn of grief-assuaging beauty). The texture is sinuous and Brahms employs the orchestra with great delicacy as well as enormous muscular energy. Klemperer's reading of this mighty work has long been famous: rugged, at times surprisingly fleet and with a juggernaut power. The superb Philharmonia are joined by their excellent Chorus and two magnificent soloists — Elisabeth Schwarzkopf offering comfort in an endless stream of pure tone and Fischer-Dieskau, still unequalled, singing with total absorption. A great performance beautifully enhanced on CD.

The pungency of a small chorus and the incisive edge provided by the orchestra of period instruments, the Orchestre Révolutionnaire et Romantique, makes for a fresh reappraisal of a work that can all too often sound turgid and dull. Gardiner has written of the work's radiance, optimism and full-bloodedness and he instils these characteristics into his performance. The reduced forces employed mean that great subtlety can be drawn out of the score — words are meticulously cared for, dynamic nuances observed and, above all, strong and secure attack ensure a genuine intensity of expression. The soloists are good too, with the young American baritone Rodney Gilfry quite outstanding, offering firm, warm and beautifully rounded tone throughout. Charlotte Margiono, set a little far back in the aural perspective, is a sweet and suitably conciliatory soprano soloist. For anyone who has in the past found Brahms's *Ein deutsches Requiem* difficult to come to terms with then this pioneering period instrument set is probably the one to win the most converts.

Frank Bridge

British 1879-1941

NEW REVIEW

Bridge. Oration — Concerto elegiaco, H174.
Britten. Cello Symphony, Op. 68. **Steven Isserlis** (vc); **City of London Sinfonia/Richard Hickox.** EMI CDM7 63909-2. From CDC7 49716-2 (5/88).

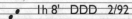

1h 8' DDD 2/92

Steven Isserlis's decision to couple these two English masterpieces on one disc was a particularly intelligent one: not only because Frank Bridge was one of Britten's most influential teachers and mentors, but also because both works reflect, in their different ways, the two composers' strong pacifist beliefs and their deep concern at man's inhumanity to man. *Oration* (subtitled *Concerto elegiaco*) dates from 1930 and is both an explicit outcry against the futility of war and a vast lament for the many friends and colleagues that Bridge had lost as a result of the Great War. Indeed, throughout its 30-minute span the work is constantly haunted by images of

Steven Isserlis *[photo: Virgin Classics/Crowthers*

war — sometimes in mocking parody (as in the central march section, or the martial fanfares that erupt violently into orchestral climaxes), and sometimes in sombre, grief-stricken episodes of moving intensity. Isserlis gives us an exceptionally fine performance that fully captures the intensity and vision of this richly rewarding and shamefully neglected masterpiece. Britten's own masterpiece in the idiom — the Cello Symphony — was composed some 30 years later, but the influence of *Oration* can be clearly discerned both in its emotional content (if perhaps less overtly displayed than in the former) and in the similar way that it eschews the conventions of a formal concerto. Again both soloist and conductor deserve the highest praise for a performance that matches the profundity and vision of the music. Well recorded.

Bridge. Suite for strings.
Butterworth. A Shropshire Lad. Two English Idylls. The Banks of Green Willow.
Parry. Lady Radnor's Suite. **English String Orchestra/William Boughton.**
Nimbus NI5068.

Ih I' DDD 10/88

No one who loves British music of the romantic period will need much introduction to the three pieces by George Butterworth that begin this programme. His poignant orchestral rhapsody *A Shropshire Lad* somehow seems to presage his death at the age of 31 in the trenches of World War I (it has been called "his own requiem") and took its inspiration from A.E. Housman's poetry, itself laden with half-suppressed longings and a passionate identification with doomed youth; and though the *Two English Idylls* and *The Banks of Green Willow* (with a folk melody introduced by the clarinet) are brighter, these too have a certain sadness along with pastoral charm. Sir Hubert Parry was another Britisher whose music reveals a sensitive heart, though he hid it under a country-squire exterior, and his *Lady Radnor's Suite* was composed in 1894 for an aristocratic friend who heard it first at her castle near Salisbury; its six movements form a sequence of neo-classical dances ending with a somewhat Irish-sounding *Gigue*. Frank Bridge was admired by his pupil, Britten, as England's foremost composer, and his Suite for strings of 1910 shows his mastery of string writing and textures. William Boughton and the English String Orchestra are persuasive advocates of this music and the recording is pleasantly resonant.

Bridge. Piano Quintet in D minor.
Elgar. Piano Quintet in A minor, Op. 84. **Coull Quartet** (Roger Coull, Philip Gallaway, vns; David Curtis, va; John Todd, vc); **Allan Schiller** (pf).
ASV CDDCA678.

Ih 10' DDD 1/90

These two endearingly evocative works are clearly linked by their characteristic tendency to refer to something unnamed outside of themselves. This was typical of Bridge's style at the time (the Quintet was composed in 1905, revised in 1912) but for Elgar in 1919 it represented a culmination of the inner doubts and public sorrows that virtually ended his compositional career. Much of Bridge's finest music is to be found in his chamber works and, besides an enormous inventiveness, he always displays in them a keen sense of just proportion. In revising the Piano Quintet, he took the opportunity to integrate the Scherzo into the slow movement, producing a more balanced structure, and resolving many of the inadequacies inherent in the work in its earlier guise. The performers here bring out that elegant shape most skilfully without undermining the passing delights to be savoured along the way. Elgar's Quintet is, for the most part, treated to a lighter touch than usual, emotional intensity being focused towards the central slow movement, and Allan Schiller's less dominating contribution allows the engineers to attain a subtle balance of strings and piano often missing in other recordings. Such an apt coupling is worth trying.

NEW REVIEW

Bridge. STRING QUARTETS. **Brindisi Quartet** (Jacqueline Shave, Patrick Kiernan, vns; Katie Wilkinson, va; Jonathan Tunnell, vc). Continuum CCD1035/6. *CCD1035* — No. 1 in E minor, H70; No. 3, H175. *CCD1036* — No. 2 in G minor, H115; No. 4, H188.

② 59', 46' DDD 5/92

Belonging to the same generation as Bax and Ireland, Bridge latterly became more adventurous stylistically than either and paid the penalty by coming to be regarded askance by the British musical establishment. Indeed, his publisher refused to take his 1928 piano piece *Gargoyle* on account of its modernity. The same suspicion caused the neglect of his Third and Fourth String Quartets, works of 1926 and 1937 in which he has been said to have "approached the early works of the Second Viennese School" with all that this implies in terms of atonality. The truth is perhaps both more complex and more interesting, namely that the extreme chromaticism of his language in these works represents a new way of looking at tonality, just as a personal use of tonality is a stylistic feature of his only pupil, Britten. In any case, Bridge's music is always 'musical' and never just theoretical, and although it can be severe there is also melodic and harmonic charm (most obviously in the two earlier quartets of 1906 and 1915) as well as an individual Englishness that is highly rewarding in its own way. Furthermore, since he was a fine viola player and professionally experienced in chamber music, as a member for some years of the English String Quartet, the writing for the four instruments is always grateful. Despite its Italian-sounding name, the Brindisi Quartet is British and they play this music with skill and understanding, while the recording brings lucidity to the often subtle textures. The two discs are accompanied by informative booklet material and are obtainable separately, but one really wants them both for a proper survey of this repertory.

NEW REVIEW

Bridge. String Quartet No. 3.
Walton. String Quartet in A minor (1945-7). **Endellion Quartet** (Andrew Watkinson, Ralph de Souza, vns; Garfield Jackson, va; David Waterman, vc). Virgin Classics VC7 91196-2.

1h 2' DDD 9/91

Frank Bridge's Third String Quartet was written 20 years before the Walton A minor, though on grounds of style alone you might expect the reverse to be the case. By the mid 1940s, Walton had settled into that gentle yet far from complacent romanticism that suited him best. There is no shortage of fast, energetic music, even so, and the whole work is built on an ample scale, requiring careful pacing from the players if the proportions of its design are to be clear, and the straightforward thematic working is to seem suitably spontaneous. The Endellion Quartet do a good job, but they come even more decisively into their own with the more challenging and dramatic music of Frank Bridge. During his lifetime (and for a while thereafter) Bridge was too often misrepresented as the pawn of sinister continental influences. As this quartet (completed in 1927) shows, he knew his Bartók, and even his Berg, but there is a textural openness and an harmonic allusiveness like no one else's, which was soon to have its effect on Bridge's star pupil, Benjamin Britten. The ideas are arresting, their development absorbing, and the vivid recording conveys the relish of this expert ensemble as its members do justice to an attractive and important score.

Bridge. Phantasie Trio in C minor.
R. Clarke. Piano Trio.
Ireland. Phantasie Trio in A minor. **Hartley Trio** (Jacqueline Hartley, vn; Martin Loveday, vc; Caroline Clemmow, pf). Gamut Classics GAMCD518.

50' DDD 9/91

The 'innocent ear' test of music is usually a good one, and this writer remembers once switching on the car radio and immediately being intrigued by the unfamiliar music being played. It was the Piano Trio by Rebecca Clarke who, like Ireland and Bridge, studied with Stanford at the Royal College of Music in London. She is less known than they, but had a personal voice, although the booklet note rightly points out her affinity with Ernest Bloch, a composer she admired and whose music also betokens a burning sincerity — incidentally, the beginning of the finale in her Trio does not sound at all British. Although she was also a professional viola player, her passionate Trio sometimes strains at the boundaries of chamber music, but for all its power it does not get out of proportion. Nor does it lack memorable ideas. One wonders whether there is any European country other than philistine Britain where such a good composer could have been ignored — she does not even rate an entry in *Grove* — and can only regret the loss of the other works that she might have given us if she had received recognition. Though better known than Clarke, Frank Bridge also never had quite the standing that he deserved, particularly after he developed a challengingly advanced harmonic language in the 1920s. His *Phantasie Trio* is an earlier piece, though, and is dramatic and well wrought. So is Ireland's attractive work of the same name, also cast in a single biggish movement. The Hartley Trio play all three of these works with love and understanding, and the recording is well balanced and faithful.

Bridge. PIANO WORKS, Volume 1. **Peter Jacobs.** Continuum CCD1016. Arabesque. Capriccios — No. 1 in A minor, H52; No. 2 in F sharp minor, H54*b*. A Dedication. A Fairy Tale Suite. Gargoyle. Hidden Fires. In Autumn. Three Miniature Pastorals — Set 1; Set 2. A Sea Idyll, H54*a*. Three Improvisations for the Left Hand. Winter Pastoral.

1h 13' DDD 9/90 ❷

Bridge. PIANO WORKS. **Kathryn Stott.** Conifer CDCF186.
A Sea Idyll, H54*a*. Capriccios — No. 1 in A minor, H52; No. 2 in F sharp minor, H54*b*. Three poems — Ecstasy, H112*b*. The Hour Glass, H148. Piano Sonata, H160. Vignettes de Marseille, H166.

1h 12' DDD 9/91 ❷

Peter Jacobs plays piano pieces composed by Bridge between 1905 and 1928. They will be unfamiliar to most listeners and are well worth exploration. It is not too much to say that they represent an English equivalent of Fauré with something of the spirit of Brahms's late pieces too. This is especially true of Bridge's pre-1914 works, where the clarity of the harmony avoids any over-lush treatment of such titles as *Sea Idyll*. The charm of the *Fairy Tale Suite* and of the *Miniature Pastorals*, both dating from 1917, belong to the world of Ravel's *Ma mère l'oye*. But the second set of *Pastorals*, composed in 1921, reflects the devastating effect the First World War had on Bridge. Delightful though they still are, these pieces have lost their innocence and are the work of a disillusioned man. During the 1920s, Bridge's harmonic style grew more radical and moved nearer to atonality, as can be heard in *A Dedication* and *In Autumn*. Jacobs's performances reflect not only his command of the technique required for this music but his total belief in its quality. He has done Bridge a service and the recording engineers have backed him to the hilt.

As well as offering an alternative choice for Bridge's piano music, Kathryn Stott's recital, equally generous in length, provides a useful complement to that of Peter Jacobs, for only three short pieces are duplicated. Her main work is the Piano Sonata, written in the early 1920s in memory of a composer friend killed in World War I: Bridge, a convinced pacifist, took three years over the writing of it and it is deeply felt music, surprisingly bold in harmonic language and with an element of angry protest as well as an elegiac mood most clearly felt in the central slow movement. It has been called "a work to be respected rather than loved" and one may feel that there are more gestures than substance, missing really memorable melody. But it makes a strong impression none the less and Kathryn Stott's committed and intense playing provides very persuasive advocacy. The other pieces are no less idiomatically done, and the early ones like the capriccios and the *Sea Idyll* show Bridge as a master like Fauré, who can say much in a short piece and whose piano writing is unfailingly graceful. The crisply drawn *Vignettes de Marseille* are no less attractive, and *The Hour Glass* adds to these qualities a freedom of language that in the 1920s placed the composer among the avant-garde in British music. The recording of the shorter pieces is a fine one and, although rather resonant, it also satisfies in the Sonata.

Benjamin Britten
British 1913-1976

Britten. Piano Concerto, Op. 13[a]. Violin Concerto, Op. 15[b]. [b]**Mark Lubotsky** (vn); [a]**Sviatoslav Richter** (pf); **English Chamber Orchestra/ Benjamin Britten.** Decca London 417 308-2LM. From SXL6512 (8/71).

1h 7' ADD 10/89 £ ⓠ ℗

NEW REVIEW

Britten/Berkeley. Mont Juic, Op. 12. [a]**Lorraine McAslan** (vn); **English Chamber Orchestra/Steuart Bedford.** Collins Classics 1123-2.

58' DDD 12/90 ⓠ ℗ ⓠ ⓢ

Just after Britten's performances were released on LP in 1971, the composer admitted with some pride that Sviatoslav Richter had learned his Piano Concerto "entirely off his own bat", and had revealed a Russianness that was in the score. Britten was attracted to Shostakovich during the late 1930s, when it was written, and the bravado, brittleness and flashy virtuosity of the writing, in the march-like finale most of all, at first caused many people (including Lennox Berkeley, to whom it is dedicated) to be wary of it, even to think it somehow outside the composer's style. Now we know his music better, it is easier to accept, particularly in this sparkling yet sensitive performance. The Violin Concerto dates from the following year, 1939, when Britten was in Canada, and it too has its self-conscious virtuosity, but it is its rich nostalgic lyricism which strikes to the heart and the quiet elegiac ending is unforgettable. Compared to Richter in the other work, Mark Lubotsky is not always the master of its hair-raising difficulties, notably in the scherzo, which has passages of double artificial harmonics that even Heifetz wanted simplified before he would play it (Britten refused), but this is still a lovely account. Fine recording, made in The Maltings at Snape.

Lorraine McAslan's disc of the Violin Concerto with the English Chamber Orchestra under Steuart Bedford is something of a *tour de force*. It comes with the *Canadian Carnival* Overture and *Mont Juic*, the set of Catalan pieces he composed together with Lennox Berkeley. McAslan is one of the illustrious band of pupils from Dorothy Delay who range from Itzhak Perlman to Cho-Liang Lin, and her performance is one of commanding eloquence and virtuosity. She and Bedford make one look at this work with new eyes. Indeed, had the first performance and its immediate successors been of this quality, its fate would surely have been very different from the long period of neglect it suffered in the 1950s and 1960s. What is even more impressive though than in the earlier recordings is the orchestral contribution under Bedford which has far greater intensity, range and urgency of feeling as well as imaginative scale than its predecessors, including the composer's own with Lubotsky. It brings home the demonic energy and fire, as well as poignancy and a sense of pain. The Collins Classics recording is of exceptional quality, wide-ranging and vivid, and to continue the litany of praise, the balance could not be bettered. For those tired of upfront larger-than-life violin sounds, this is ideal.

Britten. Cello Symphony, Op. 68[a]. Sinfonia da Requiem, Op. 20[b]. Cantata misericordium, Op. 69[c]. [a]**Mstislav Rostropovich** (vc); [c]**Sir Peter Pears** (ten); [c]**Dietrich Fischer-Dieskau** (bar); [c]**London Symphony Chorus and Orchestra**, [a]**English Chamber Orchestra**, [b]**New Philharmonia Orchestra/Benjamin Britten.** Decca London 425 100-2LM. Text and translation included. Item marked [a] from SXL6138 (12/64), [bc] SXL6175 (9/65).

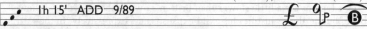

1h 15' ADD 9/89

Benjamin Britten   *[photo: Decca*

This mid-price disc offers two of Britten's finest works, the *Cello Symphony* and the *Sinfonia da Requiem*. The latter was written in 1940 and is one of the composer's most powerful orchestral works, harnessing opposing forces in a frighteningly intense way. From the opening drumbeat the *Sinfonia* employs sonata form in a dramatically powerful way, though the tone is never fierce or savage; it has an implacable tread and momentum. The central movement, "Dies irae", however, has a real sense of fury, satirical in its biting comment — the flutter-tongued wind writing rattling its defiance. The closing "Requiem aeternam" is a movement of restrained beauty. On this recording from 1964 the New Philharmonia play superbly. The Cello Symphony, written in 1963 as part of a series for the great Russian cellist Mstislav Rostropovich, was the first major sonata-form work written since the *Sinfonia*. The idea of a struggle between soloist and orchestra, implicit in the traditional concerto, has no part here; it is a conversation between the two. Rostropovich plays with a depth of feeling that has never quite been equalled in other recordings and the playing of the ECO has great bite. The recording too is extraordinarily fine for its years. The *Cantata misericordium*, one of Britten's lesser known works, was written in 1962 as a commission from the Red Cross. It takes the story of the Good Samaritan and is scored for tenor and baritone soloists, chorus, string quartet and orchestra. It is a universal plea for charity and here receives a powerful reading. This is a must for any collector of Britten's music.

NEW REVIEW

Britten. Sinfonia da Requiem, Op. 20. The Young Person's Guide to the Orchestra, Op. 34. PETER GRIMES — Four Sea Interludes; Passacaglia. **Royal Liverpool Philharmonic Orchestra/Libor Pešek.** Virgin Classics VC7 90834-2.

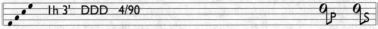
1h 3'   DDD   4/90

In the years since his appointment as musical director of the Royal Liverpool Philharmonic Orchestra, Libor Pešek has brought the city's symphony orchestra to an excellent standard and, indeed, his achievement has been compared to that of Simon Rattle in Birmingham. Here he shows also that he has a deep sympathy with the intensely felt, sometimes tortured writing in the *Sinfonia da Requiem* and the *Peter Grimes* interludes. By contrast, he and his orchestra are no less at home in the virtuoso, extrovert display of *The Young Person's Guide to the Orchestra*, and the show of youthful high spirits which, as this work reminds us, were no less part of Britten's world. The recording in the Liverpool Philharmonic Hall is quite splendid, and the colossal thumps on the bass drum and two unison timpani just before the eight-minute mark in the lamenting first movement of the *Sinfonia* have physical impact, fairly leaping out of the loudspeakers — as does the alarming, disintegrating coda to the *Dies irae* in the same work. Sometimes Pešek's tempos are a little slower than Britten's own in the recording reviewed above, but he always justifies his extra expansiveness expressively. In the Interludes, he places the Passacaglia within the sequence after *Moonlight* instead of playing it separately as is usually done, and this makes for a satisfying sequence. A thrilling disc for music, performance and sheer sound.

Britten. The Young Person's Guide to the Orchestra, Op. 34. GLORIANA — Courtly dances.
Prokofiev. Peter and the Wolf, Op. 67[a]. **Royal Philharmonic Orchestra/ André Previn** ([a]narr). Telarc CD80126. Text included where appropriate.

55'   DDD   5/87

Britten. The Young Person's Guide to the Orchestra, Op. 34[a]. Simple Symphony, Op. 4[b]. Variations on a Theme of Frank Bridge, Op. 10[c]. [a]**London Symphony Orchestra; [bc]English Chamber Orchestra/Benjamin Britten.** Decca 417 509-2DH. Item marked [a] from SXL6110 (9/64), [b] SXL6405 (6/69), [c] SXL6316 (11/67).

1h 1'   ADD   1/87

Britten. The Young Person's Guide to the Orchestra, Op. 34. Symphony for cello and orchestra, Op. 68[a]. PETER GRIMES — Four Sea Interludes, Op. 33a.
Pärt. Cantus in memory of Benjamin Britten. [a]**Truls Mørk** (vc); **Bergen Philharmonic Orchestra/Neeme Järvi.** BIS CD420.

1h 15'   DDD   6/89

In *Peter and the Wolf* André Previn is an ideal guide to the components of the orchestra, for his relaxed, friendly delivery creates just the right atmosphere, while through the magic of tape editing he also contrives to conduct a neatly characterized performance, vividly recorded. Britten's *Young Person's Guide to the Orchestra*, adapted from a theme by Purcell, came about through a film which would demonstrate to children the instruments of the orchestra. This brilliantly inventive work is excellently played by the RPO though Previn's direction is a shade reserved. The attractive Courtly dances from Britten's opera *Gloriana* complete an attractive disc.

Britten's performance of his *Young Person's Guide* wisely omits the now rather dated text. He adopts quick tempos that must be demanding even for the LSO players, along with more spacious ones for the more introspective sections. This is beautiful playing, with all kinds of memorable touches. Britten's own childhood music is also here, in the shape of the delightfully fresh *Simple Symphony*. This fine CD then ends with more variations, the young composer's tribute to his teacher Frank Bridge. It is marvellous music, of astonishing wit and often intensely serious too, and the composer's own performance with the ECO is uniquely authoritative.

The BIS issue is a well-planned disc and it was a particularly good idea to include Pärt's *Cantus*, scored for strings and a bell which tolls throughout the work to most hypnotic effect. Järvi's interpretation of Britten's Cello Symphony is more lyrical and relaxed than most, with a nostalgic touch that softens the edges of the score. But he still imparts the necessary vigour, irony and starkness to this enigmatic composition. The solo part is magnificently played by Truls Mørk, whose expressive phrasing is matched by the virtuosic brilliance of his playing. The Bergen Philharmonic gives an admirable account of the orchestral score and is also fully conversant with the *Peter Grimes* Interludes and the *Young Person's Guide*. The recording is clear and well-balanced, allowing the music to create its own atmosphere.

Britten. The Prince of the Pagodas, Op. 57. **London Sinfonietta/Oliver Knussen.** Virgin Classics VCD7 91103-2.

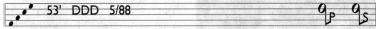

It is not surprising that this two-disc set won the 1990 *Gramophone* award in the Engineering category, for it is technically superlative (recorded in St Augustine's Church, Kilburn). But its primary importance is that Oliver Knussen has recorded the complete score of Britten's only ballet, restoring 20 minutes of music that had not previously been heard. Britten's 1957 recording for Decca had over 40 cuts, including four entire dances. It is extraordinary that the inclusion of this extra music should drastically alter the perspective of the whole work, but it does — it seems a better piece altogether, its debt to Tchaikovsky, Prokofiev and Stravinsky less obvious. Much connected with the production of the ballet at Covent Garden turned sour for Britten and this may have been reflected in his conducting of the recording. Knussen's interpretation is far more loving and effective and the playing of the London Sinfonietta is outstanding for individual virtuosity and for the richness and sparkle of the ensemble. This is that rare commodity, a disc that sheds entirely new light on a composition, and it should be in the collection of everyone who values Britten's — and British — music.

Britten. String Quartet No. 3, Op. 94.
Tippett. String Quartet No. 4 (1978). **Lindsay Quartet** (Peter Cropper, Ronald Birks, vns; Robin Ireland, va; Bernard Gregor-Smith, vc). ASV CDDCA608.

Neither Britten nor Tippett had written a string quartet for over 30 years when they returned to the medium in the 1970s. Both composed a masterpiece. In Britten's case there was the poignancy of its being the last major work he completed, yet there is no sign of declining powers in a work that pays homage to Shostakovich as well as to the special qualities of the Amadeus Quartet for whom it was written. The Lindsay Quartet's interpretation is very different; it is emotionally more intense and one can rarely be unaware of the shadow over the score, with its thematic references to Britten's last opera, *Death in Venice*. The last movement, a Passacaglia from which all passion has been drained to leave a serene air of resignation, is played very slowly. Tippett's Fourth Quartet has a lyrical and impassioned slow movement at its core and the predominant impression is one of energy and vigour. The music has such abundance that it seems to be bursting the confines of the medium and it is no surprise to learn that Tippett authorized an arrangement for string orchestra, not that the Lindsays sound at all strained by this vibrant score. The playing is masterful and the recording is admirably clear.

NEW REVIEW

Britten. Lachrymae, reflections on a song of Dowland, Op. 48[a].
Shostakovich. Viola Sonata, Op. 147[a].
Stravinsky. Elégie. **Tabea Zimmermann** (va); [a]**Hartmut Höll** (pf). EMI CDC7 54394-2.

51' DDD 3/92

Tabea Zimmermann and Hartmut Höll adopt a chillingly literal approach to the Shostakovich Viola Sonata, completed only a matter of days before the composer's death in August 1975. These players find no palliative or consolatory warmth in this spent and glacial work, which speaks not just of leave-taking, but of the outrage and sense of hopelessness revealed at the end of a lifetime's toil. This is a truly heroic reading of enormous power and musical integrity, and no finer recorded version of this grim valedictory essay has yet appeared. Zimmermann also has the true measure of Britten's *Lachrymae*, and her compelling performance reveals the hidden character of each of these fascinating diversions built around Dowland's source material. Stravinsky's *Elégie* for solo viola again suits Zimmermann's pensive and withdrawn approach, but the final direction of the music is never in any doubt. These performances excel, both in terms of superb technical mastery, and for their special insights into those aspects of human frailty and limitation which affects us all. Altogether then, a harrowing yet deeply stimulating collection of some of the most significant twentieth-century additions to the viola repertory. The recorded sound is ripe and full, and has an unexpected degree of transparency which never allows the piano to dominate in climactic passages, but which still sounds refreshingly natural and well balanced. An excellent production from every point of view.

Britten. PIANO WORKS. **Stephen Hough,** [a]**Ronan O'Hora** (pfs). Virgin Classics VC7 91203-2.
Holiday Diary, Op. 5. Three Character Pieces (1930). Night Piece (1963). Sonatina romantica (1940) — Moderato; Nocturne. 12 Variations on a Theme (1931). Five Waltzes (1923-5 and 1969). Two Lullabies (1936)[a]. Mazurka elegiaca Op. 23 No. 2[a]. Introduction and Rondo alla burlesca, Op. 23 No. 1[a].

1h 20' DDD 8/91

Though a fine pianist, Britten wrote surprisingly little for his own instrument, admitting in later life that he found it unsatisfying. Thus even with the inclusion of boyhood pieces unpublished in his lifetime there is not enough solo piano music to fill a single disc, and Stephen Hough is joined by Ronan O'Hora for three two-piano works. The biggest item here is the one that comes first, the *Holiday Diary* of 1934, four pieces of which Britten wrote to a friend a decade later, "I have an awfully soft spot for them still — they just recreate that unpleasant young thing BB in 1934 — but who

Stephen Hough   *[photo: Virgin Classics/Carnegie*

enjoyed being BB all the same!!" They have schoolboyish titles like "Early morning bathe" and "Funfair", and show an attractive youthful energy, but the final piece called "Night" is unusual in being slow and mysterious instead of a conventional brilliant finale. Stephen Hough has a coolly sharp way with this music, which is perhaps right for the buttoned-up young Britten that was revealed in the collection of his letters and diaries published in 1990. Not all the music here is distinguished, but it is well written; it is enlightening, too, to hear the influence of the composer's teacher, Ireland, in the *Three Character Pieces* and of Hindemith in the athletic *12 Variations*. Hough's playing has exemplary clarity and poise throughout, and the *Night Piece* of 1963 is beautifully atmospheric, while the two-piano music is also well delivered by thoughtful artists working well together. A clear and faithful recording complements this valuable issue.

Britten. Spring Symphony, Op. 44[a]. Cantata Academica, Op. 62[b]. Hymn to St Cecilia[c]. [ab]**Jennifer Vyvyan** (sop); [a]**Norma Procter,** [b]**Helen Watts** (contrs); [ab]**Sir Peter Pears** (ten); [b]**Owen Brannigan** (bass); [a]**Emanuel School Boys' Choir;** [a]**Chorus and Orchestra of the Royal Opera House, Covent Garden;** [bc]**London Symphony Chorus;** [b]**London Symphony Orchestra/** [a]**Benjamin Britten,** [bc]**George Malcolm.** Decca London 425 153-2LM. Texts and translation included. Item marked [a] from SXL2264 (5/61), [b] and [c] L'Oiseau-Lyre SOL60037 (10/61).

| 1h 14' ADD 1/90 | ▲ |

Britten's famous recording of the *Spring Symphony* has acquired a brightness on CD that has the effect of lightening his entire palette by a perceptible degree or two. It is a jubilantly bright piece, of course, and the enthusiasm of the performance is so great that many listeners will not object. There is now a slight acidity to the choral sound which could be a drawback for some listeners but, since this is only one of two recordings of the symphony currently available, most people will be happy to live with it. The *Cantata Academica* suffers less from this flaw and Britten's reading relishes its lightly-worn learned humour so much (and the fact that the solos were so obviously written as wittily affectionate portraits of the singers who were to record them) that it is part of the essential Britten discography. The *Hymn to St Cecilia* is also nicely done.

Britten. Les illuminations, Op. 18[a]. Simple Symphony, Op. 4. Phaedra, Op. 93[a]. [a]**Christiane Eda-Pierre** (sop); **Jean-Walter Audoli Instrumental Ensemble/Jean-Walter Audoli.** Arion ARN68035.

| 56' DDD 6/89 | 9s |

It is good to have, at last, a recording of Britten's *Les illuminations* that is sung by a French singer and played by a French orchestra under a conductor from the same country. She and her colleagues bring a clean refinement to this score, and although other performances may have more excitement and sensuous charm this is one to appreciate for its sharp intelligence and Gallic clarity of judgement. Having written that Christiane Eda-Pierre is French-speaking, one must at once add that her English in *Phaedra* is also very good. Oddly enough, Britten here set a text which was originally in French (the translation is by the American poet Robert Lowell), and his music powerfully conveys the classical intensity of Racine's play on the subject of the Greek queen who falls into a forbidden love for her stepson Hippolythus and takes poison to escape a guilt that has become intolerable. Though called a cantata, *Phaedra* is really a miniature opera for a single singer (it was written for Dame Janet Baker) and it contains some of Britten's most effective writing for the female voice. The *Simple Symphony* which separates these two vocal works is altogether different, being based on music dating from the composer's happy childhood and having a fresh and often touching quality. The recording is as crisp as the performances.

Britten. Serenade for tenor, horn and strings, Op. 31[a]. Les illuminations, Op. 18[b]. Nocturne, Op. 60[c]. [abc]**Sir Peter Pears** (ten); [c]**Alexander Murray** (fl); [c]**Roger Lord** (cor a); [c]**Gervase de Peyer** (cl); [c]**William Waterhouse** (bn); [ac]**Barry Tuckwell** (hn); [c]**Dennis Blyth** (timp); [c]**Osian Ellis** (hp); [ac]strings of the **London Symphony Orchestra,** [b]**English Chamber Orchestra**/[abc]**Benjamin Britten.** Decca 417 153-2DH. Texts included. Item marked [a] from SXL6110 (9/64), [b] SXL6316 (11/67), [c] SXL2189 (5/60).

♪♪ 1h 13' ADD 8/86   𝄽 P Ⓑ ▲

No instrument was more important to Britten than the human voice and, inspired by the musicianship and superb vocal craftsmanship of his closest friend, he produced an unbroken stream of vocal works of a quality akin to those of Purcell. Three of his most haunting vocal pieces are featured on this wonderful CD. The performances date from between 1959 and 1966 with Pears in penetratingly musical form, even if the voice itself was by now a little thin and occasionally unsteady. The ECO and LSO are superb in every way and of course Britten was his own ideal interpreter. The recordings are vintage Decca and excellent for their time.

Britten. CHORAL WORKS. **London Sinfonietta** [a]**Voices and** [b]**Chorus/ Terry Edwards.** Virgin Classics VC7 90728-2. Texts included.
A Boy was Born, Op. 3 (with St Paul's Cathedral Boys' Voices)[b]. Hymn to St Cecilia (1942)[a]. A.M.D.G. (1939)[b]. A Shepherd's Carol (1944)[b].

♪♪ 1h 4' DDD 10/88   𝄽 P 𝄽 S

Since Britten's death, a number of his works have been released from his archive which he had either suppressed or forgotten in his lifetime. All these 'discoveries' have been pure gain, but some more than others. Among the major 'lost' compositions is A.M.D.G. (*Ad maiorem Dei gloriam*), seven settings of poems by Gerard Manley Hopkins. They are difficult but very rewarding; "God's Grandeur" is an exciting song, making virtuoso demands on the choir, and in "O Deus, ego amo te", the religio-erotic fervour is striking. *A Boy was Born*, written when Britten was 19, is in some ways the most advanced choral work in his whole output. The deservedly popular and well-loved Auden setting, *Hymn to St Cecilia*, is here performed by five solo voices, a procedure which had Britten's approval and is surprisingly effective, especially in this superb performance. Recording quality is alpha-plus.

Britten. SACRED CHORAL MUSIC. [a]**Sioned Williams** (hp); **Westminster Cathedral Choir/David Hill** with [b]**James O'Donnell** (org). Hyperion CDA66220. From A66220 (12/86). Texts included.
A Ceremony of Carols, Op. 28[a]. Missa brevis, Op. 63[b]. A Hymn to the Virgin (1934). A Hymn of St Columba (1962)[b]. Jubilate Deo in E flat major (1961)[b]. Deus in adjutorum meum (1945).

♪♪ 49' DDD 2/88   𝄽 S

A Ceremony of Carols was Britten's first work for boys' voices but already shows his natural feeling for texture and rhythm. It sets nine medieval and sixteenth-century poems between the "Hodie" of the plainsong Vespers. The sole accompanying instrument is a harp, but given the right acoustic, sensitive attention to the words and fine rhythmic control the piece has a remarkable richness and depth. The Westminster Cathedral Choir perform this work beautifully; diction is immaculate and the acoustic halo surrounding the voices gives a festive glow to the performance. A fascinating *Jubilate* and *A Hymn to the Virgin*, whilst lacking the invention and subtlety of *A Ceremony*, intrigue with some particularly felicitous use of harmony and rhythm. *Deus in adjutorum meum* employs the choir without accompaniment and has an initial purity that gradually builds up in texture as the psalm (No. 70) gathers momentum. The *Missa brevis* was written for this very choir and George Malcolm's nurturing of a tonal brightness in the choir allowed Britten to use the voices in a more flexibile and instrumental manner than usual. The effect is glorious. St Columba founded the monastery on the Scottish island of Iona and Britten's hymn sets his simple and forthright prayer with deceptive simplicity and directness. The choir sing this music beautifully and the recording is first rate.

NEW REVIEW

Britten. Deus in adjutorium meum[f]. Chorale on an old French carol[f]. Cantata misericordium, Op. 69[bdfg].
Finzi. Requiem da camera[acdfg].
Holst. Psalms, H117 — No. 86[aefg]; No. 148[efg]. [a]**Alison Barlow** (sop); [b]**John Mark Ainsley** (ten); [c]**David Hoult,** [d]**Stephen Varcoe** (bars); [e]**John Alley** (org); [f]**Britten Singers;** [g]**City of London Sinfonia/Richard Hickox.** Chandos CHAN8997. Texts included.

· 1h 7' DDD 3/92

Each in his own way, all of these composers bring comfort, but first they face a world of warfare, loss, affliction, where comfort is needed. Finzi dedicated his *Requiem* to his teacher and friend, Ernest Farrar, killed in 1918 and, as its editor, Philip Thomas, writes, it is "also a meditation on the achievement of all musicians killed or blighted by the Great War". The Prelude is music of the greatest beauty, and the choral and solo settings of words by Mansfield, Hardy and W.W. Gibson are all heartfelt, the restraint of their expression being all the more moving because there is clearly such a fund of emotion to draw upon. This is a fine performance, too, interesting historically because it includes for the first time the "Time of the Breaking of Nations" completed by Thomas from a draft found in the Bodleian Library. Britten's *Deus in adjutorium meum* makes a contrast in its boldness of rhythmic and harmonic invention, yet it also brings beauty out of affliction, as Britten does again with the parable of the Good Samaritan in the *Cantata misericordium*. Holst's Psalm settings similarly turn from sombre prayer to praise. All are performed with the utmost skill and sensitivity by soloists, chorus and orchestra under Richard Hickox's always perceptive direction, and the only regrettable feature of this valuable disc is the all too common one of an insufficiently forward presence allowed the choir in the recording balance.

Britten. Saint Nicolas, Op. 42[a]. Rejoice in the Lamb, Op. 30[b]. [a]**David Hemmings,** [b]**Michael Hartnett** (trebs); [b]**Jonathan Steele** (alto); [a]**Sir Peter Pears,** [b]**Philip Todd** (tens); [b]**Donald Francke** (bass); [a]**Girls' Choir of Sir John Leman School, Beccles;** [a]**Boys' Choir of Ipswich School Preparatory Department;** [b]**Purcell Singers;** [a]**Aldeburgh Festival Choir and Orchestra/Benjamin Britten** with [a]**Ralph Downes,** [b]**George Malcolm** (orgs). Decca London mono 425 714-2LM. Texts included. Item marked [a] from LXT5060 (7/55), [b] LXT5416 (5/58).

· 1h 4' ADD 9/90 ▲

This disc is a further example of Decca's wisdom in transferring to CD its historic collection of Britten/Pears performances of the former's music; and, incidentally, it shows how extremely good the recordings were in the first place.

The performance of the cantata *Rejoice in the Lamb*, composed just after Britten returned to England from America during the war, was made in 1958 and remains unsurpassed. The mood of the work's touching setting of Christopher Smart's innocent but soul-searching poem is perfectly caught by the performers, who include George Malcolm as the organist. Britten's writing for the organ here is full of invention, whether he is illustrating Smart's cat Jeoffry "wreathing his body seven times round with elegant quickness" or the "great personal valour" of the mouse who defies Jeoffry. The Purcell Singers, impeccable in clarity of diction, and the soloists, are first-rate. *Saint Nicolas* was recorded even earlier, in Aldeburgh Church in 1955. The treble soloist is David Hemmings who had created Miles in *The Turn of the Screw* the previous year, and Pears sings the role he had created at the first Aldeburgh Festival in 1948. This disc is indispensable for the quality of the performance and as documentary evidence of the standard of the festival in its early years.

Britten. War Requiem, Op. 66. **Galina Vishnevskaya** (sop); **Sir Peter Pears** (ten); **Dietrich Fischer-Dieskau** (bar); **Simon Preston** (org); **Bach Choir**; **Highgate School Choir**; **London Symphony Chorus**; **Melos Ensemble**; **London Symphony Orchestra/Benjamin Britten.** Decca 414 383-2DH2. Texts and translations included. From SET252/3 (5/63).

② 1h 21' ADD 4/85

NEW REVIEW

Britten. War Requiem, Op. 66[a]. Sinfonia da Requiem, Op. 20. Ballad of Heroes, Op. 14[b]. [a]**Heather Harper** (sop); [a]**Philip Langridge**, [b]**Martyn Hill** (tens); [a]**John Shirley-Quirk** (bar); [a]**St Paul's Cathedral Choir; London Symphony** [ab]**Chorus and Orchestra/Richard Hickox.** Chandos CHAN8983/4. Texts and translations included.

② 2h 5' DDD 11/91

Britten's *War Requiem* is the composer's most public statement of his pacifism. The work is cast in six movements and calls for massive forces: full chorus, soprano soloist and full orchestra evoke mourning, supplication and guilty apprehension; boys' voices with chamber organ, the passive calm of a liturgy which points beyond death; tenor and baritone soloists with chamber orchestra, the passionate outcry of the doomed victims of war. The 1963 recording on Decca manages to reflect these distinctions very well indeed. The soloists for whom the work was written convey superbly the harrowing impact of the Wilfred Owen poems and under the composer's direction the performance has an unsurpassed authority. Compact Disc conveys the contrasts between the many long passages of quiet music and the awe-inspiring climaxes extremely well, of course, and the only pity is the rather high level of hiss on the original tapes. Otherwise, every aspect of the recording is quite beyond reproach.

The most recent challenger to the composer's classic Decca version offers up-to-date recording, excellently managed to suggest the various perspectives of the vast work, and possibly the most convincing execution of the choral writing to date under the direction of a conductor, Richard Hickox, who is a past master at obtaining the

Richard Hickox   *[photo: EMI/Chlala*

best from a choir in terms of dynamic contrast and vocal emphasis. Add to that his empathy with all that the work has to say and you have a cogent reason for acquiring this version even before you come to the excellent work of the soloists. In her recording swan song, Harper at last commits to disc a part she created. It is right that her special accents and impeccable shaping of the soprano's contribution have been preserved for posterity. Shirley-Quirk, always closely associated with the piece, sings the three baritone solos and duets with rugged strength and dedicated intensity. He is matched by Langridge's compelling and insightful reading, with his notes and words more dramatic than Pears's approach. The inclusion of two additional pieces, neither of them short, gives this version an added advantage even if the *Ballad of Heroes* is one of Britten's slighter works.

Britten. CURLEW RIVER. **Sir Peter Pears** (ten) Madwoman; **John Shirley-Quirk** (bar) Ferryman; **Harold Blackburn** (bass) Abbot; **Bryan Drake** (bar) Traveller; **Bruce Webb** (treb) Voice of the Spirit; **English Opera Group/ Benjamin Britten** and **Viola Tunnard.** Decca London 421 858-2LM. Text included. From Decca SET301 (1/66).

·• 1h 9' ADD 9/89   9 P

This "parable for church performance" is the first of three such works that Britten wrote in the 1960s, not long after the *War Requiem*, and it too breathes a strongly religious spirit while being far removed from conventional church music. Set in the fenland of East Anglia as a medieval Christian mystery play, it tells the story of a madwoman who, seeking the young son stolen from her, comes to, and finally crosses, the Curlew River, only to meet with the spirit of the dead boy who gives her his blessing. The story derives from a classical *Noh* play that the composer had seen in Tokyo a few years before, and following the Japanese tradition he used an all-male cast, a bold step that proved successful since he had an exceptional artist to play the Madwoman in the shape of Peter Pears. Sir Peter brings great dignity and depth to this role, one of his favourites among the many by Britten that he created, and the other principals are fine too, notably John Shirley-Quirk as the Ferryman and Bruce Webb as the Boy, both also from the original cast. The seven instrumentalists who participate are first rate, and under the composer's direction this is a moving experience and a recording of historic importance, made most atmospherically in Orford Church in Suffolk, where the work had its first performance.

Britten. THE RAPE OF LUCRETIA[a]. Phaedra, Op. 93[b]. [a]**Sir Peter Pears** (ten) Male Chorus; [a]**Heather Harper** (sop) Female Chorus; [ab]**Dame Janet Baker** (mez) Lucretia; [a]**John Shirley-Quirk** (bar) Collatinus; [a]**Benjamin Luxon** (bar) Tarquinius; [a]**Bryan Drake** (bar) Junius; [a]**Elizabeth Bainbridge** (mez) Bianca; [a]**Jenny Hill** (sop) Lucia; **English Chamber Orchestra/** [a]**Benjamin Britten,** [b]**Steuart Bedford.** Decca London 425 666-2LH2. Notes and texts included. Item marked [a] from SET492/3 (6/71), [b] SXL6847 (7/77).

·• ② 2h 4' ADD 5/90   9 P

Other transfers in this series represent a celebration of the art of Peter Pears as well as that of Benjamin Britten, but this set brings Janet Baker into the limelight. She takes the title roles in two works that, though divided by nearly 30 years, are still closely linked. Dame Janet gives of her best in strongly drawn, sympathetic portrayals of the two classical 'heroines', Phaedra and Lucretia, but, despite this, neither lady becomes particularly endearing and Britten describes their fates with an underlying coolness that countermands the immediate brilliance of the sounds he creates. Nevertheless, there is so much in both works that is typical of Britten's genius that, coupled together, they form a very significant facet of his work. *The Rape of Lucretia* was Britten's first chamber opera. *Phaedra*, based on Racine's *Phèdre*, was one of the composer's final works and capped his long-time empathy with French culture. Both receive performances that do them full justice, though the recording of the latter could be a shade more lucid for its date. Steuart Bedford's conducting matches that of Britten in the earlier recording remarkably well and the whole now presents a particularly attractive package.

Britten. A MIDSUMMER NIGHT'S DREAM. **Alfred Deller** (alto) Oberon; **Elizabeth Harwood** (sop) Tytania; **Sir Peter Pears** (ten) Lysander; **Thomas Hemsley** (bar) Demetrius; **Josephine Veasey** (mez) Hermia; **Heather Harper** (sop) Helena; **Stephen Terry** (spkr) Puck; **John Shirley-Quirk** (bar) Theseus; **Helen Watts** (contr) Hippolyta; **Owen Brannigan** (bass) Bottom; **Norman Lumsden** (bass) Quince; **Kenneth Macdonald** (ten) Flute; **David Kelly** (bass) Snug; **Robert Tear** (ten) Snout; **Keith Raggett** (ten) Starveling; **Richard Dakin** (treb) Cobweb; **John Prior** (treb) Peaseblossom; **Ian Wodehouse** (treb) Mustardseed; **Gordon Clark** (treb) Moth; **Choirs of Downside and Emanuel Schools; London Symphony Orchestra/ Benjamin Britten.** Decca London 425 663-2LH2. Notes and text included. From SET338/40 (5/67).

② 2h 24' ADD 5/90

From the first groanings of the Athenian wood, marvellously conjured by glissando strings, through to Puck's final adieu to the audience, Britten's adaptation of *A Midsummer Night's Dream* is a cascade of insight and invention, married to a clear and memorable tunefulness. Although this 1966 performance in many ways represents a definitive account of the opera, the work allows for a wide variety of interpretation. The role of Oberon, for example, is here filled with an otherworldly detachment by Alfred Deller, yet the fairy king's threatening and ambiguous sexuality has been strongly drawn by others in the opera house. A recording of the strength of this present issue does tend to inhibit the introduction on disc of other, equally viable, alternative views. Nevertheless, the transfer to CD of this performance was imperative and although the original vinyl set was splendidly vital, the recording now shines even brighter and the performance is still more lovable. There's not a weak link to be found, and the final ensemble, "Now until the break of day", retains the same power to move with its breathtaking beauty as it did when it was first recorded.

Britten. PAUL BUNYAN. **Pop Wagner** (bar) Narrator; **James Lawless** (spkr) Paul Bunyan; **Dan Dressen** (ten) Johnny Inkslinger; **Elisabeth Comeaux Nelson** (sop) Tiny; **Clifton Ware** (ten) Slim; **Vern Sutton** (ten), **Merle Fristad** (bass) Two Bad Cooks; **James Bohn** (bar) Hel Helson; **Phil Jorgenson, Tim Dahl, Thomas Shaffer, Lawrence Weller** (tens/bars) Four Swedes; **James McKeel** (bar) John Shears; **James Westbrock** (ten) Western Union Boy; **Maria Jette** (sop) Fido; **Sue Herber** (mez) Moppet; **Janis Hardy** (mez) Poppet; **Plymouth Music Series Chorus and Orchestra/Philip Brunelle.** Virgin Classics VC7 90710-2. Notes and text included.

② 1h 53' DDD 8/88

Paul Bunyan was Britten's first opera and the libretto, characteristically witty, allusive and coruscating in its dexterity, is by W.H. Auden. By an extraordinary feat of creative imagination, these two exiled young Englishmen wrote an opera that is idiomatically American. Britten's score is a dazzling achievement, with songs in the form of blues, parodies of spirituals and Cole Porter, and remarkable anticipations of his own later works. Paul Bunyan is a mythical American folk-hero, never seen on-stage and whose part is spoken. The principal singing roles are those of his assistant Johnny Inkslinger, his Swedish foreman Hel Helson, a "man of brawn but no brains", his daughter Tiny, and a collection of cooks, farmers, cats and dogs. The work was none too favourably reviewed by the Americans in 1941 and Britten was only persuaded to look at it again in 1974 as a therapeutic exercise after his serious heart operation. This is its first recording and it is an unqualified success. It is not a work that requires star voices; teamwork and a generally good standard are the chief requirements and these are forthcoming. Each individual performance is neatly characterized and there is just enough homespun quality to remind us of the work's origins. Diction is exemplary and the American accents are genuine. Philip Brunelle conducts with real affection and understanding and the booklet is a superb piece of documentation. It is difficult to imagine a better performance.

Britten. ALBERT HERRING. **Sir Peter Pears** (ten) Albert Herring; **Sylvia Fisher** (sop) Lady Billows; **Johanna Peters** (contr) Florence Pike; **April Cantelo** (sop) Miss Wordsworth; **John Noble** (bar) Mr George; **Edgar Evans** (ten) Mr Upfold; **Owen Brannigan** (bass) Mr Budd; **Joseph Ward** (ten) Sid; **Catherine Wilson** (mez) Nancy; **Sheila Rex** (mez) Mrs Herring; **Sheila Amit** (sop) Emmie; **Anne Pashley** (sop) Cis; **Stephen Terry** (treb) Harry; **English Chamber Orchestra/Benjamin Britten**. Decca London 421 849-2LH2. Notes and text included. From SET274/6 (10/64).

> 2h 18' ② ADD 6/89 〇 P

Britten's chamber-opera has found a renewed place in the public's affection since Sir Peter Hall's celebrated production at Glyndebourne in 1985. The audience was once again charmed by the freshness and joyfulness of this delightful piece, an English ensemble work if ever there was one. Based on a Maupassant short story *Le rosier de Madame Husson*, Eric Crozier's libretto transports the story from France to Britten's native East Anglia. It tells of a market town's hunt for a May Queen to be crowned at the annual May Festival. None of the female candidates pass muster, leaving the honour to a boy, Albert Herring. This hand-picked cast, directed with evident affection and incomparable skill by the composer, could hardly be bettered. Peter Pears makes a perfect Albert, hesitant, callow but ultimately dignified; Sylvia Fisher is a domineering Lady Billows; April Cantelo twitters engagingly as Miss Wordworth; Owen Brannigan is splendid as the local policeman, Superintendent Budd. Indeed there isn't a weak link. The English Chamber Orchestra play superbly and the recording sounds quite superb for its years. All in all, this is a classic performance of an enchanting piece.

Britten. THE TURN OF THE SCREW. **Sir Peter Pears** (ten) Prologue, Quint; **Joan Cross** (sop) Mrs Grose; **Arda Mandikian** (sop) Miss Jessel; **Jennifer Vyvyan** (sop) Governess; **David Hemmings** (treb) Miles; **Olive Dyer** (sop) Flora; **English Opera Group Orchestra/Benjamin Britten**. Decca London mono 425 672-2LH2. Notes and text included. From LXT5038/9 (8/55).

> ② 1h 45' ADD 5/90 ▲

Sir Colin Davis's magnificent Philips recording of *The Turn of the Screw* has yet to be transferred to CD, but Britten's own 1954 version, made with the original cast not long after the work's first performance, wants for virtually nothing — even the mono sound has a vigour and clarity that many a modern stereo recording would do well to match. Part of the lasting success of this recording is a result of Britten's use of a chamber ensemble to provide the orchestral background to the singers — this could be captured with much greater space and accuracy than would have been possible at that time with a full orchestra, and provided the opportunity to push farther the expressive potential of the chamber opera genre. Britten paces the work's chilling, insidious tale of good and evil so that it compounds, variation by variation, towards the tragic triumph of its conclusion. The key roles of Quint and the Governess, which subtly explore so many ramifications of male/female relationships, are definitively portrayed by Peter Pears and Jennifer Vyvyan, and the rest of the cast emulate the same high standard of musical distinction allied to sensitive characterization. This is, then, much more than an issue of only documentary interest.

Britten. DEATH IN VENICE. **Sir Peter Pears** (ten) Gustav von Aschenbach; **John Shirley-Quirk** (bar) Traveller, Elderly Fop, Old Gondolier, Hotel Manager, Hotel Barber, Leader of the Players, Voice of Dionysus; **James Bowman** (alto) Voice of Apollo; **Kenneth Bowen** (ten) Hotel Porter; **Peter Leeming** (bass) Travel Clerk; **Iris Saunders** (sop) Strawberry-seller; **English Opera Group Chorus; English Chamber Orchestra/Steuart Bedford.** Decca London 425 669-2LH2. Notes and text included. From SET581-3 (11/74).

② 2h 25' ADD 5/90

A special place is reserved for *Death in Venice* in the affections of most Britten aficionados, for not only is it one of his finest works but it also contains strong autobiographical associations. With his heart condition worsening as he composed, Britten feared that he might not live to complete the opera. Those troubles, coupled with his doubts about the value of what he had achieved in his life and career, found intense resonances in the plot and words of Myfanwy Piper's libretto. To us lesser mortals, his doubts might seem incomprehensible, yet they served to deepen and enrich the many layers of meaning that the music of *Death in Venice* encompasses. Recorded in The Maltings at Snape in 1974, this performance, so imaginatively and accurately directed by Steuart Bedford, brings the listener quickly to the work's chief themes. Pears's dominating presence as Aschenbach inevitably helps this process, yet much of the praise may go to the recording, which gives the singers an immediacy that, though rare in the opera house, is ideal for home listening. With magnificent support from the rest of the cast and the ECO, Pears, more than ever, seems Britten's alter ego here and the whole production a direct projection of the composer's mind.

James Bowman *[photo: Hyperion/Yanez]*

Britten. PETER GRIMES. **Sir Peter Pears** (ten) Peter Grimes; **Claire Watson** (sop) Ellen Orford; **James Pease** (bass) Captain Balstrode; **Jean Watson** (contr) Auntie; **Raymond Nilsson** (ten) Bob Boles; **Owen Brannigan** (bass) Swallow; **Lauris Elms** (mez) Mrs Sedley; **Sir Geraint Evans** (bar) Ned Keene; **John Lanigan** (ten) Rector; **David Kelly** (bass) Hobson; **Marion Studholme** (sop) First Niece; **Iris Kells** (sop) Second Niece; **Chorus and Orchestra of the Royal Opera House, Covent Garden/Benjamin Britten**. Decca 414 577-2DH3. Notes and text included. From SXL2150/52 (10/59).

③ 2h 22' ADD 4/86   ⁹ P Ⓑ ▲

NEW REVIEW

Britten. PETER GRIMES. **Jon Vickers** (ten) Peter Grimes; **Heather Harper** (sop) Ellen Orford; **Jonathan Summers** (bar) Captain Balstrode; **Elizabeth Bainbridge** (mez) Auntie; **John Dobson** (ten) Bob Boles; **Forbes Robinson** (bass) Swallow; **Patricia Payne** (mez) Mrs Sedley; **Thomas Allen** (bar) Ned Keene; **John Lanigan** (ten) Rector; **Richard Van Allan** (bass) Hobson; **Teresa Cahill** (sop) First Niece; **Anne Pashley** (sop) Second Niece; **Chorus and Orchestra of the Royal Opera House, Covent Garden/Sir Colin Davis**. Philips 432 578-2PM2. Notes and text included. From 6769 014 (3/79).

② 2h 26' ADD 11/91   £ Ⓑ

The Decca set has long been regarded as the definitive recording which, in 1958, introduced the opera to many listeners and one which has never been superseded in its refinement or insight. Britten's conducting, lithe, lucid and as inexorable as "the tide that waits for no man", reveals his work as the complex, ambiguous drama that it is. Sir Peter Pears, in the title-role which was written for him, brings unsurpassed detail of nuance to Grimes's words while never losing sight of the essential plainness of the man's speech. The rest of the cast form a vivid portrait gallery. The recording is as live and clear as if it had been made yesterday and takes the listener right on to the stage. The bustle of activity and sound effects realize nicely Britten's own masterly painting of dramatic foreground and background.

For all the authenticity of that performance, the alternative *Peter Grimes* under Sir Colin Davis's direction is also well worth considering. Jon Vickers sang the title role at the New York 'Met' in 1967 under his baton, and then they took the opera to London to give it at Covent Garden in 1969, 1971 and 1975. This 1978 recording thus sums up a long performing experience of the work and offers its own truths. One can see why the composer had reservations about Vickers's portrayal of his anti-hero, for compared to Pears the Canadian tenor makes him rougher and slower-thinking vocally, just as he was bigger and more formidable on the stage. But Vickers is sensitive in his own way, as is demonstrated in the horoscope aria "Now the Great Bear and Pleiades" in Act 1, and tellingly characterizes this lonely fisherman. Those who think Pears too gentlemanly and precise may well prefer the more forceful younger man, for example in his quarrel with Ellen Orford in Act 2. Another plus is the compassionate, mature-sounding Ellen of Heather Harper, who sang opposite Pears under Britten's direction for a BBC television production in 1969. The other principals are well chosen, and the chorus and orchestra convincingly make up a dramatic picture of a Suffolk coastal community in around 1830. The recording is vivid and atmospheric. Few collectors will fail to notice that here we have two mid-price discs while the Decca version is on three full-price ones.

Leo Brouwer   *Refer to Index*   Cuban 1939-

Max Bruch

Bruch. Violin Concerto No. 1 in G minor, Op. 26. Scottish Fantasy, Op. 46.
Cho-Liang Lin (vn); **Chicago Symphony Orchestra/Leonard Slatkin.**
CBS Masterworks CD42315. From IM42315 (3/87).

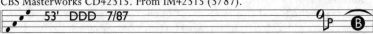

53' DDD 7/87

Bruch. Violin Concerto No. 1 in G minor, Op. 26.
Mendelssohn. Violin Concerto in E minor, Op. 64. **Scottish Chamber
Orchestra/Jaime Laredo** (vn). Pickwick IMP Red Label PCD829.

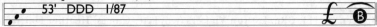

53' DDD 1/87

Bruch. Violin Concerto No. 1 in G minor, Op. 26.
Dvořák. Violin Concerto in A minor, Op. 53. **Tasmin Little** (vn); **Royal
Liverpool Philharmonic Orchestra/Vernon Handley.** Classics for Pleasure
CD-CFP4566.

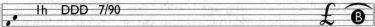

1h DDD 7/90

When the CBS disc first appeared in 1987 Edward Greenfield was moved to
write in *Gramophone*: "this is one of the most radiantly beautiful violin records I
have heard for a long time". This seems to say it all. Cho-Liang Lin's playing is
of the highest order here, with technically flawless performances of both works
performed with such consummate ease that it leaves one with a sense of
amazement. His handling of the first main subject in the Concerto's first
movement has passion and intensity without resorting to sentimentality or over-
indulgence, and a real feeling of excitement and momentum is generated as it
leads to a truly magical account of the *Adagio*, where Lin's silky smooth tone is
heard to its full advantage in the beautifully rapt and sustained melodic line.
Bravura excitement returns in the finale which couples nobility and strength with
warmth and tenderness. The *Scottish* Fantasy makes a welcome alternative to the
normal Mendelssohn Concerto coupling. This is a less known and rarely recorded
work, but is no less attractive or rewarding, especially in so persuasive and
brilliant a performance as this. Leonard Slatkin and the Chicago Symphony
Orchestra provide excellent and sympathetic support throughout. The recording
is well balanced.

For anyone seeking the inevitable coupling, the Pickwick issue offers the best
available version at any price. Laredo and the Scottish Chamber Orchestra
obviously enjoy a close rapport, and the orchestral playing is marvellously alive
and responsive, even when Laredo's attention must have been fully engaged by
the solo part. His playing is technically immaculate and his tone is pure and
sweet. In the Bruch concerto he plays with great sensitivity and sympathy and
without any spurious seeking after effect: the *Adagio*, for instance, is projected
with a quiet, reflective dignity and the finale has an abundance of natural, joyful
energy. The Mendelssohn concerto is most poetically brought off, too, with the
most natural, easy phrasing in the first movement, a beautifully shaped, most
affecting slow movement, and a finale which has the most delicious, zestful
spontaneity. It sounds very much as if Laredo and his orchestra thoroughly
enjoyed making these recordings. The recording quality is attractively warm and
clear.

The CFP disc is a most welcome issue and a fine bargain. In fact, Dvořák's
Concerto is not as well known as it should be. As a boy, the composer played
the violin for dancing in his native village, and thus he understood the instrument
well, but after he composed this work in 1879 he became discouraged when his
chosen soloist Joseph Joachim demanded revisions, and although Joachim then
played it through for him, he himself was now dissatisfied with the work and
made further changes before its première by another violinist in 1883. Today it is
hard to see what was wrong, especially when the music is played here by a very

gifted young soloist in a sympathetic partnership with an attentive conductor and the Royal Liverpool Philharmonic Orchestra in fine form. Tasmin Little's tone is rich and clear, and she shapes all this music with ardour, while the splendidly Bohemian-style finale really dances. The better known First Concerto of Bruch (another work on which the composer sought Joachim's advice) has a connection with Liverpool, for in 1881 the composer became the conductor of the city's Philharmonic Society and he directed a performance of it there in the following year. This music is also given with sweetness and considerable strength, and the recording made in the Liverpool Philharmonic Hall has good body and a natural balance.

Bruch. Kol Nidrei, Op. 47.
Lalo. Cello Concerto in D minor.
Saint-Saëns. Cello Concerto No. 1 in A minor, Op. 33. **Matt Haimovitz** (vc); **Chicago Symphony Orchestra/James Levine.** DG 427 323-2GH.

59' DDD 6/89

James Levine   [photo: DG/Lauterwasser]

Although not himself Jewish, Bruch's inspiration for *Kol Nidrei* was the Jewish prayer for the eve of Yom Kippur and the Hebrew melodies associated with it. The result is eloquent indeed, with the solo cellist acting as a kind of cantor whose music seems to speak for a whole race. Lalo's Concerto is also music that has its share of rhetoric, though much of it is in a brilliant style suited to the concerto form. Saint-Saëns offers something different again, with three linked sections of considerable charm and ingenuity.

The young cellist, Matt Haimovitz, displays a remarkable talent and an excellent recording complements the fine playing of both soloist and orchestra in all three works.

Anton Bruckner
Austrian 1824-1896

Bruckner. SYMPHONIES. **Berlin Philharmonic Orchestra/Herbert von Karajan.** DG Karajan Symphony Edition 429 648-2GSE9.
No. 1 in C minor (Linz version)[b]; No. 2 in C minor (ed. Nowak[b]. Both 2740 264, 6/82); No. 3 in D minor (1889 version, ed. Nowak[b]. 2532 007, 7/81); No. 4 in E flat major, "Romantic"[a] (2530 674, 10/76); No. 5 in B flat major[a] (2702 101, 10/78); No. 6 in A major[a] (2531 295, 11/80); No. 7 in E major[a] (2707 102, 4/78); No. 8 in C minor (ed. Haas[a]. 2707 085, 5/76); No. 9 in D minor[a] (2530 828, 6/77).

(9) 8h 40' [a]ADD [b]DDD 3/91

It is often said that the essence of good Bruckner conducting is a firm grasp of structure. In fact that's only a half-truth. Of course one must understand how Bruckner's massive statements and counterstatements are fused together, but a performance that was nothing but architecture would be a pretty depressing experience. Karajan's understanding of the slow but powerful currents that flow beneath the surfaces of symphonies like the Fifth or Nos. 7-9 has never been bettered, but at the same time he shows how much more there is to be reckoned with: strong emotions, a deep poetic sensitivity (a Bruckner symphony can evoke landscapes as vividly as Mahler or Vaughan Williams) and a gift for singing melody that at times rivals even Schubert. It hardly needs saying that there's no such thing as a perfect record cycle, and this collection of the numbered Bruckner symphonies (unfortunately Karajan never recorded "No. 0") has its weaknesses. The early First and Second Symphonies can be a little heavy-footed and, as with so many Bruckner sets, there's a suspicion that more time might have been spent getting to know the fine but elusive Sixth — and there's an irritating throw-back to the days of corrupt Bruckner editions in the first big crescendo of the Fourth Symphony (high swooping violins — nasty!) — but none of these performances is without its major insights, and in the best of them — particularly Nos. 3, 5, 7, 8 and 9 — those who haven't stopped their ears to Karajan will find that whatever else he may have been, there was a side to him that could only be described as 'visionary'. As for the recordings: climaxes can sound a touch overblown in some of the earlier symphonies, but on the whole the image is well-focused and atmospheric. A valuable set, and a landmark in the history of Bruckner recording.

Bruckner. Symphony No. 0 in D minor, "Die Nullte" (rev. 1869). Overture in G minor. **Berlin Radio Symphony Orchestra/Riccardo Chailly.** Decca 421 593-2DH.

58' DDD 1/90

It should be remembered that Bruckner wrote all his symphonies (including this one) after he was 40, indeed the bulk of *Die Nullte* that we encounter here was written after his official No. 1, and can be regarded as the progenitor of much that was to come in Bruckner's symphonic output: many of the motives can be found in later symphonies, the obvious example being the opening ostinato which later provided the underlay to the opening of the Third Symphony. Chailly's thoroughly convincing performance takes a fairly spacious view of the work, with much emphasis on nobility, poise and dynamic shaping. And if at times he comes dangerously close to sentimentality in the Andante, in the end it is his feeling of serenity and warmth that win us over. This is superbly contrasted with the exuberance and urgency that he conveys in the dance-like Scherzo. At times the strings have a tendency to sound a little thin in the trio section, but this is more than compensated for in the lyrical and graceful playing of the Berlin RSO. The Overture in G minor, dating from 1862, makes a welcome filler and receives a similarly warm and persuasive performance. The recording is warm and well balanced.

Bruckner. Symphonies — No. 1 in C minor (1866 version)[a]; No. 5 in B flat major (orig. version)[b]. **Berlin Philharmonic Orchestra/Herbert von Karajan.** DG 415 985-2GH2. Item marked [a] from 2740 264 (6/82), [b] 2702 101 (10/78).

② 2h 12' DDD/ADD 6/87

Bruckner. Symphony No. 1 in C minor (1891 version). **Berlin Radio Symphony Orchestra/Riccardo Chailly.** Decca 421 091-2DH.

54' DDD 8/88

NEW REVIEW

Bruckner. Symphony No. 1 in C minor (1866 version)[a]. Te Deum[b]. [a]**Jessye Norman** (sop); [b]**Yvonne Minton** (mez); [b]**David Rendall** (ten); [b]**Samuel Ramey** (bass); **Chicago Symphony** [b]**Chorus and Orchestra/Daniel**

Barenboim. DG Galleria 435 068-2GGA. Text and translation included. Item marked [a] from 2740 253 (10/81), [b] 2741 007 (10/81).

`1h 10'  DDD  12/91`   £ 9 p

The First Symphony is a fully mature example of Bruckner's symphonic style. The very start, with its sturdy onward treading March, broken into by a chirpy little theme, was a startling innovation and the work contains other now familiar Brucknerian trademarks. Karajan projects it in a vital, ebullient fashion with a fine control of the music's ebb and flow. By the time Bruckner completed the Fifth Symphony, his style had become more complex and he allowed his ideas to develop at considerable length. This monumental work is handled superbly by Karajan. He has an unerring grasp of the work's structure, so that it seems to flow naturally and inevitably from beginning to end. The BPO's playing is superlative, and the 1977 analogue recording is rather better than that of the First Symphony. Although Bruckner tinkered with the score of his First Symphony, it was not until 1891 that he produced a full revision. Despite leaving the overall structure of the work virtually untouched, his rethinking of the details went so far as almost to produce a new work, certainly one more akin to his last two symphonies than his earlier ones. Whereas the earlier score has a freshness and simplicity that the latter lacks, the latter has a maturity of expression and technical assurance that the previous version fails to attain. Both are most worthy of a place on the CD shelves. Chailly produces an uncompromising reading of the later version of the First. He emphasizes those features that distinguish it from the original and chooses his speeds carefully to match the weight of the orchestration and the intensity of the expression. With a full-blooded, wide-ranging recording he can afford to pull out the orchestral stops and to highlight the dynamic contrasts, knowing that the inner details will remain audible in the thickest textures and solidity of timbre will not be sacrificed in the thinnest. This is certainly the most approachable of Bruckner symphonies for the uninitiated, particularly in a performance such as this.

A Schubertian grace informs the first part of Bruckner's mighty First Symphony and this quality abounds in Barenboim's outstanding performance. His attention to detail and rhythmic accuracy, coupled with the Chicago Symphony Orchestra at their most brilliant and incisive, produces a fiery account of the work. Barenboim may lack the sweep and architectural control of Karajan but he brings a compensating wit and enthusiasm to the score — his view of the delightful scherzo, for example, is deft and appropriately capricious. The rousing finale rips along as Barenboim and his orchestra pile on the power. To further enhance this mid-price recording, Barenboim's urgent, heroic and gloriously spontaneous version of the *Te Deum* is the substantial coupling. The superb diction, dynamic discipline and overall alertness of the Chicago Symphony Chorus brings refreshing vigour to this potentially turgid work. The soloists make a superb team, blending in with the glittering array of choral and orchestral colours. The 1981 recordings shine with rich, full-bodied balance. All in all, this is a Brucknerian bargain not to be missed.

Bruckner. Symphony No. 3 in D minor (1889 version). **Berlin Philharmonic Orchestra/Herbert von Karajan.** DG 413 362-2GH. From 2532 007 (7/81).

`54'  DDD  8/84`   9 s Ⓑ

NEW REVIEW
Bruckner. Symphony No. 3 in D minor (1877 version). **Vienna Philharmonic Orchestra/Bernard Haitink.** Philips 422 411-2PH.

`1h 2'  DDD  3/91`   9 s Ⓑ

Bruckner's Third Symphony exists in three versions and Karajan opts for the final, 1889 version; not that there is anything 'late' about his reading. He conducts long stretches of the score with unusual clarity and intensity and the whole performance is very dramatic with some marvellously radiant lyrical interludes. It is also surprisingly earthy and countrified in the several peasant-like dance subjects which Bruckner winningly introduces. Some minor imprecisions in ensemble occur, the more or less inevitable by-products of what were probably long and very live takes, though the recording itself is superb. On LP it was a great threat to domestic harmony; on CD it is even more so.

Complementing Karajan's recording of the 1889 version is Haitink's account of the second version of 1877. Most Bruckner scholars regard this as the finest version of the three; the majesty of the first version is somewhat marred by the unwieldiness of its vast sprawling structure, and the 1889 rewrite has been criticized for the interference of the Schalk brothers who made various cuts and structural alterations. Haitink is a Brucknerian *par excellence* and this, his second recording of the symphony, has all the splendour and power one could wish for. The dynamic range is most impressive indeed, and this is as much an endorsement of the exceptionally fine recording as it is of Haitink's splendid control over a VPO in fine fettle. At present this is the only recording available of the 1877 version and as such no Brucknerian will want to be without it.

Bruckner. Symphony No. 4 in E flat major, "Romantic" (1888). **Philharmonia Orchestra/Otto Klemperer.** EMI Studio CDM7 69127-2. From Columbia SAX2569 (5/65).

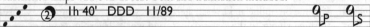

Bruckner's Fourth is the most immediately approachable of his symphonies and with its lovely horn solo has surely one of the most evocative openings of any symphony, whilst the 'Hunting' *Scherzo* uses the full horn section with rhythmical exuberance to equal atmospheric effect. The listener is ever conscious of the structural power of the piece, like a great building, with four impressive rooms, each leading to the other in perfect architectural balance. Of all conductors Klemperer most conveys this feeling of structure; its power is undeniable and he is supported by magnificent Philharmonia playing. The 1965 recording is given added brilliance in the digital remastering, but its weight and amplitude remain.

Bruckner. Symphony No. 5 in B flat major. Te Deum[a]. [a]**Karita Mattila** (sop); [a]**Susanne Mentzer** (mez); [a]**Vinson Cole** (ten); [a]**Robert Holl** (bass); [a]**Bavarian Radio Chorus; Vienna Philharmonic Orchestra/Bernard Haitink.** Philips 422 342-2PH2. Text and translation included.

Completed in 1876 and slightly modified a couple of years later, Bruckner's Fifth was not then performed in its original version until 1935. Its subsequent dissemination has done much to help our understanding of the composer's work for, being more orchestrally spartan and emotionally self-contained, it is fairly atypical of his canon of symphonies. Haitink's 1972 recording with the Concertgebouw remained for many years the yardstick by which other performances of the work could be judged, but this new version for CD looks like acceding to that role. Using the VPO here, Haitink returns the work to its roots, drawing

Bernard Haitink [photo: Philips

upon the native feel that these players have for the Austrian dance rhythms that Bruckner exploits so effectively in the Scherzo's third movement. He gives the players their collective head in the slower moments of the work, broadening the tempo to allow them to enrich expression and tonal weight. The recording also allows for this, and the result is as passionate and idiomatic as could be wished for. The coupled *Te Deum* is a glorious realization of what Bruckner considered "the pride of my life", filling to the limit the awesome Viennese acoustic.

Bruckner (ed. Haas). Symphony No. 6 in A major. **New Philharmonia Orchestra/Otto Klemperer.** EMI Studio CDM7 63351-2. From Columbia SAX2582 (9/65).

55' ADD 3/90

No Brucknerian will want to be without Klemperer's legendary performance, indeed it has long been regarded as perhaps the finest recorded interpretation of this symphony. Part of Klemperer's success lies in his unerring ability to project the symphony's architectural and organic content through Bruckner's ever changing terrain. His vigorous and resolute approach is apparent from the outset, where the opening ostinato string figure, crisp and rhythmically assured, tell us that this is no routine performance. His handling of Bruckner's frequent *fortissimo* 'blaze ups' is always dramatic, exhilarating and sonorous, whilst never destroying the beautifully clear and lucid textures he achieves throughout the symphony. The adagio is one of Bruckner's most sublime creations. Klemperer's choice of tempo may seem fast here, but is entirely justified by the resulting sense of momentum and forward drive: and you will be hard pressed to find a better rendering of the tender and expansive second theme as it burgeons out of the sombre introduction. The Scherzo, with its incessant bass and cello ostinato tread is given a subtle and evocative reading, building the tension superbly before resolving into the haunting and mysterious trio section with its Tristanesque horn calls. The recording, made in the Kingsway Hall in 1964, is excellent.

Bruckner. Symphony No. 7. **Staatskapelle Dresden/Herbert Blomstedt.** Denon C37-7286.

1h 8' DDD 8/86

Bruckner's gloriously long-breathed Seventh Symphony is, of all his works, the one most indebted to the music of Wagner. Although the Third was dedicated to this composer, it is the Seventh which is closer in spirit and tonal colour to that of Wagner. Bruckner worked on this symphony for some two years, and after a play-through on two pianos in Vienna, it received its first performance in Leipzig late in 1884 under the baton of the great Artur Nikisch. The symphony is constructed in the usual four movements, the *Adagio* second movement being the powerful core of the work — a long, richly-scored meditation that carries solemn, even funereal overtones. Herbert Blomstedt's performance of this great work is glorious — well judged, beautifully played and with just the right blend of eloquence and tension. The recording is excellent.

Bruckner. Symphony No. 8 in C minor. **Vienna Philharmonic Orchestra/ Herbert von Karajan.** DG 427 611-2GH2.

② 1h 23' DDD 10/89

As if by some strange act of providence, great conductors have often been remembered by the immediate posthumous release of some fine and representative recording. With Karajan it is the Eighth Symphony of Bruckner, perhaps the symphony he loved and revered above all others. It is the sense of the music being in the hearts and minds and collective unconscious of Karajan and every one of the 100 and more players of the Vienna Philharmonic that gives this performances its particular charisma and appeal. It is a wonderful reading, every bit as authoritative as its many predecessors and every bit as well played but somehow more profound, more humane, more lovable if that is a permissible attribute of an interpretation of this Everest among symphonies. The end of the work, always astonishing and uplifting, is especially fine here and very moving. Fortunately, it has been recorded with plenty of weight and space and warmth and clarity, with the additional benefit of the added vibrancy of the Viennese playing. The sessions were obviously sufficiently happy for there to shine through moments of spontaneous power and eloquence that were commonplace in the concert hall in Karajan's later years, but which recordings can't always be relied upon to catch.

NEW REVIEW

Bruckner. Symphony No. 9 in D minor. **Berlin Philharmonic Orchestra/ Herbert von Karajan.** DG 419 083-2GH. From 2530 828 (6/77).

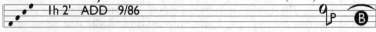
1h 2' ADD 9/86

NEW REVIEW

Bruckner. Symphony No. 9 in D minor. **Berlin Philharmonic Orchestra/ Daniel Barenboim.** Teldec 9031 72140-2. Recorded at a performance in the Philharmonie, Berlin in October 1990.

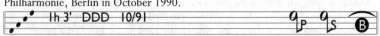
1h 3' DDD 10/91

Here is a tale of two Bruckners. The noble and the pious, the massive and the lyrical. Whichever of these two versions of Bruckner's mighty Ninth you choose, you won't regret it. Karajan's 1976 recording has long been something of a classic, capturing the maestro and the Berlin Philharmonic on top form. From the opening of the titanic first movement to the final grinding dissonance of the lofty *Adagio* Karajan's control of phrase lengths, tempo and rhythmic swing are gloriously apparent. Compared with many more recent accounts of this solemn work, Karajan's beautifully recorded performance seems refreshingly urgent, cohesive and properly threatening. Exceptionally vivid, it was sometimes difficult to tame on LP, but the CD version gives unalloyed pleasure.

This is a hard act to follow but Barenboim provides a worthy alternative. Like Karajan's reading, his is essentially a 'central' account of the score. His deeply felt reading is characterized by richly expressive tone colouring and a much more elastic way with tempos. The great climaxes of the symphony are most impressive but it's the quieter, more poetic elements which bring out the best in Barenboim's live recording; the playing is every bit as fine as it is on the Karajan recording. Teldec's sound quality is of demonstration standard and in this respect has the edge over the DG recording.

Bruckner. CHORAL WORKS. **Corydon Singers; English Chamber Orchestra Wind Ensemble/Matthew Best.** Hyperion CDA66177. Texts and translations included. From A66177 (2/86).
Mass No. 2 in E minor. Libera me in F minor (Colin Sheen, Roger Brenner, Philip Brown, tbns). Aequali for three trombones, Nos. 1 and 2 (Sheen, Brenner, Brown).

53' DDD 9/86

Bruckner's E minor Mass, unlike its two companions in D minor and F minor, employs a wind band as its instrumental base. By dispensing with the orchestra and concentrating purely on expression through human breath control Bruckner achieved a purity and translucence of texture that relate it most closely to the writing of Palestrina. The clarity of the writing and the easy unfolding of long contrapuntal lines gives the work a grandeur and feeling of architectural stability more often encountered in mghtier structures. The rich accompaniment of the wind instruments creates a powerful foundation to the spaciously conceived vocal parts. The Mass is prefaced with the *Aequali* for three trombones which date from 1847. They have a stately and somewhat sombre quality ideally suited to the work they frame, the motet, *Libera me*. This is a gentle and beautifully wrought piece using an accompaniment of three trombones, cello, double-bass and organ. The performances are extremely good, matched by a recording of the kind at which Hyperion excel.

Bruckner. SACRED CHORAL WORKS. **Bavarian Radio** [a]**Chorus and** [b]**Symphony Orchestra;** [c]**Chorus of the Deutsche Oper, Berlin;** [c]**Berlin Philharmonic Orchestra/Eugen Jochum.** DG 423 127-2GX4. Texts and translations included.
Masses[ab] — No. 1 in D minor (with Edith Mathis, sop; Marga Schiml, contr; Wieslaw Ochman, ten; Karl Ridderbusch, bass; Elmar Schloter, org. From 2720 054, 3/73); No. 2 in E minor (2720 054, 3/73); No. 3 in F minor (Maria Stader, sop; Claudia Hellmann, contr; Ernst Haefliger, ten; Kim Borg, bass; Anton Nowakowski, org. SLPM138829, 3/63). Te Deum[c] (Stader; Sieglinde Wagner, contr; Haefliger; Peter Lagger, bass; Wolfgang Meyer, org. SLPM139117/18, 5/66). Psalm 150[c] (Stader. SLPM139399, 5/69). Motets[a] — Virga Jesse; Ave Maria; Locus iste; Tota pulchra es (Richard Holm, ten; Nowakowski); Ecce sacerdos magnus (Ludwig Laberer, Josef Hahn, Alfons Hartenstein, tbns; Hedwig Bilgram, org. All from SLPM139135, 5/67); Os justi; Christus factus est; Vexilla regis (SLPM139138, 5/69); Affrentur regi (Laberer, Hahn, Hartenstein); Pange lingua (both from 2720 054).

④ **3h 47' ADD 9/88**

Bruckner's first notable composition was a Requiem in D minor and is important because it contains fingerprints of Bruckner's symphonic style, as does the Mass No. 3 in F minor. But undoubtedly the *Te Deum* is Bruckner's greatest choral work, a mighty affirmation of faith in C major but with interludes of tenderness and warmth in which a solo violin is used expressively. The performances on this disc are a notable tribute to the art of the conductor Eugen Jochum and were made between 1963 and 1972. They have been transferred to CD with total success and the singing of the respective choirs is thrilling. Maria Stader and Kim Borg are the best of the soloists in the F minor Mass, with Stader also outstanding in the *Te Deum*. The discs are invaluable, too, for containing 10 short motets, most of which will be unfamiliar to many listeners. The seraphic *Ave Maria* and a particularly touching *Pange lingua* are typical of the quality of music and performance enshrined here.

NEW REVIEW

Bruckner. SACRED CHORAL WORKS. [a]**Anne-Marie Owens** (mez); [b]**City of Birmingham Symphony Chorus;** [c]**Birmingham Symphony Orchestra Wind Ensemble/**[d]**Simon Halsey.** Conifer CDFC192. Texts and translations included.
Mass No. 2 in E minor[bcd]. Afferentur regi[bcd]. Ave Maria (1861)[bd]. Ave Maria (1882, with Peter King, org)[a]. Ecce sacerdos magnus[bcd]. Locus iste[bd]. Aequali for three trombones, No. 1 and 2[c].

1h 4' DDD 1/91

Bruckner's religious works require for their full realization an elusive combination of classical restraint and romantic fervour. In this excellent recording by the City of Birmingham Symphony Chorus and Wind Ensemble this style is captured perfectly. Under conductor Simon Halsey the chorus's finely tuned singing and rich tone is ideally suited both to the E minor Mass of 1866 and the four brief but intense motets which provide an excellent makeweight. The CBSO Wind Ensemble's accompaniment in the Mass, and solo playing in the two *Aequali* for three trombones, is well-balanced and sonorous, qualities which are also shared by Conifer's atmospheric recorded sound. These choral works display a more personal side to Bruckner's character than the mighty symphonies, and so help to round out in a unique way the musical portrait of this great composer. Thus this finely prepared CD, completed by the first ever recording of the *Ave Maria,* is an essential complement to the more well-known, and more public, works.

Ferruccio Busoni
Italian/German 1866-1924

Busoni. Piano Concerto, Op. 39. **Volker Banfield** (pf); **Bavarian Radio Chorus; Bavarian Radio Symphony Orchestra/Lutz Herbig.** CPO CPO999 017-2.

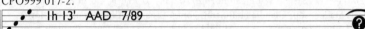
1h 13' AAD 7/89

Busoni. Piano Concerto, Op. 39. **Garrick Ohlsson** (pf); Men's voices of the **Cleveland Orchestra Chorus; Cleveland Symphony Orchestra/ Christoph von Dohnányi.** Telarc CD80207.

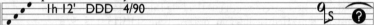
1h 12' DDD 4/90

Busoni. Piano Concerto, Op. 39. **Peter Donohoe** (pf); men's voices of the **BBC Singers; BBC Symphony Orchestra/Mark Elder.** EMI CDC7 49996-2. Recorded at a performance in the Royal Albert Hall, London on August 5th, 1988.

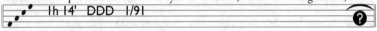
1h 14' DDD 1/91

Busoni's must be the longest piano concerto every written. Because of its length and its unusual proportions it can easily seem sprawling. Busoni gave a clue to avoiding this impression by describing the concerto in architectural terms: the central movement as a huge nave or dome, buttressed by the introduction and finale, with the scherzos envisaged as 'scenes from life', played out in the open air between the three great buildings. It is in the characterization of the music that Herbig is most successful. He is especially good at projecting Busoni's individual orchestral sound (helped by a very natural recording) and it is by this means that he makes the choral finale seem both necessary and culminatory. The sound here is quite magical. Herbig must surely have read the stage directions for the play from which Busoni drew his text; they describe Aladdin's magic cavern, with jewelled fruit growing on metal trees, and it is the rocks themselves that sing the concerto's concluding mystical hymn. The scale of Busoni's playing matches the grandeur of the work's conception, and if a few of the quieter moments lack a touch of delicacy or fantasy this is amply outweighed by his fire and virtuosity elsewhere.

Garrick Ohlsson won the Busoni Competition in Italy as long ago as 1966 and obviously believes passionately in the work. He brings to it great virtuosity and intellectual strength, while Christoph von Dohnányi and the Cleveland Orchestra (and Men's Chorus in the finale) give him excellent support. Doubts may remain as to whether this enormous structure with its mystical final message ("Lift your hearts … Feel Allah near", sings the chorus) holds up against the charge of windiness, but it is done here with such commitment and panache that even the doubters must surely salute the demonstration of a kind of genius. Ohlsson uses a Bösendorfer piano that produces just the right kind of big, craggy tone as well as being capable of delicacy when needed. The recording is outstanding, and index marks are usefully provided in the long *Pezzo serioso* which is the third movement.

However, the sense of adventure and discovery inherent in this work is nowhere better realized than in the mould-breaking 1988 Proms reading from Donohoe and Elder. Their devotion to the work is evident in every bar, and the concentration that they apply to it does not waver from start to finish: the enrapt attention of the audience bears eloquent testament to this. The price you pay for this degree of integrity, typical of live performance, is relatively slight — balance is not always ideal, especially with the mens' voices in the final movement, and the orchestral sound has a certain fullness that a studio would probably have mitigated. But be warned: this is not a performance to be sampled — it works wonderfully as a whole and once begun it seems impossible not to see it through to the end.

Busoni. Fantasia contrappuntistica (1910)[a]. Fantasia nach J. S. Bach (1909)[a]. Toccata[b]. **John Ogdon** (pf). Continuum CCD1006. Items marked [a] from Altarus AIR-2-9074 (10/88), [b] new to UK.

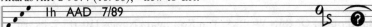

Busoni's *Fantasia contrappuntistica* is of legendary difficulty, density and length and pianists seem very reluctant to learn it. Ogdon plays it with consummate virtuosity, clarity and sustained concentration, and alongside the technical assurance there is a firm intellectual grasp of Busoni's prodigious structure and a lofty eloquence in expressing his faith. It is a formidable feat of musicianship as well as pianism. The two other pieces are more personal; many may find them even more moving. The *Fantasia nach J.S. Bach* is freer in structure than the *Fantasia contrappuntistica* and with its dedication to his father's memory it is as though Busoni has chosen particularly beloved and appropriate pages for his tribute, adding his own meditations on them. The very late *Toccata* is a resurgence of the Faustian vein that runs throughout Busoni's work, but now dark and pessimistic. The three works add up to a sort of triple self-portrait and Ogdon characterizes them finely. Busoni's piano-writing demands a huge range of sonority as well as endurance and sheer dexterity; in these performances (and this superb recording) Busoni's piano is rendered full-size.

Busoni. DOKTOR FAUST. **Dietrich Fischer-Dieskau** (bar) Doktor Faust; **William Cochran** (ten) Mephistopheles; **Anton de Ridder** (ten) Duke of Parma; **Hildegard Hillebrecht** (sop) Duchess of Parma; **Karl Christian Kohn** (bass) Wagner, Master of Ceremonies; **Franz Grundheber** (bar) Soldier, Natural Philosopher; **Manfred Schmidt** (ten) Lieutenant; **Marius Rintzler** (bass) Jurist; **Hans Sotin** (bass) Theologian; **Bavarian Radio Chorus and Symphony Orchestra/Ferdinand Leitner.** DG 20th Century Classics 427 413-2GC3. Notes, text and translation included. From 139291/3 (9/70).

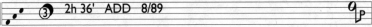

Doktor Faust has never become a popular repertory piece. Its musical subtleties, they say, are too learned for general consumption — yet those subtleties are dressed in the most alluring, indeed magical sonorities. Busoni rather too readily assumes, they say, that listeners will be as soaked in the various versions of the Faust legend as he was. He omits huge chunks of it (there is no Gretchen, for example) so that he can concentrate on the tragico-heroic essentials — but his Faust is a grander and more humane creation as a consequence. On disc especially, where its dark sayings can be mulled over at leisure, it sounds more and more like a *necessary* opera: an idealistic model of what the form is capable of, a meditation on themes, both musical and philosophical, that have never been more relevant than they are now. This excellently remastered recording is 23 years old, and the work was extensively cut to get it on to three LPs (ironically

enough its playing time is now just marginally too long for two CDs). It is a
superb performance, though, dominated by Fischer-Dieskau's grandly eloquent
assumption of the title-role. Cochran is frighteningly intense in the impossibly
high tenor role of Mephistopheles, and all the secondary characters are cast
strongly, with the exception of Hillebrecht's worn and rather squally Duchess.
Firm direction from Leitner, very accomplished choral singing, and a fine sense
of real stage space surrounding the action.

George Butterworth
Refer to Index
British 1885-1916

Dietrich Buxtehude
Danish 1637-1707

Buxtehude. ORGAN WORKS. **Ton Koopman.** Novalis 150 048-2. Played
on the Arp-Schnitger organ of St Ludgeri's, Norden.
Prelude and Ciacona in C major, BuxWV137. Eine feste Burg ist unser Gott,
BuxWV184. Passacaglia in D minor, BuxWV161. Nun komm, der Heiden
Heiland, BuxWV211. In dulci jubilo, BuxWV197. Fuga in C major, BuxWV174.
Puer natus in Bethlehem, BuxWV217. Prelude in D major, BuxWV139. Nun
lob, mein Seel, den Herren, BuxWV212. Prelude in G minor, BuxWV163. Wie
schön leuchtet der Moregenstern, BuxWV223. Prelude in G minor, BuxWV149.

> 57' DDD 6/90

A most welcome by-product of the CD revolution has been the generous
exposure given to those composers whose music, if not their names, has been
familiar only to those with specialized interest. For readers of potted histories of
music Buxtehude will be known primarily as the man whose organ playing was
considered sufficiently impressive for the young J.S. Bach to walk 400 miles to
hear. But as for his music, even organists are largely unaware of the vast amount
he wrote for that instrument. Yet there are those who would claim that, had it
not been for the towering genius of Bach, Buxtehude would today be considered
as one of the 'great' composers of the baroque age. Those of an inquisitive
disposition who would like a representative cross-section of Buxtehude's organ
music on a single disc will find this one ideal. From the big, flamboyant, virtuoso
works (such as the Prelude in G minor) to the delightful miniatures which had a
particularly strong influence on the young Bach (including a frivolous Gigue
Fugue) here is Buxtehude on top form. Ton Koopman gives them all sturdy, no-
nonsense performances on a full-blooded, earthy instrument dating from
Buxtehude's time, and the recording has great presence.

William Byrd
British 1543-1623

Byrd. MASSES AND MOTETS. **The Tallis Scholars/Peter Phillips.** Gimell
CDGIM345. From BYRD345 (5/84).
Mass for five voices. Mass for four voices. Mass for three voices. Motet — Ave
verum corpus a 4.

> 1h 7' DDD 3/86

Byrd was a fervently committed Roman Catholic and he helped enormously to
enrich the music of the English Church. His Mass settings were made for the

Peter Phillips   *[photo: Gimell/Barda]*

many recusant Catholic worshippers who held services in private. They were published between 1593 and 1595 and are creations of great feeling. The contrapuntal writing has a much closer texture and fibre than the Masses of Palestrina and there is an austerity and rigour that is allowed to blossom and expand with the text. The beautifully restrained and mellow recording, made in Merton College Chapel, Oxford, fully captures the measure of the music and restores the awe and mystery of music that familiarity has sometimes dimmed.

NEW REVIEW

Byrd. GRADUALIA — THE MARIAN MASSES. **William Byrd Choir/ Gavin Turner.** Hyperion CDA66451. Texts and translations included.
Mass Propers — Feasts of the Purification of the BVM, the Nativity of the BVM, the Annunciation of the BVM, the Assumption of the BVM; Votive Masses of the BVM: Advent, Christmas to the Purification, Purification to Easter, Easter to Pentecost and Pentecost to Advent.

Ih 20' DDD 11/91

For sheer productivity and versatility William Byrd is unrivalled among Tudor composers, and much of his impressive output is still poorly represented in the catalogue. This useful recording explores one of those shadowy corners: *Gradualia*, the cycle of motets Byrd composed for English Roman Catholics to sing in their clandestine services. He began the project soon after writing the three Masses (which date from the mid 1590s), and took ten years to bring it to completion. Like so much of Byrd's late music, the *Gradualia* motets are compact and economical in expression: miniature masterpieces that glow with the warmth of the composer's personal religious convictions, and miraculously balance exquisite musical design with the most intelligent word-setting. Their chamber-music scale is nicely captured in these performances by the William Byrd Choir, headed by a superb team of five solo voices. Everything on the disc belongs to feasts of the Blessed Virgin, many of which share texts with one another. Byrd economized by setting each text once only, and to play them in their correct liturgical order the various tracks of the CD have to be pre-selected. This is great fun to do; but the disc also makes perfectly satisfying listening when played straight through from start to finish.

John Cage

American 1912-

Cage. Sonatas and Interludes for prepared piano. **Gérard Frémy** (prepared pf). Etcetera KTC2001. From ETC2001 (12/83).

Ih 10' DDD 9/88

John Cage made two major discoveries when he invented the 'prepared piano' in 1946. The first was that to insert nuts, bolts, rubber wedges and bits of plastic between the strings of a piano does not make it sound hideously nasty but, if done with care and precision, turns it into an orchestra of delicately chiming, bright, fragile and gamelan-like sounds. The second discovery was that this 'new' instrument had to be treated with great subtlety. The result is the most mysteriously lucid score he has ever written, a sequence of quiet rituals and arabesque gestures, of silences in which hazes of resonance die away. Transparent textures and low dynamic levels predominate, but the work is by no means incidentless. There is a fairly clear progress from the briefer, quieter, more hesitant earlier Sonatas to the bigger and more dramatic gestures of Sonatas 9 to 12. To hear the Sonatas and Interludes complete and in sequence, at least once in a while, is a wonderfully ear-cleansing experience, a demonstration of how potent, beautiful and startlingly fresh the simplest of musical events can be. The discovery led Cage into an entranced contemplation of the sounds around us that we cannot accept as 'music', and these pieces raise questions about how we listen and how we hear that will not go away. Frémy's absorbed and absorbing performance has the composer's approval and the transparent clarity of the recording is ideal.

NEW REVIEW

Cage. VOCAL WORKS. **Joan La Barbara** ([a]voc/[b]perc); [c]**Scott Evans** (perc); **William Winant** ([d]pf/[e]perc); [f]**Leonard Stein** (pf). New Albion NA035CD. A flower[ad]. Mirakus[a]. Eight Whiskus[a]. The Wonderful Widow of Eighteen Springs[ad]. Nowth Upon Nacht[ad]. Sonnekus[f]. Forever and Sunsmell[ace]. Solo for Voice 49[a]. Solo for Voice 52[b]. Solo for Voice 67[a]. Music for Two (by One)[a].

· ·/ 56' DDD 9/91 ?

There was a time when Cage's impertinent theatrics and anti-art gestures served to obscure the beauty and delicacy of much of his own music. We were enjoined to experience his sound-constructions without the customary intervention of memory, taste or desire; the external noises occurring spontaneously during the performances of *his* sounds (and, notoriously, silences) had equal validity, were part of the spectacle. And yet it is possible to enjoy Joan La Barbara's carefully balanced selection — and Cage's sensitive, if unconventional, response to text — without philosophical baggage. La Barbara wants us to focus on particular aspects of Cage: "the sense of wonder, the feeling for beauty, the love of theatre, the fascination with words and sounds of all sorts and, of course, silence". The New Albion engineers surmount the various problems of balance with great skill, attempting to give each song an acoustic space appropriate to its content. And the booklet provides full texts, though it's not always easy to tell where you are as the tracks are wrongly listed on the CD itself! A pioneer of extended vocal techniques (which sounds a mite daunting), Joan La Barbara is in fact blessed with a voice of great beauty and strength. Many of the items here are for unaccompanied voice; others call for percussive or electronic effects; there is birdsong (apparently real) and piano (both the keys and the wooden case are struck). *Sonnekus* incorporates three Satie café songs. *Solo for Voice 67* is the one to shock the neighbours, with La Barbara's virtuoso grunts and squeaks punctuated by an electronic pile driver!

NEW REVIEW

Cage. The Perilous Night (1944)[a]. Four walls (1944)[b]. [b]**Joan La Barbara** (sop); **Margaret Leng Tan** ([a]prepared pf; [b]pf). New Albion NA037CD.

· ·/ 1h 11' DDD 1/91 ?

The back of the CD shows a picture of Cage beaming and congratulating Margaret Leng Tan, who is crouching on a concert platform which looks rather like a large marimba. Well might Cage look pleased — this is some of his most accessible music. No tricks, no indeterminacy, no happenings. None of the things which tend to confuse people about his intentions, when he has them. Just music. Unless, that is, you think the prepared piano is a trick? Surely not, when the Sonatas and Interludes, written shortly after the works here and recorded several times have rightly achieved the status of classics. Two strands in Cage's earlier work are concerned with his pioneering development of percussion and his invention of the prepared piano. He used both media in a particularly original way to escape from convention and find new sounds. He succeeded, and that is the joy of *The Perilous Night* and *Four walls*. *The Perilous Night* is a highly personal set of movements concerned with unhappy love, presumably reflecting Cage's own crisis. *Four walls* was written for the dancer Merce Cunningham, whose choreographic approach to measured lengths of time has influenced Cage through most of his career and gives a certain classical charm to the prepared piano music. Another important influence on Cage is Erik Satie. Anyone who enjoys the detached calm of Satie's Rosicrucian music will recognize this and respond to the meditative tranquility, the repetitions and the silences in these unfamiliar Cage works. As Cage said: "This space of time is organized. We need not fear these silences — we may love them." And he has a fine advocate in Margaret Leng Tan along with the cool, chaste tones of Joan La Barbara.

Antonio Caldara

Italian c.1670-1736

NEW REVIEW

Caldara. SOLO CANTATAS[a]. 12 Suonate da camera, Op. 2 — No. 3 in D major. 12 Suonate a 3, Op. 1 — No. 5 in E minor. [a]**Gérard Lesne** (alto); **Il Seminario Musicale.** Virgin Classics Veritas VC7 91479-2. Texts and translations included.
Cantatas: Medea in Corinto. Soffri, mio caro Alcino. D'improvviso. Vicino a un rivoletto.

Ih 8' DDD 11/91

The late baroque Venetian composer Caldara has fared much less well on disc than his more fashionable contemporaries Albinoni and Vivaldi. Yet Caldara was hardly less successful in his own lifetime which he divided between Venice, Rome and Vienna. This disc offers a glimpse of his chamber music, with four cantatas and two trio sonatas. The most impressive piece is the cantata *Medea in Corinto* whose text picks up the famous legend at that point in the story where Medea realizes that Jason intends to abandon her, and it follows through to the moment where she summons the Furies to assist her in her revenge. Caldara vividly colours this dramatic episode, effectively contrasting the moods of the Sorceress and enlivening the narrative with some splendidly declamatory recitative. The remaining cantatas, though attractive, are more modest in their expressive range and more conventional in their lovelorn Arcadian surroundings. The French countertenor, Gérard Lesne, gives technically accomplished and musical performances with dependable intonation and a fluent grasp of style. His interpretation of Medea is vividly conceived and skilfully projected with many pleasing nuances of expression. Il Seminario Musicale is a lively group which gives Lesne the necessary support though perhaps the trio-sonatas lack that finesse which Lesne unfailingly brings to his own performances. Fine recorded sound and full texts with translations are provided.

Thomas Campion

British 1567-1620

Campion. AYRES. **Drew Minter** (alto); **Paul O'Dette** (lute). Harmonia Mundi HMU90 7023. Texts included.
Beauty, since you so much desire. Love me or not. Your faire lookes. Never love unlesse you can. O never to be moved. The sypres curten of the night is spread. Awake thou spring of speaking grace. Come you pretty false-ey'd wanton. So tyr'd are all my thoughts. Fire, fire. Pin'd I am and like to dye. Author of light. See where she flies. Faire if you expect admiring. Shall I come sweet love to thee? It fell on a sommers daie. Kinde are her answers. Beauty is but a painted hell. Sweet exclude me not. Are you what your faire lookes expresse? I care not for these ladies. Never weather-beaten saile.

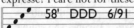 58' DDD 6/91

Thomas Campion wrote even more lute songs than John Dowland, though it must be said that, unlike Dowland, he composed nothing else. His songs are marked by a careful marriage of music with speech-rhythms but they are less demonstrative than those of Dowland, whose penchant for dramatic harmonic underlining he did not share. They are nevertheless very rewarding, beautiful in their individual way, and often catchy; another respect in which Campion differed from Dowland (and others) was that he wrote both the music and the lyrics. This recording contains a selection from Campion's published books of 1601, 1613 and 1617, and their texts range from the devout (*Never weather-beaten saile; Author of light*) to the bawdy — but subtle enough to give Mary Whitehouse no offence (*Beauty, since you so much desire; It fell on a sommers daie*), with an extensive middle ground of songs concerning the pleasure and pains of love. Drew Minter's vocal quality is excellent and Paul O'Dette's lute accom-paniments are exemplary; if Campion could do as well single-handed, he was indeed talented. Full texts are given (also in French and German) in the booklet, together with concisely informative annotation by Robert Spencer.

André Campra

French 1660-1744

Campra. Messe de Requiem. **Elisabeth Baudry, Monique Zanetti** (sops); **Josep Benet** (alto); **John Elwes** (ten); **Stephen Varcoe** (bar); **La Chapelle Royale Chorus and Orchestra/Philippe Herreweghe.** Harmonia Mundi HMC90 1251.

43' DDD 9/87

Two outstandingly beautiful *Messes des Morts* were composed in France during the late baroque period. The earlier was by Jean Gilles, the later by André Campra. Both were Provençal composers and both were connected at least by the fact that Campra directed a performance of the other's Mass at Gilles's funeral in 1705. As well as being a gifted composer of sacred music — he succeeded Lalande as composer to the Chapelle Royale — Campra was a successful and innovative theatre composer. This is reflected in his ability to handle the components of an elaborate sacred work such as this Requiem Mass in a colourful and dramatic manner. But it is the quiet intensity and profoundly contemplative character of the Requiem which more deeply affect our senses. Listeners, too, may be struck by the music's individuality which almost, perhaps, forges a link with Fauré's *Requiem* some two hundred years later. Philippe Herreweghe is attentive to points of style and has assembled a strong cast of singers among whom John Elwes and Stephen Varcoe are outstanding. The voices of La Chapelle Royale are clear in texture and pleasantly blended and the Orchestra, too, makes an effective contribution. The work is well recorded and, by-and-large, eloquently performed.

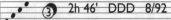

Campra. IDOMENEE. **Bernard Deletré** (bass) Idoménée; **Sandrine Piau** (sop) Electre; **Monique Zanetti** (sop) Ilione; **Jean-Paul Fouchécourt** (bass) Idamante; **Marie Boyer** (mez) Venus; **Jérôme Correas** (bass) Eole, Neptune, Jealousy, Nemesis; **Richard Dugay** (ten) Arcas; **Jean-Claude Sarragosse** (bass) Arbas, Protée; **Mary Saint-Palais** (sop) Cretan Girl; **Anne Pichard** (sop) First Shepherd; **Anne Mopin** (sop) Second Shepherd, Trojan Girl; **Les Arts Florissants Chorus and Orchestra/William Christie.** Harmonia Mundi HMC90 1396/8. Notes, text and translation included.

③ 2h 46' DDD 8/92

William Christie   *[photo: Harmonia Mundi]*

André Campra was one of the leading lights on the French musical scene between Lully's death in 1687 and Rameau's operatic début in 1733. He was a pioneer of opéra-ballet and wrote a significant corpus of sacred music and several successful *tragédies en musiques*. One of these was *Idoménée* which was first staged in 1712 and revived in 1731 in a reworked version. This later version has been chosen by William Christie for his recording. Campra's librettist was Antoine Danchet whose text was later to serve as a prime source for Mozart's *opera seria, Idomeneo*. Campra's score is an attractive one with few weak moments and the same may be said of Danchet's adaptation of Crébillon's contemporaneous play of the same name. Campra shows much skill in his writing for the human voice and a greater degree of sympathy, perhaps, than some of his fellow French composers. There are passages of finely sustained dialogue, notably between Idoménée and his son Idamante (Act 2, Scene 4), and Idoménée and Priam's daughter, Ilione. The instrumental writing, which plays a prominent part in the texture throughout the opera is also very effective; Act 3, for instance, contains a captivating sailors' dance for piccolos, drums and strings. Here is an opera which quickly proves itself deserving of the loving attention paid it by Christie and Les Arts Florissants. Supple choruses, colourful divertissements and a profusion of beguiling airs sung by a strong cast of soloists set the seal on a fine issue. Full texts and translations are included.

Campra. TANCREDE. **François Le Roux** (bar) Tancred; **Daphné Evangelatos** (contr) Clorinda; **Catherine Dubosc** (sop) Herminie; **Pierre-Yves Le Maigat** (bass-bar) Argant; **Gregory Reinhart** (bass) Ismenor; **Colette Alliot-Lugaz** (sop) Peace, Female Warrior, Dryad; **Dominique Visse** (alto) Wood-nymph; **Alison Wells** (sop) Shepherdess; **Andrew Murgatroyd** (ten) Warrior, Magician; **Christopher Royall** (alto), **Jeremy White** (bass) Magicians; **The Sixteen; Grande Ecurie et la Chambre du Roy/Jean-Claude Malgoire.** Erato Musifrance 2292-45001-2. Notes, text and translation included. Recorded at a performance in the Théâtre de l'Archevêche, Aix-en-Provence in July 1986.

② 2h 2' DDD 6/90

André Campra carried on the Lullian tradition of *tragédies en musique* but made his own distinctive contribution to the development of dramatic forms with *opéra-*

ballet. *Tancrède*, however, is a *tragédie* and proved to be one of Campra's most successful serious operas. It was first performed in 1702 and held the stage at frequent intervals until 1764. The story is loosely based on the legend of Tancred and Clorinda in Tasso's epic poem *Gerusalemme Liberata*. In its overture, prologue and five acts and its generous assortment of instrumental movements, *Tancrède* follows the pattern set by Lully. The present recording, made from a production of the work which took place during the 1986 Aix-en-Provence Festival does not include all of Campra's music but is trimmed to a two-hour entertainment. The performance is enjoyable notwithstanding a few disappointments both in the singing and playing. Catherine Dubosc, François Le Roux and Gregory Reinhart are the most impressive of the principal soloists but some of the minor roles are well sung, too. Jean-Claude Malgoire's direction is more sharply focused than in some other of his recordings and the project as a whole gives a fair account of an appealing work. Full texts are included in French, English and German.

Joseph Canteloube

French 1879-1957

Canteloube. CHANTS D'AUVERGNE, Volume 2. Triptyque. **Frederica von Stade** (mez); **Royal Philharmonic Orchestra/Antonio de Almeida.** Sony Classical CD37837. Texts and translations included. From IM37837 (7/86). Là-haut, sur le rocher. Jou l'pount d'o Mirabel. Hé beyla-z-y-dau fé. Lou boussou. Pastourelle. Malurous qu'o uno fenno. Obal, din lo coumbèlo. La pastrouletta è lou chibalié. Quand z'eyro petitoune. Pastouro sé tu m'aymo. Pastorale. La pastoura al camps. Lou diziou bé.

♪ 1h 1' DDD 10/86 Ⓑ

Frederica von Stade   *[photo: Sony Classical/Gotman*

The intriguing combination of innocence and sophistication, a favourite feature in several of the arts, is alluringly exemplified in Canteloube's now famous settings of folk-songs from his native corner of France — lusciously ornate, beautifully and ingeniously scored free arrangements of basically simple material. Von Stade's purity of tone is ideally suited to this: she tells the little tales (mostly of shepherdesses) with an engaging directness, entering with spirit into the gaiety of the song about feeding the donkey or the rollicking irony of "Unhappy he who has a wife", and providing some characterization for the mixed pathos and humour of the dialogue between Jeanneton and the hunchback. Canteloube's remarkable invention gives the RPO a real outing, providing elaborate washes of sound in the *Pastorale* (which is cognate with the celebrated *Baïlèro*) and dizzy chromaticisms in "At the Mirabel bridge". For sheer sensuous beauty, however, the prize should surely go to *Là-haut, sur le rocher* (the only one here in French: the rest are in the original *langue d'oc*). Canteloube also made various other collections of Auvergnat songs, besides composing symphonic works and two operas — none of which we ever hear. But von Stade does include here, besides 16 of the *Chants d'Auvergne*, his remarkable *Triptyque*, composed a decade earlier, ecstatic rhapsodies on pantheistic poems by Roger Frène (who ought to have been credited): the rapturous romanticism of these, sung with passion by von Stade, whets an appetite to know more of Canteloube's music.

Elliott Carter

American 1908-

Carter. Piano Concerto (1964-5)[a]. Variations for Orchestra (1954-5). [a]**Ursula Oppens** (pf); **Cincinnati Symphony Orchestra/Michael Gielen.** New World NW347-2. Recorded at performances in the Music Hall, Cincinnati, Ohio in October 1984 and October 1985.

45' DDD/ADD 4/87

Live recordings of complex contemporary works are a risky enterprise and there are certainly a few rough and ready aspects to be heard in these performances. But they are trivial in the extreme beside the excitement and commitment of artists who have read beyond the notes into the spirit of this tough but exhilarating music. Carter is so important because, while a radical in the sense of moving well beyond transitional ideas of melody and harmony, he uses his new techniques to achieve an amazing directness of expression. The Variations and the Piano Concerto complement each other very well. In the Variations, echoes of the past can still be heard, and the moods are playful and aspiring, predominantly optimistic. The Concerto is darker, with elements of the tragic represented by the tension between the soloist and the orchestral mass. The result is far from negative, even so, since the soloist's material has all the delicacy and flamboyance of Carter at his most imaginative. This music is the perfect antidote to an overdose of Philip Glass or John Adams, and the recordings, despite the occasional contributions from the audience, are perfectly adequate.

NEW REVIEW

Carter. Concerto for orchestra. Three Occasions for orchestra. Concerto for violin and orchestra[a]. [a]**Ole Böhn** (vn); **London Sinfonietta/Oliver Knussen.** Virgin Classics VC7 91503-2.

1h 3' DDD 7/92

This disc is a first-class *recording*, the sound doing as much as is technically possible to ensure that the multiple, superimposed strata of Elliott Carter's characteristically complex textures are spaced and focused to make maximum aural sense. But there is also first-class music-making to be heard here. It would be an exaggeration to say that Oliver Knussen and the London Sinfonietta play Carter's *Concerto for orchestra* (1969) as effortlessly as if it were Mozart: but the effort it takes to get this music right, and to convey its full measure of exhilarating drama, has been transformed into a marvellously positive reading of the score. Comparison with Leonard Bernstein's LP recording of the *Concerto* with the New York Philharmonic Orchestra for CBS, first issued in 1973 (not now available in any format), gives graphic evidence of how far Carter interpretation has advanced in two decades. The more recent *Occasions for orchestra* are no less characterful: music of celebration and lament showing that the originality and intensity of Carter's vision have not faded as he moves into his eighties. The Violin Concerto (1990) may not be on the same high level of inspiration as the other works on this disc but it is still an absorbing demonstration of how to 'Carterize' the solo instrument's essential lyricism and capacity for fantasy, while ensuring that it remains bracingly at odds with the orchestra.

Carter. MISCELLANEOUS WORKS. [a]**Phyllis Bryn-Julson** (sop); [b]**Heinz Holliger** (ob); [c]**Sophie Cherrier** (fl); [c]**André Trouttet** (cl); [d]**Ensemble Intercontemporain/Pierre Boulez.** Erato 2292-45364-2. Text included.
Oboe Concerto[bd]. Esprit rude/esprit doux[c]. Penthode[d]. A Mirror on which to Dwell[ad].

⸫ 1h 3' DDD 2/90 ◗ P

Elliott Carter has had a gratifyingly productive old age. Only one of the works on this disc, *A Mirror on which to Dwell*, was composed before 1980, and we can now appreciate how its beautifully refined sonorities and needle-sharp balancing of formal coherence against shapely text-setting marked the start of a new phase to which all the other works included belong. The brief flute/clarinet duet, *Esprit rude/esprit doux*, was a sixtieth-birthday gift for Boulez in 1985, and *Penthode* was completed that same year for Boulez's Ensemble Intercontemporain. The title refers to the four groups of five instruments which this rich and fascinating score explores with all Carter's characteristic subtlety of differentiation and interaction. As for the Oboe Concerto, the contrast of melody-spinning soloist and context-setting ensemble inspires Carter to an even more spontaneous outpouring of intricate yet always characterful polyphony. The performance by Heinz Holliger is quite simply definitive, and the other works are also very well done in an excellently clear and well-balanced recording.

Carter. STRING QUARTETS. **Arditti Quartet** (Irvine Arditti, David Alberman, vns; Levine Andrade, va; Rohan de Saram, vc). Etcetera KTC1065/6. *KTC1065:* String Quartets — No. 1; No. 4. *KTC1066:* String Quartets — No. 2; No. 3. Elegy.

⸫ ② 59' 45' DDD 5/89 ◗ P

The Arditti Quartet can play the most complex modern music with confidence as well as accuracy. Their performances radiate enjoyment and enthusiasm, not just a dour determination to convey what is on the printed page with maximum precision. Carter's four quartets span 35 years (1951-86) and, with the early *Elegy* of 1943, chart with exemplary clarity his spiritual and stylistic odyssey. Starting with a shapely neoclassicism quite close to that of Copland, he moved around 1950 into a world nearer that of early twentieth-century Viennese expressionism, whilst retaining an expansive form and rhythmic buoyancy which is characteristically American. In the Third Quartet you sense a kind of crisis within this expressionism, overwhelming in its unsparing vehemence and stretching the medium to breaking point. In his later works the crisis recedes and the Fourth Quartet finds room for lighter moods and calmer considerations. The Second Quartet is perhaps the jewel of the collection, but all four quartets in this finely-recorded set, performed as they are with such authority and commitment, repay repeated as well as concentrated listening.

John Casken

British 1949-

Casken. GOLEM. **Adrian Clarke** (bar) Maharal; **John Hall** (bass-bar) Golem; **Patricia Rozario** (sop) Miriam; **Christopher Robson** (alto) Ometh; **Paul Wilson** (ten) Stoikus; **Richard Morris** (bar) Jadek; **Paul Harrhy** (ten) Stump; **Mary Thomas** (sop) Gerty; **Music Projects London/Richard Bernas.** Virgin Classics VCD7 91204-2. Notes, text and translation included.

⸫ ② 1h 39' ADD 8/91 ◗ P

It is fitting that *Golem* should have won for its composer the first Britten Award for composition in 1990 — not because John Casken's music sounds remotely

like Britten's, but because the spirit of his opera does have things in common
with the humanly focused rituals of Britten's own Parables for church performance. The story of *Golem* specifically shuns a Christian context, and although it
deals with some of the same issues as, for example, the parable of the prodigal
son, it has a tragic outcome: no happy ending here. Even so, the need for human
beings to achieve a positive balance between thought and feeling is as important
in *Golem* as it is in *Curlew River*. Maharal, the embodiment of human authority,
creates a Golem — a man from clay — to serve him and society. But he fails to
anticipate or control the consequences of his action, and in the end is driven to
destroy his wayward but willing creation. As with all such symbolic tales, the
dangers of falling into alienatingly schematic formulae are considerable. But
Casken is remarkably successful in ensuring that, through his music, the story has
a convincing social context and a strong basis in human feeling. If you are so
inclined, you can approach the music by way of its associations with more
familiar idioms: here with Birtwistle, there with Maxwell Davies, sometimes
with Ligeti, Lutoslawski or Berio. But it soon becomes clear that Casken
has evolved a distinctively personal 'brew' from the rich mix of mainly
expressionist source-materials that underpin his style, and the result is a first
opera — performed and recorded with admirable conviction — that is also a
major achievement.

Mario Castelnuovo-Tedesco *Refer to Index Italian/American 1895-1968*

Emmanuel Chabrier *French 1841-1894*

NEW REVIEW
Chabrier. España. Suite pastorale.
Dukas. L'apprenti sorcier. La péri. **Ulster Orchestra/Yan Pascal Tortelier.**
Chandos CHAN8852.

57' DDD 2/91

Not many years ago, Yan Pascal Tortelier was thought of as the son of the great
cellist, but today he stands in his own right as a fine conductor who has made his
Ulster Orchestra into a splendid body of musicians, and it is no exaggeration to
say that under his baton they play this French music as to the manner born. The
programme here has been skilfully assembled, for while Chabrier's *España* and
Dukas's *L'apprenti sorcier* ("The Sorcerer's Apprentice") are popular pieces the
other works by the same composers are not, yet prove to be most rewarding
music. *La péri* is a ballet based on the Persian tale of the young Prince
Iskender (Alexander the Great) who seeks the lotus flower of immortality but
finds it guarded by a beautiful sleeping fairy with whom he falls in love, only to
see her die. This music is colourful and passionate, reminding us that Dukas won
the lasting admiration of Debussy, and the playing is no less delightful, being
shapely and at all times sensitive to the fine instrumentation. The four movements of Chabrier's *Suite pastorale* are orchestrations of his piano pieces, *Pièces
pittoresques*. They are charming and excellently crafted, and one can see why
Poulenc thought them as important in French music as Debussy's piano
Préludes — though they are unlike those impressionistic pieces in being
essentially clear and sunlit. As for the other two works, *L'apprenti sorcier* is rightly
more than a touch scary as well as brilliantly witty, while *España* has tremendous
joie de vivre and Spanish character. The recording is superbly vivid in Chandos's
best style.

Cécile Chaminade *French 1857-1944*

Chaminade. PIANO WORKS. **Eric Parkin.** Chandos CHAN8888.
Air à danser, Op. 164. Air de ballet, Op. 30. Contes bleus No. 2, Op. 122.
Danse créole, Op. 94. Etudes de concert, Op. 35 — No. 2, Automne. Feuillets
d'album, Op. 98 — No. 4, Valse arabesque. Guitare, Op. 32. La lisonjera, Op.
50. Lolita, Op. 54. Minuetto, Op. 23. Pas des écharpes, Op. 37. Pas des
sylphes: Intermezzo. Pièces humoristiques, Op. 87 — No. 4, Autrefois. Pierette,
Op. 41. Romances sans paroles, Op. 76 — No. 1, Souvenance; No. 3, Idyll;
No. 6, Méditation. Sérénade, Op. 29. Sous le masque, Op. 116. Toccata,
Op. 39.

1h 5' DDD 8/91

One doesn't have to be a feminist to regret that there have been all too few
women composers compared to, say, women novelists, at least up to the late
twentieth century. However, Cécile Chaminade was one of them and, as a fine
pianist herself, a very skilful and attractive writer of piano music who numbered
Bizet among her admirers. As Peter Dickinson rightly says in his booklet note,
writing first-class salon music is a greater achievement than producing inadequate
symphonies and sonatas, and less boring! No pianist could be a better advocate
for this music than Eric Parkin, who knows how to bring out its strength as well
as its charm and zest; readers of this *Guide* may already know his fine recordings
of piano music by Bax and Mayerl. Tempos, tone, textures, pedalling and rubato
are all splendidly judged, and one may simply say that this is music to be
enjoyed, unfailingly tuneful and telling and with plenty of variety to avoid any
tendency toward the *déjà vu* in the course of the 20 well-chosen tracks. Among
the distinguished ancestors of this music are, no doubt, Schumann, Chopin and
Fauré — no composer need be ashamed of such a lineage! — but there is a
Chaminade personality here, too, as the lilting *Sérénade*, the teasing *Guitare*, the
well-known *Automne* (a bravura concert study rather than an amateur's drawing-
room piece) and the wittily understated, neo-baroque Toccata all remind us. The
recording, made in The Maltings, Snape, offers fresh sound and a natural degree
of reverberation.

Herbert Chappell *Refer to Index* *British 1934-*

Gustave Charpentier *French 1860-1956*

G. Charpentier. LOUISE. **Ileana Cotrubas** (sop) Louise; **Plácido
Domingo** (ten) Julien; **Gabriel Bacquier** (bar) Father; **Jane Berbié** (sop)
Mother; **Michel Sénéchal** (ten) Noctambulist, King of the Fools; **Lyliane
Guitton** (mez) Irma; **Ambrosian Opera Chorus; New Philharmonia
Orchestra/Georges Prêtre.** Sony Classical CD46429. Text and translation
included. From CBS 79302 (10/76).

③ 2h 52' ADD 6/91

The generation gap, headstrong youth and 'free love', the pillars of the plot of
Louise, could suggest a subject of contemporary relevance; but the scene here is
Paris in 1900, where a naïve little seamstress (a lot more realistic than Mimì)
becomes besotted with a handsome but feckless young poet (a great deal less
sentimental than Rodolfo) with whom she goes to live, despite her parents'
opposition. Her mother, worn out by poverty, treats her sternly, but her hard-

Plácido Domingo   *[photo: DG*

working, respectable father has so deep an affection for her that, when she decides to remain with her lover although her father is ill, his final outburst against Parisian loose morals is all the more bitter. His is the most fully drawn character in this unromanticized story of ordinary working-class people (curiously, only the authentic street-vendors' cries seem contrived), and Bacquier is an almost ideal interpreter of it, capturing every nuance of the tormented father's emotions. Berbié brings distinction to her much smaller role as the mother. Cotrubas is extremely appealing, both in her tonal purity (in a technically very exacting part) and her sensitivity to words, and vividly depicts Louise's innocent charm. Julien is an entirely two-dimensional figure, but that really does not excuse his role being sung most of the time at an ardent, open-throated *forte* (thrilling as the sound is that Domingo produces). He creates several problems of balance for which the producer must shoulder some of the blame, as he should also for some ill-judged perspectives and some slips in the French. There is a vast array of small parts, on the whole very ably taken by members of the 1976 Ambrosian Opera Chorus (several of whom have since become well known in their own right), and Prêtre conducts sympathetically.

Marc-Antoine Charpentier
French c.1645-50; d.1704

Charpentier. Quatuor anni tempestatis, H335-8. PSALMS. **Françoise Semellaz, Noémi Rime** (sops); **Bernard Délétré** (bass); **Le Parlement de Musique** (Christoph Ehrsam, Patrick Blanc, recs; Eunice Brandao, Laurence Bonnal, treble viols; Sylvia Abramowicz, bass viol; Yasunori Imamura, theorbo)/ **Martin Gester.** Opus 111 OPS309005. Texts and translations included.
Psalms — Quemadmodum desiderat cervus, H174. Nisi Dominus, H231. Notus in Judea, H179.

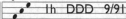 1h DDD 9/91

The main work in an attractive programme which wanders well away from the beaten track is Charpentier's *Quatuor anni tempestatis* ("The four seasons of the year"). When, or for whom Charpentier wrote these engaging little motets — there are four in all, one for each season — is not known. They draw their inspiration from the "Song of Solomon" and are scored for two sopranos and continuo. In addition "Aestas" ("Summer") has a short instrumental prelude for three recorders and continuo. Perhaps the music is not vintage Charpentier but it is none the less appealing with frequent instances of those affecting melismatic passages of which Charpentier was a distinctive master. The sopranos Françoise Semellaz and Noémi Rime are evenly matched in sound and convey a good sense of style. Not everything is immaculate but the character of the music is projected with warmth and authority. The remaining pieces are modestly scored psalms for one or two melody instruments with continuo. Of these the *Nisi Dominus* (Psalm 127) is the most striking and, perhaps the most confidently performed. The recording is clear and sympathetic and the repertoire well worth exploring. Full texts with translations included.

Charpentier. SACRED CHORAL WORKS: Canticum ad Beatam Virginem Mariam. **Le Concert des Nations/Jordi Savall.** Auvidis Astrée E8713. Texts and translations included.
Canticum in honorem Beatae Virginis Mariae inter homines et angelos, H400. Prélude a 3, H509. Pour la conception de la Vierge, H313. Nativité de la Vierge, H309. Prélude pour Salve regina a 3, H23*a*. Salve regina a 3, H23. Pour la fête de l'Epiphanie, H395. Prélude pour le Magnificat a 4, H533. Magnificat a 4, H80. Stabat mater pour des religieuses, H15. Litanies de la vierge, H83.

⟨ **1h 15′ DDD 2/90** ⟩

The music on this disc is a skilful compilation of disparate pieces by Charpentier all connected with Marian devotion. The two most extended works are the *Canticum in honorem Beatae Virginis Mariae* and the *Litanies de la vierge*; the first is intimate yet ardent in expression and takes the form of a dialogue between man and angels. Charpentier was a master of small-scale dramatic forms such as these and Jordi Savall brings passion and a lively sense of theatre to this one. The *Litanies* are more contemplative, sometimes profoundly so, but they are not without a quiet radiance and Savall convincingly explores their expressive vocabulary. Hardly less appealing is the beautiful *Stabat mater pour des religieuses*, written for soprano soloist with unison soprano chorus. Charpentier may well have composed it for the nuns of the convent of Port Royal, though Savall in fact uses male voices for the refrains retaining the soprano for the serene and ethereal solos. The remaining pieces are more modestly conceived but extremely effective in this thoughtfully constructed context. Savall creates a marvellous sense of occasion, bringing the music to life with Mediterranean verve. Lively continuo realizations, in which a theorbo plays a prominent part, are a constant delight as indeed is so much else in this captivating performance. Small vocal and instrumental insecurities matter little when interpretative skill is on such a level as this. The booklet is well documented with full texts in several languages. Faithful and vibrant recorded sound set the seal on a distinguished project.

Charpentier. SACRED CHORAL WORKS. [a]**Greta de Reyghere,** [b]**Isabelle Poulenard,** [b]**Jill Feldman** (sops); [c]**Ludwig van Gijsegem** (ten); [d]**Capella Ricercar/Jerome Léjeune** with [e]**Bernard Foccroulle,** [f]**Benoit Mernier** (orgs). Ricercar RIC052034.
Magnificat pour le Port Royal, H81[abde]. Messe pour le Port Royal, H5[abcde]. O clementissime Domine Jesu, H256[abe]. Dixit Dominus pour le Port Royal[abdf] Laudate Dominum pour le Port Royal, H227[abdf]. Stabat mater pour les religieuses, H15[bdf]. *Raison:* Pièces d'orgue[d].

⟨ **1h 7′ DDD 1/89** ⟩

There are several distinctive features about the music (composed for the nuns of Port Royal) included on this delightful disc, the most striking of them being that the vocal writing is, of course, for female voices only. That may seem a con-fining discipline but is anything but that in the hands of a composer as resource-ful as Charpentier. What is lacking in complexity and textural richness is more than compensated for by subtle inflexion, warm fervour and a radiance of sound. This is especially so in the *Magnificat*, a ravishingly beautiful setting for three voices. Here the solo sections are interspersed with a vocal ensemble refrain whose affecting suspensions haunt the memory. The most elaborate work is the *Messe pour le Port Royal* where the voices are deployed in a masterly fashion, ringing the changes between varying ensembles and vocal dispositions. Short organ solos which would have played a part in the 'Mass' were not included in Charpentier's original score since they would have probably been improvised. Sensibly, organ music by his contemporary, André Raison has been inserted at the appropriate places and very fine it sounds, too.

Charpentier. LE MALADE IMAGINAIRE. **Isabelle Poulenard, Jill Feldman** (sops); **Guillemette Laurens** (mez); **Gilles Ragon** (ten); **Michel Verschaeve, Bernard Deletré, Jean-Louis Bindi, Jean-Paul Fouchécourt** (basses); **Les Musiciens du Louvre / Marc Minkowski.** Erato MusiFrance 2292-45002-2. Notes, text and translation included.

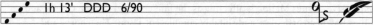

1h 13' DDD 6/90

Comédie-ballet was a dramatic form developed by Molière in which music played both an integral and incidental part. Lully was his earliest collaborator but, following a quarrel Molière turned to Charpentier to provide music. *Le malade imaginaire*, first performed in 1673, was the playwright's last *comédie-ballet* and the one to which Charpentier made his most substantial contribution. Here it is the medical profession which comes under Molière's merciless scrutiny with a hypochondriac, his deceitful wife and doctors who know everything about disease except the cure of it. This recording omits the spoken dialogue but includes almost all of Charpentier's music; and delightful it is, too, in its engaging variety of airs and dances. The orchestra is colourful, consisting of flutes, recorders, oboes and strings together with some surprising sounds in the third of three *intermèdes* which follow the prologue. Here, besides castanets, drums and tambourines, Charpentier calls for apothecary's mortars, once cast in a bell foundry and for this recording lent by a Paris antiquarian: such is the lure of authenticity these days! Marc Minkowski, Les Musiciens du Louvre and a strong ensemble of solo voices combine to give a refreshingly unbuttoned performance of the music, little of which has previously been available to record collectors. The recording is excellent and comes with full texts in French, English and German.

Charpentier. ACTEON. **Dominique Visse** (alto) Actéon; **Agnès Mellon** (sop) Diane; **Guillemette Laurens** (mez) Junon; **Jill Feldman** (sop) Arthébuze; **Françoise Paut** (sop) Hyale; **Les Arts Florissants Vocal and Instrumental Ensemble / William Christie.** Harmonia Mundi Musique d'abord HMA190 1095. From HM1095 (5/83).

47' AAD

Poor old Actaeon; if you recall, he was discovered hiding in the bushes while the goddess Diana and her followers were bathing. Without being given a chance to explain himself properly Diana turns him into a stag, whereupon he is torn to pieces by his own hounds. That is the version of the legend followed in Charpentier's opera. The score contains many ingredients of Lullian *tragédie-lyrique*, with a profusion of fine choruses and dances. William Christie and Les Arts Florissants bring stylistic unity, lively temperament and a sharp awareness of rhythmic and harmonic nuances to this music. The soloists make distinctive and accomplished contributions and the whole opera is performed with a fervour and intensity which emphasizes the poignant plot. No French text or translation are included in the CD booklet, but a useful synopsis takes their place. The recording is excellent.

Charpentier. MEDEE. **Jill Feldman** (sop) Médée; **Gilles Ragon** (ten) Jason; **Agnès Mellon** (sop) Creuse; **Jacques Bona** (bass) Créon; **Sophie Boulin** (sop) Nérine; **Philippe Contor** (bass) Oronte; **Les Arts Florissants Chorus and Orchestra/William Christie.** Harmonia Mundi HMC90 1139/41. Notes, text and translation included. From HM1139/41 (11/84).

③ 3h 2' AAD 3/85

Médée is Charpentier's dramatic masterpiece in the conventional French baroque form of a prologue and five acts and was first performed in 1693. Thomas Corneille based his libretto on the story of the sorceress Medea as told by Euripides and the opera begins after the arrival of Jason and Medea at Corinth in the "Argo"; thus the adventure of the Golden Fleece has already taken place. Charpentier's music is well able to rise to the occasion and does so with chilling effect in the memorable witchcraft scenes of Act 3. Jill Feldman's Medea contains many layers of expressive subtlety and her command of French declamation is impressive. Agnès Mellon is affecting as the innocent and sincere Creuse and Gilles Ragon an articulate and suitably complacent Jason. The chorus and orchestra of Les Arts Florissants have their rough patches but William Christie directs a thrilling performance of a work representing one of the finest achievements of French baroque musical drama. The recording was made in a lively and sympathetic acoustic but you will need a magnifying glass to read the libretto.

Ernest Chausson

French 1855-1899

NEW REVIEW

Chausson. Poème de l'amour et de la mer, Op. 19[a]. Poème, Op. 25[b].
Fauré. Pelléas et Mélisande — suite, Op. 80. Pavane, Op. 50[c]. [a]**Linda Finnie** (contr); [c]**Renaissance Singers; Ulster Orchestra/Yan Pascal Tortelier** ([b]vn). Chandos CHAN8952. Texts and translations included.

1h 9' DDD 12/91

Yan Pascal Tortelier   [photo: Chandos/Wood]

Belfast's Ulster Hall may seem an unlikely source for nearly 70 minutes worth of demure *fin de siècle* melancholia, but the Chandos engineers have secured just that from Yan Pascal Tortelier and the Ulster Orchestra, who show just how convincing they can sound in this refined and evocative music by Chausson and Fauré. They are joined by Linda Finnie in a voluptuous and often tenderly seductive reading of Chausson's *Poème de l'amour et de la mer* — a performance of clarity and winning understatement. The rich, dark-hued violin tone of Yan Pascal Tortelier, in the enigmatic *Poème* by Chausson, is an ideal foil to Finnie's crystal-line vocalization of the earlier work, and the accompaniment of both soloists reveals the Ulster Orchestra to be as sympathetic and sensitive to their needs as one could possibly wish in this music. Fauré, like Debussy, Sibelius and even

Schoenberg, perceived the musical possibilities of Maeterlinck's symbolist play
Pelléas et Mélisande, and Tortelier and his orchestra offer a memorable performance of the suite from Fauré's complete incidental music of 1898. Again, a
degree of reticence and understatement allows the elusive simplicity of expression
to come to the fore, particularly in the contributions of the Ulster wind players.
The orchestra are joined by the Renaissance Singers in the popular *Pavane*
although it has to be said that the actual text by Robert de Montesquiou makes
little impression here. With first-class sound and affecting, richly idiomatic
performances, however, this admirable recording could hardly be more
inviting.

Fryderyk Chopin
Polish 1810-1849

Chopin. Piano Concertos — No. 1 in E minor, Op. 11; No. 2 in F minor,
Op. 21. **Murray Perahia** (pf); **Israel Philharmonic Orchestra/Zubin
Mehta.** Sony Classical CD44922. Recorded at performances in the Mann
Auditorium, Tel Aviv in 1989.

| | 1h 16' DDD 6/90 | | |

Warm applause from the audience is not the only pointer to the fact that
Perahia[1]'s are live concert recordings. The playing itself is full of that
"inspirational heat-of-the-moment" long known to mean more to Perahia than
mere streamlined studio correctness. The miracle is the way his urgency of
feeling finds an outlet in playing of such super-sensitive finesse. Nearly always he
favours slightly faster tempo than many of his rivals on disc, giving the first
movements of both works a strong sense of direction in response to their *risoluto*
markings. Mehta and the Israel Philharmonic might even be thought over-
resolute, at the cost of a measure of the music's aristocratic elegance. But tonal
balance is good, and progressively in each work a close-tuned partnership is
achieved. Both rapt slow movements are sung with an exquisite tonal purity as
well as embellished with magical delicacy. Their contrasting middle sections
nevertheless bring eruptions of burning intensity. The dance-inspired finales
have a scintillating lightness and charm recalling Perahia, the fingertip magician,
in Mendelssohn. Even if not in the five-star class, the recorded sound is the
equal of anything to be heard in rival CD versions of these two endearing
reminders of the young Chopin's last year in Warsaw before leaving his
homeland for ever.

NEW REVIEW
Chopin. PIANO WORKS. **Maurizio Pollini** (pf); [a]**Philharmonia
Orchestra/Paul Kletzki.** EMI Studio CDM7 69004-2. Item marked [a] from
ASD370 (11/60), [b] ASD2577 (8/70).
Piano Concerto No. 1 in E minor, Op. 11[a]. Ballade in G minor, Op. 23[b].
Nocturnes, Op. 15 — No. 1 in F major[b]; No. 2 in F sharp minor[b]. Polonaise in
A flat major, Op. 53[b].

| | 1h 3' ADD 9/87 | | |

Pollini's disc is a classic. The concerto was recorded shortly after the 18-year-old
pianist's victory at the Warsaw competition in 1959. Nowadays we might expect
a wider dynamic range to allow greater power in the first movement's tuttis, but
in all other respects the recording completely belies its age, with a near perfect
balance between soloist and orchestra. This is, of course, very much Pollini's

disc, just as the First Concerto is very much the soloist's show, but effacing as the accompaniment is, Pollini's keyboard miracles of poetry and refinement could not have been achieved without one of the most characterful and responsive accounts of that accompaniment ever committed to tape. The expressive range of the Philharmonia on top form under Kletzki is at once, and continuously, exceptional, as is the accord between soloist and conductor in matters of phrasing and shading. The solo items, recorded in 1968, are a further reminder of Pollini's effortless bravura and aristocratic poise.

Chopin. Piano Concerto No. 2 in F minor, Op. 21[a].
Tchaikovsky. Piano Concerto No. 1 in B flat minor, Op. 23[b]. **Vladimir Ashkenazy** (pf); **London Symphony Orchestra/**[a]**David Zinman,** [b]**Lorin Maazel.** Decca Ovation 417 750-2DM. Item marked [a] from SXL6174 (9/65), [b] SXL6058 (6/63).

1h 6' ADD 1/89   Ⓑ

This coupling serves as a highly impressive showcase for Ashkenazy's talents. He was around 30 when the recordings were made and every bar reveals a maturity and relaxed mastery that many artists only achieve much later in their careers. Around 45 years separate the composition of the concertos and one is very aware in listening to them of the transition from an essentially classical form into something symphonic in scope. In the Chopin the moments of reverie are carefully divided from the heroic passages and Ashkenazy finds exactly the right concentrated mood for each. In the Tchaikovsky he avoids making the piece appear as an unequal contest between soloist and orchestra and opts for a lucid and unhurried way with the music. There is plenty of spontaneity and virtuosity in the reading as well. As in the Chopin, he regulates his piano tone with wonderful ease, so as to lend each episode its distinct character. The quality of the recorded sound really is exemplary for the date and the conductors are in complete sympathy with the aspirations of the pianist.

Chopin. PIANO WORKS. Volume 8. **Vladimir Ashkenazy** (pf). Decca 410 122-2DH. From 410 122-1DH (3/84).
Mazurkas, Op. 30 — No. 1 in C minor; No. 2 in B minor; No. 3 in D flat major; No. 4 in C sharp minor. Op. 33 — No. 1 in G sharp minor; No. 2 in D major; No. 3 in C major; No. 4 in B minor. *Nocturnes,* Op. 32 — No. 1 in B major; No. 2 in A flat major; C minor, Op. posth. Impromptu in A flat major, Op. 29. Largo in E flat major, Op. posth. Scherzo in B flat minor, Op. 31. Waltz in F major, Op. 34 No. 3. Variation No. 6 in E major, "Hexameron".

52' DDD 7/84   P Ⓑ

Though Ashkenazy's decision to offer a mix of genres on a disc instead of a chronological sequence may be questioned, the result is probably more satisfactory for listening, since one has here a real recital of varied music. It ranges from the extrovert brilliance of the B flat minor Scherzo and the F major *Grande valse brillante*, Op. 34 No. 3, through the elegantly wistful 'salon' mood of the A flat major Nocturne and the surprisingly varied and dramatic Mazurkas, to mere chips from the composer's workbench like the *Largo* in E flat major and the C minor Nocturne which were both unpublished until 1938. Ashkenazy's affinity with Chopin in all his moods is the justification for such a complete survey as this and only very occasionally might one feel a need for even more mystery and
spontaneity. As for the sound-quality, it is bright but very faithful and never

approaches harshness even in the most powerful passages. This is a noble recording.

Chopin. PIANO WORKS. **Peter Katin** (pf). Olympia OCD254.
Nocturnes — E minor, Op. 72 No. 1; C sharp minor, Op. posth. Op. 9 — No. 1 in B flat minor; No. 2 in E flat major; No. 3 in B major. Op. 15 — No. 1 in F major; No. 2 in F sharp major; No. 3 in G minor. Op. 27 — No. 1 in C sharp minor; No. 2 in D flat major. Op. 32 — No. 1 in B major; No. 2 in A flat major; C minor. Op. 37 — No. 1 in G minor; No. 2 in G major. Op. 48 — No. 1 in C minor; No. 2 in F sharp minor. Op. 55 — No. 1 in F minor; No. 2 in E flat major. Op. 62 — No. 1 in B major; No. 2 in E major.
Impromptus — No. 1 in A flat major, Op. 29; No. 2 in F sharp major, Op. 35; No. 3 in G flat major, Op. 51. Fantaisie-impromptu in C sharp minor, Op. 66.

2h 20' DDD 12/89

Here at medium price are 140 minutes of great piano music finely played. Katin is a quietly persuasive artist rather than a virtuoso and he brings an entirely appropriate sense of intimacy to this Chopin recital of nocturnes and impromptus. The approach is chronological and complete, so that in the nocturnes the E minor and the *Lento con gran espressione* in C sharp minor come first, although they were published posthumously, and we also hear the rarely played C minor (without opus number) which only came to light in 1937, a century after its composition. Rubato is used freely but tastefully and melodies really sing, so that a good balance is achieved between emotional richness and the fastidiousness that was also part of Chopin's musical nature. The impromptus are well done too, with the famous *Fantaisie-impromptu* played according to a manuscript source and so with rather fewer ornaments than usual. The recording was made in an Oslo church with a fine acoustic and an instrument that the pianist finds "exceptionally sympathetic", as the booklet tells us and his own programme notes are almost as poetic as the music itself, as when he writes of the E flat major Nocturne, Op. 55/2, that "a coda of sheer magic seems to descend from a height and passes into infinity" — which is not purple prose but a statement demonstrably true of the music and the performance.

NEW REVIEW

Chopin. PIANO WORKS. **Nikolai Demidenko**. Hyperion CDA66514.
Introduction and Variations in E major on a German air ("Der Schweizerbub").
Scherzi — No. 1 in B minor, Op. 20; No. 2 in B flat minor, Op. 31; No. 3 in C sharp minor, Op. 39; No. 4 in E major, Op. 54. Variations in B flat major on "Là ci darem la mano", Op. 2.

1h 3' DDD 1/92

"Off with your hats, gentlemen — a genius" were the percipient words of the 21-year-old Schumann on first discovering the *Là ci darem* Variations composed by Chopin when still only 17. Though well represented as originally conceived for piano and orchestra, it was left to the young Russian, Nikolai Demidenko (currently on the staff of the UK's Yehudi Menuhin School) to introduce the work to the CD catalogue as recast for solo piano. Serving as a grand finale to a recital opening with Chopin's still earlier, charmingly innocent *Swiss Boy* Variations, Demidenko's performance confirms him as a pianist of outstanding imaginative vitality as well as technical brilliance, moreover a player really able to make the piano sing throughout a wide and varied tonal range. The main musical tests nevertheless come in the four *Scherzos*, where again he surmounts all hurdles with effortless ease and poetic grace while extracting the loveliest sound from his instrument. But Chopin devotees should be warned that in making this music wholly his own he is sometimes a little idiosyncratically self-indulgent, notably in matters of lyrical relaxation, though also in No. 1, in choosing to remove the sting from Chopin's challenging opening chords. An artist to be watched none the less, here very well recorded.

NEW REVIEW

Chopin. PIANO WORKS. **Ivan Moravec.** Dorian DOR90140.
Scherzos — B minor, Op. 20; B flat minor, Op. 31; C sharp minor, Op. 39; E major, Op. 54. *Etudes,* Op. 25 — No. 1 in A flat major; No. 7 in C sharp minor. *Mazurkas* — C major, Op. 7 No. 5; C sharp minor, Op. 41 No. 1; C major, Op. 56 No. 2; F minor, Op. 68 No. 4.

57' DDD 2/92 — **B**

Here it is the shorter works that do most to explain this 62-year-old Czech pianist's enviable reputation as a Chopin player. The exquisite delicacy and finesse he brings to his concluding group of mazurkas while at the same time conveying the full potency of their folk-spirit, not least the rusticity of the last two in C, makes you long for a complete set from him. The A flat Etude is sheer magic as sound *per se*, while his intimately inflected melodic line in the laden C sharp minor Etude takes you to the innermost places of the composer's heart. Moravec plays the four scherzos with a light-fingered, mercurial, mood-of-the-moment impulse as if trying to recapture the unpredictable spontaneity and impressionability of Chopin's own playing, allegedly never the same twice. In the heat of excitement there is momentary loss of finesse in No. 2. And if copied by the younger generation, some of his rubato (especially in the more ruminative trio sections of all but No. 3) might sound mannered. So these four works are perhaps better recommended for occasional rather than everyday listening. A suspicion of boxiness in the otherwise mellow recording lessens as your ear tunes in.

Chopin. PIANO WORKS. **Martha Argerich.** DG Galleria 415 836-2GGA.
24 Preludes, Op. 28. Preludes — C sharp minor, Op. 45; A flat major, Op. posth. (all from 2530 721, 2/78). Barcarolle in F sharp major, Op. 60 (SLPM138672, 1/68). Polonaise in A flat major, Op. 53 (SLPM139317, 5/68). Scherzo in B flat minor, Op. 31 (2530 530, 6/75).

1h 2' ADD 4/88 — **P** **B**

Professor Zurawlew, the founder of the Chopin Competition in Warsaw was once asked which one of the prizewinners he would pick as having been his favourite. Looking back over the period 1927-75, the answer came back immediately: "Martha Argerich". This CD could explain why. There are very few recordings of the 24 Preludes that have such a perfect combination of temperamental virtuosity and compelling artistic insight. Argerich has the technical equipment to do whatever she wishes with the music. Whether it is in the haunting, dark melancholy of No. 2 in A minor or the lightning turmoil of No. 16 in B flat minor, she is profoundly impressive. It is these sharp changes of mood that make the performance scintillatingly unpredictable. In the *Barcarolle* there is no relaxed base on which the melodies of the right hand are constructed, as is conventional, but more the piece emerges as a stormy odyssey through life, with moments of visionary awareness. Argerich, it must be said, is on firmer ground in the *Polonaise*, where her power and technical security reign triumphant. The CD ends with a rippling and yet slightly aggressive reading of the second Scherzo. This is very much the playing of a pianist who lives in the 'fast lane' of life. The sound quality is a bit reverberant, an effect heightened by the fact that Argerich has a tendency to over-pedal.

Chopin. PIANO WORKS. **Krystian Zimerman.** (pf). DG 423 090-2GH.
Ballades — No. 1 in G minor, Op. 23; No. 2 in F major, Op. 38; No. 3 in A
flat major, Op. 47; No. 4 in F minor, Op. 52. Barcarolle in F sharp major,
Op. 60. Fantasie in F minor, Op. 49.

1h DDD 10/88

Chopin's choice of the previously
unused literary title of "ballade" for
the four great works with which this
recital begins suggests that they may
well have been inspired by tales of
his country's past. Certainly Krystian
Zimerman, a Pole himself, unfolds
all four with a rare appreciation of
their freely self-evolving narrative
style, almost as if he were composing
the music himself while going along.
His timing here and there might be
thought a little self-indulgent in its
lingerings but he never rushes his
fences. The overall impression left by
his playing is one of uncommon
expansiveness, upheld by a splendidly
full, warm, rich recording. Despite
his very slow tempo in the F minor

Krystian Zimerman   *[photo: DG/Bayat*

Fantasie he still manages to suggest that patriotic fires were very much aflame in
the composer at the time. The *Barcarolle* is as seductively sensuous as it is
passionate.

Chopin. Etudes, Opp. 10 and 25. **Maurizio Pollini** (pf). DG 413 794-2GH.
From 2530 291 (11/72).

56' ADD 5/85

The 24 *Etudes* of Chopin's Opp. 10 and 25, although dating from his twenties,
remain among the most perfect specimens of the genre ever known, with all
technical challenges — and they are formidable — dissolved into the purest
poetry. With his own transcendental technique (and there are few living pianists
who can rival it) Pollini makes you unaware that problems even exist — as for
instance in Op. 10 No. 10 in A flat, where the listener is swept along in an
effortless stream of melody. The first and last of the same set in C major and C
minor have an imperious strength and drive, likewise the last three impassioned
outpourings of Op. 25. Lifelong dislike of a heart worn on the sleeve makes him
less than intimately confiding in more personal contexts such as No. 3 in E and
No. 6 in E flat minor from Op. 10, or the nostalgic middle section of No. 5 in
E minor and the searing No. 7 in C sharp minor from Op. 25. Like the playing,
so the recording itself could profitably be a little warmer from time to time, but
it is a princely disc all the same, which all keyboard *aficionados* will covet.

Chopin. Piano Sonatas — No. 2 in B flat minor, Op. 35; No. 3 in B minor,
Op. 58. **Maurizio Pollini** (pf). DG 415 346-2GH.

52' DDD 8/86

These two magnificent romantic sonatas are Chopin's longest works for solo
piano. The passion of the B flat minor Sonata is evident throughout, as is its
compression (despite the overall length) — for example, the urgent first subject
of its first movement is omitted in the recapitulation. As for its mysterious finale,

once likened to "a pursuit in utter darkness", it puzzled Chopin's contemporaries but now seems totally right. The B minor Sonata is more glowing and spacious, with a wonderful *Largo* third movement, but its finale is even more exhilarating than that of the B flat minor, and on a bigger scale. Pollini plays this music with overwhelming power and depth of feeling; the expressive intensity is rightly often disturbing. Magisterial technique is evident throughout and the recording is sharp-edged but thrilling.

Francesco Cilea *Refer to Index*   *Italian 1866-1950*

Mikolajus Ciurlionis   *Lithuanian 1875-1911*

NEW REVIEW

Ciurlionis. Symphonic poems — The sea; In the forest. Five preludes for string orchestra. **Slovak Philharmonic Orchestra / Juozas Domarkas.** Marco Polo 8 223323.

| ♪ 51' DDD 6/91 |

Mikolajus Ciurlionis was a Lithuanian composer who studied in Warsaw and Leipzig and became deeply involved in his country's history and folk-heritage. He was also a talented visual artist, and one of his paintings, a somewhat dark and forbidding landscape, is reproduced on the cover of this CD. As a composer he was clearly influenced by the great late romantics, but he has a distinctly individual musical personality, and he handles a big orchestra with much skill and imagination. *The sea*, a tone poem completed in 1907, is cast on a very ambitious scale, and over the course of nearly half an hour maintains a high level of inspiration and concentration. The slightly earlier and shorter piece *In the forest* is a little less distinguished in invention, but still attracts through the colour of its orchestration. Ciurlionis himself transcribed the brief *Five preludes* from piano originals, and these wispy, atmospheric, and contrasted sketches show that he could work effectively on a smaller scale. The Slovak Philharmonic Orchestra's playing on this disc is efficient, but not particularly polished. Juozas Domarkas is regarded as Lithuania's leading conductor, and his performances certainly sound authoritative. The recording is very good.

Rebecca Clarke *Refer to Index*   *British 1886-1979*

Clemens non Papa   *French / Flemish c.1510-c.1556*

Clemens Non Papa. SACRED CHORAL WORKS. **The Tallis Scholars / Peter Phillips.** Gimell CDGIM013.
Missa Pastores quidnam vidistis. Motets — Pastores quidnam vidistis; Tribulationes civitatum; Pater peccavi; Ego flos campi.

| ♪ 54' DDD 12/87   ❓ ✒ |

This recording is a feast for the ear. Thanks to the Tallis Scholars a great and prolific sixteenth-century Flemish master has been rescued from almost total oblivion. Peter Phillips once pinpointed two major requirements for the performance of polyphonic music, namely, tuning and sonority. From that standpoint one can, indeed, just lean back and enjoy every moment of this recording, because it fulfils amply both requirements. One is particularly impressed by the perfection of its implementation in the long extended eight-part motet *Pater, peccavi*, which describes the confession to his father of the Prodigal Son on his return to the family home. The eight voices are so well controlled and in such perfect accord that they generate an atmosphere of total serenity and confidence consistent with the theme of the text. Similar qualities are displayed in the Scholars' performance of the parody Mass *Pastores quidnam vidistis* and of its parent motet. The crafting of the performance is matched only by the carefully-wrought structuring of the music itself. In the Mass, the tuning and the rich sonority are bound together by a series of strong, interweaving arching phrases and by a slowly descending scale passing from voice to voice towards the end of certain movements.

Louis-Nicolas Clérambault
French 1676-1749

Clérambault. DRAMATIC CANTATAS[a] — Orphée; Zéphire et Flore; Léandre et Héro. Sonata, "La Magnifique". [a]**Julianne Baird** (sop); **Music's Re-creation.** Meridian CDE84182. Texts and translations included.

1h 5' DDD 1/91

The *cantate française* was vigorously cultivated in France during the first three decades of the eighteenth century. A master, indeed *the* master of the form was Louis-Nicolas Clérambault. Like his contemporary , he was skilful in blending features of the Italian style with those of his native France. Clérambault published five books of chamber cantatas between 1710 and 1726 as well as composing some half dozen others. Julianne Baird and Music's Re-creation have chosen a captivating programme which includes Clérambault's masterpiece, *Orphée*. Baird's declamation is stylish, her diction clear and her intonation dependable. She breathes life into each of the cantatas and, notwithstanding a somewhat harsh violin tone, is sympathetically accompanied by the instruments. This is a disc which explores an important and engaging area of French baroque musical life. The performances have strengths and weaknesses but it is the former which prevail, and the music emerges with bright colours and graceful gestures. Additionally, the programme includes Clérambault's attractive but seldom-performed trio sonata *La Magnifique*. Recorded sound is effective.

Eric Coates
British 1886-1957

Coates. ORCHESTRAL WORKS. [a]**Royal Liverpool Philharmonic Orchestra/Sir Charles Groves**; [b]**London Symphony Orchestra/Sir Charles Mackerras**; [c]**City of Birmingham Symphony Orchestra/Reginald Kilbey.** Classics for Pleasure CD-CFPD4456. From CFPD414456-3 (11/86).
Saxo-Rhapsody. Wood Nymphs. Music Everywhere (Rediffusion March). From Meadow to Mayfair. The Dam Busters — march ([a] all from Columbia TWO226, 12/68); London. Cinderella — phantasy. London Again ([a] TWO321, 12/70). The Merrymakers — miniature overture. Summer Days — At the dance. By the Sleepy Lagoon. The Three Men — Man from the sea. The Three Bears — phantasy ([b] CFP40279, 3/78). Calling all Workers — march. The Three Elizabeths ([c] TWO361, 12/71).

(2) 2h 9' ADD 9/89 £ Ⓑ ▲ [b]

Eric Coates reached a vast public through the use of his music as signature tunes for radio programmes such as "In Town Tonight" ("Knightsbridge" from the

London Suite*), "Music While You Work" (*Calling all Workers*) and "Desert Island Discs" (*By the Sleepy Lagoon*). The cinema furthered the cause with the huge success of *The Dam Busters* march. There is much more to his music, though, than mere hit themes. Suites such as *London, London Again, From Meadow to Mayfair* and *The Three Elizabeths* offer a wealth of delights and are all the better for the juxtaposition of their contrasted movements. The two tone-poems for children, *Cinderella* and *The Three Bears* are splendidly apt pieces of programme music — simple to follow, ever charming, never trite. The miniature overture *The*

Sir Charles Mackerras [photo: Decca]

Merrymakers and the elegant waltz "At the dance" (from the suite *Summer Days* are other superb pieces of light music, whilst the *Saxo-Rhapsody* shows Coates in somewhat more serious mood. Throughout there is a rich vein of melody, and an elegance and grace of orchestration that makes this music to listen to over and over again with ever increasing admiration. The three conductors and orchestras featured adopt a no-nonsense approach that modestly suggests that his music should not be lingered over, never taken too seriously. Considering that the Mackerras items were first issued in 1956 (the rest being from 1968-71), the sound is of astonishingly good and remarkably uniform quality. This is a veritable feast of delightful music and, at its low price, a remarkable bargain.

Girolamo Conversi   *Refer to Index*   *Italian fl. 1571-5*

Samuel Coleridge-Taylor   *British 1875-1912*

NEW REVIEW

Coleridge-Taylor. Scenes from "The Song of Hiawatha". **Helen Field** (sop); **Arthur Davies** (ten); **Bryn Terfel** (bar); **Welsh National Opera Chorus and Orchestra/Kenneth Alwyn.** Argo 430 356-2ZH2. Notes and text included.

② 1h 59' DDD 9/91

Hiawatha's best days probably lie irrevocably in the past when the choral societies kept its publishers going with orders for copies and every year at the Albert Hall the tribes would gather for a performance in costume under Great Chief Malcolm Sargent. This new recording is at the very least an honourable reminder of those times, with choral forces that make it very clear why it was so beloved of choirs throughout the land, and orchestral playing that brings out the attractions of rhythm and colour that are also characteristic. There is an appropriately limpid, sparkling Laughing Waters in Helen Field, Arthur Davies sings the famous "Onaway, awake beloved" in fine lyrical style and Bryn Terfel makes a splendidly dramatic impression as he laments the death of Minnehaha. In short, it is a fully worthy performance under Kenneth Alwyn, and the recording is fine too. A question mark still hangs over the work itself. So often it seems to be on the verge of adventurous exploration and then to withdraw so as to remain within sound of the matinée teacups. Yet it has a genuine impulse behind it, and at times (particularly in Hiawatha's farewell) it generates emotion which one can well imagine might be almost alarmingly powerful on a grand occasion in the Albert Hall, if rather less so on an evening with the compact disc player at home.

Aaron Copland

American 1900-1990

NEW REVIEW

Copland. ORCHESTRAL WORKS. [a]**Stanley Drucker** (cl); **New York Philharmonic Orchestra/Leonard Bernstein.** DG 431 672-2GH. Recorded at performances in Avery Fischer Hall, New York in October 1989.
Clarinet Concerto[a]. Connotations. El salón México. Music for the Theatre.

Ih 14' DDD 8/91

An excellent collection of music spanning much of Aaron Copland's career as a composer, with the added bonus of Bernstein's authoritative conducting. *El salón México* gives the disc a vigorous start with the New York Philharmonic playing with plenty of character and panache. Dating from the middle 1930s this is one of Copland's most attractive works, brilliantly evoking from simple means a sound portrait of Mexico. South America also played a part in the composition of the Clarinet Concerto, which Copland started writing for Benny Goodman in Rio de Janeiro in 1947. This great twentieth-century concerto receives the finest performance on the disc, with a deeply felt interpretation of the solo part from Stanley Drucker whose command of tone, phrasing and dynamics cannot be praised too highly. This is more than a match even for the rival Benny Goodman version (CBS CD42227). The remaining works, *Music for the Theatre* and *Connotations* stand at the opposite ends of Copland's career: the first dates from 1925 and the latter from 1962. Despite this, both works have a spiky character instantly identifiable as Copland. Bernstein, who both commissioned and premièred *Connotations*, gives it a particularly strong and committed reading, and clearly enjoys the jazz influence of *Music for the Theatre.* All the recordings were taken from live performances given in 1989, but sound balance and perspective are excellent, as is the playing of the New York Philharmonic at its peak.

NEW REVIEW

Copland. ORCHESTRAL WORKS. **Detroit Symphony Orchestra/Antál Dorati.** Decca Ovation 430 705-2DM. Items marked [a] from SXDL7547 (10/82), [b] 414 457-2DH (6/86).
El salón México[a]. Dance Symphony[a]. Fanfare for theCommon Man[a]. Rodeo — Four Dance Episodes[a]. Appalachian Spring — suite[b].

Ih 14' DDD 8/91   £ Ⓑ

This glorious disc shows how well Antál Dorati assimilated the music of Aaron Copland. The big-boned swagger of "Buckaroo Holiday" from *Rodeo* with its vision of open spaces and clear blue skies is established straightaway in Dorati's performance with keen rhythmic drive and fine orchestral articulation. The "Hoe Down" is properly exciting while the other two dance episodes are wonderfully expressive. In the 1945 suite of *Appalachian Spring* Dorati secures marvellous phrasing and dynamics but tends to understate the poetic elements of the score. Decca's sound quality is exemplary and is of demonstration standard in *Fanfare for the Common Man,* as it is in the enjoyable curtain-raiser, the sturdy, big-hearted *El salón México.* Dorati's vast experience as an interpreter of Stravinsky and Bartók pays fine dividends in Copland's gruesome *Dance Symphony,* music inspired by the vampire film fantasy, *Nosferatu.* This survey of Copland's most popular orchestral works is a welcome addition to the mid-price catalogue.

Copland. ORCHESTRAL WORKS. [a]**Raymond Mase** (tpt); [a]**Stephen Taylor** (cor ang); **Orpheus Chamber Orchestra.** DG 427 335-2GH. Appalachian Spring — suite. Quiet city[a]. Short Symphony (No. 2). Three Latin-American Sketches.

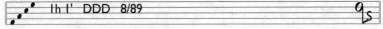

This disc will be of value to devotees of and newcomers to Copland's music alike. For the devotee, interest will be aroused not only by the *Three Latin-American Sketches*, but also by the inclusion of the 1958 version of the *Appalachian Spring* suite which uses the chamber orchestra scoring of the original ballet in place of the more frequently heard version for full orchestra. The lighter scoring gives the music a greater degree of luminosity and transparency, and also serves to highlight the crispness and buoyancy of Copland's rhythmic invention, especially when the performance is as fine as it is here; string textures are beautifully clear, and there are some wonderful solo performances from the woodwind players. The *Short* Symphony, with its obvious influences of Stravinsky (Symphony in Three Movements) and jazz is given a very rhythmically alert and vital performance, with much attention paid to subtle dynamic shading. Special mention must also be made to the solo playing of Raymond Mase and Stephen Taylor in *Quiet city* whose first-class performances create a very evocative and elegiac soundscape. With the *Three Latin-American Sketches* we return once more to the rhythmic drive that so often pervades Copland's music. The second and third dances were written in 1959; the first was added in 1971, presumably to give a more formal balance to the set, resulting in a fast-slow-fast sequence. The recorded sound is of the highest quality.

Copland. ORCHESTRAL WORKS. **St Paul Chamber Orchestra/Hugh Wolff.** Teldec 2292-46314-2. Appalachian Spring (orig. version). Music for the Theatre. Quiet City. Three Latin American Sketches.

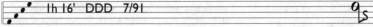

Much of what is best about Copland's vernacular music is encapsulated on this well-filled disc. Invigorating rhythms (derived from jazz, Latin-American dance, or American folk-music) and soulful musings, scored with painstaking delicacy, sit happily side-by-side in these works. *Music for the Theatre* is the earliest piece, premièred by Koussevitzky and the Boston Symphony Orchestra in 1925; its toe-tapping jauntiness reflects Copland's delight in jazz at that time, and his sidelong glances at Stravinsky and Satie. *Quiet City*, of 1940, with its effective coupling of trumpet and cor anglais, provides a reposeful heart to the programme, reflected in the simply beautiful "Paisaje mexicana", the second of the *Latin American Sketches*, finished in 1971. The original, chamber version of *Appalachian Spring* (1944) completes the disc with more dance rhythms, made all the more immediate by the use of smaller forces. The performances tie the works together through a keen sense of idiom: rhythmic lift and vitality drive the faster movements and the more meditative are either allowed to be peacefully simple or enriched by a finely poised degree of pathos that never cloys. A recording that manages to combine brightness with intimate warmth is a special bonus.

Copland. Symphony No. 3[a]. Quiet City[b]. [b]**Philip Smith** (tpt); [b]**Thomas Stacy** (cor ang); **New York Philharmonic Orchestra/Leonard Bernstein.** DG 419 170-2GH. Item marked [a] recorded at a performance in the Avery Fisher Hall, New York during December 1985.

Copland. Symphony No. 3. Music for a Great City. **Saint Louis Symphony Orchestra/Leonard Slatkin.** RCA Victor Red Seal RD60149.

Copland intended this symphony as a 'grand gesture' and there is no doubt at any point in Bernstein's performance that a big statement is being made. There is passionate earnestness in the opening movement and tremendous impact to the brass and drums at the beginning of the scherzo, the central mood of the *andantino* is one of vibrant intensity, while the finale is a public address of great splendour. It is undoubtedly the 'positive' aspects of the work that have made its reputation and they could hardly be more eloquently stated: the dance-like rhythms are crisp and springy, the *Fanfare for the common man* is magnificently sonorous and the noble conclusion of the work is vastly impressive. *Quiet City* is given a no less deeply felt reading. The symphony's live recording obviously took place before an uncommonly healthy audience: not a cough is to be heard and the sound has plenty of power and edge but not quite enough richness to the bass; high strings sometimes take on a dazzling glare. The much more reticently scored *Quiet City*, made in the studio, has no such problems.

In 1964 the London Symphony Orchestra asked Copland for a work to celebrate its sixtieth season. *Music for a Great City* refers to New York, however, not London, for instead of a new work Copland adapted music from the 1961 Carroll Baker film *Something Wild*, shot on location in New York, and he fashioned four episodes roughly in the shape of a symphony. Each 'movement'

bears a descriptive title such as "Skyline" or "Subway Jam". Leonard Slatkin obviously revels in Copland's highly expressive writing, sometimes sentimental, sometimes tense or jaggedly aggressive, and he conducts a brilliantly effective account of the score, with virtuoso playing from his Saint Louis orchestra. In the symphony he challenges Bernstein on home ground in his DG version, and with great success. Again, he is totally inside the music, and he secures playing of great precision and refinement from an orchestra which has exactly the right timbre and style. The recording has impressive range and sonority, yet detail is beautifully clear.

Leonard Slatkin   *[photo: BMG*

Copland. Billy the Kid — ballet. Rodeo — ballet. **St Louis Symphony Orchestra/Leonard Slatkin.** EMI CDC7 47382-2. From EL270398-1 (7/86).

Between 1938 and 1944 Copland wrote the three ballet scores which somehow managed to epitomize the American character in music: *Billy the Kid, Rodeo* and *Appalachian Spring*. Here we have the complete scores of the two 'Westerns', which are usually given in somewhat abridged form. *Billy* is built around a collection of cowboy ballads and is the more obviously symphonic, whilst *Rodeo* is closer to a dance suite. Slatkin and the St Louis Symphony Orchestra give spirited performances of these works, refined as well as brilliant and the recording, transferred at a rather lower level than usual, is very well defined and atmospheric, conveying both the broad horizons of the prairie and the violent exchanges to marvellous effect.

NEW REVIEW

Copland. SONGS. **Roberta Alexander** (sop); **Roger Vignoles** (pf).
Etcetera KTC1100. Texts included.
A Summer Vacation. Alone. My heart is in the East. Night. Old American Songs, Sets 1 and 2. Old Poem. Pastorale. Poet's Song. 12 Poems of Emily Dickinson.

· 1h 12' DDD 3/92

It's a joy to have one of the greatest song-cycles to an English text back in the record catalogue — and performed by such a polished team as Alexander and Vignoles. The *12 Poems of Emily Dickinson* (1950) come from Copland's finest period — after the acknowledged successes of the three folk ballets and before he began to take on aspects of serial technique, after which he composed less and less. The cycle is a wonderful match between America's great New England nineteenth-century poet and one of her greatest composers. Warm lyricism, drama, and a continuously sensitive response to the poems make this work a landmark comparable to the best of Britten's cycles. The texts (the edited versions available at the time) are provided for all the songs. The performances, in a few details, are not quite flawless but Alexander has grown in stature and vocal control since her earliest recordings. Just as delightful, if not more so, are the early Copland songs — wistful, sad, nostalgic and beautifully wrought in every way. They demonstrate an instinctive musicianship of the highest order even before Copland went to study with Boulanger in Paris. And they get superb performances worthy of the finest Lieder. The *Old American Songs* are simply some of Copland's favourite tunes, some of which he used in other works and which he often performed himself as pianist or conductor. Alexander has plenty of zip, Vignoles is perhaps a little staid, but these songs complete an excellent and well-recorded vocal anthology.

Copland. THE TENDER LAND. **Elisabeth Comeaux** (sop) Laurie; **Janis Hardy** (mez) Ma Moss; **Maria Jette** (sop) Beth; **LeRoy Lehr** (bass) Grandpa Moss; **Dan Dressen** (ten) Martin; **James Bohn** (bar) Top; **Vern Sutton** (ten) Mr Splinters; **Agnes Smuda** (sop) Mrs Splinters; **Merle Fristad** (bass) Mr Jenks; **Sue Herber** (mez) Mrs Jenks; **Chorus and Orchestra of The Plymouth Music Series, Minnesota/Philip Brunelle.** Virgin Classics VCD7 91113-2. Notes and text included.

· ② 1h 47' DDD 8/90

Aaron Copland was a father figure of American music, and Leonard Bernstein expressed a lifelong admiration when he called him "the best we have". Yet though a generation separates them, *The Tender Land* had its première in 1954 just three years before *West Side Story*. Both opened in New York, but while Bernstein's piece is set there and portrays a violent urban America, Copland's belongs to the wide Midwest and the quiet of a farming home. It was written for young singers and has a wonderful freshness, a clean 'plainness' which Copland compared to that of his ballet *Appalachian Spring*. The story tells how the young girl Laurie Moss falls in love with Martin, a travelling harvester who visits her mother's farm, and after being left by him still decides to leave home and make her own way in the world. It has been criticized as undramatic, and its partly spoken dialogue and small cast have also gone against it — Copland later wryly called opera "la forme fatale" and never wrote another — but whatever its viability on stage, on record it provides a satisfying experience and this Minnesota performance has just the right flavour, offering simplicity and sensitivity without affectation. The conductor is himself a Midwesterner who writes that his young cast "have their roots in this particular soil" which is the heartland of America. The recording is every bit as fresh as the music.

Arcangelo Corelli

Corelli. 12 Concerti grossi, Op. 6. **The English Concert/Trevor Pinnock.** Archiv Produktion 423 626-2AH2.
No. 1 in D major; No. 2 in F major; No. 3 in C minor; No. 4 in D major; No. 5 in B flat major; No. 6 in F major; No. 7 in D major; No. 8 in G minor; No. 9 in F major; No. 10 in C major; No. 11 in B flat major; No. 12 in F major.

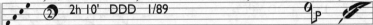
② 2h 10' DDD 1/89

In his working life of about 40 years Corelli must have produced a great deal of orchestral music, yet the 12 *Concerti grossi*, Op. 6 form the bulk of what is known to have survived. Their original forms are mostly lost but we know that those in which in which they were published in Amsterdam by Estienne Roger had been carefully polished and revised by the composer — and that they were assembled from movements that had been written at various times. The first eight are in *da chiesa* form, the last four in *da camera* form — without and with named dance movements respectively, and the number of their movements varies from four to seven. Each features the interplay of a group of soloists, the *concertino* (two violins and a cello) and the orchestra, the *ripieno*, the size of which Corelli stated to be flexible. These are masterpieces of their genre, one that was later developed by, notably, Bach and Handel, and they are rich in variety. The scores leaves scope for embellishment, not least in cadential and lining passages, and the players of The English Concert take full advantage of them. Regarding the overall performances, suffice it to say that this recording won a *Gramophone* Award in 1990.

John Corigliano

NEW REVIEW
Corigliano. Symphony No. 1. **Chicago Symphony Orchestra/Daniel Barenboim.** Erato 2292-45601-2. Recorded at performances in Orchestra Hall, Chicago in March 1990.

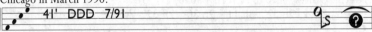
41' DDD 7/91

The symphonies of Bruckner, Mahler and Shostakovich were strongly influenced by social and political issues of the day and John Corigliano's deeply-felt First Symphony follows this line of compositional thought. Written in 1990 as a musical monument to friends who had died of AIDS — this exotically orchestrated work (complete with police whistle, vibraphone and whip) pulls no punches. It is a sombre work which in terms of style, pays partial homage to Bartók. The first movement, "Apologue: Of Rage and Remembrance" sets a test for the Chicago Symphony Orchestra's brass section which they pass with flying colours. They are also in their element in the fiery "Tarantella" where Barenboim's meticulous conducting approaches a Solti-like frenzy. Corigliano's dark orchestration and the CSO strings create a ghostly "nachtmusik" feel to the middle movement, "Giulio's Song", and the woodwind match the mood in the plaintive epilogue. This distinctive new score, which creeps in and out of tonality with cobra-like calm, becomes a classic of the present in the hands of a conductor and orchestra more closely associated with classics of the past. Erato's live recording is superb with breadth, depth and exciting perspectives. In essence, this challenging, thought-provoking disc is well worth investigating despite its rather ungenerous playing time.

William Cornysh
British d.1523

Cornysh. CHORAL WORKS. **The Tallis Scholars/Peter Phillips.** Gimell CDGIM014. Texts and translations included.
Salve regina. Ave Maria, mater Dei. Gaude virgo mater Christi. Magnificat. Ah, Robin. Adieu, adieu, my heartes lust. Adieu courage. Woefully arrayed. Stabat mater.

William Cornysh, the leading English composer of his generation, was creative, original to a degree of waywardness, sometimes tender, often ecstatic and he served both Henry VII and Henry VIII, holding the post of Master of the Children of the Chapel Royal. The highly skilled trebles he trained to tackle his own most exacting music are replaced, here, by two of the Scholars' most agile, boyish sopranos. The musical pyrotechnics they throw off with such apparent ease give one a good idea of what so delighted the ears of sixteenth-century audiences. The varied programme includes the magnificent *Salve regina*, which unfolds in never-ending volutes of melody, whilst the *Stabat mater*, depicting the sufferings of Mary, reveals Cornysh at his most powerfully imaginative. The relish with which The Scholars understand Cornysh's music makes this a disc of quite exceptional beauty.

François Couperin
French 1668-1733

F. Couperin. HARPSICHORD WORKS. **Kenneth Gilbert.** Harmonia Mundi Musique d'abord HMA190 351/60 (two triple- and two double-disc sets).
HMA 190 351/3 — Premier livre de clavecin: Ordres — 1 (from RCA LSB4067, 9/72); 2 (LSB4077, 2/73); 3 and 4 (LSB4087, 5/73); 5 (LSB4098, 8/73). *HMA190 354/6* — Deuxième livre de clavecin: Ordres — 6 and 7 (RCA LHL1 5048, 1/75); 8. L'art de toucher le clavecin (LHL1 5049, 1/75). Ordres — 9 and 10 (LHL1 5050, 2/75); 11 and 12 (LHL1 5051, 2/75). *HMA190 357/8* — Troisième livre de clavecin: Ordres — 13 (new to UK); 14 to 19 (all from RCA SER5720/23, 4/75). *HMA190 359/60* — Quatrième livre de clavecin: Ordres — 20 to 27 (LHL4 5096, 12/75).

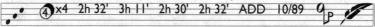

Couperin's solo harpsichord music, collected in four volumes and published between 1713 and 1730, represents one of the highest peaks of baroque keyboard repertory. Its elusive and, indeed allusive style, however, frequently gets the better of would-be performers and it is doubtless partly for this reason that only five complete versions of this music have been issued commercially. Kenneth Gilbert has long been acknowledged a master of French baroque interpretation and his performance of Couperin's 27 *Ordres* — the word implies something between a suite and an anthology — though now 21 years old, has not been surpassed. Indeed, it is no mean tribute to his informed approach that these interpretations strike today's audiences as being as stylish as when they were first issued in 1971. Gilbert scrupulously adheres to aspects of performance by which the composer himself set such store. Couperin was precise about ornamentation and related matters and Gilbert is meticulous in his observance of them. Unequal rhythms are applied discerningly but with a natural ease that variously brings out the nobility, the grandeur, and the tenderness of the music. There is, in short, a wonderful variety of affects to be found in these pieces and Gilbert seldom if ever disappoints us in his feeling for them. From among the most infinite delights to be found in this impressive and satisfying project we may, perhaps, mention the *Ordres* Nos. 6, 7, 8 and 26 in their entirety, and the exquisitely shaped seventh prelude from *L'art de toucher le clavecin* are outstanding examples of Gilbert's artistry. Small technical deficiencies in the remastering appear almost negligible in the face of so much that is rewarding. These are performances to treasure for a lifetime.

F. Couperin. HARPSICHORD WORKS. **Skip Sempé.** Deutsche Harmonia Mundi RD77219.
L'art de toucher le clavecin: Préludes — C major; D minor; G minor; B flat major; F minor; A major. *Premier livre:* Troisième ordre — Allemande La ténébreuse; Courantes I and II; Sarabande La lugubre; L'espagnolète; Chaconne La favorite. Cinquième ordre — Sarabande La dangereuse; Les ordes. *Dieuxième livre:* Sixième ordre — Les baricades mistérieuses. Huitième ordre — La Raphaéle; Allemande L'Ausoniène; Courantes I and II. Sarabande L'unique; Gavotte; Rondeau; Gigue; Passacaille. *Troisième livre:* Quinzième ordre — Le dodo ou L'amour au berçeau. *Quatrième livre:* Vingt-troisième ordre — L'arlequine. Vingtquatrième ordre — Les vieux seigneurs.

1h 12' DDD 1/91

Couperin's subtly expressive harpsichord music is amongst the most elusive in the French baroque repertory to the performer. The American, Skip Sempé, has an intuitive understanding of it and conveys to the listener the grandeur, the wit and metaphor variously present in Couperin's dances and delicately coloured character pieces. Sempé's programme is thoughtfully chosen both for its capacity to show off the composer's considerable if restrained emotional range, and in its inclusion of pieces which have helped to bring his music to a wide audience. So we find the enigmatically titled rondeau *Les baricades mistérieuses*, an enchanting pastoral "Rondeau in B flat" which Bach could not resist including in the *Music Book* for his wife Anna Magdalena, the great B minor *Passacaille* and *L'arlequine*, evoking the spirit of *commedia dell'arte* together with pieces which may be less familiar but no less rewarding on acquaintance. This is a delightful programme and an ideal introduction to Couperin's music for anyone not yet familiar with a veritable poet of the harpsichord. Sympathetically recorded and imaginatively presented.

NEW REVIEW

F. Couperin. ORGAN MASSES. **Jean-Charles Ablitzer** (org). Harmonic H/CD8613, H/CD8615. Played on the organs of [a]La Basilique Saint-Nazaire et Saint-Celse de Carcassone and [b]L'église Saint-Julien et Sainte-Basilisse de Vinça. *H/CD8613* — Messe à l'usage ordinaire des paroisses[a]. *Plainchant:* Liturgy for Easter Day (Ensemble Organum/Marcel Pérès). *H/CD8615* — Messe pour les couvents de religieux et religieuses. *Du Mage:* Livre d'orgue[b].

② 2h 12' DDD 9/91

François Couperin wrote and published his two organ masses early on in life. They comprise his complete *Pièces d'orgue* and were issued in 1689. The Masses consist of organ music for the liturgy; the *Parish Mass* is the grander of the two and was intended for use on important church feast days. The *Convent Mass*, as its title implies, is more intimate in character and shorter in length. In this recording plainchant interpolations indicated for use in conjunction with the *Parish Mass* have been included as well as a substantial Easter introit which introduces the Mass. Couperin's music does not intrinsically suffer if the plainchant is missing but its eloquence is greatly enhanced by the punctuation imposed by its presence. Jean-Charles Ablitzer, an organist with a feeling for the elusive qualities of French baroque style, plays two magnificent instruments. For the *Parish Mass* he has chosen the famous organ in the Basilica at Carcassonne, for the other an organ at Vinça in the Pyrenees. It is on this last-mentioned instrument that Ablitzer performs the *Livre d'orgue* of Couperin's contemporary Pierre du Mage. The recording is thrillingly resonant, capturing the distinctive idiom and colours of the French baroque organ school.

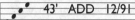

F. Couperin. Trois leçons de ténèbres[a]. Motet — Victoria! Christo resurgenti. **Judith Nelson** [a]**Emma Kirkby** (sops); **Jane Ryan** (va da gamba); **Christopher Hogwood** (chamber org). L'Oiseau-Lyre 430 283-2OH. Notes, texts and translations included. From DSLO536 (6/78).

43' ADD 12/91

Christopher Hogwood   *[photo: Decca/Broad*

Couperin's three *Leçons de ténèbres*, dating from the second decade of the eighteenth century, are masterly examples of a peculiarly French sacred musical idiom. Sung during Holy Week, their texts are drawn from the *Lamentations of Jeremiah* interspersed with ornamental melismatic phrases inspired by ritualistic Hebrew letters. The subtle blend of Italian monody with French court air, which characterizes Couperin's *Leçons* and those of his predecessor Charpentier, seems to have been appearing both at court and wider afield. Several recordings of these beautiful pieces have been made and the competition is very strong. That being said, the lightly articulated and freshsounding performances of the sopranos Emma Kirkby and Judith Nelson have lost little or nothing of their charm over the intervening years. Nelson sings the first *Leçon* and Kirkby the second, by the way. These are cooler readings than some others and, one might perhaps say, more *da chiesa* in their approach than other sensuous performances. It is well recorded and includes the radiant Easter motet, *Victoria! Christo resurgenti*. Attention to stylistic details is a major feature here; the continuo realizations are discreet, tasteful and assured and the set includes text and translations.

Bernhard Crusell

Finnish 1775-1839

NEW REVIEW

Crusell. Clarinet Concerto No. 1 in E flat major, Op. 1.
L. Koželuch. Clarinet Concerto in E flat major.
Krommer. Clarinet Concerto in E flat major, Op. 36. **Emma Johnson** (cl); **Royal Philharmonic Orchestra/Günther Herbig.** ASV CDDCA763.

1h 7' DDD 9/91

The idiom of Stockholm-based composer Bernhard Crusell embraces elements of Mozart, Spohr, Weber, Rossini and even Beethoven. But in the hands of the young woodwind virtuoso, Emma Johnson, his music has a personality all its own. Here she turns her attention to his First Clarinet Concerto which is full of engaging ideas. The slow movement is beautifully done and in the finale the soloist is at her very best — full of impulsive charm and swagger. Although the Koželuch concerto, a recent discovery, seems less distinctive, the slow movement of the Krommer is undeniably affecting and its finale bounces along in fine style. Emma Johnson plays throughout with a winning spontaneity and the RPO, arguably just a shade tubby of timbre for such music, back her up with distinction. The generous acoustic is effectively caught.

Claude Debussy

French 1862-1918

Debussy. ORCHESTRAL WORKS. **French Radio National Orchestra/ Jean Martinon.** EMI Studio CDM7 69668-2. From SLS893 (2/75).
Fantaisie for piano and orchestra (Aldo Ciccolini, pf). La plus que lente (orch. cpsr). Première rapsodie for clarinet and orchestra (Guy Dangain, cl). Rapsodie (orch. Roger-Ducasse. Jean-Marie Londeix, sax). Khamma (orch. Koechlin. Fabienne Boury, pf). Danse (orch. Ravel).

1h 15' ADD 10/89

This fourth volume of Debussy's complete orchestral works — interpreting the terms liberally to include other men's orchestrations of compositions he left in piano versions — confirms Martinon's standing as a Debussian of notable insight: perhaps the most revealing item here is his remarkably flexible and sensitive *La plus que lente*, which the composer scored, oddly enough, with a prominent part for the cimbalom. Of the three larger *concertante* works (his only other, the dances for harp and orchestra, is on a previously issued disc) the best, intrinsically, is the clarinet *Rapsodie*, written as a Conservatoire test-piece and full of delicate sensuousness, but with a Puckish final section. The three-movement *Fantaisie* with piano (which isn't allowed out on its own very much) was an early work that Debussy withdrew as uncharacteristic (moments before d'Indy was to conduct it, thus earning his permanent hostility), but its meditative Lento has an attractive languor: the saxophone *Rapsodie*, commissioned (but never received) by the lady president of the Boston Orchestral Club, found Debussy experimenting with an exotic idiom in his attempt to suit the instrument. But exoticism rampant is the characteristic of the Egyptian ballet *Khamma* (in which the heroine dances herself to death before the sun god Amon-Ra in her plea to avert the destruction of her town): the composer himself did not think much of it, but many now feel it has been under-valued, and parts of it are very lovely. The playing of orchestra and soloists is first-class throughout the disc, which never suggests that its contents were recorded in 1973/74.

Debussy. La mer[a]. Prélude à l'après midi d'un faune[a].
Ravel. Daphnis et Chloé — Suite No. 2[a]. Boléro[b]. **Berlin Philharmonic Orchestra/Herbert von Karajan.** DG Galleria 427 250-2GGA. Items marked [a] from SLPM138 923 (3/65), [b] SLPM139 010 (11/66).

1h 4' ADD 7/89

Debussy. La mer. Prélude à l'après-midi d'un faune. Jeux — poème dansé.
London Philharmonic Orchestra/Serge Baudo. EMI Eminence CD-EMX9502. From EMX2090 (8/86).

52' DDD 10/87 £ S B

Debussy. ORCHESTRAL WORKS. **Montreal Symphony Orchestra/ Charles Dutoit.** Decca 430 240-2DH.
La mer. Jeux — poème dansé. Le martyre de Saint Sébastien. Prélude à l'après-midi d'un faune.

1h 15' DDD 2/91 B

The DG disc preserves one of Karajan's finest recordings showing his deep affinity with French music and displaying a delicacy and feeling for colour that he is too often denied by his detractors. The *Daphnis* suite is magnificently conducted and played. The merest whisper of sound is lovingly tended and the climax of the great evocation of dawn is perfectly placed. The *Prélude* is a gorgeous interpretation, you can almost feel the warmth of the afternoon sun playing on the faun, and Karlheinz Zöller's flute playing is ravishing. *La mer* receives quite a powerful reading, muscular and flexible with Karajan riding the storm masterfully. The *Boléro* shows a great orchestra and conductor in perfect harmony and has remained one of Karajan's party-pieces. The sound is very fine and the performances countless times superior to Karajan's digital re-recordings. A must for admirers of French music and Karajan alike.

However, three of Debussy's most popular and most beautifully coloured works gathered on a single bargain-price disc is hard to resist, especially when Serge Baudo draws some quite exquisite playing from the LPO who have rarely sounded better. *Prélude à l'après-midi d'un faune*, in particular, has a languour and mediterranean warmth that wonderfully evokes the lines of Mallarmé's poem. This is a spectacularly recorded collection that shows that good things need not cost the most!

The undeservedly unfamiliar *Le martyre de Saint Sébastien* is undoubtedly the most compelling reason for acquiring the Decca disc. *Le martyre* is music of disturbing allure, a powerful mix of mystical and sensual rapture, dark undercurrents and strange pastoralism. The sheer sorcery of Debussy's orchestration is relished to the full by Dutoit and his players. Dutoit's *Jeux* is less successful than some in its capacity to suggest the *risqué* amorous side-play of the young man and two girls, as is the Decca sound, with its relatively distant woodwind balance in delineating the essential interplay of timbres. Dutoit's *La mer*, though, has immense drive and vitality. The listener is swept forward on a tide of bracing rhythms and cross currents. Others have found more atmosphere and enchantment in this score, but few such propulsive energy. The articulation and thrust of the lower strings at the start of the last movement has to be heard to be believed.

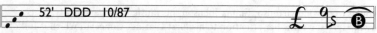

Debussy. Nocturnes[a]. Jeux — poème dansé. [a]**Collegium Musicum Amstelodamense; Concertgebouw Orchestra, Amsterdam/Bernard Haitink.** Philips 400 023-2PH. From 9500 674 (11/80).

43' ADD 6/83 P S

NEW REVIEW

Debussy. Jeux — poème dansé. Images. Musiques pour le Roi Lear (orch. Roger-Ducasse). **City of Birmingham Symphony Orchestra/Simon Rattle.** EMI CDC7 49947-2.

1h 2' DDD 3/90 P S

Debussy wrote *Jeux* in 1913 for Diaghilev's Ballets Russes and, in particular, their star dancer Nijinsky, who choreographed it as well as dancing in it. The scenario was also Nijinsky's and has a sophisticated but flimsy story of a boy and two girls, tennis players in a park at dusk who flirt, quarrel and search for a lost ball. Unfortunately, the première in May 1913 was eclipsed by that of Stravinsky's *Le sacre du printemps*, given by the same company just two weeks later, but (as the booklet says) whereas that work seems like a great statement of modern music, Debussy's elusive and far less popular score poses an immense question with its fleeting melodies, changing tempos and iridescent orchestral colour. Debussy called his *Nocturnes* an experiment with a single colour [12]—like the study of grey in painting. In their definitive form (1899) they must be numbered among his most perfect works and whether in the "Nuages", which portrays the "unchanging aspect of the sky and the slow, solemn motion of the clouds" or the vibrating, dancing rhythms of "Fêtes", Haitink succeeds in projecting their colourful atmosphere to masterly effect. Again, in *Jeux* he captures its sense of mystery and the playing of the Concertgebouw Orchestra is incomparable. This release won a *Gramophone* Award, both for the realism and naturalness of the recording and the artistry of the performance. It is one of those issues that sets a standard by which subsequent versions will be judged.

Simon Rattle and his fine Birmingham orchestra are alive to every detail of Debussy's score but do not spoil the composer's carefully contrived hazes with clinical clarity, and if his *Jeux* is a little more romantic than with some other conductors, that could win more friends for this masterpiece. The three *Images* are easier to grasp, and the playing here is no less fine, with a melancholy, poignant "Gigues" and a lambent "Rondes de printemps" framing the central and longest piece, "Ibéria". This is a superb evocation of Spain and itself a triptych with the third number ("The morning of a feast day") bringing a whole city little by little to joyful life. The two little *King Lear* pieces are rarities worth hearing, being all that Debussy wrote for a production of Shakespeare's play in 1904 which eventually used music by another composer. Rich yet delicate sound and a wide dynamic range bring all this music wonderfully to life.

Debussy (orch. Ravel). Danse. Sarabande.
Milhaud. La création du monde.
Prokofiev. Symphony No. 1 in D major, Op. 25, "Classical". Sinfonietta in A major, Op. 48. **Lausanne Chamber Orchestra / Albert Zedda.** Virgin Classics VC7 91098-2.

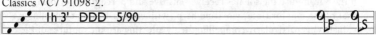

Prokofiev's *Classical* Symphony and *Sinfonietta* make ideal couplings. Their light, translucent textures and scoring, and immediately memorable tunes also make them an ideal introduction for those approaching Prokofiev's music for the first time. The *Classical* Symphony began life as an exercise in translating the formal proportions and elegance of Haydn's music into a twentieth-century style, whilst at the same time retaining an originality and spontaneity. Prokofiev said of its title: "I called it the 'Classical' symphony for the fun of it, to 'teese the geese', and in the secret hope that I would prove to be right if the symphony really did turn out to be a piece of classical music". Well, as it turned out, that's exactly what did happen, and it has been charming audiences ever since. The *Sinfonietta* predates the symphony by seven years (though it is heard on this disc in its revised version of 20 years later) but it shares the same 'classical' approach and effervescent high spirits of the symphony. Milhaud's jazz-inspired score, *La création du monde*, evolved from a collaboration with the writer Blaise Cendrars, and was given its première by the Ballet Suédois in 1923; its steamy, sultry music illustrates the creation of the world as depicted by African folklore. Ravel's two orchestrations of Debussy's piano pieces, *Sarabande* and *Danse* round off this attractive disc nicely. The Lausanne Chamber Orchestra directed by Alberto Zedda play with charm, character and warmth in performances that are amongst the finest available. The warm, slightly resonant recording is exceptionally fine.

Debussy. CHAMBER WORKS. [cd]**Roger Bourdin** (fl); [a]**Arthur Grumiaux** (vn); [d]**Colette Lequien** (va); [b]**Maurice Gendron** (vc); [d]**Annie Challan** (hp); [a]**István Hajdu**, [b]**Jean Françaix** (pfs). Philips Musica da Camera 422 839-2PC. From SAL3644 (4/68).
Violin Sonata[a]. Cello Sonata[b]. Syrinx[c]. Sonata for Flute, Viola and Harp[d].

45' ADD 1/89

Debussy. CHAMBER WORKS. **Nash Ensemble** ([e]Delphine Seyrig, narr; [bce]Philippa Davies, [e]Lenore Smith, fls; [a]Marcia Crayford, vn; [b]Roger Chase, va; [d]Christopher van Kampen, vc; [be]Marisa Robles, [e]Bryn Lewis, hps; Ian Brown, [ad]pf/[e]cel)/[e]**Lionel Friend**. Virgin Classics VC7 91148-2. Text and translation included.
Violin Sonata[a]. Sonata for Flute, Viola and Harp[b]. Syrinx[c]. Cello Sonata[d]. Chansons de Bilitis (1901)[e].

1h 8' DDD 4/91

The mystique that surrounds Debussy's late sonatas (six were intended but only three were completed before death intervened) sometimes inhibits performers from taking the music at its face value. These are direct, clean-boned compositions that benefit immeasurably from the sort of straightforward treatment they receive here from Philips. The Cello Sonata was written first, in 1915, and was followed later that year by the Sonata for Flute, Viola and Harp. The Violin Sonata was added, after a creative hiatus, in 1917 and, to some extent, it looks back to the clarity and single-mindedness that Debussy's earlier music exhibited. The flute solo, *Syrinx*, is an interloper, written in 1913 to illustrate Gabriel Mourey's *Psyche*. The playing on the Philips disc in all these works is a delight, never forced nor understated, but finding an easy balance of form and expression. The recording tidily defines the placing of the instruments across the soundstage whilst allowing just enough blending to provide a real sense of ensemble. If you've had trouble coming to terms with these works before, this disc should set you on the right path.

On the Virgin disc the sonatas receive sensitive and perceptive performances, but that of the one for flute, viola and harp (with each instrument retaining its individuality) is particularly compelling: truly affecting are the raptures of the Nash team's reading and the unaffected simplicity, "smiling through its tears", of its second movement. The 1914 war had spurred Debussy into labelling himself, proudly, as "musicien français", and the quasi-archaic, bare texture of the Cello Sonata was a symptom of his wish to evoke the glories of the golden age of French classicism. Christopher van Kampen proves himself an eloquent interpreter of it, and Marcia Crayford catches something of the elusive, intangible quality of the Violin Sonata, though the

| *Nash Ensemble* — *[photo: Virgin Classics/Vernon]*

placing of both artists (particularly the latter) in a rather hollow-sounding recording venue creates some problems of balance with their excellent pianist Ian Brown. There is a subtle, graceful sensuousness in Philippa Davies's performance. Also inspired by ancient Greece were the *Chansons de Bilitis* (written two years after Debussy's three songs of the same title), which consist of musical topping-and-tailing of a number of erotic poems, originally to accompany a performance of nude *tableaux vivants*: the music was later re-worked into the *Epigraphes antiques*. The quietly expressive reader here is the distinguished actress Delphine Seyrig, who died in October 1990: this recording is something in the nature of an *In memoriam*.

Debussy. String Quartet in G minor, Op. 10.
Ravel. String Quartet in F major. **Quartetto Italiano** (Paolo Borciani, Elisa Pegreffi, vns; Piero Farulli, va; Franco Rossi, vc). Philips Silver Line 420 894-2PSL. From SAL3643 (5/68).

57' ADD 10/88 £ Ⓑ

Coupling the Debussy and Ravel string quartets has become something of a cliché in the record industry, but these two masterpieces do make a very satisfying pair in which similarities and differences complement each other to advantage. Both composers were around 30 when they wrote them and the medium seems to have drawn from them something unusually personal and expressive which is especially intense in the slow movements, although there is ample colour and vitality in the scherzos and the brilliant finales. These performances by the Italian Quartet were hailed as superlative when they first appeared and although there have been others of comparable quality since then, this is still one of the finest of chamber music records and especially desirable at medium price. The CD transfer is excellent and catches all the nuances of the playing.

Debussy. Violin Sonata in G minor[a]. Sonata for flute, viola and harp[b].
Franck. Violin Sonata in A major[a].
Ravel. Introduction and Allegro[b]. [a]**Kyung Wha Chung** (vn); [b]**Osian Ellis** (hp); [a]**Radu Lupu** (pf); [b]**Melos Ensemble.** Decca 421 154-2DM. Items marked [a] from SXL6944 (9/80), [b] SOL60048 (9/62).

1h 7' ADD 1/90 £ ᵍ/P Ⓑ

This must be one of the best CD bargains around, with three masterpieces from the French tradition in excellent performances that have won the status of recording classics. Kyung Wha Chung and Radu Lupu are a fine duo who capture and convey the delicacy and poetry of the Franck Sonata as well as its rapturous grandeur, and never can the strict canonic treatment of the great tune in the finale have sounded more spontaneous and joyful. They are no less successful in the different world of the elusive Sonata which was Debussy's last work, with its smiles through tears and, in the finale, its echoes of a Neapolitan tarantella. The 1977 recording is beautifully balanced, with a natural sound given to both the violin and piano. The Melos Ensemble recorded the Ravel *Introduction and Allegro* 15 years before, but here too the recording is a fine one for which no allowances have to be made even by ears accustomed to good digital sound; as for the work itself, this has an ethereal beauty that is nothing short of magical and Osian Ellis and his colleagues give it the most skilful and loving performance. To talk about this disc as one for every collection savours of cliché, but anyone who does not have it may safely be urged to make its acquisition.

Debussy. Cello Sonata.
Martin. Ballade.
Poulenc. Cello Sonata. **William Conway** (vc); **Peter Evans** (pf). Linn
Records CKD002.

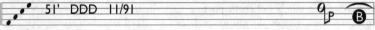

Debussy. Cello Sonata[a].
Schubert. Sonata in A minor, D821, "Arpeggione"[b].
Schumann. Fünf Stücke im Volkston, Op. 102[a]. **Mstislav Rostropovich**
(vc); **Benjamin Britten** (pf). Decca 417 833-2DH. Items marked [a] from
SXL6426 (10/70), [b] SXL2298 (1/62).

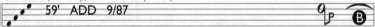

William Conway and Peter Evans enter a highly competitive arena with the
Debussy Cello Sonata, which emerges very favourably when compared with some
of the best versions on record. Many of the key figures of the French school of
cello playing have become closely identified with the work, and it is certainly an
achievement for any cellist to find his interpretation set alongside those of
Maurice Maréchal, Gendron, Rostropovich, Tortelier and Fournier! The
bewildering concentration of mood and imagery in Debussy's avowedly classical
15-minute sonata presents special challenges to the players, and Conway and
Evans have given much thought to its realization. Although they respond to every
passing bitter whim of the Pierrot ("Pierrot angry with the moon"), they also
offer animated virtuosity and brilliance in the central "Sérénade" section of this
problematic yet fascinating work. Poulenc completed his Cello Sonata in 1948,
and its richness of interest and graceful melodic charm are immediately appealing.
It is good, then, to find Conway and Evans on spirited form here in a work
which affords ample opportunities for display, in its witty three-movement
structure. Frank Martin dedicated his *Ballade* to the illustrious Pierre Fournier,
and this rarity reveals something of the results of the composer's studies with
Arnold Schoenberg. This fine recital disc was recorded in the UK at St George's
Church, Bristol, and the realism and immediacy of the sound, especially in the
Debussy, could hardly serve the needs of the music more effectively. Certainly a
disc for all cello devotees and one which will long continue to charm and
fascinate.

Benjamin Britten was also supremely gifted as conductor and pianist and on
the Decca disc we hear him interpreting the music of others. The Schubert
Sonata is an engaging work, whilst the five Schumann pieces have a rustic
simplicity and strength which these performers turn entirely to Schumann's
advantage. The main subtleties of Debussy's more intense, temperamental Sonata
reveal themselves only after many hearings. Britten and Rostropovich bring to all
these works a depth of understanding which is quite extraordinary. Certainly a
collector's item, this CD ought to be part of every chamber music collection.
The analogue recordings have transferred extremely well.

Debussy. MUSIC FOR TWO PIANOS. **Stephen Coombs, Christopher
Scott.** Hyperion CDA66468.
En blanc et noir. Prélude à l'après-midi d'un faune. Lindaraja. Trois nocturnes
(trans. Ravel). Danse sacrée et danse profane.

The number of works written for two pianos is small, perhaps because not many
concert venues past or present possess two good, well-matched instruments, and
masterpieces written for this combination of instruments is still smaller. But

| Debussy's suite *En blanc et noir* is certainly among them. Written in 1915 during

the First World War, it is one of his last works and its second movement evokes the grimness of a battle scene and is dedicated to the memory of a young friend recently killed in action. The other two movements sparkle with mysterious life, their mood elusive but compelling. Stephen Coombs and Christopher Scott are young artists who joined forces as duo pianists in 1985, and on the evidence of this playing they are extremely skilful and sensitive. This is a lovely performance, alert to every nuance of Debussy's thought. The other works are no less well done, and although with the exception of the brief Spanish-style *Lindaraja* they are all transcriptions rather than pieces originally written for two pianos, the playing is so good that we are able to forget the lack of an orchestra and enjoy them in this format. The recorded sound is admirable and atmospheric.

Debussy. Préludes — Books 1[a] and 2[b]. **Walter Gieseking** (pf). EMI Références mono CDH7 61004-2. Item marked [a] from Columbia 33CX1098 (1/54), [b] 33CX1304 (11/55).

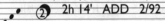

1h 10'   AAD   4/88   £ ⓠ℗ ▲

NEW REVIEW

Debussy. Préludes — Books 1[a] and 2[b]. Images[c] — Sets 1 and 2. Estampes[c].
Claudio Arrau. Philips 432 304-2PM2. Item marked [a] from 9500 676 (10/80), [b] 9500 747 (6/81), [c] 9500 965 (11/81).

② 2h 14'   ADD   2/92   ⓠ℗

Claudio Arrau   [photo: Philips

The Debussy *Préludes* have the rare distinction of appealing equally to the amateur and to the most sophisticated professional. And pianistic difficulty apart, their immediate charm as impressionistic evocations is as strong as the lasting fascination of their constructional intricacies. As repertoire pieces the technically more straightforward pieces demand considerable imaginative resources and tonal refinement, and Walter Gieseking was the epitome of this kind of artistry. His recordings of the *Préludes* have rightly remained touchstones for impressionist pianism. The subtlety of Gieseking's soft playing, his hypersensitive pedalling, his ability to separate textural strands and yet achieve an overall blended effect, are unsurpassed. Since the piano on these mid-1950s recordings is ideally regulated, since the recording quality is wholly acceptable and since both books of *Préludes* are accommodated on a single mid-price CD, it goes without saying that this is an exceptionally desirable issue.

In his two-disc set, also at medium price, Claudio Arrau offers not just the *Préludes* but also the earlier *Estampes*, Debussy's first step into a new impressionist world, and both books of *Images*. Arrau was already in his seventies when making these recordings, but his scrupulous regard for Debussy's every minute expressive marking reveals that the music was just as fresh in his mind as when he first discovered it. His range of dynamics and colouring extends from the magical fingertip delicacies of "Cloches à travers les feuilles" and "Et la lune descend sur le tempe qui fut" (both exquisitely played) to the full-bodied, opulent climaxes of pieces like "La cathédrale engloutie", "Pagodes" and "Mouvement", where his architectural shaping is no less impressive than his spellbinding atmospheric evocation throughout. Generous pedalling in a warm Philips acoustic makes for less translucent texture than we sometimes hear in this composer. Some listeners might occasionally prefer sharper-cut outlines, and now and again slightly faster — or tauter — tempo, as in "Danseuses de Delphes". But depth of sonority and spacious timing were always among this player's hallmarks, and again here he makes this music uniquely and unforgettably his own.

Debussy. PIANO WORKS. **Zoltán Kocsis.** Philips 412 118-2PH.
Suite bergamasque. Images oubliées. Pour le piano. Estampes.

55' DDD 4/85

Debussy. PIANO WORKS. **Zoltán Kocsis.** Philips 422 404-2PH.
Images, Books 1 and 2. D'un cahier d'esquisses. L'isle joyeuse. Deux arabesques. Hommage à Haydn. Rêverie. Page d'album. Berceuse héroïque.

1h 2' DDD 2/90

Three decades ago you could have counted on the fingers of one hand the performers who really had the measure of Debussy's piano style. Today there are many, but even so the Hungarian pianist Zoltán Kocsis stands out as especially idiomatic. On the first disc here, he plays four earlyish sets of pieces of which all but the *Suite bergamasque* are in the composer's favourite triptych form that he also used in *La mer*. The most 'classical' of them are the oddly titled *Pour le piano*, in which the Prelude echoes Bach's keyboard writing, and the *Suite bergamasque* with its eighteenth-century dances, but even in the latter work we find the composer's popular "Claire de lune" memorably impressionistic in its evocation of moonlight. In the *Estampes*, the last pieces played, he displayed a still more fully developed impressionism in musical pictures of the Far East, Moorish Spain and lastly a mysteriously rainswept urban garden. The rarity here is the *Images oubliées*, pieces dating from 1894 that Debussy left unpublished, doubtless because he reworked material from them in the *Estampes* and very obviously in the Sarabande of *Pour le piano*, but they are fine in their own right and here we can compare the different treatments of the similar ideas. Zoltán Kocsis brings refinement and brilliance to all this music and the piano sound is exceptionally rich and faithful.

The second Debussy recital by the same artist can be welcomed as a revealing portrait of the composer, its items discerningly offsetting the familiar with the less-known. It also brings playing not only of exceptional finesse, but at times of exceptional brilliance and fire. The main work is of course *Images*, its two sets completed in 1905 and 1907 respectively, by which time the composer was already master of that impressionistic style of keyboard writing so different from anything known before. For superfine sensitivity to details of textural shading Kocsis is at his most spellbinding in the first two numbers of the second set, "Cloches à travers les feuilles" and "Et la lune descend sur le temple qui fût". He is equally successful in reminding us of Debussy's wish to "forget that the piano has hammers" in the atmospheric washes of sound that he conjures (through his pedalling no less than his fingers) in *D'un cahier d'esquisses*. The sharp, clear daylight world of *L'isle joyeuse* reveals a Kocsis exulting in his own virtuosity and strength as he also does in the last piece of each set of *Images*, and even in the second of the two familiar, early *Arabesques*, neither of them mere vapid drawing-room charmers here. The recording is first rate. Both discs are highly recommendable.

Debussy. Etudes, Books 1 and 2; **Mitsuko Uchida** (pf). Philips 422 412-2PH.

47' DDD 7/90

Near the beginning of his career, Debussy's *Prélude à l'après-midi d'un faune* (1894) opened the door (so it is often said) for modern music. His late works, including three chamber sonatas and the set of twelve piano studies (1915), opened another door, through which perhaps only he could have stepped. But his death from cancer in 1918 at the age of 56 put paid to that prospect. The harmonic language and continuity of the *Studies* is elusive even by Debussy's standards, and it takes an artist of rare gifts to play them 'from within', at the same time as negotiating their finger-knotting intricacies. Mitsuko Uchida is such an artist. On first hearing perhaps rather hyperactive, her playing wins you over by its bravura and sheer relish, eventually disarming criticism altogether. This is not just the finest-ever recorded version of the *Studies*; it is also one of the finest examples of recorded piano playing in modern times, matched by sound quality of outstanding clarity and ambient warmth.

Debussy. MELODIES. **Anne-Marie Rodde** (sop); **Noël Lee** (pf). Etcetera KTC1048. Texts and translations included.
Jane. Caprice. Rondeau. Aimons-nous et dormons. La fille aux cheveux de lin. Calmes dans le demi-jour. Sept poèmes de Banville. Proses lyriques. Trois Poèmes de Stéphane Mallarmé.

53' DDD 4/88

Very few CDs so far have been devoted to Debussy's songs, but in any case this one is exceptional in that it includes six that he composed before the age of 20 and seven to poems by Thédore de Banville, of which this is the first recording. The sweetness and freshness of Anne-Marie Rodde's voice, her purity of intonation, her security in the high register, and not least her understanding of style and the exemplary clarity of her enunciation make her a near-ideal interpreter of this repertoire, and she is sympathetically and ably partnered by Noël Lee. In a few places the piano is on the loud side, but otherwise the recording is excellent.

NEW REVIEW
Debussy. Ariettes oubliées. Cinq poèmes de Charles Baudelaire. Chansons de Bilitis.
Ravel. Histoires naturelles. **Nathalie Stutzmann** (contr); **Cathérine Collard** (pf). RCA Victor Red Seal RD60899. Texts and translations included.

1h 7' DDD 7/92

Debussy's songs rarely insist: they suggest, sometimes with happiness, sometimes sorrow, and most often with something in between. The voice uses notes to express the meaning of words, and the pianist too must reflect the delicate nuances of the poem. Both shun exaggeration or anything conventionally operatic. All of this implies such skill, sensitivity and discipline in performance that it is not surprising to find complete success elusive. Nathalie Stutzmann and her pianist Cathérine Collard now join the select ranks, the singer's place among them being distinguished from the start by the richness and depth of her voice. Here is a rarity these days, a genuine contralto, and one who sings with all due restraint both in the deployment of her tone and in the force of her utterance. The deep voice gives unusual colouring to the *Ariettes oubliées*, while the Baudelaire settings are subtly varied and the sublimely erotic *Chansons de Bilitis* sung responsively but without self-conscious characterization. The recital ends with Ravel's witty settings of prose-sketches by Jules Renard: peacock, cricket, swan, kingfisher and guinea-fowl are depicted in turn, in performances that are vivid if perhaps a little too 'straight'. Altogether a most attractive programme, well presented and admirable in the quality of recorded sound.

Debussy. La damoiselle élue^a. Prélude à l'après-midi d'un faune. Images (1905-12) — No. 2, Ibéria. ^a**Maria Ewing** (sop) Damoiselle; ^a**Brigitte Balleys** (contr) Narrator; **London Symphony** ^a**Chorus and Orchestra/Claudio Abbado.** DG 423 103-2GH. Text and translation included.

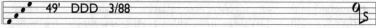
49' DDD 3/88

La damoiselle élue is scored for soprano, women's chorus and orchestra and sets verses from Dante Gabriel Rossetti's *The Blessed Damozel*. It is cast into four short movements and owes a clear debt to Wagner's *Parsifal*. The *Prélude à l'après-midi d'un faune* was Debussy's first real masterpiece and this evocation of Mallarmé's poem introduced a whole palette of new, supremely beautiful sounds, combining them into a musical structure both concise and subtly complex. Once heard it can never be forgotten. "Ibéria" is the central component of the orchestral set of *Images* and its three movements employ the rhythms and harmonies of Spanish music to conjure up a perfect picture of the Spanish/Mediterranean climate in its various moods. A fine Debussyan, Abbado penetrates to the heart of all these works and is given fine orchestral support throughout. Maria Ewing is an impressive Damoiselle and the women of the LSO chorus are in excellent voice. The recording is most successful, with good atmosphere and clarity.

NEW REVIEW

Debussy. PELLEAS ET MELISANDE. **Didier Henry** (bar) Pelléas; **Colette Alliot-Lugaz** (sop) Mélisande; **Gilles Cachemaille** (bar) Golaud; **Pierre Thau** (bass) Arkel; **Claudine Carlson** (contr) Geneviève; **Françoise Golfier** (sop) Yniold; **Philip Ens** (bass) Doctor, Shepherd; **Montreal Symphony Chorus and Orchestra/Charles Dutoit.** Decca 430 502-2DH2. Notes, text and translation included.

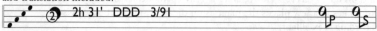
② 2h 31' DDD 3/91

NEW REVIEW

Debussy. PELLEAS ET MELISANDE. **Eric Tappy** (ten) Pelléas; **Rachel Yakar** (sop) Mélisande; **Philippe Huttenlocher** (bar) Golaud; **Jocelyne Taillon** (mez) Geneviève; **Colette Alliot-Lugaz** (sop) Yniold; **François Loup** (bass) Arkel; **Michel Brodard** (bass) Doctor, Shepherd; **Monte-Carlo National Opera Orchestra/Armin Jordan.** Erato Libretto 2292-45684-2. Notes, text and translation included. From STU71296 (10/80).

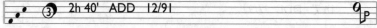
③ 2h 40' ADD 12/91

Maeterlinck's play was the inspiration for Debussy's sole masterpiece in the operatic genre. *Pelléas et Mélisande* tells of a medieval princess who falls in love with her husband Golaud's younger half-brother Pelléas, who is then killed by Golaud before Mélisande herself dies in childbirth. The story has a Wagnerian parallel in *Tristan und Isolde*, but the music is very different, being more restrained on the surface while suggesting no less powerful passions beneath. No modern performances have succeeded in replacing the classic versions conducted by Roger Desormière and Ernest Ansermet, both of which preserve a tradition of performing this elusive piece that has since been lost (the earlier of Desormière's Decca sets is due for reissue early in 1993 at medium price; the Ansermet has not been reissued). The carefully remastered 1941 Desormière recording sounds remarkably good considering it age. But it cannot, of course, compete with the wonderful achievement of this Dutoit version which has been lovingly recorded to reveal all aspects of Debussy's unique score. It boasts a cast of singers who have French as their native language and match text to music in a manner Debussy would surely have wanted. Alliot-Lugaz is adept at evincing Mélisande's strange nature. Didier Henry is a youthful, palpitating Pelléas. Cachemaille, though hard to distinguish from Henry, is a vividly tormented Golaud, Thau a suitably grave Arkel. Dutoit's handling of the score is sensitive, involved and secure. This is certainly one of the most satisfying modern versions of this undisputed materpiece currently available.

The second performance from France at once conjures up and then sustains the strange half-lit world of Maeterlinck's tale to which Debussy brought some of his most magical and memorable music. Despite the title, in some ways the chief role is that of Golaud, and Philippe Huttenlocher, who is a superb singer-actor, makes us believe in and feel for him. Rachel Yakar is mysterious, delicate and wholly feminine as Mélisande — indeed, sometimes maddeningly so, for in her passivity and reluctance to explain herself she positively invites Golaud's jealous suspicions. The role of Pelléas can be sung either by a high baritone or by a tenor: again it is the latter and Eric Tappy therefore sounds all the more youthful and innocent compared with the dark baritone quality of Golaud (he's supposed to be 20 years younger). The other principals have less to do but are also satisfying, not least the bass François Loup as the kindly old king, Arkel. The orchestra under Armin Jordan play as if inspired and the clear recording allows every word to be heard, which is what Debussy wanted but is hard to achieve in the theatre. One gladly agrees with the original *Gramophone* review which found this performance "profoundly moving" and it offer us a very agreeable mid-price alternative to the Dutoit performance.

Leo Delibes

French 1836-1891

Delibes. Sylvia — ballet suite[a]. Coppélia — ballet suite[b].
Gounod. FAUST — ballet music[a]. [a]**Budapest Philharmonic Orchestra/ János Sándor;** [b]**Berlin Radio Symphony Orchestra/Heinz Fricke.**
LaserLight 15 616. Item marked [b] from 10 073 (12/86).

57' DDD 5/90

There are some most attractive bargains to be found on various inexpensive CD labels, and this LaserLight collection provides an excellent example. It combines familiar suites from Delibes's two most popular ballet scores with the ballet music that Gounod composed for the Walpurgis Night scene of his opera *Faust*. The music is throughout supremely tuneful, always elegant, and mixing the grace and charm of, say, Delibes's ravishing waltzes with the liveliness of the Csárdás from *Coppélia* and some of the rousing *Faust* items. Whether it be Heinz Fricke and the Berlin Radio Symphony Orchestra in *Coppélia* or János Sándor and the Budapest Philharmonic in *Sylvia* or *Faust*, the interpretations are all finely judged, bringing out all that is natural in the music, without succumbing to the temptation to add extra, artificial excitement. The orchestral playing also is of a higher order of refinement. The recordings are all digital originals and are of splendid clarity, dynamic range and naturalness.

Delibes. Sylvia — ballet[a].
Massenet. LE CID — ballet music[b]. [a]**New Philharmonia Orchestra,** [b]**National Philharmonic Orchestra/Richard Bonynge.** Decca Ovation 425 475-2DM2. Item marked [a] from SXL6635/6 (6/74), [b] SXL6812 (11/76).

② 1h 58' ADD 1/90 £

If the scenario and Merante's choreography for *Sylvia* are somewhat lacking in inspiration, the same could hardly be said of Delibes's music for the ballet.

Richard Bonynge   [photo: Decca

"What charm, what elegance, what a wealth of melody, rhythm and harmony", Tchaikovsky was to write after hearing the score for the first time. With this work Delibes made a substantial advance in the lasting quality of ballet music, one that was then to be taken even further in the great masterworks of the genre by Tchaikovsky. First produced in Paris in 1876, *Sylvia* marked a new political age, the brilliance of the Second Empire which spawned *Coppélia* having recently collapsed to be replaced by a new republic. The exuberance of the earlier ballet, though still present in abundance, is now balanced by a unifying emotional undercurrent that suggests a more realistic awareness of the cost of joy.

The ballet from Massenet's opera, *Le Cid* (1885), bristles with those well-known tunes that are so often difficult to put a name to. If anything, the National Philharmonic are a touch more technically adroit here than are the New Philharmonia in the Delibes, where Richard Bonynge's hard-driven approach occasionally leaves the orchestra little space for subtlety in the quieter corners of the work. Nevertheless, both performances are first rate and excellent value.

Delibes. Coppélia — ballet. **National Philharmonic Orchestra/Richard Bonynge.** Decca 414 502-2DH2.

② 1h 32' DDD 12/86

Where other conductors may approach ballet recordings with the stage movements in mind, Bonynge sees them very much as an aural experience in their own right. He is ever ready to push the score along and provide all the excitement he can engender. For the armchair listener who may find some of the linking passages a shade tedious this may be just what is required. It may be that such numbers as the celebrated mazurka are approached a shade too aggressively and that the frequent recourse to *fortissimo* climaxes can become a shade wearying and obscure the native charm of a score such as this. On the other hand, orchestral effects such as those in the music of the automata come across with extra vividness, and set numbers such as the Act 2 "Boléro" and the "Valse des heures" achieve a quite thrilling effect. There is beautiful orchestral playing and the digital sound helps a great deal to create an overall effect of undemanding and rewarding listening.

Delibes. LAKME. **Dame Joan Sutherland** (sop) Lakmé; **Alain Vanzo** (ten) Gérald; **Gabriel Bacquier** (bar) Nilakantha; **Jane Berbié** (sop) Mallika; **Claud Calès** (bar) Frederick; **Gwenyth Annear** (sop) Ellen; **Josephte Clément** (sop) Rose; **Monica Sinclair** (contr) Miss Benson; **Emile Belcourt** (ten) Hadji; **Monte-Carlo Opera Chorus; Monte-Carlo National Opera Orchestra/Richard Bonynge.** Decca Grand Opera 425 485-2DM2. Synopsis, text and translation included. From SET387/9 (5/69).

② 2h 18' ADD 12/89

Like Pinkerton in *Madama Butterfly* (but not a cad like him), the British officer Gérald has succumbed to the exotic charm of the East: in particular, though engaged to a high-born English girl, he has become infatuated with the Brahmin priestess Lakmé, who returns his love, despite the fact that her father is bitterly hostile to the British and is plotting against them. A tragic outcome (with the help of a poisonous plant) is predictable: you might call this a Plain Tale from the Raj. This recording of Delibes's opera, though nearly 25 years old, still sounds fresh and clean. In Alain Vanzo it has a near-ideal lyric tenor hero; Gabriel Bacquier is suitably dark-hued as Lakmé's vengeful father; and in the title-role Joan Sutherland produces strikingly beautiful tone and seemingly effortless precision in florid passages (as in that famous showpiece the "Bell song"). Her words, however, are difficult to make out, owing to her weak consonants — a rare failing of hers, but one which her admirers have learnt to tolerate. In all other respects this is a very recommendable issue (especially at medium price).

Frederick Delius

British 1862-1934

Delius. Concerto for Violin and Orchestra. Suite. Légende. **Ralph Holmes** (vn); **Royal Philharmonic Orchestra/Vernon Handley.** Unicorn-Kanchana DKPCD9040. From DKP9040 (7/85).

53' DDD 9/85

NEW REVIEW

Delius. ORCHESTRAL WORKS. [a]**Tasmin Little** (vn); **Welsh National Opera Orchestra/Sir Charles Mackerras.** Argo 433 704-2ZH. Concerto for Violin and Orchestra[a]. Two Aquarelles. On hearing the first cuckoo in Spring. Summer Night on the River. FENNIMORE AND GERDA — Intermezzo. Irmelin Prelude. Dance Rhapsodies — Nos. 1 and 2.

1h 15' DDD 7/92

Two pleasing early works and a mature masterpiece make up the enterprising disc from Unicorn-Kanchana. The Suite is full of easy-going charm and the influence of Grieg is very much evident. This is the work's first (and only) recording. The *Légende* has also only been known in recent years, through Delius's own violin and piano reduction, since the original orchestral parts were lost. Fortunately the original manuscript survives and new parts have been copied. The late Ralph Holmes had a delightfully fresh and affectionate approach to both works, and the RPO and Handley lend him ideal support. In the complex and melodically inspired Violin Concerto Holmes gives an ardent, lyrical account of the solo part and Handley conducts with great sensitivity. A high quality recording captures ideally Delius's magical sound-world.

It is, however, the Argo disc of the Violin Concerto that you should play to friends who are not committed Delians; it is sure to persuade them that this concerto merits the same devotion as those by Elgar and Walton. Tasmin Little has the edge over Holmes (but only just) in coping with the work's technical difficulties; and under Mackerras's purposeful guidance, and with greater contrasts of pace between the various sections of its one movement form, the piece behaves more like a conventional concerto. If a certain amount of dream-like atmosphere is shed in the work's opening section in favour of classical rigour and vigour, at the heart of this account is the central accompanied cadenza: a minor miracle of flowing improvisation, with Mackerras and Little more freely rhapsodic than previous partnerships, and as twins in the seamless unfolding of the musical line. Argo's sound is more immediate, with a believable balance between soloist and orchestra, and better handling of the (albeit very few) orchestral climaxes. To the many shorter pieces that make up this disc's generous duration, only Beecham has brought a comparable feeling for texture and atmosphere. *Summer Night on the River*, in particular, is remarkable for its Debussian delicacy and the chamber-like intimacy of its sonorities.

Delius. Florida — suite. North Country Sketches. **Ulster Orchestra/Vernon Handley.** Chandos CHAN8413. From ABRD1150 (7/86).

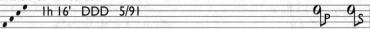

1h 7' DDD 12/86

Florida was Delius's first purely orchestral work and though a frankly derivative score, with scarcely a hint of the mature composer to be, it is skilful and attractive, with plenty of good tunes, including the well-known "La calinda". In a beautifully refined and detailed recording Handley unfolds the music easily and naturally, so that its natural warmth and charm speak to us very directly. The four *North Country Sketches*, by contrast, show the mature Delius at his very finest. Recalling youthful emotions inspired by the Yorkshire countryside, it is a work of extraordinary power and imagination. Handley is acutely sensitive to the score's numerous fine details and he understands the ebb and flow of the musical argument to perfection. He is particularly successful in achieving a good balance of textures during the climaxes and he is aided both by the refined playing of the Ulster Orchestra and the outstanding quality of recording.

Delius. Florida — suite. Paris: The Song of a Great City. Brigg Fair: An English Rhapsody. **Bournemouth Symphony Orchestra/Richard Hickox.** EMI CDC7 49932-2.

1h 16' DDD 5/91

NEW REVIEW

Delius. Paris: The Song of a Great City. Life's Dance. Dance Rhapsody No. 1. Piano Concerto[a]. [a]**Philip Fowke** (pf); **Royal Philharmonic Orchestra/ Norman Del Mar.** Unicorn-Kanchana DKPCD9108.

1h 17' DDD 3/92

NEW REVIEW

Delius. Paris: The Song of a Great City. Double Concerto[ab]. Cello Concerto[b]. [a]**Tasmin Little** (vn); [b]**Raphael Wallfisch** (vc); **Royal Liverpool Philharmonic Orchestra/Sir Charles Mackerras.** EMI Eminence CD-EMX2185.

1h 4' DDD 3/92

It has been suggested that we are in a new golden age of Delius recordings; a contention these three discs admirably bear out. Two years ago there were no stereo recordings available of Delius's *Paris*, and what these three recordings, in their different ways prove, is its status as Delius's first work of complete maturity. It is an extravagant nocturnal impression of the city where "Le grand anglais", as he was known to his friends (who included Gaugin and Eduard Munch) spent a decade of his life, during which he developed, as Eric Fenby put it, "a painter's sense of orchestral colour". Premièred in 1901 (the same year as Elgar's portrait of London, the *Cockaigne* Overture), it shows Delius relishing the full palette of his Staussian-sized orchestra to conjure an intoxicating merry-go-round of the city's night-life. Of our three contenders, Mackerras is the most physical, propelling the dancing to wild, whirling climaxes, and his balance engineers place us firmly among the excitement; Hickox, with his more opulent sounding orchestra, offers a view from the rooftops; while Del Mar's vision has grandeur and the deepest perspectives of all: Delius's own Paris (it could be by no one else) as a bygone era, the evocations coloured by distance and time.

Some 15 years earlier Delius, in his early twenties, left home to assume control of an orange plantation in Florida. Its sights and sounds, particularly of negro spirituals and dances, are incorporated in his "Tropical Scenes for Orchestra", the *Florida Suite*. Notwithstanding the echoes of Grieg and Dvořák (whose *New World* Symphony it predates by seven years), there are already characteristic Delian moods, not least in the saturated warmth, scenes of stillness and sense of wide open spaces; descriptions that are equally fitting for Hickox's EMI account of the work.

Grieg and Delius became friends and, a decade on, the former's influence in the Delius Piano Concerto is even more pronounced. But perhaps it was the Lisztian model that influenced them both. In common with the later concertos, it is a single movement work with fast and slow sections. Philip Fowke's immaculate and impassioned fingerwork, powerfully projected by Unicorn's up-front piano image is ideal for the moments of Lisztian bravura, and both he and Del Mar relax beautifully for the Griegian (and occasionally Delian) lyricism and romantic nostalgia. Some commentators have made the point that Delius's grappling with the traditional concerto form hindered his natural expression, and, with *Paris* dating from the same period as the Piano Concerto, it is difficult not to agree. The later concertos for violin (1916) and cello (1922) and the Double Concerto (1915) are all pure Delius, but have also been criticized for the soloists' dominance in what can seem like an unstructured rhapsodic outpouring of seamless melody. Their formal schemes are, in fact, supremely accomplished (close acquaintance with all three dispels any apparent waywardness of form), but as orchestral tuttis are a rare occurrence, enlivening contrasts of mood and texture are difficult to achieve. In the Cello Concerto, a personal favourite of Delius's, Raphael Wallfisch and Mackerras seek out the contrasts inherent in the score, and, for the first time on disc, its pervasive dreaminess is offset by faster decorative passages, and a genuine playfulness. In short, it dances as well as sings. They are joined by Tasmin Little for an account of the Double Concerto that has never before received teamwork of such confidence, security and unanimity of purpose. This Eminence disc is an essential acquisition for all Delians, especially at the modest asking price.

The Del Mar and Hickox discs both offer another Delian encounter with form (theme and variations) and show the wayfaring Delius responding, on this occasion, to images of his native land: nothing could be more English than the First *Dance Rhapsody*'s oboe theme. Philip Heseltine (Peter Warlock) described it as "bewitching", and its *Molto adagio* transformation in the penultimate variation as "wonderful, causing tears". A Lincolnshire folk-song provides the theme for *Brigg Fair* and Hickox's reading of this undisputed masterpiece is one of the supreme Delius recordings ever made. Time is suspended in the central interlude, a passage distilling the very essence of the English pastoral experience.

Delius. ORCHESTRAL WORKS. **Hallé Orchestra/Vernon Handley.** Classics for Pleasure CD-CFP 4568.
Brigg Fair — An English Rhapsody. In a Summer Garden. Eventyr. A Song of Summer.

56' DDD 8/90 £

Beecham laid a heavy interpretative hand on the scores of Delius, and the composer's approval of the results suggests that such adjustments of orchestral balance are essential to an idiomatic reading of this canon of works. Vernon Handley has latterly adopted Beecham's mantle in this respect, and has taken advantage of modern recording developments to lay down quite a number of the composer's chief works. His readings exalt both the hedonistic delight in life that much of Delius's music displays and intimations of the spiritual dimension that derive from the composer's pantheistic view of the world. This present disc represents remarkable value for money, combining as it does well-known works with some that few would claim to be on intimate terms with, all in a bargain package. The Hallé drive home all the points Handley wishes to make with an intuitive feel for the style and potential of the music. The recording has the fullness and clarity that is so typical of the venue, Manchester's Free Trade Hall, qualities that are normally so difficult to capture on tape. Clean CD transfers of 1981 originals make the disc doubly commendable.

NEW REVIEW

Delius. Sea Drift. Appalachia. **John Shirley-Quirk** (bar); **London Symphony Chorus; Royal Philharmonic Orchestra/Richard Hickox.** London 425 156-2LM. From ZRG934 (7/81).

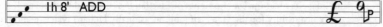

A desert island Delius disc if ever there was one: that is assuming you could cope on a desert island with *Sea Drift*'s subject matter — a sublime conjunction of poetry by Whitman and music describing love, loss and unhappy resignation, with the sea (as Christopher Palmer puts it) as "symbol and agent of parting". It is surely Delius's masterpiece: from the opening bars its spell is hypnotic and enduring, so much so that one is soon bereft of critical faculties. That must, in itself, be a tribute to the performance. Listened to with determinedly dry eyes, and ears on full scan (not easy), one could pin-point the occasional slightly imperfect pitching of the sopranos. But the taxing choral parts have never been more confidently and securely sung, and Shirley-Quirk's baritione is quite simply the noblest and most expressive the work has received on disc. *Appalachia* (the old American Indian name for North America) is a set of variations on an old Negro slave song. An earlier work (though its revision dates from 1902, the year preceding *Sea Drift*), Delius's Florida experience is here enriched by the master colourist and manipulator of the large orchestra that Delius became during his ensuing stay in Paris. This issue, recorded in 1980, is evidence that Hickox was then, as now, a perceptive and imaginative Delian; and (just as vital) that he had the full commitment of his performers. The sound has depth, warmth and brilliance in perfect proportion.

Beecham Conducts Delius. THE COMPLETE STEREO RECORDINGS. **Royal Philharmonic Orchestra/Sir Thomas Beecham.** EMI CDS7 47509–8. Items marked [a] from ASD357 (8/60), [b] ASD329 (9/60), [c] ASD518 (4/63), [d] SXLP30440 (10/80).
Over the Hills and Far Away (ed. Beecham)[b]. Sleigh Ride[a]. Irmelin — Prelude[c]. Dance Rhapsody No. 2[b]. Summer Evening (ed. and arr. Beecham)[c]. Brigg Fair: An English Rhapsody[a]. On hearing the first Cuckoo in Spring[a]. Summer Night on the River[a]. A Song before Sunrise[a]. Marche Caprice[a]. Florida Suite (ed. and arr. Beecham)[b]. Songs of Sunset (with Maureen Forrester, contr; John Cameron, bar; Beecham Choral Society)[d]. Fennimore and Gerda — Intermezzo (ed. and arr. Beecham)[a].

The names of Frederick Delius and Sir Thomas Beecham are inseparable. In the early days of Beecham's career it was Delius who convinced him that his role in life was not as pianist or composer, but as a conductor. Beecham was to more than repay his debt to the composer, for not only did he become Delius's uniquely understanding advocate, but helped to establish him as a major twentieth-century composer. The present set bears eloquent testimony in offering all the orchestral music (plus the *Songs of Sunset*) which Beecham recorded in stereo. Beecham's affinity with Delius was both instinctive and inspirational — the composer seldom made practical suggestions to him, yet expressed total

Sir Thomas Beecham   [photo: EMI

satisfaction with the conductor's magical phrasing and natural pacing. Beecham was a master of balance and this is perhaps a major reason why these early stereo recordings produce such beautiful textures of sound. Because Delius was a skilful miniaturist the shorter pieces are completely enchanting, from the veiled strings and luminous woodwind which draw a delicate watercolour of the *First cuckoo in Spring*, to the sultry, even sentient, atmosphere of *Summer Night on the River*, glowing like an impressionistic painting, while the *Sleigh Ride* has a twinkling piquancy. But it is Delius's masterpiece, *Brigg Fair*, that one remembers most of all. Here the Delian rapture is wonderfully evoked at the opening with the plaintive oboe's pastoral piping answered by the softly pliant flute. Throughout, the orchestral playing is quite marvellous and at the centre, the long-breathed string melody, finally echoed by the horn, has an unforgettable lazy somnambulance redolent of an idyllic English summer afternoon. The *Florida Suite* was written on an American orange plantation and it introduces one of the composer's most famous dance tunes, *La calinda*. Deliciously orchestrated, its mood changes from delicacy to robust high spirits, with the piece ending with a languorous horn solo. This collection presents us with a special kind of musical ecstasy, essentially innocent and wonderfully refined, which no one has since matched.

Delius. THE FENBY LEGACY. **Royal Philharmonic Orchestra/Eric Fenby.** Unicorn-Kanchana DKPCD9008/09. Texts included where appropriate. From DKP9008/09 (10/81).
Songs of Farewell (with Ambrosian Singers). Idyll (Felicity Lott, sop; Thomas Allen, bar). Fantastic Dance. A Song of Summer. Cynara (Allen). Irmelin Prelude. A Late Lark (Anthony Rolfe Johnson, ten). La calinda (arr. Fenby). Caprice and Elegy (Julian Lloyd Webber, vc). Two Aquarelles (arr. Fenby). FENNIMORE AND GERDA — Intermezzo (new to UK).

② 1h 45' DDD 12/87

It was Fenby's visit to the home of Delius in rural France that re-established the stricken composer's link with the outside world. Fenby became Delius's amanuensis and the tangible results of his French visit are offered here on a pair of CDs which make a perfect supplement to Beecham's EMI set. The *Irmelin* Prelude is the most famous but the most important are the more ambitious and equally evocative *Song of Summer*, and the *Songs of Farewell* set to words from his favourite American poet, Walt Whitman. The characteristically opaque choral textures tend to obscure the words at times, but this is of relatively small importance for Delius was mainly concerned with the sounds and colours of intertwining his ambitious chorus and equally large orchestra. The *Idyll* is an ardent love duet and its erotic element is in no doubt. The other orchestral pieces are characteristically appealing Delian miniatures, played with passionately romantic feeling and a real sense of ecstasy by the RPO; while in the choral music Fenby achieves the richest colours and wonderfully hushed *pianissimos*.

Delius. ORCHESTRAL SONGS. [a]**Felicity Lott** (sop); [b]**Sarah Walker** (mez); [c]**Anthony Rolfe Johnson** (ten); [d]**Ambrosian Singers; Royal Philharmonic Orchestra/Eric Fenby.** Unicorn-Kanchana DKPCD9029. Notes and texts included. From DKP9029 (12/84).

The song of the high hills[d]. Twilight fancies[b]. Wine roses[b]. The bird's story[a]. Let springtime come[a]. Il pleure dans mon coeur[c]. Le ciel est, par dessus le toit[a]. La lune blanche[c]. To Daffodils[b]. I-Brasil[c].

56' DDD 3/85   ♪ᵖ ♪ₛ

NEW REVIEW

Delius. ORCHESTRAL SONGS AND INSTRUMENTAL WORKS. [a]**Felicity Lott** (sop); [b]**Sarah Walker** (mez); [c]**Anthony Rolfe Johnson** (ten); [d]**Eric Fenby,** [e]**Eric Parkin** (pfs). Unicorn-Kanchana Souvenir UKCD2041. Texts and translations included.

Twilight Fancies[bd]. The Violet[ad]. In the Seraglio Garden[ad]. Silken Shoes[cd]. Autumn[bd]. Sweet Venevil[ad]. Irmelin Rose[ad]. Let Springtime Come[bd]. Il pleure dans mon coeur[cd]. Le ciel est pardessus le toit[ad]. La lune blanche[cd]. Chanson d'automne[bd]. Avant que tu ne t'en ailles[ad]. To Daffodils[bd]. So sweet is she[cd]. I-Brasil[cd] (all from DKP9022, 3/84). Three Preludes[e]. Zum Carnival — polka[e] (both from DKP9021, 7/83).

51' DDD 10/91   ♪ᵖ

The song of the high hills is one of Delius's most original masterpieces. Scored for a large orchestra and chorus it evokes with extraordinary power and beauty the grandeur and the spirit of nature. Eight of the nine songs with orchestra were scored by the composer himself, and *To Daffodils* was orchestrated by Eric Fenby. They all reflect in one manner or another Delius's favourite theme of the transience of love. The soloists are admirable, but Sarah Walker's three contributions are particularly perceptive. Fenby and the RPO accompany with total understanding and the recording is superlative.

On the second CD, there is some duplication of songs which these same artists went on to record with orchestral accompaniment a year or so later. Possibly Fenby's technical limitations influenced the choice of mainly slow songs in this recital, though the poetry (and undoubted authority) of 'the Fenby touch' provides accompaniments for these superb singers to give of their considerable best. Uniformity of mood is offset by the alternating voices; the settings which vary between German, French and English; and if Delius was not interested in exploiting piano sonority *per se*, the orchestral intention of the accompaniment has been enhanced by engineering that presents the piano spatially across the stereo spectrum. Indeed, compensation lies in the fact that the solo instrument lays bare Delius's unique harmonic idiom in the later songs. Eric Parkin's account of the four short solo piano pieces round off a modestly priced disc that has obviously been made with love and dedication.

Delius. A VILLAGE ROMEO AND JULIET. **Arthur Davies** (ten) Sali; **Helen Field** (sop) Vreli; **Thomas Hampson** (bass) The Dark Fiddler; **Barry Mora** (bar) Manz; **Stafford Dean** (bass) Marti; **Samuel Linay** (treb) Sali as a child; **Pamela Mildenhall** (sop) Vreli as a child; **Arnold Schönberg Choir; Austrian Radio Symphony Orchestra/Sir Charles Mackerras.** Argo 430 275-2ZH2. Notes and text included.

② 1h 51' DDD 12/90   ♪ᵖ

This was one of the recordings with which the Argo label was re-launched and very distinguished it proved to be. *A Village Romeo and Juliet* is the Delius opera that has held the stage while his others have appeared from time to time as curiosities. The reasons are twofold: it is dramatically the strongest and musically the most inspired. There have been two previous complete recordings (one conducted by Beecham), but this is incomparably the best, not least because the recording quality itself is so high. It was made in Vienna, with an Austrian orchestra and choir; the latter's English is impeccable. It would be insular to regard this work as English music, for it belongs to the 1900 ambience of Strauss and Mahler and that no doubt is why this cosmopolitan performance is so idiomatic. Sir Charles Mackerras conducts the opera with total authority and understanding. He demonstrates that to inspire orchestral playing as subtle and sensuous as this was not Beecham's Delian prerogative only. As the two young lovers who choose death rather than this world's worldliness, Helen Field and Arthur Davies are ideally cast, the soprano in particular giving a lustrous and moving performance. As The Dark Fiddler, the enigmatic figure whose claim to a disputed strip of land is the lynchpin of the plot, the American baritone Thomas Hampson is first-rate. The final scene of the opera, with the lovers' duet and the distant voices of "the travellers passing by", is magical as music, performance and recording.

David Del Tredici

American 1937-

Del Tredici. Steps[a] (1990). Haddock's Eyes[b] (1985). [b]**David Tel Tredici** (pf); [b]**Susan Naruki** (sop); [b]**Claire Bloom** (narr); [a]**New York Philharmonic Orchestra;** [b]**New York Philharmonic Ensemble/Zubin Mehta.** New World NW80390-2.

54' DDD

The (extraordinary) music of David Del Tredici has had relatively little exposure on disc so far, which is rather surprising given the approachability and melodious-ness of its style. Del Tredici first came to public attention in 1976 when Solti conducted the first performance of *Final Alice* — a large and colourful mono-drama scored for amplified soprano and orchestra. The subject matter of *Final Alice* — Lewis Carroll's *Alice in Wonderland* — has become an almost singular preoccupation with Del Tredici since 1968 and has formed the inspiration to nearly all of his compositions since. *Steps* for orchestra is an exception, though even here something of the surreal, dream-like quality of the *Alice* stories permeates this fascinating and richly imaginative score. *Steps* is cast in one movement, divided into four interconnected sections: "Giant Steps", "The Two-Step", "Giant Giant Steps" and "Stepping Down" and has been described by Del Tredici as "a monster — violent, powerful, inexorable ... my most dissonant tonal piece". Mehta and the New York Philharmonic give a stun-ningly virtuosic performance of this 'jabberwocky' of a piece and make a strong case for Del Tre-dici as one of America's most imaginative living composers. *Haddock's Eyes*, if the title hasn't already given it away, is one of Del Tredici's many 'Alice'-inspired works, and is a wonder-fully affectionate setting of the "White Knight's Song" from *Through the Looking-Glass* scored for soprano, narrator and chamber

Zubin Mehta *[photo:Teldec/Steiner*

ensemble. Susan Naruki's performance is a real *tour-de-force* as she spills out Carroll's words and Del Tredici's music in an ever and ever increasing hysterical frenzy. A marvellous introduction to the music of this fascinating American composer.

François Devienne   *French 1759-1803*

NEW REVIEW

Devienne. OBOE SONATAS. **Peter Bree** (ob); **Roderick Shaw** (fp). Etcetera KTC1106.
G minor, Op. 23 No. 3; C major, Op. 71 No. 3; G major, Op. 71 No. 1; D minor, Op. 71 No. 2.

1h 2' DDD 12/91

This little-known French composer was a contemporary of Mozart and it is good to make his acquaintance here. He was a wind player, though a flautist rather than an oboist, and wrote a large amount of music (including 12 concertos for flute, four for bassoon and several comic operas) before dying insane at 44. On the evidence of these four oboe sonatas, he was a man of his time who accepted the moods and structures of classicism but was aware of the new feelings coming into music in post-Revolution France and elsewhere: after all, Beethoven's *Moonlight* Sonata was written in his lifetime, though it is unlikely that he knew it. The romantic element is strongest in the slow movements, with their long and richly expressive phrases. These are played by Peter Bree with feeling as well as tonal beauty, and he brings wit and fantasy too to movements such as the *Presto* finales of the D minor and G minor Sonatas and the set of variations that ends the one in C major. Bree comes from Holland, which is also the country to which Roderick Shaw emigrated after studying at Cambridge. They play admirably as a team and both instruments sound right for this music, with the German fortepiano that is used being free of clattery quality. The recording, made in Munich, balances the oboe forwardly, but few will mind that when the playing is so good. The artists contribute an informative booklet note.

Franco Donatoni   *Italian 1927-*

Donatoni. Tema[a]. Cadeau[a].
Ligeti. Six Etudes, Book 1[b]. Trio for violin, horn and piano[c]. [bc]**Pierre-Laurent Aimard** (pf); [c]**Maryvonne Le Dizès-Richard** (vn); [c]**Jacques Deleplancque** (hn); [a]**Ensemble Intercontemporain/Pierre Boulez.** Erato 2292-45366-2.

1h 8' DDD 4/90

It's quite rare for a disc of recent music to present that often intimidating phenomenon in as appealing a manner as this one. Both composers are in their sixties, and Ligeti, the best-known of the two, is represented by two of his better later scores. The Horn Trio is perfectly conceived for this strange, Brahms-inspired combination, and Ligeti makes no technical or expressive compromises. This is music of diverse and at times dark emotions, its contrasts threatening to burst the bounds of its well-defined structures. The *Etudes* also marry technical sophistication with emotional depth, especially the staggering No. 6, "Autumn in Warsaw". Donatoni's music has been relatively rarely heard in recent years, but the two works from the 1980s recorded here reveal an infectious vitality and confidence, an infallible ear for novel sonority married to a trenchant command of well-balanced forms and an abundance of well-shaped, often witty ideas. Both pieces were written for the Ensemble Intercontemporain, and they reward the composer with highly expert performances — not that the Ligeti pieces lack this expertise either. The recording as such is very fine, even if the problems of balance created by the Horn Trio have necessitated a less natural sound than is evident elsewhere on the disc.

Gaetano Donizetti

Italian 1797-1848

NEW REVIEW

Donizetti. IMELDA DE' LAMBERTAZZI. **Floriana Sovilla** (sop) Imelda; **Andrea Martin** (bar) Bonifacio; **Diego D'Auria** (ten) Lamberto; **Fausto Tenzi** (ten) Orlando; **Gastone Sarti** (bar) Ubaldo; **Chorus and Orchestra of Swiss-Italian Radio and Television/Marc Andreae.** Nuova Era 6778/9. Notes, text and translation included.

② 2h 2' DDD 10/91

Donizetti's most original opera before *Anna Bolena* in the opinion of William Ashbrook, *Imelda de' Lambertazzi* tells of lovers kept asunder by the wars of the Guelphs and Ghibellines. Nothing particularly original about that perhaps, but it does come as something of a surprise to find that the hero is a baritone. The tenor is Imelda's brother, the bass her father, both implacably opposed to her union with Bonifacio, whose father killed her mother. The final catastrophe occurs when Bonifacio has been poisoned and Imelda tries to suck out the fatal substance. She is duly poisoned too and, rejected by her family, dies what is claimed to be the first death actually to take place on stage. Happily, the music has several points of interest and indeed some touches of inspiration. Particularly fine is the duet for Imelda and her brother in Act 2, and this also has some of the best singing, the general level of which is not that high. Most regrettable is the casting of the baritone role; Andrea Martin appears to have neither the voice nor the style for it. Still, the opportunity to hear this opera is not one to miss. It appeals at various levels, including the unintentionally comic, as when choruses telling of the sorrows of civil war and such matters swing along to a catchy tune which might almost come out of *The Pirates of Penzance*. The performance was given at Lugano "in oratorio form", and the recorded sound is more full-bodied than several in this company's catalogue.

Donizetti. L'ELISIR D'AMORE. **Katia Ricciarelli** (sop) Adina; **José Carreras** (ten) Nemorino; **Domenico Trimarchi** (bar) Dulcamara; **Leo Nucci** (bar) Belcore; **Susanna Rigacci** (sop) Giannetta; **Turin Radio Symphony Chorus and Orchestra/Claudio Scimone.** Philips 412 714-2PH2. Notes, text and translation included. From 412 714-1PH2 (2/86).

② 2h 7' DDD 6/86

The plot of *L'elisir d'amore* is a variant of the much used theme of the fake love potion. Here the potion is pedalled in a Basque village by the charlatan Doctor Dulcamara and purchased by the shy young Nemorino to help him win the love of the village girl Adina. Donizetti composed the score at high speed, and his burst of creative activity resulted in a piece of tremendous fluency and immensely fertile melodic invention. With his tender, smooth vocal production, Carreras is ideal for the part of Nemorino, culminating in a beautiful performance of the aria "Una furtiva lagrima" at the point where he finds he has truly won Adina's affection. As Adina, Katia Ricciarelli produces an equally affecting, properly

Italianate performance. Indeed the genuinely Italianate style is an aspect of the performance as a whole, and an important one in such a charmingly intimate piece as this. As Sergeant Belcore, Nemorino's rival for Adina's affections, Leo Nucci offers a performance full of verve and fun, and Domenico Trimarchi is a splendidly swaggering Doctor Dulcamara. Claudio Scimone paces the work excellently, displaying a light, buoyant touch and chorus and orchestra are splendidly full-blooded. The recorded sound is natural and open, and each act is commendably contained on a single disc of generous running time. Anyone who does not know this opera should remedy the omission forthwith. Anyone who does should need no further urging.

Donizetti. LUCIA DI LAMMERMOOR. **Dame Joan Sutherland** (sop) Lucia; **Luciano Pavarotti** (ten) Edgardo; **Sherrill Milnes** (bar) Enrico; **Nicolai Ghiaurov** (bass) Raimondo; **Huguette Tourangeau** (mez) Alisa; **Ryland Davies** (ten) Arturo; **Pier Francesco Poli** (ten) Normanno; **Royal Opera House Chorus and Orchestra, Covent Garden/Richard Bonynge.** Decca 410 193-2DH3. Notes, text and translation included. From SET528/30 (5/72).

♪ ③ 2h 20' ADD 11/85   𝄞 P

Donizetti. LUCIA DI LAMMERMOOR. **Maria Callas** (sop) Lucia; **Giuseppe di Stefano** (ten) Edgardo; **Tito Gobbi** (bar) Enrico; **Raffaele Arié** (bass) Raimondo; **Anna Maria Canali** (mez) Alisa; **Valiano Natali** (ten) Arturo; **Gino Sarri** (ten) Normanno; **Maggio Musicale Fiorentino Chorus and Orchestra/Tullio Serafin.** EMI mono CMS7 69980-2. Notes, text and translation included. From Columbia 33CX1131/2 (3/54).

♪ ② 1h 51' ADD 10/89   𝄞 P ▲

Donizetti. LUCIA DI LAMMERMOOR. **Maria Callas** (sop) Lucia; **Giuseppe di Stefano** (ten) Edgardo; **Rolando Panerai** (bar) Enrico; **Nicola Zaccaria** (bass) Raimondo; **Luisa Villa** (mez) Alisa; **Giuseppe Zampieri** (ten) Arturo; **Mario Carlin** (ten) Normanno; **Chorus of La Scala, Milan; Berlin RIAS Symphony Orchestra/Herbert von Karajan.** EMI mono CMS7 63631-2. Recorded at a performance in the Berlin State Opera on September 29th, 1955.

♪ ② 1h 59' ADD 2/91   𝄞 P ▲

Donizetti's rousing *Lucia di Lammermoor* is the greatest of his serious operas, a jewel of Italian *bel canto* writing and one of the great survivors of all changes of operatic fashion. Most notably it has the celebrated mad scene with which Sutherland made her name in 1959. Here she is at her most ravishing, with her firm, limpid soprano performing vocal acrobatics that surely cannot fail to thrill, encompassing notes that defy belief. She is supported by a remarkably fine team of singers, including one of the great tenors of our age at a relatively early stage in his career. Decca have provided a suitably clear recording to enhance the general effect, and use a music text that is absolutely complete yet not a moment too long.

Serafin was the conductor who had played such a crucial part in establishing Callas's full potential, Despite the ups-and-downs of their relationship, di Stefano was 'her' tenor, and with Gobbi she made several of the most dramatic of all duets on records. In this opera she had some of the greatest triumphs of her career, and in doing so restored to favour a whole school of opera that had come to be regarded as passé. This was 1953, and her voice had passages of rare beauty as we hear in the Love Duet, "Verranno a te", and "Soffriva nel pianto" in Act 2. The solos in Act 1 and the famous Mad Scene have that dramatic vividness and depth of feeling which at the time came as such a revelation. And, as always with Callas, any phrase of recitative is liable to go to the heart with an intensity no less penetrating than that of the great arias.

The 1955 Berlin Festival recording provides a genuine extension of the Callas Lucia known to listeners through the above studio performances. The Fountain scene is still subtler in its shadings, the verse in "Verranno a te" still more affecting in its simplicity. The Mad scene has more space and the contrasts of tone have richer dramatic effect. Di Stefano, too, sings like one inspired, and Karajan conducts with real love for the music. The recorded sound is vivid and faithful apart from an occasional distortion of upper notes. Though the applause is restricted, one knows that the spirit of deep enjoyment is abroad in the house and that when people refer to this as a "legendary performance" there is, for once, no need to reach for the salt-cellar.

NEW REVIEW

Donizetti. GIANNI DI PARIGI. **Giuseppe Morino** (ten) Gianni; **Luciana Serra** (sop) Principessa di Navarra; **Angelo Romero** (bar) Steward; **Elena Zilio** (mez) Oliviero; **Enrico Fissore** (bar) Pedrigo; **Silvana Manga** (sop) Lorezza; **Chorus and Orchestra of RAI, Milan/Carlo Felice Cillario.** Nuova Era 6752/3. Notes, text and translation included.

② 2h 3' DDD 10/91

The title-role in this early comedy of Donizetti's was written for the great tenor Rubini who, it appears, never sang it himself and pocketed the score so that nobody else should do so. It did reappear a couple of times in Donizetti's lifetime but had no success and remained unseen and unheard till the "Donizetti and his Time" Festival at Bergamo in 1988. The story is thin and the characters are pasteboard, but the music sparkles: it is a score full of attractive numbers and more than worth the rediscovery. It concerns a meeting at a country inn of the Princess of Navarre and the amiable Gianni of Paris, introduced as "un onesto borghese" but in reality the son of Philip de Valois. She pretends not to recognize him but likes him all the same, and a good deal of merriment arises out of nothing very much. There are some tuneful choruses with Rossinian crescendoes; an excellent "breakfast" duet for the tenor and buffo-bass enlivens the start of Act 2; and the arias and duets for soprano and tenor are models of grace and charm, provided that these qualities are also present in the singers. The Rubini-role is sung by a tenor who does indeed sometimes remind one of those late nineteenth-century Italian lyric tenors who lived just in time to be recorded: he is Giuseppe Morino, his voice marked by a quick vibrato, his style always sensitive and occasionally exquisite. Luciana Serra as the Princess is reputedly Italy's leading soprano leggiero (not as reassuring a recommendation as it should be). On the whole, the performance goes well and is recorded vividly enough to capture the sense of zest and pleasure in the old score happily new-found.

Donizetti. LA FILLE DU REGIMENT. **Dame Joan Sutherland** (sop) Marie; **Luciano Pavarotti** (ten) Tonio; **Spiro Malas** (bass) Sulpice; **Monica Sinclair** (contr) Marquise of Berkenfield; **Jules Bruyère** (bass) Hortensius; **Eric Garrett** (bar) Corporal; **Edith Coates** (contr) Duchess of Crakentorp; **Alan Jones** (ten) Peasant; **Chorus and Orchestra of the Royal Opera House, Covent Garden/Richard Bonynge.** Decca 414 520-2DH2. Notes, text and translation included. From SET373/4 (11/68).

② 1h 47' ADD 11/86

This is one of those obliging operas which allow you to forget just how many tuneful and charming melodies they contain, thus affording the delight of surprised recognition. On record the good humour comes through without too much underlining, and the *bravura* singing (dazzling flights of scales, staccatos, trills and high notes) puts a brilliant shine on the whole entertainment. Pavarotti has a full share in this: his solo "Ah, mes amis" is one of the most celebrated tenor recordings ever made. As so often with Sutherland one misses a firm singing-line in the simpler melodies, and there is also the depressing pronunciation, where 'fait' sounds like 'feu' and 'coquette' sounds like 'coquutte'. Still, there is much to be marvelled at, much to enjoy; a performance and an opera not to be missed.

Donizetti. DON PASQUALE. **Sesto Bruscantini** (bar) Don Pasquale; **Mirella Freni** (sop) Norina; **Leo Nucci** (bar) Dr Malatesta; **Gösta Winbergh** (ten) Ernesto; **Guido Fabbris** (ten) Notary; **Ambrosian Opera Chorus; Philharmonia Orchestra/Riccardo Muti.** EMI CDS7 47068-2. Notes, text and translation included. From SLS143436 (4/84).

② 2h 3' DDD 8/88

Mirella Freni   *[photo: EMI*

In this delightful opera Donizetti's inspiration is unfaltering, and he manages to combine sentiment and comedy in equal proportions. The somewhat hard-hearted treatment of old Pasquale's weakness for the lovely Norina, and the ruse she and Malatesta play on him are eventually dissolved in the triumph of love over cynicism. Riccardo Muti is a stickler for fidelity to the score, playing it complete and insisting on his cast singing the written notes and nothing else. Donizetti blossoms under such loving treatment. It is a reading, brisk and unvarnished, that demands one's attention throughout, and the playing of the Philharmonia is splendidly vital.

As Pasquale, Bruscantini sings with the benefit of long experience in defining line and words. Leo Nucci sings a smiling, resourceful Malatesta, at once Pasquale's friend and the author of the trick played on him. Gösta Winbergh is an accurate and fluent Ernesto, and Mirella Freni, the Norina, delivers her difficult aria with all her old sense of flirtatious fun: but when the joke has gone too far, she finds just the plaintive tone to express Norina's doubts and regret.

John Dowland
British c.1563-1626

Dowland. Lachrimae, or Seaven Teares. **Dowland Consort/Jakob Lindberg** (lte). BIS CD315. From LP315 (10/86).

1h 6' 12/86

John Dowland was described by a contemporary as "a cheerful person" but the darker side of his nature is evident in many of his works. In *Lachrimae, or Seaven Teares* he constructed seven marvellous pavans based on its opening motif and set for five viols and lute. They are followed by 14 other compositions, some of which bear dance titles whilst others are dedicated to particular persons. The melancholy consequences of technical inadequacy often suffered by viol consorts are entirely absent here and the problem of balancing the lute is solved to perfection in this marvellous recording. If Renaissance music were to be represented by only one disc it should perhaps be this one.

NEW REVIEW

Dowland. LUTE WORKS. **Robin McFarlane** (lte). Dorian DOR90148. Fantasie. P1a. Pipers Pavan, P8. Semper Dowland semper dolens, P9. Dr Cases Paven, P12. Lachrimae, P15. Captaine Digorie Piper his Galliard, P10. Dowlands Galliarde, P21. Frogg Galliard, P23a. Melancoly Galliard, P25. Doulands Rounde Battele Galliard, P39. Queene Elizabeth, her Galliard, P41. The Earl of Essex, his Galliard, P42a. The Lady Cliftons Spirit, P45. Sir John Smith his Almaine, P47. The Lady Laitones Almone, P48a. My Lady Hunsdons Puffe, P54. Mistris Winters Jumpe, P55. Mrs Whites Nothing, P56. The Shoemaker's Wife, P58. Tarletones riserrectione, P59. Orlando sleepeth, P61. Fortune, P62. Go from my windowe, P64. My Lord Willobes Wellcome Home, P66. What if a day, P79. Mr Dowland's Midnight, P99. Prelude, P102. A Fancy.

Ih 7' DDD 4/92 ❓

John Dowland wrote over 100 items for solo lute, covering every type of piece — even, a rarity at that time, a Preludium [*sic*]. Robin McFarlane's programme includes two each of the magnificent Fantasies and sets of variations but concentrates on the dance and 'character' pieces, many of them respectfully dedicated to people from whom he may have hoped for favours, though two dedications are enigmatic: Queen Elizabeth was already dead when her rather small-scale Galliard was written, and Digorie Piper was a pirate. The gift of memorable melody which marks his lute songs is no less evident in the lute solos, some of which (for instance, *Lachrimae* and *The Earl of Essex, his Galliard*) exist in both vocal and instrumental forms, and *Tarletones riserrectione* is a positive gem. This music was not meant to be played rigidly to the metronome (even if it had existed at that time!) and McFarlane avails himself of the freedom to use a measure of a rubato that humanizes the music. Dowland was the greatest lutenist of his day and this is reflected in the difficulty of many of the items, but McFarlane has nimble enough fingers to conceal the problems; this is just as well since the close recording would have revealed the slightest lapse. Recommended as a happy cross-section of this remarkable and rewarding repertory.

Dowland. SONGS. **Nigel Rogers** (ten); **Paul O'Dette** (lte). Virgin Classics Veritas VC7 90726-2. Texts included.
The First Booke of Songes — Come away, come sweet love; Come heauy sleepe; Wilt thou unkind thus reaue me of my hart:; If my complaints could passions moue; My thoughts are wingd with hopes; Awake sweet loue thou art returnd. The Second Booke of Songs — Sorow sorow stay, lend true repentant teares; Fine knacks for ladies; Flow my teares; Shall I sue, shall I seeke for grace?; I saw my Lady weepe. The Third and Last Booke of Songs — When Phoebus first did Daphne loue; Say loue if euer thou didst finde; Fie on this faining, is loue without desire; Weepe you no more, sad fountaines. A Pilgrimes Solace — Loue those beames that breede; Sweete stay a while, why will you: To aske for all thy loue; Were euery thought an eye; Shall I striue with wordes to moue.

Ih II' DDD II/88

The contents of Dowland's three *Bookes of Songes* and *A Pilgrimes Solace*, some 85 items, form the heart of the English lute-song repertoire, unexcelled expressions of the full gamut of human emotions — that of carnal desire is clothed in discreetly poetic terms. Nigel Rogers and Paul O'Dette cover the emotional range in their cross-section of all four sources. The lute accompaniments are not mere backcloths but integral parts of the musical texture; Dowland doubtless performed the songs single-handed, as do some of today's artists, but when singer and lutenist are not the same person each can concentrate on his/her own (often difficult) role, and when the partnership is felicitous — as is the present one — the songs emerge in all their expressive glory. Rogers imparts the proper ethos to every song and his pure-velvet voice is faithfully matched at every step by O'Dette's accompaniment. He liberally ornaments the lines and, though some may disagree with the practice, as each stanza is set to exactly the same music, it lends variety. The recording is crystal-clear — so much so that the printed texts provided in the inlay booklet might be regarded as a luxury.

Dowland. The Second Booke of Songs. **Emma Kirkby** (sop); **John York Skinner** (alto); **Martyn Hill** (ten); **David Thomas** (bass); **Consort of Musicke/Anthony Rooley** (lte). L'Oiseau-Lyre 425 889-2OH. Texts included. From DSLO528/9 (9/77).

⏺ 1h 10' ADD 8/91

This recording originally appeared in 1977 as part of Florilegium's complete Dowland cycle. The Second Booke of Songs dates from 1600 and contains two of Dowland's most famous compositions *Flow my teares* and *I saw my Lady weepe*, though here these are presented unusually (and not entirely convincingly) as vocal duets. In fact there is a surprisingly wide variety of vocal and instrumental combinations throughout the disc, from consort song to four-part vocal to the more familiar sound of solo voice and lute, all of which were suggested as performance possibilities by Dowland himself. It is partly as a result of this that the recording retains its freshness in spite of its age, but it would be wrong to ignore the contribution made by the intelligent and sensitive singing of Emma Kirkby and Martyn Hill, both of whom sound completely in their element.

Paul Dukas

French 1865-1935

Dukas. ARIANE ET BARBE-BLEUE. **Katherine Ciesinski** (sop) Ariane; **Gabriel Bacquier** (bar) Barbe-bleue; **Mariana Paunova** (contr) La Nourrice; **Hanna Schaer** (mez) Sélysette; **Anne-Marie Blanzat** (sop) Ygraine; **Jocelyne Chamonin** (sop) Mélisande; **Michelle Command** (sop) Bellangère; **French Radio Chorus; French Radio New Philharmonic Orchestra/ Armin Jordan.** Erato Libretto 2292-45663-2. Notes, text and translation included. From NUM750693 (10/83).

⏺ 1h 57' DDD 9/91

This is by far the longest of Dukas's works which the highly self-critical composer allowed to survive. Based on Maeterlinck's play, the opera is curiously cast in that the six most important roles are female. Barbe-bleue himself only make a brief appearance as a singer — Gabriel Bacquier nevertheless makes a strong impression in this cameo role — and the other male singers have but a line or two each. The role of Ariane, by contrast, is highly taxing for the singer, for not only is her part very wide-ranging, but she is on the stage for the whole opera. Katherine Ciesinski does not perhaps have the most attractive voice, but she is a highly resourceful artist who brings Ariane to life very vividly. The lesser role of the nurse is competently taken by Hanna Schaer, and the sopranos (Barbe-bleue's previous wives) are all first-rate. Dukas's scoring is very seductive and richly imaginative, and no performance of this opera would be successful in the hands of a lesser conductor. Armin Jordan paces the work superbly, and obtains very fine playing from the Radio France New Philharmonic Orchestra. The recording is tonally very beautiful and highly atmospheric.

Maurice Duruflé *French 1902-1986*

Duruflé. ORGAN WORKS. **John Scott.** Hyperion CDA66368. Played on the organ of St Paul's Cathedral, London.
Prélude sur l'introit de l'Epiphanie. Prélude et fugue sur le nom d'Alain, Op. 7. Suite, Op. 5. Scherzo, Op. 2. Prélude, adagio et choral varié sur le "Veni creator spiritus", Op. 4 (with the men's voices of St Paul's Cathedral Choir). Fugue sur le carillon des heures de la Cathédrale de Soissons, Op. 12.

> 1h 10' DDD 1/91

The *Requiem* is Duruflé's best-known work. But as an organist it was only natural that the bulk of his music was written for that instrument. While six pieces which comfortably fit on to a single CD may not seem much to show for a lifetime's devotion to the organ, such a meagre output is entirely the result of extreme fastidiousness: Duruflé was almost obsessively self-critical revising his compositions many times over before releasing them for publication. The result is music in which no note is superfluous and where emotional intensity has unusually direct impact. Many characteristics of the *Requiem* will be instantly picked up here by the discerning listener, not least the copious use of plainsong. A singularly beautiful addition to this recording is the use of men's voices to chant verses of *Veni creator spiritus*. But while Duruflé's deeply-felt, sometimes pained expression permeates most of this music, there are flashes of gaiety: in a simply delicious *Siciliano* (from the Suite) and in the bubbly *Scherzo*. John Scott's performances are truly exceptional. Technically he is impressive and he readily bares his sensitive musical soul to release the full beauty of these pieces. Hyperion have made a wonderful job in recording at St Paul's, achieving an ideal blend between clarity and atmosphere. The echo at this venue can have, and does here, a stunning effect: just savour that glorious aftertaste which seems to linger into eternity each time Scott's hands leave the keys.

Duruflé. Requiem[a]. Four Motets. [a]**Ann Murray** (mez); [a]**Thomas Allen** (bar); **Corydon Singers;** [a]**English Chamber Orchestra/Matthew Best** with [a]**Thomas Trotter** (org). Hyperion CDA66191. Texts and translations included. From A66191 (5/86).

> 51' DDD 4/87

The Requiem is adapted from a suite of organ pieces Duruflé based on plainsong from the Mass for the Dead. Although it expresses the same tranquility and optimism as the Fauré Requiem, Duruflé's language is firmly based in the twentieth century. The Requiem exists in three versions: one uses a full orchestra; another has just cello and organ accompaniment, while the "middle version" of 1961, used here, employs a small orchestra. The performance is admirable in its quiet expressiveness, and Matthew Best conducts with skill and sensitivity. The *Quatre Motets* inhabit a similar world to that of the Requiem and are also based on Gregorian chant. The recording is not ideally clear, but is more than adequate.

Henri Dutilleux

French 1916-

Dutilleux. Violin Concerto, "L'arbre des songes"[a].
Maxwell Davies. Violin Concerto[b]. **Isaac Stern** (vn); [a]**French National Orchestra/Lorin Maazel;** [b]**Royal Philharmonic Orchestra/André Previn.** CBS Masterworks CD42449.

> 56' DDD 2/88

This is a unique coupling in many respects, not least among them the fact that both concertos were written for this soloist. The Dutilleux Concerto, unlike the traditional bravura vehicle, is more integrated, more inward looking with the slower passages radiating a distinctive haunting beauty. The Maxwell Davies work also offers comparatively few opportunities for display, although its technical demands are virtuosic indeed, and includes numerous allusions to the dances of the Scottish highlands. Stern gives confident and involving performances of both works, projecting a wide range of colour and conveying an understanding of and confidence in their musical values. The recordings are good.

Antonin Dvořák

Czechoslovakian 1841-1904

Dvořák. Cello Concerto in B minor, B191.
Tchaikovsky. Variations on a Rococo theme, Op. 33. **Mstislav Rostropovich** (vc); **Berlin Philharmonic Orchestra/Herbert von Karajan.** DG 413 819-2GH. From SLPM139044 (10/69).

> 1h ADD 3/85

Dvořák's Cello Concerto dominates the repertoire and above all it needs a larger-than-life soloist and a balancing orchestral partnership. As an interpreter of the work Rostropovich reigns supreme and he has recorded it six times. Undoubtedly the collaboration with Karajan was the most fruitful, with these two great artists striking sparks off one another, resulting in Rostropovich's tendency to romantic indulgence seeming natural and inspirationally spontaneous against the sweep of the background canvas supplied by the Berlin Philharmonic players. It is an admirable performance, helped by a superb, naturally balanced recording. What better coupling than Tchaikovsky's elegant and tuneful *Rococo* Variations, a work displaying the composer's affinity with his beloved Mozart — there never seems to be a note too many. Again, Rostropovich and Karajan are in their element, with the Berlin orchestra providing many inimitable touches, and the result is sheer delight.

Dvořák. Violin Concerto in A minor, B108. Romance in F minor, B39.
Kyung Wha Chung (vn); **Philadelphia Orchestra/Riccardo Muti.** EMI CDC7 49858-2.

> 47' DDD 11/89

Considering the popularity of his Cello Concerto, Dvořák's concerto for violin has never quite caught on with the general public. But a top class performance can convince us that the neglect is unfair. Kyung Wha Chung plays the concerto with the right blend of simplicity and brilliance, Slavonic warmth and folk-like quality, and the Philadelphia Orchestra under Riccardo Muti give her the right kind of support, unobtrusive enough to make us forget that the orchestral writing is not Dvořák at his most instrumentally imaginative, yet positive enough to provide more than just a discreet background. Ultimately, we probably enjoy the concerto most for its Bohemian lilt, a quality we feel in the violin's very first

entry and that is present again in ample measure in the rondo finale — a movement of unfailingly dancing rhythm and considerable charm that here receives a
sparkling performance. The delicately scored Romance in F minor that completes
the programme is a slightly earlier work than the Violin Concerto and, it has
been said, suggests a leisurely walk through the Bohemian countryside with
someone who knows it well. The recorded sound is well defined and faithful,
capturing Chung's fine tonal palette.

Dvořák. Piano Concerto in G minor, B63[a].
Schumann. Introduction and Allegro appassionato, Op. 92. **András Schiff**
(pf); **Vienna Philharmonic Orchestra/Christoph von Dohnányi.** Decca
417 802-2DH. Item marked [a] recorded at a performance in the Musikverein,
Vienna during November 1986.

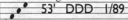

53' DDD 1/89

It seems extraordinary that the
Piano Concerto is not all that well
known. For a long time it was
thought unpianistic, but András
Schiff gives a fresh and agile account
of what is a delightful score. He is
very well partnered by Dohnányi
and the Vienna Philharmonic
Orchestra, and the playing is singularly sure for a live performance.
The music is unmistakably Dvořák's,
though in this relatively early work
we do not find the consistently
Bohemian flavour that is actually
stronger in his later music.
Schumann wrote his *Introduction*
while under the literary influence of
Byron's dramatic poem *Manfred* with
its tormented hero. Here is another
relatively neglected piece, but it has

András Schiff   *[photo: Decca/Chlala]*

considerable atmosphere and is once again persuasively performed. Clear yet
spacious recording in both works.

NEW REVIEW
Dvořák. ORCHESTRAL WORKS. **Bavarian Radio Symphony Orchestra/
Rafael Kubelík.** DG Galleria 435 074-2GGA2. Items marked [a] from 2530 593
(12/75), [b] 2530 785 (2/78), [c] 2530 712 (11/76), [d] 2530 713 (11/76).
My home, B125*a*[a]. Hussite Overture, B132[b]. In nature's realm, B168[b]. Carnival,
B169[b]. Othello, B174[b]. The water goblin, B195[c]. The noon witch, B196[c]. The
golden spinning-wheel, B197[d]. The wild dove, B198[d]. Symphonic Variations,
B70[c].

② 2h 37' ADD 11/91   £

Writing about Richard Strauss's *Don Juan*, Tovey remarked that "programme
music ... either coheres as music or it does not". Perhaps Dvořák's symphonic
poems have never attained the popularity of those by Richard Strauss because
there are a few too many seams in his musical narrative. Equally, the gruesome
local folk ballads on which they are based (and which Dvořák gleefully brings to
life) afforded him less range for depth of human characterization. But there are
lots of good reasons to value them. There's his inimitable stream of heart-easing
melody, and alongside the obvious debt to Liszt and Wagner, their harmonic

boldness and magical instrumental effects look forward to Suk, Martinů and Janáček. Indeed, in the central section of *The golden spinning-wheel*, where the wheel and assorted paraphernalia are offered to the false queen in return for the various dismembered portions of the heroine's body, the repeated patterns on muted strings sound like pure Janáček. And the exquisite closing pages of *The wild dove* could be the best thing Martinů ever wrote. Also written when Dvořák was at the height of his power (in the 1890s), these two mid-priced discs offer the chance to hear his three concert overtures — *In nature's realm, Carnival* and *Othello* — as he originally conceived them: a thematically linked three movement 'symphonic' work on the theme of nature, life and love. The earlier and no less worthy *Symphonic Variations* and *My home* and *Hussite* overtures complete a set that would be fine value in terms of minutes for your money even if the performances were mediocre. As it is you won't find a finer account at any price. Knowing when to keep this music on the move is the secret of Kubelík's success, but the mobility is always marked by freshness of spirit rather than plain drive. The whole set is informed with his burning belief in the value of the music and his experience is drawing precisely what he wants from his own Bavarian players. DG's mid-seventies recordings project this with clarity and coherence and need fear nothing from more recent digital contenders.

NEW REVIEW

Dvořák. SLAVONIC DANCES. **Bavarian Radio Symphony Orchestra/ Rafael Kubelík.** DG Galleria 419 056-2GGA. Items marked [a] from 2530 466 (11/75), [b] 2530 593 (11/75).

B83[a] — No. 1 in C major; No. 2 in E minor; No. 3 in A flat major; No. 4 in F major; No. 5 in A major; No. 6 in D major; No. 7 in C minor; No. 8 in G major. *B147*[b] — No. 1 in B major; No. 2 in E minor; No. 3 in F major; No. 4 in D flat major; No. 5 in B flat minor; No. 6 in B flat major; No. 7 in C major; No. 8 in A flat major.

1h10' ADD 8/87   Ⓑ

NEW REVIEW

Dvořák. SLAVONIC DANCES. **Czech Philharmonic Orchestra/Václav Talich.** Music and Arts mono CD658.

B83 — No. 1 in C major; No. 2 in E minor (both from HMV C2825, 3/36); No. 3 in A flat major (C2831, 4/36); No. 4 in F major (HMV B8437, 6/36); No. 5 in A major (B8471, 9/36); No. 6 in D major (C2831); No. 7 in C minor (B8471); No. 8 in G major. *B147* — No. 1 in B major (C2852, 10/36); No. 2 in E minor, (C2859, 11/36); No. 3 in F major (B8511, 12/36); No. 4 in D flat major (C2859); No. 5 in B flat minor (B8511); No. 6 in B flat major; No. 7 in C major (B8519, 1/37); No. 8 in A flat major (B8521, 2/37). Carnival — Overture, B169 (C2842, 7/36).

1h 15' AAD 6/92   Ⓑ ▲

Dvořák wrote his first set of eight *Slavonic Dances* in 1878 at the request of his publisher. They were originally cast in piano duet form, but the composer almost immediately scored them for orchestra. They achieved a great success and a further set of eight were requested. Dvořák initially doubted his ability to repeat the prescription, and it was not until 1886 that he produced a second set of eight dances. Again they were originally written for piano duet and then orchestrated, and again they proved to be very popular. Kubelík's recording was made a time when he was head of the Bavarian Radio Symphony Orchestra. As a musician steeped in the romantic traditions of his native Czechoslovakia he managed to persuade his orchestra to play Czech music almost to the manner born. His performances of the dances are brilliant, very vivacious, and highly idiomatic. The recording is very clear but slightly lacking in depth and atmosphere.

Václav Talich recorded the *Slavonic Dances* with his Czech Philharmonic Orchestra on two occasions. Music and Art's CD contains his first, pre-war cycle. Talich's Czech roots went still further back than those of Kubelík, and though energy and high spirits permeate his performances they also possess a certain old-world state atmosphere and poignancy of expression which sometimes elude Kubelík. Considerable allowances should be made for the 1935 recording quality but the effort is worthwhile. There is a bonus on this disc in the shape of a beautifully played *Carnival* Overture, though it should be added that this is only made possible by the fact that Talich's orchestra plays fewer repeats in the dances than that of Kubelík.

Dvořák. Serenades — E major, B52; D minor, B77. **Academy of St Martin in the Fields/Sir Neville Marriner.** Philips 400 020-2PH. From 6514 145 (5/82).

51' DDD 4/83

These two serenades are works full of melody and good humour, bubbling over with tuneful zest, but always inventive and skilfully scored. The gracefully elegant E major Serenade here receives a wonderfully cultivated reading which never overlooks the subtleties of the part-writing. The D minor is a slightly grittier piece and also benefits from Marriner's attentive guidance. Tempos are finely judged and well related throughout and the fast sections have a lovely zip and panache. The recording is excellent too, the strings having just the right bloom without sacrificing the music's essential intimacy.

NEW REVIEW

Dvořák. COMPLETE SYMPHONIES AND ORCHESTRAL WORKS. **London Symphony Orchestra/István Kertész.** Decca 430 046-2DC6.
Symphonies — No. 1 in C minor, B9, "The Bells of Zlonice" (from SXL6288, 10/67); No. 2 in B flat major, B12 (SXL6289, 9/67); No. 3 in E flat major, B34 (SXL6290, 5/67); No. 4 in D minor, B41 (SXL6257, 4/67); No. 5 in F major, B54 (SXL6273, 3/67); No. 6 in D major, B112 (SXL6253, 11/66); No. 7 in D minor, B141; No. 8 in G major, B163 (SXL6044, 7/63); No. 9 in E minor, B178, "From the New World" (SXL6291, 11/67). Scherzo capriccioso, B131 (SXL6348, 7/63). *Overtures* — In Nature's Realm, B168 (SXL6290, 5/67); Carnival, B169 (SXL6253, 11/66); My Home, B125a (SXL6273, 3/67).

7h 11' ADD 4/92

István Kertész recorded the Dvořák symphonies during the mid-1960s and his integral cycle was quick to achieve classic status, with his exhilarating and vital account of the Eighth Symphony (the first to be recorded in February 1963) rapidly becoming a special landmark in the catalogue. The original LPs, with their distinctive Breughel reproduction sleeves are now collectors' items in their own right, but these magnificent interpretations are now available once more, in glitteringly refined digitally remastered sound, and it is a tribute to the memory of this tragically short-lived conductor that this cycle continues to set the standard by which all others are judged. Kertész was the first conductor to attract serious collectors to the early Dvořák symphonies which, even today are not performed as often as they should be; and his jubilant advocacy of the unfamiliar First Symphony, composed in the composer's twenty-fourth year, has never been superseded. This work offers surprising insights into the development of Dvořák's mature style, as does the Second Symphony. Kertész shows that Symphonies Nos. 3 and 4 have much more earthy resilience than many commentators might have us believe, insisting that Dvořák's preoccupation with the music of Wagner and Liszt had reached its zenith during this period. The challenging rhetoric of the Fourth has never found a more glorious resolution than here, with Kertész drawing playing of gripping intensity from the London Symphony Orchestra. The Fifth Symphony, and to a still greater extent, its glorious successor, Symphony No. 6, both reveal Dvořák's clear affinity with the music of Brahms. Kertész's superb reading of the Sixth, however, shows just how individual and naturally expressive this under-rated work actually is, whilst the playing in the great climax of the opening movement and the vigorous final peroration remains tremendously exciting, even a quarter of a century after the recording first appeared. In the great final trilogy, Kertész triumphs nobly with the craggy resilience of the Seventh Symphony, and his buoyant ardour brings a dynamic thrust and momentum to the Eighth Symphony, whereas his *New World* is by turns indomitable and searchingly lyrical. The six-disc set also offers assertive and brilliant readings of the Overtures *Carnival, In Nature's Realm* and the rarely heard *My Home*, together with a lucid and heroic account of the *Scherzo capriccioso*. These definitive performances have been skilfully reprocessed, the sound is astonishingly good, even by modern standards, and the playing of the London Symphony Orchestra is often daringly brilliant under the charismatic direction of one of this century's late-lamented masters of the podium.

Dvořák. Symphony No. 5 in F major, B54. Othello, B174. Scherzo capriccioso, B131. **Oslo Philharmonic Orchestra/Mariss Jansons.** EMI CDC7 49995-2.

(♪) 1h 4' DDD 7/90 ♩ P Ⓑ

Of all the romantic composers, it is probably Dvořák who best evokes a sunlit, unspoiled and relatively untroubled picture of nineteenth-century country life. Light and warmth radiate from his Fifth Symphony, composed in just six weeks of the year 1875 when he was in his early thirties. It has been called his "Pastoral Symphony", and it is easy to see why, especially in a performance as fresh and sunny as this one. Mariss Jansons brings out all the expressiveness and heart of the music without exaggerating the good spirits and playful humour that are so characteristic of the composer, and one would single out for praise the fine wind playing of the Oslo Philharmonic Orchestra (and not least its golden-toned horns) were it not for the fact that the strings are no less satisfying. The lyrical *Andante con moto* brings out the fine interplay of the instrumental writing, the bouncy *Scherzo* is uninhibited without going over the top and the exciting finale has plenty of momentum. The other two pieces are also nicely done, the *Scherzo capriccioso* having both lilt and vigour and the rarely played *Othello* Overture (a late work) being a suitably dramatic response to Shakespeare's tragedy. The recording is warm and clear.

Dvořák. Symphony No. 6 in D major, B112.
Janáček. Taras Bulba. **Cleveland Orchestra/Christoph von Dohnányi.** Decca 430 204-2DH.

(♪) 1h 6' DDD 7/91 ♩ P

Dohnányi here turns to a radiant work that until now has been relatively neglected on CD. With its obvious echoes of Brahms's Second Symphony this is a work which, for all its pastoral overtones, gains from refined playing, and quite apart from the imaculate ensemble, the Cleveland violins play ethereally, as in the melody at the start of the slow movement. Dohnányi does not miss the earthy qualities of the writing either, and the impact of the performance is greatly enhanced by the fullness and weight of the recording. This is altogether a superb account of No. 6. There is also the bonus of an unusual makeweight, *Taras Bulba*. The account here is very Viennese in style and warmly expressive against its opulent background. However, if Janáček is your first priority, then Mackerras's version, coupled with the *Sinfonietta* (reviewed elsewhere in this Guide) is the obvious choice, for he characterfully persuades his truly Viennese musicians to sound more like Czechs, playing brilliantly with a sharp attack very apt for the composer's music. But those who want a radiant account of the Dvořák will find comparable joy in the characterful Janáček rhapsody.

Dvořák. Symphonies — No. 7 in D minor, B141[a]; No. 8 in G major, B163[b]. **Royal Concertgebouw Orchestra, Amsterdam/Sir Colin Davis.** Philips Silver Line 420 890-2PSL. Item marked [a] from 9500 132 (2/77), [b] 9500 317 (10/79).

> ♪ 1h 14'   ADD   1/89   ♩ P . £ Ⓑ

Dvořák's Seventh and Eighth Symphonies represent the peak of his symphonic creativity. The Seventh Symphony has a wider range of mood than the Eighth with its potently atmospheric opening and eloquent and life-enhancing finale. The Eighth also has its moments of strong drama but the overall mood is one of extrovert geniality. Sir Colin Davis has the full measure of both works, he finds exhilaration and vitality alongside a spontaneous lyricism. Whether in the eloquently played slow movements or the contrasted scherzos, his pacing is perfectly judged and in both finales there is flair and excitement. Not surprisingly the Royal Concertgebouw Orchestra is wonderfully responsive to his freshness of approach, and these two highly satisfying performances are superbly played. The digital remastering has been very beneficial: the orchestra is naturally balanced with detail clear within an attractively warm ambience. Offered at mid-price this reissue is an undoubted bargain.

Dvořák. Symphony No. 9 in E minor, B178, "From the New World"[a]. American Suite[b]. [a]**Vienna Philharmonic Orchestra/Kirill Kondrashin;** [b]**Royal Philharmonic Orchestra/Antál Dorati.** Decca 430 702-2DM. From [a]SXDL7510 (7/80), [b]410 735-2DH2 (3/85).

> ♪ 1h 3'   DDD   8/91   ♩ S Ⓑ

Dvořák. Symphony No. 9 in E minor, B178, "From the New World". **Cleveland Orchestra/Christoph von Dohnányi.** Decca 414 421-2DH. From 414 421-1DH (11/86).

> ♪ 41'   DDD   1/87   ♩ S Ⓑ

Dvořák. Symphony No. 9 in E minor, B178, "From the New World"[a]. Carnival Overture, B169[b]. Scherzo capriccioso, B131[c]. **London Symphony Orchestra/ István Kertész.** Decca Ovation 417 724-2DM. ·Item marked [a] from SXL6291 (11/67), [b] SXL6253 (11/66), [c] SXL6044 (7/63).

> ♪ 1h 5'   ADD   12/87   £ Ⓑ

Dvořák. Symphony No. 9 in E minor, B178, "From the New World"[a]; Symphonic Variations, B70[b]. **London Philharmonic Orchestra/Zdenek Macal.** Classics for Pleasure CD-CFP9006. Item marked [a] from CFP40382 (11/82), [b] CFP40345 (1/81).

> ♪ 1h 6'   DDD   9/87   £ Ⓑ

Kondrashin's *New World* caused something of a sensation when originally transferred to CD. Here was a supreme example of the clear advantages of the new medium over the old and the metaphor of a veil being drawn back between listener and performers could almost be extended to a curtain: the impact and definition of the sound is quite remarkable. However, Decca are never a company to rest on their laurels and in 1986 Christoph von Dohnányi provided an equally attractive and even more direct and spectacularly recorded version of the Ninth. The performance is in some respects less dramatic than Kondrashin's and has the disadvantage of omitting the first movement exposition repeat. But

Christoph von Dohnányi　　*[photo: Decca/Sayer]*

the easy lyricism of the music-making, combined with a natural vitality, brings not only great warmth in the playing but a strong affinity with the Czech idiom.

To bring yet further competition Decca have also reissued Kertész's famous LSO version from the late 1960s, a wonderfully fresh account, notable for its sense of flow and ideal choice of tempos, and the hushed intensity of the slow movement. Coupled with sparkling performances of the *Carnaval Overture* and *Scherzo capriccioso* this makes a formidable bargain at mid-price. Likewise, at not far short of 70 minutes and with a bargain price, the Macal issue might be worth considering even if the performances were of only satisfying quality. As it is, they are thrilling. The LPO play with enormous vivacity and authenticity for their Czech conductor and the sheer earthy strength and pastoral freshness of the music comes over without any lapse into crudity. The *Symphonic Variations* is a rather earlier work and is distinctly ungainly, but is here treated with ingenuity and invention as well as some humour.

Dvořák. String Sextet in A major, B80[a].
Martinů. Serenade No. 2. String Sextet (1932)[a]. **Academy of St Martin in the Fields Chamber Ensemble** (Kenneth Sillito, Malcolm Latchem, vns; Robert Smissen, [a]Stephen Tees, vas; [a]Stephen Orton, [a]Roger Smith, vcs). Chandos CHAN8771.

50' DDD 5/90

There is little which links the music of Dvořák and Martinů except a common Czech background, but the ASMF Chamber Ensemble respond well to both composers' styles and the result is a highly enjoyable, well-contrasted programme. Martinů's smart metropolitan 1930s style is encapsulated in the brief, but rather trifling *Serenade*. The Sextet is a longer and a more substantial work, still written in a busy, neoclassical style and effective in its way. These two works inspire an alert, spick-and-span response in the ASMF players. Their style in the warmly romantic Dvořák work is appropriate, too. In the first movement their tempo variations are quite marked, and the playing is highly expressive. The second movement *Dumka* has effectively strong accents and is followed by a fast, exhilarating third movement *Furiant*. The finale comprises a set of variations, each episode of which is vividly characterized in this performance. The recording was made in a church, but fortunately the acoustic is generous without having unwanted resonances and the balance is good.

NEW REVIEW

Dvořák. Piano Quintet in A major, B155[a].
Franck. Piano Quintet in F minor[b]. **Clifford Curzon** (pf); **Vienna Philharmonic Quartet** (Willi Boskovsky, Otto Strasser, vns; Rudolf Streng, va; [a]Robert Scheiwein, [b]Emanuel Brabec, vcs). Decca 421 153-2DM. Item marked [a] from SXL6043 (6/63), [b] SXL2278 (9/61).

1h 9' ADD 4/90　　　£ 🅿 Ⓑ

These are two self-recommending accounts dating from the 1960s from Clifford Curzon and the Vienna Philharmonic Quartet that long enjoyed classic status. An aristocrat of the keyboard, Curzon gives commanding accounts of both works, and his Viennese partners offer playing of great finesse and subtlety. The Dvořák is among his most endearing and captivating scores, and the Franck belongs to that master's most impassioned utterances. The quintets are separated by barely a decade (the Dvořák comes from 1888, the Franck from 1879), and it would be difficult to improve on these performances. Both are standard classics and belong in every basic collection: together in such fine performances and at such a reasonable price they offer outstanding value. The Decca sound, always very good, is as fresh and powerful as the music itself.

Dvořák. Piano Quartets — No. 1 in D major, B53; No. 2 in E flat major, B162. **Domus** (Krysia Osostowicz, vn; Timothy Boulton, va; Richard Lester, vc; Susan Tomes, pf). Hyperion CDA66287.

1h 10' DDD 3/89

Apart from the so-called *American* Quartet Dvořák's chamber music is too seldom heard. The two piano quartets are delightful works and like so much of his music seem to inhabit a world of apparently limitless melodic invention. The three movements manage to combine a sophistication of form with a folk-song-like simplicity. However, the piano's role is much more inventive in the E flat major Quartet and meets the string players as an equal partner rather than being seen merely as a subservient accompanist. Texture is uppermost in this latter work and Dvořák brings off some delicious instrumental coups. Domus is an uncommonly fine piano quartet and they bring to this music a freshness and unanimity of approach that is hugely rewarding. The recorded sound, too, is very fine.

Dvořák. String Quartet No. 12 in F major, B179, "American". Cypresses, B152 — Nos. 1, 2, 5, 9 and 11.
Kodály. String Quartet No. 2, Op. 10. **Hagen Quartet** (Lukas Hagen, Annette Bik, vns; Veronika Hagen, va; Clemens Hagen, vc). DG 419 601-2GH.

1h 1' DDD 5/87

Surely no work in the string quartet repertoire expresses so much contentment and joy as Dvořák's *American* Quartet. The very youthful Hagen Quartet penetrate the work's style, with its dance-like rhythms and open-hearted, folksy melodies, very successfully and they produce an attractively full-bodied tone-quality. With Kodály's brief Quartet No. 2 we enter a very different world. As in Dvořák's quartet there is a folk-music influence, but here it is the music of Kodály's native Hungary, which by its very nature is more introspective. The Hagen Quartet again capture the work's nationalistic flavour very adroitly. Dvořák's youthful *Cypresses* were originally voice and piano settings of poems which reflected the composer's love for a singer and are played with an affecting simplicity and warmth. The recording is a little too cavernous, but not so much as to spoil the enjoyment afforded by this excellent disc.

Dvořák. String Quartet No. 12 in F major, B179, "American"[a].
Schubert. String Quartet No. 14 in D minor, D810, "Death and the Maiden"[b].
Borodin. String Quartet No. 2 in D major — Notturno[a]. **Quartetto Italiano** (Paolo Borciani, Elisa Pegreffi, vns; Piero Farulli, va; Franco Rossi, vc). Philips Silver Line 420 876-2PSL. Items marked [a] from SAL3618 (8/67), [b] SAL3708 (5/69).

1h 15' ADD 3/89

This is a cherishable coupling of two of the finest quartets in the repertoire. The Quartetto Italiano bring to the Schubert, with its drama and passion so close to the surface, great panache and involvement. The singing theme of the second movement receives a grave intensity that is all too elusive. Similarly Dvořák's *American* Quartet is given exactly the right quality of nostalgia and ease that the work requires. The charming finale, one of Dvořák's most enchanting movements, is given a real folk-like sense of fun. As a bonus the Quartet play the celebrated *Notturno* slow movement from Borodin's Second Quartet; charming though it is it really deserves to be heard in context (refer to the Index to Reviews for a complete recording). The 1960s recordings sound well.

NEW REVIEW

Dvořák. Piano Trio in B minor, B166, "Dumky".
Schumann. Piano Trio No. 1 in D minor, Op. 63. **Oslo Trio** (Stig Nilsson, vn; Aage Kvalbein, vc; Jens Harald Brattlie, pf). Victoria VCD19020.

1h 2' DDD 10/91

Why is it that works with nicknames are so often chosen at the expense of their companion pieces, distinguished only by opus numbers? One only need think of Beethoven's *Moonlight* and *Pathétique* Sonatas, Dvořák's *New World* Symphony, Mozart's *Dissonance* and *Hunt* Quartets to name but a few, names generally imposed not by the composer but by critics, performers or audiences. Dvořák's *Dumky* Trio has been very much fêted at the expense of his other three trios. Its name derives from a Ukrainian dance form, juxtaposing lively foot-stamping tunes with quieter contemplative passages. The Oslo Trio make much of these contrasts, launching themselves into the opening with impassioned fervour; that they are all fine players in their own right is quickly shown in the many solo opportunities throughout the first movement. Their playing of the quieter Schubertian passage some six minutes into the first movement is particularly notable. In a work of many contrasts they are careful (unlike certain other groups) to maintain a feeling of dramatic continuity of tempo and mood. An altogether absorbing performance, the more desirable for being coupled with Schumann's great D minor Trio. This is vintage Schumann with thematically linked movements and an immediately recognizable impassioned ardour. Again, the Oslo prove to be very much at one with the work, balancing lyricism and drama without imposing a heart-on-the-sleeve emotionalism. Their playing of the slow third movement is particularly impressive. The insert notes provide useful information about the works and the performers and the sound is good. Highly recommended.

NEW REVIEW

Dvořák. Rondo in G minor, B171[a].
Franck (trans. Delsart/Rose). Violin Sonata in A major[b].
Grieg. Cello Sonata in A minor, Op. 36[b]. **Robert Cohen** (vc); [a]**Anthya Rael,** [b]**Roger Vignoles** (pfs). CRD CRD3391. Item marked [a] from CRD1086/8 (2/81), [b] CRD1091 (8/81).

1h 6' ADD 1/92

César Franck's majestic Violin Sonata in A major has been avidly endorsed by generations of cellists as a major addition to their repertoire, ever since Leonard Rose popularized Delsart's fine cello transcription of the work. In fact, the alterations are minimal, and the sonata emerges with renewed dramatic potency in this glorious performance from Robert Cohen and Roger Vignoles, whose stirring advocacy of the work surely belies its real identity as a violin sonata. The technical finesse and musical cohesion of their playing allow the recurring cyclic themes of this epic work to generate a craggy architectural solidity, which reaches a thrilling climax in the finale. Indeed, the playing here may well convince you that this instrumental combination serves the music more effectively than that for which it was originally intended. Cohen and Vignoles capitalize on the näive, yet always affecting Nordic sentimentality of the Grieg Cello Sonata, in a reading which is constantly sympathetic to the 'heart on sleeve' languor of its innocuous melodies. They are particularly good in the brief central *Andante*, with its reference to the "Homage March" from Grieg's incidental music to Bjornson's play, *Sigurd Jorsalfar*. This excellent recital disc ends with a dry and skittish account of the Dvořák Rondo in G minor, in which Cohen is partnered by his mother, the pianist Anthya Rael. These fine 1981 performances have superb bloom and presence, and the CD transfers are excellent.

NEW REVIEW

Dvořák. Stabat mater[a]. Psalm 149. [a]**Lívia Aghová** (sop); [a]**Marga Schiml** (contr); [a]**Aldo Baldin** (ten); [a]**Luděk Vele** (bass); [a]**Prague Children's Choir; Prague Philharmonic Choir; Czech Philharmonic Orchestra/Jiří Bělohlávek.** Chandos CHAN8985/6. Notes, texts and translations included.

② 1h 36' DDD 2/92

The *Stabat mater* is a thirteenth-century Christian poem in Latin describing the Virgin Mary standing at the foot of the Cross. It has been set to music by many Catholic composers from Palestrina to Penderecki, and Dvořák's version, first heard in Prague in 1880, soon went on to other countries including Britain, where it had a number of cathedral performances and one in the Royal Albert Hall in London in 1884 that was conducted by the composer himself and used a choir of over 800 singers — "the impression of such a mighty body was indeed enchanting", he wrote. Its ten sections are well laid out for the different vocal and instrumental forces and so avoid the monotony which might seem inherent in a contemplative and deeply sombre text. This performance was recorded by Chandos with Czech forces in Prague Castle, and in it we feel the full dignity and drama of the work, an oratorio in all but name. The four solo singers convey genuine fervour and one feels that their sound, which is quite unlike that of British singers, must be akin to what the composer originally imagined. If they are a touch operatic, that doesn't sound misplaced and they perform well together, as in the second verse quartet "Quis est home". The choral singing is no less impressive, and indeed the whole performance under Bělohlávek gets the balance right between reverent simplicity and intensity of feeling. Psalm 149 is a setting of "Sing unto the Lord a new song" for chorus and orchestra and its celebratory mood provides a fine complement to the other work.

Dvořák. RUSALKA. **Gabriela Beňačková-Cápová** (sop) Rusalka; **Wieslaw Ochman** (ten) Prince; **Richard Novák** (bass) Watergnome; **Věra Soukupová** (contr) Witch; **Drahomíra Drobková** (mez) Foreign Princess; **Jana Jonášová, Daniela Sounová-Brouková** (sops), **Anna Barová** (contr) Woodsprites; **Jindřich Jindrák** (bar) Gamekeeper; **Jiřina Marková** (sop) Turnspit; **René Tuček** (bar) Hunter; **Prague Philharmonic Chorus; Czech Philharmonic Orchestra/Václav Neumann.** Supraphon 11 03641-2. Notes, text and translation included.

③ 2h 36' DDD 7/86

Dvořák's opera contains some of his most enchanting and haunting music. It tells the tragic story of the water nymph Rusalka who falls in love with a mortal prince. Gabriela Beňačková-Cápová's Rusalka is glorious, the voice full, lithe and with a beautiful soaring legato. She sings the famous Moon song quite magically. Richard Novák is a gruff though benign Watergnome, Wieslaw Ochman an ardent prince and Věra Soukupová a splendidly ominous witch. Václav Neumann directs the Czech Philharmonic with a command of the idiom that is totally engaging. The recording is very fine and the dynamic range quite extraordinarily vivid.

Sir George Dyson

British 1883-1964

NEW REVIEW

Dyson. Three Rhapsodies (1905-12).
Howells. String Quartet No. 3, "In Gloucestershire" (1923). **Divertimenti**
(Paul Barritt, Rachel Isserlis, vns; Gustav Clarkson, va; Sebastian Comberti, vc).
Hyperion CDA66139. From A66139 (6/86).

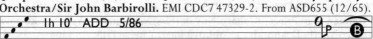

These beautiful rarities are a must for all those with an interest in English music.
Herbert Howells is perhaps better known for his choral and organ music, but he
also wrote many fine chamber works as well, of which the String Quartet No. 3,
subtitled *In Gloucestershire*, is one of the finest. Like many of the pieces of the
time (the first version dates from 1916) there are overtones of the Great War,
and like Vaughan Williams's *Pastoral* Symphony and Ivor Gurney's songs, the
tranquil images of the English countryside (in this instance Howells's beloved
Cotswolds) seem at times to be superimposed onto the battle-scarred fields of
France. The four movements are simple in design, rhapsodic in feel and
poignantly lyrical in expression. The music of George Dyson is even less well
known, though recently interest in his music has grown. The *Three Rhapsodies* for
string quartet are amongst his earliest compositions. At times the early influences
of Parry, Stanford and Richard Strauss can be heard, but on the whole they are
notable for their individuality, craftsmanship and more importantly their
spontaneity and warmth of writing. The performances are exceptionally fine and
sympathetic and the recording creates a pleasantly intimate atmosphere for the
listener to discover these little-known gems.

Werner Egk   *Refer to Index*

1901-1983

Edward Elgar

British 1857-1934

Elgar. Cello Concerto in E minor, Op. 85[a]. Sea Pictures, Op. 37[b].
[a]**Jacqueline du Pré** (vc); [b]**Dame Janet Baker** (mez); **London Symphony
Orchestra/Sir John Barbirolli.** EMI CDC7 47329-2. From ASD655 (12/65).

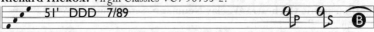

Elgar. Cello Concerto in E minor, Op. 85.
Bloch. Schelomo. **Steven Isserlis** (vc); **London Symphony Orchestra/
Richard Hickox.** Virgin Classics VC7 90735-2.

The EMI is a classic recording, offering two performances by soloists at the
turning point of their careers. Jacqueline du Pré's performance of the Elgar
Concerto is extraordinarily complete: the cello sings, cries almost, with burning
force in its upper registers; *pianissimos* barely whisper; pizzicatos ring with muted
passion; those moments of palpitating *spiccato* bowing convey more than is almost
imaginable. The LSO perform as if inspired; hardly surprising given Barbirolli's
magical accompaniment. Dame Janet Baker's *Sea Pictures* are no less masterly. The
young voice is glorious rich but agile, her diction superb whilst some of the
exquisite floated high notes simply defy description. The 1965 sound is quite
spectacular; its very immediacy and vividness grabs one at the outset and

| doesn't let go.

Nevertheless, the Virgin issue presents a brave, imaginative, highly-individual account of the Elgar Concerto — as personal in its perception of the piece as the classic Du Pré/Barbirolli recording. With Isserlis, the emotional tug is considerably less overt, the emphasis more on shadow and subtext than open heartache. Yet the inner-light is no less intense, the phrasing no less rhapsodic in manner than Du Pré. In short, understated but certainly not under-characterized. Hickox and the LSO prove model collaborators, and thanks also to an impeccably balanced recording, the give and take between soloist and orchestra in one of Elgar's most perfectly crafted scores, is seamless. Turning to the unique coupling, it almost goes without saying that the LSO bring all their well-oiled filmic skills to bear on Bloch's soulful King Solomon portrait, trumpets and horns positively outreaching themselves in the outrageous biblical climaxes. Isserlis does not stint himself, either, pouring forth his darkest and most impassioned colours, and the big Watford Town Hall acoustic opens out splendidly to accommodate it all.

Elgar. Violin Concerto in B minor, Op. 61. **Nigel Kennedy** (vn); **London Philharmonic Orchestra/Vernon Handley.** EMI CD-EMX2058. From EMX412058-1 (12/84).

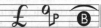

NEW REVIEW

Elgar. Violin Concerto in B minor, Op. 61[a]. Cockaigne Overture, Op. 40. [a]**Dong-Suk Kang** (vn); **Polish National Radio Symphony Orchestra/ Adrian Leaper.** Naxos 8 550489.

Even after the success of his First Symphony, Elgar's self-doubt persisted and caused his creative instincts to look inward. He could identify with his own instrument, the violin, as his own lonely voice pitted against an orchestra which might represent the forces of the outside world. Usually a concerto consisted of a big first movement, then a lyrical slow movement and a lighter finale: Elgar's finale, which balanced the first movement in weight, was unique, and at first the 50-minute-long work daunted all but the bravest soloists. Nigel Kennedy's technique is such that the work's formidable difficulties hold no terrors for him; his playing is first and foremost immaculate in its execution, and it is

Nigel Kennedy   *[photo: EMI/Jebb*

complemented by Handley's sensitive accompaniment. But it is more than that. He has a pure silvery tone-quality which is a joy to hear; his response to Elgar's vision is unfailingly sympathetic and understanding, and his projection of it is fresh and stimulating. The natural concert-hall sound is excellent in quality, with important orchestral detail always registering clearly.

Fine though EMI's version is, Naxos's more recent super-bargain issue now presents serious competition, and not merely on grounds of price. The myth that Elgar's music was unexportable British material has long been disproved, but this

fine version with a Korean soloist and a Polish orchestra does it again. As
Michael Kennedy wrote in *Gramophone*, Dong-Suk Kang plays here "as if he had
been brought up on the slopes of the Malvern Hills", but in any case, such
creators as Shakespeare and Michelangelo proved long ago that great art speaks of
human fundamentals that know no geographical or temporal frontiers. There is
ample virtuosity in this violin playing, but it is rightly always subservient to the
deep feeling of the music, and the British conductor Adrian Leaper provides him
with fully idiomatic support. The recording places Suk Kang more forwardly than
we would hear him in the concert-hall, but not exaggeratedly so, and although it
does not do quite so much justice to the orchestral sound, it allows us to hear
much of the important detail of this richly textured score. The *Cockaigne*
Overture presents Elgar in a different mood, less elegiac and more extrovert, and
Leaper's performance with the Polish orchestra has abundant vigour and humour,
as well as providing a substantial fill-up to the Violin Concerto where the
Kennedy/Handley issue has none.

Elgar. Variations on an original theme, Op. 36, "Enigma"[a]. Falstaff —
Symphonic Study, Op. 68[b]. [a]**Philharmonia Orchestra;** [b]**Hallé Orchestra/Sir
John Barbirolli.** EMI Studio CDM7 69185-2. Item marked [a] from ASD548
(11/63), [b] ASD610-11 (12/64).

> 1h 5' ADD 11/88

NEW REVIEW

Elgar. Variations on an Original Theme, Op. 36, "Enigma"[a]. Pomp and
Circumstance Marches, Op. 39[b]. [a]**London Symphony Orchestra,** [b]**London
Philharmonic Orchestra/Sir Adrian Boult.** EMI CDM7 64015-2. Item
marked [a] from HMV ASD2750 (11/71), [b] ASD3388 (10/77).

> 55' ADD 4/92

The first EMI disc restores to the catalogue at a very reasonable price two key
Elgar recordings of works which Sir John Barbirolli made very much his own.
Barbirolli brought a flair and ripeness of feeling to the *Enigma* with which Elgar
himself would surely have identified. Everything about his performance seems
exactly right. The very opening theme is phrased with an appealing
combination of warmth and subtlety, and variation after variation has a special
kind of individuality, whilst for the finale Barbirolli draws all the threads
together most satisfyingly. *Falstaff* is a continuous, closely integrated structure
and again Barbirolli's response to the music's scenic characterization is magical
while he controls the overall piece, with its many changes of mood, with a
naturally understanding flair. The original recordings perhaps sounded more
sumptuous but on CD there is more refined detail and greater range and impact
to the sound.

As one might expect, Sir Adrian Boult's 1970 recording of the *Enigma*
Variations offers similar riches to those of Barbirolli with the additional bonus of
a slightly superior recorded sound. Boult's account has authority, freshness and a
beautiful sense of spontaneity so that each variation emerges from the preceding
one with a natural feeling of flow and progression. There is warmth and affection
too coupled with an air of nobility and poise, and at all times the listener is
acutely aware that this is a performance by a great conductor who has lived a
lifetime with the music. One need only sample the passionate stirrings of
Variation One (the composer's wife), the athletic and boisterous "Troyte"
variation, or the autumnal, elegiac glow that Boult brings to the famous
"Nimrod" variation to realize that this is a very special document indeed. The
LSO, on top form, play with superlative skill and poetry and the excellent 1970
recording has been exceptionally well transferred to CD. The *Pomp and
Circumstance* Marches, recorded a year later with the London Philharmonic

Orchestra, are invigoratingly fresh and direct — indeed the performances are so full of energy and good humour that it is hard to believe that Boult was in his late eighties at the time of recording! A classic.

Elgar. The Wand of Youth — Suites Nos. 1 and 2, Opp. 1*a* and 1*b*. Nursery Suite (1931). **Ulster Orchestra/Bryden Thomson.** Chandos CHAN8318. From ABRD1079 (8/83).

♪ 1h 3' DDD 10/84

Elgar's orchestral music shows an astonishingly wide range of sensibility. The patriotic writing has all the pageantry and rumbustious vigour of an era, before the First World War, when Great Britain believed in itself and seemed to know just where it was heading. The Symphonies, which are on the grandest scale, with flowing and surging melodic lines, distil much of this confidence, yet there are already fleeting suspicions and doubts, while the Cello Concerto, the composer's *fin de siècle* masterpiece, confirms the disillusion of an age in its valedictory heart-aching intensity. Elgar's music for children remains very special, and in its innocence of atmosphere stands apart from the rest of his output. The two *Wand of Youth* Suites evoke a dream world untainted by adult unreasonableness. Vignettes like the gentle "Serenade", the delicious "Sun dance" with its dainty chattering flutes, and the fragile charm of the delicate "Fairy pipers" are utterly delightful. Orchestral textures are exquisitely radiant while the robust numbers bring elements of direct contrast, as in "Fairies and Giants" or "Wild bears", which have the bright primary colours of toy trains and nursery boisterousness. The origins of this music date from Elgar's own childhood, even though the *Nursery Suite* is quite a late work, and has the haunting nostalgia of the output from the final decade of his life. The wistful charm of "The Serious Doll" and "The Sad Doll" is unforgettable, and the approaching and departing "Wagon" shows a wonderfully sure touch in handling the orchestra. Bryden Thomson has the full measure of the disarming simplicity of Elgar's writing, and the Ulster Orchestra play this music with great affection and finesse. The warm Ulster acoustic is matched by vivid stereo projection and this fairly early digital recording has stood the test of time.

NEW REVIEW

Elgar. ORCHESTRAL WORKS. **BBC Symphony Orchestra/Andrew Davis.** Teldec British Line 9031-73279-2.
Cockaigne Overture, Op. 40. Introduction and Allegro, Op. 47. Serenade for strings in E minor, Op. 20. Variations on an Original Theme, Op. 36, "Enigma".

♪ 1h 14' DDD 3/92

For some years now Andrew Davis has been a very fine Elgar conductor. He and his orchestra are both on excellent form in this recording, which offers good value in the shape of no less than four important works. In *Cockaigne* Davis captures the music's warmth and rumbustious good humour very effectively, and he points the more reflective episodes with much skill. The *Introduction and Allegro* receives a deeply felt, richly romantic performance, though there is always a forward-moving pulse, and the work's shape and structure are clearly preserved. For the *Serenade* Davis changes the mood, and inspires a quieter, more intimate style of performance, one which evokes the work's gentle introspection very movingly. All the characters portrayed in the *Enigma* Variations are wittily, sympathetically brought to life. Every tempo seems just right, each expressive nuance is tellingly observed, and the reading as a whole is very satisfying. A well-detailed, but atmospheric recording adds still more lustre to this distinguished disc.

Elgar. Symphony No. 1 in A flat major, Op. 55. In the South, Op. 50, "Alassio". **London Philharmonic Orchestra/Leonard Slatkin.** RCA Victor Red Seal RD60380.

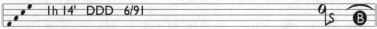

1h 14' DDD 6/91

NEW REVIEW

Elgar. Symphony No. 1 in A flat major, Op. 55. Pomp and Circumstance Marches, Op. 39 — No. 1 in D major; No. 3 in C minor; No. 4 in G major. **BBC Symphony Orchestra/Andrew Davis.** Teldec British Line 9031-73278-2.

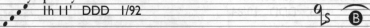

1h 11' DDD 1/92

Andrew Davis   *[photo: Teldec*

Elgar's First Symphony was one of those rare pieces of music that seemed to attain full stature and admiration from the very first public hearing. At its première in Manchester in 1908 it caused a sensation, and Elgar was received by the audience very much in the same way that the pop stars of today are. The previous successes of the *Enigma* Variations, *Gerontius* and the masterly *Introduction and Allegro* had created high hopes in the public's mind for what they felt would be the first truly great English Symphony, and they were not disappointed. Its popularity has never waned and it still holds a special place in the affections of the public today. Leonard Slatkin is a conductor whose passion for British music has become something of a crusade, and a listener hearing him play Elgar's First Symphony without knowing the artists could well think that this was a performance under a conductor such as Sir Adrian Boult. But good music knows no bounds (after all, you don't have to be Austrian to play Mozart!) and Slatkin's understanding of this composer is abundantly clear throughout. There is no trace of sentimentality in the mighty first movement, for here is real grandeur and not just grandiose utterance while the noble sadness of the coda has especial beauty. The other movements are hardly less fine, for the richly textured *Adagio* is most eloquently done and the finale is thrilling. Elgar's massive though subtle scoring can present problems for engineers; here they are magnificently solved and the sound is rich yet detailed with excellent bass. The Overture *In the South* which begins the disc is brilliantly vivid and dramatic.

Davis's account of this much-loved symphony has tremendous breadth and nobility and is full of poise and affectionate insight. The original *Gramophone* review described it as an interpretation that combined "the structural strengths of Boult with the poetic flair of Barbirolli" — on the whole this is very much a 'traditional' interpretation. At just over 20 minutes the first movement tends toward the expansive, but in the hands of so persuasive and sympathetic a conductor as Davis the music can certainly take it, and besides, he draws such wonderful performances from the orchestra. Credit must also go to the superbly natural Teldec recording, which is warm and ideally balanced. The disc also includes spirited performances of the *Pomp and Circumstance* Marches Nos. 1, 3 and 4. The choice between Davis's and Slatkin's interpretations, shaded to an extent by Davis's more overtly traditional approach, may ultimately come down to preferences in respect of the fill-ups.

Elgar. Symphony No. 2 in E flat major, Op. 63. Cockaigne Overture, Op. 40, "In London Town" **London Philharmonic Orchestra/Sir Adrian Boult.** EMI CDM7 64014-2. Item marked [a] from ASD3266 (10/76), [b] ASD2822 (9/72).

1h 8' ADD

What CD remastering reveals here in the symphony is that Boult, at the very end of his long recording career in the mid-seventies, bequeathed us a performance that has few rivals in evoking the work's passion and nostalgia, and that his familiar recording team had matched this expressive and expansive approach with sound that is spacious, bass rich and yet attentive to every detail of Elgar's miraculous orchestration. Boult's grip on the difficult structure of the first movement may not have been as sure as it once was, but just listen to the joy in the leaping violin and horn phrases; the intensity as the slow movement grasps its moments of release; the teeming inner life and vitality of the *Scherzo*; the thrust, splendour and weight after the finale has seen off its threats; and last but not least, the coda's rich impressionistic sunset glow. Boult's timing of climaxes is often daring, and more often than not heartstoppingly right. One of the best memorials to a very great Elgarian.

Elgar. MUSIC FOR STRINGS. [a]**José-Luis Garcia,** [a]**Mary Eade** (vns); [a]**Quentin Ballardie** (va); [a]**Olga Hegedus** (vc); **English Chamber Orchestra/Sir Yehudi Menuhin.** Arabesque Z6563. From ABQ6563 (1/87). Introduction and Allegro[a]. Chanson de nuit (arr. Fraser). Chanson de matin (arr. Fraser). Three Characteristic Pieces — No. 1, Mazurka. Serenade for strings in E minor. Salut d'amour (arr. Fraser). Elegy.

45' DDD 6/87

Elgar's pieces for string orchestra contain some of his greatest music and certainly the *Introduction and Allegro, Serenade* and *Elegy* included in this delightful programme embody quintessential Elgar. Sir Yehudi Menuhin's readings dig deep into the hearts of these works, drawing out the nostalgia and inner tragedy that underpins even some of the most seemingly high-spirited of Elgar's music. The lighter pieces allow relief from the intensity of the major works, thus making that intensity all the more effective. The English Chamber Orchestra is more than capable of providing first-rate soloists from its own ranks, and the quartet extracted for the *Introduction and Allegro* is suitably virtuosic. Both performers and engineers have produced an ideal integration of this solo group with the main string body, and the generally effervescent sound suits the celebratory nature of the piece. There are a number of other collections of such music available on CD, but this issue should certainly not go unsampled.

Elgar. String Quartet in E minor, Op. 83.
Walton. String Quartet in A minor. **Gabrieli Quartet** (Kenneth Sillito, Brendan O'Reilly, vns; Ian Jewel, va; Keith Harvey, vc). Chandos CHAN8474. From ABRD1185 (1/87).

56' DDD 10/87

This nicely recorded disc couples two fine English string quartets in highly accomplished performances by the Gabrieli Quartet. They are both imaginatively conceived works, powerfully projected. The Elgar Quartet is his only surviving quartet and the Gabrieli give a strong, sinuous reading revealing its toughness and range as well as its obvious beauties. Walton's String Quartet also has a similar vitality and exciting, rhythmic fervour that the composer's later reworking for string orchestra tends to dilute. The recording is faithful and exceptionally clean.

Elgar. VIOLIN WORKS. **Nigel Kennedy** (vn); **Peter Pettinger** (pf).
Chandos CHAN8380. From ABRD1099 (7/84).
Violin Sonata in E minor, Op. 82. Six Very Easy Melodious Exercises in the First
Position, Op. 22. Salut d'amour, Op. 12 (with Steven Isserlis, vc). Mot
d'amour, Op. 13. In the South — Canto popolare (In Moonlight). Sospiri,
Op. 70. Chanson de nuit, Op. 15 No. 1. Chanson de matin, Op.15 No. 2.

·· 55' DDD 8/85   ⁹P

As a violinist himself, Elgar wrote idiomatically for the instrument, and this
music shows the expressive variety that he achieved. The Sonata in E minor was
his last work for the instrument and is the centrepiece of the recital. It is the
only big work here, a dramatic utterance that the artists play with power and
poetry. If the Sonata is a key work to the understanding of this composer, so too
in its own way is the lilting piece called *Salut d'amour*, which is among his most
popular. The *Chanson de nuit* and *Chanson de matin* are charming miniatures while
the *Six Very Easy Melodious Exercises in the First Position* (written for his niece) are
tiny pieces which can surely not have received a more elegant performance.
A good digital recording catches Kennedy's fine tone and complements an
attractive issue.

Elgar. CHORAL MUSIC. **Bristol Cathedral Choir/Malcolm Archer**
([a]org), with **Anthony Pinel** (org). Meridian CDE84168.
The Apostles, Op. 49 — The Spirit of the Lord. Ave verum corpus, Op. 2
No. 1. Drakes Broughton (Hymn Tune). Give unto the Lord, Op. 74. God be
merciful unto us (Psalm 67). Great is the Lord, Op. 67 (with Stephen Foulkes,
bar; Bristol Cathedral Special Choir). Imperial March, Op. 32 (trans. Martin)[a].
Te Deum and Benedictus, Op. 34.

·· 1h DDD 10/89

When we think of Elgar's choral music we quite rightly remember the great
oratorios — *Gerontius, The Apostles, The Kingdom*. The Bristol Cathedral Choir and
their former Director of Music, Malcolm Archer, have looked to smaller-scale
pieces to fill this delightful CD. Unlike so many English composers Elgar was not
brought up in the Anglican church with its strong musical tradition: not for him
countless settings of the *Magnificat* and *Nunc Dimittis* or innumerable organ
voluntaries. Indeed he wrote only one specifically liturgical piece, the beautifully
simple setting of *Ave verum corpus*, and the *Imperial March*, which Archer plays here
with such gusto, is a transcription of a fine orchestral piece in the *Pomp and
Circumstance* tradition. Other music on this disc includes a pleasant hymn-tune, a
run-of-the-mill psalm-chant and items written for major festival occasions, such as
Te Deum and Benedictus in F and the thrilling choral showpiece *Great is the Lord*.
These 'festival' pieces were intended to have orchestral accompaniments, but
Anthony Pinel's always imaginative and skilful organ playing is a most satisfactory
alternative. The choir have been well trained for these recordings and produce
some stirring and innately sensitive performances in the pleasantly warm acoustic
of Bristol Cathedral.

NEW REVIEW

Elgar. PART-SONGS.
Vaughan Williams. Festival Te Deum in F major[a]. Mass in minor. [a]**John
Birch** (org); **Holst Singers/Hilary Davan Wetton.** Unicorn-Kanchana
DKPCD9116. Texts included.
Elgar: My Love Dwelt in a Northern Land, Op. 18 No. 3. Two Choral Songs,
Op. 71 — No. 1, The Shower; No. 2, The Fountain. Go, Song of mine,
Op. 57. Death on the Hills, Op. 72. Two Choral Songs, Op. 73 — No. 1,
Love's Tempest; No. 2, Serenade.

54' DDD 4/92

While these two great British composers are best remembered for their large-scale choral works, given performances as sensitively directed and superbly sung as these, their smaller-scale choral pieces are shown to be real masterpieces in their own right. The one accompanied piece here, Vaughan Williams's *Festival Te Deum* is a ceremonial romp evocative of the occasion for which it was written, the Coronation of George VI, and successfully combining a tangible sense of occasion with great vigour and energy. One view of Vaughan Williams's Mass is that its few moments of inspiration tend to be heavily diluted by much routine note-spinning. Perhaps its the maturity and range of these voices (above all, the Mass is more often sung liturgically by a choir of young boys and men) or Wetton's carefully-moulded approach, but nothing seems superfluous or uninspired here. And while Elgar's delightful part-songs have long been in the repertoire of amateur choirs, here they are elevated to a level of rare musical imagination and emotional scope. Listen to the impassioned appeal of the opening of "Love's Tempest" or the wonderful buoyancy of *My Love Dwelt in a Northern Land* — it seems astonishing that such colour and variety can be achieved purely by unaccompanied human voices. This is a disc of pure delight.

NEW REVIEW

Elgar. Sea Pictures, Op. 37. The Music Makers, Op. 69. **Linda Finnie** (contr); **London Philharmonic** [a]**Choir and Orchestra/Bryden Thomson.** Chandos CHAN9022.

1h 4' DDD 3/92

This was one of the late Bryden Thomson's last recordings and is arguably his finest, reminding us how grievous is the loss to British music. In *Sea Pictures* he receives orchestral playing of great sympathetic richness from veteran Elgarians, the London Philharmonic Orchestra. The second song, "In Haven" ("Capri") is wistfully treated while the accompaniment to "The swimmer" brings an over-whelming dynamic range to Elgar's evocative orchestration. Linda Finnie sings the various texts with just the right colouring of words, intelligent use of vibrato and keenness of articulation. In *The Music Makers* she identifies closely with the words of verse that is, to say the least, less than inspired and there is light, free singing from the LPO Choir, and pronounced tempo changes between sections. Thomson is equally convincing here too, and his flexible approach suits the work's moody nature, with autobiographical quotations from the *Enigma Variations*, the symphonies and *The Dream of Gerontius*. Chandos's sound quality is superb, with a wonderful bloom on the voices and depth and clarity in the orchestra. Finnie's opera-sized tone easily rides over the orchestra and is natural and comfortably distanced while the sections of *The Music Makers* are individually tracked. There is a poignancy in this posthumous release from Thomson to hear the passage, "Yea, in spite of a dreamer who slumbers, and a singer who sings no more".

Elgar. The Dream of Gerontius, Op. 38[a]. The Music Makers, Op. 69[b]. [b]**Dame Janet Baker** (mez); [a]**Helen Watts** (contr); [a]**Nicolai Gedda** (ten); [a]**Robert Lloyd** (bass); [a]**John Alldis Choir;** [ab]**London Philharmonic Choir,** [a]**New Philharmonia Orchestra;** [b]**London Philharmonic Orchestra/Sir Adrian Boult.** EMI CDS7 47208-8. Notes and texts included. Items marked [a] from SLS987 (5/76), [b] ASD2311 (5/67).

② 2h 16' ADD 1/87

Elgar. The Dream of Gerontius, Op. 38[a]. Sea Pictures, Op. 37[b]. **Dame Janet Baker** (mez); [a]**Richard Lewis** (ten); [a]**Kim Borg** (bass); [a]**Hallé Choir;** [a]**Sheffield Philharmonic Chorus;** [a]**Ambrosian Singers;** [b]**London**

Symphony Orchestra, ᵃHallé Orchestra/Sir John Barbirolli. EMI Studio
CMS7 63185-2. Texts included. Item marked ᵃ from ASD648/9 (10/65),
ᵇ ASD655 (12/65).

② 2h 2' ADD 12/89 £ Ⓑ

Elgar's best-known oratorio is the nearest he ever came to writing an opera.
The story of the anguished Gerontius in his death throes and his momentary
vision of Heaven was set by Elgar in the most graphic terms, and the
principals are like characters in music-drama. Throughout most of its history
Sir Adrian Boult was a renowned interpreter of the work, but it was only
late in his life that he came to record it. The results were both worth waiting for
and rewarding in their own right, capturing its intensity of emotion while never
allowing the structure to weaken through too much affection. Nicolai Gedda may
not be the ideal interpreter of the title-role, but Boult persuaded him to catch
something of its fervour. Helen Watts's Angel was in the best tradition of singing
that sympathetic part — warm but firm — whilst Robert Lloyd is heard to
strong effect in both bass roles. The London Philharmonic Choir and the New
Philharmonia sing and play to the top of their collective best. The spacious
recording is a fine match for the calibre of the reading.

Barbirolli's *Gerontius* is not quite so pristine, with more noticeable tape hiss
and a few glitches. Although the playing from the Hallé lacks a degree of
technical refinement, Barbirolli's direction proved inspirational and the
orchestra's legendary depth of string tone carries all before it. Richard Lewis, the
stalwart of so many concert performances, was not in best voice for this
recording, suffering from a cold, but Dame Janet and Kim Borg are more than
equal to their roles, and the composite chorus is remarkably convincing in its
urgency and commitment. Whilst this is not the version of *Gerontius* that you
might turn to for technical perfection (though you'd be hard put to it to find
fault with Janet Baker's performance here), it is an affectionate reading from
Barbirolli, and one that proves profoundly satisfying. The transcendentally radiant
account of *Sea Pictures* is still holding up unbelievably well after all this time and
makes a valuable coupling.

Elgar. The Kingdom, Op. 51ᵃ. ORCHESTRAL TRANSCRIPTIONS. ᵃ**Yvonne
Kenny** (sop); ᵃ**Alfreda Hodgson** (contr); ᵃ**Christopher Gillett** (ten);
ᵃ**Benjamin Luxon** (bar); ᵃ**London Philharmonic Choir; London
Philharmonic Orchestra/Leonard Slatkin.** RCA Victor Red Seal RD87862.
Notes and text included.
Bach (trans. Elgar): Fantasia and Fugue in C minor, BWV537. *Handel* (trans.
Elgar): Overture in D minor.

② 1h 56' DDD 3/89 ♩ₚ ♩ₛ

Elgar intended *The Kingdom* to be the second of three oratorios recounting the
events which led to the founding of the Christian church. Poor box-office returns
from the first performances of *The Apostles* and of *The Kingdom* discouraged him
from completing the project. What a shame! Hearing such a powerful performance as this, one is left in no doubt that *The Kingdom* ranks among the finest of
all oratorios. Leonard Slatkin measures his performance with a breadth and
expansiveness which suits such momentous subject matter. He isn't afraid of slow
tempos and it pays off handsomely; the climaxes, when they come, have real
impact and the essentially reflective character of the music is all the more
convincing. The orchestra and choir respond to his deeply-felt approach with
fervour and the recording, made in EMI's Abbey Road studio, is outstanding.
The two orchestral transcriptions of Bach and Handel provide slightly disappoint-
ing fillers; not because the performances are anything less than first-rate, but
simply because these are little more than Elgar fiddling around in a way which
today smacks of dubious taste.

Elgar. The Apostles[a]. The Light of Life — Meditation. [a]**Sheila Armstrong** (sop); [a]**Helen Watts** (contr); [a]**Robert Tear** (ten); [a]**Benjamin Luxon, John Carol Case** (bars); [a]**Clifford Grant** (bass); [a]**London Philharmonic Choir;** [a]**Downe House School Choir; London Philharmonic Orchestra/Sir Adrian Boult.** CMS7 64206-2. From SLS939 (4/69).

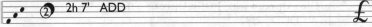

② 2h 7' ADD £

Elgar. The Apostles. **Alison Hargan** (sop); **Alfreda Hodgson** (contr); **David Rendall** (ten); **Bryn Terfel, Stephen Roberts, Robert Lloyd** (basses); **London Symphony Chorus; London Symphony Orchestra/ Richard Hickox.** Chandos CHAN8875/6. Text included.

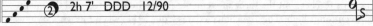

② 2h 7' DDD 12/90

Elgar was concerned that *The Apostles*, and its sequel *The Kingdom*, should seem as music drama rather than oratorio, but there are moments when the biblical texts conspire to defeat this objective; the various soloists appearing to adopt the pious "stand and deliver" manner of the oratorio tradition. It's a problem that Hickox more successfully overcomes with a more theatrical approach to the work than his only predecessor on disc, Sir Adrian Boult. Boult, of course, brought a lifetime of acquired Elgarian insights to the score; he achieves greater clarity in the elaborate interweaving of the choral parts for the multi-layered textures in "The Ascension", and his excellent late 1960s EMI recording has a more natural balance between the soloists and the main choral and orchestral forces. One of the crowning achievements of his long career, most Elgarians will consider this an essential acquisition, especially at medium price.

Newcomers, and those who love *Gerontius* but are less ready to extend indulgence for the sake of the finer moments in *The Apostles,* may well be tempted by Hickox. Of the soloists, Hickox's Alison Hargan does not match the radiant singing of Boult's Sheila Armstrong, but his men are preferable. One thinks of Bryn Terfel's magnificently sonorous St Peter, Stephen Roberts's unsanctimonious Jesus, but above all, Robert Lloyd's Judas. Judas's despair at the betrayal of Christ prompted Elgar to touch new heights of sheer human drama, and the moment where he listens with dread to the shouts of "Crucify Him" from within the temple has an impact unequalled in most opera. His final despairing words, as sung here by Lloyd, carry an unbearable tragic intensity. In

1902, the year before he completed *The Apostles*, Elgar spent a week at Bayreuth, and it's perhaps not surprising that the work contains many echoes of *Parsifal.* Chandos's policy of recording in a church really pays dividends here, and there's no denying that its wider dynamic range can cope with the extremes of, say, the rapt *pianissimo* Hickox draws from his 'mystic chorus' in preparation for the final climax, or the astonishing passage in Part One where dawn breaks and the sun rises on the morning prayers in the temple. Who could resist the floor-shaking, full blazing triple *forte* splendour that Hickox and Chandos manage here?

Sir Adrian Boult [photo: MacDominic

George Enescu
Romanian 1881-1955

Enescu. Violin Sonatas — No. 2 in F minor, Op. 6; No. 3 in A minor, Op. 25, "dans le caractère populaire roumain". Violin Sonata Movement, "Torso". **Adelina Oprean** (vn); **Justin Oprean** (pf). Hyperion CDA66484.

> 1h 4' DDD 2/92

Enescu's First Violin Sonata, written when he was 16, is said to be immature and derivative: the Second Sonata, composed two years later in 1899, is an impressive achievement for an 18-year-old. It's true that there are still Brahmsian elements, and the work is also clearly influenced by Fauré, who was then Enescu's teacher, but the three movements are well-contrasted, and the quality of invention is high. The *Torso* Sonata dates from 1911, when Enescu's style was in a state of transition. Only one movement of this work survives, and it is a long, somewhat sprawling but impassioned statement. It would seem that Enescu abandoned the composition, but it deserves much more than oblivion. In his fascinating and highly individual Third Sonata Enescu invests the work with a Romanian folk flavour, and the style of country folk-fiddlers is imitated, but all the material is of his own invention. Adelina Oprean is a highly accomplished artist, as is her brother Justin. Together they produce performances which are rich in character and highly idiomatic — both players were born and brought up in Romania, and they understand Enescu's music to perfection. The recordings are excellent.

Enescu. OEDIPE. **José van Dam** (bass-bar) Oedipus; **Barbara Hendricks** (sop) Antigone; **Brigitte Fassbaender** (mez) Jocasta; **Marjana Lipovšek** (contr) The Sphinx; **Gabriel Bacquier** (bar) Tiresias; **Nicolai Gedda** (ten) Shepherd; **Jean-Philippe Courtis** (bass) Watchman; **Cornelius Hauptmann** (bass) High Priest; **Gino Quilico** (bar) Theseus; **John Aler** (ten) Laius; **Marcel Vanaud** (bar) Creon; **Laurence Albert** (bass) Phorbas; **Jocelyne Taillon** (mez) Merope; **Les Petits Chanteurs de Monaco; Orféon Donostiarra; Monte-Carlo Philharmonic Orchestra/Lawrence Foster.** EMI CDS7 54011-2. Notes, text and translation included.

> ② 2h 37' DDD 11/90 ⓠP ⓠS ❓

It is a sad commentary on the musical world's perception that except in Enescu's native Romania this remarkable opera — not merely his masterpiece (over which he pondered for more than 15 years) but a work of international stature should have received little more than a handful of performances since it was first heard 56 years ago. Those who know Enescu only from his popular early *Romanian Rhapsodies* will here find a composer of infinitely greater stature, employing a highly individual and eclectic style that includes exotic folk elements, strong influences from his teacher Fauré, and an ultra-sophisticated harmonic idiom, subtle instrumentation and ecstatic quality akin to the music of his near-contemporary Szymanowski. The opera's plot covers the entire Greek legend, from the initial warning to Laius through the events of *Oedipus rex* to *Oedipus in Colonna*; and one of the problems of mounting the work has been that the principal personage is on the stage virtually throughout except in the prologue. In this title-role José van Dam, always an artist of the first rank, presents one of his most memorable performances, encompassing the wide range of moods (and equally varied vocal techniques) with consummate mastery. But the casting throughout — individual mention would be invidious — is superb, stars being engaged even for minor roles; and Lawrence Foster, who has consistently championed Enescu's music, draws impressive playing from the Monte Carlo orchestra, capturing the score's delicacy as well as its violence, and ensuring that its complex texture remains clear.

Juan del Encina

NEW REVIEW

Encina. ROMANCES AND VILLANCICOS. **Hespèrion XX/Jordi Savall.**
Auvidis Astrée E8707. Texts and translations included.
Romances — Una sañosa porfía. Qu'es de ti, desconsolado?. Mortal tristura me dieron (instrumental version). Triste España sin ventura. *Villancicos* — Levanta, Pascual, levanta. Amor con fortuna. Fata la parte. Ay triste, que vengo. Cucú, cucú, cucucú. A tal perdida tan triste. Quedate, Carillo, adios (instrumental version). Si abrá en este baldres. El que rigue y el regido. Mas vale trocar. Oy comamos y bebamos. Tragedia: Despierta, despierta tus fuerças, Pegaso (recited).

 | 1h 16' DDD 2/92 |

The quest for the rediscovery of Spain's Renaissance musical heritage has yielded considerable treasures on record in recent times and not the least of such treasures is this disc devoted to Encina from the Catalan musician, Jordi Savall. For a quarter of a century he has rescued countless Iberian scores from obscurity and presented them in lively and stimulating performances (seldom without excellent accompanying sleeve-notes and presentation from Auvidis which puts many another record company to shame). The success of this disc, devoted as it is to songs and music from 500 years ago, reflects Encina's important position in Spanish musical history. Born the son of a cobbler in Salamanca, he grew up to become a musician in the pay of the royal family of Aragon. Encina's songs — stirring *romances* and lighter and often more comical and even bawdy *villancicos* (try the lyrics in pieces such as "Cucú, cucú, cucucú" and "Fata la parte" for Encina's earthier side) — are strongly inflected with the nascent Spanish theatrical tradition of which he was a pivotal figure. The musical performances here (there is also a spoken elegy mourning the death of Don Juan, heir to the throne of Castille and Aragon) are all strongly characterized, the soprano Montserrat Figueras and baritone Jordi Ricart being particularly noteworthy. Savall successfully alternates the period instruments (principally early wind and brass instruments as well as violas da gamba, one of which is skilfully played by Savall himself) to match the different moods of the songs. The heights of lyric writing and composition reached half a millenium ago provide us now with a disc to be enjoyed on many levels, not least for its human passion.

Manuel de Falla
Spanish 1876-1946

Falla. El sombrero de tres picos[a]. El amor brujo — ballet[b]. [a]**Colette Boky** (sop); [b]**Huguette Tourangeau** (mez); **Montreal Symphony Orchestra/ Charles Dutoit.** Decca 410 008-2DH. From SXDL7560 (7/83).

 | 1h 2' DDD 8/83 |

Here is a partnership of charismatic music-making and engineering of great flair in a superb recording acoustic, elements which combine to produce one of Decca's most famous CDs. With the sound so wonderfully atmospheric and vivid and with seductive orchestral playing, Dutoit shows his natural feeling for Spanish Flamenco rhythms. Both scores have been recorded very successfully before, but never with more magnetism. Whether in the delicious lilt of "Pantomime" or the spectacular opening of *El sombrero de tres picos* ("The three-cornered hat"), with its voluble timpani "Olés!" and castanets, this is music-making of the most compulsive kind, projected with great realism.

Falla. El amor brujo — ballet (orig. version)[a]. El corregidor y la molinera[b].
[b]**Jill Gomez** (sop); [a]**Claire Powell** (mez); **Aquarius/Nicholas Cleobury.**
Virgin Classics VC7 90790-2. Texts and translations included.

In choosing to record here the original, chamber-orchestra version of *El amor
brujo*, Nicholas Cleobury in no way tries to compete on equal terms with the
many brilliant, full-orchestral realizations of the later ballet and suite available on
disc. He makes his effect through the new dramatic light that this more complete
version throws on the work and the increased feeling of space that is given to the
orchestral textures. *El corregidor y la molinera* is also given in its earliest mime-play
version for chamber orchestra: it was later reworked as the ballet, *El sombrero de
tres picos*. Here the later version has additions that one would not wish to be
without, but this embryonic form is pleasing enough in its own right and gives
great insights into de Falla's working methods. This CD, then, is something of a
coup, made all the more desirable by the excellent quality of the performances
from Claire Powell and Jill Gomez — both colourful and intense in their
respective roles — and Aquarius, who bring a triumph of subtlety to the reduced
orchestral parts. The recording retains their vivacity without becoming too
intimate.

NEW REVIEW

Falla. El amor brujo — ballet (complete)[a]. Nights in the gardens of Spain[b].
Rodrigo. Concierto de Aranjuez[c]. [c]**Carlos Bonnell** (gtr); [b]**Alicia de
Larrocha** (pf); [ac]**Montreal Symphony Orchestra/Charles Dutoit;**
[b]**London Philharmonic Orchestra/Frühbeck de Burgos.** Decca Ovation
430 703-2DM. Item marked [a] from SXDL7560 (7/83), [b] 410 289-2DH (10/84),
[c] SXDL7525 (7/81).

Charles Dutoit　　　　*[photo: Decca/Huf]*

This hugely enjoyable disc of
Spanish music includes
Rodrigo's most famous work,
the *Concierto de Aranjuez* which
has never lost its popularity
since its Barcelona première in
1940 and here Carlos Bonnell
imparts a wistful, intimate feeling to the work, aided by a
thoughtful accompaniment from
Charles Dutoit's stylish Montreal Orchestra. The famous
string tune in the *Adagio* enjoys
a fulsome rendition. The two
Falla items increase the attraction of this CD. Dutoit's
beautifully played interpretation
of *El amor brujo* captures the
wide range of emotions that
this fiery, mysterious piece
requires and his performance of the famous "Ritual Fire Dance" must be among
the best in the catalogue. A cooler mood is captured in *Nights in the gardens of
Spain* with Alicia de Larrocha as the distinguished soloist. Her smooth, effortless
playing matches the mood of the piece exactly and de Burgos's accompaniment
with the London Philharmonic is equally sympathetic, with ripe tone colour and
careful dynamics. Those unfamiliar with these great Spanish works will be hard
pressed to find a better introduction than this superbly recorded disc.

Falla. SPANISH OPERA ARIAS AND SONGS.
Granados. GOYESCAS — La maja y el ruiseñor[be].
Turína. SPANISH SONGS. **Victoria de los Angeles** (sop); [a]**Gerald Moore**
(pf); [b]**Philharmonia Orchestra,** [c]**London Symphony Orchestra/**[d]**Stanford
Robinson,** [e]**Anatole Fistoulari,** [f]**Walter Susskind.** EMI Références mono
CDH7 64028-2. Item marked [be] from DB21069 (12/50).
Falla: LA VIDA BREVE[bd] — Vivan los que rien!; Alli está! riyendo (both from
HMV DB6702, 6/48). Siete canciones populares españolas[a] (DB9731/2, 2/52).
Turína: Canto a Sevilla[ce] (HMV ALP1185, 11/54). Saeta en forma de Salve[bf].
Poema en forma de canciones — Cantares[bf] (HMV DA1929, 5/50).

1h 18' ADD 4/92

Victoria de los Angeles performing Spanish music on a mid-price reissue — a
self-recommending disc if ever there was one. All the recordings here date from
the late 1940s and early 1950s when los Angeles was in her mid-twenties and in
great demand by the record companies following her remarkable début in 1944.
Her interpretation of the role of Salud in Falla's *La vida breve* is unsurpassed, and
this is superbly demonstrated in the two arias recorded here, which were made
shortly after her creation of the role for the BBC. Granados's opera *Goyescas* must
be one of the only operatic works in history to have been completely constructed
from a work originally written for solo piano. The beautiful aria, "La maja y el
ruiseñor" ("The maid and the nightingale") from the opera not only provides a
rare chance to hear part of the operatic score but also offers an excellent
opportunity to sample the extraordinary tonal beauty of los Angeles's voice.
Lyricism and tonal beauty are also strong features of her recording of Turína's
Canto a Sevilla, a mixed cycle of vocal and purely orchestral movements evoking
the atmosphere of Seville as a city and arguably Turína's masterpiece, and the
two orchestral songs, *Saeta en forma de Salve* and *Cantares* which are vividly
coloured and passionately delivered. Less successful, perhaps, are her slightly
under-characterized readings of Falla's *Siete canciones populares españolas*.
Unfortunately, EMI provide neither texts nor translations. These are, however,
rather minor caveats in an otherwise indispensable and generous reissue.

Falla. EL RETABLO DE MAESE PEDRO[a]. **Matthew Best** (bass) Don
Quijote; **Adrian Thompson** (ten) Maese Pedro; **Samuel Linay** (treb) El
Trujamán; **Maggie Cole** (hpd).
Milhaud. LES MALHEURS D'ORPHEE[b]. **Malcolm Walker** (bar) Orphée;
Anna Steiger (sop) Eurydice; **Paul Harrhy** (ten) Maréchal, Le sanglier;
Patrick Donnelly (bass) Le charron; **Matthew Best** (bass) Le vannier, L'ours;
Gaynor Morgan (sop) Le renard, La soeur Jumelle; **Patricia Bardon** (sop) Le
loup, La soeur Ainée; **Susan Bickley** (mez) Le soeur Cadette.
Stravinsky. RENARD[c]. **Hugh Hetherington, Paul Harrhy** (tens); **Patrick
Donnelly, Nicolas Cavallier** (basses); **Christopher Bradley** (cimbalom)
[abc]**Matrix Ensemble/Robert Ziegler.** ASV CDDCA758. Texts and
translations included.

1h 17' DDD 7/91

Three complete operas on one disc lasting 77 minutes must be good value, and
especially so when they are important works from the first quarter of this
century. One thing they have in common is that all were commissioned by the
American-born Princess de Polignac, a patroness of music who exercised
considerable flair in her choice of gifted artists in a Paris that was then full of
them. The performances here by Robert Ziegler and his Matrix Ensemble are
full of flair and his chosen singers for the three works (who include the
convincingly Spanish boy treble Samuel Linay as El Trujamán in the Falla) sound

at home in Spanish, French and Russian in turn. As presented here, Falla's puppet-opera is full of Iberian colour and verve, and although Milhaud's piece on the Orpheus legend is not so striking or dramatic it still has beauty and is elegantly and expressively sung and played. But the best music is still to come in Stravinsky's magnificently earthy and vivid 'barnyard fable' *Renard*, not a long work but a dazzling one, where this performance of great panache simply bursts out of one's loudspeakers to transport us instantly to a farmyard of old Russia. There's excellent cimbalom playing here from Christopher Bradley. The libretto of all three works is usefully provided in the booklet, together with an English translation. The recording is first class, being both immediate and atmospheric.

Gabriel Fauré

French 1845-1924

Fauré. ORCHESTRAL WORKS. [a]**Lorraine Hunt** (sop); [b]**Jules Eskin** (vc); [c]**Tanglewood Festival Chorus; Boston Symphony Orchestra/Seiji Ozawa.** DG 423 089-2GH. Text and translation included where appropriate.
Pelléas et Mélisande (with Chanson de Mélisande — orch. Koechlin)[a]. Après un rêve (arr. Dubenskij)[b]. Pavane[c]. Elégie[b]. Dolly (orch. Rabaud).

| 56' DDD 1/88 | ♩**S** |

Fauré's music for Maeterlinck's play *Pelléas et Mélisande* was commissioned by Mrs Patrick Campbell and to the usual four movement suite Ozawa has added the "Chanson de Mélisande", superbly sung here by Lorraine Hunt. Ozawa conducts a sensitive, sympathetic account of the score, and Jules Eskin plays beautifully in both the arrangement of the early song, *Après un rêve* and the *Elégie*, which survived from an abandoned cello sonata. The grave *Pavane* is performed here in the choral version of 1901. *Dolly* began life as a piano duet, but was later orchestrated by the composer and conductor Henri Rabaud. Ozawa gives a pleasing account of this delightful score and the recording is excellent.

NEW REVIEW

Fauré. Elégie in C minor, Op. 24.
Lalo. Cello Concerto in D minor.
Saint-Saëns. Cello Concerto No. 1 in A minor, Op. 33. **Heinrich Schiff** (vc); **New Philharmonia Orchestra/Sir Charles Mackerras.** DG Privilege 431 166-2GR. From 2530 793 (2/77).

| 53' ADD 8/91 | £ ♩**P** |

The Saint-Saëns Concerto is concisely put together, and shows the composer in his wittiest and most piquant vein. Schiff responds with appropriately warm and expressive playing, and particularly in the first movement his eager, agile playing is very attractive. In the charming *Allegretto* movement his rich tone is shown off to great advantage, and in the busier sections of the finale his clean, nimble technique is very evident. Fauré's *Elégie* inhabits a vastly different world, but Schiff's noble, emotionally restrained playing captures the mood of the piece perfectly. Lalo's Concerto is not in the same class as the other two compositions, but it has a certain faded charm, and Schiff plays the work with a good deal of energy and commitment. The New Philharmonia play in a spirited and precise fashion throughout the disc under Sir Charles Mackerras's wise and experienced direction, and the late 1970s recording sounds vivid and immediate in this transfer.

Fauré. Piano Quartets — No. 1 in C minor, Op. 15; No. 2 in G minor, Op. 45. **Domus** (Krysia Osostowicz, vn; Robin Ireland, va; Timothy Hugh, vc; Susan Tomes, pf). Hyperion CDA66166. From A66166 (10/86).

> 1h 2'   DDD   10/86

Fauré. Piano Quartet No. 1 in C minor, Op. 15[a]. Piano Trio in D minor, Op. 120. **Beaux Arts Trio** (Isidore Cohen, vn; Peter Wiley, vc; Menahem Pressler, pf); [a]**Kim Kashkashian** (va). Philips 422 350-2PH.

> 53'   DDD   6/90

The First Piano Quartet reveals Fauré's debt to an earlier generation of composers, particularly Mendelssohn. Yet already it has the refined sensuality, the elegance and the craftsmanship which were always to be hallmarks of his style and it is a thoroughly assured, highly enjoyable work which could come from no other composer's pen. The Second Quartet is a more complex, darker work, but much less ready to yield its secrets. The comparatively agitated, quicksilver scherzo impresses at once, however, and repeated hearings of the complete work reveal it to possess considerable poetry and stature. Just occasionally one could wish that the members of Domus had a slightly more aristocratic, commanding approach to these scores, but overall the achievement is highly impressive, for their playing is both idiomatic and technically impeccable. The recording has an appropriately intimate feel to it and is faithful and well-balanced.

The Beaux Arts Trio are one of the most celebrated of ensembles and together with the violist Kim Kashkashian they bring the right balance of passion and poise to the C minor Quartet's first movement, one that in lesser hands can seem discursive. The wry, prickly humour of the deft scherzo and the profound yet reticent romantic feeling of the *Adagio* are fully realized here too, as is the mysterious agitation of the finale. The D minor Piano Trio dates from 1923, over 40 years after the Piano Quartet and only a year before the composer's death, and is no less moving for being sometimes elliptical and questioning in utterance; this touching yet enigmatic music, though Gallic in feeling, is unlike any other French music of its time, though we may see expressive parallels to it in aspects of the novel sequence *A la recherche du temps perdu* which Marcel Proust was bringing to completion at this time. The recording made in the Snape Maltings is on the close side but broadly satisfying, although the piano sound in the Trio is a little compressed.

Fauré. Violin Sonatas — No. 1 in A major, Op. 13[a]; No. 2 in E minor, Op. 108[a].
Franck. Violin Sonata in A major[b]. **Arthur Grumiaux** (vn); [a]**Paul Crossley**, [b]**György Sebok** (pfs). Philips Musica da Camera 426 384-2PC. Items marked [a] from 9500 534 (7/79), [b] 9500 568 (10/80).

> 1h 13'   ADD   7/90

Fauré was only 31, and on the crest of his first great love affair, when writing his radiantly lyrical A major Violin Sonata. But curiously he allowed four decades to elapse before following it up with the E minor Sonata, by which time deafness, no less than the dark background of war, had drawn him into a more recondite world of his own. As portraits of the composer in youth and full artistic maturity the two works make an ideal coupling. But here, as a bonus, we are also given César Franck's one and only Violin Sonata, written when he was 64, bringing the playing time to the very generous total of almost an-hour-and-a-quarter. It would be hard to find any two artists closer to Fauré's own heart than the intimately attuned Grumiaux and Crossley. Their original LP was immediately hailed as the best available way back in 1979. And despite fine newcomers in recent years this mellow CD transfer still triumphs over all the catalogue's rivals. An unerring sense of style goes hand in hand with very beautiful, finely nuanced tone and an immediacy of expression suggesting joyous new discovery. Even if Sebok's piano emerges a little more plummy than Crossley's, the Franck Sonata, too, appeals through its warmth of heart.

Fauré. PIANO WORKS. **Jean-Philippe Collard**, [a]**Bruno Rigutto** (pfs). EMI Rouge et Noir CZS7 62687-2.
Barcarolles, Nos. 1-13 (from CDC7 47358-2, 5/87). Impromptus, Nos. 1-5 (EMI Pathé-Marconi 2C 069 73058, 9/82). Valses-caprices, No. 1-4. Huit pièces brèves, Op. 84. Mazurka in B flat major, Op. 32. Trois romances sans paroles, Op. 17. Dolly Suite, Op. 56[a]. *Fauré/Messager:* Souvenir de Bayreuth, Op. posth[a].

② 2h 31' ADD 3/92

No composer exemplifies so-called 'English' reserve more than Fauré, a Frenchman, and compared with Beethoven, Verdi or his compatriot Berlioz he can sometimes seem pallid, lacking a strong musical personality. But when his music is really well played, as it is here by Jean-Philippe Collard, one feels its own special kind of poetry and the passion that ebbs and flows beneath its refined surface. Collard does not falsify the natural understatement of these piano works, but rather shapes them on their own terms with a wide yet subtle expressive range, and each of the 13 barcarolles, which in lesser hands can sound too alike, has its own character. (They were not written as a set, but separately

over many years.) His command of tone and texture, together with phrasing and pedalling, brings colour and vitality to these pieces, and he knows how to balance grace with strength, lyricism with vigour. He is no less telling in the other solo music, and although these performances are hardly new (the barcarolles were recorded in 1970) they are models of their kind and the sound, while a little enclosed by today's standards, is satisfying. This well-filled mid-price set also brings us two duet works, one being the charmingly melodious *Dolly Suite* and the other the *Souvenir de Bayreuth*, a mischievous pot-pourri of Wagnerian tunes which reminds us that Fauré had a sense of humour.

Jean-Phillipe Collard   *[photo: EMI/Sarrat*

Fauré. La bonne chanson, Op. 61[a]. Piano Trio in D minor, Op. 120[b]. [a]**Sarah Walker** (mez); [a]**Nash Ensemble**; [b]**Marcia Crayford** (vn); [b]**Christopher van Kampen** (vc); [b]**Ian Brown** (pf). CRD CRD3389. Text and translation included. From CRD1089 (4/81).

44' ADD 5/90

In *La bonne chanson*, generally considered the finest of Fauré's song-cycles, he perfectly matched the ecstatic moods of Verlaine's love-poems to the young girl who was to become his wife; but though the sentiments expressed are those of a man and the songs were first performed by a baritone, they are more usually sung by a female voice. Sarah Walker, with her warm, voluptuous tone, poetic sensibility, shaping of phrases and, not least, excellent French, makes an admirable interpreter of their passionate lyricism. Fauré's own arrangement of the original piano accompaniment for string quintet and piano is played with tonal finesse by the Nash Ensemble. The final song, "L'hiver a cessé", refers to the music of the previous eight, summing up the atmosphere of radiant devotion that pervades the cycle. The Piano Trio, composed 30 years later when Fauré was 77, was his penultimate work and represents him at his most direct and compact: the artists here are responsive to its subtle harmonic thinking and judge its expressive weight to a nicety, preserving the grace of this essentially elegant, if elusive, work.

Fauré. Requiem, Op. 48 (original 1894 version)[a].
Fauré/Messager. Messe des Pêcheurs de Villerville[b]. [a]**Agnès Mellon** (sop); [a]**Peter Kooy** (bar); [b]**Jean-Philippe Audoli** (vn); [a]**Leo van Doeselaar** (org); **Petits Chanteurs de Saint-Louis; Paris Chapelle Royale Chorus; Musique Oblique Ensemble/Philippe Herreweghe.** Harmonia Mundi HMC90 1292. Texts included.

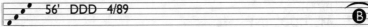

56' DDD 4/89   Ⓑ

NEW REVIEW

Fauré. Requiem, Op. 48 (revised version)[a]. Cantique de Jean Racine, Op. 11[b]. Messe basse[c].
Poulenc. Mass in G major[d]. Salve Regina. [ad]**Jonathon Bond** (treb); [c]**Andrew Brunt** (treb); [a]**Benjamin Luxon** (bar); [abc]**Stephen Cleobury** (org); [a]**Academy of St Martin in the Fields; Choir of St John's College, Cambridge/George Guest.** Decca Ovation 430 360-2DM. From ZRG841 (4/76).

1h 14' ADD 9/91   £ Ⓑ

Fauré's original conception of his Requiem was as a chamber work, but when the work was published it was scored for full orchestra. There is no evidence that Fauré did any more than acquiesce in preparing this 'concert-hall version' of his score. Even accepting that an amplification of the instrumentation is needed when the work is played in large halls, a rediscovery of the score as it existed before publication has long seemed desirable. New and convincing sources have now been discovered by the Fauré authority Jean-Michel Nectoux: a complete set of orchestral parts, apparently prepared for Fauré's use, some of them in his own hand and all corrected by him. The resulting score is as near to authentic Fauré as we shall get and this first recording by Harmonia Mundi of Nectoux's edition is ideal. It uses boys' voices in the upper parts (as did Fauré himself) and a convincingly boy-like soprano in the *Pie Jesu*. The orchestra is of ideal size and is beautifully balanced in a sympathetic acoustic. As a charming bonus we have another act of Fauréan 'restoration', the original version of what later became the *Messe basse*, with its pretty accompaniment for string quintet, wind trio and harmonium and its two long-suppressed extra movements by Messager. An enchanting record as well as an important document.

Decca's recording of the revised version of the Requiem will appeal particularly to people who dislike the large-scale sostenuto approach some conductors adopt in this work. The Choir of St John's College, Cambridge bring a clarity, purity and attention to diction and dynamics in this essentially gentle and subtle work. The big gestures we expect in Requiems by Berlioz and Verdi are absent in this piece and George Guest plays down the danger of sentimentality without skimping on taste and refinement from both the choir and the Academy of St Martin in the Fields. The initial impact of an all-male choir with boy trebles may not immediately appeal but hearing, in particular, Jonathon Bond's ethereal solo in the potentially saccharin *Pie Jesu* should dispel any such qualms. The feeling for intimacy is enhanced by Benjamin Luxon's expressive baritone and Guest's Bachian feel for Fauré's choral and orchestral part writing.

The choir are richly smooth in the mellifluous *Cantique de Jean Racine* while Andrew Brunt is a delightful soloist in the *Messe Basse*. Guest's ability to secure accurate as well as graceful singing is demonstrated in Poulenc's frisky Mass with its Stravinskian rhythms. The lusciously chromatic harmony can easily cloy, but the bright, radiant textures of the St John's singing avoids this entirely. A similar grace informs the more sombre short motet, *Salve Regina*, which rounds off this well-filled, competitively-priced disc. The recordings throughout are clear and well-balanced.

Howard Ferguson
Northern Irish 1908-

NEW REVIEW

Ferguson. Piano Sonata in F minor, Op. 8. Partita for two pianos, Op. 5b[a].
Howard Shelley, [a]**Hilary Macnamara** (pfs). Hyperion CDA66130. From A66130 (10/84).

44' DDD 1/91 ?

Although Howard Ferguson was active as a composer for over 30 years (he laid down his pen in the early 1960s, feeling that he had said all that he had to say as a composer) his published compositions number just 20. His slowness as a composer is almost entirely due to the painstaking care that he devoted to each of his compositions, and this in turn is reflected in the extremely high quality of each work. The Piano Sonata, dating from 1938-40, is dedicated to the memory of his friend and teacher, Harold Samuel, and is arguably the most intensely personal of all Ferguson's works. It is by far his most frequently performed work (though not however on disc), and the astringency of its rhythmic and harmonic writing, coupled with its classical economy and romantic gesture has given rise to Ferguson being labelled a twentieth-century romantic. Howard Shelley is both persuasive and commanding, and is particularly effective in projecting the work's overwhelming sense of despair and loss. The *Partita* for two pianos is another fine example of Ferguson's immaculate craftsmanship and concise economic style, and also underlines his allegiance to both classical and baroque forms. If this gives the impression of a rather dry, academic work, then the reader is urged to sample the seductively undulating and fantastical windswept quality of the second movement or the ebullient, reel-like energy in the outer sections of the finale. An exemplary recording from every point of view.

Gerald Finzi
British 1901-1956

Finzi. Cello Concerto, Op. 40.
Leighton. Veris gratia — suite, Op. 9[a]. **Rafael Wallfisch** (vc), [a]**George Caird** (ob); **Royal Liverpool Philharmonic Orchestra/Vernon Handley.** Chandos CHAN8471.

1h 6' DDD 10/86

Finzi wrote his Cello Concerto for the Cheltenham Festival of 1955. At this time he had suffered from leukaemia for four years and he knew that he had not long to live. This knowledge served only to enhance his deep-seated awareness of and preoccupation with questions concerning life's transience, and the result is a work which is large in scale and reflects dark, troubled emotions. Raphael Wallfisch gives a moving and eloquent account of the solo part: he plays with a rich quality of tone, and Vernon Handley provides a sympathetic accompaniment.

Kenneth Leighton was still a student when Finzi took an interest in his work. Finzi was conductor of the Newbury String Players, and for this group Leighton wrote his suite *Veris gratia*, a melodious, lyrical work in four movements, inspired by Helen Waddell's translation of *Medieval Latin Lyrics*. The performance is all that could be desired, and is set in a high quality recording.

Finzi. ORCHESTRAL WORKS. [a]**Alan Hacker** (cl); **English String Orchestra/William Boughton.** Nimbus NI5101.
Love's Labour's Lost — Suite, Op. 28. Clarinet Concerto in C minor, Op. 31[a]. Prelude in F minor, Op. 25. Romance in E flat major, Op. 11.

1h 5' DDD 12/88

There are several other Finzi issues available which include the Clarinet Concerto. Alan Hacker, however, encompasses all his colleagues' virtues, providing special insights and revelling in the brilliant writing. He also adds something extra — an almost mystical realization of the music's poetic vision which is deeply moving. This is in spite of the fact that the string-playing sometimes lacks polish and precision. Finzi wrote incidental music for a BBC production of *Love's Labour's Lost* and expanded it for a later open-air production. It is tuneful, graceful music, but one cannot feel that the stage was Finzi's world. The disc is completed by two interesting early pieces for strings, the *Prelude* and *Romance*, both wholly characteristic of the composer and very well played.

Finzi. The Fall of the Leaf, Op. 20. New Year Music nocturne for orchestra, Op. 7. **Moeran.** Sinfonietta. Serenade in G major. **Northern Sinfonia/Richard Hickox.** EMI CDC7 49912-2.

1h 2' DDD 2/90

All Saints' Church, Quayside, in Newcastle upon Tyne imparts a lively resonance to these brilliantly lit performances from the Northern Sinfonia, lending ripeness and space to the already glowing colours of such quintessentially British works. Moeran's *Serenade* and *Sinfonietta*, which frame the two shorter pieces by Finzi, are late works of direct and appealing expression. The *Serenade* is suite-like, with four dance movements plus a Prologue and Epilogue, and is brightly scored for small orchestra. The *Sinfonietta* has only three movements, though the second is a theme with six variations, and the whole is suffused with images of Radnorshire's moorland. Its darker moments tie it more closely in mood with Finzi's *The Fall of the Leaf*, a work left only partly scored at the composer's death. Howard Ferguson has made a marvellous job of completing the piece and we can but be glad that such a gloriously poignant example of Finzi's art is now available. His *Nocturne*, without being as effusively emotional, also makes a lasting impression in these strong, dedicated readings from Richard Hickox. The straightforward approach does not preclude poetry and it is difficult to think of these works receiving more sympathetic performances.

Finzi. Dies Natalis, Op. 8[a]. Farewell to Arms, Op. 9[a]. Clarinet Concerto in C minor, Op. 31[b]. [a]**Martyn Hill** (ten); [b]**Michael Collins** (cl); **City of London Sinfonia/Richard Hickox.** Virgin Classics VC7 90718-2. Texts included.

1h 1' DDD 8/88

This enterprising disc contains what can probably be regarded as Finzi's two best-known works, *Dies Natalis* and the Clarinet Concerto, and a rarity, the *Farewell to Arms*. *Dies Natalis* is a masterpiece of sustained rapture, the perfect metamorphosis into music of the metaphysical poet Traherne's Blake-like vision of the innocence and wonder with which we come into the world. Words and music belong together and the unending melody never loses its power to entrance the sympathetic listener. Martyn Hill sings beautifully and Richard Hickox's conducting ensures a memorable interpretation. The Clarinet Concerto with its elegiac slow movement inhabits a similar world. But Finzi is capable of more than pastoral reverie, as the restless first movement and the delightfully relaxed and witty *rondo-finale* demonstrate. Michael Collins is an agile, poetic and virtuosic soloist, his mellow and pleasing tone faithfully captured by the recording.

NEW REVIEW

Finzi. CHORAL WORKS. **Finzi Singers/Paul Spicer** with [a]**Harry Bicket** (org). Chandos CHAN8936. Texts included.
All this night, Op. 33. Let us now praise famous men, Op. 35[a]. Lo, the full, final sacrifice, Op. 26[a]. Magnificat, Op. 36[a]. Seven Part-songs, Op. 17. Though did'st delight my eyes, Op. 32. Three Anthems, Op. 27[a]. Three Short Elegies, Op. 5[a]. White-flowering days, Op. 37.

1h 19' DDD 9/91

Finzi Singers and Paul Spicer   [photo: Chandos/Jack

Finzi is no composer to look to for the musical counterpart of a quick fix — and how he would have abhorred that expression. To the patient spirit of the listener who seeks music in which the fastidious limitation of its means is itself some guarantee of the depth of its purposes, he will always be rewarding. This is true of all the works collected here. Some, such as the first and last, *God is gone up* and *Lo, the full, final sacrifice*, are relatively well-known, which is not to say that they will necessarily prove the most satisfying. There are some fine shorter pieces including the unaccompanied *Seven Poems of Bridges* and the *Three Drummond Elegies* that delight as word-settings. "White-flowering days", to words by Edmund Blunden, comes from *A Garland for the Queen*, the Coronation gift of ten composers in 1953, none happier than this in catching the fresh hopefulness of the time. Best of all perhaps is the *Magnificat*, which also had its first British performance in that year. It is heard here in its original version with organ, beautifully played on this disc and providing a more spiritual association than is found in the orchestral accompaniment added later. The Finzi Singers are sensitive, assured and accurate; their tone is uniformly good, and they convey a sense of personal involvement in the music. The qualities of recorded sound and presentation are well up to the rest.

Gioseffo-Hectore Fiocco   *Belgian/Italian 1703-1741*

G-H. Fiocco. Pièces de clavecin, Op. 1. **Ton Koopman** (hpd). Auvidis Astrée E7731.

② 1h 26' AAD 3/90

The Belgian-born Gioseffo-Hectore Fiocco was, in spite of his name, at least as francophile as italophile, at least to judge by these two harpsichord suites (published *c.*1730). The suites contain mixtures of French and italianate movements, as well as a few in the more *galant* style of *les goûts réünis*. Couperin's influence is evident in such external details as the titles, ornamentation — although a good proportion of that is the stylish invention of Ton Koopman — and the exquisite melancholy; but Fiocco also mastered the forms, textures and harmonic progressions epitomized by Couperin's music. And while Fiocco never surpassed the sublimity of his model, he did compose powerful and often sombre music worthy of wider circulation. Each suite is a microcosm of contemporary forms. The G major encompasses many contrasts of mood and style (*L'italiene* — surely a parody of Handel — is followed by the Couperinesque *La Françoise*). For all the French movements, Fiocco's first suite ends with a four-movement Italian sonata, in which Vivaldi might have taken pride. The D minor suite is less structured: there are dance movements graced with interesting technical challenges (especially in the Ramellian *Sauterelles*), three *rondeaux* and a lively, stylistically integrated finale (*La Frinqante*). Throughout, Koopman plays masterfully, interestingly and with unimpeachable taste. He has written the extremely informative booklet, revealing much about both the music and his approach to playing. The variety and aptness of his own ornamentation in both French and italianate movements can serve as a valuable guide: this is the crux of his performance which brings the music to life.

Antoine Forqueray   *French 1671-1745*

Forqueray. PIECES DE VIOLE. [a]**Jay Bernfield** (va da gamba); **Skip Sempé** (hpd). Deutsche Harmonia Mundi RD77262.
Allemande La Laborde[a]. La Cottin. La Portugaise[a]. La Forqueray. La Régente[a]. La Marella. Sarabande La d'Aubonne. La Ferrand[a]. La Couperin. Chaconne La Buisson[a]. Le Leclair. La Rameau. Jupiter[a].

50'   DDD   5/92

Antoine Forqueray was among the most gifted bass viol players at Louis XIV's court. His son, Jean-Baptiste-Antoine assisted him in the editing of his music and, following Antoine's death, brought out an anthology in his father's name. The collection, published in 1747, was presented in two versions, one for bass viol and continuo, the other for solo harpsichord. It is from this anthology that Skip Sempé and Jay Bernfield have compiled their attractive programme which includes pieces both for bass viola and continuo and for solo harpsichord. As with so much French instrumental music of this period the indigenous style is coloured by Italian influences and the resulting subtle interplay and juxtaposition of the two exercise lively play on our imagination. Both players are fluently versed in the particularities of French baroque style and their programme has been constructed in a manner which effectively reveals the varied colours and contrasting gestures of the music. Among the solo harpsichord pieces are delightful tributes to three of Forqueray's greatest contemporaries, Couperin, Rameau and Leclair. Outstanding among the bass viol items, perhaps, is the sensuous *La Régente*.

Cesar Franck   *Belgian/French 1822-1890*

Franck. ORGAN WORKS. **Jean Guillou**. Dorian DOR90135. Played on the organ of St Eustache, Paris.
Cantabile in B major. Chorales — No. 1 in E major; No. 2 in B minor; No. 3 in A minor. Fantaisie in A major. Fantaisie in C major. Final in B flat major.

Grande Pièce Symphonique. Pastorale in E major. Pièce Héroïque in B minor.
Prélude, Fugue et Variation. Prière in C sharp minor.

Franck. ORGAN WORKS. **Michael Murray.** Telarc CD80234. Played on
the Cavaillé-Coll organ of Saint Sernin Basilica, Toulouse.
Fantaisie in A major. Cantabile in B major. Pièce Héroïque in B minor. Fantaisie
in C major. Grande Pièce Symphonique. Prélude, Fugue et variation. Pastorale.
Prière in C sharp minor. Final in B flat major. Chorales — No. 1 in E major;
No. 2 in B minor; No. 3 in A minor.

Although Franck wrote a great many small pieces for organ it was with these 12
(the 'masterworks' as the Telarc disc styles them) that he established an organ
music tradition which French composers to this day have followed. Jean Guillou
is certainly in that tradition. He is a virtuoso organist and gifted improviser (as
was Franck) and his own organ music is in the large, colourful, symphonic mould
effectively created by Franck. As part of that living tradition Guillou obviously
doesn't feel constrained by what Franck actually wrote down. He modifies the
original almost to the point of eccentricity: much of what you hear here bears
little relation to the published text. But if you are willing to listen with an open
mind and don't believe that what the composer wrote has to be considered
sacrosanct you will be rewarded with some breathtaking virtuosity and a
spectacular recorded sound.

   Michael Murray, on the other hand, is entirely respectful of tradition. There is
about his performances something akin to reverence. He is completely faithful to
the finest detail of the score, and the authenticity of these performances is
underlined by being recorded on an instrument contemporaneous (just) with
Franck and still in virtually unaltered shape; this was the kind of organ sound that
inspired Franck to write these pieces. Authentic and respectful as they are,
Murray's performances are beautifully played. Like most American organists he
seems to have a natural gift for direct communication; a gift wholeheartedly
supported by Telarc's exceptionally fine recording.

NEW REVIEW

Franck. Symphony in D minor.
d'Indy. Symphonie sur un chant montagnard français, Op. 25ᵃ. ᵃ**Jean-Yves
Thibaudet** (pf); **Montreal Symphony Orchestra/Charles Dutoit.** Decca
430 278-2DH.

These two French masterpieces of the 1880s complement each other perfectly.
The Franck, drawing its inspiration from the other side of the Alps, is very much
in the Austro-German symphonic tradition. Its language calls to mind the vaulted
splendours and gothic interiors of many a Bruckner Symphony. D'Indy's
Symphony, in reality more of a piano concerto, is based on a folk-song he heard
whilst holidaying in the Cévennes mountains. Definitely outdoors music this, and
far more recognizably French; indeed, with its echoes of Berlioz to its pre-echoes
of Debussy and even 'Les Six', it occupies a central position in a century of
French music. Dutoit's elegant, flowing way with the Franck (marvellously
refined *espressivo* playing from the Montreal violins, and shining, incisive brass) is
ideal for those who shy away from the Brucknerian monumentalism of the work;
and Jean-Yves Thibaudet's eloquent solo playing in the d'Indy is matched by
exquisitely drawn instrumental solos from within the orchestra. Decca's spacious
Montreal sound, too, proves just as apt for the organ-like timbres of the Franck,
as for the fresh air and wide horizons of the d'Indy.

Franck. Violin Sonata in A major.
Szymanowski. Mythes, Op. 30. King Roger (trans. Kochański). Kurpian Song
(trans. Kochański). **Kaja Danczowska** (vn); **Krystian Zimerman** (pf). DG
Galleria 431 469-2GGA. From 2531 330 (6/81).

· 58' ADD 8/91

Franck's sonata, with its yearning romantic nature, makes a good foil for
Szymanowski's rather wild, rhapsodic invention. Kaja Danczowska, a pupil of
Eugenia Uminska and David Oistrakh, shows a fine technique, a beautiful tone-
quality, and plenty of temperament on this very well-recorded disc. In the
Franck Zimerman is a mite too reticent, though he plays beautifully and
impeccably, but Danczowska captures Franck's changing moods perfectly and
brings a not at all inappropriate Polish fervour to the three quicker movements.
The third movement, *Recitativo-Fantasia,* is finely characterized, too, with its
more thoughtful, inward episodes sympathetically explored. The best known of
Szymanowski's three shortish *Mythes* is the first, "La fontaine d'Arethuse", which
has often been played on its own. It has an exotic, other worldly beauty which is
very well realized by Danczowska, with Zimerman here a more positive,
purposeful partner. The second piece, "Narcisse", inhabits a similar world, but
"Dryades et Pan" is quite daring for 1915, with its use of quarter-tones.
These pieces, and the effective transcriptions, are vividly brought to life by
Szymanowski's two compatriots.

Franck. Prélude choral et fugue (1884).
Liszt. PIANO WORKS. **Murray Perahia** (pf). Sony Classical CD47180.
Mephisto Waltz No. 1, S514. Années de pèlerinage, première année, S160,
"Suisse" — Aubord d'une source; deuxième année, S161, "Italie" — Sonetto 104
del Petrarca. Two Concert Studies, S145. Rhapsodie espagnole, S254.

· 1h DDD 10/91

Having surprised many of his admirers by launching the second half of his earlier,
much-praised "Aldeburgh Recital" (reviewed in the "Collections" section of this
Guide) with a *Hungarian Rhapsody* by Liszt, Murray Perahia now leaves us in no
doubt that his encounter with this composer was no mere passing flirtation in the
course of an ever-widening exploration of the romantic repertory. 'Aristocratic'
is the adjective that first comes to mind in describing his approach. It is Liszt

playing of quite exceptional finesse,
ravishing in pellucid sonority, delicately glistening (like frost on every
individual blade of grass in early
morning winter sunshine) in sleight-
of-hand, yet not lacking strength in
the bolder climaxes of a bravura
piece such as the concluding *Rhapsodie espagnole*. Only in the *Mephisto
Waltz* is there just a slight suspicion
of caution on the dance-floor and
chasteness in the "lascivious, caressing dreams of love". Franck's *Prélude
choral et fugue* in its turn has a simplicity and dignity, free of all
arrogance or bluster very much Perahia's own. Predictably his unfailing
textural clarity is a major asset —
not least in the contrapuntal cunning

Murray Perahia   *[photo: Sony Classical*   305

of the fugue. Recorded mainly at The Maltings, Snape, but in part at the Royce Hall in Los Angeles, the sound *per se* is first-class throughout.

Franck. Les Béatitudes. **Diana Montague, Ingeborg Danz** (mezzos); **Cornelia Kallisch** (contr); **Keith Lewis, Scot Weir** (tens); **Gilles Cachemaille** (bar); **John Cheek, Juan Vasle, Reinhard Hagen** (basses); **Stuttgart Gächinger Kantorei and Radio Symphony Orchestra/Helmuth Rilling.** Hänssler 98 964. Text and translation included.

② 2h 11' DDD 7/91

Without going as far as some of Franck's disciples — d'Indy, for example, called *Les Béatitudes* "the greatest work for a long time in the development of the art" — it has to be conceded that sections of the work, such as parts four and five, contain music of great beauty, and that the rich texture and extremely effective orchestration in all of it are impressive. It was intended not as a narrative oratorio in the Handel-Haydn-Mendelssohn tradition but as a series of contemplative devotional studies; and stylistically it shows both an affinity to the Liszt-Wagner school and an anticipation of the Impressionists. The predominantly slow tempos of the Prologue and eight Beatitudes, unenterprising rhythmic invention and the structural uniformity of the sections (each consisting of high-toned but pedestrian moralistic verse followed by the Biblical quotation) flaw the impact of the oratorio as an entity; but this is a case of the parts being greater than the whole. Helmuth Rilling (if over-inclined to exaggerate ritardandos) here delivers a very fine performance, certainly superior to the two current previous recordings, with an excellent chorus and orchestra and some first-rate soloists: radiant singing from Diana Montague and incisively menacing tone from John Cheek as the voice of Satan. Good presentation material and good recording.

Robert Franz   *Refer to Index*   *German 1815-1892*

Domenico Gallo   *Refer to Index*   *Italian born c.1730*

Phillipe Gaubert   *French 1879-1941*

NEW REVIEW

Gaubert. COMPLETE WORKS FOR FLUTE AND PIANO. **Susan Milan** (fl); **Ian Brown** (pf). Chandos CHAN8981/2. Items marked [a] from CHAN8609 (11/88).
Sonata. Madrigal. Deux esquisses. Fantaisie[a]. Romance (1908). Flute Sonatas — No. 2; No. 3. Sicilienne. Berceuse. Suite. Nocturne et Allegro scherzando[a]. Romance (1905). Sonatine. Sur l'eau. Ballade.

② 2h DDD 11/91

This integral recording of the complete works for flute and piano by Philippe Gaubert commemorates the fiftieth anniversary of the death of one of the seminal figures in the history of modern flute playing. Although still revered as co-author (with Paul Taffanel) of a famous tutorial for the instrument, the majority of Gaubert's enchanting compositions will be largely unfamiliar. Fortunately, his music could hardly find more convincing advocacy than in the hands of Susan Milan and Ian Brown. Listening to these works, one cannot avoid wondering about the remainder of Gaubert's large output, which included operas, ballet scores, a symphony, several concertos, and much chamber music, all of which now seems to be forgotten. Gaubert's three sonatas are lithe, lyrical and affable, although essentially traditional in concept, but the real joys of this set are the various salon miniatures, ranging from the *Madrigal* of 1908 to such delights as *Sur l'eau* and the delectable *Sicilienne* and *Berceuse*. The *Suite* of 1921 is thoughtfully and tastefully cast, with the final "Scherzo-Valse" being particularly memorable. The playing is sparkling and witty, with the mellifluous tone of Susan Milan a lasting pleasure throughout. She is ably supported by the pianist, Ian Brown, and the recordings are beyond criticism. Strongly recommended.

George Gershwin
American 1898-1937

Gershwin. ORCHESTRAL WORKS. [a]**Earl Wild** (pf); **Boston Pops Orchestra/Arthur Fiedler.** RCA Papillon GD86519. Item marked [a] from VICS1308 (7/73), [b] new to UK, [c] SB6580 (9/64).
Rhapsody in Blue[a]. Piano Concerto in F major[b]. An American in Paris[c].
Variations on "I got rhythm"[b].

1h 10' ADD 11/87

The ideal pianist for Gershwin is one who combines the instinctive feel for Broadway musical rhythm with the control, dexterity and power of the classical virtuoso, and Earl Wild is pretty close to that ideal. The other vital ingredient is an orchestra and conductor with a similar blend of skills, and here the Boston Pops with Arthur Fiedler fits the bill as closely as any. This is one of the few symphony-orchestra versions of the *Rhapsody in Blue* which does not make one yearn for the leaner, punchier textures of the original jazz-band orchestration; and what a relief to hear the Concerto and *An American in Paris* avoiding both the constraint and the self-conscious freedom to which most classics-only orchestras are prone. The inclusion of the immensely resourceful *Variations on "I got rhythm"* gives the disc a further edge over its competitors. Recording quality is clean-cut and free from trickery, although in its somewhat constricted perspective it just falls short of the highest standards.

Gershwin. Rhapsody in Blue[a]. An American in Paris. Piano Concerto in F major[a]. **London Symphony Orchestra/André Previn** ([a]pf). EMI CDC7 47161-2. From ASD2754 (11/71).

1h 4' ADD 9/86

Gershwin. An American in Paris[a]. Rhapsody in Blue[b]. [a]**Columbia Symphony Orchestra;** [b]**New York Philharmonic Orchestra/Leonard Bernstein** (pf[a]). CBS Maestro CD42611. From Philips SABL160 (10/60).

35' ADD 11/90

Few CDs remastered from analogue LPs show an improvement in sound-quality so striking as Previn's Gershwin triptych. The digital remastering has transformed the effect of the music-making, giving both the *Rhapsody* and *An American in Paris* a vibrant, vivid clarity, without serious loss of body, and in the Concerto the strings sound particularly fresh, creating the most attractively warm timbre in the lyrical theme of the first movement. There are many felicities in these performances and *An American in Paris* is infectiously volatile, with a strong rhythmic inflection for the great blues tune when it enters on the trumpet. In the *Rhapsody* there is much chimerical detail from Previn and the lack of inflation is very telling. One is glad to see the Concerto is at last establishing itself in the concert hall for it is full of memorable tunes. Previn's version is highly distinguished, with the lyricism of the slow movement evocatively caught and the brilliant finale a *tour de force*.

Bernstein conducted and played the music of Gershwin with the same naturalness as he brought to his own music. Here, *An American in Paris* swings by with an instinctive sense of its origins in popular and film music; no stilted rhythms or four-squareness delay the work's progress, and where ripe schmaltz is wanted, ripe schmaltz is what we get, devoid of all embarrassment. *Rhapsody in Blue* is playful and teasing, constantly daring us to try to categorize its style, and then confounding our conclusions. Although the solo passages from individual players are beautifully taken, both orchestras pull together magnificently to capture the authentic flavour of Gershwin's idiom, and Bernstein pushes them to transcend the printed score. His own playing in the *Rhapsody* is tantalizingly unpredictable. The recording is clear and bright, perhaps a touch hard-edged, and a little of the richness of the original LP issue might have been preferred by some, especially as the editing is now made more obvious. The only major criticism would be of the stingy overall timing of the disc — but with these performances quality compensates.

NEW REVIEW

Gershwin (arr. Russell Bennett). PORGY AND BESS — A Symphonic Picture. **Grofé.** Grand Canyon Suite. **Detroit Symphony Orchestra/Antál Dorati**. Decca Ovation 430 712-2DM. From 410 110-2DH (5/84).

· Ih DDD 8/91

Antál Dorati was a major European conductor with a great interest in American music, particularly in his last years when he was associated with the Detroit Symphony Orchestra. His performances of Copland's music are richly enjoyable and this disc of works by Gershwin and Grofé is a worthy companion. *Porgy and Bess* is performed here in the well-known arrangement by Robert Russell Bennett. "Bess, you is my woman now" and "I got plenty o' nuthin'" appear in glitzy orchestral colours and Dorati and his orchestra revel in the colour and bring an idiomatic swing to Gershwin's distinctive melodic contours. The companion piece, Grofé's charming *Grand Canyon* Suite is also something of an American tone-poem, complete with clip-clopping mules and evocative dawns and dusks. The concluding cloudburst seems like a transatlantic answer to Richard Strauss's *Alpine* Symphony and Dorati brings a sense of structure and care for detail to the work. The recording is both full and fresh, reaching demonstration quality in the *Grand Canyon*.

Gershwin (arr. Wild). PIANO TRANSCRIPTIONS. **Earl Wild.** Chesky CD32. Fantasy on "Porgy and Bess". Improvisation in the form of a Theme and Three Variations on "Someone to watch over me". Seven Virtuoso Etudes: I got rhythm; Lady be good; Liza; Embraceable you; Somebody loves me; Fascinatin' rhythm; The man I love.

· 59' DDD 10/90

This disc is one of those remarkable contemporary documents of great pianism, to be treasured and brought out for comparison whenever the virtuosos of earlier ages are cited. Earl Wild not only matches many of the giants in technical dexterity and musical insight, but also mirrors the ability of a number to produce enthralling glosses on the music of others in the form of almost ridiculously taxing transcriptions. Here, Gershwin is the subject of Wild's wonderful flights of fancy, a particularly appropriate choice as Gershwin himself produced transcriptions of a number of his own songs, obviously considering them ideal vehicles for jazz-type transformation. Wild magically combines a modern improvisational technique with a Lisztian attention to form, development and unity, producing works that repay repeated listening. The *Porgy and Bess* Fantasy achieves what the best of Liszt's works in the genre do — it conveys the flavour of the opera to those who do not know it, prompting them to hear the original, and gives added insight into the music for those who are already familiar with it. The solid-toned Baldwin piano, captured with effective truthfulness by the recording, is the ideal instrument for such inspirational performances.

Kiri Sings Gershwin. Dame Kiri Te Kanawa (sop); **New Princess Theater Orchestra/John McGlinn.** EMI CDC7 47454-2.
Including — Somebody loves me, Love walked in, Summertime, The man I love, Things are looking up.

| ♩ 46' DDD 10/87 | ♩ p |

This recording was made possible by the discovery of a cache of scores, with original orchestrations, in the Warner Brothers warehouse in New Jersey. It is a remarkably successful disc finding Te Kanawa on sparkling form; indeed she sounds more involved here than on many of her more 'classical' recordings. The up-tempo presentation may take a little getting used to (*Love is here to stay* is really rather swift) but the disc has a wonderful verve that is quite intoxicating. *I got rhythm*, complete with its male vocal quartet, is tremendous. John McGlinn directs wholly idiomatically. The recording is a little fierce in the 'pop' style, with a slightly tiring edge lent to this already quite fizzy music. But these are treasurable mementoes of the 1920s and 1930s.

Gershwin. GIRL CRAZY. Cast includes **Lorna Luft, David Carroll, Judy Blazer, Frank Gorshin, David Garrison, Vicki Lewis, chorus and orchestra/John Mauceri.** Elektra Nonesuch 7559-79250-2. Notes and text included.

| ♩ 1h 13' DDD 2/91 | ♩ p |

George and Ira Gershwin [photo: Elektra Nonesuch

Girl Crazy is certainly one of the most hit-filled shows the Gershwins ever penned as the rousing Overture alone, with its references to "But not for me", "I got rhythm", "Bidin' my time" and "Embraceable you", immediately and irresistibly confirms. But these are not the only knockout numbers that pepper this terrific score; "Could you use me?", "Sam and Delilah" and "Treat me rough" are equally deserving of the term 'showstopper'. The show's basic setting, a Dude Ranch (where eastern playboys spent their vacation pretending to be western cowboys), may be uniquely American (which could explain why the show did not cross the Atlantic) but any unfamiliarity the overseas listener may have with the plot's finer points will in no way mar enjoyment of this completely captivating recording. One of the chief pleasures to be had from the current crop of Broadway reconstructions is the opportunity of hearing the songs with their original orchestrations, and Robert Russell Bennett's here are no exception. John Mauceri and his hand-picked orchestra respond with infectious gusto to every nuance of Bennett's delightful arrangements and throughout the score they successfully evoke the jazzy atmosphere of 1930s Broadway. Each of the soloists and chorus, too, are all just right, bringing off their respective numbers with tremendous verve and a real feel for the idiom. Packaged with an incredibly lavish and informative booklet (96 pages in all) this issue is an absolute treasure.

Gershwin. PORGY AND BESS. **Willard White** (bass) Porgy; **Cynthia Haymon** (sop) Bess; **Harolyn Blackwell** (sop) Clara; **Cynthia Clarey** (sop) Serena; **Damon Evans** (bar) Sportin' Life; **Marietta Simpson** (mez) Maria; **Gregg Baker** (bar) Crown; **Glyndebourne Chorus; London Philharmonic Orchestra/Simon Rattle.** EMI CDS7 49568-2. Notes and text included.

③ 3h 9' DDD 6/89

Gershwin. PORGY AND BESS — excerpts. **Leontyne Price, Barbara Webb, Berniece Hall, Maeretha Stewart** (sops); **Miriam Burton** (mez); **John W. Bubbles, Robert Henson** (tens); **William Warfield, McHenry Boatwright, Alonzo Jones** (bars); **RCA Victor Chorus and Orchestra/ Skitch Henderson.** RCA Victor Gold Seal GD85234. From SB6554 (1/64). Act 1 — Introduction; Summertime; A woman is a sometime thing; Gone, gone, gone. Act 2 — I got plenty o' nuttin; Bess you is my woman now; It ain't necessarily so; What you want wid Bess? I loves you Porgy. Act 3 — There's a boat dat's leavin'; Oh Bess; Oh Gawd, I'm on my way.

48' ADD 4/89

The company, orchestra and conductor from the outstanding 1986 Glyndebourne production recreate once more a very real sense of Gershwin's 'Catfish Row' community on EMI's complete recording. Such is the atmosphere and theatricality of this recording, we might easily be back on the Glyndebourne stage; you can positively smell the drama in the key scenes. From the very first bar it's clear just how instinctively attuned Simon Rattle and this orchestra are to every aspect of a multi-faceted score. The cast, too, are so *right*, so much a part of their roles, and so well integrated into the whole, that one almost takes the excellence of their contributions for granted. Here is one beautiful voice after another, beginning in style with Harolyn Blackwell's radiant "Summertime", which at Rattle's gorgeously lazy tempo, is just about as beguiling as one could wish. Willard White conveys both the simple honesty and inner-strength of Porgy without milking the sentiment and Haymon's passionately sung Bess will go wherever a little flattery and encouragement take her. As Sportin' Life, Damon Evans not only relishes the burlesque elements of the role but he really *sings* what's written a lot more than is customary. But the entire cast deliver throughout with all the unstinting fervour of a Sunday revivalist meeting. Sample for yourself the final moments of the piece — "Oh Gawd, I'm on my way" — if that doesn't stir you, nothing will.

The RCA issue is unashamedly a vehicle for the glorious voice of Leontyne Price, a notable Bess in her early career. Her voice was at its peak of form and beauty in 1963 when this disc was made and the richness and pliancy across the entire register is quite breathtaking. William Warfield's Porgy is almost overshadowed by such luxuriance of tone but it is good to have on record what was a celebrated portrayal. Another splendid assumption is John W. Bubbles's Sportin' Life, a wonderfully rounded characterization. The orchestral support is lively and theatrical and for anyone hesitant about investing in Rattle's fine complete recording of the opera, this highlights disc has a lot to offer.

Carlo Gesualdo

Gesualdo. MADRIGALS. **Les Arts Florissants** [a]**Vocal and** [b]**Instrumental Ensembles/William Christie.** Harmonia Mundi HMC90 1268. Texts and translations included.

Madrigals[a] — Ahi, disperata vita. Sospirava il mio cor. O malnati messaggi. Non t'amo, o voce ingrata. Luci serene e chiare. Sparge la morte al mio Signor nel viso. Arde il mio cor. Occhi del mio cor vita. Mercè grido piangendo. Asciugate i begli ochi. Se la mia morte brami. Io parto. Ardita Zanzaretta. Ardo per te, mio bene. *Instrumental items*[b] — Canzon francese. Io tacerò. Corrente, amanti.

⏱ 55' DDD 10/88

The music and life of Gesualdo, Prince of Venosa, have become inextricably linked for their controversy and pungency. There is a strange allure to the music of this man who murdered his wife; it drags the vocal art to extremes just as he pushed his own life to the very brink of acceptability. William Christie has gathered together a selection of Gesualdo's five-voice madrigals which ideally trace the composer's development in the realms of expression and distorted beauty. Les Arts Florissants are ever alive to the strangeness of this remarkable music and never smooth out the textures and harmonic excrescences. The clashes of tonalities, used to powerful expressive effect, are relished and the acoustic adds immensely to the fine portrayal of colour and nuance. Christie, somewhat controversially, adds some instrumental parts to the madrigals, historically defensible but stylistically questionable. That said, this is a remarkable and highly enjoyable introduction to one of the great experimenters of Western Music.

NEW REVIEW

Gesualdo. Responsoria et alia ad Officium Hebdomadae Sanctae spectantia (1611). **The Hilliard Ensemble.** ECM 843 867-2.

② 2h 4' DDD 3/92

To many, Gesualdo is known above all for the *crime passionnel* which left his wife and her lover impaled on the same sword, but the notion that his highly-charged music is the product of a tortured and unstable mind is, no doubt, over-romanticized. The exaggeratedly chromatic melodies and daring harmonic style of his late music were fully in keeping with the experimental madrigal school of the late sixteenth century. That said, Gesualdo's setting of the Responds for the Tenebrae of Holy Week is surely one of the most intense and disturbing works of the entire period. The complex service of Tenebrae is made up of the two offices, Matins and Lauds. Within Matins come the 27 responsories that were the inspiration for Gesualdo's music, in addition to which he set the "Miserere" and "Benedictus" from Lauds. At the beginning of the service the church is illumi-nated with candles, but these are extinguished one by one, hence the name *tenebrae* (darkness). It is significant that Gesualdo chose the most dramatic service of the church year, and one that is concerned with betrayal and death. The Hilliard Ensemble has not missed one ounce of the profundity of this music, and their performance is one of those rare artistic achievements that combines a heartfelt emotional response with faultless technical control. Their phrases are perfectly shaped and directed, and while it is virtually impossible to single out one particular contribution, David Beaven's ideally focused bass line should not go unmentioned. The recording is excellent, capturing the resonant acoustic of Douai Abbey, while every detail of the individual voices can be heard. Texts and translations are included, together with an extract from Hildesheimer's *Tynset*, but some explanatory notes would have been helpful.

Orlando Gibbons

British 1583-1625

Gibbons. MUSIC FOR PRINCE CHARLES.
Lupo. MUSIC FOR PRINCE CHARLES. **The Parley of Instruments/Peter Holman.** Hyperion CDA66395.
Gibbons: Two Fantasias a 4. 9 Fantasias a 3. Galliard a 3. **Lupo:** Fantasy-Airs a 3 — Nos. 16, 17 and 20. Fantasy-Airs a 4 — Nos. 5-7, 11 and 12.
Fantasies a 4 — Nos. 4 and 9.

> 59' DDD 9/91

The Parley of Instruments *[photo: Hyperion/Schillinger]*

Don't be put off by the rather forbidding titles: the terms "fantasia" and "fantasy-air" in fact conceal a wonderful mixture of the most varied music — by turns passionate, lively, languid and elegant. Peter Holman and his excellent Parley of Instruments have put together a programme which gives a snapshot of music at the beginning of the English baroque. The composers represented are two of the most eminent English musicians of the seventeenth century: Orlando Gibbons and Thomas Lupo. Both worked in the service of King Charles I during his years as the Prince of Wales, and this collection represents the type of music the Prince's household musicians wrote for him to play. Charles was a keen patron of the arts and his musical tastes were adventurous: these pieces all include parts for the violin — then a relative newcomer to the English musical scene. Beautifully-judged — and recorded — performances capture the warmth and wit of this music.

Gibbons. CHURCH MUSIC. **King's College Choir, Cambridge/Philip Ledger** with **John Butt** (org) and **ªLondon Early Music Group.** ASV Gaudeamus CDGAU123. FROM DCA514 (6/82).
Canticles — Magnificat and Nunc dimittis, "Short Service"; Magnificat and Nunc dimittis, "Second Service". *Full Anthems* — Almighty and Everlasting God; Lift up your heads; Hosanna to the Son of David. *Verse Anthems*ª — This is the record of John; See, see, the Word is incarnate; O Thou, the central orb. *The Hymnes and Songs of the Church* — Now shall the praises of the Lord be sung; O Lord of Hosts; A song of joy unto the Lord we sing; Come, kiss me with those lips of thine. *Organ works* — Voluntary; Fantasia for double organ; Fantasia.

> 53' DDD 4/86

Gibbons had close links with King's College, Cambridge, where he himself was a chorister. Little wonder, then, that the choir today frequently performs the music of one of its most illustrious musical sons! This programme is fully representative of Gibbons's output, with the two Services, several hymns, three organ pieces and examples of both his full and his verse anthems. Of these last, *This is the record of John* is particularly delectable. Michael Chance sings the alto solo with remarkable control, to the gentle accompaniment of the five viols, and in alternation with the full choir. His wonderful vocal quality 'makes' this record, but the solo trebles are notable for their poise, professionalism and first-class diction. The three organ pieces, elegantly played by John Butt, are of special interest, because of the place they hold in the development of keyboard music. Gibbons, himself renowned for his playing, was once described by the French Ambassador as 'the best finger of that age'.

Walter Gieseking   *Refer to Index*   German 1895-1956

Umberto Giordano   Italian 1867-1948

Giordano. ANDREA CHENIER. **Luciano Pavarotti** (ten) Andrea Chenier; **Leo Nucci** (bar) Gerard; **Montserrat Caballé** (sop) Maddalena; **Kathleen Kuhlmann** (mez) Bersi; **Astrid Varnay** (sop) Countess di Coigny; **Christa Ludwig** (mez) Madelon; **Tom Krause** (bar) Roucher; **Hugues Cuénod** (ten) Fleville; **Neil Howlett** (bar) Fouquier-Tinville, Major-domo; **Giorgio Tadeo** (bass) Mathieu; **Piero De Palma** (ten) Incredible; **Florindo Andreolli** (ten) Abate; **Giuseppe Morresi** (bass) Schmidt; **Ralph Hamer** (bass) Dumas; **Welsh National Opera Chorus; National Philharmonic Orchestra/ Riccardo Chailly.** Decca 410 117-2DH2. Notes, text and translation included. From 411 117-1DH3 (11/84).

② 1h 47' DDD 2/85

Andrea Chenier, set at the start of the French Revolution, is a potent blend of the social and the emotional. The three main characters, the aristocratic Maddalena, the idealistic poet Chenier and the fiercely republican Gerard, are caught up in a triangle that pits love against conscience, independence against society. The opera has many well-known set numbers high on any list of favourites must be Chenier's so-called *Improviso* in Act 1 where he bursts out in a spontaneous poem on the power of love, or Maddalena's glorious and moving "La mamma morta" in the Third Act where she describes how her mother gave up her life to save her. Giordano had a real theatrical flair for the 'big moment' and he paces the work masterfully. The tunes seem to flow endlessly from his pen and the characters have real flesh and blood. The cast is strong, with Caballé and Pavarotti making a powerful central pair. Riccardo Chailly conducts the excellent National Philharmonic with flair and feeling and the whole opera is beautifully recorded.

NEW REVIEW

Giordano. FEDORA[a]. **Magda Olivero** (sop) Fedora; **Mario del Monaco** (ten) Loris; **Tito Gobbi** (bar) de Siriex; **Leonardo Monreale** (bass) Lorek, Nicola; **Lucia Cappellino** (sop) Olga; **Virgilio Carbonari** (bass) Borov; **Silvio Maionica** (bass) Grech; **Piero de Palma** (ten) Rouvel; **Peter Binder** (bar) Kiril; **Dame Kiri Te Kanawa** (sop) Dmitri; **Riccardo Cassinelli** (ten) Desire; **Athos Cesarini** (ten) Sergio; **Pascal Rogé** (pf) Boleslao Lazinski; **Monte-Carlo Opera Chorus and Orchestra/Lamberto Gardelli.**
Zandonai. FRANCESCA DA RIMINI — excerpts[b]. [c]**Magda Oliviero** (sop) Francesca; [d]**Mario del Monaco** (ten) Paolo; [e]**Annamaria Gasparini** (mez) Biancofiore; [f]**Virgilio Carbonari** (bass) Man-at-arms; [g]**Athos Cesarini** (ten) Archer; **Monte-Carlo Opera Orchestra/Nicola Rescigno.** Decca Grand Opera 433 033-2DM2. Notes, texts and translations included. Item marked [a] from SET435/6 (3/70), [b] SET422 (1/70).

Act 2 — E ancora sgombro il campo del comune? ... Date il segno, Paolo, date ... Un'erba io m'avea, per sanare ... Onta et orrore sopra[cdfg]. Act 3 — No, Smadragedi, no! ... Paolo, datemi pace! ... Ah la parola chi i miei occhi incontrano[cd]. Act 4 — Ora andate ... E così, vada s'è pur mio destino[cde].

② 2h 12' ADD 3/92

Today the name 'Fedora' may suggest a type of hat rather than an opera, but although Giordano was overshadowed by his contemporary Puccini he was a successful composer. *Fedora* is based on a play by Victorien Sardou, the French dramatist whose *La Tosca* provided Puccini with a plot. It is set in the nineteenth century and variously in St Petersburg, Paris and Switzerland, and tells of the tragic love between the Russian Count Loris Ipanov and the Princess Fedora Romazov (Romanov), but to go into further detail of the plot, which disposes of various characters in turn and ends with the heroine herself taking poison, would take up too much space and one admires the booklet writer who has managed to produce a synopsis. *Fedora* has some Trivial Pursuits claim to be the first opera to feature bicycles in the plot! The music is richly textured orchestrally and finely written for the voices, and this recording made in 1969 is notable for the singing of Magda Olivero and Mario del Monaco, who despite being in their mid-fifties bring tremendous verve, vocal resource and dramatic skill to their roles. Tito Gobbi has less to do as the diplomat de Siriex, but gives him character, and another plus is the playing of Pascal Rogé, who performs the non-singing role of the Polish pianist and spy Boleslao Lazinski in Act 2 who, while performing, eavesdrops on a dialogue between Loris and Fedora. This exchange is a marvellous example of verismo writing and singing, and so is their final scene with her death. The set opens with excerpts from another opera, Zandonai's *Francesca da Rimini* with the same two excellent principals. The recordings are as clear and fresh-sounding as they were on the original releases.

Mauro Giuliani

Italian 1781-1829

NEW REVIEW

Giuliani. GUITAR WORKS. **David Starobin.** Bridge BCD9029.
Choix de mes Fleurs chéries, Op. 46 — Le Jasmin; Le Rosmarin; La Rose.
Etude in E minor, Op. 100 No. 13. Grande Ouverture, Op. 61. Leçons
Progressives, Op. 51 Nos. 3, 7 and 14. Minuetto, Op. 73 No. 9. Preludes,
Op. 83 Nos. 5 and 6. Rondeaux Progressives, Op. 14 Nos. 1 and 5. Six
Variations, Op. 20. Variazioni sulla Cavatina favorita, "De calma oh ciel",
Op. 101.

48' DDD 3/92

Giuliani was born and died in Italy, in between which he lived for many years in Vienna, where he scored great success in salon-music circles with his guitar virtuosity and counted many distinguished musicians amongst his friends and colleagues. He was in a sense the rival of Sor for the guitar's nineteenth-century crown but the two were 'chalk and cheese'. Giuliani the more volatile, ebullient and (as a composer) loquacious — with over 200 works as against Sor's less than 70. Giuliani's incessant desire to please his public (and to make much-needed money in the process) led to the presence of much treadmill dross amongst the gold of his best works, a thing that has contributed to his chronic undervaluation. David Starobin, playing a nineteenth-century guitar, greatly helps to redress the balance in his unfailingly musical and technically fluent playing of a selection of Giuliani's best works. Some testify to Giuliani's contribution to the student literature, the titles of others reflect the salon tastes at which they were aimed; all show that, when he took the trouble, Giuliani could be charming, polished and ingenious, all at the same time. This is a disc to charm the ear without bruising the emotions, in the nicest possible way.

Philip Glass
American 1937-

Glass. Music in 12 Parts. **Philip Glass Ensemble/Philip Glass.** Virgin Venture CDVEBX32.

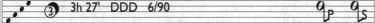

③ 3h 27' DDD 6/90

There are many who consider *Music in 12 Parts* to be one of Glass's finest works. On one level its mesmeric coruscations of sound are a kind of musical equivalent to a sensory deprivation tank (and that's not meant as an insult); on another, more serious level, it's a vast lexicon of minimalist techniques that offer the listener a fascinating insight into Glass's intellectual and aesthetic ideas. His travels in North Africa and India, and in particular his studies with Ravi Shankar's drummer Allah Rakha had a profound effect on his musical creativity, and resulted in the now familiar fingerprints of Glass's style. *Music in 12 Parts* is epic in its proportions — on CD it lasts nearly three hours, with each part roughly 20 minutes in duration (though individual parts can last considerably longer in concert performances), and its demands on the performers (keyboards, flutes, saxophones and a vocalizing soprano) are virtuosic in the extreme. The best way to experience it is in its entirety, though Glass allows (and encourages) the listener to make all manner of re-orderings and manipulations of its 12 movements. Brilliantly performed and recorded.

Alexander Glazunov
Russian 1865-1936

Glazunov. Violin Concerto[a].
Prokofiev. Violin Concerto No. 2[b].
Sibelius. Violin Concerto[c]. **Jascha Heifetz** (vn); [a]**RCA Victor Symphony Orchestra/Walter Hendl;** [b]**Boston Symphony Orchestra/Charles Münch;** [c]**Chicago Symphony Orchestra/Walter Hendl.** RCA Red Seal RD87019. Items marked [a] and [b] from GL89833 (9/86), [c] GL89832 (9/86).

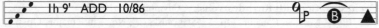

1h 9' ADD 10/86

Here are three great concertos on one CD, all of them classics which have never been equalled, let alone surpassed. Heifetz made the première recording of all

Jascha Heifetz

three concertos in the 1930s and his interpretations have particular authority. The recordings here were all issued in the early 1960s and in their digital refurbishment sound remarkably good. Heifetz's golden tone shines more brightly than ever and his technical virtuosity and profound musicianship remain dazzling. The performances can only be described as stunning and they remain an indispensable part of any collection.

Glazunov. The seasons — ballet, Op. 67.
Tchaikovsky. The Nutcracker — ballet, Op. 71[a]. [a]**Finchley Children's Music Group; Royal Philharmonic Orchestra/Vladimir Ashkenazy.** Decca 433 000-2DH2.

② 2h 11' DDD 4/92

One cannot think of a happier coupling than Glazunov's complete *Seasons* — perhaps his finest and most successful score — with Tchaikovsky's *Nutcracker*. Glazunov's delightful ballet, with even the winter's "Frost", "Hail", "Ice" and "Snow", glamorously presented, and the bitterness of a Russian winter quite forgotten are, like the scenario of the *Nutcracker*, part of a child's fantasy world, for Tchaikovsky too, in Act 2, has a wintry fairy scene and a delectable "Waltz of the snowflakes" (featuring children's wordless chorus). Glazunov's twinklingly dainty scoring of the picturesque snowy characters is contrasted with the glowing summer warmth of the "Waltz of the cornflowers and poppies", and the vigorously thrusting tune (perhaps the most memorable theme he ever wrote) of the Autumn "Bacchanale". Tchaikovsky's ballet opens with a children's Christmas party with the guests arriving, presents distributed and family dancing, in which everyone joins. Ashkenazy captures the atmosphere very engagingly; then night falls, the church clock outside strikes midnight and the magic begins. The drama of the spectacular mock battle between good and evil, the children's journey through the pine forest (to one of Tchaikovsky's most ravishing tunes) and the famous multi-coloured characteristic dances of the Act 2 Divertissement are all beautifully played by the RPO. There is much finesse and sparkle, and the lightest and most graceful rhythmic touch from Ashkenazy: the conductor's affection for the score and his feeling for Tchaikovsky's multi-hued orchestral palette is a constant delight to the ear. Yet the big *Pas de deux* brings a climax of Russian fervour. The recording is properly expansive here; made at Walthamstow, it sets everything within a glowing acoustic ambience. *The seasons* was recorded in Watford Town Hall, and again the ear is seduced by the aural richness and the glowing woodwind detail. The one minor drawback is that in the *Nutcracker* the cueing is not generous and the action not precisely related to the narrative detail. But in every other respect this is marvellous entertainment.

Glazunov. SYMPHONIES. **USSR Ministry of Culture State Symphony Orchestra/Gennadi Rozhdestvensky.** Olympia OCD100/1.
OCD100 — No. 1 in E major, Op. 5, "Slavyanskaya"; No. 7 in F major, Op. 77, "Pastoral'naya". *OCD101* — No. 4 in E flat major, Op. 48; No. 5 in B flat major, Op. 55.

② 1h 10' 1h 10' ADD 8/86

It is always easy to underestimate the Glazunov symphonies. There is no doubt that this set of performances from Rozhdestvensky and the splendid orchestra, give them a 'new look'. There is a sophistication in the playing to match the elegance of Glazunov's often highly engaging wind scoring — especially in the scherzos, always Glazunov's best movements — but there is a commitment and vitality too, which makes all the music spring readily to life. In Rozhdestvensky's hands the fine *Adagio* of No. 1 sounds remarkably mature while the *Andante* movements of Nos. 5 and 7 are romantically expansive in a very appealing way. The Fourth Symphony is a highly inventive piece throughout and held together by a moto theme; and the better-known Fifth does not disappoint when the presentation is so persuasive. On both discs the recording is brightly lit without being too brittle, and has plenty of fullness too. For anyone looking for new nineteenth-century symphonies to explore, this would be a good place to start.

Reyngol'd Glière

Russian 1875-1956

NEW REVIEW
Glière. Symphony No. 3 in B minor, Op. 42, "Il'ya Muromets". **Royal Philharmonic Orchestra/Harold Farberman.** Unicorn-Kanchana Souvenir UKCD2014/5. From PCM500-1 (8/79).

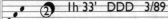 ② 1h 33' DDD 3/89

What happened to the Russian symphony between Tchaikovsky and Shostakovich? Scriabin and Rachmaninov were active of course, plus the solidly respectable Glazunov. But there was another distinctive voice, one whose interest lay in blending the heroic-saga tone of Borodin with the orchestral opulence of Wagner. This was Reyngol'd Glière, and his Third Symphony of 1912 is his undoubted masterpiece. It is a supremely late-romantic technicolour score, extreme but never uncontrolled in its excess, and always directed towards vividness of narrative rather than self-display. Now usually performed without the once-standard cuts, its four movements are fairly protracted, the more so when taken at exceptional spacious tempos as they are here by Harold Farberman (other more recent uncut recordings have clocked in at single-CD duration). But the spaciousness proves the making of the piece, giving the dimensions a truly epic feel and developing an unstoppable slow momentum. The recording quality no longer quite seems to justify the 'demonstration-class' praise originally accorded it, but it is still impressive enough.

Christoph Gluck

Bohemian 1714-1787

Gluck. LE CINESI. **Kaaren Erickson** (sop) Sivene; **Alexandrina Milcheva** (contr) Lisinga; **Marga Schiml** (contr) Tangia; **Thomas Moser** (ten) Silango; **Munich Radio Orchestra/Lamberto Gardelli.** Orfeo C178891A. Notes, text and translation included.

1h 6' DDD 1/90

Gluck's version of Metastasio's *Le cinesi* ("The Chinese ladies") was composed for the Habsburg Empress, Maria Theresa, in 1754. Within the space of a single act, the text and music of the opera-serenade brightly illuminates the relationships between the three women and the man in a series of contrasting vignettes. Using a single, exotic set, the characters devise an afternoon's entertainment; trying first a brilliantly contrived scene from a hypothetical heroic opera, then a pastorale and finally a comedy (in which the romantic undercurrents between the man and two of the women are explored), they resolve instead to dance. The Munich Radio Orchestra under Lamberto Gardelli deliver a thoroughly modern performance (replete with 'resonant' harpsichord). Of the soloists, Alexandrina Milcheva as Lisinga and Thomas Moser as Silango in particular give polished performances. Having been roused from a 200-year sleep, Gluck's jewel-like *Cinesi* seems set to attract a wide spectrum of amateur and professional performances.

Gluck. ORFEO ED EURIDICE. ORPHEE ET EURYDICE — ballet music. **Jochen Kowalski** (alto) Orfeo; **Dagmar Schellenberger-Ernst** (sop) Euridice; **Christian Fliegner** (treb) Amor; **Berlin Radio Chorus; Carl Philipp Emanuel Bach Chamber Orchestra/Hartmut Haenchen.**

Capriccio 60 008-2. Notes, text and translation included.

Orphée et Eurydice — Air de furies; Ballet des ombres heureuses; Air vif; Menuet; Chaconne.

NEW REVIEW

Gluck. ORFEO ED EURIDICE. **Michael Chance** (alto) Orfeo; **Nancy Argenta** (sop) Euridice; **Stefan Beckerbauer** (treb) Amor; **Stuttgart Chamber Choir; Tafelmusik/Frieder Bernius.** Sony Vivarte CD48040. Notes, text and translation included.

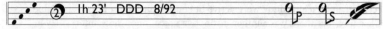

Not very long ago, the standard view of Gluck's *Orfeo ed Euridice* was that a compromise text, between the Italian original of 1762 and the French revised version of 1774, was desirable, allowing performers and listeners to have the best of both worlds. But nowadays people are beginning to realize that Gluck may have known what he was doing when he wrote these two versions, and that each has its own integrity. And certainly the more focused and more concentrated of the two is the Vienna original, in Italian. But following this means foregoing two of the most admired and striking numbers, the "Dance of the Furies" and the flute solo "Dance of the Blessed Spirits". On the Capriccio recording of the Italian version these two dances, and three others, are sensibly included as an appendix. The rich, flexible alto of Jochen Kowalski as Orfeo is very impressive; he is impassioned in the series of ariosos and recitatives that form the central part of Act 1 and his smooth and even, refined tone compels admiration. Haenchen draws very capable singing from the Berlin Radio Chorus. This version is a modern one, when period instruments might have been more appropriate, but Kowalski's very beautiful singing will be the deciding factor for many listeners.

The Sony recording also allows us to fully appreciate the beautifully balanced structure of the original version and gives us a good idea of how it might have sounded, through the use of period instruments and the fine countertenor, Michael Chance, in the castrato role. We miss out here on the well-loved dances but none the less the dramatic drive and integrity are enormous, as are the qualities of both performance and recording. The singing is, of course, first class: Chance is a revelation as Orfeo, Nancy Argenta a truly complex Euridice, a real woman rather than just a character from mythology. Performance on period instruments sets the style and (generally lively) pace of the reading, with Frieder Bernius finding just the right balance of the intriguing tonal qualities to give a special stamp to each number. With all this enhanced by an exceptionally fine recording, full of space and detail, clarity and depth, this is altogether an outstanding issue.

Gluck. IPHIGENIE EN AULIDE. **Lynne Dawson** (sop) Iphigénie; **José van Dam** (bass) Agamemnon; **Anne Sofie von Otter** (mez) Clytemnestre; **John Aler** (ten) Achille; **Bernard Delctré** (bass) Patrocle; **Gilles Cachemaille** (bass) Calchas; **René Schirrer** (bass) Arcas; **Guillemette Laurens** (mez) Diane; **Ann Monoyios** (sop) First Greek woman, Slave; **Isabelle Eschen-brenner** (sop) Second Greek woman; **Monteverdi Choir; Lyon Opéra Orchestra/John Eliot Gardiner.** Erato 2292-45003-2. Notes, text and translation included.

Gluck's first reform opera for Paris has tended to be overshadowed by his other *Iphigénie*, the *Tauride* one. But it does contain some superb things, of which perhaps the finest are the great monologues for Agamemnon. On this recording, José van Dam starts a little coolly; but this only adds force to his big moment at

Anne Sofie von Otter   *[photo: DG/Löfgren*

the end of the second act where he tussles with himself over the sacrifice of his daughter and — contemplating her death and the screams of the vengeful Eumenides — decides to flout the gods and face the consequences. To this he rises in noble fashion, fully conveying the agonies Agamemnon suffers. The cast in general is strong. Lynne Dawson brings depth of expressive feeling to all she does and her Iphigénie, marked by a slightly grainy sound and much intensity, is very moving. John Aler's Achille too is very fine, touching off the lover and the hero with equal success, singing both with ardour and vitality. There is great force too in the singing of Anne Sofie von Otter as Clytemnestre, especially in her outburst "Ma fille!" as she imagines her daughter on the sacrificial altar. John Eliot Gardiner's Monteverdi Choir sing with polish, perhaps seeming a little genteel for a crowd of angry Greek soldiers baying for Iphigénie's blood. But Gardiner gives a duly urgent account of the score, pressing it forward eagerly and keeping the tension at a high level even in the dance music. A period-instrument orchestra might have added a certain edge and vitality but this performance wants nothing in authority or drama and can be securely recommended.

Gluck. IPHIGENIE EN TAURIDE. **Diana Montague** (mez) Iphigénie; **John Aler** (ten) Pylade; **Thomas Allen** (bar) Oreste; **Nancy Argenta** (sop); **Sophie Boulton** (mez) First and Second Priestesses; **Colette Alliot-Lugaz** (sop) Diana; **René Massis** (bass-bar) Thoas; **Monteverdi Choir; Lyon Opera Orchestra/John Eliot Gardiner.** Philips 416 148-2PH2. Notes, text and translation included.

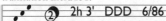

② 2h 3' DDD 6/86

Many Gluckists reckon *Iphigénie en Tauride* to be the finest of his operas; and although the claims of *Orfeo* are also very strong the breadth and grandeur of this score, the vigour of its declamatory writing, the intensity with which the situations of Iphigénie and Oreste are depicted and the ultimate integration of music and drama produce a uniquely powerful musical realization of classical tragedy. John Eliot Gardiner's sense of dramatic concentration and his intellectual control make him an ideal interpreter; the impassioned accompanied recitatives and the taut, suggestive accompaniments to the arias are particularly impressive, and the dance music is gracefully done. It might, however, have been better if a period orchestra had been used; this one, though efficient and responsive, cannot quite articulate the music as Gluck intended and tends to be string-heavy in the modern manner. Vocally, the set is distinguished above all by Diana Montague's Iphigénie, sung with due nobility and a finely true, clean middle register, and Thomas Allen's noble and passionate Oreste; John Aler's Pylade is warm and flexible and René Massis provides a suitably barbaric Thoas. In all a noble account, the best available on disc, of a remarkable opera.

Leopold Godowsky

Polish/American 1870-1938

NEW REVIEW

Godowsky. PIANO TRANSCRIPTIONS. **Rian De Waal.** Hyperion CDA66496.
Godowsky: Passacaglia. Triakontameron — Alt Wien. *Schubert:* Die schöne Müllerin, D795 — Das Wandern; Ungeduld. Winterreise, D911 — Gute Nacht. Rosamunde — Ballet Music. Moments musicaux, D780 — No. 3 in F minor. *Weber:* Invitation to the dance, J260. *J. Strauss II:* Kunsterleben, Op. 316.

58'   DDD   3/92

The pianist Leopold Godowsky acquired a legendary stature in his lifetime and remains an idol today. Small, plump and inscrutable, he was nicknamed the Buddha of the instrument and Harold Schonberg's book *The Great Pianists* refers to his possession of "the most perfect pianistic mechanism of the period". He dazzled even his greatest contemporaries, and Vladimir Horowitz, who worked at his *Passacaglia* but never performed it in public, said "it needs six hands to play it". Full marks, therefore, to the young Dutch pianist Rian de Waal, who not only plays it convincingly but also makes it sound pretty effortless; based on the opening theme of Schubert's *Unfinished* Symphony (just 12 notes in B minor), it unfolds magisterially towards a final fugue and is a fine, somewhat Brahmsian composition as well as one of virtuoso pianism. The other compositions are smaller but also worth having, particularly when they're as well played as they are here. The three transcriptions of Schubert songs become remarkable piano pieces, not least *Gute Nacht*, which is not a showpiece but a sombre tone poem. There's real charm, too, in de Waal's playing of the Strauss waltz transcription, *An Artist's Life*. There are also pieces which were originally for piano but which Godowsky further reshaped into something personal. His version of Weber's *Invitation to the dance*, here recorded for the first time, has elaborate charm as well as the romantic quality which comes out in Fokine's ballet based on it, *Le spectre de la rose*. The recital ends as it began with an original piece, the leisurely and lilting little waltz called *Old Vienna*.

Károly Goldmark

Austrian/Hungarian 1830-1915

NEW REVIEW

Goldmark. Rustic Wedding Symphony, Op. 26. Sakuntula Overture, Op. 13. **Royal Philharmonic Orchestra/Yondani Butt.** ASV CDDCA791.

1h 6'   DDD   5/92

It is good to welcome a major work by Goldmark to the *Guide*. In his lifetime, which was mostly spent in Vienna, he was thought of as the most important Hungarian composer after Liszt, and Brahms admired this work, which dates from 1876. It is something between a symphony and a sequence of symphonic poems and has an idiom not unlike Smetana or in places even Mahler in pastoral mood: tuneful, colourful and occasionally amiably pompous, as in the initial "Wedding March", which at nearly 18 minutes is the longest of the five movements. There's humour, too, as in the central "Serenade", a gentle and genial scherzo. The Royal Philharmonic Orchestra play this music with all one could ask for in the way of zest and charm under a young conductor who was born in Macao but now lives and works in Canada. The recording is rich and a touch too reverberant in climaxes, but detail is mostly clear and the string and wind sound is well captured, not least in the beautifully scored "Serenade" and the dreamy "Garden Scene" that follows. The busy, cheerful finale is a delight. *Sakuntula* was written ten years earlier, and must be among the first western pieces to be inspired by the fifth-century Indian epic called the *Mahabharata*, which Goldmark came across in a German translation; the title is the name of a woodland nymph whose love scene with King Dusjanta is rapturously melodious, and again this is played lovingly as well as skilfully by Butt and the Royal Philharmonic Orchestra.

Berthold Goldschmidt

German 1903-

NEW REVIEW

Goldschmidt. CHAMBER AND CHORAL WORKS. [a]**Mandelring Quartet** (Sebastian Schmidt, Nanette Schmidt, vns; Nora Niggeling, va; Bernhard Schmidt, vc); [b]**Jörg Gottschick** (narr); [c]**Alan Marks** (pf); [d]**Berlin Ars Nova Ensemble/Peter Schwarz.** Largo 5115. Text and translation included. String Quartets[a] — No. 2 (1936); No. 3 (1989). Belsatzar (1985)[d]. Letzte Kapitel[bcd] (1931).

♪♪ 56' DDD 11/91 ❓

After decades of neglect, the music of Hamburg-born Berthold Goldschmidt is coming back into favour and a largely forgotten grand old man (resident in the UK since 1935) has begun composing again. Older music lovers may recognize him as one of our earliest Mahler champions: he conducted the première of Deryck Cooke's full performing version of the Tenth Symphony in 1964. Like Shostakovich, whose quartet writing is not altogether dissimilar, Goldschmidt composes tonal music in which Mahler looms larger than Schoenberg, though the dominant influence is probably that of Busoni. The results are hard to describe, but sometimes remind you of Hindemith without the contrapuntal excesses. The present CD, expertly annotated, is designed to show the breadth of Goldschmidt's achievement, ranging from the trenchant, Weill-like expression of *Letzte Kapitel* to the more impressive absolute music of the quartets. Goldschmidt's writing here lacks the striking melodic charge of Shostakovich, but the committed performances and well balanced recordings make them an attractive proposition for the more adventurous collector.

Henryk Górecki

Polish 1933-

NEW REVIEW

Górecki. String Quartet No. 1, Op. 62, "Already it is Dusk"[a]. Lerchenmusik, Op. 53[b]. [b]**Michael Collins** (cl); [b]**Christopher van Kampen** (vc); [a]**Kronos Quartet** (David Harrington, John Sherba, vns; Hank Dutt, va; Joan Jeanrenaud, vc); [b]**John Constable** (pf). Elektra-Nonesuch 7559-79257-2.

♪♪ 54' DDD 9/91

The title of Górecki's String Quartet could be read as a synonym for "it's later than you think", and from one angle the work certainly seems to embody a deep resistance to the assumption that music can only progress by being ever more novel and ever more complex. But no composer who finds so much that is new and fresh in traditional tonality can be wholly despairing, and Górecki's work at it best makes a very positive creative statement. The ideas all have intense personal associations for him — he evokes Polish folk music, Catholic chant, and such icons of Western art music as Beethoven's Fourth Piano Concerto, whose opening features in *Lerchenmusik*. The subtitle of this piece, "Recitatives and

Ariosos", indicates the two poles of Górecki's style — dramatic declamation and lyric meditation — within both of which he is willing to oppose highly refined delicacy with distinctly primitive aggressiveness. His forms are not entirely non-developmental, but cumulative repetitions and strong contrasts are their principal features. Even if you are left with the suspicion that too much of what music can and should aspire to is being omitted here, Górecki's strong and immediate emotional world is difficult to ignore, and there are no drawbacks to either the performances or the recordings.

Louis Moreau Gottschalk *American 1829-1869*

NEW REVIEW

Gottschalk. PIANO WORKS. **Philip Martin.** Hyperion CDA66459.
Le bananier, RO21. Le banjo, RO22. Canto del gitano, RO35. Columbia, RO61. Danza, RO66. Le mancenillier, RO142. Mazurka in A minor, RO164. Minuit à Seville, RO170. Ojos criollos, RO184. Romance in E flat major, RO270. Sixième ballade, RO14. Souvenir de la Havane, RO246. Souvenir de Porto Rico, RO250. Union, RO269.

Ih 11' DDD 9/91   ❓

Pianistic phenomenons of the nineteenth-century European variety are two-a-penny — American ones are as rare as hens' teeth. One such phenomenon however was Louis Moreau Gottschalk. Gottschalk was born in New Orleans in 1829 at a time when America was about as far off the musical map as you could get — to most Europeans America was a place of vast open spaces, wild Indians and white barbarians but certainly not pianistic prodigies. His parents recognized his musical talents at an early age, and at 13 they sent him to Paris where, after considerable difficulty in finding anyone to take him seriously, he eventually found guidance under the tutelage of Charles Hallé and later with Charles Stamaty, who unleashed him onto an unsuspecting Paris audience (among them Chopin and Kalkbrenner) in 1845. Gottschalk's concert career, and his magnetism as a performer (he was a notorious womanizer) paralleled that of Liszt's, and he toured extensively in France, Switzerland and Spain before returning to America in 1853. He was a prolific composer of piano music (well over 100 published works) which vary from Lisztian bravura and Chopinesque musings through to lighter genre pieces of the salon *morceaux* variety. Philip Martin's generous programme presents us with a good cross section; from the immensely popular salon pieces such as *Le banjo, Le bananier* ("The banana tree") and *Columbia* (an exuberant paraphrase on Stephen Foster's *My Old Kentucky Home*)

as well as including several examples that reflect Gottschalk's love of Latin American and Creole dance rhythms. Martin concludes the recital with a spirited performance of *Union*; a brilliant concert paraphrase on national airs (including a minor key *Yankee Doodle* and a delicately harmonized *Star Spangled Banner*) where the influence of Liszt (and even Alkan) are very much in evidence. A very enjoyable disc indeed.

Charles François Gounod French 1818-1893

Gounod. Symphony No. 1 in D major. Petite symphonie.
Bizet (ed. Hogwood). L'Arlésienne — excerpts. **Saint Paul Chamber Orchestra/Christopher Hogwood.** Decca 430 231-2DH.
L'Arlésienne — Prélude; Minuetto; Entr'acte; Mélodrame; Pastorale; Carillon.

```
• 1h 7'  DDD  7/91                                    Q p
```

NEW REVIEW

Gounod. Symphonies — No. 1 in D major; No. 2 in E flat major. **Toulouse Capitole Orchestra/Michel Plasson.** EMI CDM7 63949-2. From ESD7093 (8/80).

```
• 59'  DDD  3/92                                      Q p
```

Christopher Hogwood here gives us a delightful recording of works by a pair of French composers who are well matched, for Gounod taught Bizet and spoke tearfully at his funeral. It also reminds us of Gounod's skill outside the opera house, though there is nothing especially French about this symphony that he seems to have written almost as a tribute to Mendelssohn, whom he came to know personally and admired as a musician. In other words, this is the more classical kind of nineteenth-century music and its origin in the romantic era is only revealed in its unashamed charm and elegance — the only way here, perhaps, in which Gounod shows his Gallioc nationality. Hogwood and his expert players of the Saint Paul Chamber Orchestra are perfectly at ease in this work and the performance of the *Petite symphonie* for nine wind instruments is no less stylish. In Bizet's incidental music for Daudet's play *L'Arlésienne*, Hogwood's touch is no less sure. He has gone back to the original theatre scoring rather than playing the better-known orchestral suites that were made later, which means an odd instrumental combination including seven violins but only one viola, a saxophone and a piano, plus the restoration of some original keys. The recording is spacious and detailed, and one only wishes that Decca had provided separate tracks for the six Bizet pieces.

The two Gounod Symphonies were written close together not long before his fortieth birthday and before the great success of *Faust* turned him firmly towards opera. As well as Mendelssohn Gounod admired Beethoven and Bach, and the quietly march-like second movement is akin to that of Beethoven's Seventh until a mock-Bachian fugue makes its appearance. This civilized music has elegant though impersonal manners, plumbing no depths but proving to be most agreeable company, though it's hard to believe that it was written a quarter of a century after Berlioz's wildly romantic *Symphonie fantastique*. The Second Symphony is again straight out of a classical mould, but there is nothing wrong with a melodious and well-proportioned classical symphony and in performances such as these by a fine French orchestra there is much to enjoy. The 1979 recording made in Toulouse offers satisfying sound, clear but resonant.

Gounod. FAUST — ballet music.
Offenbach (arr. Rosenthal). Gaîté parisienne — ballet. **Montreal Symphony Orchestra/Charles Dutoit.** Decca 411 708-2DH. From 411 708-1DH (3/84).

```
• 59'  DDD  7/84                                      Q p
```

The very title of Offenbach's *Gaîté parisienne* tells us that this is unashamedly music to delight. However, it is not the composer's own but rather one given to a collection of his music arranged by Ravel's pupil Manuel Rosenthal for Léonide Massine and his Ballets Russes de Monte Carlo in 1938. The ballet is set in a Parisian night club and includes many attractive dance pieces as well as the celebrated Can-can from *Orpheus in the Underworld* and the Barcarolle from *The*

Tales of Hoffman. We may forget all about Marlowe's play when we come to the *Faust* ballet, for originally Gounod's opera had no such thing as this elaborate danced section in which the *femmes fatales* of history paraded before Faust. But it seems that the Paris Opéra insisted on it. The music is in different style from Offenbach but still lilting and highly attractive. Dutoit and his excellent Montreal orchestra are admirable in this music, and if there's a trace of brashness in the noisier sections of the Offenbach that is justified by the nature of the music itself.

NEW REVIEW

Gounod. FAUST. **Richard Leech** (ten) Faust; **Cheryl Studer** (sop) Marguerite; **José van Dam** (bass-bar) Méphistophélès; **Thomas Hampson** (bass) Valentin; **Martine Mahé** (mez) Siebel; **Nadine Denize** (sop) Marthe; **Marc Barrard** (bar) Wagner; **French Army Chorus; Toulouse Capitole Choir and Orchestra / Michel Plasson.** EMI CDS7 54228-2. Notes, text and translation included.

③ 3h 24' DDD 12/91

Here we have a performance that is, at last, worthy of Gounod's concept. Plasson respects and loves the score, lavishing on it infinite care over minutiae. His affection sometimes leads him to very slow speeds but by and large the extra space is used to enhance respect for this epitome of French, nineteenth-century romantic opera. He and his orchestra light the score from within, showing how a perceptive, knowledgeable hand can restore a too-familiar picture. Plasson puts us further in his debt by playing the score complete and, as a bonus, given us, in an appendix, passages cut before the première. Leech is a near-ideal Faust, singing with lyrical, liquid tone, stylish phrasing and evincing idiomatic French. Studer, also at home in the language, produces firm, lovely tone, sensitive phrasing and encompasses every facet of the character. Van Dam is a resolute, implacable Méphistophélès who never indulges in false histrionics and sings with subtlety of accent. Plasson's Toulouse forces are wholly at home in this music and, as an added pleasure, the French Army Chorus are called in to give a touch of authenticity to the Soldiers' Chorus.

Percy Grainger
American / Australian 1882-1961

Grainger. ORCHESTRAL WORKS. **Philip Martin** (pf); [a]**Moray Welsh** (vc); **Bournemouth Sinfonietta / Kenneth Montgomery.** Chandos Collect CHAN6542. From CHAN8377 (8/85).
Youthful Suite — Rustic dance; Eastern intermezzo. Blithe Bells (free ramble on a theme by Bach, "Sheep may safely graze"). Spoon River. My Robin is to the Greenwood Gone. Green Bushes. Country Gardens (orch. Schmid). Mock Morris. Youthful Rapture[a]. Shepherd's Hey. Walking Tune. Molly on the shore. Handel in the Strand (orch. Wood).

55' ADD 2/92

None of the 13 items on this disc is longer than nine minutes, and they are carefully planned to make an attractive sequence for continuous listening. The two items from the *Youthful Suite* were composed when Grainger was but 17 years old and are quite advanced harmonically for 1898-9. *Blithe Bells* is a somewhat florid arrangement of Bach's "Sheep may safely graze", and then we have *Spoon River*, an arrangement of an old American fiddle tune. *My Robin is to the Greenwood Gone, Green Bushes* and the famous *Country Gardens* are all based on English folk-tunes, but the cheerful *Mock Morris* is an original pastiche. *Handel in the Strand* is a set of variations on Handel's *Harmonious Blacksmith* whilst the charming *Walking Tune* for wind quintet came to Grainger's mind when on a walking tour. There's no doubt that Kenneth Montgomery has a strong sympathy for Grainger's music, and he directs lively performances. The recording acoustic is a little reverberant but the sound quality is otherwise good.

Grainger. ORCHESTRAL WORKS. **Melbourne Symphony Orchestra/ Geoffrey Simon.** Koch International Classics 37003-2.
The Warriors. Hill-Song No. 1. Irish Tune from County Derry, BFMS20. Hill-Song No. 2. Danish Folk-Music Suite. **Traditional Chinese** (harmonized Yasser, arr. Grainger, orch. Sculthorpe): Beautiful fresh flower.

1h 7' DDD 11/90

It was Sir Thomas Beecham who first suggested to Percy Grainger the idea of writing a ballet, and though in the event a commission was not forthcoming Grainger went ahead with the work that was to become without doubt one of his largest and most extravagant works — *The Warriors*. Although it has only a relatively short duration — 18 minutes — its demands in every other aspect are gargantuan; in addition to an already large orchestra he calls for six horns, three pianos, a large-tuned percussion section (including wooden and steel marimbas and tubular bells), an off-stage brass section and — if necessary — three conductors! (though in this recording Geoffrey Simon takes on the task single handed), with the musical material deriving from no less than 15 themes and motifs. Grainger described the piece as "an orgy of war-like dances, processions and merry-making broken, or accompanied by amorous interludes" — a sort of "warriors of the world unite". It was described by Delius (the work's dedicatee) as "by far Grainger's greatest thing" and indeed it seems to encapsulate and condense the very essence of Grainger's wild and free-roaming spirit. The two *Hill-Songs* were a response to "the soul-shaking hillscapes" of West Argyllshire after a three-day hike in the Scottish Highlands. Like many of Grainger's compositions they exist in various scorings from the two-piano and solo piano arrangements to the chamber orchestra version of 1923 heard in this recording. Their organic, unbroken flow of melodic ideas and rhythmically complex writing create a bracing, evocative impression of the spirit of the Highlands. The remaining works on the disc consist of the attractive *Danish Folk-Music Suite*, notable for the two haunting ballads "The Power of Love" and "The Nightingale and the Two Sisters" and three short folk-song arrangements from China, Denmark and Ireland. Geoffrey Simon and the Melbourne Symphony Orchestra positively revel in this music, and the excellent recording is clear and spacious. An essential disc for those with an adventurous spirit.

Grainger. SYMPHONIC BAND MUSIC. **Michigan State University Symphonic Band/Keith Brion,** [a]**Kenneth G. Bloomquist.** Delos DE3101.
Grainger: Molly on the Shore, BFMS23. Country Gardens. The Immovable Do. Colonial Song, S1. In a Nutshell — No. 4, Gum-suckers' March[a]. Ye Banks and Braes o' Bonnie Doon, BFMS32. Children's March, "Over the Hills and Far Away", RMTB4. Country Gardens (arr. Sousa)[a]. *Fauré* (arr. Grainger): Tuscan serenade, Op. 3 No. 2. *Franck* (arr. Grainger): Chorale. *Bach* (arr. Grainger): March in D. O Mensch, bewein' dein' Sünde gross, BWV622.

57' DDD 4/91

Grainger is one of those composers who refuses to fall into any of the categories which critics use to place creative artists so as to fit them into their view of musical history. Being Australian must have helped to make him different, and although much of his musical formation was European — he studied piano with Busoni and became a friend of Grieg and Delius — he was also inspired at the Paris Exhibition of 1900 by an Indonesian *gamelan* orchestra and an Egyptian wind ensemble. His experience of wind bands was later also much enlarged by his service from 1917-19 in the US Army Band, in which he played the oboe or soprano saxophone. It seems right, therefore, that it is an American band that plays the dozen pieces on this CD, which includes such popular numbers as *Country Gardens,* in a Grainger treatment that must bring a smile of pleasure to the face of all but the most gloomy listener, with Sousa's bouncy arrangement of the same music coming later in the programme for good measure. Some of these pieces are derived from British folk music, but by no means all as the list above shows, and in fact the *Gum-suckers' March* was inspired by his home state of Victoria, Australia. This is delightful and inventive music by a real original, and the playing of the Michigan State University Symphonic Band under two good conductors does it justice, as does the clean, if sometimes slightly tubby, recording. The booklet note by the Grainger specialist Dana Perna steers us skilfully through some unfamiliar music.

Grainger. PIANO WORKS, Volume 1. **Martin Jones.** Nimbus NI5220. Andante con moto. Bridal Lullaby. Children's March. Colonial Song. English Waltz. Handel in the Strand. Harvest Hymn. In a Nutshell — suite. In Dahomey. Mock Morris. Peace. Sailor's Song. Saxon Twi-play. The Immovable Do. To a Nordic Princess. Walking Tune.

1h 12' DDD 4/90

This is the best of Percy Grainger, and it would be hard to imagine it better played. Most of these pieces are better-known in Grainger's lavish and colourful orchestrations, but they seem to have more pith and urgency to them in their piano versions, even where those were not the originals. The luscious *To a Nordic Princess* has more energy to it in this form, and the slow movement of *In a Nutshell*, far from the lyrical interlude that it can sound in orchestrated form, emerges as a very direct and almost shockingly poignant self-image of Grainger. Even the popular trifles, *Handel in the Strand* and *Mock Morris*, take on added zest at the crisp and airy tempos that Martin Jones chooses; even more importantly the haunting lyricism of *The Immovable Do* and the deep nostalgia of *Colonial Song* are liberated by restoration to Grainger's own instrument. They need something like Grainger's own flamboyantly virtuoso pianism, of course, and one of the reasons that they are far more familiar in their orchestral guise is that they make hair-raising demands of the pianist. Jones is fully equal to them; indeed, he goes well beyond meeting those demands and sounds as though he is positively enjoying himself. A hugely enjoyable collection; the rather disembodied recording is a quirk rather than a real drawback.

Enrique Granados
Spanish 1867-1916

Granados. Danzas españolas, Op. 37. **Alicia de Larrocha** (pf). Decca 414 557-2DH. From SXL6980 (3/82).

56' ADD 10/85

Not long before he drowned, in 1916, when his ship was sunk by a German submarine, Granados had felt that his compositional career was being opened up by the deep vein of genuine Spanish feeling that he was increasingly able to tap in his music. His piano suite, *Goyescas*, and the opera based on it were, perhaps, the most convincing and individual expression of that sentiment, but the numerous shorter pieces for piano that he produced, some of which were collected together in the sets of *Danzas españolas*, also showed real sparks of that same nationalism, even though they were still clearly rooted in the common European harmonic and melodic language of the later romantic period. These sparks need to be emphasized in performance by an artist who has an intuitive feel for them, and there is none better suited than Alicia de Larrocha, who has both the technical control and emotional insight to make the most of this music. Her playing, even at moments of highest constraint, has an undercurrent of powerful forces striving to be released; when the constraint is lifted, the effect is tumultuous. Thankfully, the recording can cope. The result is an almost definitive issue of this intriguing collection.

Granados. Goyescas — suite for piano. **Alicia de Larrocha** (pf). Decca 411 958-2DH. From SXL6785 (12/77).

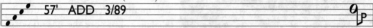

The Granados *Goyescas* are profoundly Spanish in feeling, but the folk influence is more of court music than of the flamenco or *cante hondo* styles which reflect gipsy and Moorish influence. This set of seven pieces was given its first performance by the composer in 1911, and his own exceptional ability as a pianist is evident in its consistently elaborate textures. That performance took place in Barcelona, and as Granados's compatriot and a native of that very city Alicia de Larrocha fully understands this music in its richly varied moods; a fact which tells in interpretations that have a compelling conviction and drive. Thus, she can dance enchantingly in such a piece as "El Fandango de candil", while in the celebrated "Maiden and the nightingale", No. 4 of the set, we listen to a wonderful outpouring of Mediterranean emotion, all the more moving for its avoidance of excessive rubato and over-pedalling. A splendid disc of one of the twentieth century's piano masterpieces, which was atmospherically recorded in the former Decca studios in West Hampstead in 1976 and has transferred well to CD.

Edvard Grieg

Norwegian 1843-1907

Grieg. Piano Concerto in A minor, Op. 16.
Schumann. Piano Concerto in A minor, Op. 54. **Stephen Kovacevich** (pf); **BBC Symphony Orchestra/Sir Colin Davis**. Philips 412 923-2PH. From 6500 166 (3/72).

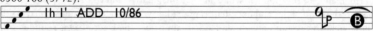

Grieg. Piano Concerto in A minor, Op. 16.
Schumann. Piano Concerto in A minor, Op. 54. **Murray Perahia** (pf); **Bavarian Radio Symphony Orchestra/Sir Colin Davis**. CBS Masterworks CD44899. Recorded at performances in the Philharmonie Gasteig, Munich during 1987 and 1988.

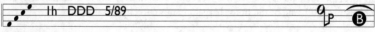

NEW REVIEW

Grieg. Piano Concerto in A minor, Op. 16[a].
Franck. Symphonic Variations[b].
Schumann. Piano Concerto in A minor, Op. 54[c]. [ab]**Clifford Curzon,** [c]**Friedrich Gulda** (pfs); [a]**London Symphony Orchestra/Øivin Fjeldstad;** [b]**London Philharmonic Orchestra/Sir Adrian Boult;** [c]**Vienna Philharmonic Orchestra/Volkmar Andreae.** Decca Headline Classics 433 628-2DSP. Item marked [a] from LW5350 (7/59), [b] SXL2173 (1/60), [c] ACL136 (5/57).

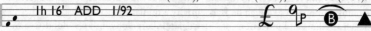

Since the advent of the LP the Grieg and Schumann concertos have been ideally paired and the performances on the Philips disc have set the standard by which

all other versions are judged. The scale of both is perfectly managed. The Grieg, with its natural charm and freshness, has power too (witness the superb first movement cadenza), but poetry dominates and climaxes must never seem hectoring, as both these artists fully understand. The romanticism of the Schumann Concerto is particularly elusive on record, with its contrasting masculine and feminine elements difficult to set in ideal balance. But here there is no sense of any problem, so naturally does the music flow, the changing moods being seen within the overall perspective. There is refinement and

Stephen Kovacevich   *[photo: Philips*

strength, the virtuosity sparkles, the expressive elements are perfectly integrated with the need for bravura. This CD remastering of a very well balanced and felicitous recording gives both performances a new lease of life.

The performances on the CBS disc are also amongst the finest. Perahia's innate sense of musicality and poetry bring out the nostalgic lyricism of these works extremely well, though he is equally at home with the more bravura passages (as for instance in the cadenza of the Grieg). Sir Colin Davis and the Bavarian RSO provide excellent support and the recordings, which were taken from public concerts in Munich (the sound is as clean as any studio recording), are warm and well balanced.

Good as both Kovacevich and Perahia are, they are matched in the Grieg by Sir Clifford Curzon's classic account from 1959 where he is most sympathetically and idiomatically accompanied by Øivin Fjeldstad and the London Symphony Orchestra. Curzon was at his finest in romantic piano concertos, and his playing achieves an exceptional balance between poetry and strength. This is a performance which clearly stakes a claim for the concerto as a work of genius. These same characteristics are also to the fore in the recording of the Franck *Symphonic Variations*, this time with Sir Adrian Boult conducting. This is probably the finest performance of this popular work on CD: imaginative and romantic with a perfect sense of style, and excellent rapport between conductor and soloist. As if these riches were not enough, and at bargain price, the Decca CD is rounded off with another extremely masterly reading, of the Schumann Concerto by Friedrich Gulda, this time dating from 1956 and with Volkmar Andreae leading the Vienna Philharmonic. This reading is absolutely in the centre of the authentic romantic style: it is both extremely personal and authoritative. Decca's recorded sound for all three performances is more than acceptable, with true piano tone throughout. This is probably one of the finest bargain issues currently available.

Grieg. Norwegian Dances, Op. 35. Lyric Suite, Op. 54. Symphonic Dances, Op. 64. **Gothenburg Symphony Orchestra/Neeme Järvi.** DG 419 2GH.

1h 8'   DDD   1/87

Grieg's music has that rare quality of eternal youth: however often one hears it, its complexion retains its bloom, the smile its radiance and the youthful sparkle remains undimmed. Though he is essentially a miniaturist, who absorbed the speech rhythms and inflections of Norwegian folk melody into his bloodstream, Grieg's world is well defined. Both the *Norwegian Dances* and the *Symphonic Dances* were originally piano duets, which Grieg subsequently scored: Järvi conducts both with enthusiasm and sensitivity. In the *Lyric Suite* he restores "Klokkeklang" (Bell-ringing), which Grieg omitted from the final score: it is remarkably atmospheric and evocative, and serves to show how forward-looking Grieg became in his late years. The recording is exceptionally fine and of wide dynamic range; the sound is very natural and the perspective true to life.

Grieg. Peer Gynt — incidental music[a]. Sigurd Jorsalfar — incidental music, Op. 22[b]. [a]**Barbara Bonney** (sop); [a]**Marianne Eklöf** (mez); [b]**Kjell Magnus Sandve** (ten); [a]**Urban Malmberg,** [a]**Carl Gustaf Holmgren** (bars); **Gösta Ohlin's Vocal Ensemble; Pro Musica Chamber Choir; Gothenburg Symphony Orchestra/Neeme Järvi.** DG 423 079-2GH2. Texts and translations included.

② 2h 4' DDD 2/88 Ⓑ

Grieg. Peer Gynt — incidental music[a]. Symphonic Dance, Op. 64 No. 2[b]. Concert Overture, Op. 11, "In Autumn"[c]. **Ilse Hollweg** (sop); **Beecham Choral Society; Royal Philharmonic Orchestra/Sir Thomas Beecham.** EMI Studio CDM7 69039-2. Item marked [a] from ASD258 (1/59); [b] ASD518 (4/63); [c] SXLP30530 (2/82).

58' ADD 1/89 Ⓑ ▲

Grieg's incidental music was an important integral part of Ibsen's *Peer Gynt*. From this score Grieg later extracted the two familiar suites but DG's issue represents the first ever complete recording of Grieg's original work. Even the music which accompanies dialogue is included, with actors speaking Ibsen's lines, and the effect enhances the music's expressive power. Texts and translations are provided, so that it is easy to put the music in its dramatic context. Room is also found for another example of Grieg's incidental music, this time for Bjørnstjerne Bjørnson's play *Sigurd Jorsalfar*. Usually we hear just the concert suite of three movements, but again Järvi has recorded for the first time the complete eight-movement original score with chorus and tenor soloist. Here is an enterprising and stimulating issue which both instructs and gives much pleasure. The recording quality is good.

Sir Thomas Beecham's recording of ten of the numbers from *Peer Gynt* goes back to 1957 but still sounds well and is most stylishly played. He includes the best known ("Anitra's Dance" is a delicate gem here) plus "Solveig's Song" and "Solveig's Cradle Song". Beecham uses the soprano Ilse Hollweg to advantage, her voice suggesting the innocence of the virtuous and faithful peasant heroine. There's also an effective use of the choral voices which are almost inevitably omitted in ordinary performances of the two well-known orchestral suites: the male chorus of trolls in the "Hall of the Mountain King" are thrilling, and the women in the "Arabian Dance" have charm. The other two pieces are worth having also; *Symphonic Dance* is a later, freshly pastoral work, while the overture *In Autumn* is an orchestral second version of an early piece for piano duet.

NEW REVIEW
Grieg. String Quartet in G minor, Op. 27.
Schumann. String Quartet No. 1 in A major, Op. 41. **English Quartet** (Diana Cummings, Colin Callow, vns; Luciano Iorio, va; Geoffrey Thomas, vc). Unicorn-Kanchana DKPCD9092.

1h 6' DDD 3/92

Grieg was in his mid-thirties when writing his G minor String Quartet (the only one he ever completed), a work with a phrase from his recently composed Ibsen setting *Spillemaend* ("Fiddlers") as its unifying motto. Frequently criticized for over-thick scoring and moments of laboured invention, it rarely turns up in concert programmes, and for a long time was conspicuous by its absence from the CD catalogue. Now, at last, it has found rescuers on disc, with this vivid performance from the English Quartet most likely to makes its disparagers think again. The music's swift-changing moods and bold dynamic contrasts are in fact caught with a surprisingly un-English intensity of feeling and temperament, not least the first movement's alternations of demonstrative vehemence and seductive lyricism. The players respond with the same imaginative immediacy to the folk-spirit of the Intermezzo's central trio, and find all the bracing brio for the saltarello-inspired finale. As a life-long Schumann devotee, Grieg would no doubt have been delighted to find his own work coupled with Schumann's First in this medium, written in a Mendelssohn-dominated Leipzig at the age of 32. Here, the English Quartet attune themselves to the music's suave lyricism with the same keen sense of style. Apart from a touch of edginess in high-lying climaxes (notably in the Grieg) the tonal reproduction is very acceptable.

Grieg. LYRIC PIECES — excerpts. **Emil Gilels** (pf). DG 419 749-2GH. From 2530 476 (3/75).
Arietta, Op. 12 No. 1. Berceuse, Op. 38 No. 1. Butterfly, Op. 43 No. 1. Solitary Traveller, Op. 43 No. 2. Album-leaf, Op. 47 No. 2. Melody, Op. 47 No. 3. Norwegian Dance, "Halling", Op. 47 No. 4. Nocturne, Op. 54 No. 4. Scherzo, Op. 54 No. 5. Homesickness, Op. 57 No. 6. Brooklet, Op. 62 No. 4. Homeward, Op. 62 No. 6. In ballad vein, Op. 65 No. 5. Grandmother's minuet, Op. 68 No. 2. At your feet, Op. 68 No. 3. Cradlesong, Op. 68 No. 5. Once upon a time, Op. 71 No. 1. Puck, Op. 71 No. 3. Gone, Op. 71 No. 6. Remembrances, Op. 71 No. 7.

`56' ADD 10/87`

This record is something of a gramophone classic. The great Russian pianist Emil Gilels, an artist of staggering technical accomplishment and intellectual power, here turns his attention to Grieg's charming miniatures. He brings the same insight and concentration to these apparent trifles as he did to towering masterpieces of the classic repertoire. The programme proceeds chronologically and one can appreciate the gradual but marked development in Grieg's harmonic and expressive language — from the folk-song inspired early works to the more progressive and adventurous later ones. Gilels's fingerwork is exquisite and the sense of total involvement with the music almost religious in feeling. This is a wonderful recording: pianistic perfection.

Grieg. LYRIC PIECES, Volume 1. **Peter Katin** (pf). Unicorn-Kanchana Souvenir UKCD2033.
Book 1, Op. 12; Book 2, Op. 38; Book 3, Op. 43; Book 4, Op. 47.

`1h 3' DDD 9/90`

Between 1867 and 1901, Grieg published ten sets of short piano pieces called *Lyric Pieces*, using an adjective which implies something expressive, songlike and on a small scale. Only one of the 29 here lasts more than four minutes and the shortest lasts just 40 seconds, yet they are not mere chips from the composer's work-bench but instead beautifully crafted miniatures in the tradition of Schumann's *Scenes from Childhood*. Although in the past pianists often played them in public, today we hardly ever hear them in the concert hall where, as Peter Katin points out in his booklet note, we usually get "far weightier fare". In fact a recorded performance is all the more welcome in that some of their intimacy is lost in an auditorium and Grieg certainly intended them to be heard in domestic surroundings. Some are 'easy' in the sense that the notes are not hard to play even for learners, but even so we gain immensely from the shaping of tone and rhythm that a fine artist can bring, especially when he so clearly loves the music. It is worth adding that there is plenty of variety here: thus Book 1 ends with a vigorous *National Song* that is very unlike the gentle little *Arietta* with which it begins. There are so many delights that it's hard to list special ones, but we would not go wrong if we lighted on the freshly charming *Butterfly, Little Bird* and *To the Spring* in Book 3, which remind us that Nature was often Grieg's inspiration. Pleasantly clean sound, with a touch of hardness in bigger passages.

Sofia Gubaidulina
Russian 1931-

NEW REVIEW
Gubaidulina. String Quartet No. 2.
Kurtág. String Quartet No. 1, Op. 1. Hommage à Milhály András, Op. 13. Officium breve in memoriam Andreae Szervánzky, Op. 28.
Lutoslawski. String Quartet. **Arditti Quartet** (Irvine Arditti, David Alberman, vns; Levine Andrade, va; Rohan de Saram, vc). Disques Montaigne 789007.

 1h 12' DDD 4/92

Recent political developments ensure that Sofia Gubaidulina's country of birth is given in the notes, not as Russia, but as the Tatar Autonomous People's Republic. Autonomy — the need for a personal tone of voice — is a quality all three of these eastern European composers well understand. Lutoslawski's quartet (1964) came at a crucial time in his development, as the first work to relate his new technique of aleatory counterpoint (in which the pitches but not necessarily the rhythms are prescribed) to a traditional, abstract genre. Compared to the best of his later works the quartet is perhaps too long-drawn-out, but this highly expressive and strongly disciplined performance makes an excellent case for it. Alongside the Lutoslawski the three works by György Kurtág sound remarkably intense and concentrated, yet with a lyricism that prevents their evident austerity from growing merely arid, and which makes the reference to a tonal melody in the *Officium breve* seem natural as well as touching. The world of consonant harmony is also evoked by Gubaidulina, not as an expression of regret for the irretrievable past but as a way of extending her own essentially modern language. There is a special sense of personal certainty and confidence about all the music on this well-recorded disc. It needs no special pleading, but the commanding authority of the Arditti Quartet's performance is still something to marvel at.

Reynaldo Hahn
Venezuelan-French 1875-1947

Hahn. Premières Valses. Le rossignol éperdu — excerpts. **Catherine Joly** (pf). Accord 20054-2.

 1h 7' DDD 5/90

The very epitome of the suave, exquisite frequenter of fashionable Paris salons, Reynaldo Hahn has until recently been little recognized as a composer except for one or two songs. Moreover, the charming *Ciboulette* (the most successful of his many stage works) and the fact that he enjoyed a reputation as a Mozart conductor and that for the last two years of his life he was music director of the Paris Opéra, prove that he was no mere dilettante. The chain of ten *Premières Valses*, it is true, reflects the atmosphere of the salons, but their wide diversity of moods and their informed passing salutations to Chopin and Schubert betoken a cultivated and inventive mind. More serious are the 25 pieces selected from the later, little-known *Le rossignol éperdu*, which are travel vignettes of a literary provenance (a pity that the introductory quotations are not given here), a kind of musical diary mostly pervaded by a dark nostalgia: in this, as elsewhere in Hahn, melody is paramount. Catherine Joly plays everything here with the utmost subtlety of dynamics, rhythm and coloration. This disc opens up a new storehouse of miniatures — only three last as long as three minutes — which will be appreciated by the discriminating.

Hahn. MELODIES. **François Le Roux** (bar); **Jeff Cohen** (pf). REM 311069. Texts and translations included.
A Chloris. Chansons grises. Les cygnes. Dans la nuit. D'une prison. Fêtes galantes. Fumée. L'incrédule. Infidélité. Mai. La nuit. L'heure exquise. Nocturne. Offrande. Paysage. Le printemps. Quand je fus pris au pavillon. Quand la nuit n'est pas étoilée. Rêverie. Séraphine. Seule. Si mers vers avaient des ailes. Sur l'eau. Tous deux. Trois jours de vendange.

| ♪ 1h 8' DDD 11/91 | ❓ |

The *mélodie* is the French equivalent of the Lied, in other words a song with piano accompaniment. But though Reynaldo Hahn wrote over 100, he was not a native of France, having been born in Venezuela of a German father and a Basque mother. However, his family moved to France and he studied at the Paris Conservatoire with Massenet. He had a good voice and became famous in high society Paris salons for performing his songs to his own piano accompaniment. The intimacy that this suggests comes across well on record, and the young baritone François Le Roux rightly avoids over-projection. The songs here are mostly on the light side (the dramatic *Dans la nuit* is an exception) and there is charm but little anguish in the setting of Verlaine's gloomy poem called *Chanson d'automne*. Even *D'une prison*, to a despairing poem which Verlaine wrote when serving a gaol sentence, is calm save for a brief climax. Yet otherwise the songs are well varied and the brighter ones have a wonderfully fresh lyricism, so that this is the sort of programme that one can listen to right through with pleasure. Le Roux is sensitive to the subtle nuances of both music and words (by 14 poets in all) and his singing is refined and expressive. There's humour, too, for example in the bouncy *Fêtes galantes*. Jeff Cohen is an understanding and supportive pianist and the recital is closely but atmospherically recorded. The booklet provides the texts and an English translation.

George Frederic Handel
German-British 1685-1759

Handel. ORGAN CONCERTOS. **Simon Preston** (org); **The English Concert/Trevor Pinnock**. Archiv Produktion 413 465-2AH2. From 413 465-1AH2 (10/84).
Op. 4 — No. 1 in G minor; No. 2 in B flat major; No. 3 in G minor; No. 4 in F major; No. 5 in F major; No. 6 in B flat major; No. 14 in A major.

| ♪ ② 1h 30' DDD 12/84 | |

Handel. ORGAN CONCERTOS. **Ton Koopman** (org); **Amsterdam Baroque Orchestra**. Erato Emerald 2292-45613-2.
Op. 4 — No. 2 in B flat major; No. 4 in F major; No. 6 in B flat major. Op 7 — No. 2; No. 4; No. 5.

| ♪ 1h 18' DDD 11/91 | |

Handel's highly acclaimed skill as a virtuoso organist was a significant factor in attracting audiences. His organ concertos are rich in catchy tunes, with some of

Simon Preston   [photo: DG

the long *allegros* sailing along with unstoppable momentum. But there are great treasures in the slow movements too — the *Andante* from Op. 4 No. 4 is full of colour and the solo part performs wonders of invention over a simple foundation of chords while the Menuet and Gavotte from Op. 7 No. 5 have great charm and elegance. Handel adapted several of these Concertos from other works — Op. 4 No. 5 comes from a recorder sonata and Op. 4 No. 6 was originally for harp — but the universality of the writing means that everything seems entirely at home in this context, especially given such compelling performances as here. Both the English Concert and the Amsterdam Baroque Orchestra use authentic instruments but while Trevor Pinnock directs a beautifully integrated dialogue between his musicians and the soloist, Ton Koopman leads his performances from the organ stool giving his disc a real feeling of intimacy which makes ideal home listening. Preston underlines the virtuosic character of the solo parts with some brilliant fingerwork and some exuberant playing, while Koopman indulges in some thoroughly convincing improvisations at points where Handel too would have given free rein to his skills as a virtuoso organist.

Handel. Concerti grossi, Op. 3. **The English Concert/Trevor Pinnock** (hpd). Archiv Produktion 413 727-2AH.

The abundant variety of these concertos is in the number and character of their movements, and in the ways in which a comparatively limited palette of instrumental colour is exploited. Collectively they show Handel's enthusiasm for the Italian style and his ability to write the good tunes it required. The recorded performances capture the youthful freshness of Handel's imagination, enhanced by graceful embellishments by the soloists where appropriate. The sound, too, is appropriate, coming from period instruments Handel would recognize, recorded with great clarity and with good balance — the continuo harpsichord is comfortably audible and, played by Pinnock himself, always worth hearing.

Handel. Concerti grossi, Op. 6 Nos. 1-4. **The English Concert/Trevor Pinnock.** Archiv Produktion 410 897-2AH. From 2742 002 (11/82).
No. 1 in G major; No. 2 in F major; No. 3 in E minor; No. 4 in A minor.

Handel. Concerti grossi, Op. 6 Nos. 5-8. **The English Concert/Trevor Pinnock.** Archiv Produktion 410 898-2AH. From 2742 002 (11/82).
No. 5 in D major; No. 6 in G minor; No. 7 in B flat major; No. 8 in C minor.

Handel. Concerti grossi, Op. 6 Nos. 9-12. **The English Concert/Trevor Pinnock.** Archiv Produktion 410 899-2AH. From 2742 002 (11/82).
No. 9 in F major; No. 10 in D minor; No. 11 in A major; No. 12 in B minor.

Handel. Concerti grossi, Op. 6 Nos. 1-12. **Guildhall String Ensemble.**
RCA Victor Red Seal RD87895/RD87907/RD87921.
RD87895 — No. 1 in G major; No. 2 in F major; No. 3 in E minor; No. 4 in
A minor. *RD87907* — No. 5 in D major; No. 6 in G minor; No. 7 in B flat
major; No. 8 in C minor. *RD87921* — No. 9 in F major; No. 10 in D minor;
No. 11 in A major; No. 12 in B minor.

③ 44' 60' 56' DDD 2/90 Ⓑ

Handel's 12 *Concerti grossi* have from four to six movements and are mostly in *da
chiesa* form, i.e. without dance movements. They were written within one month
in the autumn of 1739 (an average of two movements per day!) and when a
great composer is thus carried on the tide of urgent inspiration it usually shows,
as it does here in the flow of felicitous invention and memorable tune-smithing.
The range of musical idioms used throughout is impressive and to them all
Handel imparts his own indelible and unmistakable stamp. Trevor Pinnock's
account contains much that is satisfying: polished ensemble, effectively judged
tempos, a natural feeling for phrase, and a buoyancy of spirit which serves
Handel's own robust musical language very well. Crisp attack, a judicious
application of appoggiaturas and tasteful embellishment further enhance these
lively performances. Pinnock varies the continuo colour by using organ and
harpsichord and also includes Handel's autograph (though not printed) oboe parts
for Concertos Nos. 1, 2, 5 and 6; where they occur a bassoon is sensibly added
to fulfil the customary three-part wind texture of the period. Recorded sound is
clear and captures something of the warm sonorities of the instruments.

The ideal way to hear this music is on period instruments, but if this is not to
your taste you may with a clear conscience choose to have them on modern ones
— providing they are as well used as they are by the Guildhall String Ensemble.
This music was written to be enjoyed and that is how it is treated, stylishly and
with a fresh enthusiasm that produces some brisk tempos, in this well balanced and
clean-sounding recording. As the discs are separately available you can test the water
with a cautious toe, but having done so you are likely to opt for total immersion.

Handel. Water Music. **Simon Standage, Elizabeth Wilcock** (vns); **The
English Concert/Trevor Pinnock** (hpd). Archiv Produktion 410 525-2AH.
From 410 525-1AH (1/84).

54' DDD 2/84 Ⓑ

Handel. Water Music. **Consort of London/Robert Haydon Clark.**
Collins Classics 10152.

1h 3' DDD 6/90 Ⓑ

NEW REVIEW

Handel. Water Music. Music for the Royal Fireworks. **Concertgebouw
Chamber Orchestra/Simon Preston.** Decca Ovation 430 717-2DM.

1h 9' DDD 8/91 £ Ⓑ

The *Water Music* was written for a river journey made by King George I and his
retinue in 1717 and falls into three groups of suites in different keys (F, D and G
major). Some of the tunes such as the hornpipe are now familiar to many people
who may not even know where they come from, or who wrote them. The
English Concert play the music with a mixture of gaiety, verve and regal pomp,
using period instruments and performing practices that enable us to hear it as
closely as possible to the way it would have been heard in 1717.

Handel had earlier written a Concerto in F, which he revised and transposed
to form the first two movements of the final ('trumpet') Suite (in D major) of
the *Water Music*. In the Collins recording these two movements are added, in
their original forms, at the end of the Suite in F — which makes a pleasant

bonus, even if the King did not hear them thus. The Consort of London uses modern instruments, so that the music sounds at concert pitch ('authentic' performances emerge about half a tone lower) and they do so with the utmost intelligence — notably in the transparent sound of the strings — and alertness to good style. The pristine quality of the recorded sound helps to make this another very attractive way of hearing this much-loved music.

As the debate between authentic and modern methods of performance continues, the Preston disc comes as an intelligent compromise between points of Handelian style and contemporary concert presentation. The *Water Music* was never properly published in his lifetime. However, several manuscript scores were made, one of which was procured by the Fitzwilliam Museum, Cambridge. It is this score which Preston used for his performance with the Concertgebouw Chamber Orchestra presenting buoyant, fleet-footed accounts of the suites. The orchestral playing is polished and spruce but this modern instrument performance is light-textured and attentive to details of ornamentation. The 1991 recording is very fine as it is for Preston's lively version of the *Fireworks* music. Again textures are clean and detailed but Preston cannot resist a grand approach to "La Rejouissance" and the final minuet. This disc makes a worthy successor to previous versions by Münchinger and Marriner and provides another modern instrument alternative to the Collins Classics offering. And it is one of the few brand new recordings to be released straightaway onto a mid-price label.

Handel. Music for the Royal Fireworks. Concerti a due cori — No. 2 in F major; No. 3 in F major. **The English Concert/Trevor Pinnock.** Archiv Produktion 415 129-2AH.

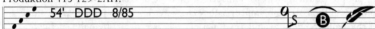

The *Concerti a due cori* (concertos for two choirs of instruments) are in fact written for a string band and two wind bands, each consisting (in the two concertos above) of oboes, horns and bassoon. The famous *Fireworks* music was written to enliven a firework display in Green Park and although King George III wanted as many warlike instruments as possible, Handel preferred to add a sizeable string band. The quality and balance of the sound are radically affected by the instruments used — period or modern. The English Concert use the former with a skill that makes this a very pleasant experience. You can enjoy this magnificent music with superb sound from the CD.

Handel. HARPSICHORD SUITES. **Scott Ross**. Erato 2292-45452-2. No. 1 in A major; No. 2 in F major; No. 3 in D minor; No. 4 in E minor; No. 5 in E major; No. 5 —Air and Variations, "The Harmonious Blacksmith"; No. 6 in F sharp minor; No. 7 in G minor; No. 8 in F minor.

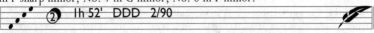

NEW REVIEW
Handel. HARPSICHORD SUITES. **Colin Tilney**. Archiv Produktion Galleria 427 170-2AGA2. Items marked [a] from 2533 169 (2/75), [b] 2533 168 (2/75). No. 1 in A major[a]; No. 2 in F major[b]; No. 3 in D minor[a]; No. 4 in E minor[b]; No. 5 in E major[b]; No. 5a —Air and Variations, "The Harmonious Blacksmith"; No. 6 in F sharp minor[a]; No. 7 in G minor[a]; No. 8 in F minor[b].

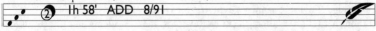

Handel published his eight harpsichord suites in 1720 though he had written much of the music earlier in his life. One of the many striking features of these pieces is that of variety. Handel's terms of reference were wide and cosmopolitan and the harpsichord suites contain many contrasting ingredients ranging from well sustained imitative part-writing on the one hand to simpler airs and dances on the

Colin Tilney   *[photo: Dorian Recordings*

other. These two aspects of Handel's art find a happy and celebrated conjunction in the air and variations affectionately known as *The Harmonious Blacksmith*. The music, displaying elements of French, Italian and German styles, reflects Handel's own cosmopolitan nature and tastes. Many readers may be as surprised to find how much of this music is unfamiliar to them as they will be delighted by its ceaseless invention and affecting idiom. To show an empathy with these diverse facets of Handel's world a performer needs a firm grasp of stylistic matters such as the rhythmic freedoms of rubato and *inégalités*, and the introduction of embellishments of various kinds; the late Scott Ross, beautifully recorded in charge of a reproduction of a French instrument of 1733, had all these attributes in abundance.

Colin Tilney is also a persuasive interpreter of this repertory, bringing a muscular strength to Handel's often complex part-writing while never complicating simpler musical ideas with misplaced rhetoric or exaggerated gestures. Preludes with their strongly improvisatory character are given just the right amount of rhythmic freedom even if *The Harmonious Blacksmith* air, though tastefully ornamented, is a shade lacking in conviviality. Tilney plays two especially fine instruments made in Hamburg during the early years of the eighteenth century. The recorded sound is sympathetic.

NEW REVIEW

Handel. THE WORLD OF HANDEL. **Various artists.** Decca 430 500-2DWO.
SOLOMON — Arrival of the Queen of Sheba (Academy of St Martin in the Fields/Sir Neville Marriner). RODELINDA — Dove sei (Marilyn Horne, mez; Vienna Cantata Orchestra/Henry Lewis). See the conquering hero comes (Handel Opera Society Chorus and Orchestra/Charles Farncombe). Water Music — Allegro; Air; Allegro deciso (London Symphony Orchestra/George Szell). SEMELE — Where'er you walk (Kenneth McKellar, ten; Royal Opera House Orchestra, Covent Garden/Sir Adrian Boult). BERENICE — Minuet from Overture (Academy of St Martin in the Fields/Sir Neville Marriner). SAMSON — Let the bright seraphim (Dame Joan Sutherland, sop; Royal Opera House Orchestra, Covent Garden/Francesco Molinari-Pradelli). ISRAEL IN EGYPT — He gave them hailstones (Handel Opera Society Chorus and Orchestra/Charles Farncombe). Organ Concerto in B flat major, Op. 4 No. 2 (George Malcolm, org; Academy of St Martin in the Fields/Sir Neville Marriner). Coronation Anthems, HWV258-61 — No. 1, Zadok the Priest (King's College Choir, Cambridge; English Chamber Orchestra/Sir David Willcocks). MESSIAH — O thou that tellest; Hallelujah (Anna Reynolds, mez; Academy and Chorus of St Martin in the Fields/Sir Neville Marriner).

1h 9' ADD 10/91

Handel was as capable of rising to the big ceremonial occasion as he was to giving voice to intimate contemplation, though it is the former which predominates in this collection of some of his best-known works. The manner in which arias and choruses from operas and oratorios, and three much-loved orchestral pieces, are delivered suggests that the affection of these performers remains undimmed, though they are probably as familiar with them as they are with the images of their own faces in the mirror. Let's imagine that you want to introduce yourself (or a friend) to Handel's music: there could be no better way to do it than this, and if you are wary of the sounds of period instruments you need not worry — they are not used in this recording.

Handel. Chandos Anthems, Volume 4 — The Lord is my light, HWV255; Let God arise, HWV256. **Lynne Dawson** (sop); **Ian Partridge** (ten); **The Sixteen Chorus and Orchestra/Harry Christophers.** Chandos Chaconne CHAN0509. Texts included.

| ♪ 49' DDD 7/90 | |

The Chandos Anthems, which Handel composed during his residence at Canons, Edgware, Middlesex, in the years around 1720, have not had a complete recording before. The Sixteen have now completed their set of these appealing pieces, church music on a modest scale composed for the Duke of Chandos's private worship. Essentially intimate in style, they nevertheless have a touch of the ceremonial about them, echoing Purcell and the English tradition but at the same time reinterpret that tradition in a broad, urbane manner, attuned to the worldliness of the Anglican establishment of the time. Probably they were intended for performance by a very small group, but Harry Christopher's ensemble is well scaled to the music and his chorus sing for the most part with spirit, especially in the quicker music. Ian Partridge sings with his usual impeccable taste and judgement in the tenor solo music; the other soloist here is the soprano Lynne Dawson, whose glowing tone and diamantine passage-work are one of the chief delights of this pleasing disc.

NEW REVIEW

Handel. Dixit Dominus, HWV232[a]. Nisi Dominus, HWV238[b]. Salve Regina, HWV241[c]. [ac]**Arleen Auger**, [a]**Lynne Dawson** (sops); [ab]**Diana Montague** (mez); [a]**Leigh Nixon**, [b]**John Mark Ainsley** (tens); [ab]**Simon Birchall** (bass); **Choir and Orchestra of Westminster Abbey/Simon Preston.** Archiv Produktion 423 594-2AH. Texts and translations included.

| ♪ 56' DDD 2/89 | 🎵P 🎵S |

Although *Dixit Dominus* is the earliest surviving large scale work by Handel (he was only 22 at the time of its composition in 1707) it displays a remarkable degree of competence and invention and also looks forward to the mature style to come. The vocal writing for both chorus and soloists is extremely ornate and embellished and requires a considerable amount of expertise and flair in order to do full justice to the music. Fortunately, Simon Preston and his team possess all the necessary requirements — indeed, this is one of the most energetic, exhilarating and purposeful performances of this work ever recorded. One need only single out the rhythmically incisive performances of the opening "Dixit Dominus Domineo meo" or the "Judicabit in nationibus" and the superbly crisp and articulate performances from the Orchestra of Westminster Abbey to realize that it is a very special recording indeed. The well thought out coupling of *Nisi Dominus* and *Salve Regina* are no less impressive, with the latter offering the listener another chance to sample the beautiful solo contributions of Arleen Auger. The recorded sound is also outstandingly fine. A delightful disc.

Handel. ITALIAN DUETS. **Gillian Fisher** (sop); **James Bowman** (alto);
The King's Consort/Robert King. Hyperion CDA66440. Texts and
translations included.
A miravi io son intento. Conservate, raddoppiate. Fronda leggiera e mobile.
Langue, geme e sospira. Nò, di voi non vuo fidarmi. Se tu non lasci amore. Sono
liete, fortunate. Tanti strali al sen. Troppo crudo.

| · Ih 4' DDD 4/91 |

Handel's duets were written for high-class domestic music-making during his
Italian years and his brief period in Hanover; then he composed some additional
ones in London in the 1740s. Mostly they consist of two or three movements in
a free contrapuntal style, the voices imitating one another, then turning each
other's ideas in a new direction, then the two coming together to round off the
section. Some are cheerful and spirited (it was from one of his duets, not on the
present disc, that Handel developed the choruses "For unto us" and "All we like
sheep" in *Messiah*); others are highly chromatic and expressive, for example, the
beautiful, heartfelt first movement of *Langue, geme e sospira* and that of *Se tu non
lasci amore*, with its languishing moans and sighs — most, of course, are about
the pleasurable pains of unrequited love. The two soloists here, both
experienced Handelians, know just how to make the most of this music, letting
their voices intertwine, dawdling faintly on the dissonances, shaping the runs
purposefully, using the words to good effect; the accompaniments are tastefully
done, with lute and organ relieving the predominant harpsichord. Altogether a
happy disc.

Handel. ITALIAN CANTATAS. **Emma Kirkby** (sop); **Michel Piguet** (ob,
rec); **Rachel Beckett** (rec); **Charles Medlam** (va da gamba); **Jane Coe** (vc
cont); **Academy of Ancient Music/Christopher Hogwood** (hpd).
L'Oiseau-Lyre Florilegium 414 473-2OH. Texts and translations included.
Tu fedel? tu costante?; Mi palpita il cor; Alpestre monte; Tra le fiamme.

| · 55' DDD 3/86 |

Three of the cantatas in this issue belong to Handel's Italian period whilst the
fourth, *Mi palpita il cor* — in its version for soprano, oboe and continuo —
probably dates from his first years in England. There is a wealth of fine music to
be found in this comparatively neglected area of Handel's output and the
composer seldom if ever disappoints us in the subtlety with which he captures a
mood or colours an image. The partnership of Emma Kirkby with solo instrumentalists and members of the Academy of Ancient Music is a rewarding one.
Her singing is light in texture, fluent and effective in phrasing, and is ideally
equipped to bring out the many nuances both of text and music. All concerned
contribute towards lively performances under the stylistically informed direction
of Christopher Hogwood.

NEW REVIEW
Handel. ITALIAN CANTATAS AND INSTRUMENTAL WORKS. [a]**Julianne
Baird** (sop); [b]**John Dornenburg** (va da gamba); [c]**Malcolm Proud** (hpd).
Meridian CDE84189. Texts and translations included.
Harpsichord Suite in F minor, HWV433[c]. Occhi mei, che faceste?[abc]. Udite il
mio consiglio[abc]. Quel fior che all'alba ride[abc]. Violin Sonata in G minor,
HWV364b[bc].

| · Ih 9' DDD 12/91 |

The chamber cantatas by Handel assembled on this disc are likely to be familiar
only to the most ardent Handelians since, until now, they have been largely if

not entirely overlooked by recording companies. The programme also includes Handel's Harpsichord Suite in F minor and his Violin Sonata in G minor, but here played on a viola da gamba — the composer seems to have had both instruments in mind at different times. Julianne Baird is one of the leading baroque sopranos but like all interesting artists there is a small element of unpredictability in her singing. In this recital her declamation is excellent and her diction commendably clear but the music, often technically demanding, finds chinks in her armour, so-to-speak. There are hints of strain in her uppermost range and an occasional tightness in the voice but the interpretations are stylish and alluring and Baird's acute ear for the pitching of notes enables her to surmount tricky chromaticisms and teasing intervals with comfortable assurance. The two instrumental pieces are very well executed by Malcolm Proud, joined by John Dornenburg in the sonata. Altogether an attractive programme. Full texts provided.

NEW REVIEW

Handel. CANTATAS FOR COUNTERTENOR[a]. Trio Sonata, Op. 5 No. 4. [a]**Gérard Lesne** (alto); **Il Seminario Musicale.** Virgin Classics VC7 91480-2. Texts and translations included.
Splende l'alba in oriente. La Lucrezia. Mi, palpita il cor. Carco sempre di gloria.

⟨ 1h 10' DDD 12/91 ⟩

NEW REVIEW

Handel. CANTATAS FOR COUNTERTENOR. **Derek Lee Ragin** (alto); **Cologne Divitia Ensemble.** Channel Classics CCS0890. Texts included.
Lungi da me pensier tiranno. Siete rose rugiadose. Udite il mio consiglio. Carco sempre di gloria. Oboe Sonatas — F major, HWV363*a*; C minor, HWV366.

⟨ 1h 1' DDD 2/92 ⟩

The French countertenor, Gérard Lesne is a sympathetic Handelian. Here he has chosen four of Handel's chamber cantatas. Two of them honour the patron saint of music, St Cecilia and these together with *Mi, palpita il cor* were written after Handel had settled in London. The remaining cantata *O numi eterni*, also known as *La Lucrezia* dates from 1709 when the composer was nearing the end of his Italian visit. Lesne's voice is able to convey a wide variety of moods and in this respect among many others he proves himself a worthy match for Handel's subtle colouring of the Italian texts. His vocal timbre inclines towards subdued rather than bright colouring and is especially well-suited to *La Lucrezia*. Florid and in other ways difficult passages are negotiated fluently and with a commendably sure sense of pitch, and the instrumentalists of Il Seminario Musicale provide lively and sympathetic support. Only in the Trio Sonata (Op. 5 No. 4) does one feel the need for a greater unanimity of ensemble and pitch but that is a small price to pay for musically sensitive performances such as these. The recorded sound is clear and the booklet contains full texts with translations.

The countertenor, Derek Lee Ragin's voice is more brightly coloured than Gérard Lesne's and, both in its range and strong projection closer, perhaps, to the sound of an eighteenth-century castrato. Each programme has hit upon the effective idea of interspersing the cantatas with one or more pieces of Handel's instrumental music. The only duplication occurs in the inclusion in each programme of the cantata *Carco sempre di gloria* which Handel wrote during the 1730s for a St Cecilia's Day celebration. Ragin declaims the texts articulately and with careful attention to detail. His approach to the music is more light-hearted (even at times mischievous) than Lesne's more guarded responses; and he is given lively support by the members of Cologne Divitia Ensemble. These are stylish performances in which the music springs to life from the printed page. Texts are provided but in Italian only, and the recorded sound is all that one could wish for.

Handel. ARIAS. **Robert White** (ten); **City of London Baroque Sinfonia/
Ivor Bolton**. Virgin Classics Virgo VJ7 91456-2. From VC7 907.
Serse: Frondi tenere — Ombra mai fù. Acis and Galatea: Love sounds the alarm;
Would you gain the tender creature. Esther: Tune your harps to cheerful strains.
Athalia: Gentle airs, melodious strains. Judas Maccabaeus: So shall the lute and
harp awake. Samson: Total eclipse. Messiah: Comfort ye — Ev'ry valley. Haman
and Mordecai: Praise the Lord with cheerful noise. The Choice of Hercules:
There the brisk sparkling Nectar. Joshua: While Kedron's brook. Rinaldo: Lascia
ch'io piange. Semele: Where'er you walk; O sleep, why dost thou leave me?
Ode for St Cecilia's Day: Sharp violins proclaim. Amadigi di Gaula: Ah! spietato.

Ih 11' DDD 12/91   £ 9s

Considering that one of the most popular pieces of classical music is Handel's
aria "Ombra mai fù" (his *Largo*), and that it is just one of a whole batch of
attractive solo airs from his operas and other music, this disc was waiting to
happen and, given the quality of Robert White's singing, a deserved winner in
Virgin's super-budget Virgo series. White's tone is warmly sweet and convincingly Italiante in the aria just mentioned, which comes first and suits him
although it lies low for tenor. He is equally idiomatic in arias taken from the
composer's English oratorios and cantatas; they form the majority of the 16
numbers here, which overall provide a satisfying range of style and mood.
Indeed, all are finely sung, and Ivor Bolton's direction of his City of London
Baroque Sinfonia, with its period instruments, is no less effective. They perform
at an 'authentic' low pitch and with an evident delight in Handel's well varied
instrumentation. One notices the skilful harpsichord playing, and several other
instrumentalists (like the oboist on track 3, the viol player on track 4, the harpist
on track 8 and the trumpeter on track 9) also get a chance to shine as they
feature in turn as obbligato players. The recording is sumptuously rich. One
might like more information on the music than the half page offered, but at this
price who's complaining?

Handel. ARIAS FOR MONTAGNANA. **David Thomas** (bass); **Philharmonia Baroque Orchestra/Nicholas McGegan**. Harmonia Mundi HMU90
7016. Texts and translations included.
Acis and Galatea — Avampo … Ferito son d'Amore. Athalia — Ah, canst thou
but prove me! Deborah — Barak, my son … Awake the ardour; They ardours
warm … Swift inundation; Tears, such as tender fathers shed. Esther — I'll hear
no more … Pluck root and branch; Turn not, O Queen; How art thou fall'n.
Ezio — Perchè tanto tormento? … Se un bell'ardire; Folle è colui … Nasce al
bosco; Che indegno! … Già risonar. Orlando — Mira, prendi l'essempio! …
Lascia Amor; Impari ognun da Orlando … O voi, del mio poter … Sorge
infausta una procella. Sosarme — Addio, principe scrupoloso … Fra l'ombre e
gli orrori; Quanto più Melo … Sento il core; Tanto s'eseguirà … Tiene Giove.
Tolomeo, re di egitto — Piangi pur.

Ih 8' DDD 8/90

Antonio Montagnana was a Venetian who sang bass parts in London in Handel's
time: which means that his voice and his capacities gave shape to many of the
bass parts Handel composed — it being the custom, in those times, for a
composer to write the music to the singer's specific abilities. And Handel's music
tells us that Montagnana was a singer quite out of the ordinary, as remarkable, in
fact, as his impersonator here, the English bass David Thomas. Some of the arias
are big, blustery pieces, suitable for unscrupulous villains or sturdy military men,
but others show Montagnana (and Thomas) as what came to be called a *basso
cantante* (listen to the eloquent one from *Tolomeo*), and there are sheer virtuoso
pieces too (conspicuously those from *Sosarme*). Some of them range from what is

practically a tenor compass right down to *basso profondo* regions. Thomas is an astonishing singer, agile to a degree, able to encompass all that Montagnana did and indeed to add apt ornamentation at times; the articulation is precise and energetic, the tone true and even across two-and-a-half octaves, and always there is a touch of wit and spirit behind the singing. Nicholas McGegan's band provides sharp, slightly choppy support.

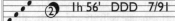

Handel. La Resurrezione, HWV47. **Nancy Argenta, Barbara Schlick** (sops); **Guillemette Laurens** (mez); **Guy de Mey** (ten); **Klaus Mertens** (bass); **Amsterdam Baroque Orchestra/Ton Koopman.** Erato 2292-45617-2. Text and translation included.

> ② 1h 56' DDD 7/91

Barbara Schlick   *[photo: DG/Fürst*

It is good to have this early Handel oratorio so richly represented on CD by Ton Koopman's colourful rendition. *La Resurrezione* was written in 1708 when Handel was 22 and working for the Marquis Ruspoli during his stay in Italy. The composer, who always had a talent for pulling the crowds, defied papal censorship and gave the part of Magdalene to a woman. A long established guardian of early music performing practices, Koopman's interpretation is as polished and expressive as one would expect; if slightly indulgent in places, it is also pleasingly spontaneous. The Amsterdam orchestra have a feel for instrumental colouring which yields rewarding results in the carefully delineated accompaniments. The soloists are very fine with Nancy Argenta giving us a particularly sensuous Magdalene which would certainly have displeased a passing cardinal! Erato's sound quality is a little top heavy in places but is typically clear and vivid.

Handel. Aci, Galatea e Polifemo[a]. Recorder Sonatas[b] — F major, HWV369; C major, HWV365; G major (trans. F major), HWV358. **Emma Kirkby** (sop) Aci; **Carolyn Watkinson** (contr) Galatea; **David Thomas** (bass) Polifemo; [b]**Michel Piquet** (rec); [b]**John Toll** (hpd); **London Baroque/Charles Medlam** ([b]vc). Harmonia Mundi HMC90 1253/4. Notes, text and translation included. Item marked [a] new to UK, [b] from HMC1190/91 (9/86).

> ② 1h 46' DDD 11/87

Handel's English pastoral *Acis and Galatea* has always been one of his most popular works, but not many of its admirers are aware that he had written a completely different treatment of the same story ten years earlier (when he was 23) for a ducal wedding in Naples. In this version modern ears need to adjust to Acis (a young shepherd lad) being represented by a soprano (originally a castrato), while the nymph Galatea is a contralto. The work is full of invention and instrumental colour, and there are several memorably beautiful items in the score, such as the opening duet (with the lovers' voices intertwining), and above all Acis's dying farewell after the jealous giant Polyphemus has crushed him under a huge rock. To suggest the giant's vast size Handel employed a prodigious vocal range of two-and-a-half octaves, which has proved the chief obstacle to performances of the work, here receiving a very enjoyable first recording. All three singers are excellent and so is the technical quality.

Handel. Acis and Galatea. **Norma Burrowes** (sop) Galatea; **Anthony Rolfe Johnson** (ten) Acis; **Martyn Hill** (ten) Damon; **Willard White** (bass) Polyphemus; **Paul Elliot** (ten); **English Baroque Soloists/John Eliot Gardiner.** Archiv Produktion 423 406-2AH2. Notes, text and translation included. From 2708 038 (9/78).

② 1h 35' ADD 8/88

John Eliot Gardiner made this recording of Handel's masque during the late 1970s when the revival of period instruments was still in a comparatively early stage. Listeners may detect weaknesses both in intonation and in ensemble from time to time but, nevertheless, Gardiner's performance is lively and stylistically assured. He paces the work dramatically revealing nuances both in the text and in the music. The solo team is a strong one and there are especially fine contributions from Norma Burrowes and Anthony Rolfe Johnson. This is an enjoyable performance of an enchanting work.

Handel. Athalia. **Dame Joan Sutherland** (sop) Athalia; **Emma Kirkby** (sop) Josabeth; **Aled Jones** (treb) Joas; **James Bowman** (alto) Joad; **Anthony Rolfe Johnson** (ten) Mathan; **David Thomas** (bass-bar) Abner; **New College Choir, Oxford; Academy of Ancient Music/Christopher Hogwood.** L'Oiseau-Lyre 417 126-2OH2. Notes and text included. From 417 126-1OH2 (11/86).

② 2h 2' DDD 2/87

Although *Athalia* was a huge success when first performed and has long been recognized as a masterly work, not only is this its first complete recording, but barely a note of it has previously appeared in the catalogues, apart from a couple of excerpts in transcriptions. With lip service constantly paid to Handel, this has been a startling neglect; but fortunately the conspiracy of silence has now been broken with a performance that does justice to this remarkable piece. Handel's treatment of form is exceptionally flexible, his characterization is vivid, and his musical invention is at its most exuberant: the opening Sinfonia (alertly played under Hogwood) immediately whets the appetite. Emma Kirkby delights by the freshness and limpidity of her tone and by the absolute precision and charm of her trills and ornamentation whilst James Bowman sings accurately but is unimaginative in his treatment of words. In the title-role Joan Sutherland makes the most of the apostate queen's vengeful outbursts, and her enunciation is much clearer than usual. There are splendid florid solos for David Thomas and Anthony Rolfe Johnson, and Aled Jones as the boy king sings his one aria with beautifully controlled tone and impeccable intonation. The chorus sings enthusiastically and makes a shattering entry in the brilliant opening of Act 2 — which is certainly the number to sample for anyone wishing to know what this fine work is like.

Handel. Alexander's Feast[a]. Concerto Grosso in C major, HWV318. [a]**Donna Brown** (sop); [a]**Carolyn Watkinson** (contr); [a]**Ashley Stafford** (alto); [a]**Nigel Robson** (ten); [a]**Stephen Varcoe** (bar); [a]**Monteverdi Choir, English Baroque Soloists/John Eliot Gardiner.** Philips 422 055-2PH2. Text included. Recorded at a performance during the 1987 Göttingen Handel Festival, Germany.

② 1h 38' DDD 11/88

Alexander's Feast was the first work Handel had set by a major English poet (Dryden) and it was also the first time he allotted the principal male part to a tenor instead of the castrato heroes of his Italian operas. These two factors, combined with much fine music, scored with great brilliance and imagination, ensured the immediate success of *Alexander's Feast*. It is strange that nowadays it is seldom performed so this recording would have been very welcome even had it not been so full of vitality and so stylishly performed (though perhaps with more sophisticated detail than the eighteenth century would have managed). The Monteverdi Choir and the soloists are all Gardiner regulars, though the pure-voiced Canadian soprano Donna Brown is a fairly recent (and welcome) acquisition; and the English Baroque Soloists have ample opportunities to shine — especially the violins, although the natural horns' lusty entry in the bucolic "Bacchus, ever fair and young" is exhilarating.

Handel. Saul. **Lynne Dawson, Donna Brown** (sops); **Derek Lee Ragin** (alto); **John Mark Ainsley, Neil Mackie, Philip Salmon, Philip Slane** (tens); **Alastair Miles, Richard Savage** (basses); **Monteverdi Choir; English Baroque Soloists/John Eliot Gardiner.** Philips 426 265-2PH3. Recorded at performances in the Stadthalle, Göttingen, Germany, in June 1989.

③ 2h 39' DDD 8/91

Saul is considered by many to be one of the most arresting music dramas in the English language, even though it is officially classed as an oratorio. In it Handel explores in some psychological depth the motivations of his characters, most notably that of the eponymous anti-hero, whose tantrums caused by envy and his searching for supernatural intervention are all vividly delineated; so is the friendship of David and Jonathan and the different characters of Saul's daughters, Merab and Michal. In yet another compelling performance of Handel under his baton, John Eliot Gardiner — in this live recording made at the Göttingen Handel Festival — fulfils every aspect of this varied and adventurous score, eliciting execution of refined and biting calibre from his choir and orchestra. The young British bass Alastair Miles captures Saul in all his moods. John Mark Ainsley and Derek Lee Ragin are both affecting as Jonathan and David; so are Lynne Dawson and Donna Brown as Michal and Merab. There are a few cuts, but they aren't grievous enough to prevent a firm recommendation.

Handel. Israel in Egypt. **Nancy Argenta, Emily Van Evera** (sops); **Timothy Wilson** (alto); **Anthony Rolfe Johnson** (ten); **David Thomas, Jeremy White** (basses); **Taverner Choir and Players/Andrew Parrott.** EMI CDS7 54018-2. Text included.

② 2h 15' DDD 2/91

If anyone needs to assure themselves as to whether the English choral tradition is alive and well, they need only buy this CD. *Israel in Egypt*, of all Handel's works, is the choral one *par excellence* — so much so, in fact, that it was something of a failure in Handel's own time because solo singing was much preferred to choral by the audiences. Andrew Parrott gives a complete performance of the work, in its original form: that is to say, prefaced by the noble funeral anthem for Queen Caroline, as adapted by Handel to serve as a song of mourning by the captive Israelites. This first part is predominantly slow, grave music, powerfully elegiac; the Taverner Choir show themselves, in what is testing music to sing, firm and clean of line, well focused and strongly sustained. The chorus have their chances to be more energetic in the second part, with the famous and vivid Plague choruses — in which the orchestra too play their part in the pictorial effects, with the fiddles illustrating in turn frogs, flies and hailstones. And last, in the third part, there is a generous supply of the stirring C major music in which Handel has the Israelites give their thanks to God, in some degree symbolizing the English giving thanks for the Hanoverian monarchy and the Protestant succession. Be that as it may, the effect is splendid. The solo work is first-rate, too, with Nancy Argenta radiant in Miriam's music in the final scene and distinguished contributions too from David Thomas and Anthony Rolfe Johnson.

Handel. L'Allegro, il Penseroso ed il Moderato. **Patrizia Kwella, Marie McLaughlin, Jennifer Smith** (sops); **Michael Ginn** (treb); **Maldwyn Davies, Martyn Hill** (tens); **Stephen Varcoe** (bar); **Monteverdi Choir; English Baroque Soloists/John Eliot Gardiner.** Erato 2292 45377-2. Notes, text and translation included. From STU71325 (11/80).

② 1h 55' DDD 7/85

Handel was the leading opera composer of the age, but when his fortunes in this sphere began to decline he started to develop other dramatic forms, notably those of the English ode and oratorio. Early in 1740 he turned to two great poems of Milton's youth and composed a masterpiece. This was the ode *L'Allegro, il Penseroso ed il Moderato*. Charles Jennens, the librettist, skilfully adjusts and alternates Milton's poems with their strongly contrasting humours to suit the best interests of the music. John Eliot Gardiner has recorded the work almost complete with a small orchestra of period instruments and a first-rate cast of soloists. Patrizia Kwella and Maldwyn Davies are memorable in the beguiling duet, "As steals the morn", one of many arias which reveal Handel's acute sensibility to the natural landscape. The Monteverdi Choir is characteristically well-disciplined in Handel's varied and evocative choruses savouring the colourful images of the poems and responding effectively to Gardiner's stylish direction. The recorded sound is clear and resonant and full texts are provided in English, French and German.

NEW REVIEW
Handel. Messiah. **Judith Nelson, Emma Kirkby** (sops); **Carolyn Watkinson** (contr); **Paul Elliott** (ten); **David Thomas** (bass); **Christ Church Cathedral Choir, Oxford; Academy of Ancient Music/ Christopher Hogwood.** L'Oiseau-Lyre Florilegium 430 488-2OH2. Notes and text included. From D189D3 (4/80).

② 2h 17' ADD 7/84 Ⓑ

Handel (arr. Mozart/Sargent). Messiah. **Elsie Morison** (sop); **Marjorie Thomas** (contr); **Richard Lewis** (ten); **James Milligan** (bass); **Huddersfield Choral Society; Royal Liverpool Philharmonic Orchestra/Sir Malcolm Sargent.** Classics for Pleasure CD-CFPD4718. From Columbia SAX2308/10 (12/59).

② 2h 24' ADD 5/91 Ⓑ ▲

NEW REVIEW
Handel. Messiah. **Joan Rodgers** (sop); **Della Jones** (mez); **Christopher Robson** (alto); **Philip Langridge** (ten); **Bryn Terfel** (bass); **Collegium Musicum 90 Chorus; Collegium Musicum 90/Richard Hickox.** Chandos Chaconne CHAN0522/3. Text included.

② 2h 21' DDD 3/92 Ⓑ

Christopher Hogwood's recording of *Messiah* was first issued on LP in 1980. Four years later it was successfully transferred to three CDs. Now, with the advance of technology the three-disc package has been supplanted by this two-disc box retaining the full texts of the original. Hogwood's version of *Messiah* conforms with a Foundling Hospital performance in 1754, directed by the composer himself. A significant difference between this recording and most others is the use of boys' treble voices in the choir as opposed to women's. That is what

Handel wanted and it is this feature of the interpretation which, perhaps more than any other makes it appealing. In contrast again with many alternative versions this one dispenses with the solo countertenor, the contralto Carolyn Watkinson singing the music often allotted to the other. She is excellent and a considerable adornment to the set. Only the Academy of Ancient Music is likely to cause occasional disappointment with playing that falls short of ideal in matters of tuning and ensemble. The acoustic is a shade reverberant but the performance comes close to the heart of the music and remains a satisfying interpretation.

For many years Sir Malcolm Sargent's *Messiah* with the Royal Choral Society was a much loved annual event which attracted a capacity audience in the Royal Albert Hall. The present recording uses a chorus of 100, which is completely contrary to the propaganda of the authenticists, who cite the smallness of the choir at Handel's own early performances. But Sargent suggests that "Handel was renowned for his big effects, for wanting twice as many voices in the chorus as usual", and goes on to describe large-scale performances of *Messiah*, with nearly 300 choristers and a huge orchestra, occurring within 25 years of Handel's death. He also tells us that under his baton "the orchestra play the original Handel string, trumpet and drum parts, plus orchestrations which I have arranged, unhesitatingly adopting any good ideas from earlier, experienced editors". In matters of scoring he is a law unto himself, using clarinets among the woodwind and commenting that "their tone colour blends well, and although it is true that they are an anachronism, I must point out that conductors who object to them are themselves an anachronism! They should not be there at all. The conductor as such was not known in Handel's day. Direction was done from the keyboard." Sargent's view of the work is unashamedly spacious and grand. His tempos are slower than we expect today, and the reason the work fits comfortably onto a pair of CDs is because he also observes traditional cuts. Sargent has splendid soloists for his recording, and they respond to his histrionic approach without losing purity of line. There is vitality here beside authority and breadth, and it is refreshing to hear this famous interpretation, recorded in 1959, emerging as such a vivid listening experience, for the transfer to CD has worked miracles with the original sound.

Richard Hickox has assembled a first-rate team for his recording. Della Jones, a gifted and experienced Handelian, gives warmly coloured and stylishly ornamented performances of her music; every note is in place and every word declaimed. Her account of "He was despised" hits just the right note of gravity and is both tender and deeply felt. Joan Rodgers has a brightly-coloured voice and an agile technique which enable her to do justice to virtuoso arias such as

Sir Malcolm Sargent [*photo: EMI*]

"Rejoice greatly". Philip Langridge is on characteristically strong form and Bryn Terfel is both resonant and commanding. The countertenor Christopher Robson, with his clearly focused voice and secure intonation, complete a notably strong solo group. It is complemented by first-rate choral singing, disciplined, athletic and responsive to textual nuances. Hickox, with his experience in voice-training has managed to blend the technical virtues of a professional choir with the spontaneity and enthusiasm with which we associate the best amateur groups. Last but by no means least is the sympathetic support given to soloists and choir alike by the orchestral players of Collegium Musicum 90, led by its leader and co-founder Simon Standage. Recorded sound is spacious with a degree of resonance that enables the ear to enjoy details of texture.

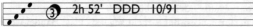 NEW REVIEW

Handel. Belshazzar. **Arleen Auger** (sop); **Catherine Robbin** (mez); **James Bowman** (alto); **Anthony Rolfe Johnson, Nicholas Robertson** (tens); **David Wilson-Johnson** (bar); **Richard Wistreich** (bass); **The English Concert Choir; The English Concert/Trevor Pinnock.** Archiv Produktion 431 793-2AH3. Notes and text included.

③ 2h 52' DDD 10/91

NEW REVIEW

Handel. Belshazzar. **Felicity Palmer** (sop); **Maureen Lehane** (mez); **Paul Esswood** (alto); **Robert Tear, Thomas Sunnegardh** (tens); **Peter van der Bilt, Staffan Sandlund** (basses); **Stockholm Chamber Choir; Vienna Concentus Musicus/Nikolaus Harnoncourt.** Teldec 2292-42567-2. Notes and text included. From EK6 35236 (2/77).

③ 2h 43' ADD 10/91

Of all Handel's oratorios *Belshazzar* is musically one of the richest; from a dramatic viewpoint it has operatic leanings, but the first performances in 1745 were received unfavourably and Handel revived it only twice. The libretto by Charles Jennens who had already supplied Handel with the text of *Messiah* draws both on classical Greek history and the Bible for its themes, central among which is the colourful account of Belshazzar's feast recorded in the Book of Daniel. Both performances have a strong cast of soloists but, excellent though the Stockholm Chamber Choir is in musical matters, its insecure grasp of English declamation invites unfavourable comparison with The English Concert Choir. Robert Tear paints a more forceful picture of Belshazzar than Anthony Rolfe Johnson but the latter projects a greater lyricism. Felicity Palmer gives a moving performance as Nitocris, Belshazzar's mother while Arleen Auger in Pinnock's recording gives a cooler, more detached reading. Paul Esswood and James Bowman are, in their different ways, arresting in their interpretation of the prophet Daniel but Maureen Lehane, an outstanding Handelian singer, makes more of the Persion Prince Cyrus than her rival Catherine Robbin. Peter van der Bilt and David Wilson-Johnson give resonant performances as the Assyrian nobleman, Gobrias. The orchestral playing in both versions is stylish though listeners may find some of Harnoncourt's mannerisms exaggerated and misplaced.

Handel. Herucles. **Jennifer Smith** (sop) Iole; **Sarah Walker** (mez) Dejanira; **Catherine Denley** (mez) Lichas; **Anthony Rolfe Johnson** (ten) Hyllus; **John Tomlinson** (bass) Hercules; **Peter Savidge** (bar) Priest of Jupiter; **Monteverdi Choir; English Baroque Soloists/John Eliot Gardiner.** Archiv Produktion 423 137-2AH3. Notes and text included. From 2742 004 (6/83).

③ 2h 33' DDD 1/88

Handel's *Hercules* is neither opera nor sacred oratorio though it contains elements of both. The story of Dejanira's jealousy of her husband Hercules and of his agonizing death on wearing a poisoned robe which she sends him is brought to life by Handel with typically vivid characterization and in an altogether masterly fashion. Dejanira is sung by Sarah Walker with intensity of feeling, and a fine sense of theatre; Handel capturing the various shades of her character with deep psychological insight and consummate musical genius. Most of the other characters, though skilfully drawn, do not develop to a comparable extent.

Jennifer Smith makes an effectively youthful and fresh-sounding princess Iole, and John Tomlinson a resonant and authoritative Hercules. The chorus reflects the varied emotions emerging as a result of the action and respond to Handel's requirements in a lively, articulate fashion. Orchestral playing on period instruments is comparably alert with clean ensemble and several fine obbligato contributions. Clear, resonant recorded sound and exemplary presentation with full text.

NEW REVIEW

Handel. Joshua. **Emma Kirkby** (sop); **Aidan Oliver** (treb); **James Bowman** (alto); **John Mark Ainsley** (ten); **Michael George** (bass); **New College Choir, Oxford; The King's Consort/Robert King.** Hyperion CDA66461/2. Text included.

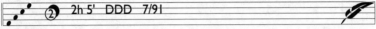

② 2h 5' DDD 7/91

NEW REVIEW

Handel. Joshua. **Julianne Baird** (sop); **D'Anna Fortunato** (mez); **John Aler** (ten); **John Ostendorf** (bass); **Palmer Singers; Brewer Chamber Orchestra/Rudolph Palmer.** Newport Classics NPD85515. Text included.

② 2h 1' DDD 7/91

After years of neglect by the record companies come two equally recommendable, but totally different versions of Handel's most successful post-*Messiah* oratorio. Typically, Handel composed *Joshua* at great speed in the summer of 1748, completing the work in a single month. It is essentially military in manner (Handel wryly observed that the English "like something they can beat time to"), and was the original setting for "See, the Conqu'ring Hero Comes". As to which of these two performances you prefer, that will depend on how you like your Handel: grand and stately in the best church music tradition, or fleet and eager in a more obviously authentic manner. Robert King's performance leans towards the former with smooth, orchestral playing and a reverberant recording from St Joseph's College in London. Palmer, with smaller crisper forces and more immediate sound quality, moves towards the latter. The choruses are equally contrasted: King's is strictly men only while Palmer prefers a mixed choir which has less polish but a greater feel for the drama of the work. For example, listen to the opening Act 3 chorus, "Hail Mighty Joshua, Hail" to hear the differences in tempo and rhythmic attack. King's version has more distinctive soloists led by the incomparable Emma Kirkby, who skilfully weaves her ravishing voice with the instrumental texture in the once popular "Oh! Had I Jubal's Lyre". Palmer's performance is more overtly theatrical with a graceful but fiery Joshua, sung by John Aler. King's Joshua, John Mark Ainsley, portrays proficient musicianship rather than characterization. With regard to ornamentation, King's sturdier performance is well judged but the dramatic flair of Palmer's conducting is hard to resist. Whichever version you choose, Handel's vision of battle and brimstone is more than adequately represented.

Handel. Solomon. **Carolyn Watkinson** (mez) Solomon; **Nancy Argenta** (sop) Solomon's Queen; **Barbara Hendricks** (sop) Queen of Sheba; **Joan Rodgers** (sop) First Harlot; **Della Jones** (mez) Second Harlot; **Anthony Rolfe Johnson** (ten) Zadok; **Stephen Varcoe** (bass) A Levite; **Monteverdi Choir; English Baroque Soloists/John Eliot Gardiner.** Philips 412 612-2PH2. Notes, text and translation included.

③ 2h 16' DDD 12/85 ⑨ P ⑨ S Ⓑ

This oratorio is a somewhat static affair but one filled with the most serene and affecting music. The three acts set forth three aspects of Solomon's majesty. The first deals with his piety and marital bliss, the second with his wisdom in his famous judgement as to which of two harlots is the mother of a child, the third to the visit of the Queen of Sheba. Handel set the scene in a wonderful contrast of pomp and ceremony with the pastoral, his choruses always apt to the mood to be depicted. The scene between the two harlots is brilliantly characterized, the airs for the other principals in Handel's most felicitous vein, while the Sinfonia depicting the Queen of Sheba's entrance is justly famous. The Monteverdi Choir sing with mellifluous tone and precise articulation and the authentic instruments of the English Baroque Soloists play for John Eliot Gardiner with style and virtuosity. The soloists are well chosen with special praise for Nancy Argenta as Solomon's Queen. The recording does full justice to every aspect of the colourful score and it would be hard to imagine a performance that was a better advocate for Handel's cause.

Handel. Susanna. **Lorraine Hunt, Jill Feldman** (sops); **Drew Minter** (alto); **Jeffrey Thomas** (ten); **William Parker** (bar); **David Thomas** (bass); **Chamber Chorus of the University of California, Berkeley; Philharmonia Baroque Orchestra/Nicholas McGegan.** Harmonia Mundi HMC90 7030/2. Notes and text included.

③ 2h 58' DDD 10/90

Susanna is one of the least often heard of Handel's oratorios. A tale, from the *Apocrypha*, of the betrayal of a beautiful and virtuous woman, in her husband's absence, by two lascivious elders when she rejects their importunities, it gives Handel opportunities for a wide range of music — there are amorous pieces for Susanna and her husband, idyllic rural ones when she is in the garden with her maid, sharply drawn pictures of the elders (one an insinuating tenor, the other a more menacing bass), and several powerful expressions of devoutness, rectitude and faith. It has been called "an opera of village life", and it does contain touches of character and comedy; but in this very fine performance one is never in doubt that it is much more than that, a deeply serious work, whose climaxes come in noble, solemn music such as Susanna's "Bending to the throne of glory" (a B minor aria with rich, five-part strings, grave yet glowing) and the chorus at the end, when she is found to be faultless, in praise of divine justice. Lorraine Hunt sings Susanna's music here with considerable power and focus of tone, rising to

the great moments, and also charming and graceful in the lesser ones such as the bathing aria in Part 2. As her husband, the gentle counter-tenor Drew Minter is sensitive and controlled, while the elders are graphically drawn by Jeffrey Thomas and David Thomas. The choral singing by this Californian group, under English direction, is clear and firm in line, direct in rhythm, and Nicholas McGegan's handling of the Baroque orchestra is live and assured, with the tempos and the sense of the music always surely judged.

NEW REVIEW

Handel. Theodora. **Roberta Alexander** (sop) Theodora; **Jard van Nes** (contr) Irene; **Jochen Kowalski** (alto) Didymus; **Hans-Peter Blochwitz** (ten) Septimius; **Anton Scharinger** (bass) Valens; **Arnold Schönberg Choir; Vienna Concentus Musicus/Nikolaus Harnoncourt.** Teldec 2292-46447-2. Notes, text and translation included. Recorded at a performance in the Grosser Saal, Konzerthaus, Vienna in March 1990.

② 2h 11' DDD 8/91

Handel's penultimate oratorio, composed in the summer of 1749, was coolly received by the London public. Its theme is the persecution and martyrdom of the Christian Theodora and her Roman lover Didymus under the Emperor Diocletian; the work's non-biblical subject, chastened tone and tragic ending all told against it. Handel, who valued *Theodora* above all his other oratorios, ruefully remarked that "the Jews will not come to it … because it is a Christian story, and the ladies will not come because it is a virtuous one". The composer's high opinion of *Theodora* is understandable: transcending Morell's mawkish, moralizing libretto, Handel created perhaps the most personal, certainly the most introspective of all his oratorios, imbued with a peculiar tenderness, idealism and spiritual serenity. The heroine is drawn with a rare compassion and insight; the Christian choruses, above all those that conclude each of the three acts, have a searching chromatic intensity. Handel's humanistic sympathy extends even to the pagans, who are presented not as bloodthirsty barbarians but as exuberant hedonists, their music characterized by catchy dance rhythms and colourful scoring. Recorded at a concert in Vienna, Harnoncourt's performance has his accustomed flair and strong feeling for drama and gesture, marred occasionally by eccentricities of tempo — the work's most famous aria, "Angels ever bright and fair", for instance, sounds uncomfortably edgy at this speed, and Harnoncourt quickens the pace further for the middle section. And there are some regrettable cuts, especially in the case of the heroine's aria, "O that I on wings could rise", designed by Handel as a resolution to the tragic "With darkness deep". But the Arnold Schönberg Choir are responsive, flexible and firm-toned, while the Concentus Musicus play with verve, finesse and much delicacy of detail — the occasional lapse of ensemble and intonation is easily overlooked in the context of a live performance. All the soloists, apart from the American Roberta Alexander, are intermittently taxed by the vagaries of English pronunciation — Anton Scharinger's formidable Roman governor suffers most here; and none makes quite enough of their words. But all give characterful, vocally assured performances, with Alexander an affecting heroine, Jochen Kowalski bringing both tenderness and a steely virtuosity to the role of Didymus and Jard van Nes singing the part of Theodora's confidante, Irene, with rich tone and a fine breadth of line. Ornamentation is generally stylish and restrained, and appoggiaturas are scrupulously observed. The recording is a shade resonant, and the audience more fidgety and bronchial than most. But no Handel-lover should miss this vivid and committed performance of a supreme and still scandalously neglected masterpiece.

Handel. Alceste[a]. Comus[b]. [a]**Emma Kirkby,** [a]**Judith Nelson,** [b]**Patrizia Kwella,** [a]**Christina Pound** (sops); [ab]**Margaret Cable,** [a]**Catherine Denley** (mezs); [a]**Paul Elliott,** [a]**Rogers Covey-Crump** (tens); [ab]**David Thomas,** [a]**Christopher Keyte** (basses); **Academy of Ancient Music/ Christopher Hogwood.** L'Oiseau-Lyre Florilegium 421 479-2OH. Texts included. Item marked [a] from DSLO581 (12/80), [b] DSLO598 (8/82).

1h 14' ADD 3/89

The *Alceste* music was written towards the end of Handel's life as masque-like interludes for a production of Tobias Smollett's play. They were never used in that form and were later employed by the composer for *The Choice of Hercules*. The musical numbers Handel created would seem to have provided a kind of musical commentary on the text of the play itself. It consists primarily of arias and choruses with occasional orchestral interludes. One of the highlights is definitely the lovely setting of "Gentle Morpheus, son of night", exquisitely sung here by Emma Kirkby. Paul Elliott, too, sings with great style. The bonus item, *Comus*, consists of three songs linked by choral refrains. They are beautifully done with the AAM playing with great style throughout, and the recordings are finely managed.

NEW REVIEW

Handel. AMADIGI DI GAULA. **Nathalie Stutzmann** (contr) Amadigi; **Jennifer Smith** (sop) Oriana; **Eiddwen Harrhy** (sop) Melissa; **Bernarda Fink** (mez) Dardano; **Pascal Bertin** (alto) Orgando; **Les Musiciens du Louvre/Marc Minkowski.** Erato 2292-45490-2. Notes, text and translation included.

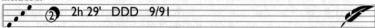

2h 29' DDD 9/91

Dating from Handel's early years in London *Amadigi* proved once more his early command in creating drama within the formalities of *opera seria*. It is the second of the composer's magical operas; set in ancient Gaul it describes how the scheming sorceress Melissa tries to entice Amadigi away from the lovely Oriana, who is also hopelessly desired by Dardano, Prince of Thrace. Although the action is dominated by these four characters, all taken by high voices (the hero originally by an alto castrato), Handel entirely avoids monotony through his skill in giving their emotions true expression in a wonderfully varied succession of numbers, every one appropriate to the situation in hand. These are all executed here in an entirely convincing, sensitive and spirited manner by the four singers — Nathalie Stutzmann is a palpitating, eager Amadigi, Bernarda Fink an appropriately earnest, forthright Daradano, Amadigi's friend, Jennifer Smith a soft-grained, plangent Oriana nicely contrasted with Eiddwen Harrhy's fiery, incisive Melissa. Minkowski's direction, lithe, direct, yet ever responsive to the emotional turbulence expressed by the principals, is consistently admirable, sailing a fair course between the Scylla of over-accentuation and the Charybdis of baroque severity, and his period-instrument Les Musiciens du Louvre play with a fluency that sounds absolutely natural.

Handel. FLAVIO. **Jeffrey Gall** (alto) Flavio; **Derek Lee Ragin** (alto) Guido; **Lena Lootens** (sop) Emilia; **Bernarda Fink** (contr) Teodata; **Christina Högman** (sop) Vitige; **Gianpaolo Fagotto** (ten) Ugone; **Ulrich Messthaler** (bass) Lotario; **Ensemble 415/René Jacobs.** Harmonia Mundi HMC90 1312/3. Notes, text and translation included.

2h 36' DDD 7/90

Flavio is one of the most delectable of Handel's operas. Although it comes from his 'heroic' period, it is not at all in the heroic mould but rather an ironic tragedy with a good many comic elements. Does that sound confusing? — well, so it is, for you never know quite where you are when King Flavio of Lombardy starts falling in love with the wrong woman, for although this starts as an amusing idle fancy it develops into something near-tragic, since he imperils everyone else's happiness, ultimately causing the death of one counsellor and the dishonour of another. The delicately drawn amorous feeling is like nothing else in Handel, and in its subtle growth towards real passion and grief is handled with consummate skill. The opera, in short, is full of fine and exceptionally varied music, and it is enhanced here by a performance under René Jacobs that, although it takes a number of modest liberties, catches the moods of the music surely and attractively, with shapely, alert and refined playing from the admirable Ensemble 415. And the cast is strong. The central roles, composed for two of Handel's greatest singers, Cuzzoni and Senesino, are done by Lena Lootens, a delightfully natural and expressive soprano with a firm, clear technique, and the counter-tenor Derek Lee Ragin, who dispatches his brilliant music with aplomb and excels in the final aria, a superb minor-key expression of passion. The singers also include Bernarda Fink as the lightly amorous Teodata and Christina Högman, both fiery and subtle in the music for her lover, and the capable Jeffrey Gall as the wayward monarch. Altogether a highly enjoyable set, not flawless but certainly among the best ever Handel opera recordings.

NEW REVIEW

Handel. GIULIO CESARE. **Jennifer Larmore** (mez) Giulio Cesare; **Barbara Schlick** (sop) Cleopatra; **Bernarda Fink** (mez) Cornelia; **Marianne Rørholm** (mez) Sextus; **Derek Lee Ragin** (alto) Ptolemy; **Furio Zanasi** (bass) Achillas; **Olivier Lallouette** (bar) Curio; **Dominique Visse** (alto) Nirenus; **Concerto Cologne/René Jacobs.** Harmonia Mundi HMC90 1385/7. Notes, text and translation included.

④ 4h 4' DDD 4/92

Handel's greatest heroic opera sports no fewer than eight principal characters and one of the largest orchestras he ever used. Undoubtedly this, and the singing of Francesca Cuzzoni (Cleopatra) and Senesino (Caesar), eighteenth-century operatic superstars, helped to launch *Giulio Cesare* into enduring popularity that it enjoys to this day. But it is primarily the quality of the music, with barely a weak number in four hours of entertainment, that has made it such a favourite choice with musicians and audiences. Surprisingly, this is the only complete performance on period instruments currently available, an immediate advantage in giving extra 'bite' to the many moments of high drama without threatening to drown the singers in *forte* passages. This performance is a particularly fine one with an excellent cast; Caesar, originally sung by a castrato, is here taken by the young mezzo, Jennifer Larmore. She brings weight and a sense of integrity to the role (which surely couldn't be matched by a countertenor), seemingly untroubled by the demands of the final triumphant aria, "Qual torrente". Occasionally her vibrato becomes intrusive, particularly near the beginning of the opera, but that is a minor quibble in a performance of this stature. Handel could just as well have called his opera *Cleopatra* as it is she who is the pivotal element in the drama, a role taken here by Barbara Schlick. One of Handel's most vividly developed characters, Schlick represents this many faceted woman with acuity and imagination, ranging from the haunting pathos of "Piangerò", where she occasionally seems stretched on the top notes, to the exuberant virtuosity of "Da tempeste" in the final act. If Cleopatra represents strength in a woman, then Cornelia is surely the tragic figure, at the mercy of events. Her first aria, "Priva son", here taken very slowly, shows Bernarda Fink to be more than equal to the role, admirable in her steady tone and dignity of character. Derek Lee Ragin's treacherous Ptolemy is also memorable, venom and fire injected into his agile voice. A first-rate cast is supported by René Jacobs and Concerto Cologne on fine form, though the continuo line is sometimes less than ideally clear. There are also occasional additions to their parts, notably when Caesar rescues Cleopatra in the last act where a series of interjections are both unnecessary and intrusive. Insert notes include translations and a useful essay from Handel scholar Winton Dean. The excellent recording completes one's pleasure in a momentous issue.

Handel. ORLANDO. **James Bowman** (alto) Orlando; **Arleen Auger** (sop) Angelica; **Catherine Robbin** (mez) Medoro; **Emma Kirkby** (sop) Dorinda; **David Thomas** (bass) Zoroastro; **Academy of Ancient Music/Christopher Hogwood.** L'Oiseau-Lyre 430 845-2OH3. Notes, text and translation included.

〇 2h 38' DDD 8/91

Handel's operas represent the greatest expanse of underexplored musical territory ever to have been written by a major composer. For cherishers of verismo the formalism of Handel's theatrical world no doubt presents a problem or two, but for listeners willing to accept the (not so very restricting) conventions within which the composer worked there are wonderful discoveries to be made. *Orlando* is as good a place as any to start looking. Its pastoral tale of unrequited love and resultant madness is retold by Handel with customary sympathy and psychological insight; and, needless to say, he provides some ravishing music along the way.

Christopher Hogwood is not, perhaps, a born opera conductor, but he has assembled a fine cast for this recording, which benefits, too, from being based on a touring production. Thus, though one might feel that there is a slight lack of dramatic weight and pacing in this performance, such faults are redeemed by the polished and confident contributions of its five experienced baroque singers. James Bowman is intelligent and passionate in the title-role, Arleen Auger frequently thrilling as the object of his hopeless love, and the remaining parts are all perfectly suited to the particular strengths of their interpreters. Definitely a Handel recording worth having.

Arleen Auger   *[photo: Virgin Classics*

Roy Harris

American 1898-1979

Harris. Symphony No. 3 (1939).
Schuman. Symphony No. 3 (1941). **New York Philharmonic Orchestra/ Leonard Bernstein.** DG 419 780-2GH. Recorded at a performance in the Avery Fisher Hall, New York in December 1985.

51' DDD 11/87

If you already know music by Gershwin and Copland and wish to explore the work of other American composers then these two symphonies provide the ideal opportunity. Harris's short Third Symphony of 1939 is in one continuous movement, which however falls into five sections — Tragic, Lyric, Pastoral, Fugue-Dramatic and Dramatic-Tragic. The style is austere without being in the least forbidding; the musical arguments are terse but easy to follow, the orchestral sound solid but not opaque. When first performed the symphony was an instant critical and popular success, as was Schuman's Third Symphony when premièred two years later. Harris's influence on his slightly younger colleague is apparent, but Schuman has a rather more brilliant orchestral style and the mood of the work, cast in two movements, each of which has two connected sections, is a

little more outgoing. The New York Philharmonic has this kind of music in its bones, and it gives superlative performances under its former chief conductor, whose sympathy and insight into the music of his older contemporaries has always been notable. The recordings are superlative.

Lou Harrison

L. Harrison. WORKS FOR GUITAR AND PERCUSSION. **John Schneider** (gtr); [a]**Janice Tipton** (ocarina); [b]**Dave Ross,** [c]**Gene Strimling** (perc); [d]**Cal Arts Percussion Ensemble/John Bergamo.** Etcetera KTC1071.
Canticle No. 3 (1941)[abd]. Suite No. 1 (1976)[bc]. Plaint and Variations on "Song of Palestine" (1978). Serenado por Gitaro (1952). Serenade (1978)[c]. Waltz for Evelyn Hinrichsen (1977).

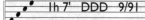 50' DDD 9/91

"The whole round world of music and instruments lives around us. I am interested in a transethnic, a planetary music." Lou Harrison is an eccentric among American composers; however, the popularity of so-called New Age and minimalist music should make us listen afresh to such apparently outmoded precursors as Harrison and his colleagues, John Cage, Harry Partch and Henry Cowell. We might just uncover an eminently approachable avant-garde. Harrison's output, which includes many works in conventional Western forms for conventional Western forces, is particularly unthreatening. Thanks to a preoccupation with oriental modes and instruments, he specializes in delicate attenuated textures which need not preclude tunes. Thus the first piece here, the sensitively percussive *Canticle No. 3* of 1941 is centred on an eerie melodic refrain. The *Suite No. 1* is about as intellectually formidable as the pop-sourced ambient music of Brian Eno. And *Plaint and Variations*, based on instantly medieval material, is not unlike Arvo Pärt for guitar. If some of John Schneider's pitching sounds unconventional — his instrument is equipped with a system of interchangeable fingerboards designed to facilitate the use of various non-standard tuning systems — all is explained in the booklet. The Esperanto-speaking Harrison may yet acquire cult status and this immaculately played and recorded disc should help.

Jonathan Harvey
Refer to Index

Joseph Haydn

Haydn. Cello Concertos — C major, HobVIIb/1; D major, HobVIIb/2.
A. Kraft. Cello Concerto in C major, Op. 4. **Anner Bylsma** (bar vc); **Tafelmusik/Jeanne Lamon.** Deutsche Harmonia Mundi RD77757.

1h 7' DDD 9/91

At best, an 'authentic' performance can only aspire to return to the spirit, rather than the letter of the period it strives to recreate, and yet the fine Dutch cellist Anner Bylsma comes as near as anyone to convincing us that this is indeed the way Haydn might have wished these sunny, yet highly sophisticated concertos to be played. Haydn composed these works for the virtuoso cellist of the Esterházy court orchestra, Anton Kraft, and the bold and adventurous solo writing reflects his fabled technical prowess and musical sensitivity. Bylsma offers a lithe, yet scrupulously classical and poised account of the C major Concerto, with a romantically inflected central *adagio* followed by a dashingly brilliant, yet suitably witty finale. His rapid passagework in higher registers is astonishing, while he reveals the stately dignity of the D major work (long attributed to Kraft) in a cultured and attractively proportioned reading of rich intensity and variety. Bylsma includes his own revisions of period cadenzas, which are never less than apposite, and deftly executed. The real discovery here, though, is the Cello Concerto by Kraft himself, which combines the expected brilliant pyrotechnics with some effective melodic writing, in a work which anticipates the styles developed during the early nineteenth century. In fact, Kraft advised Beethoven on the cello part of his Triple Concerto, and his compositions exercised great influence in the genesis of modern cello technique. Bylsma is superbly supported by the excellent Canadian ensemble, Tafelmusik, and the recording is first rate. A revealing, and often stunningly played collection — highly recommended to all cello enthusiasts.

Haydn. Horn Concerto No. 1 in D major. Symphony No. 31 in D major, "Hornsignal".
M. Haydn. Horn Concerto in D major. **Anthony Halstead** (natural hn); **Hanover Band/Roy Goodman.** Nimbus NI5190.

Ih I' DDD 11/89

This disc is something of an eulogy to the natural, valveless horn of the eighteenth century. Here it is played with panache by Anthony Halstead whose firm control of a notoriously difficult instrument together with accomplished musicianship ensures performances of assurance and finesse. The two Horn Concertos by the brothers Haydn come over well though they are not, perhaps, especially memorable pieces. Virtuoso horn playing is required and Halstead provides it with brilliant passagework, clearly articulated phrases and a characterful sound. The remaining work on the disc is Haydn's well-known Symphony No. 31, *Hornsignal*; here, the composer requires not one but four horn players who collectively make an imposing phalanx. Haydn's appealing sense of humour caters for various varieties of horn signal loudly barked out or beguilingly *piano* as the case may be. In the lyrical Adagio there is a prominent role allotted the solo violin, whilst in the finale, a set of variations, Haydn gives further solos to cello, flute, horns, violin and violone. The contributions are a little variable here but nevertheless spontaneous and affectionate playing such as this should win friends. Effective recorded sound.

Haydn. Trumpet Concerto in E flat major, HobVII*e*/1[a]. Cello Concerto in D major, HobVII*b*/2[b]. Violin Concerto in C major, HobVII/1[c]. [c]**Cho-Liang Lin** (vn); [b]**Yo-Yo Ma** (vc); [a]**Wynton Marsalis** (tpt); [a]**National Philharmonic Orchestra/Raymond Leppard;** [b]**English Chamber Orchestra/José Luis Garcia;** [c]**Minnesota Orchestra/Sir Neville Marriner.** CBS Masterworks CD39310. From IM39310 (1/85).

59' DDD 1/86

This compilation of three Haydn concertos has a different soloist and orchestra for each. The young American trumpeter Wynton Marsalis has all the fluency one could wish for and an instrument allowing a full three octaves (E flat — E flat) to be displayed in his own cadenza to the first movement. Although this is an efficient performance, it in no way approaches the class of the next one. The cellist Yo-Yo Ma is very different as a performer: though equally a master of his instrument, and indeed a virtuoso who seems incapable of producing an ugly sound or playing out of tune, one feels a deep emotional involvement in all he does. Also, the recording in this D major Cello Concerto is unusually faithful in blending the cello well into the ensemble without ever covering it. Ma is supported by the excellent English Chamber Orchestra and the qualities of integration and ensemble under their leader's direction are all that one could wish for. In the C major Violin Concerto the skilful Cho-Liang Lin has the benefit of a most sympathetic conductor in Sir Neville Marriner, but he cannot match Ma's subtlety and commitment.

Haydn. Violin Concertos — C major, HobVIIa/1; G major, Hob VIIa/4. Concerto for violin, keyboard and strings in F major, HobXVIII/6ª. ªJustin **Oprean** (pf); **European Community Chamber Orchestra/Adelina Oprean** (vn). Hyperion Helios CDH88037.

lh l' DDD l/90

Apart from his Trumpet Concerto, we don't usually associate Haydn with concerto form, but he did write a number of concertos, and not surprisingly they prove to be well worth getting to know. The three of them here are all from around his thirtieth year, and although by his standards they are a little old-fashioned and owe something to Italian models they are delightful music, tuneful and life-affirming. They are also very well written for the violin, and for the keyboard too (originally it was the organ, but here a piano is convincingly used) in the case of the Double Concerto in F major that begins the programme. The violinist Adelina Oprean has a sweet tone but plenty of attack too, and in terms of style her playing seems unfailingly right; the same may be said of her direction of this fine orchestra of strings and harpsichord and also of the cadenzas she supplies to all three works. The recording of this attractive disc was made in a North London church and it sounds very lifelike, with just a natural degree of ambience. At medium price this CD is excellent value.

NEW REVIEW

Haydn. SYMPHONIES. **Hanover Band/Roy Goodman** (hpd). Hyperion CDA66524.
No. 1 in D major. No. 2 in C major. No. 3 in G major. No. 4 in D major. No. 5 in A major.

lh 12' DDD 3/92

These five compact symphonies all date from the period 1757-61 and though there are occasional stretches of arid note-spinning (in the slow movement of No. 2, for example), each of the works here is marked by a formal assurance and a teeming physical energy that sets the young Haydn apart from his contemporaries. All but one are in three movements, though No. 5, following the old *sonata da chiesa* (church sonata) design, begins with a solemn *Adagio*; No. 3, the sole four-movement work here, is the richest of the group, with its lusty, propulsive triple-time opening movement, its rugged canonic minuet and a finale whose four-note subject and free fugal textures anticipate in a modest way the glories of Mozart's *Jupiter*. The Hanover Band's performances have a splendid verve and immediacy with light, buoyant articulation and shrewdly judged tempos. *Allegros*, never unduly precipitate, have a fine earthy exuberance (with an apt touch of majesty in the first movement of No. 2); the *Adagio* opening of No. 5 (which features some spectacular horn writing, immaculately despatched here) nicely balances elegance and gravity, while the lithe, springing *Andantes* of Nos. 1 and 3 find room for expressive shaping in the neo-baroque sequences of suspensions. Textures, as ever in the Hanover Band's cycle, are colourful and transparent, with oboes and horns clearly etched against the strings in the tuttis — the shining sonorities of No. 5, with its high-pitched A major horns, are quite thrilling. Occasionally (as in the finale of No. 1) the violins sound a shade raw;

and once or twice, as in the first movement of No. 3, Goodman seems to press the tempo uncomfortably. But for all these trifling reservations, the Hanover Band convey the self-confidence, resource and sheer *élan* of these youthful symphonies more infectiously than any other performance on disc.

Haydn. SYMPHONIES. **Philharmonia Hungarica/Antál Dorati.** Decca 430 100-2DM32. Also available as eight four-disc sets.
425 900-2DM4 (4h 30') — Nos. 1-16. *425 905-2DM4 (4h 34')* — Nos. 17-33.
425 910-2DM4 (4h 43') — Nos. 34-47. *425 915-2DM4 (4h 33')* — Nos. 48-59.
425 920-2DM4 (4h 11') — Nos. 60-71. *425 925-2DM4 (4h 29')* — Nos. 72-83.
425 930-2DM4 (4h 46') — Nos. 84-95. *425 935-2DM4 (4h 46')* — Nos. 96-104. Symphony "A" in B flat major. Symphony "B" in B flat major. Sinfonia concertante in B flat major.

| ♪ ③② 36h 31' ADD 6/91 | £ ⁹ₚ |

Though there are now two period-instrument Haydn cycles underway (from Goodman on Hyperion and Hogwood on L'Oiseau-Lyre), this pioneering modern-instrument cycle recorded by Antál Dorati and his band of Hungarian exiles between 1969 and 1973 is going to be a hard act to follow. When first issued on LP Dorati's performances won almost universal praise for their style and verve, their eager and imaginative engagement with the music's astonishing, protean inventiveness. And in their very overdue CD incarnation, in eight sets of four discs each, they still have little to fear from most of the competition. Remarkably, in such an extended project, there is hardly a whiff of routine: time and again the orchestra seems to play out of its skin for Dorati, the strings sweet-toned and luminous, the wind deft and resourceful, savouring to the full the wit and whimsy of Hadyn's writing. And though one might have reservations about this or that symphony, Dorati's actual interpretations are often exemplary, combining rhythmic resilience and a splendid overall sweep with an unusual care for detail.

Aficionados of period performances may feel that the strings, especially in the earlier symphonies, are too numerous and too liberal with vibrato. But the buoyancy of Dorati's rhythms and the crispness of the strings' articulation constantly preclude any suggestion of undue opulence. Most of the early symphonies (in which Dorati uses a discreetly balanced harpsichord continuo) are captivatingly done: *Allegros* dance and leap and slow movements are shaped with finesse and affection. Listen, for instance, to the beautiful neo-baroque D minor *Andante* in No. 4, or the grave *siciliano* in No. 12, a particularly appealing, warm-textured work. And in the second box, containing Nos. 17-33, Dorati brings a characteristic breadth and intensity of line to the opening *Adagios* of No. 21 (a notably mature and eloquent movement, this) and No. 22, the so-called *Philosopher*. The famous *Hornsignal*, No. 31, is also irresistibly done, with rollicking, ripe-toned horns; and practically the only disappointment in the first two boxes is the *Lamentatione*, No. 26, where both the tragic first movement and the quizzical final minuet are too smooth and sluggish.

A number of the minuets in the middle-period symphonies (those written between the late 1760s and the early 1780s) are also distinctly leisurely, lacking Dorati's usual rhythmic spring — cases in point are those in Nos. 43, 52 and 49 (the last funereally slow). And one or two of the passionate minor-keyed symphonies, especially Nos. 39 and 52, are, like No. 26, wanting in fire and dramatic thrust. But in many of these works of Haydn's first full maturity (several still virtually unknown) Dorati gives penetrating, shrewdly judged performances. Highlights among the rarer symphonies include No. 41, with its pealing trumpets and high horns (stunningly played), the expansive No. 42, done with real breadth and grandeur, and the subtle, lyrical No. 64, whose sublime *Largo* is sustained at the slowest possible tempo. In one or two works (notably the large-scale D major, No. 61, and the so-called *Laudon*, No. 69), Dorati might

Antál Dorati   *[photo: Decca/Wedgbury]*

seem too frothy and frolic-some. And just occasionally (as in the outrageous six-movement *Il Distratto*, No. 60) he can underplay the earthy, rumbustious side of Haydn's complex musical personality.

Two of the most desirable boxes of all are those containing Symphonies Nos. 72-83 and 84-95 — though some collectors may find it inconvenient that both the "Paris" and the "London" sets are split between boxes. Most of the pre-Paris symphonies are still underrated: but works like Nos. 76, 77 and 81 reveal a new, almost Mozartian suavity of manner and a sophistication of thematic development influenced by the Op. 33 String Quartets, while the two minor-keyed symphonies, Nos. 78 and 80, have notably powerful, concentrated first movements. If Dorati is a shade too comfortable in No. 80 he is superb elsewhere on these discs. Though the competition from rival performances now begins to hot up, he can more than hold his own in the "Paris" set: listen to the mingled grace and strength he brings to Nos. 85 and 87, with their clear, gleaming textures, or his dramatic urgency in the first movement of the misleadingly named *La Poule*, No. 83.

As for the "London" Symphonies, Dorati's readings are as detailed and attentive as any on the market, though at times he can underestimate the music's boldness, grandeur and dangerous wit. This is partly a question of tempos (some distinctly on the slow side) and accent, but also of the variable prominence accorded the brass and timpani — in several works, notably Nos. 94, 96 and, most seriously, the flamboyant, aggressive Nos. 97 and 100, these instruments are too recessed to make their full dramatic effect. Elsewhere, though, the balance is more satisfying: and in symphonies like Nos. 93, 103 and 104 Dorati combines power, incisiveness and symphonic breadth with an unusual sensitivity to the lyrical poignancy which underlies much of Haydn's later music.

The recordings, outstanding in their day, still sound pretty impressive, with a fine spaciousness and bloom, even if the violins can acquire a touch of glare above the stave. All in all, a magnificent, life-enhancing series that has contributed vastly to our deeper understanding of Haydn's genius over the last two decades. Whatever integral cycles may appear in the future, Dorati's will stand as one of the gramophone's grandest achievements.

Haydn. Symphonies — No. 6 in D major, "Le matin"; No. 7 in C major, "Le midi"; No. 8 in G major, "Le soir". **The English Concert/Trevor Pinnock** (hpd). Archiv Produktion 423 098-2AH.

1h 5' DDD 1/88

These symphonies represent the times of day; *Le matin* portrays the sunrise, and there is a storm in *Le soir*, but otherwise there is not a lot that could be called programmatic. But Haydn did take the opportunity to give his new colleagues in the princely band something interesting to do, for there are numerous solos here, not only for the wind instruments but for the section leaders — listen especially to the *Adagio* of No. 6, with solo violin and prominent flutes and cello, a delectable piece of writing. Inventively, the music is uneven; the concerto-like style was not wholly harmonious with Haydn's symphonic thinking. But there is plenty of spirited and cheerful music here, and that is well caught in these vivacious performances by Trevor Pinnock and his band, with their brisk tempos and light textures; the playing is duly agile, and the period instruments give a bright edge to the sound.

Haydn. SYMPHONIES. **Academy of Ancient Music/Christopher Hogwood.** L'Oiseau-Lyre 430 082-2OH3.
No. 21 in A major; No. 22 in E flat major, "The Philosopher"; No. 23 in G major; No. 24 in D major; No. 28 in A major; No. 29 in E major; No. 30 in C major, "Alleluja"; No. 31 in D major, "Hornsignal"; No. 34 in D minor.

③ 3h 10' DDD 12/90

As 'the father of the symphony', Haydn had over 100 children! So a complete recorded cycle is a major undertaking for any company, and the one launched with the present issue uses authentic instruments and a slightly lower pitch than modern 'concert' ones. Details of these instruments are listed in the four-language booklet, which has 70 pages including an explanation of the grouping of these works into 15 volumes — the present one, oddly enough, being No. 4 and covering the years 1764-65. The Academy of Ancient Music is usually a small orchestral body, supporting the contention expressed by Joseph Webster that Haydn's orchestra at this time was of about 13 to 16 players and that there was no keyboard continuo. In other words, there is no harpsichord to fill out textures, but although some listeners may miss it initially the playing soon convinces. The music itself cannot be summarized briefly, but as usual with Haydn, even these relatively unfamiliar pieces are inventive and often beautiful. The playing has zest, but however brisk the tempo chosen for quick movements they never degenerate into mere bustle, although other performers may take a less tense view than Christopher Hogwood. There are real discoveries to be made here, beginning with the nervous, dramatic finale to Symphony No. 21, and they also include minuets such as the enigmatic ones to Nos. 28 and 29. Similarly, slow movements have dignity, grace and often a quiet humour too, while phrasing is intelligent and affectionate and textures well balanced. Indeed, Hogwood's wind and string players alike are precise and stylish. Repeats are faithfully observed. Finally, the recording is clear and atmospheric.

Haydn. Symphonies — No. 26 in D minor, "Lamentatione"; No. 52 in C minor; No. 53 in D major, "L'Impériale". **La Petite Bande/Sigiswald Kuijken.** Virgin Classics Veritas VC7 90743-2.

1h 2' DDD 3/89

This period instrument coupling contains some sprightly and imaginative playing. Symphony No. 26, is sub-titled *Lamentatione* and the nickname alludes to Haydn's use of Gregorian chant in the first two movements. The C minor Symphony No. 52 is a dramatic work, vividly capturing a mood of restless, brooding expectancy. Symphony No. 53, *L'Impériale*, has a glorious confidence and authority to it; the title, scholars suppose, refers to the Empress Maria Theresa. It has an air of sophistication and nobility worthy of Austria's great ruler and receives a vivid and accomplished recording. The sound throughout is warm and ingratiating.

Haydn. SYMPHONIES. **The English Concert/Trevor Pinnock.** Archiv
Produktion 429 756-2AH.
No. 42 in D major; No. 44 in E minor, "Trauer"; No. 46 in B major.

· 1h 3' DDD 9/90

These are inspiriting performances of three of Haydn's greatest symphonies from
the so-called *Sturm und Drang* years of the early 1770s. Storm and stress is most
evident in the *Trauer* ("Mourning"), whose outer movements push the contemporary musical language to new limits of violent intensity; the nickname,
incidentally, derives from the sublime *Adagio*, which Haydn is said to have
wanted played at his funeral. Symphony No. 46 is probably the only eighteenth-
century symphony in the key of B major. And with the outlandish tonality go
extremes of expression: the first movement is astonishingly tense and dark-hued
for a work of this period in the major key, while the finale is Haydn at his most
bizarrely humorous. The other work on the disc, No. 42, is a real rarity, and
may well come as a revelation to many. Both the first and second movements
have an expansiveness and a harmonic breadth new in Haydn's symphonic music;
and the finale is a delightful early example of the racy, popular style which
colours so many of his later symphonies. Using an orchestra of around 20
players, as Haydn himself would have done, Pinnock gives vital, characterful
readings, with a blend of sophistication and earthiness ideally suited to the
composer. The string playing is supple and sweet-toned — no wire-wool
associations here — and the expertly played oboes and horns cut through
pungently in the tuttis. Outer movements are boldly projected, their often
exceptional rhythmic and harmonic tension powerfully controlled. All three slow
movements are done with finesse and a beautiful sense of line (none of the
exaggerated 'squeezed' phrasing favoured in some authentic performances),
though the *Adagio* of No. 44 has a slightly too easy, *grazioso* feel. More
controversial are the minuets, taken very smartly indeed, with a loss of dignity
and grandeur in Nos. 42 and 46. But these truthfully recorded performances can
be recommended to anyone who is not ideologically opposed to period
instruments.

Haydn. Symphony No. 44 in E minor, "Trauer".
Mozart. Symphony No. 40 in G minor, K550. **St John's Smith Square
Orchestra/John Lubbock.** Pickwick IMP Red Label PCD820.

· 55' DDD 8/86

Here is a performance of Mozart's No. 40 that looks deeper than the often overstated surface qualities of charm and grace, resulting in a darker and more
sinister account of this highly original work. The elusive opening is skilfully
handled, creating a fine air of expectancy. The orchestra's phrasing is always
intelligent and well articulated, and in the *Andante* they capture the restlessness of
spirit and subtle hesitations. Beautiful phrasing also pervades the *Minuet*, which
acts like an impatient upbeat to the finale, emphasized by its vague and abrupt
ending. The despairing and impassioned finale has energy and vigour as the
dramatic tension builds towards the harmonically daring development section,
notable in this performance for some excellent horn playing. Haydn's *Trauer*
Symphony receives a fine performance too, if perhaps lacking a little of the
sustained vigour and tension found in the Mozart. It is one of Haydn's finest
Sturm und Drang symphonies, and the first movement is noted for its dramatic
strength and dynamic contrast. The *Adagio* is beautifully played in this tender and
serene performance; this movement was reputed to be a particular favourite of
Haydn's, and he requested it to be played at his funeral (hence the nickname
Trauer). The finale regains the energy and vigour found in the Mozart, and the
clarity of the recording highlights the contrapuntal texture very well indeed.
Rewarding performances at a bargain price.

Haydn. Symphonies — No. 45 in F sharp minor, "Farewell"; No. 48 in C major, "Maria Theresia"; No. 102 in B flat major. **Capella Istropolitana/ Barry Wordsworth.** Naxos 8 550382.

1h 13' DDD 9/91

At the rate they're going, Barry Wordsworth and the Bratislava-based Capella Istropolitana look set to become the most recorded team of all time. But, as with their series of Mozart symphonies, their interpretations here are fresh and carefully considered; and if the violins sometimes lack the last degree of refinement, the Capella Istropolitana is a highly proficient chamber-group, with generally excellent intonation and ensemble and tangy, characterful wind — though one wishes they (and the brass in No. 102) had been balanced more forwardly in the otherwise excellent recording. Of the three works here the glittering, ceremonial No. 48 (until recently thought to have been written in honour of the Empress Maria Theresia) is perhaps the most successful. The outer movements and minuet are strong and broadly paced, their texture dominated by the brave pealings of the C alto horns; and the beautiful *Siciliano Adagio* is phrased with real delicacy and affection. The *Farewell* is given an honest, robust reading, a bit cautious in the fast outer movements (rhythms could be more incisive here), though the minuet and the programmatic final *Adagio* are both very neatly managed. At first the performance of No. 102, one of Haydn's boldest, most far-reaching works, might seem rather plain, low in emotional voltage. But

for all its deliberate pacing the opening *Vivace* is sturdily built, developing a fine cumulative tension (a thrilling crescendo from the hard-stick timpani at the outset of the recapitulation). And if Wordsworth takes the minuet at a sedate, Beechamesque tempo without quite matching Beecham's rhythmic sleight of hand, his steady approach to the finale reveals the music's robust, pawky humour more readily than the slickly virtuosic performances one sometimes hears. There may be performances of slightly greater polish and penetration in the catalogue; but at super-budget price this disc is an almost ridiculous bargain.

Capella Istropolitana   *[photo: Naxos*

Haydn. Symphony No. 49, "La passione".
Schubert. Symphony No. 5 in B flat major, D485. **St John's Smith Square Orchestra/John Lubbock.** Pickwick IMP Classics PCD819.

53' DDD 1/86

Although this reading of Schubert's charming Fifth Symphony will certainly pass muster, with straightforward playing that emphasizes the more naïve aspects of the piece, the gold on this disc is to be found in the coupled performance of Haydn's darkly urgent *La passione* Symphony. Completed in 1768, during Haydn's *Sturm und Drang* period, this work begins with a brooding *Adagio* and is followed by a vigorous, intense *Allegro di molto*. A dour *Menuetto*, with a brighter, oboe and horn dominated Trio for contrast, intervenes before the dramatic, rather brief closing *Presto*, that strangely adumbrates Mendelssohn in places. The total effect is marvellously disturbing, especially so in this involved, purposeful reading from Lubbock and the Smith Square Orchestra. They clearly have the measure of this piece and communicate its burning originality with force. Especially impressive is the way that the spirit of romanticism flourishes here without the just proportion of classicism being split asunder. The enclosed ambience of the recording intensifies the introversion of this Symphony, reflecting the isolation that Haydn welcomed at his employer's palace at Esterhaza, where he composed the work.

Haydn. Symphonies — No. 78 in C minor; No. 102 in B flat major.
Orpheus Chamber Orchestra. DG 429 218-2GH.

> 46' DDD 5/90

The Orpheus Chamber Orchestra play without a conductor, but their account of these two Haydn symphonies is splendidly precise. The key of C minor was unusual enough when No. 78 was composed in 1782 and Haydn's invention still makes the work a disturbing one, particularly when the first movement and the finale are taken at this spanking pace, surely faster than it would have been in Haydn's time but brought off well here. The quality that comes across strongly here is one of urgent energy, and even in the Adagio the articulation and dynamics keep one from cosily relaxing; but there is nothing wrong with that if the results stand on their own merits as here. We find a vivid energy also in Symphony No. 102, but although the orchestra recognize the brighter mood, sometimes one looks for more playfulness and 'smiling' quality to provide expressive contrast. Nevertheless the playing is highly skilful and though this is not a long CD, collectors wishing to investigate the relatively unfamiliar Symphony No. 78 or an alternative view of No. 102 will be rewarded, not least by the pleasing recorded quality.

Haydn. Symphonies — No. 82 in C major, "L'ours"; No. 83 in G minor, "La poule". **Concertgebouw Orchestra, Amsterdam/Sir Colin Davis.** Philips 420 688-2PH.

> 52' DDD 2/88

Haydn. Symphonies — No. 82 in C major, "L'ours"; No. 83 in G minor, "La poule"; No. 84 in E flat major. **Orchestra of the Age of Enlightenment/Sigiswald Kuijken.** Virgin Classics Veritas VC7 90793-2.

> 1h 18' DDD 2/90

Haydn's development as a symphonic composer was given a boost in the early 1780s by a commission from the Paris "Concert de la Loge Olympique". That society's orchestra was a much larger one than Haydn had written for hitherto and he was inspired to produce some of his finest works in this form, larger in scale, more complex in structure and with a wider range of expression. This is at once shown in the arresting first movement of Symphony No. 82, *The Bear*, which has something of a military character. A spacious, flowing *Allegretto* and a stately Minuet are followed by a finale which has a first subject akin to a bear dance, over a bagpipe-like drone — hence the symphony's nickname. A certain feeling of agitation pervades the minor-key first movement of Symphony No. 83, *The Hen*, whose cackling subsidiary theme gives the work its somewhat misleading nickname. A slow *Andante* then provides a sense of calm after a storm, and the Minuet and trio shows the resurgence of Haydn's good-natured optimism, with the finale positively bubbling over with high spirits. Sir Colin Davis and the Concertgebouw Orchestra unerringly go to the heart of Haydn's endearing musical personality, and the wit, the charm and the zest of each score is wonderfully realized. The recording quality is superlative.

There are a lot of happy details and interesting revelations in Kuijken's recording of three of the *Paris* symphonies on period instruments. Although the recording is decidedly on the resonant side, the symphonies come up sounding pleasantly fresh with these spruce rhythms and lively tempos and a balance that lets the woodwind detail come sharply through. Kuijken tends to use fast tempos for the minuets, which is in line with current early music orthodoxy, but he might have done well to reflect on the significance of the *allegretto* markings in those of Nos. 83 and 84, which imply something a little more measured than this. Number 84, a symphony we do not often hear, fares particularly well here, with a fine rhythm to the opening movement and an alert and pointed finale.

Haydn. Symphonies — No. 85 in B flat major, "La reine"; No. 86 in D major; No. 87 in A major. **Orchestra of the Age of Enlightenment/Sigiswald Kuijken.** Virgin Classics Veritas VC7 90844-2.

1h 19' DDD 5/90

The mention of period instruments can make people fear (with occasional good reason) that they will hear playing less notable for persuasiveness than for bluntness and sometimes roughness of interpretation and execution. If so, this recording should open minds, for the playing is clean yet fully stylish and expressive and there is no question of accepting dull string tone or poor woodwind intonation in the name of the god Authenticity. The period flavour is there all right (listen for example to the clean sound of the oboe and bassoon in Symphony No. 85, and the crisp strings and overall texture) but it convinces. So do the tempos, phrasing, dynamics and articulation, the latter being sharper than with most modern orchestras and making the latter sound heavy by comparison. To this fine playing under young the Belgian conductor you might add that these three symphonies are masterpieces of Haydn's wonderful Indian summer of his sixties, that the 1989 recording in EMI's Abbey Road Studios is atmospheric in the right degree, and that a total length of nearly 80 minutes results in a most attractive CD. The booklet gives useful details of the instruments played in each work, mostly eighteenth-century originals in the case of the strings with modern replicas for wind and nineteenth-century timpani in Symphony No. 86.

Haydn. Symphonies — No. 90 in C major; No. 93 in D major. **Orchestra of the Eighteenth Century/Frans Brüggen.** Philips 422 022-2PH. Recorded at performances in The Netherlands during 1987.

51' DDD 5/88

These performances are of a calibre which deserve to be noticed. Amongst the many delights of this recording are the mellow sound and warm textures of the wind instruments and the generally high level of technical expertise with which they are played. Haydn's wind writing is usually interesting, sometimes witty and, especially in the case of the horns, often extremely difficult to play. These fine players surmount most of the difficulties with an admirable degree of self-assurance and Brüggen's direction is always lively. Lovers of Haydn's music should find much that is rewarding in this issue.

Haydn. Symphonies — No. 92 in G major, "Oxford"; No. 104 in D major, "London". **English Sinfonia/Sir Charles Groves.** Pickwick IMP Classics PCD916.

55' DDD 6/89

Haydn. Symphonies — No. 91 in E flat major; No. 92 in G major, "Oxford". **Concertgebouw Orchestra, Amsterdam/Sir Colin Davis.** Philips 410 390-2PH. From 410 390-1PH (3/84).

51' DDD 4/85

Haydn. Symphonies — No. 102 in B flat major; No. 104 in D major, "London". **English Chamber Orchestra/Jeffrey Tate.** EMI CDC7 47462-2. From EL270451-1 (3/87).

| | 57' DDD 5/87 | | |

During his two highly successful seasons in London in 1791 and 1794 Haydn composed the twelve symphonies, known collectively as the *London* symphonies (though only the last, No. 104, bears the name of the capital), specifically for his English audiences. During the first visit, Haydn accepted an honorary doctorate from Oxford and, not having time to compose a work specially for the occasion, performed Symphony No. 92. The work has since borne the name of the University city, in honour of the event. Both the works on the Pickwick disc have, in common with the other *London* symphonies, a directness and depth of meaning that show Haydn at the very peak of his compositional powers. Typically, though, they require a lightness of touch in performance to allow the essential elegance of their idiom to make full impact. Sir Charles Groves gets the balance of intensity and shapeliness just right, and the relaxed, ideally distanced recording is the perfect complement.

Symphony No. 91 only seems less exalted by comparison with such heights, for it too shows not only the finest degree of craftsmanship of which Haydn was capable but also those hints of other-worldliness that underpin much of his greatest and most mature compositions. Sir Colin Davis and the Concertgebouw play with honesty and simple, unpretentious musicianship; an approach that makes these performances very successful. Although much work must have gone into creating such artless simplicity, it seems as though the music plays itself and the listener has a direct line with the composer's ideas. The timeless *Adagio* of the Oxford provides a fine example and Davis produces pure emotions that are very moving. With first-rate, natural sound these recordings demand a place in any collection.

Tate's *London* Symphonies have all the attributes found in his readings of Nos. 100 and 103: relaxed tempos, freshness of approach and a buoyancy that keeps the music flowing and animated. Perhaps at times there is a touch more weight in these performances, but that is as it should be, as these Symphonies are inclined towards ebulliency and grandeur — qualities that are superbly brought out in Symphony No. 104. The *Adagio* of No. 102 has suavity and elegance, and the following *Menuetto*'s dance rhythms are strongly projected, demonstrating Tate's ability to adapt to Haydn's sharply contrasting moods. Once again the recorded sound is warm and finely balanced, with perhaps a shade more bite and brilliance to the upper strings.

NEW REVIEW

Haydn. LONDON SYMPHONIES. **Concertgebouw Orchestra/Sir Colin Davis.** Philips Silver Line Classics 432 286-2PSL4.
No. 93 in D major; No. 94 in G major, "The Surprise" (both from 6514 192, 1/83); No. 95 in C minor (6514 074, 1/82); No. 96 in D major, "The Miracle" (6725 010, 6/82); No. 97 in C major (6514 074); No. 98 in B flat major (9500 678, 12/80); No. 99 in E flat major (9500 139, 4/77); No. 100 in G major, "Military" (9500 510, 3/79); No. 101 in D major, "The Clock" (9500 679, 7/81); No. 102 in B flat major (9500 679); No. 103 in E flat major, "Drumroll" (9500 303, 7/78); No. 104 in D major, "London" (9500 510).

| | ④ 5h 4' ADD/DDD 7/92 | | |

A superb achievement all round — indeed, it's nigh on impossible to imagine better 'big-band' Haydn than one encounters here on these four exceedingly well-filled CDs. Sir Colin Davis's direction has exemplary sparkle (try the superb opening movement of the *Miracle* Symphony) and sensitivity (witness his eloquent moulding of No. 98's great *Adagio*). Minuets are never allowed to plod, outer movements have an ideal combination of infectious zip and real poise, and the humour (a commodity, of course, that is never absent for too long in Haydn's music) is always conveyed with a genial twinkle in the eye. Quite marvellous, wonderfully unanimous playing from the great Amsterdam Orchestra, too (the woodwind contributions are particularly distinguished), with never a trace of routine to betray the six-year recording span of this critically acclaimed project. The Philips engineering, whether analogue or digital, is of the very highest quality throughout, offering a totally natural perspective, gloriously full-bodied tone and consistently sparkling textures within the sumptuous Concertgebouw acoustic. Invest in this set: it will yield enormous rewards for many years to come.

Haydn. STRING QUARTETS. **Lindsay Quartet** (Peter Cropper, Ronald Birks, vns; Robin Ireland, va; Bernard Gregor-Smith, vc). ASV CDDCA622. Recorded at a performance in the Wigmore Hall, London during the "Genius of Haydn" Festival in September 1987.
Op. 20: No. 2 in C major; Op. 50: No. 1 in B flat major; Op. 76: No. 2 in D minor, "Fifths".

The second of the *Sun* Quartets (Op. 20) has a gently paced but rich first movement, a dramatic *Capriccio* that gives way to a lyrical *arioso*, flowing into a far from formal Minuet and Trio, and a fugal finale which develops in whispers until vigorous homophony finally prevails. Haydn dedicated his Op. 50 set (the *Prussian* Quartets) to King Friedrich Wilhelm, an amateur cellist, and they are marked by the thematic economy typified in the first movement of No. 1. The finale is another sonata-form movement, likewise sparing with its material, en route to which is a delightful theme, three variations and coda (*Adagio non lento*), and a robust Minuet with a tip-toeing Trio. Count Joseph Erdödy was the dedicatee of the Quartets Op. 76 (1797) and are abundantly nicknamed. The whole work is a torrent of invention, Haydn at his most compelling. These recordings were made live in the Wigmore Hall, a virtual guarantee of a sympathetic acoustic: the presence of an audience can be hazardous, but here it served only to stimulate the Lindsay Quartet to performances so riveting that there isn't so much as a sniffle to be heard — only the richly earned applause at the end of each work.

Haydn. STRING QUARTETS. **Lindsay Quartet** (Peter Cropper, Robin Ireland, vns; Ronald Birks, va; Bernard Gregor-Smith, vc). ASV CDDCA582. Op. 54: No. 1 in G major; No. 2 in C major; No. 3 in E major.

All three quartets are in the usual four-movement form but with many surprises: in No. 1, the false recapitulation in the first movement, the dark modulations in the following sonata-form *Allegretto* and the Hungarian-gipsy flavour (anticipated in the Minuet) and mischievousness of the final Rondo. Number 2 has a rhapsodic fiddler in its second movement, a nostalgic Minuet with an extraordinarily anguished Trio, and an *Adagio* finale in which a *Presto* section turns out to be no more than an episode. A notable feature of No. 3 is its tenary-form *Largo cantabile*, the centre of which is more like a mini-concerto for the first violin; 'Scotch snaps' pervade the Minuet, and pedal points the finale. The performances (and the recording) are superb, marked by unanimity, fine tone, suppleness of phrasing, and acute dynamic shaping; in the second movement of No. 1 there are hushed passages whose homogeneity and quality of sound is quite remarkable. Even more remarkable would be the Haydn lover who found this recording resistible.

Haydn. STRING QUARTETS. **Gabrieli Quartet** (Kenneth Sillito, Brendan O'Reilly, vns; Ian Jewel, va; Keith Harvey, vc). Chandos CHAN8531.
Op. 54: No. 2 in C major; Op. 64: No. 5 in D major, "Lark".

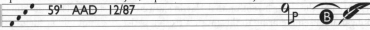

These are fabulous works, supremely inventive and remarkably innovative, with movements very much integrated into a symphonic-type structure. Few who hear the magical opening of Op. 64 No. 5 can fail to respond to Haydn's arrestingly simple opening. Few, too, could remain unmoved by the depth of emotion conveyed in Haydn's slow movements, by his impassioned melodic lines and astonishing harmonic daring. These are unquestionable masterpieces and are as central to the quartet repertoire as are the greatest essays in the medium from Mozart or Beethoven. The Gabrieli Quartet play very beautifully, demonstrating a deep understanding of both the moment and the movement.

Haydn. STRING QUARTETS. **Salomon Quartet** (Simon Standage, Micaela Comberti, vns; Trevor Jones, va; Jennifer Ward Clarke, vc). Hyperion CDA66098. From A66098 (3/84).
Op. 71: No. 3 in E flat major; Op. 74: No. 1 in C major.

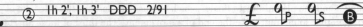

NEW REVIEW

Haydn. STRING QUARTETS. **Kodály Quartet** (Attila Falvay, Tamás Szabo, vns; Gábor Fias, va; János Devich, vc). Naxos 8 550394 and 8 550396.
8 550394 — Op. 71: No. 1 in B flat major, No. 2 in D major; No. 3 in E flat major. *8 550396* — Op. 74: No. 1 in C major; No. 2 in F major; No. 3 in G minor, "The Rider".

Kodály Quartet   *[photo: Naxos*

The two Quartets heard on the Hyperion disc are particularly fine examples of Haydn's late period. Written especially for performance in the concert hall, as opposed to the drawing room, they are much more 'public' in stance than his earlier quartets, with a deliberately more sonorous, almost orchestral, approach which is better tailored to a larger acoustic. They are more public too in having a symphonic-like opening flourish. The emotional focal point of both is the second, slow movement and it is here that Haydn produces some of his most daring harmonic innovations, his most forward-looking effects in instrumentation. The aptly-named Salomon Quartet specialize in the performance of music from the eighteenth century and they play on instruments of the period. Balancing its more serious vein, Haydn's music is elsewhere full of wit and spirit and the Salomons are very responsive to every turn he takes, revelling in his constant inventiveness. Highly recommended.

The enterprising Kodály Quartet are working their way through the middle and late Haydn Quartets and, rightly, taking their time about it. They rehearse

together privately, and then every so often turn up at the Hungaroton Studios in
Rottenbiller with a new group ready to record. They play with self-evident joy
in the music and an easy immaculateness of ensemble, which comes from
familiarity with each other's company. There is never a hint of routine and the
intercommunication is matched by enormous care for detail and clean ensemble.
In short they play as one, and project this wonderful music with enormous
dedication. Just sample the elegant *Andante* with variations which form the slow
movement of Op. 71 No. 3, or the witty Menuet which follows, or any of the
consistently inspired Op. 74 set. The hushed intensity of playing in the *Largo assai*
of Op. 74 No. 3 is unforgettable. The recordings are wholly natural and
balanced within a well-judged acoustic; the digital sound is of the highest quality
and documentation is excellent. At their modest price this pair of CDs is
irresistible.

Haydn. STRING QUARTETS. **Takács Quartet** (Gábor Takács-Nagy, Károly
Schranz, vns; Gábor Omai, va; András Fejér, vc). Decca 425 467-2DH.
Op. 76: No. 4 in B flat major; No. 5 in D major; No. 6 in E flat major.

1h 8' DDD 1/90

In these three quartets from a set of six published in 1797, one can only be
delighted by the sheer invention that Haydn showed in his sixties. This youthful
Hungarian ensemble bring to this music a freshness that does not inhibit them
from the necessary underlining of this or that point. The *Sunrise* Quartet is
invigorating in the first movement and lyrically broad in the Adagio, and the
syncopated minuet and lilting finale are no less delightful. The D major Quartet
starts with an Allegretto suggesting a set of variations but then moves into a
section in new keys before ending with a brisk coda. The slow movement's
cantabile e mesto marking is fully realized, as is the major-minor contrast of the
minuet and the playful Presto finale, which begins with an unmistakable joke of
six bars that sound more like the end of a movement. The third of these quartets
begins with variations that culminate in a fugato; the slow movement (called a
fantasia) is another original, and this is followed by a witty scherzo and a finale in
which scale fragments participate in a game of dizzy contrapuntal complexity.
The recording, made in a London church, is immediate yet atmospheric, although
with a touch of glare that tone controls will tame.

Haydn. STRING QUARTETS. **Mosaïques Quartet** (Erich Höbarth, Andrea
Bischof, vns; Anita Mitterer, va; Christophe Coin, vc). Auvidis Astrée E8799.
Op. 77: No. 1 in G major; No. 2 in F major; Op. 103: D minor (unfinished).

1h 2' DDD 2/90

Anyone who thinks that period-instrument performance means austerity and
coolness should listen to this disc. Here is a group of youngish French players,
using instruments of the kind Haydn would have heard, played (as far as we can
know) in a style he would have been familiar with: the result is a disc full of
expressive warmth and vigour. The opening of Op. 77 No. 1 is done duly
gracefully, but with a sturdy underlying rhythm and the Scherzo is as crisp and
alive as one could ask for. Then the first movement of the F major work is very
beautifully done, with many sensitive details; and the lovely second movement is
happily leisurely, so that the players have ample room for manoeuvre and the
leader makes much of his opportunities for delicate playing in the filigree-like
high music. The players show a real grasp of the structure and they know when
to illuminate the key moments, with a touch of extra deliberation or a little
additional weight of tone. These performances, clearly recorded, are competitive
ones not merely within the protected world of 'early music' but in the bigger,
'real' world too!

Haydn. The Seven Last Words of Our Saviour on the Cross (string quartet version — 1787). **Cherubini Quartet** (Christoph Poppen, Harald Schoneweg, vns; Hariolf Schlicitig, va; Klaus Kämper, vc). EMI CDC7 49682-2.

1h 17' DDD 1/90

Anyone who still regards Haydn primarily as a high-class comedy act should think again. These seven sublime *Adagios*, framed by an introduction and a concluding Earthquake, were commissioned by a canon in Cadiz and first performed in the cathedral there in Holy Week 1787. Each of the seven orchestral "Sonatas", as Haydn called them, followed a reading of Christ's words by the bishop and a discourse on their meaning; and in each the composer fashioned the opening theme to the rhythm of the Latin text. Performances of the *Seven Last Words* were always likely to be limited, and to ensure the work's wider currency Haydn later arranged it for string quartet. If the power and range of the original orchestral scoring are inevitably lost in the quartet version, and the final Earthquake distinctly muted, much of the music's poignancy, anguish and almost mystic ecstasy remains, especially in a performance as deeply considered and intensely felt as this. With their often daringly slow tempos superbly sustained, their breadth of phrasing and their unusually wide range of colour and dynamics the Cherubini Quartet make one less aware than most groups that this music was not originally conceived for string quartet — even the Earthquake has impressive dramatic force. Haydn's ornaments are always profoundly expressive, never merely elegant as in many performances, while the grief, violence and desolation of the fourth and fifth sonatas are conveyed with rare intensity, bows biting deep into the strings. The recording, made in the Haydn-Saal, Eisenstadt, is a touch close, but atmospheric and aptly resonant.

Haydn. DIVERTIMENTOS. **Ricercar Consort** (Claude Maury, Piet Dombrecht, hns; François Fernandez, [a]vn/[b]va; Alda Stuurop, vn; Ryo Terrakado, va; Philippe Pierlot, baryton; Rainer Zipperling, vc; Eric Mathot, db). Ricercar RIC067050. A minor/major, HobX/3[a]; G major, HobX/5[a]; D major, HobX/10[b]; G major, HobX/12[a].

59' DDD 9/91

Highly agreeable shavings from Haydn's workshop floor. All four works here feature the baryton, a curious, plangent-toned instrument combining gut strings and synthetic metal strings which was assiduously cultivated by Prince Nikolaus Esterhazy. Haydn satisfied the Prince's passion for this complicated (and quickly obsolete) instrument both in his long series of baryton trios and a group of seven divertimentos "for eight voices" — string quartet, baryton, double bass and two horns. Three of the set are included here. The quicker movements tend to be compact, cheerful and undemanding, though the presence of the baryton in the ensemble makes for some intriguing, dusky-hued textures and there is some quite spectacular writing for the horns, especially in the minuet finale of No. 3. But the real glory of these works lies in their intense, introspective, un-divertimento-like *Adagios*, two of which (in Nos. 3 and 7) are in the minor key, rarely favoured by Haydn for his later slow movements. There is also a noble opening *Adagio* in the fourth work on this disc, a quintet for two horns, baryton, viola and bass, arranged by Haydn from a divertimento for wind band. The playing of the Ricercar Consort, while not always immaculate in intonation, is assured, sympathetic and sensitively balanced. Fast movements are neat and spirited (though the finale of No. 2 is arguably too easygoing for a *Presto*), and the *Adagios* unfold with real breadth. The baryton player, Philippe Pierlot, deserves special praise for his expert negotiation of this excruciatingly difficult instrument; and there is consistently fine playing from the horns, not only in their high-flying virtuoso exploits but also the many places where they add a quiet, subtle gloss to the string texture. The recording is vivid and immediate, with horns and strings well separated. Definitely a disc to consider for late-night listening — though the slow movements may involve you more than you'd bargained for.

Haydn. PIANO SONATAS. **Emanuel Ax** (pf). CBS Masterworks CD44918. C minor, HobXVI/20; F major, HobXVI/23; C major, HobXVI/48; C major, HobXVI/50.

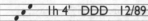

Ih 4' DDD 12/89

Emanuel Ax   *[photo: Sony Classical*

Here is another powerful antidote to the notion of Haydn as a kind of clever comedian — and it seems the point still has to be made. Emanuel Ax avoids romantic overstatement throughout these performances; the interpretation sounds as if it's felt from within the notes, rather than applied to them. Ax can bring out the high seriousness of the great C minor Sonata's first movement without trying to 'Beethovenize' the drama, while in Sonata No. 60 he can pass from childlike humour in the opening theme to taut symphonic argument without a trace of incongruity. Most impressive of all though is his feeling for dramatic shape: the slow first movement of Sonata No. 58 grows steadily to a

powerful final climax — as, with very different effect, does the C minor's opening *Moderato*: there's something truly tragic about the final resolution. The slight distant reverberation is a little disconcerting at first — as though Ax were playing to a large deserted auditorium — but it's soon accepted.

Haydn. PIANO WORKS. **Alfred Brendel** (pf). Philips 416 643-2PH4. Booklet included.
Sonatas — C minor, HobXVI/20; E flat major, HobXVI/49 (both from 9500 774, 8/81); E minor, HobXVI/34; B minor, HobXVI/32; D major, Hob XVI/42 (412 228-1PH, 8/85); C major, HobXVI/48; D major, HobXVI/51; C major, Hob XVI/50 (6514 317, 11/83); E flat major, HobXVI/52; G major, HobXVI/40; D major, HobXVI/37 (416 365-1PH, 12/86). Fantasia in C major, HobXVI/4. Adagio in F major, HobXVI/9 (412 228-1PH, 8/85). Andante with variations in F minor, Hob XVI/6 (416 365-1PH, 12/86).

④ 52' 55' 37' 61' ADD/DDD 3/87

The Sonatas collected in this set are some magnificent creations wonderfully well played by Alfred Brendel. Within the order and scale of these works Haydn explores a rich diversity of musical languages, a wit and broadness of expression that quickly repays attentive listening. It is the capriciousness as much as the poetry that Brendel so perfectly attends to; his playing, ever alive to the vitality and subtleties, makes these discs such a delight. The sophistication innate in the simple dance rhythms, the rusticity that emerges, but above all, the sheer *joie de vivre* are gladly embraced. Brendel shows in this music what makes a merely technically accomplished player a truly great one — his continual illumination of the musical ideas through intense study pays huge dividends. The recording quality varies enormously between the various works and though the close acoustic on some of the later discs could be faulted for allowing one to hear too much of the keyboard action, it certainly brings one into vivid contact with the music.

NEW REVIEW

Haydn. Arianna a Naxos. English Canzonettas. **Carolyn Watkinson** (mez); **Glen Wilson** (fp). Virgin Classics Veritas VC7 91215-2. Texts included.
A pastoral song. Despair. Fidelity. The mermaid's song. O tuneful voice. Piercing eyes. Pleasing pain. Sailor's song. She never told her love. The spirit's song. The wanderer.

1h 4' DDD 1/92

This is an absolute must for all lovers of Haydn's music. His delightful songs have been unduly neglected until relatively recently so it's a double pleasure to find such a well presented and sympathetic recording. Carolyn Watkinson's idiomatically plangent and deeply-felt singing merges the elegance of the salon with the passion and strong characterization we associate with Haydn's greatest oratorios. There is certainly a wide range of moods in these pieces, ranging from the theatrical flourishes of *Teseo mio ben!* to the purity of *The spirit's song* (Haydn gave this to Lady Hamilton on her visit to Eisenstadt with Nelson) and the buoyancy of *Sailor's song*. Glen Wilson's accompaniment in the canzonettas is tasteful and idiomatic, although the recording seems more appropriate for an orchestral performance than these essentially intimate works. However, so carefully thought-through is both Watkinson's singing and Wilson's fortepiano playing that the ear adjusts effortlessly. Virgin Classics documentation is both scholarly and entertaining.

Haydn. Mass in D minor, "Nelson"[a]. Te Deum in C major, HobXXIII*c*/2. [a]**Felicity Lott** (sop); [a]**Carolyn Watkinson** (contr); [a]**Maldwyn Davies** (ten); [a]**David Wilson-Johnson** (bar); **The English Concert and Choir/Trevor Pinnock.** Archiv Produktion 423 097-2AH. Texts and translations included.

50' ADD 2/88

The British Admiral had ousted the Napoleonic fleet at the Battle of the Nile just as Haydn was in the middle of writing his *Nelson* Mass. Although the news could not have reached him until after its completion, Haydn's awareness of the international situation was expressed in the work's subtitle, "Missa in Augustiis", or "Mass in times of fear". With its rattle of timpani, its pungent trumpet calls, and its highly-strung harmonic structure, there is no work of Haydn's which cries out so loudly for recording on period instruments; and it is the distinctive sonority and charged tempos of this performance which sets it apart from its competitors. The dry, hard timpani and long trumpets bite into the dissonance of the opening *Kyrie*, and the near vibrato-less string playing is mordant and urgent. The fast-slow-fast triptych of the *Gloria* is set out in nervously contrasted speeds, and the *Credo* bounces with affirmation. Just as the choral singing is meticulously balanced with instrumental inflection, so the soloists have been chosen to highlight the colours in Pinnock's palette. This is an unusually exciting recording.

Haydn. Stabat mater. **Patricia Rozario** (sop); **Catherine Robbin** (mez); **Anthony Rolfe Johnson** (ten); **Cornelius Hauptmann** (bass); **The English Concert and Choir/Trevor Pinnock.** Archiv Produktion 429 733-2AH.

1h 9' DDD 9/90

Haydn's deeply expressive *Stabat mater* for soloists, choir and orchestra is all too seldom performed. Composed in 1767 it hints strongly at the *Sturm und Drang* idiom that was to characterize Haydn's music over the next few years. Boldly contrasting juxtapositions, vivid dynamic shading, chromaticism, syncopation and gently sighing gestures all contribute towards an expressive intensity which affectingly complements the celebrated Latin poem. Trevor Pinnock has assembled a fine quartet of soloists whose voices, singly and in varying ensembles are sympathetically partnered by warm-sounding and stylish playing by The English Concert. The choir of The English Concert is effective, too, with well-balanced ensemble and textural clarity. One of the most alluring numbers of the work is the quartet and chorus, "Virgo virginium praeclara" in which all the various components of Haydn's forces join in a fervent, sorrowful prayer of sustained beauty. The recording is ideally resonant yet capturing many details of colour and nuance present in the character of period instruments. The booklet includes the full text of the poem in three languages.

Haydn. Die Schöpfung (sung in English). **Emma Kirkby** (sop); **Anthony Rolfe Johnson** (ten); **Michael George** (bass); **Choir of New College, Oxford; Academy of Ancient Music Chorus and Orchestra/ Christopher Hogwood.** L'Oiseau-Lyre 430 397-2OH2. Text included.

② 1h 39' DDD 3/91

NEW REVIEW

Haydn. Die Schöpfung. **Gundula Janowitz** (sop); **Fritz Wunderlich, Werner Krenn** (tens); **Dietrich Fischer-Dieskau** (bar); **Walter Berry** (bass); **Christa Ludwig** (alto) **Vienna Singverein; Berlin Philharmonic Orchestra/Herbert von Karajan.** DG 435 077-2GGA2. Text and translation included. From 2707 044 (10/69).

② 1h 49' ADD 12/91

The claims to historical authenticity made on behalf of Hogwood's performance of Haydn's oratorio *Die Schöpfung* ("The Creation"), are diffuse and overstated, but that need not worry the listener overmuch, for what counts is the performance itself. It is the second to have been recorded using period instruments but the first to use Peter Brown's new performing edition based on appropriate sources. The Academy of Ancient Music fields an orchestra expanded to 115 players together with the Choir of New College, Oxford and a strong solo vocal group. The results are mostly satisfying and the performance greatly enhanced by a sympathetic recorded balance which captures the distinctive character of period instruments. When Haydn published the first edition, it included both German and English texts and it would seem probable that he intended one or other to be sung according to the nationality of the audience. This version is sung in English, a feature that many listeners will find illuminating. All in all this is an enterprising project which has largely succeeded in achieving its aim as outlined by the Director of the performance, Christopher Hogwood "to recapture in sound, scale and text the performances conducted by the composer". The booklet contains full texts in four languages and an informative essay.

Herbert von Karajan's 1966 version of *Die Schöpfung* is something of a classic and probably one of the best recordings ever made of this joyous work. In the depiction of the chaos Karajan immediately set the atmosphere with a massive luminous tone quality from the Berlin Philharmonic, sustained fermatas and fortissimos like ocean breakers. The choir's mighty outburst in "and there was light" almost takes the roof off and the elegant accompaniment to the ensuing arias are a continuous delight. But the main glory of this recording are the soloists including Fritz Wunderlich as a brilliantly mercurial Uriel. This performance is a superb monument to the tenor whose tragically premature death occurred before the sessions were completed. Only the recitatives were left unrecorded and Werner Krenn made an excellent substitute. Walter Berry's narration of Haydn's pre-Darwinian evolution is buoyant while Gundula Janowitz's creamy soprano is a pleasure throughout. DG's recording sounds pleasantly fresh and well-balanced.

Michael Haydn   *Refer to Index*   *Austrian 1737-1806*

Christopher Headington   *British 1930-*

Headington. Violin Concerto.
R. Strauss. Violin Concerto, Op. 8. **Xue-Wei** (vn); **London Philharmonic Orchestra/Jane Glover.** ASV CDDCA780.

♪ 1h 3' DDD 12/91

Xue-Wei's penetrating and intuitive realization of Christopher Headington's Violin Concerto, written in 1959, is already commanding great admiration for this significant modern concerto, dedicated to the late Ralph Holmes, which in many respects inherits the lyric mantle of the great masterworks for the violin composed earlier in the century by Elgar and Walton. Xue-Wei also reminds the listener of the work's darker aspect, especially during the opening paragraphs of the concerto, where an affinity with the Walton Concerto is apparent. The central *Vivace* movement again has something of Walton's caustic wit, but the Headington concerto is searching and original in concept, without being overtly heroic or virtuosic. The lyrical potential of the solo writing is gloriously revealed by Xue-Wei, whose playing is superb, particularly in the lucid six-variation finale, which leads to a hushed and deeply-felt conclusion. The Violin Concerto by Richard Strauss is very much in the traditionally romantic virtuoso vein of

Christopher Headington

Wieniawski and Vieuxtemps, and although an early work it displays great pointers in the direction of Strauss's mature heroism. Xue-Wei's playing is volatile, affectionate and involving, while his rare tonal finesse has an evocative Heifetzian lustre which is always compelling. He is admirably supported throughout by the London Philharmonic, under Jane Glover, and ASV capture every nuance of the performance in the ample acoustic of London's Henry Wood Hall. The interpretation of the Headington concerto alone could well acquire classic status, and this is a disc which deserves to be heard by all who have an affinity with violin music of the twentieth century.

Hans Werner Henze   *German 1926-*

Henze. SYMPHONIES. [a]**Berlin Philharmonic Orchestra;** [b]**London Symphony Orchestra/Hans Werner Henze.** DG 20th Century Classics 429 854-2GC2. Items marked [a] from SLPM139203/4 (1/67), [b] 2530 261 (11/72). No. 1 (1947, rev. 1963)[a]; No. 2 (1949)[a]; No. 3 (1949-50)[a]; No. 4 (1955)[a]; No. 5 (1962)[a]; No. 6 (1969)[b].

♪ ② 2h 30' ADD 12/90

Hans Werner Henze is one of the few remaining composers to continue the German symphonic tradition, which make these authoritative recordings all the more invaluable and welcome. Henze was only 21 when he produced his First Symphony, and though it clearly owes much to Bartók, Stravinsky and Hindemith it is nevertheless a remarkable work for a composer so young. The Second Symphony, completed only two years after the First, is a dark and sombre work, and orchestrated in a style closer to Berg and Schoenberg than any later composer. It is here, also, that his preoccupation with the theatre begins to emerge, until in the Third, Fourth and Fifth Symphonies it becomes integrally part of the structure. The Third dates from the period when he was artistic director of the Wiesbaden Ballet, and its three movements: "Invocation of Apollo", "Dithyramb" and "Conjuring Dance" clearly evoke the spirit of the dance, within the formal structure of its symphonic argument. The Fourth and Fifth Symphonies quote heavily from his operas *König Hirsch* and *Elegy for Young Lovers*, and also begin to reflect his move from Germany to Italy, which brought about a greater feeling of 'arioso' lyricism and poetry to his style. The most radical is the Sixth, which dates from 1969 whilst Henze was living in Cuba, and we find him confronting and re-examining not only his own personal past (and political affiliations), but also the 'bourgeois' new music of the time. A valuable set that repays more and more with repeat hearings.

NEW REVIEW

Henze. Die Bassariden. **Kenneth Riegel** (ten) Dionysus, Voice, Stranger; **Andreas Schmidt** (bar) Pentheus; **Michael Burt** (bass) Cadmus; **Robert Tear** (ten) Tiresias; **William B. Murray** (bass) Captain of the Guard; **Karan Armstrong** (sop) Agave; **Celinda Lindsley** (sop) Autonoe; **Otrun Wenkel** (alto) Beroe; **Berlin Radio Chamber Choir; South German Radio Choir; Berlin Radio Symphony Orchestra/Gerd Albrecht.** Schwann Musica Mundi 314006. Notes, text and translations included.

② 2h DDD 10/91

Hans Werner Henze has by no means been under-represented on disc in the past; we have had recordings of six of his seven symphonies (reviewed above), numerous orchestral and *concertante* works and a fair quantity of chamber music. We have not, however, been given very much of the most important aspect of Henze's art — his operatic output. Many of the aforementioned works (particularly the symphonies) make reference to, or have been a fertile ground for developing material from his many operas (he has written over 15 to date), their omission from the catalogue has therefore resulted in a somewhat one-sided appreciation of Henze's output. This excellent issue goes some way to making amends. The rich, sumptuous scoring and lyrical writing in *The Bassarids* make it an ideal starting place for those exploring Henze's operatic output for the first time. The plot (after Euripides's play *The Bacchae*) concerns the power struggle and clash of moral values between the God Dionysus, and Pentheus the King of Thebes, and which culminates in the brutal murder of Pentheus at the hands of Dionysus's intoxicated followers — of which Agave, Pentheus's mother, is one. As with all Greek tragedies, the underlying message is as relevant today as it was in Ancient Greece; here the story warns of the dangers of excess, be they the excesses of wine and debauchery (Dionysus) or the excesses of fanaticism resulting from autonomy and dogmatism (Pentheus), and this is superbly brought out in W.H. Auden's and Chester Kalman's adaptation of the text. Musically the work is a perfect synthesis of Henze's operatic and symphonic writing and this is reflected in the four movement layout of the opera. The principal roles include some stunning performances headed by Andreas Schmidt, Kenneth Riegel and Karan Armstrong and praise must also go to Gerd Albrecht and the Berlin Radio

Symphony Orchestra for bringing Henze's gloriously colourful orchestration to life. Strongly recommended.

Victor Herbert
<blockquote>
American/Irish 1859-1924
</blockquote>

Herbert. Cello Concertos — No. 1 in D major, Op. 8; No. 2 in E minor, Op. 30. Five Pieces for cello and strings (trans. Dennison). **Lynn Harrell** (vc); **Academy of St Martin in the Fields/Sir Neville Marriner.** Decca 417 672-2DH.
Cello Pieces — Yesterthoughts; Pensée amoureuse; Punchinello; Ghazel; The Mountain Brook.

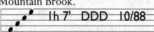 1h 7' DDD 10/88

Victor Herbert is best known nowadays as the composer of romantic American operettas. However, in his early days he was a cello virtuoso and composed many works for the instrument. The second of his two cello concertos is a powerful piece that is said to have influenced Dvořák to compose his own concerto for the instrument. The First Concerto remained in manuscript until recently and now provides a most rewarding surprise, since it offers the same characteristics of romantic warmth and subtle interplay of soloist and orchestra with even more melodic appeal. The second movement, with a sprightly scherzo section framed by an affecting andante, and ending with the soloist at the very top of the 'cello register, is a real winner. Lynn Harrell brings to the works not only virtuoso technique but an emotional intensity and variety of tone missing in previous recordings of the Second Concerto, and both accompaniment and recording are first class. The inclusion of transcriptions of five of Herbert's short pieces adds up to a very well-filled and immensely rewarding collection.

Hildegard of Bingen
<blockquote>
German 1098-1179
</blockquote>

Hildegard of Bingen. Sequences and Hymns. **Gothic Voices/Christopher Page** with **Doreen Muskett** (symphony); **Robert White** (reed drones). Hyperion CDA66039. Texts and translation included. From A66039 (7/82).
Columba aspexit. Ave, generosa. O ignis spiritus. O Jerusalem. O Euchari. O viridissima virga. O presul vere civitatis. O Ecclesia.

 44' DDD 7/85

Before 1981 Abbess Hildegard of Bingen was little more than a shadowy name in a brief paragraph in the music history text-books. Christopher Page and Gothic Voices have changed all that, revealing her to the world as one of the "greatest creative personalities of the Middle Ages". Hildegard once described herself as a "feather on the breath of God", writing and composing under divine impulsion. Now, with the arrival of this remarkable recording, a selection of her hymns and sequences has had new life breathed into it by these refreshingly unsophisticated performances. The music is all single line monody, freely composed in a modal idiom that owes much to the sort of music Hildegard was singing every day in choir. But these pieces are infused with a lyricism, sometimes even an ecstasy, that are entirely her own, and which seem to have a particular appeal to modern ears. This CD is an outright winner that merits a place in every collection.

Paul Hindemith

NEW REVIEW

Hindemith. Concerto for Orchestra, Op. 38.
Schmidt. Symphony No. 3 in A major. **Chicago Symphony Orchestra/
Neeme Järvi.** Chandos CHAN9000. Recorded at performances in Orchestra
Hall, Chicago on January 30th and February 3rd, 1991.

♪ 55' DDD 3/92

A cold shower followed by a warm bath. Hindemith's brisk 1925 Concerto is in
his defiantly anti-romantic, neo-classical vein. The composer often seems to
delight in demanding quite impossible feats of virtuosity from the violins, as
much as giving soloists and instrumental groups a fighting chance to show off.
But the real virtuosity is the composer's own. Who but Hindemith could have
written a "Basso ostinato" finale with 47 statements of its six-note theme in two
minutes and 20 seconds? Schmidt's Third Symphony, written three years later for
a competition for the best new symphony "in the spirit of Schubert", nostalgically
harks back to a bygone era through a haze of harmonic complexity. Schmidt
often tantalizes the listener with a dizzying journey of departures from his chosen
key, though wherever the undercurrents take you, the music's firm tonal foundation is never in doubt. Of all Schmidt's Austrian antecedents, the composer most
vividly recalled is Bruckner, particularly in the last two movements and in the
organ-like sonorities of the orchestration. Forgivably fallible strings in the
Hindemith apart, the Chicago Orchestra and Järvi are on top form, and these live
recordings preserve the concert-hall experience.

NEW REVIEW

Hindemith. ORCHESTRAL WORKS. [b]**Siegfried Mauser** (pf);
[a]**Queensland Symphony Orchestra,** [b]**Frankfurt Radio Symphony
Orchestra/Werner Andreas Albert.** CPO 999 005-2, 999 006-2, 999 078-2.
999 005-2[a] — Lustige Sinfonietta, Op. 4. Rag Time ("well-tempered").
Symphonische Tänze. *999 006-2*[a] — Das Nusch-Nuschi — dance suite, Op. 20.
Konzertmusik for strings and brass, Op. 50. Symphony, "Die Harmonie der
Welt". *999 078-2*[b] — Theme and Variations, "The Four Temperaments". Piano
Concerto.

♪ ③ 1h 2', 1h 4', 1h 2' DDD 12/91

The decline in status of one of this century's most prolific and versatile musical
figures is startling (Hindemith was once mentioned in the same breath as Bartók
and Stravinsky), and in the last three decades record companies have been loath
to put money into new recordings of works other than the established favourites
(the *Mathis der Maler* Symphony and the *Symphonic Metamorphosis*). There are now
signs of a revival of interest, and we are told that these discs are among the first
issues in a series that will include the "complete symphonic repertoire and a
collection of concertos". Well over half of these recordings are CD premières,
and many of these works haven't been recorded since the 1950s. The earliest
work is the *Lustige Sinfonietta*. Written in 1916, it shows the 21-year-old
Hindemith, though indebted to Reger and Richard Strauss, using a much smaller
orchestra than had been common before the war, and scoring with a freshness
and colour not always found in his later works. Sharper-tongued aphoristic wit
and hints of Hindemith, the *enfant terrible*, are found in the 1921 *Rag Time*; a
modish parodic fragmentation of Bach's C minor fugue, and a fascinating first
example of swing J.S. Bach. The same year also produced the "Burmese
marionette play", *Das Nusch-Nuschi*, and the three dances recorded here are
engagingly daft oriental burlesque, a piece of debunking very much of its period.
The gloriously robust 1930 *konzertmusik for strings and brass*, determinedly

contrapuntal and reflecting its destination (it was written for the Boston Symphony Orchestra) in its virtuoso demands and big band allusions, does not receive as idiomatic a reading as Bernstein's (see below), but it is a fine performance none the less. And the work looks forward to *Mathis* as much as the 1937 *Symphonic Dances* were obviously written in its wake, with their use of German folk-song and chorale, even the way some of the movements are constructed. British ears will delight to the frequent echoes of Walton and early Tippett. Of even greater value is the first stereo recording of the Symphony, *Die Harmonie der Welt* (1951). Like the *Mathis* Symphony, it originated in an opera project, this one devoted to the astronomer Kepler and his vision of a harmonic ordering of heavenly bodies; so, not surprisingly, the manner is grand (the scale is Brucknerian), and, equally unsurprisingly, the wide range of modern recordings allows collectors to fully savour that grandeur for the first time.

The last disc offers two concertos from the 1940s: *The Four Temperaments*, a Theme and Variations scored for piano and strings of austere beauty and finely wrought contrasts; and the Piano Concerto, with its variations gradually uncovering the theme, sumptuously scored for full orchestra, and with definite sideways glances to Bartók's night music and the rich string writing found in Prokofiev's Third Piano Concerto. Convincing proof, as are all three discs, of the diversity of Hindemith's vast output. Performances throughout are never less than good, frequently more than that, and CPO's sound is consistently smooth, airy and spacious.

Hindemith. Mathis der Maler — symphony. Trauermusik[a]. Symphonic Metamorphosis on Themes of Carl Maria von Weber. [a]**Geraldine Walther** (va); **San Francisco Symphony Orchestra/Herbert Blomstedt.** Decca 421 523-2DH.

55' DDD 10/88

Hindemith. Mathis der Maler — symphony. Symphonic Metamorphosis on Themes of Carl Maria von Weber. Konzertmusik for strings and brass, Op. 50. **Israel Philharmonic Orchestra/Leonard Bernstein.** DG 429 404-2GH. Recorded at performances in the Frederic R. Mann Auditorium, Tel Aviv in April 1989.

1h 7' DDD 5/91

The charge sometimes levelled against Hindemith of being dry and cerebral utterly collapses in the face of Blomstedt's disc. Masterly craftsmanship and virtuosity there is in plenty; but the powerful emotions of *Mathis der Maler* and the festive high spirits of the *Symphonic Metamorphosis* could not be denied except by those who wilfully close their ears. Each of the three movements of the *Mathis* symphony is based on a panel of Grünewald's great Isenheim altar. The eventual glorious illumination of "The angels" folk-tune, the poignant slow movement and the blazing triumphant Allelujas after the desperate struggle with the demons in the finale have a searing intensity in this performance, which also presents Hindemith's elaborate web of counterpoints with the utmost lucidity. For brilliant and joyously ebullient orchestral writing few works can match that based on Weber's piano duets and his *Turandot* overture: here the San Francisco woodwind and brass have a field day. In addition, this warmly recommended disc contains a heartfelt performance of the touching elegy on the death of King George V which Hindemith wrote overnight in 1936.

One can't help feeling that, had it been available, Tony Palmer would have used Bernstein's account of the *Mathis der Maler* Symphony for his South Bank Show film on Hindemith's masterpiece. Arguably the Israel woodwinds are not as spirited as Decca's version and the heart is too readily on the sleeve for the sad, withdrawn second movement, but the impact of St Anthony's torments in the finale is thrillingly graphic with Bernstein literally hurling the music's imagery at us. Here the winds of Hell blow at nothing less than hurricane force. The *Konzertmusik* and *Symphonic Metamorphosis* were both written for American orchestras, but although Bernstein was not on home ground for this recording, it's hard to imagine a more exuberant swing and swagger in the big band echoes of both works. The DG engineering is appropriately dry and clear, the balance, perhaps, co-ordinated as much from the mixing desk as the conductor, but there's no denying that the impact of the recording with the conductor's exhalations, exhortations and reinforced podium much in evidence is as physical as that of the performances. One of Bernstein's last recordings, this one unmistakably live, and a disc to treasure.

Hindemith. When Lilacs Last in the Door-yard Bloom'd (Requiem for those we love). **Jan DeGaetani** (mez); **William Stone** (bar); **Atlanta Symphony Chorus and Orchestra/Robert Shaw.** Telarc CD80132. Text included.

1h 2' DDD 7/87

Taking as his text Walt Whitman's poem, a work laden with imagery and layers of association, written to mourn the death of President Lincoln, Hindemith adds further layers of meaning to this already intense poem. He was commissioned to compose the work by Robert Shaw for his New York-based Collegiate Chorale so it is appropriate and gratifying to be recommending a recording made some 40 years later by that same Robert Shaw. Hindemith's setting of the poem perfectly moulds itself to Whitman's somewhat sectionalized approach and the virtuosity involved is balanced, if not outweighed, by the sheer power and beauty of the music. Like the lilacs of Whitman's poem the music has a pungency that lingers long after the piece has ended. Shaw's grasp of the subtleties and powerful imagery of the text is total and his experience of the work pays enormous dividends in this moving performance. William Stone is a very sympathetic and sweet-toned baritone matched by Jan DeGaetani's pure mezzo. Shaw's choral and orchestral forces point up every subtlety and the recording is first rate.

NEW REVIEW

Hindemith. CARDILLAC[a]. **Dietrich Fischer-Dieskau** (bar) Cardillac; **Leonore Kirschstein** (sop) Cardillac's daughter; **Donald Grobe** (ten) Officer; **Karl Christian Kohn** (bass) Gold dealer; **Eberhard Katz** (ten) Cavalier; **Elisabeth Söderström** (sop) Lady; **Willi Nett** (bar) Chief of Military Police; **Cologne Radio Chorus and Symphony Orchestra/Joseph Keilberth.** MATHIS DER MALER[b] — excerpts. **Dietrich Fischer-Dieskau** (bar) Mathis; **Pilar Lorengar** (sop) Regina; **Donald Grobe** (ten) Albrecht; **Berlin Radio Symphony Orchestra/Leopold Ludwig.** DG 20th Century Classics 431 741-2GC2. Item marked [a] from 139435/6 (4/70), [b] SLPM138769 (12/62).

2h 28' ADD 12/91

These discs offer you the two main facets of Paul Hindemith's music at their most convincing. *Cardillac* — the original 1926 version — is fast and furious, fitting the demonic character of the goldsmith who is so obsessed by his own creations that he kills their purchasers in order to regain them. *Mathis der Maler* — Matthias Grünewald, the painter — is introspective and idealistic, as obsessive as Cardillac but finding his way towards an ultimate serenity. Both performances are dominated by Dietrich Fischer-Dieskau, here recorded in his prime, and he is not only able to make Cardillac sound more than a mere monster, but steers clear of exaggeration and mawkishness in Mathis's more lyrical music. Supporting casts are uneven, but never fall below basic acceptability. The medium-price format means that synopses, not librettos, are provided, but given the generous duration of the discs and the (for its age) decent sound, as well as two conductors expert in articulating the tricky rythmic idiom of Hindemith's music, this is a very recommendable issue. (The *Mathis* excerpts are not to be confused with the complete recording Fischer-Dieskau made for HMV in the late 1970s, unfortunately no longer available.)

Gustav Holst
British 1874–1934

Holst. The Planets, H125. Women's voices of the **Montreal Symphony Chorus; Montreal Symphony Orchestra/Charles Dutoit.** Decca 417 553-2DH.

> 53' DDD 4/87

Holst. The Planets, H125[a]. The Perfect Fool, H150 — ballet music[b]. Egdon Heath, H127[b]. [a]Women's voices of the **London Philharmonic Choir; London Philharmonic Orchestra/**[a]**Sir Georg Solti,** [b]**Sir Adrian Boult.** Decca London 425 152-2LM. Item marked [a] from SET628 (3/79), [b] SXL6006 (9/62).

> 1h 14' ADD 12/89

Holst's brilliantly coloured orchestral suite, *The Planets*, is undoubtedly his most famous work and its success is surely deserved. The musical characterization is as striking as its originality of conception: the association of "Saturn" with old age, for instance, is as unexpected as it is perceptive. Bax introduced Holst to astrology and while he wrote the music he became fascinated with horoscopes, so it is the astrological associations that are paramount, although the linking of "Mars" (with its enormously powerful 5/4 rhythms) and war also reflects the time of composition. Throughout, the work's invention is as memorable as its vivid orchestration is full of infinite detail. No

Sir Georg Solti   *[photo: Decca/Masclet]*

recording can reveal it all but this one comes the closest to doing so. Dutoit's individual performance is in a long line of outstanding recordings.

The second Decca issue brings together three excellent Holst performances on one mid-price CD, with a total playing time of nearly 74 minutes to boot: superb value for money if ever there was. The sleeve-note to the *Planets* informs us that Solti listened to Holst's own recording of 1926 before recording this disc. Those who are familiar with Holst's account will notice that although the timings of some movements differ, Solti has remained faithful to Holst's view that rhythmic incisiveness and clarity of detail are of the utmost importance in this work. Holst said that "Mars, the Bringer of War" should sound "unpleasant and terrifying", and it is those qualities that are brought out in Solti's relentless and icy account. The rhythmic vitality of his performance is heard to great effect in

"Jupiter", with the big tune in the middle (later to be set as a hymn to the words "I vow to thee my country") sounding beautifully poised and heartfelt. Timings are at their most divergent in "Saturn, the Bringer of Old Age", where Solti adds nearly three minutes to Holst's reading, but the effectiveness of Solti's chosen tempo is undeniable. The two Boult recordings make a generous fill-up. His *Egdon Heath* is wonderfully atmospheric and the exuberance and colour of *The Perfect Fool* is vividly captured. The digital transfer is very fine indeed, with no loss of warmth or presence.

Holst. CHORAL MUSIC. **Holst Singers and ªOrchestra/Hilary Davan Wetton.** Hyperion CDA66329. Texts included.
Two psalms, H117ª. Six choruses, H186ª. The evening watch, H159. Seven Partsongs, H162ª. Nunc dimittis, H127.

Ih 5' DDD 1/90

It is incomprehensible that so much of Holst's wonderful music for chorus should still remain comparatively unknown to the general listening public. Hyperion must be particularly commended on the care and attention that have obviously been devoted to the fine recording and production here. Hilary Davan Wetton took on the mantle of Director of Music at St Paul's Girls' School in Hammersmith, the position held by Holst himself from 1905 until his death in 1934, and the spirit of the venue seems to suffuse both the performances and the recording. Featuring a chorus and orchestra dedicated to Holst's music, these readings capture exactly the sonorities that the composer implies in his scores and the spiritual world that the works inhabit. It is perhaps invidious to single out from a programme of such consistent quality a couple of items of particular merit, but the two short un-accompanied pieces for eight-part choir, *The evening watch* and the appropriately concluding *Nunc dimittis* are both outstanding and worthy of special attention.

NEW REVIEW

Holst. The Cloud Messenger, Op. 30ª. The Hymn of Jesus, Op. 37. ª**Della Jones** (mez); **London Symphony Chorus and Orchestra/Richard Hickox.** Chandos CHAN8901. Texts included.

Ih 6' DDD 5/91

When this CD was first released, the great talking point was *The Cloud Messenger*, a 43-minute work of considerable imaginative power, virtually forgotten since its disastrous première under the baton of Holst himself in 1913. It shows the composer already working on an epic scale — something which casts light on the subsequent eruption of *The Planets*. It is marvellous to have the work on disc, though it is, as you might expect, uneven. Those who admire the ascetic rigour of Holst's later music may share the reservations of Imogen Holst and find the score disappointingly 'backward'. There are certainly echoes of Vaughan Williams's *A Sea Symphony* and several older models. On the other hand, the glittering approach to the sacred city on Mount Kailasa and the stylized orientalism of the climactic dance are new to British music; another world, the world of "Venus", is foreshadowed in the closing pages. The text is Holst's own translation from the Sanskrit. Hickox's expansive account of the familiar *Hymn of Jesus* is more than a mere filler. One of the few incontrovertible masterpieces in Holst's output, it has never received a better performance on disc, although the impressively grand acoustics of London's St Jude's impart a certain warm imprecision — the choral singing itself is splendidly crisp — which can blunt the impact of Holst's acerbic harmonies.

Arthur Honegger   *French / Swiss 1892-1955*

Honegger. ORCHESTRAL WORKS. **Bavarian Radio Symphony Orchestra / Charles Dutoit.** Erato 2292-45242-2. From NUM75254 (4/86).
Symphony No. 1. Pastorale d'été. Three symphonic movements — Pacific 231; Rugby; No. 3.

| ♪ 55' DDD 12/86 | ② |

Honegger's First Symphony is a highly impressive work, concisely and effectively constructed in what might be generally described as a neoclassical style; and the scoring is attractive and skilful. His evocation of dawn on a summer's day in *Pastorale d'été*, scored for small orchestra with exquisite, quiet beauty, is surely a miniature masterpiece, and both *Pacific 231* (1924) and *Rugby* (1928) are brilliantly contrived essays in imaginative scoring and the use of cross-rhythms. Honegger was distressed by a critical notion that he was trying to imitate the sound of a steam locomotive and specific moves in a game of rugby: he insisted that the two scores conveyed only a general impression of a train journey and the atmosphere of Colombes stadium. So offended was he that he called the third companion piece merely *Mouvement symphonique No. 3*, but it is a little less effective than its two bedfellows. These vigorous performances are excellent.

Honegger. Symphonies — No. 2 for strings and trumpet; No. 3, "Liturgique".
Berlin Philharmonic Orchestra / Herbert von Karajan. DG 20th Century Classics 423 242-2GC. From 2530 068 (7/73).

| ♪ 59' ADD 6/88 | ♀℗ £ |

NEW REVIEW

Honegger. Symphonies — No. 2; No. 4, "Deliciae basiliensis". Pastorale d'été.
Prélude, arioso et fugue (on BACH). **Lausanne Chamber Orchestra / Jesús López-Cobos.** Virgin Classics VC7 91486-2.

| ♪ 1h 3' DDD 6/92 | ♀℗ |

The classic DG recording is unlikely to be surpassed. The Second Symphony is a powerfully atmospheric piece written during the grim years of the German occupation. It is a searching, thoughtful piece, appropriately dark in colouring which eventually breaks into the light with its chorale melody played on the trumpet. The *Liturgique* is a powerhouse of energy and its slow movement is among Honegger's most glorious inspirations. The playing of the Berlin Philharmonic is sumptuous in tone, vibrant with energy and encompasses an enormously wide range of dynamics and colour. One can only marvel at the quality of sound they achieve in both the beautiful slow movements and their virtuosity in the finale of No. 3. Astonishing performances and an indispensable disc for all lovers of modern music.

   The Lausanne Chamber Orchestra's coupling on Virgin is one of the best new recordings of Honegger's music to have appeared for a long time. Of course, if you want the most sumptuous and subtle of string sonorities, Karajan's account of the Second Symphony remains unrivalled but the Swiss version can hold its head high among the other recordings now in the catalogue. Jesús López-Cobos is attentive to detail in matters of phrasing, balance and dynamic nuance and gives a thoroughly idiomatic and sensitive reading of Honegger's wartime symphony. The same must also be said of the inspired *Pastoral d'été* and the (less inspired) *Prélude, arioso et fugue on BACH*, a transcription dating from 1936 of a piano piece composed four years earlier. Best of all, though, is the Fourth Symphony, written to celebrate the "delights of Basle" and composed for Paul Sacher and the Basle Chamber Orchestra. It has a lightness of touch and a responsiveness to colour and atmosphere that is most appealing. The performance itself captures the transparent, luminous quality of this sunny and enchanting score. The recording has plenty of space around the instruments and a natural, realistic balance.

Honegger. Le roi David[a]. Mouvement symphonique No. 3. La tempête — Prélude. [a]**Christiane Eda-Pierre** (sop); [a]**Martha Senn** (contr); [a]**Tibère Raffalli** (ten); [a]**Daniel Mesgiuch** (narr); [a]**Annie Gaillard** (rec); [a]**Kühn Children's Chorus; Prague Philharmonic Chorus; Czech Philharmonic Orchestra/Serge Baudo.** Supraphon CO-1412/13. Text and translation included.

② 1h 23' DDD 6/88

Honegger was thought of early in this century as a modernist as influential as Stravinsky and Bartók, but then fell into a certain neglect. However, today he is rightly seen as an important figure although with no special school or followers. *Le roi David* (1921) is a symphonic psalm in three parts that tells of the shepherd boy David who slays Goliath and becomes ruler of Israel. This music is brimful of invention, colour (sometimes oriental) and passion, and the French conductor Serge Baudo has a crisp, dramatically alert narrator in Daniel Mesgiuch as well as a heroic David in the tenor Tibère Raffalli and a fine Witch of Endor in Martha Senn. The chorus and orchestra seem completely at home with the idiom, so that such big set pieces as the "Dance before the Ark" that ends Part 2 are over-whelmingly exciting. The recording is clear yet atmospheric and encompasses the enormous climaxes. Unlike its predecessors, Honegger's Symphonic Movement No. 3 has no title, though at least one critic thought it portrayed a ski jumper! It is a lively piece, and the Prelude to Shakespeare's *Tempest* again shows the composer's skill in handling powerful ideas orchestrally. These other pieces are worth having and they help to fill the two CDs, but one may regret that at 68 minutes or so, *Le roi David* was not more economically accommodated on just one.

Honegger. Jeanne d'Arc au bûcher. **Françoise Pollet, Michèle Command** (sops); **Nathalie Stutzman** (contr); **John Aler** (ten); **Marthe Keller, Georges Wilson, Pierre-Marie Escourrou, Paola Lenzi** (narrs); **Chorus and Children's Voices of French Radio; French National Orchestra/ Seiji Ozawa.** DG 429 412-2GH. Text and translations included. Recorded at a performance in the Basilique Saint-Denis, Paris, in June 1989.

1h 9' DDD 4/91

Honegger described *Joan of Arc at the stake* as a "dramatic oratorio", but it is a work almost impossible to categorize, the two chief characters — Joan and Brother Dominc — being speaking parts, but with a chorus (now commenting on, now involved in, the action), a children's chorus, and a curiously constituted orchestra including saxophones instead of horns, two pianos and, most notably, an ondes martenot which, with its banshee shriek, bloodcurdlingly reinforces the climax as Joan breaks her earthly chains. The action is partly realistic, partly symbolic, unfolding in quasi-cinematic flashbacks. The musical techniques and styles employed by Honegger are extraordinarily varied, with humming and shouting besides singing, and with elements of polyphony, folk-song, baroque dances and jazz rhythms; yet all is fused together in a remarkable way to produce a work of gripping power and, in the final scenes, almost intolerable emotional intensity: the beatific *envoi* "Greater love hath no man ..." is a passage that catches the throat and haunts the mind for long afterwards. Ozawa fully captured the work's dramatic forces in this public performance, which has been skilfully served by the recording engineers; Marthe Keller vividly portrays Joan's bewilderment, fervour and agony, John Aler makes a swaggering Procus, and Françoise Pollet is radiant-voiced as the Virgin. Even more than *Le roi David*, this is Honegger's masterpiece.

Herbert Howells

British 1892-1983

Howells. Requiem (1936)[a]. Take him, earth, for cherishing (1963).
Vaughan Williams. Mass in G minor (1922)[b]. Te Deum in G major
(1928)[c]. [a]**Mary Seers** (sop); [ab]**Michael Chance** (alto); [ab]**Philip Salmon** (ten);
[ab]**Jonathan Best** (bass); **Corydon Singers/Matthew Best** with [c]**Thomas
Trotter** (org). Hyperion CDA66076. Texts included. From A66076 (8/83).

1h AAD 10/87

Vaughan Williams's unaccompanied Mass in G minor manages to combine the
common manner of Elizabethan liturgical music with those elements of his own
folk-music heritage that make his music so distinctive, and in so doing arrives at
something quite individual and new. The work falls into five movements and its
mood is one of heartfelt, if restrained, rejoicing. Herbert Howells wrote his
unaccompanied Requiem in 1936, a year after the death of his only son. The
work was not released in his lifetime but was reconstructed and published in

1980 from his manuscripts. It is a
most hauntingly beautiful work of an
obviously intensely personal nature.
Take him, earth, for cherishing was
composed to commemorate the
assassination of President John F.
Kennedy. The text is an English
translation by Helen Waddell of
Prudentius's fourth-century poem,
Hymnus circa Exsequias Defuncti. Again
it demonstrates the great strength of
Howells's choral writing, with a clear
outline and aptly affecting
yet unimposing harmonic twists. The
Corydon Singers give marvellous
performances of these works and the
sound is very fine indeed. An hour of
the finest English choral music and

Michael Chance   *[photo: Hyperion/Barda*   not to be missed.

Howells. SACRED CHORAL AND ORGAN WORKS. [a]**Christopher
Dearnley** (org); **St Paul's Cathedral Choir, London/John Scott.** Hyperion
CDA66260. Texts included.
Collegium regale — canticles. Six Pieces for organ — No. 3, Master Tallis's
Testament[a]. Like as the hart. Behold, O God our defender. Psalm-Preludes,
Set 2 — No. 1, De profundis[a]. Take him, earth, for cherishing. St Paul's —
canticles.

1h 2' DDD 9/88

This admirable disc is a fine tribute to the memory of Herbert Howells. The
choir has used with enormous skill everything St Paul's Cathedral has to offer in
the way of acoustical potential: space, resonance — even its echo — a lively
response to timbre and volume; all of it justly timed and finally captured in a
superb recording. The canticles for Morning Prayer (*Te Deum and Jubilate*) and
those for Evensong (*Magnificat and Nunc Dimittis*) provide a framework for the
organ pieces and the motets, all of them enhanced and enriched by the variety
of sonorities obtainable as much from the building itself as from the music.
Together, these works epitomize the life and death of this most English of

English composers. The choice and planning of the programme is particularly skilful: each piece seems to lead to the next with total inevitability. Behind that lies a measure of expertise and professionalism one rarely encounters; but it passes almost unnoticed simply because the ear is totally satisfied and charmed.

Johann Hummel

Austrian 1778-1837

Hummel. Piano Concertos — A minor, Op. 85; B minor, Op. 89. **Stephen Hough** (pf); **English Chamber Orchestra/Bryden Thomson.** Chandos CHAN8507.

1h 6' DDD 4/87

This is a staggering disc of Hummel's piano concertos played by Stephen Hough. The most obvious comparison is with the piano concertos of Chopin, but whereas those works rely on the grace and panache of the piano line to redeem an often lacklustre orchestral role, the Hummel works have finely conceived orchestral writing and certainly no shortage of original ideas. The piano part is formidable, combining virtuosity of a very high order indeed with a vigour and athleticism that does much to redress Hummel's somewhat tarnished reputation. The A minor is probably the better known of the two works here, with a thrilling rondo finale, but the B minor is no less inventive with some breathtaking writing in the piano's upper registers. This disc makes strong demands to be heard: inventive and exciting music, a masterly contribution from Stephen Hough, fine orchestral support from the ever sympathetic ECO under Bryden Thomson and, last but not least, a magnificent Chandos recording.

Hummel. Piano Quintet in E flat major, Op. 87.
Schubert. Quintet in A major, D667, "Trout". **Schubert Ensemble of London** (Jacqueline Shave, vn; Roger Tapping, va; Jane Salmon, vc; Peter Buckoke, db; William Howard, pf). Hyperion Helios CDH88010.

1h 1' DDD 6/90

Both works here offer turn-of-the-century Viennese warmth and geniality in full measure, the centuries in question being of course the eighteenth and nineteenth, and Schubert being a native of Vienna while Hummel made his home there. They are also classical in structure, and the Hummel Quintet especially so, which is not surprising since he was a pupil of Mozart and Haydn and a musical conservative compared to Beethoven, with whom he formed a lasting relationship that nevertheless had its ups and downs. The scoring of his Quintet is unusual, with the four strings featuring a double bass instead of being the usual two violins, viola and cello, and evidently this work was known to Schubert when he composed his *Trout* Quintet for the same combination, although it also reflected the instruments played by the music-loving friends in a provincial town for whom it was written. It is this work, with its famous variation-form fourth movement on the theme of the song *Die Forelle*, which begins the programme, and the playing by the Schubert Ensemble of London is vivid yet affectionate, with a recording quality that is on the full side as regards piano tone but still pleasantly natural. They are no less agreeable stylistically in the Hummel, which is more theatrical in its gestures but makes no pretence of offering romantic self-expression or real profundity, and if the first movement seems on the fast side and a touch breathless, they could argue that its marking *Allegro e risoluto assai* justifies this.

Englebert Humperdinck

German 1854-1921

Humperdinck. HANSEL UND GRETEL. **Anne Sofie von Otter** (mez)
Hänsel; **Barbara Bonney** (sop) Gretel; **Hanna Schwarz** (mez) Mother;
Andreas Schmidt (bar) Father; **Barbara Hendricks** (sop) Sandman; **Eva
Lind** (sop) Dew Fairy; **Marjana Lipovšek** (contr) Witch; **Tölz Boys' Choir;
Bavarian Radio Symphony Orchestra/Jeffrey Tate.** EMI CDS7 54022-2.
Notes, text and translation included.

(2) 1h 43' DDD 11/90

Humperdinck's delightful and ever popular fairy-tale opera is presented here in
an appealing, well paced and unsentimental performance, and though Tate brings
out the Wagnerian influence of the work (Humperdinck was greatly admired by
Wagner and was musical assistant in preparation for the first performance of
Parsifal) it is never made to sound heavyweight or protracted. Indeed, Tate's
tempos are generally faster than normal and these give the opera a persuasive
sense of flow and direction. Though carefully avoiding over-sentimentality
(especially in the "Evening Hymn" and "Dream Pantomime") Tate nevertheless
brings a natural warmth and charm to the work both in his beautifully crafted
phrasing and his subtle and sympathetic approach to the opera. The soloists are
particularly well chosen. Anne Sofie von Otter and Barbara Bonney are especially
fine in their fresh and youthful portrayal of the young children and Marjana
Lipovšek's superb performance as the Witch (avoiding the often melodramatic
and histrionic characterization found in other recordings) deserves special
mention. The beautiful warm and spacious recording is exceptionally clear and is
ideally balanced in terms of voices and orchestra. Destined to become a classic.

NEW REVIEW

Humperdinck. KONIGSKINDER. **Adolf Dallapozza** (ten) The King's Son;
Helen Donath (sop) Goose-girl; **Hermann Prey** (bar) Minstrel; **Hanna
Schwarz** (mez) Witch; **Karl Ridderbusch** (bass) Woodcutter; **Gerhard
Unger** (ten) Broom-maker; **Brigitte Lindner** (sop) Broom-maker's little
daughter; **Günter Wewel** (bass) Innkeeper; **Heidrun Ankersen** (mez)
Innkeeper's daughter; **Friedrich Lenz** (ten) Tailor; **Ortrun Wenkel** (contr)
Dairy-maid; **Tolz Boys' Choir; Bavarian Radio Chorus; Munich Radio
Orchestra/Heinz Wallberg.** EMI Studio CMS7 69936-2. Notes and text
included. From Electrola 1C 157 30698-700 (10/82).

(3) 2h 32' ADD 8/89

Humperdinck is still widely thought of as the composer of a single opera, and
that an undoubted masterpiece. Yet *Königskinder*, which had its première in 1910,
17 years after *Hänsel und Gretel*, is a wonderfully rich score and at many points
one marvels that it has not been equally popular. Like *Hänsel*, it is a fairy story,
with a witch and the two 'children' of the title, though they are in fact young
adults. Their love-story ends with a kind of Liebestod for both of them, though,
unlike Wagner and Puccini, Humperdinck seems not to have had the instinct for
theatrical timing that ensures the effectiveness of the various emotional climaxes.
The other limitation probably derives from the opera's origins as continuous
incidental music to the play-version, in which the voices were given a half-
speech, half-musical notation, anticipating Schoenberg's *Pierrot Lunaire*. Much of
the lyricism is in the orchestra, and though Humperdinck never loses contact
with song as an essential element, he often gives his most expressive writing to
instrument rather than voices. In this recording, the singers are partly compensated by being placed well in the foreground, so that the listener feels close to
the characters, as in the theatre. Helen Donath as the goose-girl heroine sings
appealingly when not under pressure or making too much of her pretty wide-

eyed innocence. Adolf Dallapozza brings charm of voice and style to the role of the Prince, Hermann Prey sings finely as the Minstrel and Hanna Schwarz is a vivid and sumptuous-voiced Witch. The smaller parts are strongly cast with the single exception of the Gaoler's daughter, whose harsh tone may nevertheless suit the unsympathetic character. Heinz Wallberg conducts a sensitive and colourful performance. The booklet has no translation of the text, but does contain a clearly posted synopsis in English, with a useful introductory essay.

Jacques Ibert   *Refer to Index*   *French 1890-1962*

Vincent d'Indy   *French 1851-1931*

NEW REVIEW

d'Indy. Poème des rivages, Op. 77. Diptyque méditerranéen, Op. 87. **Monte-Carlo Philharmonic Orchestra/Georges Prêtre.** EMI CDM7 63954-2. From Pathé 270335-1 (2/87).

49'   DDD   3/92

In old age d'Indy gained happiness and contentment from his second marriage. He now lived by the sea, which in its various manifestations inspired the two late works on this disc. Seashores are depicted in *Poème des rivages*, a symphonic suite which is made up of four 'pictures'. These illustrate respectively the Bay of Agay, where d'Indy was impressed by qualities of light and calm, the Island of Majorca, where a dark blue colour predominated, the Adriatic Coast, with its green horizons, and the mysterious Bay of Biscay. D'Indy brings all his superb craftsmanship to this score and his music reflects the varied scenes very effectively. *Diptyque méditerranéen* is a shorter but again highly skilled work in two parts, "Morning Sun" and "Evening Sun". Once more the distinctive light at Agay seems to have been an influence, as well as the mysteries and power of the sea itself. Georges Prêtre conducts idiomatic, expressive performances, but although the Monte Carlo orchestra play in committed fashion one is made aware it is not the most refined body on record. This is not an important drawback, however, and the digital sound is certainly first-class.

NEW REVIEW

d'Indy. La Forêt enchantée, Op. 8ª. Istar, Op. 42ᵇ. Wallenstein — three symphonic overtures after Schiller, Op. 12ᵇ. **Loire Philharmonic Orchestra/ Pierre Dervaux.** EMI CDM7 63953-2. Item marked ª from Pathé 2C 069 16301 (1/81), ᵇ new to UK.

1h   ADD   3/92

The refined art of Vincent d'Indy is well celebrated on this disc. *Istar* comprises a masterly set of symphonic variations on a theme which is only revealed at the end of the work. The variations also tell the tale of Istar, Goddess of Love and War, and her trials in the underworld as she attempts to rescue her lover. *Wallenstein* is a symphonic trilogy based on Schiller's drama set in the Thirty Years War. In the first part, "Wallenstein Camp", we hear rousing martial music from Wallenstein's army camped at Magdeburg. The second part, "Max et Thécla" is a tender love episode, which ends in tragedy with the death of Max. Part three, "Le mort de Wallenstein", is a most eloquent and beautiful elegy. *La Forêt enchantée* is based on a romantic ballad, and is in two parts, "Ride of Warriors through the Forest" and "Song of the Elves". Both parts are rich in colourful, inventive music. The Loire orchestra shows a good deal of skill throughout the programme, and it has just the right timbre for d'Indy's music. The experienced Pierre Dervaux conducts with flair and imagination, and the recording is very good, if not quite of today's best standards.

John Ireland   *Refer to Index*   *British 1886-1979*

Charles Ives   *American 1874-1954*

Ives. ORCHESTRAL WORKS. **New York Philharmonic Orchestra/ Leonard Bernstein.** DG 429 220-2GH. Recorded at performances in Avery Fisher Hall, New York during 1987 and 1988.
Symphony No. 2. The Gong on the Hook and Ladder. Tone Roads — No. 1. A set of 3 Short Pieces — Largo cantabile, Hymn. Hallowe'en. Central Park in the Dark. The Unanswered Question.

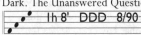 1h 8' DDD 8/90

Although Bernstein thought of Ives as a primitive composer, these recordings reveal that he had an undeniably deep affinity for, and understanding of, Ives's music. The Second Symphony (written in 1902 and first performed in 1951) is a gloriously beautiful work, still strongly rooted in the nineteenth century yet showing those clear signs of Ives's individual voice that are largely missing from the charming but lightweight First Symphony. Bernstein brings out all its richness and warmth without wallowing in its romantic elements, and he handles with utter conviction the multi-textures and the allusions to popular tunes and snatches from Bach, Brahms and Dvořák, to name but a few. The standard of playing he exacts from the NYPO, both here and in the disc's series of technically demanding shorter pieces, is remarkably high with the depth of string tone at a premium — and the engineers retain this to a degree unusual in a live recording. Altogether an essential disc for any collection.

Ives. A Symphony: New England Holidays[b]. The Unanswered Question (orig. and rev. versions)[a]. Central Park in the Dark. [a]**Adolph Herseth** (tpt); **Chicago Symphony** [b]**Chorus and Orchestra/Michael Tilson Thomas.** CBS Masterworks CD42381.

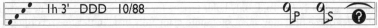 1h 3' DDD 10/88

The essential Charles Ives is here and Tilson Thomas proves a most engrossing guide. *Holidays* is a kind of American *Four Seasons* — one tone-poem per National holiday; each a wonderfully resourceful canvas from the ultimate 'American' composer. There can be no mistaking Tilson Thomas's profound affection for these scores: not least the simple home-spun honesty of the quieter reflective paragraphs — sepia memories of times past. The nostalgic winterscape of "Washington's Birthday" is most beautifully realized. So too are the opening pages of "Decoration Day", as the townsfolk of Danbury, Connecticut, gather for their annual procession to the Civil War veterans' graves. As for those rowdy Ivesian collages, the cacophonous *mêlées* of "Washington's Birthday" and, more notoriously, "The Fourth of July", Tilson Thomas and his CBS engineers have worked wonders with their keen ears and some ingenious sleight of hand at the mixing console. You'll catch more of the 'tunes' than you might have thought possible: internal clarity is most impressive, the tonal depth of the recording likewise. So don't be surprised that the Jew's harp more than holds its own during the demented "barn dance" sequence of "Washington's Birthday"! No less impressive is the conductor's concentrated way with the two remaining pieces — classics of their kind.

Ives. Symphonies — Nos. 1 and 4 (including original hymn settings). **Chicago Symphony Orchestra/Michael Tilson Thomas.** Sony Classical CD44939.

1h 17'   DDD   2/91

It could be worth asking a musical friend to listen to the start of Ives's First Symphony here and (presuming he or she doesn't already know the work) then to identify the composer. It seems almost impossible that anyone would get the answer right, for this tuneful, vigorous music hardly suggests the wild-eyed 'ornery crittur' and iconoclast represented to many listeners by much of Ives's later music; Dvořák, Mahler and Nielsen all flash through the mind, which is significant because all three drew their deepest inspiration from folk music, as did Ives himself. The explanation is that this is an early work written in 1898 as an exercise for music graduation at Yale; but make no mistake, it shows that this composer in his twenties knew a good deal about symphonic writing and (as the slow second movement, complete with Dvořákian cor anglais, demonstrates) about writing melodies as well. The Fourth Symphony with all its wild and wilful complexities is another matter, for the good tunes (which are sometimes those of hymns and Gospel songs) are interwoven with astonishing boldness into a score of daunting individuality and complexity. This disc also includes some of these hymn tunes in their original form with voices with one, however, *Beulah Land*, being an organ solo played on a modern instrument that sounds splendidly authentic. The conductor Michael Tilson Thomas has a proven affinity with Ives's music, and these authoritative performances have a touching strength, while the recording too does justice to some of the most challenging music ever to come out of America.

Ives. Symphony No. 4 (1910-16). **John Alldis Choir; London Philharmonic Orchestra/José Serebrier.** Chandos CHAN8397. From ABRD 1118 (9/85).

33'   ADD   1/86

There are wonderful accounts of the problems, both logistical and musical, involved in mounting a performance of Ives's Symphony No. 4, but the CD buyer has the opportunity with this remarkable performance to ignore all those and concentrate on what the music is about. The sound that results from that hard and dedicated work by so many people is not particularly alien or difficult to understand, however multi-layered or devious it may become. The warm, open expression of the third-movement Fugue, for example, so redolent of Mahler and early Copland, only holds terrors for those too close to it. The complexities of the final movement, not quite made fully lucid in this fine recording, do need some working at by the listener, but the rewards are great: Ives said of it that it was "an apotheosis of the preceding content, in terms that have something to do with the reality of existence and its religious experience". He wrote the Symphony between 1910 and 1916, though it was not performed in its entirety until 1965, and it marked an artistic high-point in his career, containing in its mere 33 minutes much that was best and most revolutionary about his music. This pioneering disc is a must for any collection although it is a pity that Chandos didn't provide a filler.

Ives. Piano Sonata No. 2, "Concord, Mass., 1840-60".
M. Wright. Piano Sonata (1982). **Marc-André Hamelin** (pf). New World NW378-2.

58'   DDD   9/89

From time to time composers dream of a totally free music, transcending
traditional modes of thought, floating on waves of pure untrammelled inspiration

Charles Ives, who seems to have anticipated most European developments by decades, made the dream a remarkable reality. Based on a trial-and-error approach to harmony, notated largely without bar-lines and structured only by the dictates of Ives's inner vision, the *Concord* Sonata attempts to convey the essence of writers associated with the town of Concord, Massachusetts. The music covers a colossal range of mood, from the intrepid philosophical journeys of "Emerson", to the kaleidoscopic variety of "Hawthorne", the homeliness of "the Alcotts" and finally the inner expanses of "Thoreau". Comparison with Beethoven's *Hammerklavier* may seem imprudent, but there is no clearer precedent in the piano repertoire for such a combination of visionary and technical demands. The Canadian pianist, Marc-André Hamelin, is one of the chosen few who can measure up to both aspects and Maurice Wright's Sonata is a by no means negligible fill-up. Both works are excellently recorded. A disc mainly for the adventurous, but the potential rewards of this particular adventure are immense.

NEW REVIEW

Ives. SONGS, Volume 1. **Henry Herford** (bar); **Robin Bowman** (pf). Unicorn-Kanchana DKPCD9111. Texts included.
Ann Street. Berceuse. The Children's Hour. The Circus Band. General William Booth Enters into Heaven. The Housatonic at Stockbridge. Immortality. In Flanders Fields. The Indians. In the Mornin'. Memories, A, Very Pleasant, B, Rather Sad. The New River. Paracelsus. Peaks. Pictures. The See'r. The Sideshow. Swimmers. There is a certain garden. They are there! The Things our Fathers Loved. Tom Sails Away. Two Little Flowers. West London. Where the Eagle. The White Gulls. Yellow Leaves.

1h DDD 9/91

Charles Ives   *[photo: Koch International / Tyler*

For many, the name Charles Ives is synonymous with three things — Ives the innovator and experimentalist, Ives the symphonist and Ives the composer of the kind of fiendishly difficult piano music found in the *Protests* and *Concord* Sonatas. But he was a great miniaturist also, and this is nowhere more evident than in his prolific outpourings of songs. Ives wrote songs like others keep diaries, jotting down ideas as and when they came to him — the inspiration could be great or small, domestic or global but it was always delivered with a considerable amount of care and insight for its subject matter. He also used his songs as sketchbooks for his exploratory techniques, and so one frequently encounters material found in his piano and orchestral works, as is the case in the song *The Housatonic at Stockbridge* which was later to become the third movement (minus voice) of his orchestral work *Three Places in New England*. Subject matters range from meditations and reflections on nature *(Pictures, Yellow Leaves, The White Gulls)*, through to the plight of the American Indians and even some comical observations on the expectant buzz of anticipation as an audience awaits curtain rise in the opera house *(Memories A and B)*. Excellent

performances from Henry Herford and Robin Bowman, who have made
American vocal music (especially Ives) a particular speciality. Good recording.

Leos Janáček *Czech 1854-1928*

Janáček. ORCHESTRAL WORKS[a].
Smetana. THE BARTERED BRIDE — Overture[b].
Weinberger. SCHWANDA THE BAGPIPER — Polka and Fugue[c]. **Pro Arte
Orchestra/Sir Charles Mackerras.** EMI Phoenixa CDM7 63779-2. Items
marked [a] from Pye Golden Guinea GSGC14004 (5/64), [b] CSEM75007 (12/59),
[c] CEM36014 (4/59).
Janáček: Sinfonietta. THE MAKROPOLOUS CASE — Prelude. KATA
KABANOVA — Prelude. FROM THE HOUSE OF THE DEAD — Prelude.
Jealousy.

> 1h 1' ADD 1/91 　　　　　　　　　　　　　　£ ⁹ₚ ▲

It is astonishing to think that a generation ago Janáček was still a little known
composer and that now a recorded programme of Czech music can devote most
of its space to him and use Smetana's *Bartered Bride* Overture as a fill-up! But his
music merits it, and the very first notes blared out by the brass in his *Sinfonietta*
remind us of the strength and originality of this unique musical personality, a
man born in 1854, just 13 years after Dvořák, whose music nevertheless seems
very much of the twentieth century. This is a performance of the *Sinfonietta*
which is unequivocally "red in tooth and claw", as someone wrote when it first
came out — and it sounds truthfully coarse-grained, rich and powerful in a way
that simply defies us to believe that the recording in Walthamstow Town Hall
was made in 1959. A cooler appraisal, if such a thing is desirable with this music
and playing, of course reminds us that there is some inevitable tape hiss, but it
never distracts. In the four operatic preludes (i.e. overtures) the sheer physical
and emotional heat of the playing is quite extraordinary. Indeed, this is music of
utterly abundant life-affirmation played with 110 per cent commitment by an
excellent orchestra under the young Charles Mackerras. The two fillers date from
the same 1959 sessions in London and are no less alive.

Janáček. Sinfonietta. Taras Bulba — rhapsody for orchestra. **Vienna
Philharmonic Orchestra/Sir Charles Mackerras.** Decca 410 138-2DH.
From SXDL7519 (7/81).

> 48' DDD 11/83 　　　　　　　　　　　　　　　　⁹ₛ

This has long been a favourite coupling and in these thoroughly idiomatic performances the effect is spectacular. Of course these are far more than just
orchestral showpieces. Both works were fired by patriotic fervour — *Taras Bulba*
by Czechoslovakia's struggle towards independence, the *Sinfonietta* by the city of
Brno, the composer's adopted home town. Both works display a deep-seated
passion for the basic elements of music and yield unprecedented levels of excitement. To get the most out of *Taras Bulba* you really need all its gory programmatic details (of battles, betrayal, torture and murder) to hand. The *Sinfonietta*
needs no such props; its impact is as irresistible and physically direct as a massive
adrenalin injection. If the listener is to revel in this music a corresponding sense
of abandon in the playing is even more important than precision. The Vienna
Philharmonic supplies a good measure of both and Sir Charles Mackerras's commitment and understanding are second to none, while the high-level recording
captures every detail in vivid close-up.

NEW REVIEW

Janáček. String Quartets[a] — No. 1, "Kreutzer Sonata"; No. 2, "Intimate Letters". Along an overgrown path — Suite No. 1[b]. [b]**Radoslav Kvapil** (pf); [a]**Talich Quartet** (Petr Messiereur, Jan Kvapil, vns; Jan Talich, va; Evzen Rattai, vc). Calliope CAL9699. Items marked [a] from CAL1699 (1/86), [b] CAL9206 (8/88).

Ih 13' DDD 4/89

Janáček's two string quartets stand with those of Bartók, Debussy and Ravel among the supreme masterpieces of the medium, composed during the first half of this century. Both are relatively late works: the *Kreutzer* Sonata dates from 1923 and was inspired by Tolstoy's tragic short story of the same title, depicting a women's disappointment in love both inside and outside marriage. Janáček translates the emotions of Tolstoy's story into music of intense passion. Even more immediate and personal is the Second Quartet entitled *Intimate Letters*, inspired by Janáček's infatuation at the age of 64 for his young pupil Kamila Slösslova. He poured into this quartet all his feelings for her: doubt, release, joy and despair are all graphically portrayed in Janáček's eliptical music. Inference and statement paradoxically give the quartet a wholeness which eludes other more forthright works. The Talich Quartet portray these two similar psycho-dramas with total commitment and devotion. The immense technical difficulties with which Janáček confronts his performers are set aside by the white heat of emotion clearly felt both by performers and composer. The insight of these readings fortunately even overcomes a recording perhaps too dry for Janáček's highly exposed string writing. As a bonus, Radoslav Kvapil gives an idiomatic reading of the first suite from *Along an overgrown path*, written between 1901 and 1908, and marked by the death of his daughter Olga in 1903. These short piano pieces display in embryo many of the stylistic features which were later to reappear in the two quartets. Again the performance is wholly authentic and committed, allowing Janáček's exceptional creativity to shine through without compromise. Again a rather dry recording.

NEW REVIEW

Janáček. PIANO WORKS. **Rudolf Firkušný.**DG 20th Century Classics 429 857-2GC. From 2707 055 (6/72).
Piano Sonata 1.X.1905, "From the street". Along an overgrown path. In the mists. Thema con variazioni, "Zdenka".

Ih 19' ADD 3/91

NEW REVIEW

Janáček. PIANO WORKS. **Josef Páleníček** (pf). Supraphon 10 1481-2. From 111 1481-2 (11/75).
Piano Sonata 1.X.1905, "From the street". Along an overgrown path — Suite No. 1. In the mists.

54' ADD 3/92

NEW REVIEW

Janáček. PIANO WORKS. **Mikhail Rudy.** EMI CDC7 54094-2.
Piano Sonata 1.X.1905, "From the street". Along an overgrown path. In the mists. Reminiscence. Three Moravian Dances.

Ih 19' DDD 3/91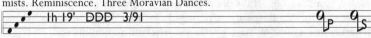

Janáček's only piano sonata has a history almost as dramatic as the events which inspired it. Its subtitle, *From the Street* commemorates a student demonstration in which a 20-year-old worker was killed, an event which so outraged Janáček that he wrote a three movement sonata as an expression of his feelings. Before the première in 1906 he burnt the third movement and after a private performance in Prague he threw the remaining movements into a river. It is only thanks to the pianist, Ludmil Tučkova, who had copied out the first two movements, that the work survives. The three pianists listed above present very different interpretations: the underlying theme of Firkušnyý's approach (who may claim historical authenticity as he studied with Janáček) is anger, turning the first movement into a defiant roar of fury whilst the slow movement has an inherent restlessness, bitterness never far below the surface. Páleníček, much freer in his handling of the music, is more introverted, full of regret as if seeing the events from a greater perspective. It is the young Russian pianist, Mikhail Rudy, however, who is the most reflective, more spacious in design and tempo. He also makes much of the contrapuntal writing, revealing details more usually concealed in Janáček's sumptuous textures.

Much of the same characteristics can be found in the other works common to each recording — *Along an overgrown path* and the masterly *In the mists*. In the former Firkušnyý is the smoother, letting the folk-song element shine through. With Páleníček (who plays only the first, and more interesting series) the delicacy with which he handles Janáček's filigree piano writing is admirable, although occasionally one longs for a little of Firkušnyý's power. But it is Rudy who gives the most insightful account of the work, catching perfectly the fleeting moods of these miniatures under their songful exterior. He does, however, make slightly too much of the detailing in *In the mists*, though the same charge could be brought against Firkušnyý who occasionally overloads these delicate little pieces with dramatic power. Páleníček, giving an unaffected reading is here the most successful. He alone adds no filler, resulting in a disc some 25 minutes shorter than his rivals. Firkušnyý adds the early Theme and Variations, conventionally romantic but impeccably played. Rudy's choice of three *Moravian dances* and a very late work, the *Reminiscence* are vintage Janáček. Programme and playing style may dictate your choice, but all three discs represent playing of the highest class with full notes and tracking details.

Janáček. The diary of one who disappeared[a]. String Quartet No. 1, "Kreutzer Sonata"[b]. [a]**Clara Wirz** (mez); [a]**Peter Keller** (ten); [a]**Lucerne Singers / Mario Venzago** (pf); [b]**Doležal Quartet** (Bohuslav Matousek, Josef Kekula, vns; Karel Doležal, va; Vladimir Leixner, vc). Accord 22031-2.

57' AAD 4/90

Both of these works reflect Janáček's innocently ecstatic love for a woman very much younger than himself, but both are also multi-layered. In the quartet the ostensible subject is Tolstoy's novella about a guilty and ultimately fatal love affair, but Janáček also described the piece as a protest against the subjection of women. The *Diary* is fascinatingly ambiguous, too: the poems on which it is based were published as the work of an unlettered peasant, all that he had left behind after abandoning home, family and friends to follow an alluring gipsy girl. There have been suggestions that the supposed authorship of the poems was a hoax, but their very mysterious anonymity makes it possible to hear the cycle both as a gripping drama and as a dream-like metaphor. That dual quality is finely conveyed in this performance of the *Diary* by a combination of directness (the dusky-voiced and intimately insinuating Clara Wirz is the gipsy Zefka to the life; the 'wordless song' at the centre of the cycle — the original poem consisted of nothing more than three suggestive asterisks — is vividly climactic) and mysterious poetry: the off-stage women's chorus both magical and real. Peter Keller has a light but ardent voice, well-suited to conveying the young man's wonder at what is happening to him and his diction is praiseworthily clear (a pity that only French translations of the Czech texts are provided). The quartet, alas, though performed with impetuous urgency and passion, receives a dry, harsh and nasal recording. But this account of the *Diary* will be a recurring pleasure.

Janáček. JENUFA. **Elisabeth Söderström** (sop) Jenůfa; **Wieslaw Ochman** (ten) Laca; **Eva Randová** (mez) Kostelnička; **Petr Dvorský** (ten) Steva; **Lucia Popp** (sop) Karolka; **Marie Mrazová** (contr) Stařenka; **Václav Zitek** (bar) Stárek; **Dalibor Jedlička** (bass) Rychtar; **Ivana Mixová** (mez) Rychtarka; **Vera Soukopová** (mez) Pastuchyňa, Tetka; **Jindra Pokorná** (mez) Barena; **Jana Janasová** (sop) Jano; **Vienna State Opera Chorus; Vienna Philharmonic Orchestra/Sir Charles Mackerras.** Decca 414 483-2DH2. From D276D3 (9/83).

② 2h 10' DDD 12/85

Lucia Popp   *[photo: EMI*

Janáček's first operatic masterpiece is a towering work which blends searing intensity with heart-stopping lyricism. It tells of Jenůfa and the appalling treatment she receives as she is caught between the man she loves and one who eventually comes to love her. But dominating the story is the Kostelnička, a figure of huge strength, pride and inner resource who rules Jenůfa's life and ultimately kills her baby. Eva Randová's characterization of the role of the Kostelnička is frightening in its intensity but also has a very human core. The two men are well cast and act as fine foils to Elisabeth Söderström's deeply impressive Jenůfa. The Vienna Philharmonic play beautifully and Mackerras directs magnificently. The recording is all one could wish for and the booklet is a mine of informed scholarship.

Janáček. THE CUNNING LITTLE VIXEN. The Cunning Little Vixen orchestral suite (arr. V. Talich)[a]. **Lucia Popp** (sop) Vixen, Young vixen; **Dalibor Jedlička** (bass) Forester; **Eva Randová** (mez) Fox; **Eva Zikmundová** (mez) Forester's wife, Owl; **Vladimir Krejčik** (ten) Schoolmaster, Gnat; **Richard Novák** (ten) Priest, Badger **Václav Zítek** (bar) Harašta; **Beno Blachut** (ten) Pásek; **Ivana Mixová** (mez) Pásek's wife, Woodpecker, Hen; **Libuše Marová** (contr) Dog; **Gertrude Jahn** (mez) Cock, Jay; **Eva Hríbiková** (sop) Frantik; **Zuzana Hudecová** (sop) Pepik; **Peter Saray** (treb) Frog, Grasshopper; **Miriam Ondrášková** (sop) Cricket; **Vienna State Opera Chorus; Bratislava Children's Choir; Vienna Philharmonic Orchestra/Sir Charles Mackerras.** Decca 417 129-2DH2. Notes, text and translation included. From D257D2 (5/82). Item marked [a] new to UK.

② 1h 49' DDD 11/86

Janáček used the most unlikely material for his operas. For *The Cunning Little Vixen* his source was a newspaper series of drawings, with accompanying text, about the adventures of a vixen cub and her escape from the gamekeeper who raised her. The music is a fascinating blend of vocal and orchestral sound — at times ludicrously romantic, at others raw and violent. Sir Charles Mackerras's Czech training has given him a rare insight into Janáček's music and he presents a version faithful to the composer's individual requirements. In the title-role, Lucia Popp gives full weight to the text while displaying all the richness and beauty of her voice. There is a well-chosen supporting cast of largely Czech singers, with the Vienna Philharmonic to add the ultimate touch of orchestral refinement. Decca's sound is of demonstration quality, bringing out all the violent detail of Janáček's exciting vocal and orchestral effects.

NEW REVIEW

Janáček. THE MAKROPOULOS AFFAIR[a]. Lachian Dances[b]. **Elisabeth Söderström** (sop) Emilia Marty; **Peter Dvorský** (ten) Albert Gregor; **Vladimir Krejčík** (ten) Vítek; **Anna Czaková** (mez) Kristina; **Václav Zítek** (bar) Jaroslav Prus; **Zdeněk Svehla** (ten) Janek; **Dalibor Jedlička** (bass) Kolenatý; **Jiří Joran** (bass) Stage technician; **Ivana Mixová** (contr) Cleaning woman; **Beno Blachut** (ten) Hauk-Sendorf; **Blanka Vitková** (contr) Chambermaid; **Vienna State Opera Chorus; Vienna Philharmonic Orchestra/Sir Charles Mackerras;** [b]**London Philharmonic Orchestra/François Huybrechts.** Decca 430 372-2DH2. Notes, text and translation included. Item marked [a] from D144D2 (10/79), [b] SXL6507 (10/71).

② 1h 58' ADD 10/91

Perhaps it was an awareness that old age was overtaking him that prompted the septuagenarian Janáček to base an opera on the subject of immortality. *The Makropoulos Affair* centres around a beautiful opera singer, Emilia Marty, who becomes involved in a prolonged law suit that arose out of an encounter many years earlier. She has managed to hide her age (at 337 she must be the oldest heroine in the history of opera) by changing her name and identity, though always keeping the initials E.M. Though the complexity of the plot makes it a problematic work to stage, *The Makropoulos Affair* works particularly well on record, with a full libretto enabling even those unfamiliar with the work to follow the finer details of the story-line. Elisabeth Söderström gives one of her finest performances as the complex, aloof yet nervous, wary yet calculating, Emilia Marty. Like Janáček's earlier operas, *Jenůfa* and *Katá Kabanová*, the drama centres around a woman but the secondary roles are also very well sung; Václav Zítek gives a forceful account of Prus, the most strongly focused male character in the opera. Special mention must also be made of Beno Blachut, in his sixties when the recording was made, but still in fine voice. His amusing character sketch of the weak Hauk-Sendorf is memorable. Sir Charles Mackerras brings all his experience and love of Janáček's operas to bear, pushing the drama inexorably forward, allowing sharp characterization of the various characters that pass before our eyes (or in this case, ears) without losing the dramatic impetus. The second disc is filled with an account of the *Lachian Dances* played by the London Philharmonic Orchestra under François Huybrechts, satisfactory but rather pedestrian after the brilliance of the opera. Full notes from John Tyrell and translations are included.

80

NEW REVIEW

Janáček. FROM THE HOUSE OF THE DEAD[a]. Mládi[b]. Nursery rhymes[c]. **Dalibor Jedlička** (bar) Goryanchikov; **Jaroslava Janská** (sop) Alyeya; **Jiří Zahradníček** (ten) Luka (Morosov); **Vladimir Krejčík** (ten) Tall Prisoner; **Richard Novák** (bass) Short Prisoner; **Antonín Svorc** (bass-bar) Commandant; **Beno Blachut** (ten) Old Prisoner; **Ivo Zídek** (ten) Skuratov; **Jaroslav Soušek** (bar) Chekunov, Prisoner acting Don Juan; **Eva Zigmundová** (mez) Whore; **Zdeněk Soušek** (ten) Shapkin, Kedril; **Václav Zítek** (bar) Shishkov; **Zdeněk Svehla** (ten) Cherevin, A Voice; **Vienna State Opera Chorus; Vienna Philharmonic Orchestra/Sir Charles Mackerras;** [c]**London Sinfonietta Chorus;** [bc]**London Sinfonietta/David Atherton.**

Decca 430 375-2DH2. Notes, texts and translations included. Item marked [a] from D224D2 (11/80), [bc] D223D5 (4/81).

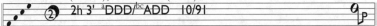

② 2h 3' [a]DDD/[bc]ADD 10/91

Shortly after completing his *Glagolitic* Mass, which scaled the heights of euphoric joy, Janáček plummeted to the depths of despair with his last opera, *From the House of the Dead*, based on a novel by Dostoyevsky and set in a Siberian prison. At first glance it seems an unlikely choice, charting the day to day misery of nameless prisoners largely identified by size or age. Janáček left the story remarkably unchanged, achieving a static quality in his music with evocative orchestration and recurring folk-tunes. In an opera where male voices predominate (there are only two female roles, one of which, the Whore, is very minor), much depends on the performers; here, surely even the composer himself would have been delighted with the results. Sir Charles Mackerras's *Gramophone* award-winning recording of the original version is now 13 years old, but remains unequalled. From the opening notes of the overture the listener is propelled into the high walled bleakness of prison life, chains rattling ominously. The story inspired Janáček to write some of his finest music; all the features of his earlier operas are here, but pared down to a minimum, laying bare the emotional impact of the drama. Much of the music is intentionally ugly, often with huge gaps between treble and bass, suggesting the emptiness of existence. Unusually for Janáček, it is very much an ensemble opera, but the part of Goryanchikov, a political prisoner representing Dostoyevsky's own experiences, stands out: Dalibor Jedlička exudes the right nobility coupled with a pleasing *cantabile* tone. Jaroslava Janská sings the part of Alyeya tenderly and with an endearing straightforwardness. In a recording without weakness it is perhaps unfair to single out individuals but mention must be made of Jiří Zahradníček's fervent characterization of the murderous Luka and Mackerras guides the Vienna Philharmonic Orchestra and Chorus through a reading of great passion and pathos. As a bonus, there are generous fillers of *Mládí* and the *Nursery rhymes*, excellently played by the London Sinfonietta under David Atherton. Whilst less well-known than *Jenůfa* and *Vixen*, this is essential listening for all fans of twentieth-century opera. Texts and translations are provided, along with an enlightening essay by Janáček scholar John Tyrrell.

Janáček. OSUD (sung in English). **Helen Field** (sop) Míla Valková; **Philip Langridge** (ten) Zivný; **Kathryn Harries** (sop) Míla's Mother; **Peter Bronder** (ten) A poet, A student, Hrazda; **Stuart Kale** (ten) Dr Suda; **Welsh National Opera Chorus and Orchestra/Sir Charles Mackerras.** EMI CDC7 49993-2. English text included.

1h 19' DDD 9/90

The story of *Osud* ("Fate") concerns a tragic relationship between a composer (Zivný) and a girl (Míla) whose mother throws both herself and her daughter to their deaths; the composer has produced an unfinished opera about his life with the girl, and as he finished explaining it to a group of his students he too is felled by a blow of fate. Composed in 1904-6, immediately after *Jenůfa, Osud* had to wait more than 50 years for its first production; and it was not until 1984 and David Pountney's staging for English National Opera that opera-goers in Britain realized they had been missing one of Janáček's most inspired works. Philip Langridge played Zivný in that production, and his singing here shows complete identification with and mastery of the role. Indeed, given the cast involved, under the guidance of the master-Janáčekian Sir Charles Mackerras, it should not be surprising that the whole performance radiates conviction and a sense of theatre. EMI's recording quality is superb and there are authoritative notes and a full libretto. Anyone who is allergic to opera in English should perhaps think carefully before buying; otherwise this can be confidently recommended, especially to anyone who thinks there is no such thing as a neglected masterpiece.

Joseph Joachim
Austrian/Hungarian 1831-1907

NEW REVIEW

Joachim. Violin Concerto in Hungarian Style, Op. 11ᵃ. Overtures — Hamlet, Op. 4; Henry IV, Op. 7. ᵃ**Elmar Oliveira** (vn); **London Philharmonic Orchestra/Leon Botstein.** Pickwick IMP Masters MCD27.

1h 14' DDD 8/91

Joachim's friendship with Brahms is well known, as is his standing as one of Europe's greatest violinists and teachers. But Joachim, the composer? These days the only compositions to receive a regular airing are his cadenzas to the Beethoven and Brahms Violin Concertos. His meeting with Brahms in 1853 coincided with a determined effort to make his mark as a composer, but after a decade (during which the works on this disc were written) he ceased to compose altogether, feeling that he could not measure up to Brahms. Well, on the evidence of this disc, perhaps not, but his Violin Concerto was hailed by Tovey as "one of the most important documents of the middle of the nineteenth century" and, predictably, it is one of the most fiendishly difficult to play. Oliveira (a gold medal winner at the 1978 Tchaikovsky Competition in Moscow) copes brilliantly with the demands; only occasionally do you feel the concerto is playing him, not the other way around, and Botstein and the LPO provide spirited support. The *Hamlet* and *Henry IV* Overtures are powerfully evocative rather than programmatic and reflect Joachim's change of allegiance from the Liszt camp to Brahms. A touch of glare apart, the sound is rich and full.

Robert Jones
British, flourished 1597-1615

NEW REVIEW

R. Jones. THE MUSES GARDIN. **Emma Kirkby** (sop); **Anthony Rooley** (lte). Virgin Classics Veritas VC7 91212-2.
What if I seeke for love of thee. Lie downe poore heart. When love on time. Farewel dear love. Love wing'd my hopes. Now what is love. Love is a bable. Loves god is a boy. When will the fountain. Flye from the world. Happy he. Goe to bed sweete Muze. Ite caldi sospiri. If in this flesh. O Thred of life. When I sit reading. Might I redeeme myne errours.

1h 1' DDD 11/91

Robert Jones was his own worst enemy, jealous of Dowland, at war with many of his contemporaries, and probably fuming posthumously at his undervaluation by the late Edmund Fellowes and in *Grove*. Though his songs neither quite scale the heights nor plumb the emotional depths of Dowland's they contain much of real value. This hand-picked selection from Jones's five songbooks makes it clear that in discarding the bath water we should not allow the baby to accompany it. Whilst it is not impossible, it is unlikely that unworthy material could draw forth such wonderfully expressive and committed performances from a singer whose experience in the field of lute-song is as long and distinguished as Emma Kirkby's; Anthony Rooley provides all the support she needs. The path of musical history is strewn with the sincere but unwise assessments of critics, some of which you may recognize as you enjoy this finely recorded recital.

Scott Joplin

American 1868-1917

Joplin. PIANO WORKS. **Dick Hyman** (pf). RCA Victor Gold Seal GD87993.
Maple Leaf Rag. Original Rags. Swipesy. Peacherine Rag. The Easy Winners. Sunflower Slow Drag. The Entertainer. Elite Syncopations. The Strenuous Life. A Breeze from Alabama. Palm Leaf Rag. Something Doing. Weeping Willow. The Chrysanthemum. The Cascades. The Sycamore.

58' ADD 10/89

The Rag is a simple dance form characterized by the device of syncopation, whereby a strong accent is displaced from its expected place on the first beat of the bar to a subsidiary beat. The effect of this is to give a lift or 'swing' to the rhythm. Traditional Negro folk and popular music provided the basis for this form, which in itself was one of the bases for the development of jazz. Scott Joplin was the most skilled composer of rags, and he wrote over 50 pieces between 1899 and 1904. In 1973 the film, *The Sting*, used Joplin's rag *The Entertainer*, and this was a strong element in a revival of his music. Dick Hyman recorded all of Joplin's rags in 1975, and this disc gives us a selection of 16 items. He manages to invest each piece with its own distinct character, and his buoyant, witty playing in a clear but slightly shallow recording is very attractive.

Josquin Desprez

French c.1440-1521

Josquin Desprez. SACRED CHORAL WORKS. **Hilliard Ensemble/Paul Hillier.** EMI CDC7 49960-2. Texts and translations included.
Missa Hercules dux Ferrariae. Pater noster/Ave Maria. Miserere mei Deus. Tu solus qui facis mirabilia. **Gombert:** Lugebat David Absalon.

1h 8' DDD 5/90

Few groups have made as consistent a contribution to early polyphony on disc as the Hilliard Ensemble under its director, Paul Hillier. Some listeners, already familiar with other versions of the *Miserere* may feel this one to be on the slow side but, on the other hand, both here and in the Mass *Hercules dux Ferrariae*, a fine product of the composer's mature period, the Hilliard Ensemble penetrates beyond the surface to reach the heart of the music. And in so doing the singers uncover many precious details and savour many nuances in Josquin's score. With great justification, perhaps, listeners might take issue with the Ensemble

Hilliard Ensemble   *[photo: EMI*

in its somewhat cool performance of the impassioned *Lugebat David Absalon*, probably by Nicolas Gombert (*c.*1500-*c.*1556); but few if any will be other than thrilled by its reading of Josquin's four-part motet *Tu solus qui facis mirabilia*. Thoughtful and thought-provoking performances, sympathetically recorded and accompanied by full texts and translations.

Josquin Desprez. Missa L'homme armé super voces musicales. Missa L'homme armé sexti toni.
Anonymous. L'homme armé. **The Tallis Scholars/Peter Phillips.** Gimell CDGIM019. Text and translation included.

> Ih 14' DDD 7/89

Towards the end of the Middle Ages it became customary to use popular secular melodies instead of the usual plainchant themes as the basis for composing poly-phonic Masses. One such was the fifteenth-century melody *L'homme armé* ("Beware of the armed man"), a melody that may have originated as a crusader song. These settings would provide endless opportunities for a composer to demonstrate his contrapuntal skills. In the first of Josquin's two settings, *Super voces musicales*, he uses the tune over and over again, beginning each time on successive ascending degrees of the six-note scale Ut-Re-Mi-Fa-Sol-La, so that it rises higher and higher as the Mass progresses. Sometimes the melody appears back to front from half way through the piece on to the end. In the *Sexti toni* Mass the tune is transposed so that F rather than G is the final note. The listener's enjoyment is in no way lessened by all this contrapuntal ingenuity. The music flows along with unsurpassed ease and beauty, displaying that unique quality of seeming inevitabil-ity which characterizes all great music. It is well matched by the expertise and enthusiasm of The Tallis Scholars and their first-class recording engineers.

Josquin Desprez. Missa Pange lingua. Missa La sol fa re mi. **The Tallis Scholars/Peter Phillips.** Gimell CDGIM009.

> Ih 2' DDD 3/87

Throughout his long life Josquin Desprez was held in enormous esteem by his contemporaries and of his 18 surviving Masses the two gathered on this disc come from different periods in his life. The *Missa La sol fa re mi* dates from 1502 and, as its name implies, is based on the notes A,G,F,D,E. From this motif the Mass emerges, a technical feat at which Josquin excelled (and of a kind which he often seemed to set himself as a challenge). The repetition of this theme is carried out with such sophistication that one is hardly aware of its recurrence so many times. The *Missa Pange lingua* is a much later work based on the plainchant written for the feast of Corpus Christi. It has a freedom of invention and harmonic richness that, at times, seem to take us far away from the restraints of a theme-based composi-tion. The eight singers of The Tallis Scholars (who, incidentally, use female voices for the soprano line) make a beautiful sound: rich, integrated but always willing to bring out the melodic subtleties presented to them in this most glorious of renaissance music. The recording matches the excellence of the performance.

Giya Kancheli

Georgian 1935-

Kancheli. Symphonies — No. 3 (1973)[a]; No. 6 (1980)[b]. [a]**Gamlet Gonashvili** (ten); [b]**Archil Kharadze,** [b]**Giya Chaduneli** (vas); **Georgia State Symphony Orchestra/Dzansug Kakhidze.** Olympia Explorer OCD401.

> Ih ADD 9/90

Kancheli. Symphonies — No. 4, "In Commemoration of Michaelangelo" (1975); No. 5 (1976). **Georgia State Symphony Orchestra/Dzansug Kakhidze.** Olympia OCD403.

> 51' ADD 4/91

Giya Kancheli is the author of seven symphonies and widely respected amongst Soviet musicians. His homeland is an entirely different entity from Russia, and in its climate, food and customs it is a far cry from most westerners' views of the Soviet Union. Bordering on the Black Sea, Turkey and Armenia, it is a land of starkly contrasted mountains and valleys, which seem to find a parallel in the inner landscape of Kancheli's music. All four symphonies on these discs are single-movement works of around 25 minutes' duration and all commute between poles of profound meditation and violent pulsating energy. In the Fourth and Fifth Symphonies the quiet music is in part a matter of explicitly childlike episodes — music-box-type ideas, or delicate, tuneful fragments of tune on a harpsichord — so that the juxtaposition with blocks of full orchestral sound (sometimes recalling Stravinsky's Russian ballets) registers as a violation of innocence. So, in common with many of his Soviet contemporaries, most famously Schnittke, Kancheli operates with extreme stylistic oppositions. But his musical personality is far more austere and more focused than Schnittke's, and the overall effect of his music is closer to the ritualistic world of the Estonian Arvo Pärt. Each of the symphonies is riveting on first hearing and each grows more and more impressive on repeated listening. Indeed, a claim could be entered for Kancheli as one of the four finest living symphonists (say, with Tippett, Simpson and Sallinen). Dzansug Kakhidze has been a friend and colleague of Kancheli since their student days in the mid-1950s. He draws performances of spellbinding intensity from his excellent Georgian orchestra, and the recordings are vivid and immediate, just as the music demands. For the record it has to be noted that the Third Symphony comes out a whole tone sharp, courtesy of less than state-of-the-art Georgian technology; but the character of the music remains 99% intact. One would hesitate to recommend one disc over the other, except to say that the Fourth Symphony is marginally less memorable than the others.

Jerome Kern

American 1885-1945

Kern. SHOW BOAT. Cast includes **Teresa Stratas, Frederica von Stade, Jerry Hadley, Bruce Hubbard, Karla Burns; Ambrosian Chorus; London Sinfonietta/John McGlinn.** EMI CDS7 49108-2. Notes and text included.

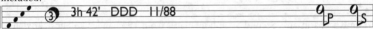

3h 42' DDD 11/88

This three-CD *Show Boat* is a remarkable, inspired achievement that is far from being an example of a musical swamped by the misguided use of operatic voices. *Show Boat* was composed on a large scale for singers of accomplishments far above those we often hear in the theatre today, and here it is given its due. "Make believe", "Ol' man river", "Can't help lovin' dat man", "Why do I love you?" and "You are love" have been sung by countless singers over the years, but in beauty and style the performances here can surely never have been rivalled. The love duets between Frederica von Stade and Jerry Hadley are stunningly beautiful and Bruce Hubbard's firm, honeyed baritone has absolutely nothing to fear from comparisons with Paul Robeson. Teresa Stratas's "Can't help lovin' dat man" is quite ravishing. But the success of this set is due above all to the enthusiasm and dedication of its conductor, John McGlinn. His avowed aim has been to include all the music Kern wrote for the piece over the years for various stage and film productions. Much of this appears in a lengthy and fascinating appendix; but the main text itself includes not only full-length versions of numbers traditionally much shortened but other magnificent items dropped during try-outs and only rediscovered in a Warner Brothers warehouse in 1982. Not least he has restored the original orchestrations of Robert Russell Bennett. The London Sinfonietta clearly revels in them, not least the jazz-flavoured elements of the final Act. The Ambrosian Chorus, too, has a field day in the rousing choral numbers. Bright, spacious recorded sound helps to make this a quite magnificent, quite irresistibly enjoyable achievement.

Aram Khachaturian

Khachaturian. Violin Concerto in D minor (1940).
Tchaikovsky (orch. Glazunov). Méditation, Op. 42 No. 1. **Itzhak Perlman** (vn); **Israel Philharmonic Orchestra/Zubin Mehta.** EMI CDC7 47087-2. From EL270108-1 (3/85).

46' DDD 7/85

The twentieth century has had its share of great violin concertos. Khachaturian's is not quite that, in the sense that it never attempts the heights and depths we find in his Soviet colleagues Prokofiev and Shostakovich; but it is a work of considerable charm, beautifully written. Shostakovich once pointed out that a "national and folk idiom" was evident in everything his friend wrote, and Khachaturian's Armenian origin is agreeably evident in the melodic and harmonic contours of the lilting second theme in the first movement and the *Andante sostenuto* that follows. It goes without saying that Itzhak Perlman plays this work with total technical command and persuasive feeling, and the result is most enjoyable even if one feels in some places, such as the first movement's long cadenza, that musical inspiration is being spread rather thin. The finale, however, is predictably exciting. The Tchaikovsky *Méditation* coupling is well worth having, both for its intrinsic quality and also because it was originally planned as the slow movement of his own Violin Concerto. Good accompaniment from Mehta and the Israel Philharmonic Orchestra and a bright recording.

NEW REVIEW

Khachaturian. Symphony No. 2. Gayaneh — suite. **Royal Scottish Orchestra/Neeme Järvi.** Chandos CHAN8945.
Gayaneh — Sabre Dance; Dance of the Rose Maidens; Lullaby; Lezghinka.

1h 4' DDD 10/91

Aram Khachaturian's Second Symphony dates from 1943 and, like Shostakovich's *Leningrad* Symphony, it deals with the suffering and torment endured by a people at war. With its epic proportions and vivid orchestration, it is never difficult to identify with the true intentions which lie behind the music, as it takes us on a harrowing journey through heroic endurance to final, hard-won victory. Neeme Järvi's recording with the Royal Scottish Orchestra is very fine indeed, and under his direction this work assumes a rare degree of gravity and purpose not matched even by the composer himself in his classic 1962 account with the Vienna Philharmonic. Järvi and his orchestra make the tumultuous opening sound massively intimidating as the grim onslaught of brass and bells summon up a vision of approaching invasion. He is equally fine in the second movement too, with its pulsing rhythms and brilliant Oriental coloration, but the inexorable tread of the invader is never far away, as we discover, in the sombre resignation of the funeral march which follows. The triumph of the finale seems more than a little empty in Järvi's hands, where the very intensity of the music-making forces us to assess the real price of victory. The recording itself has all the advantages of a resonant and brilliant Chandos production and yet it never becomes fierce or oppressive in major climaxes, and every inner detail of the scoring is clearly revealed. The disc also includes excerpts from Khachaturian's ballet score *Gayaneh* with its evocative and ever-popular "Sabre Dance", in a thrilling performance which will be hard to better. This disc does much to enhance the reputation of

Khachaturian's orchestral works and the Royal Scottish Orchestra are to be heard here at their superb best.

Khachaturian. Gayaneh — Sabre dance; Dance of the Rose Maidens; Dance of the Kurds; Lezghinka.
Offenbach/Rosenthal. Gaîté Parisienne — ballet. **Boston Pops Orchestra/Arthur Fiedler.** RCA Victrola VD87734. From SF5036 (9/59).

· 46' ADD 9/89 £ ▲

The Boston Pops are at their best here, in the sort of music they do so well. The four numbers from Khachaturian's *Gayaneh* might have benefited from the inclusion of the Lullaby but, as they stand, they form an effective short suite, played with fire and precision. The ballet, *Gaîté Parisienne*, is a compilation of items by Offenbach, taken from a richly varied array of sources from *The Tales of Hoffman* and *Orpheus in the Underworld*, through to *Le voyage dans la lune* and *Tromb al Cazar* (all, sadly, left undocumented in the minimal insert notes to this issue). Manuel Rosenthal's gloriously over-the-top orchestrations gave the

Arthur Fiedler   *[photo: BMG*

choreographer, Massine, some initial misgivings but, on the recommendation of Stravinsky, he went ahead and created the ballet that was first produced by the Ballet Russe de Monte Carlo in 1938. Percussion and brass are very much in evidence in the score and Fiedler emphasizes their role in this almost manically high-spirited reading. The extreme brightness of the recording, that verges on edginess at times, compounds the effect. The inevitable hiss from the analogue originals is not too intrusive and the whole production is carried along by the sheer vitality and rhythmic drive of the performance.

NEW REVIEW
Khachaturian. Spartacus — ballet[a]. Gayaneh — ballet[a].
Prokofiev. Romeo and Juliet — ballet, Op. 64[b]. [a]**Vienna Philharmonic Orchestra/Aram Khachaturian;** [b]**Cleveland Orchestra/Lorin Maazel.**
Decca Ovation 417 737-2DM. Items marked [a] from SXL6000 (1/63), [b] SXL6620/22 (9/73).
Spartacus — Adagio of Spartacus and Phrygia; Variation of Aegina and Bacchanalia; Scene and dance with Crotala; Dance of Gaditanae and victory of Spartacus. *Gayaneh* — Sabre dance; Aysheh's awakening and dance; Lezghinka; Gayaneh's Adagio; Gopak. *Romeo and Juliet* — Romeo; Juliet as a young girl; Dance of the knights; Balcony scene; Romeo resolves to avenge Mercutio's death; Death of Tybalt; The last farewell.

· 1h 11' ADD £

Pulsating rhythms (many high-speed oompahs) and streamers of highly-spiced colours; not forgetting that lush, sweeping and most yearning of string tunes from the *Spartacus* Adagio (which, for more mature collectors, will be impossible to listen to without memories of an aerial camera circling and panning down broadside onto the resplendent white sea-faring craft of BBC TV's "The Onedin

Line"), and for which the Vienna Philharmonic strings produced their most sensuous tones, appropriately laden with vibrato and slides. The music could be by no one else. This lovable 1962 Khachaturian coupling has transferred well to CD, with increased clarity of texture and dynamic range, though with a loss of bass richness, and with the close balance and exaggerated stereo separation now more obvious. But the extra sharpness of focus also confirms how much the Vienna Philharmonic must have enjoyed these sessions. Timings are generously extended by the inclusion of the *Romeo and Juliet* excerpts from Maazel's complete Cleveland set (Decca 417 510-2DH2, reviewed in the 1992 edition of this *Guide*).

Gideon Klein
Czechoslovakian 1919-1945

NEW REVIEW

Klein. String Trio. Fantasie a Fuga. Piano Sonata[a]. String Quartet, Op. 2.
Ullmann. String Quartet No. 3, Op. 43. **Hawthorne Quartet** (Roman Lefkowitz, Si Jing Huang, vns; Mark Ludwig, va; Sato Knudsen, vc); [a]**Virginia Eskin** (pf). Channel Classics CCS1691.

1h 8' DDD 12/91 ❓

This CD is devoted to music by two Jewish musicians incarcerated in the Theresienstadt ghetto camp established by the Nazis in November 1941. On the evidence of the works recorded here, Gideon Klein and Viktor Ullmann were substantial figures whose music needs no special pleading. In stylistic terms, Ullman is perhaps the more predictable of the two. His Third Quartet shows him remaining true to Schoenbergian expressionism within a tonal context. Klein, deported to the camp at the age of 21, was by all accounts an astonishingly accomplished musician. His own music shows unmistakable signs of potential greatness even if the major influences — including Schoenberg, Janáček and Bartók — are not fully assimilated within a definitive creative profile. The bravely invigorating String Trio, completed only nine days before Klein's disappearance, receives a magnificent performance from members of the Hawthorne Quartet, a group drawn from the Boston Symphony Orchestra. Virginia Eskin gives a powerful account of the hard-hitting Piano Sonata, humming along discreetly as she plays. Channel Classics deserve high praise for these ideally balanced recordings which document a form of spiritual resistance we can barely begin to comprehend.

Zoltán Kodály
Hungarian 1882-1967

NEW REVIEW

Kodály. ORCHESTRAL WORKS. **Philharmonia Hungarica/Antál Dorati.**
Decca Ovation 425 034-2DM. From SXLM6665-7 (9/74).
Háry János Suite. Dances from Galánta. Variations on a Hungarian folk-song, "The Peacock". Dances from Marosszék.

1h 16' ADD

Four of Kodály's most famous and best loved orchestral works on one mid-priced disc is a rare treat. Dorati conduct an exceptionally vivid and colourful account of the *Háry János* suite, and one that really draws the listener into the hero's elaborate and fantastic story telling. Particularly effective are the *Song* (the orchestral version of the love duet of Háry and Orzse from the opera) and the popular *Intermezzo*, both featuring excellent playing from an uncredited cimbalom player. Like his fellow compatriot, Bartók, Kodály was an avid collector and transcriber of Hungarian folk material and there is hardly a work in his output in which his efforts in this field are not put to some use. The *Dances from Marosszék* and the *Dances from Galánta* together with the colourful and highly enjoyable *Peacock* Variations are perhaps three of the finest examples of his use of folk material, and these can be heard in particularly engaging and affectionate performances from the Philharmonia Hungarica. The superb 1974 recordings still sound exceptionally fresh and have transferred well to CD.

Charles Koechlin *Refer to Index* French 1867-1950

Joonas Kokkonen Finnish 1921-

NEW REVIEW

Kokkonen. Cello Concerto[a]. Symphonic Sketches. Symphony No. 4. [a]**Torleif Thedéen** (vc); **Lahti Symphony Orchestra/Osmo Vänskä.** BIS CD468.

• 1h 2' DDD 12/91

Joonas Kokkonen [photo: Anderson]

The Finnish composer Joonas Kokkonen belongs to the same generation as Robert Simpson and Peter Racine Fricker in England, and first came to wider attention in the 1960s with his Third Symphony. His style is essentially neoclassical and he has fully assimilated the influences of Hindemith and Bartók without resembling either. His music has an unfailing sense of logic and a finely disciplined craftsmanship to commend it and the three works recorded on this disc form an admirable introduction to his art. The Cello Concerto, composed shortly after the death of his mother, has a strong elegiac element particularly in the slow movement. The *Adagio* is obviously deeply-felt even though its main idea rather overstays its welcome and the emotional effect is weakened. The remarkable young Swedish soloist Torleif Thedéen, still in his twenties at the time of this recording, plays superbly; indeed he must be one of the finest cellists of his generation now before the public. His account has an eloquence, all the more powerful for being understated and restrained. The *Symphonic sketches* (1968), written immediately after the Third Symphony, possess that powerful forward current and logical development that characterize this composer at his best. And the three-movement fourth Symphony also makes a powerful impression. The playing of the Lahti Symphony Orchestra for Osmo Vänskä is alert and responsive, and the BIS recording team certainly do justice to them. The balance is exemplary and there is just the right amount of air around the instruments.

Erich Wolfgang Korngold   *Austrian/Hungarian 1897-1957*

NEW REVIEW

Korngold. Baby Serenade, Op. 24. Cello Concerto, Op. 37[a]. Symphonic
Serenade, Op. 39. [a]**Julius Berger** (vc); **North West German Philharmonic
Orchestra/Werner Andreas Albert.** CPO 999 077-2.

1h 6' DDD/ADD 10/91

NEW REVIEW

Korngold. Symphony in F sharp minor, Op. 40. Theme and Variations,
Op. 42. Straussiana. **North West German Philharmonic Orchestra/
Werner Andreas Albert.** CPO 999 146-2.

1h 8' DDD/ADD 10/91

These are two extremely useful CDs which bring together all of Korngold's post-
war music, when he was trying to re-establish himself in Europe and escape his
acquired reputation as a master composer of film music. All of Korngold's music
to a greater or lesser degree has similar characteristics: virtuoso orchestration
which always surprises and delights, memorable lyricism which combines
optimism and regret in similar quantities (a quality shared with his beloved
Johann Strauss) and rhythmic dynamism which creates tremendous forward
motion. The first CD kicks off with the 1928 *Baby Serenade* written to mark the
birth of his second son George, who later repaid the compliment by initiating
the renaissance of his father's music in the 1960s and 1970s. With a breezy banjo
and three vigorous saxophones there is more than a hint of America and jazz in
this entertaining piece. The Cello Concerto, which receives a committed
performance of the solo part from Julius Berger, is a reworking of the music for
a major Bette Davis vehicle of 1946 entitled *Deception*. Like all his film music it
is both memorable and atmospheric — indeed a miniature masterpiece of only
16 minutes in length. The Symphonic Serenade was premièred by no less than
Wilhelm Furtwängler and the Vienna Philharmonic in December 1950; but
despite its similarity in mood to Richard Strauss's *Metamorphosen*, it failed to
establish itself in the repertoire. Werner Andreas Albert's well prepared and
sympathetic reading makes up for this extraordinary situation.

Like the Serenade, Korngold's greatest post-war work, the Symphony in F
sharp was simply out of its time when completed in 1952 — it had to wait for
over a decade for its first public performance. In a bizarre way it merges the
sound worlds of Mahler and the large-scale Hollywood extravaganza — the tragic
Adagio rises to several impassioned climaxes using themes from the film *Anthony
Adverse*. A great work, which like all of Korngold's music, including the
scintillating final orchestral pieces, Theme and Variations and *Straussiana*, should
now come into their own as historical taste and influence can be put to one side.
All the performances by the North West German Philharmonic Orchestra under
Albert are fully up to Korngold's considerable demands, and CPO's recordings
are warmly atmospheric with particularly well-judged balance throughout. Highly
recommended.

Leopold Koželuch   *Refer to Index*   *Bohemian/Austrian 1747-1818*

Anton Kraft   *Refer to Index*   *Bohemian 1749-1820*

Johann Ludwig Krebs

German 1713-1780

Krebs. CHORALE AND FANTASIAS. [a]**William Bennett** (fl); [b]**Neil Black** (ob/ob d'amore); [c]**Michael Laird** (tpt/clarino); [d]**Michael Thompson** (hn); **Peter Hurford** (org). Argo 430 208-2ZH. Played on the organ of Gloucester Cathedral.

Es ist gewisslich an der Zeit (*c.*1743)[d]. Fantasia in C major[a]. Fantasia in F minor[b]. Fantasia on "Wachet auf"[c]. Fantasias[b] — No. 1 in F major; No. 2 in F major. Gott der Vater wohn uns bei (1745)[c]. Herr Jesu Christ, meins Lebens Licht (1743)[c]. Herzlich lieb hab ich dich, o Herr (1743)[c]. In allen meinen Taten (*c.*1743)[c]. Jesu, meine Freude (1743)[d]. Meine Seel, ermuntre dich (1751)[b]. O Gott, du frommer Gott (1742)[b]. Treuer Gott, ich muss dir klagen (*c.*1746)[b]. Wachet auf, ruft uns die Stimme[c] — versions I, II and III (1743).

· 1h 4' DDD 9/91

This disc contains a selection of Lutheran chorales and fantasies for organ with a solo instrument. A few of Krebs's contemporaries treated Lutheran hymn tunes in a similar way but none succeeded to the extent demonstrated by this gifted pupil of J.S. Bach. Many of the chorale melodies will be familiar to readers acquainted with Bach's organ music and church cantatas and few will be disappointed by the inventive character of the fantasias. One of the finest of these is the Fantasia in F minor, happily included in Peter Hurford's recital. Here the chosen partner to the organ is the oboe, beautifully played by Neil Black. All the performers turn in polished performances though there is a lack of unanimity in matters of style. Neil Black's restrained playing with its tightly controlled vibrato, for example, is in stark contrast to the wide vibrato and greater romanticism of William Bennett's flute playing. Peter Hurford is a stylish interpreter and the organ of Gloucester Cathedral sounds magnificent. Fine recorded sound and informative notes.

Fritz Kreisler *Refer to Index*

Austrian 1875-1962

Franz Krommer

Bohemian 1759-1831

Krommer. WIND OCTETS. **Sabine Meyer Wind Ensemble** (Sabine Meyer, Reiner Wehle, cls; Diethelm Jonas, Thomas Indermühle, obs; Bruno Schneider, Klaus Frisch, hns; George Klütsch, Sergio Azzolini, bns; Klaus Lohrer, cbn). EMI CDC7 54383-2.
F major, Op. 57; E flat major, Op. 71; C major, Op. 76; B flat major, Op. 78.

· 1h 9' 5/92

Born in Czechoslovakia as František Kramář, this composer changed his name to Krommer when he lived in Vienna. Though a contemporary of Mozart, he outlived Beethoven and Schubert and was a major Viennese figure in his time, although to compare him to Haydn (as a contemporary did in 1813) is going too far, for to judge from what we know of his enormous output of music he was a fluent, gifted musician but no genius. The music played here was published under various names, such as partita and Harmonie-musik, which suggest suites for wind players, and although the intended scoring remains unclear the sound of the Sabine Meyer Wind Ensemble is completely convincing. This is the kind of repertory that we hardly ever hear in the concert hall, and we are lucky to have it on record although, to be candid, it earns performance less for its own merit than because it provides a splendid vehicle for fine players. Nevertheless, the performances here will give much satisfaction if you can derive sufficient delight from the artistry of the playing and do not expect too much of the works themselves, and though depth may be lacking in Krommer's music, there is vigour, wit and charm. These qualities are demonstrated most fully in the E flat major and F major Octets which comes third and fourth in this programme. The playing of this fine ensemble is unfailingly stylish, while the recording does justice to its tone and is well balanced.

György Kurtág *Refer to Index* *Romanian 1926-*

Michel Lalande *French 1657-1726*

NEW REVIEW

Lalande. Dies irae, S31. Miserere mei Deus secundum, S27. **Linda Perillo, Patrizia Kwella** (sops); **Howard Crook** (alto); **Herve Lamy** (ten); **Peter Harvey** (bass); **Chorus and Orchestra of La Chapelle Royale/Philippe Herreweghe.** Harmonia Mundi HMC90 1352.

⸬ 1h 2' DDD 12/91

Grands motets are sacred compositions for solo voices and chorus with instruments which epitomize an aspect of courtly life at Versailles during the reign of Louis XIV, the 'Sun King'. Lalande and his older contemporary Charpentier in their very different ways brought the *grand motet* to an expressive peak. The two works on this disc are especially fine examples of Lalande's skill in this sphere of composition. The *Dies irae* contains some wonderfully descriptive movements from among which we might single out the declamatory "Tuba mirum" whose music breathes the air of the opera house, and the chromatic, tenderly affecting "Lacrimosa". The *Miserere* continues a prevailing C minor tonality and, like the *Dies irae* is a grief-laden utterance. Philippe Herreweghe and the Choir of La Chapelle Royale give fervent performances and there are strong contributions above all from Howard Crook and Linda Perillo. The recording is clear and spacious and the accompanying booklet contains full texts with translations.

Lalande. Te Deum, S32. Super flumina. Confitebor tibi, Domine. **Véronique Gens, Sandrine Piau, Arlette Steyer** (sops); **Jean-Paul Fouchécourt, François Piolino** (tens); **Jérôme Corréas** (bass); **Les Arts Florissants/ William Christie.** Harmonia Mundi HMC90 1351. Texts and translations included.

⸬ 1h 4' DDD 7/91

Lalande was the greatest court musician of his generation and a gifted composer of *grands motets*, some 64 of which survive. William Christie has chosen three of them for his recording and in varying ways they illustrate Lalande's considerable strengths when working in this medium. These performances are full of affecting gestures, and telling insights to the music and it is all stylishly interpreted though some listeners might take issue over details. Christie's shaping of phrases is eloquent and his articulation crisp though the latter is not always helpfully served by a recording which tends to diffuse the larger sound of singers and instruments rather than focus it. There are some notable solo contributions, outstanding among which is that of the soprano, Sandrine Piau; she is well-matched by another soprano, Véronique Gens though the *haute-contre* or high tenor, Jean-Paul

Fouchécourt, sounds a little strained in his uppermost notes. A rewarding disc in spite of a few rough edges in both singing and playing.

Edouard Lalo
French 1823-1892

NEW REVIEW

Lalo. Cello Concerto in D minor[a].
Saint-Saëns. Cello Concerto in A minor, Op. 33[b].
Schumann. Cello Concerto in A minor, Op. 129[a]. **János Starker** (vc);
London Symphony Orchestra/[a]**Stanislaw Skrowaczewski,** [b]**Antál
Dorati.** Mercury 432 010-2MM. Items marked [a] from Philips SAL3482 (3/65), [b] SAL3559 (7/66).

1h 5' ADD 4/92 £ 9 p

János Starker recorded for the Mercury label on several occasions during the 1960s, and the results provide a vivid document of an extraordinary artist heard at the peak of his career. Starker's outward intensity belies a formidable intellectual mastery of Schumann's Cello Concerto, a work whose tangible mood of paranoia and mingled heroism has perplexed generations of players and listeners alike. Interpretations as zealous and charismatic as this are certainly to be treasured, as much for a clarification of the composer's intention, as for the valiant heroism of Starker's playing. He brings a similar clear-sighted gravity of purpose to the Lalo concerto, with a suitably massive opening movement contrasted effectively by a charmingly realized intermezzo and a finale of quicksilver brilliance. The sheer dynamism and drama of this reading has never been bettered, and Starker also succeeds in making Saint-Saëns's First Concerto sound a good deal more substantial than it really is, in a reading of exemplary mastery coupled with scrupulous attention to every requirement of the score. Mercury's original masters traditionally set new standards of fidelity and dynamic range, but in their digitally refurbished form it seems scarcely possible that these classic performances are now almost 30 years old, whilst from a musical standpoint, these individual and occasionally provocative readings remain as enthralling as ever.

NEW REVIEW

Lalo. Symphonie espagnole, Op. 21.
Saint-Saëns. Introduction and Rondo capriccioso, Op. 28.
Vieuxtemps. Violin Concerto No. 5 in A minor, Op. 37. **Shlomo Mintz** (vn); **Israel Philharmonic Orchestra/Zubin Mehta.** DG 427 676-2GH. Recorded at performances in the Frederic R. Mann Auditorium, Tel Aviv in October 1988.

1h DDD 3/92

For violin lovers who want a change from the great concertos of Mendelssohn, Beethoven and Brahms, this captivating collection of lighter, but no less distinctive fare, could be just the thing. Lalo's *Symphonie espagnole* gets the substantial performance it deserves: Shlomo Mintz plays the piece with fine panache, his sweet-toned phrasing always conveying the excitement and sheer enjoyment of this colourful music. Zubin Mehta and the Israel Philharmonic bring keen rhythmic attack to the *Carmen*-like tuttis and pin-point accuracy and tonal balance to the lively orchestration (in the Intermezzo Mehta matches Mintz in his outstanding handling of Lalo's complex cross-rhythms). The Vieuxtemps is no less successful. Composed in 1861, the Fifth Concerto is a comparatively short but rewarding work in the Paganini mould, with a moody, bittersweet aspect which Mintz captures perfectly. Again, there's an almost insolent ease in the way he tackles all these double stops, scales and portamentos. All great virtuosos revel in Saint-Saëns's *Introduction and Rondo capriccioso* and Mintz is no exception. Mehta and the Israel Philharmonic also give Mintz a run for his money in the richly sounded big tuttis. The recording is slightly larger than life with plenty of inner clarity. The overall balance perhaps works best in the Lalo but the general sound quality is very satisfying.

Constant Lambert
British 1905-1951

NEW REVIEW

Lambert. Rio Grande[a]. Summer's Last Will and Testament[b]. Aubade héroïque. [a]**Sally Burgess** (mez); [b]**William Shimell** (bar); [a]**Jack Gibbons** (pf); [a]**Opera North Chorus;** [b]**Leeds Festival Chorus; English Northern Philharmonia/ David Lloyd-Jones.** Hyperion CDA66565. Texts included.

• 1h 15' DDD 6/92 ❓

Constant Lambert was a man of so many talents — conductor, writer, speaker (not merely social but professional, as in the first recording of Walton's *Façade*) — that in his own lifetime it was not always clear how far his greatest gift lay in composition. Even the success of his *Rio Grande* in 1928 hindered him from being taken quite seriously, for, although it was (as the *Musical Times* reported) "the hit of the season", it was also the work of a 22-year-old, brilliant but modish, and considered "a hotch-potch of good and bad" rather than a sound and solid achievement. When *Summer's Last Will and Testament* appeared in 1936 it disappointed those who hoped for another *Rio Grande*, and failed to satisfy the serious ones who wanted something more 'difficult' and 'progressive' in idiom. It became, in Malcolm Arnold's words, "one of the undiscovered treasures of the English choral repertoire" and so remained, for many listeners, until the issue of this excellent recording. What this reveals is a work of varied moods, including the desperate seriousness of black comedy, and of unvarying distinction. It draws its title and text from Thomas Nashe's entertainment written after the plague in 1592, and Lambert incorporates "Spring, the sweet spring" and "Adieu, farewell, earth's bliss", the two best-known lyrics, interposing the *Rondo Burlesca* or "King-Pest", most original of the movements. David Lloyd-Jones conducts a performance which is both powerful and sensitive, and he also gives an additional tautness to the *Rio Grande*, in which Jack Gibbons (a Gershwin specialist) is the outstanding pianist. The third work, *Aubade héroïque*, is an elegiac piece of great beauty, written after Lambert and the Sadlers Wells Ballet Company had been trapped in Holland after the German invasion in 1940. This issue should correct once and for all the notion that Lambert was anything other than an extraordinary and multifarious talent.

Orlando Lassus
Franco/Flemish 1532-1594

Lassus. SACRED CHORAL WORKS. **The Tallis Scholars/Peter Phillips.** Gimell CDGIM018. Texts and translations included.
Missa Osculetur me. Motets — Osculetur me; Hodie completi sunt; Timor et tremor; Alma Redemptoris mater a 8; Salve regina mater a 8; Ave regina caelorum Il a 6; Regina coeli a 7.

• 49' DDD 7/89

The Tallis Scholars have produced another winner with this recording, performing a fairly recently discovered and relatively unknown masterpiece: the melliflu-

The Tallis Scholars   *[photo: Gimell/Barda]*

ous *Missa Osculetur me*, built on the composer's own motet of the same title. The Mass, with its two alternating and interlocking choirs and its two solo quartets, presents a fascinating study in the use of vocal textures. Indeed, this is equally true of the motets, variously scored for six, seven and eight voices. The Pentecost motet *Hodie completi sunt*, sung by men's voices, is particularly effective. It bursts into its final "alleluias" after a sustained crescendo of tremendous power. The weirdly chromatic *Timor et tremor* presents a rich, full sound, lightened when the sopranos indulge in lively syncopation towards the end. Such variety is exploited to the full by the Scholars: the listener can hear each strand of the web, and enjoy not only the final blend but also the sheer quality of each and every voice.

Antonio Lauro   *Venezuelan 1917-1986*

NEW REVIEW

Lauro. GUITAR WORKS. **Jesus Castro Balbi** (gtr). Etcetera KTC1110. Suite Venezolana. Carora. El Marabino. Variaciones sobre un Tema Infantil Venezolano. Cuatro Valses Venezolanos. Sonata. Tripitco. Maria Luisa. Angostura.

Ih DDD 11/91

Among the ethnic ingredients of South American music it is the Spanish one which predominates in Venezuela, particularly evident in the juxtaposition of 3/4 and 6/8 times (the hemiola), characteristic of many of the renaissance dances taken there by the Spanish conquerors, *c.*1500. The many *valses* of Antonio Lauro owe more to this inheritance than to the Viennese waltz, though their melodies are scarcely less winsome than those of Strauss; several are named after members of Lauro's family or after places in his own country. The *Suite Venezolano* is 'regional' only in its first movement, a depiction of the people from one area who chatter incessantly. A few of his guitar works, here the Sonata and the Variations, are cast in European moulds but their accent is Venezuelan — the slow movement of the Sonata is a *canción* (song), the last a *bolera*. Lauro's music was never more seductively played than by the composer himself but, as he is no longer able to do so, Balbi makes a very satisfying substitute in this clearly recorded selection of polished, charming and tuneful music.

Ludwig Lebrun   *Refer to Index*   *German 1752-1790*

Jean-Marie Leclair

Leclair. FLUTE SONATAS. **Barthold Kuijken** (fl); **Wieland Kuijken** (va da gamba); **Robert Kohnen** (hpd). Accent ACC58435/6D. From ACC8435/6 (7/85).
ACC58435D — Op. 1: No. 2 in C major. Op. 2: No. 1 in E minor; No. 3 in C major; No. 5 in G major. *ACC58436D* — Op. 1: No. 6 in E minor. Op. 2: No. 8 in D minor; No. 11 in B minor. Op. 9: No. 2 in E minor; No. 7 in G major.

② 50' 59' DDD 2/86

Leclair's Flute Sonatas are technically among the most advanced of their period; only Bach's make comparable demands on the soloist. The music is subtle and much of its charm lies in the successful assimilation and juxtaposition of French and Italian styles. In Leclair's hands the "reunion of tastes" is considerably and brilliantly advanced. Fast movements are outwardly clad in Italian dress, yet French dance measures sometimes lie concealed within. Slow movements are usually of a more overtly French character brought out in ornamentation, gesture and the rhythmic inflexions of courtly dances such as the menuet and gavotte. Kuijken gives fluent and stylistically assured performances, chasing the elusive qualities of the music with unhurried grace and a warm rounded tone. His is a baroque flute and on occasion he is inclined to be smothered by an over-assertive continuo team; but Kuijken's feeling for gesture, his informed use of unequal rhythms and his quietly passionate affair with this great flute literature assures performances that are enduringly satisfying.

Leclair. SCYLLA ET GLAUCUS. **Donna Brown** (sop) Scylla; **Howard Crook** (ten) Glaucus; **Rachel Yakar** (sop) Circé; **Catherine Dubosc** (sop) Dorine, Sicilian girl; **Françoise Golfier** (sop) Cupid; **Agnès Mellon** (sop) Venus; **René Schirrer** (bar) Licas; **Elisabeth Vidal** (sop) Temire; **André Murgatroyd** (ten) Propetide I; **Nicolas Robertson** (ten) Propetide II; **Philip Salmon** (ten) Shepherd; **Elizabeth Priday** (sop) Shepherdess; **Richard Stuart** (bar) Sylvan; **Francis Dudziak** (bar) Hecate, Sylvan; **Monteverdi Choir; English Baroque Soloists/John Eliot Gardiner.** Erato 2292-45277-2. Notes, text and translation included.

③ 2h 50' DDD 4/88

Leclair was foremost an instrumental composer and *Scylla et Glaucus* was his sole contribution to the French operatic stage. There are three principal characters in the drama and they have been strongly cast in Donna Brown (a warmly appealing Scylla), Howard Crook (effortlessly negotiating the highest reaches of his tessitura) and in Rachel Yakar (as Circé). Circé is Leclair's most colourful role and the potency of her magic is vividly captured in the music of Act 4. The Monteverdi Choir and English Baroque Soloists under the informed and lively direction of John Eliot Gardiner set the seal on a splendid achievement. The recorded sound is clear and a full libretto is legibly presented in the accompanying booklet.

Franz Lehár

Lehár. DIE LUSTIGE WITWE. **Josef Knapp** (bar) Baron Mirko Zeta; **Hanny Steffek** (sop) Valencienne; **Eberhard Waechter** (bar) Graf Danilo Danilowitsch; **Elisabeth Schwarzkopf** (sop) Hanna Glawari; **Nicolai Gedda** (ten)

Camille Rosillon; **Kurt Equiluz** (ten) Vicomte Cascada; **Hans Strohbauer** (ten) Raoul de St Brioche; **Franz Böheim** (buffo) Njegus; **Philharmonia Chorus and Orchestra/Lovro von Matačić.** EMI CDS7 47178-8. Notes, text and translation included. From Columbia SAN101/2 (5/63).

② 1h 20' AAD 4/86 **B**

The Merry Widow contains some marvellous melodies and although versions have come and gone none have ever managed to oust the classic 1962 recording with Elisabeth Schwarzkopf. She is a merry widow without equal, conveying with her rich and alluring voice the ebullience and glamour of the character as in no other recording. EMI's preference for a baritone (rather than tenor) Danilo in successive recordings has not always been successful, but here Eberhard Waechter encompasses the role without difficulty and gives a rousing portrayal of the play-boy embassy *attaché*. As the second couple, Nicolai Gedda is in typically radiant voice, whilst Hanny Steffek makes a charming and vibrant Valencienne. Josef Knapp is a spirited ambassador. If von Matačić's tempos are at times a little on the fast side, this is fully justified by the extra excitement achieved. At the same time there are moments of tenderness, as in the beautifully paced "Vilja" song, which comes off to perfection with Schwarzkopf's beautifully held final note. The contribution of the "Königliche-Pontevedrinische Hof-Tamburrizzakapelle" to provide authentic Balkan atmosphere at Hanna's party is just one of the delightful touches of Walter Legge's production that go to make this a very special recording. The pity is that the score is given less than absolutely complete and that the CD changeover comes in the middle of Act 2. However, the artistry and sheer enjoyment of the recording are unmatched. It is one of those occasions when everything seems to come off perfectly.

Kenneth Leighton   *Refer to Index*   *British 1929-1989*

Ruggero Leoncavallo   *Italian 1857-1919*

Leoncavallo. PAGLIACCI[a]. **Joan Carlyle** (sop) Nedda; **Carlo Bergonzi** (ten) Canio; **Giuseppe Taddei** (bar) Tonio; **Ugo Benelli** (ten) Beppe; **Rolando Panerai** (bar) Silvio.
Mascagni. CAVALLERIA RUSTICANA[a]. **Fiorenza Cossotto** (mez) Santuzza; **Adriane Martino** (mez) Lola; **Carlo Bergonzi** (ten) Turiddu; **Giangiacomo Guelfi** (bar) Alfio; **Maria Gracia Allegri** (contr) Lucia; **Chorus and Orchestra of La Scala, Milan/Herbert von Karajan.**
OPERA INTERMEZZOS. **Berlin Philharmonic Orchestra/Herbert von Karajan.** DG 419 257-2GH3. Notes, texts and translations included. Items marked [a] from SLPM139205/07 (10/66), [b] SLPM139031 (6/69).
Verdi: La traviata — Prelude, Act 3. *Puccini*: Manon Lescaut — Intermezzo. Suor Angelica — Intermezzo. *Schmidt*: Notre Dame — Intermezzo. *Massenet*: Thaïs — Meditátion (with Michel Schwalbé, vn). *Giordano*: Fedora — Intermezzo. *Cilea*: Adriana Lecouvreur — Intermezzo. *Wolf-Ferrari*: I gioiello della Madonna — Intermezzo. *Mascagni*: L'amico Fritz — Intermezzo.

③ 3h 18' ADD 10/87 **B**

Cav and Pag as they are usually known have been bedfellows for many years. Lasting for about 75 minutes each, they have some similarities. Both works concern the passions, jealousies and hatred of two tightly-knit communities — the inhabitants of a Sicilian town and the players in a travelling troupe of actors. *Cavalleria rusticana* ("Rustic chivalry") concerns the triangular relationship of mother, son and his rejected lover. Played against a rich musical tapestry,

Carlo Bergonzi   [photo: Decca

sumptuously orchestrated, the action is played out during the course of an Easter day. Bergonzi is a stylish, ardent Turiddu whose virile charms glitter in his every phrase and Fiorenza Cossotto makes a thrilling Santuzza motivated and driven by a palpable conviction; her contribution to the well-known Easter hymn scene is gripping. But the real hero of the opera is Karajan, whose direction of this powerful work is magnificent. Conviction and insight also instil *Pagliacci* with excitement and real drama. A troupe of actors arrive to give a performance of a *commedia dell'arte* play. The illustration of real love, life and hatred is portrayed in the interplay of Tonio, Silvio, Nedda and her husband Canio. As the two rivals, Bergonzi and Taddei are superb. Taddei's sinister, hunchbacked clown, gently forcing the play-within-the-play closer to reality until it finally bursts out violently is a masterly assumption, and Karajan controls the slow build-up of tension with a grasp that few conductors could hope to equal. The Scala forces respond wholeheartedly and the 1965 recording sounds well. The third disc is filled by a selection of very rich, very soft-centred opera intermezzos.

Anatoli Liadov   Russian 1855-1914

Liadov. ORCHESTRAL WORKS. **Slovak Philharmonic Orchestra/ Stephen Gunzenhauser.** Marco Polo 8 220348.
Baba-Yaga, Op. 56. Intermezzo in B flat major, Op. 8 No. 1. Pro starinu — Ballade in D major, Op. 21b. The enchanted lake, Op. 62. Village scene by the inn — Mazurka, Op. 19. Nénie, Op. 67. Polonaise, Op. 49. Polonaise in D major, Op. 55. Kikimora, Op. 63. From the Apocalypse, Op. 66.

> 58'   DDD   10/86   ?

Liadov was a superb miniaturist and as a professor of composition at the St Petersburg Conservatory he had an interestingly potent influence on the music of his younger contemporaries. His finest works are jewel-like in the depth and luminosity of colour they embody and the finesse with which they are worked. His short tone-poem, *The enchanted lake*, immediately establishes in a few delicate strokes the dank mystery of his subject; *Baba-Yaga* conjures up in only three minutes the menace of the mythical witch in flight; *Kikimora*, so well admired by Stravinsky, summons from out of hushed menace the demon wife of the house spirit, Domovoi. Listening to Liadov's works in succession highlights his problem with more protracted formal structures, but a programme such as this one is worth dipping into for the choice morsel or two. Each of these performances drives straight to the heart of the mood Liadov has in mind and the recording more than adequately captures the sparkle and solidity of the orchestral sound. For anyone interested in Liadov or the flowering of late-romanticism in music, this disc is well worth sampling.

Gyorgy Ligeti

NEW REVIEW

Ligeti. String Quartet No. 1.
Lutoslawski. String Quartet.
Schnittke. Kanon in memoriam I. Stravinsky. **Hagen Quartet** (Lukas Hagen, Rainer Schmidt, vns; Veronika Hagen, va; Clemens Hagen, vc). DG 431 686-2GH.

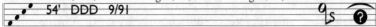

54' DDD 9/91

You won't find Ligeti and Lutoslawski subscribing to the conventional view of the string quartet as requiring four 'symphonic' movements. Ligeti's extended single movement has 17 kaleidoscopically-interacting sub-sections, and Lutoslawski's two main sections are also mosaic-like in form, with a wide variety of different ideas emerging and, on occasion, conflicting. Both quartets — not least because they are superbly imagined for the medium, and finely played on this disc — make fascinating listening, and Ligeti's subtitle ("Nocturnal Metamorphoses") would not be wholly inappropriate for the Lutoslawski as well. There's a dark quality, many rustlings and flickerings, which Ligeti balances against a more fantastic, sardonic tone, and which Lutoslawski leads into both highly dramatic and poignantly lyrical regions. The Ligeti is an early work, beholden to Bartók but bursting with its own very definite ideas about both form and content. The Lutoslawski is more mature, less adventurous, but far from cautious either. With Schnittke's austere, grief-stricken tribute to Stravinsky as a bonus, and with admirably natural yet spacious recorded sound, this is a disc which anyone sceptical about the rewards of modern chamber music can approach with confidence.

NEW REVIEW

Ligeti. VOCAL WORKS. **Groupe Vocale de France/Guy Reibel.** EMI CDC7 54096-2.
Lux aeterna (1966). Drei Phantasien (1982). Loneliness (1946). Pápainé (1953). Night (1955). Morning (1955). Three Hungarian études (1983). Three Hungarian Folk-songs. Mátraszentimre songs (1955). Pietykazo asszonyok. Haj, ifjuság!.

54' DDD 10/91

This disc brings together, with the exception of a few early unpublished works, all of Ligeti's unaccompanied choral works to date. The most familiar item for many listeners will be *Lux aeterna*, which became famous as part of the soundtrack for the cult movie *2001: A Space Odyssey*. For many people it was their first introduction to the strange, atmospheric sounds of this highly original and inventive composer, and its inclusion almost certainly brought Ligeti's music to the attention of a far greater audience than it would otherwise have found. Its dense, cloud-like pillars of shifting sound became, for a time, the unmistakable trademark of Ligeti's style, but as this disc clearly reveals, there are more sides to Ligeti's creativity than the sound sculptures of the mid to late 1960s. Of greater interest to the enthusiast perhaps, will be the more recent pieces such as *Drei Phantasien* and the *Three Hungarian études* on poems by Sandor Weöres. The densely packed, highly chromatic textures of works such as *Lux aeterna* and the Requiem are still in evidence, but here we find Ligeti placing greater emphasis on harmony and melody, which in turn give rise to even greater complexities. The *Hungarian études* (which have a certain parallel with the avant-garde madrigals of the sixteenth century) are an excellent example — the "Canon-miroir" is a marvellously descriptive tone-painting of a thawing icicle, whose 12-part canon opens with each voice 'plip-plopping' as the water drips to the ground, and later disintegrates as into long points of repose as the water transforms into a pool. The remaining pieces consist mainly of early works, whose style lies somewhere between Kodály and Bartók, which although not representative of the Ligeti we know today are no less enjoyable and provide a fascinating insight into the formation of Ligeti's more mature style. A must for all Ligeti enthusiasts. Well recorded.

NEW REVIEW

Ligeti. LE GRAND MACABRE. **Eirian Davies** (sop) Chief of the Secret Police (Gepopo), Venus; **Penelope Walmsley-Clark** (sop) Amanda; **Olive Fredericks** (mez) Amando; **Kevin Smith** (alto) Prince Go-Go; **Christa Puhlmann-Richter** (mez) Mescalina; **Peter Haage** (ten) Piet the Pot; **Dieter Weller** (bar) Nekrotzar; **Ude Krekow** (bass) Astradamors; **Johann Leutgeb** (bar) Ruffiak; **Ernst Salzer** (bar) Schobiak; **Laszlo Modos** (bar) Schabernack; **Herbert Prikopa** (spkr) White Minister; **Ernst Leopold Strachwitz** (spkr) Black Minister; **Austrian Radio Chorus; Arnold Schönberg Choir; Gumpoldskirchner Spartzen; Austrian Radio Symphony Orchestra/Elgar Howarth.** Wergo WER6170-2. Notes, text and translations included.

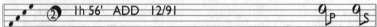

Contemporary operas can be a risky business for an opera house at the best of times, and even if they do attract sizeable audiences at their first performance, the prospect of future productions is never guaranteed. Ligeti's *Le grand macabre*, however, has been an exception and since its première in Stockholm over 13 years ago it has been produced in well over a dozen different opera houses world-wide. Chronologically it occupies a place between Ligeti's earlier, more experimental works such as the Requiem, *Adventures I & II* and *Clocks and Clouds*, and his more recent compositions which have favoured a superficially more traditional approach. Its intriguing plot is certainly not for those of a prudish disposition: Nekrotzar (the Tsar of Death) visits the dilapidated, imaginary principality of Breughelland in order to announce the imminent destruction of the world. Along the way he encounters various colourful inhabitants: the local inebriate Piet the Pot (whom he enlists as his horse), two star-struck lovers Amando and Amanda (who spend most of their time in mortal love-lock) and the royal astrologer Astradamors and his nymphomaniac wife Mescalina — the latter bestially fulfilled by Nekrotzar. On his arrival at the royal palace of the childish glutton Prince Go-Go he declares the end of the world and … well, that would be telling, but needless to say, in an opera as bizarre and "Jarryesque" as this anything might happen. Of course a certain amount of visual impact has been lost in its transfer to CD, but then what the eye loses the imagination gains and can run riot with. Excellent performances and a magnificent recording.

Franz Liszt

Hungarian 1811-1886

NEW REVIEW

Liszt. Piano Concertos — No. 1 in E flat major, S124; No. 2 in A major, S125. Totentanz, S126. **Krystian Zimerman** (pf); **Boston Symphony Orchestra/Seiji Ozawa.** DG 423 571-2GH.

The Polish pianist gives us performances in the grand manner here. Where some of his colleagues play for safety in the recording studio, knowing that every detail is under scrutiny, he sounds wholly spontaneous and even brave. Thus the difficult octaves at the start of the First Concerto leave you gasping at a powerfully heroic musical gesture rather than just admiring well-schooled arms, hands and fingers. Yet there's something beyond this virtuosity which is just as important, namely Zimerman's poise, finesse and tonal subtlety, not least in the many lyrical sections of this work and the more consciously poetic (though hardly less demanding) Second Concerto. He reminds us, too, that this is a young man's music. Add to this fine solo playing the excellent support of Ozawa and his Boston orchestra and we have a great pair of performances. Furthermore, where some discs have just these two concertos, here we get the *Totentanz* as well. And what a superb bonus it is, music inspired by some grisly Italian frescos depicting the triumph of Death and using the famous *Dies irae* plainchant melody in a set of diabolically glittering variations that are intended to scare as well as thrill. This is playing to make your hair stand on end! As for the sound, both the piano and orchestra have an impressive presence and tonal depth.

Liszt. ORCHESTRAL WORKS. ªShura Cherkassky (pf); **Berlin Philharmonic Orchestra/Herbert von Karajan.** DG 415 967-2GH2.
Fantasia on Hungarian Folk-themes, S123ª. Mazeppa, S100 (both from 138 692, 9/61). Les préludes, S97 (139 037, 6/69). Mephisto Waltz No. 2, S111 (2530 244, 10/72). Hungarian Rhapsodies: No. 2 (2530 698, 8/76), No. 4, S359 (135 031, 4/68); No. 5 (2530 698, 8/76). Tasso, lamento e trionfo, S96 (2530 698, 8/76).

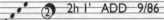 ② 2h 1' ADD 9/86 Ⓑ

Shura Cherkassky   *[photo: DG*

It was Liszt who first used the term "symphonic tone-poem" to describe the orchestral pieces he composed depicting stories and events. This set is a compilation of Liszt recordings made by Karajan over a period of some 15 years, and it is apparent that here is a composer who constantly stimulates the BPO's conductor to his freshest and most imaginative performances. There is a remarkable consistency of style in the playing, which is everywhere fresh, alert and has an abundance of energy and spirit, and the orchestra respond to their director with virtuoso playing of a high order. The *Fantasia* is an ideal vehicle for Cherkassky's brilliant, improvisatory style and although this particular recording was made 32 years ago the piano tone and indeed the orchestral sound are very good. In fact the recordings all sound excellent, despite the difference in their dates of origin.

NEW REVIEW

Liszt. A Faust Symphony, G108. **Kenneth Riegel** (ten); **Tanglewood Festival Chorus; Boston Symphony Orchestra/Leonard Bernstein.** DG Galleria 431 470-2GGA. From 2707 100 (4/78).

⌐ 1h 17' ADD 8/91 £

NEW REVIEW

Liszt. A Faust Symphony, G108. **Gösta Winbergh** (ten); **Westminster College Choir Male Chorus; Philadelphia Orchestra/Riccardo Muti.** EMI CDC7 49062-2. From HMV SLS143570-2 (12/83).

⌐ 1h 17' DDD 10/91

Goethe's *Faust* provided a source of inspiration for numerous symphonic, operatic, literary and stage works and, indeed, its influence is hardly diminished even in the late twentieth century. With its heroic and undeniably visionary qualities, it is hardly surprising that many romantic composers seized upon Goethe's text; one of the most lucid presentations of the original drama is found the work offers a huge range of interpretative possibilities and both Muti and Bernstein concentrate upon presenting differing aspects of Faust's character as the opening movement develops. Muti and the Philadelphia Orchestra dwell at length upon Faust, the man of action, and they are especially successful in the more martial areas of the score, as a tangible portrait of heroism emerges. With the formidable virtuosity of the Philadelphia at his command, he makes the most of the dramatic potential of Liszt's great score.

By contrast an altogether more mystical and philosophical Faust is revealed by Bernstein in his 1977 performance with the Boston Symphony Orchestra. A final choice between these two superb readings will depend upon what you ultimately regard as priorities in Goethe's drama, and how these are best portrayed within each performance. It is left to Bernstein to add the extra dimensions of real musical perception and true dramatic mastery to Liszt's concoction of sinister diablerie. Equally, Muti brings a thrilling and no less charismatic degree of authority to the symphony in a vivid, if occasionally hard-driven modern recording. The 1977 DG sound for Bernstein is excellent in its remastered form and this disc has the added advantage of being mid-price. If on the other hand you prefer your Faust to be red in tooth and claw, then the panache and flair of Muti may well prove hard to resist.

Liszt. HUNGARIAN RHAPSODIES, S244 — Nos. 1-19. **Roberto Szidon** (pf). DG Galleria 423 925-2GGA2. From 2720 072 (10/73).
No. 1 in C sharp minor; No. 2 in C sharp minor; No. 3 in B flat major; No. 4 in E flat major; No. 5 in E minor, "Héroïde-Elégiaque"; No. 6 in D flat major; No. 7 in D minor; No. 8 in F sharp minor, "Capriccio"; No. 9 in E flat major, "Carnival in Pest"; No. 10 in E major; No. 11 in A minor; No. 12 in C sharp minor; No. 13 in A minor; No. 14 in F minor; No. 15 in A minor, "Rákóczy"; No. 16 in A minor, "For the Munkascy festivities in Budapest"; No. 17 in D minor; No. 18 in F sharp minor, "On the occasion of the Hungarian Exposition in Budapest"; No. 19 in D minor.

② 2h 23' ADD 3/89 *£*

NEW REVIEW
Liszt. HUNGARIAN RHAPSODIES, S244. Csárdás obstiné. **Alfred Brendel** (pf). Vanguard Classics 08 4024 71. From VCS10035 (7/72).
No. 2 in C sharp minor; No. 3 in B flat major; No. 8 in F sharp minor, "Capriccio"; No. 13 in A minor; No. 15 in A minor, "Rákóczy"; No. 17 in D minor.

46' ADD 2/92 *£*

Liszt's 19 *Hungarian Rhapsodies* contain some formidably difficult music of tremendous flavour and colour. Liszt first encountered gipsy music when he returned to Hungary in 1840 and he was quite entranced with the abandon and ecstasy it seemed capable of inspiring. Although the rhapsodies are perfectly able to stand on their own they can also be seen as an entity, a work with disparate but linked elements. The first 15 pieces (the last four date from the 1880s) therefore form a unified creation. The clash of tempo, tonality and rhythm has a strong place in Liszt's rhapsodies and the colours and timbres of the gipsy band are beautifully captured by this wizard of the keyboard with almost diabolic accuracy. The last four rhapsodies, in common with his other works from late in his career, have a haunted, introspective quality that makes them sound more abstract than their earlier counterparts. Szidon's recording has always been highly

regarded and hearing it again on CD it is easy to understand why. There is a
panache and verve that is so vital for the inner life of this music.

Brendel's selection from the *Hungarian Rhapsodies* is extremely satisfying and
will suit collectors who don't wish to purchase two discs so as to have them all.
Like the Szidon recording, it originally appeared in the 1970s, but the playing has
a timeless mastery and the digital transcription is worthy of it. Brendel has long
been a champion of this composer and it was he who introduced many of us to
unfamiliar late pieces such as the brief Seventeenth Rhapsody and the chunky,
enigmatic *Csárdás obstiné*. The latter provides a useful fill-up after the six
rhapsodies, and while one would have welcomed more in this disc lasting only 46
minutes, it reflects the content and format of the original LP. Brendel includes
the Second Rhapsody which is the most famous of the set, and his is a splendid
performance which balances aristocratic authority with gipsy charm and fire. The
Rákóczy March which begins the recital (Rhapsody No. 15) is grand and powerful,
too. As always, this pianist brings a certain weight to the music, so that it's
never flashy, yet retains the necessary feeling of spontaneity. Indeed, the whole
sequence is most enjoyable, while the piano tone has ample body and sounds
very faithful. The issue is made even more attractive by Brendel's booklet essay,
which tells us more about Liszt in five stylish pages than many writers would
achieve in 50.

Liszt. PIANO WORKS. **Alfred Brendel** (pf). Philips 410 040-2PH. From
6514 147 (11/82).
Piano Sonata in B minor, S178. Légendes, S175 — St François d'Assise: la
prédication aux oiseaux; St François de Paule marchant sur les flots. La lugubre
gondola Nos. 1 and 2, S200/1-2.

> Ih 2' DDD 10/83

Liszt. PIANO WORKS. **Maurizio Pollini.** DG 427 322-2GH. Items marked
[a] recorded at a performance in the Grosser Saal, Musikverein, Vienna on May
30th, 1988.
Piano Sonata in B minor, S178. Nuages gris, S199[a]. Unstern: sinistre, disastro,
S208. La lugubre gondola I, S200[a]. R. W. — Venezia, S201[a].

> 46' DDD 7/90

Liszt's Piano Sonata is one of the monuments of the romantic period and is the
only sonata which the greatest pianist of musical history wrote for his instrument.
It is in one long movement that has its component parts contained within a
mighty sonata structure. Unfortunately it is also a work that has often been
misunderstood and when treated chiefly as a virtuoso warhorse and vehicle for
self-display the Sonata loses its dignity and poise. Alfred Brendel has lived with
this music for decades, and his love and understanding of it are evident.
Technically it is not flawless, but the blend of the various qualities needed —
power, dignity, dexterity, sheer excitement, charm and above all structural
cohesion is admirable. The two *St Francis* Legends and the funereal *Gondola* pieces
are more than a fill-up and enhance this fine disc, revealing as they do other
aspects of the composer.

Pollini is also one of the select few pianists who can keep all the Sonata's
diverse elements in balance, so that his reading has a sense of wholeness rarely
encountered in this work, even though others may have been even more
illuminating in one or other aspect. Deutsche Grammophon's recording is of the
highest quality. It would be unwise to expect too much of the late pieces,
however. These are widely held to be prophetic of early twentieth-century
modernism, but Pollini's way with them is rather detached (though pianistically
judged to perfection) and the recording mixes live and studio performances to
disconcerting effect.

Liszt. PIANO WORKS. **Stephen Hough.** Virgin Classics VC7 90700-2. Mephisto Waltz No. 1, S514. Venezia e Napoli, S162 — Tarantella. Rhapsodie espagnole, S254. Harmonies poétiques et religieuses, S173 — Bénédiction de Dieu dans la solitude; Pensée des morts. Légendes, S175 — St François d'Assise: la prédication aux oiseaux.

`1h 15'  DDD  6/88` ⑨ₛ

Liszt. PIANO WORKS. **Jorge Bolet.** Decca 411 803-2DH. Venezia e Napoli, S162. Années de pèlerinage. Troisième année, S163 — No. 4, Les jeux d'eaux à la Villa d'Este. Harmonies poétiques et religieuses, S173 — Bénédiction de Dieu dans la solitude. Ballade No. 2 in B minor, S171.

`58'  DDD  12/85`

The most popular of the virtuoso pieces on the Hough disc is of course the first *Mephisto Waltz,* played here with pronounced contrasts of dazzling diablerie and seductive lyricism. The Italy-inspired *Tarantella* confirms Hough's technical brilliance in breathtakingly fast repetition of single notes, while throughout the dance he preserves an exceptional textural clarity. Characterization in the *Rhapsodie espagnole*'s variations is enhanced by a wide range of tone colour, though just once or twice his scintillating prestidigitation militates against breadth. But there is certainly no lack of that quality in *Pensée des morts*, the fourth and most introspectively searching of the *Harmonies poétiques et religieuses*, whose broodings are sustained with quite exceptional intensity as well as expanding into a magnificently sonorous climax. The simple holiness of *St François d'Assise: la prédication aux oiseaux* is conveyed with pellucid delicacy. Finally comes the deeply consolatory *Bénédiction de Dieu dans la solitude*, where Hough is even able to convince us that its "heavenly lengths" (over 17 minutes) are not a moment too long. The excellent recording artfully contrasts the crispness of the three virtuoso pieces with Hough's more sustained sonority in religious reflection.

The Decca recital also gives an unusually well-rounded picture of Liszt's piano writing, what with the flurries of *Les jeux d'eaux à la Villa d'Este* (the most important single precursor of French pianistic impressionism), the devotional inwardness of *Bénédiction de Dieu* and the easy flowing grace of "Gondoliera" and "Canzona" from *Venezia e Napoli*. Jorge Bolet's spacious approach allows the ear to savour every detail, never at the expense of musical flow and only at some small cost to physical exhilaration in the display pieces. The impression of warm, consoling lyricism is enhanced by the faithfulness of an exceptionally fine recording.

NEW REVIEW

Liszt. PIANO WORKS, Volume 15 — SONG TRANSCRIPTIONS. **Leslie Howard.** Hyperion CDA66481/2.
Beethoven: Adelaïde, S466. Sechs geistliche Lieder, S467. An die ferne Geliebte, S469. Lieder von Goethe, S468. **Mendelssohn:** Lieder, S547.
Dessauer: Lieder, S485. **Franz:** Er ist gekommen in Sturm und Regen, S488. Lieder, S489. **Rubinstein:** Two songs, S554. **Schumann:** Lieder von Robert und Clara Schumann, S569. Provenzalisches Lied, S570. Two songs, S567. Frühlingsnacht, S568. Widmung, S566.

`② 2h 27'  DDD  4/92`

Few composers have ever shown a more insatiable interest in the music of others than Liszt, or devoted more time to transcribing it for the piano. In this radio-cum-gramophonic age, such activity might even be deemed time wasted. But in Liszt's day it was a godsend for music-lovers and composers alike, and all praise to Leslie Howard for including it in his mammoth pilgrimage through the composer's complete keyboard works. Here, he plays 60 of Liszt's 100 or so song transcriptions, including several by the lesser-known Dessauer, Franz and (as composers) Anton Rubinstein and Clara Schumann, alongside Beethoven, Mendelssohn and Robert Schumann. The selection at once reveals Liszt's variety of approach as a transcriber no less than his unpredictability of choice. Sometimes, as most notably in Beethoven's concert aria, *Adelaïde*, the keyboard virtuoso takes over: he links its two sections with a concerto-like cadenza as well as carrying bravura into an amplified coda. Mendelssohn's *On wings of song* brings imitative subtleties all his own, while the fullness of heart of Schumann's *Dedication* and *Spring Night* is likewise allowed to expand and overflow. But after the dazzling pyrotechnics of many of his operatic arrangements, the surprise here is the self-effacing simplicity of so much included. The five songs from Schumann's *Liederalbum für die Jugend* are literal enough to be played by young children. Even his later (1880) fantasy-type transcriptions of Rubinstein's exotic *The Asra* has the same potent economy of means, characterizing his own original keyboard music in advancing years. Howard responds keenly to mood and atmosphere, and never fails, pianistically, to emphasize the 'singer' in each song — in response to the actual verbal text that Liszt was nearly always conscientious enough to write into his scores. The recording is clean and true.

Liszt. 12 Transcendental Studies, S139. **Claudio Arrau** (pf). Philips 416 458-2PH. From 6747 412 (2/78).

> 1h 7' ADD 6/86

Liszt published the *Douze Etudes en Douze Exercices* in 1826, when he was 15. He later expanded all but one to form the basis of his horrendously difficult *Grandes etudes* of 1838 (24 were intended but only 12 completed). Sensitivity to the technical limitations of other virtuosos eventually overcame him, and in 1852 he published a revised, 'easy' version, entitled the *Douze Etudes d'Exécution Transcendante*, which he dedicated to his teacher, Carl Czerny. It is in this (fiendishly difficult) form, with its fanciful titles for ten of the pieces, that the work is usually performed today. Only a very few pianists of each generation can begin to make music of these works in the way Liszt expected. The technique required goes well beyond simple virtuosity and all too often performances sink in a tumultuous sea of the scales and arpeggios that Liszt intended should only provide a background tint. Maintaining speed is the other major problem, for the great melodies must flow and sing as though the myriad of other notes that interpose are hardly there. Arrau has for many years been one of the select band capable of this work and in this stable, well-defined recording from the mid 1970s he gives us this performance against which most others are judged.

Liszt. ORGAN WORKS. **Gunther Kaunzinger.** Novalis 150 069-2.
Recorded on the organ of the Stiftsbasilika, Waldsassen, Germany.
Prelude and Fugue on the name B-A-C-H, S260. Evocation à la Chapelle Sixtine, S658. Variations on "Weinen, Klagen, Sorgen, Zagen", S673. Fantasia and Fugue on "Ad nos, ad salutarem undam", S259.

> 1h 12' DDD 2/91

Liszt's prodigious skill at the piano was legendary. But he was also a most capable organist and in the later years of his life he turned more and more to the organ, making transcriptions and reworkings for it of his own and other composers' music. As for original organ compositions he wrote a mere handful. The *Fantasia and Fugue* on the chorale *Ad nos, ad salutarem undam* (from Meyerbeer's opera *La Prophète*) is a work of considerable stature and virtuosity almost unparalleled in the organ's repertory. Although barely a third the length of the *Fantasia and Fugue*, the *Prelude and Fugue on the name B-A-C-H* is also a virtuoso showpiece paying homage to the composer who Liszt regarded as a supreme master. Homage is also paid to Bach in the Variations on *Weinen, Klagen, Sorgen, Zagen*, a theme Liszt took from Bach's Cantata No. 21. The *Evocation* of the Sistine Chapel combines Allegri's *Miserere* and Mozart's *Ave verum* in a deeply religious work which was, for Liszt, a profound statement of faith. Gunther Kaunzinger gives an outstanding performance of the *Fantasia and Fugue*, and in the other pieces his playing has great authority. He is served by a fine, if rather thick-sounding instrument, and a clean, full-blooded recording.

Liszt. ORGAN WORKS.
Reubke. Sonata on the 94th Psalm. **Thomas Trotter** (org). Argo 430 244-2ZH. Played on the organ of the Münster zur Schönen Unsrer Lieben Frau, Ingolstadt, Germany.
Liszt: Prelude and Fugue on the name B-A-C-H, S260. Gebet, S265 (arr. Gottschalg). Orpheus S98 (arr. Schaab). Prometheus, S99 (trans. Guillou).

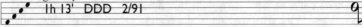
1h 13' DDD 2/91

This is a spectacular organ record, made on a big modern instrument in the very resonant acoustic of the Church of Our Lady, at Ingolstadt in Germany, which Thomas Trotter plays with great flair. The music is no less spectacular, belonging as it does to the nineteenth century and a full-blooded romantic tradition. The longest piece is the Reubke Sonata, music by a composer who died at 24 and is virtually unknown except to organists, and even to them by just this one work. It is a mighty one-movement sonata which reflects the influence of his teacher Liszt, to whom he went in 1856 shortly after the older man completed his great Piano Sonata, and was inspired by the powerful text of *Psalm* No. 94, which calls for God's judgement upon the wicked. Liszt himself is represented here by another work of surging strength, the *Prelude and Fugue* on the letters of the name Bach (the notes B flat, A, C, B natural), which make for a tightly chromatic motif yielding great harmonic and contrapuntal possibilities, not least in the fugue. This work begins the recital, and is followed by the same composer's serene tone poem in praise of music which he called *Orpheus*. Then comes the Reubke, and the other Liszt items follow it and thus make a sort of triptych with the longest work (the Sonata) as the centrepiece. Though two of the Liszt pieces are transcriptions rather than original organ works, they are effective in this form.

Theo Loevendie

Dutch 1930-

Loevendie. MISCELLANEOUS WORKS. [a]**Rosemary Hardy** (sop); [b]**Jard van Nes** (mez); [c]**John Snijders** (pf); [d]**Nieuw Ensemble/Ed Spanjaard.** Etcetera KTC1097.
Venus and Adonis[d]. Strides[c]. Six Turkish Folk Poems[ad]. Music for flute and piano[b]. NAIMA[bd] — A man of life upright; As fast as thou shalt wane. Back Bay Bicinium[d].

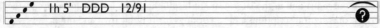
1h 5' DDD 12/91

Theo Loevendie is a Dutch composer who has turned from jazz to more 'serious' composition, with fascinating results. Far from simply juxtaposing two different musical worlds, Loevendie seems to have absorbed the old into the new, so that lightness of touch, flexibility of form and clarity of texture are all prominent features of the works recorded here. In general, the longer, more abstract pieces are the least interesting, although the early *Strides* for solo piano, *Music for flute and piano* and the evocatively titled *Back Bay Bicinium* for seven instruments are all well worth hearing. But Loevendie comes into his own with vocal and theatre music. The two pieces derived from his music for Shakespeare's *Venus and Adonis* grab and sustain the attention, while the two songs to English texts from the opera *Naima* are notable for their fresh and vivid sonorities — there's a hint of the later Stravinsky here. One of the most enjoyable items is the set of *Six Turkish Folk Poems*, brilliantly sung by Rosemary Hardy, and showing Loevendie's ability to allude to ethnic music without resorting to parody. Overall, this disc is technically first rate, and likely to provide pleasures and surprises even for listeners who think they know their way about the contemporary music scene.

Henry Litolff   *Refer to Index*   French 1818-1891

Albert Lortzing   German 1801-1851

Lortzing. UNDINE. **Monika Krause** (sop) Undine; **Josef Protschka** (ten) Hugo; **Christiane Hampe** (sop) Bertalda; **John Janssen** (bar) Kühleborn; **Klaus Häger** (bass) Tobias; **Ingeborg Most** (contr) Marthe; **Heinz Kruse** (ten) Veit; **Andreas Schmidt** (bass) Hans; **Günter Wewel** (bass) Heilmann; **Dirk Schortemeier** (spkr) Messenger; **Cologne Radio Chorus and Orchestra/Kurt Eichhorn.** Capriccio 60 017-2. Text and translation included.

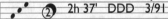

② 2h 37' DDD 3/91

Andreas Schmidt   *[photo: DG/Bayat*

A pity, in a way, that this couldn't have been a video recording, for *Undine*, a curious mixture of the fantastic and the prosaically bourgeois, has one of the most spectacular (though enormously difficult to stage) endings in all opera: the knight Hugo's castle is (in full view) inundated, and he and his living waternymph Undine (who has been put on earth to find out whether humans, who have souls, are superior to nature-spirits, who have none) are united in a crystal palace at the bottom of the sea. A lot more than he deserved, for having fallen in love with this pretty and ingenuous creature and married her, he had been faithless; but Lortzing allowed himself to be persuaded to give the work a happy ending. His setting of this fable is undemandingly melodious, frequently folk-like, and extremely skilfully scored; and the veteran Kurt Eichhorn secures first-class orchestral playing and choral singing. The sopranos — Undine and the haughty princess who is discovered to be low-born — are less impressive than the men, who are extremely well cast. Protschka as the fickle knight excels in his big 'nightmare' aria in Act 4, Janssen makes a menacing Prince of the Waters, and Kruse is efficient, if sounding over-classy for a mere squire with a weakness for the bottle. Gaps left between the ends of musical numbers and the ensuing dialogues (which are well produced) rather weaken the dramatic flow; but all in all this first complete recording for 25 years of this romantic opera is greatly to be welcomed.

Antonio Lotti

Italian 1667-1740

Lotti. MADRIGALS.
A. Scarlatti. MADRIGALS. **The Consort of Musicke/Anthony Rooley.**
Deutsche Harmonia Mundi RD77194.
Lotti: Moralità d'una perla. Inganni dell'umanità. Lamento di tre amanti. La vita caduca. ***A. Scarlatti:*** Sdegno la fiamma estinse. O selce, o tigre, o ninfa. Intenerite voi, lacrime mie. Arsi un tempo e l'adore. O morte, agli altri fosca, a me serena. Mori, mi dici. Cor mio, deh, non languire.

52' DDD 11/91

Most histories of music will tell you that the madrigal — one of the most popular vocal genres of the renaissance and early baroque — fell into disuse in the 1630s. Well, here is proof that the form was still alive and kicking at least 60 years after that. The two composers featured on this disc are not figures you would automatically think of as madrigalists — both were much more at home with the vocal forms of their own day, such as opera and cantata (Scarlatti's tally alone ran to something like 700 such works). But perhaps it was their interest in writing dramatic vocal music that drew them back to the madrigal. These are highly-charged miniatures, in which every nuance of the texts is reflected in a corresponding musical image — producing music of, at times, incredible intensity: Scarlatti's setting of *Cor mio, deh non languire*, for example — scored for five female voices — almost burns you with its white-hot dissonances and chromaticisms, all depicting the languishing pains of a heart consumed by love. And Lotti's highly expressive, *La vita caduca*, comparing the transience of human existence to the fragile beauty of a rose, was so admired in its own day that it became famous across Europe. The Consort of Musicke, accompanied in some of the pieces by a small group of continuo players, make light work of the technical difficulties in this repertoire: tuning, blend and balance are all immaculate. Anthony Rooley directs the group, distributes a characteristically well-researched programme-note and, as ever, succeeds in lifting the music off the page and bringing it vividly to life.

Hermann Løvenskiold

Danish 19th century

Løvenskiold. La Sylphide — ballet. **Royal Danish Orchestra/David Garforth.** Chandos Collect CHAN6546. From ABRD1200 (2/87).

1h 12' DDD 4/92

La Sylphide is one of the classic themes of romantic ballet, a story of a Scotsman enticed away from his wedding celebrations by a winged spirit (the Sylphide). It was originally danced at the Paris Opéra by Marie Taglioni in 1832, and it was seen there by the choreographer Auguste Bournonville, who produced his own version in Copenhagen in 1836. This has remained ever since in the repertory of the Royal Danish Ballet. The original Parisian version had music by Schneitzhoeffer, but Bournonville commissioned a new score from Herman Severin Løvenskiold, a young Norwegian of aristocratic background. It has remained his masterpiece. The score uses the standard conventions of the time, incorporating a prominent solo violin part for the music of the Sylphide. If ultimately it makes no greater pretensions than most scores of its kind, it has very agreeable tunes, several of which are paraded in its jolly overture. This is the most extended recording of the score, including an extra *pas de deux* as an appendix. Performance and recorded sound alike are excellent, and no ballet lover should be without such an important score in such a fine version at such a reasonable price.

Jean-Baptiste Lully

Italian-French 1632-1687

Lully. ATYS. *Prologue* — **Bernard Deletré** (bass) Le Temps; **Monique Zanetti** (sop) Flore; **Jean-Paul Fouchécourt** (bass), **Gilles Ragon** (ten) Zephirs; **Arlette Steyer** (sop) Melpomene; **Agnès Mellon** (sop) Iris. *Tragédie-lyrique* — **Guy de Mey** (ten) Atys; **Agnès Mellon** (sop) Sangaride; **Guillemette Laurens** (mez) Cybèle; **Françoise Semellaz** (sop) Doris; **Jacques Bona** (bass) Idas; **Noémi Rime** (sop) Mélisse; **Jean-François Gardeil** (bass) Célénus; **Gilles Ragon** (ten) Le sommeil; **Jean-Paul Fouchécourt** (ten) Morphée, Trio; **Bernard Deletré** (bass) Phobétor, Sangar; **Michel Laplénie** (ten) Phantase; **Stephan Maciejewski** (bass) Un songe funeste; **Isabelle Desrochers** (sop) Trio; **Véronique Gens** (sop) Trio; **Les Arts Florissants Chorus and Orchestra/William Christie.** Harmonia Mundi HMC90 1257/9. Notes, text and translation included.

③ 2h 50' DDD 7/87

Once upon a time Lully's melodies were the property of the common people. Not so today when, apart from occasional revivals and broadcasts, his operas are largely forgotten. *Atys* is reputed to have been Louis XIV's favourite opera and here William Christie and a fine line-up of soloists bring the work to life in a most compelling way. There are some beautiful choruses and ensembles throughout the opera which should make wide and immediate appeal; but it is in the Third Act where Lully treats his audience to a *sommeil* or sleep scene that much of the most arresting and original music is contained. Recorded sound is effective and the booklet contains the full libretto.

Thomas Lupo   *Refer to Index*

British d.1628

Witold Lutoslawski

Polish 1913-

Lutoslawski. ORCHESTRAL WORKS. [a]**Louis Devos** (ten); [b]**Roman Jablónski** (vc); [b]**Katowice Radio Symphony Orchestra;** [ad]**Warsaw National Philharmonic Orchestra;** [cd]**Jan Krenz;** [ab]**Witold Lutoslawski.** Polskie Nagrania Muza PNCD042. Paroles tissées[a]. Cello Concerto[b] (both from EMI 1C 165 03231/6, 7/79). Postlude I[bc]. Livre pour orchestre[d].

1h 4' ADD 9/90

This volume featuring CD transfers of ageing recordings stands up to today's competition better than most. Although they date from between 1964 and 1976, the recordings still retain much of the clarity and detail of these first-rate performances. Jan Krenz makes a fine job of the intricate textures of that concentrated masterpiece, *Livre pour orchestre* and the somewhat similarly structured Cello Concerto, dedicated to Rostropovich, finds here a committed advocate in Roman Jablónski. These two works date from 1968 and 1970 respectively. *Paroles tissées* predates the first of these by three years and, superficially, seems very different in style with open textures and chamber-music balances. If the tenor here, Louis Devos, lacks the poetry of Sir Peter Pears, for whom the work was written, he nevertheless does the work justice and points its many delights. The first of the three Postludes (1958-63), which opens the disc, shows Lutoslawski's musical antecedents much more clearly than the other works, but it is still a remarkable piece for a composer who, only a few years before, had been producing music that only too well complied with the requirements of a Poland still in the cultural grip of Stalinist dictates.

Lutoslawski. Partita for violin, orchestra and obbligato solo piano (1985)[a]. Chain 2 for violin and orchestra (1984)[b].
Stravinsky. Violin Concerto in D[c]. **Anne-Sophie Mutter** (vn); [a]**Phillip Moll** (pf); [ab]**BBC Symphony Orchestra/Witold Lutoslawski;** [c]**Philharmonia Orchestra/Paul Sacher.** DG 423 696-2GH.

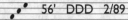 56' DDD 2/89

Anne-Sophie Mutter   *[photo: DG*

This disc contains some spellbinding violin playing in a splendidly lifelike recording, and it's a bonus that the music, while unquestionably 'modern', needs no special pleading: its appeal is instantaneous and long-lasting. Anne-Sophie Mutter demonstrates that she can equal the best in a modern classic — the Stravinsky Concerto — and also act as an ideal, committed advocate for newer works not previously recorded. The Stravinsky is one of his liveliest neoclassical pieces, though to employ that label is, as usual, to underline its rough-and-ready relevance to a style that uses Bach as a springboard for an entirely individual and unambiguously modern idiom. Nor is it all 'sewing-machine' rhythms and pungently orchestrated dissonances. There is lyricism, charm, and above all humour: and no change of mood is too fleeting to escape the razor-sharp responses of this soloist and her alert accompanists, authoritatively guided by the veteran Paul Sacher. Lutoslawski's music has strongly individual qualities that have made him perhaps the most approachable of all contemporary composers. This enthralling collaboration between senior composer and youthful virtuoso is not to be missed.

Sergey Lyapunov   *Russian 1859-1924*

NEW REVIEW

Lyapunov. TRANSCENDENTAL STUDIES, Op. 11. **Malcolm Binns** (pf). Pearl SHECD9624.
No. 1 in F sharp major, "Berceuse"; No. 2 in D sharp minor, "Rondes des fantômes"; No. 3 in B major, "Carillon"; No. 4 in G sharp minor, "Terek"; No.

5 in E major, "Nuit d'été"; No. 6 in C sharp minor, "Tempête"; No. 7 in A major, "Idylle"; No. 8 in F sharp minor, "Chant épique"; No. 9 in D major, "Harpes éoliennes"; No. 10 in B minor, "Lesghinka"; No. 11 in G major, "Rondes des Sylphes"; No. 12 in E minor, "Elégie en mémoire de François Liszt".

$\cdot$ 1h 12' DDD 5/92

The 12 Transcendental Studies by Sergey Lyapunov have long been admired and respected in pianistic circles, and yet strangely enough have been almost totally neglected both in the concert-hall and on disc. Two previous complete recordings — both by the late Louis Kentner — have long since vanished, which makes this recording from Malcolm Binns an extremely welcome issue indeed. The studies were composed between 1897 and 1905 as an affectionate homage to Liszt — to whom the late nineteenth-century Russian school of piano composition owed so much — and were designed to complete the key sequence (major and minor sharp keys) that was begun in Liszt's own set of 12 Transcendental Studies of 1852. However, although the debt of Liszt can be clearly heard both in the structural and pianistic aspects of the set their harmonic language and use of folk material are unmistakeably Russian in origin. The technical demands (which are exceptionally severe) range from the overtly virtuosic — as in the Studies No. 4, *Terek* (depicting the course of the River Terek through the Georgia mountains), No. 10, *Lesghinka* (a sibling of Balakirev's *Islamey*) and No. 6, *Tempête* — through to those whose difficulties are of a much more subtle and altogether delicate nature such as No. 1, *Berceuse* and No. 7, *Idylle*. Malcolm Binns, a stalwart champion of neglected piano music of the romantic era and long-term supporter of the Lyapunov cause, proves an excellent guide through this attractive and rewarding music. Not to be missed.

Edward MacDowell

American 1860-1908

MacDowell. Piano Concerto No. 2 in D minor, Op. 23[a]. Woodland Sketches, Op. 51 — No. 1, To a Wild Rose[b].
Schumann. Piano Concerto in A minor, Op. 54[c]. **Van Cliburn** (pf); **Chicago Symphony Orchestra/[a]Walter Hendl, [c]Fritz Reiner.** RCA Victor Van Cliburn Collection GD60420. Item marked [a] from SB2113 (8/61), [b] new to UK, [c] SRA6001 (1/62).

$\cdot$ 1h ADD 10/91

A brilliant pianist himself, MacDowell was still only in his mid-twenties when writing his Second Piano Concerto. Even if lacking an immediately recognizable face of its own, it upholds the grand, later-nineteenth century romantic tradition with enough warmth, verve and virtuosity to explain why the now legendary Van Cliburn could not keep his hands off it. We're told it was the first concerto he ever played professionally with an orchestra (in 1952, when he was 18), and that it was one of the six works with which he toured the Soviet Union in 1960 after winning the first International Tchaikovsky Competition two years before. Also dating from 1960, when he was 26, his recording with Walter Hendl has an irresistible youthful urgency, intensity and élan matching that of the music itself. Though inevitably betraying its age, the sound has been skilfully enough remastered to make the disc something of a collector's piece. The Schumann coupling, recorded early the following year, has a similarly endearing ardour and freshness reminding us that this composer, too, was still then in his prime. Only the slow movement occasionally seems to need phrasing of a more intimately confidential kind.

Guillaume de Machaut

French c.1300-1377

Machaut. Messe de Nostre Dame.
Anonymous. Plainsong Prayers for the Feast of the Nativity of Our Lady.
Taverner Consort and Choir/Andrew Parrott. EMI Reflexe CDC7 47949-2. Notes, texts and translations included. From ASD143576-1 (3/84).

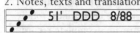 51' DDD 8/88

Machaut. Messe de Nostre Dame. Je ne cesse de prier (lai "de la fonteinne").
Ma fin est mon commencement. **Hilliard Ensemble/Paul Hillier.** Hyperion
CDA66358. Texts and translations included.

54' DDD 3/90

Machaut's *Messe de Nostre Dame* is the earliest known setting of the Ordinary Mass
by a single composer though we cannot be certain either that Machaut wrote it
at one time or even that he initially intended to bring its six movements
together. The music is splendid but though each of these performances seeks
'authenticity' the chosen path towards it is markedly different. Paul Hillier is the
more modest of the two directors in the extent to which he 'reconstructs', and
he employs two voices only to a part. Andrew Parrott, on the other hand, places
the Mass in a liturgical context with Propers, bells and celebrants; furthermore,
he transposes the music down a fourth employing only tenors and basses as
soloists. Each performance has its own strengths and weaknesses and you should
try both, if possible, before making a decision. Listeners will probably find that
the textures achieved by the Hilliard Ensemble are lighter and more expressive
than those of the other, transposed down a fourth. But the notion of presenting
the music in the context of a Mass, thereby allowing for important contrasts
between chant and polyphony is effective, and Parrott's reconstruction contains
an engaging and proper sense of occasion. Both versions include texts and
translations and both should be heard.

Roman Maciejewski

Polish 1910-

Maciejewski. Missa pro defunctis. **Zdzislawa Donat** (sop); **Jadwiga Rappé**
(contr); **Jerzy Knetig** (ten); **Janusz Niziolek** (bass); **Warsaw Philharmonic
Choir and Orchestra/Tadeusz Strugala.** Polskie Nagrania Muza PNCD039.

② 2h 11' DDD 9/90

This Requiem was Roman Maciejewski's attempt to come to terms with the
catastrophic events of the Second World War and also with his disillusionment
with the pre-war avant-garde. It took him until 1959 to finish it, and it had to
wait another 16 years for its first performance in Los Angeles — apparently a
very emotional event. One of the most extraordinary things about the Requiem
though is the way that it anticipates recent developments in music, particularly
the rejection of difficult atonalism in favour of sensuous modal harmonies and
hypnotic repetitions. Occasionally one may be reminded of the Holst of *Neptune*
or the *Rig Veda* hymns — and that's a significant comparison, because whatever
else he is, Maciejewski is not a minimalist. In the most beautiful movements —
the "Graduale", "Tractus" or "Recordare" for instance — the patterns provide the
background to some finely expressive vocal and instrumental writing. It is in
these meditative movements rather than in the big apocalyptic numbers that
Maciejewski really shows his strength, but he manages to keep the listener
hooked right to the end. Performances and recording may lack the final layer of
polish, but intense feelings are communicated. A real discovery.

Elizabeth Maconchy

British 1907-1990

Maconchy. String Quartets — Nos. 5-8. **Bingham Quartet** (Stephen Bingham, Mark Messenger, vns; Brenda Stewart, va; Miriam Lowbury, vc). Unicorn-Kanchana DKPCD9081.

· · 1h 9' DDD 6/90

NEW REVIEW

Maconchy. String Quartets — Nos. 9-12; No. 13, "Quartetto Corto". **Mistry Quartet** (Jagdish Mistry, Charles Sewart, vns; Caroline Henbest, va; Susan Monks, vc). Unicorn-Kanchana DKPCD9082.

· · 1h 4' DDD 2/91

Elizabeth Maconchy was a pupil, and later a lifelong friend, of Vaughan Williams. But her music owes little to the British nationalist tradition inspired by folk-song; rather, she has always shown a natural inclination towards what she calls the "difficult and challenging medium" and "impassioned debate" of the string quartet, with its form and interplay between four balanced voices. This second disc in Unicorn-Kanchana's enterprising series of these works brings us music written between 1948 and 1967, played with intelligence and commitment by a young British ensemble. The fact that Quartets Nos. 5-8 all fit on to a single CD itself tells us something about their terse, pithy nature; Bartók is the most obvious model (and sometimes too obvious for comfort, as in the finale of No. 5 and the form of No. 7), but we also often find, in the slow movements particularly, a quiet, edgy lyricism that is very much an aspect of the composer's own voice and an attractive one. The recording has warm yet detailed sound. In the accompanying booklet, the composer is usefully informative and her daughter's biographical note is also valuable, though making rather extravagant claims.

The final issue in the Maconchy quartet cycle more than fulfils the promise of its predecessors. The Quartets Nos. 9-13 take the story from 1968 to 1984, and show how the composer's earlier Bartókian models are modified by the more advanced but no less approachable musical language established in No. 8. The single-movement structures of Nos. 10 and 11 are particularly impressive, with No. 11 challenging its own continuities and symmetries to striking effect. Even the late No. 13 shows no loss of cogency or vitality, revealing new aspects of that principle of continuous discourse among the players that has always been at the heart of Maconchy's quartet style. The young members of the Mistry Quartet clearly relish the music's idiomatic though often testing string writing, and the recording has admirable range and definition.

Pierre du Mage

Refer to Index

French c.1676-1751

Albéric Magnard

French 1865-1914

NEW REVIEW

Magnard. CHAMBER WORKS AND SONGS. [a]**Artis Quartet** (Peter Schuhmayer, Johannes Meissl, vns; Herbert Kefer, va; Othmar Müller, vc) and various artists. Accord 20075-2. Texts included. Item marked [a] also available separately on 22060-2 (39'), [b] 20010-2 (1h 11').
Violin Sonata in G major, Op. 13 (Robert Zimansky, vn; Christoph Keller, pf). Three Piano Pieces, Op. 1. En Dieu mon espérance (Keller). Cello Sonata in A major, Op. 20 (Thomas Demenga, vc; Keller). Promenades, Op. 7 (Keller). Piano and Wind Quintet in D minor, Op. 8[b] (Anna-Katharina Graf, fl; Roman

Schmid, ob; Elmar Schmid, cl; Jiri Flieger, bn; Keller). Piano Trio in F minor, Op. 18[b] (Adelina Oprean, vn; Demenga; Keller). Six poèmes, Op. 3 (Eva Csapo, sop; Christoph Homberger, ten; Niklaus Tüller, bar; Keller). Quatre poèmes, Op. 15 (Tüller; Keller). A Henriette (Homberger; Keller). Suite dans le style ancien in G minor, Op. 2 (arr. composer. Katharina Weber, Keller, pf duet). String Quartet in E minor, Op. 16[a].

⑤ 4h 33' DDD 3/90

Those who care about French music and regret the neglect of Magnard will be thankful for this survey of his music for smaller vocal and instrumental forces. There are many good things here, and this is the kind of material that rewards repeated hearings. Fortunately, the several artists performing all show sympathy with the music and there are no weaknesses, which is just as well since five full-price discs represent quite an outlay for those wishing to explore this composer. However, if you are daunted by it, the String Quartet is available on its own, a restless and complex work owing something to Franck, and so is the more generous pairing of the Piano and Wind Quintet and the Piano Trio, attractive if not altogether memorable music persuasively played. Much of this is probably due to the pianist Christoph Keller, who really understands this idiom, as he also shows elsewhere in the Violin Sonata with Robert Zimansky, the passionate Cello Sonata with Thomas Demenga (another fine artist for this music) and the solo piano pieces called *Promenades*, which agreeably evoke walks in and around Paris. The songs on the last of the five discs are also well performed and worth getting to know for their strong personal feeling: eight of them have texts by the composer himself. These recordings were made over some five years in the 1980s and the sound is acceptable although not outstanding.

Gustav Mahler

Austrian 1860-1911

Mahler. SYMPHONIES. **Bavarian Radio Symphony Orchestra/Rafael Kubelík.** DG 429 042-2GX10.
Symphonies — No. 1 (from SLPM139331, 5/68); No. 2, "Resurrection" (Edith Mathis, sop; Norma Procter, contr; Bavarian Radio Chorus 139332/3, 4/70); No. 3 (Marjorie Thomas, contr; Tölz Boys' Choir; Bavarian Rad. Chor. SLPM139337/8, 9/68); No. 4 (Elsie Morison, sop. SLPM139339, 12/68); No. 5 (2720 033, 10/71); No. 6 (139341/2, 11/69); No. 7 (2720 033); No. 8 (Martina Arroyo, Erna Spoorenberg, Mathis, sops; Júlia Hamari, Procter, contrs; Donald Grobe, ten; Dietrich Fischer-Dieskau, bar; Franz Crass, bass; Regensburg Cathedral Boys' Choir; Munich Motet Choir; Bavarian Rad. Chor; North German Radio Chorus; West German Radio Chorus, 2720 033); No. 9 (SLPM139 345/6, 12/67); No. 10 — Adagio (139341/2).

⑩⑩ 10h 51' ADD 5/90 £ p

There are nearly 250 recordings of Mahler's symphonies listed in the current *Classical Catalogue*, so anyone approaching them for the first time is faced with the daunting problem of which versions to acquire. This reissue may well be something of a solution. Here we have a distinguished and highly commendable cycle of the symphonies at bargain price that provides an excellent opportunity for the newcomer to explore the symphonies at a relatively low cost. Kubelík's cycle is still one of the most completely satisfying on disc. There is a breadth and consistency of vision in these interpretations, that comes only from a conductor who has a deep understanding and a long association with this music. The most successful performances are perhaps Symphonies Nos. 1, 4, 5, 7 and 9. The First, notable for its fresh, youthful account and clearly defined textures, is still one of the finest versions available. The Fourth is equally as impressive, with

Rafael Kubelík   [photo: DG / Feinburg]

lively tempos and excellent orchestral playing. There is a strong sense of direction and structural unity in this perfor-mance and Elsie Morison's warm and poetic performance in the finale is a real delight. Kubelík's reading of Symphonies Nos. 5 and 7 have not always met with the credit that they deserve. The Fifth is a very individual perfor-mance, though certainly not lacking in intensity or power. Kubelík avoids dwelling too much on the tragic elements in the first movement of the Seventh and instead tries to build out of the devastation of the Sixth Sym-phony's finale. The Ninth is a very strong performance indeed, with great clarity of detail and a strong sense of architecture. It would of course be foolish to suggest that Kubelík's cycle is without flaws — the Second Symphony, although not without intensity, lacks perhaps the drama and spirituality of, say, Klemperer or Rattle and the same could be said of the Third. The Eighth is a fine performance superbly recorded and with some excellent singing from the soloists, but is ultimately outclassed by the superb award-winning Tennstedt recording (reviewed further on). The recordings are all clear, spacious and naturally balanced and were recorded in the warm and resonant acoustic of the Munich Herkulessaal between 1967 and 1971. A considerable bargain.

Mahler. Symphony No. 1. **Concertgebouw Orchestra, Amsterdam/ Leonard Bernstein.** DG 431 036-2GBE. Recorded at performances in the Concertgebuw, Amsterdam in October 1987.

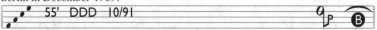

· 56' DDD 3/89   *q* P Ⓑ

NEW REVIEW

Mahler. Symphony No. 1. **Berlin Philharmonic Orchestra/Claudio Abbado.** DG 431 769-2GH. Recorded at a performance in the Philharmonie, Berlin in December 1989.

· 55' DDD 10/91   *q* P Ⓑ

The first DG disc gives us a great performance from a great Mahlerian impressively caught 'in the act' at Amsterdam's Concertgebouw. Bernstein's view of the piece has changed comparatively little over the years and fundamentals such as tempos remain more or less consistent. And yet the whole experience sounds newer, fresher; certain phrases have filled out, the expression is appreciably freer and easier now. How acutely Bernstein still *hears* Mahler's early-morning 'silence' at the outset: the dewy haze of string harmonics, the richly harmonized horns, their dreamy reveries broken only by sudden *fortissimo* pizzicatos (like startled animals) in the violins. All this is most beautifully and subtly chronicled by the Royal Concertgebouw players. In the bucolic inner movements, Bernstein characteristically relishes the coarse-cut sonorities. Accenting is trenchant and weighty in the lumbering scherzo, and the corny gipsy-cum-café music of the third movement is ideally tawdry. Furthermore, Bernstein's inspired account of the finale is a performance like no other — in atmosphere, in galvanic energy, in repose or in triumph. The recording, like the performance, is vivid and immediate. A very hard act to follow.

But not impossible, as is shown by Claudio Abbado's live recording (also by DG) with the Berlin Philharmonic Orchestra. While Bernstein's vision of the symphony is intense, with every corner of the work stamped with his personality, Abbado directs a technically immaculate account. Combined with his own particular insight this performance conveys more a sense of Mahler's sound world rather than, as previously, Mahler and Bernstein's. The playing of the BPO combined with DG's extraordinarily vivid and well balanced recording takes the performance of this work into a new league. Perhaps orchestras are only now fully able to realize Mahler's music in the way that they have been able to with, for instance, Beethoven's for years. There is here a confidence, familiarity and precision that is most unusual and deeply impressive. Added to its technical perfection is Abbado's assured control of tempos, phrasing and dynamics. These define very strongly both the character and atmosphere of each movement which are much more clearly delineated than has usually been the case in the past. The overall result is a major symphonic work at last coming into true focus: both weaknesses, such as its episodic nature, and strengths, its tremendous originality and character, stand fully revealed. Warts and all, this is an outburst of young musical genius fully realized by another, interpretative, genius. Try both recordings if you can. There is little to separate them in sound quality, both being first-class, so your choice will be a difficult one.

Mahler. Symphony No. 2, "Resurrection". **Arleen Auger** (sop); **Dame Janet Baker** (mez); **City of Birmingham Symphony Chorus and Orchestra/ Simon Rattle.** EMI CDS7 47962-8. Text and translation included. From EX270598-3 (10/87).

② 1h 26' DDD 12/87

The folk-poems from *Des knaben Wunderhorn*, with their complex mixture of moods and strong ironic edge, formed the basis of Mahler's inspiration for the Second Symphony. It is a work of huge scope, emotionally as well as physically taxing, and here it receives a performance that remarkably rekindles the feeling of a live performance with a quite breathtaking immediacy. The CBSO play magnificently and Rattle's attention to the letter of the score never hinders his overall vision of this masterpiece. The recording is superb.

Mahler. Symphony No. 3. **Norma Procter** (contr); **Wandsworth School Boys' Choir; Ambrosian Singers; London Symphony Orchestra/Jascha Horenstein.** Unicorn-Kanchana Souvenir UKCD2006/07. Text and translation included. From RHS302/03 (12/70).

② 1h 37' ADD 11/88

Every now and again, along comes a Mahler *performance* that no serious collector can afford to be without. Horenstein's interpretation of the Third Symphony is an outstanding example and its reissue on CD at mid-price is a major addition to the Mahler discography. No other conductor has surpassed Horenstein in his total grasp of every facet of the enormous score. Even though the LSO strings of the day were not as powerful as they later became, they play with suppleness and a really tense sound, especially appropriate in the kaleidoscopic first movement, where changes of tempo and mood reflect the ever-changing face of nature. Horenstein gives the posthorn solo to a flügelhorn, a successful experiment. His light touch in the middle movements is admirable, and Norma Procter is a steady soloist in "O Mensch! Gib acht!", with the Wandsworth School Boys' Choir bimm-bamming as if they were all Austrian-born! Then comes the *Adagio* finale, its intensity and ecstasy sustained by Horenstein without dragging the tempo. The recording is not as full and rich in dynamic range as some made recently, but it is still a classic.

Mahler. Symphony No. 4 in G major. **Kathleen Battle** (sop); **Vienna Philharmonic Orchestra/Lorin Maazel.** CBS Masterworks CD39072. From IM39072 (3/85).

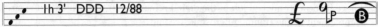

Mahler. Symphony No. 4 in G major. **Felicity Lott** (sop); **London Philharmonic Orchestra/Franz Welser-Möst.** EMI Eminence CD-EMX2139. Text and translation included.

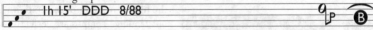

"With sincere and serene expression" says Mahler's footnote in the finale — "absolutely without parody!" And that is exactly how Lorin Maazel, Kathleen Battle and the Vienna Philharmonic Orchestra respond to this music: the grotesqueries of the scherzo are nicely underplayed; the darker outbursts of the slow movement are not overloaded with *Angst*; and there is nothing wry or sentimentally nostalgic about "Die himmlischen Freuden". Instead, there is warmth, tenderness and, especially in the closing movement, a kind of heart-easing simplicity, enhanced by the purity and uncloying sweetness of Kathleen Battle's singing. The recording is warm-toned and beautifully balanced and the dynamic range is impressive, though never unrealistic.

Franz Welser-Möst, however, sheds new light on this Symphony with a reading that is the most expansive on disc so far. This has the effect of placing the work more in the context of Mahler's symphonic line. 'Expansive' is very much the word, the slow movement being the most controversial in this respect. Welser-Möst takes a leisurely 25 minutes here (most performances average 19 or 20 minutes) but the effect is quite magical and convincing, with never a hint of sluggishness, and the final climax and closing pages of this movement are truly revelatory and uplifting. The phantasmagoria of the first movement is well captured too, from the optimistic opening to the fairy-tale horror of the development's climax, where the trumpet's fanfare looks both back to the Second and Third Symphonies and forward to the opening of the Fifth. The LPO's performance is top rate, with some ravishing and full-bodied string playing, and Welser-Möst's meticulous attention to detail is highlighted by a spacious and well-defined recording.

Mahler. Symphony No. 5. **Vienna Philharmonic Orchestra/Leonard Bernstein.** DG 431 037-2GBE. Recorded at a performance in the Alte Oper, Frankfurt during September 1987.

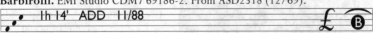

Mahler. Symphony No. 5. **New Philharmonia Orchestra/Sir John Barbirolli.** EMI Studio CDM7 69186-2. From ASD2518 (12/69).

Mahler's Fifth begins with a funeral march, in which the military bugle-calls he heard as a boy sound through the textures, leading to a central *scherzo* full of nostalgia for Alpine lakes and pastures, a soulful *Adagietto* for strings which we now know was a love-letter to his future wife and ends with a triumphant, joyous *rondo-finale*. It has been called Mahler's *Eroica* and that is not a far-fetched description. In recent years Bernstein tended to go 'over the top' in Mahler, but here he is at his exciting best and the Vienna Philharmonic responds to him as only it can to a conductor with whom it has a special relationship. The recording is exceptionally clear and well-balanced, so that many subtleties of detail in the scoring emerge but are not over highlighted. The symphony again sounds like the daringly orchestrated piece that bewildered its first audiences, only now we realize the genius of it all. Structure, sound and emotion are held in ideal equilibrium by Bernstein in this enthralling performance.

Barbirolli's Mahler No. 5 has a special place in everybody's affections: a performance so big in spirit and warm of heart as to silence any rational discussion of its shortcomings. Despite some controversially measured tempos and ensemble in the vehement second movement that is not all it should be, this reading has a unity and strength of purpose and an entirely idiomatic response to Mahlerian colour and cast. But most important of all, it has that very special Barbirolli radiance, humanity — call it what you will — the celebrated *Adagietto* is, needless to say, in very caring hands indeed. Something of a classic, then (and EMI have made a wonderful job of the digital remastering), though one to regard as a supplement to the stunning Bernstein account.

Mahler. Symphony No. 6 in A minor[a]. Five Rückert Lieder[b]. [b]**Christa Ludwig** (mez); **Berlin Philharmonic Orchestra/Herbert von Karajan.** DG 415.099-2GH2. Notes, texts and translations included. Item marked [a] from 2707 106 (7/78), [b] 2707 082 (12/75).

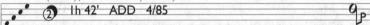

② 1h 42' ADD 4/85

Mahler. Symphony No. 6. **City of Birmingham Symphony Orchestra/ Simon Rattle.** EMI CDS7 54047-2.

② 1h 26' DDD 11/90

Mahler. Symphony No. 6. Kindertotenlieder[a]. [a]**Thomas Hampson** (bar); **Vienna Philharmonic Orchestra/Leonard Bernstein.** DG 427 697-2GH2. Recorded at a performance in the Grosser Saal, Musikverein, Vienna in September and October 1988

② 1h 55' DDD 1/90

Mahler's tragic Sixth Symphony digs more profoundly into the nature of man and Fate than any of his earlier works, closing in desolation, a beat on the bass drum, a coffin lid closing. Karajan's reading of this great work is superb, profoundly observed and imaginatively coloured. The *Rückert Lieder*, which complete the set, show how Mahler's song writing changed as he moved away from the folk-song world of *Des Knaben Wunderhorn* to the sparer, emotionally tauter and spiritually more concentrated poetic world of Friedrich Rückert. Christa Ludwig brings her rich, burnished tones to these glorious songs and is sensitively accompanied by Karajan, whose handling of the important wind lines is masterly. It restores one's taste for life after the bleakness of the symphony's close.

Rattle is also a natural Mahlerian and his emotional and intellectual grasp of

the first movement of the Sixth is outstanding. Tempos are perfectly judged and there's a tremendous feeling of architectural unity here. The beautiful *Alma* theme is played with a great deal of elation and affection, with inner parts superbly detailed (the descanting horns sound wonderful) and upper strings are perfectly phrased and radiant. Rattle has strong feelings about the ordering of the central movements, belonging to the school of thought that Mahler originally intended the *Andante* to precede the *Scherzo* (most conductors perform them as published — *Scherzo* first, *Andante* second) so it comes as no surprise to find the more controversial

Simon Rattle   [photo: EMI/Mihich

order in Rattle's recording (it's only fair to mention that EMI have split these movements between the two discs, thus ruling out any ideas listeners may have of craftily altering the sequence). Rattle's account of the *Andante* is extraordinarily beautiful — magical in the extreme, with some particularly intense and lovely solos from the players of the CBSO, and in the finale Rattle calculatingly builds the intensity and anguish to an almost unbearable degree when we reach the third and final hammer blow (which Rattle reinstates in this performance) after which all is darkness until the spine-chilling final chord in A minor. The recording is well balanced and superbly engineered.

Bernstein's reading was a live recording at a concert, with all the electricity of such an occasion, and the Vienna Philharmonic Orchestra respond to the conductor's dark vision of Mahler's score with tremendous bravura. Fortunately, the achingly tender slow movement brings some relief, but with the enormous finale lasting over 30 minutes we must witness a resumption of a battle to the death and the final outcome. The coupling is a logical one, for the *Kindertotenlieder* takes up the theme of death yet again. But it is in a totally different, quieter way: these beautiful songs express a parent's grief over the loss of a child, and although some prefer a woman's voice, the sensitive Thomas Hampson makes a good case here for a male singer. The recording of both works is so good that one would not know it was made 'live', particularly as the applause is omitted.

Mahler. Symphony No. 7. **Chicago Symphony Orchestra/Claudio Abbado.** DG 413 773-2GH2. From 413 773-1GH2 (3/85).

(2) 1h 19' DDD 4/85

Mahler provided no programme for this Symphony but it can be logically viewed as a progression through various shades of darkness until a finale is reached, providing light and hope. Abbado's performance has a clear-sighted lucidity which serves this work well. The first movement has a fine coherence, and a forward-moving thrust; the distinctive separate characters of the inner movements are sharply drawn, and throughout the symphony Abbado draws playing of brilliance and refinement from the Chicago orchestra. The recording has an ideal clarity too, and a presence which boldly illuminates Mahler's fantastic scoring.

Mahler. Symphony No. 8. **Elizabeth Connell, Edith Wiens, Felicity Lott** (sops); **Trudeliese Schmidt, Nadine Denize** (contrs); **Richard Versalle** (ten); **Jorma Hynninen** (bar); **Hans Sotin** (bass); **Tiffin Boys' School Choir; London Philharmonic Choir and Orchestra/Klaus Tennstedt.** EMI CDS7 47625-8. Notes, text and translation included. From EX270474-3 (3/87).

(2) 1h 22' DDD 5/87

Mahler's extravagantly monumental Eighth Symphony, often known as the *Symphony of a Thousand*, is the Mahler symphony that raises doubts in even his most devoted of admirers. Its epic dimensions, staggering vision and sheer profligacy of forces required make it a 'difficult work'. Given a great live performance it will sway even the hardest of hearts; given a performance like Tennstedt's, reproduced with all the advantages of CD, home-listeners, too, can be mightily impressed (and so, given the forces involved, will most of the neighbourhood!) — the sheer volume of sound at the climax is quite overwhelming. The work seeks to parallel the Christian's faith in the power of the Holy Spirit with the redeeming power of love for mankind and Tennstedt's performance leaves no doubt that he believes totally in Mahler's creation. It has a rapt, almost intimate, quality that makes this reading all the more moving. The soloists are excellent and the choruses sing with great conviction.

Mahler. Symphony No. 9. **Berlin Philharmonic Orchestra/Herbert von Karajan.** DG 410 726-2GH2. Recorded at performances in September 1982 at the Berlin Festival.

| | ② | 1h 25' | DDD | 8/84 | | P | Ⓑ |

Mahler: Symphony No. 9. **Berlin Philharmonic Orchestra/Sir John Barbirolli.** EMI Studio CDM7 63115-2. From ASD596/7 (9/64).

| | 1h 18' | ADD | 11/89 | £ | P | Ⓑ |

<u>NEW REVIEW</u>

Mahler. Symphony No. 9[a].
Wagner. Siegfried Idyll[b]. [a]**New Philharmonia Orchestra;** [b]**Philharmonia Orchestra/Otto Klemperer.** EMI Studio CMS7 63277-2. Item marked [a] from Columbia SAX5281/2 (9/67), [b] SAX2455/6 (11/62).

| | ② | 1h 45' | ADD | 1/90 | | P | Ⓑ |

Mahler's Ninth is a death-haunted work, but is filled, as Bruno Walter remarked, "with a sanctified feeling of departure". Rarely has this Symphony been shaped with such understanding and played with such selfless virtuosity as it was by Karajan and the Berlin Philharmonic in a legendary series of concerts in 1982. The performance is electric and intense, yet Karajan — ever the enigmatic blend of fire and ice — has the measure of the symphony's spiritual coolness. Karajan had previously made a fine studio recording of the Ninth but this later concert performance is purer, deeper, and even more dauntingly intense. The digital recording has great clarity and a thrilling sense of actuality; no symphony in the repertoire benefits more than this one from the absolute quietness that CD allows. When the history of twentieth-century music-making comes to be written this performance will be seen as one of its proudest landmarks.

Barbirolli's famous recording of Mahler's Ninth Symphony has also long been considered as one of the finest accounts on disc. It is reputed that Barbirolli spent over 50 hours rehearsing this Symphony when he first conducted it with the Hallé Orchestra in 1954. This recording, made ten years later with the Berlin Philharmonic, certainly contains all the hallmarks of a conductor who possesses a deep understanding of and affection for the work. The result is very special indeed. Barbirolli took great pains over this recording, even to the point of rearranging the recording schedules so that the last movement *Adagio* was recorded in one of the evening sessions, giving the players a chance to "get in the right mood" as he put it. The first movement is primed with intensity and emotion, and Mahler's vast arch-like structure is never allowed to flag or falter for a moment. Contrapuntally this movement is the most complex that Mahler ever wrote, and Barbirolli's handling of these textures is imbued with a clarity and sense of purpose seldom found. The sarcasm and irony of the central movements are superbly drawn, and the *Rondo Burleske* has a savage ferocity of demonic proportions. The stoical *Adagio*-finale is given a reading of transcendental beauty, intensity and passion. The recording, like the playing, is warm, sumptuous and atmospheric and apart from some faint tape hiss, shows little sign of ageing. Highly recommended.

Otto Klemperer's approach to the Ninth stands at an opposite pole to those of Karajan and Barbirolli. Where the latter imbue this deeply melancholic work with a very intense level of personal feeling, Klemperer appears to stand back, letting the music speak simply for itself. The result is different but equally powerful: the two majestic outer movements have a stoic grandeur quite different from other interpretations. And the great benefit of this approach is seen in the central scherzos, both of which have a genuine rustic vigour — almost mocking the finer feelings of the rest of this extraordinary work, and by implication, death itself. Klemperer's interpretation has an objective power and passion which is becoming increasingly rare today: and it may be worth noting that of the three conductors in question, he was the only one to have worked closely with Mahler himself. His conducting therefore has a stamp of authority inevitably lacking elsewhere. The New Philharmonia play well for him, if not quite with the acute tonal refinement of the Berlin Philharmonic, and EMI's recording is clear if a little antiseptic. An added bonus to this issue is Klemperer's fine performance of Wagner's *Siegfried Idyll*. Mahler's Ninth is such a great masterpiece that it can only benefit from three such different interpretations: each reading reveals varied facets of one of the key works of the early twentieth century.

Mahler (ed. Cooke). Symphony No. 10. **Bournemouth Symphony Orchestra/Simon Rattle.** EMI CDC7 54406. From HMV SLS5206 (12/80).

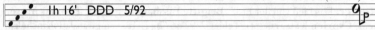

Rattle's superb interpretation of Cooke's performing version of the Tenth Symphony now sweeps the board. His achievement is in a special class, empowering the music with such emotional clout that you forget the scholarly debates. There are in fact several adjustments to Schirmer's published score which Rattle explained in the splendid booklet which accompanied the original LP issue. Unfortunately, this has not been included with this CD reissue. One example of his innovatory approach is his merging of the drum stroke which ends the fourth movement with the one which triggers the fifth; furthermore the opening pages of the finale are truly awesome here. Tempos are unfailingly appropriate and the Bournemouth band is second to none. This is music-making of extraordinary fervour, with excellent sound. It is altogether an essential purchase.

Mahler. LIEDER.
Wolf. LIEDER. **Anne Sofie von Otter** (mez); **Ralf Gothóni** (pf). DG 423 666-2GH. Texts and translations included.
Mahler: Des Knaben Wunderhorn — No. 2, Verlorne Müh; No. 7, Rheinlegendchen; No. 9, Wo die schönen Trompeten blasen; No. 10, Lob des hohen Verstands. Lieder und Gesang — No. 1, Frühlingsmorgen. No. 2, Erinnerung. No. 4, Serenade aus Don Juan. No. 5, Phantasie aus Don Juan No. 7, Ich ging mit Lust durch einen grünen Wald. No. 8, Aus! Aus!. *Wolf:* Heiss mich nicht reden (Mignon I). Nur wer die Sehnsucht (Mignon II). So lasst mich scheinen (Mignon III). Kennst du das Land (Mignon). Frühling übers Jahr. Frage nicht. Die Spröde. Der Schäfer. Gesang Weylas.

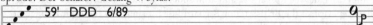

Anne Sofie von Otter's first record of Lieder proved an outright winner. She obviously owes something of a debt to Christa Ludwig and Brigitte Fassbaender, but she nonetheless establishes a personality and style of her own. Technically she is virtually faultless, and she brings to her performance a nice combination of interpretative insight and emotional involvement. These assets are at once evident in the four settings by Hugo Wolf of Mignon's enigmatic utterances from *Wilhelm Meister*. Each is perceptively characterized by von Otter and her admirable partner Ralf Gothóni, bringing before our eyes the suppressed grief and longing of the sad waif so unerringly portrayed by Wolf. They then find, by contrast, a pleasing simplicity for the next three songs before returning to a more intense manner for the marvellous *Gesang Weylas*. For the Mahler the pair adopt another style and just the right one. Humour and lightness, where relevant, rightly dominate their accounts of the pieces from *Des Knaben Wunderhorn*. Von Otter's singing is playful without ever becoming coy or mannered. In the more serious "Ich ging mit Lust" the singer's melding of line and tone is near-ideal. "Wo die schönen Trompeten blasen" may be taken at a dangerously slow tempo, but this in a way enhances the mesmeric mood of the song. The seldom-heard settings from Molina's *Don Juan*, especially the alluring "Serenade", are precisely tuned to the music in hand. Altogether a delightful disc.

Mahler. Das Lied von der Erde. **Christa Ludwig** (mez); **Fritz Wunderlich** (ten); **Philharmonia Orchestra, New Philharmonia Orchestra/Otto Klemperer.** EMI CDC7 47231-2. From SAN179 (1/67).

1h 4' ADD 12/85

Mahler. Das Lied von der Erde. **Maureen Forrester** (contr); **Richard Lewis** (ten); **Chicago Symphony Orchestra/Fritz Reiner.** RCA Victor Gold Seal GD60178. Text and translation included. From VICS6200 (10/69).

1h 3' ADD 10/91

Mahler. Das Lied von der Erde. **Brigitte Fassbaender** (mez); **Thomas Moser** (ten); **Cyprien Katsaris** (pf). Teldec 2292-46276-2. Text and translation included.

1h 1' DDD 6/90

One of the great orchestral song cycles grew, like the Ninth Symphony, out of Mahler's sense of the imminence of his own death. The text is based on poems from the Chinese T'ang dynasty and their delicate sense of the transience of things chimed perfectly with Mahler's mood. His music is luminously beautiful but shot through with a recurring sense of irony, anguish and imminent loss. Of the recordings on CD Otto Klemperer's 1966 version remains one of the best sung, best played, and most characterfully and illuminatingly conducted of all. Walter Legge's recording is admirably balanced, allowing us to hear every word and nuance of Wunderlich's incomparable singing. Christa Ludwig also benefits from the unvarnished clarity of the recording; like Wunderlich, she gives a performance which for beauty of tone and truth of inflexion remains unsurpassed in living memory. Klemperer's reading is cast in the stoic vein and is uniquely chilly in the haunting second movement. But for all its grimness and gauntness and sharply etched detailing, Klemperer's is also a reading of great compassion. Above all, it is that rare thing: a performance in which the work seems to be being discovered anew in every bar.

At mid-price Fritz Reiner's interpretation presents a fitting alternative to Otto Klemperer's. If anything Reiner's orchestra — the Chicago Symphony — has a slight edge over the New Philharmonia: string tone is rich and sumptuous, the woodwind playing is equally as subtle and in general phrasing and dynamics are extremely well observed. And RCA's recording, dating from 1959, retains a competitive degree of warmth and atmosphere. Reiner's soloists are experts in their repertoire: the British tenor Richard Lewis brings just the right balance of naïvety and irony to his three songs, as well as great tonal refinement. Maureen Forrester is a fine contralto soloist who has all the vocal and interpretative resources required for this demanding work: different in style and approach from Christa Ludwig under Klemperer but just as compelling. And finally there is Reiner himself: one of the great conductors of the twentieth century who, like Klemperer, opts for the objective style with Mahler, rather than Bruno Walter's 'heart on the sleeve' approach. Both are equally valid, and when combined with such an excellent orchestra as the Chicago Symphony and two fine soloists, the result is both memorable and compelling.

The première recording of the composer's own piano version of *Das Lied von der Erde* provides us with a valuable insight into Mahler's creative processes. As Stephen E. Hefling's informative booklet-notes point out this is not just a piano transcription of the orchestral score, but a valid performing version in its own right; an observation reinforced not only by Mahler's own remark that "*what* one writes has always seemed to me more important than what it is scored *for*" but also by the fact that he worked on both the piano and orchestral versions almost simultaneously. The orchestral version of *Das Lied von der Erde* (a symphony in all but name) represents a perfect synthesis of the two genres that occupied his entire creative career — the symphony and the song, which make it all the more fitting to have the opportunity to hear the more intimate keyboard setting

presented here. Any lingering doubts one may still have about the validity or
necessity for such a recording are soon dispelled by the commitment and
persuasiveness of the performances. Thomas Moser and Brigitte Fassbaender give
intense and moving performances throughout (Fassbaender's "Der Abschied" is
particularly impressive) and both respond well to the more subtle approach
required for this more intimate, almost Lieder-like version. Cyprien Katsaris
deserves much praise too for his sympathetic and virtuoso performance of the
piano part. An essential purchase for any serious Mahlerian.

Mahler. Des Knaben Wunderhorn. **Elisabeth Schwarzkopf** (sop); **Dietrich
Fischer-Dieskau** (bar); **London Symphony Orchestra/George Szell.** EMI
CDC7 47277-2. From SAN218 (1/69).

| 48' ADD 11/88 |

NEW REVIEW

Mahler. Des Knaben Wunderhorn. **Ann Murray** (mez); **Thomas Allen**
(bar); **London Philharmonic Orchestra/Sir Charles Mackerras.** Virgin
Classics VC7 91432-2. Texts and translations included.
Der Schildwache Nachtlied. Verlor'ne Müh'. Trost im Unglück. Wer hat dies
Liedlein erdacht?. Das irdische Leben. Des Antonius von Padua Fischpredigt.
Rheinlegendchen. Lied des Verfolgten im Turme. Wo die schönen Trompeten
blasen. Lob des hohen Verstandes. Revelge. Der Tambourg'sell.

| 51' DDD 11/91 |

Mahler's reputation rests primarily on his ten symphonies, but running alongside
these magnificent works are his great song cycles. The poems of *Des Knaben
Wunderhorn* ("The youth's magic horn") are drawn from a collection written in a
deliberately 'folk' style. They are often humorous, ironic (as in the military
settings), surreal or eerily strange. Mahler's use of the orchestra is delicate and
sensitive; he rarely employs its full might but conjures from it a wide variety of
colours and sounds. Schwarzkopf and Fischer-Dieskau sing the songs magnificently, drawing from the texts every verbal nuance and subtle shading and Szell's
accompaniments are outstanding.

Virgin's 1991 recording presents a worthy foil to this earlier (1968) classic.
Sir Charles Mackerras leads the London Philharmonic in a jauntily extrovert style
which offers a freer and more
'open air' alternative to Szell's
intense and precise direction.
Thomas Allen's singing shares
the same characteristics as
Mackerras's conducting and if
he does not possess all of
Fischer-Dieskau's lifetime of
insights into Mahler's songs,
tonally he offers strong competition. Similarly Ann Murray's
beautiful mezzo voice has a
plangent naturalness that contrasts well with Schwarzkopf's
occasional archness. Virgin's
recorded sound does not quite
possess the atmosphere of
Walter Legge's EMI recording
but the difference is not so
great as to prevent this newer
issue from presenting an

Elisabeth Schwarzkopf   [photo: EMI/Wilson]

attractive alternative to Szell with its own distinctive approach to Mahler's unique and evocative sound world.

Mahler. Das klagende Lied (complete version including "Waldmärchen"). **Susan Dunn** (sop); **Markus Baur** (alto); **Brigitte Fassbaender** (mez); **Werner Hollweg** (ten); **Andreas Schmidt** (bar); **Städtischer Musikverein Düsseldorf; Berlin Radio Symphony Orchestra/Riccardo Chailly.** Decca 425 719-2DH. Text and translation included.

1h 4' DDD 2/92

Even the musically acute listener would be unlikely to realize that *Das klagende Lied* is the work of a teenager. Mahler's first significant work is as self-assured as anything he was to write in later life. Indeed enthusiastic Mahlerians will ecognize here passages which crop up in other works, most notably the Second Symphony. Those same enthusiastic Mahlerians might not recognize much of this recording, however, since only two movements of *Klagende Lied* are usually performed: the 30-minute first movement is considered too rambling. But no one could possibly arrive at that conclusion from this tautly directly, electrifying performance, and it contains some wonderfully imaginative music, including some delightful forest murmurs, which it seems tragic to miss out. For this movement alone this CD is a must for any Mahler fan, but more than that this is a spectacular recording of a one-in-a-million performance. The soloists, choir and orchestra achieve near perfection under Chailly's inspired direction, and the decision to substitute for the marvellous Brigitte Fassbaender a boy alto (Markus Baur) to represent the disembodied voice of the dead brother is a stroke of pure genius. His weird, unnatural voice provide a moment of sheer spine-tingling drama.

Mahler. Kindertotenlieder[a]. Rückert Lieder[b]. Lieder eines fahrenden Gesellen[a]. **Dame Janet Baker** (mez); [a]**Hallé Orchestra;** [b]**New Philharmonia Orchestra/Sir John Barbirolli.** EMI CDC7 47793-2. Texts and translations included. Items marked [a] from ASD2338 (2/68), [b] ASD2518/19 (12/69).

65' ADD 12/87

The songs of the *Lieder eines fahrenden Gesellen* ("Songs of a Wayfarer") are directly quoted from Mahler's First Symphony and the same fresh, springtime atmosphere is shared by both works. The orchestration has great textural clarity and lightness of touch. The *Kindertotenlieder*, more chromatically expressive than the earlier work, tap into a darker, more psychologically complex vein in Mahler's spiritual and emotional make-up. The *Rückert Lieder* are not a song cycle as such but gather in their romantic awareness and response to the beauties of the poetry a unity and shape that acts to bind them. Together, Baker and Barbirolli reach a transcendental awareness of Mahler's inner musings. Barbirolli draws from the Hallé playing of great delicacy and precision and establishes a clear case for having this CD in your collection.

Gian Francesco Malipiero
Italian 1882-1973

Malipiero. STRING QUARTETS. **Orpheus Quartet** (Charles-André Linale, Emilian Piedicuta, vns; Emil Cantor, va; Laurentiu Sbarcea, vc). ASV CDDCD457.

No. 1, "Rispetti e strambotti"; No. 2, "Stornelli e ballate"; No. 3, "Cantari alla madrigalesca"; No. 4; No. 5, "dei capricci"; No. 6, "L'arca di Noè"; No. 7; No. 8, "per Elisabetta".

② 2h 5' DDD 2/92 ❓

Gian Francesco Malipiero belonged to that post-Puccinian phase of Italian music in which composers sought to be taken as seriously for instrumental and symphonic composition as for opera. Though an almost exact contemporary of Stravinsky, Malipiero was never a wholehearted neoclassicist: rather, there is a lively, unsentimental romanticism in his music that may suggest affinities with composers as different as the later Janáček, the later Bartók and even the earlier Tippett. Malipiero may only rarely achieve an expressive depth comparable to these masters at their greatest. But he hardly ever lapses into mere note-spinning. Even though his forms seem to shun sonata principles with conscious consistency, there is a fluency and spontaneity in his materials and forms (which often come across as sequences of dance-like and song-like episodes) that make for enjoyable, refreshing listening. Malipiero's characteristically light touch is especially apparent in the Sixth Quartet, *L'arca di Noè* ("Noah's Ark"), though it would seem to be the pleasure of the animals at being saved from the flood rather than farmyard noises that the music represents. The Orpheus Quartet are to be warmly commended for devoting such care and commitment to this unfamiliar repertory. The recording is on the close side, but this never becomes oppressive.

Marin Marais
French 1656-1728

NEW REVIEW

Marais. ALCYONE. **Jennifer Smith** (sop) Alcyone; **Gilles Ragon** (ten) Ceyx; **Philippe Huttenlocher** (bar) Pélée; **Vincent Le Texier** (bass-bar) Pan, Phorbas; **Sophie Boulin** (sop) Ismène, First Sailor; **Bernard Delétré** (bass) Tmole, High Priest, Neptune; **Jean-Paul Fouchécourt** (alto) Morpheus; **Véronique Gens** (sop) Second Sailor, Priestess; **Les Musiciens du Louvre/ Marc Minkowski.** Erato MusiFrance 2292-45522-2. Notes, text and translation included.

② 2h 34' DDD 4/92 ❓

Today, Marin Marais is remembered almost entirely for his legacy of music for the bass viol. But in his own day Marais was recognized as a talented opera composer, too. *Alcyone*, first performed in 1706, was his dramatic *chef d'oeuvre* and held the stage at intervals for more than half a century. Though he followed in Lully's footsteps, Marais spoke with a voice of his own and nowhere is this more apparent than in *Alcyone*, which contains in its Fourth Act one of the great moments in French opera literature — a tempest, judged so successful by his contemporaries that not only was it performed as a separate item at court, at the express command of the king, but also found its way into a revival of a Lully opera early in the eighteenth century. The plot centres on the thwarted love of Alcyone for Ceyx, a *tragédie* which moves, however, to a happy ending. Marais's music explores a wide range of emotions. Catchy instrumental pieces — the sailors' dance in Act 3 is especially captivating — supple choruses and touching airs abound, several foreshadowing Rameau in their colourful orchestration. The mainly strong cast is headed by the soprano, Jennifer Smith, in the title role, with lively performances by Sophie Boulin as Ismène, Phorbas's partner in crime, and Gilles Ragon as Ceyx. Minkowski directs with stylish conviction and a good sense of pace. A few rough edges count for little where so much else is enlightened. The vivid recording comes with full texts and translations.

Frank Martin

Swiss 1890-1974

Martin. Cello Concerto[a]. Les quatre éléments[b]. [a]**Jean Decross** (vc);
Concertgebouw Orchestra/Bernard Haitink. Preludio PRL2147.
43' ADD 10/91

Two works from the 1960s which fill in the picture of the composer after such
works as the *Petite symphonie concertante* or the Concerto for seven wind
instruments. *The four elements* (1963-64) was designed as an eightieth birthday
present for Ernest Ansermet, a lifelong champion of the composer, and the Cello
Concerto (1966) was written for the great French cellist Pierre Fournier. (It says
much for the swinging, shallow 1960s that their appearance made scarcely any
impact at the time.) *The four elements* is a short work of just under 20 minutes
but is music of substance and powerful imaginative vision. It was the "world in
the original state, without movement" as Martin experienced it in the uppermost
part of Northern Norway and Iceland that inspired the first movement, "Earth".
"Water" has plenty of movement, and is scored with wonderful delicacy and
resource; "Air" is all lightness and transparency and "Fire" is wonderfully evoked.
The Cello Concerto is a real discovery, a strong work and vintage Martin. The
slow movement has the character of a Sarabande and is particularly haunting.
Both in substance and the orchestral presentation, this is inventive and resourceful music. The performances emanate from radio tapes and though the recordings
are not perfect, they are very good indeed as one would expect given the
Concertgebouw's acoustic, and the balance is excellent. The audience is generally
quiet and attentive throughout, and applause is retained at the end of the two
works. At under 44 minutes this is open to the charge of short measure even at
mid price. But if it is short on quantity, it is long on quality.

Martin. Concerto for seven wind instruments, timpani, percussion and string
orchestra. Petite symphonie concertante[a]. Sechs Monologe aus "Jedermann"[b].
[b]**Gilles Cachemaille** (bar); [a]**Eva Guibentif** (hp); **Christiane Jaccottet** (hpd);
[a]**Ursula Riuttimann** (pf); **Suisse Romande Orchestra/Armin Jordan.**
Erato 2292-45694-2. Notes, texts and translations included.
1h 2' DDD 11/91

Martin. Concerto for seven wind instruments, percussion and string orchestra
(1949). Polyptique (1972-3)[a]. Etudes (1955-6). [a]**Marieke Blankestijn** (vn);
Chamber Orchestra of Europe/Thierry Fischer. DG 435 383-2GH.
1h 6' DDD 6/92

Here at long last we have a really satisfying modern version of the Martin *Petite
symphonie concertante* with all the benefits of good modern sound. Armin Jordan's
reading has a sense of space and atmosphere that draws you immediately into
Martin's world and his command of the architecture of the piece and its pacing is
impressive. The excellent recorded balance enables the three soloists to come
through their transparent string texture. The Concerto for seven wind instruments finds the Orchestre de la Suisse Romande in very good form indeed and
this splendidly recorded new account supersedes other recordings of the work.
The *Sechs Monologe aus "Jedermann"* (Six Monologues from Hofmannsthal's
"Everyman"), written at the height of the Second World War and orchestrated
three years after its conclusion, is arguably Martin's masterpiece. It is surely one
of the most subtle and profound vocal works of our time. While it does not
displace the classic 1963 account by Fischer-Dieskau and the Berlin Philharmonic

under the composer (reviewed below), it is very impressive sonically. Gilles Cachemaille proves a perceptive and powerful advocate of this remarkable score, while the orchestra is recorded with great presence and detail. This disc would make an ideal starting-point for anyone wanting to explore this remarkable composer's world.

This is a disc of exceptional excellence. These three pieces have all been recorded before but never as well — and they have certainly never been better played! In the concerto the virtuosity and sophistication of the wind of the Chamber Orchestra of Europe is so effortless and their accents far lighter in touch than their rivals. Their playing has real delicacy and clarity of articulation and the slow movement for once really sounds as it is marked, mysterious and yet elegant, while the muted strings have a lightness of sonority and colour which greatly enhances the atmosphere. The artistry of the strings is everywhere in evidence in the Etudes and they quite outclass other performances in their sensitivity of response and range of colour. The *Polyptique* for violin and two string orchestras dates from the last year of Martin's life, when he was 83. It was

inspired by a polyptych, a set of very small panels that Martin saw in Sienna representing various episodes in the Passion. The work is inward-looking and powerfully searching, and is played with great beauty and purity of tone, and rapt concentration by Marieke Blankestijn and the Chamber Orchestra of Europe. The recording is one of the best from this (or any other) source. It is completely natural, truthful in timbre and has remarkable clarity and presence. The perspective is very musically judged and both producer and engineer deserve a special mention for the refinement and quality of the sound they have captured.

Armin Jordan   *[photo: Erato / Sarrat]*

NEW REVIEW

Martin. Petite symphonie concertante[a]. Maria-Triptychon[b]. Passacaglia (transc. comp.)[c]. [b]**Irmgaard Seefried** (sop); [b]**Wolfgang Schneiderhan** (vn); [a]**Eva Hunziker** (hp); [a]**Germaine Vaucher-Clerc** (clavecin); [a]**Doris Rossiaud** (pf); [ab]**Suisse Romande Orchestra;** [c]**Berlin Philharmonic Orchestra / Frank Martin.** Jecklin Disco mono JD645-2.

57' ADD 10/91

Frank Martin's own recording of the *Petite symphonie concertante* comes from a Swiss Radio broadcast in 1970 and confirms the suspicion that most performances and recordings are too fast. He takes the opening at the speed he marked; it is slower and much more concentrated in atmosphere, and the *Adagio* section later on gains from a similar breadth. Two of the soloists, Germaine Vauchet-Clerc and Doris Rossiaud, took part in Ansermet's pioneering recording (Decca mono 430 003-2DM, reviewed in the 1992 edition of this *Guide*). This is a most convincing and atmospheric account of this masterly score. But be warned, the 1970 Swiss Radio recording is mono, which is not in itself worrying, but the sound is less than state-of-the-art even by the standards of the 1960s and 1970s. Nor is the *Maria-Triptychon* very much better. The work was written in the late 1960s in response to a request from Wolfgang Schneiderhan for a work for violin, soprano and orchestra that he could perform with his wife, Irmgaard Seefried. The "Magnificat", which constitutes the middle movement, originally stood on its own, the two outer movements ("Ave Maria" and "Stabat Mater") being added later. There are moments of great vision during the course of the piece but the monochrome recording will undoubtedly limits its appeal somewhat. Martin's refined and imaginative orchestral transcription of the 1944 *Passacaglia* for organ is a rarity: (the 1952 version for string orchestra he made for Karl Münchinger is more commonly encountered). But it is beautifully played under Martin's own direction and readers with a special interest in this remarkable composer should consider investigating this issue for its documentary interest.

Martin. CHAMBER WORKS. **Zurich Chamber Ensemble** (Brenton Langbein, [ab]Andreas Pfenninger, vns; [a]Cornel Anderes, [bc]Jürg Dähler, vas; Raffaele Altwegg, [a]Luciano Pezzani, vcs); [bd]**Hanni Schmid-Wyss** (pf). Jecklin Disco JD646-2. Pavane couleur du temps[a]. Piano Quintet[b]. String Trio[c]. Trio sur des mélodies populaires irlandaises[d].

· 1h 6' ADD 10/91

This disc is valuable in filling in a gap in our knowledge of a still much underrated master. All four works come from the period 1919-36 before Martin found the mature style of *Der Cornet, Le vin herbé* and the *Six "Everyman" monologues*. They are presented chronologically, the earliest and longest being the Piano Quintet (1919), written as the composer was approaching 30. The influence of Ravel is strongest in the minuet (particularly the trio), and in the finale, though in the first movement he seems even closer to the language of late Fauré. There is a serious, almost elegiac quality about this writing and a sustained poignant eloquence which resurfaces in the slow movement though the finale is not quite the equal of the opening movement. The string quintet from the following year is a short piece lasting seven minutes. Its title, *Pavane couleur du temps*, derives its title from the fairy story by Charles Perrault, *Peau d'âne* ("Donkey skin") in which a young girl wishes for "a dress the colour of time", and the piece has a grave courtly quality that is charming. The two other works are both trios. The *Trio sur des mélodies populaires irlandaises* comes from the mid-1920s and is the more familiar of the two. It is an ingenious and witty piece whereas Martin himself says "everything is achieved through rhythm and melody", and it is this rhythmic ingenuity that lends it so strong an appeal. The String Trio is made of sterner stuff and its harmonic language is far more astringent than any of the companion works. It is short, barely 15 minutes in length, concentrated in feeling, economical in its gesture and with no notes wasted. The performances are all highly accomplished and the excellent, well-balanced 1989 recordings emanate from analogue originals made presumably for Zurich Radio. A valuable and rewarding addition to the growing discography of this composer, this disc is strongly recommended.

Martin. Sechs Monologe aus "Jedermann"[a]. DER STURM[a] — Overture; Mein Ariel!; Hin sind meine Zaubere'in.
Egk. La tentation de Saint Antoine[b]. [b]**Dame Janet Baker** (mez); [a]**Dietrich Fischer-Dieskau** (bar); [b]**Koeckert Quartet** (Rudolf Koeckert, Willi Buchner, vns; Oskar Reidl, va; Josef Merz); [b]strings of **Bavarian Radio Symphony Orchestra/Werner Egk**; [a]**Berlin Philharmonic Orchestra/Frank Martin.** DG 20th Century Classics 429 858-2GC. Texts and translations included. Item marked [a] from SLPM138871 (4/64), [b] SLPM139142 (2/67).

· 1h 5' ADD 10/91

A desert island disc in more senses than one! Martin's opera *Der Sturm* ("The Tempest") comes from the early 1950s. The text used is Schlegel's German translation, not Shakespeare's original — Martin's first language was French and he spoke only a little English. The Overture is quite magical and evokes the mysterious atmosphere of the island and the sea. If the pale, moonlit colouring of *Pélleas* can at times be detected in some of his earlier works, *The Tempest* inhabits a wholly individual sound world and one which puts you immediately and lastingly under its spell. Dietrich Fischer-Dieskau sings the two excepts from Act 3 of the opera, Prospero's aria, "My Ariel!/Hast thou, which art but air,/A touch, a feeling of their afflictions ..." and the Epilogue, "Now my charms are all o'erthrown", with his usual authority and poetic feeling, and though he is more closely balanced than is ideal, that is the only reservation to be made about the sound, which is first class. Martin's *Sechs Monologe aus "Jedermann"* is arguably his greatest song-cycle (apart from his extraordinary setting of Rilke's *Der Cornet*) and one of the great song cycles of this century. Hofmannsthal's verse gives expression both to the fear of death and the doctrine of the resurrection through love. Martin himself spoke of the wonderful harmony of this dramatic poem, its deep psychological penetration and beauty of language and form as "the curtain lifts on the interior life of each listener, on his spirit in which the drama of life and death, and sin and forgiveness, takes place". This classic recording has been matched by others but never surpassed and it still sounds as powerful as ever. The German composer Egk composed his *La Tentation de Saint Antoine* ("Temptation of St Anthony") in 1945; it is a folksy and accessible work, not anywhere near the same quality or stature as the Martin but worth an occasional hearing, particularly given the distinction of the soloist here. The Martin pieces are indispensable.

Martin. Mass for double chorus.
Poulenc. Mass in G major. Quatre petites prières de Saint François d'Assise. Salve regina. **Christ Church Cathedral Choir, Oxford/Stephen Darlington.** Nimbus NI5197. Texts included.

59' DDD 12/89

This recording of the Poulenc Mass stands up well against its competitors, with a sense of artistic finish, absolute security in the singing and an attractive forwardness and freshness of sound: specially notable is the beautifully tranquil *Benedictus*. The smaller Poulenc pieces are also expressively performed; but the chief attraction of the disc is the little-known Mass by Frank Martin, which he wrote in the 1920s while still completing his lengthy studies. It is a deeply impressive work, its eight-part *a cappella* texture richly contrapuntal, with strong overtones of plainchant in the *Kyrie* though elsewhere highly original (for example, in the impressionistic bell-sounds of the *Sanctus*): not until later did Martin adopt his individual brand of dodecaphony. The Christ Church Cathedral Choir (whose trebles are very likeable) sing splendidly — flexible and well moulded in their phrasing, stirring in their capture of the feelings of utter joy in *Et resurrexit*. The recording gives just the right amount of reverberation. A notable addition to the recorded repertoire.

Martin. Requiem. **Elisabeth Speiser** (sop); **Ria Bollen** (contr); **Eric Tappy** (ten); **Peter Lagger** (bass); **Lausanne Women's Chorus; Union Chorale; Ars Laeta Vocal Ensemble; Suisse Romande Orchestra/Frank Martin.** Jecklin Disco JD631-2. Text and translation included. Recorded at a performance in Lausanne Cathedral on May 4th, 1973. From Jecklin 190 (12/85).

47' ADD 1/90

If Frank Martin were to be represented by one work, it should be this one. The Requiem is a remarkable and beautiful score. It comes from Martin's last years, and was written after a Mediterranean cruise he made in 1971 and was inspired by three cathedrals, St Mark's in Venice, the Montreale in Palermo and the Greek temples of Paestum near Naples. It is a work of vision and elevation of spirit and casts a strong spell. There is a dramatic power and a serenity that are quite new. The short *In Paradisum* is inspired and has a luminous quality and a radiance that is quite otherworldly. The 83-year-old composer conducts a completely dedicated and authoritative performance: it might well be improved upon at one or two places in terms of ensemble or security, but the spirit is there. The Swiss Radio recording is eminently truthful and well-balanced and offers a natural enough acoustic, the audience reasonably unobtrusive. It is a sorry comment on our times that music of this calibre has so far enjoyed so little exposure: it deserves to be heard every bit as often as the Fauré Requiem.

Vicente Martín y Soler · Spanish 1754-1806

NEW REVIEW

Martín y Soler. UNA COSA RARA. **Maria Angeles Peters** (sop) Queen Isabella; **Ernesto Palacio** (ten) Prince Giovanni; **Montserrat Figueras** (sop) Lilla; **Gloria Fabuel** (sop) Ghita; **Iñaki Fresán** (bar) Lubino; **Fernando Belaza-Leoz** (bass-bar) Tita; **Stefano Palatchi** (bass) Podestà; **Francesc Garrigosa** (ten) Corrado; **La Capella Reial de Catalunya; Le Concert des Nations/Jordi Savall.** Auvidis Astrée E8760. Notes, text and translation included. Recorded at performances in the Gran Teatro del Liceo, Barcelona during February and March 1991.

③ 2h 54' DDD 2/92 ❓ ✒

"Bravi! Cosa rara!", exclaims Leporello in the supper scene of *Don Giovanni*, immediately recognizing the tune struck up by the Don's hired band. Martín y Soler's *opera buffa*, premièred in Vienna in November 1786, may be remembered today only because of Mozart's quotation; but in its day it far eclipsed both *Figaro* and *Don Giovanni*, scoring a runaway success in Vienna (where the ladies dressed and did their hair 'alla cosa rara') and was soon hailed throughout Europe, from Madrid to St Petersburg. Like *Figaro* and *Don Giovanni, Una cosa rara* ("A rare thing") exploited the Viennese taste for all things Spanish, with the Valencian-born composer spicing his score with snatches of popular songs and a couple of tangy folk-dances. Da Ponte's libretto, a leisurely, loosely woven tale of Spanish village life, has several ingredients in common with his operas for Mozart, including a cynical, lecherous nobleman thwarted by his peasant rival, a wily, minx-like village girl (country cousin to Despina) and a scene of nocturnal confusion and mistaken identities recalling the finale of *Figaro*. The score of *Una cosa rara* has countless fleeting reminders of Mozart, though if, say, eight bars might be taken for the master himself, the following eight will demonstrate the gulf between an agreeable talent and transcendent genius. There's much inventive, colourful wind scoring here, including some sensuous writing for the clarinets; the characterization is deft; and Martín y Soler has a fetching vein of frank, often touching lyricism. But he lacks staying power: his melodic invention, for all its charm, is inclined to be short-breathed and repetitive, his harmonies are often confined to tonic, dominant and subdominant, while his extended act finales seem almost casually assembled, with little of Mozart's supreme command of dramatic pacing, timing and cumulative growth.

Still, there's much undemanding entertainment here, and this première recording, taken from live performances in Barcelona, gives a pretty fair account of the work. The period-instrument orchestra, under the alert direction of Jordi Savall, is responsive to the colour and variety of the score (some splendidly rude

Jordi Savall   *[photo: Auvidis/Catahy]*

sounds from the natural horns); the recitatives, accompanied by the guitar to add a dash of extra Spanish flavour, are done with real dramatic flair; and the cast is uniformly strong on the male side (Ernesto Palacio singing with style and firm, ring-ing tone as the Prince, Stefano Palatchi displaying a fine, fruity bass as the village elder). Less reli-able, though, are the sopranos — Montserrat Figueras sings the role of Lilla, the heroine, with tremulous, rather unvaried tone, while Maria Angeles Peters as the benevolent Queen is sometimes uncomfortably flat. The recording is slightly constricted and favours the orchestra over the singers. But this set can be recommended to all explorers of eighteenth-century operatic byways, and anyone who wants to set Mozart's own Da Ponte operas in a broader perspective.

Bohuslav Martinů   *Czech 1890-1959*

NEW REVIEW

Martinů. Cello Concertos — No. 1; No. 2. Cello Concertino. **Raphael Wallfisch** (vc); **Czech Philharmonic Orchestra/Jiří Bělohlávek.** Chandos CHAN9015.

♪ ● 1h 16' DDD 4/92

Following his centenary year in 1990, Bohuslav Martinů has been returning to favour, although, as the composer of almost 30 concerto-type works, he cannot always escape the charge of flatulent note-spinning that attaches itself to such fertility. On the present disc, his unique imaginative vision is most obvious in the Cello Concerto No. 1. The central slow movement in particular finds Martinů at his best, a deeply moving threnody with a potent nostalgic quality which will be instantly recognizable to admirers of the later symphonies. There is an improvisa-tory freedom about the Second Concerto which makes it harder to grasp and the thematic material has rather too much in common with other, better scores. The much earlier *Concertino* is in Martinů's playful, more overtly neoclassical vein. You may notice some vamp-until-ready eighteenth-century scrubbing in the concertos, but here the younger composer is preoccupied with the lighter aspects of the style. There's a Stravinskian wit and elegance about the writing and the chamber scoring reflects both the fashionable trends and the economic constraints of life in 1920s Paris. In the First Concerto, Raphael Wallfisch is rather backwardly balanced *vis-à-vis* the Czech Philharmonic, whose regular conductor, Jiří Bělohlávek, is of course totally inside this music. At the same time, the resonant Spanish Hall of Prague Castle provides an agreeable ambient glow which does not mask too much detail. Make no mistake: this is a most attractive proposition for those already familiar with the idiom. Adventurous beginners should perhaps start elsewhere.

NEW REVIEW

Martinů. ORCHESTRAL WORKS. **Czech Philharmonic Orchestra/Jiří Bělohlávek.** Supraphon 10 4140-2.
The parables. Estampes. Overture. La rhapsodie, "Allegro symphonique".

| 58' DDD 6/91

Estampes and *The parables* are both descriptive three-movement works written near the end of the composer's life. At this stage Martinů's fertile imagination was quite undiminished, and each piece teems with imaginative, colourful neo-romantic invention and brilliant orchestral effects. The subjects of the three *Parables* are described respectively as a sculpture, a garden and a navire, but it's best simply to enjoy the music as it is without attempting to look further into hidden meanings: the three movements of the *Estampes* are in fact given tempo indications rather than titles. In the busy Overture of 1953 Martinů uses more of a formal neoclassical style to great effect. The *Rhapsodie* dates from 1928, and was written to celebrate ten years of Czech independence. This work has an outgoing, joyful spirit and trumpet and drums are very much to the fore. Jiří Bělohlávek conducts all these works with a great deal of flair and imagination, and the Czech Philharmonic support their chief conductor with highly accomplished, resourceful playing. Supraphon's recording is warm, atmospheric and attentive to detail.

Martinů. SYMPHONIES. **Bamberg Symphony Orchestra/Neeme Järvi.** BIS CD362/3, CD402.
CD362 — No. 1 (1942); No. 2 (1943). *CD363* — No. 3 (1944); No. 4 (1945).
CD402 — No. 5 (1946); No. 6 (1953).

| ③ 61' 63' 59' DDD 9/87 12/88

Martinů began composing at the age of ten and later studied and lived in Paris, America and Switzerland. Despite his travels he remained a quintessentially Czech composer and his music is imbued with the melodic shapes and rhythms of the folk-music of his native homeland. The six symphonies were written during Martinů's years in America and in all of them he uses a large orchestra with distinctive groupings of instruments which give them a very personal and unmistakable timbre. The rhythmic verve of his highly syncopated fast movements is very infectious, indeed unforgettable, and his slow movements are often deeply expressive, most potently, perhaps, in that of the Third Symphony which is imbued with the tragedy of war. The Bamberg orchestra play marvellously and with great verve for Järvi, whose excellently judged tempos help propel the music forward most effectively. His understanding of the basic thrust of Martinů's structures is very impressive and he projects the music with great clarity. The BIS recordings are beautifully clear, with plenty of ambience surrounding the orchestra, a fine sense of scale and effortless handling of the wide dynamic range Martinů calls for. Enthusiastically recommended.

Martinů. Nonet (1959). Trio in F major (1944). La Rêvue de Cuisine. **The Dartington Ensemble** (William Bennett, fl; Robin Canter, ob; David Campbell, cl; Graham Sheen, bn; Richard Watkins, hn; Barry Collarbone, tpt; Oliver Butterworth, vn; Patrick Ireland, va; Michael Evans, vc; Nigel Amherst, db; John Bryden, pf. Hyperion CDA66084.

| 50' DDD

The last few years or so have seen a steadily increasing interest in the music of Martinů. This beautifully balanced programme of chamber music may not be wholly representative of his style, but it's certainly an enjoyable and entertaining disc, and is as good a starting place as any for those approaching his music for the first time. His style has often been described as eclectic; his early works reveal the influence of Debussy and impressionism, and later, in the 1920 and 1930s, jazz and neoclassicism play an increasingly important role in his work. The concert suite from the ballet *La Rêvue de Cuisine* ("The Kitchen Review") dates from 1930 when he lived in Paris. There are plenty of high jinks and comedy in this agreeable and unpretentious work and the sound and influence of the Paris jazz bands are clearly discernible in the dance-inspired movements. The outer movements of the Trio in F major inhabit a similarly bright and cheerful world, and these are contrasted well with the lyrical beauty of the central *Adagio*. The *Nonet*, completed shortly before his death in 1959, is a serene and sunny work, neoclassical in design with its Haydnesque themes and its clarity of texture with a deep nostalgia for his Czech homeland from which he had been separated for so many years. The Dartington Ensemble give fine, committed performances and the recording has warmth and perspective. An essential disc for enthusiasts and toe-dippers alike.

Martinů. The epic of Gilgamesh. **Eva Depoltová** (sop); **Stefan Margita** (ten); **Ivan Kusnjer** (bar); **Ludek Vele** (bass); **Milan Karpíšek** (spkr); **Slovak Philharmonic Choir; Slovak Philharmonic Orchestra/Zdeněk Košler.** Marco Polo 8 223316. Translation included.

56' DDD 4/91

Gilgamesh is a long Assyrian-Babylonian poem recorded on cuneiform tablets in or before the seventh century BC which predates Homer by at least 1,500 years. Martinů was fascinated not only by the poem, the oldest literature known to mankind, but its universality — "the emotions and issues which move people have not changed ... they are embodied just as much in the oldest literature known to us as in the literature of our own time ... issues of friendship, love and death. It is dramatic; it pursues me in my dreams", he wrote. It certainly inspired in him music of extraordinary vision and intensity as well as enormous atmosphere. The *Epic* tells how Gilgamesh, King of Uruk, hears about the warrior Enkidu, a primitive at home among the works of nature with only animals as friends. He sends him a courtesan to whom he loses his innocence; the King then befriends him but they quarrel and fight before their friendship is really cemented. The second and third parts of the oratorio centre on the themes of death and immortality; the second tells of Enkidu's death and Gilgamesh's grief, his plea to the gods to restore Enkidu and his search for immortality, and the third records his failure to learn its secrets. *Gilgamesh* deals with universal themes and is Martinů at his most profound and inspired. There are no weaknesses in the cast (and the Gilgamesh of Ivan Kusnjer is very impressive indeed), and the chorus and orchestra respond very well to Zdeněk Košler's direction. The recording maintains a generally natural balance between the soloists, narrator, chorus and orchestra, and the somewhat resonant acoustic is used to good advantage. Those who do not know this extraordinary work of Martinů's last years should investigate it without delay.

Jules Massenet

French 1842-1912

Massenet. MANON[a]. **Victoria de los Angeles** (sop) Manon; **Henri Legay** (ten) Des Grieux; **Michel Dens** (bar) Lescaut; **Jean Borthayre** (bass) Comte des Grieux; **Jean Vieuille** (bar) De Brétigny; **René Hérent** (ten) Guillot; **Liliane Berton** (sop) Poussette; **Raymonde Notti** (sop) Javotte; **Marthe Serres** (sop) Rosette; **Chorus and Orchestra of the Paris Opéra-Comique/Pierre Monteux.**

Chausson. Poème de l'amour et de la mer[b]. **Victoria de los Angeles** (sop); **Lamoureux Orchestra/Jean-Pierre Jacquillat.** EMI [a]mono/[b]stereo CMS7 63549-2. Notes and text included. Item marked [a] from HMV ALP1394/7 (11/56), [b] ASD2826 (3/73).

③ 3h 9' ADD 8/90 ▲

This has always been the classic version of Massenet's most popular opera. Pierre Monteux was one of the most eminent interpreters of French music in the gramophone's history, and he here draws authentically idiomatic playing from the Opéra-Comique Orchestra. The tradition they embody between them has been more-or-less lost in the interim which made the reappearance of this set that much more welcome and important. And who could resist de los Angeles in the title role? She embodies to perfection, as she did on stage, Manon's endearing, sensual and flirtatious characteristics, and manages to convert them into a reading

Victoria de los Angeles　　　　　　*[photo: EMI]*

that is true to all Massenet's copious demands on his singers. Add to that the sheer beauty of the soprano's voice at the time and you have a good enough reason for acquiring these discs. Henri Legay's Des Grieux is hardly less affecting. He is the amorous, highly charged and obsessed lover to the life and matches his Manon in obedience to Massenet's requirements. As the smaller parts are cast with other French singers familiar with Massenet's idiom every need is fulfilled. The recording sounds very reasonable for its day. Chausson's *Poème* makes an apt filler if by the early seventies the tonal bloom on de los Angeles's voice was much less in evidence.

Massenet. WERTHER. **Alfredo Kraus** (ten) Werther; **Tatiana Troyanos** (mez) Charlotte; **Matteo Manuguerra** (bar) Albert; **Christine Barbaux** (sop) Sophie; **Jules Bastin** (bass) Bailiff; **Philip Langridge** (ten) Schmidt; **Jean-Philippe Lafont** (bar) Johann; **London Philharmonic Orchestra/Michel Plasson.** EMI CMS7 69573-2. Notes and text included. From SLS5183 (2/80).

② 2h 17' ADD 4/89 £

Massenet. WERTHER. **José Carreras** (ten) Werther; **Frederica von Stade** (mez) Charlotte; **Thomas Allen** (bar) Albert; **Isobel Buchanan** (sop) Sophie; **Robert Lloyd** (bass) Bailiff; **Paul Crook** (ten), **Malcolm King** (bass) Bailiff's friends; **Linda Humphries** (sop) Katchen; **Donaldson Ball** (bar) Bruhlmann; **Children's Choir; Royal Opera House Orchestra, Covent Garden/Sir Colin Davis.** Philips 416 654-2PH2. Notes, text and translation included. From 6769 051 (10/81).

② 2h 11' ADD 2/87

Werther is considered by many to be Massenet's outright masterpiece. Here he reaches his zenith in the supple combination of a lyrical and a parlando style. Based faithfully on Goethe's novel, the work exposes movingly the feelings of the

lovelorn poet Werther and those of his beloved Charlotte. The EMI recording
benefits from Michel Plasson's instinctive feeling for the very individual shape of
a Massenet phrase and for impassioned identification with the work's direct
emotions. He draws sensuous and eloquent playing from the LPO. Alfredo Kraus
has been for many years a leading interpreter of the title role, which he understands to the full. He is to the life the self-pitying, tortured poet, obsessed by his
love for the unattainable Charlotte and delivers Werther's many solos with an
innate feeling for the poet's predicament. His Charlotte is the equally admirable
Tatiana Troyanos, who perfectly catches the undercurrent of emotional conflict in
Charlotte's being. Hers is a big-hearted, committed interpretation, but one that
doesn't want for subtlety or interpretation. The two principals are well supported by the singers of the secondary roles, especially Christine Barbaux's
properly eager and girlish Sophie. The recording is full and natural.

   In Sir Colin Davis's recording the changing seasons, which form a backdrop to
Werther's own manic swings between dream and reality, joy and despair, are
recreated in exuberant and vibrant detail. The Royal Opera Orchestra play at
their very best: the solo detail, in every sentient responsive to Massenet's
flickering orchestral palette, operates as if with feverishly heightened awareness.
Carreras sees the force of the will to self-destruction in the character as
dominating even the passages of brooding lyricism. Charlotte, struggling between
the responsibilities of her bourgeois home life and the emotional turmoil in which
she sees much of herself reflected in Werther, is sung by Frederica von Stade
with winning simplicity and idiomatic French style. Young Sophie, whom
Massenet made more important than Goethe did, becomes a true *oiseau d'aurore*
in the voice of Isobel Buchanan, while Thomas Allen, characteristically, finds
unusual breadth in the role of poor, spurned Albert.

NEW REVIEW

Massenet. DON QUICHOTTE[a]. Scènes alsaciennes.[b]. **Nicolai Ghiaurov**
(bass) Don Quichotte; **Régine Crespin** (sop) Dulcinée; **Gabriel Bacquier**
(bar) Sancho Panza; **Michèle Command** (sop) Pedro; **Annick Duterte** (sop)
Garcias; **Peyo Garazzi** (ten) Rodriguez; **Jean-Marie Fremeau** (ten) Juan;
Suisse Romande Chorus and Orchestra/Kazimierz Kord; [b]**National
Philharmonic Orchestra/Richard Bonynge.** Decca 430 636-2DM2. Notes,
text and translation included. Item marked [a] from D156D3 (11/79), [b] SXL6827
(12/77).

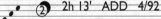

Massenet's operas are patchily represented in the catalogue, and this heroic
comedy, which was his last big success (in 1910, when he was 67) is most
welcome. People who think of him as only a salon composer, lacking the vigour
and depth of a Berlioz or a Debussy, should listen to the start of Act 1, set in a
Spanish town square at fiesta time; the opening music bursts out of the
loudspeakers like that of Verdi's *Otello*, although here the mood is joyous, with
tremendous rhythmic verve and gusto. In fact, this opera is closer to Verdi's
Falstaff, with the same admixture of gentler serious moments amidst the comic
bustle and intrigue, and of course, here again the central character is a comic yet
lovable figure. The recording, made by a British team in Geneva in 1978, still
sounds well although orchestral detail could be clearer. As for the performance
by mainly Swiss forces under Kazimierz Kord, and with a Bulgarian bass in the
title role (written for Chaliapin), one can only praise it for its idiomatic
realization of a 'Spanish' opera by a gifted French composer for the theatre.
Though Régine Crespin may be too mature vocally for Dulcinée, the object of
the elderly Don Quixote's adoration, she sings splendidly and few will find this a
serious weakness. Nicolai Ghiaurov rightly makes Quixote himself a real person,

touching and dignified as well as comic, and Gabriel Bacquier gives a rounded portrayal of his servant Sancho Panza, so that Quixote's death scene in the company of his old friend is particularly strong. The booklet provides a synopsis plus the French text and a translation. This is a fine mid-price issue, and the lively and tuneful *Scènes alsaciennes* with a British orchestra under Richard Bonynge make a fine fill-up.

Sir Peter Maxwell Davies

British 1934-

Maxwell Davies. Symphony No. 4[a]. Trumpet Concerto[b]. [b]**John Wallace** (tpt); [a]**Scottish Chamber Orchestra/Sir Peter Maxwell Davies.** Collins Classics 1181-2.

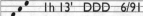 1h 13' DDD 6/91

Sir Peter Maxwell Davies has survived the transition from *enfant terrible* to *éminence grise* with equanimity — perhaps because he was always less 'terrible' than he seemed, and is still far from seriously 'grise'. From his earliest works to his most recent — the Trumpet Concerto and Fourth Symphony date from the late 1980s — he has used his delight in system-building to generate ambitious and complex structures that vibrate with no less complex but utterly uninhibited emotions. The Concerto is the immediately accessible of the two: the nature of the solo instrument, and Maxwell Davies's willingness not to jettison all the conventions of the concerto genre see to that. The work was written for John Wallace, and while it would be wrong to say that he makes light of its difficulties — at times you could swear that only a flautist could get round such florid writing — he succeeds brilliantly in demonstrating that the difficulties serve musical ends. The Symphony has less immediately arresting ideas, but when the music is savoured, returned to, and allowed time to weave its spells, its rewards become progressively more apparent. These recordings capture the composer's own highly-charged readings with commendable fidelity.

Maxwell Davies. Miss Donnithorne's Maggot[a]. Eight Songs for a Mad King[b]. [a]**Mary Thomas** (sop); [b]**Julius Eastman** (bar); **The Fires of London/Sir Peter Maxwell Davies.** Unicorn-Kanchana DKPCD9052. Texts included. Item marked [a] new to UK, [b] from RHS308 (12/71).

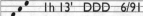 1h 7' ADD/DDD 3/88

King George III in his madness sang the music of his beloved Handel; he also used a miniature mechanical organ in attempts to teach caged birds to sing for him. Eliza Donnithorne, on the other hand, was jilted at the church door and reacted by making the rest of her life an endless wedding-morning. She did not sing, so far as we know, but her crazed monologues are as haunted, in Maxwell Davies's phantasmagoria, by memories of martial music and by overtones of all those Italian opera heroines who went 'mad in white satin' as the King's are by distorted Handel, by folk-songs and the twittering of birds and by grotesque foxtrots. The range of vocal effects required of the two soloists is punishing: howls and screeches and extremes of pitch for the vocalist in *Eight Songs*, burlesque coloratura warblings and swoopings for the soprano in *Miss Donnithorne*. The hysterical intensity of the music is pretty taxing for the listener, too, but he is rewarded in *Eight Songs* by a breathtaking kaleidoscope of vivid allusion, invention and parody, and in *Miss Donnithorne* by a harsh poignancy as well. Both pieces are vehicles for virtuoso performance, from the instrumentalists as well as the singers, and one can scarcely imagine either being done better than it is here. The very immediate recording adds substantially to their uncomfortable impact.

Nicholas Maw

British 1935-

NEW REVIEW

Maw. Odyssey (1972-85, rev. 1989-90). **City of Birmingham Symphony Orchestra/Simon Rattle.** EMI CDS7 54277-2.

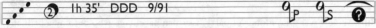

Nicholas Maw's *Odyssey* is a musical voyage of extraordinary emotional conviction. Given its wellnigh 20-year gestation, it is also a composition of remarkable coherence, a super-symphony in a single span which sustains its forward movement and sense of direction over an hour and a half with formidable skill. The listener is undoubtedly helped by a formal design that sets up plentiful associations with the grand symphonic structures of the late romantic era, particular Mahler and Strauss. But Maw is no parodist: his is a late twentieth-century affirmation of belief in certain fundamental musical truths, especially the abiding need for contrast between consonance and dissonance, and the consequently inescapable relevance of tonality. The whole enterprise, like the title itself, could have yielded an embarrassing pretentiousness. Yet the actual effect is rather to reinforce awareness of the difficulties the composer had to surmount in bringing *Odyssey* to a convincing conclusion — a conclusion that seems to express fulfilment and apprehension in equal measure. Simon Rattle, the CBSO and the EMI recording team are all equal to the composer's imaginative vision. A studio recording might have managed an even richer sound, but the impact of this live event is overwhelming in a very special way.

NEW REVIEW

Maw. Life Studies[a].
Bennett. Spells[b]. [b]**Jane Manning** (sop); [a]**Academy of St Martin in the Fields/Sir Neville Marriner;** [b]**Bach Choir;** [b]**Philharmonia Orchestra/Sir David Willcocks.** Continuum CCD1030.

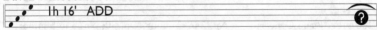

Nicholas Maw's *Life Studies* for 15 solo strings have rightfully taken their place in the lineage of great English string works which began with Elgar's *Introduction and Allegro*. Their importance cannot be understated. On one level they are a marvellous sequence of virtuosic studies (eight in all) exploring the many possibilities of texture, timbre and sonority; but they also possess a strong sense of communication and an extremely wide emotional range, making them an ideal introduction to Maw's highly individual and warmly expressive language. The Academy of St Martin in the Fields (for whom they were composed in 1973) gives an outstanding performance. Richard Rodney Bennett's *Spells*, for soprano, chorus and orchestra, is an evocative and highly colourful set of magical incantations to words by Kathleen Raine, which successfully blends an English tradition of choral writing with the more astringent, atonal aspect of Bennett's musical style. The orchestra is used to great effect in bringing out the dreamy, supernatural overtones of the poems, and in the movement entitled "Love Spell" Jane Manning gives a wonderfully dramatic and literally spellbinding performance of Bennett's melismatic vocal writing. Both works, which originally appeared on the Argo label in the late 1970s, are exceptionally well recorded and have been beautifully transferred to CD.

Billy Mayerl

British 1902-1959

Mayerl. PIANO WORKS. **Eric Parkin.** Chandos CHAN8848.
Four Aces Suite (1933) — No. 1, Ace of Clubs; No. 4, Ace of Spades. Mistletoe
(1935). Autumn crocus (1932). Hollyhock (1927). White heather (1932). Three
Dances in Syncopation, Op. 73. Sweet William (1938). Parade of the Sandwich-
Board Men (1938). Hop-O'-My-Thumb (1934). Jill all alone (1955). Aquarium
Suite (1937). **Mayerl/Croom-Johnson:** Bats in the Belfry (1935). Green tulips
(1935).

50' DDD 11/90 ❷

Billy Mayerl was a Londoner of partly German parentage who became a brilliant
pianist and a composer whose piano pieces, immensely popular between the
wars, successfully bridge the gap between ragtime and, let's say, Frank Bridge
and John Ireland in their lighter piano moods. In this way, he was a middle-of-
the-road figure like Eric Coates, and for that reason he later came to be
neglected by jazz aficionados and classical buffs alike as representing no pure
'tradition'. Today, it's a delight to return to tuneful music which has such
originality, wit, and sparkle as well as being superbly written for the piano.
Listen to the very first number (the *Ace of Clubs*), and you at once hear the charm
and sharp sophistication of Mayerl's style, which is worthy of his contemporaries
Noël Coward and Cole Porter, to say nothing of Gershwin. Though it's a pity
we don't have all the 'Aces' of this four-part suite here, that's because Eric
Parkin recorded the other two on an earlier CD devoted to this composer on
which we also find the famous piece *Marigold* (CHAN8560). Parkin is right inside
this music and his playing is stylistically spot on in its tonal warmth, crisp
articulation and rhythmic zest. This is a delightful disc. Quite a few classical
music lovers, if given a one-way ticket to a desert island and a medium-size
suitcase, would gladly sacrifice some Schoenberg for modern music as attractive
and well played as this.

Nikolay Medtner

Russian 1880-1951

92
NEW REVIEW

Medtner. Piano Concertos — No. 2 in C minor, Op. 50; No. 3 in E minor,
Op. 60. **Nikolai Demidenko** (pf); **BBC Scottish Symphony Orchestra/
Jerzy Maksymiuk.** Hyperion CDA66580.

1h 14' DDD 4/92 ❷

This is a splendid issue of two piano concertos by a neglected Russian master,
with fine recording, good orchestral playing from a Scottish orchestra under a
Polish conductor and, above all, truly coruscating and poetic playing from the
brilliant young Russian pianist Nikolai Demidenko. It also bids fair to do a
splendid rehabilitation job for Nikolay Medtner, a composer who did not feature
at all in last year's edition of this *Guide* but who is steadily coming in from the
cold after half a century of neglect. He was a contemporary and friend of
Rachmaninov who settled in Britain in the 1930s, and like Rachmaninov (to
whom the Second Concerto is dedicated and who returned the compliment with
his own Fourth) he was an excellent pianist. But while the other composer
became immensely popular, Medtner languished in obscurity, regarded (if
thought about at all) as an inferior imitation of Rachmaninov who wrote gushing
music that was strong on gestures but weak on substance. The fact is that he can
be diffuse (not to say long-winded) and grandiose, and memorable tunes are in

short supply, so that his music needs to be played well to come off. But when it is there's much to enjoy and the strong Russian flavour of the ornate writing is evident, as is the composer's masterly understanding of the piano.

Felix Mendelssohn
German 1809-1847

Mendelssohn. PIANO CONCERTOS. **Murray Perahia; [a]Academy of St Martin in the Fields/Sir Neville Marriner.** CBS Masterworks CD42401. Items marked [a] from IM76376 (7/75), [b] IM37838 (5/85).
Piano Concertos[a] — No. 1 in G minor, Op. 25; No. 2 in D minor, Op. 40. Prelude and Fugue in E major/minor, Op. 35 No. 1[b]. Variations sérieuses in D minor, Op. 54[b]. Andante and Rondo capriccioso, Op. 14[b].

Ih 10' ADD/DDD 11/87

Though conflict and suffering, the experiences on which Beethovenian music is supposed to feed, were foreign to Mendelssohn's nature, ardour, inspiration, soulfulness and fiery energy he had in abundance. So although both these concertos, products of the composer's twenties, are in minor keys, they have little of the pathos or drama that that might lead one to expect. It is for their consummate ease and naturalness, their ability to make the listener feel as though he is soaring, that they are valued. Not too many pianists are suited by temperament, or indeed equipped by technique, for such music. Murray Perahia undoubtedly is. His dazzling fingerwork and his sensitivity to the direction of harmony are delightful, and he knows just how to step aside to let the more relaxed slow movements make their point. Slight fizziness on the string sound and a less than ideally regulated piano detract but little from one's enjoyment; and CBS have made partial amends by adding 26 minutes from a solo Mendelssohn recital which shows Perahia on top form.

Mendelssohn. Violin Concertos — E minor, Op. 64; D minor. **Viktoria Mullova** (vn); **Academy of St Martin in the Fields/Sir Neville Marriner.** Philips 432 077-2PH.

50' DDD 5/91

Since the competition is strong to say the least, new accounts of 'the' Mendelssohn Violin Concerto have to be rather special to make their way in the catalogue, but that of Viktoria Mullova and the ASMF under Sir Neville Marriner falls into the category of distinguished additions. The deliberate mention of the orchestra and conductor here is because this work is emphatically not a showpiece for a soloist in the way that Paganini's or Wieniawski's violin concertos are. Instead it offers a real dialogue with orchestra although there are plenty of opportunities for violin virtuosity as well. Mullova's sweet and somehow youthful tone is beautifully matched here by Marriner and his orchestra, which in turn does not sound so big as to overwhelm the often intimate character of the music. The recording helps, too, with its natural balance between the soloist and the orchestral body. The reference above to this E minor work as 'the' Mendelssohn Violin Concerto is because after his death it was found that as a boy of 13 he also composed the one in D minor which here makes a useful coupling. Of course it shows the influence of classical models, including Mozart, but the slow movement has an attractive warmth and the finale a zest and drive that owes something to gipsy music. Maybe in less than expert hands it could sound ordinary, but not when it is done as stylishly as here.

Mendelssohn. OVERTURES. **Bamberg Symphony Orchestra/Claus Peter Flor.** RCA Victor Red Seal RD87905.
Die Hochzeit des Camacho, Op. 10. A Midsummer Night's Dream, Op. 21 (from RD87764, 10/88). Meeresstille und glückliche Fahrt, Op. 27. Ruy Blas, Op. 95. Athalie, Op. 74. The Hebrides, Op. 26, "Fingal's Cave".

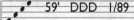

Claus Peter Flor   *[photo: BMG*

The Marriage of Camacho Overture was written in 1825, two years before the masterly evocation of *A Midsummer Night's Dream*, with its gossamer fairies, robust mortals and pervading romanticism, and already demonstrates the teenage composer's enormous musical facility and organizational skills, together with the high quality of his invention. *Calm sea and prosperous voyage* (1828) anticipates *The Hebrides* of a year later, and celebrates an ocean voyage on a sailing ship. *Ruy Blas* is a jolly, slightly melodramatic, but agreeably tuneful piece and *Athalie* is also attractive in its melodic ideas. *Fingal's Cave* with its beauty and dramatic portrayal of Scottish seascapes matches the Shakespearian overture in its melodic inspiration (the opening phrase is hauntingly unforgettable) and shows comparable skill in its vivid orchestration. Flor directs wonderfully sympathetic and spontaneous performances, with the Bamberg Symphony Orchestra playing gloriously. There is abundant energy and radiant lyrical beauty in the playing and each piece is unerringly paced and shaped. The glowing recording gives a wonderful bloom to the orchestral textures without preventing a realistic definition. There has never been a collection of Mendelssohn's overtures to match this and it will give enormous pleasure in every respect.

Mendelssohn. SYMPHONIES AND OVERTURES. **London Symphony Orchestra/Claudio Abbado.** DG 415 353-2GH4.
Symphonies — No. 1 in C minor, Op. 11; No. 2 in B flat major, Op. 52, "Lobgesang" (with Elizabeth Connell, Karita Mattila, sops; Hans-Peter Blochwitz, ten); No. 3 in A minor, Op. 56, "Scottish"; No. 4 in A major, Op. 90, "Italian"; No. 5 in D major, Op. 107, "Reformation". Overtures — The Hebrides, Op. 26, "Fingal's Cave"; A Midsummer Night's Dream, Op. 21. The Fair Melusina, Op. 32. Octet in E flat major, Op. 20 — Scherzo.

This is a most valuable collection and Abbado impresses at once in the First Symphony by his serious yet lively account of the score: his approach to the *Lobgesang* is warm and joyful and though he cannot quite rid the work of its Victorian flavour, his performance is fresh and restores the music's charm and innocence. He has a good chorus at his disposal and three dedicated, skilful soloists. In the more familiar *Scottish* Symphony Abbado again invests the work with warmth and stature, never rushing or driving too hard: the familiar *Italian* Symphony, too, gains from his affectionate, respectful yet sparkling approach. Even the *Reformation* Symphony, which can seem even more coloured by Victorian religious sentiment than the *Hymn of Praise*, emerges as a vigorous, uplifting work, with the hymn tunes played in cheerful, direct fashion. Only in the three overtures, where Abbado's tempos and phrasing are strangely idiosyncratic (though never less than interesting), do the performances depart from a very high standard indeed. Throughout the set the LSO respond to Abbado with lean, virile playing. The recordings have a pleasing, natural sound, with a particularly good balance in the choral item.

NEW REVIEW

Mendelssohn. STRING SYMPHONIES. **London Festival Orchestra/Ross Pople.** Hyperion CDA66561/3. Items marked [a] from CDA66196 (6/87), [b] CDA66318 (11/89), others new to UK.
No. 1 in C major; No. 2 in D major; No. 3 in E minor; No. 4 in C minor; No. 5 in B flat major[b]; No. 6 in E flat major; No. 7 in D minor[b]; No. 8 in D major[b]; No. 9 in C minor[a]; No. 10 in B minor[a]; No. 11 in F major; No. 12 in G minor[a].

③ 3h 23' DDD 12/91

"Mendelssohn — twelve years old — promises much": this prophetic entry made by Beethoven in one of his conversation books, shortly after his first encounter with the young genius, is certainly vindicated in the astonishing cycle of 12 symphonies for string orchestra. These youthful works chart the composer's mastery of symphonic genre and total command of formal classicism over a period of barely two years, and Ross Pople is eager to communicate his own tangible sense of wonderment and deepening incredulity throughout this excellent integral cycle. Whilst Pople himself confirms this ongoing revelation in his performances, Hyperion have ensured that the layout of the discs conform to the chronology of the works themselves. Symphonies Nos. 1 and 2 were evidently compositional studies directed by Mendelssohn's private tutor, Zelter, but they have charm and true melodic interest, whereas No. 3 clearly owes much to the turbulence of Haydn's *Sturm-und-drang-Periode*. The spirit of the high baroque is revealed in the Handelian *Grave* introduction to Symphony No. 4, whilst its successor is evidently something of a fusion of baroque and early classical styles. The central works of the cycle reveal a greater sense of assurance and individuality, but as Pople avidly demonstrates, they have a growing emotional impetus and architectural potency also. Equally, the influence of other composers is diminishing as the later symphonies assume a traditional four-movement form, of increasing complexity and cohesion, and Pople directs a memorably vigorous account of Symphony No. 8, with its astonishing *Scherzo* and ingenious double fugue. If one senses more than ever the forward looking innovation of the last three symphonies, then this is as much a tribute to the sheer excellence of these performances as to the actual resources of the music itself, for Pople conveys all the joy and wonderment of each fresh discovery, and the London Festival Orchestra clearly share in his delight as they unfold the true genius of these extraordinary works. Very highly recommended.

NEW REVIEW

Mendelssohn. Symphony No. 2 in B flat major, Op. 52, "Lobgesang". **Barbara Bonney, Edith Wiens** (sops); **Peter Schreier** (ten); **Leipzig Radio Choir; Leipzig Gewandhaus Orchestra/Kurt Masur.** Teldec 2292-44178-2. Text and translation included.

59' DDD 4/90

In this memorable performance of one of Mendelssohn's lesser-known but highly rewarding symphonies, Kurt Masur carries forward a tradition of music-making of which Mendelssohn was himself a part, through his conducting of the Leipzig Gewandhaus Orchestra. The *Hymn of Praise* stands under the shade of Beethoven's *Choral* Symphony, with its considerable length and choral and solo contributions, both here extremely well delivered, but it does not reach similar heights of sublimity. What it does possess is an unassuming lyricism, vitality and elegance throughout that is highly attractive. Popular with choral societies during the last century, this is an interesting part of Mendelssohn's symphonic canon. Masur's performance is perfectly attuned to the work's character, the orchestral playing is excellent with an assured sense of style, and the recording is spacious. Well worth investigating.

Mendelssohn. Symphonies — No. 3 in A minor, Op. 56, "Scottish"; No. 4 in A major, Op. 90, "Italian". **London Symphony Orchestra/Claudio Abbado.** DG 3D-Classics 427 810-2GDC. From 415 353-2GH4 (1/86).

> Ih II' DDD 2/90 £ P B

Mendelssohn. Symphonies — No. 3 in A minor, Op. 56, "Scottish"; No. 4 in A major, Op. 90, "Italian". **London Classical Players/Roger Norrington.** EMI Reflexe CDC7 54000-2.

> Ih 5' DDD II/90 P B

NEW REVIEW

Mendelssohn. Symphonies — No. 3 in A minor, Op. 56, "Scottish"; No. 4 in A major, Op. 90, "Italian". **Chamber Orchestra of Europe, Nikolaus Harnoncourt.** Teldec 9031-72308-2.

> Ih 9' DDD 5/92 P S B

There have already been individual discs extracted from Abbado's well-thought of set of Mendelssohn's orchestral music, but this well-filled issue is probably the most generally appealing, coupling two of the best loved works in two of the most astute performances of the set — and all at bargain price. Although there are many more challenging readings of these two symphonies elsewhere on CD, Abbado's is a soundly middle-of-the-road view, drawing refined, understated playing from the LSO that is especially effective, for example, in the more brooding moments of the first movement of the *Scottish*. Abbado captures keenly here the ambience of the ruined chapel of Holyrood House in Edinburgh, so imbued with the tragedy of Mary, Queen of Scots, that first inspired Mendelssohn in this work. The restrained recording suits this symphony better than it does the brilliant lights of the *Italian*, though even there the understated playing makes its own, peculiarly poignant effect. At the price, then, this is certainly an issue to consider.

In any performance of the *Scottish* Symphony on period instruments there are bound to be losses: the modern symphony orchestra is wonderfully capable of realizing the brooding mists and powerful outbursts of the first movement in a way that lighter-toned instruments cannot hope to emulate. But turn to the *Scherzo* on the Norrington disc and the validity of using authentic instruments becomes immediately apparent. Here, the wind timbres are so intriguing in themselves, the woodwinds so individual, the horns so ruggedly outdoor, that another level of meaning within this music is revealed to us. The *Adagio* now becomes much more classical, shorn of its late-romantic Angst, rendering the intimations of full-blooded romanticism to become all the more telling. The opening of the *Italian* is predictably vivacious, with soft-timbred flutes blending with the strings rather than trying to compete, and when they come to the fore again in the *Saltarello*, playing a breathy duet, the effect is magical. Lively speeds adopted by Norrington in both works may seem hurried on first hearing, but their rightness for the forces used and the acoustic of the venue establishes itself with repeated listening. A well-balanced, not too brightly lit recording serves both symphonies well.

It is tempting to suggest that Harnoncourt, with his small modern instrument orchestra ('classical' trumpets excepted) playing in an historically aware manner

— i.e. shorter, more eventual phrasing, rationed vibrato, horns that rasp like their valveless antecedents, and sharply defined timpani — occupies the middle ground between Abbado and Norrington, and has the best of both worlds. What really impresses here is how well Harnoncourt has chosen his tempos, not only for ease of articulation, but to attend to the music's illustrative poetry. The *Italian*'s pilgrims, for example, tread more reverentially than either Abbado's or Norrington's and although the finale is faster than Norrington's, instead of Abbado's exhilarating whirlwind, Harnoncourt reminds us of its minor key — its ambiguity is caught to perfection. Impressive too is how Harnoncourt manages to suggest a Beethovenian strength in much of Mendelssohn's inspiration, and attend as successfully to its unique graceful, tripping, light-as-air quality. The Chamber Orchestra of Europe are at their unassailable best, and the sound is superb.

Mendelssohn. Symphony No. 5 in D major, Op. 107, "Reformation"[a].
Schumann. Symphony No. 3 in E flat major, Op. 97, "Rhenish"[b]. **Berlin Philharmonic Orchestra/Herbert von Karajan.** DG Galleria 419 870-2GGA. Item marked [a] from 2720 068 (12/73), [b] 2720 046 (9/72).

> 1h 9' ADD 4/88 £

This is just the sort of repertoire at which Karajan excels; his Schumann is strongly characterized, firmly driven and beautifully shaped and his Mendelssohn often achieves a delicacy of touch that belies the size of orchestra employed. Karajan's set of the Schumann symphonies made in 1971 was a notable success and the *Rhenish* speaks for them all. Here the powerful thrust of the work is gorgeously conveyed by the Berlin strings and the spontaneity of the music-making is striking. The Mendelssohn makes an ideal companion, since in scale the *Reformation* embraces wide vistas and far horizons. Laden with references to Protestant worship, Mendelssohn paints a picture of security and solidity achieved over many years and much struggle. Karajan maybe overemphasizes the epic qualities of the work but the playing of the orchestra is superb. The recordings have 'dried-out' a little in the transfer, but still sound well.

NEW REVIEW
Mendelssohn. A Midsummer Night's Dream — incidental music, Opp. 21 and 61. **Edith Wiens** (sop); **Christiane Oertel** (mez); **Friedhelm Eberle** (spkr); **Leipzig Radio Chorus; Leipzig Gewandhaus Orchestra/Kurt Masur.** Teldec 2292-46323-2. Text and translation included.

> 1h 3' DDD 5/92

To have a recording of Mendelssohn's incidental music with linking dialogue is an advantage, for the shorter pieces in particular make more of an impact when performed in the appropriate dramatic context. Teldec's recording was made in conjunction with a concert performance. Friedhelm Eberle speaks his lines in German, but no matter, for the insert notes contain Shakespeare's original English text set alongside the German translation. Of more concern is the fact that Eberle takes all the parts, occasionally going into falsetto for female roles. Edith Wiens and Christiane Oertel both sing their brief parts very capably, and in German, and the choral and orchestral contributions are first-rate. Masur's conception of the score is a little more serious and a little tougher than usual, but there is a good deal of personality in his conducting, and plenty of poetic expression. He takes the *Scherzo* a little more slowly than is the norm, but there is still a lightness of touch: the "Wedding March", by contrast, goes at a cheerfully fast pace. Throughout the performance, in fact, textures are kept very clear, and rhythms are appropriately light-footed. The recording quality is fully up to today's best standards.

Mendelssohn. Octet in E flat major, Op. 20. String Quintet No. 2 in B flat major, Op. 87. **Academy of St Martin in the Fields Chamber Ensemble.** Philips 420 400-2PH. From 9500 616 (3/80).

1h 3' ADD 11/87

Mendelssohn was as remarkable a prodigy as Mozart and one can only speculate with sadness what marvels he might have left us had he lived longer. Had death claimed him at 20 we would still have this glorious Octet, a work of unforced lyricism and a seemingly endless stream of melody. The Academy Chamber Ensemble, all fine soloists in their own right, admirably illustrate the benefits of working regularly as an ensemble for they play with uncommon sympathy. The string quintet is a work of greater fervour and passion than the Octet but it is characterized by the same melodiousness and unfettered lyricism with plenty of opportunities for virtuoso playing, which are well taken. The recordings, made in 1978, give a pleasant and warm sheen to the string colour of the ensemble.

Mendelssohn. String Quintet No. 1 in A major, Op. 18[a]. Octet in E flat major, Op. 20. **Hausmusik** ([a]Monica Huggett, [a]Pavlo Beznosiuk, Paull Boucher, Jolianne von Einem, vns; [a]Roger Chase, [a]Simon Whistler, vas; [a]Anthony Pleeth, Sebastian Comberti, vcs). EMI CDC7 49958-2.

1h 3' DDD 9/90

Hausmusik is an impressive chamber group, led by Monica Huggett, with Anthony Pleeth the principal cellist. They use original instruments, and create fresh, transparent textures, yet there is no lack of warmth and those horrid bulges on phrases which disfigure some early music performances are mercifully absent. Mendelssohn's miraculous Octet was written in 1825 when the composer was 16 and the almost equally engaging Quintet, with its gently nostalgic *Intermezzo* dates from a year later. The performances here fizz with vitality in outer movements where pacing is brisk and sparkling, yet never sounds rushed. The famous *Scherzo* in the Octet is wonderfully fleet, and articulated with a disarming, feather-light precision, and the *Presto* finale has real exhilaration. Yet the expressive music sings with unforced charm. Excellent, realistic recording, with enough resonance for bloom without clouding. If you are only familiar with the Octet the Quintet could prove a real bonus.

NEW REVIEW

Mendelssohn. String Quartets — No. 1 in E flat major, Op. 12; No. 2 in A minor, Op. 13. **Gabrieli Quartet** (John Georgiadis, Brendan O'Reilly, vns; Ian Jewel, va; Keith Harvey, vc). Chandos CHAN8827.

59' DDD 2/92

Chandos have sensibly programmed Quartet No. 2 before No. 1, and thus they restore the order of composition. The Second Quartet dates from 1827, when Mendelssohn was something of a veteran composer at the age of 18. It is a beautiful, perfectly mature work, as is the First Quartet, which was written two years later. There is a tendency for modern groups to drive Mendelssohn's quartets too hard, but the highly experienced Gabrieli Quartet avoid this fault, and instead bring out each work's joyful, spring-like quality. In Quartet No. 2 they take the first movement's main *allegro vivace* section at a moderate tempo, letting plenty of air into rhythms and phrasing. If the second *Adagio* movement is more serious, the Gabrieli do not darken its mood too much, and their playing is very affectionate. Even in the finale, initially marked *Presto*, the playing is still appropriately light in accents. Similar qualities inform the performance of Quartet No. 1, whose finale, for instance, marked *molto allegro e vivace*, is played purposefully but with elegance and good humour. The recording has an appropriately intimate acoustic, but is still pleasantly roomy.

Mendelssohn. Piano Trios — No. 1 in D minor, Op. 49; No. 2 in C minor, Op. 66. **Guarneri Trio** (Mark Lubotsky, vn; Jean Decroos, vc; Daniele Dechenne, pf). Globe GLO5007.

57' DDD 9/89

The First Piano Trio is a beautifully crafted work, richly melodious yet not without moments of tension and drama. His only other trio, in C minor, was composed six years later, and this too is an impressive piece, which uses a solemn chorale theme known to Bach (*Vor deinem Thron tret' ich*) to express his longing for a better world. But although the finale of the D minor is rather serious, neither of these works is at all tragic despite their minor keys, and neither has a really slow movement, while the two scherzos dance along in the composer's best fairy-playful manner, that of the Second Trio taken here at a pace which must tax even these skilful players. The Guarneri Trio play this music with wit and expressive force, keeping the right balance between romantic feeling and classical poise. The recording is a model of clarity, with well-judged slight reverberation.

Mendelssohn. Violin Sonatas — F minor, Op. 4; F major (1838). **Shlomo Mintz** (vn); **Paul Ostrovsky** (pf). DG 419 244-2GH.

51' DDD 8/87

The surprise here is the early F minor Violin Sonata, which is a work of strong character and an amazing achievement for a boy of 14. It is true that the sonata bears the influence of Beethoven and Mozart, but these influences are somehow assimilated and translated in a way that results in the work having its own very distinct personality. Obviously Mintz and Ostrovsky believe strongly in the work, and rightly do not play it down as a piece of juvenilia. Their response to the slow central movement is equally sensitive and beautifully phrased, and the last movement *Allegro agitato* is taut and well-argued. The F major Sonata shows all the elements of Mendelssohn's mature style, and is an altogether more urbane work than its predecessor. Again the soloists deserve high praise for their sympathetic response to the score. The excellent recording does full justice to Mintz's beautiful violin tone.

NEW REVIEW

Mendelssohn. Songs without Words. Kinderstücke, Op. 72. **Daniel Barenboim** (pf). DG 423 931-2GGA2. From 2740 104 (12/74).

② 2h 13' ADD

Mendelssohn's piano music in general, and the *Songs without Words* in particular, are all too often dismissed as 'mere' salon music, not to be mentioned in the same breath as the Octet and the Violin Concerto, works of undoubted genius. Certainly there is engaging intimacy and fine craftsmanship coupled with a fastidious attention to detail that is found in the very finest salon music. But many of the pieces rise to far greater heights, the famous *Duetto* Op. 38 No. 6 beloved of Dame Myra Hess for example, or the hunting song vigour of Op. 19 No. 3. The latter sets of *Songs* become ever more questing in their variety; in Op. 62 we find the gossamer lightness of No. 6 (reminiscent of his *Dream* music) set against No. 2 where clusters of notes demand a sure touch and an agile technique. Daniel Barenboim gives performances combining great sensitivity and musical imagination, the eloquence of his readings allowing the unaffected beauty of these miniatures to shine through. This is equally true of the other works in this two-disc set, particularly *Kinderstücke*, reminiscent of Schumann's *Kinderszenen*, though perhaps less deeply personal. Barenboim also enchants in his seductively sun-drenched *Gondellied*. The remastered sound has just the right degree of resonance and it is difficult to believe that this recording is nearly 21 years old. Useful insert notes including an enlightening essay by Joan Chissell.

Mendelssohn. PIANO WORKS. **Murray Perahia** (pf). CBS Masterworks CD37838. From IM37838 (5/85).
Piano Sonata in E major, Op. 6. Prelude and Fugue in E minor/major, Op. 35 No. 1. Variations sérieuses in D minor, Op. 54. Andante and Rondo capriccioso in E minor, Op. 14.

```
50'  DDD
```

This is a beautifully controlled and very welcome glimpse of a side of Mendelssohn rarely encountered in the concert-hall. Perahia's exquisitely fleet fingerwork and finely controlled pianism matches the weight of the music ideally. The four pieces represented here are not of equal stature but there are certainly some fine things. The *Variations sérieuses* is Mendelssohn's best-known work for the piano — as the title might imply there is a darker, maybe even melancholy flavour to the theme and the subsequent variations have real substance. Here and in the other works, particularly the delightful *Rondo capriccioso*, Perahia's performance overlooks nothing in mood or atmosphere.

NEW REVIEW
Mendelssohn. LIEDER. **Nathalie Stutzmann** (contr); **Dalton Baldwin** (pf). Erato 2292-45583-2. Texts and translations included.
Der Blumenstrauss, Op. 47 No. 5. Pagenlied. Des Mädchens Klage. Die Liebende schreibt, Op. 86 No. 3. Suleika, Op. 34 No. 4. Suleika, Op. 57 No. 3. Reiselied, Op. 34 No. 6. Erster Verlust, Op. 99 No. 1. Auf Flügeln des Gesanges, Op. 34 No. 2. Andres Maienlied ("Hexenlied"), Op. 8 No. 8. Der Blumenkranz. Ferne, Op. 9 No. 9. Scheidend, Op. 9 No. 6. Reiselied, Op. 19 No. 6. Herbstlied, Op. 84 No. 2. Venetianisches Gondellied, Op. 57 No. 5. Schlafloser Augen Leuchte. Neue Liebe, Op. 19a No. 4. Der Mond, Op. 86 No. 5. An die Entfernte, Op. 71 No. 3. Die Sterne schau'n, Op. 99 No. 2. Frühlingslied, Op. 47 No. 3. Nachtlied, Op. 71 No. 6. Volkslied, Op. 47 No. 4.

```
59'  DDD  5/91                                          9 P
```

Nathalie Stutzmann, the young French contralto, has rapidly established herself as one of the most interesting and intelligent Lieder singers of her generation. Here she devotes herself to the songs of Mendelssohn, which have been too long neglected. The composer may not have plumbed the emotional depths of the greatest of his predecessors and successors in his field, but he was unusually faithful to the shape and meaning of the poetry and covered quite a wide range of mood with an unerring sense of the appropriate setting. There are a number of arresting pieces here, such as *Reiselied, Die Liebende schreibt* and *Der Mond*, that are peculiarly Mendelssohnian in style. To these, and to the lighter songs, Stutzmann brings a welcome spontaneity of approach allied to a firm tone and expressive diction that make her singing consistently vital. She is splendidly partnered by the experienced Baldwin.

Nathalie Stutzmann   *[photo: Erato/Sarrat]*

Mendelssohn. Elijah. **Elly Ameling** (sop); **Annelies Burmeister** (contr); **Peter Schreier** (ten); **Theo Adam** (bass); **Leipzig Radio Chorus; Leipzig Gewandhaus Orchestra/Wolfgang Sawallisch.** Philips 420 106-2PH2. Text and translation included. From SAL3730/32 (9/69).

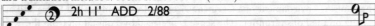

② 2h 11' ADD 2/88

Mendelssohn's *Elijah* received its first performance (in its English version) in Birmingham in 1846; thanks to the vigour and excitement of the writing the occasion was a resounding success, requiring of its performers encore after encore. This 1968 recording made with the Leipzig Gewandhaus Orchestra (which Mendelssohn himself conducted) uses the German version and the performance is quite simply superb. Sawallisch clearly believes in every note of this score and his team of soloists, with Theo Adam outstanding in the title-role, is very fine, as are the chorus. The recording wears its years lightly. This is one of the great choral records of recent decades.

Saverio Mercadante
Italian 1795-1870

NEW REVIEW

Mercadante. Flute Concerto in E minor.
Mozart. Flute Concerto No. 2 in D major, K314/285d.
Stamitz. Flute Concerto in G major. **Irena Grafenauer** (fl); **Academy of St Martin in the Fields/Sir Neville Marriner.** Philips 426 318-2PH.

1h DDD 11/91

Given that the flute and the soprano voice share the attributes of flexibility and tonal purity, it is hardly surprising that it should enter the mind of an Italian composer of some 60 operas and a player of the flute, as Mercadante was, to write a few flute concertos; nor is it entirely eyebrow-raising that, despite their classical form, they should sound like winsome, extended showcases for agile divas in libretto-less operas. Flautists are beginning to rediscover these works, to their and our benefit. Mozart told his father that he hated the flute but he wrote so wonderfully for it that it is hard to take his statement seriously. Though he was a great composer of operas he was no less prolific in his purely instrumental output; no operatic air hangs over his flute concertos. Neither does it over those of Stamitz, who wrote no opera — and, though he wrote splendidly for it, did not play the flute. Grafenauer is one of the very best young flautists to appear in recent years and she brings freshness (and two of her own cadenzas) to these attractive works; the ASMF are never slow to respond to a good and stimulating soloist, and they make no exception here.

Olivier Messiaen
French 1908-

NEW REVIEW

Messiaen. Quatuor pour la fin du temps[a]. Le merle noir[b]. [b]**Karlheinz Zöller** (fl); [a]**Erich Gruenberg** (vn); [a]**Gervase de Peyer** (cl); [a]**Anthony Pleeth** (vc); [a]**Michel Béroff**, [b]**Aloys Kontarsky** (pfs). EMI CDM7 63947-2. Item marked [a] from ASD2470 (8/69), [b] new to UK.

51' ADD 3/92

With its eight sections lasting not far short of 50 minutes, Messiaen's *Quartet for the end of time* is a milestone in twentieth-century chamber music, both for the originality of its language (sometimes complex and sometimes boldly simple) and for a mystical fervour unique in Western music. The other astonishing thing about it is its early date (1941) and the circumstances of its composition, for it was written and first performed by the composer and three friends in the unpromising environment of a German prisoner of war camp called Stalag VIII at Görlitz on the Polish frontier. The score is prefaced by a quotation from the Revelation of St John the Divine describing an angel descending from Heaven to announce that "the mystery of God will be accomplished" and the music as a whole represents Messiaen's response, as a devout Catholic, to what he called "the harmonious silence of the heavens ... the ascent of man towards his God". One might think that this could make for too private a vision, but the invention is so powerful and varied that a sympathetic listener, whether believer or no, can find the work utterly compelling. This was the first recording of the work and it remains among the best, with the four players (who appear more as individuals than in conventional ensemble) bringing to it a rapt intensity. *Le merle noir* ("The blackbird") was written a decade later for a flute competition at the Paris Conservatoire and evokes the birdsong which was a lifelong preoccupation of this composer. This is another fine performance, and both works are well recorded.

NEW REVIEW

Messiaen. Turangalîla-symphonie[a]. Quatuor pour la fin du temps[b]. [b]**Saschko Gawriloff** (vn); [b]**Siegfried Palm** (vc); [b]**Hans Deinzer** (cl); [b]**Aloys Kontarsky**, [a]**Peter Donohoe** (pfs); [a]**Tristan Murail** (ondes martenot); [a]**City of Birmingham Symphony Orchestra/Simon Rattle.** EMI CDS7 47463-8. Item marked [b] from Deutsche Harmonia Mundi 065 99711 (8/79).

② 2h 10' [a]DDD/[b]ADD 12/87

No longer a rarity in the concert-hall, Messiaen's epic hymn to life and love has been lucky on record too, with Rattle's performance staying just ahead of the pack. Messiaen's luxuriant scoring presents a challenge for the engineers as much as the players and the EMI team come through with flying colours. Tristan Murail's ondes martenot is carefully balanced here — evocative and velvety, neither reduced to inaudibility nor over-miked to produce an ear-rending screech. Peter Donohoe's piano obbligato is similarly integrated into the orchestral tapestry yet provides just the right kind of decorative intervention. Rattle is at his best in the work's more robust moments like the jazzy fifth movement and the many rhythmic passages which recall Stravinsky's *Le Sacre*. But those unfamiliar with Messiaen's extraordinary score should perhaps start with the central slow movement, the beautiful *Jardin du sommeil d'amour*, exquisitely done by the Birmingham team. Unlike at least one rival account, this *Turangalîla* spills on to a second CD, which leaves room for a distinguished *Quatuor pour la fin du temps* as a makeweight. The music-making here lacks the youthful spontaneity of the main work, but is notable for an unusually slow and sustained performance of the movement with cello solo.

Messiaen. Des canyons aux étoiles (1974)[a]. Oiseaux exotiques (1956). Couleurs de la cité céleste (1963). **Paul Crossley** (pf); [a]**Michael Thompson** (hn); [a]**James Holland** (xylorimba); [a]**David Johnson** (glockenspiel); **London Sinfonietta/Esa-Pekka Salonen.** CBS Masterworks CD44762.

② 2h 2' DDD 2/89

Anyone who has ever responded to Messiaen's *Turangalîla* Symphony should certainly experience its counterpart. *Des canyons aux étoiles* is an awed contemplation of the marvels of the earth and the immensity of space, both seen as metaphors and manifestations of divinity. And yet of the two works it is *Des canyons* that most startlingly conjures up visual, physical images in sound. It is often ravishing music but also often hard-edged and dazzlingly bright. The two shorter works in the collection make interesting points of reference. In *Oiseaux exotiques* Messiaen delights in intensifying birdsong by transposing it to quite un-birdlike instruments: brass, percussion and the piano. And if you imagine that an exclusively religious meditation like *Couleurs de la cité céleste* will be hushed, prayerful and mysterious, watch out. It speaks of rainbows and of trumpets, abysses and measureless spaces, blinding light and jewel-like colour, and the work is scored accordingly for strident clarinets, xylophones, brass and metal percussion: it is one of the loudest scores he has ever written. Both these sound-tributaries flow into *Des canyons aux étoiles*, one of this century's masterpieces of instrumental writing, and it is good to have such a virtuoso performance of it. Paul Crossley produces prodigies of brilliant dexterity throughout all three works and he is worthily backed by Salonen and the Sinfonietta players. The recording is as clear as can be, but not without atmosphere.

Messiaen. Catalogue d'oiseaux — Books 1-3. **Peter Hill** (pf). Unicorn-Kanchana DKPCD9062.
Book 1 — Le Chocard des Alpes; Le Loriot; Le Merle bleu. Book 2 — Le Traquet Stapazin. Book 3 — Le Chouette Hulotte; L'Alouette Lulu.

59' DDD 5/88

Messiaen describes himself as 'ornithologist-musician', but he is a landscape-painter of genius as well. Though each piece in his catalogue bears the name of a single bird, each is really an evocation of a particular place (very often at a particular season and time of day), and most of the pieces contain the carefully transcribed and meticulously labelled songs of many birds. His imagery is naïve but the catalogue's huge range of sonority and gesture, its eloquently visionary intensity and its descriptive power make it one of the peaks of twentieth-century piano literature. It is so long (the complete catalogue plays for about two-and-three-quarters hours) and so difficult that the peak is seldom scaled. The work is fortunate to have found such an interpreter as Peter Hill. He is a complete master of its rhythmic complexity and its finger-breaking defiance of the pianistically possible, but he never loses sight of the fact that the cycle's main objective is to evoke a sense of place, of light and temperature even, and thereby to awake awe in the listener at the majesty and sublimity of creation.

NEW REVIEW

Messiaen. Préludes[a]. Vingt regards sur l'enfant Jésus[b]. **Michel Béroff** (pf). EMI CMS7 69161-2. Item marked [b] from SLS793 (11/70).

② 2h 26' AAD 3/92

Messiaen's death in 1992 at the age of 83 took from us the last musical giant of the twentieth-century, into which his lifetime fitted almost exactly since he was born eight years after its beginning and died eight years before its end. The year 2000 also marks the millennium, and with his apocalyptic vision and fervent Catholic faith this composer seems like a present-day Messianic prophet whose musical utterance is a kind of revelation, meditative and exuberant by turns. Listeners who have thus far found the *Vingt regards sur l'enfant Jésus* self-indulgent and syrupy could well try again with this fine disc. Michel Béroff was actually a protégé of Messiaen and studied with the composer's wife Yvonne Loriod, and he recorded the work as long ago as 1969, when he was only 19. His performance balances intensity with reverent restraint and his freshness and pianistic resource together avoid the *longueurs* that lesser pianists can bring to this lengthy and sometimes very slow-moving music. The eight *Préludes* were recorded a decade later and are among Messiaen's earliest works. Although they are superficially rather too similar in their hothouse quietude (at least until the extrovert last one), they are exquisitely written for the piano and should present no problems to listeners who enjoy Debussy. The recording is very acceptable.

Messiaen. La nativité du Seigneur[a]. Le banquet céleste[b]. **Jennifer Bate** (org). Unicorn-Kanchana DKPCD9005. Played on the organ of Beauvais Cathedral. Item marked [a] from DKP9005 (6/82), [b] DKP9018 (2/83).

> 1h 2' DDD 2/88

La nativité du Seigneur comprises nine meditations on themes associated with the birth of the Lord. Messiaen's unique use of registration gives these pieces an extraordinarily wide range of colour and emotional potency and in Jennifer Bate's hands (and feet) it finds one of its most persuasive and capable advocates. Bate is much admired by the composer and is so far the only organist to have recorded his complete works for the instrument. *Le banquet céleste* was Messiaen's first published work for the organ and is a magical, very slow-moving meditation on a verse from St John's Gospel (VI, 56). The very faithful recording captures both the organ and the large acoustic of Beauvais Cathedral to marvellous effect.

NEW REVIEW

Messiaen. Méditations sur le mystère de la Sainte Trinité. **Hans-Ola Ericsson** (org). BIS CD464. Played on the Grönlund organ of Luleå Cathedral, Sweden.

> 1h 18' DDD 3/92

At the time of his death Messiaen could point to tangible evidence of international stature as a composer of organ music. Several recordings of his organ works were either complete or in the throes of completion including this one from the 35-year-old Swedish organist, Hans-Ola Ericsson. Using the organ of Luleå Cathedral, an instrument which had to be modified in order to be more faithful to Messiaen's score, Ericsson shows a consistently strong command of both the technical and inspirational aspects of this unique body of organ music. Dating from 1969 the principal strands of Messiaen's diverse sources of musical inspiration coalesce in this remarkable work. Precisely annotated birdsong perches happily alongside Greek and Indian rhythms, but the central element throughout is plainsong; Messiaen may have been strongly influenced by exotic elements, but his profound faith and firm Catholic background remained his principal channel of expression. Ericsson's performance is clean, precise and flawless in its technical delivery although, perhaps, Messiaen's mystic vision might seem just a little too sharply focused.

Messiaen. Livre du Saint Sacrement. **Jennifer Bate** (org). Unicorn-Kanchana DKPCD9067/8. Recorded on the organ of L'Eglise de la Sainte-Trinité, Paris.

> ② 2h 9' DDD 10/87

The crowning achievement of Messiaen's unique cycle of music for the organ, the *Livre du Saint Sacrement* is also his largest work for the instrument. It is an intensely personal score based on the cornerstone of Messiaen's Catholic faith, the Blessed Sacrament, and spans a wide range of emotions from hushed, private communion to the truly apocalyptic. Jennifer Bate gave the British première of the work in 1986, following which Messiaen invited her to record it using his own organ at the Trinity Church in Paris. He was on hand throughout the sessions as he so often was. The recording is a model of clarity and it is hard to imagine the complex and often very subtle textures of this music being better conveyed. This is a magnificent achievement and should be heard by all who profess an interest in the music of our time.

Messiaen. ORGAN WORKS, Volume 1. **Hans-Ola Ericsson.** BIS CD409.
Played on the organ of Lulea Cathedral, Sweden.
L'Ascension. Le banquet céleste. Apparition de l'église éternelle. Diptyque.

Ih 4' DDD

This disc contains Messiaen's first organ works written between 1928 and 1934,
and they are among his most expressive and attractive pieces. The titles bear
testament to his profound Christian faith and his visionary approach to music. His
earliest composition, *Le banquet céleste* represents the Holy Communion with long
drawn-out manual chords supporting a pedal line which represents the drops of
Christ's blood. *Diptyque* is subtitled "essay on earthly life and eternal happiness"
and after a bustling, rather sour opening the transformation to the celestial peace
is quite unnerving. Most visionary of all, the *Apparition de l'eglise éternelle* portrays
the coming into view among swirling clouds of the eternal church and then its
subsequent fading away. Incessant hammer blows can be heard from the organ
pedals. *L'Ascension* was the first of Messiaen's large-scale cycles for the instrument, and was itself a transcription of an orchestral work. Hans-Ola Ericsson has
a richly romantic vein in his soul which he willingly bares here. He produces
some lovely playing, especially in the slower pieces, and is supported by a
mellow organ tone which is well captured in this fine recording.

NEW REVIEW

Messiaen. Trois petites liturgies de la Présence Divine[a]. Cinq Rechants[b].
O sacrum convivium[c]. [a]**Cynthia Miller** (ondes martenot); [a]**Rolf Hind** (pf);
[a]**London Sinfonietta** [a]**Chorus and** [bc]**Voices;** [a]**London Sinfonietta/Terry
Edwards.** Virgin Classics VC7 91472-2. Notes, texts and translations included.

Ih DDD 11/91

Even if, as Messiaen himself insisted, he was pre-eminently a 'theological'
composer, dedicated to celebrating the divine presence in his music, that music
often seems to embrace the sensuous as wholeheartedly as the spiritual. Indeed,
one suspects that anyone listening to the *Trois petites liturgies de la Présence Divine*
in ignorance of the content of the text would assume that the chanted phrases
and opulent consonances of the all-female chorus, coupled with the swooning
tonal quality of the ondes martenot, which is so prominent in the instrumental
accompaniment, were hymning an essentially physical union after the manner of
Stravinsky's *Les Noces*. In *Cinq Rechants* the secularity is more explicit, though
hidden to a degree within Messiaen's own rather surrealistic texts. Here the
musical focus is even more directly on the voices, now unaccompanied, and the
panache and polish of the London Sinfonietta Chorus are remarkably well
sustained. For the ultimate in refined control of a slow moving, quiet choral
texture, the short motet *O sacrum convivium* is the ideal foil to the larger, more
dramatic compositions, and the recordings are exemplary in ensuring that each
vocal strand is clear without any artificial spotlighting.

Messiaen. La nativité du Seigneur[a]. La Transfiguration de Notre Seigneur Jésus-
Christ[b]. [b]**Michael Sylvester** (ten); **Paul Aquino** (bar); [b]**Westminster
Symphonic Choir;** [b]**Wallace Mann** (fl); [b]**Loren Kitt** (cl); [b]**János Starker**
(vc); [b]**Frank Ames** (marimba); [b]**Ronald Barnett** (vibraphone); [b]**John Kane**
(xylorimba); [b]**Yvonne Loriod** (pf); [a]**Simon Preston** (org); [b]**Washington
National Symphony Orchestra/Antál Dorati.** Decca Enterprise 425 616-
2DM2. Notes, text and translation included. Item marked [a] played on the organ
of Westminister Abbey and from Argo ZRG5447 (3/66), [b] HEAD1-2 (5/74).

② 2h 30' ADD 9/90 £

Considering that *La Transfiguration de Notre Seigneur Jésus-Christ* represents one of
the most important landmarks in Messiaen's output, it is somewhat surprising

that this pioneering account from the 1970s remains the only recording of this work — and even this remained out of circulation for some time. Its neglect undoubtedly has something to do with the work's monumental proportions and equally monumental forces required for performance (it requires an orchestra of over 100 players, a choir of 100 voices as well as a group of seven instrumental soloists). The texts centre around the Gospel narrative of the Transfiguration, interspersed with meditative movements drawn from various biblical and theological texts. Messiaen's fondness for formal symmetry dictates the structure; the work is divided into two groups of seven pieces, which in turn contain internal symmetries and reflections within each part. Stylistically it contains all the ingredients that we have come to associate with Messiaen's music — plainsong, Indian and Greek rhythms and birdsong, in this case a staggering 80 different species. At the time of its composition it represented the summation of Messiaen's art and achievement. Dorati's structural control over this immense work is little short of miraculous, and there are some deeply committed performances from the instrumental soloists too; particularly notable are Yvonne Loriod and János Starker. Not content with giving us just one bargain, Decca have also included as an added bonus Simon Preston's marvellous 1965 recording of *La nativité du Seigneur*. Both works are exceptionally well recorded.

Nikolay Miaskovsky *Russian 1881-1950*

NEW REVIEW

Miaskovsky. Cello Concerto in C minor, Op. 66.
Shostakovich. The Limpid Stream, Op. 39 — Adagio.
Tchaikovsky. Variations on a Rococo Theme in A minor, Op. 33. Nocturne, Op. 19 No. 4. **Julian Lloyd Webber** (vc); **London Symphony Orchestra/ Maxim Shostakovich.** Philips 434 106-2PH.

Ih 3' DDD 5/92

Maxim Shostakovich   [photo: Philips

Miaskovsky won a Stalin Prize for his Cello Concerto in 1946. It is a beautifully crafted and finely structured piece, scored for an orchestra that Brahms might have used. It shares a certain introspection with the Elgar Cello Concerto, though its autumnal mood is pervaded by an essentially Russian brooding and melancholy; qualities that are drawn out with sensitivity by Lloyd Webber and Shostakovich at slower tempos. Lloyd Webber lingers lovingly over the Tchaikovsky *Rococo* Variations as well, and opts for the original version which restores a cut variation and reverts to the composer's first thoughts on how the Variations should be ordered. His smooth, rich tone and sense of line are a joy to hear, though one could possibly wish for a little more virtuosic projection in, say, the final variation and coda. The *Limpid Stream* Adagio, too, is an original, and preferable version (and a world première recording) of a seven minute piece that turns up with bolstered orchestration in Shostakovich's Ballet Suite No. 2. Philips supply spacious sound, with a very full bass; and the soloist is placed within the orchestra, though slightly left of centre in the Miaskovsky. A valuable and rewarding disc.

Luis de Milán

Milán. Libro de musica de vihuela de mano, "El maestro" — excerpts. **Hopkinson Smith** (vihuela). Auvidis Astrée E7748. Texts and translations included.

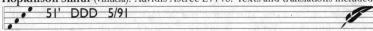

`51' DDD 5/91`

Luis Milán's anthology of vihuela music, *El maestro* was printed in 1535 or 1536 and was the first of its kind for the instrument. It contains villancios and romances, sets of diferencias, dances, transcriptions of sacred and secular polyphony, fantasias and tientos. Some of the pieces can easily be sung as well as played and in such cases in the manuscript the melody appears in red figures to assist the singer. This disc, however, contains only pieces for solo vihuela including four of Milán's six beautiful pavanas, nine fantasias and three tientos. Hopkinson Smith is a skilled and sympathetic player who has given careful thought to his programme, laying it out in four groups corresponding to the modes carefully documented in Milán's imaginative anthology. All in all it makes for fascinating listening, and the disc is very well recorded allowing us to appreciate the subtleties of the gut-string sound of the instrument.

Ernest Moeran

NEW REVIEW
Moeran. Symphony in G minor. Overture to a Masque. **Ulster Orchestra/ Vernon Handley.** Chandos CHAN8577.

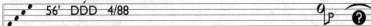

`56' DDD 4/88`

It has been suggested that Moeran's Symphony is "among the five or six most original [symphonies] to appear between the two world wars". Original? The Anglo-Irish Moeran all too obviously knew and loved his Sibelius, and the stylistic imprints of just about every major British composer from and including Elgar onwards are here too. So why does the symphony exert such a powerful spell? The bracing *allegros* of the outer movement frame and punctuate some of the most sublime land and seascape imagery ever composed. Folk melody is richly and unashamedly deployed (never mind the derivations, what a supreme melodist Moeran was!) yielding legendary echoes, and a yearning lyricism. The orchestration throughout, even when undercurrents erupt into moments of violence, has lucidity of texture, a light-as-air quality. Perhaps the marvel of this symphony is that Moeran has fused his derivations into something completely personal. It is a disturbing work, disquiet lingering in the memory long after its final chords, which, though commanding, resolve nothing. Handley, the Ulster Orchestra and Chandos have done so much for music from these shores. Never have they made a better disc.

Federico Mompou

NEW REVIEW
Mompou. PIANO WORKS. **Paul Komen** (pf). Globe GLO6004. Suburbis. Cants mágics. Pessebres. Paisajes. 10 Preludes. Impresiones intimas.

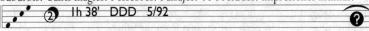

`② 1h 38' DDD 5/92`

Since the death of this Catalan composer six years ago at the age of 94, interest in his music has increased and this new recording will deservedly win admirers. He was a fine pianist in his youth, but excessive shyness kept him away from a concert career and he devoted much of his creative energy to composing piano pieces that are short but invariably telling. The first one here, No. 1 of the five *Suburbis*, recalls Debussy (whom he admired) in its gentle eloquence although there is also an unmistakable Spanish quality. That Spanish, or more precisely that Catalan voice, pervades some of the other music here, but it is never laid on too thickly, and indeed a chief characteristic of the Mompou style is a certain inwardness and elusiveness. Yet there is no lack of charm or inventiveness, and the more one listens to this music, the more one realizes that this composer was a master and no mere miniaturist. He has been championed by other pianists, notably his compatriot Alicia de Larrocha, but it is good to see him being taken up by an artist of another nationality and generation, and the young Dutchman Paul Komen is totally inside the idiom. Mompou may be a 'one-off' composer like Delius or Satie, not belonging to any school, but his music is rewarding for that very reason as well as for its introspection, stillness and quiet humanity. To see if it appeal to you, try the three *Paisajes* ("Landscapes") which are among his later works. This finely recorded recital is most welcome.

Claudio Monteverdi   *Italian 1567-1643*

Monteverdi (ed Parrott/Keyte). Vespro della Beata Vergine. **Taverner Consort; Taverner Choir; Taverner Players/Andrew Parrott.** EMI CDS7 47078-8. From EX270129-3 (5/85).

♪ ② 1h 52' DDD 10/85

For a generation, performances have revelled in the colossal aspect of this work: huge choirs, generously-sized orchestras of modern instruments and lavish interpretations, all of which go hand in hand with a such a view of the music. Without question, splendour was part of Monteverdi's conception, but it was the splendour of ritual that he had in mind. It is this ritualistic aspect that Andrew Parrott restores in this special recording. Plainchant and instrumental sonatas mix authentically with Monteverdi's music; changes are made to the printed order of items to conform to the requirements of the *Vespers* service; several movements are transposed downwards to make them easier on the voice. If the result undermines the conventional view of the *Vespers* as an unbroken chain of glorious concert pieces, culminating in the huge, high-pitched Magnificat, then it does so to the advantage of Monteverdi's original intentions. Parrott brings together the cream of today's early-music specialists and both the playing (entirely on period instruments) and the singing are of the highest order. Few liturgical reconstructions on record have worked so well as this one does. It is a noble and moving experience.

Monteverdi. SACRED VOCAL MUSIC. [a]**Emma Kirkby** (sop); [b]**Ian Partridge** (ten); [c]**David Thomas** (bass); **The Parley of Instruments/Ray Goodman** (vn) with **Peter Holman** (chbr org). Hyperion CDA66021. From A66021 (10/81). La Maddalena — Prologue: Su le penne de'venti[c]. Confitebor tibi, Domine[abc]. Iste confessor Domini sacratus[b]. Laudate Dominum, Omnes gentes[c]. Confitebor tibi, Domine[ab]. Confitebor tibi, Domine[a]. Ab aeterno ordinata sum[c]. Nisi Dominus aedificaverit domum[abc]. Deus tuorum militum sors et corona[abc].

♪ 43' DDD 7/85

This is a delightful selection of lesser-known shorter sacred pieces. There are five psalm settings, each one perfectly distinct from the others; a setting of a passage from *Proverbs* depicting a fantastic vision of creation, two hymn settings and finally, the Prologue to a liturgical drama, *La Maddalena*. The writing has much in common with the madrigalian style: in the first place, it is episodic; it also vividly dramatizes the sense of the words and demands a sensitive response on the part of the singers. For example, the phrase "sanctum et terribile nomen eius" is highlighted by a dignified, slow-moving theme at "sanctum" followed by speedy vocal jittering on "terribile"! The singers have countless opportunities to display both their mastery of vocal techniques and their sensitivity to the text. In general they show restraint and avoid overdoing the pyrotechnics: the music never seems to deviate from its sacred purpose, always retaining a sense of decorum.

Thomas Morley
British 1557-1602

NEW REVIEW

Morley. JOYNE HANDS. **Red Byrd; Musicians of Swanne Alley/Paul O'Dette; Lyle Nordstrom.** Virgin Classics Veritas VC7 91214-2. Texts included. *Morley:* Joyne hands. A lieta vita. O griefe, even on the bud. Our bonny bootes could toote it. Pavan (arr. Cutting). Galliard. Sleepe slumbr'ring eyes. Thirsis and Milla Sacred End Pavin (arr. Rosseter). Galliard to Sacred End (arr. Baxter). Pavin and Galliard. A painted tale. Faire in a morne. Sayd I that Amarillis. Now is the gentle season. Harke; Alleluia cheerely. Hard by a cristall fountaine. Now is the month of maying (arr. Rosseter). **P. Philips:** Philips Paven and Galliard. *Conversi:* Sola soletta (arr.? Morley). **Strogers:** In Nomine Pavin and Galliard. *Anonymous:* O mistresse mine (vocal and consort versions). La Coranto (all arr.? Morley). Monsieurs Almaine. My Lord of Oxenfordes March.

1h 12' DDD 1/92 ❓

Thomas Morley was a central figure in English renaissance music, a composer of the first rank, an arranger of his own and other people's music, and a publisher who greatly helped to spread the gospel of Italian style on these shores. His major contribution to instrumental music was his two books (1599 and 1611) of "Lessons" for that most English of bands, the 'broken consort', an ingenious and flexible combination of blown, bowed and plucked instruments (here the Musicians of Swanne Alley) which grew out of the Elizabethan theatre. The music of the "Lessons" was of both instrumental and vocal origin and included only one arrangement known to be by Morley, that which gives this album its title. His books of vocal music (again mostly by others) were numerous and it is in these that his helping hand to Italian music was strongest. The traffic was two-way: Morley's music, including some of the lute solos in this recording, was also arranged and published by others. When the Musicians of Swanne Alley play in concert you can see that they are enjoying themselves; on record you can *hear* it just as easily, and this recording is no exception. Very little of the music is to be had in any other recording, and hearing it you may well wonder why. These magnificent performances are a worthy tribute to the multi-faceted work of a man of no small importance.

Wolfgang Amadeus Mozart
Austrian 1756-1791

Mozart. Sinfonia concertante in E flat major, K364/K320*d*[a]. Concertone in C major for two violins, oboe, cello and orchestra, K190/K186*e*[b]. **Itzhak Perlman** (vn); **Pinchas Zukerman** ([a]va, vn); [b]**Chaim Jouval** (ob); [b]**Marcel Bergman** (vc); **Israel Philharmonic Orchestra/Zubin Mehta.** DG 415 486-2GH. Item marked [a] from 2741 026 (11/83), [b] new to UK.

1h DDD 12/85 Ⓑ

The first of these works was recorded in 1982 at a concert in Tel Aviv, and represents live music making at its best. Itzhak Perlman's colleague Pinchas

Zukerman is, like him, a violinist of international reputation, but in the last decade or so he has also played the viola, and since they have a similar approach to the *Sinfonia concertante,* they make for possibly the most desirable pair of soloists that one could hope to bring together for a performance of this melodious work. All is of the finest quality, but the exquisite slow movement stands out memorably even so, "with the silvery image of the violin set against the richer viola tone" as it has been said. Zubin Mehta accompanies sensitively too, with an Israel Philharmonic seemingly inspired by the occasion, and this Mozart playing is exceptional even by today's high standards. The recording is excellent although the soloists sound closer than they would in the concert hall, and audience noise is minimal with no applause. Recorded in the studio, the *Concertone* is another unusually named work, written when Mozart was 18, and has two solo violins plus roles for oboe and cello; this too is most enjoyable and the oboist Chaim Jouval plays with firm yet sweet tone.

Mozart. Sinfonias concertante — E flat major, K364/320*d*[a]; E flat major, KAnh9/C14·01/297*b*[b]. [b]**Stephen Taylor** (ob); [b]**David Singer** (cl); [b]**Steven Dibner** (bn); [b]**William Purvis** (hn); [a]**Todd Phillips** (vn); [a]**Maureen Gallagher** (va); **Orpheus Chamber Orchestra.** DG 429 784-2GH.

⠶ · ♪ 1h 3' DDD 4/91   **Ⓑ**

The Orpheus Chamber Orchestra have made several successful Mozart records. The soloists in the *Sinfonia concertante* for violin and viola are well blended with the orchestral body yet are distinguishable from it and from each other, while the playing in the *Allegro maestoso* first movement is energetic yet not over-emphasized or forced along and the cadenza here is finely shaped. The beautiful central slow movement is warm yet gentle, with a quiet unflagging strength underlying the sensitivity of the soloists in their thoughtful dialogue, and the finale is vivid without breathlessness. The other work with four wind soloists is also very pleasing, with no weaker member in the solo quartet; here is a good tonal, rhythmic and interpretative blend. If in comparison with some other performances it may seem a trifle understated in places, that is no serious fault in music such as this, which speaks pretty eloquently for itself, and the players miss none of the wit of the cheery variation-form finale. The recording accorded to both these sinfonias concertantes, which was made at the State University of New York, is both natural and pleasing.

Mozart. Sinfonia concertante in E flat major, K296*b*[a]. Horn Quintet in E flat major, K407/386*c*[c]. Quintet in E flat major for piano and wind, K452[c]. [ac]**Derek Wickens** (ob); [ac]**Robert Hill** (cl); [ac]**Martin Gatt** (bn); [b]members of the **Gabrieli Quartet** (Kenneth Sillito, vn; Kenneth Essex, va; Kenneth Harvey, vc); [c]**John Ogdon** (pf); [a]**English Chamber Orchestra/Barry Tuckwell** ([bc]hn). Decca 421 393-2DH. From 410 283-1DH3 (8/84).

⠶ · ♪ 1h 13' DDD 9/88   **Ⓑ**

This is a happily chosen compilation of three lesser-known Mozart works, offering a handy way of adding them to a collection without duplication. The *Sinfonia concertante* is not the one featuring violin and viola as soloists, but a delectable lightweight work with wind instruments to the fore. Playing here is smiling and stylish, the lovely slow movement has the lightest touch and is elegantly gracious. The Horn Quintet with its spirited finale, will appeal to anyone who enjoys the concertos while the Piano and Wind Quintet is one of Mozart's masterpieces. Mozart had a very special way with blending woodwind (and horn) and here with the piano as a dominating catalyst he gives us a three movement piece which is infectiously inventive from the first bar to the last. Barry Tuckwell is the personality common to all three performances, and it is he who dominates the Horn Quintet; elsewhere he takes his place with his colleagues, but also directs the *Sinfonia concertante*. The digital recording is very realistic, the players might well be sitting at the end of your listening room.

Mozart. Clarinet Concerto in A major, K622[a]. Clarinet Quintet in A major, K581[b]. **Thea King** (basset cl); [b]**Gabrieli String Quartet** (Kenneth Sillito, Brendan O'Reilly, vns; Ian Jewel, va; Keith Harvey, vc); [a]**English Chamber Orchestra/Jeffrey Tate.** Hyperion CDA66199. From A66199 (3/86).

1h 4'   DDD   9/86   Ⓑ

Mozart. Clarinet Concerto in A major, K622[a]. Flute and Harp Concerto in C major, K299/297c[b]. [a]**Emma Johnson** (cl); [b]**William Bennett** (fl); [b]**Osian Ellis** (hp); **English Chamber Orchestra/Raymond Leppard.** ASV CDDCA532. From DCA532 (6/85).

54'   DDD   Ⓑ

Emma Johnson   *[photo: ASV*

The two works on the Hyperion disc are representative of Mozart's clarinet writing at its most inspired; however, the instrument for which they were written differed in several respects from the modern clarinet, the most important being its extended bass range. Modern editions of both the Concerto and the Quintet have adjusted the solo part to suit today's clarinets, but on this recording Thea King reverts as far as possible to the original texts, and her playing is both sensitive and intelligent. Jeffrey Tate and the ECO accompany with subtlety and discretion in the Concerto, and the Gabrielli Quartet achieve a fine sense of rapport with King in the Quintet. Both recordings are clear and naturally balanced, with just enough distance between soloist and listener.

The ASV recording followed swiftly on the success of Emma Johnson as the BBC's 1984 "Young Musician of the Year", and it certainly bears out her success. This is tasteful and fluent playing: rather less a performance memorable for special beauty and subtlety of tone and delivery or the revelatory quality which is impossible to define but easily recognized when present — though the *Adagio* has a simple eloquence. However, it is still admirably sure and direct. The Concerto for Flute and Harp brings together two instruments of exquisite beauty. Not surprisingly, the music is delightful, with the two soloists pouring forth golden melody and rippling arpeggios. William Bennett and Osian Ellis are among today's finest players, too, and the recording is very natural, although one might have liked a little more brightness to their sound and could feel that the well-modulated orchestral playing under Raymond Leppard could have more sheer sparkle. Only your preference in respect of coupling can determine the choice between these two recordings

Mozart. Flute Concerto No. 1 in G major, K313/285c. Andante in C major, K315/285e. Flute and Harp Concerto in C major, K299/297c[a]. **Susan Palma** (fl); [a]**Nancy Allen** (hp); **Orpheus Chamber Orchestra.** DG 427 677-2GH.

58'   DDD   3/90   Ⓟ

Mozart described the flute as "an instrument I cannot bear" in 1778 before composing his G major Flute Concerto for the Dutch amateur Ferdinand DeJean.

However, he was incapable of writing poor music and this is a work of much charm and some depth that comes up with admirable freshness in this performance by Susan Palma. She is a remarkably gifted player and a member of the no less skilled Orpheus Chamber Orchestra, a conductorless ensemble of 24 players who shape the music with unfailing skill and unanimity so that everything is alert, lithe and yet sensitive. Palma's tone is liquid and bright, and she offers fine tonal nuances too, while her cadenzas are no less well imagined. The Concerto for Flute and Harp, written for another amateur player (the Count de Guines) to play with his harpist daughter, combines these two beautiful instruments to celestial effect; again the soloists are highly skilled and beyond that, they are perfectly matched. Palma is as delightful as in the other work and the spacious *Andante* in C major that separates the two concertos, while Nancy Allen makes an exquisite sound and also articulates more clearly than many other harpists in this work. The balance between the soloists and the orchestra is natural and the recording from New York's State University has a very pleasing sound.

Mozart. HORN CONCERTOS. **Dennis Brain** (hn); **Philharmonia Orchestra/Herbert von Karajan.** EMI Références mono CDH7 61013-2. From Columbia 33CX1140 (10/54).
No. 1 in D major, K412; No. 2 in E flat major, K417; No. 3 in E flat major, K447; No. 4 in E flat major K495.

55' ADD 2/88 £ 9p ⓑ ▲

Mozart. HORN CONCERTOS. **English Chamber Orchestra/Barry Tuckwell** (hn). Decca 410 284-2DH. From 410 284-1DH3 (8/84).
No. 1 in D major, K412; No. 2 in E flat major, K417; No. 3 in E flat major, K447; No. 4 in E flat major K495.

52' DDD 11/84 9p ⓑ

Dennis Brain set the yardstick by which all subsequent performances of these concertos would be measured. The security of his technique, the smooth, easy tone and subtle, almost understated expression were all exceptional for the early 1950s, and only the leading horn players of subsequent generations have been able to approach his degree of finesse. Karajan was the ideal accompanist and together they produced performances of great humanity. Although the mono sound is now somewhat lacking in string warmth, it is clean and detailed enough to allow the years to fall away, and for Brain to speak directly to us.

Barry Tuckwell proves that he is one of only a meagre handful of players who can equal Brain's artistry in these works. For some, Brain's view, always urbane and intuitively Mozartian, will remain a first choice, whilst others will prefer the more up-to-date sound of the later recording — despite the comparative thickness of the horn timbre engendered by close miking — and Tuckwell's more overtly virtuosic approach and broader tone quality. The ECO, always the most sensitive of accompanists, are on fine form, their effectiveness limited only by an acoustic that traps lower middle-register detail. With excellent insert notes from Lionel Salter, and Barry Tuckwell himself, this is an issue that may be safely recommended to all wanting a first, second, or subsequent version of these works for their collection.

Mozart. Oboe Concerto in C major, K314/285.
R. Strauss. Oboe Concerto in D major. **Douglas Boyd** (ob); **Chamber Orchestra of Europe/Paavo Berglund.** ASV CDCOE808. From COE808 (7/87).

44' DDD 11/87

This coupling links two of the most delightful oboe concertos ever written. Mozart's sprightly and buoyant work invests the instrument with a chirpy, birdlike fleetness encouraging the interplay of lively rhythm and elegant poise. Boyd's reading of this evergreen work captures its freshness and spontaneity beautifully. If the Mozart portrays the sprightly side of the instrument's make-up the Strauss illustrates its languorous ease and tonal voluptuousness. Again Boyd allows himself the freedom and breadth he needs for his glowing interpretation; he handles the arching melodies of the opening movement and the witty staccato of the last with equal skill. Nicely recorded.

Mozart. PIANO CONCERTOS. **English Chamber Orchestra/Daniel Barenboim** (pf). EMI CZS7 62825-2.
No. 1 in F major, K37; No. 2 in B flat major, K39; No. 3 in D major, K40; No. 4 in G major, K41 (all from SLS5031, 1/76); No. 5 in D major, K175 (ASD2484, 11/69); No. 6 in B flat major, K238 (ASD3032, 11/74); No. 8 in C major, K246 (ASD3033, 1/75); No. 9 in E flat major, K271 (ASD2484); No. 11 in F major, K413/387*a* (ASD2999, 9/74); No. 12 in A major, K414/385*p* (ASD2956, 2/74); No. 13 in C major, K415/387*b* (ASD2357, 4/68); No. 14 in E flat major, K449; No. 15 in B flat major, K450 (both ASD2434, 11/68); No. 16 in D major, K451 (ASD2999); No. 17 in G major, K453 (ASD2357); No. 18 in B flat major, K456 (ASD2887, 7/73); No. 19 in F major, K459 (ASD2956); No. 20 in D minor, K466 (ASD2318, 7/67); No. 21 in C major, K467 (ASD2465, 2/69); No. 22 in E flat major, K482 (ASD2838, 11/72); No. 23 in A major, K488 (ASD2318); No. 24 in C minor, K491 (ASD2887); No. 25 in C major, K503 (ASD3033); No. 26 in D major, K537, "Coronation" (ASD3032); No. 27 in B flat major, K595 (ASD2465). Rondo in D major, K382 (ASD2838).

(10) **11h1' ADD 6/90** £

Here are all 27 of Mozart's piano concertos plus the D major Rondo, K382, on ten medium-priced discs giving a total of eleven hours listening. The skills of Daniel Barenboim and the English Chamber Orchestra in this repertory are well proven, and his account of these concertos, directed from the keyboard, is spacious and satisfying. This artist has always been a master of clean exposition and structure, and from the early Concertos to the late masterpieces such as Nos. 21, 24 and 27 he is a sure guide with a full awareness of Mozart's inventive and expressive range. Sometimes one may feel that he allows a rather romantic self-indulgence to creep in, and in the more dramatic music (e.g. in the D minor and C minor concertos) he may be thought to be too powerfully Beethovenian and, incidentally, he uses a Beethoven cadenza, as arranged by Edwin Fischer, in the first movement of the first of these. Ideally, too, we might prefer a smaller body of strings than was used in these performances from the late 1960s and early 1970s. But these are only small reservations, given the high overall standard, and certainly this is a major achievement. The recordings sound well, with mellow piano tone and good balance.

Mozart. Piano Concertos — No. 15 in B flat, K450; No. 16 in D major, K451. **English Chamber Orchestra/Murray Perahia** (pf). CBS Masterworks CD37824.

50' DDD 9p 9s

It is difficult to do justice to interpretations of this calibre in a short review. Perahia's delicious shaping of even the most elaborate phrases and his delicacy and refinement of tone impress throughout these performances. The two works are admirably contrasted: K450 is on the whole light and high-spirited, while the first movement of K451 is almost Beethovenian in its grandeur and purposeful-ness, and both concertos have typically beautiful slow movements. Recordings are superb: an overly attentive microphone could have done irreparable damage to

Perahia's legato, but here the distance is finely judged and the soloist/orchestra balance is exemplary.

Mozart. Piano Concertos — No. 19 in F major, K459; No. 27 in B flat major, K595. **András Schiff** (pf); **Salzburg Mozarteum Camerata Academica/ Sándor Végh.** Decca 421 259-2DH.

59'	DDD	3/89	**Q** P

Listening to this disc one is immediately struck by a quality rarely encountered in so much music-making today. It is civilized, urbane, 'old fashioned' even, but always alive to the inner vitality of the music. It is also pleasant to encounter music-making where both soloist and conductor evidently enjoy playing together and achieve an almost chamber-music intimacy. Sándor Végh conducts with sympathy, panache and an evident love of the music. His hand-picked orchestra are quite outstanding with some remarkable wind playing. András Schiff responds with equal amounts of sympathy, giving razor-sharp articulation to the music. It is subtle pianism, performed with taste. The recording is generous, initially slightly disconcerting (reverberance somewhat diminishing the piano's impact) but one soon adjusts, aided by perceptive musicianship at its very best.

Mozart. PIANO CONCERTOS. **English Chamber Orchestra/Murray Perahia** (pf). CBS Masterworks CD42241 and CD42243. Items marked [a] from 76651 (4/78), [b] 76731 (5/80), [c] 76481 (5/76).
CD42241 — No. 20 in D minor, K466[a]; No. 27 in B flat major, K595[b].
CD42243 — No. 11 in E major, K413[a]; No. 12 in A major, K414[b]; No. 14 in E flat major, K449[c].

②	1h 2'	1h 10'	ADD/DDD	9/87

These discs happily epitomise some of the best qualities of the complete Perahia/ ECO set. Always intelligent, always sensitive to both the overt and less obvious nuances of this music, Perahia is firstly a true pianist, never forcing the instrument beyond its limits in order to express the ideas, always maintaining a well-projected singing touch. The superb ECO reflect his integrity and empathy without having to follow slavishly every detail of his articulation or phrasing. K414 and K413 are charming and typically novel for their time, but do not break new ground in quite the way that K449 does. Here, Mozart's success in the theatre may have suggested a more dramatic presentation and working of ideas for this instrumental genre. K595 is a work pervaded by a serenity of acceptance that underlies its wistfulness. Mozart had less than a year to live, and the mounting depression of his life had already worn him down, yet there is still a sort of quiet joy in this music. The vast range of styles, emotions, and forms that these few works encompass are evocatively celebrated in these performances, and admirably captured in civilized recordings.

Mozart. Piano Concertos — No. 20 in D minor, K466; No. 21 in C major, K467. **Mitsuko Uchida** (pf); **English Chamber Orchestra/Jeffrey Tate.** Philips 416 381-2PH.

1h 2'	DDD	7/86	**B**

Mozart. Piano Concertos — No. 20 in D minor, K466; No. 27 in B flat major, K595. **Sir Clifford Curzon** (pf); **English Chamber Orchestra/ Benjamin Britten.** Decca 417 288-2DH. From SXL7007 (2/83).

1h 5'	ADD	10/86	**B**

Mitsuko Uchida's Mozart is quite without parallel. Her manner is strong and intense but free from any kind of romantic excess. For her every note matters,

Jeffrey Tate   [*photo: EMI/Steiner*]

even when the piano writing is largely decorative, and yet her playing never sounds sententious. In the shaping of the tiniest phrase, or in the pacing of the longest movement, she shows the same remarkable insight and sensitivity. As a result, her performances are elegant as well as moving. She is fortunate in having Jeffrey Tate, another perceptive and deeply serious Mozartian, as a musical partner. Their obvious rapport adds considerably to the impact of the D minor Concerto and to the more intimate charm of the C major. Fine recordings, with soloist and orchestra convincingly balanced.

Sir Clifford Curzon's playing is also extraordinarily alert and concentrated: shaping and shading of even the minutest details is superbly subtle, while each movement as a whole has a sense of grand inevitability. This ability to focus intently upon foreground detail without losing the sense of the overall shape is one of the hallmarks of Curzon's genius, and one could be thankful that he was able to find such an understanding and sympathetic accompanist as Benjamin Britten. Their partnership in this music radiates a sense of shared joy in music-making. There is a quick fade-in at the start of K595, slightly blunting the effect of the opening tutti, but otherwise the transfers are excellent.

NEW REVIEW

Mozart. PIANO CONCERTOS. **Robert Casadesus, ªGaby Casadesus** (pfs); **ᵇCleveland Orchestra, Columbia Symphony Orchestra/George Szell; ªPhiladelphia Orchestra/Eugene Ormandy.** Sony Legendary Interpretations CD46519.
No. 21 in C major, K467ᵇ (from SBRG72234, 7/65); No. 22 in E flat major, K482; No. 23 in A major, K488 (both 61021); No. 24 in C minor, K491ᵇ (SBRG72234, 7/65); No. 26 in D major, K537, "Coronation"; No. 27 in B flat major, K595 (both SBRG72107, 4/63). Concerto for two pianos in E flat major, K365ª (SBRG72008, 5/62).

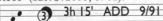 ③ **3h 15′ ADD 9/91** Ⓑ ▲

It's good to welcome back to the catalogue these refreshingly direct, unfussy performances of a selection of Mozart concertos by Robert Casadesus. Despite their age, these successfully remastered early 1960s recordings have come up well. There is a clear, cool logic in Casadesus's pianism, which harbours an unhurried, old-world charm all its own. He has a superb foil in George Szell and the Cleveland Orchestra, whose accompaniments blaze with an operatic intensity Mozart might well have enjoyed. In the popular Concerto No. 21 Casadesus is deft and elegant, with clear passagework and an engaging simplicity. He imparts a Bachian severity to the F sharp minor *Adagio* of No. 23 and his playing of No. 24 is both powerful and profound. Szell's conducting throughout is lively and polished. The odd one out here is Casadesus's Concerto for two pianos where he is joined by his wife, Gaby. Here, their sympathetic playing gets rather stolid support from Ormandy and the Philadelphia Orchestra. Despite consistent background hiss, the recordings are full-bodied, beautifully balanced and surprisingly detailed. At mid-price this three-CD set is certainly worth investigating and could be a fine introduction to these timeless masterpieces.

Mozart. Piano Concertos — No. 21 in C major, K467; No. 25 in C major, K503. **Stephen Kovacevich** (pf); **London Symphony Orchestra/Sir Colin Davis.** Philips Concert Classics 426 077-2PC. From 6500 431 (4/74).

59' ADD 2/90 £ p B

Mozart. Piano Concerto No. 21 in C major, K467[a].
Schumann. Piano Concerto in A minor, Op. 54[b]. **Dinu Lipatti** (pf); [a]**Lucerne Festival Orchestra;** [b]**Philharmonia Orchestra/ Herbert von Karajan.** EMI Références mono CDH7 69792-2. Item marked [a] recorded at a performance in the Kunsthaus, Lucerne on August 23rd, 1950 and from Columbia 33C1064 (1/61), [b] LX1110/3 (11/48).

58' ADD 7/89 p B ▲

The Philips disc may contain fairly standard readings but Stephen Kovacevich makes the concertos sparkle with crystalline tone, perfectly even, though shapely passagework, and a total dedication to conveying the music's directness of expression. In the *Andantes*, his absorption with the sheer perfection of the sound ideally transmits the inner light of the work, and in the faster movements he delights in their fluidity and rhythmic vitality. Sir Colin Davis seems well in tune with the soloist's intentions but, though the LSO generally provides a pleasingly coherent accompaniment, the whole is let down on occasions by obtrusive width of vibrato and moments of sour chording from the woodwind. That aside, there is little here that is other than delightful. The recording sets the soloist fairly far forward and provides plenty of orchestral detail, so any anomalies are particularly obvious: Kovacevich's playing blooms under these conditions, his avoidance of overstatement made all the more pertinent.

Lipatti recorded the Schumann Concerto in 1948 and the sound is more true to life, and better balanced, than anything heard in Mozart's K467 taken from a concert performance two years later. But it's the playing that counts. There was only one Lipatti, as a younger generation of CD collectors can now, happily, discover for themselves. He is known to have expressed doubts about his readiness to record the Schumann and after its emergence, he wondered if his playing might have been a little too "confined". Such fears were groundless. The reading combines spontaneous youthful freshness and élan with absolute truthfulness to the letter of the score. The music's poetry is conveyed without self-conscious 'interpretation' and its sentiment never degenerates into sentimen-tality. When undertaking the Mozart in Lucerne in 1950, the miraculous reprieve wrought by cortisone was ending. But nearly 40 years on, the vitality and commitment of the performance make it impossible to believe that leukaemia was to claim his life in less than four months. It's a collector's piece, despite less than ideal reproduction, all the more so for allowing us to hear Lipatti's own cadenzas in the first movement and the last.

Mozart. Piano Concertos — No. 22 in E flat major, K482[a]; No. 23 in A major, K488[b]. **English Chamber Orchestra/Daniel Barenboim** (pf). EMI CDM7 69122-2. Item marked [a] from ASD2838 (11/72), [b] ASD2318 (7/67).

1h 2' ADD 6/88 B

These two concertos make a good coupling, especially in these affecting, elegant readings from Barenboim and the ECO. What Barenboim may have lacked in authenticity of instruments or style when recording these concertos, he more than made up for in authenticity of spirit and musicianship. Both the slow movements of these works are especially fine, poised, shapely, and heartfelt: Barenboim employs both great subtlety and great simplicity, keeping the listener on the edge of his seat waiting for even the slightest of gestures that can open the way to new meanings. The faster, outer movements are ideally paced and although dexterity obviously plays a part in their successful realization, it never intrudes. We have here two performances of the highest calibre from a soloist and orchestra of the front rank. They will bear much repetition, and the close yet well-spaced recordings lend an easy, genial feel to the proceedings.

NEW REVIEW

Mozart. Piano Concertos[a] — No. 23 in A major, K488; No. 24 in C minor, K491.
Schubert. Impromptus[b] — G flat major, D899; A flat major, D899. **Sir Clifford Curzon** (pf); **London Symphony Orchestra/István Kertész.** Decca 430 497-2DWO. Items marked [a] from SXL6354 (11/68), [b] SXL6135 (11/64).

Ih 9' ADD 10/91 · · B

These two piano concertos succeed one another in Mozart's catalogue but could hardly be more different, the A major being a sunny work (at least in its outer movements) and the C minor one of storm and distress. Thus the coupling is attractive. Attentively partnered by his conductor and orchestra, Sir Clifford Curzon takes a serene, unusually spacious view of the first movement of the A major which allows every detail to tell and yet does not lose sight of the whole. The lovely *Adagio* (in F sharp minor, the only instance of Mozart using this key) is not beautified tonally but its slight understatement makes it all the more poignant, and the bustling finale is all of a piece with the rest of the interpretation in being distinctly unhurried. The performance of the C minor Concerto is again typical of this fine pianist in that nothing is exaggerated and no 'effects' are sought: what we have instead is quietly artistic and sensitive playing, much less urgent and dramatic than some other performances but equally satisfying in its own way; predictably, the oasis of calm that is the slow movement has a quiet simplicity. The two Schubert impromptus make an unusual fill-up, but receive attractive performances, though the sound has a good deal of background hiss. In the concertos, the piano sound could have more brilliance and the orchestral violins are somewhat whiskery; but this need not be a major consideration when the performances are of this quality.

NEW REVIEW

Mozart. Double Piano Concertos[a] — E flat major, K365/316a; F major, K242, "Lodron". Andante and Variations in G major, K501. Fantasia in F minor, K608 (arr. Busoni). **Murray Perahia, Radu Lupu** (pfs); [a]**English Chamber Orchestra.** Sony Classical CD44915.

Ih 2' DDD 10/91 · ·

NEW REVIEW

Mozart. Double Piano Concerto in E flat major, K365/316a. Double Piano Sonata in D major, K448/375a. Fugue in C minor, K426. **Alfred Brendel, Walter Klien** (pfs); **Vienna State Opera Orchestra/Paul Angerer.** Tuxedo TUXCD1028. From STPL510780 (5/61).

50' ADD 2/92 · · P ▲

Since each of the pianists on the Sony disc is a fine Mozartian, it will attract many collectors, who should not be disappointed despite a couple of reservations listed below. The recording of the two concertos derives from a packed-out concert at The Maltings, Snape, during the 1988 Aldeburgh Festival and has a live immediacy, but the microphone placing does not allow a spacious sound. The playing itself is also immediate, and in the famous Concerto for two pianos there is a consistent feeling of energy in the outer movements. Less expectedly, we note it also in the central *Adagio*, which could have been more restfully done, particularly as the piano tone is close and full throughout. But there it is, the

Wolfgang Amadeus Mozart

performance is all of a piece and its vigour certainly does not exclude grace, while the English Chamber Orchestra play with its customary skill. The less memorable *Lodron* Concerto was originally a triple piano concerto written for Countess Lodron and her two daughters and is here done in the composer's own duo transcription. The other two pieces on the disc were recorded a year later in London's Abbey Road Road Studio No. 1 and are skilfully done, but the beautiful and dramatic F minor Fantasia for mechanical organ loses much in Busoni's tubby arrangement for two pianos, particularly as Perahia and Lupu choose a deliberate tempo for the outer sections. However, the G major *Andante and Variations* for piano duet, presented here in a somewhat restrained performance, are both graceful and attractive.

It is over 30 years since Alfred Brendel, then in his late twenties, made the Tuxedo recordings with his fellow-Austrian Walter Klien; they earned praise then and still deserve it now. The performance of the Double Piano Concerto has freshness coupled with sensitivity, and the playing of both these artists is beautifully matched, as are their two instruments. Indeed, one cannot tell which is which unless one has a score or knows the work well — musically speaking, that is, for the stereo separates them clearly to left and right. The Vienna State Opera Orchestra play well under Paul Angerer. Brendel and Klein are also crisp and enjoyable in the D major Sonata and the Fugue in C minor. The digital remastering of these classic performances is pleasing, although by modern standards the piano sound is lacking in edge and bloom and there is noticeable tape hiss in the sonata. This is a very attractive disc, but given its age and shortish duration, together with the mere 12 lines of English booklet notes, collectors may feel that a budget price tag would have made it even more so.

Mozart. Violin Concertos — No. 3 in G major, K216; No. 4 in D major, K218; No. 5 in A major, K219. **Christian Altenburger** (vn); **German Bach Soloists/Helmut Winscherman.** LaserLight 15 525.

1h 15' DDD 5/90   £ Ⓑ

The violin concertos remind us that, apart from being one of the leading pianists of his day, Mozart was also a more-than-capable violinist. Whilst working with the court orchestra of the Prince-Archbishop of Salzburg, he completed, in 1775, five prime examples of the genre; these were intended as entertainment music for the court, and were to feature himself as soloist. The concertos have much in common with Mozart's cassations, divertimentos and serenades, which also highlight the solo violin and have other concerto-like elements in them. But their lightweight means of expression in no way diminishes their long-term appeal, for Mozart could not but fill them to the brim with wonderful ideas. High spirits are much in evidence in Christian Altenburger's performance of the last three of these concertos, and the restrained size of the accompanying ensemble, along with its crisp, unfussy playing, makes for a relaxed, celebratory atmosphere. The engineers have kept the performers in agreeable balance, placing the soloist far enough forward for his sound to retain its immediacy and vivacity, yet still keeping the German Bach Soloists in sharp focus. Stripped of the usual romantic overkill that they receive from most of the big-name soloists, these concertos now emerge as surprisingly refreshing, youthful works of great charm.

Mozart. Serenade in B flat major for 13 wind instruments, K361. **Academy of St Martin in the Fields Wind Ensemble/Sir Neville Marriner.** Philips 412 726-2PH.

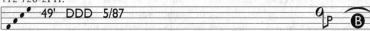

Here is the finest of Mozart's open-air works for wind ensemble. Although the title of "Gran Partita" on the original manuscript may not be Mozart's own the serenade's length of almost 50 minutes fully justifies such a title. Mozart himself described the work, rather more aptly, as "a great wind piece of a very special kind". Sir Neville Marriner is at his very best in repertoire such as this, and he has at his disposal some of Britain's finest wind players. Together they create a performance which reflects Mozart's inspiration to ideal effect. Tempos are all beautifully judged to give the music a good forward momentum and coherence while providing ample room for the most elegant phrasing, and the score's variations in mood are skilfully drawn out. The recording is warm and falls naturally and pleasantly on the ear.

Mozart. Serenade in D major, K250/248*b*, "Haffner". **Josef Suk** (vn); **Prague Chamber Orchestra/Libor Hlaváček.** Supraphon Gems 2SUP0006.

54' AAD 12/87

Mozart. Serenade in D major, K250/248*b*, "Haffner"[a]. March in D major, K249, "Haffner". [a]**Iona Brown** (vn); **Academy of St Martin in the Fields/ Sir Neville Marriner.** Philips 416 154-2PH. From 416 154-1PH (3/86).

58' DDD 9/86

The Serenade in D, subtitled after its dedicatee Elizabeth Haffner, is one of Mozart's most joyful and festive works. Its eight movements encompass a wide range of emotions and the essentially dance-based structure is enriched, as is often found in Mozart's serenades, by the interpolation of what amounts to a miniature violin concerto at its heart. Josef Suk has a very positive approach to his solo role, his tone being firm, his decorative trills very clear-cut. His manner is reflected by the playing of the Prague Chamber Orchestra as a whole — Hlaváček drawing from them correspondingly precise and robust playing, suitably festive, pointing up the celebratory purpose for which the work was conceived. Some may prefer a lighter musical approach with perhaps more variety in the phrasing but this is a very acceptable version and a good introduction to one of the composer's most utterly charming works.

Marriner's is a desirable disc even if you already possess the *Haffner* Serenade, for playing such as this brings out the genial warmth of Mozart's inspiration to the full. The little March that precedes the main work seems to wear a smile for all its rhythmical neatness and precision, and that too is surely as it should be. Recorded in London in 1984, the Academy of St Martin in the Fields is in top form and Iona Brown is an immaculate violinist in the solo role which surfaces in what is in effect a kind of violin concerto that Mozart incorporated into the eight movements that make up the larger whole of the Serenade. It has a particularly lovely *Andante*, which is the Serenade's second movement, and a bustling and brilliant rondo-finale. The sound is full yet detailed, with natural reverberation.

Mozart. Wind Serenades — E flat major, K375; C minor, K388/384*a*. Wind soloists of the **Chamber Orchestra of Europe/Alexander Schneider.** ASV CDCOE802. From COE802 (6/85).

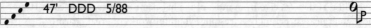

NEW REVIEW

Mozart. Wind Serenades — E flat major, K375; C minor, K388/384*a*. **Orpheus Chamber Orchestra.** DG 431 683-2GH.

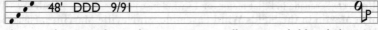

These two big pieces for wind instruments are well-contrasted although they share the same title. Indeed, the use of a minor key for the four-movement K388 tells us at once that it is no ordinary serenade and certainly not just music for casual entertainment — in fact it is quite stormy in character, and the DG booklet notes go so far as to call it "dramatic and sombre". Why Mozart called it a serenade we do not know: but at any rate it has a tense first movement and a terse finale in variation form, and in between them a minuet with some ingenious counterpoint for oboes and bassoon. As for the E flat major Serenade, K373, this has delicacy as well as expressive qualities (the *Adagio* is notably eloquent), and the finale really dances. Although a collection of wind serenades may possibly be too much of a good thing, the alertness of the playing on the ASV disc prevents any musical or tonal monotony. The Chamber Orchestra of Europe players have an excellent tonal blend and interpretative unanimity and their musical style too is good, being vital yet flexible.

The Orpheus Chamber Orchestra plays without a conductor, and very well too, for the artists who make up this American orchestra evidently understand each other completely as well as being fine executants in their own right. Few artists or orchestral bodies who regularly contribute to the record catalogue can claim an unbroken record of success, but the Orpheus is so far among them. The oboes, clarinets, bassoons and horns of this fine ensemble blend together so well that one's only regret may be the feeling that Mozart himself can never have heard such sensitive playing of this music, and the recording in a New York location is no less worthy of it.

Mozart. Divertimentos — B flat major, K287/271*h*; D major, K205/167*a*. **Salzburg Mozarteum Camerata Academica/Sándor Végh.** Capriccio 10 271.

Mozart's Divertimento, K287 is a six-movement work cast on quite a large scale, and is scored for two violins, viola, two horns and bass, a combination which presents some difficulties of balance. One solution is to use a full orchestral string section, as did Toscanini and Karajan in their recordings, but this can bring its own problems, for Mozart demands playing of virtuoso standard in this score, and anything less than this is ruthlessly exposed. Sandor Végh's smallish string band is of high quality, and has a pleasantly rounded tone quality. The engineers have managed to contrive a satisfactory balance which sounds not at all unnatural, and the sound quality itself is very good. Végh directs an attractive, neatly-pointed performance of the work, one which steers a middle course between objective classicism and expressive warmth. The Divertimento, K205, has five movements, but none lasts longer than five minutes, and the work is much shorter and more modest than K287. Scoring in this case is for violin, viola, two horns, bassoon and bass, to provide another difficult but well resolved problem for the engineers. Végh directs another characterful, delightful performance, to round off a very desirable disc.

Mozart. Divertimentos — D major, K205/167*a*[a]; D major, K334/320*b*[b].
March in D major, K290/167*ab*[a]. **Franz Liszt Chamber Orchestra/**[a]**János Rolla,** [b]**Frigyes Sándor.** Hungaroton White Label HRC080.

1h 7' ADD 5/90 £

The Franz Liszt Chamber Orchestra of Budapest is a fine ensemble, and here they play two of Mozart's divertimentos with a crisp, lithe style and pleasant and well varied tone. The bigger work here is the first, K334, which has a Theme (in D minor) and Variations as its second movement and a well known Minuet as its third. The earlier Divertimento, also in D major, is preceded by the little March, K290, which was also evidently played at its first performance at a garden party in 1773. Neither work is deep music, as the title tells us, but each entertains delightfully and the minuets, of which there are four in all, dance with both gravity and grace. Excellent recording in a resonant acoustic that does not obscure detail and of course the price is another attraction, while there is an informative booklet note provided too.

Mozart. Cassations — G major, K63; B flat major, K99/63*a*. Adagio and Fugue in C minor, K546. **Salzburg Camerata/Sándor Végh.** Capriccio 10 192.

51' DDD 3/88

Mozart's cassations, a term usually applied to music that was intended for performance in public, often outdoors, are works of great charm and vitality. How lovely it must have been to catch this graceful, elegant music floating out into the night air. The solemn *Adagio and Fugue*, K546, written originally around a two-piano composition and later arranged for strings, shows Mozart looking back to the baroque era, and the great form of that age, the fugue. It has a solemnity and gravity beautifully captured by this fine band of musicians. Sándor Végh, one of the most celebrated chamber-musicians of our age, brings a wealth of musical understanding to these rarely heard works imbuing them with an old-world humanity.

NEW REVIEW

Mozart. ORCHESTRAL WORKS. [a]**Arvid Engegard** (vn); **Salzburg Mozarteum Camerata Academica/Sándor Végh.** Capriccio 10 302.
Serenade in D major, K185/167*a*[a]. March in D major, K189/167*b*. Five Contretanze, K609. Notturno in D major, K286/269*a*.

1h 6' DDD 10/91

The main work here is the big Serenade, K185, commissioned by the Antretter family of Salzburg and first performed in August 1773 to celebrate the end of the university year. Like other works of its kind it incorporates a miniature two-movement violin concerto within a loose symphonic framework: an *Andante* designed to display the instrument's powers of cantilena, and a brisk *contredanse* with plenty of opportunities for ear-catching virtuosity. There is also a violin solo in the glum D minor trio of the second minuet. But perhaps the finest movements are the sensuous A major *Andante grazioso*, with its *concertante* writing for flutes and horns, and the rollicking 6/8 finale, preceded by an unexpectedly searching *Adagio* introduction. The performance by Végh and his hand-picked Salzburg players is affectionate, rhythmically alive and beautifully detailed, with an imaginative, subtly coloured solo violin contribution from Arvid Engegard. The tempo and specific character of each movement is shrewdly judged: the two minuets, for example, are vividly differentiated, the first properly swaggering, with a nice lilt in the trio, the second spruce and quick-witted. Only in the finale is Végh arguably too leisurely, though here too the style and rhythmic lift of the playing are infectious. Végh follows the serenade with deft, colourful readings of five contredanses from Mozart's last year and a beguiling performance of the *Notturno* for four orchestras, exquisitely imagined open-air music, with its multiple echoes fading into the summer night. All in all a delectable disc, offering a varied concert of Mozart's lighter music performed with exceptional flair and finesse. The recording, too, is outstandingly vivid, with the spatial effects in the *Notturno* beautifully managed.

Mozart. ORCHESTRAL WORKS. **Orpheus Chamber Orchestra.** DG 429 783-2GH.

Ein musikalischer Spass, K522. Contredanses — C major, K587, "Der Sieg vom Helden Koburg"; D major, K534, "Das Donnerwetter"; C major, K535, "La Bataille"; G major, K610, "Les filles malicieuses"; E flat major, K607/605a, "Il trionfo delle donne". Gallimathias musicum, K32. German Dances — K567; K605; C major, K611, "Die Leyerer". March in D major, K335 No. 1.

1h 9' DDD 4/91

After all the Mozart with which we were bombarded during his bicentenary year, it is a mark of his greatness that an issue such as this comes up with an incomparably engaging freshness. The celebrated *Musikalischer Spass* ("Musical Joke") which begins the disc is never so crudely funny that it wears thin, but make no mistake, the jokes are there in just about every passage, whether they are parodying third-rate music or wobbly playing, and oddly enough sound still more amusing when the performance is as stylishly flexible as this one by the conductorless Orpheus Chamber Orchestra. One of the tunes here (that of the finale on track four) is that of the BBC's *Horse of the Year* programme — and what a good tune it is, even at the umpteenth repetition as the hapless composer finds himself unable to stop. The rest of this programme is no less delightful and includes miniature pieces supposedly describing a thunderstorm, a battle, a

hurdy-gurdy man and a sleigh-ride (with piccolo and sleigh-bells). There is also a *Gallimathias musicum*, a ballet suite of dainty little dances averaging less than a minute in length, which Mozart is supposed to have written at the age of ten. Whatever the case this CD, subtitled "A Little Light Music", provides proof of his genius, though differently from his acknowledged masterpieces. The recording is as refined as anyone could wish yet has plenty of impact.

Orpheus Chamber Orchestra   [*photo: DG/Steiner*]

Mozart. DANCES, MARCHES AND OVERTURES. [a]**Staatskapelle Dresden/Hans Vonk;** [d]**Salzburg Mozarteum Orchestra/Hans Graf.** Capriccio 10 809. Items marked [a] from 10 070, [b] new to UK, [c] 10 253 (11/89). Five Minuets, K461/448a[bd]. *Contredanses*[bd] — Six, K462/448b; D major, K534, "Das Donnerwetter"; C major, K535, "La Bataille"; C major, K587, "Der Sieg vom Helden Koburg"; Two, K603. Two Minuets with Contredanses (Quadrilles), K463[bd]. *German Dances*[bd] — Six, K509; Six, K600; Three, K605. *Marches*[cd] — D major, K52; D major, K189/167b; C major, K214; D major, K215/213b; D major, K237/189c; F major, K248; D major, K249; Two in D major, K335/320a; C major, K408 No. 1/383e; D major, K408 No. 2/385a; C major, K408 No. 3/383F; D major, K445/320c. *Overtures*[a] — Die Zauberflöte; Le nozze di

Figaro; Ascanio in Alba; Idomeneo; Der Schauspieldirektor; Così fan tutte; Die Entführung aus dem Serail; La finta giardiniera; Lucio Silla; La clemenza di Tito; Don Giovanni. Idomeneo — Marches[cd]: Nos. 8, 14 and 25. Le nozze di Figaro: March[cd]: No. 23.

③ 3h 2' DDD 10/91

The first of these discs offers 11 operatic overtures and a convenient means of surveying Mozart's contribution to this form, ranging from the bustle of *Le nozze di Figaro* ("The marriage of Figaro") to the profundities of *Die Zauberflöte* ("The Magic Flute") — although that too has its elements of vivacity, befitting music which was always intended to capture the attention of an audience before the stage action began. Hans Vonk and his Dresden orchestra play these overtures with a light touch, and the recording in the Dresden Lukaskirche is clear yet atmospheric. The second disc, with different forces recorded in the composer's native city of Salzburg, has no less than 17 marches, but some of them, like the one on track two, have such a spring in their step that they are more akin to dance music than to military drill; it is thanks not only to Mozart's invention but also to the neat, alert playing of the Salzburg Mozarteum Orchestra under Hans Graf that monotony and boredom are never allowed to set in here. The same artists bring equal stylishness to the dances and minuets on the third disc, some of which have earthy peasant rhythms and humour, while the programmatic *Contredanses* are no less enjoyable. One is called *The Thunderstorm* and anticipates Beethoven's similar movement in his Sixth Symphony by including a piccolo. There's also a *Battle* and the disc ends thoughtfully with a *German Dance* called *The Sleighride* which features two posthorns, drums and tambourines. The Salzburg recording of all these pieces is satisfying if rather reverberant.

NEW REVIEW

Mozart. OVERTURES. Serenade in G major, K525, "Eine kleine Nachtmusik". **Tafelmusik/Bruno Weil.** Sony Classical Vivarte CD46695.
Overtures — Idomeneo; Die Entführung aus dem Serail; Der Schauspieldirektor; Le nozze di Figaro; Don Giovanni; Così fan tutte; La clemenza di Tito; Die Zauberflöte.

1h DDD 5/92 ⁹ₚ ⁹ₛ Ⓑ

These exhilarating accounts of the overtures to eight of Mozart's greatest stage works come from the Canadian ensemble Tafelmusik, conducted by Bruno Weil. The fresh vigour and *élan* of these period-instrument performances reveal these works in an altogether grander light than some and Bruno Weil's dynamic interpretations never fail to generate a powerful impression of what would follow in complete productions of the operas. The challenging gravity and intimidating momentum of the overture to *Don Giovanni* leaves little unsaid, whilst the masonic pomp which opens *Die Zauberflöte* could not be more telling. Weil's relaxed tempo for *Le nozze di Figaro* may not generate the impetus and galvanism of those conductors who dash through this overture in barely three-and-a-half minutes, but the chance to luxuriate in the genius of Mozart's scoring is all the more welcome when all the parts are clearly audible and well balanced. In the remaining overtures, too, the advantages of period instruments are constantly brought to the fore, as fresh instrumental details leap from these scores with renewed clarity and emphasis, whilst the antiphonal division of first and second violins allows each contrapuntal surprise to register powerfully. The disc also includes an articulate rendition of the ever-popular G major Serenade, *Eine kleine Nachtmusik*; again superbly played by the Tafelmusik strings, and with a total lack of contrived artifice. These performances combine thrilling and dramatic musicianship with refined period sensibilities in a recording of the highest technical quality, and this excellent disc will fascinate and challenge the preconceptions of any Mozart enthusiast.

Mozart. SYMPHONIES. **Prague Chamber Orchestra/Sir Charles Mackerras.** Telarc CD80256, CD80272/3.

CD80256 — No. 1 in E flat major, K16; F major, K19a; No. 4 in D major, K19; No. 5 in B flat major, K22; No. 6 in F major, K43; B flat major, KAhn214/45b; No. 7 in D major, K45. *CD80272* — No. 8 in D major, K48; No. 9 in C major, K73/75a; D major, K73l/81; D major, K73m/97; D major, K75n/95; D major, K73n/95; D major, K73q/84. *CD80273* — No. 10 in G major, K74/73p; C major, K111b/96; F major, K75; G major, K75b/110; No. 13 in F major, K112.

③ 1h 13', 1h 1', 58' DDD 11/91

These three discs present the earliest, least-known of Mozart's symphonic works. The numbers are useful for identification only, as the symphonies were not written in the numbered order and several (not included in these CDs) have been established as the works of others. The value of resuscitating composers' juvenilia is often called into question. After all, when he composed the earliest of these works (in London, during a period when his father was ill and required him not to practise the piano) Mozart had reached the grand old age of eight; these discs follow his symphonic music up to the age of 16. But Mozart is, as usual, a case apart, and in listening to these symphonies one can learn not only a great deal about the context from which his mature masterpieces were to develop but also discover many movements which are enchanting in their own right. Inevitably, the music is patchy — some is extremely repetitive — but take the tender *Andantino* third movement of No. 42, or the spirited second movement *Allegro* of No. 10 and it becomes clear that there is much to enjoy here, and music which seems little short of miraculous for a composer of such tender years. There are also some surprises for those unfamiliar with these little-known works, most notably in the very first symphony. The second movement presents, over a gentle triplet accompaniment, a four-note theme on the horns which seems uncomfortably familiar. It is academic whether Mozart remembered it consciously, unconsciously or not at all when he trotted it out again as the basis of the last movement of *Jupiter* (No. 41). Throughout the recordings Sir Charles Mackerras and the Prague Chamber Orchestra give affectionate performances which are full of sparkle and precision. Devotees of period performance will not find original instruments here, but the Prague orchestra combines the best of both worlds, reduced vibrato and lively tempos, without the tendency towards scrawny tone of some period performances, giving a clear-cut, lean quality which brings to life even the music's less imaginative moments. First and second violins are positioned on opposite sides, to left and right, which enhances antiphonal effects, and the harpsichord continuo is kept in the background where it provides unobtrusive crispness. The recorded sound is resonant, but beneficially so, complementing the orchestra's admirable clarity.

Mozart. SYMPHONIES. **The English Concert/Trevor Pinnock** (hpd). Archiv Produktion 431 679-2AH.

No. 25 in G minor, K183/173db; No. 26 in E flat major, K184/161a; No. 29 in A major, K201/186a.

53' DDD 7/91

The bicentenary year brought so many Mozart issues (and reissues) that there is a danger that with its passing some of them may quickly be forgotten. However, this one has enough personality to keep its place in the catalogue, and that quality comes across instantly at the start of Symphony No. 26, which is played first. Admittedly the marking is *molto presto*, but even so the listener may be startled by the brisk pace and the near-aggressive vigour of this sound. This is a performance with period instruments (note the veiled string tone in quiet passages), yet there is also something modern about the spotless efficiency of it all and one wonders whether Mozart heard or intended performances like this and if Trevor Pinnock's penchant for pace and sheer energy is sometimes excessive. Set aside that doubt, however, and one must admire the polish and ensemble of this playing, and make no mistake, there is sensitivity too, as the *Andante* shows. This miniature symphony lasts less than nine minutes and its three movements are played without a break. Predictably, Pinnock brings out all the "storm and stress" drama of the G minor Symphony, but there is mystery too in the strangely gliding slow movement and the quiet start of the finale. The elegantly genial A major is nicely shaped, too, and only in the finale might one wish for more space for the music to sound. A vivid and well balanced recording complements this expert playing.

Mozart. SYMPHONIES. **Capella Istropolitana/Barry Wordsworth.** Naxos 8 550113, 8 550119, 8 550164, 8 550186, 8 550264 and 8 550299.
8 550113 (65 minutes): No. 25 in G minor, K183/173*dB*; No. 32 in G major, K318; No. 41 in C major, K551, "Jupiter". *8 550119* (69 minutes): No. 29 in A major, K201/186*a*; No. 30 in D major, K202/186*b*; No. 38 in D major, K504, "Prague". *8 550164* (61 minutes): No. 28 in C major, K200/189*k*; No. 31 in D major, K297/300*a*, "Paris"; No. 40 in G minor, K550. *8 550186* (62 minutes): No. 34 in C major, K338; No. 35 in D major, K385, "Haffner"; No. 39 in E flat major, K543. *8 550264* (65 minutes): No. 27 in G major, K199/161*b*; No. 33 in B flat major, K319; No. 36 in C major, K425, "Linz". *8 550299* (62 minutes): No. 40 in G minor, K550; No. 41 in C major, K551, "Jupiter".

⑥ 6h 24' DDD 4/91 £ Ⓑ

Collectors who complain about the price of CDs will find their prayers answered in this marvellous Naxos set of the 15 greatest symphonies of Mozart, digitally recorded, yet offered at super-bargain price. Moreover, for those who do not need them all, Naxos have combined the two greatest, No. 40 in G minor and the *Jupiter* on a single disc, which at its modest price should surely find a place in every collection, for it is exceptionally satisfying in every respect. The Capella Istropolitana was founded in 1983, drawing for its players on members of the Slovak Philharmonic Orchestra. The orchestra has already recorded a wide range of baroque music for Naxos and through these discs is gaining a reputation for freshness of musical presentation and polish of ensemble that recalls the early days of the Academy of St Martin in the Fields. Like the first series of Argo ASMF recordings, the impression is that the players really care about the music; there is not a whiff of routine about the music-making. And, as observed in the original *Gramophone* review, "there is an inescapable feeling of fine players enjoying themselves". They are fortunate to have a musical director as sensitive in matters of style and phrasing as Barry Wordsworth, a British conductor, who began his conducting career with the Royal Ballet. His star is ascending very quickly into the firmament, and these discs represent his finest achievement so far. His gift of spontaneity in the recording studio is of course helped by the natural response of his orchestra, which is surely exactly the right size for Mozart. One of his greatest gifts is his sense of pacing, which seems unerring. One has only to turn to the two most famous works (Nos. 40 and 41) to find that tempos are perfectly interrelated. Yet one can go back to the delightful early G minor Symphony (No. 25) and find the *Allegro con brio*, exactly that, and the following *Andante* bringing balm to the senses, with a warmly relaxed *espressivo*. Yet there is never a feeling that the momentum is flagging, for a gently sustained tension beneath the surface of the music keeps it flowing onwards. This is even more striking in the poignant elegy of the *Andante* of No. 29, with its exquisitely gentle cantilena in the violins, while the gracious melodies of the *Andantes* of the *Haffner* (No. 35) and the *Prague* (No. 38) are shaped with disarming beauty. The

Introduction of the first movement of the *Prague* is particularly imposing (clearly Mozart wanted to make a strong impression at its first performance): then follows a bright, alert *Allegro*, here full of the spirited momentum one also finds in the finale of No. 29 and the brightly, vivacious outer movements of No. 28. This is an early masterpiece that has only recently been receiving its full due from the general public. Symphony No. 39, a great favourite of many, has another portentous introduction, made the more impressive here by the hard-sticks used on the timpani. Its merry finale (comparable with the genial *Allegro molto* of No. 34) almost anticipates Mendelssohn in its sparkle, and the bright colours from the woodwind. The key of A major means that in the *Allegros* of No. 29 the horns are pitched high, and how wonderfully they shine out over the strings in the finale. Indeed, another aspect of these discs is their excellent balance, with the orchestra believably set out in front of the listener in a natural concert hall acoustic that is warm, yet not too resonant for clarity. Barry Wordsworth is wholly sensible in the matter of repeats, observing them in the expositions of first movements (where they are needed so that the main themes register firmly with the listener, before the argument of their development begins), and in the finales only where they are necessary to establish the appropriate character of the work. As in the *Jupiter*, where the repeat emphasizes the power and breadth of the closing movement, with its great culminating fugal denouement. In all this is a superb set, among the very finest new offerings made during the Mozart bicentennial. To quote further from the original *Gramophone* review, "In every way these are worthy rivals to the best full-price versions". Unless you insist on original instruments they will give very great satisfaction. There are adequate notes (only the disc with Nos. 28, 31 and 40 is deficient in this respect) and they currently cost around £22 for the six discs, which provide around five-and-a-half hours of the greatest music ever written.

Mozart. Symphonies — No. 25 in G minor, K183/173*dB*; No. 28 in C major, K200/189*k*; No. 29 in A major, K201/186*a*. **Prague Chamber Orchestra/ Sir Charles Mackerras.** Telarc CD80165.

♪ 1h 18' DDD 9/88

Here are three symphonies from Mozart's late teens, written in his native Salzburg, in crisply articulated performances. The first of them is a *Sturm und Drang* piece in a key that the composer reserved for moods of agitation. Mackerras takes the orchestra through the big opening *Allegro con brio* of No. 25 with drive and passion, although it is unlikely that Mozart would have expected a Salzburg orchestra in the 1770s to play as fast as this skilful body of Czech players. The gentle *Andante* comes therefore as a relief, though here too Mackerras keeps a firm rhythmic grasp on the music, and indeed a taut metrical aspect is a feature of all three symphonies as played here, so that minuets dance briskly and purpose-fully and finales bustle. However, the sunlit warmth of the beautiful A major Symphony, No. 29, comes through and the bracing view of the other two symphonies is a legitimate one, though giving little or nothing in the direction of expressive lingering, much less towards sentimental indulgence. The Prague Chamber Orchestra is an expert ensemble, not over-large for this style of music and the recording is admirably clear although a little reverberant. A well-filled disc.

Mozart. Symphonies — No. 27 in G major, K199/161*b*; No. 28 in C major, K200/189*k*; No. 34 in C major, K338. **English Sinfonia/Sir Charles Groves.** Pickwick IMP Classics PCD933.

♪ 1h 3' DDD 3/90

Most music lovers are familiar with half a dozen or so of the Mozart symphonies, but there are others worth exploring too, and this account of three of them is most agreeably done. In the quicker movements, Sir Charles Groves and the English Sinfonia are deft yet alert, but they also respond to nuance, while in the slow movements the playing is quietly expressive. There is an unforced quality about the interpretation overall that is attractive, though some listeners might feel that individual works need fuller characterization. Nevertheless, the playing is always stylish and faithful, and No. 34 is well projected in its sturdy utterance. One curious fault, at least on the copy reviewed here, is that the track for the bustling finale of this latter symphony (Track 10) begins too early and takes in the last phrase of the *Andante di molto*; however, this will not be noticed if the two are played consecutively, as that phrase, ending with a perfect cadence in F major, is followed by an appropriate small pause. The recording has a natural balance and reverberation.

Mozart. Symphonies — No. 29 in A major, K201/186*a*; No. 32 in G major, K318; No. 33 in B flat major, K319. **English Sinfonia/Sir Charles Groves.** Pickwick IMP Classics PCD922.

Ih I' DDD II/89   Ⓑ

Mozart. Symphonies — No. 29 in A major, K201/186*a*; No. 33 in B flat major, K319. **English Baroque Soloists/John Eliot Gardiner.** Philips 412 736-2PH. From 412 736-1PH (4/86).

44' DDD 8/86   Ⓑ

Sir Charles Groves

The bright and attractive performances of Sir Charles Groves are crisply articulated and yet with the right degree of lyricism, even in quick movements. The quality of playing that comes across above all is élan, but this 'dash' is never allowed to drive the music forward so that we overlook delights on the way, and overall one feels that Sir Charles gets the balance right between 'just playing the notes' and allowing them to sound mannered. The slow movements remind us of the excellence of the wind players in the English Sinfonia, and the strings sing most fetchingly. Tempos are well judged too, and how good it is to hear the *Allegro moderato* first movement of Symphony No. 29 (which some conductors bustle through) presented with poise, delicacy and even tenderness — and yet also with the necessary feeling of energy. The recording is clear yet with enough atmosphere to suggest an expert band in rococo surroundings. The medium price is another attraction. Sir Charles, who died in 1992, will be sadly missed.

The Philips performances on period instruments sound entirely idiomatic and John Eliot Gardiner has taken pains to avoid anything anachronistic. But perhaps the most striking effect of playing this music on 'authentic' instruments is the gain in textural clarity and the improved orchestral balance: the woodwind stand out distinctly without microphonic assistance and it is no longer necessary to subdue the horns. Performances are marvellously fresh and vital, and the attentive and sympathetic recordings ensure that nothing is lost. Both works are highly inventive and rich in melodic interest, although it is the earlier symphony, No. 29, which impresses most — an astonishing achievement for an 18 year old!

Mozart. Symphonies — No. 31 in D major, K297, "Paris" (first version);
No. 34 in C major, K338. **English Baroque Soloists/John Eliot Gardiner.**
Philips 420 937-2PH.

48' DDD 7/88

Mozart. Symphonies — No. 31 in D major, K297, "Paris"; No. 33 in B flat
major, K319; No. 34 in C major, K338. **Prague Chamber Orchestra/Sir
Charles Mackerras.** Telarc CD80190.

1h 5' DDD 3/90

The three-movement *Paris* Symphony was written during Mozart's visit to the capital
in 1778. A request for a slow movement that was less complex than the first he
produced spurred him to compose one of his finest works in the genre, showing
a new structural tension, with all superfluous material, however fine, pared away.
On both of these recordings, we have the chance directly to compare the old and
new slow movements, as they are played consecutively. The less blatant Symphony
No. 34 is performed on the Philips disc with the addition of the Minuet K409,
which may have been intended for the work's Viennese revival two years after
the Symphony's composition. Both of Gardiner's versions of the symphonies are
performed on period instruments, with a keen sense of their significance but
without any undue aggrandizement. There is a natural ease and flow in his readings
that allows the listener simply to sit back and enjoy the music's glorious charm and
shapeliness. The recording provides fine scope for the subtleties of the playing,
especially in the more exposed sections for woodwinds, to be fully appreciated.

Although Sir Charles Mackerras does not choose to use period instruments, he
is a most dedicated Mozartian, going to a variety of original manuscripts and
orchestral parts in order to provide what he considers to be the composer's final
thoughts on each of the works coupled here. He also uses a reduced-scale
orchestra and harpsichord continuo to help recreate these masterworks. The
performances themselves need no further validation, though, for Mackerras
infuses all with a vitality and style that easily keeps his audience on the edge of
their seat, eager to miss no inspired detail or well-turned phrase. The Prague
Chamber Orchestra rise to the challenge he sets them with fleet dexterity in the
faster movements and poised, heartfelt expression in the *Andantes*, all produced
against a backcloth of adroit textural balance. The open, large-scale acoustic tends
to upset these best endeavours in the loudest passages, but elsewhere the sound
is first-class, with a fine feeling of space in Prague's characterful Castle of Dobris.

Mozart. Symphonies — No. 31 in D major, K297, "Paris"; No. 38 in
D major, K504, "Prague". **English Sinfonia/Sir Charles Groves.** Pickwick
IMP Classics PCD892.

55' DDD 9/88

Groves's no-nonsense approach to music of the classical era pays dividends with
these two masterworks. He loves this music but, rather than harbouring too
precious an infatuation, he greets it with the warm embrace of long acquaintance,
letting his natural sense of style control any romantic excess that might otherwise
ensue. He brings to these performances the poise of a great performer, unhurried
even in the fastest sections, palpably delighting in the fact that repeats provide
the opportunity to hear more of this wonderful music. The three movements of
both these symphonies require careful balancing if they are not to seem too
lightweight and too close to the operatic-overture beginnings of the genre. Sir
Charles achieves this by bringing out the warmth of the slow movements, with
their elegant phrasing, and avoiding an overdriven and frenetic feel to the finales,
by the use of well-judged tempos. The recording, agreeable in most respects,
lacks impact in the loudest sections but the overall result is still a happy example
of music-making at its best.

Mozart. Symphonies — No. 35 in D major, K385, "Haffner"[a]; No. 36 in
C major, K425, "Linz"[a]. Rondo for violin and orchestra in B flat major, K269[b].
[a]**Bavarian Radio Symphony Orchestra/Rafael Kubelík;** [b]**Saint Paul
Chamber Orchestra/Pinchas Zukerman** (vn). CBS Masterworks CD44647.

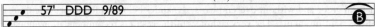

57' DDD 9/89   **B**

These are very satisfying accounts of the *Linz* and *Haffner* Symphonies. Kubelík's
ability to project a strong sense of architecture and formal balance is remarkable,
and this is reflected on the small scale too, with melodic phrases beautifully
shaped and refined. The outer movements of both works are consistently well
paced with plenty of rhythmic drive, vitality and drama, with Kubelík never
allowing his grip on the symphonic argument to falter or slacken. His unfussy
approach in the *Andante* of the *Haffner* allows the pastoral freshness of this
movement to surface with ease, and in the *Menuetto* much is made of the contrast
between loud and soft, emphasizing the Haydnesque qualities of this movement.
The Bavarian orchestra respond well to Kubelík's approach with playing that is
warm, full-toned and very assured. The disc also contains an extra bonus in the
shape of the *Rondo* in B flat, originally written as an alternative finale to the
Violin Concerto No. 1, K207, and is played here in a very attractive performance. The recorded sound has warmth and presence.

Mozart. Symphonies — No. 36 in C major, K425, "Linz"; No. 38 in D major,
K504, "Prague". **English Chamber Orchestra/Jeffrey Tate.** EMI CDC7
47442-2. From EL270306-1 (1/86).

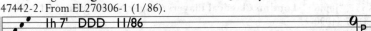

1h 7' DDD 11/86   **⁹ₚ**

Mozart. Symphonies — No. 36 in C major, K425, "Linz"; No. 38 in D major,
K504, "Prague". **Prague Chamber Orchestra/Sir Charles Mackerras.**
Telarc CD80148.

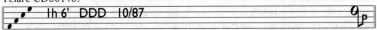

1h 6' DDD 10/87   **⁹ₚ**

Mozart. Symphonies — No. 38 in D major, K504, "Prague"; No. 39 in E flat
major, K543. **Bavarian Radio Symphony Orchestra/Rafael Kubelík.** CBS
CD44648.

56' DDD 2/90   **⁹ₚ**

Mozart wrote his *Linz* Symphony in great haste (five days to be precise), but
needless to say there is little evidence of haste in the music itself, except perhaps
that the first movement has all the exuberance of a composer writing on the
wing of inspiration. The slow movement with its siciliano rhythm certainly has
no lack of serenity, although it has drama too. The *Prague* Symphony was written
only three years later, yet Mozart's symphonic style had matured and the work is
altogether more ambitious and substantial. It has a superbly expansive *Andante*,
most imaginatively orchestrated, which Tate makes the very most of by observing
the repeat. There is no minuet and the *Presto* finale provides a sparkling release of
tension. For those who enjoy Mozart on a sensible scale, yet using modern
instruments, Tate's performances will surely seem near ideal, for they match
finesse and warmth of phrasing with vitality and a fine sense of overall structure.
The digital recording is forward and clear, yet has plenty of body.

A glorious spaciousness surrounds Sir Charles's performances. The recording
venue is reverberant, yet there is no loss of detail, and the fullness of the sound
helps to add weight to climaxes without going beyond the bounds of volume that
Mozart might have expected. Sir Charles captures the joy and high spirits that
these symphonies embody without in any way undermining their greatness. This
vivacity is emphasized by the east-European sound of the Prague Chamber
Orchestra, with the out-of-doors timbre of its winds which provides a pleasing
contrast both with those of the standard British and Germanic orchestras and

specialist, authentic ensembles. Mackerras does, however, adopt some aspects of the modern approach to Mozart performance: he includes harpsichord continuo, his minuets are taken trippingly, one-to-a-bar, and he prefers bowing that is crisper, more detached, and pointed. Phrasing and articulation are taken with a natural grace and without overemphasis, dynamics being graded to provide drama at the right moments. The very rightness of the result is recommendation enough.

Symphony No. 39 has a more expansive, four-movement structure than No. 38 that draws attention to its great stature. Mozart substituted two clarinets for the more usual oboes in this work and his use of them gives the Symphony a distinctive colouring that frequently shapes the nature of the melodic lines and harmonic balance. In the relaxed, clean CBS recordings, Kubelík shows himself alive to the subtleties of emphasis that give these two works their individual personalities, and the Bavarian Radio orchestra displays both the technique and empathy required to give them weighty meaning without the intrusion of heavy articulation. Both first movements find a fine sense of direction and the finales fairly dance along.

Mozart. Symphonies — No. 39 in E flat major, K543[a]; No 41 in C major, K551, "Jupiter"[b]. **Staatskapelle Dresden/Sir Colin Davis.** Philips 410 046-2PH. Item marked [a] from 6514 205 (7/83), [b] 6514 206 (9/83).

| | 1h 6' | DDD | 6/84 |

Mozart. Symphonies — No. 39 in E flat major, K543; No. 41 in C major, K551, "Jupiter". **London Classical Players/Roger Norrington.** EMI Reflexe CDC7 54090-2.

| | 1h 6' | DDD | 6/91 |

Disc buyers who like their Mozart free from romantic exaggeration and other dubious traditional accretions but who don't warm to the experiments of the period instruments school need look no further than the Sir Colin Davis recording. These are direct, no-nonsense performances, steering a confident middle path between overly personal interpretation on the one hand and clinical intellectualism on the other. Each instrumental line is elegantly shaped and the orchestra respond warmly to Davis's stylish direction. Recordings are clear and well balanced, with the weight and distance of the horns, trumpets and timpani (always a problem in conventional instrument performances) judged to a nicety.

Roger Norrington's performances of the classical repertory usually carry a few surprises. This CD starts off with one: the slow introduction to the E flat Symphony is no broad, dignified prelude but an impassioned, almost hectic piece of rhetoric, shot through with the fierce thwacks of the period timpani; and

when the main *Allegro* comes its tuttis, full of sharp accents, are restless and brilliant in effect. There is an alert, quickish account of the *Andante*, a powerfully propelled minuet and a finale which forswears the usual wit in favour of sturdiness and seriousness. It's a new view of the work, not particularly a period-instrument one, nor a specially sympathetic one, but it is certainly riveting and brings out unfamiliar aspects of the music. The *Jupiter* is again rather hard driven in the outer movements, and not readily responsive to mood, and there are one or two seeming lapses of taste; but

Roger Norrington [*photo: EMI/Leighton*]

although the *Andante* is none too *cantabile*, and decidedly on the quick side, the tone of unease, almost of menace, behind it is telling. These are not, then, conventional performances, nor beguiling ones, but a tough and original view of the music, often very dramatic, and always invigorating. If you like your Mozart docile and soothing, don't try it.

Mozart. Symphonies — No. 40 in G minor, K550; No. 41 in C major, K551, "Jupiter". **English Chamber Orchestra/Jeffrey Tate.** EMI CDC7 47147-2. From EL270154-1 (2/85).

1h 4' DDD 7/85   Ⓑ

Mozart. Symphonies — No. 40 in G minor, K550; No. 41 in C major, K551, "Jupiter". **Bavarian Radio Symphony Orchestra/Rafael Kubelík.** CBS Masterworks CD44649.

58' DDD 9/89   £ Ⓑ

Mozart. Symphonies — No. 40 in G minor, K550; No. 41 in C major, K551, "Jupiter". **Prague Chamber Orchestra/Sir Charles Mackerras.** Telarc CD80139.

1h 11' DDD 5/87   Ⓑ

Jeffrey Tate's approach to both these works is fresh and vigorous and, while he has obviously laboured long and hard over these scores, there isn't the faintest suggestion of contrivance or self-conscious novelty-seeking. His lucid articulation and attention to detail give the music a distinctive textural clarity. There is a monumental quality about these interpretations but this by no means precludes expressive intimacy, for human interest is there too. The playing of the English Chamber Orchestra is a constant delight, and the recording is admirably clear and realistically balanced. Kubelík's account of Mozart's Symphony No. 40 is noble and poised; cool, and yet not without feeling or emotion. Some may wince at the way he teases out phrase lengths (purists beware!) especially the drooping semitone string figures in the exposition, but others will find them beautifully turned and elegant. He brings an aloofness to this work that is not entirely out of place; the intense and melancholic *Andante* has a veiled, far-off quality, as if suspended between two worlds. The Menuetto is given an unusually slow and deliberate tempo (no brusqueness or ebullience here) which has an unsettling and disquieting effect that seems totally apt before it launches into the troubled spirit of the finale; here Kubelík is suitably restless and impetuous, as the Symphony speeds headlong towards its destiny — the *Jupiter*. This receives a strong, if perhaps less individual performance, and like his recordings of the *Haffner* and *Linz* Symphonies there is a fine sense of architectural balance; the outer movements are brisk and alert in tempo, with the contrapuntal textures in the finale superbly controlled. The recording is very fine.

Sir Charles Mackerras observes all repeats in these works but adopts lively tempos, establishing the balanced weighting of sections as Mozart wanted without allowing the whole to become over-ponderous. His method is not, however, to dash headlong at the various movements, but to allow space and light into the textures and to retain an underlying feeling of repose in the most urgent sections. Even the fastest movements, then, are not rushed and the intensity of expression never becomes overdone. The results are sometimes startling, but Mackerras and the Prague Chamber Orchestra have the innate musicianship to bring off these innovations with an unerring sense of style. The easy flow and delight of these pieces are reminiscent of Sir Thomas Beecham's approach to music-making, even though the interpretations are far removed from his world. Just listening to this sportive, yet exultant performance of the finale of the *Jupiter*, with its dazzling contrapuntal devices, the listener is prompted to recall that Mozart's greatness lay so much in his ability to rise above the misery of his situation to create music that, whilst profoundly meaningful, could still retain a strong element of childlike playfulness.

Mozart. 17 Church Sonatas. **Ian Watson** (org); **Classical Orchestra of the King's Consort/Robert King** (org). Hyperion CDA66377.

` 1h DDD 11/90 `

At the age of 16 Mozart was appointed Konzertmeister to the Prince-Archbishop of Salzburg. Opportunities for composing large-scale church music in this post were rather restricted since the Archbishop had ruled that music for the Mass had to be kept to an absolute minimum: the whole service could not exceed 45 minutes. One area where a brief musical interlude was required was between the readings of the Epistle and Gospel. Normally for this Mozart would improvise on the organ, but on special occasions he made use of an instrumental ensemble. These 17 Epistle Sonatas were the result. Most composers would have found little scope in such short pieces (none lasts much more than four minutes). Mozart, the supreme genius, came up with 17 tiny yet perfectly-proportioned gems, full of interest, originality and charm. The later sonatas use the organ in something approaching a solo role; indeed the last one, K336, is like a self-contained concerto movement complete with cadenza. In this recording Ian Watson is a most agile and stylish soloist. As ever Robert King and the King's Consort show total involvement in the music and play with refreshing enthusiasm.

NEW REVIEW

Mozart. COMPLETE EDITION, Volume 14 — PIANO QUINTET, QUARTETS, TRIOS, etc. [a]**Aurèle Nicolet** (fl); [ac]**Heinz Holliger** (ob); [a]**Eduard Brunner**, [b]**Jack Brymer** (cls); [a]**Hermann Baumann** (hn); [a]**Klaus Thunemann** (bn); [cd]**Bruno Hoffmann** (glass harmonica); [b]**Patrick Ireland**, [c]**Karl Schouten**, [e]**Bruno Giuranna** (vas); [c]**Jean Decroos** (vc); [ef]**Beaux Arts Trio** (Isidore Cohen, vn; Bernard Greenhouse, vc; Menahem Pressler, pf); [a]**Alfred Brendel**, [b]**Stephen Kovacevich** (pfs). Philips Mozart Edition 422 514-2PME5.
Quintet in E flat major for piano and wind, K452[a] (from 420 182-2PH, 8/87). Clarinet Trio in E flat major, K498, "Kegelstatt"[b] (6500 073, 2/71). Adagio and Rondo in C minor, K617[c] (9500 397, 5/78). Adagio in C major, K356/617d[d] (Vox STPL512880, 6/65). Piano Quartets[e] — No. 1 in G minor, K478; No. 2 in E flat major, K493 (both from 410 391-1PH, 10/84). Piano Trios[f] — B flat major, K254; D minor, K442 (cpted. Stadler and Marguerre); G major, K496; B flat major, K502; E major, K542; C major, K548; G major, K564 (all from 422 079-2PH3, 11/88).

` 4h 34' ADD/DDD 9/91 `

These recordings come from different locations and dates, ranging from 1969 to 1987. Four discs out of the five offer the two piano quartets and seven piano trios, played by the Beaux Arts Trio who are joined in the quartets by the viola player Bruno Giuranna; these are clearly the centrepiece of the issue and the playing of this fine ensemble is strongly characterful yet thoughtful. These are alert, direct and yet refined performances and earn only praise, although the recording in Philips's favoured Swiss location of La-Chaux-de-Fonds could have placed a little more distance between the players and the listener (we also hear the odd intake of breath). But otherwise this clear sound suits the music, and Menahem Pressler's piano tone is well captured. The D minor Trio which ends the series is not wholly authentic, being mainly Maximilian Stadler's compilation from existing material found by Mozart's widow Constanze after his death. Before we come to the piano quartets and piano trios, the first disc also has important works in fine performances in which Alfred Brendel and Heinz

Holliger are just two of the artists involved (the Quintet for piano and wind was among the composer's favourite works). The first disc also offers two pieces featuring the ravishing sound of the glass harmonica (musical glasses), which is played by its leading exponent, Bruno Hoffmann, and the solo *Adagio* in C major is quite ethereally beautiful if rather closely recorded. This unique instrument is usefully described and illustrated in the booklet.

NEW REVIEW

Mozart. COMPLETE EDITION, Volume 11 — STRING QUINTETS. **Arthur Grumiaux, Arpad Gérecz** (vns); **Georges Janzer, Max Lesueur** (vas); **Eva Czako** (vc). Philips Mozart Edition 422 511-2PME3. From 6747 107 (1/76). B flat major, K174; C minor, K406/516*b*; C major, K515; G minor, K516; D major, K593; E flat major, K614.

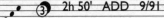

NEW REVIEW

Mozart. STRING QUINTETS. **Simon Whistler** (va); **Salomon Quartet** (Simon Standage, Micaela Comberti, vns; Trevor Jones, va; Jennifer Ward Clarke, vc). Hyperion CDA66431/2.
CDA66431 — C major, K515; D major, K593. *CDA66432* — G minor, K516; E flat major, K614.

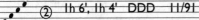

Of the six works which comprise Mozart's complete *oeuvre* for string quintet, that in B flat major, K174, is an early composition, written at the age of 17. It is a well-made, enjoyable work, but not a great deal more than that. The C minor work, K406, is an arrangement by Mozart of his Serenade for six wind instruments, K398. It is difficult not to feel that the original is more effective, since the music seems to sit a little uncomfortably on string instruments. But the remaining four works, written in the last four years of Mozart's life, are a different matter. The last string quintets from Mozart's pen were extraordinary works, and the addition of the second viola seems to have encouraged him to still greater heights. It has been suggested that Mozart wrote K515 and K516 to show King Friedrich Wilhelm II of Prussia that he was a better composer of string quintets than Boccherini, whom the King had retained as chamber music composer to his court. There was no response, so he offered these two quintets for sale with the K406 arrangement to make up the usual set of three. K593 and K614 were written in the last year of his life. Arthur Grumiaux and his colleagues recorded their survey in 1973. Refinement is perhaps the word that first comes to mind in discussing these performances, which are affectionate yet controlled by a cool, intelligent sensitivity. The recordings have been well transferred, the quality is warm and expansive and Grumiaux's tone, in particular, is a delight to the ear but all the playing is alert and stylish. In all, this Philips release is one to earn a strong recommendation, offering as it does Mozart playing of fine quality allied to very decent sound.

The Hyperion discs are the first ever period-instrument recordings of Mozart's four mature string quintets and the Salomon display their now familiar virtues: a pure, refined sound, warmed here and there by a discreet use of vibrato; precise, buoyant articulation from the shorter, lighter period bows; unusual clarity in Mozart's often complex textures and first-class ensemble, with a close and careful matching of tone and phrasing. And, as always, the group is led with uncommon flair and eloquence by Simon Standage. But even if you're used to the drier, sharper-edged sound of the period string quartet you may be surprised at the difference between these versions and modern-instrument performances: with the rather austere, dusty timbre of the old violas the eighteenth-century string quintet as heard here distinctly lack that dark, saturated quality familiar from more traditional performances. There are, though, abundant compensations for any lack of sheer tonal richness, especially in the performances of the three major-keyed quintets. The first movement of K515, for instance, one of Mozart's grandest conceptions, receives a noble, spacious reading, remarkable both for its finesse of detail and its command of his vast structural span. And in the two final quintets, with their more open textures and surface lightness of manner, the Salomon's springy rhythms and crisp, airy articulation pay particular dividends. It's strange, though, that in K593 the Salomon, with their authentic credentials, should opt for the zig-zag version of the finale's main theme that has long been recognized as an editorial simplification of Mozart's slithering chromatic opening. In the famous G minor Quintet the Salomon's grace, gentle eloquence and textural transparency bring many rewards but for all their poise and delicacy, their readings of the slow movement and the *Adagio* introduction to the finale will strike many as too cool and objective for such disquieting, even anguished music. Also, in an otherwise exemplary recording, the balance seems tipped slightly in favour of the first violin. But despite any reservations, these are accomplished and at times revelatory performances of this inexhaustible music. Both Hyperion discs, but particularly that containing K515 and K593, can be commended to all but the most implacable opponents of authentic instruments.

NEW REVIEW

Mozart. COMPLETE EDITION, Volume 12 — STRING QUARTETS. **Quartetto Italiano** (Paolo Borciani, Elisa Pegreffi, vns; Piero Farulli, va; Franco Rossi, vc). Philips Mozart Edition 422 512-2PME8.
G major, K80/73f; D major, K155/134a; G major, K156/134b (with additional original Adagio); C major, K157 (all from 6500 142, 12/71); F major, K158; B flat major, K159; E flat major, K160/159a; F major, K168 (6500 172, 12/72); A major, K169; C major, K170; E flat major, K171; B flat major, K172; D minor, K173 (6747 097, 9/74); G major, K387; D minor, K421/417b (SAL3632, 10/67); E flat major, K428/421b; B flat major, K458, "Hunt" (SAL3633, 10/67); A major, K464; C major, K465, "Dissonance" (SAL3634, 10/67); D major, K499; D major, K575 (6500 241, 7/72); B flat major, K589; F major, K590 (6500 225, 7/73).

⑧ 7h 54' ADD 8/91

These are classic performances which have won praise ever since they began to appear back in 1967. Admittedly, a little allowance has to be made for the sound since the recordings date from between 1966 and 1973. For example, it is a touch heavy and close in the 1966 recording of the D minor Quartet that is one of the wonderful set of six that Mozart dedicated to Haydn. In a way, this accords to some extent with the playing of the Quartetto Italiano, which is at times rather earnest — and in the first movement of this work, rather deliberate in its pace. But these are really the only criticisms of a generally splendid issue, and the innate seriousness of these fine Italian artists is almost always a plus feature: indeed, they bring an overall intelligence, refinement and, above all, range of interpretative values to this often superb and always attractive music. As for quality of ensemble, they are impeccable. This is undeniably still the best general survey of Mozart's string quartets available, and at mid-price the eight discs represent a safe investment that should yield many years of pleasure.

Mozart. String Quartets — D major, K575; F major, K590. **Salomon Quartet** (Simon Standage, Micaela Comberti, vns; Trevor Jones, va; Jennifer Ward Clarke, vc). Hyperion CDA66355.

1h 1' DDD 4/91

It is not always that the sound of a string quartet is as easy on the ear as here, and although the recording has fine clarity and bloom it really seems as if this is

Salomon Quartet   *[photo: Hyperion*

thanks to the unusually sensitive playing of the four artists using modern replicas of fine period instruments. The result sounds authentic, in the best sense of that much-misused word, and an attractive warmth is imparted to the music. Along with that the members of the Salomon Quartet phrase thoughtfully and affectionately, articulate springily and exercise good judgement in their choice of tempos, not least that of the opening *Allegretto* of the D major Quartet, an unusual pace for a Mozart first movement. Just here and there one might wish for the greater humour, vigour and momentum that other ensembles find, say in the finale of the same work, but the playing is still highly enjoyable and it is a further plus that repeats are faithfully observed. The quartets themselves are the first and third of his three *Prussian* quartets written in 1789-90 for the cello-playing King Friedrich Wilhelm of Prussia — hence their sometimes prominent cello writing and also, probably, the not excessive technical demands placed upon the players. The recording has already been praised and it remains only to add that although it is a little close, lacking really soft dynamics, the intimacy of the playing style still pleases and the instruments are well balanced.

Mozart. String Quartets — G major, K387; D minor, K421/417*b*. **Bartók Quartet** (Peter Komlos, Sandor Devich, vns; Géza Németh, va; Károly Botvay, vc). Hungaroton White Label HRC129.

59' ADD 10/89

Mozart. String Quartets — D minor K421/417*b*; C major, K465, "Dissonance". **Salomon Quartet** (Simon Standage, Micaela Comberti, vns; Trevor Jones, va; Jennifer Ward-Clarke, vc). Hyperion CDA66170. From A66170 (12/85).

1h 3' DAD 4/87

Although the string quintet is usually cited as the chamber-music medium into which Mozart poured his most profound thoughts, his canon of some 23 string quartets contains so much that is typical of his genius that to write those works off as being of lesser interest would be to mistake their importance and stature. Quartets Nos. 14-19, effusively dedicated to Haydn, are rightfully the most famous, for in these works Mozart was successfully able to combine, as never before, elements of both the string quartet's entertaining, public face and its more intimate aura of friends relaxing in genial music-making. The Bartók Quartet innately emphasizes this last element, for each of the players produces a distinctively different timbre and adopts an intriguingly individual approach to the technical posers set by the composer. As a whole, their view of the music, though not without its moments of surprising interpretation, always maintains a restrained awareness of its idiomatic bounds and the recording similarly conveys immediacy without over-inflation.

The thoughtful, warm yet often incisive playing (the violin tone altogether lacks gloss) on the Hyperion recording, with period instruments, leads to performances that are finely shaped and beautifully clear in detail. The minuets tend to be quickish by modern standards, which is in line with the latest thinking about how they were done in Haydn and Mozart's time, and makes good musical sense. These performances may not represent the ultimate word on the music but they have real integrity and are very satisfying.

Mozart. "HAYDN" STRING QUARTETS. **Chilingirian Quartet** (Levon Chilingirian, Mark Butler, vns; Nicholas Logie, va; Philip de Groote, vc). CRD CRD3362/4. From CRD1062/4 (12/80).
CRD3362 — G major, K387; D minor, K421/417b. *CRD3363* — E flat major, K428/421b; B flat major, K458, "Hunt". *CRD3364* — A major, K464; C major, K465, "Dissonance".

③ 59' 56' 68' ADD 9/90

Though the Chilingirian may yield to quartets like the Melos and the Alban Berg in sheer virtuosity, their performances of these six inexhaustible works represent some of the most thoughtful, naturally expressive Mozart playing in the catalogue. Unlike some of their more high-powered rivals their manner is essentially private, devoid of both surface gloss and self-conscious point-making. Tempos tend to be rather slower than average, especially in the outer movements of the *Hunt* and the *Dissonance* and in some of the minuets. But any lack of bite and brio is more than offset by the Chilingirian's breadth of phrase and unusual care for inner detail. The A major, Beethoven's favourite among Mozart's quartets, is especially successful, done with a gentle, luminous intensity, the minuet spare and absorbed, the variations shaped with a real sense of cumulative growth. If the 6/8 *Andantes* of K421 and K428 are a touch too deliberate (the latter hardly *con moto* as Mozart asks), the Chilingirian's profound reflective tenderness, here and in the other slow movements, brings its own rewards. The quality of the interpretations is matched by that of the recordings, which is intimate, truthful and rounded, with the four instruments nicely separated.

Mozart. FLUTE QUARTETS. **William Bennett** (fl); **Grumiaux Trio** (Arthur Grumiaux, vn; Georges Janzer, va; Eva Czako, vc). Philips Musica da Camera 422 835-2PC. From 6500 034 (6/71).
D major, K285; G major, K285a; C major, KAnh171/285b; A major, K298.

49' ADD 10/89

Mozart. FLUTE QUARTETS. [a]**János Szebenyi** (fl); [b]**Béla Kovács** (cl); [a]**András Kiss** (vn); [a]**László Bársony**, [b]**Géza Németh** (vas); [a]**Károly Botvay** (vc); [b]**Ferenc Rados** (pf). Hungaroton White Label HRC128.
D major, K285; G major, K285a; C major, KAnh171/285b; A major, K298. Clarinet trio in E flat major, "Kegelstatt", K498[b].

1h 10' ADD 10/89

Though he confessed that he did not much like the flute, Mozart was incapable of writing dull or poorly constructed music, and as it happens we know that he gave especial attention to the D major Flute Quartet, rewriting part of its finale, while its *Adagio* with its pizzicato accompaniment has a liquid beauty that utterly suits the instrument. This is all attractive music, and the four pieces played on the Philips disc include two charming sets of variations. The playing is of a high order, for William Bennett is an agile and sensitive flautist with a sure sense of the Mozart style, while the Grumiaux Trio, always reliable in this composer, blend beautifully with him tonally. Tempos are well judged also, always a good test of the understanding of the music. The recording dates from 1969, but nothing in the sound suggests this save perhaps a lack of real *pianissimo,* while the instruments are nicely balanced by the Philips engineers in a slightly (but not excessively) reverberant acoustic.

Hungaroton's generously filled disc gives us the Clarinet Trio as well as the four flute quartets. The Clarinet Trio acquired its nickname (meaning 'skittle alley') because Mozart is supposed to have conceived it while bowling. The performances of the flute quartets are less consciously refined than those of William Bennett and the Grumiaux Trio but sound delightfully spontaneous — though that word is not intended to suggest any lack of precision, and indeed the ensemble is excellent, for example in the difficult pizzicato accompaniment in the *Adagio* of the D major Quartet. János Szebenyi has a fine tone, rich yet delicate, and that of the clarinettist Béla Kovács in the Trio is pleasing too. With good playing and a natural recorded balance, this is an attractive bargain.

Mozart. Divertimento in E flat major for string trio, K563[a]. Six Preludes and Fugues (after Bach), K404*a*[b] — No. 1 in D minor; No. 2 in G minor; No. 3 in F major. **Grumiaux Trio** (Arthur Grumiaux, vn; Georges Janzer, va; Eva Czako, vc). Philips 416 485-2PH. Item marked [a] from SAL3664 (8/68), [b] 6500 605 (5/75).

1h 2' ADD 11/87

Mozart. Divertimento in E flat major for string trio, K563. Duos for violin and viola — G major, K423; B flat major, K424. **Dénes Kovács** (vn); **Géza Németh** (va); **Ede Banda** (vc). Hungaroton White Label HRC072.

1h 13' ADD 5/90 £

NEW REVIEW
Mozart. Divertimento in E flat major for string trio, K563. Six Preludes and Fugues (after Bach), K404*a* — No. 1 in D minor; No. 2 in G minor; No. 3 in F major; No. 6 in F minor. **L'Archibudelli Trio** (Vera Beths, vn; Jürgen Kussmaul, va; Anner Bylsma, vc). Sony Classical Vivarte CD46497.

1h 3' DDD £

There cannot be many major works by great composers that are undoubted masterpieces and yet remain still relatively little known, but Mozart's Divertimento for string trio is certainly one of them. The late Arthur Grumiaux leads his Trio in a very skilful and sensitive performance, and they bring out the tragic power of the *Andante* in a way that cannot fail to impress and move a sympathetic listener. This is a work that all who love Mozart should know, and this performance is persuasive and very well recorded, so that one would not guess that the date of the sessions was 1967. The three Preludes followed by Fugues in three contrapuntal parts were recorded in 1973 and while not personal in the obvious sense they have a special interest of their own for students of this composer.

Though the Hungaroton performance of the Divertimento is less subtle than that of the Grumiaux Trio, it is fresh and clean and at a bargain price and a length of over 70 minutes this CD is most recommendable, particularly as the recording is well balanced and has a natural sound. With his sweet, clear tone, the violinist Dénes Kovács also leads positively in the two duos with viola, which are too attractive and substantial to be thought of as miniatures or curiosities — those wishing to sample may try the slow movement of either work. Incidentally, the *Duo*, K424, is in B flat major, not B major as the booklet states: Mozart never used the latter as a main key for a work, though Haydn did.

The Divertimento receives a searching and sublime performance from the period instrument ensemble L'Archibudelli, the brainchild of the cellist Anner Bylsma. These highly accomplished players present this startlingly original late masterwork with an elevated gravity of purpose, and an overall objectivity which demands concentrated attention from the outset. Their performance reveals the mastery and majesty of the Divertimento through the medium of authentic instrumental styles, which somehow refine the tonal colouration and formal precision of each of the six movements with unerring skill and textural integrity.

L'Archibudelli's arrangements of the Preludes and Fugues are similarly daring in concept and offer fascinating insights into Mozart's innovative use of original material; if, indeed, he was actually responsible for the transcriptions (which still remains unclear). This budget-priced CD can be unhesitatingly recommended to all period instrument devotees.

NEW REVIEW

Mozart. COMPLETE EDITION, Volume 18 — PIANO VARIATIONS, RONDOS, etc. [a]**Ingrid Haebler**, [b]**Mitsuko Uchida** (pfs); [c]**Ton Koopman** (hpd). Philips Mozart Edition 422 518-2PME5.
Variations — G major, K24[a]; D major, K25[a]; C major, K179/189*a*[a]; G major, K180/173*c*[a]; C major, K264/315*d*[a]; C major, K265/300*e*[a]; F major, K352/374*ca*[a]; E flat major, K353/300*f*[a]; E flat major, K354/299*a*[a]; F major, K398/416*e*[a]; G major, K455[a] (all from 6747 380, 6/79); A major, K460/454*a*[c] (new to UK); B flat major, K500[a]; D major, K573[a]; F major, K613[a] (6747 380).
Minuets — F major, K1*d*[c]; G major/C major, K1/1*e*/1*f*[c]; F major, K2[c]; F major, K4[c]; F major, K5[c]; D major, K94/73*h*[c]; D major, K355/576*b*[b] (all new to UK).
Fantasia in D minor, K397/385*g*[b] (412 123-1PH, 7/84). *Rondos* — D major, K485[b] (420 185-2PH, 7/87); A minor, K511[b] (412 122-1PH, 11/84). Adagio in B minor, K540[b]. Gigue in G major, K574[b] (both from 412 616-1PH, 4/85).
Klavierstück in F major, K33*B*[c]. Capriccio in C major, K395/300*g*[c]. March No. 1 in C major, K408/383*e*[c]. Prelude and Fugue in C major, K394/383*a*[c].
Allegros — C major, K1*b*[c]; F major, K1*c*[c]; B flat major, K3[c]; C major, K5*a*[c]; G minor, K312/590*d*[c]; B flat major, K400/372*a* (cpted Stadler)[c]. Suite in C major, K399/385*i*[c]. Kleine Trauermarsch in C minor, K453*a*[c]. Andante in C major, K1*a*[c]. Fugue in G minor, K401/375*e*[c] (with Tini Mathot, hpd. All new to UK).

(5) 4h 34' ADD/DDD 10/91

Mitsuko Uchida   *[photo: Philips*

These five mid-price discs offer music of fine and often superb quality in a convenient format. The piano was Mozart's own instrument (though he also played the violin) and he composed much music for it besides the sonatas and concertos. Of the three artists here, two are generally fine and satisfying, though the third is more controversial. Ingrid Haebler was recorded back in 1975, but the piano sound is good and little tape background remains, and her performances of the variation sets, which take up the first three discs, are delicate without cuteness, effortlessly encompassing the music's wide range of moods. Mitsuko Uchida, on the fourth disc, performs individual pieces including the two rondos and the beautiful *Adagio* in B minor (the only piece Mozart wrote in this key) in a highly refined manner, a touch over-sophisticated perhaps but still beautiful and expressive and taking full, unashamed advantage of the sound of a modern grand. By contrast, Ton Koopman's disc of minuets and other miscellaneous things is played on a harpsichord at a semitone below modern concert pitch and offers a recording of such immediacy that some listeners will regard it as too bright. Koopman puts gusto into everything he does, but not always to good effect. However, even if grace is in short supply in his performances, they undeniably offer ample personality and such reservations as one may have about his playing should not affect the desirability of the set as a whole.

Mozart. SONATAS FOR KEYBOARD AND VIOLIN. **Szymon Goldberg** (vn); **Radu Lupu** (pf). Decca 430 306-2DM4. From 13BB 207/12 (11/75). C major, K296; G major, K301/293*a*; E flat major, K302/293*b*; C major, K303/293*c*; E minor, K304/300*c*; A major, K305/293*d*; D major, K306/300*l*; F major, K376/374*d*; F major, K377/374*e*; B flat major, K378/317*d*; G major, K379/373*a*; E flat major, K380/374*f*; B flat major, K454; E flat major, K481; A major, K526; F major, K547.

④ 4h 42' ADD 9/91 £

This set of Mozart's violin sonatas has acquired something like classic status since it was released on six vinyl discs in 1975. Now on four mid-price CDs, it represents fine value. Szymon Goldberg and Radu Lupu make an excellent partnership, for the inherent vigour of the violinist's playing is tempered by the innate warmth of the pianist in such a way that their various qualities appear to advantage according to the nature of each sonata as well as individual movements. In other words, Lupu is still there as a personality in his own right, which is as it should be when one remembers that, strictly speaking, these are sonatas designated as "for piano and violin" but he is never over-assertive. There's much to enjoy here, such as the agreeable quiet charm with which the artists handle the finale of the two-movement Sonata in G major, K301, and the elegance of the finale in the late A major Sonata, K526, one of the finest of all as well as the most challengingly difficult. But similar examples of their empathy abound in the 42 movements (and 16 sonatas) that are played, and even if some collectors may feel that the minuets in K303 and K377 are a touch too dreamy, this is a most desirable set, clearly yet warmly recorded in London's Kingsway Hall.

Mozart. Double Piano Sonata in D major, K448/375*a*.
Schubert. Fantasia in F minor, D940. **Murray Perahia, Radu Lupu** (pfs), CBS Masterworks CD39511. From IM39511 (3/86).

42' 10/86

One of the highlights of concert-going at Snape in the 1980s was to hear Lupu and Perahia, two of the greatest pianists of our era, performing together as one, and yet retaining their own, very individual identities. This disc is a happy reminder of that experience; it was recorded live at The Maltings and it captures exactly that peculiarly characterful, wayward acoustic that has been the bane of so many recording engineers. Having an audience present makes the job infinitely simpler, yet the task is still not an easy one. The performances that are so admirably conveyed here are not of the conventional block-buster type. Neither of these pianists has made tickets to their recitals as difficult to grasp as the Grail by producing virtuosic histrionics. Perfect tone control, total dedication to the inner life of the music, satisfying originality of vision, and a beguiling spontaneity have made their solo performances special; together they show themselves to be selfless chamber musicians of the highest order, capable of lifting already great music to a higher plain. Despite the warm tone of the instruments and ambience, their Mozart is totally classical in ethos, their Schubert divinely other-worldly. One of the desert island's life-sustaining Eight.

Mozart. PIANO WORKS. **András Schiff.** Decca 421 369-2DH.
Variations on "Ah, vous dirai-je, maman", K265/300*e*. Andante in F major, K616. Rondo in A minor, K511. Adagio in C major, K356/617*a*. Minuet in

D major, K355/576b. Gigue in G major, K574. Adagio in B minor, K540.
Variations on "Unser dummer Pöbel meint", K455.

1h 12' DDD 10/88

This young Hungarian can boast fingers second to none when dazzling prestidigitation is the order of the day. Here, however, we meet him not as a virtuoso but as a musician. Nothing in the recital makes heavy technical demands, but since everything dates from Mozart's last decade, each note in a sense is laden. And Schiff brings this home with a rare understanding of the eloquence of simplicity. The Variations themselves testify to Mozart's ever-burgeoning ingenuity of invention as time ran on — and out. In the field of the so-called miniature, surely no composer has ever written anything more profound than the A minor *Rondo* and B minor *Adagio*, both beautifully timed and shaded here. The harmonically audacious *Minuet* in D and the teasing G major *Gigue* in their turn bring just the right contrast from the *Andante* in F for Mechanical Organ and the *Adagio* in C for Glass Harmonica, which in their Elysian purity touch the heart just that much more for having both grown from Mozart's very last spring. In sum, a disc to be treasured.

NEW REVIEW

Mozart. COMPLETE EDITION, Volume 17 — PIANO SONATAS. **Mitsuko Uchida** (pf). Philips Mozart Edition 422 517-2PME5.
C major, K279/189d (from 412 617-1PH, 1/86); F major, K280/189e; B flat major, K281/189f; E flat major, K282/189g; G major, K283/189h (all from 420 186-1PH, 4/88); D major, K284/205b (420 185-1PH, 7/87); C major, K309/284b; A minor, K310/300d; D major, K311/284c (412 174-1PH, 4/86); C major, K330/300h (412 616-1PH, 4/85); A major, K331/300i; F major, K332/300k (412 123-1PH, 7/84); B flat major, K333/315c (412 616-1PH); C minor, K457 (412 617-1PH); F major, K533/494; C major, K545 (412 122-1PH, 11/84); B flat major, K570 (420 185-1PH); D major, K576 (420 617-1PH); Fantasia in C minor, K475 (412 617-1PH).

5h 25' DDD 9/91

By common consent, Mitsuko Uchida is among the leading Mozart pianists of today, and her recorded series of the piano sonatas won critical acclaim as it appeared and finally *Gramophone* Awards in 1989 and 1991. Here are all the sonatas, plus the Fantasia in C minor, K475, which is in some ways a companion piece to the sonata in the same key, K457. This is unfailingly clean, crisp and elegant playing, that avoids anything like a romanticized view of the early sonatas such as the delightfully fresh G major, K283. On the other hand, Uchida responds with the necessary passion to the forceful, not to say *Angst*-ridden, A minor Sonata, K310. Indeed, her complete series is a remarkably fine achievement, comparable with her account of the piano concertos. The recordings were produced by Erik Smith in the Henry Wood Hall in London and offer excellent piano sound; thus an unqualified recommendation is in order for what must be one of the most valuable volumes in Philips's Complete Mozart Edition. Do not be put off by critics who suggest that these sonatas are less interesting than some other Mozart compositions, for they are fine pieces written for an instrument that he himself played and loved.

Mozart. MASONIC MUSIC. [a]**Werner Krenn** (ten); [b]**Tom Krause** (bar); [c]**Edinburgh Festival Chorus; György Fischer** ([d]org/[e]pf); [f]**London Symphony Orchestra/István Kertész.** Decca Serenata 425 722-2DM. Texts and translations included. From SXL6409 (10/69).
Lobegesang auf die feierliche Johannisloge, K148[ae]. Dir, Seele des Weltalls, K429/K468a[acf]. Lied zur Gesellenreise, K468[ae]. Die Maurerfreude, K471[acf].

Maurerische Trauermusik, K477[f]. Zerfliesset heut', geliebte Brüder, K483[acd]. Ihr unsre neuen Leiter, K484[acd]. Die ihr des unermesslichen Weltalls, K619[ae]. Laut verkünde unsre Freude, K623[abcf]. Lasst uns mit geschlungnen Händen, K623*a*[cd].

53' ADD 11/90

In the late eighteenth century, the Freemasons' belief in a human brotherhood and mutual responsibility that was independent of birth or wealth was a force for social change which proved so strong and influential that Masonry was banned in Austria not long after Mozart's death. Since he, Haydn and Beethoven were all Masons, it is clear that this secretive society meant much to several major artists, and in Mozart's case this is reflected in the many Masonic works he composed, of which the opera *Die Zauberflöte* is the most celebrated. This disc offers a number of other Masonic pieces, mostly little known, some of which were actually used in Viennese Lodges. They begin with a simple tenor hymn in praise of brotherhood, and include several other vocal pieces, some honouring God the 'Great Architect'; there is also the powerful *Masonic Funeral Music* of 1785, written for an unusual orchestral body (including a double-bassoon) just 11 months after the composer was admitted to the Viennese Lodge 'Beneficence', with its name implying the doing of good works. These performances sound dedicated as well as being skilful, with the tenor soloist Werner Krenn sounding particularly suited to the music with its touch of solemn earnestness. The recording does not show its age and balances the various vocal and instrumental forces well.

Mozart (ed. Maunder). Mass in C minor, K427/417*a*. **Arleen Auger, Lynne Dawson** (sops); **John Mark Ainsley** (ten); **David Thomas** (bass); **Winchester Cathedral Choir; Winchester College Quiristers; Academy of Ancient Music/Christopher Hogwood.** L'Oiseau-Lyre Florilegium 425 528-2OH. Text and translation included.

51' DDD 7/90

NEW REVIEW

Mozart (ed. Eder). Mass in C minor, K427/417*a*. **Arleen Auger, Barbara Bonney** (sops); **Hans Peter Blochwitz** (ten); **Robert Holl** (bass); **Berlin Radio Chorus; Berlin Philharmonic Orchestra/Claudio Abbado.** Sony Classical CD46671. Text and translation included.

53' DDD 10/91

Mozart left unfinished the work that ought to have been the choral masterpiece of his early Viennese years but there is enough of it to make up nearly an hour's music — music that is sometimes sombre, sometimes florid, sometimes jubilant. Christopher Hogwood avoids any charge of emotional detachment in his steady and powerful opening *Kyrie*, monumental in feeling, dark in tone; and he brings ample energy to the big, bustling choruses of the *Gloria* — and its long closing fugue is finely sustained. The clarity and ring of the boys' voices serve him well in these numbers. There is a strong solo team, headed by Arleen Auger in radiant, glowing voice and, as usual, singing with refined taste; Lynne Dawson joins her in the duets, John Mark Ainsley too in the trio. But this is essentially a "soprano mass" — Mozart wrote it, after all, with the voice of his new wife (and perhaps thoughts of the much superior one of her sister Aloysia) in his mind — and Auger, her voice happily stealing in for the first time in the lovely "Christe", excels in the florid and expressive music of the "Et incarnatus" (where Richard Maunder has supplied fuller string parts than usual, perhaps fuller than Mozart would have done had he finished the work). Hogwood directs with his usual spirit and clarity.

Abbado, with the Berlin Philharmonic, presents the great work on a larger scale, but not so as to smother it either in grandeur of sound or in alien romanticism. This is a good 'central' performance, thoroughly observant in detail and responsive to all that is joyous, tender, penitent or (in the "Qui tollis") unrelenting in mood, but without exaggeration. The recorded sound matches this: it is generous, reverberant rather than dry, yet not so as to impair clarity. Auger also features here as soprano soloist but is joined now by Barbara Bonney who contributes some exquisitely pure singing in the "Et incarnatus est", her voice having just the right degree of similarity and distinctiveness when the two sing together in the blissfully competitive "Domine Deus". It is also good to hear the choir given due prominence in the balance. The edition is Helmut Eder's, created with reconstruction from the *Credo* onwards.

NEW REVIEW

Mozart (cptd Süssmayr). Requiem in D minor, K626. **Sylvia McNair** (sop); **Carolyn Watkinson** (contr); **Francisco Araiza** (ten); **Robert Lloyd** (bass); **Chorus and Academy of St Martin in the Fields/Sir Neville Marriner.** Philips 432 087-2PH. Text and translation included.

50' DDD 12/91

NEW REVIEW

Mozart (cptd Süssmayr). Requiem in D minor, K626. **Yvonne Kenny** (sop); **Alfreda Hodgson** (contr); **Arthur Davies** (ten); **Gwynne Howell** (bass); **Northern Sinfonia and Chorus/Richard Hickox.** Virgin Classics Virgo VJ7 91460-2.

47' DDD 12/91

Alongside those old musical teasers, "Who wrote Haydn's *Toy* Symphony?" (Leopold Mozart) and "Who wrote Purcell's Trumpet Voluntary?" (Jeremiah Clarke) can be added "Who wrote Mozart's Requiem?". Mozart's pupil Süssmayr was responsible for much of the work as most modern audiences would recognize it, but exactly how much was Mozart's, how much Süssmayr's, and how much anybody else's is anyone's guess. But performers don't seem unduly perturbed by this masterpiece's less than certain provenance, and there is no shortage of first-rate CD versions. Sir Neville Marriner's interpretation stands out as one of towering authority with a nobility and emotional impact few performances outside the concert-hall could expect to muster. From the stately opening "Requiem aeternam" to the Requiem's emotional climax, the "Agnus Dei", Marriner's musicians produce superlative performances. The chorus is remarkably well disciplined (just listen to the beautifully incisive singing with its dramatic dynamic contrasts in the "Domine Jesu"), and from the soloists Robert Lloyd's resonant "Tuba mirum" is a stunning contribution to a disc of exceptional quality.

Richard Hickox's version is far more than a mere super-budget priced alternative. As a performance in its own right it stands proudly alongside Marriner's and, indeed, in many respects Hickox has mustered an even finer team of soloists. The Northern Sinfonia play with sensitivity, although it must be said the recording slightly favours the very exuberant choral forces who sing with great gusto throughout.

Sylvia McNair   *[photo: Philips/Steiner]*

Mozart. CONCERT ARIAS. [a]**Lena Lootens** (sop); [b]**Christoph Prégardien** (ten); **La Petite Bande/Sigiswald Kuijken.** Virgin Classics Veritas VC7 90753-2. Texts and translations included.

Misero! o sogno ... Aura che intorni spiri, K431/425b[b]. A questo seno deh vieni ... Or che il cielo, K374[a]. Si mostra la sorte, K209[b]. Voi avete un cor fedele, K217[a]. Clarice cara, K256[b]. Va, dal furor portata, K21/19c[b]. Ah, lo previdi! ... Ah, t'invola agl'occhi miei ... Deh, non varcar, K272[a]. Se al labbro mio non credi, K295[b]. Bella mia fiamma ... Resta, oh, cara, K528[a].

1h 14' DDD 8/89

While much has been written and said about authentic instruments over these last few years, the subject of 'authentic voices' is altogether more elusive — for obvious reasons, the most obvious one being that none survive from the eighteenth century. The two young artists represented on this appealing disc would sound a good deal more like the singers for whom Mozart composed than do most of the singers who fill, and whose voices fill, our large opera houses. Lena Lootens, a sweet and unspoilt soprano, shows graceful phrasing and clean, light coloratura in the early aria *Voi avete un cor fedele*; but in one for the distraught Andromeda, *Ah, lo previdi!*, she produces ample histrionic power, and she also distinguishes herself in the demanding *Bella mia fiamma*, an aria written, it seems, to test the powers of an old friend of Mozart's with its chromaticisms and its high-lying music. Christoph Prégardien, a tenor with a real gift for shapely phrasing, shows a command of Mozartian line in the elegant cantilena of *Misero! o sogno* and again in the sympathetically written *Se al labbro mio non credi*. With the alert, rhythmic accompaniments provided by Sigiswald Kuijken and his Petite Bande, this is altogether an appealing disc.

Mozart. LIEDER. **Barbara Hendricks** (sop); [a]**Goran Söllscher** (gtr); [b]**Maria João Pires** (pf); [c]**Lausanne Chamber Orchestra/Mika Eichenholz.** EMI CDC7 54007-2. Texts included.

Abendempfindung, K523[b]. Als Luise die Briefe, K520[b]. An Chloe, K524[b]. Ch'io mi scordi di te ... Non temer, amato bene, K505[bc]. Dans un bois solitaire, K308/295b[b]. Ich würd, auf meinem Pfad, K390/340c[b]. Die ihr des unermesslichen Weltalls, K619[b]. Die kleine Spinnerin, K531[b]. Komm, liebe Zither, komm, K351/367b[a]. Das Lied der Trennung, K519[b]. Un moto di gioia, K579[b]. Oiseaux, si tous les ans, K307/284d[b]. Ridente la calma, K152/210a[b]. Sehnsucht nach dem Frühling, K596[b]. Sei du mein Trost, K391/340b[b]. Das Veilchen, K476[b]. Die Verschweigung, K518[b]. Der Zauberer, K472[b]. Die Zufriedenheit, K473[b].

1h 3' DDD 7/91

Few would claim that Mozart was one of the great composers of Lieder; it fell to Schubert, Schumann and Brahms to perfect this particular genre. Mozart himself never really seemed entirely happy with the form and in all he wrote only 33 individual songs. Perhaps this is a little surprising since in his operas Mozart showed himself to be a supreme composer for the human voice. Indeed this CD ends with a delightful performance of the concert aria *Ch'io mi scordi di te* in which both the singer and pianist are projected as soloists above the orchestra in an enchanting re-working of material from *Idomeneo*. But while his solo songs certainly don't contain his best music, his wonderful gifts of lyrical expression shine through: provided, of course, they are given sensitive and intelligent performances. They most certainly are here. Barbara Hendricks sings with poise and elegance and is beautifully supported by Maria João Pires. They never try to overstate their case by underlining too heavily the touches of genius in Mozart's subtle word-painting at the expense of the fundamentally simple and open character of the songs. All in all a captivating disc, although it is something of a disappointment that EMI have chosen not to include translations of the Italian, French and German texts.

Mozart. ARIAS. **Elisabeth Schwarzkopf** (sop); [a]**London Symphony Orchestra/George Szell;** [bcd]**Philharmonia Orchestra/**[bc]**Carlo Maria Giulini,** [d]**Sir John Pritchard.** EMI CDC7 47950-2. Texts and translations included. Items marked [a] from ASD2493 (3/70), [b] Columbia SAX2381/4 (6/61), [c] SAX2369/72 (2/61), [d] Columbia mono 33CX1069 (12/53). Concert arias[a] — Ch'io mi scordi di te, K505 (with Alfred Brendel, pf); Vado ma dove?, K583; Alma grande e nobil core, K578; Nehmt meinem Dank, K383. LE NOZZE DI FIGARO — Porgi amor[b]; E Susanna non vien! … Dove sono[b]; Non so più[d]; Voi che sapete[d]; Giunse alfin il momento … Deh vieni, non tradar[d]. DON GIOVANNI — Ah, fuggi il traditor[c]; In qual eccessi … Mi tradi quell'alma ingrata[c]; Batti, batti, o bel Masetto[d]; Vedrai, carino[d]; Crudele? … Non mi dir[d]. IDOMENEO — Zeffiretti lusinghieri[d].

1h 12' ADD 11/87

This superb collection gathers together some of the finest Mozart singing heard in the last four decades. The shading and shaping Schwarzkopf brings to this glorious music everywhere displays a style and panache only achieved by study aided by insight. Take for example her majestic but human Countess and her sympathetic Donna Elvira. Both are unmannered and have a depth of personality so often missing in today's interpreters. Given the luxury of so fine a pianist as Alfred Brendel in the celebrated *Ch'io mi scordi di te*, this is five-star Mozart interpretation indeed.

NEW REVIEW

Mozart. ARIAS. **Cecilia Bartoli** (mez); [a]**András Schiff** (pf); **Peter Schmidtl** ([b]basset cl and [c]basset hn); **Vienna Chamber Orchestra/György Fischer.** Decca 430 513-2DH. LE NOZZE DI FIGARO — Non so più; Voi che sapete; Giunse alfin il momento … Deh vieni. COSI FAN TUTTE — E'amore un ladroncello. DON GIOVANNI — Vedrai, carino. LA CLEMENZA DI TITO — Parto, parto[b]; Deh, per questo; Ecco il punto, o Vitellia … Non piu di fiori[c]. Concert Arias — Chi sa, chi sa, qual sia, K582; Alma grande e nobil core, K578; Ch'io mi scordi di te?, K505[a].

58' DDD 12/91

Mozart wrote some of his most appealing music for the mezzo-soprano voice with the roles of Cherubino and Susanna in *Le nozze di Figaro*, Dorabella in *Così fan tutte* and Zerlina in *Don Giovanni* each boasting at least one memorable aria. Alongside these this disc includes a handful of concert arias including "Ch'io mi scordi di te?" which was written for the farewell performance of the great mezzo Nancy Storace with Mozart himself playing the concertante piano role. Here with as innate an interpreter of Mozart's piano writing as András Schiff and a voice so remarkably self-assured as Cecilia Bartoli's the electricity of that first, historic performance seems almost to be recreated. And, here as elsewhere, György Fischer directs the splendid Vienna Chamber Orchestra with disarming sensitivity while the recording is wonderfully warm and vibrant. Cecilia Bartoli boasts a voice of quite extraordinary charm and unassuming virtuosity: her vocal characterizations would be the envy of the finest actresses and her intuitive singing is in itself a sheer delight. But she also brings to these arias a conviction and understanding of the subtleties of the language which only a native Italian could. Listen to the subtle nuances of "Voi che sapete", the depth of understanding behind Dorabella's seemingly frivolous "E'amore un ladroncello"; these are not mere performances, but interpretations which penetrate to the very soul of the music. No Mozart lover should be without this CD.

Mozart. LE NOZZE DI FIGARO. **Claudio Desderi** (bar) Figaro; **Gianna Rolandi** (sop) Susanna; **Richard Stilwell** (bar) Count Almaviva; **Felicity Lott** (sop) Countess Almaviva; **Faith Esham** (mez) Cherubino; **Anne Mason** (sop) Marcellina; **Artur Korn** (bass) Bartolo; **Ugo Benelli** (ten) Don Basilio; **Alexander Oliver** (ten) Don Curzio; **Federico Davià** (bass) Antonio; **Anne Dawson** (sop) Barbarina; **Glyndebourne Chorus; London Philharmonic Orchestra/Bernard Haitink** with **Martin Isepp** (hpd). EMI CDS7 49753-2. Notes, text and translation included.

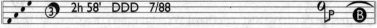

Mozart. LE NOZZE DI FIGARO. **Giuseppe Taddei** (bar) Figaro; **Anna Moffo** (sop) Susanna; **Eberhard Waechter** (bar) Count Almaviva; **Elisabeth Schwarzkopf** (sop) Countess Almaviva; **Fiorenza Cossotto** (mez) Cherubino; **Dora Gatta** (sop) Marcellina; **Ivo Vinco** (bass) Bartolo; **Renato Ercolani** (ten) Don Basilio, Don Curzio; **Piero Cappuccilli** (bass) Antonio; **Elisabetta Fusco** (sop) Barbarina; **Philharmonia Chorus and Orchestra/Carlo Maria Giulini.** EMI CMS7 63266-2. Notes, text and translation included. From Columbia SAX2381/4 (6/61).

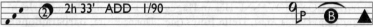

NEW REVIEW

Mozart. LE NOZZE DI FIGARO. **Sesto Bruscantini** (bar) Figaro; **Graziella Sciutti** (sop) Susanna; **Franco Calabrese** (bass) Count Almaviva; **Sena Jurinac** (sop) Countess Almaviva; **Risë Stevens** (mez) Cherubino; **Monica Sinclair** (contr) Marcellina; **Ian Wallace** (bass) Bartolo; **Hugues Cuénod** (ten) Don Basilio; **Daniel McCoshan** (ten) Don Curzio; **Gwyn Griffiths** (bar) Antonio; **Jeanette Sinclair** (sop) Barbarina; **Glyndebourne Festival Chorus and Orchestra/Vittorio Gui.** Classics for Pleasure CD-CFPD4724. From HMV ALP1312/15 (1/56).

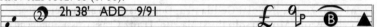

Le nozze di Figaro ("The marriage of Figaro") is comically inventive (though subtly spiked with irony), musically fleet and theatrically well-nigh perfect. The plot revolves around the domestic arrangements of the Count and Countess and their servants Figaro and Susanna, and more specifically around the male/female struggle in the household. Plots involving disguise and much hiding lead effortlessly through this most enchanting of operas to a rousing chorus when, in true Mozartian style, the world is restored to rights and everyone is just that bit chastened and a little wiser. With a cast of very accomplished singers Haitink recreates a real sense of ensemble and shared music-making. The LPO play delightfully and Martin Isepp's witty continuo playing is a joy. A lovely set.

Giulini stresses the opera's Italian virtues of line and ebullience of spirit, and with a largely Italian (or Italian-descended) cast Da Ponte's words are given due attention. At the centre is Schwarzkopf's Countess, done with exceptional grace and pathos, and matched in weight by Waechter's imposing, irascible Count. There is a strong, darkish Figaro from Taddei, a vivacious Susanna from Moffo and from Cossotto a Cherubino of unusual fullness. But it is Giulini who is the real star here, in his immaculate pacing of the score, his constant concern, above all, with a shapely, beautiful and carefully timed musical line as well as luminous orchestral textures, nowhere sacrificing the music to the senses as more modern performances are often inclined to do. The virtues may be old-fashioned ones, but the musical experience is of a high order.

The Gui set is an outright bargain. Although the performance hasn't quite the dramatic drive or vocal glamour of the Giulini it has a lively, intimate ambience deriving from performances at Glyndebourne and boasts the loveliest of all Countesses in Jurinac and a vitally idiomatic Figaro in Bruscantini. The recording is more than adequate. The impecunious newcomer should hurry to catch this set while it's available — such reissues have the habit of not lasting long in the catalogue.

Mozart. DON GIOVANNI. **Thomas Allen** (bar) Don Giovanni; **Carol Vaness** (sop) Donna Anna; **Maria Ewing** (mez) Donna Elvira; **Elizabeth Gale** (sop) Zerlina; **Keith Lewis** (ten) Don Ottavio; **Richard Van Allan** (bass) Leporello; **John Rawnsley** (bar) Masetto; **Dimitri Kavrakos** (bass) Commendatore; **Glyndebourne Festival Chorus; London Philharmonic Orchestra/ Bernard Haitink.** EMI CDS7 47037-8. Notes, text and translation included. From SLS143665-3 (7/84).

③ 2h 52' DDD 12/84

Mozart. DON GIOVANNI. **Eberhard Waechter** (bar) Don Giovanni; **Dame Joan Sutherland** (sop) Donna Anna; **Elisabeth Schwarzkopf** (sop) Donna Elvira; **Graziella Sciutti** (sop) Zerlina; **Luigi Alva** (ten) Don Ottavio; **Giuseppe Taddei** (bar) Leporello; **Piero Cappuccilli** (bar) Masetto; **Gottlob Frick** (bass) Commendatore; **Philharmonia Chorus and Orchestra/Carlo Maria Giulini.** EMI CDS7 47260-8. Notes, texts and translation included. From Columbia SAX2369/72 (2/61).

③ 2h 42' ADD 12/87

Mozart. DON GIOVANNI. **Håkan Hagegård** (bar) Don Giovanni; **Arleen Auger** (sop) Donna Anna; **Della Jones** (mez) Donna Elvira; **Barbara Bonney** (sop) Zerlina; **Nico van der Meel** (ten) Don Ottavio; **Gilles Cachemaille** (bar) Leporello; **Bryn Terfel** (bass-bar) Masetto; **Kristinn Sigmundsson** (bass) Commendatore; **Drottningholm Theatre Chorus and Orchestra/Arnold Ostman.** L'Oiseau-Lyre 425 943-2OH3. Text and translation included.

③ 2h 51' DDD 12/90

NEW REVIEW

Mozart. DON GIOVANNI. **Nicolai Ghiaurov** (bass) Don Giovanni; **Claire Watson** (sop) Donna Anna; **Christa Ludwig** (mez) Donna Elvira; **Mirelli Freni** (sop) Zerlina; **Nicolai Gedda** (ten) Don Ottavio; **Walter Berry** (bar) Leporello; **Paolo Montarsolo** (bass) Masetto; **Franz Crass** (bass) Commendatore; **New Philharmonia Chorus and Orchestra/Otto Klemperer.** EMI CMS7 63841-2. Notes, text and translation included. From HMV SAN172/5 (11/66).

③ 3h ADD 9/91

NEW REVIEW

Mozart. DON GIOVANNI. **Ingvar Wixell** (bar) Don Giovanni; **Martina Arroyo** (sop) Donna Anna; **Dame Kiri Te Kanawa** (sop) Donna Elvira; **Mirella Freni** (sop) Zerlina; **Stuart Burrows** (ten) Don Ottavio; **Wladimiro Ganzarolli** (bar) Leporello; **Richard Van Allen** (bass) Masetto; **Luigi Roni** (bass) Commendatore; **Chorus and Orchestra of the Royal Opera House, Covent Garden/Sir Colin Davis.** Philips Mozart Edition 422 541-2PME3. Notes, text and translation included. From 6707 022 (11/73).

③ 2h 44' ADD 1/92 £

Haitink's is a performance of assured musical pacing which, with a vividly matched team of soloists, is refined in a sturdily well-balanced recording. Those familiar with the production will recognize at once its chillingly saturnine Don Giovanni as portrayed by Thomas Allen who conveys a sensuousness which knows no true tenderness. His women are unusually strongly characterized. Donna Anna and Donna Elvira face each other as fearfully contrasted victims of both Giovanni and themselves. Richard Van Allan's chiaroscuro of wit, audacity and sulking petulance, of foreground servility and background resentment, make this one of the most entertaining and thought-provoking Leporellos on disc. And the same imaginative response to every nuance of Mozart's musical subtext runs like an electric current through this performance's recitatives. With Martin Isepp's tingling harpsichord continuo acting as invisible director and stage

Barbara Bonney   *[photo: DG/Bayat*

manager, it is here that the musical and dramatic heart of the work really beats; and for private listening on this count alone the performance can hardly be bettered.

Nevertheless, Giulini's version has always been most recommendable and here he captures all the work's most dramatic characteristics, faithfully supported by the superb Philharmonia forces of that time. Then he had one of the most apt casts ever assembled for the piece. Waechter's Giovanni combines the demonic with the seductive in just the right proportions, Taddei is a high-profile Leporello, who relishes the text and sings with lots of 'face'. Elvira was always one of Schwarzkopf's most successful roles: here she delivers the role with tremendous intensity. Sutherland's Anna isn't quite so full of character but it is magnificently sung. Alva is a graceful Ottavio. Sciutti's charming Zerlina, Cappuccilli's strong and Italianate Masetto and Frick's granite Commendatore are all very much in the picture. The recording still sounds well.

The L'Oiseau-Lyre issue is Mozart opera with a difference — and for once the difference is not a gimmick but the feeling that we really are closer to the original. Ostman's Don Giovanni is a young man and the other characters are no less human beings living at a dangerous pace, so that there is urgency as well as realism in his treatment of the score. The effect is as powerful as if one had cleaned away accretions of dust from a picture, and makes one feel that Ostman has removed inappropriate later traditions from this summit of music drama. Håkan Hagegård and Gilles Cachemaille, although both baritones, are fully contrasted as the Don and his servant-confidant Leporello, though indeed Ostman thinks of them as in a sense brothers belonging to different classes. Also fine are the ladies who in their different ways react to Giovanni's charm and self-will: listen, for example to "La ci darem la mano" (CD1, track 15), to hear outstanding singing and characterization. In fact these singer-actors are real to a degree that we sometimes despair of finding in more conventional accounts of this opera, and it seems no surprise when we learn that the 'real' Giovanni and Zerlina (Barbara Bonney) were married shortly after the recording. The orchestra, playing period instruments, are no less fine. The third CD includes the alternative or additional material that Mozart wrote for the Viennese production following the Prague première. This is a *Don Giovanni* to delight, and it has been beautifully recorded.

Otto Klemperer's granite-like, magisterial reading is well worth consideration at mid-price. For instance, nobody quite equals Klemperer in the power and inevitability of Giovanni's downfall; he is just as impressive in the demonic Act 1 finale. Ghiaurov is a superb Giovanni, possibly the best on any version, apart from Pinza. He is nicely set off by Berry's sardonic Leporello and Gedda is a suave, though ill-tuned Ottavio. The ladies, though less impressive, have their moments, with Freni a supple, inviting Zerlina. The recording is exemplary.

Another very tenable choice (now at medium price) is the 1970s performance conducted by Colin Davis, which has much to commend it, not least Davis's lean, taut, impassioned reading. Wixell is a properly commanding and seductive Giovanni. Te Kanawa is a distraught, passionate Elvira, in 1973 at the peak of her dramatic powers. Arroyo is a firm, serious Anna. Ganzarolli is a characterful, never exaggerated Leporello, Freni the most delightful of Zerlinas, Burrows the most lyrical of Ottavios. Roni's imposing Commendatore completes an excellent cast. The sound remains exemplary. But then this cast is singing under one of the great Mozart conductors of our age, who has the full measure of the score. His acquaintance with the work, even in 1973, stretched back more than 20 years.

Mozart. COSI FAN TUTTE. **Elisabeth Schwarzkopf** (sop) Fiordiligi; **Christa Ludwig** (mez) Dorabella; **Hanny Steffek** (sop) Despina; **Alfredo Kraus** (ten) Ferrando; **Giuseppe Taddei** (bar) Guglielmo; **Walter Berry** (bass) Don Alfonso; **Philharmonia Chorus and Orchestra/Karl Böhm.** EMI CMS7 69330-2. Notes, text and translation included. From SAN103/6 (5/63).

Mozart. COSI FAN TUTTE. **Karita Mattila** (sop) Fiordiligi; **Anne Sofie von Otter** (mez) Dorabella; **Elzbieta Szmytka** (sop) Despina; **Francisco Araiza** (ten) Ferrando; **Thomas Allen** (bar) Guglielmo; **José van Dam** (bass-bar) Don Alfonso; **Ambrosian Opera Chorus; Academy of St Martin in the Fields/Sir Neville Marriner.** Philips 422 381-2PH3. Notes, text and translation included.

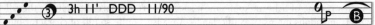

Così fan tutte has been very lucky on disc, and besides the delightful EMI set there have been several other memorable recordings. However, Böhm's cast could hardly be bettered, even in one's dreams. The two sisters are gloriously sung — Schwarzkopf and Ludwig bring their immeasurable talents as Lieder singers to this sparkling score and overlay them with a rare comic touch. Add to that the stylish singing of Alfredo Kraus and Giuseppe Taddei and the central quartet is unimpeachable. Walter Berry's Don Alfonso is characterful and Hanny Steffek is quite superb as Despina. The pacing of this endlessly intriguing work is immaculate. The emotional control of the characterization is masterly and Böhm's totally idiomatic response to the music is without peer. It is as close as you could wish to get to ideal Mozart, and its mid price only serves to makes this a truly desirable issue.

Nevertheless, Marriner's set ranks as a strong modern alternative. His pacing is naturally and firmly paced throughout, and he manages more successfully than other recent conductors to create a sense of the opera house in the studio. With his own smallish band in alert and responsive form and the instruments well balanced with the singers, one can sit back and enjoy some finely articulated and lively singing of six well-integrated voices. There is no weakness in the cast, but the Ferrando of Araiza (technically secure in his three, difficult arias) and the Guglielmo of Thomas Allen are particularly successful as regards Mozartian style and refined, seductive tone. Their voices blend well as do those of Mattila and von Otter as the girls. If one has a passing doubt about Mattila's sense of pitch, she consoles us with her warm, even tone. Von Otter bubbles with fun and her tone is fresh and firm. Van Dam is a keen-voiced and wily Alfonso, Szmytka a vivid Despina. All enter willingly into the high spirits and the sentiments of Mozart's flawless, ever-fascinating opera, and together make up a splendid ensemble.

NEW REVIEW

Mozart. APOLLO ET HYACINTHUS. **Christian Günther** (alto) Apollo; **Sébastien Pratschke** (treb) Hyacinthus; **Markus Schäfer** (ten) Oebalus; **Christian Fliegner** (treb) Melia; **Philippe Cieslewicz** (alto) Zephyrus; **Christian Immler** (bass) Priest of Apollo; **Nice Baroque Ensemble/ Gerhard Schmidt-Gaden.** Pavane Prestige ADW7236/7. Notes, text and translation included.

(2) 1h 21'   DDD   11/91

Mozart. APOLLO ET HYACINTHUS — COMPLETE EDITION, Volume 26.
Cornelia Wulkopf (mez) Apollo; **Edith Mathis** (sop) Hyacinthus; **Anthony Rolfe Johnson** (ten) Oebalus; **Arleen Auger** (sop) Melia; **Hanna Schwarz** (mez) Zephyrus; **Salzburg Chamber Choir; Salzburg Mozarteum Orchestra/Leopold Hager.** Philips Mozart Edition 422 526-2PME2. Notes, text and translation included. From DG 2707 129 (3/82).

(2) 1h 22'   AAD   11/91

Mozart was 11 when this first of his stage works had its première at Salzburg University. It is a 'comedy intermezzo' lasting around 80 minutes, to a text written by a Benedictine monk and teacher called Dom Rufinus Widl, which modifies a Greek legend into an improving tale, not least because the original singers were choirboys. It is far from dull, for it shows a born operatic composer discovering himself and his excitement comes across. But choosing between these two versions of it means considering roundabouts and swings. Neither gets it on to a single disc, and while the Pavane set is at full price it is also fully digital, whereas the Philips recording dating from 1981 is not, though the sound is good. But the chief point at issue is whether you want experienced artists with cultivated voices or something nearer vocal authenticity. Philips have fine soloists in Arleen Auger, Edith Mathis and Anthony Rolfe Johnson, but they are in some ways upstaged by the Pavane Prestige issue in which four principal roles are played by boys, aged 12 and 13, of the Bad Tölz Choir. Neither Cornelia Wulkopf nor Hanna Schwarz, playing Apollo and Zephyrus for Philips, sound masculine, and nor are they very dissimilar; in both these respects the alto and treble on the other recording are more satisfying. Above all, we must remember that the boy Mozart was writing for boys' voices and accept Pavane Prestige's claim that this is the recording première of the original version. Those seeking fine singing above all may go to Philips, but for an extra freshness you can choose Pavane Prestige — where the death of the boy Hyacinthus is all the more moving for being sweetly sung by the treble Sébastien Pratschke. Their recording has a small-sounding but effective orchestra and a pleasing acoustic and balance. It also has more tracks than the Philips issue, making access to the various numbers that much easier.

NEW REVIEW

Mozart. COMPLETE EDITION — LA FINTA SEMPLICE. **Barbara Hendricks** (sop) Rosina; **Siegfried Lorenz** (bar) Don Cassandro; **Douglas Johnson** (sngr) Don Polidoro; **Ann Murray (mez)** Giacinta; **Eva Lind** (sop) Ninetta; **Hans-Peter Blochwitz** (ten) Fracasso; **Andreas Schmidt** (bar) Simone; **C.P.E. Bach Chamber Orchestra/Peter Schreier.** Philips Mozart Edition 422 528-2PME2. Notes, text and translation included.

(2) 2h 27'   DDD   11/91

The "finta semplice" or "feigned simpleton" is a clever woman who, so as to smooth the path of the young lovers, hoodwinks the objectionable people who stand in their way. These are two brothers, one a bully, the other a nitwit, and they provide the main touch of originality in a story that could be considered both silly and heartless (despite deriving from a comedy by Goldoni). The point in its favour is that it provides good situations for musical numbers, including the kind of sustained finale which was to be a special feature of Mozart's mature masterpieces. Not that there is anything notably immature about the finales of Acts 1 and 2 in the work of the 12-year-old on exhibition here. It was his first *opera buffa*, written in 1768, a massive achievement in terms of length alone, yet eventually put aside without performance. This is not its first recording, but it does in almost every respect improve on its predecessor, not least in shortening the recitatives and reducing the number of discs from three to two. The quartet of lovers are fresh-voiced and sprightly, and the title-role is well sung by Barbara Hendricks. Siegfried Lorenz hardly succeeds in turning the bully-brother into a genuine comic character, but Douglas Johnson is good as the nincompoop and sings well when he has the chance. Peter Schreier encourages a lively sense of rhythm and attention to detail in his players. The recorded sound is clear and well balanced. But above all else is the miracle of composition. Not simply the degree of technical mastery but the depth of feeling attained by the 12-year-old genius, working in a comic genre too, becomes more astounding every time one listens.

Mozart. IDOMENEO. **Anthony Rolfe Johnson** (ten) Idomeneo; **Anne Sofie von Otter** (mez) Idamante; **Sylvia McNair** (sop) Ilia; **Hillevi Martinpelto** (sop) Elettra; **Nigel Robson** (ten) Arbace; **Glenn Winslade** (ten) High Priest; **Cornelius Hauptmann** (bass) Oracle; **Monteverdi Choir; English Baroque Soloists/John Eliot Gardiner.** Archiv Produktion 431 674-2AH3. Notes, text and translation included. Recorded at performances in the Queen Elizabeth Hall, London on June 8th, 11th and 19th, 1990.

③ 3h 31' DDD 6/91

This is unquestionably the most vital and authentic account of the opera to date on disc. We have here what was given at the work's first performance in Munich plus, in appendices, what Mozart wanted, or was forced, to cut before that première and the alternative versions of certain passages, so that various combinations of the piece can be programmed by the listener. Gardiner's direct, dramatic conducting catches ideally the agony of Idomeneo's terrible predicament — forced to sacrifice his son because of an unwise row. This torment of the soul is also entirely conveyed by Anthony Rolfe Johnson in the title role to which Anne Sofie von Otter's moving Idamante is an apt foil. Sylvia McNair is a diaphanous, pure-voiced Ilia, Hillevi Martinpelto a properly fiery, sharp-edged Elettra. With dedicated support from his own choir and orchestra, who have obviously benefited from a long period of preparation, Gardiner matches the stature of this noble *opera seria*. The recording catches the excitement which all who heard the live performances will recall.

NEW REVIEW

Mozart. DIE ENTFUHRUNG AUS DEM SERAIL. **Lynne Dawson** (sop) Konstanze; **Marianne Hirsti** (sop) Blonde; **Uwe Heilmann** (ten) Belmonte; **Wilfrid Gahmlich** (ten) Pedrillo; **Gunther von Kannen** (bass) Osmin; **Wolfgang Hinze** (spkr) Bassa Selim; **Academy of Ancient Music Chorus and Orchestra/Christopher Hogwood.** L'Oiseau-Lyre 430 339-2OH2. Notes, text and translation included.

② 2h 24' DDD 11/91

This is the first recording of Mozart's delectable harem *Singspiel* to use period instruments, and very persuasive it is too. Hogwood's direction is fresh and unfussy, high on comic energy but always allowing his cast ample room for manoeuvre. If the string sound is sparer and dustier than with some other period groups, Mozart's wonderful, sometimes exotic scoring for wind in this opera has never been more tellingly realized, from the piping, piercing piccolo in the overture and the 'Turkish' numbers to the rasping brass in the Act One finale and the dark, nutty basset-horns in Konstanze's sorrowful *Traurigkeit*. Hogwood uses a fortepiano continuo, following the composer's own practice; and his musical text is absolutely complete, restoring the optional cuts Mozart made in several arias, and including for good measure a little march in Act One that has only recently come to light. Though other recordings have fielded starrier casts, Hogwood's singers are aptly and appealingly youthful, and characterize their roles with flair. Pride of place goes to Uwe Heilmann's elegant, ardent Belmonte, a Mozartian of real distinction, with plenty of sap in the voice and a honeyed *mezza voce*. His Konstanze is Lynne Dawson, less grand and impassioned than some exponents of the role but singing with grace, warmth and all the agility Mozart demands; and she and Heilmann bring a rare poignancy to their final duet. Marianne Hirsti makes a delicious, quick-witted Blonde, Wilfrid Gahmlich a likeable Pedrillo, though his intonation falters in the romance, "Im Mohrenland". And though others have brought a juicier, more rotund bass to the plum role of Osmin, Gunther von Kannen has ample weight for Mozart's subterranean writing, articulates vividly and relishes the gleeful malice of "Ach, wie will ich triumphieren". The dialogue is delivered naturally by the singers themselves (many other recordings bus in actors for this, thereby causing a frequent sense of culture shock), while Wolfgang Hinze brings nobility and some pathos to the spoken role of the Bassa Selim. Altogether a fetching, colourful and involving reading of this most lovable of Mozart's operas, captured in a clear, crisp, if slightly dry, recording.

NEW REVIEW

Mozart. LA CLEMENZA DI TITO. **Anthony Rolfe Johnson** (ten) Tito; **Julia Varady** (sop) Vitellia; **Anne Sofie von Otter** (mez) Sesto; **Catherine Robbin** (mez) Annio; **Sylvia McNair** (sop) Servilia; **Cornelius Hauptmann** (bass) Publio; **Monteverdi Choir; English Baroque Soloists/John Eliot Gardiner.** Archiv Produktion 431 806-2AH2. Notes, text and translation included. Recorded at performances in the Queen Elizabeth Hall, London in June 1991.

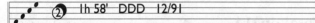 ② 1h 58' DDD 12/91

This matches the twin recording of the *Gramophone* award-winning *Idomeneo* as an almost ideal interpretation of *opera seria*. There is nothing marmoreal or static about Gardiner's reading which suggests a taut and vivid drama unfolding before the listener, enhanced by a sense of an occasion and of an ensemble dedicated to the work in hand. Tempos are keenly judged and related unerringly to each other. The playing of the period instruments is disciplined, phrasing keen and well pointed. Rolfe Johnson makes a convincingly sensitive, clement Emperor who dispatches his runs with imperial finesse. Beside him, von Otter is superb in her taxing arias, using her runs to expressive purpose. Their rapport is heartening. Varady makes a bitingly vengeful and jealous Vitellia, also sensual and eventually remorseful. Sylvia McNair is a sweetvoiced, slightly bland Servilia, Catherine Robbin a stylistically and vocally secure Annio. The recitatives (by Süssmayr) are substantially cut, probably an advantage in a recording.

Anthony Rolfe Johnson   [photo: DG/Holt

Mozart. DIE ZAUBERFLOTE. **Ruth Ziesak** (sop) Pamina; **Sumi Jo** (sop)
Queen of Night; **Uwe Heilmann** (ten) Tamino; **Michael Kraus** (bar)
Papageno; **Kurt Moll** (bass) Sarastro; **Andreas Schmidt** (bar) Speaker; **Heinz
Zednik** (ten) Monostatos; **Lotte Leitner** (sop) Papagena; **Adrianne Pieczo-
nka** (sop), **Annette Kuettenbaum, Jard van Nes** (mezs) First, Second and
Third Ladies; **Max Emanuel Cencic, Michael Rausch, Markus Leitner**
(trebs) First, Second and Third Boys; **Wolfgang Schmidt** (ten), **Hans
Franzen** (bass) Two Armed Men; **Clemens Bieber** (ten), **Hans Joachim
Porcher** (bar) Two Priests; **Vienna Boys' Choir; Vienna State Opera
Concert Choir; Vienna Philharmonic Orchestra/Sir Georg Solti.** Decca
433 210-2DH2. Notes, text and translations included.

② 2h 32' DDD 10/91 P Ⓑ

Sir Georg Solti's *Flute* is a lively enticement, with the promise of fun and
adventure. He showed this very well in his first recording, in 1969, but the new
version has still more spring in its step, and probably a better cast of singers too.
The high and low of it, Sumi Jo as the Queen of Night, Kurt Moll as Sarastro,
have spirit to match Solti's as well as the vocal and technical qualities necessary
for the mastery of their daunting roles. Ruth Ziesak, the Pamina, may not suit all
tastes (hers is a brighter voice than generally heard), but beauty and intelligence
distinguish much of her singing, and the Tamino (Uwe Heilmann) and Papagena
(Michael Kraus) are excellent. If Andreas Schmidt makes a somewhat youthful-
sounding Speaker of the Temple, that is in keeping with the performance as a
whole, where the spirit of youth prevails: in the players, the ever-youthful
veteran conductor, and indeed in Sarastro himself, whose exposition of the 'holy
halls' is less the usual solemn recitation than a genial and sensible provider of
useful information.

Moritz Moszkowski

Polish 1854-1925

Moszkowski. Piano Concerto in E major, Op. 59.
Paderewski. Piano Concerto in A minor, Op. 17. **Piers Lane** (pf); **BBC
Scottish Symphony Orchestra/Jerzy Maksymiuk.** Hyperion CDA66452.

1h 12' DDD 2/92 ❓

How the music-loving public suffer at the hands and whims of the musical
literati. Twenty years ago the concertos on this disc were enjoying something of
a revival thanks to the sterling efforts of such pianists as Earl Wild and Michael
Ponti and enterprising record companies like Vox, Candide and Genesis. Then
came the 1980s when once again such works found themselves very much out of
favour. However, with the launch of a new series from Hyperion entitled "The
Romantic Piano Concerto" we now seem set to enjoy an exciting new revival.
These concertos may not be masterpieces in the accepted sense (though they're
certainly masterpieces of their genre) but do all pieces of music have to be earth-
shatteringly great to be appreciated? Listening to these wonderfully exhilarating
and tuneful works the answer has to be a resounding no! Both the Moszkowski
and Paderewski concertos take the listener back to a time when pianist-composers
weren't afraid of wearing their hearts on their sleeves, but let no one try to convince you that these are empty vessels. The slow movements of both are beautifully
constructed and contain some of the most gorgeous melodies to be encountered
anywhere and the outer movements are full of sunny optimism and brilliance. To
add icing to an already very tasty cake Piers Lane gives performances of exceptional poetry and virtuosity and the recording is first class. Strongly recommended.

John Mundy Refer to Index British c.1555-1630

Modest Mussorgsky Russian 1839-1881

Mussorgsky. Pictures at an Exhibition (orch. Ravel). A night on the Bare Mountain (arr. Rimsky-Korsakov). **Cleveland Orchestra/Lorin Maazel.** Telarc CD80042. From 10042 (3/80).

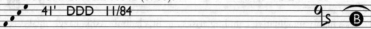

Mussorgsky. Pictures at an Exhibition (orch. Ravel). A night on the Bare Mountain (arr. Rimsky-Korsakov).
Ravel. Valses nobles et sentimentales. **New York Philharmonic Orchestra/ Giuseppe Sinopoli.** DG 429 785-2GH.

It would be unthinkable for any collection of outstanding CDs to omit the Telarc disc, one of the first and still one of the most spectacular demonstrations of how first-rate recording can enhance the realism of a big nineteenth-century orchestra. The closing climax of "The Great Gate of Kiev", at the end of Mussorgsky's *Pictures*, has an amplitude and impact of the kind to send a tingle of excitement to the nape of the listener's neck: the splendidly sonorous Cleveland brass produce an effect that is quite riveting. This is not to minimize the contribution of the orchestra itself, which play superbly throughout, for Maazel's reading is strongly characterized, from the chattering children in "Tuileries" to the sinister "Catacombs" sequence, with the trombones again featured arrestingly. The acoustic is admirably suited to this music, allowing the *fortissimos* to expand gloriously and providing a glowing warmth to the gentler moments. Just one grumble: as this was an early CD the separate 'pictures' are not cued.

Sinopoli's recording of *Pictures at an Exhibition* has great panache and is full of subtle detail and sharply characterized performances. Of course none of this would be possible without the marvellous virtuosity of the New York Philharmonic, whose brass section play with a wonderful larger-than-life sonority (just what's needed in this colourful extravaganza) and whose woodwind section produce playing of considerable delicacy and finesse, as for example in "Tuileries" and the "Ballet of the Unhatched Chicks". Sinopoli clearly revels in the drama of this work and this is nowhere more noticeable than in his sinister readings of "Catacombs" and "Baba-Yaga". *A night on the Bare Mountain* is no less impressive, where again the flair and dazzling virtuosity of the NYPO have an almost overwhelming impact. Less successful are Ravel's *Valses nobles et sentimentales* which are perhaps a little too idiosyncratic for an individual recommendation despite some superb performances and moments of great beauty. The sound is beautifully balanced and engineered.

Mussorgsky. Pictures at an Exhibition — original piano version[a].
Mussorgsky (orch. Ashkenazy). Pictures at an Exhibition[b]. [b]**Philharmonia Orchestra/Vladimir Ashkenazy** ([a]pf). Decca 414 386-2DH. Item marked [a] from SXDL7624 (4/83), [b] 410 121-1DH (11/83).

Mussorgsky. Pictures at an Exhibition — original piano version.
Tchaikovsky (arr. Pletnev). The Sleeping Beauty, Op. 66   excerpts.
Mikhail Pletnev (pf). Virgin Classics VC7 91169-2.
The Sleeping Beauty — Introduction; Danse des pages; Vision d'Aurore;

Andante; La feéargent; Le chat botté et la chatte blanche; Gavotte; Le canari qui chante; Chaperon rouge et la loup; Adagio; Finale.

1h 4' DDD 4/91

NEW REVIEW

Mussorgsky. Pictures at an Exhibition — original piano version.
Stravinsky. Three movements from "Petrushka".
Tchaikovsky. Dumka: Russian rustic scene in C minor, Op. 59. **Yefim Bronfman** (pf). Sony Classical CD46481.

56' DDD 1/92

Decca's highly imaginative coupling arises out of Vladimir Ashkenazy's dual career as a pianist and conductor. In fact he appears here in yet another role, that of transcriber for orchestra; for as he tells us revealingly in his informative notes, he always thinks in orchestral colours when he plays the piano, and now his imagination has allowed him to realize those colours in orchestral terms as well, and with success, drawing sharper lines than Ravel in his famous transcription. It is worth saying too that he has been able to correct "a number of textual errors" in Ravel's score that occurred because they were in the only piano copy available to the French composer. There's tremendous personality in Ashkenazy's piano playing, although some listeners may find the almost metallic intensity of his sound as here recorded a bit overwhelming at times, in the opening of the *Pictures*, the heavy ox-wagon tread of "Bydlo", "The Market at Limoges" and "Baba-Yaga". A tiny point which should make musicologists think is that tempos are mostly slower in the orchestral version although the same artist is in charge — entirely convincingly, but one wonders why. Certainly this is great Russian music performed by a great Russian artist, and the recordings which were both made in London's Kingsway Hall in 1982 are very fine.

  Mikhail Pletnev brings a strong personality to whatever he does, and his *Pictures* are no exception, with subtlety and intensity in such quieter pieces as "The Old Castle" and a tremendous urgency and sense of space in the really big numbers like "Baba-Yaga" and of course the monumental final "Great Gate of Kiev". In both these latter pieces, and most obviously the "Gate", the pianist adds some notes of his own which sound musically convincing; although purists with an eye on Mussorgsky's score will shake their heads and say that he has gone over the top, others will forgive him for being, as it seems, simply carried away by the sheer dynamic sweep of performance. Pletnev's mastery of atmosphere is also well illustrated by the conversation of the two Jews, Goldenberg and Schmuyle, and his evocation of the black "Catacombs". All this is enhanced by a wonderfully vivid recording. The Tchaikovsky ballet transcriptions made by Pletnev himself are much more than a fill-up. They are splendidly conceived in piano terms and his playing here is so stylish as to be in a class quite of its own.

  Pictures has so many facets that no one performance can reveal them all and there is always room for another of the quality of the one by Yefim Bronfman. Like so many pianists from the former Soviet

| *Yefim Bronfman*   [photo: Feingold

Union, he cares deeply about this music, such a cornerstone of the Russian piano repertory, and worked from a facsimile of Mussorgsky's manuscript when preparing this recording. He doesn't add a single note to it either, unlike one or two of his contemporaries, saying "I think it is such a work of genius just as it is — it really wasn't necessary", and the performance proves his point. He takes a broad view of the work, less forceful than that of his compatriot Vladimir Ashkenazy, but that enables its leisurely, intense passages (as in "The Old Castle" and some of the "Promenades") to make a better contrast with the more virtuoso ones such as "Baba-Yaga". This is a distinguished performance, with the aristocratic roughly primitive elements of the score kept in a fine balance and a final "Great Gate of Kiev" that is majestic rather than merely noisy. Another great attraction on the Sony Classical issue is the other music offered. Bronfman thinks Stravinsky's *Three Movements from Petrushka* "the most difficult piece written for the piano" — and this remark comes from someone who has recorded Rachmaninov's Third Concerto! The layout for the hands is consistently awkward, quite apart from the difficulty of matching up to the orchestral colours implicit in the score. But he gives a tremendous performance, full of colour and excitement. The Tchaikovsky *Dumka* is not often played, but it is profoundly Russian in feeling and Bronfman does it full justice. His playing in these great Russian works is matched throughout by rich and spacious sound.

Mussorgsky. SONGS. **Boris Christoff** (bass); [a]**Alexandre Labinsky,** [b]**Gerald Moore** (pfs); **French Radio National Orchestra/**[a]**Georges Tzipine.** EMI Références mono CHS7 63025-2. [a] from ALP1652/5 (1/59), [b] DB21383 (2/52). Notes, texts and translations included.
Sadly rustled the leaves; Where art thou, little star; Hour of Jollity; Tell me why; I have many palaces and gardens; What are words of love to you?; King Saul; Old man's song; But if I could meet thee again; Wild wind blows; Night; Kalistratushka; Salammbô — Balearic Song; Prayer; Outcast; Lullaby; Dear one, why are thine eyes?; From my tears; Gopak; Darling Savishna; Seminarist; Hebrew Song; Magpie; Gathering mushrooms; Feast; Ragamuffin; He-Goat; Garden by the Don; Classicist; Orphan; Child's song; Nursery; Eremushka's lullaby; Peepshow; Evening song; Forgotten; Sunless; Songs and Dances of Death; Epitaph; Sphinx; Not like thunder; Softly the spirit flew; Is spinning man's work; It scatters and breaks; Vision; Pride; Wanderer; On the Dnieper; Song of the flea.

〰 ③ 3h 11' ADD 8/89 ⸬ £ ♭ P Ⓑ ▲

This set is undoubtedly one of the all-time glories. Unavailable on LP for many years, its welcome reappearance on CD should make it a 'must' for any worthwhile collection on account of both its content and execution. Listening through the set without interruption gives one a wonderful idea of the range and variety of Mussorgsky's writing and leaves one amazed at the virtuosity of Christoff's singing. This is unquestionably the famous bass's most importance legacy to music simply because one cannot imagine another singer attempting so many of these songs so successfully. The composer's range of characterization is veritably Dostoyevskian. Even on the first disc, in the earlier and slightly less remarkable songs, he offers a range of personalities and emotions until then unexplored in Russian song. In their interpretation, Christoff brings before us a whole cast of characters portrayed with an amazing palette of sound-colours, everything from the utterly ferocious to the gentlest whisper. The second disc brings many of the better-known songs, all arrestingly interpreted, and the *Nursery* cycle, in which Christoff manages to adapt his dark tone miraculously to a convincing impersonation of a small boy. On the final disc, we hear predictably penetrating performances of the other two cycles. Christoff catches the bleak gloom of *Sunless* and the histrionic force of *Songs and Dances of Death* (though unfortunately a corrupt orchestration is used), some lesser songs and finally a

rollicking *Song of the Flea*. Labinsky is a vivid, imaginative pianist. All in all, a set
to treasure.

NEW REVIEW

Mussorgsky. KHOVANSHCHINA. **Aage Haugland** (bass) Ivan Khovansky;
Vladimir Atlantov (ten) Andrey Khovansky; **Vladimir Popov** (ten) Golitsin;
Anatolij Kotscherga (bar) Shaklovity; **Paata Burchuladze** (bass) Dosifey;
Marjana Lipovšek (contr) Marfa; **Brigitte Poschner-Klebel** (sop) Susanna;
Heinz Zednik (ten) Scribe; **Joanna Borowska** (sop) Emma; **Wilfried
Gahmlich** (ten) Kouzka; **Vienna Boys' Choir; Slovak Philharmonic
Choir; Vienna State Opera Chorus and Orchestra/Claudio Abbado.**
DG 429 758-2GH3. Recorded at performances in the Vienna State Opera during
September 1989. Notes, text and translation included.

③ 2h 51' DDD 11/90

The booklet essay with this issue suggests that, like Dostoevsky's novels,
Mussorgsky's music constantly poses a question to his Russian compatriots: "What
are the causes of our country's continuing calamities, and why does the state
crush all that is good?". Anyone who follows today's news from Russia and then
experiences this opera will understand what is meant, and while we observe with
sympathy we seem no nearer than the citizens of that great, tormented country
to finding solutions for its endemic problems. However, Mussorgsky was not the
least of those Russian musicians who found lasting beauty in her history and he
expressed it in a powerfully dramatic idiom that drew on folk-music and had
both epic qualities and deep humanity as well as an occasional gentleness. There
is also an element here of Russian church music, since *Khovanshchina* has a
political and religious theme and is set in the 1680s at the time of Peter the
Great's accession. Since the work was unfinished when Mussorgsky died,
performances always involve conjectural work, and the version here — which
works convincingly — is mostly that of Shostakovich with the choral ending that
Stravinsky devised using Mussorgsky's music. The cast in this live recording is
not one of star opera singers, but they are fully inside the drama and the music,
as is the chorus and the orchestra under Abbado, and the result is deeply and
compellingly atmospheric. The booklet has the Russian text and a translation as
well as informative essays on the music.

Mussorgsky. BORIS GODUNOV. **Alexander Vedernikov** (bass) Boris
Godunov; **Vladislav Piavko** (ten) False Dmitri; **Irina Arkhipova** (mez)
Marina; **Vladimir Matorin** (bass) Pimen; **Artur Eizen** (bass) Varlaam; **Andrei
Sokolov** (ten) Prince Shuisky; **Anatoli Mishutin** (ten) Missail; **Yuri
Mazurok** (bar) Rangoni; **Glafira Koroleva** (mez) Feodor; **Elena
Shkolnikova** (sop) Xenia; **Nina Grigorieva** (mez) Nurse; **Ludmila
Simonova** (mez) Hostess; **Janis Sporgis** (ten) Simpleton; **Alexander
Voroshilo** (bar) Shchelkalov; **Yuri Elnikov** (ten) Lavitsky, Khrushchov, Boyar;
Vladimir Silaev (bar) Chernikovsky; **Spring Studio Children's Chorus;
USSR TV and Radio Large Chorus and Symphony Orchestra/Vladimir
Fedoseyev.** Philips 412 281-2PH3. Notes, text and translation included. From
412 281-1PH4 (12/84).

③ 3h 18' ADD 3/85

Boris is often regarded as the quintessential Russian opera as it embodies in a
highly-charged dramatic scheme the best of Russian folk idioms and word setting.
After the composer's death, Rimsky-Korsakov extensively reworked the opera
and it is in various versions of his revised score that the work is best known
today. But although he did a great service in keeping the opera in the repertoire,
many would regard Mussorgsky's original version to be superior. To have an all-

Russian production for this opera has not always been of such benefit as one might expect, with the delight in watery vocal tone and wide vibrato sometimes obscuring the music's direction, but on this recording the overall dedication and empathy of the performers produces a vital and soul-searching interpretation that easily compensates for lack of the stage's visual drama. Much of the opera's success lies with the strength of the title-role and here Alexander Vedernikov scores with a psychologically penetrating account of the great Tsar's mental, spiritual, and physical decline. Fedoseyev conducts with complete understanding of the essence of each scene, and draws excellent singing and playing from the chorus and orchestra. Though the wide-spread recording sessions have not been fully integrated, the overall effect is appropriate to the sequence of events and in no way distracts from this moving production.

Josef Mysliveček
Bohemian 1737-1781

NEW REVIEW

Myslivecek. IL BELLEROFONTE. **Celina Lindsley** (sop) Bellerofonte; **Gladys Mayo** (sop) Argene; **Douglas Ahlstedt** (ten) Ariobate; **Raúl Giménez** (ten) Atamante; **Krisztina Laki** (sop) Briseide; **Stefan Margita** (ten) Diomede; **Czech Philharmonic Chorus; Prague Chamber Orchestra/Zoltán Peskó.** Supraphon 11 0006-2. Notes, text and translation included.

③ 2h 52' DDD 3/92

Though the Bohemian-born Mysliveček is now all but forgotten outside his native land, he was one of the most renowned *opera seria* composers of his day. Affectionately dubbed *Il Boemo* in Italy, where he spent much of his creative life, he was one of the few contemporary composers to earn the wholehearted admiration of Mozart — though whether Wolfgang was influenced by Czech folk elements in Mysliveček's music, as the booklet claims, is highly dubious. *Il Bellerofonte*, first performed in Naples in 1767 to celebrate the birthday of King Carlos III of Spain, was the third of his 27 operas, and its brilliant success made his reputation in Italy and beyond. Of the ancient myth of Bellerophon little remains, apart from the hero's slaying of a local monster with a partiality for noble maidens. Instead we have a familiar series of *opera seria* situations, involving intrigue, treachery and thwarted love and culminating in a happy-ever-after ending achieved against improbable odds. Neither Mysliveček's invention nor his dramatic pacing is consistently compelling, with overlong tracts of recitative (not helped by their often deliberate, foursquare treatment here) and, in Act One, too many arias in similar mood and tempo. But he frequently adapts the conventional *de capo* aria form to telling effect, and many of the numbers reveal a fluent, confident technique and a distinctive melodic gift. These include the expressive extended duet that closes Act One, a passionate C minor aria for Diomede and a sensuous slow aria, coloured by flutes and high horns, for the heroine, Argene, who later has a spectacular coloratura number complete with horn obbligato. Delivery of the recitatives apart, this recording, made in Prague, makes a persuasive case for the opera. The orchestral playing under the Hungarian conductor, Zoltán Peskó, is spruce and alert, with springing rhythms and lucid textures; and the singers, while not uniformly distinguished, cope well with Mysliveček's often taxing coloratura demands, with specially fine contributions from Celina Lindsley in the formidable title role (originally written for castrato), Krisztina Laki as the Cretan princess Briseide and Douglas Ahlstedt in the principal tenor role of Ariobate whose creator, Anton Raaff, would later be Mozart's first Idomeneo. With clear natural recorded sound this is a set to be recommended to anyone with a taste for eighteenth-century operatic rarities.

Ernesto Nazareth *Refer to Index* *Brazilian 1863-1934*

Carl Nielsen *Danish 1865-1931*

Nielsen. Violin Concerto, FS61[a].
Sibelius. Violin Concerto in D minor, Op. 47[b]. **Cho-Liang Lin** (vn);
[a]**Swedish Radio Symphony Orchestra,** [b]**Philharmonia Orchestra/Esa-Pekka Salonen.** CBS Masterworks CD44548.

1h 9' DDD 1/89

Nielsen. Violin Concerto, FS61[a]. Flute Concerto, FS119[b]. Clarinet Concerto,
FS129[c]. [d]**Toke Lund Christiansen** (fl); **Niels Thomsen** (cl); [a]**Kim Sjøgren**
(vn); **Danish National Radio Symphony Orchestra/Michael
Schønwandt.** Chandos CHAN8894.

1h 20' DDD 4/91

Cho-Liang Lin   *[photo: Feingold]*

Oddly enough no one has previously recorded the two greatest Nordic violin concertos on one disc and the result on the CBS disc is a triumphant success. This is the best recording of the Sibelius Concerto to have appeared for more than a decade and probably the best ever of the Nielsen. Cho-Liang Lin brings an apparently effortless virtuosity to both concertos. He produces a wonderfully clean and silvery sonority and there is no lack of aristocratic finesse. Only half-a-dozen years separate the two concertos, yet they breathe a totally different air. Lin's perfect intonation and tonal purity excite admiration and throughout them both there is a strong sense of line from beginning to end. Esa-Pekka Salonen gets excellent playing from the Philharmonia Orchestra in the Sibelius and almost equally good results from the Swedish Radio Symphony Orchestra. This should take its place among the classic concerto recordings of the century.

Nielsen's six symphonies range over the best part of his creative life and have inevitably overshadowed his other work. The well-filled Chandos CD brings all three concertos together: the Violin Concerto comes from the period of the Third Symphony and the two wind concertos were written after the Sixth during the last years of his life. Nielsen planned to write five concertos, one for each member of the Copenhagen Wind Quintet. Kim Sjøgren may not command the purity of tone of Cho-Liang Lin but he has the inestimable advantage of totally idiomatic orchestral support: Michael Schønwandt has an instinctive feeling for this music — and this shows throughout the whole disc. The perspective between soloist and orchestra is well-judged (Sjøgren is never larger than life) and so is the internal balance. In the Flute Concerto, which veers from Gallic wit to moments of great poetic feeling, Toke Lund Christiansen is an excellent soloist. He has no want of brilliance or authority and his performance also has plenty of character. Niels Thomsen's account of the Clarinet Concerto is one of the very finest now before the public. If there is any music from another planet, this is it! There is no attempt to beautify the score nor to overstate it: every dynamic nuance and expressive marking is observed by both the soloist and conductor. Thomsen plays as if his very being is at stake and Michael Schønwandt secures playing of great imaginative intensity from the Danish Radio Orchestra.

Nielsen. Symphonies — No. 1 in G minor, FS16; No. 6, "Sinfonia semplice", FS116. **San Francisco Symphony Orchestra/Herbert Blomstedt.** Decca 425 607-2DH.

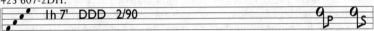

1h 7' DDD 2/90

Nielsen. Symphony No. 1 in G minor, FS16. Flute Concerto, FS119[a]. An imaginary trip to the Faroe Islands — rhapsody overture, FS123. [a]**Patrick Gallois** (fl); **Gothenburg Symphony Orchestra/Myung-Whun Chung.** BIS CD454.

1h 3' DDD 8/90

Nielsen always nurtured a special affection for his First Symphony — and rightly so, for its language is natural and unaffected. It has great spontaneity of feeling and a Dvořákian warmth and freshness. Blomstedt's recording is one of the best to have appeared for some years. It is vital, beautifully shaped and generally faithful to both the spirit and the letter of the score. The recording, too, is very fine: the sound has plenty of room to expand, there is a very good relationship between the various sections of the orchestra and a realistic perspective. Blomstedt gives a powerful account of the Sixth, too, with plenty of intensity and an appreciation of its extraordinary vision. It is by far the most challenging of the cycle and inhabits a very different world from early Nielsen. The intervening years had seen the cataclysmic events of the First World War and Nielsen himself was suffering increasingly from ill health. Blomstedt and the fine San Fransisco orchestra convey the powerful nervous tension of the first movement and the depth of the third, the *Proposta seria*. He is splendidly served by Decca's recording team.

Nielsen's symphonies cover the same period as those of Sibelius though the two composers developed very differently. The First Symphony (1892) bears the imprint of Brahms, Dvořák and Svendsen but Nielsen never disowned it — and rightly so. A young man's work written while he was still a member of the Royal Danish Orchestra, it remains wonderfully fresh and full of ardour. Myung-Whun Chung conducts as if he were born and bred in Denmark. There is a splendid sense of line, and he is always attentive to phrasing but never fussy or narcissistic. Throughout the piece he knows how to build up to a climax and keep detail in the right perspective. As always the Gothenburg Orchestra play with enthusiasm and spirit, and though they must have lived with this music all their lives, they play with the enthusiasm of first discovery. The rhapsody overture is not one of Nielsen's best works but the Flute Concerto most emphatically is. This performance is most strongly characterized by Patrick Gallois who plays with effortless virtuosity and an expressive eloquence that is never over or understated. His purity of line is quite striking, his dynamic range wide, the tone free from excessive vibrato and his approach fresh. Nielsen himself spoke of the conflict between the Arcadian solo instrument which "prefers pastoral atmospheres; the composer is therefore obliged to submit to its sweetness — if he does not wish to be branded as a barbarian", and Gallois splendidly conveys this spirit. The wonderful acoustic of the Gothenburg Hall is vividly captured and the engineering is first class.

Nielsen. Symphonies — No. 2, FS29, "The Four Temperaments"; No. 3, FS60, "Sinfonia espansiva"[a]. [a]**Nancy Wait Fromm** (sop); [a]**Kevin McMillan** (bar); **San Francisco Symphony Orchestra/Herbert Blomstedt.** Decca 430 280-2DH.

1h 7' DDD 8/90

This disc couples two of Nielsen's most genial symphonies, both of which come from the earliest part of the century, in performances of the very first order. The Second (1902), inspired by the portrayal of *The Four Temperaments* (Choleric, Phlegmatic, Melancholic, Sanguine) that he had seen in a country inn, has splendid concentration and fire and, as always, from the right pace stems the right character. Moreover the orchestra sounds as if it is fired at having encountered this music, for there is a genuine excitement about their playing. Indeed Blomstedt's accounts are by far the most satisfying to have appeared for some time. The Third *Espansiva*, is even more personal in utterance than *The Four Temperaments*, for during the intervening years Nielsen had come much further along the road of self-discovery. His melodic lines are bolder, the musical paragraphs longer and his handling of form more assured. It is a glorious and richly inventive score whose pastoral slow movement includes a part for two wordless voices. Blomstedt gives us an affirmative, powerful reading and in the slow movement, the soprano produces the required ethereal effect. The Decca sound is very detailed and full-bodied, and in the best traditions of the company. Blomstedt's *Espansiva* has greater depth than most rival accounts; the actual sound has that glowing radiance that characterizes Nielsen, and the tempo, the underlying current on which this music is borne, is expertly judged — and nowhere better than in the finale. Blomstedt is an experienced guide in this repertoire and this shows, while his orchestra play with refreshing enthusiasm.

Nielsen. Symphony No. 3, FS60, "Sinfonia espansiva"[a]. Clarinet Concerto, FS129[b]. MASKARADE — Overture. [a]**Pia Raanoja** (sop); [a]**Knut Skram** (bar); [b]**Olle Schill** (cl); **Gothenburg Symphony Orchestra/Myung-Whun Chung.** BIS CD321.

1h 8' DDD 8/86

This is vivid and idiosyncratic music. Here at times is not so much a sublimation of human thought and feeling as a deliberate voicing and portrayal of personal whims and traits, warts and all — as in the Clarinet Concerto. It will startle anyone hoping for an elegant flow of liquid melody but there is some fun and much skill on display. The *Maskarade* Overture is easier stuff: it belongs to a comic opera and sets the scene well enough, but is so brief at under five minutes that it sounds rather abrupt on its own. As for the Third Symphony it has much of the vigour and purpose that the title suggests. These performances are vivid and the recording is good.

Nielsen. Symphonies — No. 4, FS76, "Inextinguishable"; No. 5, FS97. **San Francisco Symphony Orchestra/Herbert Blomstedt.** Decca 421 524-2DH.

1h 12' DDD 10/88

This Decca recording presents two of Nielsen's most popular and deeply characteristic symphonies on one CD. Both are good performances that can hold their own with any in the present catalogue, and as recordings they are better. The Fourth Symphony occupied Nielsen between 1914 and early 1916 and reveals a level of violence new to his art. The landscape is harsher; the melodic lines soar in a more anguished and intense fashion (in the case of the remarkable slow movement, "like the eagle riding on the wind", to use the composer's own graphic simile). The title *Inextinguishable* tries to express in a single word what only the music alone has the power to fully express: "the element will to life". Blomstedt's opening has splendid fire: this must sound as if galaxies are forming; he is not frightened of letting things rip. The finale with its exhilarating dialogue between the two tympanists comes off splendidly. The Fifth Symphony of 1922 is impressive, too: it starts perfectly and has just the right glacial atmosphere. The climax and the desolate clarinet peroration into which it disolves are well handled. The recording balance could not be improved upon: the woodwind are decently recessed (though clarinet keys are audible at times), there is an almost ideal relationship between the various orchestra sections and a thoroughly realistic overall perspective. Blomstedt has a good rapport with his players who sound in excellent shape and respond to these scores to the manner born.

NEW REVIEW

Nielsen. CHAMBER MUSIC. [a]**Bergen Wind Quintet** (Gro Sandvik, fl[fgh], rec[i]; [c]Steinar Hannevold, ob; [be]Lars Kristian Holm Brynildsen, cl; [de]Vidar Olsen, hn; Per Hannevold, bn[e], rec[i]); [f]**Turid Kniejski** (hp); [h]**Lars Anders Tomter** (va); [e]**Sally Guenther** (vc); [e]**Torbjorn Eide** (db); [bcd]**Lief Ove Andsnes** (pf). BIS CD428.
Wind Quintet, FS100[a]. Fantasy Piece for clarinet and piano, FS3h[b]. Fantasy Pieces for oboe and piano, FS8[c]. Canto serioso for horn and piano, FS132[d]. Serenata in vano, FS68[e]. The Mother, FS94 — The fog is lifting[f]; The children are playing[g]; Faith and Hope are playing[h]. Allegretto for two recorders, FS157[i].

56' DDD 9/89

The Wind Quintet was one of the first works to spread Nielsen's fame outside Denmark on 78s in the classic account by its dedicatees, the Wind Quintet of the Royal Orchestra, Copenhagen whose Mozart playing had so delighted Nielsen in the early 1920s. Before the vogue for his music of the 1950s got under way, it remained Nielsen's visiting card in the record catalogues together with the Second Symphony. It is still generously represented in the catalogue but there are few versions of it that are so logically coupled as this BIS account by the Bergen Wind Quintet or, for that matter, better recorded. The Norwegian players are all principals of the Bergin Philharmonic and are completely at home in this repertoire. Their collection also offers the remainder of Nielsen's chamber music for wind. There is a delightful account of the slight but charming *Serenata in vano* for clarinet, bassoon, horn, cello and double bass and the Op. 2 *Fantasy Pieces* as well as an earlier *Fantasy Piece* for clarinet and piano, written when he was 16 years old.

Nielsen. SAUL AND DAVID. **Aage Haugland** (bass) Saul; **Peter Lindroos** (ten) David; **Tina Kiberg** (sop) Mikal; **Kurt Westi** (ten) Jonathan; **Anne Gjevang** (contr) Witch of Endor; **Christian Christiansen** (bass) Samuel; **Jørgen Klint** (bass) Abner; **Danish National Radio Choir and Symphony Orchestra/Neeme Järvi.** Chandos CHAN8911/12. Notes, text and translation included.

② 2h 4' DDD 3/91

Although Scandinavia has produced a number of great dramatists and an abundance of world-famous singers, scarcely a handful of operas have reached the international repertoire. *Saul and David* is one of them. It comes from the period immediately preceding the Second Symphony and inhabits much the same world. Nielsen served in the Orchestra of the Royal Theatre for many years and became its conductor when Svendsen retired, and so knew the operatic reper- toire from the inside. Before he began work on Saul he wrote, "The plot must be the 'pole' that goes through a dramatic work; the plot is the trunk; words and sentences are fruits and leaves, but if the trunk is not strong and healthy, it is no use that the fruits look beautiful". His librettist, Einar Christiansen certainly provided a strong 'pole', and in this splendid Chandos version sung in the original Danish we are at last able to hear it as both author and composer intended. However intelligent and sensitive a translation may be, something valuable is lost when the original language is abandoned (as it is when Mussorgsky, Janáček or Debussy are sung in translation). It is on Saul that the opera really focuses: his is the classic tragedy of the downfall of a great man through some flaw of character and it is for him that Nielsen (and the splendid Aage Haugland) mobilizes our sympathy. Haugland's portrayal is thoroughly full-blooded and three-dimensional, and he builds up the character with impressive conviction. The remainder of the cast is also good and the Danish Radio Choir does justice to the powerful choral writing, some of it strongly polyphonic, which distinguishes the score. The action is borne along effortlessly on the essentially symphonic current of Nielsen's musical thought. What is, of course, so striking about this piece is the sheer quality and freshness of its invention, its unfailing sense of line and purpose! No attempt is made at stage production but thanks to the committed performers under Neeme Järvi, the music fully carries the drama on its flow. The conductor paces the work to admirable effect and the Chandos recording made in collaboration with the Danish Radio is well-balanced and vivid.

Otto Nicolai
German 1810-1849

NEW REVIEW

Nicolai. ORCHESTRAL WORKS. **Bamberg Symphony Orchestra/Karl Anton Rickenbacher.** Virgin Classics VC7 91079-2.
Overtures — Die lustigen Weiber von Windsor; Der Tempelritter; Die Heimkehr des Verbannten; Weihnachtsouvertüre (with chorus). Symphony in D major.

1h 12' DDD 3/90

Nicolai's overture *Die lustigen Weiber von Windsor* ("The Merry Wives of Windsor") has enchanted generations of music lovers, and this enterprising collection provides an overdue opportunity to discover to what extent that work was just a flash in the pan. Here we are offered overtures to two other operas, of which *Der Tempelritter* is based on Walter Scott's *Ivanhoe*. If neither is so fluently captivating as *The Merry Wives of Windsor*, both have memorable themes, original twists and gracious, cultured instrumental writing that at times vividly recalls the more familiar model. Perhaps the youthful *Weihnachtsouvertüre* ("Christmas Overture"), complete with chorus, is somewhat overblown; but the symphony proves well worth getting to know — a strongly melodic, vivacious work that recalls Berwald or Weber, as well as having highly individual ideas of its own. The slow movement is a delight, and there is some highly effective writing for horn in the finale, which parades earlier themes to considerable effect. Karl Anton Rickenbacher conducts the whole with an enthusiasm of joyous discovery that it is easy to share.

NEW REVIEW

Nicolai. DIE LUSTIGEN WEIBER VON WINDSOR. **Ruth-Margret Pütz** (sop) Mistress Ford; **Gisela Litz** (mez) Mistress Page; **Edith Mathis** (sop) Ann Page; **Gottlob Frick** (bass) Sir John Falstaff; **Ernst Gutstein** (bar) Ford; **Kieth Engen** (bass) Page; **Fritz Wunderlich** (ten) Fenton; **Friedrich Lenz** (ten) Slender; **Carl Hoppe** (bass) Dr Caius; **Bavarian State Opera Chorus; Bavarian State Orchestra/Robert Heger.** EMI CMS7 69348-2. Notes and text included. From EMI ASD580/81 (5/64).

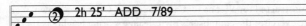

② 2h 25' ADD 7/89   £ 9 ₚ

Shakespeare's *The Merry Wives of Windsor* has survived on the operatic stage in Verdi's *Falstaff* setting; but there are those people (and not only Germans) who prefer Otto Nicolai's earlier setting. Almost everyone knows its overture — a sparkling, melodic piece of music that is obviously the product of a highly cultured musician. Yet the opera as a whole is every bit as delicious. It is quite simply one musical treat after another, and with this performance it is difficult to find fault. The men are uniformly superb, with Gottlob Frick a massive-voiced Falstaff, Fritz Wunderlich an ardent, god-like Fenton, and Ernst Gutstein, Kieth Engen, Friedrich Lenz and Carl Hoppe providing uniformly rich male support. Among the women, Ruth-Margret Pütz and Gisela Litz are sprightly-voiced, dependable and enjoyable, with the young Edith Mathis a sweet, confident and characterful Ann Page. The work fits conveniently on to two generously-filled CDs, and even after nearly 30 years the recording still comes up with sparkling clarity, offering a perfect balance between singers and orchestra.

Michael Nyman

British 1944-

Nyman. String Quartets — No. 1 (1985); No. 2 (1988); No. 3 (1990). **Balanescu Quartet** (Alexander Balanescu, Jonathan Carney, vns; Kate Musker, va; Anthony Hinnigan, vc). Argo 433 093-2ZH.

1h 3' DDD 8/91   ?

The liveliness of Michael Nyman's musical imagination here combines with the Balanescu Quartet's sparkling performance style to create one of the most enticing recitals of new chamber music released in recent years. Those who associate Nyman with pastiche, parody and wit will feel particularly at home with the First Quartet, which takes as its starting point a piece by the Elizabethan virginalist John Bull. A loose variation form binds together various acts of dismemberment and reassembly, some of them reverent, others emphatically not so. The Second Quartet, designed for dance and loosely inspired by Indian models of cyclic rhythm, is gritty where its predecessor is cheeky. In complete contrast, the Third Quartet models itself on Nyman's soundtrack for a BBC documentary on the 1988 Armenian earthquake; a solemn nobility here replaces the vivacity of the two partner pieces. Those who view Nyman as a lightweight or a mere joker need look no further than this piece to have their views put into disarray.

Jacques Offenbach

German/French 1819-1880

NEW REVIEW

Offenbach. ORCHESTRAL WORKS. **Philharmonia Orchestra/Antonio de Almeida.** Philips 422 057-2PH.
Le Voyage dans la lune — Overture and Snowflakes ballet. Die Rheinnixen — Overture. Monsieur et Madame Denis — Overture. Orphée aux enfers — Overture and Pastoral ballet. Le roi Carotte — Overture. Maître Péronilla — Overture.

59' DDD 10/88   ?

Most Offenbach orchestral collections offer his music in arrangements and scoring inflated for German orchestras. Not so here. Here everything is as the composer himself left it, so that the *Orpheus in the Underworld* overture, for instance, is not the familiar one constructed for Vienna by Carl Binder but Offenbach's own. Yet this is no academic exercise: the composer's own, leaner scoring heightens the native sparkle of the music, and even in unfamiliar titles the listener will recognize familiar melodies. The overture to *Le Voyage dans la lune*, for instance, contains the theme that, 23 years after Offenbach's death, was turned into "Scintille, diamant" in *The Tales of Hoffmann*, while the overture to *Die Rheinnixen* contains the very first appearance of the celebrated *Hoffmann* barcarolle. There is other music that will be familiar from Manuel Rosenthal's *Gaîté Parisienne* ballet score. Throughout, the music sparkles and delights, and Antonio de Almeida obtains from the Philharmonia Orchestra performances (complete with wind machine in the "Snowflakes Ballet" from *Le Voyage dans la lune*) that ooze enjoyment.

Offenbach. LA BELLE HELENE. **Jessye Norman** (sop) Hélène; **John Aler** (ten) Paris; **Charles Burles** (ten) Menelaus; **Gabriel Bacquier** (bar) Agamemnon; **Jean-Philippe Lafont** (bar) Calchas; **Colette Alliott-Lugaz** (mez) Orestes; **Jacques Loreau** (bar) Achilles; **Roger Trentin** (ten) Ajax I; **Gérard Desroches** (ten) Ajax II; **Nicole Carreras** (sop) Bacchis; **Adam Levallier** (spkr) Slave; **Toulouse Capitol Chorus and Orchestra/Michel Plasson.** EMI CDS7 47157-8. Notes, text and translation included. From EX270171-3 (12/85).

⊙ 1h 46' DDD 9/86

La Belle Hélène is Offenbach's satirical treatment of the story of Helen of Troy. Though others of his operettas may show individual aspects of his genius to greater effect, there is perhaps none that combines so well the charm, the sparkle, the melodic verve and the musical humour that are his musical trademarks. Despite having American singers in the two leading roles, this is nonetheless a very French version, and there is excellent support from a team of seasoned French performers. Plasson knows how to keep an Offenbach score tripping along, and such rousing ensemble numbers as the "March of the Kings" and the Act 2 finale help to make this a joyful and exciting experience.

Jessye Norman   *[photo: EMI/Philips*

NEW REVIEW

Offenbach. LA PERICHOLE. **Régine Crespin** (sop) La Périchole; **Alain Vanzo** (ten) Piquillo; **Jules Bastin** (bass) Don Andrès; **Gérard Friedmann** (ten) Miguel de Panatellas; **Jacques Trigeau** (bar) Don Pedro; **Aimé Besançon, Paul Guigue** (tens) First and Second Notaries; **Rebecca Roberts** (sop) Guadalena, Manuelita; **Eva Saurova** (sop) Berginella, Ninetta; **Geneviève Baudoz** (mez) Mastrilla, Frasquinella; **Ine Meister** (mez) Bramdilla; **Rhine Opera Chorus; Strasbourg Philharmonic Orchestra/Alain Lombard.** Erato Libretto 2292-45686-2. Notes, text and translation included. Recorded in 1976.

⊙ 1h 26' ADD 5/92

Of all Offenbach's operetta scores, *La Périchole* is perhaps the one that oozes the greatest charm. The satirical touch is there, to be sure, but the edge is less sharp. One detects a vein of genuine feeling for the fate of the Peruvian street-singer forced to marry a man she only later discovers is her own true love, that one never does with Eurydice, Helen, or the Grand-Duchess of Gerolstein. The splendid songs Offenbach composed for her (the "Letter Song", "Ah! quel dîner", "Ah! que les hommes sont bêtes" and "Je t'adore, brigand" head up a richly melodic score. Régine Crespin is a somewhat matronly Périchole, but she knows how to tease the best out of the textual and melodic phrases. Her Piquillo, Alain Vanzo, is the ideal Offenbach tenor, gliding lightly over the score, while Jules Bastin brings experience to the role of the Viceroy, if perhaps not quite capturing all its comic possibilities. Alain Lombard directs sympathetically. The absence of spoken dialogue to provide atmosphere is unfortunate, but Erato have generously provided a full libretto, which also includes a linking narration by Alain Decaux that featured in the original LP recording but has been edited out of the CD reissue. This is a fine opportunity to fall under the spell of this captivating score.

Offenbach. LES BRIGANDS. **Tibère Raffalli** (ten) Falsacappa; **Ghislaine Raphanel** (sop) Fiorella; **Colette Alliot-Lugaz** (sop) Fragoletto; **Michel Trempont** (bar) Pietro; **Christian Jean** (ten) Carmagnola; **Francis Dudziak** (ten) Domino; **Pierre-Yves le Maigat** (bass-ten) Barbavano; **Valérie Millot** (sop) Princess of Granada; **Michel Fockenoy** (ten) Adolphe de Valladolid, A page; **Jean-Luc Viala** (ten) Comte de Gloria-Cassis; **Thierry Dran** (ten) Duke of Mantua; **François le Roux** (bar) Baron de Campotasso; **Bernard Pisani** (ten) Antonio; **René Schirrer** (bar) Captain of the Carabinieri; **Jacques Loreau** (bar) Pipo; **Chorus and Orchestra of the Lyon Opéra / John Eliot Gardiner.** EMI CDS7 49830-2. Notes, text and translation included.

♪ ② 1h 45' DDD 2/90	♀

If *Les Brigands* does not count amongst the best-known of Offenbach's works, it has a consistently attractive score and some outstanding individual numbers. It also has one of the wittiest of the librettos supplied by the masters Meilhac and Halévy. The comment that "one should steal according to the position that one occupies in society" is as valid a comment on corruption today as it was in the final throes of Second Empire Paris. As for anyone interested in influences on Gilbert and Sullivan (specifically *The Pirates of Penzance*), they might note not only the comic carabinieri who always arrive too late to capture their prey but also the beautiful double chorus in Act Three. W.S. Gilbert in fact wrote an English version of the work, which was staged to considerable effect in London a few years back. The piece has generally remained much better known on the continent, though, and this recording is based upon a production at Lyon in 1988. It fully shows the benefits of stage preparation, with John Eliot Gardiner directing with an attractive lightness of touch, allowing Offenbach's scoring and tempo markings to whip up the excitement as required. Of the singers, the light tenor Tibère Raffalli leads the way admirably as the brigand chief, whilst Ghislaine Raphanel is no less attractively sweet-voiced as his daughter Fiorella. Bernard Pisani pulls off the treasurer's hilarious song with splendid aplomb, and there is also the usual fine bunch of supporting characters. The recording is clear and natural, with some excellent action effects to complete a splendid representation of a typical Offenbach *tour de force*.

Offenbach. LES CONTES D'HOFFMANN. **Plácido Domingo** (ten) Hoffmann; **Dame Joan Sutherland** (sop) Olympia, Giulietta, Antonia, Stella; **Gabriel Bacquier** (bar) Lindorf, Coppélius, Dapertutto, Dr Miracle; **Huguette Tourangeau** (mez) La Muse, Nicklausse; **Jacques Charon** (ten) Spalanzani; **Hugues Cuénod** (ten) Andres, Cochenille, Pitichinaccio, Frantz;

André Neury (bar) Schlemil; **Paul Plishka** (bass) Crespel; **Margarita Lilowa** (mez) Voice of Antonia's Mother; **Roland Jacques** (bar) Luther; **Lausanne Pro Arte Chorus; Du Brassus Chorus; Suisse Romande Chorus and Orchestra/Richard Bonynge.** Decca 417 363-2DH2. Notes, text and translation included. From SET545/7 (11/72).

② 2h 23' ADD 11/86

Offenbach died after finishing the piano score of *The Tales of Hoffmann* plus the orchestration of the First Act and a summary of the scoring of the rest, which was then completed by Ernest Guiraud. The work became an instant popular success, but not exactly as the composer conceived it. Bonynge's recording returns to Offenbach's original conception as far as seems practicable, but includes certain desirable extra numbers such as the inserted arias for Dapertutto and Coppélius — both of which would be sorely missed — and restores a fine missing quartet to climax the Epilogue. It is essential that the four main soprano roles are taken by one singer, here Dame Joan Sutherland in superb form, and the four faces of villainy (Lindorf, Coppélius, Dapertutto and Dr Miracle) must also be given to a single artist, here the magnificent Gabriel Bacquier. Plácido Domingo is outstanding as Hoffmann (and it is not easy to be convincing in a role that demands ingenuous amorous liaisons with first a clockwork doll, then a courtesan and finally an opera star, determined to sing herself to death). He sings with optimistic fervour throughout all his disappointments, while Huguette Tourangeau is most appealing as his companion and confidante, Nicklausse. Bonynge directs with splendid vitality and romantic feeling and finds the right lightness of touch for the doll scene. The whole performance goes with a swing and Decca's recording, vividly atmospheric, is fully worthy of it.

Carl Orff
German 1895-1982

Orff. Carmina burana. **Sheila Armstrong** (sop); **Gerald English** (ten); **Thomas Allen** (bar); **St Clement Danes Grammar School Boys' Choir; London Symphony Chorus and Orchestra/André Previn.** EMI CDC7 47411-2. Text and translation included. From ASD3117 (10/75).

1h 3' DDD 12/86

There are at least 20 digital recordings of Orff's flamboyant and inspired cantata, using Latin texts taken from a thirteenth-century manuscript, and it is a work that particularly benefits from the range and clarity of digital techniques. Never-theless, Previn's 1975 version sweeps the board. Not only has the performance a unique bite and exuberance, plus at times an infectious joy, but the three soloists are outstanding and the recording has been most effectively remastered to seem fresher than ever. For once all three soloists are splendid. If Thomas Allen especially catches the attention, the tenor, Gerald English, is excellent too and the soprano, Sheila Armstrong, is suitably ravishing in her love songs, with words explicitly conveying that they are about physical love-making. The boys, too, obviously relish the meaning of the lyrics, which they put over with much gusto. Indeed, this pantheistic celebration of life's earthy pleasures could hardly be more vividly projected: the recording is a triumph.

Ignacy Paderewski
Refer to Index
Polish 1860-1941

Niccolo Paganini

Paganini. Violin Concertos — No. 1 in D major, Op. 5; No. 2 in B minor, Op. 7, "La campanella". **Salvatore Accardo** (vn); **London Philharmonic Orchestra/Charles Dutoit.** DG 415 378-2GH. From 2740 121 (11/75).

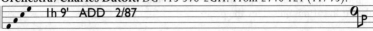

NEW REVIEW

Paganini. Violin Concerto No. 1 in D major, Op. 5[a].
Saint-Saëns. Violin Concerto No. 3 in B minor, Op. 61[b]. **Zino Francescatti** (vn); [a]**Philadelphia Orchestra/Eugene Ormandy;** [b]**New York Philharmonic Orchestra/Dimitri Mitropoulos.** CBS Masterworks Portrait mono CD46728. From Philips SBL5219 (4/58).

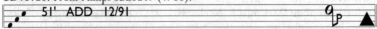

Paganini's violin music was at one time thought quite inaccessible to lesser mortals among the violin-playing fraternity, but as standards of technique have improved master technicians are now able to do justice to such works as these concertos. Salvatore Accardo is certainly among them, and we can judge his skill as early as the opening violin solo of the First Concerto. This is typical of the style, with its authoritative and rhetorical gestures and use of the whole instrumental compass, but so is the second theme which in its refinement and songlike nature demands (and here receives) another kind of virtuosity expressed through a command of tone, texture and articulation. Dutoit and the London Philharmonic Orchestra have a mainly subordinate role, certainly when the soloist is playing, but they fulfil it well and follow Accardo through the kind of rhythmic flexibilities which are accepted performing style in this music and which for all we know were used by the virtuoso performer-composer himself. The 1975 recording is faithful and does justice to the all-important soloist.

   Zino Francescatti's mid-price recording of the First Concerto on CBS dates from 1950 and stylistically comes from an earlier era. Technically immaculate, Francescatti's playing has a barnstorming approach closer to that of the great virtuosos of the first half of the century. Fully acknowledging the extrovert style of the concerto, he gives a reading full of high spirits, in which all of Paganini's numerous technical hurdles are faced and overcome with great musical relish. The Philadelphia Orchestra under Eugene Ormandy fully enter into the spirit of Francescatti's performance, and the recorded sound is remarkably clear for its age. The coupling, Saint-Saëns's Third Violin Concerto, was perhaps closer to home territory for Francescatti: his innately elegant French style of playing is here allowed full scope and the result is extremely attractive. With Dimitri Mitropoulos and the New York Philharmonic Orchestra providing a full-blooded accompaniment, the performance as a whole lifts this attractive concerto onto a higher plane than is usually encountered. Again the recorded sound is good for its age.

Paganini. 24 Caprices, Op. 1. **Itzhak Perlman** (vn). EMI CDC7 47171-2. From SLS832 (6/72).

This electrifying music with its dare-devil virtuosity has long remained the pinnacle of violin technique, and they encapsulate the essence of the composer's style. For a long time it was considered virtually unthinkable that a violinist should be able to play the complete set; even in recent years only a handful have produced truly successful results. Itzhak Perlman has one strength in this music that is all-important, other than a sovereign technique — he is incapable of playing with an ugly tone. He has such variety in his bowing that the timbre of the instrument is never monotonous. The notes of the music are despatched with a forthright confidence and fearless abandon that are ideal. The frequent double-stopping passages hold no fear for him. Listen to the fire of No. 5 in A minor and the way in which Perlman copes with the extremely difficult turns in No. 14 in E flat; this is a master at work. The set rounds off with the famous A minor Caprice, which inspired Liszt, Brahms and Rachmaninov, amongst others, to adapt it in various guises for the piano.

Giovanni Palestrina
Italian c.1525/6-1594

Palestrina. SACRED CHORAL WORKS. **Christ Church Cathedral Choir, Oxford/Stephen Darlington.** Nimbus NI5100. Texts and translations included. Missa Dum complerentur. *Motets* — Super flumina Babylonis; Exsultate Deo; Sicut cervus; O bone Jesu, exaudi me a 8; Dum complerentur a 6.

55' DDD 11/88

The full potential of this choir gradually unfolds as they sing through the movements of Palestrina's parody mass *Dum complerentur dies pentecostes* — one of the 22 masses the composer based on one of his own earlier motets. The choir's approach to the Pentecost mass is generally restrained and they find greater scope in the five motets, ending with a brilliant performance of *Dum complerentur* upon which the Mass is built. They clearly revel in its cascading descending phrases in all six voices, which they pour forth jubilantly. Darker, more sombre colours are displayed in *Super flumina Babylonis*, whilst rejoicing and exuberance characterize *Exsultate Deo*, with its crisp treble lead. Anyone coming fresh to this type of music will benefit by following the excellent notes.

Palestrina. SACRED CHORAL WORKS. **Westminster Cathedral Choir/James O'Donnell.** Hyperion CDA66316. Texts and translations included. *Masses* — Viri Galilaei; O Rex gloriae. *Motets* — Viri Galilaei; O Rex gloriae.

1h 8' DDD 1/90

This is music in which Westminster Cathedral Choir excel: their response to the richly reverberant acoustic is warm and generous; they perform with the ease and freedom of kinship — a far cry from the studied perfection of many other choirs. Each motet is heard before its reworking as a Mass. The six-part scoring of *Viri Galilaei* (two trebles, alto, two tenors and bass) invites a variety of

combinations and textures, culminating in the joyful cascading Alleluias at the end of Part I and the jubilant ascending series in Part II. In the Mass the mood changes from triumph to quiet pleading — a change partly due to revised scoring: the two alto parts beneath the single treble produce a more subdued sound. The Choir clearly relishes this exploration of the deeper sonorities: in the *Creed* one entire section is entrusted to the four lowest voices. The four-part motet *O Rex gloriae* is lithe and fast-moving. The corresponding Mass, largely syllabic in style, gives the Choir the chance to demonstrate their superb

James O'Donnell [photo: Hyperion

command of phrasing and accentuation: the Latin comes over with intelligibility and subtlety. Listen, also, to the wonderful solo boys' trio in the "Crucifixus", and for the carefully crafted canons in the *Benedictus* and the *Agnus Dei*.

Sir Andrzej Panufnik
Polish/British 1914-1991

NEW REVIEW

Panufnik. Sinfonia sacra[a]. Arbor cosmica[b]. [a]**Royal Concertgebouw Orchestra;** [b]**New York Chamber Symphony/Andrzej Panufnik.** Elektra-Nonesuch 7559-79228-2.

59' DDD 5/91

Panufnik's *Sinfonia sacra* of 1963 is a tribute to his native Poland. The work is cast in two movements, the first of which divides into "Three visions". Four trumpets provide an opening fanfare; then a contemplative atmosphere is provided in a section for strings alone. Finally the full orchestra combines to evoke a mood of agitation and war. The second movement is based on an old Polish hymn called the *Bogurodzica*. This work very much needs a virtuoso orchestra to make its full effect, and Panufnik, an experienced conductor who studied with Felix Weingartner, gets very disciplined, high quality playing from the Concertgebouw. *Arbor cosmica*, written in 1983 for string orchestra, reflects Panufnik's lifelong affinity with trees, and in 12 sections depicts contrasted moods and feelings experienced by the composer when in contact with the phenomenon of photosynthesis. Each section is brief, but each also clearly poses very difficult problems for the string players. The New York Orchestra rise to the occasion brilliantly. *Sinfonia sacra* enjoys a very clear, spacious 1987 recording; the other 1988 New York recording has an appropriately closer acoustic.

Hubert Parry
British 1848-1918

NEW REVIEW

Parry. Symphony No. 1 in G major. From Death to Life. **English Symphony Orchestra/William Boughton.** Nimbus NI5296.

1h 4' DDD 5/92

Parry wanted to write a symphony even in his student days, but he waited until the age of 32, when at last he felt sure of his technique, before tackling full symphonic form. The result was certainly a fully mature composition, constructed with much skill, and beautifully orchestrated. In manner the First Symphony is an urbane, civilized work, whose optimism perhaps reflected English upper-class confidence in 1880. The best movement is the second, an elegant, warmly expressive *Andante*. Elsewhere the Symphony's invention is pleasing to the ear without being very memorable. Thirty four years later the elderly Parry's world had changed for ever with the outbreak of world war. *From Death to Life*, cast in two connecting movements, moves from despair, "Via mortis", to a certain optimism, "Via vitae". Here Parry reaches greater depths than in the First Symphony. William Boughton conducts both works efficiently and very sympathetically, though sometimes they could benefit from a greater sense of urgency in performance. The orchestra sounds fairly small in numbers, but plays very well. The recording is somewhat over-reverberant, but the quality is otherwise very good.

Parry. Symphony No. 2 in F major, "Cambridge". Symphonic Variations (1897). **London Philharmonic Orchestra/Matthias Bamert.** Chandos CHAN8961.

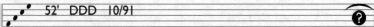

· 52' DDD 10/91

Matthias Bamert and the London Philharmonic score another important first here with these fine recordings of the *Cambridge* Symphony and the *Symphonic Variations* by Parry. Like its predecessors in the splendid Chandos/Parry series, this disc also offers some surprises, for its seems incredible that this music has remained virtually unknown for the best part of a century! The Second Symphony has no particular link with Cambridge, save for the fact that it received its première there in 1883. Bamert and the London Philharmonic offer a revelatory performance here in which the real qualities of the music are allowed to shine through any reverential backward glances at the works of Brahms, Dvořák and Schumann. Parry was enthusiastic, however, about Dvořák's *Symphonic Variations* and Brahms's *Haydn* Variations, and followed the example of both in his own set for orchestra. It is also fascinating to speculate about the impact made upon Parry by Wagner, whom he met in 1877, for much of the music here has a broad conception and often employs sumptuous orchestration with much emphasis upon grand gestures. The London Philharmonic are captured here on vibrant form and the Chandos sound is especially full-bodied and resonant. Matthias Bamert directs these performances with energy and vision and like his other Parry discs this deserves the strongest recommendation.

Parry. Symphonies — No. 3 in C major, "English"; No. 4 in E minor. **London Philharmonic Orchestra/Matthias Bamert.** Chandos CHAN8896.

· 1h 16' DDD 1/91

It has been encouraging to find the Swiss conductor, Matthias Bamert, championing Parry's music in the Chandos cycle of the symphonies and some choral works of which this was the first issue. He is clearly a convinced enthusiast and brings to the music a probing passion that eluded Boult in his last years when he recorded some Parry with the same orchestra. The discovery here is the Fourth Symphony, first performed (conducted by Hans Richter) in 1889, revised in 1910, performed twice in its new version and then forgotten for nearly 80 years. It is a deeply personal work, almost confessional in its repressed passion. The first movement (16 minutes) is on an immense scale, covering an emotional range comparable with Elgar's Second (which it preceded). The Third Symphony is more conventional, an English equivalent of Schumann's *Rhenish*. Its sunny exuberance and the lightness of the scoring make it highly attractive. Performance and recording are both admirable. Highly recommended.

Parry. Symphony No. 5 in B minor, "Symphonic Fantasia 1912". From Death to Life (1914). Elegy for Brahms (1897). **London Philharmonic Orchestra/ Matthias Bamert.** Chandos CHAN8955.

· 57' DDD 9/91

Parry's Fifth Symphony dates from 1912 and like so much of his output this substantial work reveals the composer's enduring devotion to the music of Brahms. However, Parry was fascinated by the idea of writing a programmatic symphony, in the Lisztian mould, and thus each of the four linked movements have titles which relate strongly to his personal ethical outlook. The finale, entitled "Now" culminates with an expansive review of material from earlier in the work, and here it is clearly a sense of confidence and affirmation, expressed in grandiose Edwardian musical rhetoric, which concludes Parry's symphonic cycle. The remaining movements, "Stress", "Love" and "Play" also serve to remind us of the clear romantic origins of this splendid and inexplicably neglected British symphony. Also included on this disc are two shorter, although no less weighty Parry rarities, and the Symphonic Poem *From Death to Life* shares much common ground with the Fifth Symphony, at least in terms of its general subject matter. The orchestral parts have been reconstructed only recently, and the work receives its first modern performance on this disc. Both the Symphony and the *Elegy for Brahms* were recorded by Sir Adrian Boult, a great champion of Parry's music, in 1978. By then Sir Adrian was nearing the end of a long career of course, and it was left to Matthias Bamert to take up the cause, which he has done with notable distinction. Bamert reveals the true fire and dignity which colours the music of this remarkable composer and the London Philharmonic respond with tremendous conviction and brilliance.

Parry (ed J. Dibble). Nonet in B flat major[a].
Stanford. Serenade (Nonet) in F major, Op. 95[b]. **Capricorn** ([b]Elizabeth Layton, [b]Iain King, vns; [b]Paul Silverthorne, va; [b]Timothy Mason, vc; [b]Judith Evans, db; [ab]Helen Keen, fl; [a]Christopher O'Neal, [a]Katie Clemmow, obs; [ab]Anthony Lamb, [a]Julian Farrell, cls; [ab]Gareth Newman, [a]Jean Owen, bns; [ab]Michael Baines, [a]Stephen Bell, hns). Hyperion CDA66291.

53' DDD 9/89

Those who are fond of the nonets by Spohr and Rheinberger might well like to try Stanford's Serenade, Op. 95, scored for an almost similar line-up of winds and strings. Like those two greater works, it inhabits a world of grace and melodic charm, only occasionally essaying more turbulent emotions. Written in 1905, the work was immediately admired both for its spontaneity and clean structural lines. Parry's Nonet for winds, composed in 1877, was more of a student work and owes allegiances to Brahms's Op. 16 Serenade, which Parry had studied in fine detail. Whilst it lacks the glorious tunefulness of Dvořák's D minor Serenade, completed in the following year, it is by no means without interest and has many moments of well-judged scoring, harmonic surprise, and melodic shapeliness. Capricorn give both Nonets the solidity of a dedicated performance, allowing the richness of resonance that comes from expert chording, and the subtlety of understated, yet well-turned phrasing, to draw the listener's attention towards the best qualities of the works. All is revealed in a typically first-class recording from Hyperion, that does not shout its quality but gets on with its job unobtrusively.

NEW REVIEW

Parry. Violin Sonata in D major (1889). 12 Short Pieces (1894). Fantasie-sonata in B minor (1878). **Erich Gruenberg** (vn); **Roger Vignoles** (pf). Hyperion CDA66157. From A66157 (11/85).

59' DDD 9/91 ❓

Hyperion originally released this collection of works by Parry for violin and piano in 1985. These sensitive and stimulating performances from Erich Gruenberg and Roger Vignoles now sound even finer in a superb CD transfer, which is notable for the excellent balance between the players and for the affectionate warmth of the sound. None of the music offered here has found its way into the repertoire, and yet much of it is of real quality. Gruenberg and Vignoles are especially committed in the Violin Sonata of 1889, and this work, like the single movement *Fantasie-sonata* of a decade earlier, demonstrate Parry's deep understanding of the form. Sadly, the latter work was withdrawn after its frosty initial reception, but like the D major sonata, this attractive work is thoughtfully played, and makes a welcome addition to this disc. The set of 12 short pieces make for refreshing and undemanding listening, each miniature recalling a different member of Parry's family. These musical portraits are engagingly played, and complement the broader gestures of the sonatas particularly well. This disc will be welcomed by anyone with a taste for the unfamiliar, and will certainly reward the curiosity of the adventurous collector — warmly recommended.

Parry. The Soul's Ransom — sinfonia sacra[a]. Choric song from Tennyson's "The Lotos Eaters". **Della Jones** (mez); [a]**David Wilson-Johnson** (bar); **London Philharmonic Choir and Orchestra/Matthias Bamert.** Chandos CHAN8990. Texts included.

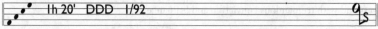

The renaissance of British music goes on apace, and it is good to see this conductor from another tradition in charge of a Parry series of which this disc was recorded under the auspices of the Vaughan Williams Trust. Parry was one of Vaughan Williams's teachers and the younger man admired him, but today he is chiefly known for his setting of *Jerusalem* and for his coronation anthem *I was glad*. His 'sacred symphony' *The Soul's Ransom* (1906) is subtitled "A Psalm for the Poor" and symbolizes his humanism, and though most of the text comes from the Bible he himself wrote that of the final chorus which describes the eternal power of the human spirit and includes the line, "Truth will not die". The music is rather earnest, but it does not lack colour and the two soloists project their contribution strongly. The *Choric song* from *The Lotos Eaters* was written earlier (1892) and is a setting of part of Tennyson's poem of that name. It was one of Parry's own favourites among his own works and has a quite different character that befits a text describing the delight of Odysseus's sailors on an island whose sense of paradise is induced by an "enchanted stem laden with flower and fruit", in other words the opiate that puts them into a drug-induced half-dream. The languorous hedonism of the words is so well captured that one forgets that this is Victorian music and regrets that although Elgar conducted it in 1902 it was then largely forgotten. There's plenty of variety of mood and the choral writing is imaginative. This compelling and convincing performance is given a rich recording.

Arvo Pärt
Estonian 1935-

Pärt. TABULA RASA. [ad]**Gidon Kremer,** [d]**Tatjana Grindenko** (vns); [a]**Keith Jarrett** (pf); [d]**Alfred Schnittke** (prepared pf); [b]**Stuttgart State Orchestra/ Dennis Russell Davies;** [c]**cellists of the Berlin Philharmonic Orchestra;** [d]**Lithuanian Chamber Orchestra/Saulus Sondeckis.** ECM 817 764-2. Item marked [d] recorded at a live performance in Bonn in 1977.
Fratres[a]. Cantus in memory of Benjamin Britten[b]. Fratres for 12 cellos[c]. Tabula rasa[d].

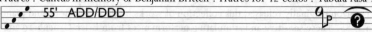

If Reich, Adams and Glass represent the so-called composers of minimalist music there is a strong case to be made for the Estonian-born Arvo Pärt as a composer who has blended the most alluring elements of that 'school' with his own individual musical voice and a definite message. His strongly held religious beliefs find frequent expression in his music; indeed, a discernible relationship can be made between his 'works of suffering' and the society that emerged under the former Soviet régime. These four works were composed between 1974 and 1976. *Fratres* appears twice: once in a version for piano and violin and again in a

Gidon Kremer   *[photo: DG/Bayat*

version for 12 cellos. They both comprise variations on a theme which formed the original version. The piece is constructed in strict metrical and mathematically conceived units but none the less possesses a freedom of utterance that is totally beguiling. The *Cantus* is no less bewitching, spinning a long cantilena with enormous simplicity. *Tabula rasa* is the most substantial piece on the disc, some 26 minutes long, employing two violins, prepared piano and chamber orchestra. Across a great chasm the lower registers of the piano seem to cry out to the upper harmonics of the violins. The effect is quite extraordinary. Gidon Kremer, who was deeply involved in the work's creation, clearly inspired his colleagues to give their utmost to produce a performance of great luminosity and intensity. The recording is well balanced and offers a fascinating picture of a composer whose language is direct, profound and hauntingly beautiful.

Pärt. Passio Domini nostri Jesu Christi secundum Johannem (1982). **Michael George** (bass) Jesus; **John Potter** (ten) Pilate; **Hilliard Ensemble** (Lynne Dawson, sop; David James, alto; Rogers Covey-Crump, ten; Gordon Jones, bass — Evangelist quartet; Elizabeth Layton, vn; Melinda Maxwell, ob; Elisabeth Wilson, vc; Catherine Duckett, bn; Christopher Bowers-Broadbent, org); **Western Wind Chamber Choir/Paul Hillier.** ECM New Series 837 109-2. Text and translation included.

1h 11' DDD 2/89

It's a mark of the extent to which Arvo Pärt identifies with the distant musical past that in setting the words of the St John Passion he should look not to J.S. Bach for his model, but rather to the ritualistic severity of plainchant and polyphony of the pre-Baroque era. The *Passion* is, indeed, an austere work even by Pärt's own standards. Without question it is the sheer restraint of the music, combined with the tension that gradually accumulates over a vast span of time that lends the work its special nobility and pathos. Pärt relies on simple but potent recitation formulae, which he entrusts to small consorts of voices variously accompanied by a tiny (but tellingly handled) instrumental ensemble. So underplayed is most of the narration that the tiniest emphasis, piquancy of harmony or addition of colour makes its presence felt, often to exquisite and moving effect. Add to this a committed performance by a superb team, an evocatively resonant church acoustic and a quite unexpected bonus — the sound of the wind haunting the building — and the net effect is one of the most powerful twentieth-century musical responses to a Christian theme currently available.

NEW REVIEW

Pärt. Miserere[a]. Festina lente[b]. Sarah was ninety years old[c]. [a]**Western Wind Choir; [ac]Hilliard Ensemble/Paul Hillier; [b]Bonn Beethovenhalle Orchestra/Dennis Russell Davies.** ECM New Series 847 539-2. Texts and translations included.

1h 6' DDD 1/92

Like so many of Pärt's works, these three pieces convey a sense of monumentality that is quite out of proportion to the economical means to achieve it. Each pitch, each duration, each colour is carefully chosen and meticulously placed; nothing is superfluous or wasted. At first the music seems sparse to the point of emptiness: the dull, unhurried thudding of drums in *Sarah was ninety years old*, for instance, might have been lifted straight out of some Buddhist ritual; the shards of unaccompanied melody running through the *Miserere* are leaner than even the simplest Gregorian chant. Yet the cumulative effects are devastating. Climaxes, slow to build, are cathartic; the voids that follow them must surely rank among the most profound silences ever devised by a Western composer. Minimalistic techniques — the cyclic rotation of musical material according to strict, simple rules — play a vital role: by taking responsibilities out of the composer's hands, they add to the solemn impersonality of the rites. Everything about the disc — performances, production, presentation — is outstanding.

Flor Peeters

Belgian 1903-1986

NEW REVIEW

Peeters. ORGAN WORKS. **Jozef Sluys.** Prezioso CD820 204. Played on the organ of St Saviour's Cathedral, Bruges.
Entrata festiva, Op. 93 (with Paul Voet, Peter Lejaeghere, tpts; Dominique Vanhaegenberg, Mick De Cooman, tbns). Prelude and Fugue in A major, Op. 72 No. 3. Concert Piece, Op. 52a. Abdijvrede, Op. 16a. Suite Modale, Op. 43. Ten Chorale Preludes, Op. 39 — No. 2, Hirten, er ist geboren; No. 3, Nun sei willkommen, Jesu, lieber Herr; No. 4, Uns ist geboren ein Kindelein; No. 5, Maria sollte nach Bethlehem gehn. Chorale Preludes on Well-known Hymns, Op. 68 — No. 2, O Gott, du frommer Gott; No. 3, Nun ruhen alle Wälder; No. 4, Ach blieb' mit Deiner Gnade; No. 7, Wie schön leuchtet der Morgenstern.

 Ih I' DDD 9/91

One of this century's most prolific composers for the organ was Flor Peeters. His compositions range from large-scale symphonic type works to a seemingly innumerable collection of small-scale chorale and hymn-tune preludes. From this vast body of music Jozef Sluys has planned a programme which gives as representative a cross-section as is possible on a single CD of Peeter's prodigious output. The four-movement *Suite Modale* is perhaps the finest example of his inimitable style mixing French (as in an invigorating final Toccata) and German (in the opening Choral) elements with the light-hearted (a bubbling *Scherzo*) and the intensely beautiful (a gorgeous *Adagio*). But there is also the dazzlingly virtuosic *Concert Piece*, an arrangement by Peeters himself of a movement from one of his two organ concertos, a selection of chorale-preludes and the jubilant *Entrata festiva* where the organ is joined by a brass quartet. The performances and recording do more than justice to this tiny glimpse of a truly phenomenal compositional career.

Francisco de Peñalosa

Spanish c.1470-1528

NEW REVIEW

Peñalosa. MOTETS. **Pro Cantione Antiqua** (Michael Chance, Timothy Penrose, altos; James Griffett, Ian Partridge, tens; Stephen Roberts, bar; Michael George, Adrian Peacock, basses)/**Bruno Turner.** Hyperion CDA66574. Texts and translations included.
Inter vestibulum et altare. Tribularer, si nescirem. Ne reminiscaris, Domine.

Versa est in luctum. Domine, secundum actum meum. Adore te, Domine Jesus
Christe. Ave, verum corpus natum. Nigra sum, sed formosa. Sancta Maria. Unica
est colomba mea. Ave, vera caro Christi. Ave, vere sanguis Domini. In passione
positus. Precor te, Domine Jesu Christe. Pater noster. Ave Regina caelorum.
Sancta Mater, istud agas. O Domina sanctissima. Emendemus in melius. Deus,
qui manus tuas. Domine Iesu Christe, qui neminem. Transeunte Domino Jesu.

Ih 18' DDD 7/92

Peñalosa was one of a number of Spanish composers of outstanding skill and
individuality who surfaced at the end of the fifteenth century, a time when
Spanish polyphonists were under strong Flemish influence. From 1517-1525 he
was in Rome, a member of the papal choir, a long absence during which even
Pope Leo X could not persuade Peñalosa's employers in Madrid to continue to
pay his salary; on his return, however, he became the Cathedral Treasurer. In his
compositional fluency and grace he most closely resembled Josquin Desprez, but
in the smoothness of its face his music is nearer to that of Jean Mouton, his close
contemporary. The bulk of his output was sacred music, including the 22 motets
in this recording; several others dubiously ascribed to him are omitted, thereby
ensuring an academically sound programme and a well filled disc. There is
considerable variety within this music, which places expressivity above contrapuntal virtuosity. The warm maturity of Pro Cantione Antiqua's performances make
this a fine contribution to the overdue and, in "Columbus Year", timely exposure
of some of the finest — but hitherto neglected Spanish polyphony, balm to the
most troubled soul.

Krzysztof Penderecki   *Refer to Index*   Polish 1933-

Giovanni Pergolesi   *Italian 1710-1736*

Pergolesi. Stabat mater[ab]. Salve regina in A minor[a]. In coelestibus regnis[b].
[a]**Gillian Fisher** (sop); [b]**Michael Chance** (alto); **King's Consort/Robert
King.** Hyperion CDA66294.

54' DDD 11/88

Pergolesi. Stabat mater[a]. Salve regina in C minor. **Emma Kirkby** (sop);
[a]**James Bowman** (alto); **Academy of Ancient Music/Christopher
Hogwood.** L'Oiseau-Lyre Florilegium 425 692-2OH. Texts and translations
included.

52' DDD 2/90

Pergolesi's *Stabat mater*, written in the last few months of his brief life, enjoyed a
huge popularity throughout the eighteenth century. But modern performances
often misrepresent its nature, either through over-romanticizing it or by transforming it into a choral work. Of the various versions available, the Hyperion
performance is one of the most successful and the most rewarding. The two
soloists are excellent, Gillian Fisher combining tonal purity and finesse of
phrasing, and Michael Chance showing himself an alto of outstanding accomplishment and artistry; and the ensemble of solo strings with archlute and organ
(Robert King himself) is exemplary. Pergolesi's emotional effects, such as his
piled-up suspensions or broken rhythms, have an intensity that is admirably
caught — but never exaggerated — in this stylish and tasteful performance. The
disc also includes some sweet legato singing in the *Salve regina* in A minor, and a
very brief cheerful motet about the blissful abode of the saints. First-class
recording too.

None of the *Stabat mater*'s qualities is overlooked in Hogwood's affecting performance, for Emma Kirkby and James Bowman are well-versed in the stylistic conventions of baroque and early classical music — and their voices afford a pleasing partnership. Both revel in Pergolesi's sensuous vocal writing, phrasing the music effectively and executing the ornaments with an easy grace. Singers and instrumentalists alike attach importance to sonority, discovering a wealth of beguiling effects in Pergolesi's part writing. In the *Salve regina* in C minor, the better known of two settings by Pergolesi, Emma Kirkby gives a compelling performance, pure in tone, expressive and poignant, and she is sympathetically supported by the string ensemble. The recording is pleasantly resonant and does justice to Pergolesi's translucent textures. Full texts are included.

Pérotin
French c.1160-c.1225

Pérotin. SACRED CHORAL WORKS. **Hilliard Ensemble** (David James, alto; John Potter, Rogers Covey-Crump, Mark Padmore, Charles Daniels, tens; Gordon Jones, bar)/**Paul Hillier** (bar). ECM New Series 837 751-2. Texts included.
Pérotin: Viderunt omnes. Alleluia, Posui adiutorium. Dum sigillum summi Patris. Alleluia, Nativitas. Beata viscera. Sederunt principes. *Anonymous Twelfth Century:* Veni creator spiritus. O Maria virginei. Isias cecinit.

1h 8' DDD 2/90

Today the music of a great choirmaster of Notre Dame in Paris is accessible to all of us thanks to the dedication, stylistic flair and remarkable skill of the seven male singers who make up the Hilliard Ensemble. There are nine pieces here, of which three are anonymous. Five of them are in *conductus* style, with one rhythm even if there is more than one vocal part, and the others in *organum* with more independent writing — an example of *conductus* is *Beata viscera*, a flowing meditation on the Virgin birth for solo countertenor above a quiet drone bass, while the opening *Viderunt omnes* in four parts is in *organum,* as is the rhythmically remarkable *Allelulia, Posui Adiutorium*. Such music as this evokes the great gothic cathedrals of France such as Notre Dame and Chartres, buildings of the same period, and its intense luminous quality has something of the power of their architecture, carving and stained glass, giving a great craftsmanship and a sense of lofty grandeur that is allied to simplicity of faith. There's an excellent booklet note by Paul Hillier. The recording was made in Boxgrove Priory and, rightly, it has plenty of reverberation.

Peter Philips   *Refer to Index*
British 1560-1628

Gabriel Pierné
French 1863-1937

NEW REVIEW

Pierné. Images — ballet, Op. 49 (1935). Viennoise (1932, earlier version of Images). Paysages franciscains. Les cathédrales — Prélude. **Loire Philharmonic Orchestra/Pierre Dervaux.** EMI CDM7 63950-2. From Pathé 2C 069 16302 (1/81).

54' ADD 3/92

Pierné is a most underrated composer whose best work is on the same level as that of Massenet or d'Indy. Here are three virtually unknown compositions, all of which offer considerable rewards. In 1915 Pierné wrote incidental music to accompany a staged dramatic poem, *Les cathédrales*, by Eugene Morand. We hear only the Prélude on this disc, a most dignified solemn piece. *Paysages franciscains*, written in 1920, was inspired by the travel journals of Johennes Joergensen. The first scene depicts a convent garden, the second recalls the olive trees at Assisi, and the last describes a festival procession in Italy. The musical style here is something like Respighi with a French accent — colourful, superbly scored and highly atmospheric. The genesis of the ballet *Images*, first produced in 1935, is curious, since the first version contained *Viennoise*, a sequence of waltzes and cortèges-blues. This was then replaced by another work which had been written a few years earlier, *Divertissement sur un thème pastoral*, and this was then coupled to an Introduction to make up the ballet in its second version. The disc contains both the complete ballet score in its revised version, and also the discarded *Viennoise*. All the music is written in Pierné's most elegant, positive manner, and is excellently played by the Loire orchestra under the imaginative direction of Pierre Dervaux. The recording quality is very good.

Walter Piston

USA 1894-1976

Piston. Symphony No. 2 (1943)[a].
Ruggles. Sun-treader (1926-31)[b].
Schuman. Violin Concerto (1959)[c]. [c]**Paul Zukofsky** (vn); **Boston Symphony Orchestra/Michael Tilson Thomas.** DG 20th Century Classics 429 860-2GC. Items marked [a] and [c] from 2530 103 (7/71), [b] 2530 048 (4/71).

Ih 15' ADD 1/91

Michael Tilson Thomas [photo: Sony Classical/Friedman

Though British collectors know their Gershwin, Copland, Bernstein, and maybe some Ives, Carter, Glass or Adams, there are still unfamiliar areas of American music and the composers here are major figures. The most radical is Ruggles, whose music is as uncompromising as Ives's though without that composer's folksy quality; not surprisingly, he was long neglected and *Sun-treader* waited 35 years for its American première at the time of his ninetieth birthday. This tough, big-scale piece is played first, and with considerable expressive force, under Michael Tilson Thomas, who was in his twenties when these recordings were made but had already made a name as a conductor willing to explore unfamiliar repertory, and the sound needs no apology for its age, being detailed and satisfying. Schuman and Piston are later figures than Ruggles, and both were distinguished teachers though in no way academic in their composing styles. The Schuman Concerto has violin writing that is lively as well as sometimes calmly lyrical (although the orchestration tends to be heavy), and Paul Zukofsky is a strong soloist. But Piston's Second Symphony, though a shorter work, has more to offer with its melodic sweep and well varied textures (the *Adagio* second movement has climaxes worthy of Shostakovich) and an element of lightness and even tunefulness that the Schuman lacks, while the structure convinces, too, as being well thought out. An important and well filled issue, and one that is especially desirable at medium price.

Amilcare Ponchielli

Italian 1834-1886

Ponchielli. LA GIOCONDA. **Maria Callas** (sop) La Gioconda; **Fiorenza Cossotto** (mez) Laure Adorno; **Pier Miranda Ferraro** (ten) Enzo Grimaldo; **Piero Cappuccilli** (bar) Barnaba; **Ivo Vinco** (bass) Alvise Badoero; **Irene Companeez** (contr) La Cieca; **Leonardo Monreale** (bass) Zuane; **Carlo Forte** (bass) A Singer, Pilot; **Renato Ercolani** (ten) Isepo, First Distant Voice; **Aldo Biffi** (bass) Second Distant Voice; **Bonaldo Giaiotti** (bass) Barnabotto; **Chorus and Orchestra of La Scala, Milan/Antonio Votto.** EMI mono CDS7 49518-2. Notes, text and translation included. From Columbia SAX2359/61 (11/60).

③ 2h 47' DDD 2/88 ▲

Ponchielli's old warhorse has had a bad press in recent times, which seems strange in view of its melodic profusion, his unerring adumbration of Gioconda's unhappy predicament and of the sensual relationship between Enzo and Laura. But it does need large-scale and involved singing — just what it receives here on this now historic set. Nobody could fail to be caught up in its conviction. Callas was in good and fearless voice when it was made, with the role's emotions perhaps enhanced by the traumas of her own life at the time. Here her strengths in declaiming recitative, her moulding of line, her response to the text are all at their most arresting. Indeed she turns what can be a maudlin act into true tragedy. Ferraro's stentorian ebullience is most welcome. Cossotto is a vital, seductive Laura. Cappuccilli gives the odious spy and lecher Barnaba a threatening, sinister profile, whilst Vinco is a suitably implacable Alvise. Votto did nothing better than this set, bringing out the subtlety of the Verdi-inspired scoring and the charm of the "Dance of the Hours" ballet. The recording sounds excellent for its age.

Francis Poulenc

French 1899-1963

Poulenc. Concerto in D minor for two pianos and orchestra[a]. Piano Concerto. Aubade. **François-René Duchable,** [a]**Jean-Philippe Collard** (pfs); **Rotterdam Philharmonic Orchestra/James Conlon.** Erato 2292-45232-2. From NUM75023 (2/86).

59' DDD 8/88

The *Aubade* is a most delicious ballet score, with clear-cut rhythms, aggressive Stravinskian harmonic clashes, and an abundance of good melodies, some jolly, some sentimental. Duchable and Conlon give a good account of the score, though they are sometimes a little too straight-faced. The Concerto for two pianos is another brilliant *divertissement*. The first movement has a superficially neoclassical style, but pert little tunes crop up to dispel any temporary seriousness. There follows a *Larghetto* which possesses genuine elegance and melodic beauty, and then there is a final energetic romp. The shortish Piano Concerto is another *jeu d'esprit* in three movements, but the style is noticeably that of the later Poulenc. Though the recording tends to favour the soloists it is otherwise very satisfactory.

NEW REVIEW

Poulenc. Organ Concerto in G minor[a]. Concert champêtre[b]. Piano Concerto[c]. [a]**Gillian Weir** (org); [b]**Maggie Cole** (hpd); [c]**Jean-Bernard Pommier** (pf);

City of London Sinfonia/Richard Hickox. Virgin Classics VC7 90799-2.

⠶ 1h 10' DDD 4/90

From the concerto's first, huge organ chord (thundering here from London's
Royal Festival Hall as dramatically as one could wish for) you might get the
impression that Poulenc's Organ Concerto is a work of almost Gothic pretensions. But even in his darkest hour Poulenc could never remain serious for long,
and moments of simple pathos and disarming humour constantly bubble to the
surface. Gillian Weir reflects these ever-changing moods admirably in her
superbly controlled performance, entering into a dialogue with Richard Hickox
and the City of London Sinfonia which bounces along with remarkable agility.
The *Concert champêtre* sets the spindly harpsichord against a surprisingly large
orchestra, but a careful balance has been achieved by the Virgin team, and
Maggie Cole's deft fingerwork, scuttling along like an energetic spider, is always
perfectly audible. Poulenc wrote this concerto for the famous harpsichordist
Wanda Landowska who was renowned for her volatile personality, by turns
playful and aggressive, and this is mirrored in his music. On the other hand the
Piano Concerto is pure fun. Written for an American audience Poulenc
attempted to charm them with the inclusion, in the finale, of the song *Swanee
River*. The joke fell rather flat among the Boston audience in 1949, but this
sprightly performance (slightly muffled by a boomy acoustic) is sure to lift
anyone's spirits.

Poulenc. CHAMBER MUSIC. [a]**Paris Wind Quintet** (Jacques Castagner, fl;
Robert Casier, ob; André Boutard, cl; Gérard Faisandier, bn; Michel Bergès, hn)
and various artists. EMI CZS7 62736-2. Items marked [b] from EMSP553 (3/76),
[c] EMI Pathé Marconi 2C 165 12519-22 (2/81).
Violin Sonata[b] (Sir Yehudi Menuhin, vn; Jacques Février, pf). Cello Sonata[b]
(Pierre Fournier, vc; Février). Trio for oboe, bassoon and piano[c] (Février;
Robert Casier, ob; Gérard Faisandier, bn). Sextet for piano and wind quintet[ac]
(Février). Flute Sonata[b] (Michel Debost, fl; Février). Oboe Sonata[b] (Maurice
Bourgue, ob; Février). Clarinet Sonata[b] (Michel Portal, cl; Février). Elégie for
horn and piano[b] (Alan Civil, hn; Février). Sonata for two clarinets[b] (Portal,
Maurice Gabai, cl). Sonata for clarinet and bassoon[b] (Portal, Amaury Wallez,
bn). Sonata for horn, trumpet and trombone[b] (Civil; John Wilbraham, tpt; John
Iveson, trbn).

⠶ ② 2h 25' ADD 12/89 £ 9[p]

Except for his works with voice, this collection contains the whole of Poulenc's
chamber music, from the 1918 Sonata for two clarinets to the 1962 oboe and
clarinet Sonatas; and though there is plenty of evidence of his frivolous side (as in
the early Sonata for three brass instruments and the scherzo of the Cello Sonata),
the conspectus also reveals the melancholy which underlay several of his best
works. Three were specifically elegiac — the Oboe Sonata in memory of his
friend Prokofiev, that for clarinet for Honegger, and the horn *Elégie* for Dennis
Brain; but it is worth noting that the first movement of the Flute Sonata is also
marked *Allegro malinconico*. The standard of performance throughout this set, by a
number of distinguished French and British artists, is of the highest: while
Poulenc was happiest with wind instruments, Menuhin and Fournier are both
most persuasive even against the composer's exuberant piano parts. His piano
writing is such that not even so understanding a player as Février can help
dominating too much in the Sextet (a diffuse work); but apart from this, and a
decidedly too close positioning of the two wind instruments in the Trio for oboe,
bassoon and piano, the recording quality of the set is very acceptable. At medium
price this valuably comprehensive survey is a bargain.

Poulenc. PIANO WORKS. **Pascal Rogé.** Decca 417 438-2DH.
Les soirées de Nazelles (1930-36). Deux novelettes — No. 1 in C major (1927);
No. 2 in B flat minor (1928). Novelette "sur un thème de M de Falla" (1959).
Pastourelle (arr. pf). Trois mouvements perpétuels (1918). Valse (1919).
15 Improvisations (1932-59) — No. 1 in B minor; No. 2 in A flat major; No. 3
in B minor; No. 6 in B flat major; No. 7 in C major; No. 8 in A minor; No. 12
in E flat major, "Hommage à Schubert"; No. 13 in A minor; No. 15 in C minor,
"Hommage à Edith Piaf". Trois Pièces (1928).

1h 7' DDD 7/87

Poulenc. PIANO WORKS. **Pascal Rogé.** Decca 425 862-2DH.
Humoresque (1934). Nocturnes (1929-38). Suite in C (1920). Thème varié
(1951). Improvisations — No. 4 in A flat major (1932); No. 5 in A minor
(1932); No. 9 in D major (1934); No. 10 in F major, "Eloge des gammes"
(1934); No. 11 in G minor (1941); No. 14 in D flat major (1958). Two
Intermezzos (1934). Intermezzo in A flat major (1943). Villageoises (1933).
Presto in B flat major (1934).

1h 3' DDD 4/91

These beautifully recorded and generously filled discs offer a rich diversity of
Poulenc's output. On the first disc, the masterly *Soirées de Nazelles* were
improvised during the early 1930s at a country house in Nazelles as a memento
of convivial evenings spent together with friends. It paints a series of charming
portraits — elegant, witty and refined. The *Trois mouvements perpétuels* are, like so
many of the works represented here, light-hearted and brief, improvisatory in
flavour and executed with a rippling vitality. The *Improvisations* constantly offer up
echoes of the piano concertos with their infectious rhythmic drive — the
"Hommage à Schubert" is a tartly classical miniature in three-time played with
just the right amount of nonchalant ease by Pascal Rogé. The "Hommage à Edith
Piaf" is a lyrical and touching tribute — obviously deeply felt.

The *Humoresque* which opens the second recital is open-air and open-hearted in
style, yet songlike too in its melodic richness. The simplicity of this music is
deceptive, as is that of the warmly caressing C major Nocturne that follows, for
both pieces need subtle phrasing, rubato and the kind of textures only obtainable
through the most refined use of the sustaining pedal. Rogé has these skills, and
he is also fortunate in having an excellent piano at his disposal as well as a
location (the Salle Wagram in Paris) that gives the sound the right amount of

reverberation. There are many
delights in this music and the
way it is played here: to mention just one, listen to the
masterly way that the composer
and pianist together gradually
bring around the flowing freshness of the C major Nocturne
towards the deeply poignant
feeling of the close. Both discs
hold the listener's attention
effortlessly from one piece to
the next, and though suitable
for any time of day they make
perfect late-night listening.
They should especially delight,
and to some extent reassure,
anyone who deplores the
absence of charm and sheer
romantic feeling in much of our
century's music.

| *Pascal Rogé*   *[photo: Decca/Loca*

Poulenc. CHORAL WORKS. **The Sixteen/Harry Christophers.** Virgin
Classics VC7 91075-2. Texts and translations included.
Figure humaine. Quatre motets pour un temps de pénitence. Laudes de Saint
Antoine de Padoue. Quatre motets pour le temps de Noël. Quatre petites prières
de Saint François d'Assise.

•	1h 2' DDD 3/90		**9** **P**

Poulenc. CHORAL WORKS. [a]**Donna Carter** (sop); [b]**Christopher Cock**
(ten); **Robert Shaw Festival Singers/Robert Shaw.** Telarc CD80236. Texts
and translations included.
Mass in G major[a]. Quatre motets pour le temps de Noël. Quatre motets pour un
temps de pénitence. Quatre petites prières de Saint François d'Assise[b].

•	52' DDD 10/90		**9** **P**

Poulenc made a particularly substantial contribution to the body of twentieth-
century French works for *a capella* chorus, and one of his finest works for the
medium receives a splendid performance on the Virgin disc. *Figure humaine*,
described as a Cantata, a setting of eight poems by Paul Eluard, was written
during the Second World War as an expression of the urgent, libertarian feeling
of a nation suffering under an oppressive yoke. Poulenc stretches the technical
resources of the double mixed chorus to its maximum in order to convey the
profundity of the emotions rawly displayed in the verse, and it is the triumph of
this performance that The Sixteen not only cope with these difficulties with
seeming ease but allow the music to soar, a symbol of the transcendence of the
human spirit in the face of adversity. The coupled motets, littered with
remarkable, jewel-like delights of affecting harmonic shifts, contrasts of chordal
placings, and melodic twists, receive a similarly thoughtful and technically expert
treatment from this front-ranking chorus. The recording is well balanced, with
the basses allowed to make a solid, full effect that is to some tastes, but may be
a little overdone for other listeners.

Telarc's fine account of Poulenc's sacred music was recorded in the church
of St Pierre de Gramat, near Rocamadour in the south of France. It was there
that Poulenc, following the death of a friend, rediscovered his Catholic faith.
The Robert Shaw Festival Singers comprise a homogeneous-sounding, highly
professional group. The soloists Donna Carter and Christopher Cock are effective, too. But perhaps what makes this disc special, apart from its touching
association with the composer, himself, is the skilful way in which Robert Shaw
places his forces at the service of the church's ample resonance. In this way his
singers are able to bring a subtle range of emotions to the music, delicately
coloured and almost infinitely varied. Not that everything here fares equally well
in such a spacious acoustic, but it would be hard to imagine more affecting
performances than these under similar circumstances.

Poulenc. Gloria[a]. Piano Concerto[b]. Les biches — ballet suite[c]. [a]**Norma
Burrowes** (sop); [b]**Cristina Ortiz** (pf); **City of Birmingham Symphony
Orchestra and** [a]**Chorus/Louis Frémaux.** EMI CDM7 69644-2. Items marked
[ab] from SQ ASD3299 (12/76), [c]ASD2989 (5/74).

•	1h 2' ADD 1/89	

Poulenc is a difficult figure to classify, and the frivolities and Gallic charm of
his music go hand in hand with a deep if unorthodox religious feeling and an
occasional sadness. His admiration for light music and for classical figures as
different as Schubert and middle-period Stravinsky are reflected in the melodic
richness and rhythmic bounce of his music, so that a movement such as the
"Laudamus te" of his *Gloria* sounds at first as if Stravinsky's *Symphony of Psalms*
had been rewritten by a twentieth-century Offenbach, while the soprano solo

"Dominus Deus" that follows has a Franckian fervour. But like Stravinsky, Poulenc made everything he borrowed delightfully his own. The Piano Concerto and the ballet suite *Les biches* are no less delightful and touching. This is music to give pleasure, not to be intellectualized or analysed. Good performances and satisfying digital transfer from 1970s originals.

Michael Praetorius   *German 1571-1621*

Praetorius. Terpsichore — excerpts. **New London Consort/Philip Pickett.** L'Oiseau-Lyre Florilegium 414 633-2OH.

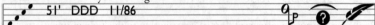

For the full range of late Renaissance instruments, impressively played and brimming over with good humour, this is unquestionably the finest disc in the catalogue. Schryari, racketts, crumhorns, sorduns, theorboes, archlutes, viols, regal: all these and lots more, played by some of Britain's finest exponents and recorded with dazzling clarity. Moreover, should you be at all unsure about the difference between the sound of a shawm and a rauschpfeife, for example, you will find all the instruments used carefully itemized for each of the 31 different dances presented here. And the insert reproduces the pictures of these instruments that Praetorius himself published in his massive *Syntagma musicum*. The dances themselves are chosen from over 300 that Praetorius published in his *Terpsichore* of 1612. They are the perfect vehicle for this array of machinery. Pickett and his musicians go to work on them with considerable verve and the result fairly fizzles.

Sergey Prokofiev   *Russian 1891-1953*

Prokofiev. Piano Concertos. **Vladimir Ashkenazy** (pf); **London Symphony Orchestra/André Previn.** Decca 425 570-2DM2. From 15BB 218 (10/75). No. 1 in D flat major, Op. 10. No. 2 in G minor, Op. 16. No. 3 in C major, Op. 26. No. 4 in B flat major, Op. 53, "for the left hand". No. 5 in G major, Op. 55.

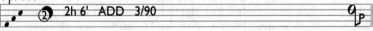

NEW REVIEW
Prokofiev. Piano Concertos[a] — No. 1 in D flat major, Op. 10; No. 3 in C major, Op. 26. Piano Sonata No. 7 in B flat major, Op. 83. **Mari Kodama** (pf); [a]**Philharmonia Orchestra/Kent Nagano.** ASV CDDCA786.

  1h 4' DDD 4/92

While it's true that the Prokofiev piano concertos are an uneven body of work, there's enough imaginative fire and pianistic brilliance to hold the attention even in the weakest of them, while the best by common consent Nos. 1, 3 and 4 have stood the test of time very well. As indeed have these Decca recordings. The set first appeared in 1975, but the sound is fresher than many contemporary digital issues, and Ashkenazy has rarely played better. Other pianists have matched his brilliance and energy in, say, the Third Concerto, but few very few have kept up such a sure balance of fire and poetry. The astonishingly inflated bravura of the Second Concerto's opening movement is kept shapely and purposeful even the out-of-tune piano doesn't spoil the effect too much. And the youthful First has the insouciance and zest its 22-year-old composer plainly intended. Newcomers to the concertos should start with No. 3: so many facets of Prokofiev's genius (including that wonderfully piquant lyricism) are here, and Ashkenazy shows how they all take their place as part of a kind of fantastic story. But there are rewards everywhere, and the effort involved in finding them is small. Why hesitate?

The First and Third are the most popular of the concertos, the Seventh the most popular of the sonatas; together they make an excellent sampler, recommendable to anyone looking for just a taste of Prokofiev's piano style. In fact Mari Kodama's performances on the ASV disc are rather more special than that. She is not a hugely powerful player and she wisely avoids the barnstorming approach more usually associated with this composer. Instead she turns her gifts for nuance and shading (she is French-trained) to her advantage, and the music's. With the close collaboration of her husband Kent Nagano, and of the Philharmonia Orchestra at its most refined, she draws out the playfulness and chamber music interplay in the concertos, and lets the sonata dance along rather than steamroller everything in its path. This is perhaps a disc to have in addition to more mainstream accounts like Ashkenazy's in the concertos or Maurizio Pollini's reading of the Seventh Sonata (reviewed in the Collections section, refer to the Index to Reviews) rather than instead of them — the slow movement of the sonata in particular misses out on its true depth of emotion (its lyricism is deceptive). But the concertos are a refreshing experience and the entire programme has the benefit of outstandingly fine recorded sound.

Prokofiev. Piano Concerto No. 3 in C major, Op. 26[a].
Tchaikovsky. Piano Concerto No. 1 in B flat major, Op. 23[b]. **Martha Argerich** (pf); [a]**Berlin Philharmonic Orchestra/Claudio Abbado;** [b]**Royal Philharmonic Orchestra/Charles Dutoit.** DG 415 062-2GH. Item marked [a] from 138349 (2/68), [b] 2530 112 (10/71).

. .	1h 3' ADD 5/85			P	Ⓑ

By general consensus Martha Argerich's 1971 recording of Tchaikovsky's B flat minor Piano Concerto is still among the best of the currently available recordings. The opening of the first movement sets the mood of spaciousness and weight, with the lovely secondary material bringing poetic contrast. The *Andantino* has an appealing delicacy, with the centrepiece dazzling in its light-fingered virtuosity to match the exhilaration of the last movement. The admirably balanced recording has plenty of spectacle, the strings are full and firm and the piano image is strikingly real and tangible. The unexpected but inspirational coupling was one of Argerich's début recordings, and for those less familiar with Tchaikovsky's twentieth-century compatriot, the music itself will come as a refreshing surprise. The apparent initial spikiness soon dissolves with familiarity and Prokofiev's concerto reveals itself as very much in the romantic tradition. Its harmonies are more pungent than those of Tchaikovsky, but the melodic appeal is striking and the sheer vitality of the outer movements is irresistible as projected by Martha Argerich's nimble fingers.

NEW REVIEW

Prokofiev. Piano Concerto No. 4 in B flat major, Op. 53[a].
Reger. Piano Concerto in F minor, Op. 114[b]. **Rudolf Serkin** (pf); **Philadelphia Orchestra/Eugene Ormandy.** CBS Masterworks Portrait CD46452. Item marked [a] from SBRG72109 (5/63), [b] SBRG72399 (6/66).

. .	1h 2' ADD 12/91	

Prokofiev's Fourth Piano Concerto was written for the Austrian pianist, Paul Wittgenstein, after he lost his right arm; his other commissions included similar works from Ravel and Britten — quite a formidable array! In this pioneering recording, which dates from 1958, Rudolf Serkin gives a most captivating performance; he expertly balances Prokofiev's staccato style of piano writing with beautiful legato playing of his long-limbed romantic melodies. The recorded sound is very good for its age: rich and atmospheric. The pairing of the Prokofiev with Reger's rarely heard Piano Concerto is an unusual decision which pays off handsomely. Although the work itself is not one of Reger's best — it has a rather four-square character and the level of musical invention does not hold one's attention throughout, Serkin gives a most valiant performance, making light of Reger's handfuls of notes. The accompaniments by Eugene Ormandy and the Philadelphia Orchestra in both recordings are highly expert. Not only is Ormandy extraordinarily punctilious, he also draws from his orchestra stylistically varied and appropriate playing in both concertos. This is a CD which, especially at medium price, is well worth investigation.

Prokofiev. Piano Concerto No. 5 in G major, Op. 55[a].
Rachmaninov. Piano Concerto No. 2 in C minor, Op. 18[b]. **Sviatoslav Richter** (pf); **Warsaw Philharmonic Orchestra/[a]Witold Rowicki, [b]Stanislaw Wislocki.** DG 415 119-2GH. Item marked [a] from 138075 (3/60), [b] 138076 (1/60).

> 58' ADD 6/85

Prokofiev was to find no more dedicated an advocate for his keyboard works than Richter. So how good that this artist's now legendary account of the Fifth Piano Concerto has been granted a new lease of life on CD. Although it has never enjoyed the popularity of Prokofiev's Nos. 1 and 3, here, however, attention is riveted from first note to last. Richter delights in the music's rhythmic vitality and bite, its melodic and harmonic unpredictability. Both piano and orchestra are so clearly and vividly reproduced that it is difficult to believe the original recording dates back to 1959. Though betraying its age slightly more, notably in the sound of the keyboard itself, Rachmaninov's No. 2 is no less gripping. Not all of Richter's tempos conform to the score's suggested metronome markings, but his intensity is rivalled only by his breathtaking virtuosity. Never could the work's opening theme sound more laden, more deeply and darkly Russian.

Prokofiev. Violin Concertos — No. 1 in D major, Op. 19; No. 2 in G minor, Op. 63. **Dmitry Sitkovetsky** (vn); **London Symphony Orchestra/Sir Colin Davis.** Virgin Classics VC7 90734-2.

> 49' DDD 12/88

NEW REVIEW

Prokofiev. Violin Concertos — No. 1 in D major, Op. 19[a]; No. 2 in G minor, Op. 63[a].
Stravinsky. Violin Concerto in D major. **Kyung-Wha Chung** (vn); **London Symphony Orchestra/André Previn.** Decca Ovation 425 003-2DM. Items marked [a] from SXL6773 (3/77), [b] SXL6601 (5/73).

> 1h 12' ADD 7/90

Sitkovetsky rediscovers page after page of these concertos and the First is little short of revelatory. Rarely can the tenuous balance between the lyrical and the diabolical have proved so unsettling. From the 'once upon a time' opening, with its beautiful spun-silk melody, to the disruptive, increasingly agitated development which ensues, Sitkovetsky never once sacrifices accuracy for drama or vice versa. His technical prowess throughout is extraordinary. At the other end of the expressive spectrum, the long *Romeo and Juliet*-like cantabile of the Second Concerto's *Andante* is gloriously true and free — almost as if the line were being created in the playing of it. Sir Colin Davis proves the ideal collaborator, his firm rhythmic arm much in evidence. If the recording is somewhat close and overbearing, with soloist and orchestra thrown into sharp foreground relief, in the light of such marvellous music-making, there is no need to quibble.

The balance is better on the Decca disc, though the well integrated image of the Stravinsky work does betray an element of solo spotlighting in the Prokofiev, noticeably in the Second Concerto. No matter: this is Chung at her most compelling, never deliberately attention seeking, yet riveting attention from the first bar. Her deft mastery of the solo sword-play in the First Concerto's *Scherzo* defies criticism, yet it is the contemplative moments one remembers most of all: the very start of the First Concerto, for example, with tone of extraordinary delicacy and finesse; and the withdrawn, initially almost whispered delivery of the opening melody of the Second Concerto's slow movement. The LSO were audibly inspired by the example and by the time the Prokofiev concertos were made, Previn was already a proven Prokofievian and Chung's most frequent partner on disc. The Stravinsky was an earlier collaboration. The concerto is in Stravinsky's most diamond-edged neoclassical manner. It finds Chung at her most incisive and high spirited, and Previn relishing the sonorities and the syncopations.

Prokofiev. ORCHESTRAL WORKS. [a]**Sting** (narr); [b]**Stefan Vladar** (pf); **Chamber Orchestra of Europe/Claudio Abbado.** DG 429 396-2GH. Peter and the wolf, Op. 67[a]. Symphony No. 1 in D, Op. 25, "Classical". March in B flat minor, Op. 99. Overture on Hebrew Themes, Op. 34*bis*[b].

50' DDD 4/91

Abbado and the multi-talented Sting offer a lively and beautifully crafted account of Prokofiev's ever popular *Peter and the wolf*. The choice of Sting as narrator is clearly aimed at a younger audience who would otherwise never give this delightful work a second glance. Any fears that the original freshness of Prokofiev's creation may be lost in favour of a less formal approach are soon dispelled — Sting is an effective and intelligent story-teller capable of capturing the imagination of adults and children alike, and there is never a feeling of

contrivance or mere gimmickry. The orchestral playing is a real delight too; sharply characterized and performed with great affection. The *Overture on Hebrew Themes* is more commonly heard in its drier, more acerbic version for clarinet, piano and string quartet, but makes a welcome and refreshing appearance on this disc in Prokofiev's own arrangement for small orchestra. Abbado's elegant and graceful reading of the *Classical* Symphony is one of the finest in the catalogue, and is particularly notable for its beautifully shaped phrasing, clarity of inner detail and crisp articulation.

Claudio Abbado   [photo: DG/Bayat

Prokofiev. Romeo and Juliet, Op. 64 — ballet suite. Chout, Op. 21 — ballet suite. **London Symphony Orchestra/Claudio Abbado.** Decca Ovation 425 027-2-2DM. From SXL6286 (5/67).

— 54' ADD 6/91 — Ⓑ

It was an excellent idea to couple a suite of nine items from the familiar *Romeo and Juliet* ballet score with a similar sequence from the unjustly neglected *Chout* — the blackly comic tale of a village trickster, the Buffoon of the alternative title. *Romeo and Juliet* is more popular than ever these days, but Abbado's mid-sixties selection — less predictable than most — retains its freshness and appeal; only his sluggish *Dance of the girls with lilies* lacks something in charm. The sound is pretty good, the brass very immediate. While *Chout* has that rather sadistic plot — and the audiences of 1921 had ultra-modern cubist sets, costumes and choreography to object to — its neglect seems unaccountable today, given the quality of the music. Here, Prokofiev was clearly inspired by Stravinsky's *Petrushka*. Even if there remains some loosely-written connective tissue, there is also a fund of melodic invention that could only have come from the younger man. The orchestration glitters throughout, sharp-edged and totally distinctive. Decca's analogue recording remains impressive with the scintillating textures clearly defined.

Prokofiev. Romeo and Juliet, Op. 64 — ballet: excerpts. **Montreal Symphony Orchestra/Charles Dutoit.** Decca 430 279-2DH.
Introduction; Romeo; The street awakens; Morning Dance; The Quarrel; The Fight; The Prince gives his order; Juliet, as a young girl; Arrival of the guests; Mask; Dance of the Knights; Romeo and Juliet; Folk Dance; Friar Laurence; Dance; Tybalt and Mercutio fight; Mercutio dies; Romeo decides to avenge Mercutio's death; Romeo fights Tybalt; Introduction to Act 3; The last farewell; Dance of the girls with the lilies; Juliet's funeral; Death of Juliet.

— 1h 15' DDD 9/91 — Ⓢ Ⓑ

Prokofiev's *Romeo and Juliet* is one of the greatest of all Russian ballets and a masterly successor to Tchaikovsky's works. The melodic invention, always consistently inspired, the harmonic flavour, often pungent, and the individual and brilliantly colourful orchestration bring the ear constant diversity and stimulation. Charles Dutoit's 1991 recording is extremely attractive: by judicious selection he compresses the epic span of the ballet into 24 separate items from the original score. The playing of the Montreal Symphony Orchestra is spectacular with very fleet strings and brass playing of imposing weight and tragic pungency. Dutoit's interpretation is highly theatrical: the lighter excerpts from the score are pointed and witty, while the more romantic elements are given full expression and the variety of Shakespeare's and Prokofiev's dramatic vision is most expertly recreated by Dutoit. The recording is top class, not only expertly balanced but capturing the wide dynamic range and finesse of the splendidly virtuoso Montreal orchestra.

Prokofiev. Symphonies — No. 1 in D major, Op. 25, "Classical"; No. 4 in C major, Op. 112 (rev. 1947 version). **Scottish National Orchestra/Neeme Järvi.** Chandos CHAN8400. From ABRD1137 (11/85).

— 52' DDD 3/86 — Ⓟ Ⓑ

Prokofiev. Symphonies — No. 3 in C minor, Op. 44; No. 4 in C major, Op. 47 (original 1930 version). **Scottish National Orchestra/Neeme Järvi.** Chandos CHAN8401. From ABRD1138 (11/85).

| 59' DDD 5/86 | P B |

Prokofiev. Symphonies — No. 1 in D major, Op. 25, "Classical"; No. 5 in B flat major, Op. 100. **Los Angeles Philharmonic Orchestra/André Previn.** Philips 420 172-2PH.

| 58' DDD 11/87 | P B |

NEW REVIEW

Prokofiev. Symphonies — No. 1 in D major, Op. 25, "Classical"; No. 7 in C sharp minor, Op. 131. The Love for Three Oranges — Suite, Op. 33*a*. **Philharmonia Orchestra/Nicolai Malko.** Classics for Pleasure CD-CFP 4523. From HMV CLP1044 (6/55).

| 57' ADD | £ P B ▲ |

Few twentieth-century symphonies have quite the immediate melodic appeal of Prokofiev's *Classical* Symphony. It is so familiar that its perfect proportions, its effervescent high spirits and its striking originality tend to be taken for granted. Järvi gives an altogether exhilarating account of it. The slow movement has real tenderness and the finale is wonderfully high spirited. It is coupled with a rarity, the Fourth Symphony, which draws on material from his ballet, *The prodigal son*. The balletic origins of the symphony are obvious, both in terms of its melodic substance and organization. Prokofiev drastically revised the score in 1947 and the extent of this overhaul will be evident from the fact that the 1930 version takes 23 minutes and the revision 37. The first two movements are much expanded, the orchestration is richer and among other things a piano is added. Järvi's totally committed accounts of both versions are recorded with remarkable fidelity and presence. Järvi is also entirely at home with the Third Symphony (a reworking of ideas from the opera *The fiery angel*) and is particularly successful in conveying the sense of magic and mystery in the *Andante*. The opening idea is austere but lyrical, and the music to which it gives rise is extraordinarily rich in fantasy and clothed in an orchestral texture of great refinement and delicacy. With its whirlwind of activity, the scherzo evokes the strange, supernatural and 'possessed' atmosphere of the opera.

Prokofiev is a composer with whom Previn has a strong natural affinity and his recording is an almost unqualified success. Once an artist has found the speed which ideally suits his view of a work, details of phrasing, articulation and colour fall naturally into place. Thus the first movement of the Fifth Symphony seems to be exactly right, everything flowing naturally and speaking effectively, sweeping up to an exhilarating and high-spirited scherzo. In the slow movement Previn gets playing of genuine eloquence from the Los Angeles orchestra. He also gives an excellent account of the *Classical* Symphony, this perennially fresh score sounding beautifully natural with impressive detail, range and body. This is a splendid issue and must rank among the finest versions now available; highly recommended.

Malko's readings of Prokofiev's most charming symphonies have an assured place in gramophone history. These were in fact EMI's first stereo recordings — made as long ago as 1955 in the ideal acoustic of Kingsway Hall, London — and very good they sound too, only fractionally thin on top, superbly balanced within an attractively resonant acoustic space. Malko's view of No. 7 is warm and obliging, superbly played by the Philharmonia but not over-characterized. It may disappoint those who look for darker currents even in this most wistful of symphonies, but perhaps we should not look for a political statement in every nook and cranny of Soviet symphonism. Prokofiev, gravely ill and under pressure from Stalin's regime, wrote the work with an audience of children in mind. Malko, himself a Soviet *émigré*, was responsible for its British première. The

Classical Symphony goes similarly well (at a fairly moderate pace), and the bonus items from *The Love for Three Oranges* demonstrate Malko's legendary care for clarity and balance of sonority. This is music that can easily sound raucous and facile. Not so here: the famous March is irresistible, the love scene genuinely moving. All in all, this disc is a remarkable bargain.

NEW REVIEW

Prokofiev. Symphony No. 2 in D minor, Op. 40. Romeo and Juliet, Op. 64 — Suite No. 1. **Scottish National Orchestra/Neeme Järvi.** Chandos CHAN8368. From ABRD1134 (9/85).

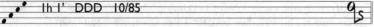

1h 1' DDD 10/85

Prokofiev's Second Symphony very much reflects the iconoclastic temper of the early twenties, and the violence and dissonance of its first movement betrays his avowed intention of writing a work "made of iron and steel". It is obvious that he was keen to compete with Mossolov's Steel Foundry from the *Symphony of Machines* or the Honegger of *Horace Victorieux* or *Pacific 231* in orchestral violence. In its formal layout (but in no other respect) the symphony resembles Beethoven's Op. 111 Sonata in being in two movements, the second of which is a set of variations. It is the latter that more than compensates for the high decibel quotient of its companion. It is rich in fantasy and some of the variations are wonderfully atmospheric — indeed Nos. 2 and 3 are altogether magical. In this it almost recalls the "Night" movement from the *Scythian Suite*. Neeme Järvi has a real flair for the music of this composer and produces altogether excellent results from the Scottish Orchestra. Moreover the Chandos recording has admirable detail, presence and body, and is a clear first choice. The *Romeo and Juliet* suite comes off well, too, and the Scottish Orchestra play with as much character here as in the companion work.

Prokofiev. Symphony No. 6 in E flat minor, Op. 111. Waltz Suite, Op. 110 — Nos. 1, 5 and 6. **Scottish National Orchestra/Neeme Järvi.** Chandos CHAN8359. From ABRD1122 (5/85).

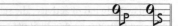

57' DDD 7/85

Although it appeared after the end of the war, the Sixth Symphony reflects much of the anguish and pain of those years, and it certainly strikes a deeper vein of feeling than any of its companions. It begins in a way that leaves no doubt that it is made of sterner stuff, the brass and lower strings spitting out a few notes that are so striking and bitter that the relatively gentle main theme comes as a surprise. Järvi has an intuitive understanding of this symphony, and indeed the whole Prokofiev idiom, and he shapes the details as skilfully as he does its architecture. The various climaxes are expertly built and the whole structure is held together in a masterly fashion. As a fill-up there are three movements from the *Waltz Suite*, in which Prokofiev draws from the ballet, *Cinderella*, and the opera, *War and Peace*. The recording is remarkably vivid and well detailed with a particularly rich bass.

Prokofiev. Symphony No. 7 in C sharp minor, Op. 131. Sinfonietta in A major, Op. 48. **Scottish National Orchestra/Neeme Järvi.** Chandos CHAN8442. From ABRD1154 (4/86).

51' DDD 7/86

The two pieces on this disc come from the opposite extremes of Prokofiev's career, the *Sinfonietta* from the beginning and the Symphony from the end. Both have that blend of wit and fantasy that Prokofiev so made his own. The Seventh Symphony is a relaxed and genial composition, some of whose ideas recall the fairy-tale atmosphere of *Cinderella*. The *Sinfonietta* is a tuneful, delightful piece that ought to be as popular as the *Classical* Symphony or *Peter and the Wolf*. Järvi is totally inside this music and the Scottish National Orchestra play splendidly for him. The recording has great range and depth, effectively conveying the impression of a concert hall experience.

Prokofiev. String Quartets — No. 1 in B minor, Op. 50; No. 2 in F major, Op. 92. **American Quartet** (Mitchell Stern, Laurie Carney, vns; Daniel Avshalomov, va; David Geber, vc). Olympia OCD340.

50' ADD 2/90

Prokofiev's wider popularity has never extended to his chamber music. Of his two quartets, the Second is by far the better-known and comes from the war years when Prokofiev was evacuated to the Caucasus, where he made a study of the musical folklore of Kabarda — indeed, it is sometimes known as the "Kabardinian" Quartet. Although the material is folk-derived, it is completely absorbed into Prokofiev's own melodic bloodstream and doesn't sound in the least bit 'folksy'. The second movement quotes a Kabardinian love song of great lyrical beauty, and at one point in the slow movement, the accompaniment imitates a Caucasian stringed instrument, the kamancha. It is a work of real quality which has the astringent flavouring and poetic flair that characterizes Prokofiev at his best. Although the First Quartet, written at the behest of the Library of Congress in 1930, is not so immediately appealing it, too, is a work of substance which grows on the listener. Prokofiev's friend and colleague, Nikolay Miaskovsky, who composed 13 string quartets and more than twice as many symphonies, particularly admired the last movement, and encouraged Prokofiev to score it for full strings. The American Quartet communicate conviction and belief in this music: theirs is a persuasive account, sensitive and yet full-blooded, and they are very well recorded.

Prokofiev. Violin Sonatas — No. 1 in F minor, Op. 80; No. 2 in D major, Op. 94a. **Shlomo Mintz** (vn); **Yefim Bronfman** (pf). DG 423 575-2GH.

56' DDD 2/89

Prokofiev. Violin Sonata No. 2 in D major, Op. 94a.
Ravel. Violin Sonata (1927).
Stravinsky. Divertimento. **Viktoria Mullova** (vn); **Bruno Canino** (pf). Philips 426 254-2PH.

1h 1' DDD 8/90

Both Prokofiev sonatas are wartime pieces; both follow the classical four-movement plan and both must be numbered among Prokofiev's very finest achievements. There the similarities end, for the First is declamatory, agonized and predominantly introspective, whereas the Second, originally for flute and piano, is untroubled, intimate and consoling. This essential difference in character presents a challenge which not all duos have risen to. Mintz and Bronfman have got right to the heart of the matter, however, and if their First Sonata is still marginally the finer that is only because it is on a truly rare level of insight. Both players deploy a wide range of colour and accent, superbly captured in a bright but not over-reverberant acoustic, and they are united in their nuanced response to Prokofiev's lyricism and motoric drive. In the extraordinary first movement coda of the First Sonata, they create an atmosphere of almost hypnotic numbness, and it is a pity that one terrible edit breaks the spell here (the violin tone changes abruptly in mid-bar). But that is the only serious defect in what is a truly outstanding recital.

Shlomo Mintz   *[photo: DG/Steiner]*

Prokofiev's Second Sonata needs a performance that is fully committed to its violin garb. It receives that in force on the Philips disc, Mullova relishing its challenge. Stravinsky's Divertimento is a 1933 transcription of music from his enchanting ballet, *Le baiser de la fée*, which is in turn founded on the music of Tchaikovsky. Mullova and Canino take it 'as found' rather than being beholden to its origins, allowing the work's own logic to sustain emotional impact. The superb security of their playing, coupled with an acute sense of the work's direction, makes a strong case for it being included in every violinist's recital repertoire. The Ravel Sonata, finished in 1927, is characterized by a strident 'Blues' second movement, followed by a *Perpetuum mobile* finale which serve, on reflection, to set the more conventional opening movement in stark relief. Some may find this reading a touch too solid to reflect the impressionism of Ravel's idiom, but its purposefulness cannot be doubted. In all three works, Canino is an ideally sensitive, but far from passive, accompanist and together these superb musicians create an engrossing recital that is well worth investigating.

NEW REVIEW

Prokofiev. PIANO SONATAS, Volume 1. **Murray McLachlan.** Olympia OCD255.
Piano Sonatas — No. 1 in F minor, Op. 1; No. 4 in C minor, Op. 29; No. 5 in C major (revised version), Op. 135; No. 9 in C major, Op. 103; No. 10 in E minor, Op. 137.

1h 10'   DDD   3/90

The first volume of Murray McLachlan's complete survey of the Prokofiev Piano Sonatas contains some very fine performances indeed. A suitably bold and youthfully exuberant account of the romantic First Sonata Op. 1 is followed by a particularly thoughtful and probing reading of the introverted and less frequently heard Fourth Sonata — the slow movement is especially intense and poetic. Indeed, one of McLachlan's strengths, both here and in the other sonatas on this disc, is his ability to bring out the poetry and lyricism of these pieces that so often get overlooked by pianists in favour of the more abrasive and dissonant aspects. The Fifth Sonata (again most persuasively handled) is heard here in its revised version of 1953, which used to be the accepted version among pianists but which is now taking something of a back seat in favour of the original 1938 version. However, the real gem of the disc lies in McLachlan's performance of the much underrated Ninth Sonata. Richter (to whom it was dedicated) described it as "intimately chamber in character, concealing riches which are not immediately obvious to the eye". Performed as it is here, with a great deal of poetry and insight, the concealed riches become more readily apparent and one is left wondering why the sonata has remained neglected for so long. The disc concludes with the tiny fragment (a mere 27 bars) that would have become the Tenth Sonata had Prokofiev's death not intervened. Excellent sleeve notes from Murray McLachlan.

NEW REVIEW

Prokofiev. PIANO WORKS. **Barry Douglas.** RCA Victor Red Seal
RD60779.
Piano Sonatas — No. 2 in D minor, Op. 14; No. 7 in B flat major, Op. 83.
The Love for three oranges — March, Op. 33*ter*. Ten Pieces from Cinderella,
Op. 97 — No. 10, Waltz. Six Pieces from Cinderella, Op. 102 — No. 4,
Amoroso. Three Pieces, Op. 96 — No. 1, Waltz from War and Peace.

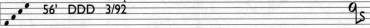

There has often been a tendency with Prokofiev's piano music for pianists to
overplay the percussive, steely qualities of the piano writing at the expense of the
lyrical aspects. Barry Douglas, however, attains the perfect blend — muscular
and athletic where power and agility are called for, but ever alert to the lyricism
which lies beneath the surface. The Second Sonata is a prime example. Douglas
has the full measure of this youthful, energetic masterpiece, and one feels that he
has fully assimilated this piece before committing it to disc. The first movement
with its restless oscillation between expressive melody and ruminative figuration
is thoughtfully fashioned, and the knockabout scherzo and fleet-footed energetic
finale are delivered with much vigour and flair. The Seventh Sonata (the central
work of Prokofiev's "War Trilogy") is impressive too, with Douglas fully in
command of its bristling difficulties. As for the rest of the disc, Douglas offers
some of the less frequently heard piano transcriptions, of which the delirious
'love' Waltz from *Cinderella* and the March from *The Love for three oranges* crave
particular attention. The recording is beautifully engineered and balanced.

Prokofiev. Piano Sonata No. 6 in A major, Op. 82.
Ravel. Gaspard de la nuit. **Ivo Pogorelich** (pf). DG 413 363-2GH. From
2532 093 (6/83).

Although Prokofiev's Sixth Sonata is less well known than its successors, it is
every bit as brilliant and if anything more inventive. Ivo Pogorelich has remarkable technical address, as is evident from these performances, and he plays with a
mixture of abandon and discipline that is enormously exhilarating. Ravel's evocations of Aloysius Bertrand's prose poems in *Gaspard de la nuit* is a *tour de force*,
one of the most totally pianistic works in the whole keyboard repertoire.
Pogorelich produces a remarkable range of keyboard colour and the recording
does justice to his dynamic range. His account of "Le gibet" is particularly
imaginative and chilling.

Prokofiev. Visions fugitives, Op. 22.
Scriabin. PIANO WORKS. **Nikolai Demidenko** (pf). Conifer CDCF204.
Scriabin: Piano Sonatas — No. 2 in G sharp minor, Op. 19, "Sonata-fantasy";
No. 9 in F major, Op. 68, "Messe noire". Etudes — F sharp minor, Op. 8
No. 2; B major, Op. 8 No. 4; E major, Op. 8 No. 5; F sharp major, Op. 42
No. 3; F sharp major, Op. 42 No. 4; F minor, Op. 42 No. 7. Four Pieces,
Op. 51. Vers la flamme, Op. 72.

The remarkable talent of Nikolai Demidenko is heard here to its full advantage.
The Scriabin items not only display the breadth of Demidenko's expressive
powers, but also serve to illustrate Scriabin's astonishing transition from post-
romantic to the visionary modernist. The early *Sonata-fantasy* of 1892-7 (surely
one of his most beautiful and sensuous pieces) is played here with much poetry
and affection, and the final movement (an exhilarating *Presto* in 3/4 time) is a
fine example of Demidenko's precision, clarity and immaculate pedal control.

With the six etudes and the *Four Pieces*, Op. 51 that follow the listener is taken on a fascinating journey that culminates in the volatile sound-worlds of the Ninth Sonata and *Vers la flamme*. These nebulous, shadowy works are delivered with an extraordinary degree of intensity and perception. His account of Prokofiev's *Visions fugitive* is in a class of its own. Each tiny miniature is jewelled to perfection, and his acute sense of colour and tonal variation make this one of the finest performances on disc. A remarkable début recording in every respect.

NEW REVIEW

Prokofiev (ed. Palmer). Ivan the Terrible — concert scenario. **Linda Finnie** (contr); **Nikita Storojev** (bass-bar); **Philharmonia Chorus and Orchestra/ Neeme Järvi.** Chandos CHAN8977.

· 59' DDD 11/91

Christopher Palmer is a scholar, stylish writer, and above all a skilful and enthusiastic musician, and he has done a major service to Prokofiev by arranging this performing concert scenario from his music to Sergei Eisenstein's epic 1940s film *Ivan the Terrible* with its view of an episode in Russia's turbulent history. When the director began work on it in 1941, he had recently produced Wagner's *Die Walküre* at the Bolshoi Theatre in Moscow, and he brought to it a spectacular operatic treatment. In turn, Prokofiev's music heightened the drama to fever pitch and provided plenty of big set pieces such as arias and choruses, Russian liturgical music, a wedding scene and a lullaby. From all this music, Palmer has created a satisfying musical sequence of 13 sections which also follows the drama. The performance under Neeme Järvi is immensely atmospheric, and while his male solo singer Nikita Storojev is predictably idiomatic, the fine contralto Linda Finnie sounds no less Russian. Though the Philharmonia Chorus cannot quite match them in this respect, they sing strongly and expressively throughout. This is inspired music which sweeps the listener along irresistibly, and Chandos's recording is worthy of it, capturing the full-blooded primitivism and primary colours of Prokofiev's score with its powerful writing for voices and its bold instrumentation. The booklet has a translation of the text as well as an informative essay by Palmer himself.

Prokofiev. Alexander Nevsky — cantata, Op. 78[a].
Rachmaninov. The Bells, Op. 35[b]. [b]**Sheila Armstrong** (sop); [a]**Anna Reynolds** (mez); [b]**Robert Tear** (ten); [b]**John Shirley-Quirk** (bar); **London Symphony Chorus and Orchestra/André Previn.** EMI Studio CDM7 63114-2. Item marked [a] from ASD2800 (7/72), [b] ASD3284 (12/76). Texts and translations included.

· 1h18' ADD 10/89   9 p £

NEW REVIEW

Prokofiev. Alexander Nevsky — cantata, Op. 78[a]. Scythian Suite, Op. 20.
[a]**Linda Finnie** (contr); **Scottish National** [a]**Chorus and Orchestra/Neeme Järvi.** Chandos CHAN8584. Text and translation included.

· 1h DDD 5/88   9 p 9 s

One of the remarkable musical partnerships of the seventies was that of André Previn and the London Symphony Orchestra, for their special blend of communication and enthusiasm produced electrifying results. Some of their finest recordings were made for EMI, two of which have been combined on this CD reissue. Previn's account of Prokofiev's *Alexander Nevsky* has tremendous energy and power, which is aided and abetted by the dramatic and colourful singing of the LSO chorus. Anna Reynolds's solo in the "Field of the Dead" is very fine too, where her rich, velvety tone and plangent reading create a moving contrast to the excitement of "The Battle on the Ice" movement. Rachmaninov's choral symphony *The Bells* was recorded four years later, but is no less impressive or compelling. This is certainly one of the most satisfying performances on disc, with splendid performances from orchestra, chorus and soloists. The wonderfully crisp and detailed orchestral playing is noticeable from the very beginning and the first appearance of the chorus is guaranteed to send tingles down any listener's spine. Both performances on this disc are served with outstandingly good recorded sound and at 78 minutes this mid-price CD offers exceptional value for money.

However, if *Alexander Nevsky* is your main concern, and money is no object, then Järvi's Chandos disc must earn top recommendation. As recorded sound, this is stunning. The ample acoustics of Caird Hall, Dundee add extra atmosphere for the wide icy expanses and chill of the Russian winter and the huge dynamic range allows an overwhelming force in the "Battle on the Ice". On first hearing, the chorus's frenzied war cries could well induce heart failure. The only small blot on the landscape is the slightly inflated prominence given to Linda Finnie's already rich contralto in the "Field of the Dead". All this would amount to naught were not Järvi and his Scottish forces to give the performance of a lifetime (surely, both singers and players must have some slavic blood coursing their veins?). Järvi, never afraid to intensify the drama with a few ideas of his own, does just that at the start of the "Battle of the Ice" with a gradual acceleration for the advancing forces. It's not in the score, but it is a master-stroke. The earlier *Scythian Suite*, with its more complex textures and spicier harmonies to suit the blood-drinking, pagan god worshipping Scythians, makes an ideal coupling. Try the end — the sun-god appearing to a crescendo of metal and searing, stratospheric woodwind — at a realistic volume setting, and deafness is almost guaranteed. Järvi, teeth bared and nostrils flared, probably gets closer than anyone to the core of this brutal, but mesmerizing score.

Prokofiev. THE LOVE FOR THREE ORANGES (sung in French). **Gabriel Bacquier** (bar) King of Clubs; **Jean-Luc Viala** (ten) Prince; **Hélène Perraguin** (mez) Princess Clarissa; **Vincent Le Texier** (bass-bar) Leandro; **Georges Gautier** (ten) Truffaldino; **Didier Henry** (bar) Pantaloon, Farfarello, Master of Ceremonies; **Gregory Reinhart** (bass) Tchelio; **Michèle Lagrange** (sop) Fata Morgana; **Consuelo Caroli** (mez) Linetta; **Brigitte Fournier** (sop) Nicoletta; **Catherine Dubosc** (sop) Ninetta; **Jules Bastin** (bass) Cook; **Béatrice Uria Monzon** (mez) Smeraldina; **Chorus and Orchestra of Lyon Opéra/Kent Nagano.** Virgin Classics VCD7 91084-2. Notes, text and translation included.

② 1h 42' DDD 12/89

This is a wonderfully zany story about a prince whose hypochondriac melancholy is lifted only at the sight of a malevolent witch tumbling over, in revenge for which she casts on him a love-spell for three oranges: in the ensuing compli-cations he encounters an ogre's gigantic cook who goes all gooey at the sight of a pretty ribbon, princesses inside two of the oranges die of oppressive desert heat, and the third is saved only by the intervention of various groups of 'spectators' who argue with each other on the stage. The music's brittle vivacity matches that of the plot, and though there are no set-pieces for the singers and there is practically no thematic development — the famous orchestral March and Scherzo are the only passages that reappear — the effervescent score is most engaging. The performance, conducted by the musical director of the Lyon Opéra, is full of zest, with lively orchestral playing and a cast that contains several outstanding members and not a single weak one; and the recording is extremely good. Those desirous of so doing can delve into the work's symbolism and identify the objects of its satire — principally Stanislavsky's naturalistic Moscow Arts Theatre: others can simply accept this as a thoroughly enjoyable romp.

Giacomo Puccini

Italian 1858-1924

Puccini. OPERA ARIAS. **Leontyne Price** (sop); **New Philharmonia Orchestra/Edward Downes.** RCA RD85999. Texts and translations included. Items marked [a] from SER5674 (12/73), [b] ARL1 0840 (4/76), [c] SER5589 (1/71), [d] new to UK.
LA BOHEME[a] — Sì, mi chiamano Mimì; Donde lieta uscì; Quando me'n vo'soletta. EDGAR[a] — Addio, mio dolce amor. LA RONDINE[a] — Ore dolce e divine. TOSCA[a] — Vissi d'arte. MANON LESCAUT[a] — In quelle trine morbide; Sola, perduta, abbandonata. LE VILLI[a] — Se come voi. MADAMA BUTTERFLY — Bimba, bimba, non piangere (with Elizabeth Bainbridge, mez; Plácido Domingo, ten; New Philh/Nello Santi)[b]; Un bel dì, vedremo[a]. LA FANCIULLA DEL WEST[a] — Laggiù nel Soledad. GIANNI SCHICCHI[c] — O mio babbino caro (London Symphony Orchestra/Downes). TURANDOT[d] — In questa reggia (Daniele Barioni, ten; Ambrosian Opera Chorus; New Philh/Santi).

· 1h 11' ADD 2/88

Puccini. OPERA ARIAS. **Montserrat Caballé** (sop); **London Symphony Orchestra/Sir Charles Mackerras.** EMI CDC7 47841-2. Texts and translation included. From ASD2632 (2/71).
TURANDOT — Signore, ascolta; Tu che di gel sie cinta. MADAMA BUTTERFLY — Un bel dì vedremo; Tu, tu, piccolo iddio. MANON LESCAUT — In quelle trine morbide; Sola, perduta, abbandonata. GIANNI SCHICCHI — O mio babbino caro. TOSCA — Vissi d'arte. LA BOHEME — Sì, mi chiamano Mimì; Donde lieta uscì. LE VILLI — Se come voi. LA RONDINE — Chi il bel sogno di Doretta.

· 44' ADD 10/87

These two immensely cherishable discs show off a couple of the most beautiful voices of recent decades. Leontyne Price's smokey soprano is gloriously displayed and even in roles one would not expect of her, such as Turandot, her artistry and feeling for line reaps rich rewards. The rarely heard aria from *Edgar* proves a fine vehicle for Price's fluidly-produced legato line and her sure-footed building of climax. Montserrat Caballé's lighter voice is also used to ravishing effect in a similarly wide-ranging programme. She focuses primarily on Puccini's 'little women', singing the role of Liù rather than Turandot, capturing her vulnerability as well as her resolve. She offers the *Rondine* aria that Price passes over and sings it for all it is worth. Her phrasing is quite superb and always used to illuminate the characterization. Mackerras, sensitively aided by the London Symphony Orchestra, accompanies with feeling.

Puccini. MANON LESCAUT. **Maria Callas** (sop) Manon Lescaut; **Giuseppe di Stefano** (ten) Des Grieux; **Giulio Fioravanti** (bar) Lescaut; **Franco Calabrese** (bass) Geronte; **Dino Formichini** (ten) Edmondo; **Fiorenza Cossotto** (mez) Singer; **Carlo Forti** (bass) Innkeeper; **Vito Tatone** (ten) Dancing-master; **Giuseppe Maresi** (bass) Sergeant; **Franco Ricciardi** (ten) Lamplighter; **Franco Ventrigilia** (bass) Captain; **Chorus and Orchestra of La Scala, Milan/Tullio Serafin.** EMI CDS7 47393-8. Notes, text and translation included. From EX290041 (3/86).

· ② 2h ADD 9/86 **℗** ▲

Manon Lescaut is not by any means the most lucidly constructed of Puccini's works, but the youthful ardour of it all combined with his already evident skill as an orchestrator make it an attractive work to encounter both in the theatre and
on disc. Manon herself needs a touch of the capriciousness of a spoilt child in her

portrayal and only Maria Callas has really encompassed all its needs; she is the character to the life, her verbal pointing subtle as always. As Des Grieux, Giuseppe di Stefano is her ardent partner, and their duets are as impassioned and desperate as they should be. Serafin's conducting is attuned to the needs of Puccini's score. His pacing is exemplary, serving the cause of the work's overall shape and the intricate detail of the scoring, drawing authentic sounds from the forces of La Scala. The sound may leave something to be desired but that hardly seems important bearing in mind the arresting nature of the performance.

Puccini. LA BOHEME. **Jussi Björling** (ten) Rodolfo; **Victoria de los Angeles** (sop) Mimì; **Robert Merrill** (bar) Marcello; **Lucine Amara** (sop) Musetta; **John Reardon** (bar) Schaunard; **Giorgio Tozzi** (bass) Colline; **Fernando Corena** (bass) Benoit, Alcindoro; **William Nahr** (ten) Parpignol; **Thomas Powell** (bar) Customs Official; **George de Monte** (bar) Sergeant; **Columbus Boychoir; RCA Victor Chorus and Orchestra/Sir Thomas Beecham.** EMI mono CDS7 47235-8. Notes, text and translation included. From ALP1409/10 (1/57).

⓶ 1h 48' ADD 6/87 P Ⓑ ▲

To recommend a 30-year-old mono recording of *La bohème* over all the more glamorously star-studded and sumptuously recorded versions that have appeared since may seem perverse, but the Beecham version is a true classic which has never been surpassed. This intimate opera is not about two super-stars showing off how loudly they can sing their top Cs, but about a poverty-stricken poet's love for a mortally-ill seamstress. De los Angeles's infinitely-touching Mimì and Björling's poetic, ardent Rodolfo are backed by consistently fine and characterful ensemble work making this the most realistic version ever recorded. The recording of course shows its age, but this is scarcely noticeable as page after page of the score come freshly alive again: not a *tour de force* of vocalism, not a sequence of famous arias with bits of dialogue between but a lyric tragedy of wrenching pathos and truth.

Puccini. TOSCA. **Maria Callas** (sop) Floria Tosca; **Giuseppe di Stefano** (ten) Mario Cavaradossi; **Tito Gobbi** (bar) Baron Scarpia; **Franco Calabrese** (bass) Cesare Angelotti; **Angelo Mercuriali** (ten) Spoletta; **Melchiorre Luise** (bass) Sacristan; **Dario Caselli** (bass) Sciarrone, Gaoler; **Alvaro Cordova** (treb) Shepherd Boy; **Chorus and Orchestra of La Scala, Milan/Victor de Sabata.** EMI mono CDS7 47175-8. Notes, text and translation included. From Columbia 33CX1094/5 (12/53).

⓶ 1h 48' ADD 9/85 P Ⓑ ▲

NEW REVIEW

Puccini. TOSCA. **Nelly Miricioiu** (sop) Floria Tosca; **Giorgio Lamberti** (ten) Mario Cavaradossi; **Silvano Carroli** (bar) Baron Scarpia; **Andrea Piccinni** (bass) Cesare Angelotti; **Miroslav Dvorsky** (ten) Spoletta; **Jozef Spacek** (bar) Sacristan; **Jan Durco** (bass) Sciarrone; **Stanislav Benacka** (bass) Gaoler; **Slovak Philharmonic Chorus; Czecho-Slovak Radio Symphony Orchestra, Bratislava/Alexander Rahbari.** Naxos 8 660001/2. Notes and text included.

⓶ 1h 56' DDD 10/91 £ Ⓑ

In the course of *Tosca*'s history there have been many notable interpreters, but few have been able to encompass so unerringly the love, jealousy and eventual courage of Tosca as well as Maria Callas. Her resinous, sensuous tone, her wonderful diction, and her inborn passion filled every phrase of the score with

Maria Callas   *[photo: EMI/Steiner]*

special and individual meaning. In 1953 she was in her early prime, the tone seldom prey to those uneasy moments on high that marred her later recordings, and with the vital, vivid conducting of Victor de Sabata, her performance has rightly attained classic status. Giuseppe di Stefano is the ardent Cavaradossi, his tone forward and vibrant in that way peculiar to Italians. Tito Gobbi's cynical, snarling Scarpia, aristocratic in manner, vicious in meaning, remains unique in that part on record. The mono recording stands up well to the test of time.

The 1990 Naxos recording presents a strong challenge at bargain price. Whilst not possessing the elemental grandeur of de Sabata's reading, Alexander Rahbari's direction has a properly theatrical feel about it and vocally the performance is of a similar calibre to that of many top Italian opera houses. The undoubted star of the set is Nelly Miricioiu as Tosca. She possesses all the technical requirements demanded by Puccini's graceful vocal writing, and adds a particular brand of pathos which is highly appealing. Giorgio Lamberti's Cavaradossi is very much of the 'stand and deliver' school, but he exploits his big arias to the full. Even more robust is Silvano Carroli's Scarpia. This is a really melodramatic portrayal with every vocal inflexion luxuriously relished; however, there are signs of wear and tear showing from time to time. All the smaller parts are competently taken and the Bratislava Radio Symphony and Chorus have no problems securing a properly Italianate style. Rahbari's choice of tempos are judicious, and he possesses a good sense of dramatic pace, building suitably powerful climaxes in each of the three acts. Naxos's recording is excellent: full and clear. Taken together these factors add up to the kind of performance which has made *Tosca* one of the best loved operas in the repertoire, not overly subtle but powerful and direct.

Puccini. MADAMA BUTTERFLY. **Renata Scotto** (sop) Madama Butterfly; **Carlo Bergonzi** (ten) Pinkerton; **Rolando Panerai** (bar) Sharpless; **Anna di Stasio** (mez) Suzuki; **Piero De Palma** (ten) Goro; **Giuseppe Morresi** (ten) Prince Yamadori; **Silvana Padoan** (mez) Kate Pinkerton; **Paolo Montarsolo** (bass) The Bonze; **Mario Rinaudo** (bass) Commissioner; **Rome Opera House Chorus and Orchestra/Sir John Barbirolli.** EMI CMS7 69654-2. Notes, text and translation included. From SAN184/6 (9/67).

② 2h 22' ADD 5/89   P Ⓑ

This is not quite the best sung *Butterfly* available but Barbirolli ensures that it is the most richly and enjoyably Italianate. Italian opera was in his blood and as a cellist at Covent Garden, playing under Puccini's direction, and as a conductor whose formative years were spent in the theatre (his Covent Garden début was in this very opera), Barbirolli's pleasure in returning to the world of opera is audible throughout this recording. The rapport between him and the Italian orchestra is close and affectionate; it is a heart-warming performance, subtle and supple in the pacing of the love duet, urgently passionate in the great outbursts. Scotto is a touching Butterfly, with all the tiny and crucial details of characterization delicately moulded. There have been more dashing Pinkertons than

Bergonzi, but not many who have so effectively combined suavity of sound with neatness of phrasing and good taste. Panerai is a first-class Sharpless and di Stasio a sympathetic Suzuki; there are no weak links elsewhere, and the recording is decent enough for its date, if a bit narrow in perspective and with the singers rather forwardly placed. Barbirolli's *Butterfly* has several distinguished rivals on CD, but for a performance that will remind you of the first time you fell in love with this opera it has permanent value and great eloquence.

Puccini. LA FANCIULLA DEL WEST. **Carol Neblett** (sop) Minnie; **Plácido Domingo** (ten) Dick Johnson; **Sherrill Milnes** (bar) Jack Rance; **Francis Egerton** (ten) Nick; **Robert Lloyd** (bass) Ashby; **Gwynne Howell** (bass) Jake Wallace; **Paul Hudson** (bass) Billy Jackrabbit; **Anne Wilkens** (sop) Wowkle; **Chorus and Orchestra of the Royal Opera House, Covent Garden/Zubin Mehta.** DG 419 640-2GH2. Notes, text and translation included. From 2709 078 (9/78).

2h 10' ADD 11/87

Puccini. LA FANCIULLA DEL WEST. **Renata Tebaldi** (sop) Minnie; **Mario del Monaco** (ten) Dick Johnson; **Cornell Macneil** (bar) Jack Rance; **Piero de Palma** (ten) Nick; **Silvio Maionica** (bass) Ashby; **Giorgio Tozzi** (bass) Jake Wallace; **Dario Caselli** (bass) Billy Jackrabbit; **Biancamaria Casoni** (mez) Wowkle; **Santa Cecilia Academy Chorus and Orchestra, Rome/Franco Capuana.** Decca Grand Opera 421 595-2DM2. Text and translation included. From SXL2039/41 (12/58).

2h 13' ADD 1/89 £ ▲

This opera depicts the triangular relationship between Minnie, the saloon owner and 'mother' to the entire town of gold miners, Jack Rance, the sheriff and Dick Johnson (alias Ramerrez), a bandit leader. The music is highly developed in Puccini's seamless lyrical style, the arias for the main characters emerge from the texture and return to it effortlessly. The vocal colours are strongly polarized with the cast being all male except for one travesti role and Minnie herself. The score bristles with robust melody as well as delicate scoring, betraying a masterly hand at work. On the DG recording Carol Neblett is a strong Minnie, vocally distinctive and well characterized, whilst Plácido Domingo and Sherrill Milnes make a good pair of suitors for the spunky little lady. Zubin Mehta conducts with real sympathy for the idiom and the orchestra respond well.

Franco Capuana conducts a performance that never forces the pace or overplays a climax, and as a company production it is an admirable piece of work. Of the three principals, Tebaldi as 'the girl' might be expected to constitute the main attraction, del Monaco as the hero the main liability, with Macneil as nasty Jack Rance something in between. In the event, the men do very well indeed, for both are well-suited and del Monaco is both thrilling and surprisingly tender. Tebaldi, by contrast, is a mixed blessing. Cackling at the miners' confusion about the Old Testament and still more at the idea of any man wanting water with his whisky, she establishes the tough side of Minnie's character, but does not make it immediately clear why everyone is so fond of her. She gives a good standard performance, but her best singing comes near the end of the opera in Minnie's touching appeal to the miners before riding off into the sunset.

Puccini. SUOR ANGELICA. **Ilona Tokody** (sop) Suor Angelica; **Eszter Póka** (mez) Princess; **Zsuzsa Barlay** (mez) Mother Superior, Lay Sister II; **Maria Teresa Uribe** (mez) Sister Superior; **Tamara Takács** (mez) Mistress of the Novices, Sister of the Infirmary; **Katalin Pitti** (sop) Suor Genovieffa; **Magda Pulveri** (sop) Suor Osmina; **Zsuzsa Misura** (sop) Suor Dolcina, Lay Sister I; **Janka Békás** (sop) First Nursing Sister; **Margit Keszthelyi** (sop)

Second Nursing Sister; **Ildikó Szönyi** (sop) Novice; **Hungarian State Opera Chorus and Orchestra/Lamberto Gardelli.** Hungaroton HCD12490-2.

| 52' DDD |

Suor Angelica risks sentimentality, telling of a young nun confined to a convent to atone for the scandal of having given birth to a child out of wedlock. She is visited by her aunt, the frosty Princess, who tells Angelica of the death of her son. Angelica resolves on suicide and as her life ebbs away sees a vision of the Holy Virgin. The orchestration is lush and the texture can become monotonous with its preponderance of female voices. The lament "Senza mamma" is the opera's 'hit', and when sung in so winning a way as here by Ilona Tokody, achieves a moving sense of the young girl's spiritual innocence and nobility of purpose. The other parts are sung competently and the choral passages are nicely balanced. Gardelli directs a highly sympathetic performance, never overlooking the score's felicitous detail. The recording is clear if a little generous of acoustic.

Puccini. TURANDOT. **Dame Joan Sutherland** (sop) Princess Turandot; **Luciano Pavarotti** (ten) Calaf; **Montserrat Caballé** (sop) Liù; **Tom Krause** (bar) Ping; **Pier Francesco Poli** (ten) Pang, Prince of Persia; **Piero De Palma** (ten) Pong; **Sir Peter Pears** (ten) Emperor Altoum; **Nicolai Ghiaurov** (bass) Timur; **Sabin Markov** (bar) Mandarin; **Wandsworth School Boys' Choir; John Alldis Choir; London Philharmonic Orchestra/Zubin Mehta.** Decca 414 275-2DH2. From SET561 (9/73).

| ② 1h 57' ADD 5/85 |

Turandot is a psychologically complex work fusing appalling sadism with self-sacrificing devotion. The icy Princess of China has agreed to marry any man of royal blood who can solve three riddles she has posed. If he fails his head will roll. Calaf, the son of the exiled Tartar king Timur, answers all the questions easily and when Turandot hesitates to accept him, magnanimously offers her a riddle in return — "What is his name?". Liù, Calaf's faithful slave-girl, is tortured but rather than reveal his identity kills herself. Turandot finally capitulates, announcing that his name is Love. Dame Joan Sutherland's assumption of the title role is statuesque, combining regal poise with a more human warmth, whilst Montserrat Caballé is a touchingly sympathetic Liù, skilfully steering the character away from any hint of the mawkish. Pavarotti's Calaf is a heroic figure in splendid voice and the chorus is handled with great power, baying for blood at one minute, enraptured with Liù's nobility at the next. Mehta conducts with great passion and a natural feel for Puccini's wonderfully tempestuous drama. Well recorded.

Henry Purcell

British 1659-1695

Purcell. SONATAS, Volume 3. **Purcell Quartet** ([a]Catherine Mackintosh, Elizabeth Wallfisch, vns; Richard Boothby, va da gamba; [b]Robert Woolley, org). Chandos CHAN8763.
Ten Sonatas in Four Parts, Z802-11 — No. 3 in A minor; No. 4 in D minor; No. 5 in G minor; No. 6 in G minor; No. 7 in G major; No. 8 in G minor (with two variant movements); No. 9 in F major; No. 10 in D major. Organ Voluntaries, Z717-20[b] — No. 2 in D minor; No. 4 in G major. Prelude for Solo Violin in G minor, ZN773[a].

| 1h 3' DDD 12/89 |

For Purcell lovers this recording promises an hour of sheer delight. The
performers play upon instruments of choice, one violin (Jan Bouwmeester, 1669)

being contemporary with the composer, the other a fine-toned eighteenth-century Italian instrument. Both gamba and chamber organ are modern reconstructions based on seventeenth-century English models. The acoustics of Orford Church where the recording took place ensure warmth and clarity and even give you the extraordinary feeling that the players are actually present in your sitting-room, with the strings close beside you and the organ only a step away. Many listeners will be familiar with Purcell's *Sonatas in Four Parts*: generations of young fiddlers have been brought up on pieces like the *Golden* Sonata (No. 9) or the famous Chaconne (No. 6). This performance, with its sensitivity, ease and wit should therefore arouse happy memories. It all seems so simple, yet what perfection of detail! — small points, such as the choice of the order in which the sonatas are played, ensuring smooth transitions and apt contrasts; the adoption of appropriately graded tempos; the delicacy, grace and elegance of the music, but also the mysteriously expressive chromaticism and certain moments of unexpected exploratory harmony.

Purcell. AYRES FOR THE THEATRE. **The Parley of Instruments/Peter Holman.** Hyperion CDA66212.
Abdelazer, Z570 — suite. Timon of Athens, Z632 — No. 1, Overture; No. 20, Curtain tune. The Gordion Knot Unty'd, Z597 — suite. Bonduca, Z574 — suite. The Virtuous Wife, Z611 — suite. Chacony in G minor, Z730.

`57' DDD 9/87`

This well recorded disc gathers some of Purcell's most delightful incidental music for the many theatrical productions his music graced. Listeners familiar with Britten's *The Young Person's Guide to the Orchestra* will recognize the theme plucked from *Abdelazer* and here given a very sprightly gait. There is some outstanding instrumental playing — with some virtuoso natural trumpet playing from Crispian Steele-Perkins — and tempos are consistently crisper and more alert than normal. The collection also includes Purcell's well-known *Chacony* in a brisk performance — it may have originated in the theatre anyway and so makes a logical addition. This delightful disc is far more generously cued than the sleeve would have one believe, and makes for pleasing listening in an intimate recording acoustic.

Purcell. CHORAL WORKS. **Taverner Choir; Taverner Players/Andrew Parrott.** EMI Reflexe CDC7 49635-2. Texts included.
Ode for St Cecilia's Day, 1683 — Welcome to all the pleasures, Z339 (with John Mark Ainsley, Charles Daniels, tens). Funeral Sentences — Man that is born of a woman, Z27; In the midst of life, Z17a; Thou know'st, Lord, Z58b. Ode for Queen Mary's Birthday, 1694 — Come ye sons of art, away, Z323 (Emily Van Evera, sop; Timothy Wilson, alto; Ainsley, Daniels; David Thomas, bass). Funeral Music for Queen Mary — March and Canzona, Z860. Thou know'st, Lord, Z58c.

`55' DDD 2/90`

This is a satisfying anthology of vocal music by Purcell which includes the masterly and memorable *Come ye sons of art, away*. Andrew Parrott, as so often, has some surprises in store for the unsuspecting listener; here he performs the famous duet "Sound the trumpet" not with two countertenors but with two voices of contrasting timbres and registers: a countertenor and a tenor, albeit a high one. This has been achieved by a choice of low pitch for the entire work and the results are convincing. Likewise, the air "Sound the viol", traditionally countertenor's property, has been allotted to a high tenor. Parrott brings this beautiful work to life with insight, affection and rigorous attention to all aspects of style. Much else on the disc is comparably successful and, if the music does

557

not always maintain the dizzy heights of *Come ye sons of art* it is never far below. Outstanding from a musical and interpretative standpoint are the profoundly affecting *Funeral Sentences* and *Funeral Music for Queen Mary* both of which are notably well served by EMI in its sympathetic recording.

Purcell. THEATRE MUSIC. **Joy Roberts, Judith Nelson, Emma Kirkby, Elizabeth Lane, Prudence Lloyd** (sops); **James Bowman** (alto); **Martyn Hill, Paul Elliott, Alan Byers, Peter Bamber, Rogers Covey-Crump, Julian Pike** (tens); **David Thomas, Christopher Keyte, Geoffrey Shaw, Michael George** (basses); **Taverner Choir; Academy of Ancient Music/ Christopher Hogwood** (hpd). L'Oiseau-Lyre 425 893-2OM6. Texts included. Abdelazar, Z570. Distressed Innocence, Z577. The Married Beau, Z603. The Gordian Knot Unty'd, Z597 (all from DSLO504, 6/76). Sir Anthony Love, Z588. Bonduca, Z574. Circe, Z575 (DSLO527, 2/78). The Virtuous Wife, Z611. The Old Bachelor, Z607. Overture in G minor, Z770. Amphitryon, Z572 (DSLO55Q, 12/79). The Comical History of Don Quixote, Z578 (DSLO534, 11/78). The Double Dealer, Z592. The Richmond Heiress, Z608. The Rival Sisters, Z609. Henry the Second, King of England Z580. Tyrannic Love, Z613 (DSLO561, 4/81). Overture in G minor, Z772. Theodosius, Z606. The Libertine, Z600. The Massacre of Paris, Z604. Oedipus, Z583 (DSLO590, 3/82). Overture in D minor, Z771. The History of King Richard II, Z581. Sir Barnaby Whigg, Z589. Sophonisba, Z590. The English Lawyer, Z594. A Fool's Preferement, Z571. The Indian Emperor, Z598. The Knight of Malta, Z599. Why, my Daphne, why complaining?, Z525. The Wifes' Excuse, Z612. Cleomenes, Z576. Regulus, Z586. The Marriage-hater Match'd, Z602 (414 173-1OH, 7/85). Love Triumphant, Z582. Rule a Wife and have a Wife, Z587. The Female Virtuosos, Z596. Epsom Wells, Z579. The Maid's Last Prayer, Z601. Aureng-Zebe, Z573. The Canterbury Guests, Z591. The Fatal Marriage, Z595. The Spanish Friar, Z610. Pausanias, Z585. The Mock Marriage, Z605. Oroonoko, Z584 (414 174-1OH, 9/85). Pavans — A major, Z748; A minor, Z749; B flat major, BWV750; G minor, BWV751; G minor, Z752. Trio Sonata for violin, bass viol and organ, Z780. Chaconne, Z730 (DSLO514, 10/77).

⑥ 6h 54' ADD/DDD 4/91

This six-CD anthology of vocal and instrumental music by Purcell is as rich and rewarding in its variety as it is indispensable to our picture of this English genius. Although Restoration England continued to take an interest in theatre music from abroad towards the end of the seventeenth century she began to develop staged

musical entertainments along hybrid lines of her own. Most of the music contained here dates from the last six years of Purcell's life when plays, from Shakespeare to Shadwell were seldom staged without songs, instrumental interludes and dances. Purcell's legacy to the Restoration stage contains jewels of almost price-less worth and these are lovingly burnished by Christopher Hogwood, the Academy of Ancient Music and an excellent group of vocalists; choruses are imaginatively sung by the Taverner Choir under Andrew Parrott's direction. It would be difficult to isolate any particular songs and dances from such a vast

Emma Kirkby *[photo: Sclater*

treasure-trove but few may be able to resist Emma Kirkby's saucy "Lads and Lasses, blithe and gay" (*Don Quixote*), Martyn Hill's "Thus to a ripe, consenting maid" (*The Old Bachelor*), the ravishing trio "With this sacred charming wand" (*Don Quixote*) or the "Scotch tune" from *Amphitryon*. Performances are lively and stylish if not always polished but that, one suspects, is as authentic a touch as anything else here. The booklet contains texts of all the songs and the discs are pleasantly recorded.

Purcell. Hail, bright Cecilia. **Emma Kirkby** (sop); **Michael Chance, Kevin Smith** (altos); **Rogers Covey-Crump, Charles Daniels, Paul Elliott, Neil Jenkins, Andrew King** (tens); **Michael George, Simon Grant, David Thomas, Richard Wistreich** (basses); **Robert Woolley** (org); **Taverner Choir and Players/Andrew Parrott.** EMI Reflexe CDC7 47490-2. Text included.

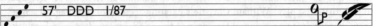

57' DDD 1/87

Purcell's Ode in praise of the patroness of music is but one of a whole series of such works written by various composers between 1683 and 1703 for festivities held at the Stationer's Hall in London. Purcell had written the first ode for these gatherings and was later asked to make a setting of words by the Royal Chaplain Nicholas Brady. Throughout its 13 sections poet and composer hymn the praises of the various instruments of music. Purcell's limpid music beautifully and tastefully adorns this most gracious of poetry and vividly observes both its vigour and sublimity. The Taverner Consort, Choir and Players comprise some of the finest musicians in the early-music field and with such fresh and versatile voices as Emma Kirkby's, Rogers Covey-Crump's and Michael Chance's, to single out but three, singing the praises of music, who could complain? The recording is clear, spacious and natural-sounding.

Purcell. DIDO AND AENEAS. **Dame Janet Baker** (sop) Dido; **Patricia Clark** (sop) Belinda; **Eileen Poulter** (sop) Second Woman; **Raimund Herincx** (bass) Aeneas; **Monica Sinclair** (contr) Sorceress; **Rhianon James** (mez) First Witch; **Catherine Wilson** (mez) Second Witch; **John Mitchinson** (ten) Sailor; **Dorothy Dorow** (sop) Spirit; **St Anthony Singers; English Chamber Orchestra/Anthony Lewis.** Decca Serenata 425 720-2DM. From L'Oiseau-Lyre 1961 SOL60047 (3/62).

53' ADD 12/90

This now historic recording has never really been surpassed in excellence. It is arguably the best performance of Purcell's tightly-constructed opera — better even than Flagstad's and Schwarzkopf's rendering in the 1950s and certainly equal to more recent recordings. It is a collector's item, with Janet Baker, in the role of Dido, rising to the height of her vocal powers. Her first aria, "Ah! Belinda I am prest", is full of tender foreboding and her final lament powerfully grief-stricken. She is well supported by Patricia Clark, Dido's light-hearted confidante. Monica Sinclair reveals herself as a truly sinister, though somewhat unevenly-voiced Sorceress. The hero's role in the opera is minimal, but Raimund Herincx matches up well to the heroine in their famous final duet. The St Anthony Singers give ample proof of their versatility producing, as required by the score, cackling witches, boozy sailors and rabble or merely a crowd of gently gossiping English courtiers running for shelters from the elements. The strings of the English Chamber Orchestra are supported by Thurston Dart on the harpsichord continuo — a definite plus, this, and a reminder of the tragically early death of a brilliant performer who combines, here as always, both discretion and inspired imagination.

Purcell. THE FAIRY QUEEN. **Nancy Argenta, Lynne Dawson, Isabelle Desrochers, Willemijn van Gent, Veronique Gens, Sandrine Piau, Noéme Rime** (sops); **Charles Daniels, Jean-Paul Fouchécourt, Mark le Brocq, Christophe le Paludier** (altos); **Bernard Loonen, Françoise Piolino, Thomas Randle** (tens); **François Bazola** (bar); **Jérôme Corréas, George Banks-Martin, Bernard Deletré, Thomas Lander, Richard Taylor** (basses); **Les Arts Florissants/William Christie.** Harmonia Mundi HMC90 1308/9. Notes and text included.

② 2h 8' DDD 1/90

Purcell's *The Fairy Queen*, loosely based by an anonymous seventeenth-century literary hack on Shakespeare's *A Midsummer Night's Dream*, was one of the composer's last works. Like all his other works for the London public theatres, *The Fairy Queen* is not so much an opera in the accepted sense, but more a sequence of masque-like interludes together with dances and instrumental music designed to punctuate the play. William Christie's exciting account of this magical score grew directly from a staging of the piece at the 1989 Aix-en-Provence Festival, and it retains all the immediacy and conviction of an interpretation born of genuine theatrical experience. The orchestra is large for the period, but it allows Christie to exploit all the nuances of Purcell's writing, from the wit of the Scene

of the Drunken Poet to the delicate sadness of the Act Five Plaint, wistfully delivered by Lynne Dawson. The high point is the deliciously comic exchange between Bernard Deletré and Jean-Paul Fouchécourt in the dialogue between Corydon and Mopsa, sharply characterized and given an added humorous edge by the remaining traces of Gallic pronunciation. This is a sheer delight to listen to, and a must for anyone keen to hear some of the finest English music of the seventeenth century.

The Fairy Queen   *[photo: Harmonia Mundi/Ely*

Henri Rabaud
French 1873-1949

NEW REVIEW

Rabaud. MAROUF, SAVETIER DU CAIRE — Dances. ORCHESTRAL WORKS. **Loire Philharmonic Orchestra/Pierre Dervaux.** EMI CDM7 63951-2. From Pathé 2C 069 16303 (1/81).
Eglogue — Virgilian poem for orchestra, Op. 7. Divertissement on Russian Songs, Op. 2. La procession nocturne — symphonic poem, Op. 6.

49' ADD 3/92

Rabaud was an experienced conductor, who headed the Boston Symphony Orchestra for two years, and who in fact recorded all the works on this disc. His gifts as a creator of orchestral colour were probably stimulated initially by a period of study with Massenet, and later by his practical experience on the rostrum. *Maroûf*, an opera based on tales from the Arabian Nights, was produced at the Paris Opéra in 1914. It contains a set of lively dances with a quasi-oriental flavour, which are played with great dash and enthusiasm by the Loire orchestra under Pierre Dervaux. The other three pieces date from the mid to late 1890s, when Rabaud was still in his twenties. The short and contemplative *Eglogue*, based on a poem by Virgil, is a most delightful piece: the *Divertissement* explores various Russian airs in a very jolly fashion; and *La procession nocturne*, based on an episode from Lenau's *Faust* is a mysterious, atmospheric piece with something of a Franckian flavour. Dervaux conducts all these pieces with imagination and flair, the orchestral playing is highly idiomatic, and the recorded sound is warm and spacious.

Sergey Rachmaninov
Russian / American 1873-1943

Rachmaninov. Piano Concerto No. 1 in F sharp minor, Op. 1[a]. Rhapsody on a Theme of Paganini, Op. 43[b]. **Vladimir Ashkenazy (pf); [a]Concertgebouw Orchestra, Amsterdam, [b]Philharmonia Orchestra/Bernard Haitink.** Decca 417 613-2DH.

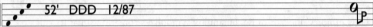

52' DDD 12/87

Showpiece that it is, with its lush romantic harmonies and contrasting vigorous panache, the First Concerto has much to commend it in purely musical terms and although its debts are clear enough (most notably perhaps to Rimsky-Korsakov), it stands on its own two feet as far as invention, overall design and musical construction are concerned. The *Paganini* Rhapsody is one of the composer's finest works and arguably the most purely inventive set of variations to be based on Paganini's catchy tune ever written. The wealth of musical invention it suggested to Rachmaninov is truly bewildering and his control over what can in lesser hands become a rather laboured formal scheme is masterly indeed. Ashkenazy gives superb performances of both works and the Concertgebouw and the Philharmonia are in every way the perfect foils under Bernard Haitink's sympathetic direction. There is weight, delicacy, colour, energy and repose in equal measure here and it is all conveyed by a full-bodied and detailed recording.

Rachmaninov. Piano Concerto No. 2 in C minor, Op. 18. Rhapsody on a Theme of Paganini, Op. 43. **Vladimir Ashkenazy (pf); London Symphony Orchestra/André Previn.** Decca Ovation 417 702-2DH. From SXLF6565/7 (9/72).

58' ADD 7/87

Rachmaninov. Piano Concerto No. 2 in C minor, Op. 18. **Cristina Ortiz (pf); Royal Philharmonic Orchestra/Moshe Atzmon.** Decca 414 348-2DH. From 414 348-1DH (5/86).
Addinsell: Warsaw Concerto. *Litolff:* Concerto symphonique No. 4 in D minor, Op. 102 — Scherzo. *Gottschalk* (orch. Hazell): Grande fantaisie triomphale sur l'hymne national brésilien, RO108.

58' DDD 9/86

Rachmaninov. Piano Concertos — No. 2 in C minor, Op. 18[a]; No. 3 in D minor, Op. 30[b]. **Sergei Rachmaninov (pf); Philadelphia Orchestra/ [a]Leopold Stokowski; [b]Eugene Ormandy.** RCA Red Seal mono RD85997. Item marked [a] from HMV DB1333/7 (11/29), [b] DB5709/13 (12/40).

1h 6' ADD 10/88

Rachmaninov. Piano Concerto No. 3 in D minor, Op. 30[a]. PRELUDES[b].
Vladimir Ashkenazy (pf); [a]**London Symphony Orchestra/André Previn.**
Decca Ovation 417 764-2DM. Item marked [a] from SXLF6565/7 (9/72), [b] 5BB
221/2 (2/76).
Preludes — C sharp minor, Op. 3 No. 2; B flat major, Op. 23 No. 2; G minor,
Op. 23 No. 5; B minor, Op. 32 No. 10; D flat major, Op. 32 No. 13.

> 1h 10' ADD 10/88 £ Ⓑ

Rachmaninov. Piano Concertos — No. 2 in C minor, Op 18; No. 3 in
D minor, Op. 30. **Earl Wild** (pf); **Royal Philharmonic Orchestra/Jascha
Horenstein.** Chandos Collect CHAN6507. First released on Reader's Digest in
1966.

> 1h 6' ADD 2/91 Ⓟ Ⓑ

Rachmaninov. Piano Concerto No. 2 in C minor, Op. 18. Rhapsody on a
Theme of Paganini, Op. 43. **Jenö Jandó** (pf); **Budapest Symphony
Orchestra/György Lehel.** Naxos 8 550117.

> 58' DDD 10/90 £ Ⓑ

The C minor Concerto of Rachmaninov symbolizes romanticism at its ripest.
Its combination of poetry and sensuous warmth with languorously memorable
melodic lines balanced by exhilarating pianistic brilliance happily avoids any
suggestion of sentimentality. The simple chordal introduction from the soloist
ushers in one of the composer's most luscious tunes, yet the slow movement
develops even greater ardour in its melodic contour, and the composer holds
back a further haunting expressive idea to bring lyrical contrast to the scintillating finale. Ashkenazy's 1972 performance with Previn is a superb mid-price
bargain, coupled with an exhilarating performance of the *Rhapsody on a theme of
Paganini*, where the famous Variation No. 18 blossoms with passionate fervour.
The Concerto is no less involving, the first movement building to an engulfing
climax, the *Adagio* radiantly beautiful, perhaps the finest on disc. The recording
represents Decca vintage analogue sound at its best and the remastering is
extremely successful, rich, well balanced and vivid.

However, Decca have since produced a highly-recommendable digital
alternative from Ortiz and the RPO. The couplings are apt. The genuinely
inspired pastiche *Warsaw Concerto* by Richard Addinsell has a principal theme
worthy to stand alongside those of Rachmaninov and its layout shows satisfying
craftsmanship. Ortiz plays this main theme with great affection and she is equally
beguiling in the delicious Litolff *Scherzo*. The effect here is of elegance rather than
extrovert brilliance: this is reserved for the Gottschalk *Grande fantaisie triomphale*,
which is played with a splendid panache that almost covers its inherent vulgarity
and certainly emphasizes its ingenuous charm. Throughout the recording balance
is realistic and the reverberation adds the most attractive bloom.

·The RCA recordings sound every bit as old as they are, ill-defined in the
bass and decidedly short on tonal allure from either piano or orchestra. So it
takes a rather special kind of performance to earn this CD a place in this *Guide*.
To have the composer's own view of two such familiar works is valuable enough
in itself and to many listeners brought up on more modern styles of playing
Rachmaninov's interpretations will seem startlingly different. Not that they are
freer or more romantic; rather the reverse — tempos are generally faster,
expressive lingerings generally avoided. The end result is to reveal more clearly
the architecture of the music and its dynamic force rather than its communication
of feeling.

The fourth disc here again features the Ashkenazy/Previn/LSO partnership.
Ashkenazy's recording of the Third Concerto complements the composer's own.
It is more conspicuously expressive, more heroic and more yielding by turns; it
is uncut, includes the more massive of the first movement cadenzas, and it enjoys
a full-blooded modern recording. There is a tendency to bang away when the

chords are coming thick and fast and to overdo expressive lingerings; also, Previn's accompaniment is fine but not outstandingly idiomatic. But these points do not outweigh the advantages of what, especially at mid-price, is one of the top recommendations for this concerto. A selection of five of Rachmaninov's most popular Preludes enhances the attractions of the disc.

Wild's 1965 recording with Horenstein comes into the connoisseur category. All the urgent bravura is here, and the heart-on-the-sleeve emotions, but a strong discipline controls the overall framework. Excessive fluctuations in speed and mawkish poring over details are carefully avoided to produce an almost classical structural poise. The Third Concerto, with its sometimes overplayed degree of introspection, particularly benefits from this approach and together these readings illustrate the best qualities of Rachmaninov's work in this genre.

The highly recommendable Naxos coupling did much to establish the reputation of its Hungarian soloist, Jenö Jandó as an artist of distinction, and at the same time shows that a super bargain label could offer a quality of music-making and recording to compare with the finest issues at premium price. The Concerto opens simply, and Jandó shows a natural feeling for the ebb and flow of the Rachmaninovian phrase The *Adagio* is beautifully played by soloist and orchestra alike and the finale brings exhilarating zest and a ripe romantic blossoming for its famous lyrical melody. The *Rhapsody on a Theme of Paganini* is even finer: it has all the necessary flamboyance and bravura, yet there is no sense of virtuosity just for its own sake, and the work's detail and variety of mood are revealed in the most spontaneous way, not least the plangent arrival of the *Dies irae*. The romantic expansiveness at Variation No. 18 is followed by a postlude of gentle nostalgia from the soloist; then he sets off again in sparkling fashion and there is plenty of excitement in the closing Variations. György Lehel's accompaniments are splendidly supportive in both works, while the recorded sound is first rate in every way. The individual Variations are not cued, but this remains an astonishing bargain.

Rachmaninov. ORCHESTRAL WORKS. **London Symphony Orchestra/ André Previn.** EMI Studio CDM7 69025-2. Items marked [a] from ASD3259 (9/76), [b] ASD3284 (12/76), [c] ASD3369 (8/77).
Symphonic Dances, Op. 45[a]. The isle of the dead, Op. 29[a]. Vocalise, Op. 34 No. 14[b] (arr. composer). ALEKO[c] — Intermezzo; Women's Dance.

| ●●● | 1h 11' ADD 9/87 | ♀♂ |

André Previn's affinity with the music of Rachmaninov is evident and few people give the symphonic works the same weight of authority or attention to detail. This issue gathers some of his finest performances. The *Symphonic Dances* have a rhythmic crispness that Previn willingly softens where the string writing gains in texture and fullness. The elegant waltz theme is laid over the sprightly accompaniment with just the right nonchalance. *The isle of the dead* receives an appropriately mysterious interpretation and the *Vocalise* is prepared for even the most addicted sweet-tooth. The programme closes with the two extracts from *Aleko* — nicely shaded and beautifully shaped. The LSO play superbly and the recording has been finely remastered.

Rachmaninov. SYMPHONIES. **Concertgebouw Orchestra, Amsterdam/ Vladimir Ashkenazy.** Decca 421 065-2DM3. Item marked [a] from SXDL7603 (11/83), [b] SXDL7563 (7/82), [c] SXDL7531 (6/83).
Symphonies — No. 1 in D minor, Op. 13[a]; No. 2 in E minor, Op. 27[b]; No. 3 in A minor, Op. 44[c]; Youth Symphony[c].

| ●●● ③ | 2h 30' DDD 12/87 | ♀♂ |

NEW REVIEW

Rachmaninov. SYMPHONIES AND ORCHESTRAL WORKS. **Royal Philharmonic Orchestra/Andrew Litton.** Virgin Classics VC7 90830/32-2. *VC7 90830* — Symphony No. 1 in D minor, Op. 13. The isle of the dead, Op. 29. *VC7 90831* — Symphony No. 2 in E minor, Op. 27. Vocalise, Op. 34 No. 14. *VC7 90832* — Symphony No. 3 in A minor, Op. 44. Symphonic Dances, Op. 45.

③ 1h 7', 1h 10', 1h 18' DDD 5/90

NEW REVIEW

Rachmaninov. Symphony No. 2 in E minor, Op. 27. **Orchestre de Paris/ Semyon Bychkov.** Philips 432 101-2PH.

58' DDD 9/91

Rachmaninov's symphonies possess a melodic memorability and lyrical ardour to match the piano concertos. The Second in E minor was the first to gain general recognition, with its sweeping string melodies and gloriously expansive slow movement; No. 3, written some 20 years after the Second Symphony, has hardly less melodic appeal, and is notable for a hauntingly nostalgic *molto cantabile* melody which acts as secondary theme in the first movement. His First was a failure at its première and Rachmaninov abandoned it in despair; it languished unplayed for two decades but has now gained universal acceptance for its emotional power and the rugged strength of the finale. Ashkenazy is particularly successful in bringing this fine work vibrantly to life. Here, as in the other symphonies, his volatile tempos and passionately spontaneous control of rubato within the spacious romantic paragraphs create the most involving ebb and flow of tension, with the lyrical melodies always blossoming readily. Throughout all three symphonies the expressive urgency of the playing of the Concertgebouw, with moments of serenity and glowing expansiveness to balance the ardour, give the utmost satisfaction to the listener. Each work moves forward with striking spontaneity and the splendid digital recording is vividly detailed and gloriously full in its textures; the slight edge of the strings in the Second Symphony adds bite to the performance, rather than detracting from the interpretation. As a bonus Ashkenazy offers the early *Youth* Symphony composed when Rachmaninov was 18, immature in its Tchaikovskian influences, but pleasingly fresh in invention.

Apart from Ashkenazy's complete cycle of the symphonies there have been few conductors (save perhaps Previn) who have shown such a consummate under-standing of Rachmaninov's symphonic language and thought processes. However, in 1990, Andrew Litton came along with a cycle that proved, in one giant stride, that he too can rightfully take his place alongside some of the finest Rachmaninov interpreters on disc. The ill-fated First Symphony receives a truly weighty and magnificent performance that should lay to rest for once and all the vitriolic notices that at one times caused it to languish as a mere footnote to Rach-maninov's output — Litton's account has fire, spontaneity and nobility tempered with that particular brand of restless yearning that pervades so much of Rachmaninov's music. The Second Symphony faces particularly stiff competition from both Ashkenazy and Bychkov, but Litton absolves himself marvellously. The expansive first movement has rarely sounded so fresh and engaging as it does here (incidentally Litton observes the exposition repeat), and the lush, nostalgic romanticism of the gorgeous *Adagio* is exquisitely captured. In Litton's hands, the Third Symphony doesn't perhaps achieve the same heart-wrenching nostalgic glow as Ashkenazy's account, but it's nevertheless a performance of great beauty and perception. A suitably dark and inwardly brooding account of *The isle of the dead* comes coupled with the First Symphony, and a very fine, sparkling account of the *Symphonic Dances* with the Third.

Semyon Bychkov's account of the Second Symphony on Philips may be rather ungenerous regarding value (no couplings), but what it lacks in length it more

Semyon Bychkov   *[photo: Philips/Holt*

than makes up for in quality. With Previn's classic account currently out of the catalogue, Bychkov's reading may well lay strong claims to being the finest version on disc. Here is an account that is both full-blooded and romantic, never overindulgent, and refreshingly direct. The *Adagio* is given a very dignified, almost stoical reading which never lapses into maudlin sentimentality as it sometimes can, and from which Bychkov coaxes from his players some extremely telling and subtle performances. Unlike Litton, Bychkov omits the exposition repeat in the first movement, but makes none of the other cuts that have sometimes plagued this score. Stunningly recorded.

Rachmaninov. Symphony No. 3 in A minor, Op. 44[a].
Shostakovich. Symphony No. 6 in B minor, Op. 54[b]. **London Symphony Orchestra/André Previn.** EMI Studio CDM7 69564-2. Item marked [a] from ASD3369 (8/77), [b] ASD3029 (12/74).

1h 15'   ADD   12/88   £

Previn's highly praised recording of Rachmaninov's Third Symphony came at the peak of a very successful period in the EMI studios, the Shostakovich, hardly less fine, was done three years earlier. They make a splendid and distinguished mid-price coupling showing the symbiosis Previn had with the LSO at that time. The string section play Rachmaninov's lyrical themes with a rapturous romantic sweep and the nervous intensity of the reading is immensely gripping. The first movement of the Shostakovich Sixth is an expansive *Largo*, longer than the other two movements put together, especially when Previn's treatment is so eloquently spacious; the scherzo which follows is full of wit, and the ebullient finale seems optimistic, but maybe things are not what they seem. Previn is clearly deeply involved in this powerful score and so are his players and the remastered recording is full and clear without too much loss of ambience in the clarification process.

NEW REVIEW

Rachmaninov. Symphony No. 3 in A minor, Op. 44[a]. The isle of the dead, Op. 29[b]. Vocalise, Op. 34 No. 14 (arr. composer)[c]. **Philadelphia Orchestra/ Sergey Rachmaninov.** Pearl GEMMCD9414. Item marked [a] from HMV DB5780/4 (3/41), [b] and [c] HMV D2011/3 (10/31).

59'   AAD   ▲

The composer's own recording of the Third Symphony is an essential companion to any modern recording. Rachmaninov himself considered it to be one of his finest works and he was both mystified and disappointed by the somewhat unenthusiastic reception it received at its first performance in 1937. Indeed, critics of the time were almost unanimous to a man in predicting an early demise (heaven protect the public from music critics!), but Rachmaninov was determined to record the work so as to allow for a greater time for a reappraisal. Two years later he fulfilled his ambition, though it is only in recent years that the symphony has achieved anything like the recognition it so richly deserves, and it is now even beginning to rival the popularity of the much loved Second Symphony. As one can imagine, Rachmaninov makes a powerfully convincing case for the work, and many conductors recording the work today still return to the composer's authoritative interpretation for inspiration. Rachmaninov certainly brings a special kind of warmth and nostalgia to this work (which speaks so longingly of his homeland) that few conductors have rivalled since. The composer's own recordings of the symphonic tone poem *The isle of the dead* and his own orchestration of *Vocalise* are no less moving. The transfers from 78s are excellent though the vintage of the recordings still demands a certain tolerance.

Rachmaninov. PIANO MUSIC FOR FOUR AND SIX HANDS. **Brigitte Engerer, Oleg Maisenberg.** Harmonia Mundi HMC90 1301/02.
Russian Rhapsody in E minor. Suites — No. 1, Op. 5, "Fantaisie-tableaux"; No. 2, Op. 17. Polka italienne (1906). Romance in G major (1893). Six Duets, Op. 11. Two pieces for six hands (with Elena Bachkirova). Symphonic Dances, Op. 45*a*.

② 2h 11' DDD 3/90

Rachmaninov's four- and six-hand piano music covers his whole composing career, from the *Russian Rhapsody* of 1891 to the *Symphonic Dances* of nearly 50 years later (the latter being better known in Rachmaninov's orchestral version). It is a rewarding repertoire, even if it is only with the *Symphonic Dances* that it is appropriate to speak of a masterpiece. One reason why these works get so much less exposure than the solo piano music is the inherent problem of the two-piano or duet medium — the need to synchronize the instantaneous attacks of two pianists can easily stifle their expressive freedom (and to leave attacks unsyn-chronized can sound terribly amateurish). Engerer and Maisenberg have a shared understanding of the idiom which helps them around this problem, and their performances are fluent, warmly expressive and cleanly recorded. Recording quality gourmets should note that not all the pieces were recorded on the same occasion or with the same set-up of instruments — in the second movement of the First Suite the two pianos even appear to swap channels. It should also be said that the Second Suite, a favourite with students and adventurous amateurs, is a little less exciting as a performance than the rest of the programme. Apart from those things, this is an exceptionally fine issue.

Rachmaninov. Piano Sonatas — No. 1 in D minor, Op. 28; No. 2 in B flat minor, Op. 36 (original version). **Gordon Fergus-Thompson** (pf). Kingdom KCLCD2007.

1h 13' DDD 6/89

Familiar though Rachmaninov is as a composer of piano concertos, his two Piano Sonatas have not attained anything like the same level of popularity. But here is a recording that couples them together in performances that are both persuasive and masterly. Gordon Fergus-Thompson has the technique and the temperament to do full justice to this music. In his later life, Rachmaninov made considerable cuts in his Second Sonata, but today the tendency is to return to his original, which is what Fergus-Thompson does here to good advantage. In this form the Sonata lasts some 28 minutes, but it does not outstay its welcome; and as a matter of fact the First Sonata is longer at nearly three-quarters of an hour. Both sonatas contain thrilling and highly personal music, and they have been well recorded.

Rachmaninov. 24 Préludes[a]. Piano Sonata No. 2 in B flat minor, Op. 36[b]. **Vladimir Ashkenazy** (pf). Decca 414 417-2DH2. Item marked [a] from 5BB 221/2 (2/76), [b] SXL6996 (9/82).

(2) 1h 46' ADD 11/85

These recordings were outstanding on LP and they sound even better in CD format. Ashkenazy gets as close as possible to making the C sharp minor *Prelude* sound fresh, and one might also note the becalmed melancholy of Op. 23 No. 1, the exquisite management of the different threads in the texture of Op. 23 No. 4, the supple flow of Op. 23 No. 6. Superficially the two sets of *Preludes* are similar, yet in reality they are a lot different. Closely linked to the quality of Ashkenazy's interpretations is the fact that he brings to this music a technique perfectly adapted to Rachmaninov's way of writing for the piano in these works, a good illustration being Op. 23 No. 9, which is an *étude* rather than a prelude. The Sonata also receives a magnificent performance, though one whose recorded sound is less sumptuous than that of the *Preludes*. These two CDs of Ashkenazy's are unlikely to be surpassed in terms of sheer mastery of this composer's music.

Rachmaninov. The bells, Op. 35[a]. Vocalise, Op. 34 No. 14[b]. **Tchaikovsky**. Romeo and Juliet (orch. Taneyev) — duet[ac]. Festival Coronation March in D major. [abc]**Suzanne Murphy** (sop); [ab]**Keith Lewis** (ten); [a]**David Wilson-Johnson** (bar); **Scottish National** [a]**Chorus and Orchestra/Neeme Järvi.** Chandos CHAN8476. Notes and English texts included.

1h 3' DDD 2/87

Rachmaninov had grown up in a land where different kinds of church bells were often heard, and their sound evoked in him vivid childhood memories. Edgar Allan Poe's evocation of four human states and their bell connotations seemed to Rachmaninov an ideal basis for a four-part choral symphony. This is well realized by Järvi, though perhaps the urgency of the "Loud Alarum Bells" could be expressed more vehemently. The soloists are not ideal, but a rich, atmospheric recording provides a suitable vehicle for some lusty though well-disciplined choral singing. *Vocalise* is reasonably well sung, as is the Tchaikovsky *Romeo and Juliet* duet. After Tchaikovsky's death Taneyev discovered and then put together sketches for the operatic duet recorded here: no doubt he was aided by the fact that the duet re-uses material from the Fantasy overture. *The Festival Coronation March* was written to celebrate the 1883 crowning of Tsar Alexander III.

Rachmaninov. Vespers, Op. 37. **Corydon Singers/Matthew Best.** Hyperion CDA66460. Text and translation included.

1h 6' DDD 7/91

Rachmaninov's piano concertos and solo pieces are among the most popular of classical works, but he covered a wider range than this and his setting of the Vespers (or to use his own title, *All-night vigil*) has long been admired by the few outside Russia who knew it. It uses a liturgical text of the Russian Church for the services of Vespers (starting at sunset), Matins and The First Hour (Prime), and is deeply religious in feeling, for although the composer did not always adhere to the faith of his childhood he was married in church and thought much about the beliefs of his forefathers. After he wrote this work in a mere two weeks of 1915, one of his friends said that basses who could sing a low C, to say nothing of the B flat at the end of the fifth section, "were as rare as asparagus at Christmas" and that was in Russia, famous for its low basses! Nevertheless, Matthew Best and his Corydon Singers rise (or rather fall) splendidly to this occasion, and overall their style, tonal quality and pronunciation are alike convincingly authentic, with fine alto and tenor soloists; indeed, hearing John Bowen in the *Nyne Otpushchaeshi* ("Nunc dimittis") one could imagine oneself at a real Orthodox service, especially as the recording was made in a church. There's an excellent booklet note and the text is given in a transliteration from the original Cyrillic script into our own Roman alphabet, with an English translation. This is music of spiritual beauty that fully embodies the Russian Orthodox saying that "the mind should enter the heart".

André Raison   *Refer to Index*   *French; before 1650-1790*

Jean-Philippe Rameau   *French 1683-1764*

NEW REVIEW

Rameau. HARPSICHORD WORKS. **Christophe Rousset** (hpd).
L'Oiseau-Lyre 425 886-2OH2.
Premier livre de pièces de clavecin. Pièces de clavecin. Nouvelles suites de pièces de clavecin. Les petits marteaux de M Rameau. La Dauphine.

② 2h 9' DDD 12/91

Christophe Rousset's recording of Rameau's solo harpsichord music outdistances the competitors currently available on CD in the UK. Rousset does not include everything that Rameau wrote for the instrument but he does play all the music contained in the principal collections of 1706, 1724 and *c.*1728 as well as *La Dauphine*. Rousset's phrasing is graceful and clearly articulated, the inflexions gently spoken and the rhythmic pulse all that one might wish for. Tempos are, for the most part, well-judged and the playing admirably attentive to detail and delightfully animated. Only occasionally does Rousset perhaps just miss the mark with speeds that are uncomfortably brisk and lacking that choreographic poise which is such a vital ingredient in French baroque music. But Rousset at his strongest is irresistible and this is how we find him in "Les niais de Sologne" and its variations, the reflective "L'entretien des Muses", the animated "Les cyclopes", "La poule", "L'enharmonique" and the dazzling A minor Gavotte and variations. In these and in many other of the pieces, too, Rousset's impeccable taste and seemingly effortless virtuosity provide the listener with constant and intense delight. The quality of the recording is ideal as are the two instruments which Rousset has chosen to play.

NEW REVIEW

Rameau. LES INDES GALANTES — *Prologue:* **Claron McFadden** (sop) Hébé; **Jérôme Corréas** (bar) Bellone; **Isabelle Poulenard** (sop) L'Amour. *Le Turc généreux:* **Nicolas Rivenq** (bass) Osman; **Miriam Ruggieri** (sop) Emilie; **Howard Crook** (ten) Valère. *Les Incas du Pérou:* **Bernard Delétré** (bass) Huascar; **Poulenard** (Phanie); **Jean-Paul Fouchécourt** (ten) Carlos. *Les fleurs:* **Fouchécourt** (Tacmas); **Corréas** (Ali); **Sandrine Piau** (sop) Zaïre; **Noémi Rime** (sop) Fatime. *Les sauvages:* **Rivenq** (Adario); **Crook** (Damon); **Delétré** (Don Alvar); **McFadden** (Zima); **Les Arts Florissants/William Christie.** Harmonia Mundi HMC90 1367/9. Notes, text and translation included.

③ 3h 23' DDD 2/92

Les Indes galantes was Rameau's first *opéra-ballet*. He completed it in 1735 when it was performed at the Académie Royale in Paris. *Opéra-ballet* usually consisted of a prologue and anything between three and five entrées or acts. There was no continuously developing plot but instead various sections might be linked by a general theme, often hinted at in the title. Such is the case with *Les indes galantes* whose linking themes derives from a contemporary taste for the exotic and the unknown. Following a prologue come four entrées, "Le Turc généreux", "Les Incas du Pérou", "Les fleurs" and "Les sauvages". William Christie and Les Arts Florissants give a characteristically warm-blooded performance of one of Rameau's most approachable and endearing stage works. Christie's control of diverse forces — his orchestra consists of some 46 players — his dramatic pacing of the music, his recognition of Rameau's uniquely distinctive instrumental palette and his feeling for gesture and rhythm contribute towards making this a lively and satisfying performance. The choir is alert and well-disciplined and the orchestra a worthy partner in respect of clear textures and technical finesse; this can be readily appreciated in the splendid, spaciously laid out and tautly constructed orchestral Chaconne which concludes the work. The booklet contains full texts in French, English and German and the music is recorded in a sympathetic acoustic.

Rameau. PLATÉE. **Gilles Ragon** (ten) Platée; **Jennifer Smith** (sop) La Folie, Thalie; **Guy de Mey** (ten) Thespis, Mercure; **Vincent le Texier** (bass-bar) Jupiter, A satyr; **Guillemette Laurens** (mez) Junon; **Bernard Deletré** (bass) Cithéron, Momus; **Véronique Gens** (sop) L'Amour, Clarine; **Michel Verschaeve** (bass) Momus; **Françoise Herr Vocal Ensemble; Musiciens du Louvre/Marc Minkowski.** Erato MusiFrance 2292-45028-2. Notes, text and translation included.

② 2h 15' DDD 9/90

Marc Minkowski [photo: Erato/Sarrat]

The *comédie-lyrique, Platée* is one of Rameau's masterpieces. It dates from 1745 when it was performed at Versailles as part of the celebrations for the Dauphin's marriage to the Infanta Maria-Theresa of Spain. The story concerns Platée, a nymph of unprepossessing appearance who is the butt of a cruel joke which leads her to believe that she will be the bride of Jupiter, no less. The theme may appear heartless but the music most certainly is not, and the charades, disguises and comic figures, evoking Carnival spirit, provides Rameau with almost unparalleled opportunities to display his unique genius as an orchestrator. There is hardly a weak moment in the score and anyone hitherto intimidated by this giant of the French baroque will find in *Platée* an enchanting introduction to Rameau's music. The performance under Marc Minkowski's direction is full of life and mischievous little insights. The solo cast is strong with Gilles Ragon in the high tenor travesti role of Platée and Jennifer Smith dazzlingly virtuosic and high-spirited as La Folie. This is, in short, a robust and well-paced account of a captivating work. The score is presented without cuts and with only a very few repeats omitted. The recorded sound is bright and effective and the accompanying booklet contains full texts in French, English and German.

Rameau. ZOROASTRE. **John Elwes** (ten) Zoroastre; **Greta de Reyghere** (sop) Amélite; **Mieke van der Sluis** (sop) Erinice; **Agnès Mellon** (sop) Céphie; **Gregory Reinhart** (bass) Abramane; **Jacques Bona** (bar) Oramasés, Voice from the Underworld; **Michel Verschaeve** (bass) Zopire; **François Fauché** (bass) Narbanor; **Philippe Cantor** (ten) God of Revenge; **Ghent Collegium Vocale; La Petite Bande/Sigiswald Kuijken.** Deutsche Harmonia Mundi Editio Classica GD77144. Notes, text and translation included. From HM1999813 (5/84).

⠆ ⟨3⟩ 3h 4' ADD 7/90

Zoroastre was first performed in Paris in 1749 and was Rameau's penultimate serious opera or *tragédie en musique*. It was fairly well received but not without criticism concerning, above all, the librettist, Cahusac's text. When the work was revived in 1756 shifts of emphasis were made within the plot and it is this later version which is performed here. The story deals with the conflict between Light (Good) and Darkness (Evil) central to Zoroastrianism. Rameau brings to life the chief protagonists Zoroastre and Abramane with consummate skill and his characteristic feeling for colour is seldom absent from the many fine choruses, airs and instrumental dances. John Elwes (tenor) sings the title role with a firm grasp of the French baroque idiom, while Gregory Reinhart (bass) makes a formidable opponent in the person of Abramane with clear diction and a commanding vocal presence. The three principal female roles are sung with equal assurance though their voices are perhaps insufficiently distinctive from one another to make the strong contrasts implicit in their characters. Agnès Mellon as the innocent Céphie is, nonetheless, a particularly happy piece of casting. Sigiswald Kuijken directs the performance with insight into and affection for Rameau's subtle art and the recording comes with an informative booklet in French, English and German.

Maurice Ravel

French 1875-1937

Ravel. Piano Concerto in G major.
Rachmaninov. Piano Concerto No. 4 in G minor, Op. 40. **Arturo Benedetti Michelangeli** (pf); **Philharmonia Orchestra/Ettore Gracis.** EMI CDC7 49326-2. From ASD255 (10/58).

⠆ 47' ADD 9/88

Temperamentally it might seem that neither piece on this disc is ideally suited to the aloof, magisterial image that Michelangeli cultivates. The Ravel is a witty, jazzy-influenced score; the Rachmaninov is full of big-hearted nostalgia and heroic virtuosity. Michelangeli's achievement is to let those elements speak for themselves, and, by his refinement and awareness of long lines of musical thought, to bring out a sense of wholeness which is absent from the vast majority of other interpretations — apart from which the sheer virtuosity is breathtaking. Two passages stand out as examples of indisputably great music-making — the climax of Rachmaninov's first movement, prepared with gripping dramatic intensity and unleashed with astonishing force, and the exquisitely refined unfolding of the solo opening to Ravel's sublime slow movement. The Philharmonia, obviously sensing a special presence at the keyboard, play out of their skins; EMI have lavished all the care on the digital remastering that the performance deserve.

Ravel. Daphnis et Chloé — ballet[a]. Rapsodie espagnole[b]. Pavane pour une
infante défunte[b]. [a]**Chorus of the Royal Opera House, Covent Garden;**

London Symphony Orchestra/Pierre Monteux. Decca Historic 425 956-2DM. Item marked [a] from SXL2164 (12/59), [b] SXL2312 (7/62).

Ih 14' ADD 5/90

Ravel. Daphnis et Chloé — ballet. **Montreal Symphony Chorus and Orchestra/Charles Dutoit.** Decca 400 055-2DH. From SXDL7526 (6/81).

56' DDD 3/83

Diaghilev's ballet *Daphnis et Chloé*, based on a pastoral romance by the ancient Greek poet Longus, was first produced in June 1912, with Nijinsky and Karsavina in the title roles and choreography by Mikhail Fokine. Pierre Monteux conducted the first performance, and 47 years later he recorded his peerless interpretation for Decca. Though the Second Suite from the ballet is familiar to concert-goers and makes an effective piece in its own right, the full score, with wordless chorus, conveys still greater atmosphere and magic. No work of more sheer sensual beauty exists in the entire orchestral repertoire, and Monteux was its perfect interpreter. He conducts with a wonderful sense of clarity and balance: every important detail tells, and there is refinement of expression, yet inner strength too. The LSO play with superlative poetry and skill, and the chorus is magnificent in its tonal blend and colour. The *Rapsodie espagnole* and *Pavane* are also given ideal performances, and the recordings show off Decca's exceedingly high standards during the late 1950s and early 1960s. On the second Decca disc the ballet is given not only a gloriously rich and understanding performance but a sumptuous recording to match. This swiftly became the CD medium's most cherished demonstration recording and indeed the sound is not only refined in its texturing of detail, but is beautifully balanced and warmly co-ordinated. Dutoit's reading is both brilliant and ardently committed, with the celebrated crescendo of "Daybreak" sounding radiant.

Ravel. Alborada del gracioso. Rapsodie espagnole. La valse. Boléro. **Montreal Symphony Orchestra/Charles Dutoit.** Decca 410 010-2DH. From SXDL7559 (9/82).

51' DDD 8/83

Ravel. Alborada del gracioso. Rapsodie espagnole. Le tombeau de Couperin. La valse. **Orchestre de Paris/Herbert von Karajan.** EMI Studio CDM7 63526-2. From ASD2766 (3/72).

57' ADD 11/90

Ravel's *Boléro* is now so popular and universally familiar that it is easy to forget its originality. Dutoit plays it magnetically as a steady, remorseless crescendo and its power and marvellous command of orchestral colour are freshly revealed. The glittering *Alborada del gracioso* and the sensuous and exciting *Rapsodie espagnole* readily demonstrate the special feeling French composers had for the Spanish idiom, with diaphanous textures to capture the sultry quality of the Mediterranean evening and offset the sparkle of the Flamenco dance rhythms. *La valse* begins in the mists and expands to a breathtaking climax with a vision of countless dancing couples whirling round in an intoxicating infinity of space; then cruelly and abruptly the imagery disintegrates into silence. This CD is a model of its kind while the music-making combines a feeling for spectacle with the utmost refinement of detail.

Purists might argue that Karajan's Ravel was impressionistic on the surface and romantic at its core, with no room for the symbolist currents that so distinguish the composer's style. Yet it is still so alluringly attractive to listen to that we would be foolish to ignore it for those reasons. His collection of popular works illustrates exactly Karajan's ability to combine his fascination with sonic beauty and his keen sense of structure: details are important here, but only to give substance to the long-term meaning of the music. The Orchestre de Paris play magnificently.

Their intonation is not always as positive as that of some other major orchestras, but the spirit of the music is unerringly captured and the French tones are distinctively presented, even in those works that evoke Spain and Vienna. The woodwind playing in *Le tombeau de Couperin* is wistfully redolent of an earlier age and its pastoral context, and in *La valse* the impressionistic mists that Karajan summons are entirely appropriate, even cited by the composer in his commentary on the work. A spacious, warm recording is the cherry on the top of this delicious gateaux.

Ravel. ORCHESTRAL WORKS. **Montreal Symphony Orchestra/Charles Dutoit.** Decca 410 254-2DH. From 410 254-1DH (8/84).
Ma mère l'oye — ballet. *Pavane pour une infante défunte. Le tombeau de Couperin. Valses nobles et sentimentales.*

> • 1h 7' DDD 11/84 ⓆⓅ Ⓑ

There is no more magical score than Ravel's *Ma mère l'oye* ("Mother Goose"). It has the elegance and perfection of Mozart, yet the translucence of the scoring is a Ravelian hallmark. *Le tombeau de Couperin* also shows the composer at his most elegant. This neoclassical evocation again demonstrates an affinity with a different age from Ravel's own, yet the delicious orchestral colour essentially belongs to the twentieth century. The *Valses nobles et sentimentales*, more melodically diffuse, have comparable subtlety. This is a very different work from *La valse* and much more characteristic of the essence of the composer. The Montreal orchestra show a natural rapport with these scores and their playing is warmly sympathetic yet not indulgent, so that the delicacy of texture is never over-laden. It is difficult to think of many other discs where everything comes together so perfectly to serve the composer's inspiration.

Ravel. ORCHESTRAL WORKS. **Orchestre de Paris/Jean Martinon.** EMI Studio CDM7 69565/6-2. From SLS5016 (10/75).
CDM7 69565-2 — Boléro. Shéhérazade — Ouverture de féerie. Rapsodie espagnole. Menuet antique. La valse. *CDM7 69566-2* — Daphnis et Chloé — ballet (with Paris Opéra Chorus). Valses nobles et sentimentales.

> • ② 1h 4' 1h 13' ADD 12/88 £ ⓆⓅ Ⓑ

Appropriately enough, the best performance and recording here are of the finest work, the complete *Daphnis et Chloé* ballet. Martinon was a conductor of impeccable taste who fully understood this music and who here shapes the glorious score with great delicacy, seductiveness and tingling energy: it is a reading to rank among the most recommendable now available. The *Rapsodie espagnole* is perhaps less atmospheric, but clean-cut and lucid. The obstinately popular *Boléro* often proves difficult for conductors to find its right pace, but Martinon manages it admirably, on the way extracting some wry humour in its cumulative repetitions. The two Viennese-inspired works here come off less well because of their recorded quality, *Valses nobles et sentimentales* shrill in its *fortissimos, La valse* too harsh. A rarely-heard curiosity in this collection is the early *Shéhérazade* overture.

NEW REVIEW

Ravel. String Quartet in F major.
Vaughan Williams. On Wenlock Edge[ab]. String Quartet No. 1 in G minor.
[a]**Philip Langridge** (ten); [b]**Howard Shelley** (pf); **Britten Quartet** (Peter Manning, Keith Pascoe, vns; Peter Lale, va; Andrew Shulman, vc). EMI CDC7 54346-2.

> • 1h 18' DDD 2/92 ⓆⓅ ⓆⓈ

This outstanding disc from the Britten Quartet brings together several works which share far more in common than one might at first imagine. Vaughan

Williams spent a short study vacation in Paris during 1908 hoping, on his own admission, to acquire "a little French polish" from Ravel, who himself took part in the French première of his student's song cycle, *On Wenlock Edge*. Ravel's String Quartet receives a provocative, and yet totally convincing reading from the Britten Quartet, who choose to dwell upon the polarization of tonal and melodic content in this work to a greater degree than any of their rivals on disc, all of whom offer the more usual coupling in the shape of the Debussy Quartet. *On Wenlock Edge*, a setting of six poems selected from A.E. Houseman's set of 63 poems, *A Shropshire Lad*, is heard here in a quite exceptional performance from the tenor, Philip Langridge, joined by pianist Howard Shelley and the Britten Quartet. Langridge recognizes the irony and understatement of Houseman's verse, whilst exploiting its more sinister undertones with searching skill, as he does in the uncanny dialogue between the living and the dead, in "Is my team ploughing", bringing chilly pallor to his delivery of the opening stanza in particular. It would be difficult to match the communicative power of this performance even in the concert-hall. The Brittens also excel in a crystalline and devoted account of Vaughan Williams's underrated G minor Quartet, which sounds more than usually weighty and musically coherent in this fluid and sharply perceived reading. The technical aspects of the playing are second to none, while its added sensitivity contributes to an involving and frequently moving musical experience. The recorded sound is brilliant and immediate, and this disc is a clear triumph from every conceivable viewpoint!

Ravel. MUSIC FOR TWO PIANOS. **Louis Lortie, Hélène Mercier** (pfs). Chandos CHAN8905.
Boléro. Introduction and Allegro. La valse. Ma mère l'oye. Rapsodie espagnole.

1h 5' DDD 3/91

Ravel. MUSIC FOR TWO PIANOS. **Stephen Coombs, Christopher Scott** (pfs). Gamut Classics GAMCD517.
Frontispice. Introduction and Allegro. La valse. Rapsodie espagnole. Sites auriculaires — Entre cloches. Shéhérazade — Ouverture de féerie.

56' DDD 2/91

Louis Lortie is an excellent Ravel pianist and he and his fellow-Canadian Hélène Mercier have played as a duo since their student days in Montreal. Their performance of *Ma mère l'oye* is as delicate and tender as befits a piece written for children, but it also has the passion which is also part of a child's world, not least in the deep sense of joyful wonder of the final movement called "The Fairy Garden", which opens up to our inner vision the kind of childhood paradise that for all but the rarest mortals is forever lost, like innocence, as we reach adulthood. The *Rapsodie espagnole* is also done with great refinement, and although some collectors might like it more overtly sensual this is a performance to place beside the more familiar orchestral version of the same music. So is the *Boléro* in Ravel's own two-piano transcription, for although the piece might seem to depend wholly on orchestral colour it comes off well when played as excitingly as this at a fairly taut tempo. Again, the *Introduction and Allegro* may seem to depend on the sound of a chamber ensemble including harp, but this keyboard transcription made by the composer is beautiful. The programme ends with an account of *La valse* which offers playing that can only be described in superlatives or in terms of Dionysiac frenzy; this is a glowing, sumptuous dream-turning-to-nightmare that should not be missed by anyone who cares about Ravel's music and yet again reveals what an extraordinarily unsettling masterpiece this is. The recording made in the Snape Maltings is outstanding, detailed yet atmospheric.

Stephen Coombs and Christopher Scott formed a duo in 1985 and their outstanding début recording of Debussy will be found elsewhere in the *Guide* (refer to the Index to Reviews). Here they turn their attention to Ravel, and the result is equally satisfying. They play with such style and sensitivity that the works in the composer's own piano transcriptions have more than documentary interest, while *Entre cloches* and *Frontispice* are original works for two pianos. One notes, however, that *Ma mère l'oye* is not here, and nor is *Boléro*; the latter work was recorded and edited, but finally the artists and producer decided that it did not succeed in keyboard form, which one may regret since other duos, like Lortie and Mercier, have recorded it successfully. The richly atmospheric yet delicate recording is another plus for this attractive disc.

Ravel. PIANO WORKS, Volume 1. **Vlado Perlemuter.** Nimbus NIM5005.
Items marked [a] from 2102 (7/79), [b] 2101 (7/79).
Miroirs[a]. Jeux d'eau[b]. Pavane pour une infante défunte[b]. Gaspard de la nuit[b].

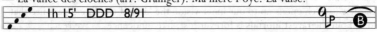

59' AAD 1/84

It would be foolish to deny that technical wizardry is essential to the performance of Ravel's piano music, so much of which was intended to stretch the limits of virtuosity, but depth of imagination and poetry are, if anything, even more important to its successful recreation. It is with this latter quality that Vlado Perlemuter scores so heavily. In his performances you can lose yourself, absorbed totally by the worlds he summons. His technical mastery lies less with fleet fingers than with supple pedalling and the enormous range of tone colours that he employs, with *pianissimo* chords that are distant soundings, and semiquaver passagework that ripples and scintillates. As one who studied with Ravel, Perlemuter has much to say about these works that is of archival as well as artistic value, but in, say, "Oiseaux tristes" from *Miroirs*, how Ravel might have wanted the work played on one or two occasions in the past is not as important as the depth of natural insight that this pianist brings to the score. Nimbus's preferred resonant acoustic suits both this music and Perlemuter's style of playing well, supporting the textures warmly without limiting clarity where it is required. The recording contributes substantially to the success of this altogether unique project.

Ravel. VOCAL AND ORCHESTRAL WORKS. [a]**Maria Ewing** (mez); **City of Birmingham Symphony Orchestra/Simon Rattle.** EMI CDC7 54204-2.
Text and translation included.
Fanfare pour "L'éventail de Jeanne". Shéhérazade[a]. Alborada del gracioso. Miroirs
— La vallée des cloches (arr. Grainger). Ma mère l'oye. La valse.

1h 15' DDD 8/91

A paean of British critical praise greets almost every new issue from this team with monotonous regularity, so it is gratifying, in this instance, to note *Diapason*'s (the French contemporary to *Gramophone*) reviewer finding Rattle's *Ma mère l'oye* of a "striking delicacy" and "releasing an indescribable emotion" (apologies to Rémy Louis for a wholly inadequate translation). In the past there have been instances of Rattle's intensive preparation for setting down a much loved masterpiece precluding spontaneity in the end result. Not here. Along with the customary refinement and revelation of texture, there is a sense of Rattle gauging the very individual fantasy worlds of this varied programme with uncanny precision: an aptly child-like wonder for *Ma mère l'oye*'s fairy tale illustrations; the decadence and decay that drive *La valse* to its inevitable doom; and the sensual allure of the Orient in *Shéhérazade* providing a vibrant backdrop for soprano Maria Ewing's intimate confessions. Space does not permit enthusing about the three shorter items that make up this indispensable (and generously filled) disc, recorded with stunning realism. Try it for yourself and marvel at the astonishing range of Ravel's imagination.

Ravel. L'HEURE ESPAGNOLE. **Jane Berbié** (sop) Concepción; **Jean Giraudeau** (ten) Torquemada; **Gabriel Bacquier** (bar) Ramiro; **José van Dam** (bass-bar) Don Inigo Gomez; **Michel Sénéchal** (ten) Gonzalve; **French Radio National Orchestra/Lorin Maazel.** DG 423 719-2GH. Notes, text and translation included. From SLPM138 970 (10/65).

46' ADD 3/89

For genuinely witty operas *L'heure espagnole* is in a class of its own; and to do it justice it needs a conductor with an alert ear for all Ravel's minutely judged and ingeniously scored jests (the automata in the shop, the story of the toreador's watch, the jangling of the pendulum as the grandfather clock is hoisted on to the muleteer's brawny shoulder) and no conductor is more mentally alert than Maazel. It also requires a cast which relishes the verbal nuances and adopts the

quasi-parlando style that the composer asked for; and these desiderata are met in this classic, and unequalled, 1965 performance. All the singers give excellent characterizations — Berbié as the frustrated and exasperated young wife, Bacquier as the simple, somewhat bemused muleteer who is happy to oblige, Sénéchal as the poet whose head is too far in the clouds to attend to practicalities, van Dam as the fatuous portly banker, and Giraudeau as the doddery old watchmaker who at the end shows an unexpectedly astute business sense. A delicious work, in a performance to savour.

Lorin Maazel   *[photo: Decca*

Ravel. L'ENFANT ET LES SORTILEGES. **Françoise Ogéas** (sop) Child; **Jeanine Collard** (contr) Mother, Chinese cup, Dragonfly; **Jane Berbié** (sop) Sofa, She Cat, Squirrel, Shepherd; **Sylvaine Gilma** (sop) Fire, Princess, Nightingale; **Colette Herzog** (sop) Bat, Little Owl, Shepherdess; **Heinz Rehfuss** (bar) Armchair, Tree; **Camille Maurane** (bar) Grandfather Clock, Tom Cat; **Michel Sénéchal** (ten) Teapot, Little Old Man (Mr Arithmetic), Frog; **Chorus and Children's Voices of French Radio; French Radio National Orchestra/Lorin Maazel.** DG 423 718-2GH. Notes, text and translation included. From SLPM138675 (6/61).

43' ADD 3/89

This is a Desert Island Disc if ever there was one. Every musical and verbal point in Ravel's brilliantly ingenious, deliciously witty and entirely enchanting score is brought out by a well-nigh perfect cast, backed by orchestral playing of the first class; and the recording is as vivid as anyone could wish. The story is that of a petulant brat who breaks the china, pulls the cat's tail, pricks the pet squirrel with a pen-nib, puts the fire out by upsetting the kettle on it, tears the wallpaper and his books and snaps off the pendulum of the grandfather clock — only to find that all these come to life and turn on him. Their anger is appeased only when he tends the squirrel's paw; and finally the naughty child, having seen the error of his ways, falls tearfully into his mother's arms. Everyone will have their own favourite passages but the last pages of the opera, in particular, are hauntingly beautiful. An absolute gem of a disc.

Thomas Ravenscroft

British c.1590-c.1633

Ravenscroft. THERE WERE THREE RAVENS. **Consort of Musicke/ Anthony Rooley.** Virgin Classics Veritas VC7 91217-2. Texts included.
A Round of three Country dances in one. A wooing Song of a Yeoman of Kents Sonne. Browning Madame. The crowning of Belphebe. The Cryers Song of Cheape-Side. Laboravi in gemitu meo. The Marriage of the Frogge and the Mouse. Martin said to his man. Musing mine owne selfe all alone. Ne laeteris inimica mea. Of all the birds that ever I see. There were three ravens. Three blinde Mice. To morrow the Fox will come to towne. Wee be Souldiers three. The wooing of Hodge and Malkyn. Yonder comes a courteous knight.
Instrumental works — Fancy No. 1. Fantasia No. 4. Viol Fancy a 5.

 Ih I' DDD 8/91

Thomas Ravenscroft was a learned musician (even a pedant in some respects) who is perhaps best known for his 1621 collection of psalms; and to illustrate that side of him this disc contains two deeply expressive Latin motets and some attractive and skilfully written fantasias for viols. However, as a likeable and lively-minded person, he also delighted in writing music for entertainment, "mirth and jocund melody", and in 1609 printed the first known collection in England of catches and rounds, under the title *Pammelia*. From this and two similar subsequent volumes the Consort of Musicke have made a selection which they themselves obviously thoroughly enjoyed performing and whose enjoyment is infectious. (The assumption of a variety of accents, from Cockney for a Cheapside crier's song to a Somerset-dialect wooing dialogue for once does not seem an irritating gimmick.) Anthony Rooley has skilfully arranged the programme to present a diversity of types, pace and scoring; but among the highlights here are the melancholy *Musing mine owne selfe all alone* and *There were three ravens* and the merry *The Marriage of the Frogge and the Mouse* and the saucy *Yonder comes a courteous knight*.

Max Reger

Refer to Index

German 1873-1916

Reger. Variations and Fugue on a Theme of J.A. Hiller, Op. 100. Eine Ballettsuite, Op. 130. **Bavarian Radio Symphony Orchestra/Sir Colin Davis.** Orfeo CO90841A. From SO90841A (2/85).

 59' DDD 4/87

Mention of Reger's name in 'informed' circles is likely to produce a conditioned reflex: "Fugue!". In his day he was the central figure of the 'Back to Bach' movement, but he was also a romantic who relished all the expressive potential of the enormous post-Wagnerian orchestra. Then came the slender acerbities of the next generation of neoclassicist, and Reger's backward glances were deemed inflated and in shocking taste. Until recently he has proved largely unexportable from his native Germany. Times are changing though, and collectors who respond to the musical ingenuity of Elgar's *Enigma* Variations should give Reger's *Hiller* Variations a try. As in his excellent disc of Reger's *Mozart* Variations reviewed above, Sir Colin Davis ensures sufficient contrast between the ravishingly scored slower variations and the bouncing contrapuntal energy and interplay of the faster ones. And the engineers avoid the danger of over-egging the pudding: the textures here are light, airy and transparent. In *Eine Ballettsuite* Reger wished "to write something infinitely graceful, subtle in tone, dainty musically and cobweb-fine". That he succeeded is a tribute, in no small measure, to the love and dedication (felt in every bar) of these Bavarian players.

Reger. Variations and Fugue on a Theme of Mozart, Op. 132.
Hindemith. Symphonic Metamorphosis on Themes of Carl Maria von Weber.
Bavarian Radio Symphony Orchestra/Sir Colin Davis. Philips 422 347-2PH.

♪ 55' DDD 9/90

Debussy once dismissed variation technique as "an easy way of making a lot
out of a little". It is certainly astonishing what Reger manages to make out of
Mozart's little theme (one of those tunes you know, even if you didn't know
that you knew it) and the long journey to the inevitable king-sized fugue is full
of late romantic nostalgia, fantasy and an enlivening lightness of touch. If, to
quote Wilfred Mellers, Reger's "chromatic elaboration did not follow Tristan
into a transfigured night", his writing for strings is surely as sensuous as in
Schoenberg's early masterpiece. The flavour of Davis's performance of
Hindemith's *Symphonic Metamorphosis* is more Anglo-Bavarian than American but,
as in the Reger, the playing is superb and the sound very natural.

Steve Reich

American 1936-

Reich. Different Trains (1988)[a]. Electric Counterpoint (1987)[b]. [a]**Kronos
Quartet** (David Harrington, John Sherba, vns; Hank Dutt, va; Joan Jeanrenaud,
vc); [b]**Pat Metheny** (gtr). Elektra-Nonesuch 7559-79176-2.

♪ 42' DDD 6/89

The name 'minimalist' clings to Steve Reich, but in fact there's little that can be
called minimal in works of the richness and comparative complexity of *Octet* or
The Desert Music, where all that's left of his earlier style is a taste for pulsating
rhythms, short-term circular repetitions and a sonorous harmoniousness. *Different
Trains* also combines strong ideas with superb craftsmanship, and it is carried
out with total confidence. The programme is autobiographical: Reich evokes
his long childhood train journeys across America in the aftermath of the
Second World War, and ponders on the parallel but enforced train journeys
undertaken by Jewish refugees in Europe. A tinge of melancholy darkens the
otherwise excited mood of music, which draws most of its imagery from the
driving motor-rhythms of steam trains, constantly punctuated by the evocative
sound of whistles, and scraps of recorded interviews. *Different Trains* is given an
exemplary reading by the Kronos Quartet, and it is nicely complemented by
Pat Metheny's performance of the short *Electric Counterpoint* for live and multi-
tracked acoustic guitars.

Franz Reizenstein

German/English 1911-1968

NEW REVIEW

Reizenstein. Piano Quintet in D major, Op. 23[a]. Sonata for Violin and Piano,
Op. 20[b]. Sonatina for Oboe and Piano, Op. 11[c]. [a]**Melos Ensemble** (Emanuel
Hurwitz, Ivor McMahon, vns; Cecil Aronowitz, va; Terence Weil, vc; Lamar
Crowson, pf). [b]**Eric Gruenberg** (vn); [b]**David Wilde** (pf); **Janet Craxton**
(ob); [c]**Lamar Crowson** (pf). Continuum CCD1024. From L'Oiseau-Lyre
SOL344 (7/75).

♪ 1h 11' ADD 11/91

Franz Reizenstein's uproarious contributions to the ever popular Hoffnung
concerts quickly achieved a degree of notoriety which overshadowed virtually all

of his remaining output, and this excellent Continuum disc offers pioneering recordings of several of his finest chamber works, fittingly played by some of his closest associates. The Melos Ensemble, with the pianist Lamar Crowson, are heard in a definitive reading of Reizenstein's Piano Quintet in D major, a finely structured and readily approachable work which deserves renewed attention today. This expansive composition is finely presented by the Melos players, all of whom excel in the irascible *moto perpetuo* Scherzo; the highlight of an obscure and neglected work which will not disappoint the adventurous listener. Reizenstein's mildly ironic style is evident, too, in the central movement of his Violin Sonata which is engagingly realized by Eric Gruenberg and David Wilde. The constant melodic interest and harmonic coloration makes the sonata sound refreshingly inventive, in a performance of great authority from two of the composer's staunchest advocates. The final work here is the delightful Oboe Sonatina, heard in a reading which is by turns witty and plangent, from the late Janet Craxton, who is joined at the piano by Lamar Crowson. The recordings sound a touch brittle and a little dated, but given the excellence of these authoritative and affectionate performances, there is much to enjoy here.

Ottorino Respighi *Italian 1879-1936*

Respighi. Symphonic Poems — Pines of Rome; Fountains of Rome; Roman Festivals. **Montreal Symphony Orchestra/Charles Dutoit.** Decca 410 145-2DH. From SXDL7591 (9/83).

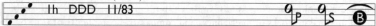

Respighi. Symphonic Poems — Pines of Rome; Fountains of Rome. The birds — suite[a]. [a]**William Bennett** (fl); **London Symphony Orchestra/István Kertesz.** Decca Weekend 425 507-2DC. From SXL6401 (7/69).

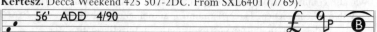

Respighi's three orchestral showpieces inspired by Rome have often been dismissed as merely musical picture-postcards, but in ripely committed performances like Dutoit's, stunningly recorded, there are few works to match them in showing off the glories of a modern orchestra in full cry. Dutoit's performance is as brilliant as any, but it also finds a vein of warm expressiveness in the writing as well as rhythmic point, so adding to the vividness of atmosphere. This is a work which benefits more than most from CD, when quite apart from the quality of recording over the widest range of dynamics and frequency, the perils of LP end-of-side distortion are eliminated, and separate bands allow you to pick out individual movements in each work, even though the music is continuous.

The musicality and keen attention to detail of Kertesz's performances stand out against some of the more superficially glossy and brilliant versions on disc. The joy and exuberance of children playing is marvellously evoked in the 'Petrushka'-like opening movement of *Pines*, and in the sensuous and lovely "Pines of the Janiculum" Kertész creates a magical nocturnal atmosphere in which there are some seductively expressive solos from the clarinet, violin and cello. "Pines on the Appian Way" lacks perhaps the sheer excitement of Dutoit's recording, but nevertheless succeeds in its objective of sending tingles up and down the spine. *Fountains* is equally as impressive; the serenity of the gently flowing "Fountains of the Valle Guilia at dawn" is gorgeously captured, and the full virtuosity of the LSO can be heard in the stormier waters of "The Fountain of Trevi at Mid-day". The ever popular suite *The birds* provides an excellent contrast to the richly scored symphonic poems. These delightful and charming arrangements of compositions by seventeenth and eighteenth century composers

(Rameau, Pasquini, etc.) receive superb performances, with some exceptionally fine playing from the wind section. The recording is vividly realistic with a very wide dynamic range. A classic recording.

NEW REVIEW

Respighi. WORKS FOR VIOLIN AND ORCHESTRA. **Ingolf Turban** (vn); [a]**Neil Black** (ob); [a]**Graham Ashton** (tpt); [a]**Stephen Williams** (db); [a]**Ian Watson** (pf); [b]**English Chamber Orchestra/Marcello Viotti.** Claves CD50-9017.
Chaconne (after Vitali: 1908)[b]. Pastorale in C major (after Tartini: 1908)[b]. Concerto all'antica (1923)[b]. Concerto a cinque (1933)[a].

• 1h 19' DDD 10/91

An enterprising disc — both concertos are world première recordings — and one which offers further examples of Respighi's desire to relate the best of bygone eras to modern ears. Or, to be more precise, to modern ears if you happened to be listening in the first three decades of this century. Even then you might have been surprised at the warmth of the most neoclassical works here, the 1933 *Concerto a cinque* (a sort of Corellian *concerto grosso*), given the astringency that is generally associated with neoclassicism. The *Concerto all'antica* is a much earlier work, a beautifully crafted, highly engaging mish-mash of styles from Bruch and Mendelssohn back to the baroque, with hardly an identifiably Respighian fingerprint in earshot. But with music as lucid and graceful as this, few will complain. Inevitably, given the music's unfamiliarity, there are a few tentative moments in the playing. Though one craves, say, a Heifetz in the Vitali transcription, Turban is an accomplished violinist and corporate commitment is rarely in doubt. The sound, ideally distanced, has bloom and warmth.

Respighi. The birds. Ancient airs and dances for lute. **Australian Chamber Orchestra/Christopher Lyndon Gee.** Omega OCD191007.

• 1h 13' DDD 8/89

Respighi's skill as a transcriber of other men's music sometimes makes us forget his own real creative gifts as exemplified in his evocative *Pines of Rome* and other orchestral works. *The birds* is a suite consisting of something between transcriptions of older music and original pieces, rather as happens in Stravinsky's *Pulcinella*, and the result is delightful. Thus, "The Dove", a seventeenth-century lute piece by Jacques Gallot, is transformed into an expressive oboe solo (beautifully played here) with a delicate, twittering accompaniment, while "The Hen" comes from a keyboard piece by Rameau and "The Nightingale" is an atmospheric nocturnal arrangement of an old English folk-tune. The scoring is charmingly imaginative and a wide variety of instruments are heard, including brass, harp and metallophones. The *Ancient airs and dances* are rather more straightforward as transcriptions, but even here there is charming invention. The Australian Chamber Orchestra under the stylish direction of Christopher Lyndon Gee proves to be an expert, refined body of players and the recording, made in Sydney, is successfully balanced with good texture and dynamic range.

Respighi. Violin Sonata in B minor.
R. Strauss. Violin Sonata in E flat major, Op. 18. **Kyung-Wha Chung** (vn); **Krystian Zimerman** (pf). DG 427 617-2GH.

• 52' 2/90

This is wonderful violin playing, as richly romantic as both works often demand, but with a wide range of colour to underline the subtleties and the varying tones

Kyung-Wha Chung   [photo: DG

of voice that both employ. To add to the coupling's appeal, Kyung-Wha Chung's pianist is a musician of exceptional subtlety who is clearly as intent as she is to demonstrate that both sonatas deserve a position much closer to the centre of the repertory than they have so far been given. In the Strauss in particular they succeed eloquently. It is often described as the last work of his apprentice years, but in this performance the mature Strauss steps out from the shadow of Brahms so often and so proudly that its stature as his 'real' Op. 1 seems confirmed. The Respighi is a lesser piece, no doubt, but its melodies and its rhapsodic manner are attractive, and Chung's warm response to Respighi's idiomatic way with the instrument (he was a violinist himself) is infectious. Good and natural-sounding balance between violin and piano is not easy to achieve, but the recording here, significantly helped by Zimerman's combination of poetry and alert responsiveness, is outstandingly successful.

NEW REVIEW

Respighi. Gli uccelli. Il tramonto[a]. Adagio con variazioni[b]. Trittico botticel-liano. [a]**Linda Finnie** (contr); [b]**Raphael Wallfisch** (vc); **Bournemouth Sinfonietta/Tamás Vásáry.** Chandos CHAN8913.

Ih 5'   DDD   3/92

Five harpsichord pieces from the seventeenth and eighteenth centuries, all but one having bird subjects, form the basis of the suite *Gli uccelli* ("The birds"). Respighi's arrangements for small orchestra are unashamedly picturesque and romantic, and Tamás Vásáry secures alert, affectionate playing from the Bourne-mouth Sinfonietta. Three Botticelli paintings housed in a Florence gallery inspired Respighi to write his *Trittico botticelliano* ("Three Botticelli Pictures"). The music is again richly colourful in tone paintings depicting "The Spring", "The Adoration of the Magi", and "The Birth of Venus", and once more Vásáry conducts in a spirited, characterful fashion. *Il tramonto*, for voice and string orchestra (or string quartet), is a vivid setting of Shelley's poem *The sunset*, in an Italian translation. Linda Finnie sings beautifully, even if her Italian pronunciation is a little Anglicized. The *Adagio con variazioni* was originally written for cello and piano, and later orchestrated by the composer. This pleasant, well-ordered work is sensitively played by Raphael Wallfisch. The four works on offer here make up a nicely contrasted programme, and Chandos have provided an attractively rich sound quality.

Julius Reubke   *Refer to Index*   *German 1834-1858*

Nicolay Rimsky-Korsakov   *Russian 1844-1908*

Rimsky-Korsakov. Scheherazade, Op. 35. Capriccio espagnol, Op. 34.
London Symphony Orchestra/Sir Charles Mackerras. Telarc CD80208.

Ih   DDD   10/90

Rimsky-Korsakov. Scheherazade, Op. 35[b]. [a]**Beecham Choral Society; Royal Philharmonic Orchestra/Sir Thomas Beecham.**
Borodin. PRINCE IGOR — Polovtsian Dances[a]. EMI CDC7 47717-2.
Item marked [a] from SXLP30171 (10/74), [b] ASD251 (10/58).

58' ADD 9/87 | P Ⓑ ▲

Sir Charles Mackerras throws himself into this music with expressive abandon, but allies it to control so that every effect is realized and the London Symphony Orchestra play this familiar music as if they were discovering it afresh. Together they produce performances that are both vivid and thoughtful, while the solo violin in *Scheherazade*, who represents the young queen whose storytelling skills prolong and finally save her life in the court of the cruel Sultan Shahriar (portrayed by powerful brass), is seductively and elegantly played by Kees Hulsmann, not least at the wonderfully peaceful end to the whole work. The finale featuring a storm and shipwreck is superbly done, the wind and brass bringing one to the edge of one's seat and reminding us that Rimsky-Korsakov served in the Russian Navy and well knew the beauty and danger of the sea. This sensuous and thrilling work needs spectacular yet detailed sound, and that is what it gets here, the 1990 recording in Walthamstow Town Hall being highly successful and giving us a CD that many collectors will choose to use as a demonstration disc to impress their friends. The performance and recording of the *Capriccio espagnol* is no less of a success, and this issue is worth every penny of its full price.

Beecham's classic version of *Scheherazade* deserves a special place in every discerning CD collection. Over 35 years have elapsed since this recording, but the passage of time has had no detrimental effect, and it is still capable of holding its own against even the most recent of digital rivals. This is a spell-binding performance of considerable depth and power, made even greater by a recording that has warmth, clarity and wide dynamic range. The wonderfully exotic atmosphere is captured exceedingly well, helped by some marvellous orchestral playing: the solo bassoon's characterful portrait of the Prince in the opening of the second section; the beautiful arabesque woodwind passages, and not least the beguiling performance of the solo violin (played here by Steven Staryk) representing Scheherazade's voice as it leads us through this colourful landscape. Beecham's performance of Borodin's "Polovtsian Dances" have great energy and vitality, but the recorded sound is less flattering here with an element of coarseness and a noticeable amount of tape hiss.

NEW REVIEW

Rimsky-Korsakov. SYMPHONIES AND ORCHESTRAL WORKS. **Gothenburg Symphony Orchestra/Neeme Järvi.** DG 423 604-2GH2.
Symphonies — No. 1 in E minor, Op. 1; No. 2 (Symphonic Suite), Op. 9, "Antar"; No. 3 in C major, Op. 32. Russian Easter Festival Overture, Op. 36. Capriccio espagnol, Op. 34.

② 2h 5' DDD 2/89

No one is going to claim Rimsky's First and Third Symphonies to be neglected masterpieces. He came to refer to his First (partly written whilst the young naval officer was on duty!) as a "disgraceful composition", and along with the other two symphonies, it was subjected to extensive revision by the later learned master of musical technique. As the equally learned, entertaining and informative essay accompanying this set points out, the opening of the symphony could have been a trial run for the opening of Schumann's Fourth (and a very fine one, too!). It's the beautifully lyrical second theme which reminds us that Rimsky was reared in the country and had the early advantage of a good soaking in folk song. Though the debt to Glinka is obvious, to our ears classical concerns seem uppermost throughout, and the music is free from anything that could be called exoticism. Not so the Second. Rimsky was a member of the 'Mighty Five', a group of composers (including Mussorgsky, Balakirev and Borodin) sworn to the nationalist cause, professing horror at anything tinged with German academicism and ever searching for subjects on which they could lavish a preference for orchestral colour above form. Rimsky's *Antar* combined these ideals, and more. Our hero of the title is allocated a Berliozian *idée fixe*, an oriental location (the desert of Sham) and the joys of vengeance, power and love from the grateful fairy Gul-Nazar as a gift for saving her from a winged monster. It is, in every way, an antecedent of *Sheherazade* and, after hearing Järvi's rich and eloquently descriptive account, one wonders why it has never attained anything like the same popularity. His Third Symphony reverts to a more academic manner. In 1871 he was invited to join the theory and composition faculty at the St Petersburg Conservatory and, in Tchaikovsky's words, "from contempt of schooling he had turned all at once to the cult of musical technique". Despite a paucity of truly memorable ideas, it is a symphony to admire for its construction and light-as-air orchestration. The set is completed with urgent, vibrant accounts of the *Capriccio espagnol* and the *Russian Easter Festival Overture*, quite the most colourful and exciting versions on disc, and they confirm that the less familiar symphonies could not be in better hands. DG's engineers resist the temptation to glamorize the music and offer a lucid and spacious panorama of sound.

NEW REVIEW

Rimsky-Korsakov. OVERTURE AND SUITES FROM THE OPERAS. **Scottish National Orchestra/Neeme Järvi.** Chandos CHAN8327/8/9. From DBRD3004 (12/84).

May Night — Overture. Suites: The Snow Maiden; Christmas Eve; Mlada; The Invisible City of Kitezh; Le Coq d'Or; The Tale of Tsar Saltan.

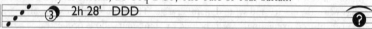

③ 2h 28' DDD

Taking the moral and musical high ground, one should treat with suspicion the output of a composer who is quoted as having said "I am of the opinion that art is essentially the most enchanting, intoxicating lie". But to write off Rimsky as an insincere conjurer of decorous realms of fantasy, you would have to indict Ravel for the same crime; he also took a certain pride in his "artificial" nature. They shared more than a common creed too: just consider the echoes of *Scheherazade*'s "Festival at Baghdad" in the final bacchanal of Ravel's *Daphnis et Chloé*. Rimsky was a prolific opera composer, writing 15 operas between 1872 and 1907. The best music is contained in the purely orchestral suites, principally because the achievement of the opera lies in Rimsky's handling of orchestral colour and texture rather than his writing for the human voice. Rimsky was, in fact, less interested (and less successful) in dramatizing human emotions than in dealing with pantheistic or non-human subjects.

The highlights are all here: the *Tsar Saltan* Suite with its famous "Flight of the Bumble Bee"; the "Dance of the Tumblers" from *The Snow Maiden* and the "Procession of the Nobles" from *Mlada*, taken very broadly here, with an unprecedented pomp and splendour. And the less familiar items have no less facility to excite and fascinate: the *Christmas Eve* Suite with murmuring strings evoking a snow-laden landscape above which glittering stars dance a mazurka (delightfully cosy imagery after Shostakovich's symbolic icy wastelands). But the set is also valuable because it enables us to put Rimsky in an historical perspective. *Christmas Eve*'s grand Polonaise might have danced out of one of Tchaikovsky's ballets; and it is difficult to imagine Rimsky imagining the *Kitezh* without having first heard Wagner's "Forest Murmurs". More importantly, would Stravinsky have given us his *Firebird* without knowledge of Rimsky's *Golden Cockerel*, or Prokofiev his *Alexander Nevsky* unaware of the Tartar invasion in *Kitezh*? Such speculation is part and parcel of the musical enjoyment. And should we turn away from Rimsky simply because Stravinsky, his most starry pupil, chose to eradicate his influence? Järvi has few peers in this kind of music.

Although it was an early collaboration with the Scottish National Orchestra, whose string section was soon to acquire fuller tone and greater finesse (and Chandos were soon better able to tame the occasionally fierce edge of the orchestra's brass section), anyone who wishes to investigate Rimsky beyond *Scheherazade* and the *Spanish Caprice* will find these three discs a musical treasure trove.

Joaquin Rodrigo

Spanish 1901-

Rodrigo. Concierto de Aranjuez. Fantasía para un gentilhombre. **John Williams** (gtr); **Philharmonia Orchestra/Louis Frémaux.** CBS Masterworks CD37848. From IM37848 (7/84).

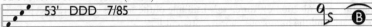

Rodrigo. Concierto de Aranjuez. Fantasía para un gentilhombre.
Villa-Lobos. Guitar Concerto. **Göran Söllscher** (gtr); **Orpheus Chamber Orchestra.** DG 429 232-2GH.

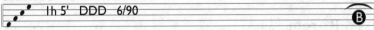

The *Concierto de Aranjuez* is a romantic work whose success remains unparalleled. Rodrigo's recipe for both works on this recording is to express his reverence for past traditions in terms of his own, neoclassical musical language — lush tunes and harmonies, some courtly formality and a soupçon of mischievous spikiness. The *Fantasía* (the *Gentilhombre* is Segovia) pays its respects also to a great guitarist of the seventeenth century, Gaspar Sanz, some of whose themes are winsomely reworked by Rodrigo. Both works call for a high degree of virtuosity but difficulties present no problem to John Williams, who brings to both pieces the proper blend of expressiveness and poise. To describe a recording as 'vivid' has become a cliché but in this case it is inevitable.

All three works on the DG issue contain elements of Latin fire and temperament, fully exploited by many other soloists, but Söllscher, a Swede of aristocratic musicality, also shows the other side of their coin in his sensitive, thoughtful and immaculately played performances. The Orpheus Chamber Orchestra manage wonderfully well without a conductor (so too did their eponym!), following Söllscher with the attentiveness of members of a string quartet, and the recording engineers are equally alert to everyone else concerned. These are 'the thinking man's' versions of these three works.

Sigmund Romberg

Hungarian/American 1887-1951

THE STUDENT PRINCE (Romberg/Donelly). Cast includes **Marilyn Hill Smith, Rosemary Ashe, Diana Montague, David Rendall, Bonaventura Bottone, Neil Jenkins, Jason Howard, Norman Bailey, Donald Maxwell; Ambrosian Chorus; Philharmonia Orchestra/John Owen Edwards.** TER Classics CDTER2 1172.

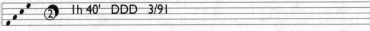

Although we think of the 1920s as a period of great success for the musical comedies of the Gershwins and Rodgers and Hart it was, too, a glorious decade for Sigmund Romberg, who scored three personal triumphs with his operettas *The Student Prince*, *The Desert Song* and *New Moon*. Each of these scores exudes an air of confidence both in the sweep of their melodic lines, and the vigorous choral writing that has stood the test of time rather better than the flimsy story lines that support them. In order to include as much of Romberg's score as feasible, it has been necessary to include some rather embarrassing cues that certainly defeats one of the more senior members of the cast, which in the main is the same team that was assembled by TER for their outstanding recording of *Kismet*, with John Owen Edwards once again drawing assured playing from the Philharmonia. In addition to David Rendall sporting boyish good humour in the title role, there are distinctive contributions from Bonaventura Bottone leading the Drinking song, Norman Bailey in "Golden days" and a lovely version of the Lehár-like duet, "Just we two" from Diana Montague and Steven Page. The one slight disappointment in this line-up is Marilyn Hill Smith who on this occasion can't escape a charge of blandness, and a touch of shrillness on the high Cs of "Come boys, let's be gay boys". That apart, there is no hesitation in extending a warm welcome to this much-needed new recording which surprises more than once by the charm of its lesser known numbers: the Act 2 gavotte, for instance, and the sophistication of Romberg's handling of the score's big duet, "Deep in my heart" and the humorous chorus, "Student life".

Ned Rorem   *Refer to Index*   *American 1923-*

Antonio Rosetti   *Bohemian c.1750-1792*

NEW REVIEW

Rosetti. Horn Concertos — E major, K3:42; E major, K3:44; E flat major, K3:39. **English Chamber Orchestra/Barry Tuckwell** (hn). Classics for Pleasure CD-CFP4578.

53' DDD 8/91

Barry Tuckwell   *[photo: EMI/Holt]*

Although Rosetti's contemporaries ranked him with Haydn and Mozart, posterity has been less kind. Born near Prague in 1750, he was christened Franz Anton Rössler, but preferred the Italianized form of his name, Rosetti ("little roses"), for professional use. He was a prolific composer, mostly of orchestral and chamber music, but is remembered for his wind concertos. His idiomatic writing for horn, in particular, greatly contributed to the development of a melodic style for the instrument. This disc is something of a labour of love. All three of the concertos were edited by John Humphries, from the printed parts in the possession of various libraries, especially for the recording. To be honest, the concertos are not in the same league as Mozart's, though they should be snapped up by all horn *aficionados* and explorers of musical byways. Not only is the asking price very modest, but their challenge brings some stunning playing from one of the world's greatest horn virtuosos. The English Chamber Orchestra react well to him and the recording has exactly the right mix of intimacy and space with plenty of headroom for Tuckwell's most forthright bursts of tone.

Luigi Rossi
Italian c.1597-1653

NEW REVIEW

Rossi. ORFEO. **Agnès Mellon** (sop) Orfeo; **Monique Zanetti** (sop) Euridice; **Dominique Favat** (mez) Nutrice, Bacco; **Sandrine Piau** (sop) Aristeo; **Nicholas Isherwood** (bass) Satiro; **Caroline Pelon** (sop) Amore; **Noémi Rime** (sop) Venere, Vittoria; **Jean-Paul Fouchécourt** (ten) Vecchia, Giove; **Jérôme Corréas** (bar) Endimione; **Marie Boyer** (mez) Giunone; **Cécile Eloir** (mez) Gelosia; **Bernard Deletré** (bass) Augure, Plutone; **Benoît Thivel** (alto) Apollo, Mercurio; **Jean-Marc Salzmann** (bar) Caronte, Momo; **Donatienne Michel-Dansac** (sop) Proserpina; **Beatrice Malleret** (sop) Himeneo; **Les Arts Florissants/William Christie.** Harmonia Mundi HMC90 1358/60. Notes, text and translation included.

③ 3h 39' DDD 3/92

Luigi Rossi spent most of his career in Rome, but in 1646 he was invited by Cardinal Mazarin to the Parisian Court. Shortly after he arrived, and while he was working on his second opera *Orfeo*, he received the tragic news of his wife's death in Italy. Small wonder, then, that he produced such profound and affecting music for the subject of this opera. Francesco Buti's libretto consists of three acts, with a prologue and postlude in praise of Louis XIV — dramatically, quite inapposite. Buti supplemented the mythological characters with a host of minor roles, many of them comic figures to lighten the mood. With these resources, Rossi was able to intersperse the recitatives and arias with ensembles, choruses, and dance music, no doubt to appeal to French taste. This recording is most welcome, not just because it is the only one available, but more because it is so impeccably performed. William Christie achieves the finest musical precision as well as giving a powerful dramatic thrust to the whole. He has a crack orchestra, with some admirably fleet cornetts and very polished continuo playing. Of the soloists, Agnès Mellon handles the title role beautifully, and her interpretation of "Lagrime, dove sete?", which Orfeo sings on hearing of Euridice's death, is particularly moving. What emotive and perfectly crafted music this is; and how deeply Rossi must have felt it. Monique Zanetti is appropriately sweet-toned as Euridice — very poised in her death scene; and Sandrine Piau's interpretation of the complex character of Aristeo is particularly admirable. One or two of the minor roles are not so strong, and Buti's interpolations do tend to interrupt the dramatic thread, but these are insignificant quibbles. It is an absolutely first-rate recording of a work which deserves to be better known.

Gioachino Rossini
Italian 1792-1868

Rossini. OVERTURES. **Orpheus Chamber Orchestra.** DG 415 363-2GH.
Tancredi. L'italiana in Algeri. L'inganno felice. La scala di seta. Il barbiere di Siviglia. Il Signor Bruschino. La cambiale di matrimonio. Il turco in Italia.

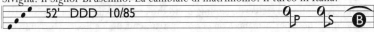

52' DDD 10/85

Rossini. OVERTURES. **Philharmonia Orchestra/Herbert von Karajan.**
EMI CDM7 63113-2. Items marked [a] from Columbia SAX2378 (3/61), [b] SAX2274 (9/59).
L'italiana in Algeri[a]; Semiramide[a]; Il barbiere di Siviglia[a]; Guillaume Tell[a]; La scala di seta[a]; La gazza ladra[a]. GUILLAUME TELL — Overture; Pas de trois et choeur tyrolien[b].

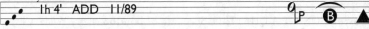

1h 4' ADD 11/89

NEW REVIEW

Rossini. OVERTURES. **London Classical Players/Roger Norrington.**
EMI Reflexe CDC7 54091-2.
La scala di seta. Il Signor Bruschino. L'italiana in Algeri. Il barbiere di Siviglia. La
gazza ladra. Semiramide. Guillaume Tell.

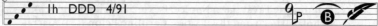

1h DDD 4/91

In 1824 the English essayist Leigh Hunt wrote that Rossini possessed "the genius
of sheer animal spirits", and certainly few composers can rival his gaiety and life-
affirmation. Whatever the story of a Rossini opera (and he even wrote an *Otello*),
geniality is the keynote of the music, not least because he enjoyed writing it. He
felt himself to be "born to comic opera" and was also quintessentially Italian, with
no gloomily German spiritual doubts: the Italian writer Luigi Barzini could have
had Rossini in mind when he declared that the pleasures of his countrymen came
from "living in a world made by man for man on human measurements". There
are numerous collections of Rossini overtures in the catalogue, but the DG one is
special: not only is the recording first-rate, presenting the orchestra with a
splendidly tangible sense of presence, but the performances exude life and delight
in the music. The Orpheus CO plays without conductor, yet the ensemble is exact,
expression and tempo fluctuations are beautifully fluid, and balance is just right
for these very theatrical works. Rossini would rarely have had a large orchestra
available to him in the Italian theatre pit of his time, and the wind-dominated
texture that is heard from this chamber ensemble is probably closer to his expectations than the string-heavy balance of most symphony orchestras. The woodwind
playing here is warm and full of individuality, and each work is driven by a lively
sense of rhythm that only flags on the odd few occasions. What is perhaps most
refreshing about this issue is the way the inherent humour of the music is
allowed to raise an ongoing chuckle, rather than being forced to a belly laugh.

Background hiss is one of the few indicators of the age of Karajan's otherwise
vivacious and full-bodied recordings. This is vintage Karajan, at ease with the
orchestra and the music, prepared to rest on his heels and let the natural good
humour of the music make its own effect. He takes the traditional, concert view
of these overtures, treating them as mini tone-poems. The performances are none
the worse for that, and they provide ideal home listening, with lashings of
dynamic contrast and well-paced crescendos, full-toned woodwind solos and
weighty string playing. The "Pas de trois et choeur tyrolien" from *Guillaume Tell*,
added to make up time on this CD, make an effective intermezzo for the
programme and provide the listener who only knows the Overture with an
intriguing taste of the opera's other delights. The Philharmonia plays all with
practised ease, obviously pleased to find their conductor in such an affable mood.

The seven overtures on the Norrington disc are played in the order of
composition and show Rossini in witty and boisterous mood, but each one also
has its own character and plenty of internal variety as well. Thus the cut-and-
thrust opening of *La scala di seta,* which begins this disc, immediately gives way
to mellifluous woodwind writing, and the famous galloping tune in the closing
work, *William Tell* (which was his last opera before he retired to gastronomy) is
the companion to gentle or grand pastoral music. These pieces feature the famous
Rossini crescendo, like a kettle coming up to the boil, and their vivacity is vastly
enhanced by these performances on period instruments under Roger Norrington.
One can only agree with the critic who wrote admiringly of his "cooing or
bitching wind, burping horns, Rumpole-like bassoons" and of his drummer's
"murderous thwacks". The recording is as vivid as the music. This is a disc to
bring a smile to the lips and make you appreciate life.

NEW REVIEW

Rossini. SONATE A QUATTRO. **Serenata of London** (Barry Wilde, Clive
Lander, vns; Roger Smith, vc; Michaël Brittain, db). ASV CDDCA767.

No. 1 in G major; No. 2 in A major; No. 3 in C major; No. 4 in B flat major; No. 5 in E flat major; No. 6 in D major.

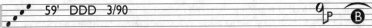

lh 18' DDD 10/91

Rossini's six string sonatas are usually heard performed by a string orchestra, although they were in fact composed for a quartet of two violins, cello and double bass. This issue, which gives us for the first time on CD the original instrumentation, is therefore most welcome. The sonatas, which display amazing musical dexterity and assurance may date from 1804, when Rossini was only 12. The world of eighteenth-century opera is never far away, with the first violin frequently taking the role of soprano soloists, particularly in the slow movements. Written for Rossini's friend Agostino Triosso, who was a keen double bass player, the sonata's bass parts are full of wit and suavity. The performances by the Serenata of London are full of elegance and polish. Rossini's youthful high spirits are always to the fore and some of the fearsome string writing clearly holds no terrors for the members of this group. ASV's resonant recording adds the final touch of satisfaction to a most welcome recording.

Rossini. Stabat mater. **Helen Field** (sop); **Della Jones** (mez); **Arthur Davies** (ten); **Roderick Earle** (bass); **London Symphony Chorus; City of London Sinfonia/Richard Hickox.** Chandos CHAN8780. Text and translation included.

59' DDD 3/90

This used to be a ripe nineteenth-century favourite, and many a proudly bound vocal score at present languishing in a pile of second-hand music would testify to a time when its owner felt enabled, with its help, to combine the pleasure of church-going with the duty of attendance at the opera. The words are those of Jacapone da Todi's sacred poem, but Rossini's music is dramatic, exciting and sometimes almost indecently tuneful. Certainly the soloists have to be recruited from the opera company; the soprano who launches out into the "Inflammatus" must be generously supplied with high Cs as well as the power to shoot them over the heads of full choir and orchestra, while the tenor at one alarming moment is asked for a top D flat and has to ring out the melody of his "Cujus animam" with tone to match the trumpets which introduce it. In all four soloists, grace and technical accomplishment are as important as range and power; they must also have the taste and discipline to work harmoniously as a quartet. In this recording they certainly do that, and neither are they lacking in range or technique; if there is a limitation it is rather in richness of tone and in the heroic quality which the solos mentioned above ideally need. Even so, individually and collectively, they compare well with most of their competitors on record, and the choral and orchestral work under Hickox is outstanding.

Rossini. Petite messe solennelle. **Helen Field** (sop); **Anne-Marie Owens** (mez); **Edmund Barham** (ten); **John Tomlinson** (bass); **David Nettle, Richard Markham** (pfs); **Peter King** (harmonium); **City of Birmingham Symphony Orchestra Chorus/Simon Halsey.** Conifer CDCF184. Text and translation included.

lh 18' DDD 10/90

Of Rossini's later works, none has won such affection from the general listening public as the *Petite messe solennelle*. He called it "the final sin of my old age" and, as with the other of his *pêches de vieillesse*, he declined to have it published. Editions issued in 1869, the year after his death, failed to retain his original scoring and contained numerous inaccuracies, yet these have been the basis of most subsequent recordings of the work. This disc presents the mass in a revelatory new Oxford University Press edition by Nancy Fleming, using two pianos in addition to a fine, French harmonium. That alone would mark it out for prime consideration, even if the reading were only passable, but here we have the bonus of dedicated, heartfelt performances from all involved. Above all, the scale of the work is finely captured — it was intended for chamber performance and both writing and scoring reflect the intimacy of Rossini's ideas. Much praise must go to Simon Halsey for so clearly establishing the parameters for this performance, and to the recording engineers for making it all seem so convincing. The whole issue establishes a new benchmark for assessing recordings of this work.

NEW REVIEW

Rossini. HEROINES. **Cecilia Bartoli** (mez); [a]**Chorus and Orchestra of the Teatro La Fenice, Venice/Ion Martin.** Decca 436 075-2DH.
ZELMIRA — Riedi al soglio[a]. Le nozze di Teti e di Peleo — Ah, non potrian reistere. MAOMETTO II — Ah! che invan su questo ciglio; Giusto ciel, in tal periglio[a]. LA DONNA DEL LAGO — Tanti affetti in tal momento[a].
ELISABETTA, REGINA D'INGHILTERRA — Quant' è grato all'alma mia[a]; Fellon, la penna avrai[a]. SEMIRAMIDE — Serenai vaghirai ... Bel raggio lusinghier[a].

59' DDD 2/92

This sparkling disc brings together a collection of arias composed by Rossini for one of the great prima donnas of the nineteenth century, who was also his wife, Isabella Colbran. It is tempting to wonder whether even she had a voice to match that of Cecilia Bartoli, one of the newest, luscious, most exciting voices in opera. All those dazzling chromatic runs, leaps, cadenzas and cascading coloraturas are handled with consummate ease. Throughout, Bartoli sounds as if she's enjoying the music; there is always an engaging smile in the voice, although she is properly imperious in the extracts from *Elisabetta* and disarmingly simple in the

prayerful "Giusto ciel, in tal periglio" ("Righteous heaven in such danger") from *Maometto II*. The orchestral and choral forces bring a delightful intimacy to the proceedings, with some cheeky woodwind solos and fruity brass passages. The recording, produced at the Teatro La Fenice by Decca veteran Christopher Raeburn, favours the voices but gives it just enough distance to accommodate high Cs and astounding A flats at the bottom of the range. The orchestral perspective is changeable but satisfactory. For Rossini and Bartoli fans alike, this disc is a must.

Cecilia Bartoli   *[photo: Decca*

Rossini. OPERA ARIAS. **Della Jones** (mez); [a]**Richard Hickox Singers; City of London Sinfonia/Richard Hickox.** Chandos CHAN8865. Texts and translations included.
L'ITALIANA IN ALGERI — Quanta roba! ... Cruda sorte! Amor tiranno![a]. LA DONNA DEL LAGO — Mura felici ... O quante lacrime finor versai. IL SIGNOR BRUSCHINO — Ah, voi condur volete ... Ah, donate i caro sposo. ADELAIDE DI BORGOGNA — Soffri la tua sventura; Salve, Italia, un dì regnante[a]. OTELLO — Assisa apiè d'un salice (with Carol Smith, sop). IL BARBIERE DI SIVIGLIA — Una voce poco fà. BIANCA E FALLIERO — Tu non sai qual colpo atroce. LA CENERENTOLA — Nacqui all'affanno ... Non

più mesta[a] (Smith; Katherine Steffan, mez; Harry Nicholl, Gerard Finley, tens; Simon Birchall, bass).

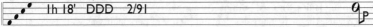 1h 18' DDD 2/91

In the court of the mezzo-soprano, Rossini would be composer-laureate. He wrote for the mezzo voice most extensively and excitingly, providing opportunities for comedy and pathos, for a pure, even melodic line and for brilliant displays of virtuosity. He exploited the whole vocal range, two octaves or more, yet was considerate in keeping the 'lie' or *tessitura* of the notes within the comfortable middle of the voice, avoiding strain at either extreme. Above all, he put the mezzo-soprano into the centre of the stage: for once, she, and not the full, high soprano, would be the star. Over the last 30 or 40 years many famous singers have been associated with these roles. Marilyn Horne and Teresa Berganza perhaps come to mind first, while most recently added to the line has been Cecilia Bartolli. None has coped more ably with the technical demands than Della Jones. She is fluent and precise, and exercises an easy mastery over the most difficult passage-work. She can express tenderness and concern (as in *La cenerentola*), but most of all these are *spirited* performances, some of them, too, in little-known music such as the arias from *Adelaide di Borgogna* and *Bianca e Falliero*. The acoustic may be a trifle too reverberant, but both the singing and the playing are so well defined that any loss of clarity is minimal.

Rossini. IL SIGNOR BRUSCHINO. **Bruno Praticò** (bar) Gaudenzio; **Natale di Carolis** (bass-bar) Bruschino padre; **Patrizia Orciani** (sop) Sofia; **Luca Canonici** (ten) Florville; **Pietro Spangnoli** (bar) Filiberto; **Katia Lytting** (mez) Marianna; **Fulvio Massa** (ten) Bruschino figlio, Commissario; **Turin Philharmonic Orchestra/Marcello Viotti.** Claves CD50-8904/5. Text included.

② 84' DDD 10/89

It may take a wise father to know his own son, but even a fool can recognize a complete impostor: that, roughly, is the upshot of this little comedy in which the young Rossini tried out several ideas that were going to come in handy later on, and which is still revived from time to time to act as a pleasant part of a double-bill or a curtain-raiser. It is a pity that this recording could not have run in harness, for 84 minutes on two discs hardly constitutes good value these days. Still, the performance is likeable and at present has no competitor on CD. The singers are young and fresh-voiced; they miss a few tricks which their elders might have brought to the catch-phrases and the supposedly unexpected turn of events, but we are spared the conventional buffo clowning, with its exaggerated diction and falsetto squeaks. The best feature is the playing of the accomplished Turin orchestra under Marcello Viotti. The score is delightfully melodious and inventive, and the delicacy of orchestral texture as well as the spring of its rhythms can be well appreciated here, starting, of course, with the Overture and its famous raps of the second violins' bows on their music-stands which brought the musicians out on strike at the première in 1813.

Rossini. IL TURCO IN ITALIA. **Maria Callas** (sop) Fiorilla; **Nicolai Gedda** (ten) Narciso; **Nicola Rossi-Lemeni** (bass) Selim; **Mariano Stabile** (bar) Poet; **Franco Calabrese** (bass) Geronio; **Jolanda Gardino** (mez) Zaida; **Piero De Palma** (ten) Albazar; **Chorus and Orchestra of La Scala, Milan/ Gianandrea Gavazzeni.** EMI mono CDS7 49344-8. Notes, text and translation included. From Columbia 33CXS1289, 33CX1290/91 (10/55).

② 1h 53' ADD 12/87 £ 9 P ▲

The triumph of *L'italiana in Algeri* in 1813 prompted Rossini to write a successor the following year. The ideas are similar, the basic propositions being that foreigners are funny (especially if from the Middle East or the wrong side of the Mediterranean) and that old gentlemen must look out for trouble if they associate with young ladies who are both pretty and witty. The orchestral score sparkles and charms, the principal roles demand plenty of personality as well as vocal accomplishment, and the ensembles gather momentum with the madcap exhilaration of a fairground roundabout. It may seem strange to come upon Maria Callas in the midst of all this, for comedy may not appear to be an element in which she would thrive. But in fact she succeeds brilliantly, not only in her solos and in the deft inflections of recitative but also in ensemble-work as a member of the company, playing her part in happy collaboration with the others. These include the veteran Mariano Stabile and the young Nicolai Gedda, neither of whom has as much to do as one would wish; Rossi-Lemeni as the Turk and Franco Calabrese as the old husband sing with zest, and all take heart from the practised skill of Gavazzeni at the helm. The old recording comes up like new, and though some cuts have been made in the score they hardly detract from the enjoyment of so polished an entertainment.

Rossini. IL BARBIERE DI SIVIGLIA. **Thomas Allen** (bar) Figaro; **Agnes Baltsa** (mez) Rosina; **Domenico Trimarchi** (bar) Dr Bartolo; **Robert Lloyd** (bass) Don Basilio; **Francisco Araiza** (ten) Count Almaviva; **Matthew Best** (bass) Fiorello; **Sally Burgess** (mez) Berta; **John Noble** (bar) Official; **Ambrosian Opera Chorus; Academy of St Martin in the Fields/Sir Neville Marriner** with **Nicholas Kraemer** (fp). Philips 411 058-2PH3. Notes, text and translation included. From 6769 100 (6/83).

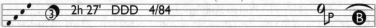

The Overture gives the clue: this is to be a real *Barbiere* on the boards. Incisive, sprung rhythms, cheeky, rather than seductive, woodwind and a sense of fun as much as of intrigue characterize this performance from start to finish. It has a lot to do with Marriner's phrasing and rollicking sense of Rossinian style, to which the orchestra of the Academy respond so readily. But the barometer of this performance is its recitatives, and with Nicholas Kraemer's astute playing of a sweet-toned fortepiano in place of a spidery harpsichord, the voltage of the Rosina/Figaro encounters and the comic timing of Bartolo and Basilio is excitingly high. It keeps the soloists on their toes, too; and they are a strong team. The outstanding recommendation of this *Barbiere,* though, is its Rosina. From the first bars of "Una voce poco fa", Agnes Baltsa shows that this "dolce amorosa" can turn to the sting of a viper, too: the dark recesses of her chest voice and the brilliance of her high register flash in turn to follow every volatile mood of the role in a searching performance of superb dramatic timing.

NEW REVIEW
Rossini. L'ITALIANA IN ALGERI. **Lucia Valentini-Terrani** (contr) Isabella; **Francisco Araiza** (ten) Lindoro; **Enzo Dara** (bass) Taddeo; **Wladimiro Ganzarolli** (bass) Mustafà; **Jeanne Marie Bima** (sop) Elvira; **Lucia Rizzi** (contr) Zulma; **Alessandro Corbelli** (bar) Haly; **Cologne West German Radio Male Chorus; Cappella Coloniensis/Gabriele Ferro.** CBS Masterworks CD39048. Notes, text and translation included. From M3 39048 (11/84).

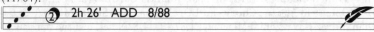

NEW REVIEW
Rossini. L'ITALIANA IN ALGERI. **Marilyn Horne** (mez) Isabella; **Ernesto Palacio** (ten) Lindoro; **Domenico Trimarchi** (bar) Taddeo; **Samuel Ramey** (bass) Mustafà; **Kathleen Battle** (sop) Elvira; **Clara Foti** (mez) Zulma; **Nicola Zaccaria** (bass) Haly; **Prague Philharmonic Chorus; I Solisti Veneti/**

Claudio Scimone. Erato Libretto 2292-45404-2. Notes and text included.
From STU7 1394 (3/81).

⊘ 2h 20' ADD 1/92 £

Written within the space of a month during the spring of 1813, and with help
from another anonymous hand, Rossini's *L'italiana in Algeri* was an early success,
and one which went on to receive many performances during the nineteenth
century, with an increasingly corrupt text. A complete reconstruction was
undertaken by Azio Corghi and published in 1981; both these recordings use this
new edition which corresponds most closely to what was actually performed in
Venice in 1813. *L'italiana* is one of Rossini's wittiest operas, featuring as did a
number of his most successful works a bewitching central character, in this case
Isabella, who makes fun of her various suitors, with the opera ending with a
happy escape with her beloved, Lindoro, a typical *tenorino* role. Both these fine
recordings have considerable strengths; Gabriele Ferro's reading on CBS
emphasizes the drama of the score, while Claudio Scimone's on Erato has plenty
of vocal polish.

Scimone's biggest asset is Marilyn Horne as Isabella: possibly the finest Rossini
singer of her generation and a veteran in this particular role, she sings Rossini's
demanding music with great virtuosity and polish. Her liquid tone and artful
phrasing ensure that she is a continuous pleasure to listen to. She is strongly
supported by the rest of the cast: Kathleen Battle, making an early (1981)
operatic appearance, is a beguiling Elvira, Domenico Trimarchi a most humorous
Taddeo, and Samuel Ramey a sonorous Bey of Algiers — Isabella's opponent and
pursuer. Ernesto Palacio's Lindoro, however, has patches of white tone and is
correct rather than inspiring. Scimone's conducting is likewise efficient if at times
slightly lacking in sparkle.

By contrast Ferro's conducing on CBS is full of vigour right from the first
note of the overture: his reading is imbued with the spirit of the theatre, as are a
number of the principal performers. Wladimiro Ganzarolli as the Bey gives a
rollicking performance, if tonally somewhat woolly: one can almost hear his eyes
rolling! Francisco Araiza is an ardent and mellifluous Lindoro, and Enzo Dara a
suave Taddeo. The principal role of Isabella is taken by Lucia Valentini-Terrani
whose interpretation tends to the placid rather than the dynamic: however her
tone and phrasing are always wholly acceptable. A considerable advantage to the
CBS set is the lively playing of the German 'authentic' performance orchestra
from Cologne — and a spacious and well-balanced recording. Both recordings
will give considerable pleasure: Erato provides much fine singing and conducting
that might be described as correct rather than inspired, while CBS's performance
contains more fun and dynamic musical direction, if at the expense of vocal
polish.

Rossini. ARMIDA. **Cecilia Gasdia** (sop) Armida; **William Matteuzzi** (ten)
Goffredo, Carlo; **Bruce Ford** (ten) Ubaldo, Gernando; **Chris Merritt** (ten)
Rinaldo; **Charles Workman** (bar) Eustazio; **Ferruccio Furlanetto** (bass)
Idraote, Astarotte; **Ambrosian Opera Chorus; I Solisti Veneti/Claudio
Scimone.** Europea Musica 350211. Notes and Italian text included.

⊘ 2h 33' DDD 12/91

The story of Armida the sorceress must be one of the most popular in the
history of opera. Monteverdi tackled it in the seventeenth century, Handel,
Haydn and Glück in the eighteenth, and here in the nineteenth Rossini gives it
full-blown Italianate treatment, complete with crescendos, ballet music and
virtuoso vocal lines. It provides one of the few opportunities in Rossini for the
soprano to head the cast; and considering the demands of this role and the
scenario's opportunities for spectacle (descending clouds for example) it is

perhaps surprising that it is not more frequently performed. There are fewer memorable melodies than, for instance, in the *Barber of Seville*, but nevertheless some of the music is appropriately enchanting, with particularly luscious orchestration, as in the Act 2 nymphs' chorus, and a glorious duet for Armida and Rinaldo in the same act, with obbligato cello. Armida is admirably sung with command, clarity and stunningly articulated consonants by Cecilia Gasdia. Her Rinaldo, Chris Merritt, is an excellent match, and there is much fine singing from the supporting cast which includes Ferruccio Furlanetto, Bruce Ford and Charles Workman, though William Matteuzzi sounds a little strained when contending with the full orchestra, not aided by the resonant acoustic. The Ambrosian Opera Chorus, directed by John McCarthy, is superbly mellifluous, and from I Solisti Veneti and the conductor Claudio Scimone comes enthusiastic and wonderfully fresh playing with fine soloists for the obbligatos. The whole performance has much warmth, tenderness and spirit. The one quibble concerns the booklet. No English translation is provided, and no full synopsis; and it would have been better to insert track numbers beside the Italian text instead of identical black boxes at the start of each track, which do not help you to keep your place.

NEW REVIEW

Rossini. LA CENERENTOLA. **Teresa Berganza** (mez) Angelina; **Luigi Alva** (ten) Don Ramiro; **Renato Capecchi** (bar) Dandini; **Paolo Montarsolo** (bar) Don Magnifico; **Margherita Guglielmi** (sop) Clorinda; **Laura Zannini** (contr) Tisbe; **Ugo Trama** (bass) Alidoro; **Scottish Opera Chorus; London Symphony Orchestra/Claudio Abbado.** DG 423 861-2GH2. Notes, text and translation included. From 2709 039 (6/72) and 415 698-2GH3 (9/86).

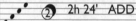

② 2h 24' ADD

Teresa Berganza   [photo: Erato/Estrada]

Rossini's Cinderella is a fairy-tale without a fairy, but no less bewitching for the absence of a magic wand. In fact the replacement of the winged godmother with the philanthropic Alidoro, a close friend and adviser of our prince, Don Ramiro, plus the lack of any glass slippers and the presence of a particularly unsympathetic father character, makes the whole story more plausible. *La Cenerentola*, Angelina, is more spunky than the average pantomime Cinders, not too meek to complain about her treatment or to beg to be allowed to go to the ball. She herself gives Don Ramiro one of her pair of bracelets, charging him to find the owner of the matching ornament and thus taking in hand the control of her own destiny. Along the way, Don Ramiro and his valet Dandini change places, leading to plenty of satisfyingly operatic confusion and difficult situations. This recording, when originally transferred to CD, was spread across three discs, but it has now been comfortably fitted into two. It gives a sparkling rendition of the score with a lovely light touch and well-judged tempos from Abbado and the London Symphony Orchestra and virtuoso vocal requirements are fully met by the cast. The chief delight is Teresa Berganza's Angelina, gloriously creamy in tone and as warm as she is precise.

The supporting cast is full of character, with Luigi Alva a princely Don Ramiro, Margherita Guglielmi and Laura Zannini an affected and fussy pair of sisters, and Renato Capecchi as Dandini, gleeful and mischievous as he takes on being prince for a day. Although the recording was made in 1972 it has survived its technological transfers more than usually well.

Rossini. LA GAZZA LADRA. **Katia Ricciarelli** (sop) Ninetta; **William Matteuzzi** (ten) Giannetto; **Samuel Ramey** (bass) Gottardo; **Bernadette Manca di Nissa** (contr) Pippo; **Luciana d'Intinto** (mez) Lucia; **Ferruccio Furlanetto** (bar) Fernando Villabella; **Roberto Coviello** (bass) Fabrizio Vingradito; **Oslavio di Credico** (ten) Isacco; **Pierre Lefebre** (ten) Antonio; **Francesco Musinu** (bass) Giorgio; **Marcello Lippi** (bass) Ernesto; **Prague Philharmonic Choir; Turin Radio Symphony Orchestra/Gianluigi Gelmetti.** Sony Classical CD45850. Notes, text and translation included. Recorded at performances in the Teatro Rossini, Pesaro in August 1989.

③ 3h 14' DDD 10/90

Recorded live during the 1989 Rossini Opera Festival in Pesaro, and suffused with the atmosphere of the venue, this performance sports a first-class line-up of soloists, a strong chorus and an enthusiastic orchestra. Ricciarelli, though perhaps a little rich-toned for the role of a country girl, stylishly ornaments her part and brings great authority and conviction to the role. Similarly, Samuel Ramey, as the Mayor, is particularly telling; but even the smallest parts are effectively done. The score employed here is unusually close to that used when this "Melodrama in due atti" first saw the light of day at La Scala in 1817, and as such gives us a good idea of Rossini's intentions for the work, unencumbered by the 'improvements' of later hands; the sentiments of the original play by d'Aubigny and Caigniez, that so moved Parisian audiences of 1815 and 1816, are once again made vital and relevant. Most importantly, the conductor, Gianluigi Gelmetti, must be commended for pacing the opera so astutely: Act 1 seems relatively low-key at first hearing, but emotion steadily builds in the long Act 2 to culminate in a stunning finale.

Rossini. SEMIRAMIDE. **Dame Joan Sutherland** (sop) Semiramide; **Marilyn Horne** (mez) Arsace; **Joseph Rouleau** (bass) Assur; **John Serge** (ten) Idreno; **Patricia Clark** (sop) Azema; **Spiro Malas** (bass) Oroe; **Michael Langdon** (bass) Ghost of Nino; **Leslie Fryson** (ten) Mitrane; **Ambrosian Opera Chorus; London Symphony Orchestra/Richard Bonynge.** Decca 425 481-2DM3. Notes, text and translation included. From SET317/19 (10/66).

③ 2h 48' ADD 2/90

Wagner thought it represented all that was bad about Italian opera and Kobbe's *Complete Opera Book* proclaimed that it had had its day — but then added what looked like second thoughts, saying that "were a soprano and contralto to appear in conjunction in the firmament the opera might be successfully revived". That was exactly what happened in the 1960s, when both Sutherland and Horne were in superlative voice and, with Richard Bonynge, were taking a prominent part in the reintroduction of so many nineteenth-century operas which the world thought it had outgrown. This recording brought a good deal of enlightenment in its time. For one thing, here was vocal music of such 'impossible' difficulty being sung with brilliance by the two principal women and with considerable skill by the men, less well-known as they were. Then it brought to many listeners the discovery that, so far from being a mere show-piece, the opera contained ensembles that possessed quite compelling dramatic intensity. People who had heard of the duet "Giorno d'orroré" (invariably encored in Victorian times) were surprised to find it remarkably unshowy and even expressive of the ambiguous feelings of mother and son in their extraordinary predicament. It will probably be a long time before this recording is superceded, admirably vivid as it is in sound, finely conducted and magnificently sung.

Rossini. IL VIAGGIO A REIMS. **Cecilia Gasdia** (sop) Corinna; **Katia Ricciarelli** (sop) Madama Cortese; **Lella Cuberli** (sop) Contessa di Folleville; **Lucia Valentini Terrani** (mez) Marchesa Melibea; **Edoardo Gimenez** (ten) Cavalier Belfiore; **Francisco Araiza** (ten) Conte di Libenskof; **Samuel Ramey** (bass) Lord Sidney; **Ruggero Raimondi** (bass) Don Profondo; **Enzo Dara** (bar) Barone di Trombonok; **Leo Nucci** (bar) Don Alvaro; **Prague Philharmonic Chorus; Chamber Orchestra of Europe/Claudio Abbado.** DG 415 498-2GH3. Notes, text and translation included. Recorded at performances at the 1984 Rossini Opera Festival, Pesaro, Italy.

③ 2h 16' DDD 1/86

Composed as an elaborate and sophisticated entertainment for the coronation of Charles X, *Il viaggio a Reims* marked Rossini's début in Paris as the international superstar which his dazzling and innovative Italian career had justly made him. Musically it is bewitching: an intoxicant that gives sustained sensuous pleasure quite independent of the libretto. The rediscovery and assembly of the complete score, which Rossini partially dismantled and expertly reallocated to *Le Comte Ory*, is the brilliant scholarly achievement of Janet Johnson and Philip Gosset. The set is also a triumph for Claudio Abbado, the finest Rossini conductor of our day, and for DG whose munificence helped make possible the assembly of that dazzling array of vocal talent which the piece needs. The recording is a miracle of clarity and brilliance, with the kind of electricity in the atmosphere which is virtually impossible to reproduce in studio conditions.

Rossini. LE COMTE ORY. **John Aler** (ten) Comte Ory; **Sumi Jo** (sop) Adèle; **Gille Cachemaille** (bar) La Gouverneur; **Diana Montague** (mez) Isolier; **Gino Quilico** (bar) Raimbaud; **Raquel Pierotti** (mez) Ragonde; **Maryse Castets** (sop) Alice; **Francis Dudziac** (ten) First Chevalier; **Nicholas Rivenq** (bar) Second Chevalier; **Chorus and Orchestra of Lyon Opera/ John Eliot Gardiner.** Philips 422 406-2PH2. Notes, text and translation included.

② 2h 12' DDD 10/89

NEW REVIEW

Rossini. LE COMTE ORY. **Juan Oncina** (ten) Comte Ory; **Sari Barabas** (sop) Adèle; **Ian Wallace** (bass) Gouverneur; **Cora Canne-Meijer** (mez) Isolier; **Michel Roux** (bar) Raimbaud; **Monica Sinclair** (contr) Ragonde; **Jeannette Sinclair** (sop) Alice; **Dermot Troy** (ten) Nobleman; **Glyndebourne Festival Chorus and Orchestra/Vittorio Gui.** EMI Rossini Edition mono CMS7 64180-2. Notes, text and translation included. From HMV ALP1473/4 (7/57).

② 1h 53' ADD 5/92

Rossini's last comedy had its première in 1828 and for English audiences it came delightfully to new life at Glyndebourne in 1955. More than most, it is an opera that needs to be seen, especially the part where Ory and his men disguised as nuns are solicitously cared for by the ladies whom they hope to vanquish in the few hours remaining before their husbands return from the Crusades. Still, all is played vividly, and the ear catches the infection of laughter much as sight does in the theatre. Gardiner's direction has pace and point, and his young-sounding cast have a natural grace and lightness of touch. Outstanding among them is the Korean-born soprano Sumi Jo, charming in tone and style, highly accomplished in the rapid scale-work and high coloratura abounding in her part. Her duet with Ory in Act 2 is one of the high-spots; one among many, it has to be added, for all of the principal singers add something distinctive and delightful when their turn comes. Best of all perhaps is the concerted work of the whole company in the finale of Act 1: the very essence of Rossinian comedy is here, and one can hardly imagine a performance more happily combining refinement and exhilaration.

The EMI recording, made by the cast of the 1955 Glyndebourne production, captures much of the essence of this frothy comedy. There are no heroes here, but a collection of cuddly characters delighting in the deceptions of their companions and themselves. Although the digitally remastered sound is obviously older and therefore less slick that than of the Philips recording, a certain dryness of acoustic helps to give great clarity to the voices and their diction. The singers are characteristically and fittingly light, with the charm of Juan Oncina's very high tenor matched by the delightfully outraged white coloratura of Sari Barabas as Countess Adèle. Even without the visual effect, many of the gags (classic farce material for the most part) are really very funny. The Act 2 scene, where the count and friends, disguised as nuns, switch instantaneously from their drinking session song into piety as one of their unsuspecting hostesses crosses the stage, is particularly successful. Several passages are omitted from the recording, not least the scene in which the page Isolier reveals to Countess Adèle the true nature of the 'nuns' — crucial to the story — but happily the text makes all omissions clear and fills in the narrative gaps. The trio of mistaken identities before the finale is Rossini at his most tenderly insouciant and the warmth of this performance should ensure that it remains a favourite alongside more modern recordings.

Rossini. GUILLAUME TELL. **Gabriel Bacquier** (bar) Guillaume Tell; **Montserrat Caballé** (sop) Mathilde; **Nicolai Gedda** (ten) Arnold; **Kolos Kovacs** (bass) Walter Furst; **Gwynne Howell** (bass) Melcthal; **Mady Mesplé** (sop) Jemmy; **Jocelyne Taillon** (mez) Hedwige; **Louis Hendrikx** (bass) Gessler; **Charles Burles** (ten) Fisherman; **Ricardo Cassinelli** (ten) Rudolph; **Nicholas Christou** (bar) Leuthold; **Ambrosian Opera Chorus; Royal Philharmonic Orchestra/Lamberto Gardelli.** EMI CMS7 69951-2. Notes and text included. From SLS970 (11/73).

④ 3h 58' ADD 3/89

Rossini's last opera was not only his grandest but also the very epitome of operatic grandeur. In length alone it involves a formidable commitment, but more fundamental are the span of the scenes, the amplitude of the forces employed and the range of mood and feeling from simple rustic happiness to a passionate affirmation of liberty hard-won in the face of cruelty and personal loss. Near the end of the whole epic work, as the sky clears, literally and figuratively, there comes a passage of inspired sublimity, with an effect worthy of *Fidelio*; it also is built with Rossini's favourite device of the crescendo, but having its excitement now transfigured and ennobled, so that even if Rossini had composed more operas one feels he could hardly have gone beyond this. Though frequently given in Italian, it was written to a French text and the language gives a strong initial advantage to this recording over its notable rivals. Among the principals Bacquier is a dignified, elderly-sounding Tell, Caballé a tender yet patrician Mathilde, Gedda a lyrical Arnold who fortifies his voice manfully for the heroic passages. Gardelli conducts with control and flexibility; the orchestral playing and chorus work are alike admirable, as are the clarity and sense of presence in the recorded sound.

Albert Roussel

French 1869-1937

Roussel. Symphonies — No. 1 in D minor, Op. 7, "Le poème de la forêt";
No. 3 in G minor, Op. 42. **French National Orchestra/Charles Dutoit.**
Erato 2292-45254-2. From NUM75283 (2/87).

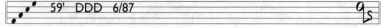

59' DDD 6/87

Roussel's First Symphony is not a symphony in the usual sense at all, but more a
cycle of four tone-poems. When the first of these, "Soir d'été", was performed
Roussel did not envisage any further seasonal depictions of nature, but after
"Renouveau" was written it was quickly followed by "Forêt d'hiver" and "Faunes
et Dryades" — this last piece having autumnal connotations to complete
Roussel's own 'Four Seasons'. The completed Symphony was Roussel's first
major orchestral work, and although it is more romantic than his later works it
already has characteristic fingerprints in his use of the orchestra. The Third
Symphony is a very outgoing work in conventional four movement form, with
characteristic 'motor' rhythms, and breezy, rather terse melodies — except in
the *Scherzo*, which almost has the air of a jaunty popular song. Dutoit's performances are quite admirable in their clarity and understanding of Roussel's
contrasted styles. The orchestra have just the right timbre and the recording is
superb.

Roussel. Symphonies — No. 2 in B flat major, Op. 23; No. 4 in A major,
Op. 53. **French National Orchestra/Charles Dutoit.** Erato 2292-45253-2.

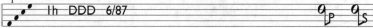

1h DDD 6/87

This disc couples one of Roussel's most often-played symphonies with one of his
least. The Fourth Symphony is a late work written only a few years before his
death, and is a delightful score, the product of a richly-stocked imagination. It
has a dark and powerful slow movement, a most infectiously engaging scherzo
and a captivating finale. The Second Symphony is a rarity. It is abundantly
resourceful and full of colour, and the scoring is refined and opulent. Dutoit gets
playing of great vitality from this great French orchestra, dynamic markings are
scrupulously observed but it is not just the letter but the spirit of the score that
is well served. The Erato engineers do full justice to the dark and richly-detailed
orchestral textures and the sound is particularly imposing in the definition of the
bottom end of the register. Not to be missed.

Edmund Rubbra

British 1901-1986

Rubbra. ORCHESTRAL WORKS. **Philharmonia Orchestra/Norman Del
Mar.** Lyrita SRCD202.
Symphonies — No. 3, Op. 49; No. 4, Op. 53. A Tribute, Op. 56. Resurgam
— overture, Op. 149.

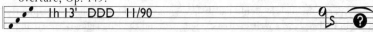

1h 13' DDD 11/90

These are the only recordings of either symphony after half-a-century of
indifference and neglect! Yet the opening of the Fourth Symphony is one of the
most beautiful things not just in Rubbra but in all present-day English music. It is
often said that Rubbra's music is "not of our time but could not have been
written at any other", to which one might add that it could not have been
composed anywhere other than England. It is predominantly pastoral in feeling

Norman Del Mar   [photo: Hammonds

but there is little sense of what Constant Lambert called the 'cow-pat' school (though as the seventieth-birthday tribute included on this disc shows, Rubbra certainly revered Vaughan Williams). It is obvious from the first bars of each work that this music possesses eloquence and nobility and clearly tells of deep and serious things. The opening pages of the Fourth Symphony are free from any kind of artifice and their serenity and quietude resonate long in the memory. The overture, *Resurgam*, is a late work, also of great beauty, written in response to a commission from the Plymouth Orchestra, and another first recording. It commemorates the rebuilding of the Church of St Andrew, destroyed by Nazi bombers in 1941. Only its tower remained intact on whose north door of its tower stood one word, *Resurgam* ("I will rise again"). The performances by the Philharmonia Orchestra under Norman Del Mar are dedicated and the recorded sound offers superb clarity and presence with transparent well-defined textures. An important and rewarding issue.

Anton Rubinstein   *Refer to Index*   *Russian 1829-1894*

Poul Ruders   *Danish 1949*

NEW REVIEW

Ruders. Violin Concerto No. 1[a]. Concerto for clarinet and twin-orchestra[b]. Drama-Trilogy — Cello Concerto, "Polydrama"[c]. [a]**Rebecca Hirsch** (vn); [b]**Niels Thomsen** (cl); [c]**Morten Zeuthen** (vc); **Odense Symphony Orchestra/Tamás Vetö.** Unicorn-Kanchana DKPCD9114.

1h DDD 4/92

In recent years Poul Ruders has emerged as one of the leading and most imaginative younger Danish composers of our time. This CD collects three of his works, all of them concertos, from the 1980s. He has an excellent feeling for colour and his textures even at their most complex, are never thick or cluttered. The most powerful and atmospheric of the three is the Clarinet Concerto (1985) written for Niels Thomsen (who has, incidentally, made an impressive recording of the Nielsen concerto). It is a short one-movement work in which (to quote the composer), the soloist is a Pierrot-like figure "in a vice of orchestral onslaught"; the overall effect is of conflict and turbulence. The effect, both here and in the Cello Concerto, at times is almost surrealistic. The Concerto No. 1 for violin, harp and harpsichord (1981) was inspired by a visit to Amalfi and has warmth and colour; it is an appealing piece, simpler in style than its companions, with brief echoes of Vivaldi's *Primavera*. It is perhaps best described as a blend of

neoclassicism and minimalism. The performances by the Odense Orchestra are
both expert and dedicated and the recordings are very good too.

Carl Ruggles   *Refer to Index*   *American 1876-1971*

Camille Saint-Saëns   *French 1835-1921*

Saint-Saëns. PIANO CONCERTOS. **Pascal Rogé** (pf); [a]**Philharmonia
Orchestra,** [b]**Royal Philharmonic Orchestra,** [c]**London Philharmonic
Orchestra/Charles Dutoit.** Decca 417 351-2DH2. From D244D3 (10/81).
No. 1 in D major, Op. 17[a]; No. 2 in G minor, Op. 22[b]; No. 3 in E flat
major, Op. 29[c]; No. 4 in C minor, Op. 44[a]; No. 5 in F major, Op. 103,
"Egyptian"[b].

② 2h 21' ADD 12/86

NEW REVIEW

Saint-Saëns. PIANO CONCERTOS. **Aldo Ciccolini** (pf); **Orchestre de
Paris/Serge Baudo.** EMI Rouge et Noir CMS7 69443-2. From SLS 802 (6/71).
No. 1 in D major, Op. 17; No. 2 in G minor, Op. 22; No. 3 in E flat major,
Op. 29; No. 4 in C minor, Op. 44; No. 5 in F major, Op. 103, "Egyptian".

② 2h 18' ADD 3/92   £

Saint-Saëns's First Concerto was written when the composer was 23 years old,
and it is a sunny, youthful, happy work conventionally cast in the traditional
three-movement form. A decade later he wrote the Second Concerto in a period
of only three weeks. This concerto begins in a mood of high seriousness rather in
the style of a Bach organ prelude; then this stern mood gives way to a jolly fleet-
footed scherzo and a *presto* finale: it is an uneven work, though the most popular
of the five concertos. The Third Concerto is perhaps the least interesting work,
whilst the Fourth is the best of the five. It is in effect a one-movement work cast
in three ingeniously crafted sections. Saint-Saëns wrote his last, the *Egyptian*, in
1896 to mark his 50 years as a concert artist. Mirroring the sights and sounds of
a country he loved, this is another brilliant work. Pascal Rogé has a very secure,
exuberant sense of rhythm, which is vital in these works, as is his immaculate,
pearly technique. Dutoit is a particularly sensitive accompanist and persuades all
three orchestras to play with that lean brilliance which the concertos demand.
The recordings are true and well-balanced.

We should not underestimate Saint-Saëns, any more than Ravel did when he
coupled his name with a greater one and said that his own G major Piano Concerto was "written in the spirit of Mozart and Saint-Saëns". The five concertos
here remind us that he was an excellent pianist, but although the virtuosity that
they demand shows Liszt's influence there's also plenty of individuality and each
work has its own character — not least No. 5, the *Egyptian*. Aldo Ciccolini was
born in Naples, but he moved to France as a young man in 1949 and is totally in
sympathy with this music; like Rogé, his playing is brilliant and warmly lyrical by
turns, and one always feels that he listens to the orchestra and collaborates with
his fellow artists rather than seeking to dominate them. The attentive Serge
Baudo is a fine partner in these concertos and under his direction the Orchestre
de Paris play with verve and sensitivity. They are not profound works in the
German tradition, nor do they aim to be; instead, they are beautifully crafted,
melodious and never, but never, a bore! Try the finale of the Second Concerto
to hear Saint-Saëns at his most infectiously sparkling. These EMI recordings date
from 1970, but the sound is perfectly enjoyable and at budget price this makes a
delightful and rewarding alternative to the Decca set, although the Third
Concerto is divided between the two discs.

Saint-Saëns. SYMPHONIES. [a]**Bernard Gavoty** (org); **Orchestre National de l'ORTF/Jean Martinon.** EMI CZS7 62643-2.
A major; F major, "Urbs Roma"; No. 1 in E flat major, Op. 2; No. 2 in A minor, Op. 55; No. 3 in C minor, Op. 78, "Organ"[a].

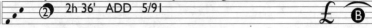

② 2h 36' ADD 5/91 £ Ⓑ

Saint-Saëns's four early symphonies have rather tended to be eclipsed by the popularity of his much later *Organ* Symphony. It's easy to see why the latter, with its rich invention, its colour and its immediate melodic appeal has managed to cast an enduring spell over its audiences, but there is much to be enjoyed in the earlier symphonies too. The A major dates from 1850 when Saint-Saëns was just 15 years old and is a particularly attractive and charming work despite its debt to Mendelssohn and Mozart. The Symphony in F major of 1856 was the winning entry in a competition organized by the Societé Sainte-Cécile of Bordeaux but was immediately suppressed by the composer after its second performance. The pressures of writing for a competition no doubt contribute to its more mannered style but it nevertheless contains some impressive moments, not least the enjoyable set of variations that form the final movement. The Symphony No. 1 proper was in fact written three years before the *Urbs Roma* and shares the same youthful freshness of the A major, only here the influences are closer to Schumann and Berlioz. The Second Symphony reveals the fully mature voice of Saint-Saëns and in recent years has achieved a certain amount of popularity which is almost certainly due in part to this particularly fine recording. Inevitably we arrive at the *Organ* Symphony, and if you don't already have a recording then you could do a lot worse than this marvellously colourful and flamboyant performance. Indeed, the performances throughout this generous set are persuasive and exemplary. A real bargain and well worth investigating.

Saint-Saëns. Symphony No. 3 in C minor, Op. 78, "Organ". **Peter Hurford** (org); **Montreal Symphony Orchestra/Charles Dutoit.** Decca 410 201-2DH. From SXDL7590 (3/83).

34' DDD 3/84 ⑨s Ⓑ

Saint-Saëns. Symphony No. 3 in C minor, Op. 78, "Organ". **Daniel Chorzempa** (org); **Berne Symphony Orchestra/Peter Maag.** Pickwick IMP Red Label PCD847.

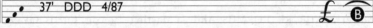

37' DDD 4/87 £ Ⓑ

Saint-Saëns completed his Third Symphony at the peak of his career, in 1886, the same year in which he composed the *Carnaval of the Animals* (although this latter work was not given public performance until after his death). He was a renowned virtuoso pianist, had been described by Liszt as the world's greatest organist, and was recognized abroad, and especially in England, as France's leading composer; it was for a Philharmonic Society's commission that he produced this Symphony. It is packed with splendour. Its huge orchestra, including triple woodwind and a generous brass section, is joined by piano duet and greatly enriched by the majestic organ part. It is the presiding presence of the organ which quickens the listener's heartbeat and which inevitably makes this the *Organ* Symphony. The magnificent finale is all highly artificial and theatrical, but wholly absorbing every time. It is a perfect demonstration piece. Dutoit spaces his dynamic effects for maximum clarity, so that nothing is ever missed. Compact Disc opens up the score amazingly: it is impossible to resist turning towards the timpani and the triangle.

Pickwick's issue presents a performance of great charm and vigour in a work that can easily become over-heavy or too studied. The use of the organ has given rise to many problems in recording the work, especially ones of balance and tuning. Here the producer, Tony Faulkner, has overcome these difficulties with alacrity and the Berne orchestra are given the freedom to produce both powerful blocks of sound and delicately controlled textures. The much under-recorded veteran Swiss conductor, Peter Maag, controls all with an innate understanding of the work's overall structure. Dutoit's version may have more sumptuous or arresting sound, but this must be a first choice at its price.

NEW REVIEW

Saint-Saëns. SAMSON ET DALILA. **Plácido Domingo** (ten) Samson; **Elena Obraztsova** (mez) Dalila; **Renato Bruson** (bar) Priest; **Pierre Thau** (bass) Abimelech; **Robert Lloyd** (bass) Old Hebrew; **Gérard Friedmann** (ten) Messenger; **Constantin Zaharia** (ten) First Philistine; **Michel Hubert** (bass) Second Philistine; **Chorus and Orchestre de Paris/Daniel Barenboim.** DG 413 297-2GX2. Notes, text and translation included. From 2531 050 (10/79).

② 2h 6' ADD 11/91

Surviving the shafts of Bernard Shaw, bans by the Lord Chamberlain, and cries of "oratorio" from New York pundits, this impressive, subtly composed work continues to hold the attention of the opera-going public whenever and wherever it is performed mainly because of its discreet combination of the pagan and the religious, the exotic and the erotic. Within a framework of the struggle between the Jews and Philistines, Delilah's overpowering sexuality and her dark soul are magnificently portrayed as are the proud, sensual and eventually tragic sides of Samson, while the High Priest is a vengeful, preening, frustrated figure. Their well-defined characters are depicted against a background of splendidly written choruses for Jews and Philistines. Barenboim realized most of the sensuousness and vigour of the score in a reading notably well played by his Paris forces following a live performance at the Arena in Orange in 1978. Obraztsova, although occasionally harsh in voice, suggests the double-dealing nature of Delilah, the heart of a devil inside a nubile body although her French is a doubtful quantity. Domingo, at the height of his powers, delivers Samson's defiance and love with equal aplomb, showing a particular affinity with Samson's downtrodden state in Act 3. Bruson hectors effectively as the High Priest.

Antonio Salieri
Italian 1750-1825

Salieri. AXUR, RE D'ORMUS. **Andrea Martin** (bar) Axur; **Curtis Rayam** (ten) Atar; **Eva Mei** (sop) Aspasia; **Ettore Nova** (bass) Biscroma, Brighella; **Ambra Vespasiani** (mez) Fiammetta, Smeraldina; **Massimo Valentini** (bass) Arteneo; **Michele Porcelli** (bar) Altamor; **Mario Cecchetti** (ten) Urson; **Sonia Turchetta** (contr) Elamir; **Giovanni Battista Palmicri** (ten) Arlecchino; **Guido d'Arezzo Choir; Russian Philharmonic Orchestra/René Clemencic.** Nuova Era 6852/4. Notes, text and translation included. Recorded at performances in the Teatro di Rinnovati, Sienna between August 19th-23rd, 1989.

③ 2h 44' DDD 12/90

This work, which has good claims to be reckoned Salieri's masterpiece, was composed in 1787, the time of *Don Giovanni*, with which it shares the librettist, Da Ponte. Unlike Mozart's work, *Axur* is a serious opera, and indeed it had originally been a *tragédie lyrique*, written for Paris; this Italian reworking, for Vienna, retains much of the nobility of manner and exalted style associated with the French form, especially in the music for the central characters. Listen for example to the big two-part aria in the second act for the hero, Atar, or the thrilling scene for him in Act 3 — a link, this, between the operas of Salieri's mentor Glück and the serious operas of Rossini. Do not look here for the human quality, the wit, the warmth, of a Mozart; Salieri was a different kind of composer, and his music is lofty and solemn, also occasionally stilted, pretentious and dry. But it is skilful music, bold in harmony and inventive in orchestration and is well worth trying. The plot is rather a silly one, not much helped by its passages of comic relief. But the singing here serves it well. Curtis Rayam is outstanding as Atar, with his smooth, graceful and expressive tenor; Eva Mei gives pleasure too in the *prima donna* role of Aspasia, with an attractive glow to her voice and no shortage of passion. René Clemencic's direction, if not ideally stylish or disciplined, nevertheless gives a very fair idea of an opera that truly merits an occasional revival. The live recording evokes, sometimes almost too vividly, the atmosphere of an Italian opera house.

Aulis Sallinen

Finnish 1935-

NEW REVIEW

Sallinen. THE HORSEMAN. **Matti Salminen** (bass-bar) Antti; **Taru Valjakka** (sop) Anna; **Eero Erkkilä** (ten) Merchant of Novgorod; **Anita Valkki** (contr) Merchant's Wife; **Martti Wallén** (bass) Judge; **Tuula Nieminen** (mez) Woman; **Usko Viitanen** (bar) Yeoman; **Heikki Toivanen** (bass) Matti Puikkanen; **Savonlinna Opera Festival Chorus and Orchestra/Ulf Söderblom.** Finlandia FACD101. Notes, text and translation included. Recorded at a performance in Savonlinna in July 1975. From Finnlevy SFX41/3 (10/79).

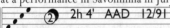

② 2h 4' AAD 12/91

NEW REVIEW

Sallinen. THE RED LINE. **Jorma Hynninen** (bar) Topi; **Taru Valjakka** (sop) Riika; **Usko Vitanen** (ten) Puntarpaa; **Jaakko Hietikko** (bass) Simana Arhippaini; **Erkki Aalto** (bass-bar) Young priest; **Ulla Maijala** (contr) Kaisa; **Harri Nikkonen** (bass) Jussi; **Helena Salonius** (sop) Tiina; **Antti Salmen** (ten) Vicar; **Kauko Vayrynen** (ten) Epra; **Finnish National Chorus and Orchestra/Okko Kamu.** Finlandia FACD102. Notes, text and translation included. Recorded at performances in Helsinki in November 1978.

② 1h 56' ADD 12/91

Accessible modern operas are not plentiful. Indeed the renaissance of opera during the 1970s in Finland, not a country renowned for a strong operatic tradition, was an encouraging and positive phenomenon. Aulis Sallinen has a very good sense of theatre and an eclectic musical palette. Finlandia have now transferred his first two operas to CD. *The Horseman* was something of a landmark in the resurgence of opera in the North and was greeted in extravagant terms at its first appearance. One distinguished critic hailed it as "without shadow of doubt a masterpiece" and even if that may be putting it too strongly, it is a highly effective work. *The Horseman* does not tell a conventional story and can be seen as "an image of a small country, ever the battleground between mighty powers, but — even more than that — it tells of the constantly shifting relationship between man and woman". The music itself is both compelling and strongly atmospheric. At times, as in the Third Symphony with which it is roughly contemporaneous, it calls Britten to mind but its sound world with the fascination for bells is hauntingly imaginative. The advantage of CD means that it can be heard with only one break (between Scenes 4 and 5 of Act 1). The gap in its companion work comes just between Scenes 3 and 4 of Act 1.

The Red Line, followed only three years later and is in some ways an even stronger piece of theatre, distinguished by a powerful sense of dramatic purpose and direction. It is set in 1907, a watershed in Finnish history, at a time when the country was struggling against Russian domination. It has been described as "a study of man's struggle for survival in an inhospitable environment". There is some obvious symbolism — the poor crofter and his wife living in the bleak northern Finnish backwoods are beset by a marauding bear, a symbol of a hostile nature — and some effective stage work. Excellent and authoritative live performances with some stage noises which add atmosphere. The performances were rightly praised at the time and although the acoustic is on the dryish side the sound is very acceptable.

Pablo Sarasate
Spanish 1844-1908

NEW REVIEW

Sarasate. Zigeunerweisen, Op. 20.
Wieniawski. Violin Concertos — No. 1 in F sharp minor, Op. 14; No. 2 in D minor, Op. 22. Légende, Op. 17. **Gil Shaham** (vn); **London Symphony Orchestra/Lawrence Foster.** DG 431 815-2GH.

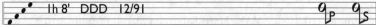

Sarasate's *Zigeunerweisen* brings forth one of those voluptuous gipsy tunes that insist on gorgeous tone, a temperamental warmth of feeling and a naturally seductive line. Then comes the fireworks, fizzling and effervescing; here the soloist needs to be enormously dashing and exuberant, yet at the same time relaxed, so that the listener senses no real effort. Gil Shaham takes naturally to all the demands made on his technique and musicianship, entrancing the listener with his provocative phrasing, and easy panache. Wieniawski's *Légende* has another melting violinistic melody and a livelier central section before the more gentle reprise of the main theme. Again Shaham is completely at home, the melodic line flowing ravishingly. But these pieces are merely encores for the two Wieniawski Violin Concertos of which the First is much less often played than the Second. Yet the lyrical theme of the first movement has a touch of magic on Shaham's bow and he is no less bewitching in the slow movement *Preghiera*, while the Paganinian pyrotechnics and the finale's dance rhythms are hardly less enticing. Lawrence Foster and the LSO, who until now have been simply providing a faultless backcloth for their young soloist, now come into their own in their imposing introduction for the Second Concerto, and Shaham's contribution is hardly less winning than in the earlier work, especially in the comparative innocence of the Romance. Another volatile zigeuner finale is thrown off with entertaining panache by all concerned. Excellent DG sound throughout.

Erik Satie
French 1866-1925

Satie. PIANO WORKS. **Anne Queffélec.** Virgin Classics VC7 90754-2.
Six Gnossiennes. Véritables préludes flasques (pour un chien). Vieux séquins et vieilles cuirasses. Chapitres tournés en tous sens. Three Gymnopédies. Embryons desséchés. Je te veux valse. Sonatine bureaucratique. Heures séculaires et instantanées. Le Picadilly. Avant-dernières pensées. Sports et divertissements.

Ih 16' DDD 5/89 Ⓑ

Satie. PIANO WORKS. **Pascal Rogé** (pf). Decca 410 220-2DH. From 410 220-1DH (6/84).
Three Gymnopédies. Je te veux valse. Quatre préludes flasques. Prélude en tapisserie. Nocturne No. 4. Vieux séquins et vieilles cuirasses. Embryons desséchés. Six Gnossiennes. Sonatine bureaucratique. Le Picadilly.

Ih I' DDD 10/84 Ⓑ

Satie. PIANO WORKS. **Peter Dickinson.** Conifer CDCF183.
Chapitres tournés en tous sens. Croquis et agaceries d'un gros bonhomme en
bois. Je te veux valse. Le Picadilly. Pièces froides. Le piège de Méduse. Poudre
d'or. Préludes du fils des étoiles. Prélude en tapisserie. Sonatine bureaucratique.
Sports et divertissements. Three Gymnopédies. Véritables préludes flasques (pour
un chien). Vexations.

1h 17' DDD 12/90 ⒷⒷ

Satie is a composer who defies description. His piano music has the same quirky
originality as his life and his love of flying in the face of convention are
crystallized in these fascinating miniatures. Anne Queffélec has made an excellent
selection of Satie piano music starting with the famous and well-loved *Gnossiennes*
and also including the *Gymnopédies*, works of a chaste almost ritualistic stillness.
Also included are the wicked *Véritables préludes flasques (pour un chien)* containing
his celebrated parody of Chopin's funeral march, credited typically à la Satie as a
quotation "from the famous mazurka by Schubert". The programme ends with the
whimsical and charming *Sports et divertissements* played with just the right air of
mock seriousness. The recorded quality is good. It is a hard-hearted and humour-
less listener who cannot respond to the often childlike charm and evident warm
and guileless heart of this very individual composer. Pascal Rogé plays these short
pieces with the right kind of (again one must use the word) childlike gravity and
sensuousness and the 1983 recording made in London's Kingsway Hall is excellent.

Peter Dickinson also succeeds admirably in his selection; the gravity and/or
humour of these pieces is perfectly caught and conveyed, and as regards the
latter quality the slightly understated playing in, say, *Le piège de Méduse* is right for
this enigmatic composer. The three *Gymnopédies* provide a good test of Satie

performance as well as being his most
popular work, and Peter Dickinson is
dead on target in his blend of gravity,
sadness and tenderness — one almost
writes "suppressed tenderness", given
that their rarely understood titles
evokes ceremonial dances of ancient
Sparta performed by naked boys.
There's also charm in plenty in the
café-concert waltzes called *Poudre d'or*
and *Je te veux*, and though not distinguished as music they have a fetching
Gallic variety of schmaltz, while the
Rosicrucian music of *Le fils des étoiles* is
impressively serious. The recording has
piano sound that is immediate yet well
Erik Satie textured.

Alessandro Scarlatti
Italian 1660-1725

NEW REVIEW

A. Scarlatti. Venere e Adone: Il giardino d'amore. **Catherine Gayer** (sop);
Brigitte Fassbaender (mez); **Munich Chamber Orchestra/Hans
Stadlmair.** Archiv Produktion Galleria 431 122-2AGA. Text and translation
included. From SAPM198344 (8/65).

59' ADD 10/91 ⒼⒸ

This performance of Scarlatti's engaging Serenata based on the legend of Venus
and Adonis was recorded during the mid 1960s. Many aspects of baroque

interpretation have changed since then but a musically enlightened and imaginative approach such as that captured on this disc has an enduring appeal. And deservedly so since both singing and playing are first rate. Catherine Gayer makes a spirited, ardent-sounding Adonis while Brigitte Fassbaender is wonderfully alluring and passionate throughout. Her "Augelletti, si cantate" is irresistible and her radiant duet with Adonis at the conclusion of the work something to treasure. The instrumental accompaniment reflects much that was best in baroque performance during the 1950s and 1960s with fine contributions from Hans-Martin Linde (sopranino recorder). In short this is music making of a kind which brings Scarlatti's score — and what a ravishing score it is — to life affectionately and convincingly. The recorded sound is almost all that one could wish for and full texts with translations are included.

NEW REVIEW

A. Scarlatti. CANTATAS AND ARIETTAS. **Nancy Argenta** (sop); **Chandos Baroque Players.** EMI Reflexe CDC7 54176-2. Texts and translations included.
Cantatas — Cantata pastorale per la nascità di Nostro Signore Gesù Cristo; Là dove a Mergellina; Quella pace gradita; Hor che di Febo ascosi. *Ariettas* — Dove voli, o mio pensiero?; Aure leggiere, fermate il volo. IL PIRRO E DEMETRIO — Le violette.

1h 10'   DDD   9/91

Alessandro Scarlatti was a gifted and prolific exponent of the Italian chamber cantata yet this important aspect of his work is slenderly represented on disc. Nancy Argenta has chosen four from among some 800 surviving cantatas further including three arias from Scarlatti's operas. Baroque chamber cantata texts usually concern the pangs of unrequited love suffered by nymphs and shepherds dwelling in Arcadia. The exception in this recital is the beautiful *Cantata pastorale per la nascità*. It is the most elaborately scored and perhaps the most immediately attractive of the pieces on the disc with parts for two violins, viola and continuo. Scarlatti's inspiration is drawn in part from the music of the shepherds who converged on Rome each Christmas from outlying countryside to play at the crib. The setting is intimate, tender and very appealing. Argenta's natural, fresh-sounding and well-focused singing with its innocent quality suits both music and text perfectly and she is complemented with lively instrumental support from the Chandos Baroque Players. The remaining works are more darkly coloured but full of harmonic interest and everywhere demonstrating Scarlatti's deft and imaginative word-painting. Full texts with translations are included.

A. Scarlatti. Variations on "La folia"ª. Cantatasᵇ — Correa nel seno amato; Già lusingato appieno. ᵇ**Lynne Dawson** (sop); **Purcell Quartet** (Catherine Mackintosh, Elizabeth Wallfisch, vns; Richard Boothby, va da gamba; ªRobert Woolley, hpd). Hyperion CDA66254. Texts and translations included.

52'   DDD   3/90

To their series devoted to *La folia* variations, the Purcell Quartet have added this CD of music by Alessandro Scarlatti, who set the familiar tune in startlingly original harpsichord couplets. Robert Woolley plays 30 of them — many with striking touches of chromaticism — in glorious fashion; it is hard to imagine a performance that could match his wonderfully disciplined yet witty virtuoso one, which culminates in arpeggiated harp effects. Most of this disc, however, is devoted to two 'unfoliated' cantatas in which the Purcell Quartet is joined by the bewitching voice of Lynne Dawson. *Correa nel seno amato* is a pastoral cantata, the natural imagery of the text beautifully reflected in the music. The opening sinfonia and lyrical opening recitative are characterful and sensitively paced. Both singer and quartet capitalize on the chromatic inflexions and echoes in "Idolo amato". "Già lusingato appieno" is unusual for its textual references to an 'English hero' — possibly James II — bidding farewell to his family as he goes into exile. Among the highlights are the movements of collaboration between voice and strings, as in "Cara sposa" with its concertante violins, and "Sento l'aura", in which slow trills and echoes are made to sound like "whispering breezes". Just as in "Correa nel seno amato", Dawson commands the listener's attention from the very first notes of recitative with her beautifully weighted projection of the text. Both cantatas end with magical epilogues cast in recitative.

Domenico Scarlatti

Italian 1685-1757

D. Scarlatti. KEYBOARD SONATAS. **Virginia Black** (hpd). CRD CRD3442.
A major, Kk113; E major, Kk380; E major, Kk381; D minor, Kk213; D major, Kk119; D minor, Kk120; C major, Kk501; C major, Kk502; F minor, Kk466; G major, Kk146; F sharp major, Kk318; F sharp major, Kk319; A major, Kk24.

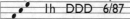 1h DDD 6/87

D. Scarlatti. KEYBOARD SONATAS. **Trevor Pinnock** (hpd). CRD CRD3368. From CRD1068 (5/81).
G major, Kk124; C minor, Kk99; G major, Kk201; B minor, Kk87; E major, Kk46; C major, Kk95; F minor/major, Kk204a; D major, Kk490; D major, Kk491; D major, Kk492; G major, Kk520; G major, Kk521; C major, Kk513.

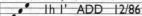 1h 1' ADD 12/86

D. Scarlatti. KEYBOARD SONATAS, Volume 25. **Gilbert Rowland** (hpd). Keyboard KGR1025CD.
D minor, Kk9; E major, Kk46; E minor, Kk98; C minor, Kk129; A major, Kk208; A major, Kk209; B flat major, Kk360; B flat major, Kk361; G major, Kk454; G major, Kk455; C major, Kk514; C major, Kk515.

51' DAD 10/89

D. Scarlatti. KEYBOARD SONATAS. **Vladimir Horowitz** (pf). CBS Masterworks CD42410. Items marked [c] recorded at a concert in Carnegie Hall, New York in 1968. Items marked [a] from SBRG72117 (7/63), [b] SBRG72274 (8/65), [c] 72720 (1/69).
D major, Kk33[b]; A major, Kk39[b]; A minor, Kk54[b]; G major, Kk55[c]; D major, Kk96[b]; G major, Kk146[b]; E major, Kk162[b]; E minor, Kk198[b]; A major, Kk322[a]; E major, kk380[c]; G major, Kk455[a]; F minor, Kk466[b]; E flat major, Kk474[b]; F minor, Kk481[b]; D major, Kk491[b]; F major, Kk525[b]; E major, Kk531[a].

1h 1' AAD 5/89

D. Scarlatti. KEYBOARD SONATAS. **Elaine Thornburgh** (hpd). Koch International Classics 37014-2.
D minor, Kk52; A major, Kk211; A major, Kk212; B flat major, Kk248; B flat major, Kk249; B major, Kk261; B major, Kk262; E minor, Kk263; E major, Kk264; F sharp major, Kk318; F sharp major, Kk319; G minor, Kk347; G major, Kk348; D major, Kk416; D minor, kk417; D major, kk490; D major, Kk491; D major, Kk492.

1h 12' DDD 10/91

D. Scarlatti. KEYBOARD SONATAS, Volume 1. **Andreas Staier** (hpd). Deutsche Harmonia Mundi RD77224.

G minor, Kk108; D major, Kk118; D major, Kk119; D minor, Kk141; E minor, Kk198; E minor, Kk203; G major, Kk454; G major, Kk455; D major, Kk490; D major, Kk491; D major, Kk492; C major, Kk501; C major, Kk502; D minor, Kk516; D minor, Kk517; F major, Kk518; F minor, Kk519.

1h 10'   DDD   2/92

A highly accomplished harpsichordist, Domenico Scarlatti's influence on keyboard composition was enormous giving the short sonatas a freedom of form, range of expression and technical complexity quite unlike anything previously written for the medium. His sonatas call for extremes of virtuosity and a quick-silver technique. Virginia Black proves herself a worthy exponent and offers in her well-balanced recital three pairs of sonatas as well as five separate sonatas. Though much of the music demands a powerful sense of momentum and furious brilliance from the player, Black shows how expressive much of the music can be if treated with sensitivity, gently introducing a little rubato and allowing the music to breathe more freely. The harpsichord is beautifully recorded and altogether this programme offers a vivid and most enjoyable introduction to the art of Scarlatti.

Pinnock presents 13 of these very varied pieces with all the vivacity and panache his admirers have learned to expect. One advantage of this particular compilation is that it avoids some very well-known sonatas to introduce others of equal character and invention. Though the recording is close and on the harsh side it should not deter anyone from an interesting and useful issue in which the last sonata of all, Kk513, is especially charming and evocative with its lilting siciliana rhythm and musette effects.

Volume 25 of Gilbert Rowland's complete Scarlatti sonata series contains eight Kirkpatrick-paired sonatas and four singletons, offering an enjoyable cross-section of Scarlatti's output in this genre — as astonishing in its stylistic variety as in its quantity. If you are a keyboard player you will recognize the ways Scarlatti tested his pupils' technique; whether you are or not, you can thoroughly enjoy his musical creativity — and share Rowland's love for it.

Horowitz's chosen 17 at once prove the point made in the booklet that this composer's music is not just "mostly fast, light and requiring only articulation and dexterity". He finds room for more than a few that are "poetic, nostalgic and even dreamy, very much in the bel canto style". Whatever the tempo or mood, his playing is as memorable for its pin-point precision and textural clarity as it is for its potency of characterization. All in all it would be difficult to imagine these works played with a keener reconciliation of the demands of period style and the resources of the modern piano, with its richer range of colour. The CD transfer is excellent.

With 555 harpsichord sonatas to choose from it is unlikely that any recitalist will duplicate another's programme. And such is the fertility of Scarlatti's imagination that no chosen anthology is in any danger of being either dull or repetitive. Florid passages, cascading arpeggios, daring hand-crossing, syncopation, dissonance, chromaticism and an arsenal of percussive effects are all present in the American harpsichordist, Elaine Thornburgh's carefully chosen programme. She demonstrates Scarlatti's many-sided genius in sonatas which awaken strongly contrasting emotions in the listener. There is a welcome absence of empty virtuosity in this playing, but no lack of vivacity, lyricism and insight to the music. Included in her recital are several of the least frequently performed sonatas while also including a handful of those which, like the great D major triptych (Kk490/491/492) are justly popular.

Andreas Staier's recital demonstrates yet again that Scarlatti's keyboard sonatas are substantial and inventive enough to make stimulating listening, and each of the 17 here brings something fresh and exciting to the listener in a well chosen sequence of pieces. As an Italian who spent the latter part of his life in Spain, Scarlatti learned much in his adopted country and there are things in this music that probably show it, including vigorous rhythms, virtuosity and seductive

Elaine Thornburgh   *[photo: Koch International*

charm. People have found the sound — or at least the spirit — of quick Spanish dances in such pieces as the F minor Sonata (track 11) and the one in D major which ends the recital, as well as a suggestion of street processions in the two ceremonial ones in the same key that precede it. Maybe there's also something of those typically Spanish instruments, the guitar and castanets, in the rattling, thrumming D major Sonata on track 3. Scarlatti used the technical resources of harpsichordists and the instrument itself to the full, as the brilliant repeated notes in the D minor Sonata on track 1 immediately show us. Staier responds splendidly, throwing himself with zest into the whirlwind finger dexterity and rapid leaps demanded in the sonatas Kk517 and 108, which follow each other. The sound of his instrument, which is tuned about a semitone lower than modern pitch, is wonderfully rich, and the recording has great immediacy without the glaring and clangorous tone that disfigures some harpsichord recordings.

Giacinto Scelsi   *Italian 1905-1988*

Scelsi. CHAMBER WORKS. [a]**Michiko Hirayama** (sop); [a]**Frank Lloyd** (hn); [a]**Maurizio Ben Omar** (perc); **Arditti Quartet** (Irvine Arditti, David Alberman, vns; Levine Andrade, va; Rohan de Saram, vc)/[a]**Aldo Brizzi.**
Salabert Actuels SCD8904/05.
String Quartets Nos. 1-5. String Trio. Khoom[a].

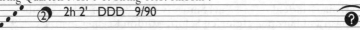

② 2h 2' DDD 9/90

Even in the twentieth century, an age of rampant musical individualism, Giacinto Scelsi stands out as an independent spirit. One authority claims convincingly that he was neither "a sublime visionary" nor "a bungling amateur" so much as "an inspired naïf", similar in some ways to Charles Ives except that there is nothing Ivesian about the pared-down luminosity of Scelsi's later works. The five String Quartets chart a remarkable journey from the relatively traditional expansiveness and assured technique of No. 1 (1944) to the later styles which, in a nutshell, seek (with even greater assurance) as many subtle — often microtonal — inflexions of as few notes as possible. As a result there's an intensity to which so-called minimalism rarely aspires and what might seem impersonal experiments with pure sound take on compelling shapes and forms. Apart from the Quartets this admirable set contains the seminal String Trio of 1958 and a striking vocal work from the early 1960s, *Khoom.* Authoritatively performed, effectively recorded, and well annotated, the set provides an ideal introduction to an authentically modern and still too little known composer, who has many of the attributes of genius.

Johann Heinrich Schmelzer   *Refer to Index*   *Austrian c.1620/23*

Franz Schmidt

Austrian 1874-1939

NEW REVIEW

Schmidt. Symphony No. 4 in C major[a].
Schoenberg. Chamber Symphony No. 1, Op. 9[b]. [a]**Vienna Philharmonic Orchestra,** [b]members of the **Los Angeles Philharmonic Orchestra/Zubin Mehta.** Decca Enterprise 430 007-2DM. Item marked [a] from SXL6544 (2/73), [b] SXL6390 (8/69).

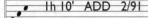

Franz Schmidt and Arnold Schoenberg were born in the same year (1874), Schoenberg's parents having moved to Vienna from Pressburg, where Schmidt was born. Both composers then spent much of their careers in Vienna. Yet it was developments in twentieth century music, with Schoenberg at the forefront, that decreed that Franz Schmidt's music should run into something of a backwater. His Fourth Symphony, though, is surely one of the symphonic masterpieces of the twentieth century. Inspired by the death of his only daughter, it is in one continuous sequence, mournful and yet full of determination to overcome adversity, continuously arresting, and enriched by the bewitching orchestral sonorities that typify Schmidt's music. The work begins and ends with a trumpet solo, and along the way there are tender and haunting solos for violin, cello and other instruments. The Vienna Philharmonic has made something of a speciality of Schmidt's music, and Zubin Mehta captures admirably the contrasting strands to be found in it. The more pungent harmonies of Schoenberg's First Chamber Symphony provide a provocative, but apt, companion piece, and the 20-year-old recordings wear extremely well.

Alfred Schnittke

Russian 1934-

Schnittke. Concerto Grosso No. 1[a]. Quasi una sonata[b]. Moz-Art à la Haydn[c]. [ac]**Tatiana Grindenko** (vn); **Yuri Smirnov** ([a]hpd/[a]prep pf/[b]pf); **Chamber Orchestra of Europe/**[a]**Heinrich Schiff,** [bc]**Gidon Kremer** ([a]vn). DG 429 413-2GH. Recorded at a performance in the Kammermusiksaal, Berlin in September 1988.

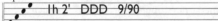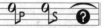

For a single representative of Alfred Schnittke's work you could choose nothing better than the first *Concerto Grosso* of 1977. Here are the psychedelic mélanges of baroque and modern, the drastic juxtapositions of pseudo-Vivaldi with pseudo-Berg, producing an effect at once aurally exciting and spiritually disturbing. The piece has been recorded several times over, but never with the panache of Gidon Kremer and friends and never with the vivid immediacy of this live DG recording (in fact the solo violins are rather too closely miked for comfort, but that's only a tiny drawback). *Quasi una sonata* was originally composed in 1968 for violin and piano and it was something of a breakthrough piece for Schnittke as he emerged from what he called "the puberty rites of serialism", letting his imagination run riot for the first time. No-one could call it a disciplined piece, but if that worries you, you should leave Schnittke alone anyway. The transcription for solo violin and string orchestra is an ingenious one and Kremer again supplies all the requisite agonized intensity. *Moz-Art à la Haydn* is a very slight piece of work, and it really depends on visual theatricality to make its effect. Still, it complements the other two pieces well enough, and the disc as a whole makes an excellent introduction to a composer currently enjoying an enormous vogue.

NEW REVIEW

Schnittke. Concerti grossi — No. 3; No. 4/Symphony No. 5. **Royal Concertgebouw Orchestra/Riccardo Chailly.** Decca 430 698-2DH.

59' DDD 2/92

Although the Concertgebouw and Chailly gave the 1988 première of Schnittke's *Concerto grosso* No. 4/Symphony No. 5 they were pre-empted in the recording world by the Gothenburg Symphony and Neeme Järvi. That BIS recording was strongly recommended in last year's *Good CD Guide*: but this new Decca version is even finer. As more and more of Schnittke's music appears on CD it becomes clear that this work is a synthesis of his achievements, just as the title itself suggests a synthesis of his main preoccupations as a composer. The idea is to start in the world of the neo-baroque *concerto grosso* (with barely concealed references to Stravinsky and Prokofiev) and to end up as a full-blown tragic Mahlerian symphony. Each stage on this musical journey is riveting, and the performance is wholly authoritative. The earlier *Concerto grosso* leaves more room for doubt, though it too offers the wary listener plenty of familiar jumping-off points. Recording quality is in the very best Decca/Concertgebouw tradition.

NEW REVIEW

Schnittke. Viola Concerto[a]. Trio Sonata (arr. Bashmet)[b]. [a]**London Symphony Orchestra/Mstislav Rostropovich;** [b]**Moscow Soloists/Yuri Bashmet** ([a]va). RCA Victor Red Seal RD60446.

1h 2' DDD 2/92

Just like Shostakovich, to whom he is in many ways the natural successor, Schnittke has been inspired by the cream of Russia's string virtuosos. The Viola Concerto was written in 1985 for Yuri Bashmet, a charismatic musician who himself can claim to be carrying on where Oistrakh left off. Its three movements are characteristically extreme in their emotional intensity, alternately brooding and explosive, and there is an especially memorable episode when the fast central movement gives way to bleak images of past innocence — that should strike a chord with anyone who enjoys Russian art films. Bashmet and Rostropovich interpret the music to the manner born. The coupling is both apt and poignant — Bashmet's arrangement of the String Trio is his expression of thanks for the Concerto and at the same time a get-well present after the composer's near-fatal stroke. It too is magnificently played, and both works are superbly recorded.

Schnittke. String Quartets — No. 1 (1966); No. 2 (1980); No. 3 (1983). **Tale Quartet** (Tale Olsson, Patrik Swedrup, vns; Ingegerd Kierkegaard, va; Helena Nilsson, vc). BIS CD467.

1h 2' DDD 7/90

Schnittke's achievement — and you can hear him acquiring increasing mastery of it through these three quartets, covering a 17-year period — is to stay on the right side of the fine line that separates expressionistic modernism from self-indulgent musical chaos. The First Quartet risks the most in its eagerness to equal if not to outdo the most extravagant devices that the avant-garde style (in 1966) had to offer. By 1980 Schnittke was sadder, wiser and much more responsive to the long shadow of history. In the Third Quartet, in particular, that responsiveness initially involves a riveting dialogue between Schnittke himself and the disparate but formidable trio of Lassus, Beethoven and Shostakovich, and gradually develops into a compelling meditation on the associations and incompatibilities of past and present. Nobody in their right minds would want to hear all three quartets at a sitting. Schnittke's music needs the contrast of something more classically restrained and consolatory in character — the quartets of Haydn or Mozart, perhaps. Yet even if Schnittke's Quartets are too immediate, too unmediated to demand instant elevation to the category of 'Masterwork', they are memorable in a manner that, unlike much modern music, puts no barriers between composer and listener, and they are brilliantly performed and recorded here.

NEW REVIEW

Schnittke. Piano Sonata (1987).
Stravinsky. Piano Sonata (1924). Serenade in A (1925). Piano-rag-music (1919). **Boris Berman** (pf). Chandos CHAN8962.

55' DDD 10/91

This is a disc to encourage thoughts about what might have been. In particular: if Stravinsky had launched his great neoclassical initiative from within the Soviet Union in the 1920s, and if that regime had continued to encourage free artistic expression, would the kind of reborn Russian late romanticism we associate with Shostakovich, and now with Schnittke, ever have come about? These are futile questions, of course. Yet what is clear from this strongly projected, cleanly recorded recital is that a positive conjunction between a high degree of self-consciousness (the constant hints of other composers' music) and an instinctive, strongly personal expressive impulse, is present in and crucial to both Schnittke and Stravinsky. Berman probes Stravinsky's piano works for their innate eloquence, to a degree which not all listeners will accept. Certainly, if you like your Stravinsky objectively light and airy you will need to look elsewhere. But the effect here is to build a bridge to Schnittke's large-scale, wide-ranging sonata design, in which simple beginnings usually escalate to imposingly intense climaxes: and while Schnittke would not be Schnittke without a touch of melodrama, Berman moulds the potentially wayward outpourings with convincing and never merely coercive control.

Arnold Schoenberg

Austrian/Hungarian 1874-1951

Schoenberg. Verklärte Nacht, Op. 4. Variations for Orchestra, Op. 31.
Berlin Philharmonic Orchestra/Herbert von Karajan. DG 415 326-2GH.
From 2711 014 (3/75).

52' ADD 3/86

The decadence of German culture in the 1920s and 1930s is already very apparent in the saturated romanticism of *Verklärte Nacht* (1899), the most lusciously sentient work ever conceived for a string group. By comparison the *Variations for Orchestra* comes at the peak of the composer's atonal period and is perhaps the most impressive and imaginative demonstration of the possibilities of this compositional method. Thus the two works on this CD are pivotal in Schoenberg's career and Karajan and the Berlin Philharmonic make the very best case for both works. It is impossible not to respond to the sensuality of *Verklärte Nacht* in their hands, while the challenging *Variations* also make a profound impression. The recording matches the intensity of the playing brilliantly.

Schoenberg. Chamber Symphonies — No. 1, Op. 9; No. 2, Op. 38.
Verklärte Nacht, Op. 4 (arr. string orch). **Orpheus Chamber Orchestra.** DG 429 233-2GH.

1h 9' DDD 7/90

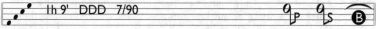

Schoenberg. Serenade, Op. 24[a]. Chamber Symphony No. 1, Op. 9[b].
[a]**Thomas Paul** (bass); **Marlboro Festival Chamber Ensemble/**[a]**Leon Kirchner.** Sony Classical CD45894. Item marked [a] recorded 1966, [b] 1982. Both new to UK.

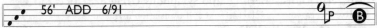

56' ADD 6/91

In the late twentieth century there's increasing evidence that the early twentieth century's most radical music is becoming so easy to perform that it may at last be losing its terrors for listeners as well as players. This can only be welcomed, provided that performances do not become bland and mechanical, and the unconducted Orpheus Chamber Orchestra triumphantly demonstrate how to combine fluency with intensity. If you like your Schoenberg effortful — to feel that the players are conquering almost insuperable odds — these recordings may not be for you. But if you like spontaneity of expression that is never an end in itself, and communicates Schoenberg's powerfully coherent forms and textures as well as his abundant emotionalism, you should not hesitate. The DG disc is the first to place Schoenberg's two Chamber Symphonies alongside *Verklärte Nacht*, whose original version for string quartet was the prime mover of so many later developments, in Schoenberg and others. Here, in *Verklärte Nacht*, is Schoenberg the late-romantic tone poet, the equal of Richard Strauss: the First Chamber Symphony shows Schoenberg transforming himself from late-romantic into expressionist, while in the Second the recent American immigrant, in the 1930s, looks back to his romantic roots and forges a new, almost classical style. With superb sound, this is a landmark in recordings of twentieth-century music.

An earlier set of live performances from the 1966 Marlboro Festival pairs the First Chamber Symphony with the Serenade, Op. 24, which dates from 1924. Under the direction of conductor Leon Kirchner the distinguished ensemble from Marlboro gets right to the heart of the Serenade. Schoenberg's early use of the 12-tone row in this work, whose layout follows that of the traditional Serenade, can at times result in rather coarse performances, but Kirchner's distinguished team of soloists knock all the rough edges off the piece, and present it in shining primary colours. The similarly clear reading of the First Symphony whips up a lot of emotional energy in this tempestuous work. In style this performance leans more to earlier exploratory readings than that of, say, the Orpheus Chamber Orchestra, but both approaches are completely valid. The main bonus of the Sony disc lies in the sense of discovery that permeates both these fine Marlboro recordings.

Schoenberg. PIANO MUSIC. **Maurizio Pollini.** DG 20th Century Classics 423 249-2GC. From 2530 531 (5/75).
Three Piano Pieces, Op. 11. Six Little Piano Pieces, Op. 19. Five Piano Pieces, Op. 23. Piano Suite, Op. 25. Piano Pieces, Opp. 33*a* and 33*b*.

50' ADD 6/88

When Pollini claims these as probably the most important piano pieces of the twentieth century he does so with good reason. For example, the Op. 11 pieces are generally reckoned to be the first wholly atonal work and the Prelude of Op. 25 was Schoenberg's first 12-note piece. Not surprisingly they are tough going for the uninitiated. Schoenberg expects the listener to come all the way to meet him, however uninviting the journey may appear; and getting to the sense behind the notes has defeated plenty of would-be exponents, for it tolerates no weakness of technical or musical equipment. Fortunately, Pollini is just about the ideal guide across Schoenberg's bleak ridges and past his sudden avalanches, and for combined intellectual and pianistic mastery he stands unchallenged. DG's recording is clear and lifelike and at mid-price this CD is superb value.

Schoenberg. Gurrelieder. **Susan Dunn** (sop); **Brigitte Fassbaender** (mez);
Siegfried Jerusalem, Peter Haage (tens); **Hermann Becht** (bass); **Hans
Hotter** (narr); St Hedwig's Cathedral Choir, Berlin; Dusseldorf
Musikverin Chorus; Berlin Radio Symphony Orchestra/Riccardo
Chailly. Decca 430 321-2DH2. Text and translation included.

Riccardo Chailly   [*photo: Decca/Swinkels*]

"Every morning after sunrise, King Waldemar would have a realization of the renewing power of nature, and would feel the love of Tove within the outward beauty of Nature's colour and form" (thus said Leopold Stokowski, who made the first ever recording of *Gurrelieder*). This vast cantata, here more than ever experienced as a direct descendant of Wagnerian music-drama, was for the turn-of-the-century musical scene in general, more the ultimate gorgeous sunset. Schoenberg started work on it in 1899, the same year as his *Verklärte Nacht* (see above), but delayed its completion for over a decade, by which time some of his more innovatory masterpieces were already behind him. But there is little here to upset those who shy away from the forbidding father of the atonal 12-note technique. Indeed nothing could be more tonal than the shining C major to which the final chorus ascends with the words "behold the sun", and there are few moments in music of such cumulative power and radiance. Schoenberg's forces are, to put it mildly, extravagant. As well as the six soloists and two choruses, the orchestra sports such luxuries as four piccolos, ten horns and a percussion battery that includes iron chains; and so complex are some of the textures that, to achieve a satisfactory balance, a near miracle is required of conductor and recording engineers. Decca have never been mean with miracles where large scale forces are concerned: one thinks immediately of Solti's *Götterdämmerung*, and this set is no exception. In fact much of the black majesty of the "gathering of the vassals" scene from Act 2 of the latter is recalled here, both musically and sonically, in Waldemar's nocturnal hunt with his male chorus of 'un-dead' warriors. It is but one of many highlights in Chailly's and Decca's superbly theatrical presentation of the score. The casting of the soloists is near ideal. Susan Dunn's Tove has youth, freshness and purity on her side. So exquisitely does she float her lines that you readily sympathize with King Waldemar's rage at her demise. Siegfried Jerusalem has the occasional rough moment but few previous Waldemars on disc have possessed his heroic ringing tones and range of expression. And Decca make sure that their trump card, the inimitable Hans Hotter as the speaker in "The wild hunt of the summer wind", is so tangibly projected that we miss not one single vowel or consonant of his increasing animation and excitement at that final approaching sunrise.

Franz Schreker

Austrian 1878-1934

Schreker. DIE GEZEICHNETEN. **Charles van Tassel** (bass) Adorno/
Capitaneo di Giustizia; **Sigmund Cowan** (bar) Count Tamare; **Wout**

Oosterkamp (bass) Podestá; **Marilyn Schmiege** (mez) Carlotta; **William Cochran** (ten) Alviano; **Hein Meens** (ten) Guidobald; **Frieder Lang** (ten) Menaldo; **Ernst Daniel Smid** (bar) Michelotto; **Math Dirks** (bar) Gonsalvo; **Emile Godding** (bass) Julian; **Lieuwe Visser** (bass) Paolo; **Ellen Bollongino** (sop) Ginevra/A maiden; **Michael Austin** (ten) A youth; **Alex Vermeulen** (ten) First Senator; **Hans van Heiningen** (bar) Second Senator; **Traian Aga** (bass) Third Senator; **Dutch Radio Philharmonic Chorus and Orchestra/ Edo de Waart.** Marco Polo 8 223328/30. Notes, text and translation included. Recorded at performances and rehearsals in the Concertgebouw, Amsterdam between February 26th and March 3rd, 1990.

③ 2h 27' DDD 12/91

A contemporary of Richard Strauss who earned the respect of Schoenberg and Berg, Schreker is far less well-known although his operas were performed in Austria and Germany until they were suppressed by the Nazis as decadent (he was also Jewish). His music owes much to the German tradition and sometimes recalls Strauss, but in his sumptuous orchestral writing and tendency towards hothouse operatic subjects he most resembles the Polish composer Szymanowski. The title of this opera, written to his own libretto in 1913-15, means something like *The Branded Ones* and tells of a sixteenth-century Genoese prince of great ugliness who makes a private island called Elysium into an erotic paradise for his friends, where abducted young girls are debauched and sometimes die before the tormented Prince Alviano himself goes mad. The music suits this melodramatic and improbable tale, and is at its most lurid in Act 3, set in the pagan 'paradise garden' of Elysium with its fauns and fountains, where the vocal forces and large orchestra depict a powerfully sensuous scene. This Dutch performance recorded in the Amsterdam Concertgebouw is a strong one, and if William Cochran's Alviano is too heavily declamatory and wobbly to be attractive that may be acceptable in this role and his lengthy mad scene is effective. The other soloists, chorus and orchestra under Edo de Waart are clearly in sympathy with the style, and only purists need mind that some cuts have been made in Act 3. The booklet has the libretto in German and English.

Franz Schubert

Austrian 1797-1828

Schubert. SYMPHONIES. **Chamber Orchestra of Europe/Claudio Abbado.** DG 423 651-2GH5.
Symphonies — No. 1 in D major, D82; No. 2 in B flat major, D125; No. 3 in D major, D200; No. 4 in C minor, D417, "Tragic"; No. 5 in B flat major, D485; No. 6 in C major, D589; No. 8 in B minor, D759, "Unfinished"; No. 9 in C major, D944, "Great". Grand Duo in C major, D812 (orch. J. Joachim). Rosamunde, D644 — Overture, "Die Zauberharfe".

⑤ 5h 20' DDD 2/89

For this covetable box-set Abbado has had original sources researched in order to restore bars and details that have been missed out by later editors and to expurgate those added by some, Brahms included, who felt Schubert's originals did not quite balance! For those who know these Symphonies in the later, corrupted versions, these performances can be startling at times, and real eye-openers. The balance of the first movement of the Fourth Symphony, for example, where eight bars added by Brahms to the exposition have been cut, is so radically altered that the effect persists throughout the work, and changes its meaning. Such dedication to Schubert's intentions must be applauded, and the more so because Abbado also draws from his small orchestra of brilliant young performers playing of the utmost sympathy and commitment. The whole set sounds like a labour of love. It has the occasional weaker point but, as a whole, it sustains a remarkably high standard, and the admirably-detailed recordings permit an unstrained appreciation of the finer qualities of the playing.

Schubert. Symphonies — No. 1 in D major, D82; No. 5 in B flat major, D485. Overtures — D major, D590, "In the Italian Style"; "Des Teufels Lustschloss", D84. **English Sinfonia/Sir Charles Groves.** Pickwick IMP Classics PCD944.

Ih 18' DDD 11/91 £ Ⓑ

Young master Schubert had not yet turned 16 when he penned his First Symphony (1813); he then embarked immediately on an opera called *Des Teufels Lustschloss* ("The Devil's Pleasure Castle"). What matters is not that the models are obvious (Haydn, Mozart and Beethoven in the symphony) but the music's mix of confidence and daring experimentation: the symphony's majestic writing for woodwind and brass in the highest registers; and the high drama of the overture (complete with threatening timpani crescendos and a strange central *Largo* for trombones). Two years on Schubert gave us his sunny Fifth Symphony, "a pearl of great price" as Tovey put it, banishing the percussion and most of the brass; and the following year saw one of Schubert's reactions to the Rossini mania that was sweeping through Vienna at the time with his *Overture in the Italian Style*. Sir Charles Groves, like Abbado (reviewed above), uses a small orchestra of modern instruments to obtain the textural clarity of period performances without what some feel as the rawness of authentic instruments. He may not have as polished an ensemble of players as Abbado, but freshness of spirit makes up for any lack of elegance of execution. The sound is excellent, the duration generous — a fine bargain.

Schubert. Symphonies — No. 3 in D major, D200[a]; No. 5 in B flat major, D485[a]; No. 6 in C major, D589[b]. **Royal Philharmonic Orchestra/Sir Thomas Beecham.** EMI Studio CDM7 69750-2. Items marked [a] from HMV ASD345 (6/60), [b] Columbia 33CX1363 (9/56).

Ih 18' ADD 8/90 Ⓠ/P ▲

Beecham was well into his seventies when he made these recordings with the Royal Philharmonic, the orchestra he had founded in 1946. His lightness of touch, his delight in the beauty of the sound he was summoning, the directness of his approach to melody, and his general high spirits will all dominate our memory of these performances. But listening again, we may be reminded that Beecham could equally well dig deep into the darker moments of these works. Schubert's elation was rarely untroubled and the joy is often compounded by its contrast with pathos — Beecham had that balance off to a tee. It should be noted that Beecham does not take all the marked repeats and he doctored some passages he considered over-repetitive. However, these recordings may also serve as a reminder of the wonderful heights of musicianship that his players achieved, as in the Trio of the Third Symphony's *Minuet*, where a simple waltz-like duet between oboe and bassoon attains greatness by the shapeliness, ease and poig-nancy of its execution. Despite some signs of age, these recordings still preserve the brilliance of their readings and the tonal quality of this orchestra. Altogether, a disc to lift the heaviest of spirits.

Schubert. Symphonies — No. 4 in C minor, D417, "Tragic"; No. 6 in C major, D589. **London Classical Players/Roger Norrington.** EMI Reflexe CDC7 54210-2.

Ih DDD 5/92 ✒

It makes sense that the private, or semi-private music-making for which Schubert's first six symphonies were destined, should be performed by a small orchestra of instruments of the period, rather than given the full blown modern symphony orchestra treatment. The subtitle of the Fourth, *Tragic*, and its minor key, have led many an interpreter, encouraged by the extra weight of modern instruments, to invest it with a profundity (tragedy to triumph on a Beethovenian scale) it manifestly does not possess. Norrington's tempos are expertly judged to give natural expression to its passion and melancholy; its theatrical, rather than genuinely tragic concerns. And the swing into the major at the end of the finale here is a memorable *coup de théâtre*; only period brass and timpani can respond with this degree of enthusiasm without masking the rest of the orchestra. Again, in the *Scherzo* of the Sixth (with its unmistakable echoes of the one in Beethoven's Seventh), the reduced density of period instruments allows sharp accenting without the threat of over-emphasis. Its springing vitality is as irresistible as are the period woodwind colours for the rest of the Symphony's Rossinian charm, humour and high spirits. With lucid sound, there will be little here to offend, and plenty to enchant even the most die-hard traditionalist.

NEW REVIEW

Schubert. Symphonies — No. 5 in B flat major, D485; No. 8 in B minor, D759, "Unfinished". **London Classical Players/Roger Norrington.** EMI Reflexe CDC7 49968-2.

49' DDD 12/90

This recommendation may seem rather perverse, particularly as Norrington's urgency in Schubert's "charming symphony in B flat major" puts a noticeable strain on his players in the first movement. The romantic warmth of the sunny Schubert Five that we have always known and loved, and which remains intact in other period instrument performances of the work, is here replaced with a restless, almost *Sturm und Drang*, seriousness. After one has recovered from the initial shock of such a presentation, it remains a thoroughly plausible view, and a consistently stimulating one. Which is why it merits a recommendation. The Eighth was discovered and became popular long after its period, and interpreters throughout the ages have been tempted to compensate for its "unfinished" state by investing its two existing movements with a weight and breadth that was probably not originally envisaged. They can, of course, withstand this. But a less expansive view, such as Norrington's, does not diminish their stature. Indeed, the resulting concentration of Schubert's symphonic argument, with classical proportions and a true 'sense of line' restored, is very compelling. Together with the very determined pointing of accents, and a magically withdrawn pianississimo in the second movement, this is an *Unfinished* that, based on fidelity to the score, realizes a great deal more of the music's expressive potential than many a modern instruments version. The sound is firm and superbly focused.

NEW REVIEW

Schubert. Symphony No. 8 in B minor, D759, "Unfinished".
Schumann. Symphony No. 4 in D minor, Op. 120. **North German Radio Symphony Orchestra/Günter Wand.** RCA Victor Red Seal RD60826. Recorded at performances in the Musikhalle, Hamburg in April 1991.

57' DDD 5/92

Wand's is a traditionally unhurried unfolding of Schubert's *Unfinished*, and one which does not exploit its troubled lyrical expanses, bar by bar, for the utmost drama. Perceptible deviations from his well maintained pulse give heightened expressiveness to crucial moments in the 'symphonic' drama, such as the fearful start of the first movement's development section, and the second movement's haunting central transition. But the quality here that is most easy to recognize, and just as impossible to analyse, is its spirituality. The live origins may help to explain this, as they do a few trifling imprecisions in the playing. His Schumann Fourth has impressive cumulative power; something the composer obviously intended with all four movements linked and sharing common themes. Wand's purposeful manner does not preclude many individual touches early in the work (the *Romanze* is darkly coloured and beautifully phrased), but as Schumann's thematic unity in continuity becomes more established, so Wand tightens his grip: the finale's introductory "darkness to dawn", for example, is here no interpolated episode, but an amassing of energies already in the air. The sound is full, deep and natural.

NEW REVIEW

Schubert. Symphony No. 9 in C major, D944, "Great". **London Classical Player/Roger Norrington.** EMI Reflexe CDC7 49949-2.

58' DDD 4/90

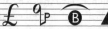

NEW REVIEW

Schubert. Symphony No. 9 in C major, D944, "Great". **North German Radio Symphony Orchestra/Günter Wand.** RCA Victor Red Seal RD60978. Recorded at performances in the Musikhalle, Hamburg in April 1991.

53' DDD 1/92

NEW REVIEW

Schubert. Symphony No. 9 in C major, D944, "Great".[a]
Schumann. Symphony No. 4 in D minor, Op. 120[b]. **London Symphony Orchestra/Josef Krips.** Decca Historic 425 957-2DM. Item marked [a] from SXL2043 (1/59), [b] SXL2223 (8/60).

1h 17' ADD 10/90

Josef Krips   *[photo: Follet]*

We now know that Schubert's *Great* C major was not a farewell offering from the last year of his life (1828), but written two or three years earlier, shortly after the *Unfinished*, at white heat, and with a new found confidence and maturity. "Forget all that 'Schubert with one foot in the grave' rubbish — the thing's so *alive!*" remarked Roger Norrington in a *Gramophone* interview. And so it proves in Norrington's extraordinary disc, which admirably bears out the validity of his dictum "it's only by being a bit purist to begin with, that you can allow later freedom". The freedoms are here, for example, in the relaxing of tempo for the awestruck response to the slow movement's central crisis, and in many dynamic inflexions throughout, but they will pass by those who crave the kind of distortions of tempo perpetrated on poor Schubert by revered podium luminaries from the past as the *sine qua non* for enjoyment of this symphony. And if the propulsive energy generated by Norrington's speeds, and say, the gentle pianissimo for the slow movement's second theme, or the precisely registered (and hugely effective) pianississimo at the start of the finale's momentous coda, are example of purism, then long may it reign in this work. The disc also offers convincing proof that period instruments do help to realize Schubert's intentions: Tovey remarked that the woodwind melody of the Trio needed a double wind band to be heard, or the string accompaniment damped down till it lost its energy of character. Here you can have both; a gloriously full and detailed woodwind sound and a splendidly energetic accompaniment. The balance, in fact, offers textural revelations in virtually every bar.

If you feel that the work's "heavenly lengths" are too protracted by the observance of every single repeat, or that Schubert's scheme implied a greater variety of tempo within each movement, or are simply allergic to the sound of period instruments and the insistent vitality that their use seems to encourage, then Wand's disc merits serious consideration. He slows for the first two movements' second themes, for transitions, and for the *Scherzo*'s Trio, but the variations of speed are accomplished without damaging the flow (even though, after Norrington, the manoeuvring is very obvious). It's an approach that is perhaps more consciously seeking out contrasts of emotion, and, at the same time, exploring the Symphony's structural possibilities; a *great* C major, that may not have all the answers (no single performance of any symphonic masterwork can claim that) but one which adventures further than most. As with his *Unfinished* (see above), this was recorded before a well behaved audience, with good presence and natural perspectives.

It's hard to believe the Krips version was recorded back in 1958, such is the transparency of the sound. It is also gratifying to note that the single tempo philosophy was not discovered by the authenticists: apart from the traditionally slow introduction and coda of the first movement, Krips maintains steady tempos throughout. They are, though, generally more relaxed than Norrington's. Krips was born in Vienna, and this performance is imbued with a recognizable Viennese charm and lyrical grace. Nothing is forced; "Everything I try to do as if it were by Mozart" he once declared. Far from diminishing the stature and power of this Symphony, his approach removes a lot of the unappealing weight it can acquire on modern instruments, and, more importantly, it rises to the exciting challenge of the first two movements' climaxes, and all of the finale, with a wholly natural intensification. In the finale, the superb LSO strings leap for joy, and Krips rightly reserves his maximum thrust for the thrice repeated octave Cs to thrilling effect. Like Wand, Krips ignores the repeats, but Decca, unlike RCA, offer a generous coupling. The Schumann Fourth Symphony was recorded two years earlier. The sound is generally less well defined, with thin violins and a boomy bass. As for the performance, it is more for connoisseurs of the conductor's art, and for those who mourn the passing of an age of elegance in music-making. But the Schubert alone makes this disc an irresistible bargain.

Schubert. Octet in F major, D803. **Academy of St Martin in the Fields Chamber Ensemble** (Kenneth Sillito, Malcolm Latchem, vns; Stephen Shingles, va; Denis Vigay, vc; Raymund Koster, chbr bass; Andrew Marriner, cl; Timothy Brown, hn; Graham Sheen, bn). Chandos CHAN8585.

lh DDD 8/88

Schubert used material from previous years in composing this work which ostensibly has a serenade-like character, but shows a great depth of feeling, almost pathos at times. Schubert was already afflicted with the illness which was to dog the rest of his short life, and in the six-movement Octet he looked back nostalgically to happier days. It is one of his great masterpieces. The ASMF Chamber Ensemble have recorded the Octet on two occasions, but this Chandos version is considerably the better of the two. The engineers have succeeded in resolving problems of balance posed by the unequal power of solo strings and wind with great skill, and the sound itself is superlatively fine. The players respond eagerly to the Octet's song-like spontaneity, and they manage to capture its relaxed, Viennese flavour in a very authentic style, but they also understand and express with rare eloquence the work's underlying profundity of expression.

Schubert. String Quintet in C major, D956. **Cleveland Quartet** (Donald Weilerstein, Peter Salaff, vns; Atar Arad, va; Paul Katz, vc) with **Yo-Yo Ma** (vc). CBS Masterworks CD39134. From IM39134 (4/85).

| 54' | DDD | 8/86 | Ⓑ |

The String Quintet is extraordinarily fertile in melodic invention and Schubert frames it in a rich harmonic language alive to the many rhythmic subtleties. The Cleveland Quartet and Ma capture the urgency and ardour of the long first movement but also take the beautiful second subject at the requested *pp* — a rare but welcome observation. The intense second movement with its pizzicato bass line is well done too and greatly helped by the recording, which is attentive without being too close (there's no excessive breathing): the five players are well spread across the stereo image. The closing *Allegretto*, the shortest movement, is nicely sprung, giving it a slightly folk-like gait. A fine disc in an already well-represented catalogue.

Schubert. Piano Quintet in A major, D667, "Trout"[a]. String Trios[b] — B flat major, D471; B flat major, D581. **Grumiaux Trio** (Arthur Grumiaux, vn; Georges Janzer, va; Eva Czako, vc); [a]**Jacques Cazauran** (db); [a]**Ingrid Haebler** (pf). Philips Musica da Camera 422 838-2PC. Item marked [a] from SAL3621 (10/67), [b] SAL3782 (6/70).

| 1h 3' | ADD | 10/89 | Ⓑ |

Schubert. Piano Quintet in A major, D667, "Trout"[a]. String Quartet in D minor, D810, "Death and the Maiden"[b]. [a]**Sir Clifford Curzon** (pf); [a]members of the **Vienna Octet** (Willi Boskovsky, vn; Gunther Breitenbach, va; Nikolaus Hübner, vc; Johann Krump, db); [b]**Vienna Philharmonic Quartet** (Boskovsky, Otto Strasser, vns; Rudolf Streng, va; Robert Scheiwein, vc). Decca 417 459-2DM. Item marked [a] from SXL2110 (6/59), [b] SXL6092 (5/64).

| 1h 11' | ADD | 6/88 | £ Ⓑ ▲ |

Schubert. Piano Quintet in A major, D667, "Trout". **Clemens Hagen** (vn); **Veronika Hagen** (va); **Lukas Hagen** (vc); **Alois Posch** (db); **András Schiff** (pf). Decca 411 975-2DH. From 411 975-1DH (2/85).

| 44' | DDD | 4/85 | Ⓑ |

Schubert composed the *Trout* Quintet in his early twenties for a group of amateur musicians in the town of Steyr in Upper Austria, which lies upon the River Enns which was then noted for its fine fishing and keen fishermen. The Quintet was certainly tailored for special circumstances, but like all great occasional music it stands as strongly as ever today, with its freshly bubbling invention and sunny melodiousness. Arthur Grumiaux is always a stylish violinist, but his natural refinement never inhibits the natural high spirits of the music, while Ingrid Haebler is no less stylish. The single movement for string trio that is D471 was written even earlier in the composer's short life, in 1816, while the four-movement Trio in the same key followed it a year later; these too are played deftly yet with the right kind of simplicity. The recordings are satisfactory but have a little residual tape hiss; in the trios it may be useful to make some treble reduction, since the sound here is brighter.

Willi Boskovsky's gentle and cultured mind is very much responsible for the success of these performances of Schubert's two best-known chamber works. In the delectable *Trout* Quintet there is real unanimity of vision between the players, as well as an immaculate attention to the details of the scoring. Clifford Curzon's part in the performance is memorable especially for his quiet playing — the atmosphere is magical in such moments. Everywhere there is a great awareness of the delicacy and refinement of Schubert's inventiveness. The *Death and the Maiden* Quartet is no less successful. Schubert's strikingly powerful harmonies, together with a sustained feeling of intensity, all go to heighten the urgency of the first movement. Despite this, string textures are generally kept light and feathery. In the *Andante* all is subtly understated and although a mood of tragedy is always lurking in the background, never is it thrown at the listener. Boskovsky's understanding of the music is very acute and the performance cannot fail to satisfy even the most demanding. These are two vintage recordings and in the quartet the quality of sound is quite remarkable.

Schubert's *Trout* Quintet is played on the later Decca recording by a professional Viennese family group, joined by the naturally musical András Schiff, and the result combines freshness with concentration to hold the listener in rapt attention from the first note to the last. To emphasize that this is a team project, the Decca engineers have perceptively balanced the piano within the string group, and that adds to the feeling of spontaneous musical integration. The recorded sound is eminently vivid and realistic.

Schubert. String Quartets — D minor, D810, "Death and the Maiden"; C minor, D703, "Quartettsatz". **Lindsay Quartet** (Peter Cropper, Ronald Birks, vns; Robin Ireland, va; Bernard Gregor-Smith, vc). ASV CDDCA560. From DCA560 (7/86).

· 52' DDD 3/87

Der Tod und das Mädchen ("Death and the Maiden") Quartet is a work composed entirely in the minor key and draws its title from the song based on the poem by Matthias Claudius which Schubert had set in 1817. Not unlike the famous song *Erlkönig, Der Tod und das Mädchen* takes the form of a dialogue between life and death, here the maiden and the scythe-bearing figure of death. Schubert uses this song as the basis for the second movement's set of variations. How much he intended the mood of the poem to permeate the entire quartet is impossible to tell; suffice it to say that performing tradition has tended to emphasize the dark, death-centred character of the piece. The Lindsay Quartet bring their usual intense and febrile approach to what is appropriately Schubert's most intense chamber work. If at times the expression threatens to become orchestral in scope it never obscures the composer's vision. The recording allows plenty of air around the players without diminishing their powers of attack.

NEW REVIEW

Schubert. Piano Trios — B flat major, D28 (Sonata in one movement); B flat major, D898. Notturno in E flat major, D897. **Trio Zingara** (Elizabeth Layton, vn; Felix Schmidt, vc; Annette Cole, pf). Collins Classics 1215-2.

· 1h 1' DDD 10/91

Schubert was a mere schoolboy of 15 when writing his Sonata Movement in B flat, D28, in 1812. Yet curiously he allowed some 14 years to elapse before producing his two full-scale masterpieces in this medium, likewise the independent *Adagio* in E flat, posthumously published under the title *Notturno*. Here, we're given three of the four in performances as mellow in feeling as in actual sound — not for nothing was the chosen recording venue The Maltings at Snape. So hopefully it will not be too long before this musicianly young team goes back there to complete its cycle with the big E flat major Trio. The occasionally audible intakes of breath betray the extent of their involvement. Yet there is no self-conscious attempt to hold any listener captive. The predominant impression left by their playing is of complete naturalness, of total absence of special pleading, just as if they were in the relaxed atmosphere of Joseph von Spaun's drawing-room on 28th January 1828, when the B flat Trio is thought to have had its first performance in the presence of the composer himself.

Schubert. Duo in A major, D574. Rondo brillant in B minor, D895. Fantasy in C major, D934. **Gidon Kremer** (vn); **Valery Afanassiev** (pf). DG 431 654-2GH.

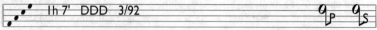

Few indeed are the recital discs which can offer the listener such unalloyed pleasure as this gloriously played and generously conceived Schubert recording from Gidon Kremer and Valery Afanassiev. Rarer yet by far, though, are releases capable of generating the kind of communicative ambience more normally revealed by the intimacy of live music making. The very opening bars of Afanassiev's piano introduction at the start of the *Duo* in A major, D574, with its restrained yet expectant dignity of utterance would mesmerize the heart of the sternest critic, whilst Kremer exhibits charm, wit, understatement and sheer delight in this work, quite possibly Schubert's most frequently played composition for violin and piano. The B minor Rondo and the magnificent Fantasy in C major were written a decade after the *Duo* and were both intended to display the talents of the composer's friend, the Czech violinist, Josef Slavic, who had settled in Vienna during 1826. Neither work found favour at the time, and quite possibly the dark premonitions of the Rondo, whose emotional sympathies recalled those of the *Unfinished* Symphony, were inappropriate for Viennese popular tastes. However, although Kremer's approach avoids mere rhetoric here, this superb recording is surely crowned by a magisterial performance of the C major Fantasy. This account combines bravura, elegance and a deep affinity with the Schubertian genre, captured with splendid realism by a recording which is technically beyond criticism.

Schubert. Impromptus — D899; D935. **Murray Perahia** (pf). CBS Masterworks CD37291. From 37291 (1/84).

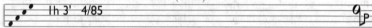

Schubert. Impromptus — D899; D935. **Krystian Zimerman** (pf). DG 423 612-2GH.

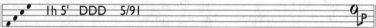

Though an able pianist, Schubert was not a concert-giving virtuoso out to conquer an international public with large-scale bravura works. The music-making he most enjoyed was at informal parties (they came to be known as Schubertiads) in the homes of music-loving friends, hence the very large number of miniatures — with the *Impromptus* among them — that flowed unceasingly from his pen. Whereas so much of what he wrote was never published in his lifetime, he had the satisfaction of seeing all eight *Impromptus* in print the year before he died. And their popularity has never waned, as the quickest glance at any catalogue at once makes clear. Inevitably Murray Perahia has strong rivals all equally deserving of a place in this *Guide*. His own version nevertheless constantly enchants with its pellucid tone and spontaneous spring-like freshness. Note the rippling lightness of the triplets in No. 2 in E flat and the pinpoint clarity of his semiquaver articulation in No. 4 in A flat in the first set, likewise the dancing lilt he brings to the variations of No. 3 in B flat and his respect for the *scherzando* expressively qualifying the *allegro* in No. 4 in F minor in the second set. None are 'over-loaded'. The recording is no less pleasing.

Zimerman's searching and very personally committed account of these eight pieces comes as a keen reminder that they are as representative of the composer in full maturity as any of the later piano sonatas. With his wide tonal range and bold response to climaxes, he sometimes even brings to mind how this music might have sounded had Schubert chosen to score it for an orchestra of that day. The recording itself very faithfully reproduces the mellow warmth of his own sound-world. Zimerman's desire to shed new light on the familiar has sometimes in recent years made us too aware of an interpreter at work. That danger is not wholly averted in his elasticity of pulse in the emotionally ambivalent D899 No. 1 in C minor/major, and equally his coquetry in some of the variations of D935 No. 3 in B flat. But for the most part it is a joy to hear these pieces at once so intensely experienced and lyrically sung. Though the earlier version from Perahia will always keep its place on library shelves, this new issue can now join it.

Schubert. PIANO WORKS. **András Schiff.** Decca 425 638-2DH.
Allegretto in C minor, D915. Drei Klavierstücke, D946. 12 Ländler, D790. Vier Impromptus, D935.

1h 14' DDD 7/90

Throughout his life Schubert was as irresistibly drawn to the keyboard miniature as he was to the realm of song. On this disc András Schiff assembles a choice assortment of these shorter pieces, playing them with the youthful freshness and charm with which Schubert himself must so often have delighted his friends. Most familiar, of course, are the last four *Impromptus*, dating from the year before he died but inexplicably left unpublished for the next 12 years. For these Schiff favours fleeter tempos than we often hear (notably for the Second in A flat), giving each piece an effortless lyrical flow. The three *Klavierstücke* of his

András Schiff   [photo: Decca/Chlala]

last year, with their strong internal contrasts, are richly characterized, yet again Schiff resists all temptation to over-interpret or emotionally inflate. The minor/major bittersweetness of the C minor *Allegretto*, written for Schubert's "dear friend", Ferdinand Walcher, on his departure from Vienna in April 1827, is brought home with the same disarming simplicity. Lighter relief comes in the 12 *Ländler* of 1823 (always so dear to Brahms, who owned the manuscript and eventually arranged for their publication), where Schiff prefers imaginative vitality to *schmalz*. The recording (made in Vienna's Konzerthaus) respects his light-fingered textural clarity.

Schubert. Fantasy in C major, D760, "Wanderer".
Schumann. Fantasia in C major, Op. 17. **Murray Perahia** (pf). CBS Masterworks CD42124.

52' DDD 12/86

The *Wanderer* Fantasy is a work in four linked movements using a motto theme that is variously transformed as the work proceeds, a technique that we find later in such works as Liszt's Piano Concertos and Franck's Symphony. It is a vigorous piece and in some ways somewhat classical and symphonic in utterance, strong in rhetoric as well as poetry. On the other hand, Schumann's *Fantasia*, written some 16 years later around 1837, is more obviously pianistic (of the two composers it was he who was the better pianist) and inspired more clearly by the romantic spirit that had already developed in music during Schubert's lifetime. Both works are major landmarks of the piano repertory, and Murray Perahia plays them with an unerring sense of their different styles as well as impeccable technical command. He is unfailingly exciting and uplifting in the quicker music, but it is probably in the slower and more expressive sections that his nobly personal eloquence is most strikingly revealed. Two different American locations were used for these performances, but the second of them (for the Schumann) allows a richer and more atmospheric piano sound.

NEW REVIEW

Schubert. Piano Sonata in C minor, D958. Impromptus, D899. Deutsche Tänze, D783. **Imogen Cooper** (pf). Ottavo OTRC78923.

⟨ 1h 10' DDD 2/92 ⟩

This is in fact the last of Imogen Cooper's six-disc cycle of the piano music of Schubert's last six years, a cycle launched in 1988 hard on the heels of similar cycles given on the concert platform in both London and Amsterdam. Like its predecessors, it confirms her as a Schubert player of exceptional style and finesse. Intuitively perceptive phrasing and a willingness to let the music sing within a wholly Schubertian sound-world are prime virtues. And though (like her erstwhile mentor, Alfred Brendel) she is no slave to the metronome when contrasting first and second subjects in sonata expositions, she still makes the music her own without the self-consciously mannered kind of interpretation heard from one or two more recent rivals in this strongly competitive field. Her urgent yet poised performance of the late C minor Sonata certainly confirms her admission (in a 1988 *Gramophone* interview) that the comparatively clinical atmosphere of an audience-less recording venue worries her not at all. In London's Henry Wood Hall her Yamaha is as clearly and truthfully reproduced (save for a slight suspicion of pedal-haze in the sonata's demonically driven finale) as most else in the series. The Impromptus reveal an acutely sensitive response to Schubert's dynamic subtleties and surprises of key, while the 16 *German Dances* tell their own simple Viennese tale without any suggestion of applied make-up.

Schubert. Piano Sonata in A minor, D845. Drei Klavierstücke, D946. **Alfred Brendel** (pf). Philips 422 075-2PH.

⟨ 1h 1' DDD 10/89 ⟩

Schubert. Piano Sonatas — A minor, D845[a]; G major, D894[b]. **Radu Lupu** (pf). Decca 417 640-2DH. Item marked [a] from SXL6931 (12/79), [b] SXL6741 (5/76).

⟨ 1h 14' ADD 6/87 ⟩

The coupling of Brendel and Schubert inspires confidence. Though love of the music alone, as pianists know, is not enough to master these pieces, it is essential, and in this big A minor Sonata (a key that was somehow especially important to Schubert) Brendel presents us with a drama that is no less tense for being predominantly expressed in terms of shapely melody. There is a flexibility in this playing that reminds us of the pianist's own comment that in such music "we feel not masters but victims of the situation". he allows us plenty of time to savour detail without ever losing sight of the overall shape of the music, and the long first movement and finale carry us compellingly forwards, as does the scherzo with its urgent energy, while the *Andante* second movement, too, has the right kind of spaciousness. In the *Three Piano Pieces* which date from the composer's last months, Brendel is no less responsive and imaginative. Richly sonorous digital recording in a German location complements the distinction of the playing on this fine Schubert disc.

Radu Lupu also understands Schubert's style as do few others and the way in which he is able to project this essentially private world is extraordinary. His tone is unfailingly clear, and this adds substantially to the lucidity of the readings. The simplicity of the opening themes of the A minor Sonata is a marvel of eloquence and when it is reset in the development section of the first movement one is amazed to hear Lupu transforming it into something far more urgent and full of pathos. The G major Sonata again fires Lupu's imagination and in the Minuet third movement he uses a considerable amount of rubato for the dance; its solid rhythmic pulse is an ideal foil to offset the extraordinary transitions of the finale that follows. The recorded sound does full justice to the colour of the pianist's tone.

Schubert. Piano Sonatas — D major, D850; A minor, D784. **Alfred Brendel** (pf). Philips 422 063-2PH.

· Ih 3' DDD 11/88

There is an extraordinary amount of highly experimental writing in Schubert's piano sonatas. The essence of their structure is the contrasting of big heroic ideas with tender and inner thoughts; the first impresses the listener, the second woos him. The two works on this CD are in some ways on a varying scale. The D major lasts for 40 minutes, the A minor for around 23. However, it is the latter that contains the most symphonically inspired writing — it sounds as if it could easily be transposed for orchestra. Alfred Brendel presents the composer not so much as the master of lieder-writing, but more as a man thinking in large forms. Although there are wonderful quiet moments when intimate asides are conveyed with an imaginative sensitivity one remembers more the urgency and the power behind the notes. The A minor, with its frequently recurring themes, is almost obsessive in character whilst the big D major Sonata is rather lighter in mood, especially in the outer movements. The recorded sound is very faithful to the pianist's tone, whilst generally avoiding that insistent quality that can mar his loudest playing.

Schubert. Piano Sonatas — A major, D959; B flat major, D960. **Melvyn Tan** (fp). EMI Reflexe CDC7 49631-2.

· Ih 7' DDD 9/89

Schubert. Piano Sonata in B flat major, D960. **Stephen Kovacevich** (pf). Hyperion CDA66004. From A66004 (2/83).

· 42' DDD 4/87

Schubert. Piano Sonata in B flat major, D960. Fantasia in C major, D760, "Wanderer". **Alfred Brendel** (pf). Philips 422 062-2PH.

· 58' DDD 1/90

Readers should perhaps be reminded that Melvyn Tan is only in his thirties. In years to come he will probably play the last two and greatest of Schubert's keyboard sonatas with a deeper poise. But for the moment we can be grateful for his refreshing reminder that when writing them, Schubert (albeit with only another two months to live) was not an elderly philosopher but like Tan himself, a highly impressionable young man. To meet the composer still more closely on his own ground he uses a reproduction by Derek Adlam of an 1814 Nannette Streicher fortepiano, which comes over with vibrant warmth in a recording made in the Long Gallery of Doddington Hall, Lincoln. The most controversial feature of the disc is the unusually brisk tempo he adopts for both slow movements, as if trying to lighten their sorrow. In other contexts, such as the second subject of the A major Sonata's first movement, there are occasional rhythmic idiosyncrasies which might, after repeated hearings, begin to sound a little mannered. Yet the spontaneity of his youthful response to passing marvels remains irresistible, likewise his virility in both Scherzos and his strong sense of direction in the B flat major Sonata's finale.

Stephen Kovacevich offers a deeply felt and comprehensive experience of Schubert's last Piano Sonata seemingly acknowledging all shades of meaning, yet retaining a marvellous sense of wholeness (and a marvellous pianistic poise as well). In this context his heart-stopping withdrawals of tone (especially in the first two movements) are profoundly moving. At full price, without coupling, and with slightly veiled sound-quality, this may seem like an extravagant purchase — but musical riches of this kind are impossible to put a price on. Brendel meets Schubert on his own ground, exulting in the *con fuoco* panache of the earlier work, and just as keenly revealing the 'other-worldliness' of Schubert's farewell. For immediacy of response, it would be hard to name any player more aware of Schubert's own impressionability — the impressionability of a composer who died young enough to have known only "the poignancy and rapture of first sensations". Some might feel that Brendel's reaction to the mood of the moment at times results in over-elasticity of pulse, as in his drastic slowings-down for the lyrical second subject in the *Wanderer*'s first movement. But never mind. Whatever he does is done with enough conviction to make you feel, at the moment of listening, that there could be no other way. The recording is both rich and clear.

Schubert. LIEDER. **Felicity Lott** (sop); **Graham Johnson** (pf). Pickwick IMP Classics PCD898.
Die Forelle, D550. An Sylvia, D891. Heidenröslein, D257. Du bist die Ruh, D776. Der Musensohn, D764. An die Musik, D547. Auf dem Wasser zu singen, D774. Sei mir gegrüsst, D741. Litanei, D343. Die junge Nonne, D828. Ave Maria, D839. Im Frühling, D882. Gretchen am Spinnrade, D118. Nacht und Traüme, D827. Ganymed, D544. Mignon und der Harfner, D877. Seligkeit, D433.

· 1h 5'   DDD   10/88   𝄞 ℗ £

Felicity Lott   [photo: EMI / Hickey]

This mid-price disc of Schubert Lieder presents many of his best-loved songs in attractive, fresh performances. Felicity Lott shows her complete command of the genre. Secure tone, confident phrasing, exemplary control of breathing, combined with an understanding of the idiom are evident throughout. They help to make songs such as *Du bist die Ruh*, *Nacht und Träume* and *Ganymed* a pleasure from start to finish. Throughout she cleverly varies her tone and style: for instance, light for *Ganymed*, smiling for *Seligkeit*, sombre for *Litanei*. The more dramatic songs are dealt with strongly and in *Die junge Nonne*, she creates the right sense of unease conquered by serenity. In everything she is superbly supported by Graham Johnson's pertinent and perceptive playing, which recalls that of his mentor Gerald Moore in its softness of touch and clarity of detail.

Schubert. LIEDER. **Nancy Argenta** (sop); **Melvyn Tan** (fp). EMI Reflexe CDC7 54175-2. Texts and translations included.
Gott im Frühlinge, D448. Nachtviolen, D752. Der Wanderer an den Mond, D870. Der Musensohn, D764. An die Nachtigall, D497. Der Schmetterling, D633. Abendstern, D806. Schwestergruss, D762. Der Wachtelschlag, D742.

Nacht und Träume, D827. Liebhaber in alien Gestalten, D558. Auf dem Wasser
zu singen, D774. Die Forelle, D550. Kennst du das Land, D321. Heiss mich
nicht reden, D877 No. 2. So lasst mich scheinen, D877 No. 3. Nur wer die
Sehnsucht kennt, D877 No. 4. Heimliches Lieben, D922. An die Entfernte,
D765. Seligkeit, D433. Erster Verlust, D226. Rastlose Liebe, D138. Der Hirt
auf dem Felsen, D965 (with Erich Hoeprich, cl).

Ih I4' DDD 7/91

Here is a collection of Schubert Lieder performed by two highly respected
musicians who have a remarkably close musical partnership. What makes this CD
unusual is that Nancy Argenta is rarely heard in music of this period. The use,
not of a modern piano, but of a fortepiano (the kind of instrument more familiar
to Schubert) is also of particular interest here. It is an utter delight to hear
Argenta's interpretations of such familiar repertoire. It's almost as if she is discovering it for the first time and her enthusiasm and enjoyment of each new song
is most infectious. The fortepiano has a nimble, sprightly quality which gives an
extra dimension of buoyancy in *Der Wanderer an den Mond* and *Der Musensohn*. There
is a danger that it can become a little too twangy to our twentieth century ears,
but we must not forget that Melvyn Tan is one of the foremost exponents of the
fortepiano and knows exactly how to measure his accompaniments so that we
quickly forget that this is not the instrument we hear almost every day of our lives.

NEW REVIEW

Schubert. LIEDER. **Cheryl Studer** (sop); **Irwin Gage** (pf). DG 431 773-
2GH. Texts and translations included.
Am See, D746. Auf dem Wasser zu singen, D774. Auflösung, D807. Der Fluss,
D693. Die Forelle, D550. Ganymed, D544. Die Gebüsche, D646. Im Abendrot,
D799. Im Frühling, D882. Klage der Ceres, D323. Das Lied im Grünen, D917.
Nacht und Träume, D827. Die Rose, D745. Die Vögel, D691. Wehmut, D772.

Ih 5' DDD I0/91

We know that it is not necessary to have one of the best voices in the world to
sing Schubert, but it helps. Here the sheer beauty of sound is one of the recital's
principal assets in a highly competitive field. Cheryl Studer comes to Lieder on
record after making her name in the world's leading opera houses, but she is no
novice: her teachers included two of the most honoured Lieder singers of an
earlier generation (Hans Hotter and Irmgard Seefried) and she was a prizewinner
of the Schubert Institute in Vienna. She is also working with one of the most
interesting and insightful of accompanists, and Irwin Gage's touch in these songs
always helps to add distinction. There are limits too: a kind of formality inhabits
the sense of a smiling presence in songs such as *Auf dem Wasser zu singen*, and
Nacht und Träume sounds like what it is — a song which puts the technique to a
very severe test. But there are lovely things. *Das Lied im Grünen* has an infectious
enthusiasm; *Auflösung* gains much from the ability of this voice to soar; *Die
Gebüsche* is given a most lovely performance, with great sensitivity on the part of
both artists and a ravishing quality of tone in the voice. The programme itself is
thoughtfully arranged, its theme a Wordsworthian one of nature and emotions,
its contents an enjoyable mixture of the famous and the less familiar.

Schubert. LIEDER, Volume 1. **Dame Janet Baker** (mez); **Graham Johnson**
(pf). Hyperion CDJ33001. Texts and translations included.
Der Jüngling am Bache, D30. Thekla, D73. Schäfers Klagelied, D121 (first
version). Nähe des Geliebten, D162 (second version). Meerestille, D216. Amalia,
D195. Die Erwartung, D159 (second version). Wandrers Nachtlied, D224. Der
Fischer, D225 (second version). Erster Verlust, D226. Wonne
der Wehmut, D260. An den Mond, D296. Das Geheimnis, D250. Lied,

D284. Der Flüchtling, D402. An den Frühling, D587 (second version). Der Alpenjäger, D588 (second version). Der Pilgrim, D794. Sehnsucht, D636 (second version).

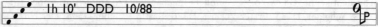

Schubert. LIEDER, Volume 6. **Anthony Rolfe Johnson** (ten); **Graham Johnson** (pf). Hyperion CDJ33006. Texts and translations included.
Die Nacht, D534 (completed by Anton Diabelli). Jagdlied, D521 (with chorus). Abendstern, D806. Abends unter der Linde, D235. Abends unter der Linde, D237. Der Knabe in der Wiege, D579. Abendlied für die Entfernte, D856. Willkommen und Abschied, D767. Vor meiner Wiege, D927. Der Vater mit dem Kind, D906. Des Fischers Liebesglück, D933. Die Sterne, D939. Alinde, D904. An die Laute, D905. Zur guten Nacht, D903 (chorus).

Schubert. LIEDER, Volume 7. **Elly Ameling** (sop); **Graham Johnson** (pf). Hyperion CDJ33007. Texts and translations included.
Minona, D152. Der Jüngling am Bache, D192. Stimme der Liebe, D187. Naturgenuss, D188. Des Mädchens Klage, D191. Die Sterbende, D186. An den Mond, D193. An die Nachtigall, D196. Die Liebe (Klärchens Lied), D210. Meeresstille, D215a. Idens Nachtgesang, D227. Von Ida, D228. Das Sehnen, D231. Die Spinnerin, D247. Wer kauft Liebesgötter?, D261. An den Frühling, D283. Das Rosenband, D280. Liane, D298. Idens Schwanenlied, D317. Luisens Antwort, D319. Mein Gruss an den Mai, D305. Mignon, D321. Sehnsucht, D310 (two versions).

Schubert. LIEDER, Volume 8. **Sarah Walker** (mez); **Graham Johnson** (pf). Hyperion CDJ33008. Texts and translations included.
An den Mond, D259. Romanze, D114. Stimme der Liebe, D418. Die Sommernacht, D289. Die frühen Gräber, D290. Die Mondnacht, D238. An den Mond in einer Herbstnacht, D614. Die Nonne, D208. An Chloen, D462. Hochzeit-Lied, D463. In der Mitternacht, D464. Trauer der Liebe, D465. Die Perle, D466. Abendlied der Fürstin, D495. Wiegenlied, D498. Ständchen, D920 (with chorus). Bertas Lied in der Nacht, D653. Der Erlkönig, D328.

Schubert. LIEDER, Volume 10. **Martyn Hill** (ten); **Graham Johnson** (pf). Hyperion CDJ33010. Texts and translations included.
Der Sänger, D149. Auf einen Kirchhof, D151. Am Flusse, D160. An Mignon, D161. Vergebliche Liebe, D177. An die Apfelbäume, wo ich Julien erblickte, D197. Seufzer, D198. Auf den Tod einer Nachtigall, D201. Der Liebende, D207. Adelwold und Emma, D211. Der Traum, D213. Die Laube, D214. Der Weiberfreund, D271. Labetrank der Liebe, D302. An die Geliebte, D303. Harfenspieler I, D325.

Schubert. LIEDER, Volume 11. **Brigitte Fassbaender** (mez); **Graham Johnson** (pf). Hyperion CDJ33011. Texts and translations included.
An den Tod, D518. Auf dem Wasser zu singen, D774. Auflösung, D807. Aus Heliopolis I, D753. Aus Heliopolis II, D754. Dithyrambe, D801. Elysium, D584. Der Geistertanz, D116. Der König in Thule, D367. Lied des Orpheus, D474. Nachtstück, D672. Schwanengesang, D744. Seligkeit, D433. So lasst mich scheinen, D727. Thekla, D595. Der Tod und das Mädchen, D531. Verklärung, D59. Vollendung, D989. Das Zügenglöcklein, D871.

Schubert. LIEDER, Volume 14. **Thomas Hampson** (bar); **Graham Johnson** (pf). Hyperion CDJ33014. Texts and translations included.
An die Leier, D737. Amphiaraos, D166. Gruppe aus dem Tartarus, D396. Gruppe aus dem Tartarus, D583. Hippolits Lied, D890. Memnon, D541. Fragment aus dem Aeschylus, D450. Philoktet, D540. Uraniens Flucht, D554. Hektors Abschied, D312. Antigone und Oedip, D542 (both with Marie McLaughlin, sop). Lied eines Schiffers an die Dioskuren, D360. Orest auf Tauris, D548. Der entsühnte Orest, D699. Der zürnenden Diana, D707. Freiwilliges Versinken, D700. Die Götter Griechenlands, D677.

1h 20' DDD 4/92

The Hyperion Schubert Edition goes from strength to strength and all the discs here are outstanding. Dame Janet Baker has always espoused the cause of rare Schubert since the early days of her career and here she seems rejuvenated and inspired by Johnson to recapture all her old sense of questing as she tackles many songs that must be new to her. The selection is made entirely from settings of Goethe and Schiller, and Baker responds strongly to some often quite taxing songs. Right through she demonstrates again her unerring ability to seize the mood and character of a song and project it with imaginative bravura. In each case she makes you listen to the familiar as much as the unfamiliar with an enthusiasm that matches her own adventurous approach. In support Graham Johnson illustrates Schubert's mastery of the piano.

The Rolfe Johnson volume is devoted to nocturnal matters and it finds the mellifluous tenor in his most inspired form. The soft grain of his tone and his perceptive phrasing are to the fore throughout his long recital. The variety in the readings match the variety in the music and very few points go unremarked: intensity and sensitivity here go hand in hand.

As they do on the equally recommendable disc that features Ameling and Johnson. Once again the pianist and the originator of the series picks songs that are suited to the singer in the limelight. Ameling has made many very special Schubert recitals on disc over the years but here she seems inspired in the many rare and marvellous songs chosen for her to surpass even her own achievements. She sheds the years in producing performances that are of particular beauty and eloquence, not forgetting her total command of technique and phrasing. Again there is a judicious mixture of the familiar and the unfamiliar, with the latter eliciting several forgotten masterpieces.

On Volume 8, with the theme of "Schubert and the Nocturne", are many marvels, not least a wondrous setting of *An den Mond in einer Herbstnacht* where Schubert minutely reflects the detail of a lovely poem about the moon being, as Johnson comments in his interesting notes, "all-seeing and all-encompassing". The Klopstock setting, *Die Sommernacht*, is another moon-saturated piece, where recitative and melody ideally match the cut of the poem. In more extrovert vein there is the gothic horror of Goethe's *Die Nonne* and the dreadful story of Rosalie von Montavert's interment in *Romanze*. To match these eerie ballads are Schubert's first settings of Goethe's beautiful *An den Mond* and the magically lilting *Ständchen* (Grillparzer) for mezzo and men's chorus. Yet another vein is struck in the still, timeless *Die Mondnacht* (Kosegarten). To crown the achievement comes a hair-raising version of *Der Erlkönig*. All these varying moods and types of setting are unerringly voiced by Sarah Walker (at home in the dramatic as she is in the lyrical or pensive) and played by Johnson, superb in *Erlkönig*. Both excel themselves. The recording is well balanced.

Johnson's choice of songs on Volume 10 are all well suited to Hill's plaintive tenor and slightly reticent manner. And what songs they are! It remains a mystery why so many outright masterpieces should have been neglected for so long, most notably perhaps the settings of the poet Ludwig Hölty, in all of which Hill's subtle word-painting and Johnson's finely shaped playing are unassumingly right. Many might have been written for this partnership to interpret. The two

Goethe settings are on a similar level of inspiration. Then there is the first recording ever of the 27-minute narrative, *Adelwold und Emma*, a cornucopia of Schubertian invention, here fully realized. With a generous timing of 74 minutes this is a recital that will afford long-lasting and deep pleasure.

In Volume 11 of the series, we are given highly individual performances typical of Fassbaender in their intensity of manner. Graham Johnson has devised for her a programme with an emphasis on Death, with a capital 'D'. The songs range in breadth and colour from the eloquent swansong, *Nachtstück*, through the black humour of *Geistertanz*, the mystery of *Mignon (So lasst mich scheinen)*, the impassioned exaltation of *Aus Heliopolis I*, to the majestic power of *Auflösung*. This series of thoughts about eternity and the Promised Land reaches its zenith in the quirky but magnificent Schiller view of heaven in *Elysium*, a cantata influenced by Beethoven. Fassbaender also throws new light on two songs usually associated with lighter voices — *Auf dem Wasser zu singen* and *Seligkeit*. As in other discs in this series, Johnson contributes well-varied playing and authoritative notes.

"Schubert and the Classics" is the subtitle of Volume No. 14. It comprises settings of poems based on Greek and Latin mythology, as depicted in ancient literature, which the composer found, in Graham Johnson's phrase, "a rejuvenating force for modern literature". These include the grand, searching compositions drawn from Schiller's poetry on the Ancients and a whole collection of Mayrhofer settings, among them the 18-minute ballad *Uraniens Flucht*, not great Schubert but with its fascinating moments. Hampson's achievement in that narrative and in more rewarding songs comes from total command over his pleasing, well-focused, ample baritone, supplemented by his impeccable phrasing and enunciation. These are heard in some of Schubert's most imposing songs, such as *Gruppe aus dem Tartarus* (Schiller) and *Memnon* (Mayrhofer), both reasonably familiar. Hampson and Johnson are just as riveting in many discoveries such as the extraordinary discourse between Antigone and Oedipus, another Mayrhofer setting, where they are joined by Marie McLaughlin. Here Hampson's weary, reawakened, blinded father movingly answers his daughter's urgency. Nothing here is easy to perform or understand, but these performers are ever enlightening in guiding the persevering listener to probe into this rarefied world.

Schubert. LIEDER[a].
Schumann. LIEDER[b]. **Elly Ameling** (sop); **Jörg Demus** (fp). Deutsche Harmonia Mundi Editio Classica GD77085. Texts and translations included. Items marked [a] from BASF BAC3088 (2/75), [b] Deutsche Harmonia Mundi 1C 065 99631 (11/78).
Schubert: Der Hirt auf dem Felsen, D965 (with Hans Deinzer, cl). Seligkeit, D433. Gretchen am Spinnrad, D118. Du liebst mich nicht, D756. Heimliches Lieben, D922. Im Frühling, D882. Die Vögel, D691. Der Jüngling an der Quelle, D300. Der Musensohn, D764. **Schumann:** Myrthen, Op. 25 Widmung; Der Nussbaum. Aufträge, Op. 77 No. 5. Sehnsucht, Op. 51 No. 1. Frage, Op. 35 No. 9. Mein schöner Stern, Op. 101 No. 4. Lieder Album für die Jugend, Op. 79 — Schmetterling; Käuzlein; Der Sandmann; Marienwürmchen; Er ists's; Schneeglöckchen. Erstes Grün, Op. 35 No. 4. Die Sennin, Op. 90 No. 4. Sehnsucht nach der Waldgegend, Op. 35 No. 5. Jasminenstrauch, Op. 27 No. 4. Liederkreis, Op. 39 — Waldesgespräch. Loreley, Op. 53 No. 2. Die Meerfee, Op. 125 No.]1.

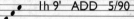 1h 9' ADD 5/90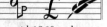

This recital has been compiled from two LPs dating from the mid 1960s when the soprano, Elly Ameling was at the height of her career. The older and perhaps more beautiful of the two is the Schubert recital in which Elly Ameling is accompanied on a fortepiano by Jörg Demus. It was an early gesture towards 'authenticity' and this is reflected both in the choice of piano and in the early clarinet played by Hans Deinzer in the most celebrated of the songs *Der Hirt auf*

dem Felsen. But whatever the merits of the approach, and they are in this instance considerable, it is the superlative singing of Elly Ameling that sets the seal of distinction on this beautiful recital. *Gretchen am Spinnrad* is exquisitely felt, *Im Frühling* fervent, wistful and perhaps unrivalled in its freshness of tone and warmth of sentiment. This is a performance to treasure for a lifetime, leaving an indelible mark upon the sensibilities. There is not one disappointment here and the atmosphere one imagines to have suffused a Schubertiad is at times almost unbearably strong. The Schumann songs are no less well sung but, with a more up-to-date sounding piano the atmosphere is somewhat less heady. But these are affecting performances and no-one with a love of the repertory could fail to be enchanted by them. Full texts are provided in German and English and the sound, capturing much that was most attractive in recording techniques of the period, is appealing. An outstanding achievement.

Schubert. LIEDER. **Peter Schreier** (ten); **András Schiff** (pf). Decca 425 612-2DH. Texts and translations included.
Schwanengesang, D957. Herbst, D945. Der Wanderer an den Mond, D870. Am Fenster, D878. Bei dir allein, D866 No. 2.

Ih 3' DDD 6/90

NEW REVIEW

Schubert. LIEDER. **Brigitte Fassbaender** (mez); **Aribert Reimann** (pf). DG 429 766-2GH. Texts and translations included.
Schwanengesang, D957. Sehnsucht, D879. Der Wanderer an den Mond, D870. Wiegenlied, D867. Am Fenster, D878. Herbst, D945.

Ih 8' DDD 6/92

Though *Schwanengesang* is not a song-cycle but a collection of Schubert's last (or 'swan') songs by their first publisher, it is generally felt to form a satisfying sequence, with a unity of style if not of theme or mood. This is certainly not weakened by the addition on the Decca disc of the four last songs which were originally omitted, all of them settings of poems by Johann Seidl. Seidl is one of the three poets whose work Schubert used in these frequently sombre songs and it is strange to think that all concerned in their creation were young men, none of the poets being older than Schubert. The listener can scarcely be unaware of a shadow or sometimes an almost unearthly radiance over even the happiest (such as "Die Taubenpost", the last of all) and that is particularly true when the performers themselves have such sensitive awareness as here. Peter Schreier is responsive to every shade of meaning in music and text; graceful and charming in

Peter Schreier   [photo: Decca/Purdom]

"Das Fischermädchen", flawlessly lyrical in "Am Meer", he will sometimes risk an almost frightening rawboned cry as in the anguish of "Der Atlas" and "Der Doppelgänger". András Schiff's playing is a miracle of combined strength and delicacy, specific insight and general rightness. One of the great Lieder recordings, and not merely of recent years.

Fassbaender and Reimann offer something equally compelling but rather different in their account of *Schwanengesang*. Fassbaender's interpretation, idiosyncratic in every respect, pierces to the heart of the bleak songs with performances as daring and challenging as the playing

629

of her partner. More than anyone, these two artists catch the fleeting moods of these mini-dramas, and their searing originality of concept. Even the lighter songs have a special individuality of utterance. This is a starkly immediate interpretation that leaves the listener shattered. The extra Seidl settings, rarely performed, are all worth hearing. The true lover of Lieder will need to have both these notable partnerships, superb in their own, searching ways.

Schubert. LIEDER. **Elisabeth Speiser** (sop); **John Buttrick** (pf). Jecklin Disco JD630-2. Texts and translations included.
Abendbilder, D650. Abschied, D475. Am Grabe Anselmos, D504. An mein Herz, D860. Beim Winde, D669. Frühlingsglaube, D686. Ganymed, D544. Strophe aus Die Götter Griechenlands, D677. Gretchen am Spinnrade, D118. Heimliches Lieben, D922. Im Abendrot, D799. Der Knabe, D692. Lachen und Weinen, D777. Lied der Anne Lyle, D830. Nachtstück, D672. Die Rose, D745. Schlaflied, D527. Sehnsucht, D879. Der Wanderer an den Mond, D870. Wanderers Nachtlied, D224. Der Winterabend, D938.

1h 15' ADD 2/91 **B**

Sometimes it is a less well-known artist who yields more gratifying insights into a composer's music than a more familiar one. That is the case here where Elisabeth Speiser, a soprano who has been unassumingly on the scene for some time now, calls on her experience to look into the heart of a group of Schubert songs, familiar and unfamiliar, on a very well-filled CD. Time and again she goes to the heart of the matter through the thoughtfulness of her phrasing and the acuity of her verbal emphases. That would be of little avail if it were not for the sheer beauty of Speiser's singing. Though she recalls at times Irmgard Seefried and Margaret Price, she has a plaintive quality in her tone very much her own. All this makes her ideally fitted to the programme she has chosen, which has the sub-title *Schöne Welt, wo bist du ...?* ("Beautiful world, where are you ...?"). She and her admirable pianist John Buttrick have chosen well from Schubert's many songs dealing with the search for a peace and happiness mostly just beyond reach. For instance, the grief of *Am Grabe Anselmos*, the longing of *Der Wanderer an den Mond*, the unease amidst happy surroundings of *Frühlingsglaube* are moods all caught and held, with speeds ideal, line clear and accents precisely placed. These are typical of the whole.

Schubert. Die schöne Müllerin, D795. **Olaf Bär** (bar); **Geoffrey Parsons** (pf). EMI CDC7 47947-2. Text and translation included.

1h 5' DDD 8/87 **P B**

Schubert. Die schöne Müllerin, D795. **Dietrich Fischer-Dieskau** (bar); **Gerald Moore** (pf). DG 415 186-2GH (9/85).

1h 2' ADD 9/85 **P B**

Schubert. Die schöne Müllerin, D795. **Siegfried Lorenz** (bar); **Norman Shetler** (pf). Capriccio 10 220. Texts included.

1h 8' DDD 5/90 **P B**

Schubert. Die schöne Müllerin, D795. **Peter Schreier** (ten); **András Schiff** (pf). Decca 430 414-2DH. Texts and translations included.

1h 3' DDD 5/91 **P S B**

The 20 songs of *Die schöne Müllerin* portray a Wordsworthian world of heightened emotion in the pantheistic riverside setting of the miller. The poet, Wilhelm Müller, tells of solitary longings, jealousies, fears and hopes as the river rushes by, driving the mill-wheel and refreshing the natural world. Olaf Bär has a most

beautiful voice: warm and flexible and, more importantly, possessing the interpretative means of expressing the poetry. Fischer-Dieskau brings experience and
intelligence to the inner life of both poetry and music. His flexible but distinctive
tone-quality is fined down for the reflective songs and swelled to stentorian
directness for the more resonant ones. On both recordings the accompanists
bring insight and flair; sound quality is clean and natural.

Siegfried Lorenz and his dynamic accompanist, Norman Shetler, steals a march
on much of the rest of the field by presenting the work with such unadorned
freshness, captured in a recording of ideally distanced intimacy. Lorenz has a
youthful vocal quality that accords beautifully with the sentiment of the verse, yet
his maturity allows him to bring out the universal resonances that underpin the
cycle, without having to resort to overemphasis. Norman Shetler is hardly an
accompanist, for he ensures that the important piano part equals that of the
vocalist, without in any way unduly dominating it: the result is an ideal musical
partnership of give and take. Both performers have a lively sense of rhythm and a
long-sighted view of pacing and balance within the cycle, so the prospects look
good for this version to hold up well under the onslaught of repeated listening.
Try before you buy, but if this is not possible you will not be disappointed with
this recommendation.

However, Schreier's partnership with a notable Schubert pianist, András Schiff,
surpasses all its predecessors and should be part of any worthwhile collection of
Lieder. With his plangent tone, now more disciplined than ever, allied to his
poignant and finely accented treatment of the text, Schreier gives moving expression to the youth's love and loss, nowhere more so than in his colloquy with the
stream, "Der Müller und der Bach". Everything in his reading has been carefully
thought through yet the result sounds wholly spontaneous and natural. To his
role Schiff brings an inquiring mind, deft and pliant fingers and an innate feeling
for Schubertian phraseology. He probes as deep into the music's meaning,
perhaps deeper than any before him yet without giving the accompaniment undue
prominence or calling attention unduly to the piano. More than anything, it is as
a unified concept that this reading achieves its greatness. It is recorded with an
ideal balance between voice and piano, in a sympathetic acoustic.

Schubert. Winterreise, D911[a]. Piano Sonata in C major, D840, "Reliquie"[b].
Peter Schreier (ten); **Sviatoslav Richter** (pf). Philips 416 289-2PH2. Text
and translation included. Item marked [a] from 416 194-1PH2 (2/86) — recorded
at a performance in the Semperoper, Dresden on February 17th, 1985; [b] 416
292-1PH (2/86) — recorded at a performance in Leverkusen, West Germany on
December 12th, 1979.

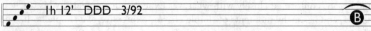

NEW REVIEW
Schubert. Winterreise, D911. **Sir Peter Pears** (ten); **Benjamin Britten** (pf).
Decca 417 473-2DM. Text and translation included. From SET270/1 (7/65).

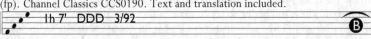

NEW REVIEW
Schubert. Winterreise, D911. **Andreas Schmidt** (bar); **Rudolf Jansen** (pf).
DG 435 384-2DG. Text and translation included.

NEW REVIEW
Schubert. Winterreise, D911. **Max van Egmond** (bar); **Jos van Immerseel**
(fp). Channel Classics CCS0190. Text and translation included.

Schubert. Winterreise, D911. **Brigitte Fassbaender** (mez); **Aribert Reimann** (pf). EMI CDC7 49846-2. Text and translation included.

`70' DDD 7/90` ⓟ Ⓑ ❓

Winterreise can lay claim to be the greatest song cycle ever written. It chronicles the sad, numbing journey of a forsaken lover, recalling past happiness, anguishing over his present plight, commenting on how the snow-clad scenery reflects or enhances his mood. Although the songs were written for a tenor, very often in recent years they have been sung by lower voices, which made the appearance of Peter Schreier's recording all the more welcome, particularly as he was partnered by Sviatoslav Richter. Schreier's plangent tenor and finely moulded phrasing are supported by almost limitless breath control. Richter's playing is communicative in a refined and subtly modulated way. The live recording has the attendant drawback of coughs at the most untoward moments, but the feeling of being present at a real occasion overrides it. Richter offers Schubert's *Reliquie* Sonata as a substantial filler in a mesmeric performance.

The mid-price Pears/Britten version remains an astonishing and unique experience in the sense of the 'oneness' of the interpretation achieved by two artists working together over a lifetime. In that sense it is a more unified interpretation than the Schreier/Richter. Pears's diction is almost as piercingly intense as Schreier's, Britten's playing notable for a fellow-composer's special insights into Schubert's writing. Two baritone versions are also well worth having although they are different in concept. Schmidt suggests a youthful, agonized traveller, not at all resigned to his fate. He sings the cycle impeccably with consistently firm, beautiful tone and immaculate phrasing while Jansen's piano playing is never less than probing. Van Egmond and Immerseel give a bleaker, greyer reading that is just as valid as the other versions. It is notable for the fortepiano's plain speaking.

Although we normally hear a man sing this cycle, there is a precedent for a female interpreter in the past (Elena Gerhardt) and it has been followed by at least three mezzos today. Undoubtedly the most compelling among them is Brigitte Fassbaender whose reading is full of the agony of the soul portrayed by Schubert. However idiosyncratic she may be, Fassbaender's subtleties of phrase and verbal nuance always arise from the inner meaning of the poems and their settings. Her bold and arresting performance makes the listener hear this most searing of all cycles anew, and she is supported in her highly individual reading by the searching and frequently revelatory playing of Aribert Reiman. This isn't an easy or comforting interpretation, but it is one that consistently reaches the heart of the matter.

Schubert. Masses — G major, D167[a]; E flat major, D950[b]. [a]**Dawn Upshaw,** [b]**Benita Valente** (sops); [b]**Marietta Simpson** (mez); [a]**David Gordon,** [b]**Jon Humphrey,** [b]**Glenn Siebert** (tens); [a]**William Stone** [b]**Myron Myers** (bars); **Atlanta Symphony Chamber Chorus; Atlanta Symphony Chorus and Orchestra/Robert Shaw.** Telarc CD80212. Text and translation included.

`1h 18' DDD 9/90`

Schubert's second Mass, D167, was written in six days during 1815 when he was 18. This small-scale, tuneful work, given only a light accompaniment of strings and organ, conformed closely with what was expected of Schubert by his teacher, Salieri, and has many moments of simple charm, expressive of a simple faith. The Mass in E flat was completed, along with *Tantum Ergo* and the *Offertorium*, in the autumn of 1828, the year of Schubert's death, and is clearly the work of a composer at the height of his powers, intent on extending the boundaries of expression whilst still having to retain some of the conventions of formal liturgical structure. The accompaniment here is for the full orchestra of the time, minus flutes, and the dramatic impact of these resources is exploited to the full.

Dawn Upshaw   *[photo: Elektra Nonesuch*

Yet more than this, it is the revolutionary harmonic ideas that single this Mass out for special note, orchestral colours emphasizing the drastic shifts and subtle slides. The composer's faith had, by this time, become more individual, less conformist, and there are hints in this work of that reassessment. Robert Shaw and his Atlanta forces set the two works in stark contrast, underlining the individual qualities of each. The choral singing is of a high order and there is an underlying detachment in their approach that fits well with the intended use of this music; operatic emotion would hardly have been in keeping.

Schubert. FIERRABRAS. **Josef Protschka** (ten) Fierrabras; **Karita Mattila** (sop) Emma; **Robert Holl** (bass) Charlemagne; **Thomas Hampson** (bar) Roland; **Robert Gambill** (ten) Eginhard; **László Polgár** (bass) Boland; **Cheryl Studer** (sop) Florinda; **Brigitte Balleys** (contr) Maragond; **Hartmut Welker** (bar) Brutamonte; **Arnold Schönberg Choir; Chamber Orchestra of Europe/Claudio Abbado.** DG 427 341-2GH2. Notes, text and translation included. Recorded at performances in the Theater an der Wien, Vienna in May 1988.

②   2h 24'   DDD   10/90

The pathetic comment that Schubert "wrote more beautiful music than the world has time to know" is gradually being corrected as more of his almost completely neglected works are being brought to light. This opera was commissioned in 1823 in Vienna but, because of the Rossini craze, the departure of several German singers and a consequent managerial upheaval, not produced, and Schubert received no payment for it, either: it remained in limbo until it was published almost 60 years after his death. The 1988 performances in Vienna, from which this recording was taken, revealed the riches of his score, which — especially in Act 2, contains an astonishing sequence from a lovely duet for two girls and a forceful quintet to an unaccompanied chorus and a moving recognition scene — are overwhelming. The plot, a complicated web of medieval chivalry, love, honour and war at the courts of Charlemagne and a defeated but vengeful Moorish prince (whose daughter is secretly in love with the Frankish knight Roland, and his son Fierrabras with Charlemagne's daughter who, however, has been dallying with the knight Eginhard), would have been enough to defeat an experienced operatic composer; and Schubert, without a hand to guide him, allowed his matchless lyrical invention to swamp dramatic pace, though there *is* drama too, in the rescue by the Moorish princess of Roland and his fellow ambassadors for peace from the prison in which they have basely been thrown. The orchestral writing is splendid and very characteristic, and Abbado misses no opportunity to underline its strength — perhaps a trifle at the expense of the voices, who are not always ideally balanced in ensembles: the choruses are brilliantly handled. The well-integrated cast is very satisfactory: chief honours go to Karita Mattila as Charlemagne's daughter, to Josef Protschka as the noble Moorish prince ready to sacrifice himself to shield her, and to Robert Gambill as the guilt-ridden Eginhard. The spoken dialogue is omitted but printed in full in the admirably produced booklet.

William Schuman   *Refer to Index*   *American 1910-*

Robert Schumann   *German 1810-1856*

Schumann. Violin Concerto in D minor, Op. posth. Fantasie in C major, Op. 131.
Thomas Zehetmair (vn); **Philharmonia Orchestra/Christoph Eschenbach.**
Teldec 2292-44190-2.

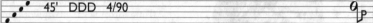

Schumann had barely six months of normal working life left to him when writing
his only two works for violin and orchestra in the autumn of 1853. Both were
inspired by the 22-year-old Joachim, who though immediately taking the *Fantasie*
into his repertory, subsequently decreed that the Concerto was unworthy of its
composer and should be suppressed. However, his great-niece, Jelly d'Aranyi,
secured its publication and performance in 1938 and we now know that any shortcomings in the finale are more than redeemed by the quality of the first two
movements, particularly the nostalgically beautiful *Langsam*. For Thomas Zehetmair's
rapt playing of that movement alone, the disc would be invaluable. Though
questionably deliberate in tempo in the finale, the performance as a whole emerges
as a labour of love from soloist, orchestra and conductor alike, very sumptuously
recorded. All musicians were grateful for the Concerto's coupling with the *Fantasie*,
a work which until the appearance of this recording, had been unobtainable on CD.
Here the disposition of the solo part and its interplay with the orchestra suggest that
Joachim himself may have proffered a few helpful performing suggestions. Though
not wholly seamless, the sonata-form argument is memorable for its recall of the
inspired introductory theme in both the development section and coda. With their
close attunement and fine balance, the warmly lyrical Zehetmair and Eschenbach
certainly explain Joachim's own enthusiasm for this now unjustly neglected work.

Schumann. SYMPHONIES. **Staatskapelle Dresden/Wolfgang Sawallisch.**
EMI Studio CDM7 69471-2, CDM7 69472-2. From SLS867 (2/74).
CDM7 69471-2 — No. 1 in B flat major, Op. 38, "Spring"; No. 4 in D minor,
Op. 120. Overture, Scherzo and Finale, Op. 52. *CDM7 69472-2* — No. 2 in C
major, Op. 61; No. 3 in E flat major, Op. 97, "Rhenish".

② 1h 17' 1h 11' ADD 11/88 5/89   £ Ⓑ

Schumann's symphonies come in for a lot of criticism because of his supposed cloudy
textures and unsubtle scoring, but in the hands of a conductor who is both skilful
and sympathetic they are most engaging works. These two mid-price CDs, brightly
transferred, return to circulation the contents of a much admired set. Sawallisch's
conducting is sensible, alert and very pleasing and he achieves great lightness in the
First and Fourth Symphonies. The Second and Third Symphonies, larger and more
far-reaching in their scope, again benefit from Sawallisch's approach. The Dresden
orchestra play superbly, with a lovely veiled string sound and a real sense of ensemble.
These are real bargains and with the *Overture, Scherzo and Finale* thrown in for
good measure, definitely not to be missed.

Schumann. Symphonies — No. 1 in B flat major, Op. 38, "Spring"; No. 4 in
D minor, Op. 120. **Royal Concertgebouw Orchestra/Riccardo Chailly.**
Decca 425 608-2DH.

1h 3' DDD 12/90   ♩ S Ⓑ

Recent recordings of Schumann Symphonies have sought to bring new insights
often at the expense of beauty of tone, or the composer's perceived romanticism.

Here is one which triumphantly proves that Schumann, played on modern instruments without radical interpretative standpoints, need not be a stale or bloated experience. Listening to this disc, one wonders why critics used to constantly berate poor Schumann for his inept orchestration. The lean, but wonderfully expressive, Concertgebouw strings are equal partners with the fresh and characterful woodwind (rarely, if ever, has this balance been so well managed); Chailly's direction is warm, precise, both taut and yielding in all the right places. Sawallisch's indispensable set of the seventies on EMI (reviewed above) offers playing of more energy and determination in the Fourth, but the recording lacks the detail and transparent textures of this newcomer. Indeed the pristine clarity and three dimensional depth of Decca's sound is one of this disc's principal joys.

Schumann. Symphonies — No. 3 in E flat major, Op. 97, "Rhenish"; No. 4 in D minor, Op. 120. **London Classical Players/Roger Norrington.** EMI CDC7 54025-2.

57' DDD 3/91

Spearheading the authentic brigade's excursion into romantic repertoire, it's surprising how euphonious Roger Norrington's ensemble sounds here. Gone is the braying brass obscuring fragile strings that was often a feature of period performance. As in his recent Schubert discs, Norrington controls his forces with an acute ear and intelligence for what is germane to the music, and the brass only 'open up' where structure demands it, or where the overall balance would be unaffected. The strength of purpose, separated violin desks and close balance are often reminiscent of the best of Klemperer's work for EMI in the sixties. There is too a similar lack of concern for mere beauty of sound. Textural revelations aside (they are too numerous to mention), the most striking feature of these accounts is their strict adherence to Schumann's explicit indications of tempo: the middle movements of both symphonies are much faster than usual. Some collectors may initially feel short changed on graceful singing lines and variety of moods but compensation lies in the revitalization of the music's rhythms, and its sense of direction. The Fourth Symphony, in particular, is experienced in one single sweep. It's a pity, here, in music that should be continuous, that the CD contains breaks between the first three movements.

Schumann. WORKS FOR CELLO. **Yo-Yo Ma** (vc); [b]**Emanuel Ax** (pf); [a]**Bavarian Radio Symphony Orchestra/Sir Colin Davis.** CBS Masterworks CD42663.
Cello Concerto in A minor, Op. 129[a]. Fantasiestücke, Op. 73[b]. Adagio and Allegro in A flat major, Op. 70[b]. Funf Stücke im Volkston, Op. 102[b].

1h 11' DDD 10/88

While others couple Schumann's endearing Concerto with other concertos, Yo-Yo Ma adopts the most logical course and gives us the rest of Schumann's music for cello and piano. His account of the Concerto is keenly affectionate and Sir Colin Davis gives him the most sympathetic support. Both soloist and conductor are in harmony and thoroughly attuned to the sensibility of this music. The Concerto comes from 1850, the same period as the *Rhenish* Symphony, and so is a relatively late work. Schumann called it a "Concert piece for cello with orchestral accompaniment", and is particularly successful in balancing the roles of both. The CBS recording is particularly successful with nicely rounded and mellow tone: the balance between soloist and orchestra is just about right and the various elements in the orchestral picture blend admirably. The sound suits Schumann's well-upholstered scoring. The three pieces that complete this disc are well projected and full of feeling with sensitive and well-characterized playing from Emanuel Ax. This belongs in any self-respecting Schumann collection and even though Ma exaggerates his *pianissimo* tone once or twice, his is playing of great refinement which serves this lovely music well.

NEW REVIEW

Schumann. Piano Quintet in E flat major, Op. 44[a]. Piano Quartet in E flat major, Op. 47[b]. **Beaux Arts Trio** (Isidore Cohen, vn; Bernard Greenhouse, vc; Menahem Pressler, pf) with [a]**Dorf Bettelheim** (vn); [ab]**Samuel Rhodes** (va). Philips 420 791-2PH. From 9500 065 (5/76).

58' ADD 2/88

After devoting the first ten years of his composing life to the piano (not only his own but also his beloved Clara's instrument), a self-confessed desire to spread his wings led Schumann in turn to song (1840), the orchestra (1841), and in 1842 to chamber music. And no sooner had the ink dried on his E flat major Piano Quintet in October of that year than he plunged at once into a Piano Quartet in that selfsame key. Whereas the Quintet at once established itself as a repertory work, the Quartet has too often been left to blush unseen — despite a slow movement as meltingly beautiful as any of the composer's Clara-inspired love-songs, as the Beaux Arts team so eloquently remind us here. They are not the only artists brave enough to offer the two works for reappraisal on a single CD. But they win all hearts with the little extra breathing-time, in other words feeling-time, they allow both slow movements, but also with their nimbleness in the two Scherzos and their grace and colour in the bigger flanking movements. The warmth of the remastered sound is ample compensation for any hint of its original age.

Schumann. Violin Sonatas — No. 1 in A minor, Op. 105; No. 2 in D minor, Op. 121. **Gidon Kremer** (vn); **Martha Argerich** (pf). DG 419 235-2GH.

49' DDD 1/87

The rapidity of composition of the two violin sonatas (four and six days respectively) is nowhere evident except perhaps in the vigour and enthusiasm of the music. Argerich and Kremer, both mercurial and emotionally charged performers, subtly balance the ardent Florestan and dreamily melancholic Eusebius elements of Schumann's creativity. This is even more striking in the Second Sonata, a greater work than its twin, thematically vigorous with a richness and scope that make it at once a striking as well as ideally structured work. Kremer and Argerich have established a close and exciting duo partnership and this fine recording shows what like minds can achieve in music so profoundly expressive as this.

Schumann. Piano Sonata No. 1 in F sharp minor, Op. 11. Fantasia in C major, Op. 17. **Maurizio Pollini** (pf). DG 423 134-2GH. From 2530 379 (5/74).

1h 3' ADD 5/88

These works grew from Schumann's love and longing for his future wife Clara. Both performances are superb, not least because they are so truthful to the letter of the score. By eschewing all unspecified rubato in the *Fantasia*, Pollini reminds us that the young Schumann never wrote a more finely proportioned large-scale work; this feeling for structure, coupled with exceptional emotional intensity, confirms it as one of the greatest love-poems ever written for the piano. His richly characterized account of the Sonata is refreshingly unmannered. Certainly the familiar charges of protracted patterning in the faster flanking movements are at once dispelled by his rhythmic *élan*, his crystalline texture and his ear for colour. The sound re-emerges with all its original clarity on CD.

Schumann. Kinderszenen, Op. 15. Kreisleriana, Op. 16. **Martha Argerich**
(pf). DG 410 653-2GH. From 410 653-1GH (3/84).

52' DDD 5/84

Schumann. Kinderszenen, Op. 15[a]. Faschingsschwank aus Wien, Op. 26[b].
Carnaval, Op. 9[b]. **Daniel Barenboim** (pf) DG Privilege 431 167-2GR. Item
marked [a] from 2531 079 (6/79), [b] 2531 089 (7/79).

1h 13' ADD 8/91 £

The extremely fine DG budget price CD recital of three of Schumann's finest
works finds Daniel Barenboim at the peak of his pianistic power. Recorded in
1979, Barenboim achieves both the virtuosity and interpretative prowess
necessary to fully realize the brilliant miniatures within each work. Above all it is
the strong sense of character which he imparts to Schumann's individual sound
world that makes the disc as a whole so successful. The *Kinderszenen* ("Scenes
from Childhood") contain some of Schumann's most eloquent and intimate piano
writing and Barenboim brings a wonderful delicacy and wistfulness to this music.
The more robust *Faschingsschwank aus Wien* ("Carnival Jest from Vienna") is given
a performance of great vitality, more than sufficient to hide the work's occasional
weaknesses. The crowning glory of the disc as a whole is a splendidly vibrant and
intense performance of *Carnaval* which perfectly captures the extrovert intentions
of Florestan, while equally successfully portraying the poetic side of Eusebius.
The climax, with Schumann triumphing against the Philistines, is extraordinarily
exhilarating. DG's sound is fully worthy of this magnificent example of romantic
interpretation.

An effective performance of Schumann's 13 little pieces must be spontaneous
and fresh-sounding yet sensitive to every detail. Martha Argerich fulfils these
requirements for the most part, although some may find her treatment of certain
of the *Kinderszenen* a little brisk. The *Kreisleriana,* however, is especially suited to
her natural impetuosity; its sections are capricious and tenderly song-like by
turns. Both works are marvellous examples of piano romanticism and the
recording is delightfully natural.

Schumann. Dichterliebe, Op. 48. Liederkreis, Op. 39. **Olaf Bär** (bar);
Geoffrey Parsons (pf). EMI CDC7 47397-2. From EL270364-1 (6/86).

54' DDD 9/86

The 16 songs of *Dichterliebe* ("A
poet's love") form not so much a
cycle as a sequence of *tableaux*
charting the many emotions of the
lover, from the wonder at the
beauties of nature to the stoic
resignation at love's fickleness. This
is young man's music — ardent,
vigorous and heartfelt. From Olaf
Bär we have a young man's
response — virile, firm of tone and
warmly beautiful, never hectoring
or over-insistent. This is mature
singing of surpassing elegance. In
the softer, dusky contours of the
Liederkreis Bär demonstrates his fine
legato and again impresses with his
varied expressive range, capturing
both the sense of mystery and the

Olaf Bär [photo: EMI/Brood]

bitter-sweet quality of such songs as "Zwielicht" or "Wehmut". Geoffrey Parsons offers sensitive accompaniments and the recording assists Bär's immaculate diction, though never at the piano's expense.

NEW REVIEW

Schumann. Das Paradies und die Peri, Op. 50. **Edith Wiens, Sylvia Herman** (sops); **Anne Gjevang** (contr); **Robert Gambill, Christoph Prégardien** (tens); **Hans-Peter Scheidegger** (bar) **Lausanne Pro Arte Choir; Suisse Romande Chamber Choir and Orchestra/Armin Jordan.** Erato 2292-45456-2. Text and translation included.

② 1h 36' DDD 4/90

"An oratorio — not for an oratory but for bright, happy people" was how Schumann once described *Das Paradies und die Peri*, his first venture into the choral field at the age of 33. The text (taken from Thomas Moore's *Lalla Rookh*) in fact appealed to him not only for its moral message but just as strongly for its eastern exoticism as the Peri (a fallen angel) journeys to India, Egypt and Syria in search of the "gift most dear to heaven". Neither the blood of a hero slain in freedom's cause, nor the last sigh of a maiden choosing to die alongside her plague-stricken lover, suffice. Not until she returns with the tear of a sinner moved to repentance by the sight of a child at prayer do the gates of Paradise reopen to let her in. With its stirring battle music and seductive choruses of Egyptian genii of the Nile and Syrian houris as well as such treasures as "Schlaf' nun und ruhe" for soprano and choir (which if he had written nothing else would still have made Schumann one of the immortals) the work won an immediate success before virtually disappearing from the concert repertory in the early years of this century. Now no less than three fine performances are currently available on CD. That of Armin Jordan and his Swiss forces (first to reach the catalogue and winner of the 1990 *Gramophone* Choral Award) still heads the list for its judiciously chosen tempos, its effortless continuity and its well-judged balance of voices and orchestra. Jordan, eminently stylish, never over-dramatizes or over-sentimentalizes this heartfelt music and his collaborators (with a caring cast of soloists headed by Edith Wiens in the title role) do not let him down.

Schumann. Szenen aus Goethes Faust. **Elizabeth Harwood, Jenny Hill, Jennifer Vyvyan, Felicity Palmer** (sops); **Meriel Dickinson, Margaret Cable, Pauline Stevens** (mezs); **Alfreda Hodgson** (contr); **Sir Peter Pears, John Elwes, Neil Jenkins** (tens); **John Noble, Dietrich Fischer-Dieskau, John Shirley-Quirk** (bars); **Robert Lloyd** (bass); **Wandsworth School Choir; Aldeburgh Festival Singers; English Chamber Orchestra/ Benjamin Britten.** Decca 425 705-2DM2. Notes, text and translation included. From SET567/8 (12/73).

② 1h 58' ADD 7/90

It was with Goethe's mystical closing scene, never approached by any composer before, that Schumann began his *Scenes from Faust* in 1844, when around the age of 34. The impending Goethe centenary celebrations sufficiently rekindled his life-long enthusiasm for the subject for three Gretchen-inspired scenes to follow in the summer of 1849, and three more Faust-inspired scenes the next year. But it was not until 1853 that he finally added the overture, and the work was never performed in its entirety until six years after his death. Even today it remains enough of a rarity for Benjamin Britten's revelatory revival in June 1972, to stand out as one of the most memorable of all his Aldeburgh Festival's many glories. So hats off to Decca for this CD reissue of the LP recording made at The Maltings in Snape shortly afterwards, with some, if not all, of the festival cast — incidentally a recording happily timed for first release on Britten's sixtieth birthday in November 1973. Whereas in Goethe's closing scene (Part 3) we are reminded of the lyrical Schumann, the great surprise of the work is the drama of the subsequently composed Parts 1 and 2. Not for nothing had Schumann by this time moved from a Mendelssohn-dominated Leipzig to a Wagner-stirred Dresden. The late and still sorely lamented Elizabeth Harwood is a touchingly vulnerable, pure toned Gretchen, while Fischer-Dieskau responds with quite exceptional immediacy and intensity to Faust's blinding, visionary dreams and moment of death. As Mephistopheles and Ariel, John Shirley-Quirk and Sir Peter Pears are equally outstanding for their sensitive tonal shading and shapely line. Under Britten's inspired direction all soloists are splendidly upheld by the ECO, and last but not least, by the Aldeburgh Festival Singers and Wandsworth School Choir who sing with as much flexibility and character in their various guises as anyone on the platform. The CD reproduction is excellent.

NEW REVIEW

Schumann (arr. Beecham). Manfred — incidental music, Op. 115. **Gertrud Holt** (sop); **Claire Duchesneau** (mez); **Glyndwr Davies, Ian Billington** (tens); **Niven Miller** (bar); **Laidman Browne, Jill Balcon, Raf de la Torre, David Enders** (spkrs); **BBC Chorus; Royal Philharmonic Orchestra/Sir Thomas Beecham.** Sir Thomas Beecham Trust mono BEECHAM4. From Fontana CFL1026/7 (2/59).

Ih 18' ADD 9/91 £ **q**p ▲

Schumann was haunted by Byron's autobiographically-inspired dramatic poem, *Manfred*, from a very early age. When eventually writing his incidental music for it (15 numbers and an overture) in 1848-9 he confessed to never having devoted himself to any composition before "with such lavish love and power". No one in this country has ever done more for it than Sir Thomas Beecham, who even staged it at the Theatre Royal, Drury Lane, London, way back in 1918, some 36 years before reviving it for the BBC and at the Festival Hall in performances leading to this now legendary recording. Score-followers will at once note Beecham's appropriation and scoring of two of the composer's roughly contemporaneous keyboard miniatures as additional background music for the guilt-wracked, soliloquizing Manfred. But their choice and placing is so apt that even Schumann himself might have been grateful. By present-day standards Laidman Browne might be thought a shade too overtly emotional in the title-role. But speakers (including a splendidly awesome Witch of the Alps and rustic chamois-hunter), like singers, orchestra and the magnetic Sir Thomas himself, are all at one in vividness of atmospheric evocation. Splendid remastering also plays its part in making this medium-priced disc a collector's piece.

Schumann. LIEDER. **Peter Schreier** (ten); **Christoph Eschenbach** (pf). Teldec 2292-46154-2. Texts and translations included.
Liederkreis, Op. 24. Liederkreis, Op. 39. Dichterliebe, Op. 48. Myrthen, Op. 25 — No. 1, Widmung; No. 2, Freisinn; No. 3, Der Nussbaum; No. 7, Die Lotosblume; No. 15, Aus den hebräischen Gesängen; No. 21, Was will die einsame Träne?; No. 24, Du bist wie eine Blume; No. 25, Aus den östlichen Rosen; No. 26, Zum Schluss, Lieder-Album für die Jugend, Op. 79 — No. 4, Frühlingsgruss; No. 7, Zigeunerliedchen; No. 13, Marienwürmchen; No. 26, Schneeglöckchen. Zwölf Gedichte, Op. 35 — No. 3, Wanderlied; No. 4, Erstes Grün; No. 8, Stille Liebe; No. 11, Wer machte dich so krank?; No. 12, Alte Laute. Liebesfrühling, Op. 37 — No. 1, Der Himmel hat eine Träne geweint; No. 5, Ich hab in mich gesogen; No. 9, Rose, Meer und Sonne. Fünf Lieder, Op. 40. Mein schöner Stern!, Op. 101 No. 4. Nur ein lächelnder Blick, Op. 27 No. 5. Geständnis, Op. 74 No. 7. Aufträge, Op. 77 No. 5. Meine Rose, Op. 90 No. 2. Kommen und Schneiden, Op. 90 No. 3. Lieder und Gesange,

Op. 51 — No. 1, Sehnsucht; No. 3, Ich wandre nicht. An den Mond, Op. 95
No. 2. Dein Angesicht, Op. 127 No. 2. Lehn deine Wang, Op. 142 No. 2. Der
arme Peter, Op. 53 No. 3.

③ 2h 45' DDD 6/91

This is a very fair conspectus of Schumann's genius as a Lieder composer and all
the offerings are authoritatively performed. They include recommendable
accounts of the three cycles appropriate for a male singer to tackle. Schreier with
Eschenbach, who has made a special study of the composer, make the most of
Dichterliebe and the two *Liederkreise*, identifying themselves with the various moods
and characters depicted within. Schreier's idiomatic and pointed diction and
accents allied to Eschenbach's exploratory and imaginative way with Schumann's
highly individual writing for piano would be hard to better. The remainder of
these three well-filled CDs is given over to single songs and to discerning choices
from groups other than the cycles. Here are the most telling pieces from *Myrthen*
and from the 12 Kerner settings, Op. 35. Late Schumann is acknowledged to be
a more doubtful quantity, but he could still write great songs such as the
poignant *Meine Rose* and the lovely Heine setting, *Dein Angesicht*. To these, as to
the delightful *Zigeunerliedchen*, and much else, this pair of superb performers
bring their unfailing artistry, always seeking and finding the heart of the matter.
The well-balanced recording is an unobtrusive support.

Schumann. LIEDER. **Eberhard Waechter** (bar); **Alfred Brendel** (pf).
Decca 425 949-2DM. Texts and translations included. From SXL2310 (6/62).
Dichterliebe, Op. 48. Liederkreis, Op. 24 — Schöne Wiege meiner Leiden; Mit
Myrten und Rosen. Lehn deine Wang an meine Wang, Op. 142 No. 2. Mein
Wagen rollet langsam, Op. 142 No. 4.

41' ADD 6/91

This recording of *Dichterliebe*, 31 years old and somewhat overlooked when first
issued, is one of the most satisfying ever made of the cycle, by virtue of
Waechter's total identification with the jilted man's sorrow expressed in warm,
vibrant, wholehearted, never self-conscious singing. Here the romantic thoughts,
melancholy, anger, torment, resignation, so memorably achieved in Schumann's
setting of Heine, receives an answering identification on Waechter's part.
Nowhere else in Schumann's output are the voice and piano so closely entwined
as if in a single outpouring of inspiration. Here that achievement is fully realized
through Brendel's discerning, probing execution. Always achieving rapport with
his partner, Brendel is here caught before he became the famous pianist he is
today. Anybody listening to his marvellously perceptive accounts of Schumann's
ingenious postludes would hear what a masterly pianist he already was. The extra
songs are given with just as much illumination on both sides.

NEW REVIEW

Schumann. LIEDER. **Brigitte Fassbaender** (mez); **Irwin Gage** (pf). DG
415 519-2GH.
Frauenliebe und -leben, Op. 42. Tragödie, Op. 64 No. 3. Liederkreis, Op. 24.
Abends am Strand, Op. 45 No. 3. Lehn' deine Wang, Op. 142 No. 2. Mein
Wagen rollet langsam, Op. 142 No. 2.

57' DDD 2/86

Schumann's cycle, *Frauenliebe und -leben*, depicting a woman's adoring relationship
with her perfect man, who marries her, gives her a child, then dies prematurely
can seem a trifle sentimental in the wrong hands — or voice. Fassbaender wholly
avoids any pitfall in her typically intense and individual reading, one that projects

all the subjective ardour and infatuation of the early songs, catches the contented centre of the middle ones and the inner tragedy and emptiness of the finale after the husband's death. She is ably supported by Gage, who also is perceptive in the Op. 24 *Liederkreis*. This isn't a true cycle but a collection of settings of Heine texts. Fassbaender is equally at home here in the dramatic and reflective songs, once more going to the heart of the matter through her probing approach to note and text. The three late Schumann songs are welcome bonuses on this well-filled and excellently recorded disc.

Heinrich Schütz   *German 1585-1672*

Schütz. SACRED CHORAL WORKS. **Monteverdi Choir; English Baroque Soloists; His Majesties Sagbutts and Cornetts/John Eliot Gardiner.** Archiv Produktion 423 405-2AH. Texts and translations included. Freue dich des Weibes deiner Jugend, SWV453 (with Frieder Lang, ten). Ist nicht Ephraim mein teuer Sohn, SWV40. Saul, Saul, was verfolgst du mich, SWV415. Auf dem Gebirge, SWV396 (Ashley Stafford, Michael Chance, altos). Musicalische Exequien, SWV279-81 (Lang).

51' DDD 11/88

Unlike so much of Schütz's huge output, made up largely of short motet-like settings, the *Musicalische Exequien* is a work of ample proportions; the opening "concerto in the form of a burial Mass" alone runs to more than 20 minutes of music. But it is not mere size that makes this work so striking. It is also a work of impressive solemnity. For all the exuberance trained into him through early contact with Venice in the age of the Gabrielis, in his mature works Schütz's distinguishing quality is his sobriety and austere nobility. Without question the climax of the *Musicalische Exequien* comes in the concluding "Nunc dimittis", an extraordinary setting in which a semi-chorus, half-heard from the dark recesses of the church, punctuates the main text with its own exquisite words, "Blessed are the dead which die in the Lord". Both here and in the selection of four short motets, the Monteverdi Choir sing with authority and great beauty, revealing in the process the true colours of music which in the wrong hands all too often is made to seem grey.

James Scott   *Refer to Index*   *American 1885-1938*

Alexander Scriabin   *Russian 1872-1915*

Scriabin. Piano Concerto in F sharp minor, Op. 20[a]. Prometheus, Op. 60[b]. Le poème de l'extase, Op. 54[c]. [ab]**Vladimir Ashkenazy** (pf); [b]**Ambrosian Singers;** [ab]**London Philharmonic Orchestra,** [c]**Cleveland Orchestra/Lorin Maazel.** Decca 417 252-2DH. Items marked [a] and [b] from SXL6527 (1/72), [c] SXL6905 (9/79).

1h 6' ADD 4/89

This CD gives us the essential Scriabin. The Piano Concerto has great pianistic refinement and melodic grace as well as a restraint not encountered in his later music. With *Le poème de l'extase* and *Prometheus* we are in the world of *art nouveau* and Scriabin in the grip of the mysticism (and megalomania) that consumed his later years. They are both single-movement symphonies for a huge orchestra: *Prometheus* ("The Poem of Fire") calls for quadruple wind, eight horns, five trumpets, strings, organ and chorus as well as an important part for solo piano in which Ashkenazy shines. The sensuous, luminous textures are beautifully conveyed in these performances by the LPO and the Decca engineers produce a most natural perspective and transparency of detail, as well as an appropriately overheated sound in the sensuous world of *Le poème de l'extase*.

Scriabin. ORCHESTRAL WORKS. **Philadelphia Orchestra/Riccardo Muti.** EMI CDS7 54251-2. Text and translation included.
Symphonies — No. 1 in E major, Op. 26 (with Stefania Toczyska, mez; Michael Myers, ten; Westminster Choir. From EL270270-1, 3/86); No. 2 in C minor, Op. 29 (CDC7 49859-2, 11/90); No. 3 in C minor, Op. 43, "Le divin poème" (CDC7 49115-2, 4/89). Le poème de l'extase, Op. 54 (Frank Kaderabek, tpt. CDC7 54061-2). Prometheus, Op. 60, "Le poème du feu" (Dmitri Alexeev, pf; Philadelphia Choral Arts Society, CDC7 54112-2).

③ 3h 8' DDD 7/91

Harken all hedonists! Herein are contained all Scriabin's symphonies — the *Poem of Ecstasy* and *Prometheus* couldn't possibly be referred to by anything as mundane as mere symphonic numbers — at last in performances that mingle dramatic fervour with an ability to float all those gorgeous *cantabiles*; and achieve climaxes that radiate enlightenment and, yea, cause the very earth to move. The first two Symphonies find the budding luminary still bound by the fetters of tradition (such stars in the firmament as Liszt, Tchaikovsky and Wagner exerting a strong gravitational pull). *The Divine Poem* (No. 3) shows Scriabin's universe magnific-ently broadening, using an enormous orchestra (to match the expanded mission), whilst the single movement *Poem of Ecstasy* and *Prometheus* represent the full flowering of his genius, and manage some startling musical innovations in the process. High Priest Riccardo Muti has at his command an orchestra whose opulent tones are here at their legendary best and a group of technical acolytes who see to it that the mystical waves of sound are aptly tidal.

Scriabin. Symphony No. 3 in C minor, Op. 43, "Le divin poème". Le poème de l'extase, Op. 54. **New York Philharmonic Orchestra/Giuseppe Sinopoli.** DG 427 324-2GH.

1h 10' DDD 6/89

NEW REVIEW
Scriabin. Symphony No. 3 in C minor, Op. 43, "Le divin poème".
Arensky. Silhouettes (Suite No. 2), Op. 23. **Danish National Radio Symphony Orchestra/Neeme Järvi.** Chandos CHAN8898.

1h 6' DDD 10/91

Scriabin's "Divine Poem" is a gorgeous tapestry of shot colours and sinuous arabesques, portraying languorous and ecstatic emotions, visionary states and scarcely com-municable ecstasies, but it is also a piece of music with a beginning, a middle and an end. What makes Sinopoli's account so special is his refined care for balance, both of texture and of tempo, and his choice of the *Poem of Ecstasy* as the obvious coupling. There is a fine sense, in both works, that you

Giuseppe Sinopoli   [photo: DG/Umboh

really are hearing every note that Scriabin wrote, and that foreground and background are both audible but never confused with each other. The secret seems to be a very precise control of the subtle slackenings and hastenings of tempo that are essential to Scriabin's idiom, and after one has relished all the impossible richnesses of this music it is an absorbing experience to go back for a repeat hearing to work out how Sinopoli does it. He couldn't have done it, of course, without orchestral playing of great subtlety and responsiveness and a recording that combines richness with exceptional clarity. Here he has both, and the result is both sumptuous and vital.

Much in evidence, too, on the Chandos disc is Järvi's preference for, and control of those same slackenings and hastenings, and his uncanny instinct for judging exactly how much and when they should be applied. Järvi's credo: "our business is to help the composer" finds him adopting swifter tempos than Sinopoli throughout. In the 25 minute first movement many will find this a welcome relief, and not surprisingly, it's a performance more in the Russian tradition with fervour and urgency replacing Sinopoli's, at times, almost Brucknerian grandeur. There's nothing arbitrary about Järvi's coupling: Scriabin was Arensky's pupil at the Moscow Conservatoire for theory and composition, and the teacher's wholly delightful character pieces provide the perfect antidote to the pupil's symphonic striving for the stars. Together, both works continue the post-Tchaikovskian Moscow tradition of identifying with the European mainstream. The Danish Radio Orchestra strings are occasionally overawed by the brass, but the sound is firm, airy and unfussy and offers, unusually for Chandos, very much the modern concert-hall experience.

NEW REVIEW

Scriabin. PIANO WORKS. **Roberto Szidon.** DG 20th Century Classics 431 747-2GC3. Items marked [a] from 642104 (11/69), [b] 2707 053 (2/72), [c] 2707 058 (6/72).
Fantaisie in B minor, Op. 28[c]. Piano Sonatas — No. 1 in F minor, Op. 6[c]; No. 2 in G sharp minor, Op. 19, "Sonata-fantasy"[c]; No. 3 in F sharp minor, Op. 23[c]; No. 4 in F sharp major, Op. 30[a]; No. 5, Op. 53[b]; No. 6, Op. 62[b]; No. 7, Op. 64, "White Mass"[b]; No. 8, Op. 66[b]; No. 9, Op. 68, "Black Mass"[b]; No. 10, Op. 70[b]. Sonata in E flat minor[c]. Sonate-fantaisie in G sharp minor[c].

③ 3h ADD 4/92 £ 9 P

Although these recordings date from the late 1960s and early 1970s they remain some of the finest accounts in the catalogue and should be an obligatory purchase for any Scriabin enthusiast. The earlier sonatas (Nos. 1-4) are admittedly a little uneven both in terms of recorded quality and interpretation (Nos. 2 and 4 being surprisingly lacklustre), but Szidon's spell-binding and authoritative accounts of the late sonatas (Nos. 6-10) have rarely been equalled. The late sonatas all date from Scriabin's mystical, quasi-religious, quasi-occult period; the Sixth for example is a truly terrifying work both in its technical demands and its demonical, malevolent outpourings, and it is said to have scared Scriabin so much that he never performed it publicly or even encouraged its playing — in the expert and imaginative hands of Szidon one can easily see why! Empathy with these strange and highly individual sonatas is of course a mandatory requirement for the pianist, but they also need a considerable technical armament as well if they are to be brought off successfully — Szidon, in equal measures, possesses both. Also included in this three-disc mid-price set are two rarely heard early, though by no means unimportant, sonatas dating from 1886 and 1887-89 and the equally rare *Fantaisie* in B minor, Op. 28. The latter, dating from Scriabin's ultra-romantic period, is full of unbridled virtuosity and passion of the late nineteenth-century variety and deserves to be heard far more frequently than it is. An excellent bargain.

Scriabin. PIANO WORKS. **Graham Scott.** Gamut Classics CD520.
Piano Sonatas — No. 3 in F sharp minor, Op. 23; No. 9 in F, Op. 68, "Black
Mass". Three Pieces, Op. 2 — No. 1, Etude in C sharp minor; No. 2, Prelude
in B major. Five Preludes, Op. 16. Four Preludes, Op. 22. Two Preludes,
Op. 27. Four Preludes, Op. 31. Four Preludes, Op. 33. Five Preludes, Op. 74.

1h 7' DDD 10/91

This is an exceptionally well played and carefully thought-out recital of Scriabin's
piano music. The first half of the disc is devoted to a selective survey of
Scriabin's Preludes which, when heard in chronological order as they are here,
provide an excellent opportunity for the listener to experience the astonishing
trajectory of Scriabin's musical development; from the early Chopinesque musings
of Opp. 2 and 16, and the more rhythmically complex and harmonically
adventurous Preludes of Opp. 31 and 33, through to the theosophical and quasi-
atonal utterances of the Five Preludes, Op. 74. Scriabin was a master of
economy, and some of these Preludes are tiny in the extreme ("as short as a
Sparrow's beak" as Tolstoy once remarked), yet contained within their diminutive
frames there lies a wealth of emotion and experience. Scott brings to them an
outstanding degree of intensity and concentration and his delicacy of touch and
beautifully singing *cantabile* are much to be admired. There are several fine
performances of the Ninth Sonata *Black Mass* in the catalogue at present, but
Scott's impressive and exhilarating account bears comparison with the finest; the
build up of tension before the desolation of the closing bars is delivered with
considerable *frisson*, and Scott reveals an instinctive feel for Scriabin's complex
layering of individual strands. The final item brings us full circle to the stormily
romantic Scriabin of 1897 and an impassioned and beautifully crafted account of
the Third Sonata. The sound is well balanced and engineered.

Peter Sculthorpe

Australian 1929-

Sculthorpe. PIANO WORKS.
W. Stanley (ed. Sculthorpe). Rose Bay Quadrilles. **Max Cooke, Darryl
Coote, Linda Kouvaras, Robert Chamberlain, Gudrun Beilharz, Alex
Furman, Michael Hannan, Peter Sculthorpe** (pfs). Move MD3031.
Four Little Pieces — Morning song; Sea chant; Little serenade; Left Bank waltz
(1979). Callabonna. Night Pieces — Snow; Moon; Flowers; Night; Stars.
Mountains. Djilile. Nocturnal. Sonatina. Koto I. Koto II. Landscape. Sea chant
(trans pf.) Left Bank waltz (1958).

1h 15' ADD/DDD 3/92

Peter Sculthorpe, now in his early sixties, is Australia's leading composer. His
music gives expression to aspects of Australia's landscape and history and in many
ways it feels as different from that of European composers as many American
composers do. There's a continental sense of space, an awareness of aboriginal
culture and myth and a commitment to preserving the environment. This
collection of piano pieces is an enjoyable source-book drawn from four decades
of the composer's life, starting when he was a student at Melbourne University.
It includes Sculthorpe's own playing of his charming *Left Bank waltz* plus a team
of seven other pianists to cope with the rest, including piano duets. Two pieces
called *Koto* emphasize the oriental component in Sculthorpe — Japan is much
closer than Europe — and his use of the piano played directly on the strings is
poetic and sensitive. There's a strong atmosphere, too, in each of the *Night
Pieces*. Sculthorpe's arrangement of the *Rose Bay Quadrilles* by the mid-nineteenth

century composer William Stanley adds zest to the collection. Overall the
recorded quality is variable but this Sculthorpe retrospective is an ideal
introduction to his personality and his larger works now on CD.

Dmitry Shostakovich   *Russian 1906-1975*

Shostakovich. Cello Concertos — No. 1 in E flat major, Op. 107; No. 2,
Op. 126. **Heinrich Schiff** (vc); **Bavarian Radio Symphony Orchestra/
Maxim Shostakovich.** Philips 412 526-2PH. From 412 526-1PH (8/85).

Ih 1' DDD 10/85

These two concertos make an obvious and useful 'coupling' for they are both
vintage Shostakovich. Indeed, the First occupies a commanding position in the
post-war repertory and is probably the most often-heard modern cello concerto.
If the Second Concerto has not established itself in the repertory to anywhere
near the same extent, the reason may be that it offers fewer overt opportunities
for display. It is a work of grave beauty, inward in feeling and spare in its
textures. It is pensive, intimate and withdrawn and on first encounter its ideas
seem fugitive and shadowy, though the sonorities have a characteristic asperity.
The recording's balance is generally excellent: very natural yet very clear, and
there is quite outstanding definition and realism.

Shostakovich. Concerto in C minor for piano, trumpet and strings, Op. 35ᵃ.
Piano Concerto No. 2 in F major, Op. 102. The Unforgettable Year 1919, Op.
89 — The assault on beautiful Gorky. **Dmitri Alexeev** (pf); ᵃ**Philip Jones**
(tpt); **English Chamber Orchestra/Jerzy Maksymiuk.** Classics for Pleasure
CD-CFP4547. From CFP414416-1 (11/83).

48' DDD 1/89

Shostakovich's Piano Concertos were written under very different circumstances,
yet together they contain some of the composer's most cheerful and enlivening
music. The First, with its wealth of perky, memorable tunes, has the addition of
a brilliantly-conceived solo trumpet part (delightfully done here by Philip Jones)
that also contributes to the work's characteristic stamp. The Second Concerto
was written not long after Shostakovich had released a number of the intense
works he had concealed during the depths of the Stalin era. It came as a sharp
contrast, reflecting as it did the optimism and sense of freedom that followed the
death of the Russian dictator. The beauty of the slow movement is ideally
balanced by the vigour of the first, and the madcap high spirits of the last. The
poignant movement for piano and orchestra from the Suite from the 1951 film
The Unforgettable Year 1919, "The assault on beautiful Gorky", provides an
excellent addition to this disc of perceptive and zestful performances by Alexeev.
He is most capably supported by the ECO under Maksymiuk, and the engineers
have done them proud with a recording of great clarity and finesse. A joyous
issue.

Shostakovich. Violin Concertos — No. 1 in A minor, Op. 99; No. 2 in C
sharp minor, Op. 129. **Lydia Mordkovitch** (vn); **Scottish National
Orchestra/Neeme Järvi.** Chandos CHAN8820.

Ih 9' DDD 4/90

These two heartfelt violin concertos are fine examples of Shostakovich's genius. It
is the First, composed in 1948 for David Oistrakh, that is the better known and

Lydia Mordkovitch   *[photo: Chandos/Curzon]*

some people think it the finer work; but the Second was written for the same violinist two decades later and Lydia Mordkovitch, who studied with him in Moscow, reveals its sparer lines no less successfully than the big romantic gestures of No. 1. Her tone has a dark warmth that suits the soliloquizing lyrical music of these pieces admirably, but she is also not afraid to be uncompromisingly rough and tough (more so than Oistrakh himself) in the delivery of the scherzo and finale of the First Concerto as well as its great cadenza. Neeme Järvi is himself a committed performer of the Shostakovich symphonies who well understands the composer's style, and the Scottish National Orchestra sounds as Russian as anyone could wish, even to the tone of its brass section, which has the fine principal horn that both concertos require. The recording of the solo violin is closer than one would hear in the concert hall — Glasgow's City Hall in this case — and at times (for example, the cadenza of the First Concerto) positively tactile and percussive in effect, but with playing such as this few will complain. The orchestral sound is rich in the Chandos tradition and if it occasionally almost overwhelms the ear that is maybe what the composer intended. An exciting disc.

NEW REVIEW

Shostakovich. Symphonies — No. 1 in F minor, Op. 10; No. 7 in C major, Op. 60, "Leningrad". **Chicago Symphony Orchestra/Leonard Bernstein.** DG 427 632-2GH2. Recorded at performances in Chicago Hall, Chicago in June 1988.

②   2h   DDD   1/90

Both these symphonies caused an immediate sensation. The First, the 19-year-old composer's graduation piece from the then Leningrad Conservatory in 1926, may be indebted to Stravinsky, Prokofiev, Tchaikovsky and even Scriabin. But viewed with hindsight of the later symphonies, it rarely sounds like anything other than pure Shostakovich. Bernstein relishes its eagerness, wit and nervous intensity. Predictably he takes his time for expressive pointing, and some may feel that this disrupts the work's sense of direction, and with it, the underlying unease. But it is both those qualities that are so remarkably maintained here in the *Leningrad* Symphony. Composed in haste as the Nazis sieged and bombarded the city in 1941, the stitches and seams are more apparent than usual; though Michael Oliver in his original *Gramophone* review commented that in this performance "the Symphony sounds most convincingly like a symphony, and one needing no programme to justify it". Added to which, and no disrespect is intended by this observation, the work's epic and cinematic manner has surely never been more fully and powerfully realized. These are live recordings, with occasional noise from the audience (and the conductor), but the Chicago Orchestra has rarely sounded more polished or committed under any conditions. A word of caution: set your volume control carefully at the Symphony's start; it is scored for six of both trumpets and trombones, and in the first movement's notorious "invasion" episode, no other recording has reproduced them so clearly, and to such devastating effect.

NEW REVIEW

Shostakovich. Symphonies[a] — No. 2 in B major, Op. 14, "To October"; No. 3 in E flat major, Op. 20, "The first of May". The Age of Gold — suite, Op. 22*a*[b]. **London Philharmonic [a]Choir and Orchestra/Bernard Haitink.** Decca 421 131-2DH. Texts and translations included. Items marked [a] from SXDL7535 (7/82), [b] D213D2 (11/80).

> 1h 12'   DDD   6/88

Slamming the door noisily on the First Symphony, which he quickly came to regard as too traditional, Shostakovich, in his early twenties, embarked on two symphonies which married "abstract experimentalism" (his own term) with choral finales whose revolutionary poems demanded simple and direct settings (the two styles distinctly unhappy bedfellows). But those looking for symphonic continuity and coherence need read no further. For this is music that daringly turns conventions upside down and inside out. His innate lyricism occasionally allows us to come up for air in between the wildly over the top gestural rhetoric. So why include this disc in the *Guide*? Simply because in both works the untamed creative energy is more often exhilarating than exhausting, but also, particularly in the Third, much of the language of the later symphonies is explicitly foreshadowed. With the prankster's antics of *The Age of Gold* Suite providing a welcome contrast, Haitink and the LPO, undaunted by any of the challenges, and one of Decca's most spectacular early digital recordings, it is a disc that does more than merely fill a gap in your Shostakovich collection.

Shostakovich. Symphony No. 4 in C minor, Op. 43. **Scottish National Orchestra/Neeme Järvi.** Chandos CHAN8640.

> 1h 1'   DDD   12/89

Shostakovich withdrew the Fourth Symphony before its first performance and one can readily see why: Stalin would have loathed it. It is a work of extraordinary bitterness and anger, curdled with dissonance, raucous derision and eerie unease, the very model of what a Soviet symphony should not be, but at the same time the teeming cauldron from which much of the troubling ambiguity of Shostakovich's later style was cast. It needs a performance that takes risks, not least of setting the listener's teeth on edge and of terrifying him out of his wits. Järvi is prepared to allow his orchestra to yell at times to allow the occasional ugly, poisoned sound in a work that boils with discontent but also with sheer unreleased creative energy. No one who admires the Fifth Symphony should be without a recording of the Fourth that presents its towering frustration and disquiet at full strength. Järvi does so more successfully than any other conductor. Both his orchestra and the recording engineers hang on like grim death. The effect can only be described as magnificently appalling.

Shostakovich. Symphony No. 5 in D minor, Op. 47. Ballet Suite No. 5, Op. 27*a*. **Scottish National Orchestra/Neeme Järvi.** Chandos CHAN8650.

> 1h 16'   DDD   4/90   (B)

Shostakovich. Symphony No. 5 in D minor, Op. 47[a]. Cello Concerto No. 1 in E flat major, Op. 107[b]. [a]**New York Philharmonic Orchestra/Leonard**

Bernstein; [b]**Yo-Yo Ma** (vc); [b]**Philadelphia Orchestra/Eugene Ormandy.**
CBS Maestro CD44903. Item marked [a] from 35854 (12/80), [b] 37840 (3/84).

Ih I7' DDD 4/90 £ Ⓑ

Shostakovich. Symphony No. 5 in D minor, Op. 47. Five Fragments, Op. 42.
Royal Philharmonic Orchestra/Vladimir Ashkenazy. Decca 421 120-
2DH.

56' DDD 6/88 Ⓑ

NEW REVIEW

Shostakovich. Symphonies — No. 5 in D minor, Op. 47; No. 9 in E flat
major, Op. 70. **USSR Ministry of Culture State Symphony Orchestra/
Gennadi Rozhdestvensky.** Olympia OCD113.

Ih I3' DDD 5/89 Ⓑ

NEW REVIEW

Shostakovich. Symphony No. 5 in D minor, Op. 47. **Hallé Orchestra/
Stanislav Skrowaczewski.** Pickwick IMP Classics PCD940.

48' DDD 8/91 Ⓑ

There are more Shostakovich Fifths than you can shake a stick at in the CD
catalogue at present, and several of them are very good. Järvi's makes perhaps
the safest recommendation of them all: it has a generous coupling (which cannot
be said of many of its rivals), it has no drawbacks (save, for some tastes, a slight
touch of heart-on-sleeve in the slow movement) and a number of distinct
advantages. A profound seriousness, for one thing, and an absolute sureness about
the nature of the finale, which many conductors feel the need to exaggerate,
either as brassy optimism or as bitter irony. Järvi takes it perfectly straight,
denying neither option, and the progression from slow movement (the overtness
of its emotion finely justified) to finale seems more natural, less of a jolt than
usual. The SNO cannot rival the sheer massiveness of sound of some of the
continental orchestras who have recorded this work, but while listening one
hardly notices the lack, so urgent and polished is their playing. A very natural
and wide-ranging recording, too, and the lengthy Suite (eight movements from
Shostakovich's early ballet *The Bolt*, forming an exuberantly entertaining essay on
the various modes that his sense of humour could take) makes much more than a
mere fill-up.

Bernstein's overall approach to the Fifth is unashamedly warm and romantic,
and is certainly one of the most weighty and impressive performances in the
catalogue. Drama and tension are superbly sustained throughout the first
movement, and it comes as no surprise to find the Mahlerian qualities of the
work strongly projected both here and in the following *Allegretto*. The hushed and
expressive playing from the NYPO strings at the beginning of the *Largo* is quite
extraordinary, and Bernstein conveys the tragic intensity and introspective mood
of this movement with consummate skill. The finale, avoiding any trace of irony
or sarcasm, brings the Symphony to a triumphant and optimistic conclusion. The
recording conveys all the electricity and presence of a live performance, while
also having the clarity and precision one normally only finds in a studio
recording. Yo-Yo Ma's intense, compelling account of the First Cello Concerto is
perhaps second only to Rostropovich's world première recording. Technically Ma
is without flaw in this work. The outer movements are full of fire and rhythmic
vitality, and in the slow movement and following cadenza he plays with great
lyrical beauty and intensity. The recording is warm and well balanced. A
remarkable bargain.

The collaboration of a Russian-born conductor and a Western orchestra works
splendidly on the Decca issue. There have been more spectacular orchestral
displays and more spectacular recording qualities, but rarely a more convincing
alliance of idiomatic detail and structural insight. If one movement has to be

singled out let it be the *Largo*, often regarded as the emotional core of the work and interpreted here with intense inwardness and no trace of artificiality. Best results will be obtained at a slightly higher volume setting than usual, and even then glamorous orchestral sounds should not be expected — they're not what this music is about. The *Five Fragments* contain some of Shostakovich's quirkiest invention and are a rare and welcome bonus to a fine disc.

Some of Rozhdestvensky's interpretations in his Shostakovich cycle on Olympia are quirky in the extreme. In the Fifth Symphony he is at his most restrained, and the result is one of the finest accounts on CD of this much-recorded work. Listening to it you wonder why so many conductors fail to achieve a natural flow, and why those who do achieve it often sound bland. Rozhdestvensky gives us just about the best of both worlds, as he does in the Ninth Symphony — a kind of not-the-Ninth-Symphony, written in 1945 in a spirit of deliberate non-celebration and full of black humour and evasiveness. Neither playing nor recording are in the highest class, but the communicative instincts are in the right place throughout and the coupling is a generous one.

Skrowaczewski presents yet another valid alternative for those who like their Shostakovich sane and explicit. A consummate technician, his period with the Hallé Orchestra was often underrated by the critics. His No. 5 may be less highly charged than Ashkenazy's, but it is arguably better played, more startlingly immediate as sound. The luminous recording was made in the unlikely venue of Huddersfield Town Hall. Skrowaczewski is more faithful to the letter of the score than most of his rivals. Hence the first movements takes time to catch fire, and the final *Allegro non troppo* is launched at a comparatively deliberate pace — just what Shostakovich asks for in the score. A performance to live with.

Shostakovich. Symphonies — No. 6 in B minor, Op. 54; No. 11 in G minor, Op. 103, "The year 1905"[a]. Overture on Russian and Kirghiz Folk Themes, Op. 115[b]. **Concertgebouw Orchestra, Amsterdam/Bernard Haitink.** Decca 411 939-2DH2. Item marked [a] from 411 939-1DH2 (6/85), [b] SXDL7577 (6/83).

② 1h 45' DDD 8/85

Shostakovich's Sixth and Eleventh Symphonies are both real challenges to the interpreter. The Sixth consists of a sombrely noble but deeply uneasy slow movement enigmatically followed by two scherzos but no apparent finale. The Eleventh, a sequence of bold, poster-like images of the abortive 1905 uprising in Russia, makes extensive use of a number of tunes that are not Shostakovich's own (revolutionary songs of the period, mostly) and are not wholly suited to a symphonic structure on such a scale. The orchestral playing throughout both works is of the utmost splendour: the darkly glittering sonorities of the Sixth Symphony finely judged, the exhausting demands of its two fast movements heroically met; the sheer power and attack of the Eleventh, of the strings especially, rendered with precision as well as weight. The recording is very clean, natural and spacious.

NEW REVIEW

Shostakovich. Symphony No. 8 in C minor, Op. 65. **Leningrad Philharmonic Orchestra/Evgeni Mravinsky.** Philips 422 442-2PH. Recorded at a performance in Leningrad in February 1982.

1h ADD 6/89

Dedicated to Mravinsky, the Eighth Symphony, written in 1943, two years after the *Leningrad*, offers a wiser, more bitterly disillusioned Shostakovich. The heroic peroration of the Seventh's finale is here replaced by numbed whimsy and eventual uneasy calm. Whether the grim visions that the journey there depicts

Evgeni Mravinsky

are wartime or peacetime ones, rarely can a performance have presented them with more lacerating force. The solo cor anglais, after the first movement's central climax, plays as if his very life depended on his lament being heard at the other side of the world. Speeds are generally faster than we are used to from western interpreters, and the standard of playing, given the risks taken, and that this is a one-off live performance, defies criticism. Only a restricted dynamic range mars an excellent piece of engineering. The Leningrad audience, clearly immobilized, maintain an awed silence.

NEW REVIEW

Shostakovich. Symphony No. 10 in E minor, Op. 93. **Berlin Philharmonic Orchestra/Herbert von Karajan.** DG Galleria 429 716-2GGA. From SLPM139020 (1/69).

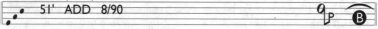

Stalin died on 5 March 1953, the same day as Prokofiev. In the summer of that year Shostakovich produced a symphony which can be taken as his own return to life after the dark night of dictatorship — the last two movements included, for the first time in his output, his personal DSCH signature (the notes D, E flat, C, B natural, in the German spelling). In the West the Tenth Symphony is now widely regarded as the finest of the cycle of 15, not just for its sheer depth of personal feeling, but because it finds the purest and subtlest musical representation of that feeling. Perhaps this is why it is less dependent than some of Shostakovich's major works on a conductor steeped in the Russian idiom. Karajan's profound grasp of the overall drama unites with a superb instinct for atmosphere and mood to put the earlier of his two recordings into a class of its own. It is a performance of compelling integrity and sweep, with an almost palpable sense of what is at stake emotionally. The recording sounds a little bass-heavy in this digital remastering but is still far more realistic than Karajan's 1982 remake.

NEW REVIEW

Shostakovich. Symphony No. 13, "Babi Yar". **Marius Rintzler** (bass); male voices of the **Concertgebouw Orchestra Choir; Concertgebouw Orchestra/Bernard Haitink.** Decca 417 261-2DH. Notes, texts and translations included.

In 1962 Shostakovich, setting Yevtushenko's poetry, made a bold public statement about concerns close to his heart. One of his most unambiguous works, the symphony's five movements are powerful, impassioned statements on anti-semitism, the indestructible power of humour, Russian women "who have endured everything", fears of the informer, and finally, artistic integrity. With its direct and simple (though never plain) appeal, and the texts divided between a solo bass and a unison male chorus, it is Shostakovich at his most Mussorgskian. It is a pity that Marius Rintzler isn't as passionate in manner as he is sonorous of tone, but worries that the Dutch chorus may lack the range and richness of

Russian men, or that the woodwinds' humour may not be sharp-edged enough are confounded in Haitink's vividly characterized account. Decca, superseding their own previous triumphs in the Concertgebouw, produce spectacularly ample and spacious sound; full and firm in the bass (so many of the themes are for cellos and basses) and able to resolve the massive tuttis as clearly and coherently as the work's frequent chamber-like textures.

NEW REVIEW

Shostakovich. Symphony No. 14[a]. Six Poems of Marina Tsvetayeva[b]. [a]**Julia Varády** (sop); [b]**Ortrun Wenkel** (contr); [a]**Dietrich Fischer-Dieskau** (bar); **Concertgebouw Orchestra/Bernard Haitink.** Decca 417 514-2DH. Texts and translations included. Item marked [a] from SXDL7532 (1/82), [b] 414 410-1DH2 (5/86).

Ih I3' DDD 3/87

"I'll follow my career in such a way that I'm not following it" sings the soloist at the end of the Thirteenth Symphony, followed by the exquisitely private sound of solo violin and viola. And so it was to be. There were no more public statements. The Fourteenth is not a symphony at all, but a song cycle on the theme of Death, for a soprano and bass with a small complement of strings and light percussion; and the Fifteenth is a series of unresolved riddles. This is a unique and logical coupling: the poems of the symphony are sung here in the original languages (a version which had the composer's approval); and both the Symphony and the Tsvetayeva cycle are essentially private expressions. The expressions, though, of scorn, bitterness and, in the symphony, violence, are as potent as ever, the more so for their needle-sharp presentation by a small ensemble. There are one or two moments in the symphony where Haitink does not live dangerously enough and, arguably, the recording over-projects Fischer-Dieskau and Varády, but this is the most consistently satisfying version currently available. As ever, the Concertgebouw acoustic supplies atmosphere in abundance without ever impeding clarity.

NEW REVIEW

Shostakovich. Symphony No. 15 in A major[a]. From Jewish Poetry, Op. 79[b]. [b]**Elisabeth Söderström** (sop); [b]**Ortrun Wenkel** (contr); [b]**Ryszard Karcykowski** (ten); [a]**London Philharmonic Orchestra,** [b]**Concertgebouw Orchestra/Bernard Haitink.** Decca 417 581-2DH. Notes, text and translation included. Item marked [a] from SXL6906 (3/79), [b] 414 410-1DH2 (5/86).

Ih I3' AAD 4/87

By the end of the 1960s Shostakovich was an ill and troubled man and it seemed that his death-haunted Fourteenth Symphony of 1969 would be his last. Instead, in 1971 he produced this surprising successor, with a definite key of A major but also enigmatic quotations from Rossini's *William Tell* Overture and Wagner's *Ring* cycle besides several from his own music and his favourite DSCH (D, E flat, C, B) motto. The Rossini was bouncy, and the Wagner profoundly gloomy — but what did it all mean? Later the composer offered some clues, for example saying that the first movement represents a toyshop at night with the toys coming to life, but the suspicion remains that the work has other darker secrets. Bernard Haitink understands this Russian world in which the childishly playful and the grimly grotesque co-exist, and his Dutch orchestra play the music as to the manner born, with fine work from the important percussion section of 12 instruments besides timpani which include vibraphone and bells. The other work is earlier: it was written in 1948 after Shostakovich found a book of Jewish poetry and felt that a vocal cycle could help combat the increasing anti-Semitism that he saw around him. It was not, in fact, performed until 1955, during the cultural thaw that came after Stalin's death, and was orchestrated later. "Jews were tormented for so long that they express despair in dance music", said the composer, but though this big cycle hardly makes for cosy listening it has a fine semitic character and the performance and recording are splendid.

Shostakovich (arr. Atovm'yan). The gadfly — suite, Op. 97*a*. **USSR Cinema Symphony Orchestra/Emin Khachaturian.** Classics for Pleasure CD-CFP4463. From EMI ASD3309 (2/77).

> 42' ADD 4/89 £

This film score belongs to the 1950s, a period when the composer produced some of his finest and most characteristic work, and if this is hardly profound or very personal Shostakovich it is still often striking, usually charming and unmistakably his. In a way the bargain price goes with the music: this is emphatically not top-drawer Shostakovich but it is worth having and the 1962 Melodiya recording has come up well in the present digital remastering. Sample No. 6 in the Suite, the entertaining "Galop", to see how the composer could be absolutely simple yet effective; sample the following "Introduction into the Dance" to hear how he could turn conventional phrases into something genuinely touching. The Suite shows how much music from the film was worth preserving and it has been well arranged by Lev Atovm'yan from the original score. The USSR Cinema Symphony Orchestra plays it as to the manner born.

Shostakovich. String Quartets — No. 1 in C major, Op. 49; No. 3 in F major, Op. 73; No. 4 in D major, Op. 83. **Brodsky Quartet** (Michael Thomas, Ian Belton, vns; Paul Cassidy, va; Jacqueline Thomas, vc). Teldec 2292-46009-2.

> 1h 12' DDD 6/90

The young Brodsky Quartet are in the course of issuing a complete cycle of Shostakovich's string quartets and on this evidence it should be well worth collecting. The First, Third and Fourth Quartets make a particularly absorbing coupling, with hinted depths and plans for further exploration clearly audible beneath the acknowledgements to quartet tradition in the First (which also has a touch of very likeable open-eyed naïvety to it), an enormous step forward to the grandeur of the Third's impassioned slow movement and a path forward firmly indicated by the troubled ambiguities and poignancies of the Fourth. The Brodsky will have the range for the complete cycle, there seems no doubt of that; already there is a fine balance between bigness of gesture and an expressive but strong lyricism. They are especially good at pacing and concentration over a long span, too, and they leap the technical hurdles with ease. A very clean and direct but rather close recording; but the sense of being amidst such responsive players, almost watching their intentness, has its own rewards.

Shostakovich. String Quartet No. 8 in C minor, Op. 110.
Tippett. String Quartet No. 3. **Duke Quartet** (Louise Fuller, Martin Smith, vns; John Metcalfe, va; Ivan McCready, vc). Factory Classical FACD246.

> 51' DDD 1/90

Shostakovich's Eighth is his most 'public' quartet, a sustained and bitter outcry at oppression and inhumanity. Its official dedication is "in memory of the victims of fascism and war"; but its copious self-quotations and its incessant use of the composer's musical monogram DSCH (D, E flat, C, B in German notation) makes it clear that the work is 'about' far more than the aftermath of the Second World

War. Tippett's Third, by contrast, is in a sense his most private quartet, a prolonged and at times visionary wrestling with the shade of Beethoven, containing audacious formal experiments. By choosing for their recording début two of the most technically and expressively demanding works in the repertory, the young Duke Quartet certainly nailed their colours to the mast. They are powerfully communicative players, with what seems like a burning desire to convey the protesting grief of the Shostakovich and the sometimes inward, sometimes ecstatic musings of the Tippett. They have the virtuoso technique and the ample tone to achieve this. No less important, they have a very firm sense of the music's impulse; whether the movement is fast or slow, there is a strong feeling of forward impetus and clearly perceived destination. The recording, appropriately enough, brings these passionately urgent readings very close to the listener.

Shostakovich. Piano Quintet in G minor, Op. 57[a]. String Quartets — No. 7 in F sharp minor, Op. 108; No. 8 in C minor, Op. 110. [a]**Sviatoslav Richter** (pf); **Borodin Quartet** (Mikhail Kopelman, Andrei Abramenkov, vns; Dmitri Shebalin, va; Valentin Berlinsky, vc). EMI CDC7 47507-2. From EL270338-1 (11/85).

1h 10' ADD 10/87

The Seventh and Eighth Quartets are separated by only one opus number and both works inhabit a dark and sombre sound world. The Seventh is dedicated to the memory of his first wife, Nina, who died in 1954 and is one of his shortest and most concentrated quartets. The Eighth Quartet provides a perfect introduction to Shostakovich's music. It is very much an autobiographical work. The Piano Quintet is almost symphonic in its proportions, lasting some 35 minutes and has been popular with audiences ever since its first performance in 1940. Much of its popularity stems from Shostakovich's highly memorable material, particularly in the boisterous and genial Scherzo and finale movements. The Borodin Quartet play with great authority and conviction and in the Seventh Quartet there is a fine sense of poetry and intimacy. Richter's performance of the Piano Quintet matches the grandeur of the work, with playing that has tremendous power and strength. The recording, taken from a live performance, is rather dry with a slightly hard piano sound, but this does little to distract from so commanding a performance as this. The earlier studio recordings of the string quartets are well recorded. An excellent introduction to the chamber music of Shostakovich.

NEW REVIEW

Shostakovich. Piano Trio No. 1 in C minor, Op. 8.
Tchaikovsky. Piano Trio in A minor, Op. 50. **Chung Trio** (Kyung-Wha Chung, vn; Myung-Wha Chung, vc; Myung-Whun Chung, pf). EMI CDC7 49865-2.

1h DDD 3/90

Before Shostakovich's great cycle of 15 string quartets, begun in the late 1930s, Russian chamber music lagged well behind its symphonic and operatic traditions. But Tchaikovsky's A minor Piano Trio, composed in 1881-82 in memory of the pianist-pedagogue Nikolai Rubinstein, comes from somewhere near the top drawer of his inspiration. It falls into two large movements and needs all the exuberance and variety the Chung Trio bring to it. They are among the few ensembles to play the work without cuts, and amongst the even fewer who can justify doing so. To clinch the exceptional value of the disc they include the rarely heard single-movement Trio, Op. 8 by the teenage Shostakovich — a heartfelt work composed at the time of his first amorous attachment. Recording quality is on the mellow side of ideal but, more importantly, the balance between the instruments is excellent.

Shostakovich. 24 Preludes and Fugues, Op. 87. **Tatyana Nikolaieva** (pf). Hyperion CDA66441/3.

③ 2h 46' DDD 3/91 ⑨ P ❓

Even if you didn't know that Shostakovich had written his 24 Preludes and Fugues specially for Tatyana Nikolaieva it would be difficult not to sense the unique authority. The playing isn't without the odd small blemish here and there (memory lapses?) and the reverberant acoustic adds a sustaining pedal effect of its own in one or two places, but for playing of such strength, character and insight one would willingly put up with far worse. Inevitably, particular pieces linger in

the memory — the impassioned F sharp minor Fugue, the dancing A major Prelude or the haunted stillness of the B flat minor Fugue — but the most impressive aspect of Nikolaieva's interpretation is the way she communicates her belief that these 24 small pieces add up to a complete musical experience — after this it's very difficult to disagree: the monumental D minor Fugue really does feel like the final stage in a long and fascinatingly varied process. If you still think that Shostakovich's contribution to piano literature is relatively insignificant, try this.

Tatyana Nikolaieva   *[photo: Hyperion/Schillinger*

Jean Sibelius
Finnish 1865-1957

Sibelius. Violin Concerto in D major, Op. 47 (original 1903-04 version and final 1905 version). **Leonidas Kavakos** (vn); **Lahti Symphony Orchestra/ Osmo Vänskä.** BIS CD500.

1h 15' DDD 4/91 ⑨ P ⑨ S ❓

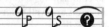

In the 1950s the BBC Third Programme regularly broadcast a series called "Birth of an opera" which traced the evolution of an operatic masterpiece from gestation to first performance. This disc could almost be called "Birth of a Concerto", for it offers Sibelius's first thoughts alongside the final version of the Violin Concerto. After its unsuccessful first performance in Helsinki in 1904, the composer decided to overhaul it and putting the two versions alongside each other is an absorbing experience. One is first brought up with a start by an incisive figure just over a minute into the proceedings after which the orchestra does all sorts of 'unexpected' things! In the unaccompanied cadenza 21 bars later there is some rhythmic support while to the next idea on cellos and bassoon (figure 2), the soloist contributes decoration. And then at seven bars before figure 3 a delightful new idea appears which almost looks forward to the light colourings of the later *Humoresques*. Although it is a great pity that it had to go, there is no doubt that the structural coherence of the movement gains by its loss both here and on its reappearance. It is the ability to sacrifice good ideas in the interest of structural coherence that is the hallmark of a good composer. The fewest changes are in the slow movement which remains at the same length. As in the case of the Fifth Symphony where the revision is far more extensive than it is here the finished work tells us a great deal about the quality of Sibelius's artistic judgment, and that, of course, is what makes him such a great composer. This disc offers an invaluable insight into the workings of his mind, and even in its own right, the 1904 version has many incidental beauties to delight us. Leonidas Kavakos and the Lahti Orchestra play splendidly throughout and the familiar concerto which was struggling to get out of the 1903-04 version emerges equally safely in their hands.

Sibelius. ORCHESTRAL WORKS. **Berlin Philharmonic Orchestra/ Herbert von Karajan.** DG 413 755-2GH. From 413 755-1GH (10/84). Finlandia, Op. 26. Legends, Op. 22 — No. 2, The swan of Tuonela. Kuolema, Op. 44 — Valse triste. Tapiola, Op. 112.

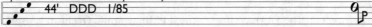

Sibelius. ORCHESTRAL WORKS. **Philharmonia Orchestra/Vladimir Ashkenazy.** Decca Ovation 417 762-2DM. From 417 378-1DM5. Finlandia, Op. 26. Karelia Suite, Op. 11. Tapiola, Op. 112. En Saga, Op. 9.

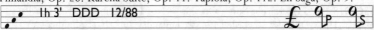

Karajan was a lifelong Sibelian and his CD brings us what is arguably his greatest account of *Tapiola*, that extraordinary vision of the primaeval Northern forests — though to be frank you can't go far wrong with any of his performances of it! But never has it sounded more mysterious or its dreams more savage; never have the wood-sprites "weaving their magic secrets" come more vividly to life and never has the build-up to the storm ever struck a more chilling note of terror. Once in his later years Sibelius spoke of Karajan having a very special feeling for his music and listening to his account of *The swan* you can see why! He captures its powerful, brooding atmosphere to perfection and the remaining two pieces, *Valse triste* and *Finlandia* are hardly less impressive. At 44 minutes playing-time this may seem short measure, but if it is short on quantity, it is long on quality and that applies to the recording too.

More than 30 years separate *En Saga* and *Tapiola*, yet both works are quintessential Sibelius. The latter is often praised for the way Sibelius avoided 'exotic' instruments, preferring instead to draw new and inhuman sounds from the more standard ones; and the former is, in many ways, just as striking in the way Sibelius's orchestration evokes wind, strange lights, vast expanses and solitude. Both works suggest some dream-like journey; *En Saga* non-specific though derived from Nordic legend; *Tapiola* more of an airborne nightmare in, above and around the mighty giants of the Northern forests inhabited by the Green Man of the Kalevala, the forest god Tapio (the final amen of slow, bright major chords brings a blessed release!). Ashkenazy's judgement of long term pacing is very acute; the silences and shadows are as potent here as the wildest hurricane. And Decca's sound allows you to visualize both the wood and the trees: every detail of Sibelius's sound world is caught with uncanny presence, yet the overall orchestral image is coherent and natural. In addition, his *Finlandia* boasts some of the most vibrant and powerful brass sounds on disc.

Sibelius. ORCHESTRAL WORKS. **Gothenburg Symphony Orchestra/ Neeme Järvi.** BIS CD312. Pohjola's daughter, Op. 49. Rakastava, Op. 14. Tapiola, Op. 112. Andante lirico.

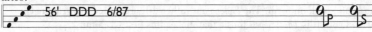

This disc offers two of Sibelius's most powerful and concentrated symphonic poems together with one of his most affecting works, *Rakastava* for strings, timpani and triangle. *Tapiola* is his last major work, a terrifying evocation of the vast forests of the North and the spirits that dwell within them. *Pohjola's daughter* is one of the greatest examples of the genre, having all the narrative power of a Strauss tone poem and yet the concentration and organic cohesion of a symphonic movement. *Rakastava* began life as a work for unaccompanied male voices in 1894 but Sibelius reworked it at about the time of the Fourth Symphony (1911) to striking effect. The *Andante lirico*, alternatively known as the Impromptu for string orchestra, is a rarity from 1893 (the year after the *Kullervo* Symphony and before *The Swan of Tuonela*), which draw for its material on the last two of the Impromptus, Op. 5. Persuasive and splendidly recorded performances by the Gothenburg Orchestra under Neeme Järvi.

Sibelius. ORCHESTRAL WORKS. [a]**Royal Philharmonic Orchestra;** [b]**BBC Symphony Orchestra;** [c]**London Philharmonic Orchestra/Sir Thomas Beecham.** EMI Beecham Edition mono CDM7 63397-2.
The Tempest — incidental music, Op. 109 (from Philips ABR4045, 12/55)[a]. Scènes historiques: Op. 25 — No. 3, Festivo; Op. 66 (both from Columbia 33C1018, 11/53)[a]. Karelia Suite, Op. 11 — No. 1, Intermezzo; No. 3, Alla marcia (HMV DB6248. Recorded 1945)[b]. Finlandia, Op. 26 (Columbia LX704, 4/38)[c].

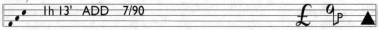
1h 13' ADD 7/90 £ 9 p ▲

Sibelius. ORCHESTRAL WORKS. **Royal Philharmonic Orchestra/Sir Thomas Beecham.** EMI Beecham Edition CDM7 63400-2.
Pelléas et Mélisande — incidental music, Op. 46. The Oceanides, Op. 73. Symphony No. 7 in C major, Op. 105 (all from HMV ASD468, 7/62). Tapiola, Op. 112 (ASD518, 4/63).

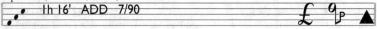
1h 16' ADD 7/90 £ 9 p ▲

NEW REVIEW

Sibelius. ORCHESTRAL WORKS. [a]**London Philharmonic Orchestra,** [b]**Royal Philharmonic Orchestra/Sir Thomas Beecham.** EMI Beecham edition mono CDM7 64027-2.
Symphonies — No. 4 in A minor, Op. 63[a] (from HMV DB3351/5, 3/38); No. 6 in D minor, Op. 104[b] (DB6640/42, 6/50). The Tempest — incidental music, Op. 109: Prelude[a] (DB3894, 12/39). Legends, Op. 22 — Lemminkäinen's Homeward Journey[a] (DB3355/6, 3/38). The bard, Op. 64[a] (DB3891, 12/39).

1h 19' ADD 3/92 £ 9 p ▲

In 1925 Sibelius was commissioned to write incidental music for a lavish production of Shakespeare's *The Tempest* at the Royal Theatre, Copenhagen. As this theatre also houses the Royal Danish Opera, he had a large orchestra at his disposal. After its successful production the following year he arranged two suites from the music, publishing the Prelude separately. Beecham's 1955 recording of the two suites has long enjoyed legendary status — and has never really been equalled, let alone surpassed. (Beecham omits the Prelude here, perhaps because it appears in truncated form at the end of the Second Suite.) The "Oak Tree" is haunting and the "Chorus of the Winds" is pure magic in his hands: it is a joy to hear the rapt *ppp* string tone he secured and in the Intermezzo that follows. The 1952 performances of four of the *Scènes historiques* have a similar ring of authenticity that transcend sonic limitations — which, incidentally, are few. The *Karelia* Intermezzo recorded in 1945 is curiously cavalier but the "Alla marcia" finds him back on form. The *Finlandia* is rather drily recorded but grippingly played. But it is *The Tempest* music that makes this first CD a must.

One of the special things about Beecham's Sibelius was its sheer sonority: there was a fresh, vernal sheen on the strings quite different from the opulence of Koussevitzky or Karajan but with all their flexibility and plasticity of phrasing, and a magic that is easier to discern than define. Moreover his feeling for atmosphere in Sibelius was always matched by a strong grip on the architecture. The second CD collects some of his greatest performances from the early days of stereo — *Pelléas, Tapiola* and *The Oceanides*. His *Pelléas* is glorious and remains unsurpassed in atmosphere and poetic feeling, though Karajan some three decades later runs it pretty close. But Beecham conveys that pale wintry light in the "Pastorale", when the strings enter, as does no other conductor. When he visited Sibelius in 1955 shortly before his ninetieth birthday, the composer asked him to record *The Oceanides*, and his performance remains altogether special in its handling of light and colour, as well as the control of climax. Beecham recorded *Tapiola* twice, once immediately after the war and then again in 1955, and though he did not actually pass the present recording for publication it is still pretty superb. He makes the magic of the forest depths very telling and though his account of the Seventh Symphony does not quite match it, this CD still remains an indispensable part of a Sibelius collection. Amazing sound for its period.

The recordings on the third disc are a good deal earlier than those listed above. No need in this day and age to dwell on the merits of his celebrated 1937 account of the Fourth Symphony, which has enormous concentration and power. It is totally uncompromising and in both its poetic feeling and dramatic tension remains unequalled to this day. Sibelius and Beecham corresponded about its interpretation and we can take it that this reading comes very close to the composer's wishes. In addition to the Fourth this disc restores two important recordings that have not been in circulation for some 40 or 50 years: the celebrated 1947 account of the Sixth Symphony, and the pre-War 1938 version of the Prelude to *The Tempest*. Despite frequent rumours that it was to be issued on LP, the Sixth never appeared. It was said during the early 1950s to be Sibelius's favourite recording of any of his symphonies, and is indeed a performance of eloquence and powerful atmosphere. Beecham judges the tempo and mood of both the middle movements perfectly. The Prelude to *The Tempest* is quite terrifying; one feels completely drained after exposure to it. As mentioned above, his later 1955 version of the two *Tempest* suites omitted it. Nor has there ever been a more exciting account of *Lemminkäinen's Homeward Journey*, in which the steed gallops hell for leather to the crack of the whip, through the cold northlands. An indispensable part of any self-respecting Sibelius collection and still sounding marvellous.

NEW REVIEW

Sibelius. Four Legends, Op. 22. **Gothenburg Symphony Orchestra/ Neeme Järvi.** BIS CD294.

49' DDD 6/86

In later life Sibelius spoke of the Op. 22 *Legends* as "a kind of Kalevala symphony", though the four tone poems do not have the organic cohesion of the four movements of the First and Second symphonies. He revised them twice, once in 1897 and then again in 1900, though only *The Swan of Tuonela* and *Lemminkäinen's Homeward Journey* entered the repertoire. (The other two remained tucked away in a drawer until the 1930s: indeed, the whole work was not performed in its entirety until after the Second World War.) The very opening of the first one, *Lemminkäinen and the maidens of the island* establishes an entirely new voice in music as, for that matter does *The Swan*, which was originally the Prelude to a projected opera, *The Building of the Boat*. Neeme Järvi gives a passionate and atmospheric account of this lovely movement and his performance of *The Swan* is altogether magical. He takes a broader view of *Lemminkäinen in Tuonela* than many of his rivals and builds up an appropriately black and powerful atmosphere, showing the Gothenburg brass to excellent advantage. The recording quality is impressive with splendid range and presence — and it is good to hear the two solo violins towards the end of the first *Legend* sounding so naturally life-size — and not larger than life! All four pieces are very well played and the complete naturalness of the recorded balance is admirable. This Gothenburg version can hold its head high in the company of all the performances recorded in the last decade or so.

NEW REVIEW

Sibelius. Scaramouche — incidental music, Op. 71. The Language of the Birds — wedding march. **Gothenburg Symphony Orchestra/Neeme Järvi.** BIS CD502.

| 1h 8' DDD 4/92 |

Scaramouche is Sibelius's longest uninterrupted orchestral work and this is its first complete recording — and something of a discovery. In all it runs to some 65 minutes of music and though there are some passages deficient in inspiration, the score contains much music that is touched by both distinction and vision. Indeed, the first Act is quite captivating. He composed it in 1913 with much reluctance on a commission from the Danish publisher, Wilhelm Hansen, thinking that it would not involve the composition of more than a few dance numbers. However the idea of the Danish writer, Poul Knudsen was a dance pantomime and Sibelius was furious with himself when it suddenly dawned on him that he had bound himself to compose a full-length ballet! Some of its music recalls the lighter Sibelius of the *Suites mignonne* and *Champêtre* but if the music is occasionally thin (particularly the Second Act) there are some moments of great poetic feeling, almost evoking the luminous colouring of the world of the *Humoresques* for violin and orchestra that were to follow in 1917. (We also glimpse ideas that were

Jean Sibelius

forming in his mind for use in *The Oceanides* the following year and, in the music where solo viola and cello depict Scaramouche's hypnotic viola playing, a figure that was to emerge in the Seventh Symphony.) The wistful gentle sadness of the first Act casts a strong spell, and its charms grow stronger on each hearing. *The Language of the Birds* was a play by Adolf Paul for whose *King Christian II* Sibelius had provided the music, but he never thought well enough of the Wedding March to publish it. It is quite an attractive piece and like *Scaramouche* itself is given very persuasively and affectionately by Neeme Järvi and the Gothenburg Symphony Orchestra and splendidly recorded.

Sibelius. SYMPHONIES. **Philharmonia Orchestra/Vladimir Ashkenazy.** Decca 421 069-2DM4.
Symphonies — No. 1 in E minor, Op. 39 (from 414 534-1DH, 5/86); No. 2 in D major, Op. 43 (SXDL7513, 11/80); No. 3 in C major, Op. 52 (414 267-1DH, 8/85); No. 4 in A minor, Op. 63 (SXDL7517, 5/81); No. 5 in E flat major, Op. 82 (SXDL7541, 1/82); No. 6 in D minor, Op. 104 (414 267-1DH, 2/85); No. 7 in C major, Op. 105 (SXDL7580, 8/83).

| ④ 3h 52' ADD/DDD 12/87 |

Of all the cycles of Sibelius's symphonies recorded during recent years this is one
of the most consistently successful. Ashkenazy so well understands the thought

processes that lie behind Sibelius's symphonic composition just as he is aware,
and makes us aware, of the development between the Second and Third Symphonies. His attention to tempo is particularly acute and invariably he strikes just
the right balance between romantic languor and urgency. The Philharmonia play
for all they are worth and possess a fine body of sound. The recordings are
remarkably consistent in quality and well complement the composer's original
sound-world.

Sibelius. Symphony No. 1 in E minor, Op. 39. Karelia — suite, Op. 11.
Philharmonia Orchestra/Vladimir Ashkenazy. Decca 414 534-2DH.

| ♪ 57' DDD 5/86 | Ⓑ |

NEW REVIEW

Sibelius. Symphonies — No. 1 in E minor, Op. 39[a]; No. 6 in D minor,
Op. 104[b]. **Berlin Philharmonic Orchestra/Herbert von Karajan.** EMI
CDD7 63896-2. Item marked [a] from ASD4097 (9/82), [b] EL270407-1 (8/86).

| ♪ 1h 9' DDD 7/91 | Ⓟ Ⓑ |

The First Symphony has strong Tchaikovskian echoes, even though the
colouring and personality of Sibelius are still greatly in evidence. Ashkenazy and
the Philharmonia Orchestra give a strongly projected account of the score: the
first movement has real grip and this performance conveys a powerful sense of its
architecture. Throughout the work Ashkenazy evokes the Sibelian landscape with
instinctive sympathy and the sheer physical excitement this score engenders is
tempered by admirable control. The recording has superb detail and clarity of
texture, and there is all the presence and body one could ask for. The playing of
the Philharmonia Orchestra is of the very first order. The popular *Karelia* Suite
makes an admirable make-weight and is beautifully played and recorded.

   Karajan's coupling is more generous. He had a particular affinity with the
Sixth Symphony and this, his final recording, is only marginally less magical than
his 1960s classic for DG (reviewed below). Karajan seems a little fleeter of foot
this time round, but the atmosphere is just as remote and otherworldly, making a
strong contrast with his extrovert approach to No. 1. Here the conductor gives
full rein to the opulence and virtuosity of the Berlin Philharmonic and there is a
particularly impressive account of the finale, very grand yet always pressing for
home. The Berlin strings are quite glorious in their big tune. The only drawback
is the recording, an early digital production which now sounds a trifle hollow
and unnatural, no match for Ashkenazy's superb sonics. The Sixth fares better in
this respect and the package is certainly an attractive alternative at the price.

Sibelius. Symphony No. 2 in D major, Op. 43. Romance in C major, Op. 42.
Gothenburg Symphony Orchestra/Neeme Järvi. BIS CD252.

| ♪ 48' DDD 10/84 | Ⓑ |

The Second Symphony possesses a combination of Italianate warmth and Nordic
intensity that has ensured its wide popular appeal. None of Sibelius's other
symphonies has enjoyed such immediate and enduring success. If it inhabits much
the same world as the First, it views it through more subtle and refined lenses.
As in the First Symphony, it is the opening movement that makes the most
profound impression. Its very air of relaxation and effortlessness serves to mask
its inner strength. Järvi's version has sinew and fire and the Gothenburg orchestra
are splendidly responsive and well disciplined. There is an unerring sense of
purpose and direction: the momentum never slackens and yet nothing seems
over-driven. The performance is concentrated in feeling and has freshness and
honesty. The short but charming *Romance* in C for strings, written at about the
same time, is an excellent fill-up.

Sibelius. Symphonies — No. 3 in C major, Op. 52; No. 7 in C major, Op. 105. **City of Birmingham Symphony Orchestra/Simon Rattle.** EMI CDC7 47450-2. From EL270496-1 (4/87).

♪ 51' DDD 8/87

Sibelius's Third Symphony is a striking advance on his first two; whilst they speak the same language as the music of Tchaikovsky and Grieg, the Third strikes us because of its spareness of texture and concentration of ideas. The weight of string tone associated with Sibelius is here apparent and carries tremendous expressive power. The finale, in particular, is a remarkable movement possessing a power and inevitability that evolve from the Symphony's unusual structure. Sibelius's last symphony, also in C major, shows how far his gift for concentration had taken him. It is his shortest symphony; a single 23-minute movement originally entitled *Fantasia Sinfonica*. Its brevity by no means impedes its scale and scope and in it Sibelius weaves together a series of motivic ideas that fuse and gain in strength as the work unfurls. Both performance and recording are very fine.

Sibelius. Symphonies — No. 4 in A minor, Op. 63[a]; No. 6 in D minor, Op. 104[b]. **Berlin Philharmonic Orchestra/Herbert von Karajan.** DG 415 107-2GH. Item marked [a] from SLPM138974 (6/66), [b] SLPM139032 (10/68).

♪ 1h 3' ADD 6/85   ⓆP

Sibelius. Symphonies — No. 4 in A minor, Op. 63; No. 5 in E flat major, Op. 82. **San Francisco Symphony Orchestra/Herbert Blomstedt.** Decca 425 858-2DH.

♪ 1h 8' DDD 7/91   ⓆP   ⓆS

NEW REVIEW

Sibelius. Symphony No. 4 in A minor, Op. 63. The Tempest, Op. 109 — Suite No. 1. **Danish National Radio Symphony Orchestra/Leif Segerstam.** Chandos CHAN8943.

♪ 1h 5' DDD 8/91   ⓆP   ⓆS

Both of the symphonies on the DG disc are dark almost sombre pieces, lacking the harmonic colouring and textural richness of many of the other compositions from this period. The Fourth is cast in greys and silvers rarely employing the orchestral resources at their most opulent, preferring instead a sparer, more restrained weave. Sibelius employs a motto theme which, like so many works that seem to lie under a shadow cast by Fate, adds to its powerful sense of internal unity. The Sixth Symphony, too, is a work of restraint and sombre colour. Again the composer eschews vibrant surface life to dig deep in the soul and the music receives a strong sense of unity through the use of motifs but here they have a rich modal flavour that place the work apart as a product of the carefree 1920s. Karajan has long been a champion of Sibelius's music and the icy depths of the Berlin strings, their peerless winds and dark, baying brass add a powerful sense of inevitability to these two scores. The early 1960s recording are very good.

Herbert Blomstedt's performances are very impressive indeed. First, he gets exactly the right kind of sound from the San Francisco orchestra: the strings are cultured without being too sumptuous, the wind and brass are beautifully blended and the overall sound is lean and refined. Secondly, the music unfolds so naturally and logically, and in a totally unforced way. This is impressive in both symphonies, and so is the feeling for texture Blomstedt shows. In both the first and the slow movement of the Fourth Symphony there is an impressive sense of communion with nature. It is never possible to say that one recording is the 'best', particularly when there are so many fine versions of both symphonies in circulation, but there is no doubt that this is one of the best discs of both symphonies to have appeared for a very long time, and the recording is altogether state-of-the-art.

Of the Finnish conductors now before the public, Leif Segerstam is in many ways the most naturally gifted. He has a highly developed feeling for texture, and this colours his account of Sibelius's darkest symphony. The powerful opening pages are imposing as is the savagery of the brass outburst a little later on. The weakest movement is the scherzo which he disturbs with some disruptive exaggerations of tempo. This apart, the performance is otherwise highly responsive to atmosphere. The finale is generally first-rate and he scores over Blomstedt here in using glockenspiel rather than tubular bells. He also character-izes the closing woodwind dialogue (which according to the composer's son-in-law, the conductor Jussi Jalas, alludes to Peter's denial of Christ before cockcrow) in masterly fashion, though his very closing bars soften perhaps the matter-of-fact ending this symphony should have. As a fill-up Segerstam brings us the first suite that Sibelius made of his music for the 1926 Copenhagen production of *The Tempest*. He really has the measure of "Der Eichbaum" ("The oak-tree"), one of Sibelius's most inspired miniatures, and the celebrated "Intrada" and "Berceuse". If Segerstam does not distil quite the same powerful magic that Beecham achieved (see below) he comes very close to it. This is by far the most powerful modern recording of his music for *The Tempest* and the Chandos recording, made in collaboration with Danish Radio, is very good indeed.

Sibelius. Symphonies — No. 5 in E flat major, Op. 82[a]; No. 7 in C major, Op. 105[b]. **Berlin Philharmonic Orchestra/Herbert von Karajan.** DG 415 108-2GH. Item marked [a] from SLPM138973 (9/65), [b] SLPM139032 (10/68).

The Fifth Symphony, like the Seventh, is epic and heroic in character, and the finale has a tremendous feeling of momentum as well as an awe-inspiring sense of the majesty of nature. The one-movement Seventh is the most extraordinary of his symphonies and the most sophisticated in its approach to form. Karajan has recorded the Fifth no fewer than four times and the best is undoubtedly this DG version made in 1965. It has grandeur and nobility and, it goes without saying, superlative orchestral playing. The transfer to CD is so successful that it would be difficult to guess its age. This is a classic account of the Fifth.

Sibelius. Piano Quintet in G minor (1890)[a]. String Quartet in D minor, Op. 56, "Voces intimae". **Gabrieli Quartet** (John Georgiadis, Brendan O'Kelly, vns; Ian Jewel, va; Keith Harvey, vc) with [a]**Anthony Goldstone** (pf). Chandos CHAN8742.

Only a few months after its composition in 1890, Sibelius dismissed his Piano Quintet as "absolute rubbish". It is far from that, though Busoni's description of it as "wunderschön" is rather overdoing things. The first movement is probably the finest though the *Andante,* too, has a lot of good music in it, if let down by a rather lame, march-like second theme. The scherzo is attractive and very neatly played. To maximize contrast, these artists reverse the order of the scherzo and the *Andante* so that the two slow movements are separated. Although the finale is less satisfactory in terms of structure, it has a good deal of spirit and some memorable ideas. Anthony Goldstone is consistently imaginative and intelligent throughout and the Gabrielis play with conviction. The *Voces intimae* Quartet comes from Sibelius's maturity — between the Third and Fourth symphonies. It is a masterly score and is selflessly played. The fourth movement certainly needs more bite and forward movement; yet the scherzo could not be done with greater delicacy and finesse — and no one comes closer than they to the spirit of this music in the closing bars of the slow movement or the celebrated bars that Sibelius marked "voces intimae".

Sibelius. SONGS. **Anne Sofie von Otter** (mez); **Bengt Forsberg** (pf). BIS CD457. Texts and translations included.
Arioso, Op. 3. Seven Songs, Op. 17. Row, row duck. Six Songs, Op. 36. Five Songs, Op. 37. Pelleas and Melisande, Op. 46 — The three blind sisters. Six Songs, Op. 88. Narcissus.

57' DDD 6/90

In all, Sibelius composed about 100 songs, mostly to Swedish texts but his achievement in this field has, naturally enough, been overshadowed by the symphonies. Most music-lovers know only a handful like "Black roses", Op. 36 No. 1, and "The Tryst" and the most popular are not always the best. Sibelius's output for the voice has much greater range, diversity and depth than many people suppose. For collectors used to hearing them sung by a baritone, the idea of a soprano will seem strange but many of them were written for the soprano Ida Ekman. Anne Sofie von Otter not only makes a beautiful sound and has a feeling for line, but also brings many interpretative insights to this repertoire. The very first song from the Op. 17 set is a marvellous Runeberg setting, "Since then I have questioned no further" and it was this that Ida Ekman sang for Brahms. Von Otter captures its mood perfectly and has the measure of its companions too. Her account of "Black roses" is particularly thrilling and she is very persuasive in the weaker Op. 88 set. She sings throughout with great feeling for character and her account of "Astray", Op. 17 No. 6, has great lightness of touch and charm. The Opp. 36 and 37 sets are among the finest lyrical collections in the whole of Sibelius's song output, and they completely engage this artist's sensibilties. These are performances of elegance and finesse; Bengt Forsberg proves an expert and stylish partner and both artists are well recorded.

Robert Simpson
British 1921-

Simpson. Symphony No. 3[a]. Clarinet Quintet[b]. [b]**Bernard Walton** (cl); [b]**Aeolian Quartet** (Sydney Humphreys, Raymond Keenlyside, vns; Margaret Major, va; Derek Simpson, vc); [a]**London Symphony Orchestra/Jascha Horenstein.** Unicorn-Kanchana Souvenir UKCD2028. Item marked [a] from UNS225 (9/70), [b] UNS234 (8/71).

1h 6' ADD 6/90

The British have been accused of chauvinism, but by no way of thinking can this be said to apply to British opinion of native composers, which has often been disparaging, as both Elgar and Britten found to their cost until the pendulum swung the other way, and it is disgraceful that Robert Simpson has only recently been recognized as the major figure that he is although he has been a symphonist for 40 years and not long ago wrote his Tenth Symphony. This is not the place to apportion blame, but rather to say that many of us are doing some belated catching up with this composer who proves that one doesn't have to be a serialist or minimalist to write music that is personal and worth hearing. His Third Symphony (1962) is not easy listening, though, for it offers an uncompromising argument forcefully scored, but it also reveals real purpose and repays the close acquaintance that a recording allows. The sound here is from 1970 and has a rather cramped acoustic quality, but it is still acceptable and the performance by the LSO under Horenstein, an early Simpson champion, brings out the strength of the writing, not least in the big second movement (there are only two) which the composer calls "Nature music, in a sense" and which, after a hushed start on violins, steadily grows in pace and excitement though ending quietly. The Clarinet Quintet (·1968) is in five connected sections, and though it has some dourness it is finely written and well played here, so that careful listening brings rewards. Both works were recorded under the composer's supervision.

Simpson. Symphony No. 9. **Bournemouth Symphony Orchestra/Vernon Handley.** Hyperion CDA66299. Also includes an illustrated talk on the work by the composer.

> 1h 8' DDD 12/88

Simpson's Ninth Symphony made a tremendous impact on its appearance in 1987 and this CD is excellent in every way. As in the Sixth and Seventh Symphonies, Simpson's mastery of musical motion takes the breath away. The sense of power and energy in reserve is almost tangible at the very outset and once hooked the attention is held through a patiently unfolded 'chorale prelude', a battering scherzo, a disembodied slow movement and an awe-inspiring finale. A superb modern symphony, an excellent performance, self-effacing sound-quality, informative sleeve-notes, a fascinating illustrated talk by the composer — what more could you want?

NEW REVIEW

Simpson. MUSIC FOR BRASS BAND. **Desford Colliery Caterpillar Band/ James Watson.** Hyperion CDA66449.
Energy — symphonic study. The Four Temperaments. Introduction and Allegro on a Bass by Max Reger. Volcano — symphonic study. Vortex.

> 1h 9' DDD 9/91

No one who has his *Canzone* for brass consort which he wrote in 1958 (Chandos CHAN6573) will need reminding that Robert Simpson writes for brass instruments with quite impressive grandeur. Of course, like Nielsen he played the cornet himself as a boy and his experience playing in brass bands has furnished him with enormous expertise in handling the medium. Yet he did not write his first piece for full band until he was 50. This was *Energy* (1971) which was a response to a commission from the World Brass Band Championships. The *Introduction and Allegro* (1987), based on a motive that occurs in Max Reger's D minor organ Fantasia and Fugue, Op. 135*b*, is every bit as awesome and impressive. There is some extraordinary music on this disc including one masterpiece, *The Four Temperaments* (1983), a four-movement 22-minute symphony of great imaginative power, resourcefully laid out for the band. It packs quite a punch and it is not only the music that is extraordinary, so is the playing! One is

Desford Colliery Caterpillar Band   [*photo: Hyperion*

used to hearing brass bands of some virtuosity but the Desford Colliery Caterpillar Band under James Watson really are in a class of their own, to use an overworked phrase. The acoustic is just a shade on the dry side but all the detail comes across clearly and with great presence. This disc is for those who think they don't like brass band music. It is also mandatory listening for those who respond to real symphonic thinking.

Simpson. String Quartets — No. 3[a]; No. 6[a]. String Trio (Prelude, Adagio and Fugue). **Delmé Quartet** (Galina Solodchin, [a]John Trusler, vns; John Underwood, va; Jonathan Williams, vc). Hyperion CDA66376.

1h 12' DDD 7/90

Simpson has said that if he were restricted to writing only one kind of music it would have to be string quartets, and his cycle of 14 such works to date is gradually becoming recognized as a major contribution to the genre. It is something of a shock to hear the familiar bounding momentum and knotty, argumentative tone of the recent Simpson so fully formed no less than 39 years ago in the Third Quartet; the shock consists partly of amazement that the quality of this music took so long to dawn on so many critics. Twenty years later the Sixth Quartet is the last of a trilogy closely modelled on Beethoven's three *Razumovsky* Quartets — a curious exercise, but one which produces fascinating results, especially in the haunting slow movement. Another jump, this time of 12 years, takes us to the String Trio of 1987. This resourceful work is cast in an apparently baroque mould of Prelude, Adagio and Fugue, but in fact sounds wholly modern in its combative energy. Clean, well-balanced playing from the Delmé Quartet, backed up by the same virtues in Hyperion's engineering.

Simpson. String Quartets. **Delmé Quartet** (Galina Solodchin, Jeremy Williams, vns; John Underwood, va; Stephen Orton, vc). Hyperion CDA66117, CDA66127. Items marked [a] from A66117 (9/84), [b] A66127 (11/84).
CDA66117 — No. 7[a]; No. 8[a]. *CDA66127* — No. 9[b].

② 51' 58' ADD 2/90

Robert Simpson's main musical preoccupation has been with the restoration of a sense of forward motion — one of the principal achievements of the great Viennese classics. And it is natural that this preoccupation should have been worked out in those classical genres *par excellence*, the symphony and string quartet. The Seventh and Eighth Quartets reflect the astronomical and entomological interests of their respective dedicatees, whilst the Ninth is a piece of unashamed creative virtuosity — 32 variations and a fugue on the minuet from Haydn's Symphony No. 47, and all of them, like the original theme, palindromic (that is, they go backwards from the halfway point — the challenge being to make the music sound as good both ways). The Delmé Quartet's dedicated performance reveal all three works as major contributions to the quartet literature. The recordings, though less than ideal in 'bloom', are adequate.

Edith Sitwell *Refer to Index*   *British 1887-1964*

Bedrich Smetana   *Bohemian 1824-1884*

Smetana. Má vlast. THE BARTERED BRIDE — Overture; Polonaise; Furiant; Skočná. **Vienna Philharmonic Orchestra/James Levine.** DG 419 768-2GH2.

② 1h 36' DDD 10/87

Smetana. Má vlast. **Royal Liverpool Philharmonic Orchestra/Libor Pešek.** Virgin Classics VC7 91100-2.

1h 16' DDD 7/90

Smetana. Má vlast. **Czech Philharmonic Orchestra/Rafael Kubelík.**
Supraphon 11 1208-2. Recorded at a performance in the Smetana Hall, Prague in
May 1990.

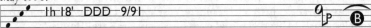

Ih·18'   DDD   9/91

Smetana's great cycle of six tone-poems, *Má vlast*, celebrating the countryside and
legendary heroes and heroines of Bohemia, in Levine's recording receives the
performance it had been waiting for since the long deleted version by Karel
Ančerl. This is a work of immense national significance encapsulating many of the
ideals and hopes of that country. The Overture and dances from Smetana's *The
bartered bride* make a vivid and popular coupling. The VPO play this music for all
it is worth and the recording is clear and open.

   Libor Pešek is himself a native of Prague and brings great affection and
strength to this music, and the Royal Liverpool Philharmonic Orchestra of, which
he is Music Director, play as if to the manner born, while the recording, made
in Liverpool's Philharmonic Hall, is vivid but very natural. Though the second
piece, *Vltava,* is the best known of this great cycle, to appreciate it fully one
should really hear it right through for its nobly cumulative effect, as this 76-
minute CD allows, and when one does so Smetana's use of the powerful Hussite
hymn melody "You who are God's warriors" in the last two pieces is all the
more moving, not least at this time of great changes and major challenges in
Czechoslovakia.

   What a triumphant occasion it was when Rafael Kubelík returned to his native
Czechoslovakia and to his old orchestra after an absence of 42 years and
conducted *Má vlast* at the 1990 Prague Spring Festival. Supraphon's disc captures
that live performance — not perfectly, since the sound is efficient rather than
opulent — but well enough to show off what is arguably the finest performance
on record since Talich's early LP set. You would never imagine that Kubelík had
emerged from five years of retirement and a recent serious illness, such is the
power and eloquence of his conducting. Typically he takes a lyrical rather than a
dramatic view of the cycle, and if there is strength enough in more heroic
sections there is also a refreshing lack of bombast. Kubelík's intimate knowledge
of the score (this is his fifth recording of it) shows time and time again in the
most subtle touches. Even the weakest parts of the score are most artfully
brought to life, and seem of much greater stature than is usually the case.
"Vltava" flows beautifully, with the most imaginative flecks of detail, and in
"From Bohemia's Woods and Fields" there are vivid visions of wide, open spaces.
The orchestra, no doubt inspired by the occasion, reward their former director
with superlative playing.

Smetana. String Quartets — No. 1 in E minor, "From my life"; No. 2 in D
minor. **Smetana Quartet.** Supraphon C37S-7338. From 411 2130 (3/80).

46'   ADD   1/86

Although we think of Smetana as first and foremost an operatic composer, his
two string quartets are also important. The First is frankly programmatic and
autobiographical: the call of destiny in the first movement; the lilting second
reminiscing on his carefree youth and the last, the recognition of "national
awareness in art" and the first warning of impending deafness. The work is
almost as central to the chamber-music repertoire as Dvořák's *American* Quartet
or Borodin's Second — and every bit as tuneful. The Second comes from 1882-
83 when deafness had overtaken him and is, as Smetana himself put it, "the
presentation of the whirl of music in a man who has lost the power of hearing".
The eponymous Smetana Quartet have long championed both works and this
recording remains the classic version of these pieces.

NEW REVIEW

Smetana. THE BARTERED BRIDE. **Gabriela Beňačková** (sop) Mařenka;
Peter Dvorsk 〰ten) Jeník; **Miroslav Kopp** (ten) Vašek; **Richard Novák**
(bass) Kecal; **Jindřich Jindrák** (bar) Krušina; **Marie Mrázová** (contr) Háta;
Jaroslav Horáček (bass) Mícha; **Marie Veselá** (sop) Ludmila; **Jana Jonášová**
(sop) Esmeralda; **Alfréd Hampel** (ten) Circus master; **Karel Hanuš** (bass)
Indian; **Czech Philharmonic Chorus and Orchestra/Zdeněk Košler.**
Supraphon 11 3511-2. Notes, text and translation included. From 1116 3511 (7/82).

③ 2h 17' DDD 10/91 ⑨P

There is something special about a Czech performance of *The bartered bride* and
this one is no exception. The hint of melancholy which runs through the work is
wonderfully evoked, as well as its marvellous gaiety. Zdeněk Košler has the
rhythm and lilt of the music in his bones, like any Czech conductor worth his
salt. The Czech Philharmonic has long had one of the finest of all woodwind
sections, and especially in this music they play with a sense of their instruments'
folk background, with phrasing that springs from deep in Czech folk-music. This
sets the musical scene for some moving performances. The warm, lyrical quality
of Gabriela Beňačková's voice can lighten easily to encompass her character's
tenderness in the first duet, "Věrné milováni", or "Faithful love", the considerable
show of spirit she makes when Jeník appears to have gone off the rails. Her
Act 1 lament is most beautifully song. Peter Dvorský ýýý as Jeník plays lightly with
the score, as he should, or the character's maintaining of the deception can come
to seem merely cruel. Even old Kecal comes to new life, not as the conventional
village bumbler, but as a human character in his own right as Richard Novák
portrays him — quite put out, the old boy is, to find his plans gone astray. In
fact, all of the soloists are excellent. The chorus enjoy themselves hugely, never
more so than in the Beer chorus. Altogether a delightful, touching and warming
performance.

Ethel Smyth

British 1858-1944

Smyth. Mass in D major[a]. THE BOATSWAIN'S MATE — Suppose you mean
to do a given thing. March of the Women[b]. **Eiddwen Harrhy** (sop); [a]**Janis
Hardy** (contr); [a]**Dan Dressen** (ten); [a]**James Bohn** (bass); **Plymouth
Festival** [ab]**Chorus and Orchestra/Philip Brunelle.** Virgin Classics VC7
91188-2. Texts and translation included.

1h 15' DDD 8/91

Dame Ethel Smyth's Mass was performed by the Royal Choral Society under Sir
Joseph Barnby in 1893, when *Musical Opinion* found in it "many pages of supreme
beauty, for which parallels must be sought in the masterpieces of the great choral
writers". *The Musical Times* detected royal patronage, which "explained all, prevented the action of the committee from being assailed, and revealed Miss Smyth
in the character of a very fortunate person". Whatever the cause, her good
fortune then deserted her, for the Mass was not heard again till 1924, when
The Musical Times decided after all that "its genuine character and its vehemence
make it intrinsically worth hearing". Now in 1991 it gains its first recording, not
from London or Birmingham (where the second performance took place) but
Minnesota. Time, certainly, has done nothing to weaken its effects. "Parallels ...
in the masterpieces of the great choral writers" do indeed come to mind, most
notably the Beethoven of the *Missa solemnis*, but what impresses now is the
individuality and scale of the achievement. The *Kyrie*, for instance, may start like
a text-book fugue with echoes of Bach's B minor Mass, but it soon develops
along its own lines, and the declamatory use of the choir, the quickening pace,
growing intensity and unforeseen turns of form and style are expressions of an

almost fiercely independent spirit at work. Each movement has its special strength, and the *Gloria*, transposed from its normal place in the Mass, provides a joyfully rumbustious finale. The attractive solo from *The Boatswain's Mate* makes one wish to hear the rest of the opera (and the other five), while the *March of the Women* or *Suffragettes' Battle Hymn* recalls another part of that contentious and vigorous life. The performances carry conviction; recorded sound is adequate except that, as usual, one would like the choir to be more forward.

Antonio Soler

Spanish 1729-1783

NEW REVIEW

Soler. KEYBOARD SONATAS. **Maggie Cole** ([a]fp/[b]hpd). Virgin Classics Veritas VC7 91172-2.
No. 18 in C minor[a]; No. 19 in C minor[a]; No. 41 in E flat major[a]; No. 72 in F minor[a]; No. 78 in F sharp minor[a]; No. 84 in D major[b]; No. 85 in F sharp minor[b]; No. 86 in D major[b]; No. 87 in G minor[a]; No. 88 in D flat major[b]; No. 90 in F sharp major[b]. Fandango.

1h 11' DDD 5/91

If Soler's name is not widely known, that is doubtless because this eighteenth-century Spanish monk devoted much of his creative time to writing 120 keyboard sonatas which have been overshadowed by those of his predecessor Domenico Scarlatti — who was also his teacher. But they have a character of their own and are longer and more elaborate than Scarlatti's. Maggie Cole takes into account the fact that Soler knew both the fortepiano and harpsichord and sensibly divides the 12 here into two parts, playing the first six on the former and the second on the older instrument. The overriding character of the music is energy, and pieces such as Sonatas Nos. 84 and 88 (played on a three-manual Goble harpsichord after a Hamburg instrument of 1740) fairly burst out of the loudspeakers in a recording that will be too closely-miked for some tastes but is undeniably realistic. Still, there's enough variety in the invention for listening in sequence — though nothing is especially Spanish-sounding save for the *Fandango* on track 7. The fortepiano (by Derek Adlam and based on a Viennese instrument) is more expressive than many, as the gravely melancholy Sonata No. 18 demonstrates. This piece is one of the longest at nearly ten minutes, and is nicely complemented by the shorter and bouncier No. 19 that follows. Maggie Cole's playing is wonderfully crisp and clean, and by using discreet rhythmic flexibility (and tonal shading in the fortepiano pieces) she never allows busy passagework to become merely mechanical.

Fernando Sor

Spanish 1778-1839

Sor. GUITAR WORKS. **Lex Eisenhardt.** Etcetera KTC1025. From ETC1025 (11/85).
Variations on the Scottish Air, "Ye banks and braes", Op. 40. Six Airs from Mozart's "Die Zauberflöte", Op. 19. Le calme — caprice, Op. 50. Sonata in C minor, Op. 25.

49' DDD 1/89

In May 1819 *Die Zauberflöte* was performed in London and it may have been there that Sor heard it — and was stimulated to write his famous Variations (Op. 9) on *Das klinget so herrlich*, published in 1821; two years later, when he was living in Russia, he made simple, charming settings of six more airs from the

opera which he sent to his publisher in Paris. Variations were in the salon-
musical air that Sor regularly breathed and those on *Ye banks and braes* may have
resulted from his hearing the tune in London, or perhaps, reflected the contemporary continental taste for Scottish melodies, shared by Beethoven, Haydn
and (in London) J.C. Bach. By 1832 Sor had returned to Paris, where he
dedicated the elegant little Caprice *Le calme* to one of his lady students. Of the
few guitar composers of the time who ventured to write full-scale sonatas, Sor
was the most lyrical, adventurous in departing from the guitar's most grateful
keys, and fastidious in his craftsmanship; the Sonata Op. 25 is the finest of his
works in this genre. Lex Eisenhardt plays all this music most persuasively and is
clearly recorded in a generous acoustic.

NEW REVIEW

Sor. GUITAR WORKS **Eduardo Fernández.** Decca 425 821-2DH.
Grand solo, Op. 14. Fantasia élégiaque, Op. 59. Sonatas — C major, Op. 15
No. 2; C minor, Op. 25. Etudes — Op. 6 Nos. 4, 6 and 8; Op. 29 No. 25;
Op. 35 Nos. 16 and 17; Op. 21. "Les adieux".

1h 9' DDD 11/91

Although best known for his guitar music Sor wrote much for other mediums; it
was through his ballet music that he visited Russia. Stylistically, his music sits
between that of Mozart and Beethoven, and little of it shows any trace of his
Hispanic origins. Of his several sonata-form works, Op. 25 is the most developed
of its time for the guitar, and the *Grand solo* is in effect one sonata-form
movement. The *Fantasia élégiaque* is a lament on the death of his friend Charlotte
Beslay — above the final bars is written "Charlotte! Adieu" and it is arguably the
most moving piece written for the guitar before this century. Sor also wrote
numerous pieces for didactic purposes (which they serve without sacrifice of
musical appeal), including 97 studies under five opus numbers, of which there is
a selection in this recording. Though the quest after authenticity has marched
beyond the date of Sor's death, no recording of this music on a nineteenth-
century guitar and played with period technique is yet available; Fernández's
clean performances complement Eisenhardt's and both provide an excellent
introduction to Sor's music as it is perceived by today's guitarists.

Kaikhosru Shapurji Sorabji   *British 1892-1988*

NEW REVIEW

Sorabji. Piano Sonata No. 1. **Marc-André Hamelin.** Altarus AIR-CD9050.

22' DDD 5/91

Imagine the perfumed mysticism of Scriabin combined with the mind-bending
jazz arabesques of Art Tatum, and you have some idea of the character of this
music. Son of a Parsi father and a Spanish-Sicilian mother, Kaikhosru Shapurji
Sorabji lived for many years as a recluse in England, deliberately discouraging
performance of his own music. In 1919 Sorabji played his First Sonata to his idol
Busoni, who aptly summed it up as being "like a tropical forest" (although by the
standards of his later works it is restrained in both its musical language and its
dimensions — his most famous piano extravaganza, *Opus Clavicembalisticum,* fills
some four and a half hours!). Marc-André Hamelin describes the sonata as "a
thrilling magic-carpet ride, hurtling from splendour to splendour". That's well
put, and the young Canadian's playing fully lives up to his description. It is a
pianistic *tour de force* which should appeal to anyone with adventurous tastes.
Recording quality is beautifully clean. Even the duration of the disc seems quite
appropriate to the unusual density of the music.

Louis Spohr

German 1784-1859

NEW REVIEW

Spohr. JESSONDA. **Julia Varady** (sop) Jessonda; **Renate Behle** (sop)
Amazili; **Kurt Moll** (bass) Dandau; **Thomas Moser** (ten) Nadori; **Dietrich
Fischer-Dieskau** (bar) Tristan d'Acunha; **Peter Haage** (ten) Pedro Lopes;
**Hamburg State Opera Chorus; Hamburg Philharmonic Orchestra/
Gerd Albrecht.** Orfeo C240912H. Notes, text and translations included.

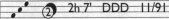

Kurt Moll   [photo: Decca/Purdom]

Spohr is generally association with the pieties of *The Last Judgement* and the prettiness of a few songs and chamber pieces, but his opera set among the Brahmins and bayadères enjoyed considerable success in its time (it appeared in 1823, the same years as Weber's *Euryanthe*) and it generally receives respectful, if brief, mention in the history books. This is its first recording. The music is mild in its orientalism, as in most things else. Mourning for the late Rajah quickly cheers up along the lines of "He's gone to Heaven", with a jolly chorus in compound time suggestive of later times of Gilbert and Sullivan. The natives take part in a war-dance, which is as decorous as a gavotte, and when the hero and heroine have their love duet there is nothing remotely erotic about it. Even so, the music is graceful, unfailingly workmanlike and notably well-orchestrated. At a rather late stage in the drama, which poses the familiar love-or-duty dilemma and ends with a last-minute rescue by the gallant Portuguese just as the heroine is about to be sacrificed to Brahma, some real inspiration arises and Jessonda's final aria achieves something not far short of sublimity. In the recording it is helped by the exquisite singing of Julia Varady, who brings distinction to everything she touches. As much can usually be said of Kurt Moll also, but on this occasion, though the depth and quality of his voice are impressive as ever, he makes little pretence of thinking this a dramatic as well as a musical entertainment. Renate Behle sings well and Fischer-Dieskau does nothing by half-measures. Thomas Moser, playing Nandori, a Brahmin with liberal tendencies, makes the most of his opportunities. Gerd Albrecht conducts a spirited performance, bringing one more near-forgotten work down from the shelves and giving it a new chance of survival as living sound.

Charles Villiers Stanford

Irish/British 1852-1924

NEW REVIEW

Stanford. Symphony No. 2 in D minor, "Elegiac". Clarinet Concerto in
A minor, Op. 80[a]. [a]**Janet Hilton** (cl); **Ulster Orchestra/Vernon Handley.**
Chandos CHAN8991.

Though Stanford is best known as the teacher of Vaughan Williams, Holst, Bliss
and Ireland, this Irish composer is an important figure in his own right. Trained
at Cambridge and then in Germany, where he became a lifelong admirer of

Brahms, Stanford was essentially conservative, but that does not mean a lack of quality and in listening to the Second Symphony one immediately detects links with Elgar, though he lacks Elgar's passion and pathos. Perhaps it is only in Britain that a work as good as this should have lain unperformed for over a century — that is, between 1883 and 1990, when it was revived by the Ulster Orchestra. Their performance here under the sympathetic direction of Vernon Handley (who has already recorded five of Stanford's seven symphonies) brings out the warmth of the music, which is melodious, shapely and finely scored. The subtitle refers to the lines from Tennyson's *In Memoriam* with which the composer prefaced the score, but the prevailing mood is more positive than sombre and the slow second movement is satisfyingly serene. The vigorous scherzo has been likened to the music of Beethoven, but it is Dvořák who comes more readily to mind, while the spacious finale may recall Brahms — but even if there is no special individuality or innovation, this is fine music. So is the Clarinet Concerto, which is better known since players are glad to have this well written piece in a smallish concerto repertory. It is in three linked movements, played fluently and persuasively by Janet Hilton, whose rich tone is a delight, not least in the central *Andante con moto*. The recording of both these works is unspectacular but pleasing.

Stanford. Symphony No. 3 in F minor, Op. 28, "Irish". Irish Rhapsody No. 5 in G minor, Op. 147. **Ulster Orchestra/Vernon Handley.** Chandos CHAN8545.

♪ 56' DDD 1/88

The Third Symphony is marvellously well written and incorporates traditional Irish folk melodies in a rich palette of ideas, presenting these ingredients in a Brahmsian orchestral environment which nevertheless retains a perfectly individual voice. Few can resist the deft jig-scherzo of its second movement or can remain unmoved by the beautiful slow movement. The coupling is the *Irish Rhapsody* No. 5. Written some 30 years after the symphony it again draws heavily on Irish tunes and inflexions, with vigorous outer sections and a seamlessly beautiful, nostalgic central episode. The Ulster Orchestra play magnificently, giving a performance that would be hard to match let alone surpass, and the recording is a truly magnificent example of the art.

Stanford. Symphony No. 4 in F major, Op. 31. Irish Rhapsody No. 6, Op. 191[a]. Oedipus tyrannus, Op. 29 — Prelude. [a]**Lydia Mordkovitch** (vn); **Ulster Orchestra/Vernon Handley.** Chandos CHAN8884.

♪ 1h 5' DDD 3/91

Chandos's exploration of the wilder — or, at any rate, unfamiliar — shores of British music has led them to record all the Stanford symphonies in excellent sound. The Fourth Symphony was commissioned by Berlin, where it was first performed in 1889. Its first audience would no doubt have recognized the twin influences of Brahms and Dvořák, but if they had any sense would have put them to the back of their minds as they enjoyed the light and luminous orchestration. Although the finale is the weakest moment, it is melodically enchanting. The Sixth *Irish Rhapsody* is a rarity, dating from 1922, two years before the composer's death when he was out of fashion and knew it. Perhaps this accounts for the sense of isolation in this haunting piece for violin and orchestra, played most eloquently by Lydia Mordkovitch and conducted with rare understanding by Vernon Handley. The Ulster Orchestra's playing of all the music on the disc is admirable.

William Stanley *Refer to Index* Australian 19th Century

Wilhelm Stenhammar *Swedish 1871-1927*

Stenhammar. Serenade, Op. 31 (with the "Reverenza" movement). **Gothenburg Symphony Orchestra/Neeme Järvi.** BIS CD310.

> 44' DDD 2/87

The Serenade for Orchestra is without doubt Stenhammar's masterpiece, an imaginative and magical work, full of memorable ideas and delicate orchestral colours. But it was not an immediate success and after the appearance of his Second Symphony Stenhammar returned to the Serenade, removing one of the movements and revising the outer ones. The jettisoned *Reverenza* survives in the Swedish Royal Academy Archives and Järvi has chosen to restore the movement to its original place. The *Reverenza* has some of the melancholy charm of Elgar and its refined texture enriches this wholly enchanting piece. The performance here is eloquent and committed. Glorious music, sensitively played and finely recorded, this CD is strongly recommended.

Stenhammar. SONGS. [a]**Anne Sofie von Otter** (mez); [b]**Håkan Hagegård** (bar); [a]**Bengt Forsberg,** [b]**Thomas Schuback** (pfs). Musica Sveciae MSCD623. Texts included.
In the forest[a]. Ingalill[b]. Fylgia[a]. My ancestor had a great goblet[b]. I was dear to you[b]. The girl came from meeting her lover[a]. The girl tying on Midsummer's Eve[a]. A fir tree stand alone[a]. The ballad of Emperor Charles[b]. Leaning against the fence[a]. The girl to her aged mother[a]. To a rose[a]. Under the maple tree at dusk[b]. Were I a small child[b]. A barrel-organ ballad[b]. Melody[a]. Star eye[a]. At the window[a]. Old dutchman[b]. Moonlight[a]. Adagio[a]. The Wanderer[b]. The Star[b]. Mistress Blond and Mistress Brunett[b]. A ship is sailing[b]. When through the room[b]. Why so swift to retire?[b]. Voyage to the happy country[b]. Prince Aladdin of the lamp[b]. Love song[b].

> 1h 14' DDD 7/90 ❓

Alongside his many accomplishments as composer and conductor Stenhammar was a pianist of some renown. He played with most of the major conductors of his day including Hans Richter and Richard Strauss, and was a noted interpreter of the Brahms concertos as well as his own. His late Beethoven was also much admired, as was his chamber music playing. What is less well-known is that he was much in demand as an accompanist, and toured extensively in that capacity. At home in his childhood, the family could muster a vocal quartet, for which he composed a number of small pieces though most of his youthful output was for solo voice, for which he wrote throughout his life. This CD brings no fewer than 30 songs into the catalogue and is the most comprehensive survey yet to appear. They cover his whole career from *In the forest*, written when he was only 16, through to his very last work, a love song from 1924. The bulk come from the 1890s and 1900s including *The girl came from meeting her lover* (or "The Tryst") made famous by Sibelius's slightly later setting. (In this instance Stenhammar's is the more subtle setting.) Some of the earlier songs are a bit conventional but they never fall below a certain level of distinction, and some are captivating. They can be original and forward-looking as in *Prince Aladdin of the lamp*, or have an unaffected naturalness and charm as in *A barrel-organ ballad*, both of which are good tracks to sample. But they are all beautifully fashioned with not a note out of place and the product of a man of fastidious taste and poetic feeling. The majority are allotted to Håkan Hagegård and Thomas Schuback, who accompanies

superbly. Anne Sofie von Otter is a joy throughout. The original texts are all
given with detailed summaries in English, and there is an authoritative and
scholarly essay, which is a model of its kind.

Karlheinz Stockhausen

German 1928-

NEW REVIEW

Stockhausen. Mantra. **Yvar Mikashoff, Rosalind Bevan** (pfs); **Ole Orsted**
(electronics). New Albion NA025CD.

· 1h 10' DDD 1/91

A mantra is "a sacred text used as an incantation"; but although the two pianists
in Stockhausen's fascinating composition do occasionally call out to one another
the work is predominantly a sustained and highly original exploration of
instrumental sonority, which confirms the richness of Stockhausen's aural
imagination in the late 1960s, before he embarked on the grandiose operatic
project that continues to absorb all his compositional energies today. *Mantra*
offers you a gripping musical argument, but not in terms of normal piano sound.
The consistent use of ring modulation either distorts or enriches that sound,
depending on your point of view. Stockhausen's attitude is that only through the
use of such weird and wonderful technological advances can the innate spirituality
of music be enhanced, and he has consistently sought to escape the mundane and
embrace the transcendental in his compositions. *Mantra* is typical of his work in
that its spiritual ambitions make enormous demands on the performers, and the
composer's earthly messengers, in the form of Yvar Mikashoff and Rosalind
Bevan, realize his intentions with both brilliance and dedication. Beyond the
spirituality, there is enormous excitement in the way the music builds to its
dazzling concluding toccata, and the recording does the whole enterprise full
justice.

Stockhausen. Stimmung. **Singcircle/Gregory Rose.** Hyperion CDA66115.
Text and translation included. From A66115 (10/84).

· 1h 10' DDD 2/87

Stimmung relies totally on vocal harmonics formed from six notes centred around
various words. The six voices work closely together following a leading singer
into sympathetic treatments of tempo, rhythm and dynamic. When the voices
have achieved an 'identity' another singer leads into the next section. Of the 51
sections of the work (all individually cued on this CD) 29 employ a 'magic
name' drawn from a diversity of cultures, others employ erotic poetry written by
the composer himself. The variety of timbres created by the quite extraordinarily
virtuosic group Singcircle is astonishing — the mesmerizing web of sounds at
times seems to reject any association with the human voice. This is a very
acquired taste but really does deserve to be heard. Fascinating!

Johann Strauss I

Austrian 1804-1849

Johann Strauss II

Austrian 1825-1899

Josef Strauss   *Austrian 1827-1870*

NEW YEAR'S DAY CONCERT IN VIENNA, 1987. [a]**Kathleen Battle** (sop);
Vienna Philharmonic Orchestra/Herbert von Karajan. DG 419 616-
2GH. Recorded at a performance in the Grosser Saal, Musikverein, Vienna on
January 1st, 1987.
J. Strauss I: Beliebte Annen-Polka, Op. 137. Radetzky March, Op. 228.
J. Strauss II: DIE FLEDERMAUS — Overture. Annen-Polka, Op. 117.
Vergnügungszug-Polka, Op. 281. Unter Donner und Blitz-Polka, Op. 324.
Frühlingsstimmen-Waltz, Op. 410[a]. An die schönen blauen Donau-Waltz, Op.
314. *J. Strauss II/Josef Strauss:* Pizzicato Polka. *Josef Strauss:*
Sphärenklänge-Waltz, Op. 235. Delirien-Waltz, Op. 212. Ohne Sorgen-Polka,
Op. 271.

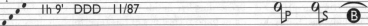

Kathleen Battle   *[photo: DG/Steiner*

This has claims to being the finest Johann Strauss compilation ever recorded. It was the first time Karajan had conducted a New Year concert in Vienna and before he did so he prepared himself by returning to the scores for a period of intensive study. In the famous *Radetzky March* the audience was allowed to join in with the traditional hand-claps, but Karajan had only to glance over his shoulder and the sound was almost instantaneously quelled, so that the lyrical strains of the piece were not drowned. Throughout, the performances have the spontaneity of the most memorable live occasion. The Waltzes, *Delirien* and *Sphärenklänge*, are superb and in *Frühlingsstimmen* Kathleen Battle's deliciously radiant roulades are wonderfully scintillating, yet lyrically relaxed. The polkas, too, have irrepressible flair and high spirits. But it is at the arrival of the great *Blue Danube* that the magic of magic arrives. The horns steal out of the silence with their famous arpeggio theme and the strings take it up with an almost voluptuous richness. The rhythmic lilt has a special feeling unique to the VPO and at the end one is left quite overwhelmed by the experience, as if hearing the piece for the very first time. The recording is quite superb, with the acoustic of the Musikverein adding bloom and richness without robbing the definition of its natural clarity; few live occasions have been caught on the wing like this. An indispensable disc.

**NEW YEAR'S DAY CONCERT IN VIENNA, 1989. Vienna Philharmonic
Orchestra/Carlos Kleiber.** Sony Classical CD45938. Recorded at performances in the Grosser Saal, Musikverein, Vienna on December 31st 1988 and
January 1st, 1989. From CBS CD45564 (7/89).
Johann Strauss I: Radetzky March, Op. 228. *J. Strauss II:* Accelerationen -
Waltz, Op. 234. Bauern-Polka, Op. 276. DIE FLEDERMAUS — Overture.
Künstlerleben-Waltz, Op. 316. Eljen a Magyar!-Polka, Op. 322. Im
Krapfenwald'l-Polka française, Op. 336. Frühlingsstimmen-Waltz, Op. 410.
RITTER PASMAN — Csárdás. An die schönen blauen Donau-Waltz, Op. 314.

J. Strauss II / Josef Strauss: Pizzicato Polka. **Josef Strauss:** Die Libelle-Polka Mazur, Op. 204. Moulinet-Polka française, Op. 57. Plappermäulchen-Polka schnell, Op. 245. Jockey-Polka schnell, Op. 278.

⸱ 1h 16' DDD 2/91 ⓟ Ⓑ

The special ingredient added in 1989 to Vienna's usual New Year's Day confection of waltzes and polkas from the Strauss family was Carlos Kleiber. He brought a depth of flavour to the expected spice and froth without making the mixture too heavy, and the result delighted even the most particular gourmets. Captured on disc, the concert retains much of the sparkle of the occasion and some of Kleiber's individual contribution to Strauss interpretation, but the issue as a whole is perhaps best heard as a record of a special event that incidentally meets a demand that most of the standard, run-of-the-mill collections of Strauss waltzes only half-heartedly fulfil. The Sony recording is surprisingly good considering the problems of recording live in this venue and whilst the sound does not equal the best of some studio recordings of this repertoire, it does sizzle with authenticity.

J. Strauss I. Radetzky March, Op. 228.
J. Strauss II. WALTZES AND POLKAS. **Vienna Philharmonic Orchestra / Willi Boskovsky** (vn). Decca Ovation 417 747-2DM. From Decca recordings made between 1958-74.
J. Strauss II: DIE FLEDERMAUS — Overture. Perpetuum mobile, Op. 257. Accelerationen-Waltz, Op. 234. Unter Donner und Blitz-Polka, Op. 324. Morgenblätter-Waltz, Op. 279. Persischer Marsch, Op. 289. Explosionen-Polka, Op. 43. Wiener Blut-Waltz, Op. 354. Egyptischer Marsch, Op. 335. Künstl erleben-Waltz, Op. 316. Tritsch-Tratsch-Polka, Op. 214. **J. Strauss II / Josef Strauss:** Pizzicato Polka.

⸱ 1h 5' ADD Ⓑ

There have been no finer recordings of Johann Strauss than those by Boskovsky and the Vienna Philharmonic. The velvety sheen and elegance of the orchestra's sound, combined with the unique lilt that comes so naturally to Viennese players, produced magical results. For this compilation Decca have sensibly mixed seven of the most famous waltzes and polkas from those sessions with other popular Strauss compositions in various rhythms, from the celebrated *Die Fledermaus* Overture, through popular polkas and novelty pieces (for *Perpetuum mobile* Boskovsky himself can be heard explaining that it has no ending) to the ever-popular *Radetzky March*. The recorded sound is not up to the most modern digital standards, but reprocessing has produced a remarkably homogeneous sound for recordings originating over a 15-year period.

NEW REVIEW

J. Strauss II. WALTZES AND OVERTURES. **London Philharmonic Orchestra / Franz Welser-Möst.** EMI CDC7 54089-2.
Künstlerleben-Waltz, Op. 316. Rosen aus dem Süden-Waltz, Op. 388. DER ZIGEUNERBARON — Overture. G'schichten aus dem Wienerwald-Waltz, Op. 325. Kaiser-Waltz, Op. 437. DIE FLEDERMAUS — Overture. An die schönen, blauen Donau-Waltz, Op. 314.

⸱ 1h 6' DDD 12/91 Ⓑ

This Johann Strauss collection offers five of the most popular waltzes and the two most popular operetta overtures in interpretations in the best symphonic style. That is to say the performances make the very most of the miniature tone poems that Strauss provided as introductory sections to his waltzes, with the actual waltz sections themselves full of the hesitations, inflexions and tempo changes that would make the music impossible to dance to, but make it so much more effective in the concert-hall. What matters most is that all the rubato and dynamic changes evolve utterly naturally and with a delightful lilt. As the accompanying notes suggest, Welser-Möst's Austrian background gives him an advantage in evoking the special colour, gaiety and melancholy of Strauss's music, and in addition the LPO rise superbly to the lead he sets. There is a sparkle to the playing, and the instrumental solos are expertly and delicately played. All these virtues are well shown in the opening sections of *Rosen aus dem Süden* (for older music lovers always associated with radio's sometime "Grand Hotel" programme), though the fourth waltz section is somewhat rushed. Some potential buyers may regret the lack of rustic authenticity created by the absence of a zither in *G'schichten aus dem Wienerwald*, but the string alternative is beautifully played.

NEW REVIEW

J. Strauss II. DIE FLEDERMAUS. **Elisabeth Schwarzkopf** (sop) Rosalinde; **Rita Streich** (sop) Adele; **Nicolai Gedda** (ten) Eisenstein; **Helmut Krebs** (ten) Alfred; **Erich Kunz** (bar) Doctor Falke; **Rudolf Christ** (ten) Orlovsky; **Karl Dönch** (bar) Frank; **Erich Majkut** (ten) Blind; **Luise Martini** (sop) Ida; **Franz Böheim** (bar) Frosch; **Philharmonia Chorus and Orchestra/ Herbert von Karajan.** EMI CHS7 69531-2. From Columbia 33CX1309-10 (11/55).

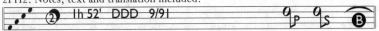

NEW REVIEW

J. Strauss II. DIE FLEDERMAUS. **Dame Kiri Te Kanawa** (sop) Rosalinde; **Edita Gruberová** (sop) Adele; **Wolfgang Brendel** (bar) Eisenstein; **Richard Leech** (ten) Alfred; **Olaf Bär** (bar) Doctor Falke; **Brigitte Fassbaender** (mez) Orlovsky; **Tom Krause** (bar) Frank; **Anton Wendler** (ten) Blind; **Karin Göttling** (sngr) Ida; **Otto Schenk** (spkr) Frosch; **Vienna State Opera Chorus; Vienna Philharmonic Orchestra/André Previn.** Philips 432 157-2PH2. Notes, text and translation included.

NEW REVIEW

J. Strauss II. DIE FLEDERMAUS[a]. NEW YEAR'S DAY CONCERT IN VIENNA, 1951[b]. **Hilde Gueden** (sop) Rosalinde; **Wilma Lipp** (sop) Adele; **Julius Patzak** (ten) Eisenstein; **Anton Dermota** (ten) Alfred; **Alfred Poell** (bar) Doctor Falke; **Sieglinde Wagner** (mez) Orlovsky; **Kurt Preger** (bar) Frank; **August Jaresch** (ten) Blind; **Vienna State Opera Chorus; Vienna Philharmonic Orchestra/Clemens Krauss.** Decca Historic Series mono 425 990-2DM2. Text and translation included. Item marked [a] from LXT2550/51 (2/51), [b] LXT2645 (1/52).
J. Strauss II: G'schichten aus dem Wienerwald-Waltz, Op. 325. Im Krapfenwald'l-Polka française, Op. 336. Eljen a Magyar!-Polka, Op. 332. Egyptischer Marsch, Op. 335. Vergnügungszug-Polka Galop, Op. 281.
J. Strauss II/Josef Strauss: Pizzicato Polka. **Josef Strauss:** Mein Lebenslauf ist Lieb und Lust-Waltz, Op. 263. Die Libelle-Polka mazur, Op. 204. Jockey-Polka schnell, Op. 278.

Anyone less concerned with modernity of sound than with enjoying a well-proven, classic interpretation of Strauss's operetta masterpiece can readily be recommended to EMI's 1955 recording. Herbert von Karajan, whose preference for slow tempos and beauty of sound above all else was then still in the future, here directs with affection and *élan*. Amongst the principals Elisabeth Schwarzkopf leads the cast majestically and ravishingly. Notably in the *csárdás*, her firm lower notes swell gloriously into a marvellously rich and individual register. As her maid, Adele, Rita Streich is an agile-voiced, utterly charming foil, launching her "Laughing Song" with deliciously credible indignation. Nicolai Gedda also enters

Nicolai Gedda   *[photo: EMI*

into the fun with supreme effect. Throughout he sings with youthful ardour and freshness, but he also has a high old time impersonating the stammering Blind in the Act 3 trio. Erich Kunz's rich, characterful baritone is also heard here to good effect as Doctor Falke, the character who arranges the 'bat's revenge' which forms the story of *Die Fledermaus*. Unconventionally, the young Prince is played by a tenor rather than the mezzo-soprano for whom the role was written. Purists may object, but the result is dramatically convincing, and musically could hardly be bettered when the singer is the sweet-toned Rudolf Christ. Altogether this set can still rival any later one in theatrical effectiveness and EMI have done a good job in refurbishing it, with the disc-break sensibly placed between Acts 1 and 2.

For those seeking a more contemporary performance, André Previn's 1991 recording for Philips can be strongly recommended as an alternative to Karajan's classic interpretation. Previn's strength lies very much on the distaff side: Dame Kiri Te Kanawa is superbly elegant as Rosalinde, combining rich tone throughout with consistent vocal high spirits. Brigitte Fassbaender is a 'natural' as Prince Orlovsky and invests her singing with just the right degree of frosty hauteur. As Rosalinde's maid, Adele, Edita Gruberová is simply delicious, giving a performance full of champagne-like charm. On the male side the set is slightly less assured: Wolfgang Brendel forces occasionally as Eisenstein, and Olaf Bär has some way to go before rivalling Erich Kunz as the manipulative Doctor Falke. However, the more minor roles are cast from strength with Tom Krause excellent as Frank, Richard Leech a full-throated Alfred, and the Stage Director, Otto Schenk, an *echt-Wienerisch* gaoler Frosch. Previn secures extremely rich playing from the Vienna Philharmonic. His conducting is always assured, if without the final degree of individuality that conductors such as Clemens Krauss or Karajan are able to bring to this immortal score. Philips's recording is of the highest standard: exceptionally well detailed, finely balanced and with a strong sense of atmosphere.

Another highly recommendable version of this delightful operetta, if you want only the music, is the famous historic performance of 1951 conducted — irresistibly — by Clemens Krauss. Nobody knew better than he how this score should go and he had under him a cast that has seldom if ever been surpassed, authentically Viennese in all respects. It represents a performance of a kind that has now passed into history and has never been emulated in the studio. It has in Krauss one of the supreme conductors of the genre. Here we have the lift, the insouciance, the rhythmic discipline, the control of subtle rubato that cannot be learnt but were an essential part of this born-and-bred Viennese. Patzak's heady, charming Eisenstein, Gueden's witty Rosalinde, Loose's charming Adele, Dermota's ardent Alfred, Poell's wry Falke, Dönch's comic Frank are all endearing portraits that haven't staled with the passing years; on the contrary they remain models of style. They form an unbeatable ensemble. The recording has plenty of presence and isn't overblown or over-reverberant in the modern manner, although the digital transfer only emphasizes the papery sound of the strings. No dialogue is included, but does that really matter in a performance that creates its own stage by musical means alone? The second CD is completed with excerpts from the first Decca New Year Concert, studio-made not live. Krauss inaugurated the idea in the dark days of the war to cheer up Vienna. He presided over the event until his untimely death in 1954, and nobody has yet surpassed him in terms of champagne sparkle and rhythmic bite.

Richard Strauss

German 1864-1949

R. Strauss. Horn Concertos[a] — No. 1 in E flat major, Op. 11; No. 2 in E flat major. Oboe Concerto in D major[b]. Duett-Concertino[c]. [a]**Peter Damm** (hn); [b]**Manfred Clement** (ob); [c]**Manfred Weise** (cl); [c]**Wolfgang Liebscher** (bn); Staatskapelle Dresden/**Rudolf Kempe**. EMI Studio CDM7 69661-2. From SLS5067 (10/76).

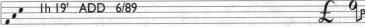

R. Strauss. Horn Concertos[a] — No. 1 in E flat major, Op. 11; No. 2 in E flat major.
Hindemith. Horn Concerto[b]. **Dennis Brain** (hn); **Philharmonia Orchestra**/[a]**Wolfgang Sawallisch**; [b]**Paul Hindemith**. EMI CDC7 47834-2. Items marked [a] Columbia mono 33CX1491 (11/57), [b] from HLS7001 (3/72).

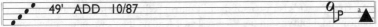

Kempe's disc is a skilful compilation, bringing together Strauss's finest solo concertos. The First Horn Concerto has great panache, not surprising for a 19-year-old whose father was principal horn in the Munich Court Orchestra. It is a graceful piece and one which nevertheless has considerable humour. The other works on the disc date from Strauss's maturity and they all share his exquisitely vocal style of composition: fluid, subtle and unrestrainedly melodious. The Oboe Concerto is particularly fine and could quite easily be seen as an instrumental equivalent of the delicious *Four Last Songs*. The soloists, all drawn from the ranks of the Staatskapelle Dresden, play with consummate skill and a real feel for Strauss's idiom. Kempe conducts superbly.

The First Horn Concerto was already typical in many respects of the mature composer to be. The Second Concerto dates from 1942 and looks back to his early years. The later concerto shows an obviously much more experienced hand at work: the scoring is more resourceful and adventurous, the structure of the work more sophisticated. Hindemith wrote his only horn concerto in 1949 for Dennis Brain, whose score he later inscribed with the words "To the unsurpassed original performer of this piece from a grateful composer". The work is quite short and unusual in construction, with two two very brief quicker movements succeeded by a longer slow movement in the form of a palindrome. After Strauss's warm romanticism Hindemith's work seems a little severe at first, but it has its own very distinct character and wit. It would be difficult to imagine more accomplished, more confident and exuberant performances than these by Dennis Brain. The Hindemith was recorded in stereo, and is in good sound: the Strauss concertos were recorded in mono only, and the orchestral sound was never good for its date. This transfer has even less body than the original LP, but fortunately Brain's unique and instantly recognizable tone quality comes through unscathed.

R. Strauss. Don Juan, Op. 20[a]. Tod und Verklärung, Op. 24[b]. Also sprach Zarathustra, Op. 30[c]. **Vienna Philharmonic Orchestra/Herbert von Karajan.** Decca Ovation 417 720-2DM. Item marked [a] from SXL2269 (5/61), [b] SXL2261 (4/61), [c] SXL2154 (8/59).

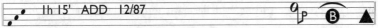

The orchestral playing here is magnificent — the sheer ecstatic fervour of the violins brings out all the sexuality of the glorious *Don Juan* love-music, while at the end the feeling of the desolate ebbing away of all feeling is marvellously conveyed. *Also sprach Zarathustra* is full of subtle detail, and the CD background quiet brings the most potent atmospheric feeling, as is immediately instanced by the hushed string entry of "The dwellers in the world beyond". The punch of the brass and again the soaring violins in "Of joys and passions"

compensates for any lack of amplitude while the "Dance Song" has a special rhythmic lilt from an orchestra famous for their feeling for the dance idiom. The transfiguration theme of *Tod und Verklärung* is another instance where the leonine timbre of the VPO brings a new dimension. All in all, this is a splendid triptych, confirming Karajan as a great and indeed uniquely perceptive Straussian.

NEW REVIEW

R. Strauss. Don Juan, Op. 20. Don Quixote, Op. 35[a]. [a]**Franz Bartolomey** (vc); [a]**Heinrich Koll** (va); **Vienna Philharmonic Orchestra/André Previn.** Telarc CD80262.

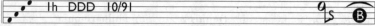

Strauss's two Dons make an obvious coupling. There are versions of *Don Juan* where "youth's fiery pulses race" like a tornado sweeping through the entire orchestra. Previn's isn't one of them. Control is the keynote here, a certain nobility and dignity, with the Vienna strings lending their own inimitable brand of sweetness and vibrancy to the love music. Similarly, there are versions of *Don Quixote* which place the principal characters (cello and viola) emphatically down at the footlights. Previn and Telarc respect the composer's original intentions and use the principals of the orchestra who are quite clearly balanced within the orchestra. It's a patient and considered reading full of warmth and humanity that does not yield all its treasures on first hearing but will only initially disappoint if you have become used to the piece being recorded as a double concerto. There have also been recordings that render the sound of the Vienna Philharmonic with more richness and gloss, but momentary suspicions of the woodwind in *Don Juan*, to borrow Debussy's phrase, "sending out distress signals from the back of the orchestra" are the only blot on a superbly natural, ideally distanced sound from Telarc.

R. Strauss. Don Quixote, Op. 35[a]. Le bourgeois gentilhomme — suite, Op. 60[b]. [a]**Leonard Rubens** (va); [a]**Paul Tortelier** (vc); **Royal Philharmonic Orchestra/Sir Thomas Beecham.** EMI Great Recordings of the Century mono CDH7 63106-2. Item marked [a] from HMV DB6796/800 (4/49), [b] DB6643, DB6646/8 (11/49).

Although *Don Quixote* has been well served on record, this recording must be chosen for its special qualities of insight. It combines the youthful freshness of the young soloist at the beginning of his career, who only a few years earlier had played the work under Strauss himself, with the wisdom and maturity of a lifelong advocate of the composer. Moreover, the composer was present not only during the recording of *Don Quixote* but also during some of the movements from *Le bourgeois gentilhomme*, which are given with such sparkle here. Beecham was one of the few conductors to bring a rare kind of delicacy and lightness to Strauss's scores, nowhere more so than in *Le bourgeois gentilhomme*. Tortelier brings to *Don Quixote* nobility and great poetic insight and no reader of whatever generation is likely to be disappointed by the quality of the orchestral playing. Indeed it is pretty electrifying, with the newly-formed RPO on their best form.

R. Strauss. Aus Italien, Op. 16. Don Juan, Op. 20. **Berlin Philharmonic Orchestra/Riccardo Muti.** Philips 422 399-2PH.

Muti's interpretation of *Aus Italien*, Strauss's early 'symphonic fantasy', composed after a holiday in Italy, glows and glistens with Southern warmth and colour. The

Berlin Philharmonic revels in the masterly scoring and its rich sound is fully captured by the Philips recording. Muti achieves a splendid balance and one can
almost feel the heat of the sun as the young Strauss glories in his first experience
of the land that has inspired so many composers. The performance of *Don Juan* is
also extremely good, but Muti's interpretation favours excessively slow tempos in
the romantic episodes.

R. Strauss. Eine Alpensinfonie, Op. 64. **Concertgebouw Orchestra,
Amsterdam/Bernard Haitink.** Philips 416 156-2PH. From 416 156-1PH
(4/86).

50' DDD 7/86

R. Strauss. Eine Alpensinfonie, Op. 64. Don Juan, Op. 20. **San Francisco
Symphony Orchestra/Herbert Blomstedt.** Decca 421 815-2DH.

1h 10' DDD 6/90

The *Alpine* Symphony is the last of Richard Strauss's great tone-poems and is in
many ways the most spectacular. The score is an evocation of the changing
moods of an alpine landscape and the huge orchestral apparatus of over 150
players encompasses quadruple wind, 20 horns, organ, wind machine, cowbells,
thunder machine, two harps and enhanced string forces. Its pictorialism may be
all too graphic but what virtuosity and inspiration Strauss commands. Haitink
gives a magisterial account of this long underrated score and the playing of the
Concertgebouw Orchestra is of the highest order of virtuosity. The recording
reproduces every strand in the complex texture with clarity and does full justice
to its wide dynamic range.

Herbert Blomstedt's *Eine Alpensinfonie* also penetrates beyond the pictorialism
into the work's deeper elements. It emerges as a gigantic hymn to nature on a
Mahlerian scale. Tempos are slower, but these are justified by the noble
expansiveness of the final pages, towards which the whole performance moves
with impressive inevitability. The San Francisco Symphony's playing is magnificent, with subtle use of vibrato by the strings and superb performances, individual
and corporate, by the wind sections. The recording is on a spacious scale to
match the performance, the big climaxes really thrilling and the whole well
balanced. The *Don Juan* performance is fine too.

R. Strauss. Symphonia domestica, Op. 53. **Berlin Philharmonic
Orchestra/Herbert von Karajan.** EMI Studio CDM7 69571-2. From
ASD2955 (4/74).

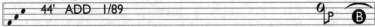

44' ADD 1/89

What this disc lacks in total playing time, it more than makes up for by the
quality and dedication of the performance. This is a classic reading of Op. 53
from Karajan and the Berlin Philharmonic, embodying their special affinity for
Strauss's music. The work lays powerful traps for the unwary conductor — the
domestic delights can, all too easily, acquire the amateur triviality of the home
movie but Karajan allows the sentiments to ring true by letting them speak for
themselves. The domestic incidents are vividly portrayed but not parodied, the
more romantic sections are allowed their head, but not overdriven. Karajan also
has a clear idea of the music's direction, and passing details are not permitted to
hinder his path or obscure his view. With refined playing typical of the Berlin
Philharmonic's standard and a wide-ranging, subtle recording, this issue does not
put a foot wrong.

R. Strauss. Metamorphosen for 23 solo strings. Tod und Verklärung, Op. 24. Drei Hymnen, Op. 71ᵃ. ᵃ**Felicity Lott** (sop); **Scottish National Orchestra/ Neeme Järvi.** Chandos CHAN8734. Texts and translations included.

> 1h 12' DDD 3/90

R. Strauss. Metamorphosen for 23 solo strings. Tod und Verklärung, Op. 24. **Berlin Philharmonic Orchestra/Herbert von Karajan.** DG 410 892-2GH. From 2532 074 (5/83).

> 52' DDD 2/84

There is plenty of competition among recordings of *Metamorphosen* and *Tod und Verklärung*, but what makes this Chandos disc so attractive is that it contains the only CD recording of the *Drei Hymnen*, Op. 71, settings of poems by Hölderlin about aspects of love, not erotic love so much as love of nature and one's country. They were composed in 1921 for the Wagnerian soprano Barbara Kemp and require a very large orchestra. In their outpouring of soprano ecstasy, they anticipate the *Four Last Songs* and would be as well known were they not so difficult to perform. Felicity Lott is no Wagnerian, but she has the Straussian qualities of silvery tone and expressive radiance. Although she is occasionally tested by the sustained intensity of these songs, she sings them rapturously while Järvi and the Scottish orchestra give her fine support. Järvi's interpretation of *Metamorphosen* is urgent and compelling and the performance of *Tod und Verklärung* likewise. The recording is up to Chandos's high standard for its Järvi/Strauss cycle, although the resonance of the hall used for the recordings may not be to every collector's liking.

In Karajan's handling of *Metamorphosen* power is held in reserve, until the climactic C major eruption just before the coda, with thrilling effect — everything, one feels, has been in some way a preparation for this moment, and the final turn to the minor acquires greater poignancy and dramatic force as a result. The playing of the Berlin Philharmonic strings is magnificent, and the recording manages to be both spacious and intimate. After this, the prospect of another long stretch of C minor may seem a little daunting, but *Tod und Verklärung* provides a strong contrast to the much later *Metamorphosen*, and once again Karajan's superbly controlled and intense reading ensures a gripping musical experience.

NEW REVIEW

R. Strauss. Ein Heldenleben, Op. 40ᵃ. Macbeth, Op. 23ᵇ. **Staatskapelle Dresden/Rudolf Kempe.** EMI Studio CDM7 69171-2. Item marked ᵃ from SLS880 (6/74), ᵇ SLS861 (10/73).

> 1h 4' ADD 5/88   q P Ⓑ

NEW REVIEW

R. Strauss. Ein Heldenleben, Op. 40. Till Eulenspiegels lustige Streiche, Op. 28. **Chicago Symphony Orchestra/Daniel Barenboim.** Erato 2292-45621-2.

> 1h 3' DDD 8/91   q P q S Ⓑ

The premature death of Rudolf Kempe in 1976 robbed us of one of the twentieth century's greatest conductors, whose career would no doubt have blossomed into an elder statesmanship equal to Karl Böhm or Herbert von Karajan. Kempe was not a prolific recording artist, but the interpretations he did commit to disc captured him at his greatest. This glorious performance of *Ein Heldenleben*, beautifully recorded by EMI in 1972, is one of the best ever made, with the Dresden State Orchestra imparting a silky, old world resonance to the piece. Kempe's Hero is noble and chivalrous, if slightly taciturn, and his critics really are a picky, pedantic lot. The smooth violin of Peter Mirring enhances the soundscape, while Kempe attends to every nook and cranny of Strauss's potentially congested orchestration. This is essentially a symphonic view of the work, with a strong sense of architecture. "The Hero's Battle" plays by Queensberry rules, but Kempe's slightly understated approach makes the great interludes and epilogues all the more moving.

Barenboim's recording presents a more impetuous, more overtly romantic hero and gives the Chicago Symphony Orchestra a free rein to bring their customary flair and virtuosity to the work. The battle sequence is properly exciting while Samuel Magad's violin solo is sweet

Rudolf Kempe   [photo: Allen

and seductive. Erato's wide-angle recording is very fine, with plenty of inner detail and for sheer splendour and opulence it surpasses the EMI version. It kicks off with Barenboim's suave, lightweight version of *Till Eulenspiegel* while the EMI fill-up is a somewhat Brahmsian account of the lesser known tone poem, *Macbeth*. Although no Straussian should be without Kempe's poetic interpretation, Erato's disc is now a major claimant for supremacy.

NEW REVIEW

R. *Strauss*. LIEDER. OPERA EXCERPTS. **Lisa della Casa** (sop); **Vienna Philharmonic Orchestra/ªKarl Böhm; ᵇRudolf Moralt, ᶜHeinrich Hollreiser.** Decca Historic mono 425 959-2DM. Texts and translations included. Four Last Songs, AV150 (from LW5056, 12/53)[a]. ARABELLA — Er ist der Richtige nicht (with Hilde Gueden, sop. LW5029, 10/53)[b]; Der Richtige so hab ich stets zu mir gesagt (Paul Schoeffler, bass-bar. LXT5017, 4/55)[c]; Das war sehr gut, Mandryka (Alfred Poell, bar. LW5029)[b]. ARIADNE AUF NAXOS — Es gibt ein Reich[c]. CAPRICCIO — Closing scene (Franz Bierbach, bass. Both LXT5017)[c].

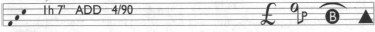

$\cdot$ 1h 7' ADD 4/90   £ ♪ ℗ Ⓑ ▲

NEW REVIEW

R. *Strauss*. Four Last Songs, AV150. VOCAL WORKS. **Elisabeth Schwarzkopf** (sop); **Philharmonia Orchestra/Herbert von Karajan.** EMI CDM7 63655-2. New to UK. Recorded at a performance in the Royal Festival Hall, London in June 1956.
Bach: Cantata No. 199, "Mein Herze schwimmt im Blut" (Schwarzkopf; Philharmonia/Thurston Dart. New to UK. 1958). Mass in B minor, BWV232 — Christe eleison; Laudamus te; Et in unum Dominum (Schwarzkopf, Kathleen Ferrier, contr; Vienna Philharmonic Orchestra/Karajan. New to UK. 1950). *Mozart:* Nehmt meinen Dank, K383 (Schwarzkopf; Philharmonia/Alceo Galliera. New to UK. 1955). *Gieseking:* Kinderlieder (Schwarzkopf/Walter Gieseking, pf. New to UK. 1955).

$\cdot$ 1h 19' ADD 12/90   £ ♪ ℗ Ⓑ ▲

NEW REVIEW

R. *Strauss*. LIEDER. **Dame Kiri Te Kanawa** (sop); **ªVienna Philharmonic Orchestra/Sir Georg Solti** (ᵇpf). Decca 430 511-2DH. Texts and translations included.
Four Last Songs, AV150[a]. All' mein Gedanken, Op. 21 No. 1[b]. Allerseelen, Op. 10 No. 8[b]. Begegnung, AV72[b]. Cäcilie, Op. 27 No. 2[b]. Hat gesagt, Op. 36

No. 3[b]. Madrigal, Op. 15 No. 1[b]. Malven, Op. posth[b]. Morgen, Op. 27 No. 4[b]. Muttertändelei, Op. 43 No. 2[b]. Die Nacht, Op. 10 No. 3[b]. Schlechtes Wetter, Op. 69 No. 5[b]. Ständchen, Op. 17 No. 2[b]. Zueignung, Op. 10 No. 1[b].

50' DDD 9/91

R. Strauss. Four Last Songs, AV150[a]. Tod und Verklärung, Op. 24[b].
Wagner. GOTTERDAMMERUNG[c] — Dawn and Siegfried's Rhine Journey; Siegfried's Death and Funeral Music. [a]**Lucia Popp** (sop); [ab]**London Philharmonic Orchestra;** [c]**Berlin Philharmonic Orchestra/Klaus Tennstedt.** EMI Digital CDD7 64290-2. Items marked [ab] from HMV ASD4182 (2/83), [c] ASD3985 (10/81).

1h 10' DDD 8/92

Strauss's *Four Last Songs* are a perfect summation of the composer's lifelong love-affair with the soprano voice deriving from the fact that he married a soprano, Pauline Ahna. They are also an appropriate and deeply moving farewell to his career as a composer and to the whole romantic tradition. They have inspired many glorious performances so that there is no reason to apologize for listing as many as four different interpretations. In recent times there has been a tendency to linger unnecessarily over what are already eloquent enough pieces. Lisa Della Casa, in her naturally and lovingly sung performance under Karl Böhm (the first-ever recording of the pieces back in 1953) makes no such mistake. In this new incarnation this is a wonderful offering at medium price backed by other invaluable Strauss interpretations from the Swiss diva. Her particular gift is to sing the pieces in a natural, unforced manner with gloriously unfettered tone. Her and Böhm's tempos tend to be faster than those employed by most of her successors. Schwarzkopf's reading is more detailed, more intimate, slightly more studied. Of her three recordings, this live one, only recently come to light, with Karajan catches her at her most spontaneous. Her version also includes rewarding additions to her discography, not least the delightful children's cycle by pianist Walter Gieseking and items from a rehearsal, conducted by Karajan, of Bach's Mass in B minor.

For those looking for a modern performance Decca have brought together Sir Georg Solti, a conductor who has devoted much of his career to the service of this composer, an orchestra which has Strauss in its very bones, and one of the most justly revered sopranos of our time, Dame Kiri Te Kanawa. Her fine-tuned, soaring sound and rapturous performance lingers long in the memory. Meanwhile, Sir Georg ensures that spontaneity never lapses into sentimentality, with the peerless Vienna Philharmonic on top form, with some glorious horn playig and a deeply-felt solo violin intermezzo in "Beim Schlafengehan". The Decca sound is highly distinguished and this glorious recording should find a place in the affections of every Straussian. Another choice in modern sound is Lucia Popp with Klaus Tennstedt. She, perhaps, gives the most deeply moving, valedictory performance of all. Hers is a truly inspired reading of the *Four Last Songs*, undoubtedly enhanced by the London Philharmonic's splendid playing. The Decca disc also includes other Strauss songs where Dame Kiri and Sir Georg inspire each other to loving interpretations. The EMI Popp disc has a moving, very recommendable account of Strauss's *Tod und Verklärung* and some rousing chunks of Wagner.

R. Strauss. LIEDER[a]. Metamorphosen for 23 solo strings. [a]**Gundula Janowitz** (sop); **Academy of London/Richard Stamp.** Virgin Classics VC7 90794-2. Texts and translations included.
Lieder — Ruhe, meine Seele, Op. 27 No. 1; Waldseligkeit, Op. 49 No. 1; Freundliche Vision, Op. 48 No. 1; Morgen!, Op. 27 No. 4; Befreit, Op. 39 No.

4; Meinem Kinde, Op. 37 No. 3; Winterweihe, Op. 48 No. 4; Wiegenlied, Op.
41 No. 1; Die heiligen drei Könige aus Morgenland, Op. 56 No. 6.

·· 1h DDD 2/91 ⓠₚ ⓠₛ

Gundula Janowitz has given some of the most beautiful performances of the
music of Richard Strauss in the last three decades. Why no one asked her to
record more songs during her heyday is a great mystery, but here is a quite
lovely collection that shows her musicality and fine feeling for the Strauss idiom
at its best. Obviously, given the passing of the years, she is happiest in the gentler, more legato numbers where her quite exquisite breath control and beauty of
tone reap rich rewards — the floated line in *Wiegenlied* is absolutely ravishing and
her feeling for words has, if anything, deepened over the years. She instils appropriate drama into the ecstatic *Die heiligen drei Könige aus Morgenland*, a lovely
song. Throughout the disc the Academy of London play with great feeling and a
good regard for the sound-world that Richard Strauss's music demands. As a very
substantial fill-up, Richard Stamp and his orchestra offer a sensitive reading of
Strauss's heartrending *Metamorphosen*, that threnody for the great opera-houses of
Germany destroyed by Allied bombing during the Second World War. The
complex lines are interwoven with care and sensitivity, and the work's true
character emerges powerfully in this passionate performance. The recording is
rich and clear. A delightful disc.

R. Strauss. LIEDER.
Wolf. LIEDER. **Barbara Bonney** (sop); **Geoffrey Parsons** (pf). DG 429
406-2GH. Texts and translations included.
R. Strauss: Du meines Herzens Krönelein, Op. 21 No. 2; Meinem Kinde,
Op. 37 No. 3; Ich schwebe wie auf Engelsschwingen, Op. 48 No. 2; Die Nacht,
Op. 10 No. 3; Morgen, Op. 27 No. 4; Allerseelen, Op. 10 No. 8; Mein Auge,
Op. 37 No. 4; Schön sind, doch kalt die Himmelssterne, Op. 19 No. 3; Ich
wollt' ein Sträusslein binden, Op. 68 No. 2; Ständchen, Op. 17 No. 2. **Wolf:**
Mörike Lieder — Der Knabe und das Immlein; Er ist's; Das verlassene
Mägdlein; Begegnung; Nimmersatte Liebe; Verborgenheit. Eichendorff Lieder —
Verschwiegene Liebe. Italienisches Liederbuch — Auch kleine Dinge. Spanisches
Liederbuch — In dem Schatten meiner Locken. Bescheidene Liebe.

·· 55' DDD 8/90 ⓠₚ

Bonney's clear, bell-like tone and faultless technique are heard at their most
appealing here. Adding to her purely vocal accomplishments is the imagination
behind the singing. Cannily choosing some of Wolf's most approachable songs,
she proceeds to interpret them with unaffected, stylish singing. She finds truth in
simplicity, avoiding the need for any over-detailed word painting; at the same
time she unerringly finds the right mood and timbre for each piece. *Das·verlassene
Mägdlein* is properly empty and weary, *Begegnung* smiling and playful, *Nimmersatte
Liebe* sensuous, *Verschwiegene Liebe* easily playful. Her Strauss might sometimes
benefit from more flowing tempos, but the phrasing is as inevitable and natural
as it is in the Wolf. Most attractive here is the conjuring up of unnamed threats
in *Die Nacht* and the proper rapture in *Ständchen*. Parsons is at his most free-
ranging and keen. Both artists are well supported by an open, forward recording.
Anyone wanting a representative choice of these composers' songs need look no
further.

R. Strauss. SALOME. **Birgit Nilsson** (sop) Salome; **Eberhard Waechter**
(bar) Jokanaan; **Gerhard Stolze** (ten) Herod; **Grace Hoffman** (mez) Herodias;
Waldemar Kmentt (ten) Narraboth; **Josephine Veasey** (mez) Page; **Tom
Krause** (bar) First Nazarene; **Nigel Douglas** (ten) Second Nazarene; **Zenon
Koznowski** (bass) First Soldier; **Heinz Holecek** (bass) Second Soldier;

Theodore Kirschbichler (bass) Cappadocian; **Vienna Philharmonic Orchestra/Sir Georg Solti.** Decca 414 414-2DH2. Notes, text and translation included. From SET228 (3/62).

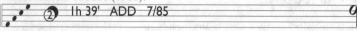

② 1h 39' ADD 7/85

NEW REVIEW

R. Strauss. SALOME. **Cheryl Studer** (sop) Salome; **Bryn Terfel** (bar) Jokanaan; **Horst Hiestermann** (ten) Herod; **Leonie Rysanek** (sop) Herodias; **Clemens Bieber** (ten) Narraboth; **Marianne Rørholm** (contr) Page; **Friedrich Molsberger** (bass) First Nazarene; **Ralf Lukas** (bass) Second Nazarene; **William Murray** (bass) First Soldier; **Bengt Rundgren** (bass) Second Soldier; **Klaus Lang** (bar) Cappadocian; **Orchestra of the Deutsche Oper, Berlin/Giuseppe Sinopoli.** DG 431 810-2GH2. Notes, text and translation included.

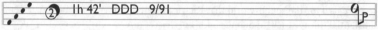

② 1h 42' DDD 9/91

With the Vienna Philharmonic in full cry and the Decca engineers capturing the violently erotic splendour of the sound, this set, like the opera, caused something of a stir when it first appeared and one can hear why even more vividly on CD. Nilsson marvellously captures Salome's decadent sensuality and produces a softer grain to her voice than some at the time thought her capable of, while the well-known solidity of her singing was unimpaired. Gerhard Stolze makes a suitably fevered, unhinged sound as the near-crazed Herod, Eberhard Waechter is a forceful, visionary-sounding John the Baptist, Waldemar Kmentt a properly ardent Narraboth (the soldier so infatuated with Salome's charms that he commits suicide when she shows no interest in him). The supporting cast, recruited from the Vienna State Opera and Covent Garden, is strong.

The DG version is also a magnificent achievement. Studer, her voice fresh, vibrant and sensuous, conveys exactly Salome's growing fascination, infatuation and eventual obsession with Jokanaan, ending in the arresting necrophilia of the final scene. She expresses Salome's wheedling, spoilt nature, strong will and

Bryn Terfel   *[photo: Harlequin*

ecstasy in tones apt for every aspect of the strenuous role. She is supported to the hilt by Sinopoli's incandescent conducting and by Bryn Terfel's convincing Jokanaan, unflaggingly delivered, by Hiestermann's neurotic Herod, not quite so outlandish a reading as Stolze's, and Rysanek's wilful Herodias. The playing is excellent. The recording, while not so multi-coloured as the Decca, has breadth and warmth. These two readings are equally recommendable. For a newcomer to the work, Studer's superb portrayal just tips the balance in favour of the more recent set. She has all her rival's accomplishments and something more.

R. Strauss. ELEKTRA. **Birgit Nilsson** (sop) Elektra; **Regina Resnik** (mez) Klytemnestra; **Marie Collier** (sop) Chrysothemis; **Tom Krause** (bar) Orestes; **Gerhard Stolze** (ten) Aegisthus; **Pauline Tinsley** (sop) Overseer; **Helen Watts** (contr), **Maureen Lehane, Yvonne Minton** (mezs), **Jane Cook, Felicia Weathers** (sops) First, Second, Third, Fourth and Fifth Maids; **Tugomir Franc** (Tutor); **Vienna Philharmonic Orchestra/Sir Georg**

Solti. Decca 417 345-2DH2. Notes, text and translation included. From
SET354/5 (11/67).

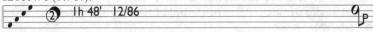

R. Strauss. ELEKTRA. **Inge Borkh** (sop) Elektra; **Jean Madeira** (mez)
Klytemnestra; **Marianne Schech** (sop) Chrysothemis; **Fritz Uhl** (ten)
Aegisthus; **Dietrich Fischer-Dieskau** (bar) Orestes; **Ilona Steingruber** (sop)
Overseer; **Cvetka Ahlin** (contr), **Margarete Sjöstedt, Sieglinde Wagner**
(mezs), **Judith Hellwig, Gerda Scheyrer** (sops) First, Second, Third, Fourth
and Fifth Maids; **Fred Teschler** (bass) Tutor; **Dresden State Opera Chorus;
Staatskapelle Dresden/Karl Böhm.** DG 431 737-2GX2. Notes, text and
translation included. From SLPM138690/91 (11/61).

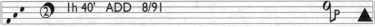

Elektra is the most consistently inspired of all Strauss's operas and derives from
Greek mythology, with the ghost of Agamamenon, so unerringly delineated in the
opening bars, hovering over the whole work. The invention and the intensity of
mood are sustained throughout the opera's one-act length, and the characterization
is both subtle and pointed. It is a work peculiarly well-suited to Solti's gifts and
he has done nothing better in his long career in the studios. He successfully maintains the nervous tension throughout the unbroken drama and conveys all the power
and tension in Strauss's enormously complex score which is, for once, given complete.
The recording captures the excellent singers and the Vienna Philharmonic in a
warm, spacious acoustic marred only by some questionable electronic effects.

Although it makes the traditional theatre cuts (probably sanctioned by Strauss),
the Böhm recording is also recommendable. At mid-price it represents very good
value. Böhm and the Staatskapelle are perhaps even more conversant with the
Strauss idiom than their Viennese counterparts. Böhm's reading is beautifully shaped
and timed — swift in execution as befits the pell-mell character of the score.
Borkh's crazed fanatical Elektra is quite the equal of Nilsson on Decca and perhaps
searches even deeper into Elektra's psyche. Schech is an articulate, appropriately
fevered Chrysothemis, Madeira a commanding, unexaggerated Klytemnestra. If
you add in Fischer-Dieskau's affecting, superbly sung and enuniciated Orestes you
have a formidable combination in a recording that wears its years lightly.

R. Strauss. DER ROSENKAVALIER. **Elisabeth Schwarzkopf** (sop) Die
Feldmarschallin; **Christa Ludwig** (mez) Octavian; **Otto Edelmann** (bass)
Baron Ochs; **Teresa Stich-Randall** (sop) Sophie; **Eberhard Waechter** (bar)
Faninal; **Nicolai Gedda** (ten) Italian Tenor; **Kerstin Meyer** (contr) Annina;
Paul Kuen (ten) Valzacchi; **Ljuba Welitsch** (sop) Duenna; **Anny Felber-
mayer** (sop) Milliner; **Harald Pröghlöf** (bar) Notary; **Franz Bierbach** (bass)
Police Commissioner; **Erich Majkut** (ten) Marschallin's Majordomo; **Gerhard
Unger** (ten) Faninal's Majordomo, Animal Seller; **Karl Friedrich** (ten)
Landlord; **Loughton high School for Girls and Bancroft's School Choirs;
Philharmonia Chorus and Orchestra/Herbert von Karajan.** EMI CDS7
49354-2. Notes, text and translation included. From Columbia SAX2269/72 (11/59).

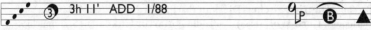

R. Strauss. DER ROSENKAVALIER. **Dame Kiri Te Kanawa** (sop) Die
Feldmarschallin; **Anne Sofie von Otter** (mez) Octavian; **Kurt Rydl** (bass)
Baron Ochs; **Barbara Hendricks** (sop) Sophie; **Franz Grundheber** (bar)
Faninal; **Richard Leech** (ten) Italian Tenor; **Claire Powell** (mez) Annina;
Graham Clark (ten) Valzacchi; **Julia Faulkner** (sop) Duenna; **Sabine Brohm**
(sop) Milliner; **Alfred Sramek** (bar) Notary; **Bodo Schwanbeck** (bass) Police
Commissioner; **Ferry Gruber** (ten) Marschallin's Majordomo; **Michael Kraus**

(ten) Faninal's Majordomo; **Heinz Zednik** (ten) Landlord; **Armin Ude** (ten)
Animal Seller; **Dresden Kreuzchor; Dresden State Opera Chorus;
Staatskapelle Dresden/Bernard Haitink.** EMI CDS7 54259-2. Notes, text
and translation included.

Der Rosenkavalier concerns the transferring of love of the young headstrong aristocrat
Octavian from the older Marschallin (with whom he is having an affair) to the young
Sophie, a girl of *nouveau riche* origins who is his generation. The portrayal of the
different levels of passion is masterly and the Marschallin's resigned surrender of her
ardent young lover gives opera one of its most cherishable scenes. The comic side of
the plot concerns the vulgar machinations of the rustic Baron Ochs and his attempts
to seduce the disguised Octavian (girl playing boy playing girl!). The musical
richness of the score is almost indescribable with stream after stream of endless
melody, and the final trio which brings the three soprano roles together is the
crowning glory of a masterpiece of our century. The magnificent 1957 recording,
conducted with genius by Karajan and with a cast such as dreams are made of,
has a status unparalleled and is unlikely to be challenged for many a year. The
Philharmonia play like angels and Elisabeth Schwarzkopf as the Marschallin gives one
of her greatest performances. The recording, lovingly remastered, is outstanding.

However, EMI's 1991 recording, conducted by Bernard Haitink, provides
worthy competition to Karajan's now historic recording. The principal difference
between the two is Haitink's superbly vigorous direction. With the Dresden
Staatskapelle providing a level of orchestral virtuosity which it would be hard to
equal, Haitink digs deeply into Strauss's superb score, producing time after time
memorable flashes of insight as well as inspiration. This is opera conducting of a
standard rarely encountered on disc or in the theatre. Haitink has a brilliant cast
at his disposal. Dame Kiri Te Kanawa delivers a statuesque and suitably regal
interpretation of the Marschallin: not as finely detailed as Elisabeth Schwarzkopf
but well characterized and warmly sung. Equally appealing is Anne Sofie von
Otter as the young Octavian: the slight pressure which she has to apply to
encompass the full vocal range of the part perfectly describes the ardour and
impetuosity of the opera's central character. Barbara Hendricks gives an assured if
slightly sophisticated performance as Sophie, while Kurt Rydl and Franz
Grundheber are solidly reliable as Baron Ochs and Herr von Faninal, respectively, both mercifully rejecting the temptation to indulge in vocal caricature. All
the minor roles are highly characterized, with Richard Leech giving a particularly
well judged portrayal of the Italian Tenor. EMI's recording here is exceptionally
rich: the overall relationships have been acutely judged, allowing the full sweep
of Strauss's rich orchestral writing to be heard in perfect balance to the individual
voices. Thanks principally to Bernard Haitink's magnificent conducting this set is
an excellent modern alternative to Karajan's Philharmonia recording, and in its
extraordinary insight may well for many provide a more truthful and well-
balanced interpretation of Strauss's operatic masterpiece.

R. Strauss. ARIADNE AUF NAXOS. **Jessye Norman** (sop) Ariadne; **Juia
Varady** (sop) Composer; **Edita Gruberová** (sop) Zerbinetta; **Paul Frey** (ten)
Bacchus; **Dietrich Fischer-Dieskau** (bar) Music Master; **Olaf Bär** (bar)
Harlequin; **Gerd Wolf** (bass) Truffaldino; **Martin Finke** (ten) Scaramuchio,
Dancing Master; **Eva Lind** (sop) Naïad; **Marianne Rørholm** (contr) Dryad;
Julie Kaufmann (sop) Echo; **Rudolf Asmus** (spr) Major-domo; members of
the **Leipzig Gewandhaus Orchestra/Kurt Masur.** Philips 422 084-2PH2.
Notes, text and translation included.

Not everybody finds Jessye Norman a truly Straussian soprano, but the sheer
opulence of her singing, its dignity and poise, are to be cherished. Julia Varady's

Composer is full of fire and, where required, tenderness and although she is perhaps not quite at her best here, it is still a formidable performance, bright, incisive and crystalline in the trills in the big aria. Outstanding among the men are Olaf Bär as Harlequin — the best on disc — and Fischer-Dieskau as a gruff Music Master. Many *Ariadne* performances have foundered on the singing of Bacchus, but Paul Frey recalls the achievements of Helge Roswaenge in the role and makes the final duet the climactic experience that Strauss intended. Exquisite playing by the instrumentalists from the Leipzig Gewandhaus Orchestra and inspired conducting by Kurt Masur make this a highly successful issue.

NEW REVIEW

R. Strauss. DIE FRAU OHNE SCHATTEN. **Julia Varady** (sop) Empress; **Plácido Domingo** (ten) Emperor; **Hildegard Behrens** (sop) Dyer's Wife; **José van Dam** (bar) Barak the Dyer; **Reinhild Runkel** (contr) Nurse; **Albert Dohmen** (bar) Spirit-Messenger; **Sumi Jo** (sop) Voice of the Falcon; **Robert Gambill** (ten) Apparition of a Young Man; **Elzbieta Ardam** (mez) Voice from above; **Eva Lind** (sop) Guardian of the Threshold; **Gottfried Hornik** (bar) One-eyed Brother; **Hans Franzen** (bass) One-armed Brother; **Wilfried Gahmlich** (ten) Hunchback Brother; **Vienna Boys' Choir; Vienna State Opera Chorus; Vienna Philharmonic Orchestra/Sir Georg Solti.** Decca 436 243-2DH3. Notes, text and translation included.

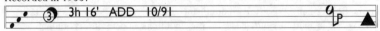

NEW REVIEW

R. Strauss. DIE FRAU OHNE SCHATTEN. **Leonie Rysanek** (sop) Empress; **Hans Hopf** (ten) Emperor; **Christel Goltz** (sop) Dyer's Wife; **Paul Schoeffler** (bar) Barak the Dyer; **Elisabeth Höngen** (contr) Nurse; **Kurt Böhme** (bass) Spirit-Messenger; **Judith Hellwig** (sop) Voice of the Falcon; **Karel Terkal** (ten) Apparition of a Young Man; **Hilde Rössl-Majdan** (mez) Voice from above; **Emmy Loose** (sop) Guardian of the Threshold; **Harald Pröglhöf** (bass) One-eyed Brother; **Oskar Czerwenka** (bass) One-armed Brother; **Murray Dickie** (ten) Hunchback Brother; **Vienna State Opera Chorus; Vienna Philharmonic Orchestra/Karl Böhm.** Decca Historic 425 981-2DM3. Notes, text and translation included. From GOS554/7 (4/68). Recorded in 1955.

This was the most ambitious project on which Strauss and his librettist Hugo von Hofmannthal collaborated. It is both fairy tale and allegory with a score that is Wagnerian in its scale and breadth. The Solti version presents the score absolutely complete in an opulent recording that encompasses every detail of the work's multi-faceted orchestration. Nothing escapes his keen eye and ear or that of the Decca engineers. The cast boasts splendid exponents of the two soprano roles. Behrens's vocal acting suggests complete identification with the unsatisfied plight of the Dyer's Wife and her singing has a depth of character to compensate for some tonal wear. Varady gives an intense, poignant account of the Empress's taxing music. The others, though never less than adequate, leave something to be desired. Domingo sings the Emperor with customary vigour and strength but evinces little sense of the music's idiom. José van Dam is likewise a vocally impeccable Barak but never penetrates the Dyer's soul. Runkel is a mean, malign Nurse as she should be though not as interesting as her predecessors in this part.

These roles are very well understood on the pioneering 1955 Decca version, still sounding well. Schoeffler's Barak is unsurpassed in its eloquent accents. Höngen is a fiercely articulate Nurse, Hopf a true Heldentenor Emperor. Rysanek's inward-looking, moving Empress is a treasurable performance, equal to if different from Julia Varady's. Goltz is an involved though vocally uningratiating Dyer's Wife. Nobody has surpassed Karl Böhm in his understanding of the score, which he conducts more flowingly than does Solti. He makes a few, not very serious excisions. Both versions benefit from glorious, dedicated playing by the Vienna Philharmonic Orchestra.

NEW REVIEW

R. Strauss. FRIEDENSTAG. **Roger Roloff** (bass) Commandant; **Alessandra Marc** (sop) Maria; **William Wildermann** (bass) Sargeant; **Max Wittges** (bass-bar) Corporal; **George Shirley** (ten) Private Soldier; **Peter van Derick** (bar) Musketeer; **Paul Schmidt** (bass) Bugler; **Stephen Lusmann** (bar) Officer, Front-line Officer; **Ruben Broitman** (ten) A Piedmontese; **Terry Cook** (bass) Holsteiner; **Richard Cassilly** (ten) Burgomaster; **James Wood** (bass) Bishop; **Karen Williams** (sop) A Woman; **New York City Gay Men's Chorus; Collegiate Chorale and Orchestra/Robert Bass.** Koch International Classics 37111-2. Notes, text and translation included. Recorded at a performance in Carnegie Hall, New York on November 19th, 1989.

· · 1h 20' DDD 1/92

First produced in Munich in 1938 with Hans Hotter as the commandant, Strauss's one-act opera *Friedenstag* has never become widely known, doubtless because it has an austere theme compared to others such as *Salome* and *Der Rosenkavalier*. Set in a seventeenth-century fortress under siege during the Thirty Years War, it tells of a military commander who resolves to die rather than surrender but then, as news of peace arrives, vows with his former enemy to work for a better world. Strauss himself said that this moral tale did not suit him and was "a tiring assignment", but it has qualities of its own and with its mainly male roles and the importance of the chorus it has a special place among his works. Furthermore, the collaboration of the Jewish writer Stefan Zweig and the anti-war feeling of the opera (it declares that "the enemy are human beings like us" and hails peace) makes it all the more interesting as a work created in Nazi Germany. Straussians will want to invest in this first recording which fits some 80 minutes of music on to one disc, especially since from the little march at the very opening of the work it has a character all of its own. If a few little noises intrude to remind us that it was recorded during a live performance, there are compensations too in that the singing and playing have urgency and spontaneity and the sound is well balanced. The soloists and chorus sing throughout in idiomatic German. As for the predominance of male voices, it proves as acceptable as it is in Britten's *Billy Budd*, also set in a fighting community, though here it's relieved by the lengthy aria for the commander's young wife Maria on track 10. There are 21 tracks in all, but the booklet libretto with translation does not show where they begin and collectors may want to write them in for themselves.

R. Strauss. CAPRICCIO. **Elisabeth Schwarzkopf** (sop) The Countess; **Eberhard Waechter** (bar) The Count; **Nicolai Gedda** (ten) Flamand; **Dietrich Fischer-Dieskau** (bar) Olivier; **Hans Hotter** (bass-bar) La Roche; **Christa Ludwig** (mez) Clairon; **Rudolf Christ** (ten) Monsieur Taupe; **Anna Moffo** (sop) Italian Soprano; **Dermot Troy** (ten) Italian Tenor; **Karl Schmitt-Walter** (bar) Major-domo; **Philharmonia Orchestra/Wolfgang Sawallisch.** EMI mono CDS7 49014-8. Notes, text and translation included. From Columbia 33CX1600/02 (3/59).

· · ② 2h 15' ADD 9/87 ▲

The plot of *Capriccio* centres on the Countess and her two suitors, a poet and a composer. The opera moves as surefootedly as one would expect of this master, to its closing scene, one of Strauss's most magical, in which the Countess speculates on her predicament. Right from the opening notes of this classic performance, where the string sextet evokes the mood so delicately, one can

sense that this is a recording that will never be equalled. There is not a weak
link in the chain and the cast couldn't be more perfectly matched. Though the
recording is in mono it sounds quite magnificent.

Igor Stravinsky

Russian/French/American 1882-1971

NEW REVIEW

Stravinsky. Orpheus. Jeu de cartes. **Royal Concertgebouw Orchestra/
Neeme Järvi.** Chandos CHAN9014.

53' DDD 3/92

Here are two well contrasted neoclassical ballets, both collaborations with the
choreographer Balanchine. *Jeu de cartes* (1937) has the dancers as cards in a game
of poker which is perpetually disturbed by the entry of the joker. And the jokes
in Stravinsky's score come as he looks back with humour and raids the scores of
past masters for affectionate parodies. From Stravinsky's love of Greek mythology
came *Orpheus* (1948), less well known as not everyone responds to its remote-
ness, its "mimed song" (Stravinsky's own words); and the fact that in half an
hour's duration, the music only rises above mezzo-forte for a matter of seconds.
The music's timeless, other-worldly stillness, and gentle spirit are beautifully
evoked in this performance (helped by the Concertgebouw's wide open acoustic)
though some may prefer the composer's own sharper focus for his characteristic
motor rhythms (reviewed as part of the Stravinsky Edition). There are no
worries on that account in Järvi's *Jeu de cartes*, a reading of grace, humour and
high contrasts; and in the final 'deal', at a faster pace than either Abbado or the
composer (see below), tremendous agility. The acoustic adds an unfamiliar but
welcome richness to Stravinsky's timbres, particularly the tuba and spectacular
bass drum, without blurring essential rhythmic definition.

NEW REVIEW

Stravinsky. The Rite of Spring. Apollo. **City of Birmingham Symphony
Orchestra/Simon Rattle.** EMI CDC7 49636-2.

1h 5' DDD 11/89

Recordings of *The Rite of Spring* are
legion, but it is rare to find Stravinsky's most explosive ballet score
coupled with *Apollo*, his most serene.
The result is a lesson in creative
versatility, confirming that Stravinsky
could be equally convincing as
expressionist and neoclassicist. Yet
talk of lessons might suggest that
sheer enjoyment is of lesser importance, and it is perfectly possible to
relish this disc simply for that personal blend of the authoritative and
the enlivening that Simon Rattle's
CBSO recordings for EMI so consistently achieve. Rattle never rushes
things, and the apparent deliberation
of *The Rite*'s concluding "Sacrificial
Dance" may initially surprise, but in
this context it proves an entirely

Igor Stravinsky

appropriate, absolutely convincing conclusion. Rattle sees the work as a whole, without striving for a spurious symphonic integration, and there is never for a moment any hint of a routine reading of what is by now a classic of the modern orchestral repertoire. The account of *Apollo* has comparable depth, with elegance transformed into eloquence and the CBSO strings confirming that they have nothing to fear from comparison with the best in Europe or America. The recordings are faithful to the intensity and expressiveness of Rattle's Stravinsky, interpretations fit to set beside those of the composer himself.

NEW REVIEW

Stravinsky. The Firebird — ballet. Scherzo à la russe (versions for jazz ensemble and orchestra). Quatre études (1952 version). **City of Birmingham Symphony Orchestra/Simon Rattle.** EMI CDC7 49178-2.

| · · | 1h 5′ DDD 4/89 | 9 P Ⓑ |

NEW REVIEW

Stravinsky. The Firebird — complete ballet[a]. Le chant de rossignol — symphonic poem[b]. Fireworks, Op. 4. Scherzo à la russe. Tango. **London Symphony Orchestra/Antál Dorati.** Mercury 432 012-2MM. Item marked [a] from EMI Mercury AMS16038 (5/60), [b] Philips 6585 003 (5/72). Others new to UK.

| · · | 1h 14′ ADD 11/91 | 9 P Ⓑ |

Diaghilev chose *The Firebird* as the subject of the first ballet which he himself created for his own company. Lyadov's tardiness in delivering the musical score caused the great impresario to take a risk in transferring his commission to a young and inexperienced composer, but Stravinsky seized his first important opportunity to great effect, and the result was an early masterpiece. Simon Rattle emphasizes the work's romantic influences rather than those elements which suggest a composer who would soon take a radically new path. We are reminded that Rimsky-Korsakov was Stravinsky's teacher, and that he was influenced at the time by Scriabin and Glinka. On its own terms it is a very fine, illuminating performance, brilliantly colourful and superbly played by the Birmingham orchestra. The four *Etudes*, completed in 1929, are neoclassical in style and Rattle delivers these pithy, pungent little pieces with wit and clarity. It's interesting to hear both the original orchestral version of *Scherzo à la russe*, written in 1944, and the composer's own arrangement of this poker-faced piece for Paul Whiteman's band, made later the same year. Both seem equally effective in their different ways. The recording is very good indeed to match a high-quality, highly sympathetic performance.

Dorati made his famous Mercury recording of Stravinsky's *Firebird* ballet in Watford Town Hall in June 1959. It was an extraordinary musical and technical achievement. The performance, one of the very finest the conductor ever committed to disc, has a pervading feeling of freshness and spontaneity. The LSO play with marvellously sympathetic precision, and Dorati's ear for detail is especially telling in the score's long opening sequence which begins with gently growling lower strings, and then produces a galaxy of iridescent flashes of orchestral colour to intrigue and captivate the ear. The intensity of the playing prevents any feeling of fragmentation, rather a kaleidoscopic series of glittering images, and the warmth and atmosphere of the sound increases the feeling of magic. There is a sense of ecstasy that is almost Ravelian in the "Firebird's supplication", textures are lusciously transparent when the "Enchanted maidens" appear, while the "Lullaby" is captivating in its glowing simplicity. Yet later Kastchei brings malignant drama, and the glorious closing sequence of the celebration of the marriage of the Prince and Princess is thrillingly expansive. As a curtain raiser to the ballet we have the early *Fireworks*, no less dazzling and even more indebted to the composer's Rimsky-Korsakovian inheritance, and after the ballet concludes comes the sardonic *Tango* and the deliciously bizarre *Scherzo à la russe*. The programme closes with the exotic *Chant de rossignol* with its brilliantly phantasmagorical Chinoiserie. All this music is played with great panache and the Mercury recording team have provided a recording which totally defies the intervening years.

NEW REVIEW

Stravinsky. Petrushka (1911 version)[a]. Scènes de ballet. [a]**Philip Moll** (pf); **Berlin Philharmonic Orchestra/Bernard Haitink.** Philips 422 415-2PH.

52' DDD 10/91

NEW REVIEW

Stravinsky. Petrushka (1947 version)[a]. Symphony in Three Movements. [a]**Peter Donohoe** (pf); **City of Birmingham Symphony Orchestra/Simon Rattle.** EMI CDC7 49053-2.

57' DDD 5/88

Stravinsky's second great ballet score has been well served on disc from the earliest days of LP. He recorded it himself (rather indifferently) but there is in any event a good case for preferring the brilliance and clarity of digital sound in this of all works. Should this be your priority, Bernard Haitink's stunning (if synthetically recorded) Berlin Philharmonic version makes a plausible first choice. The engineers come in close and every detail tells, even though Haitink uses the less transparent 1911 scoring. As in his previous recording taped in London, Haitink's presentation of the rage and hysteria of Stravinsky's puppet protagonists is deliberately unexaggerated: you may find more intensity and drama in rival accounts. Nevertheless, it is hard to argue with the solidity, bite and precision of the playing on offer here, and the final scene is among the most persuasive on disc with each dance episode superbly delineated. The rarely heard *Scènes de Ballet* make a welcome if not over-generous makeweight. Stravinsky intended the score for a Billy Rose revue. In the end, not all the music was used on Broadway, but Stravinsky made the most of the opportunity; there are intriguing pointers to the *Symphony in Three Movements* completed the following year.

Simon Rattle chooses that score as the coupling for his own recording of *Petrushka* in its 1947 guise. He is marginally more histrionic than Haitink in the ballet, though the performance is most notable for its fresh look at details of scoring and balance, with pianist Peter Donohoe making a strong impression. The results are robust and persuasive, though one sometimes has·the impression that the characters are being left to fend for themselves. The atmospheric sound with its generous middle and bass is certainly more natural than DG's for Haitink. The symphony too is eminently recommendable, sounding more grateful and high spirited than it sometimes has, with Rattle particularly relishing the jazzy bits.

NEW REVIEW

Stravinsky. The Rite of Spring. Perséphone[a]. [a]**Anthony Rolfe Johnson** (ten); [a]**Anne Fournet** (narr); [a]**Tiffin Boys' Choir; London Philharmonic** [a]**Choir and Orchestra/Kent Nagano.** Virgin Classics Duo VCK7 91511. Notes, text and translation included.

(2) 1h 23' DDD 6/92

The American composer Elliott Carter described *Perséphone* as "a humanist *Rite of Spring*", so this makes a logical and thought-provoking coupling (timings are not generous on the two CDs but they do come at mid-price). Although 20 years separate both works they could not be more different. The primal energy of the earlier *Rite of Spring*'s very naturalistic setting of scenes from pagan Russia is almost wholly absent from the cool, hieratic beauty of *Perséphone*'s ritual, and predominantly lyrical mode of address. The latter fuses elements of melodrama (literally, speech with music), oratorio and ballet, is set in classical Greece and has a text that is spoken and sung in French. Nagano's recording is the first to have appeared since Stravinsky's own 1966 account (part of the Stravinsky Edition but not one of the items to be made available separately) and is, in many ways, finer. A modern dynamic range predictably benefits the thrilling theatre of the choral invocation for Perséphone's return from the underworld in the third part of the work (culminating in a triple *forte* cry of "Printemps" as powerful as anything in the *Rite*); and both Anne Fournet in the spoken role of Perséphone, and Anthony Rolfe Johnson as the priest of the Eleusinian mysteries are preferable to their predecessors. Nagano's tempos are swifter than Stravinsky's which, in music that is predominantly slow moving, will be welcomed by many. Nagano's *Rite* is balletic and sharply emphatic; closely miked in a way often reminiscent of Stravinsky's own, with strongly projected woodwind and a crisp, forceful, though never heavy presence for the percussion. Other versions may remind us more powerfully of the work's extremism, but Nagano is often strikingly individual — one thinks of the almost reptilian coiling of clarinets at the end of the "Ritual of the Ancestors" — with more expressive phrasing and pacing than usual in the work's mysterious moments.

NEW REVIEW

Stravinsky. Pulcinella — ballet (rev. 1947)[a]. Jeu de cartes. [a]**Teresa Berganza** (mez); [a]**Ryland Davies** (ten); [a]**John Shirley-Quirk** (bar); **London Symphony Orchestra/Claudio Abbado.** DG Galleria 423 889-2GGA. Text and translation included. Item marked [a] from 2531 087 (6/79), [b] 2530 537 (8/57).

1h 2' ADD 1/89

Claudio Abbado's 1970s recordings of these two so-called neoclassical ballet scores are very tempting at mid-price. "So called" because *Jeu de cartes* ("Game of cards"), one of Stravinsky's wittiest concoctions, contains a dash of Beethoven, Rossini, Johann Strauss, Ravel and even Stravinsky himself. Leaving pedantry aside, not even the composer himself achieved Abbado's combination of rapier-like pointing of accents (the snap in those rhythmic displacements), of humour in the instrumental interplay and of grace in the singing lines. Remastering has revealed slightly edgy violin tone in *Jeu de cartes*, but the bright sound is wholly suitable for the diamond edged profile of Stravinsky's orchestration.

Stravinsky. Concerto in E flat major, "Dumbarton Oaks". Pulcinella[a] — ballet (with original inspirations). [a]**Bernadette Manca di Nissa** (mez); [a]**David Gordon** (ten); [a]**John Ostendorf** (bass); **St Paul Chamber Orchestra/ Christopher Hogwood.** Decca 425 614-2DH.
Inspirations — **Gallo:** Trio Sonatas — No. 1 in G major: Moderato; No. 2 in B flat major: Presto, Presto; No. 7 in G minor: Allegro (Romuald Tecco, Thomas Kornacker, vns; Peter Howard, vc; Hogwood, hpd). **Pergolesi:** Cello sinfonia (Howard, Joshua Koestenbaum, vcs; Hogwood).

1h 6' DDD 6/90

Both *Dumbarton Oaks* and *Pulcinella* are deeply involved with the eighteenth century and the benefit of involving an eighteenth-century specialist in performing them is, firstly, that he will adopt a scholarly attitude to both pieces (Hogwood has sorted out one or two textual problems in *Dumbarton Oaks* by going back to the sources, just as if Stravinsky were an obscure composer of concerti grossi) and secondly that he will be likely to try out some of what he knows of period performing practice on these products of Stravinsky's kleptomaniac (his own word) forays into the eighteenth century. So, we have on the whole non-legato, eighteenth-century style bowing among the strings (expressive slurs and slides only where Stravinsky asks for them), an implicit assumption that if a note appears in the score it is intended to be heard and a feeling, in both works, of an inherently vocal, Italianate grace to the sustained lines. Together with clean, crisp rhythms (this music dances more often than it pounds) and a deft pointing of accents it makes for great freshness and zest and a clear demonstration of Stravinsky's deep love for and understanding of the past and of the wholly twentieth-century creative response it awoke in him. The fragments of eighteenth-century music that Stravinsky used as a basis for *Pulcinella* make an entertaining supplement, but how one misses his inspired 'distortions' while listening to them. Admirable playing throughout, acceptable soloists and a first-class recording.

NEW REVIEW

Stravinsky. SONGS. [a]**Phyllis Bryn-Julson** (sop); [b]**Ann Murray** (mez); [c]**Robert Tear** (ten); [d]**John Shirley-Quirk** (bar); **Ensemble Intercontemporain/Pierre Boulez.** DG 20th Century Classics 431 751-2GC. Texts and translations included. From 2531 377 (7/82).
Pastorale[a]. Deux poèmes de Paul Verlaine[d]. Two poems of Konstantin Bal'mont[a]. Three Japanese lyrics[a]. Three little songs, "Recollections of my childhood"[a]. Pribaoutki[d]. Cat's Cradle Songs[b]. Four Songs[a]. MAVRA — Chanson de Paracha[a]. Three Songs from William Shakespeare[b]. In memoriam Dylan Thomas[c]. Elegy for J.F.K.[d]. Two Sacred Songs (after Wolf)[c].

• 58' ADD 2/92

It may be true that this disc lacks the focus of a single major work, but it is also much more than a random compilation of unrelated miniatures. Principally, it offers an aurally fascinating contrast between two groups of pieces: Stravinsky's relatively early Russian settings, as he worked through his own brand of nationalism, reaching from the salon style of *Pastorale* to the folk-like vigour of a work like *Pribaoutki*; then the late serial compositions, written in America, which prove that the rhythmic vitality and melodic distinctiveness of the early works survived undimmed into his final years. Stravinsky may have regarded texts as collections of sounds whose natural rhythms had no role to play in their musical setting, but the essential meaning still comes through unerringly, whether it is that of the plaintive Paracha's song from the opera *Mavra* or the sombre *Elegy for J.F.K.* (to an Auden text). The disc is rounded off by the very late Wolf arrangements, and whilst one might quibble here and there about Boulez's choice of tempo, or the balance of voice and instruments, the disc as a whole is immensely satisfying as a comprehensive survey of an important repertory.

NEW REVIEW

Stravinsky. SACRED CHORAL WORKS. [a]**John Mark Ainsley** (ten); [b]**Stephen Roberts** (bar); **Westminster Cathedral Choir;** [c]**City of London Sinfonia/ James O'Donnell.** Hyperion CDA66437. Texts and translations included.
Symphony of Psalms[c]. Pater noster. Credo. Ave Maria. Mass[c]. Canticum sacrum[abc].

• 1h 8' DDD 9/91

It is no ordinary cathedral choir that can cope with the music of Stravinsky. The relatively traditional style of the *Symphony of Psalms* and the Mass provide plenty of challenges, especially in the pitching of those dissonant yet still tonal chords, while the *Canticum sacrum* offers even fewer familiar landmarks for singers who spend most of their time with the euphonious polyphony of Palestrina or Victoria. Yet the Westminster Cathedral Choir is remarkably assured throughout this disc. There is no sense of strain, rather a genuine sense of style, reinforcing the rightness of the composer's instincts in arguing the case for all-male singers in these works. Just occasionally, indeed, one might welcome a more wholehearted response to the weight and urgency of the music. Overall,

nevertheless, there is a clarity and poise which underline Stravinsky's concern with the timeless rituals of religious observation, and the sense that sacred music is above all a celebration of belief. There is admirable support from the soloists and the City of London Sinfonia, and the recording avoids the excessive resonance that often afflicts the cathedral environment. The conductor James O'Donnell merits particular praise for the disciplined flexibility of the performances.

John Mark Ainsley   [photo: Hyperion/Chlala]

Stravinsky. Les noces[a]. Mass[b]. [a]**Anny Mory** (sop); [a]**Patricia Parker** (mez); [a]**John Mitchinson** (ten); [a]**Paul Hudson** (bass); **English Bach Festival Chorus;** [b]**Trinity Boys' Choir;** [a]**Martha Argerich,** [a]**Krystian Zimerman,** [a]**Cyprien Katsaris,** [a]**Homero Francesch** (pfs); [a]**English Bach Festival Percussion Ensemble;** [b]members of the **English Bach Festival Orchestra/ Leonard Bernstein.** DG 20th Century Classics 423 251-2GC. Texts and translations included. From 2530 880 (2/78).

44' ADD 6/88   £ 9 P

Like *Les noces*, the *Mass* presents a fundamental ritual experience, here the sacrament of worship rather than marriage. It does so in a similar depersonalized way but with the emphasis on stillness and awe rather than driving rhythmic energy. In its austerity the *Mass* is the gateway to the later serial Stravinsky of the 1950s and 1960s. The English Bach Festival Chorus, joined by the Trinity Boys' Choir in the *Mass*, carry the burden of the all-important choral parts, and do so triumphantly. The glamorous line-up of pianists (Argerich, Zimerman, Katsaris, Francesch) supplies the expected panache in *Les noces* and the vocal soloists are first-rate. Bernstein co-ordinates the ensemble superbly and ensures that the sense of wonder underlying both works is fully conveyed. In DG's digital remastering the original analogue recording sounds in mint condition.

The three reviews which follow comprise part of "The Complete Edition" [Sony Classical CD46290, medium price, 22 CDs, ADD, 7/91]. The items reviewed here were subsequently issued as separate sets.

NEW REVIEW
Stravinsky. THE COMPLETE EDITION. **Various artists/Igor Stravinsky.** Sony Classical SM3K46292 (Volume 2).
Apollo (Columbia Symphony Orchestra From SBRG72355, 11/65). Agon (Los Angeles Festival Symphony Orchestra. SBRG72438, 8/66). Jeu de cartes (Cleveland Orchestra). Scènes de ballet (CBC Symphony Orchestra). Bluebird — Pas de deux (Columbia Symphony Orchestra. All from SBRG72270, 5/65). Le baiser de la fée (Columbia Symphony Orchestra. SBRG72407, 5/66). Pulcinella (Irene Jordan, sop; George Shirley, ten; Donald Gramm, bass; Columbia Symphony Orchestra. SBRG72452, 7/66). Orpheus (Chicago Symphony Orchestra. SBRG72355).

(3) 3h 30'   9 P

Volume 2 of Sony's Stravinsky Edition comprises ballets written between 1919 and 1957. *Pulcinella* was based on music originally thought to have been written by Pergolesi, but now known to be the work of various eighteenth-century composers. In 1919 Stravinsky had not long embraced neoclassical style, but here was a brilliant example of old wine in new bottles, with the melodies sounding as if they come from the pen of Stravinsky himself. The composer conducts a lively, sharply-accented account of the score. 1928 saw the production of two Stravinsky ballets. *Appolo*, a mainly quiet, contemplative score, written for string orchestra, has many passages of great beauty. Stravinsky the conductor does not linger over these, but allows the work's cool classical elegance to speak for itself. In *Le baiser de la fée* Stravinsky used themes by Tchaikovsky as the basis for his score. Once again, the music seems quite transformed, and the result is a most captivating work. Stravinsky's watchful, affectionate performance is perfectly proportioned. His arrangement of the "Pas de deux" from Tchaikovsky's *Sleeping Beauty* is no more than a reduction for small pit orchestra, however, and a mere curiosity.

In *Jeu de cartes*, which dates from 1936, Stravinsky used music by Rossini and others, but here the references are only fleeting, and merely enhance the humour of this robust, outgoing score. His performance brings out all the work's vigour and personality very effectively, but here and there rhythms become slightly unstuck, and a slightly hectic quality manifests itself. *Scènes de ballet* was written in 1944, and possesses a slightly terse quality in the main, though there are some more lyrical passages. Stravinsky does nothing to soften the work's edges in his performance, and it emerges as a strong, highly impressive piece. *Orpheus* was completed in 1947, and shows Stravinsky's neoclassical style at its most highly developed. Much of the music is quiet, after the manner of *Apollo*, but then the orchestra suddenly erupts into a passage of quite savage violence. Stravinsky conducts this passage with amazing energy for a man in his eighties, and elsewhere his performance has characteristic clarity and a very direct means of expression typical of a composer performance. Finally *Agon*, written in 1957, attracts the listener with its colourful opening fanfares, and then pursues an increasingly complex serial path in such a brilliant and highly rhythmical fashion that one is hardly aware that the technique is being used. This work, brilliantly conducted by Stravinsky, is an ideal introduction to his late style, and to the serial technique itself. Remastering has been carried out with the greatest skill, and all the recordings in this set sound very well indeed for their age.

NEW REVIEW

Stravinsky. THE COMPLETE EDITION. **Various artists/Igor Stravinsky.** Sony Classical SM2K46294 (Volume 4).
Symphonies — No. 1 in E flat major (Columbia Symphony Orchestra SBRG72569, 11/67). Stravinsky in rehearsal. Stravinsky in his own words (GM31). Symphony in Three Movements (Columbia Symphony Orchestra. SBRG72038, 9/62). Symphony in C (CBC Symphony Orchestra). Symphony of Psalms (Toronto Festival Singers, CBC Symphony Orchestra. SBRG72181, 8/64).

② 2h 23'

The word 'symphony' appears in the title of each work on these two discs, but this term covers some very diverse material. Stravinsky was in his mid-twenties when he wrote his Symphony in E flat, and the score is very much in the style of his teacher Rimsky-Korsakov. It has genuine colour and flair, however, and the octogenarian conductor brings paternalistic affection and a good deal of vigour to his performance. The *Symphony in C* dates from 1940, when Stravinsky was in his neoclassical phase. The work has many beautiful pages, as well as much pungent wit. In this performance Stravinsky drives the music much harder than he did in his 1952 mono recording with the Cleveland Orchestra, and although there are some exciting moments the music does tend to lose its elements of grace and charm. The performance of the *Symphony in Three Movements* is also characterized by the use of fastish tempos. But this violent work, written in 1945, and inspired by events in the Second World War, responds more readily to a strongly driven interpretation. Stravinsky wrote his *Symphony of Psalms* in 1930, and this composition reflects his deep religious convictions in varied settings from the Book of Psalms. His use of a chorus is interestingly combined with an orchestra which lacks upper strings. Stravinsky conducts a fervent, serious, beautifully balanced performance. All the 1960s recordings in this set sound very well in their new CD transfers. In some quarters the elderly Stravinsky has been wrongly portrayed as a frail, inadequate figure who only took over performances when works had been thoroughly rehearsed for him. Nothing could prove more clearly that this was not true than the rehearsal excerpts in this set, which show a vigorous, alert octogenarian very much in control of proceedings, and rehearsing passages in some detail.

Stravinsky. THE RAKE'S PROGRESS (THE COMPLETE EDITION). **Alexander Young** (ten) Tom Rakewell; **Judith Raskin** (sop) Anne Truelove; **John Reardon** (bar) Nick Shadow; **Regina Sarfaty** (mez) Baba the Turk; **Kevin Miller** (ten) Auctioneer; **Jean Manning** (mez) Mother Goose; **Don Garrard** (bass) Truelove; **Peter Tracey** (bar) Keeper of the Mad House; **Sadler's Wells Opera Chorus; Royal Philharmonic Orchestra/Igor Stravinsky.** Sony Classical SM2K46299 (Volume 9).

Stravinsky's only full-length opera was inspired by a viewing of Hogarth's *Rake's Progress* paintings in 1947. The composer asked W.H. Auden to supply an English text in verse form, and with the librettist he evolved a series of scenes depicting the feckless Tom Rakewell's meeting with the Devil in the form of Nick Shadow, his journey to London in pursuit of promised fortune, separation from his faithful fiancée Anne Truelove in favour of the dubious Baba the Turk, his financial failure, and his demise in Bedlam. The music is cast in classical forms, and was in fact Stravinsky's last important composition in neoclassical style. The composer directs a strong, dramatic, sharply-accented performance, with excellent playing from the RPO, and good singing from the Sadler's Wells Chorus. Alexander Young brings out Tom's blustering weakness and subsequent bewilderment very tellingly in a finely sung, strongly characterized performance. John Reardon plays the part of Nick Shadow in an appropriately ingratiating, wheedling manner, and Judith Raskin's performance as the rejected but single-minded Anne Truelove is very touching. The other parts are all more than adequately taken, and the well-balanced 1964 recording has come out very vividly on CD.

Nicholas Strogers   *Refer to Index*   *British fl. 1560-1575*

Josef Suk   *Bohemian 1874-1935*

Suk. Asrael — Symphony, Op. 27. **Royal Liverpool Philharmonic Orchestra/Libor Pešek.** Virgin Classics VC7 91221-2.

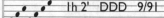

To use large scale symphonic form for the purging of deep personal grief carries the danger that the result will seriously lack discipline. In 1904-5 Suk's world was shattered by two visits from *Asrael* (the Angel of Death in Muslim mythology): he lost his father-in-law (and revered teacher) Dvořák, and his beloved wife, Otylka. Forgivably, Suk does perhaps linger a little too long in the fourth movement's gentle, mainly lyrical portrait of Otylka, but elsewhere the progress is as satisfying psychologically as it is symphonically. Much of the music has a concentrated dream-like quality; at the extremes, spectral nightmare visions merge with compensatory surges of lyrical ardour. It would be easy to cite the presence of Mahler in the former and Richard Strauss in the latter, but Suk's language remains identifiably Czech, not least in the woodwind colouring, the moments of consolation in nature. To define the symphony as employing a very sophisticated use of the Lisztian cyclic principle of construction is to deaden with dusty analysis a work whose every bar communicates experiences worth communicating with an intensity that Mahler would certainly have envied. It's not just an eloquent funeral oration. It was, for the composer, a piece that had to be written ("I was saved by music") and is the perfect example of music taking over where mere words are inadequate — and universalizing the experience. Pešek and his Liverpool musicians deserve our gratitude for their faith and commitment, Virgin Classics for supporting the enterprise with a wide-ranging recording that does Suk's sound world full justice.

Arthur Sullivan

British 1842-1900

Sullivan. TRIAL BY JURY[a]. **Ann Hood** (sop) Plaintiff; **Thomas Round** (ten) Defendant; **Kenneth Sandford** (bar) Counsel; **John Reed** (bar) Judge; **Donald Adams** (bass-bar) Usher; **Anthony Raffell** (bass-bar) Foreman of the Jury; **D'Oyly Carte Opera Chorus; Orchestra of the Royal Opera House, Covent Garden/Isidore Godfrey.** From SKL4579 (4/64).
Sullivan. THE YEOMEN OF THE GUARD. **Anthony Raffell** (bass-bar) Sir Richard Cholmondeley; **Philip Potter** (ten) Col Fairfax; **Donald Adams** (bass-bar) Sergeant Meryll; **David Palmer** (ten) Leonard Meryll, First Yeoman; **John Reed** (bar) Jack Point; **Kenneth Sandford** (bar) Wilfred Shadbolt; **Thomas Lawlor** (bass) Second Yeoman; **Elizabeth Harwood** (sop) Elsie Maynard; **Ann Hood** (sop) Phoebe Meryll; **Gillian Knight** (mez) Dame Carruthers; **Margaret Eales** (sop) Kate; **D'Oyly Carte Opera Chorus, Royal Philharmonic Orchestra/Sir Malcolm Sargent.** Decca 417 358-2LM2. From SKL4624-5 (11/64).

⏺ ② 2h 5' ADD 1/90 £ 9 P

The D'Oyly Carte Opera Company's 1964 recording of *Yeomen of the Guard* was one of the finest of all their recordings and certainly the most desirable CD version. For it Decca imported Sir Malcolm Sargent, who directs an interpretation of Sullivan's most imposing comic opera score that is at once spacious and commanding but at the same time breathes far more life than his earlier version for EMI. Decca also brought in the much lamented Elizabeth Harwood to display the beauties of the soprano writing that Sullivan provided for the role of Elsie Maynard. In support, the traditional D'Oyly Carte musical theatre style of performance is preserved through the contribution of various leading members of the permanent company of the time, including Ann Hood, Kenneth Sandford, Donald Adams and Gillian Knight, and John Reed as Jack Point. As if this fine performance could not stand up on its own, Decca have generously coupled a *Trial by Jury* recording of similar vintage, conducted in sparkling fashion by Isidore Godfrey and featuring Thomas Round as a suitably caddish defendant. The recorded sound in both cases remains remarkably good, making an altogether irresistible coupling of two of Sullivan's finest stage scores.

NEW REVIEW

Sullivan. THE PIRATES OF PENZANCE. **Eric Roberts** (bar) Major-General Stanley; **Malcolm Rivers** (bar) Pirate King; **Gareth Jones** (bar) Samuel; **Philip Creasy** (ten) Frederic; **Simon Masterton-Smith** (bass) Sargeant of Police; **Marilyn Hill Smith** (sop) Mabel; **Patricia Cameron** (sop) Edith; **Pauline Birchall** (mez) Kate; **Susan Gorton** (contr) Ruth; **D'Oyly Carte Opera Chorus and Orchestra/John Pryce-Jones.** TER CDTER2 1177.

② 1h 25' DDD 9/90

The revival of the D'Oyly Carte Opera Company has produced the first digital recordings of complete Gilbert and Sullivan scores, and this TER set is a very happy example. Philip Creasy is an engaging and vocally secure Frederic, and Marilyn Hill Smith trips through "Poor wandering one" with a delectable display of vocal ability and agility. The couple's interplay with the chorus in "How beautifully blue the sky" is quite enchanting, and their exchanges in "Stay, Frederic, stay" splendidly convincing. Eric Roberts makes the Major-General a thoroughly engaging personality, and the dotty exchanges between Simon Masterson-Smith's Sargeant of Police and his police force are sheer joy. Even such details as the girls' screams at the appearance of the pirates in Act 1 have a rare effectiveness. John Pryce-Jones keeps the score dancing along. Those who want the dialogue as well as the music must look elsewhere, but this version is certainly to be recommended for its musical and acting values as well as its fine modern sound.

NEW REVIEW

Sullivan. THE MIKADO. **Donald Adams** (bass) The Mikado; **Anthony Rolfe Johnson** (ten) Nanki-Poo; **Richard Suart** (bar) Ko-Ko; **Richard Van Allan** (bass) Pooh-Bah; **Nicholas Folwell** (bar) Pish-Tush; **Marie McLaughlin** (sop) Yum-Yum; **Anne Howells** (mez) Pitti-Sing; **Janice Watson** (sop) Peep-Bo; **Felicity Palmer** (mez) Katisha; **Welsh National Opera Chorus and Orchestra/Sir Charles Mackerras.** Telarc CD80284. Notes and text included.

1h 19' DDD 5/92

It is generosity indeed to be offered *The Mikado* complete on a single CD, and with full libretto, even if we have to do without spoken dialogue and the overture, whose purpose in the home is obviously less significant than in the theatre, and which anyway was put together by one of Sullivan's assistants. What is more, the performance is an outstanding one of a work that has not always fared too well in recordings. Sullivan has been among the diverse specialities of Sir Charles Mackerras ever since he arranged *Pineapple Poll* over 40 years ago, but

this is the first time he has committed any of the comic operas to disc. That we have waited far too long is soon evident from he way he brings out not only the familiar delicacies of Sullivan's score but also very many points of fine detail — the "short, sharp shock" in "I am so proud" for instance, and a chilling shriek in "The criminal cried". His tempos are generally on the quicker side, except for Richard Suart's Ko-Ko, who is here somewhat lacking in character though agreeably musical. Anthony Rolfe Johnson is a delicious Nanki-Poo, shading his voice to delightful effect, and Felicity Palmer is an absolutely magnificent Katisha. Marie McLaughlin is a good Yum-Yum, and Anne Howells a ravishing Pitti-

Arthur Sullivan

Sing. Donald Adams has here recorded the title role for the second time — no less than 33 years after the first — and generally the years seem to have stood still.

Sullivan. The GONDOLIERS. Overture di Ballo (1870 version). **Richard Suart** (bar) Duke of Plaza-Toro; **Philip Creasey** (ten) Luiz; **John Rath** (bass) Don Alhambra; **David Fieldsend** (ten) Marco; **Alan Oke** (bar) Giuseppe; **Tim Morgan** (bar) Antonio; **David Cavendish** (ten) Francesco; **Toby Barrett** (bass) Giorgio; **Jill Pert** (contr) Duchess of Plaza-Toro; **Elizabeth Woollett** (sop) Casilda; **Lesley Echo Ross** (sop) Gianetta; **Regina Hanley** (mez) Tessa; **Yvonne Patrick** (sop) Fiametta; **Pamela Baxter** (mez) Vittoria; **Elizabeth Elliott** (sop) Giulia; **Claire Kelly** (contr) Inez; **D'Oyly Carte Opera Chorus and Orchestra/John Pryce-Jones.** TER CDTER2 1187.

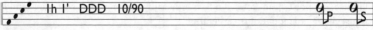
② 1h 49' DDD 5/92

This is one of a new series of recordings by the new D'Oyly Carte Opera Company that offers a vastly better quality of sound than any of its ageing competitors. Orchestral detail is the most immediate beneficiary, and the overture serves to demonstrate John Pryce-Jones's lively tempos and lightness of touch. Outstanding among the singers are perhaps John Rath, who gives Don Alhambra's "I stole the prince" and "There lived a king" real presence, and Jill Pert, a formidable Duchess of Plaza-Toro. Richard Suart not only provides the leading comedy roles with exceptionally clear articulation and musicality, but also adds considerable character to his portrayals; his "I am a courtier grave and serious" is a sure winner. David Fieldsend and Alan Oke provide attractive portrayals of the two gondoliers, and Lesley Echo Ross and Regina Hanley are also most agreeable. Seasoned listeners may note numerous changes of detail as a result of the purging of the performance material of changes made to the parts around the time of the 1920s Savoy Theatre revivals. There is no dialogue, but added value is provided by Sullivan's sunniest comic opera score being accompanied by the sparkling *Overture di Ballo*, played in its original version with some traditional cuts opened up.

Franz von Suppé

Austrian 1819-1895

Suppé. OVERTURES. **Academy of St Martin in the Fields/Sir Neville Marriner.** EMI CDC7 54056-2.
Leichte Kavallerie. Tantalusqualen. Die Irrfahrt um's Glück. Die Frau Meisterin. Ein Morgen, ein Mittag, ein Abend in Wien. Pique-Dame. Wiener Jubel. Dichter und Bauer.

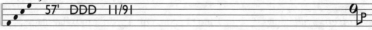
1h 1' DDD 10/90

Suppé. OVERTURES. **Royal Philharmonic Orchestra/Gustav Kuhn.** Eurodisc RD69226.
Die Irrfahrt um's Glück. Donna Juanita. Fatinitza. Das Modell. Der Gascogner. Wiener Jubel. Die Frau Meisterin.

57' DDD 11/91

Suppé's overtures are delightful creations brimming with melodic invention, and Marriner brings out all their warmth and infectious vitality in his highly successful interpretations. The orchestra respond to their conductor's obvious enthusiasm for this music with great aplomb, their expressive playing breathing new life into the more familiar items, like *Leichte Kavallerie* ("Light Cavalry") and *Dichter und Bauer* ("Poet and Peasant"). But what makes this winning collection so valuable is the inclusion of four Suppé rarities, *Tantalusqualen*, *Die Irrfahrt um's Glück*, *Wiener Jubel* and *Die Frau Meisterin*, all of which are constructed with great skill and deserve to be more widely known. Sparkling, crisp recorded sound provides the final icing on the cake.

Kuhn offers a refreshingly individual approach to Suppé's overtures, with particularly spacious slower sections building up to glorious climaxes. Not everything comes off altogether convincingly, and some sections seem altogether too slow. However, the beauties of the playing and the shaping of the themes are readily evident in, for example, the jaunty build-up and rousing conclusion of the familiar *Fatinitza*. Elsewhere, an attraction of this CD, as on the Marriner, is that the contents are anything but oft-played. The overture to *Die Irrfahrt um's Glück* is a fine early Suppé overture, while that to *Das Modell* was evidently one of the last things Suppé composed, the operetta being left unfinished at his death. The *Wiener Jubel* overture is a particularly marvellous discovery, with one theme especially that darts irresistibly hither and thither. *Donna Juanita* is a longer and generally more subdued overture, with a beautiful violin solo and delightfully intertwining woodwind, and Kuhn's command over the music is nowhere shown to better effect than in the major theme towards the end, which he alternately holds back and then moves on to captivating effect. This is not a collection to be acquired in preference to that by Marriner, but one that admirably complements it.

NEW REVIEW

Suppé. Requiem. **Ouliana Tchaikovsky** (sop); **Danielle Michel** (mez); **Gilles Vitale** (ten) **Jean-Louis Bindi** (bass); **Franco-German Choir, Lyon; Bonn Youth Symphony Orchestra/Wolfgang Badun.** BNL BNL112774.

1h 6' DDD 1/92

A requiem by Suppé may come as a surprise, but in fact the composer of all those rousing overtures composed a good deal of religious music. He had a thorough musical training, and much of his musical heritage came through his 'uncle' Donizetti. Thus it is hardly surprising that his Requiem should be in the Italian operatic line of such works that runs from Mozart through Donizetti to Verdi. Suppé composed it in 1855 in memory of Franz Pokorny, the theatre manager for whom he wrote his early theatrical music. Particularly noteworthy are the two sections in which the bass solo joins the chorus — the "Tuba mirum" and the "Hostias". Both have imposing brass openings, and the former features a striking choral passage over a haunting string figure. The "Agnus Dei" is a choral funeral march embellished with marvellous instrumental effects and enlivened by one of Suppé's typically gorgeous melodies. Do not be put off by the unfamiliar artists or the participation of a youth orchestra. The orchestra comprises highly accomplished musicians ranging in age from 16 to 22, and their conductor has been in charge of many major orchestras. The choral contribution is full-blooded, and the bass soloist, Jean-Louis Bindi, is especially imposing. The recorded sound has just the right amount of reverberation.

Johann Svendsen
Norwegian 1840-1911

NEW REVIEW

Svendsen. Symphonies — No. 1 in D major, Op. 4; No. 2 in B flat major, Op. 15. Two Swedish folk-melodies, Op. 27. **Gothenburg Symphony Orchestra/Neeme Järvi.** BIS CD347.

1h 11' DDD 11/87

The justified popularity of Grieg's music has perversely obscured that of his contemporary Svendsen, for no impression of Norwegian music of Grieg's time

can be complete without experiencing the freshness and joyous exuberance of
Svendsen's rich invention. Where Grieg concentrated mainly on miniature forms,
it was Svendsen who explored larger structures. His two symphonies have
justifiably been described as being, together with Berwald's, the finest to appear
in Scandinavia before Sibelius. The first is a youthful work, but one of remarkable freshness and assurance, its *scherzo* a gloriously infectious piece, deliciously
orchestrated. Everything there finds a worthy counterpart in the mature Second
Symphony, which builds up to a sparkling finale. These captivating works are
here given first-class, sensitive and lively performances, with excellent digital
sound. As if to reassert the affinity with Grieg, the CD offers a fill-up of string
arrangements of two Swedish folk-tunes, the second of which became the
Swedish National Anthem.

Karol Szymanowski *Polish 1882-1937*

Szymanowski. String Quartets[a] — No. 1 in C major, Op. 37; No. 2, Op. 56.
Lutoslawski. String Quartet[b].
Penderecki. String Quartet No. 2[b]. **Varsovia Quartet** (Boguslaw Bruczkow-
ski, Krzysztof Bruczkowski, vns; Artur Paciorkiewicz, va; Wojciech Walasek, vc).
Olympia OCD328. Items marked [a] from Pavane ADW7118 (10/85), [b]new to
UK.

> 1h 8'   AAD   6/89   ❓

NEW REVIEW

Szymanowski. String Quartets — No. 1 in C major, Op. 37; No. 2, Op. 56.
Webern. Slow Movement (1905). **Carmina Quartet** (Matthias Enderle,
Susanne Frank, vns; Wendy Champney, va; Stephan Goerner, vc). Denon CO-
79462-2.

> 45'   DDD   3/92   ❓

Szymanowski's sound world is totally distinctive: there is an exotic luxuriance, a
sense of ecstasy and longing, a heightened awareness of colour and glowing,
almost luminous textures. The two quartets are separated by a decade: the First,
whose sense of ecstasy and longing permeates its opening, is a subtle and deeply-
felt performance and much the same must be said of the Varsovia account of
No. 2. Again heady perfumes and exotic landscapes are in evidence, though with
his increasing interest in folk-music, the finale has slight overtones of Bartók.
There are magical things in both works and the Varsovia play marvellously
throughout. Lutoslawski's Quartet has a highly developed and refined feeling for
sonority and balance, and generally speaking succeeds in holding the listener,
whereas the Penderecki is perhaps less substantial and for much of its time the
sound world seems to aspire to the condition of electronic music. The Varsovia
Quartet play excellently and are recorded in a warm and fresh acoustic. A most
rewarding issue.

The Denon disc presents a pleasing alternative to the Varsovia Quartet's
performances of the two Szymanowski quartets if Lutoslawski and Penderecki are
not to your taste. In terms of playing time, however, the single Webern piece
provides a less generous coupling. The Swiss-based Carmina Quartet play both
Szymanowski works with great understanding and emotional involvement, and
technically they are quite brilliant. If we associate Webern with brief, highly
compressed atonal and serial works, the Slow Movement for String Quartet
shows the composer in his early twenties still writing in a late-romantic style,
appropriately enough for a piece which reflects for Webern the pleasures of a
walk through Austrian woods with his future wife. The Movement sprawls a
little, but is very pleasingly written. The Carmina Quartet give a sympathetic,

warm-hearted performance of this piece, and the sound obtained by Denon's largely Japanese team throughout the disc is very detailed, but also has a very attractive bloom.

Szymanowski. PIANO WORKS. **Dennis Lee.** Hyperion CDA66409.
Four Studies, Op. 4. Metopes, Op. 29. Fantasy, Op. 14. Masques, Op. 34.

Ih 4' DDD 7/91

Szymanowski is to Polish music what Bartók was to Hungarian, in that he revived his country's musical creativity and enriched its repertory in the early part of this century. Like Bartók, too, he was attracted to Richard Strauss's harmonic and instrumental opulence, and sometimes drew upon his native folk-music and allowed it to influence his works. But here the resemblance ends, for this Pole was a hothouse romantic more akin to Scriabin, and his piano music resembles his in being characteristically luxuriant and decadent in a *fin de siècle* way. Like Scriabin's, his earlier pieces owe much to Chopin, as we hear at once in the Four Studies. Dennis Lee plays them persuasively, and these studies (of which the melodiously poignant third was a favourite of Paderewski) have charm as well as brilliance. But already in No. 4 we find the more chromatic style to which Szymanowski's music was soon to adhere and into which we are immediately plunged in "Isle of the Sirens", the first of the *Metopes* of 1915: their title suggests scenes depicted in antique Greek friezes. Here are what someone has called "swarms of notes", and this lushness is characteristic of the other works too, but though the constant runs and trills and the shifting harmony may cloy some palates, in certain moods this music can carry one away into a world of mystery, especially when it is played with this quiet authority. A valuable Szymanowski anthology, with piano sound that is pleasing though not in the demonstration class.

NEW REVIEW

Szymanowski. Harnasie, Op. 55[a]. Mandragora, Op. 43[b]. [a]**Jozef Stępień,** [b]**Paulus Raptis** (tens); **Polish National Opera** [a]**Chorus and Orchestra/ Robert Satanowski.** Schwann Musica Mundi 311064.

Ih 2' DDD 12/91

After the First World War Szymanowski's musical language underwent a striking change: the heavy exoticism of the First Violin Concerto and Third Symphony was enriched by his encounter with the folk-music of the Polish highlands (or Tatras). Its accents inform the melodic character of the Mazurkas for piano, Op. 50, which have an extraordinary refinement and melancholy and are all pervasive in his choral ballet, *Harnasie*. The exotic luxuriance, the familiar sense of ecstasy and longing, the glowing colours and luminous textures are still strongly in evidence but they are tempered by an altogether earthier melodic language. Szymanowski worked on *Harnasie* for the best part of a decade (1923-32). It calls for enormous forces, including a large orchestra and chorus, and lasts only 35 minutes. Small wonder that few ballet companies outside Poland can afford to put it on. It is set in the High Tatras and the colourful plot centres on a bridal abduction by a band of highland brigands, the Harnasie, who take their name from their leader, Harnas, a kind of Robin Hood about whom there were many folk legends. It is all heady, intoxicating stuff and no one who enjoys the rich luxuriant textures in which Szymanowski's scores abound, should miss it. While Szymanowski laboured over *Harnasie*, he polished off *Mandragora* in ten days. By contrast this harlequinade is for chamber forces and designed for a performance of Molière's *Le Bourgeois Gentilhomme*. It is far less characteristic and sounds rather more like Prokofiev than Szymanowski. The performances have plenty of colour and spirit and the recording is naturally balanced with plenty of detail and presence.

Toru Takemitsu

NEW REVIEW
Takemitsu. ORCHESTRAL, CHAMBER AND INSTRUMENTAL WORKS.
John Williams (gtr); [a]**Sebastian Bell** (alto fl); [b]**Gareth Hulse** (ob d'amore);
[c]**London Sinfonietta/Esa-Pekka Salonen.** Sony Classical CD46720.
To the Edge of Dream[c]. Folios — I, II and III. Toward the Sea[a]. Here, There
and Everywhere. What a Friend. Amours Perdues. Summertime. Vers, l'Arc-en-
ciel, Palma[bc].

1h DDD 1/92

Toru Takemitsu is an original, refined composer and something of a latter-day
impressionist, as titles like *To the Edge of Dream* suggest. It may therefore come as
a surprise to find him arranging songs by Lennon and McCartney, Gershwin and
others, for solo guitar. Yet these prove to have attractive touches of the subtlety
found in Takemitsu's own compositions, and they also provide useful contrast to
the more substantial works on this beguiling disc. *Folios*, the earliest composition
included, already reveal Takemitsu's musical catholicity in its reference to a Bach
chorale. *Toward the Sea* and *Vers, l'Arc-en-ciel, Palma* are both more expansive

mood pieces, the former (for guitar
and alto flute) almost too reticent and
hesitant beside the richer textures of
the latter, which is enhanced by the
additional solo role given to the oboe
d'amore as well as its beautifully laid
out orchestral accompaniment. *To the
Edge of Dream* is in effect a guitar
concerto, with a wider range of mood
and an even more developed role for
the orchestra than *Vers, l'Arc-en-ciel,
Palma*. It provides a particularly satisfying focus for a sensitively performed
and well recorded disc. Even if we
hear rather more of the guitar relative
to the orchestra than we would in the
concert-hall, there is nothing unreason-

John Williams   *[photo: Sony Classical/Nieman]*   ably artificial about the result.

NEW REVIEW
Takemitsu. CHAMBER WORKS. [a]**Paul Crossley** (pf); **London
Sinfonietta/Oliver Knussen.** Virgin Classics VC7 91180-2.
Rain Coming (1982). Rain Spell (1982). riverrun (1984)[a]. Tree Line (1988).
Water-ways (1977).

55' DDD 9/91

Ever since the 1889 Paris Exhibition which introduced Debussy to the marvels of
the Javanese Gamelan, European composers have looked East for alternative
approaches to musical expression and technique. The process can work the other
way about too. Toru Takemitsu, for many years Japan's leading composer, has
found his niche by uniting oriental sensibility with various aspects of European
styles. Debussy is a figure to whom he is often likened; Scriabin, Berg and
Messiaen may also come to mind as you listen to this disc of his chamber
orchestral works. But the overriding impression is of that fragile blend of
formality, timelessness and beauty peculiar to a Japanese garden. It is no
coincidence that the titles all have to do with nature, and the predominantly
aquatic evocations suggest something of a latter-day Ravel *Miroirs*. This is music

for active meditation, if that isn't a contradiction in terms. If you have any curiosity about music in our time the wavelength is not all that difficult to find, especially when the playing is as perceptive and the recording as fine as they are here.

Takemitsu. PIANO WORKS. **Roger Woodward** (pf). Etcetera KTC1103. Items marked [a] recorded at a performance in the Art Gallery of New South Wales, Sydney on September 16th, 1990.
Corona[a]. The Crossing[a]. Far Away. Les yeux clos. Litany. Pause uninterrupted. Piano Distance. Rain Tree Sketch.

Ih 18' DDD 6/91 ❓

The piano works on this disc illustrate particularly well the three stages in Takemitsu's development as a composer. The early pieces such as *Pause uninterrupted* of 1952-9 and *Piano Distance* (1969) reveal the influences of Scriabin, Debussy and Messiaen together with more modernist hints of composers such as Boulez and Stockhausen, whilst *Corona, The Crossing* and *Far Away* reveal his interest in the experimental music of composers such as John Cage. The remaining works, *Rain Tree Sketch, Litany* and *Les yeux clos* date from 1980-90 and represent his return to a more traditional, less radical style of composition. Despite his varied approach to writing Takemitsu has always maintained a distinct personal voice, and his unique, skilful blend of eastern aesthetics with western contemporary trends has earned him a prominent position in the world of contemporary music. His music is always highly coloured, sensuous and even when he is at his most extreme, as in *Corona* or *Far Away*, there is always a great sense of beauty and poetry. Roger Woodward has had a long association with Takemitsu and plays his music with authority and affection.

Thomas Tallis
British c.1505-1585

Tallis. SACRED CHORAL WORKS. **The Hilliard Ensemble/Paul Hillier.** ECM New Series 833 308-2. From 833 308-1 (4/88).
Lamentations of Jeremiah the Prophet a 5. Salvator mundi II a 5. O sacrum convivium a 5. Mass a 4. Absterge Domini a 5.

54' DDD

The Hilliard Ensemble appear here in sombre mood. They sing with restraint and gravity a programme of quite uncommon beauty, in the main austere and penitential. Apart from the Mass for Four Voices, most of these pieces would have been written during the reign of Elizabeth I, when Latin had ceased, in England, to be the official language of liturgy. *Salvator mundi* and *O sacrum convivium* are short five-part antiphons from the feasts of the Exaltation of the Cross and Corpus Christi respectively. The singers respond to both with perfect objectivity, appearing to have greater affinity with the final piece, *Absterge Domine,* which is forward-looking in its delicate sensitivity to the words. The whole performance is distinguished by the careful shaping of every musical phrase and the impressive vocal quality — a glorious richness devoid of any vibrato.

Tallis. SACRED CHORAL WORKS. [a]**Taverner Consort;** [b]**Taverner Choir/Andrew Parrott.** EMI Reflexe CDC7 49555-2, CDC7 49563-2. Texts and translations included.
CDC7 49555-2 — Videte miraculum[b]. Homo quidam[b]. Audivi vocem[a]. Candidi facti sunt Nazarei[b]. Dum transisset Sabbatum[b]. Honor, virtus et potestas[b]. Hodie

nobis[a]. Loquebantur variis linguis[b]. In pace, in idipsum[a]. Spem in alium (with Wim Becu, bass sackbut; Paul Nicholson, Alan Wilson, orgs)[ab]. *CDC7 49563-2* — Gaude gloriosa Dei mater[ab]. Te lucis ante terminum … Procul recedant somnia I[a]. Miserere nostri[a]. Salvator mundi I[a]. Salvator mundi[b]. Lamentations of Jeremiah[a]. O sacrum convivium[b]. Suscipe, quaeso Domine[b]. O nata lux[b]. In jejunio et fletu[a].

② 1h 2' 1h 8' DDD 5/89

Tallis, one of the greatest composers of sacred music, has been sympathetically and generously acknowledged by Andrew Parrott and the Taverner Choir with two separately available discs of Latin church music. They include 12 pieces from the Cantiones Sacrae of 1575, the two *Lamentations of Jeremiah*, and the masterly 40-part responsary *Spem in alium* written, it would seem, in reply to a similarly ambitious one by Tallis's Italian contemporary, Alessandro Striggio. The performances are characterized by translucent textures, a wonderful feeling for structure and a fluent understanding of the composer's contrapuntal ingenuity. Certainly there are occasional hints of vocal strain in the uppermost reaches of the part writing but they do little to spoil an affectionate, technically assured account of thrilling music. Among many impressive features to be found in these discs is the performance of the *Gaude gloriosa Dei mater*, spacious in dimension, rich in counterpoint and concluding with an extended "Amen". Parrott illuminates the music with his own deep understanding of it, but above all with the skilful deployment of vocal talent that he has at his command.

Tallis. MOTETS. **The Tallis Scholars/Peter Phillips.** Gimell CDGIM006. Spem in alium. Salvator mundi (I, II). Sancte Deus, sancte fortis. Gaude gloriosa Dei mater. Miserere nostri. Loquebantur variis linguis.

43' DDD 3/86   Ⓟ Ⓑ

In Thomas Tallis's celebrated *Spem in alium* the Roman Catholic composer pleads to his queen for tolerance of his faith in the language he knows best, the tongues of collected voices. The result is humbling, overwhelming and quite lovely. The Tallis Scholars directed by Peter Phillips offer this monumental work in their glorious Tallis programme. The blend of voices, capped by a penetrating soprano line, makes a versatile and tremendously powerful instrument. *Gaude gloriosa* deploys the choir with a richness of texture and gradual accumulation of voices that are used to hymn Queen Mary for being "the means of salvation", the restorer of the faith. The recording, made in Merton College Chapel, Oxford, is beautifully handled. The space and shape of the building virtually appear before one's ears and eyes as the music unfolds.

Tallis. Missa Salve intemerata virgo.
Taverner. Mass a 4, "Western Wynde". Song, "Western Wynde". **St John's College Choir, Cambridge/George Guest.** EMI Eminence CD-EMX2155.

58' DDD 2/90

The St John's College Choir, Cambridge under its now retired Director, George Guest here gives fervent and firmly structured performances of Masses by two great masters of English sixteenth-century sacred vocal music. Taverner, the earlier composer of the two was innovative in his use of a secular cantus firmus, the tune of *Western Wynde* throughout the Mass. In the present performance, a solo tenor introduces the listener to this famous and beautiful sixteenth century song which in the Mass is treated to 36 variations. Tallis's five-part Mass *Salve intemerata virgo* is based on his own motet of that name. Its masterly counterpoint is lucidly sustained and is balanced in such a way as to highlight details in vocal character and texture. Nowhere, perhaps, is this more movingly demonstrated than in the second *Agnus Dei* where the four lower voices pursue a course of vocalization on the syllable 'O' of "nobis". This and the re-entry of the trebles for the final invocation is affectingly realized by Guest and his accomplished choir. The recording is sympathetic but the booklet omits the Latin texts.

Giuseppe Tartini *Refer to Index* *Italian 1692-1770*

NEW REVIEW

Tartini. Violin Concertos — E minor, D56; A major, D96; A minor, D113. **Uto Ughi** (vn); **I Solisti Veneti/Claudio Scimone.** Erato Emerald 2292-45380-2.

53' DDD 11/91

Tartini used to be known to the musical public at large as the composer of the *Devil's Trill* Sonata (echoes of Paganini). His output is surprisingly underexplored on record, but this is music surely due for a revival. This highly rewarding triptych demonstrates its quality. None of these violin concertos contains routine gestures and Uto Ughi makes a real case for their return to the repertoire. Outer movements have genuine vitality and all three slow movements are expressively appealing. The A major Concerto even offers an alternative, a particularly lovely *Andante*. I Solisti Veneti give persuasively polished accompaniments and the whole atmosphere of the collection is of cultivated music-making and enjoyment. This disc is a real find: all three concertos are beautifully played and the sound is excellent — sweet and full. A lovely disc for the late evening.

John Tavener *British 1944-*

NEW REVIEW

Tavener. The Protecting Veil[a]. Thrinos. *Britten.* Solo Cello Suite No. 3, Op. 87. **Steven Isserlis** (vc); [a]**London Symphony Orchestra/Gennadi Rozhdestvensky.** Virgin Classics VC7 91474-2.

1h 14' DDD 3/92

The Protecting Veil is one of the feasts of the Mother of God, according to the ritual of the Orthodox Church. John Tavener's ability to transfer such a concept into a concert work of wide appeal and proven impact is indeed remarkable, even if its success has more to do with the simple, direct emotionalism of the music than with its specific religious connotations. Direct emotionalism, certainly — but the music's predominantly slow pace and sustained lyricism, offset by occasional, striking dramatic gestures of sorrow and lamentation, make huge demands on the stamina and technique of the performers. Both Steven Isserlis and Gennadi Rozhdestvensky, not normally one of the more self-effacing of conductors, deserve high praise for the way they sink themselves into the music's contemplative but far from monotonous ethos, and refugees from the battering of more complex contemporary music need look no further for solace and consolation. The brief lament of the unaccompanied cello piece *Thrinos* is no less affecting, while the Britten suite provides valuable contrast through music from which the intense and unshakeable religious faith of Tavener's work is conspicuous by its absence. Even by modern standards, the recording quality is

outstandingly good.

Tavener. Ikon of Light (1984)[a]. Funeral Ikos[b]. Carol — The Lamb[c]. [a]Members of the **Chilingirian Quartet** (Mark Butler, vn; Csaba Erdelyi, va; Philip de Groote, vc); **The Tallis Scholars/**[ab]**Peter Phillips,** [c]**John Tavener.** Gimell CDGIM005. Texts and translations included. From 1585-05 (12/84).

55' DDD 6/91

John Tavener first met with critical acclaim in 1968 with his dramatic cantata on biblical (and not so biblical) texts — *The Whale*. There followed a series of works (*Ultimos Ritos, Celtic Requiem* and the opera *Therese* to name but three) in which he seemed to be re-examining and questioning the very nature of his faith and his relationship with his creator, and this culminated in his being received, in 1977, into the Russian Orthodox Church. Since then many of his works have been inspired by Russian Orthodox texts and the quietly omnipotent image of the ikon. One such work, and argu-

Chilingirian Quartet   *[photo: Chandos/Curzon]*

ably an important turning point in his approach to composition, is the *Ikon of Light*. This penetrating and visionary work is a setting of the "Mystic Prayer to the Holy Spirit" by mystical poet St Simeon, the New Theologian. To describe the opening as luminous would be an understatement. Five repetitions of the word *Phos* ("Light"), each proportionally longer than the previous, are interspersed by the sound of a distant string trio (representing the Soul's yearning for God) before dissolving into the radiantly polyphonic music of the second movement "Dhoxa" ("Glory"). As an expression of faith in contemporary art it is without doubt one of the most important works of the last 20 years, and deserves to win many friends and renewed recognition for this often undervalued and extraordinarily gifted composer. The austere and simple, yet equally moving *Funeral Ikos* — a setting of the Greek funeral sentences for the burial of priests — and the gentle stillness of the now popular carol *The Lamb* complete this richly rewarding disc. Beautifully performed and vividly recorded.

John Taverner
British c.1490-1545

Taverner. Missa Gloria Tibi Trinitas. Kyrie a 4, "Leroy". Dum transisset Sabbatum. **The Tallis Scholars/Peter Phillips.** Gimell CDGIM004. From 1585-04 (12/84).

47' DDD 7/86

Taverner's Mass *Gloria Tibi Trinitas* is a gloriously rich work showing a strong awareness of continental styles that was a hallmark of the cultural life encouraged by Henry VIII until he broke with Rome. Taverner was appointed the first choir-master of Cardinal College, Oxford (now Christ Church) and it seems almost certain that the Mass was composed for that choir. Musicians today accept the work's superiority and though there are several excellent recordings currently in the catalogue, Peter Phillips's recording with The Tallis Scholars is perhaps the most exciting, splendidly recorded in the chapel of Merton College, Oxford.

Pyotr Ill'yich Tchaikovsky *Russian 1840-1893*

Tchaikovsky. Piano Concerto No. 1 in B flat minor, Op. 23[a]. Violin Concerto in D major, Op. 35[b]. [a]**Emil Gilels** (pf); [a]**New York Philharmonic Orchestra/Zubin Mehta;** [b]**Pinchas Zukerman** (vn); [b]**Israel Philharmonic Orchestra/Zubin Mehta.** CBS Masterworks CD44643. Item marked [a] from 36660 (5/81), [b] IM39563 (10/85).

| 1h 9' DDD 9/89 | £ | p | B |

Tchaikovsky. Piano Concerto No. 1 in B flat minor, Op. 23.
Dohnányi. Variations on a Nursery Song. **András Schiff** (pf); **Chicago Symphony Orchestra/Sir Georg Solti.** Decca 417 294-2DH. From 417 294-1DH (10/86).

| 59' DDD 12/86 | p | B |

The factor of cost which sometimes worries people buying CDs is put into perspective here, with a mid-price disc lasting nearly 70 minutes and containing Tchaikovsky's two most popular concertos, works which we would in the past normally have bought on separate LPs, and played by top-class artists who for all their virtuosity put expression first and foremost and bring considerable charm to the music. The Piano Concerto No. 1 is a 1979 live performance from New York, and has all the excitement which that implies, a kind of urgency that keeps you at the edge of your seat. Emil Gilels is in his best form, which is saying something, and the New York Philharmonic under Zubin Mehta are caught up in this fine music-making. The recording does not bring the piano as close as we are accustomed to, perhaps, but that is no bad thing, and though there are some noticeable audience noises, few people will consider this too high a price to pay for being present, as it were, on a memorable occasion. In the Violin Concerto, Pinchas Zukerman joined the same conductor in Tel Aviv in 1984 and here, too, we have a thrilling live performance of one of the great violin concertos by a soloist and conductor entirely in sympathy with the music. Applause follows both performances, but sensibly it is faded fairly quickly.

Schiff's reading of the Tchaikovsky war-horse is very competitive, with the piano finely integrated with the orchestra in the tuttis and picking a telling line above the texture in the quieter moments. His reading is not as aggressive as some, and this provides a useful alternative view of the work. But if that is not enough to tempt you, the coupling of Dohnányi's *Variations on a Nursery Song* makes this issue even more attractive. From its portentous opening, through its bathetically simple theme, to the joyous delights of the finale, this is a work that, for all its humour, is not to be underestimated. Schiff and Solti certainly could not be accused of that, for they give it their all, treating each idea with utter conviction. Schiff's immaculate fingerwork is particularly effective in the filigree passagework and Solti's firm hand on the tiller ensures that the whole functions as a rounded and balanced structure. The clean recording allows all performers to take the dynamic range to its limits, allowing even the snowflake delicacy of Variation No. 5 to be deliciously sustained, whilst the opening of Variation No. 11 has all the power and impact you could hope for.

Tchaikovsky. Violin Concerto in D major, Op. 35[a]. WORKS FOR VIOLIN AND PIANO[b]. **Itzhak Perlman** (vn); [b]**Janet Goodman Guggenheim** (pf); [a]**Israel Philharmonic Orchestra/Zubin Mehta.** EMI CDC7 54108-2. Recorded at performances in [a]Philharmonic Hall, Leningrad in May, 1990 and [b]Tchaikovsky Hall, Moscow in April, 1990.
Bazzini: La ronde des lutins, Op. 25. *Bloch:* Baal shem — Nigun. *Kreisler:* Liebeslied. *Prokofiev* (arr. Heifetz): The Love for Three Oranges — March.

Tartini: Violin Sonata in G minor, "The devil's trill". **Tchaikovsky** (arr. Kreisler): String Quartet No. 1 in D major, Op. 11 — Andante. **Wieniawski** (arr. Kreisler): Caprice in A minor.

> ♪ 1h 12' DDD 2/91 — B

NEW REVIEW

Tchaikovsky. WORKS FOR VIOLIN AND ORCHESTRA. **Xue-Wei** (vn); **Philharmonia Orchestra/Salvatore Accardo.** ASV CDDCA713.
Violin Concerto in D major, Op. 35. Sérénade mélancolique in B minor, Op. 26. Souvenir d'un lieu cher, Op. 42 — No. 3, Mélodie (orch. Glazunov). Valse-scherzo in C major, Op. 34.

> ♪ 54' DDD 9/90 — B

EMI's recording has a special interest in that it provides a memento of Itzhak Perlman's first visit to the Soviet Union in 1990, which happens also to have been the first visit of the Israel Philharmonic Orchestra and the conductor Zubin Mehta. There is a sense of immediacy that belongs to a live performance before an audience, and for this most collectors will accept the debit side, which frankly includes a fair amount of audience noise including applause not only at the end of pieces — note that in Russia, the slow handclap is a mark of special enthusiasm! — but, for example, when the violinist announces some of the pieces he played at his Moscow concert with piano (this occupies the seven tracks after the three that are taken up with the Tchaikovsky Concerto, played in Leningrad). Judging by the odd murmurs, rustles and bumps, Soviet concert audiences who are obviously enjoying themselves are none too silent either while the music is actually happening, and if you think this could matter a lot to you, try to listen to the slow movement of the concerto before purchasing this CD. Otherwise, there's little to fear and much to delight, for the violin playing is masterly in its vibrant eloquence and bravura, and Mehta and the orchestra accompany most attentively in the concerto although the recording (excellent of Perlman) could ideally have captured more detail of their contribution. The wonders of violin virtuosity in the final piece with piano by Bazzini draw gasps of delighted amazement from the Moscow audience, as well they might!

If the audience noise in Perlman's live performance of the Tchaikovsky Concerto on EMI distracts you, then all is quiet in the studio version featuring Xue-Wei as soloist. In fact, the recording quality is conspicuously good, with an unusually sensible balance struck between soloist and orchestra. This disc is also notable for the Philharmonia's particularly expressive and sensitive playing under Salvatore Accardo, whose knowledge of these works as a soloist must have been a great boon to his fellow violinist. Xue-Wei plays the first movement of the concerto with plenty of feeling, generosity of phrase and a beautiful quality of tone. The *Canzonetta* is notable for a high degree of concentration and expressive warmth on the part of the soloist, and a particularly close rapport between him and his conductor: in the finale virtuosity and high spirits are apt partners. The three shorter pieces make appropriate pendants to the concertos — two charming, melodious sweetmeats flanking the lively *Valse-scherzo*. Playing and conducting in these fill-ups are as winning as in the main work.

Tchaikovsky. 1812 — Overture, Op. 49. Capriccio italien, Op. 45. MAZEPPA — Cossack Dance. **Cincinnati Symphony Orchestra/Erich Kunzel.** Telarc CD80041. From DG10041 (4/80).

> ♪ 35' DDD 12/83 — S B

Kunzel's recording of the *1812* is an unashamed hi-fi spectacular, so much so that purchasers are warned that the cannon at the end can damage loudspeakers with their extreme volume. At the time of the recording it is claimed that windows nearby were shattered. In the *Capriccio italien* too, another colourful popular favourite, this version uses the full range of high-fidelity digital sound with the bass drum very prominent and astonishingly vivid in its exploitation of the lowest register. The forwardness of such effects may detract from the purely musical qualities of the performances, which are strong and energetic without being so perceptive or so exciting as some, though very well played. Particularly enjoyable is the third item, the vigorous and colourful "Cossack Dance".

NEW REVIEW

Tchaikovsky. Serenade in C major, Op. 48. Souvenir de Florence, Op. 70. **Vienna Chamber Orchestra/Philippe Entremont.** Naxos 8 550404.

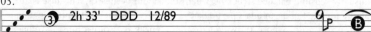

This is one of the many CDs now on the market that dispel the myth once and for all that only full-price recordings contain really outstanding performances. The Naxos label is just about as 'bargain' as you will get, and here they have given us superlative performances of two of Tchaikovsky's most endearing works. The Serenade in C contains a wealth of memorable and haunting music, beautifully and inventively scored and guaranteed to bring immense pleasure and delight to those dipping their toes in to the world of classical music for the first time. Philippe Entremont and the Vienna Chamber Orchestra give a marvellously polished and finely poised performance full of warmth, affection and high spirits, and the famous second movement Waltz in particular is played with much elegance and grace. The *Souvenir de Florence*, originally written for string sextet, makes a welcome appearance here in Tchaikovsky's own arrangement for string orchestra. This is a delightfully sunny performance, full of suavity, exuberance and romantic dash, but always alert to the many subtleties of Tchaikovsky's skilful and intricate part-writing. The *Adagio cantabile* is particularly notable for some extremely fine and poetic solo playing from the violin and cello principals of the VPO. The beautifully spacious recording does ample justice to the performances. A magnificent bargain.

Tchaikovsky. Swan Lake, Op. 20 — ballet. **Royal Opera House Orchestra, Covent Garden/Mark Ermler.** Royal Opera House Records ROH301/03.

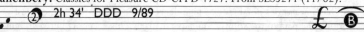

Tchaikovsky. Swan Lake, Op. 20 — ballet. **Philharmonia Orchestra/John Lanchbery.** Classics for Pleasure CD-CFPD 4727. From SLS5271 (11/82).

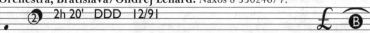

NEW REVIEW

Tchaikovsky. Swan Lake, Op. 20 — ballet. **Slovak Radio Symphony Orchestra, Bratislava/Ondrej Lenárd.** Naxos 8 550246/7.

It is a measure of its greatness that *Swan Lake* has survived the many trials and tribulations of its chequered history. Its first performance met with only moderate success in 1877; critics found its form and orchestration original, but generally considered it unsuitable for dance. It remained in the repertoire, however, until 1883, during which time it had undergone gross distortions at the hands of various choreographers, even to the point of having nearly a third of Tchaikovsky's music replaced by music from other composers's ballets. It was not until two years after Tchaikovsky's death that a truly successful production was mounted and today *Swan Lake* is rightfully recognized as a masterpiece, greatly loved by dancers and audiences alike.

The Orchestra of the Royal Opera House, Covent Garden, must have performed this music more times than they care to remember. However, this is no routine performance; in fact, the result is very special indeed. Their playing glows with a freshness of an orchestra performing the music for the first time and you would be hard put to find a recording where the strings play so beguilingly or with such romantic fervour as they do here, with every phrase beautifully crafted and elegant. The brass sound splendid too, playing with great panache and sonority. All this is helped by the marvellously sumptuous recording, set in a warmly resonant acoustic. Ermler's tempos are generally more expansive than his rivals, adding about ten minutes to the overall duration, although the decision of Conifer (who distribute this label) to spread the ballet over three discs seems rather curious, as it could easily have been fitted on to two well filled CDs. That aside, this is still the first choice and is a recording that the orchestra can be very proud of.

Lanchbery's recording is near complete and even though two (identical) numbers which frame Act 2 had to be omitted for space reasons, these are very like a similar treatment of the same famous oboe tune, as used by the composer to end Act 1. What is included is the extra music — the *pas de deux* danced by the Prince and Odile — which Tchaikovsky added to Act 3, after the first performance. This interpolation is not included in the Naxos set, which is otherwise complete. But, now reissued on Classics for Pleasure, the Lanchbery recording is a clear first choice in the bargain range. It is played here with immense affection and rhythmic gusto by the Philharmonia Orchestra under a conductor who has over 30 years of experience directing ballet in the theatre and knows just how to pace a scene for maximum effect. The accompanying booklet gives a full synopsis of the action and lists the various numbers which each occupy a separate track.

In the super-bargain area the Naxos set from the Slovak Radio Symphony Orchestra, Bratislava, under Ondrej Lenárd, with its bold sense of drama and urgent tempos has a character all of its own. The conductor's pacing is brisk, and the effect is essentially that of a vibrant concert performance, rather than evoking the ballet theatre. But the orchestral solo playing is felicitous — especially the all-important oboe — and there is warmth and lilt in the waltzes as well as plenty of dash in the more vigorous numbers. The concert-hall acoustic helps a believable balance and the digital recording is certainly faithful. This makes stimulating listening and has considerable finesse. It is not an opulent account to wallow in like Ermler's, but is still well worth considering when it costs about a quarter of the price of the Conifer set.

Tchaikovsky. Romeo and Juliet — Fantasy Overture. The Nutcracker — ballet suite, Op. 71a. **Berlin Philharmonic Orchestra/Herbert von Karajan.** DG 410 873-2GH. From 410 873-1GH (2/84).

44' DDD 4/84

It might be argued that *Romeo and Juliet* is the most successful symphonic poem in the repertoire, economically structured, wonderfully inspired in its melodies and with the narrative and final tragedy depicted with imaginative vividness. Karajan brings out all the intensity of the composer's inspiration and the playing of the Berlin Philharmonic creates much excitement. *The Nutcracker* shows the other side of the composer's personality, the most wonderfully crafted light music, and the suite is utter perfection. Each of the *danses caractéristiques* is a miracle of melody and orchestration and their charm never cloys, especially when they are played so winningly and with such polish. The recording is admirably clear and well balanced and though a little more warmth would have made the upper strings sweeter in the ballet music, this remains a very recommendable disc.

Tchaikovsky. ORCHESTRAL WORKS. **Royal Liverpool Philharmonic Orchestra/Sian Edwards.** EMI Eminence CD-EMX2152.
1812 — Overture, Op. 49. Romeo and Juliet — Fantasy Overture. Marche slave, Op. 31. Francesca da Rimini, Op. 32.

1h 6' DDD 12/89   £ *q*p *q*s Ⓑ

It is an extraordinary achievement that the young British conductor, Sian Edwards, should have made her recording début with a Tchaikovsky programme of such distinction. She immediately achieves a splendid artistic partnership with the Royal Liverpool Philharmonic Orchestra, whose playing is so full of vitality, and whether in *1812* with its vigour and flair, its cluster of lyrical folk melodies, and a spectacular finale with thundering canon, or in *Marche slave*, resplendently patriotic, in a uniquely Russian way, together they bring the music tingling to life in every bar. *Romeo and Juliet*, on the other hand, needs a finely judged balance between the ardour and moonlight of the love music, the vibrant conflict of the battle, and the tragedy of the final denouement, which is uncannily well managed. Most intractable interpretatively is *Francesca da Rimini*, with its spectacularly horrifying picture of Dante's inferno which the composer uses to frame the central sequence depicting the lovers, Francesca and Paolo, and the doom-laden atmosphere which surrounds their intense mutual passion. Edwards's grip on this powerfully evocative sequence of events is unerringly sure, and she takes the orchestra through the narrative as only an instinctive Tchaikovskian could. The work opens with an unforgettable sense of nemesis and ends with a truly thrilling picture of the whirlwinds of Hell, into which the lovers are cast, still in their final passionate embrace. All in all this is one of the best Tchaikovsky discs in the mid-price catalogue and the fine EMI Eminence recording combines weight and sonority with brilliance, and brings a most attractive ambient effect.

Tchaikovsky. ORCHESTRAL WORKS. [a]**Carl Pini,** [b]**Pinchas Zukerman** (vns); [a]**Philharmonia Orchestra/Michael Tilson Thomas;** [b]**Israel Philharmonic Orchestra/Zubin Mehta.** CBS Digital Masters CD46503.
Orchestral Suites[a] — No. 2 in C major, Op. 53; No. 4 in G major, Op. 61, "Mozartiana". Sérénade mélancolique in B minor, Op. 26[b]. Mélodie in E flat major, Op. 42 No. 3[b].

1h 12' DDD 8/91

Pinchas Zukerman   [photo: BMG/Swope]

The musical 'marriage' of Tchaikovsky and Mozart might seem odd in that it allies a full-blooded romantic composer with one of an incomparable classical poise. But when one remembers that the Russian composer's ballet music has an equally admirable grace and elegance, and that he adored Mozart, it is less surprising that he succeeded when he chose three of Mozart's piano pieces (a gigue, a minuet and a theme with variations) and his choral *Ave verum* as the basis of the Fourth Orchestral Suite. *Mozartiana* is enjoyable music, and represents what Tchaikovsky called "the past revisited in a contemporary work". However, the effect is lush because of the orchestration, which includes a solo violin, harp and cymbals, and that is emphasized by Michael Tilson Thomas's slowish tempos (at least until the finale) and the rich recording — indeed, it's surprising how romantic Mozart's virtually unaltered classical notes become. The Second Suite is all Tchaikovsky and even more delightful, with characteristically fine scoring and a wealth of tunes; it has an eloquence and drama more reminiscent of the composer's ballets than of his symphonies — indeed, the second movement is a waltz, while the fourth is called "A Child's Dream" and could have come from *The Nutcracker*. Tilson Thomas brings charm and zest to this music, and Zubin Mehta, with a different orchestra, is no less successful in the other two pieces, in which the superbly polished violin playing of Pinchas Zukerman is a considerable bonus.

Tchaikovsky. The Nutcracker, Op. 71 — ballet[a]. QUEEN OF SPADES — Duet of Daphnis and Chloë[b]. [b]**Cathryn Pope** (sop); [b]**Sarah Walker** (mez); [a]**Tiffin Boys' School Choir; London Symphony Orchestra/Sir Charles Mackerras.** Telarc CD80137.

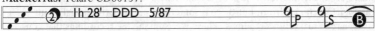

Tchaikovsky. The Nutcracker, Op. 71 — ballet[a].
Rossini/Respighi. La boutique fantasque[b]. [a]**Suisse Romande Orchestra/ Ernest Ansermet;** [b]**Israel Philharmonic Orchestra/Sir Georg Solti.** Decca Weekend 425 509-2DC2. Item marked [a] from SXL2092/3 (4/59), [b] SXL2007 (10/58).

The *Nutcracker* ballet shows Tchaikovsky's inspiration at its most memorable and the orchestration creates a unique symbiosis with the music. The ballet is based on a grotesque tale by E.T.A. Hoffmann, but in the ballet it becomes more of a fairy story, with only the eccentric Drosselmeyer who provides the heroine, Clara, with the Nutcracker at a Christmas party, reflecting anything of the mood of the original narrative. Tchaikovsky's music, a stream of wonderful tunes, radiantly, piquantly or glitteringly scored, as the character of each demands, contains much that enchants the listener which is not included in the famous Suite, notably the "Waltz of the Snowflakes" (with its wordless chorus) and the glorious climbing melody that accompanies the journey through the pine forest to the Magic Castle. Under Mackerras the music glows with colour and has superb vitality; the stunningly rich Telarc recording helps too. This is a wonderful entertainment from the first bar to the last and the documentation is admirable. As a bonus we are offered a charming duet from the *Queen of Spades*.

Whilst the *Nutcracker* from the Suisse Romande and Ansermet may not feature dazzling technical display from the orchestra or the rich sonic kaleidoscope of the Telarc production, its interpretative qualities still keep it a firm favourite. Ansermet's knack of fixing on just the right tempo for each of the multifarious sections helps not just every individual section make sense, but it also shapes the overall form so that the complete ballet acquires a satisfying structure. Outside the theatre, *The Nutcracker* can seem to be just a motley collection of unrelated numbers, but not in this performance. Less than 30 years separated the first production of *The Nutcracker* (1892) and Respighi's arrangement of pieces by Rossini for his one act ballet, *La boutique fantasque* (1919). Yet, even though the original music used for the latter is firmly of the nineteenth century and Respighi makes obvious allusion to later romantic ballet idioms, there is still a world of difference between the two. This contrast is strongly drawn by Solti's dynamic reading of the Respighi, its primary-colour brilliance forcing the Israel Philharmonic to pull out all the stops. The close recording is the ideal complement.

Tchaikovsky. SYMPHONIES. [abc]**Philharmonia Orchestra,** [d]**New Philharmonia Orchestra/Vladimir Ashkenazy.** Decca 425 586-2DM3. No. 4 in F minor, Op. 36[a] (from SXL6919, 12/79); No. 5 in E minor, Op. 64[b] (SXL6884, 5/78); No. 6 in B minor, Op. 74, "Pathétique"[c] (SXL6941, 8/81). Manfred Symphony, Op. 58[d] (SXL6853, 9/78).

③ 3h 12' ADD 3/90 £ ♀ P Ⓑ

NEW REVIEW

Tchaikovsky. SYMPHONIES. [a]**New Philharmonia Orchestra,** [b]**Philharmonia Orchestra/Riccardo Muti.** EMI CZS7 67314-2.
Symphonies — No. 1 in G minor, Op. 13, "Winter Daydreams"[a] (from ASD3213, 7/76); No. 2 in C minor, Op. 17, "Little Russian"[b] (ASD3488, 6/78); No. 3 in D major, Op. 29, "Polish"[b] (ASD3449, 5/78); No. 4 in F minor, Op. 36[b] (ASD3816, 3/80); No. 5 in E minor, Op. 64[b] (ASD3717, 6/79); No. 6 in B minor, Op. 74, "Pathétique"[b] (ASD3901, 11/80). Romeo and Juliet — fantasy overture[b] (ASD3488).

④ 4h 32' ADD 9/91 £ ♀ P Ⓑ

There are many fine recordings of Tchaikovsky's last three symphonies in the catalogue to choose from, but there is something particularly special about Ashkenazy's marvellous readings. These were among the recordings that confirmed Ashkenazy's status as a conductor of considerable powers. Repackaged as they are here on three mid-price CDs they represent exceptional value for money. Despite having been recorded over a period of three years, there is a remarkable consistency in style, quality and approach. Particularly striking is the way in which he underplays the obvious emotional qualities of these works by avoiding any over sentimentality or self indulgence. Instead we are given strong, dramatic and purposeful readings that are unafraid to probe beneath the surface of these most intimate utterances. The Philharmonia's string playing has a wonderful pureness of tone and there is some delicious wind playing too, particularly in the scherzos, where lightness, accuracy and crisp articulation are required. The Fourth Symphony has plenty of vigour and dramatic weight, but there is subtlety too, especially in his close attention to dynamic shading. The transition from *Scherzo* to finale is splendid and the finale itself is a real *tour de force*. A remarkably warm and lyrical reading of the Fifth Symphony follows and in the *Pathétique* it is once again his freshness and spontaneity, together with a strong sense of forward momentum and purpose, that makes this so compelling a performance. And for desert — simply one of the finest readings of the *Manfred* Symphony on disc. The vivid analogue recordings (some of Decca's very best) have lost none of their lustre or clarity in their transfer to CD. Strongly recommended.

Recorded between 1975 and 1979, Riccardo Muti's Tchaikovsky's cycle has come up very vividly, neatly fitted on to four mid-price CDs. All the numbered symphonies are included, and for once the set is sensibly laid out, with *Romeo and Juliet* a splendid bonus and only the Fourth Symphony unavoidably split between the second and third disc. Muti tends to favour fast speeds, but, apart perhaps from the big tune in the first movement of the *Pathétique*, there is no feeling of undue haste. By and large, his youthful ardour pays off in such oft-recorded music. This is Tchaikovsky as he ought to be played: reliably fresh and direct, aptly passionate without lapsing into sentimentality. Tchaikovsky's balletic inner movements are always delightfully sprung, though Muti's rustic brand of charm is less svelte and sophisticated than some others. His finales are positively incendiary. The Philharmonia regained its old title and much of its prestige in the course of these sessions. And Muti proved more than an excellent orchestral trainer: his interpretations stand the test of time, consistently alive in a thrusting, post-Toscanini manner. The analogue recordings, not as detailed as some, have been expertly remastered to sound consistently bold and full, which matches the music-making to perfection.

Tchaikovsky. Symphonies — No. 1 in G minor, Op. 13, "Winter daydreams"[a]; No. 2 in C minor, Op. 17, "Little Russian"[b]; No. 3 in D major, Op. 29, "Polish"[c]. **Concertgebouw Orchestra/Bernard Haitink.** Philips 420 751-2PM2. Item marked [a] from 9500 777 (4/81), [b] 9500 444 (6/79), [c] 9500 776 (8/81).

(2) 2h 4' ADD 6/90

All too often conductors approach these early symphonies with the hindsight of the later, more passionate symphonies in mind, often resulting in an over-indulgence that seems inappropriate in these earlier, more optimistic symphonies. Haitink however, responds in a much more sympathetic and direct manner, with clean-limbed performances that have poise, nobility and great charm, coupled with a freshness of approach that allows the music to speak for itself. Symphony No. 1, *Winter daydreams*, is given a marvellously atmospheric reading, especially in the sub-titled first and second movements — "Reveries of a Winter Journey" and "Land of Desolation, Land of Mists" and his choice of tempos throughout are perfectly judged. The Second Symphony, *Little Russian*, is amongst the finest in the catalogue at any price. Here Haitink responds in a most persuasive way to Tchaikovsky's symphonic structure and draws from the Concertgebouw perform-ances of remarkable clarity and detail. The Third is also very fine and again it is his direct and fresh approach that is most convincing. If, perhaps, it lacks the passion found in some performances, it is more than compensated for in the charm and eloquence of the playing. For the collector who already possesses the more popular symphonies Nos. 4, 5 and 6, this set provides the perfect oppor-tunity to complete the cycle with performances of the highest quality at medium price. The recordings are exceptionally fine and have lost none of their warmth in this transfer to CD. Strongly recommended.

Tchaikovsky. Symphony No. 3, Op. 29, "Polish". **Oslo Philharmonic Orchestra/Mariss Jansons.** Chandos CHAN8463.

45' DDD 7/86

Unusually, this symphony has five movements: the first is the longest, and consists of a subdued introduction followed by a bracing, very positive *Allegro brillante*. A graceful, waltz-like intermezzo follows and then there is the slow movement proper, marked *Andante elegiaco*. The *Scherzo* is a bouncing, whirling affair, with delicate, wispy figurations. A final quicker movement with a rousing climax brings the symphony to a confident conclusion. This is not an easy work to bring off effectively in performance, for the material is not always so im-mediately memorable as in other Tchaikovsky symphonies, and it is sometimes awkwardly constructed. Mariss Jansons comes through the test with flying colours. He secures playing of high virtuosity from the Oslo orchestra, and the recording has splendid clarity and presence.

Tchaikovsky. Symphony No. 4 in F minor, Op. 36. **Oslo Philharmonic Orchestra/Mariss Jansons.** Chandos CHAN8361. From ABRD1124 (7/85).

42' DDD 9/85

Tchaikovsky. Symphonies — No. 4 in F minor, Op. 36[a]; No. 5 in E minor, Op. 64[b]; No. 6 in B minor, Op. 74, "Pathétique"[c]. **Leningrad Philharmonic Orchestra/Evgeny Mravinsky.** DG 419 745-2GH2. Items marked [a] from SLPM138657 (6/61), [b] SLPM138658 (10/61), [c] SLPM138659 (11/61).

(2) 2h 9' ADD 8/87

A high emotional charge runs through Jansons's performance of the Fourth, yet this rarely seems to be an end in itself. There is always a balancing concern for the superb craftsmanship of Tchaikovsky's writing: the shapeliness of the phrasing; the superb orchestration, scintillating and subtle by turns; and most of all Tchaikovsky's marvellous sense of dramatic pace. Rarely has the first movement possessed such a strong sense of tragic inevitability, or the return of the 'fate' theme in the finale sounded so logical, so necessary. The playing of the Oslo Philharmonic Orchestra is first rate: there are some gorgeous woodwind solos and the brass manage to achieve a truly Tchaikovskian intensity. Recordings are excellent: at once spacious and clearly focused, with a wide though by no means implausible dynamic range.

Mravinsky's classic 1960s recordings make a fine, and reasonably priced, alternative to Jansons's superb Chandos issues. Mravinsky's control of his orchestra is total, and the sheer energy he can unleash at climaxes is breathtaking. His rhythmic control is remarkable and is used at all times to follow the letter of the score. The sincerity and spirit of the music-making is without question. The recordings have an immediacy and depth that has greatly benefited from the remastering.

Tchaikovsky. Symphony No. 5 in E minor, Op. 64. **Oslo Philharmonic Orchestra/Mariss Jansons.** Chandos CHAN8351.

· 43' DDD 3/85

Tchaikovsky. Symphony No. 5 in E minor, Op. 64. EUGENE ONEGIN — Tatiana's letter scene[a]. [a]**Eilene Hannan** (sop); **London Philharmonic Orchestra/Sian Edwards.** EMI Eminence CD-EMX2187.

· 59' DDD 1/92

Many of the remarks made about Mariss Jansons's performance of the Fourth Symphony also apply here, though it should be stressed that there isn't the vaguest hint of sameness about his interpretations. One's impressions in the Fifth are very different: the rich dark tones of the clarinets in the first movement's introduction, the beautiful tone and elegant phrasing of the horn in the *Andante cantabile*, the ardent, sweeping intensity of the strings at climaxes and, above all, Jansons's extraordinarily coherent vision of the Symphony as a complete utterance. This is a most recommendable version of the Fifth, despite the lack of a fill-up.

Sian Edwards's account of the Fifth combines fiery drama, most compelling in the thrusting first movement, with romantic warmth in the *Andante*, opening with an exceptionally well-played horn solo. Phrases are lovingly moulded, particularly in the slow movement which here receives a very measured tempo. This is a somewhat more expansive reading than Jansons's. As well as the advantage of coming at mid-price, Edwards offers the bonus of an unusual coupling — Tatiana's Letter scene from *Eugene Onegin*. The Australian soprano, Eilene Hannan offers an ideal combination of girlish enthusiasm and assured strength to give a characterful portrayal of the young Tatiana. EMI Eminence's sound quality is ripe, clear and naturally distanced.

Tchaikovsky. Symphony No. 6 in B minor, Op. 74, "Pathétique". Marche slave, Op. 31. **Russia National Orchestra/Mikhail Pletnev.** Virgin Classics VC7 91487-2.

· 53' DDD 1/92

There's no denying that Russian orchestras bring a special intensity to Tchaikovsky, and this Symphony in particular. But, in the past, we have had to contend with lethal, vibrato-laden brass, and variable (to say the least) Soviet engineering. Not any more. Pianist Mikhail Pletnev formed this orchestra in 1990 from the front ranks of the major Soviet orchestras, and in 1991 Virgin Classics brought them to London for these tapings. The result has all the makings of a classic. The brass still retain their penetrating power, and an extraordinary richness and solemnity (without the unappealing wobble) before the Symphony's coda; the woodwind (soft, veiled flute tone; dark-hued bassoons) make a very melancholy choir; and the strings possess not only the agility to cope with Pletnev's aptly death-defying speed for the third movement march, but beauty of tone for Tchaikovsky's yearning cantabiles, and their lower voices add thunderous black density to the first movement's development's shattering intrusion. All this would count for little, were it not for Pletnev's inspired shaping of the work. He exerts the same control over his players, as he does over his fingers, to imaginatively realize the meaning behind the notes, and draws supremely expressive playing at both ends of a huge dynamic range; one that is comfortably reproduced here with clarity, natural perspectives, a sense of instruments playing in a believable acoustic space, and a necessarily higher volume setting than usual. *Marche slave*'s final blaze of triumph, under the circumstances, seems apt.

NEW REVIEW

Tchaikovsky. Symphony No. 7 in E flat major (orch./ed S. Bogatyryev)[a]. Variations on a Rococo Theme for cello and orchestra, Op. 33[b]. [b]**Leonard Rose** (vc); **Philadelphia Orchestra/Eugene Ormandy.** CBS Masterworks Portrait CD46453. Item marked [a] from SBRG72042 (9/62), [b] SBRG72296 (6/55).

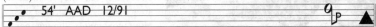

54' AAD 12/91

Tchaikovsky's Seventh Symphony is a reconstruction from various sources of a symphony which he started to compose in 1892 and put aside before commencing the *Pathétique*. Like the latter, the Seventh has a brooding atmosphere, but also contains some very vigorous and exciting music; it certainly deserves rediscovery and recognition. Eugene Ormandy conducted the Western première of the Seventh in 1962 and the excitement of this occasion is fully caught in this excellent studio recording. Ormandy jumps out of his normally reserved musical shell to deliver a performance of real panache. He whips his trusty orchestra into a considerable frenzy at the work's impressive climaxes and in general makes out the strongest possible case for this strange, not wholly legitimate work. The fill-up is generous and also of high quality: Leonard Rose's elegant and highly adroit reading of the *Rococo* Variations; the beauty of Tchaikovsky's solo writing is ideally realized by Rose, and Ormandy's accompaniment is extremely sympathetic. The recorded sound of both these Philadelphia performances is very acceptable: a rich sense of atmosphere with considerable depth.

Tchaikovsky. Manfred Symphony, Op. 58. **Oslo Philharmonic Orchestra/ Mariss Jansons.** Chandos CHAN8535.

53' DDD 5/88

This Symphony "in Four Scenes" was inspired by a reading of Byron's dramatic poem. Tchaikovsky seems to have felt great affection for the work but was unsure of its structural validity. It has proved difficult to bring off successfully in performance, despite the straightforward appeal of much of its melodic invention. In this performance, Jansons selects rather fast tempos for the most part and manages to bring out the warmth of the melodic writing whilst holding the whole work together most convincingly. The Oslo Philharmonic responds with adroit vivacity. Spectacularly open sound complements all the best qualities of this performance, securing here what is likely to be a prime recommendation for quite some time to come.

Tchaikovsky. String Quartets — No. 1 in D major, Op. 11; No. 2 in F major, Op. 22; No. 3 in E flat minor, Op. 30. Souvenir de Florence, Op. 70ª. **Borodin Quartet** (Mikhail Kopelman, Andrei Abramenkov, vns; Dmitri Shebalin, va; Valentin Berlinsky, vc) with ªYuri Bashmet (va); ªNatalia Gutman (vc). EMI CDS7 49775-2.

② 2h 20' ADD 8/88

Tchaikovsky's writing for string quartet shows considerable mastery, and all three works have an open-hearted fluency and a high quality of invention. There are no hints of constraint, and it seems that Tchaikovsky enjoyed the task of writing for a gentler medium. The Third Quartet has an elegiac quality throughout, with a particularly deeply-felt slow movement. The First Quartet, with the famous *Andante cantabile* slow movement, has a delightfully spring-like, outgoing lyrical character, and is the most popular of the three: the Second Quartet has a slightly greater range of expression, and the movements are more contrasted in mood. The Borodin Quartet play these works with a fine sense of style, and their readings are totally free of mannerisms and interpretative quirks. They are particularly impressive in the way that they float the long melodies in Tchaikovsky's slow movements, though they can play with plenty of brilliance when required. In *Souvenir de Florence* the two extra players combine happily with the Quartet. The recordings have plenty of presence and warmth.

Yuri Bashmet   [photo: BMG/Lewis

Tchaikovsky. EUGENE ONEGIN. **Bernd Weikl** (bar) Onegin; **Teresa Kubiak** (sop) Tatyana; **Stuart Burrows** (ten) Lensky; **Júlia Hamari** (mez) Olga; **Nicolai Ghiaurov** (bass) Gremin; **Anna Reynolds** (mez) Larina; **Enid Hartle** (mez) Filippyevna; **Michel Sénéchal** (ten) Triquet; **Richard Van Allan** (bass) Zaretsky; **William Mason** (bass) Captain; **John Alldis Choir; Orchestra of the Royal Opera House, Covent Garden/Sir Georg Solti.** Decca 417 413-2DH2. Notes, text and translation included. From SET596/8 (6/75).

② 2h 23' ADD 8/87

In *Eugene Onegin* the young, sensitive Tatyana falls in love with the blasé dandy Onegin only to be bluntly rejected. Onegin's emotional insensitivity leads to the death of his friend Lensky in a duel, but he realizes his mistake and confronts his true feelings for Tatyana. The seven scenes of *Onegin* do not follow the usual narrative progression of a Mozart or Verdi opera, but rather present a series of situations like cartoon pictures, concentrated and emotionally precise. Tchaikovsky's intense sympathy with Tatyana's unrequited love is evident and in the famous Letter scene he gives her some of his most exquisite music, highlighting every emotional twist and turn she encounters. This recording is well conceived and sounds very good in this transfer.

Tchaikovsky. THE QUEEN OF SPADES. **Wieslaw Ochman** (ten) Hermann; **Stefka Evstatieva** (sop) Lisa; **Penka Dilova** (mez) Countess; **Ivan Konsulov** (bar) Count Tomsky; **Yuri Mazurok** (bar) Prince Yeletsky; **Stefania Toczyska** (mez) Paulina; **Angel Petkov** (ten) Chekalinsky; **Peter Petrov** (bass) Surin; **Mincho Popov** (ten) Chaplitsky, Major-domo; **Stoil Georgiev** (bass) Narumov; **Wesselina Katsarova** (mez) Governess; **Rumyana Bareva** (sop) Masha; **Elena Stoyanova** (sop) Prilepa; **Gouslarche Boys' Choir; Svetoslav Obretenov National Chorus; Sofia Festival Orchestra/Emil Tchakarov.** Sony Classical CD45720. Notes, text and translation included.

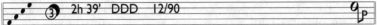

Recordings of what many consider to be Tchaikovsky's greatest opera have been few and far between, and none too satisfactory so that this excellent performance is a most welcome addition to the catalogue. It is one of a series of Russian operas issued by Sony and conducted by Tchakarov, who rises magnific-ently to the challenge of this work's astonishing originality of concept and struc-ture. He is splendidly supported by his Bulgarian forces, his Bulgarian chorus and orchestra singing and playing with vigour tempered by sensitivity. The set has been care-fully cast. Ochman's anguished, intensely subjective, slightly crazed Hermann could hardly be bettered in either interpretation or singing. Evstatieva makes a vibrant, highly strung Lisa, just right. Mazurok's authoritative Yeletsky and Konsulov's properly gruff Tomsky are other assets. Dilova's old Countess may not be as characterful as some but the part is well sung, as are the smaller roles, including Toczyska's Paulina. The recording is full of the right, haunted atmosphere in the private scenes, big scale in the public ones.

Georg Philipp Telemann

German 1681-1767

Telemann. ORCHESTRAL WORKS. **Stephen Preston** (fl); **John Turner** (rec); **Clare Shanks** (ob d'amore); **Friedmann Immer, Michael Laird, Iain Wilson** (tpts); **Monica Huggett** (va d'amore); **Academy of Ancient Music/Christopher Hogwood** (hpd). L'Oiseau-Lyre Florilegium 411 949-2OH. From DSDL701 (1/83).
Concerto in D major for three trumpets, strings and continuo. Quadro in B flat major. Concerto in E minor for recorder and flute. Concerto polonois. Concerto in E major for flute, oboe d'amore, viola d'amore, strings and continuo.

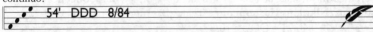

Telemann's distinctive eclecticism, uniting Italian energy and brilliance with French delicacy of expression, is often irresistibly appealing. Sometimes, too, his music is seasoned with Polish folk rhythms, melodies which had always fascinated the composer. Telemann claimed to have found difficulty in writing concertos but he nevertheless composed well over a hundred of them. This modest selec-tion contains two of his finest works in the form, the Concertos in E major and E minor. The delicately blended textures of the first provide a wonderful example of Telemann's instrumental writing in which the solo parts are clearly outlined in registers that emphasize their individual character. In the second, the partnership of flute and recorder creates an engagingly subtle tonal palette, especially in the slow movements while the finale is a swirling dance in Telemann's best Polish manner. The performances capture the spirit of the music delightfully with Christopher Hogwood providing stylish direction.

Telemann. ORCHESTRAL WORKS. **Cologne Musica Antiqua/Reinhard Goebel.** Archiv Produktion 413 788-2AH.
Suite in C major. Concertos — B flat major; F major; A minor.

49' DDD 3/85

Telemann's love for the French overture suite is in little doubt, if only because he wrote so many of them. A notably fine example of his skill in this medium exists in the Suite in C major. The programmatic element is a strong one and most of its movements have titles relating to figures from classical myth. Reinhard Goebel and Cologne Musica Antiqua vividly evoke the aquatic fun and games of Aeolus, Thetis, Neptune, Zephyr, Tritons, Naiads and the like in a varied sequence of French dance movements. These are prefaced by a splendid Overture in the French manner. The remainder of the disc is given over to three of Telemann's concertos for pairs of treble recorder and oboes, with bassoon and strings. They are attractive pieces, two of them having not been previously recorded and the crisp woodwind playing makes the most of this graceful, unassuming repertoire. Clear recorded sound and informative presentation.

NEW REVIEW

Telemann. RECORDER WORKS. **Peter Holtslag** (rec); **The Parley of Instruments/Peter Holman, [a]Roy Goodman.** Hyperion CDA66413.
Suite in A minor[a]. Concertos — F major; C major. Sinfonia in F major[a].

1h 6' DDD 10/91

Telemann professed a working knowledge of most of the standard instruments of his day and consequently wrote rewardingly for them. This is especially true in his treatment of woodwind instruments for which he has left a generous legacy. This disc, as well as containing two concertos, includes a suite and a sinfonia. The Suite in A minor is Telemann's best-known work for treble recorder; indeed, it is to recorder players what Bach's B minor Orchestral Suite is to flautists. The soloist, Peter Holtslag, is an accomplished player whose sensibilities exert a favourable influence over matters of texture, articulation and phrasing. He is a good judge of tempos and, almost alone among his competitors on disc, hits on an effective pace for the beautifully constructed French overture with which the Suite begins. The concertos are attractive pieces, too, that in F major concluding with an engaging pair of menuets. The Sinfonia, unusually scored for recorder, viola da gamba, cornett, three trombones, strings and continuo with organ introduces a distinctive splash of colour. The recording is most sympathetic.

Telemann. Musique de table — Productions I-III. **Vienna Concentus Musicus/Nikolaus Harnoncourt.** Teldec Das Alte Werk 2292-44688-2.

④ 4h 21' DDD 10/89

Telemann. Musique de table — Productions I-III. **Cologne Musica Antiqua/Reinhard Goebel.** Archiv Produktion 427 619-2AH4.

④ 4h 14' DDD 10/89

By some curious quirk of fate Archiv Produktion and Teldec have managed not once but twice simultaneously to issue complete recordings of Telemann's three-part orchestral and instrumental anthology *Musique de table*. Notwithstanding what must have seemed commercially bad timing we should be grateful to both companies for instigating performances which, though uneven in places are by and large outstandingly successful. Both Nikolaus Harnoncourt and Reinhard Goebel direct ensembles of period instruments but what each does with them is in striking contrast with the other. In matters of instrumental finesse Goebel's

Musica Antiqua Cologne has the edge on the Vienna Concentus Musicus and listeners will hardly fail to recognize disciplined and lively playing of a high order throughout this set. Nevertheless rigorous precision of this kind is sometimes at the cost of spontaneity and lyricism and it is in these respects that Harnoncourt's performances may well strike a more sympathetic chord in the listener.

Nowhere are the two approaches more divergent, perhaps, than in the beautiful G major Quartet of the First Production of the *Musique de table*. There Harnoncourt captures the gently sighing, *galant* gestures of the opening movement with sympathy and insight while Goebel is rhythmically stiff, and self-consciously mannered. But the positions are frequently reversed especially at such times when Harnoncourt's group sounds comparatively rough in ensemble or when occasionally it makes heavy weather over rhythmic patterns. To conclude on a positive note, neither version of Telemann's *magnum opus* is likely to cause disappointment. Ultimately it must be a question of taste and temperament. It may well be some while before such performances as these are equalled let alone bettered. Fine recorded sound and helpful documentation are features of both issues.

NEW REVIEW

Telemann. Fourth Book of Quartets. **American Baroque** (Stephen Schultz, fl; Elizabeth Blumenstock, vn; Roland Kato, va; Roy Whelden, va da gamba; Cheryl Ann Fulton, hp; Charles Sherman, hpd). Koch International Classics 37031-2.
No. 1 in D major; No. 2 in F major; No. 3 in A major; No. 4 in C major; No. 5 in G major; No. 6 in D minor.

· 54' DDD 1/92

The six quartets in this recording were published as *Quatrième Livre du Quatuors* under Telemann's name in Paris, probably in 1752. There is some doubt concerning their authenticity, yet the likelihood is that they are early exercises in quartet writing from Telemann's pen. Previous publications of his quartets had gone down well in Paris and it is possible that Telemann sanctioned the publication of these owing to popular demand. Be that as it may, the music is performed with imagination and sensibility by American Baroque. The pieces are scored for flute, violin, viola and bass but, rather than use a harpsichord continuo throughout, a triple harp is sometimes substituted. There is no precedence for this yet the resulting colours are undeniably attractive and it is hard to believe that Telemann himself would have other than approved. The group's ensemble and intonation is excellent throughout and the individual players respond affectionately to the composer's finely wrought textures and delicate tracery. Telemann or no the programme is an attractive one not least for the many engaging slow movements. The recorded sound is clear, complementing the chamber character of the music.

Telemann. 12 Fantaisies for transverse flute. **Barthold Kuijken** (transverse fl). Accent ACC57803D.

· 48' DDD 9/85

Telemann's music reached full maturity during the 1730s and in the flute *Fantaisies* we find pieces of sustained concentration, varied invention and easy grace. As so often with this composer the idiom is frequently forward-looking, hinting not only at the incipient 'galant' style but also at the acutely sensitive style (*emfindsamer Stil*) later developed above all in the keyboard music of Telemann's godson and successor at Hamburg, C.P.E. Bach. Barthold Kuijken plays a baroque flute which is strikingly different in sound from a present day instrument. His technique is secure, his articulation clear and communicative, and his phrasing pleasingly shaped. He is able to feel beyond what is written on the printed page and this pays off handsomely in movements such as the *Largo* of the B minor *Fantaisie*. Set in contrast with 'affective' pieces such as these are captivating little dances like the pastoral finale of the *Fantaisie* No. 5. Recorded sound is first-rate.

Telemann. Ino[a]. Overture-Suite in D major. [a]**Barbara Schlick** (sop); **Cologne Musica Antiqua/Reinhard Goebel.** Archiv Produktion 429 772-2AH. Text and translation included.

54' DDD 4/91

Telemann's dramatic cantata, *Ino,* is the product of an Indian summer which the composer enjoyed during the decade 1755-1765. He was, in fact, 84 when he composed *Ino* but we could easily be forgiven for believing it to be the work of a composer half his age. The Enlightenment poet Ramler's text is based on one of Ovid's *Metamorphoses* and concerns Ino, daughter of Cadmus and Hermione. She married Athamos who went mad, murdered one of their sons and attempted murder on the other. Ino, with husband in hot pursuit hurls herself into the sea clutching her child. Neptune comes to her aid, transforms her into the goddess Leukothea and her son into the god Palaemon. Telemann, with music wonderfully fresh in spirit, brings the tale to life in a manner hardly equalled and never surpassed by any of his earlier dramatic works. Barbara Schlick sounds cool in the face of such adversity as Ovid and Ramler place in her path, but there is an underlying passion in her interpretation and the result is musically satisfying. That is also true of Cologne Musica Antiqua under the informed and enthusiastic direction of Reinhard Goebel. This stylish ensemble comes into its own in a performance of another product of Telemann's Indian summer, the Overture-Suite in D major. A feast for lovers of this composer's music and one which offers delights that no baroque music enthusiast should overlook. Outstanding.

NEW REVIEW

Telemann. Missa brevis[a]. Deus judicium tuum[b]. Alles redet jetzt und singet[c]. [bc]**Barbara Schlick,** [b]**Martina Lins** (sops); [b]**Silke Weisheit** (contr); [a]**David Cordier** (alto); [b]**Christoph Prégardien** (ten); [bc]**Stephen Varcoe** (bar); [b]**Hans-Georg Wimmer** (bass); [b]**Rheinische Kantorei; Das kleine Konzert/Hermann Max.** Capriccio 10 315. Texts and translations included.

1h 3' DDD 11/91

This programme contains three strongly contrasting vocal works dating from different periods in the composer's long life. Earliest by far is the Lutheran Mass — in B minor, as it happens —— which Telemann may have composed even as early as his student days at Leipzig during the early years of the eighteenth century. The cantata *Alles redet jetzt und singet* is a setting of the spring song from an enormously long poem by the Hamburg poet and senator, Barthold Heinrich Brockes, who was also the author of a Passion text set by Handel, Telemann and others. This piece belongs to Telemann's Frankfurt period (1712-1721) while the remaining work, the motet *Deus judicium tuum* was a product of the composer's visit to Paris in 1737-38. Musically this is the most consistently satisfying of the three compositions. Telemann modelled it on the French *grand motet* with chorus, vocal ensembles and instruments, doubtless in deference to his hosts. They seem to have liked it since it was twice heard at the Paris Concert Spirituel. The performances are engaging and affectionate with notably strong contributions from the vocal soloists. Both the chorus and the orchestra respond in a lively manner to Hermann Max's direction and the recorded sound is clear and pleasingly resonant.

Telemann. Der Tag des Gerichts[a]. PIMPINONE[b]. Paris Quartets Nos. 1 and 6[c]. [a]**Gertraud Landwehr-Herrmann** (sop); [a]**Cora Canne-Meijer** (contr); [a]**Kurt Equiluz** (ten); [a]**Max van Egmond** (bass); [a]**Vienna Boys' Choir**, [a]**Hamburg Monteverdi Choir**, [a]**Vienna Concentus Musicus/Nikolaus Harnoncourt**; [b]**Ute Spreckelsen** (sop) Vespetta; [b]**Siegmund Nimsgern** (bass) Pimpinone; [b]**Ensemble Florilegium Musicum/Hans Ludwig Hirsch** with [b]**Herbert Tadiezi** (hpd). [c]**Quadro Amsterdam** (Frans Brüggen, fte; Jaap Schröder, vn; Anner Bylsma, vc; Gustav Leonhardt, hpd). Teldec 2292-42722-2. Text and translations included. From Telefunken Das Alte Werk SAWT9484-5 (3/67).

③ 3h 7' ADD

NEW REVIEW

Telemann. PIMPINONE. **John Ostendorf** (bass) Pimpinone; **Julianne Baird** (sop) Vespetta; **St Luke's Baroque Orchestra/Rudolph Palmer.** Newport Classics NCD60117. Notes, text and translation included.

1h 7' DDD 1/92

Julianne Baird [photo: Hamilton]

It says much for Harnoncourt's performing style that his recording of Telemann's last oratorio comes across as freshly and stylishly today as it did on its first appearance in the 1960s. The soloists include Kurt Equiluz and Max van Egmond, and van Egmond's declamation of Devotion's aria, "Da kreuzen verzebrende Blitze" ("consuming lightnings cross each other") is just one among many thrilling details in this vivid realization of Telemann's music. The remainder of the cast is impressive too, with outstanding contributions from two soloists of the Vienna Boys' Choir. This is Harnoncourt at his best. Telemann's comic intermezzo, *Pimpinone* was probably first performed between the acts of Handel's *Tamerlano* in Hamburg in 1725. Pimpinone, an elderly bachelor, is looking for a maid. He engages Vespetta who persuades him to marry her, only to play fast and loose with his affections and his cash. This is a stylish performance under the direction of Hans Ludwig Hirsch, with especially fine singing from Nimsgern. Two of Telemann's *Paris* Quartets make a delightful filler.

The Newport Classics recording of *Pimpinone* is also stylish and it is fluently sung. The soprano Julianne Baird is well cast in the role of Vespetta which she enlivens with appropriately coquettish and waspish singing. Her intonation is not always secure but her vivacious characterization and pleasing vocal timbre are a constant delight. The bass John Ostendorf turns in an endearing performance, eager, lustful but, as the story unfolds, increasingly irritable and not without self-pity. A weaker element is provided by the St Luke's Baroque Orchestra for whom period instruments pose problems still to be overcome. The interpretative ideas are good but ensemble is sometimes untidy and the string sound lustreless and weakly projected. But this is a largely successful enterprise and the animated exchanges which take place between the two vocal protagonists are well sustained. The text, partly in German, partly in Italian, is printed in full with English translations. This recording of *Pimpinone* is a worthy alternative to the three-disc set reviewed above.

Michael Tippett

Tippett. Concerto for double string orchestra. Fantasia concertante on a Theme of Corelli[a]. Songs for Dov[b]. [b]**Nigel Robson** (ten); [a]**John Tunnell,** [a]**Rosemary Ellison** (vns); [a]**Kevin McCrae** (vc); **Scottish Chamber Orchestra/Sir Michael Tippett.** Virgin Classics VC7 90701-2. Texts included.

Ih II' DDD 6/88

Tippett. Concerto for double string orchestra. Fantasia concertante on a Theme of Corelli. Little Music for strings. **Academy of St Martin in the Fields/Sir Neville Marriner.** Decca London 421 389-2LM. From ZRG680 (1/72).

56' ADD 8/89

A recording by the composer is always an event and the enterprising Virgin release finds Sir Michael at the helm of a very responsive and finely-recorded Scottish Chamber Orchestra. The Concerto receives a very broad reading, one sensitive to the complexity of texture and dynamic, drawing it very much away from the tradition of the English string serenade. The *Corelli* Fantasia too has a breadth and textural concern. The soloists are good and because of the small forces involved it has a crispness it so importantly needs. The highlight on the disc is undoubtedly the strange but haunting *Songs for Dov* in a quite outstanding interpretation by Nigel Robson who has obviously worked long and hard on them. He integrates the barking and howling into the vocal line so well and really captures the spirit of these songs (do persevere with them, they are difficult at first!). The recording is very good.

Marriner's disc of the works for strings is certainly not second best. Indeed, in the *Corelli* Fantasia, his version allows clearer perception of the concertino group (solo violins and cello) within the main string choirs. It's partly a question of microphone positioning, but mainly due to the Academy's fuller and more unanimous string tone. And what an astonishing range of tone these players possess. Dynamic shading and phrasing, and the sheer energy of these performances are irresistible. You won't hear a more rhythmically vital performance of the Double Concerto in a lifetime of CD listening or concert going. Digital remastering has sharpened up the music's positional exchanges. It has also revealed a slightly steely edge to upper strings at full stretch, and that the *Corelli* Fantasia's rich harmonies would have benefited from a fuller bass foundation. But these are tiny grumbles. On LP this programme was always essential to any Tippett collection; on CD and at mid-price it is as desirable as ever.

Tippett. ORCHESTRAL WORKS. [c]**Heather Harper** (sop); [abc]**London Symphony Orchestra/Sir Colin Davis;** [d]**Chicago Symphony Orchestra/ Sir Georg Solti.** Decca London 425 646-2LM3.
Symphonies — No. 1[a] (from Philips 9500 107, 10/76); No. 2[b] (Argo ZRG535, 1/68); No. 3[c] (Philips 6500 662, 1/75); No. 4[d], Suite in D for the Birthday of Prince Charles[d] (both from Decca SXDL7546, 8/81).

(3) 2h 51' ADD/DDD 7/90

These four symphonies comprise one of the most considerable contributions to the genre by a British composer this century. Numbers 1 and 2 are examples of Tippett's earlier, still relatively traditional language, while Nos. 3 and 4 are more radical. Bounding energy is the predominant quality of Nos. 1 and 2, an energy whose individual attributes are by no means diminished by association with Stravinsky. But Tippett's more personal, magical lyricism is also prominent, especially in the marvellous slow movement of No. 2, and this lyricism forms a clear link to the more reflective passages of No. 3. This glorious, 55-minute work evolves from purely instrumental arguments about active and reflective states of mind into a series of songs (for soprano) that confront some of the most urgent social issues of our time. Though arguing the need to counter violence and repression with tolerance and love, the music offers its own irreconcilable confrontation between allusions to Beethoven's Ninth and Bessie Smith-style blues, swept up into a stark coda as uncompromising in its modernism as anything in Tippett's output. After this the Fourth Symphony is less hectic, though no less diverse in its materials, a half-hour single movement of dazzling colours and vivid emotions. Although the performances occasionally remind us of the difficulties Tippett presents to his interpreters, and the recordings are not, on the whole, of the latest digital vintage, this is — thanks mainly to the commitment and persuasiveness of Sir Colin Davis — a set of considerable distinction.

Tippett. CHORAL WORKS. **Christ Church Cathedral Choir/Stephen Darlington.** Nimbus NI5266. Texts included.
Dance, Clarion Air. The Weeping Babe. Plebs angelica. Bonny at Morn (with Michael Copley, Maurice Hodges, Evelyn Nallen, recs). Crown of the Year (Medici Quartet — Paul Robertson, David Matthews, vns; Ivo-Jan van der Werff, va; Anthony Lewis, vc; Copley, Hodges, Nallen; John Anderson, ob; Colin Lawson, cl; Graham Ashton, tpt; Peter Hamburger, Martin Westlake, Jeremy Cornes, perc; Martin Jones, pf). Music (Jones, pf). A Child of Our Time — Five Negro Spirituals.

51' DDD 1/91 *Q*ₚ

Here is choral singing of the very highest order sumptuously recorded in the mellow surrounds of the Abbey at Dorchester-on-Thames. Under Stephen Darlington the men and boys of Christ Church Cathedral Choir sing with precision, immaculate control and great sensitivity. They achieve an almost perfect blend: no voice stands out in isolation, there are no rough edges and the whole effect is of a single, immensely versatile musical instrument. Of course there is a price to be paid: any individuality or character in the voices has had to be subjugated. So it's probably something of a mistake to project singers from the choir as soloists in the four Spirituals from *A Child of Our Time*. There are no reservations about anything else on this lovely disc. The principal work, *Crown of the Year*, was written in 1958 for a children's choir supported by very economical instrumental resources, Surprisingly this hasn't been recorded before; yet as this performance demonstrates most vividly, it is a colourful and vibrant work full of joy and vigour and incorporating such familiar tunes as "For he's a jolly good fellow". With the exception of the captivating *Bonny at Morn*, which uses a trio of fluttering recorders as a descant to a beautifully sung unison line, the other pieces on this CD are unaccompanied. The music is Tippett in his most simple and magical vein. Performed and recorded with such excellence the whole thing is a delight to the ear.

Tippett. A Child of Our Time. **Jessye Norman** (sop); **Dame Janet Baker** (mez); **Richard Cassilly** (ten); **John Shirley-Quirk** (bar); **BBC Singers; BBC Choral Society; BBC Symphony Orchestra/Sir Colin Davis.** Philips 420 075-2PH. Text included. From 6500 985 (11/75).

1h 4' ADD 11/87 Ⓑ

A Child of Our Time takes as its narrative kernel the shooting in 1938 of a minor German diplomat by a 17-year-old Jew, Herschel Grynspan, and so causing one of the most savage anti-Jewish pogroms seen in Nazi Germany. But the universality of the dilemma of an individual caught up in something he cannot control gives it a much broader relevance. Just as Bach used the Lutheran hymns for the chorale sections within his Passions, so Tippett uses the negro spiritual to tap a similarly universal vein. The soloists provide the narrative thread against the more reflective role of the chorus but they come together forcefully in the spirituals. Sir Colin Davis directs a powerful and atmospheric performance and his soloists are very fine. The 1975 recording sounds well.

Tippett. The Mask of Time. **Faye Robinson** (sop); **Sarah Walker** (mez); **Robert Tear** (ten); **John Cheek** (bass); **BBC Singers; BBC Symphony Chorus and Orchestra/Andrew Davis.** EMI CDS7 47705-8. From EX270567-3 (5/87). Recorded at a performance in the Royal Festival Hall, London, in March 1986.

2 | 1h 32' | DDD | 10/87

A huge work in two parts, each lasting some 45 minutes, *The Mask of Time* comprises ten 'scenes', the five in Part One more obviously mythological in character and moving from the 'creation' of the cosmos to the emergence of civilization and an earthly paradise, and those in Part Two more to do with the individual in history. The work calls for four soloists, chorus and large symphony orchestra and presents all manner of difficulties in performance and recording with its contrasting of full-blown episodes (with typically thrilling brass and percussion writing) and intimate chamber-like ensembles. There are many unforgettable moments in this deeply felt and thought-provoking score, and none more moving than Tippett's post-Hiroshima threnody for "those who have never had a life". This performance is superb, Andrew Davis demonstrating a fine grasp of the overall structure as well as the fine detail of this complex work. The live recording, too, is first-rate. This is by no means an easy work to assimilate, but those prepared to give it open-minded consideration will find themselves richly rewarded.

Tippett. KING PRIAM. **Norman Bailey** (bar) Priam; **Heather Harper** (sop) Hecuba; **Thomas Allen** (bar) Hector; **Felicity Palmer** (sop) Andromache; **Philip Langridge** (ten) Paris; **Yvonne Minton** (mez) Helen; **Robert Tear** (ten) Achilles; **Stephen Roberts** (bar) Patroclus; **Ann Murray** (mez) Nurse; **David Wilson-Johnson** (bar) Old man; **Peter Hall** (ten) Young guard; **Kenneth Bowen** (ten) Hermes; **Julian Saipe** (treb) Paris, as a boy; **Linda Hirst** (sop) Serving woman; **London Sinfonietta Chorus; London Sinfonietta/David Atherton.** Decca London 414 241-2LH2. Notes and text included. From D246D3 (11/81).

2 | 2h 8' | DDD | 1/90

Sir Michael Tippett [*photo: Decca*]

King Priam is the exception among Tippett's five operas in taking its plot from existing literature. But the text itself is Tippett's own, and the dramatic themes — the horrors of war, the torments of families whose destinies and choices create only tragedy — reverberate in various ways in many of his other works, though never again with the stark immediacy and sense of despair embodied here. It is astonishing how so uncompromising an opera can leave the listener more exhilarated than depressed: it must be something to do with witnessing human creativity asserting its power so convincingly. And Tippett's power here extends well beyond the blood and gore of the Trojan War. Even more moving and compelling is the mutual compassion of those who share bereavement, and the tortured hope of the one character (Achilles) who imagines what life might be like "after the war" — though he too will die in battle. No praise can be too high for this performance, in which a fine cast and the matchless London Sinfonietta are galvanized by David Atherton into an account which achieves maximum expressive fidelity while also affirming the opera's great structural strength. The recording does not seek to reproduce a theatrical ambience, but it is totally convincing in its own terms.

NEW REVIEW

Tippett. THE ICE BREAK. **David Wilson-Johnson** (bar) Lev; **Heather Harper** (sop) Nadia; **Sanford Sylvan** (bar) Yuri; **Carolann Page** (sop) Gayle; **Cynthia Clarey** (mez) Hannah; **Thomas Randle** (ten) Olympion; **Bonaventura Bottone** (ten) Luke; **Donald Maxwell** (bar) Lieutenant; **Christopher Robson** (alto) and **Sarah Walker** (mez) Astron; **London Sinfonietta Chorus; London Sinfonietta/David Atherton.** Virgin Classics VC7 91448-2. Notes and text included.

Ih 14' DDD 2/92

When *The Ice Break* was first performed in 1977, it was widely regarded as too modern for its own good. The story of a Solzhenitsyn-like writer exiled to a New York-like urban jungle where his son is almost killed in race riots but is finally, miraculously reborn, could indeed have been an all-too-simplistic piece of musical reportage, not least because the libretto is so liberally spiced with slang and colloquialisms, jostling against more poetic passages. Nevertheless, now that time has brought some distance to both story and music, the deeper resonances implicit in the opera's title, which refers both to the writer's memories of the beginning of the Russian spring as well as to the need to rebuild relationships in a new world, can be properly appreciated. That the music — and the drama — supports and strengthens these deeper resonances is abundantly clear from this exemplary performance, guided by David Atherton with a compelling blend of energy and restraint. The recording ensures that the vivid instrumental detail (and occasional, essential sound effects) do not submerge the voices. So, even if *The Ice Break* remains a problem in the theatre, this recording makes the best possible case for it as music drama.

Michael Torke

American 1961-

Torke. CHAMBER AND ORCHESTRAL WORKS. **Michael Torke** (pf); [a]**Edmund Niemann, Nurit Tilles** (pf, four hands); [b]**James Pugliese** (xylophone); [c]**Gary Schall** (marimba); **London Sinfonietta/**[d]**Kent Nagano,** [e]**David Miller.** Argo 430 209-2ZH.
The Yellow Pages[e]. Slate[abcd]. Adjustable Wrench[d]. Vanada[d]. Rust[e].

55' DDD 12/90

This début disc provides an excellent opportunity to explore the music of this talented young American composer. Michael Torke's unique blend of minimalist techniques and popular styles (that range from hip-hop to jazz) have created some of the most successful cross-over music in recent years. The upbeat pieces such as *Adjustable Wrench* and *The Yellow Pages* are the most obvious examples of his pop-inspired works; though the subtle influence of composers like Copland and Stravinsky can also be heard in the rhythmic drive and fastidious scorings. *Vanada* and *Slate* reveal greater complexities at work, though with no loss of immediacy or attractiveness. *Rust* (the title alludes to both a pitted texture and the colour) is a concerto for piano, winds and electric bass and displays the energy and rhythmic drive of this young composer at its most compelling; raunchy brass interjections, sleazy saxophone breaks and a funky off-beat electric bass line are led by the seemingly boundless energy of the solo piano. The performances, by members of the London Sinfonietta under the direction of Kent Nagano and David Miller, match the energy and vitality of the music, and one senses a genuine feeling of enjoyment and involvement in their playing. A well balanced recording, with clear and natural sound.

Charles Tournemire French 1870-1939

NEW REVIEW

Tournemire. ORGAN WORKS. **Torvald Torén.** Opus 3 CD8901. Played on the Grölunds organ of the Hedvig Eleonora Church, Stockholm.
L'orgue mystique: Cycle de Pâques, Op. 56 — No. 14, Quinquagesima: Verrière; No. 18, Quasimodo: Toccata sur un choral. Cycle après la Pentecôte, Op. 57 — No. 35, In Assumptione BVM: Prélude a l'Introit; Offertoire; Elévation; Communion; Paraphrase-Carillon. Suite évocatrice, Op. 74. Deux fresques symphoniques sacrées, Opp. 75 and 76.

`1h 7'  AAD  1/92`

The name of Charles Tournemire may be unfamiliar to most music-lovers, but he was an extraordinarily prolific composer whose compositions included four operas, eight symphonies, several large oratorios, and countless songs, chamber works and piano pieces. His greatest contribution, though, was in the field of organ music. His *magnum opus* for the instrument was the gargantuan *L'orgue mystique* which consists of 51 five-movement suites each based on the plainsong proper for the Sundays and Feast Days of the Church's year. This CD includes one complete suite as well as single movements from two of the others, the *Suite évocatrice* which takes the form of a modern version of the Classical French organ suite, and his last compositions, the two *Fresques symphoniques sacrées* which were inspired by the church of St Julien-le-Pauvre in Paris and Beauvais Cathedral respectively. While Tournemire's music is often somewhat obscure and improvisatory in nature these persuasive performances, crisply recorded on a bright, clear voiced organ unravel much of the mystery of Tournemire's writing while preserving a fine sense of atmosphere: Torvald Torén makes the music readily accessible for the first-time listener while established Tournemire-hands will relish these rewarding and thoroughly stimulating interpretations of a well-chosen cross-section of this vast output.

NEW REVIEW

Tournemire. Suite Evocatrice, Op. 74.
Vierne. Symphony No. 3, Op. 28.
Widor. Symphonie Gothique, Op. 70. **Jeremy Filsell** (org). Herald HAVPCD145. Played on the Harrison and Harrison organ of Ely Cathedral.

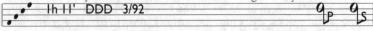

Compared with, say, the symphonies of Tchaikovsky or Sibelius the organ symphonies of Widor and his pupil Vierne are not particularly long. But in terms of organ music they are among the longest single works in the repertory. Within their five-movement form the composers set out to exploit the full expressive range of the organ and it was no coincidence that the organ symphony developed in turn of the century France. The great French organ builder Aristide Cavaillé-Coll was then producing instruments capable of hitherto undreamt-of colour and expression. Both Widor (at St Sulpice) and Vierne (at Notre Dame) had at their disposal the finest instruments in Paris and they indulged themselves fully in their symphonies. The subtitle of Widor's Ninth (*Gothic*) says it all. The structure is vast, intricately detailed, and almost forbidding in its grandness. Vierne's Third also presents an awesome spectacle, full of complex music and technically demanding writing, while Tournemire's neoclassical Suite provides a moment almost of light relief in such heavyweight company. Jeremy Filsell is an outstanding virtuoso player with a gift for musical communication and, in the Ely Cathedral organ, an instrument which produces the range of the great French instruments, but within an altogether clearer acoustic. These are performances of exceptional quality captured in a recording of rare excellence from the small independent company, Herald.

Eduard Tubin
Estonian-Swedish 1905-1982

Tubin. Symphony No. 3; Symphony No. 8. **Swedish Radio Symphony Orchestra/Neeme Järvi.** BIS CD342. Recorded in association with the Estonian Church Foundation, Vancouver.

♪ 1h 3' DDD 9/88

Tubin's Third Symphony comes from 1940, six months after Stalin had "incorporated" Estonia into the Soviet Union. Not surprisingly, it is strongly nationalist in feeling, reflecting the mood of a nation that had just lost its independence. The first two movements are full of imaginative and individual touches, the listener borne along on a current of movement. The finale is not wholly free from rhetoric and bombast, but all the same it is a strong piece and those who have the Second and Fourth Symphonies will find familiar resonances. The Eighth Symphony, however, is possibly his masterpiece: it is the darkest in colouring and most intense in feeling of all his symphonies. It comes from 1966 and the opening movement has a sense of vision and mystery whose atmosphere stays with you long afterwards. There is an astringency and a sense of the tragic that leaves a strong impression. Järvi's tireless championship of Tubin puts us much in his debt and the playing of the Swedish Radio Symphony Orchestra displays real commitment. The recording has quite exceptional body, clarity and definition.

Tubin. Symphonies — No. 4, "Sinfonia lirica"[a]; No. 9[b]. Toccata[b]. [a]**Bergen Symphony Orchestra,** [b]**Gothenburg Symphony Orchestra/Neeme Järvi.** BIS CD227. Item marked [a] from LP227 (12/83), [b] LP264 (3/85).

♪ 1h 4' AAD 10/86

The atmosphere of the Fourth Symphony is predominantly pastoral, a mixture of the Slavonic and the Nordic, with a strongly Sibelian feel to much of it. It is immediately accessible music, with real imaginative vitality and a strong feeling for structure. A quarter of a century separates it from the Ninth Symphony, where the mood is elegiac and the gently restrained melancholy of the slower sections makes a strong emotional impact. The fluid harmonies are quite haunting but as always Tubin's musical language is direct, tonal and, in its way, quite personal. Though there is an overriding sadness and resignation about this music, there is not a trace of self-pity. The exuberant and inventive *Toccata* for orchestra is also an enjoyable piece. The orchestral playing is first-class and the recorded sound splendidly firm and rich.

Viktor Ullmann   *Refer to Index*   *Austrian/Hungarian 1898-1944*

Joaquin Turína   *Refer to Index*   *Spanish 1882-1949*

Edgard Varèse   *French/American 1883-1965*

Varèse. VARIOUS WORKS. [a]**Rachel Yakar** (sop); [b]**Lawrence Beauregard** (fl); [c]**New York Philharmonic Orchestra;** [d]**Ensemble Intercontemporain** /[e]**Pierre Boulez.** Sony Classical CD45844. Texts and translations included. Ionisation (1929-31)[ce]. Amériques (1921)[ce]. Arcana (1925-7. All from CBS 76520, 6/78)[ce]. Density 21·5 (1936)[b]. Offrandes (1921)[ade]. Octandre (1923)[de]. Intégrales (1924-5. All from IM39053, 3/85)[de].

1h 17' ADD/DDD 10/90

These classic recordings make a welcome return to the catalogue, especially since the music of Varèse has been so poorly represented on disc and in the concert hall in recent years. Quite why so important a figure in twentieth-century music should be neglected like this is hard to say, and even more difficult to comprehend when one samples the quality of the music presented here. Varèse was a pioneer, a quester and above all a liberator. Music for him was a form of twentieth century alchemy — the transmutation of the ordinary into the extraordinary, an alchemical wedding of intellectual thought with intuitive imagination. Indeed, it was the writings of the fourteenth century cosmologist and alchemist Paracelsus that formed the inspiration behind his orchestral work *Arcana*, a vast canvas of sound built entirely out of one melodic motive. Discernible are echoes of Stravinsky and others, but the totality of *Arcana* is pure Varèse. The same is true of *Amériques*, a title that Varèse emphasized was not to be taken as "purely geographical but as symbolic of discoveries — new worlds on earth, in the sky or in the minds of men". Here romanticism and modernism seem to coexist side by side, where allusions from works such as *La mer* and *The Firebird* seem like racial memories carried into his brave new world. The remaining items consist of smaller chamber works which display Varèse's most radical, though equally rewarding, styles. Boulez and his players give committed, virtuosic performances of these challenging and intriguing works. Well worth exploring.

Ralph Vaughan Williams   *British 1872-1958*

Vaughan Williams. WORKS FOR STRING ORCHESTRA. [a]**Maurice Bourgue** (ob); **English String Orchestra/William Boughton.** Nimbus NI5019.
Fantasia on a Theme by Thomas Tallis. Oboe Concerto in A minor[a]. Concerto grosso. Fantasia on Greensleeves. Five Variants of "Dives and Lazarus".

1h 4' DDD 6/85

The Oboe Concerto consists of a *Rondo pastorale* in the composer's most fresh, open-air manner; a very short, high stepping *Minuet and Musette*, and a finale in the form of a scherzo with two trios, the second of which is grave and reflective. It is an immediately enjoyable piece, and Maurice Bourgue gives a good, idiomatic account and is well accompanied by the orchestra. Boughton's account of the *Tallis* Fantasia is good, though it lacks the spirituality and eloquence of the readings of Boult and Marriner. If the *Concerto grosso* is not a major work its five short movements are characteristically warm and vivacious. In the *Dives and Lazarus* Variants a harp adds piquancy to the rich string texture, and the variations are on a tune most will know as *The star of the County Down*. The *Greensleeves* Fantasia is a simple but poignant arrangement of the folk-tune and a second tune called *Lovely Joan*. All these works receive good performances by Boughton and his orchestra and the sound calls for no reservation.

Vaughan Williams. Job — a masque for dancing. **David Nolan** (vn); **London Philharmonic Orchestra/Vernon Handley.** EMI Eminence CD-EMX9506. From EMX412056-1 (8/84).

48' DDD 10/87 £

The work of William Blake was close to the heart of Vaughan Williams, and from Blake's *21 Illustrations to the Book of Job*, he produced a ballet score that came to represent a watershed in his career, looking backwards to the pastoral, folk-song idiom of his Third Symphony and forwards to the violence and vigour of the Fourth. *Job* requires an orchestra that is particularly flexible, with full and poignantly-toned soloists and a string body that can produced a rounded, consistent timbre with great depth. The London Philharmonic display all those qualities here, and a good deal more besides, and all is captured in a spacious, characterful acoustic and in a full-bodied recording that can handle equally well the hushed opening of the work and the enormities of the sixth scene. This highly persuasive performance is a particularly good bargain.

Vaughan Williams. A London Symphony. Fantasia on a Theme by Thomas Tallis (1910). **London Philharmonic Orchestra/Bernard Haitink.** EMI CDC7 49394-2.

1h 6' DDD 7/88

Vaughan Williams. A London Symphony. Concerto Grosso. **London Symphony Orchestra/Bryden Thomson.** Chandos CHAN8629.

1h 5' DDD 10/89

A London Symphony presents a vision of the capital far removed from the busy cosmopolitan metropolis it has become today. The London Vaughan Williams knew then was more elegant and less hectic though, alas, its Edwardian charm would soon be changed for ever by the First World War. At the beginning of the work slow Westminster chimes signal the beginning of the day; the main section of the first movement then evokes London's hustle and bustle. In the second *Lento* movement we explore some quieter byways, while the *Scherzo-Nocturne* third movement depicts the city at night. The finale looks at several city scenes and its epilogue portrays the River Thames as evening draws in. Bernard Haitink obtains excellent playing from the LPO, and he is particularly successful in bringing out the Symphony's contrasts and colour. Some details emerge more clearly than ever before in this very fine recording and there is an impressively powerful quality in Haitink's conducting. His sense of structure and line also bring powerful dividends in the *Tallis* Fantasia.

Whilst the LSO are not quite on best form on the Chandos issue, with some moments of suspect intonation, the clear layout of their performance, so finely aimed at the climax of the final movement and then sustained into the magical Epilogue, carries all before it. The succulent recording admirably reflects Thomson's delight in the sheer beauty of sound that Vaughan Williams can summon, and it is agreeably wide-ranging for the coupled *Concerto Grosso* of 1950, performed with an equal empathy for its idiom.

Vaughan Williams. A Sea Symphony. **Felicity Lott** (sop); **Jonathan Summers** (bar); **Cantilena; London Philharmonic Choir and Orchestra/ Bernard Haitink.** EMI CDC7 49911-2. Text included.

| · 1h 11' DDD 1/90 | ∅ P |

A firm hand on the tiller is needed to steer a safe course through this, Vaughan Williams's first and most formally diffuse symphony, completed in 1909. Haitink is clearly an ideal choice of helmsman and he is helped by a remarkably lucid recording that resolves details that would rarely be revealed in live performance. What might be more unexpected here is the obvious affinity he shows for this music: whilst never transgressing the bounds of Vaughan Williams's characteristically English idiom, he manages to place the work in the European mainstream, revealing a whole range of resonances, from Bruckner and Mahler to the Impressionists. Not all the glory should go to the conductor, of course. Both soloists are particularly fine, the vulnerability behind the spine-tingling power of Felicity Lott's voice providing excellent contrast to the staunch solidity of Jonathan Summers. The LPO Chorus, aided by Cantilena, are on top form and the whole enterprise is underpinned by the London Philharmonic's total commitment and expertise. Here is the recording of this glorious work for which the catalogue was waiting.

Vaughan Williams. Sinfonia antartica. **Sheila Armstrong** (sop); **London Philharmonic Choir and Orchestra/Bernard Haitink.** EMI CDC7 47516-2. From EL270318-1 (10/85).

| · 42' DDD 1/87 | ∅ P | ∅ S |

Scored for wordless soprano solo and chorus plus a large orchestra, this Seventh Symphony was based on the composer's music for the film *Scott of the Antarctic*. It comprises five movements; the Prelude, which conveys mankind's struggle in overcoming hostile natural forces; a *Scherzo*, which depicts the whales and penguins in their natural habitat; "Landscape", which portrays vast frozen wastes; Intermezzo, a reflection of the actions and thoughts of two members of the party; and "Epilogue", describing the final tragic assault on the South Pole. Bernard Haitink's conducting is highly imaginative, very concentrated and very committed and the LPO respond to him with some wonderfully atmospheric playing, full of personality and colour. Sheila Armstrong's eerie disembodied soprano voice and the remote chorus heighten the atmosphere, so that the score emerges as a powerful, coherent essay in symphonic form. Every detail has been captured by a magnificently sonorous and spacious recording.

Vaughan Williams. A Pastoral Symphony[a]. Symphony No. 4 in F minor[b]. [a]**Heather Harper** (sop); **London Symphony Orchestra/André Previn.** RCA Gold Seal GD90503. Item marked [a] from GL89691 (1/86), [b] GL89692 (1/86).

| · 1h 13' ADD 11/86 |

Previn's view of these symphonies is very sharp and clear with the LSO giving incisive, vital performances. It was an interesting idea to couple *A Pastoral Symphony*, where the composer is at his most inward and poetic, with the abrasive, angry Fourth Symphony. Previn's way with the *Pastoral* detracts in no way from the work's stature and his is a most persuasive performance. In the Fourth Symphony he does not tear into the work as some (including the composer) have done; he has an eye for its structure. The energy is very much there, with buoyant rhythms and sharp accents, but it is more controlled. The transfers are most successful and only a very slight lack of fullness in the sound indicates that the recordings are from the late 1960s and early 1970s.

Vaughan Williams. Symphony No. 5 in D major. Flos campi — suite[a].
[a]**Christopher Balmer** (va); [a]**Liverpool Philharmonic Choir; Royal
Liverpool Philharmonic Orchestra/Vernon Handley.** EMI Eminence CD-
EMX9512. From EMX2112 (8/87).

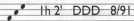 1h 2' DDD 3/88 £ Ⓑ

This disc is a bargain, both artistically and economically. The recording is full-
toned and carefully balanced, preserving the luminous qualities of two of
Vaughan Williams's most visionary and subtly devised scores; and the RLPO's
playing under Vernon Handley is totally in sympathy with the music. The performance of *Flos campi* is outstandingly good. This work is deeply influenced by
Ravel and has marvellous use of a wordless choir to intensify the erotic and
sensuous longing of the music inspired by the *Song of Solomon*. The viola's impassioned and lyrical outpouring is beautifully played by Christopher Balmer, with
excellent woodwind soloists in support, and the Liverpool Philharmonic Choir
sings with secure intonation and flexible dynamic range. Handley's interpretation
of the Fifth Symphony emphasizes the strength and passion in this music. His
control of the architectural splendour of the first movement is masterly and he
allows the ecstasy of the slow movement to unfold most naturally.

Vaughan Williams. Symphony No. 6 in E minor. Fantasia on a Theme by
Thomas Tallis. The Lark Ascending[a]. [a]**Tasmin Little** (vn); **BBC Symphony
Orchestra/Andrew Davis.** Teldec British Line 9031-73127-2.

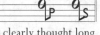 1h 2' DDD 8/91 q p q s

*Tasmin Little, Andrew Davis and Mrs Ralph Vaughan
Williams   [photo: Teldec/Koettlitz*

Andrew Davis has clearly thought long
and hard before committing this enigmatic and tragic symphony to disc,
and the result is one of the most spontaneous and electrifying accounts of
the Sixth Symphony available. The
urgency and vigour of the first and
third movements is astonishing, leaving
one with the impression that the work
might have been recorded in one take.
His treatment of the second subject's
reprise in the closing pages of the first
movement is more underplayed and
remote than the beautifully sheened
approach of some recordings, but is
arguably more nostalgic for being so.

The feverish, nightmare world of the *Scherzo* is a real *tour de force* in the hands of
an inspired BBC Symphony Orch-estra, and the desolate wasteland of the eerie
final movement has rarely achieved such quiescence and nadir as here. Davis's
searchingly intense *Tallis Fantasia* is finely poised with a beautifully spacious acoustic.
The disc concludes on a quietly elevated note with Tasmin Little's serene and
gently introspective reading of *The Lark Ascending*. The recording is excellent.

Vaughan Williams. String Quartets — No. 1 in G minor; No. 2 in A
minor. Phantasy Quintet[a]. **English Quartet** (Diana Cummings, Colin Callow,
vns; Luciano Iorio, va; Geoffrey Thomas, vc) with [a]**Norbert Blume** (va).
Unicorn-Kanchana DKPCD9076.

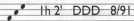 1h 1' DDD 9/89

See the word 'Phantasy' or its like in the title of some British chamber work of
the early years of this century, and you would rarely lose money betting that it

was produced for the wealthy patron, Walter W. Cobbett, who was fascinated by the Elizabethan form. He commissioned Vaughan Williams's Quintet through the Worshipful Company of Musicians in 1912, and received a short piece in four sections, played without break. The scoring is highly effective and the players here lose no opportunity to bring out the music's richly evocative atmosphere, perceptively varying tone-colour and vibrato to add an extra dimension to the notes of the score. They capture the contrasting moods of the First and Second String Quartets, of 1908 and 1944 respectively, with a very keen awareness of the different backgrounds to these pieces. Quartet No. 1, with its overtones of Ravel (with whom Vaughan Williams had been studying), is the most lighthearted of these three works, whilst No. 2 has a flavour of wartime darkness, emphasized by the dominance of the viola — it was dedicated to the violist of the Menges Quartet, Jean Stewart. These front-ranking performances are set in a pleasing, resonant acoustic that lends a genial ease to the proceedings.

Vaughan Williams. VOCAL WORKS. [a]**Elizabeth Connell**, [a]**Linda Kitchen**, [a]**Anne Dawson**, [a]**Amanda Roocroft** (sops); [a]**Sarah Walker**, [a]**Jean Rigby**, [a]**Diana Montague** (mezs); [a]**Catherine Wyn-Rogers** (contr); [a]**John Mark Ainsley**, [a]**Martyn Hill**, [a]**Arthur Davies**, [a]**Maldwyn Davies** (tens); [acd]**Thomas Allen**, [a]**Alan Opie** (bars); [a]**Gwynne Howell**, [a]**John Connell** (basses); [b]**Nobuko Imai** (va); [bcd]**Corydon Singers; English Chamber Orchestra/Matthew Best.** Hyperion CDA66420. Texts included.
Serenade to Music[a]. Flos campi[b]. Five mystical songs[c]. Fantasia on Christmas carols[d].

| 1h 8' DDD 9/90 |

In 1938 Sir Henry Wood celebrated his 50 years as a professional conductor with a concert. Vaughan Williams composed a work for the occasion, the *Serenade to Music*, in which he set words by Shakespeare from Act 5 of *The Merchant of Venice*. Sixteen star vocalists of the age were gathered together for the performance and Vaughan Williams customized the vocal parts to show off the best qualities of the singers. The work turned out to be one of the composer's most sybaritic creations, turning each of its subsequent performances into a special event. Hyperion have gathered stars of our own age for this outstanding issue and Matthew Best has perceptively managed to give each their head whilst melding them into a cohesive ensemble. A mellow, spacious recording has allowed the work to emerge on disc with a veracity never achieved before. The coupled vocal pieces are given to equal effect and the disc is substantially completed by Nobuko Imai's tautly poignant account of *Flos campi*, in which the disturbing tension between viola solo and wordless chorus heighten the work's crypticism. Altogether, an imaginative issue that is a must for any collection.

Giuseppe Verdi
Italian 1813-1901

Verdi. OVERTURES AND PRELUDES. **Berlin Philharmonic Orchestra/ Herbert von Karajan.** DG 419 622-2GH. From 413 544-1GX2 (2/86).
Nabucco; Ernani; I Masnadieri; Macbeth; Il Corsaro; La Battaglia di Legnano; Luisa Miller; Rigoletto; La Traviata; I Vespri Siciliani; Un Ballo in maschera; La Forza del Destino; Aida.

| 1h 13' ADD 10/87 |

Karajan was one of the most adaptable and sensitive of dramatic conductors. His repertoire in the theatre is extraordinarily wide being at home equally in Verdi,

Wagner, Richard Strauss and Puccini. In this selection from his celebrated 1976 collection of all of Verdi's overtures, he gives us some fine insights into the composer's skill as an orchestrator, dramatist and poet. Though Karajan had only recorded *Aida* complete his dramatic instincts bring some fine performances of the lesser known preludes. The earliest, *Nabucco* from 1842 (the collection is arranged chronologically), already shows a mastercraftsman at work, with a slow introduction promising much. *La Traviata* shows a quite different skill — the delcate creation of a sensitive poet working in filigree. The final four preludes are great works fully worthy of this individual presentation. Even the lesser known Preludes are enhanced by Karajan's dramatic instincts. Good recordings, though less than outstanding.

Verdi. Messa da Requiem[a]. OPERA CHORUSES. [a]**Susan Dunn** (sop); [a]**Diane Curry** (mez); [a]**Jerry Hadley** (ten); [a]**Paul Plishka** (bass); **Atlanta Symphony Chorus and Orchestra/Robert Shaw.** Telarc CD80152. Texts and translations included.
Opera choruses: DON CARLOS — Spuntato ecco il dì. MACBETH — Patria oppressa. OTELLO — Fuoco di gioia. NABUCCO — Va, pensiero, sull'ali dorate. AIDA — Gloria all'Egitto.

② 1h 53' DDD 3/88 **B**

Verdi. Messa da Requiem[a]. Quattro pezzi sacri[b]. [a]**Maria Stader** (sop); [a]**Oralia Dominguez** (mez); [a]**Gabor Carelli** (ten); [b]**Iván Sardi** (bass); [b]**Berlin RIAS Chamber Choir; St Hedwig's Cathedral Choir, Berlin; Berlin Radio Symphony Orchestra/Ferenc Fricsay.** DG Dokumente mono 429 076-2GDO2. Texts and translations included. Item marked [a] recorded at a performance in Berlin on October 23rd, 1960, [b] January 14th, 1952.

② 2h 12' ADD 11/89 **B** ▲

Of all nineteenth-century choral works, Verdi's setting of the Requiem Mass seems to be the most approachable. The choral writing is of the utmost splendour and conviction, and is a very personal statement of belief although written by an unbeliever. In many sections soloists and chorus are intermingled in a masterly fashion, and the writing for the orchestra is always appropriate to the text. Robert Shaw directs a performance that avoids histrionics and display and impresses by sheer musicianship. Tempos are well judged and for once rarely depart from the composer's markings. The team of soloists are well blended. The chorus are well drilled and full bodied and contribute lustily to the operatic choruses included as a bonus. The recording is very fine, spacious yet clear.

In his performance, recorded live like Toscanini's, Ferenc Fricsay came very close to equalling the former's achievement in a performance that matches lyrical intensity with tragic force (the conductor *must* have been influenced by the fact that he knew he hadn't long to live). The discipline here on all sides also matches Toscanini's and the choral singing, better recorded, is marginally superior. Fricsay's account of the *Four Sacred Pieces* is more than a fill-up: it's an arresting and moving interpretation of Verdi's last work for chorus.

Verdi. OPERA CHORUSES. **Chicago Symphony Chorus and Orchestra/ Sir Georg Solti.** Decca 430 226-2DH. Texts and translations included.
NABUCCO — Gli arredi festivi giù cadano infranti; Va, pensiero, sull'ali dorate. I LOMBARDI — Gerusalem!; O Signore, dal tetto natio. MACBETH — Tre volte miagola; Patria oppressa. I MASNADIERI — Le rube, gli stupri. RIGOLETTO — Zitti zitti. IL TROVATORE — Vedi! le fosche notturne spoglie; Squilli, echeggi la tromba guerriera. LA TRAVIATA — Noi siamo zingarelle ... Di Madride nio siam mattadori (with Marsha Waxman, mez; David Huneryager, Richard Cohn, basses). UN BALLO IN MASCHERA — Posa in

pace. DON CARLOS — Spuntato ecco il dí. AIDA — Gloria all'Egitto.
OTELLO — Fuoco di gioia. REQUIEM — Sanctus.

1h 10' DDD 4/91   qp qs B

Verdi. OPERA CHORUSES. **Slovak Philharmonic Choir; Slovak Radio Symphony Orchestra/Oliver Dohnányi.** Naxos 8 550241.
NABUCCO — Gli arredi festivi giù cadano infranti; Va, pensiero, sull'ali dorate.
MACBETH — Patria oppressa. IL TROVATORE — Vedi! le fosche notturne
spoglie; Ora co'dadi, ma fra poco. LA TRAVIATA — Noi siamo zingarelle; Si
ridesta in ciel (with Alena Cokova, mez; Stanislav Vrabel, bass). DON CARLOS
— Spuntato ecco il dì d'esultanza. AIDA — Gloria all'Egitto. OTELLO —
Fuoco di gioia. LA BATTAGLIA DI LEGNANO — Deus meus, pone illos ut
rotam (Eva Jenisova, sop; Cokova); Giuramento (L'udovit Ludha, ten). ERNANI
— Si rideste il Leon di Castiglia. LA FORZA DEL DESTINO — Rataplan!
rataplan! (Ida Kirilová, mez).

56' DDD 4/91   £ qp B

Verdi's choruses occupy a special place in his operas. They are invariably red-
blooded and usually make a simple dramatic statement with great impact. Such is
their immediacy and communicative force that they have sometimes produced an
influence on listeners, over and above that pertinent to the plot, especially where
the audience has already been primed with patriotic nationalistic feeling by local
events outside the theatre. The arresting "Chorus of the Hebrew Slaves" ("Va,
pensiero") from *Nabucco* is a prime example. Probably the best-known and most
popular chorus in the entire operatic repertoire, it immediately tugs at the heart-
strings with its gentle opening cantilena, soon swelling out to a great climax.
Solti, in his splendidly vibrant Decca collection, with the Chicago Symphony
Chorus, shows just how to shape the noble melodic line which soars with firm
control, yet retaining the urgency and electricity in every bar. He is equally good
in "Gli arredi festivi", from the same opera, not only in the bold opening
statement, shared between singers and the resplendent sonority of the Chicago
brass, but also later when the mood lightens, and women's voices are heard
floating over seductive harp roulades. The dramatic contrasts at the opening of
"Gerusalem!" from *I Lombardi* are equally powerfully projected, and the brass
again makes a riveting effect in "Patria oppressa" from *Macbeth*. But, of course,
not all Verdi choruses offer blood and thunder: the volatile "Fire chorus" from
Otello flickers with an almost visual fantasy, while the wicked robbers in *I
Masnadieri* celebrate their excesses (plunder, rape, arson and murder) gleefully,
and with such rhythmic jauntiness that one cannot quite take them seriously. The
"Gypsies chorus" from *La Traviata* has a nice touch of elegance, and the scherzo-
like "Sanctus", from the *Requiem*, which ends the concert, is full of joy. But it is

the impact of the dramatic moments
which is most memorable, not least the
big triumphal scene from *Aida*, complete
with the ballet music, to provide a
diverse interlude in the middle. Throughout we have demonstration-worthy
sound from the Decca engineers in the
suitably resonant acoustic of Chicago's
Orchestra Hall, and the back-up documentation includes full translations.

It might be thought that after such a
degree of spectacle the alternative super-
bargain collection by the Slovak forces
under Oliver Dohnányi might sound a
little flat. Not so! Even though this is
such a modestly priced CD, costing
about a third as much as the Decca disc,

Sir Georg Solti   *[photo: Decca/Masclet*

the digital sound is first class and the singing of the Slovak chorus has plenty of Verdian fervour. The singers are placed rather more backwardly in the overall Naxos sound picture, but the effect is in some ways more natural, with no lack of vocal splendour. Indeed in the "Grand March" scene from *Aida* (which omits the ballet sequence) the direct impact is most telling, with the fanfare trumpets blazing out on either side of the chorus with great presence. Dohnányi, too, finds a light touch to pick up the fantasy of the "Fire Chorus", while the Slovak brass are splendid in "Patria oppressa". This collection is shorter than Solti's, but it includes some attractive items not in the Decca programme from *Ernani, La Forza del destino*, and two vintage choruses from *La battaglia de Legnano*. The documentation is good, but omits translations, but this seems reasonable for a disc that costs so little.

Verdi. I DUE FOSCARI. **Piero Cappuccilli** (bar) Francesco Foscari; **José Carreras** (ten) Jacopo Foscari; **Katia Ricciarelli** (sop) Lucrezia; **Samuel Ramey** (bass) Jacopo Loredano; **Vincenzo Bello** (ten) Barbarigo; **Elizabeth Connell** (sop) Pisana; **Mieczyslaw Antoniak** (ten) Officer; **Franz Handlos** (bass) Doge's servant; **Austrian Radio Chorus and Symphony Orchestra/ Lamberto Gardelli.** Philips 422 426-2PM2. Notes, text and translation included. From 6700 105 (4/78).

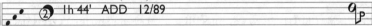

1h 44' ADD 12/89

This is one of the most impressive of Verdi's early scores, a dark, dour drama of a dynastic and family drama played out on a historic plane. The performance is worthy of the piece. Gardelli has always been a loving exponent of Verdi's 'galley-years' opera and here his conducting brings out the colour and character of the piece unfussily yet with innate eloquence. Tempos, dynamics and rhythmic emphasis are all ideally adumbrated; so is the depth of feeling in the score. He is blessed with a near-ideal cast, all three principals being at the peak of their achievement in 1978 when the set was made. Cappuccilli is absolutely in his element as the gloomy old Doge and father, a portrait to set alongside his superb Boccanegra. His breath control and line in his first aria, "O vecchio cor", is a classic of Verdian singing. Carreras, as the condemned Jacopo, sings with the right feeling of sincerity and desperation in his Prison scene. Ricciarelli offers the role of Lucrezia with lustrous tone and unflinching attack, one of her best performances on disc. She and Cappuccilli make the most of their wonderful duet in the last act. The recording is true and well balanced.

Verdi. ATTILA. **Samuel Ramey** (bass) Attila; **Cheryl Studer** (sop) Odabella; **Giorgio Zancanaro** (bar) Ezio; **Neil Shicoff** (ten) Foresto; **Ernesto Gavazzi** (ten) Uldino; **Giorgio Surian** (bass) Leone; **Chorus and Orchestra of La Scala, Milan/Riccardo Muti.** EMI CDS7 49952-2. Notes, text and translation included.

1h 49' DDD 5/90

This is one of the most successful of the collaborations between Muti and the La Scala forces. The raw vigour of Verdi's early triumph is splendidly captured by Muti's fiery yet sensitive direction, with his forces fired to great things. Tenor excepted, this cast couldn't be bettered anywhere today. Samuel Ramey is an incisive, dark-hued Attila, singing with accuracy and confidence. His main adversary is the indomitable Odabella, here taken with spirit, vital attack and well-fashioned phrasing by Cheryl Studer, who might now give us the Norma for which we have all been waiting. Giorgio Zancanaro can be rough as Ezio but he is dramatically well in the picture, and Neil Shicoff is never less than honourable in tone and line. The recording, though not ideal in every respect, gives the voices their rightful prominence.

Verdi. STIFFELIO. **José Carreras** (ten) Stiffelio; **Sylvia Sass** (sop) Lina; **Matteo Manuguerra** (bar) Stankar; **Wladimiro Ganzarolli** (bass) Jorg; **Ezio di Cesare** (ten) Raffaele; **Maria Venuti** (mez) Dorotea; **Thomas Moser** (ten) Federico; **Austrian Radio Chorus and Symphony Orchestra/Lamberto Gardelli.** Philips 422 432-2PM2. Notes, text and translation included. From 6769 039 (10/80).

② 1h 49' ADD 3/90

This work is gradually gaining the reputation it deserves as companies and audiences realize its quality (it gains its first performance at Covent Garden in the 1992-3 season). It tells of Stiffelio, a Protestant clergyman, in a Catholic country, whose wife Linda has committed adultery and finds it in his heart, after her father has killed her lover, to forgive her. The work has elements that pre-echo *Otello* and is yet another example of Verdi finding the specific music for a specific predicament. This performance, firmly conducted by Gardelli, has an involved, involving assump-tion of the title-role by Carreras. This role is a gift for an accomplished tenor and he catches the moral fervour and uncertainties of the part with his open-hearted, spontaneous performance. Sylvia Sass also offers a rewarding, strongly emotional performance as Linn.

Verdi. MACBETH. **Piero Cappuccilli** (bar) Macbeth; **Shirley Verrett** (mez) Lady Macbeth; **Nicolai Ghiaurov** (bass) Banquo; **Plácido Domingo** (ten) Macduff; **Antonio Savastano** (ten) Malcolm; **Carlo Zardo** (bass) Doctor; **Giovanni Foiani** (bass) Servant; **Sergio Fontana** (bass) Herald; **Alfredo Mariotti** (bass) Assassin; **Stefania Malagú** (mez) Lady-in-waiting; **Chorus and Orchestra of La Scala, Milan/Claudio Abbado.** DG 415 688-2GH3. Notes, text and translation included. From 2709 062 (10/76).

③ 2h 34' ADD 9/86

Verdi's lifelong admiration for Shakespeare resulted in only two operas based on his plays. *Macbeth*, the first, originally written in 1847, was extensively revised in 1865. Without losing the direct force of the original, Verdi added greater depth to his first ideas. Once derided as being un-Shakespearian, it is now recognized as a masterpiece for its psychological penetration as much as for its subtle melodic inspiration. Abbado captures perfectly the atmosphere of dark deeds and personal ambition leading to tragedy, projected by Verdi, and his reading holds the opera's disparate elements in the score under firm control, catching its interior tensions. He is well supported by his Scala forces. Shirley Verrett may not be ideally incisive or Italianate in accent as Lady Macbeth, but she peers into the character's soul most convincingly. As ever, truly inspired by Abbado, Cappuccilli is a suitably haunted and introverted Macbeth who sings a secure and unwavering legato. Domingo's upright Macduff and Ghiaurov's doom-laden Banquo are both admirable in their respective roles.

Verdi. RIGOLETTO. **Tito Gobbi** (bar) Rigoletto; **Giuseppe di Stefano** (ten) Duke; **Maria Callas** (sop) Gilda; **Nicola Zaccaria** (bass) Sparafucile; **Adriana Lazzarini** (mez) Maddalena; **Giuse Gerbino** (mez) Giovanna; **Plinio Clabassi** (bass) Monterone; **William Dickie** (bar) Marullo; **Renato Ercolani** (ten) Borsa; **Carlo Forti** (bar) Count Ceprano; **Elvira Galassi** (sop) Countess Ceprano; **Chorus and Orchestra of La Scala, Milan/Tullio Serafin.** EMI mono CDS7 47469-8. Notes, text and translation included. From Columbia 33CXS1324, 33CX1325/6 (2/56).

② 1h 58' ADD 2/87 Ⓑ ▲

The story of the hunchbacked jester Rigoletto at the court of a licentious Duke who seduces the Fool's daughter Gilda by masquerading as a poor student, and

the consequent attempts at revenge on the part of Rigoletto, produced from
Verdi one of the most telling of his mid-period triumphs. His identification with
each of the characters and the sheer energy and sensuous ardour of the score is
quite remarkable. Nowhere else on record have these characterizations been
delineated with such intelligence and commitment as by Gobbi, Callas and di
Stefano on this 37-year-old set. Over all Serafin presides with an unerring grasp
of Verdian timing.

Verdi. LA TRAVIATA. **Maria Callas** (sop) Violetta Valéry; **Alfredo Kraus**
(ten) Alfredo Germont; **Mario Sereni** (bar) Giorgio Germont; **Laura Zanini**
(mez) Flora Bervoix; **Maria Cristina de Castro** (sop) Annina; **Piero De
Palma** (ten) Gaston; **Alvero Malta** (bar) Baron Douphol; **Vito Susca** (bass)
Marquis D'Obigny; **Alessandro Maddalena** (bass) Doctor Grenvil; **Manuel
Leitao** (ten) Messenger; **Chorus and Orchestra of the Teatro Nacional de
San Carlos, Lisbon/Franco Ghione.** EMI mono CDS7 49187-8. Notes, text
and translation included. Recorded at a performance in the Teatro Nacional de
San Carlos, Lisbon on March 27th, 1958. From RLS757 (10/80).

② 2h 3' ADD 11/87 ᵖ Ⓑ ▲

Verdi. LA TRAVIATA. **Renata Scotto** (sop) Violetta Valéry; **Alfredo Kraus**
(ten) Alfredo Germont; **Renato Bruson** (bar) Giorgio Germont; **Sarah
Walker** (mez) Flora Bervoix; **Cynthia Buchan** (mez) Annina; **Suso Mariate-
gui** (ten) Gaston; **Henry Newman** (bar) Baron Douphol; **Richard Van Allan**
(bass) Marquis d'Obigny; **Roderick Kennedy** (bass) Doctor Grenvil; **Max-
René Cosotti** (ten) Giuseppe; **Christopher Keyte** (bass) Messenger;
**Ambrosian Opera Chorus; Band of HM Royal Marines; Philharmonia
Orchestra/Riccardo Muti.** EMI CDS7 47538-8. Notes, text and translation
included. From SLS5240 (5/82).

② 2h 9' DDD 11/87 ᵖ Ⓑ

Verdi. LA TRAVIATA (sung in English). **Valerie Masterson** (sop) Violetta;
John Brecknock (ten) Alfredo; **Christian du Plessis** (bar) Germont; **Della
Jones** (mez) Flora; **Shelagh Squires** (mez) Annina; **Geoffrey Pogson** (ten)
Gaston; **John Gibbs** (bar) Baron; **Denis Dowling** (bar) Marquis; **Roderick
Earle** (bass) Doctor; **Edward Byles** (ten) Giuseppe; **John Kitchiner** (bar)
Messenger; **English National Opera Chorus and Orchestra/Sir Charles
Mackerras.** EMI CMS7 63072-2. Notes and text included. From SLS5216 (10/81).

② 1h 58' ADD 10/89 ᵖ Ⓑ

Most sopranos in the part of Violetta (forced to give up her true love for the
sake of convention) make you cry in the last act; Callas also made you cry in the
second. A fullness of heart and voice informs everything she does in the long
colloquy with the elder Germont. The sorrow and emptiness that enters her tone
when she realizes she will have to give up her beloved Alfredo is overwhelmingly
eloquent. Then the final scene is almost unbearable in its poignancy of expression: the reading of the letter so natural in its suggestion of emptiness. However,
the sense of sheer hollowness at "Ma se tornando …" proves the most moving
moment of all as Violetta knows nothing can save her life. All that and so much
else suggests that Callas more than anyone understood what the role is about.
To add to one's pleasure the young Kraus is as appealing as any tenor on disc as
Alfredo. His Schipa-like tone, his refinement of phrase, especially in his duets
with Callas, and his elegant yet ardent manner are exactly right for the part.
Mario Sereni may not be in his colleagues' class, but his elder Germont is
securely, sincerely and often perceptively sung. Franco Ghione is a prompt and
alert conductor and the mono recording has plenty of theatrical presence.
  Renata Scotto, also, was always an affecting Violetta on stage and her portrayal
on Muti's disc displays utmost understanding for its deep emotions. She is aptly

partnered by Renato Bruson and Alfredo Kraus, who once again shows an innate feeling for Verdian line and phraseology and blends his voice cleanly with Scotto's. Riccardo Muti gives us the score complete (the Callas recording is cut) and ensures faithfulness to Verdi's tempos and dynamic markings. The recording, too, has great theatrical feeling.

"ENO at its very best" was the verdict when their recording first appeared in 1981. This *Traviata* provided eloquent testimony to the standards of their more workaday occasions, with a popular opera at the very heart of the Italian repertoire and a representative cast, the strength of which lay not simply in the three main roles but in having such excellent artists as Della Jones and the veteran Denis Dowling in secondary parts. Mackerras, a former Musical Director of the company and always closely associated with it, brings to the performance his customary care for detail and feeling for overall cohesion, and both orchestra and chorus are admirably responsive. Views on opera in translation will always vary, and such encouragement from the chorus as "That's how to take it! Splendid!" may suggest the ethos of Lords rather than that of the Palais-Royal; still, the advantages of immediate intelligibility are undeniable and the enunciation is remarkably clear. Similarly, the English style of singing has the merits of clean, well-placed tone and scrupulous attention to the score, even if some of the richness and emotional fervour of Italian tradition is lacking. Valerie Masterson's assured technique is matched by the vividness of her characterization; she gives a touching and accomplished performance.

Verdi. IL TROVATORE. **Maria Callas** (sop) Leonora; **Giuseppe di Stefano** (ten) Manrico; **Rolando Panerai** (bar) Count di Luna; **Fedora Barbieri** (mez) Azucena; **Nicola Zaccaria** (bass) Ferrando; **Luisa Villa** (mez) Ines; **Renato Ercolani** (ten) Ruiz, Messenger; **Giulio Mauri** (bass) Old Gipsy; **Chorus and Orchestra of La Scala, Milan/Herbert von Karajan.** EMI mono CDS7 49347-2. Notes, text and translation included. From Columbia 33CXS1483, 33CX1484/5 (11/57).

② 2h 9' ADD 12/87   ⑨ P Ⓑ ▲

Written in between *Rigoletto* and *La traviata*, *Il trovatore* has its own distinct identity. Pictorially, the nightscape of its action is penetrated by the watchman's torch, the gipsy's campfire and the cruel flame of the witch's stake. Dramatically, the passions of the present flare up among the shadows of a death-ridden past. Musically, the melodies surge to the background of an uneasy chromaticism, with taut rhythms and a predominantly minor tonality. A great performance can be exhilarating, but an indifferent one will often appear depressingly shabby. This recording finds Callas in fine voice and liable at any moment to bring a special thrill of conviction and individuality. As so often when one returns to reissues of her recordings, it is to find her quite remarkably restrained for most of the time: then a moment of rapt lyricism or fierce declamation produces a tingling effect with its feeling of spontaneous intensity and personal involvement. Her collaboration with Karajan is also among the most distinguished on record, and it often seems that his more calculated procedure with its care for the dignity of the score acts as both a foil and a balance to her impulsively emotional approach. Among the other singers, the most impressive is Fedora Barbieri, giving here her most inspired performance on record and Rolando Panerai, whose dark vibrancy suits the character of the Count di Luna. If di Stefano has neither the requisite steel in his voice nor the nobility of style, he is best in the full-voiced passion of the final scene.

Verdi. I VESPRI SICILIANI. **Cheryl Studer** (sop) Elena; **Chris Merritt** (ten) Arrigo; **Giorgio Zancanaro** (bar) Montforte; **Ferruccio Furlanetto** (bass) Procida; **Gloria Banditelli** (contr) Ninetta; **Enzo Capuano** (bass) De Béthune; **Francesco Musinu** (bass) Vaudemont; **Ernesto Gavazzi** (ten) Danieli; **Paolo**

Barbacini (ten) Tebaldo; **Marco Chingari** (bass) Roberto; **Ferrero Poggi**
(ten) Manfredo; **Chorus and Orchestra of La Scala, Milan/Riccardo
Muti.** EMI CDS7 54043-2. Notes, text and translation included. Recorded at
performances in La Scala,·Milan during December 1989 and January 1990.

③ 3h 19' DDD 1/91

Verdi's French opera, here given in its more familiar Italian guise, is a difficult
work to bring off. Verdi felt he had to try to accommodate Parisian taste for the
grand and theatrically exciting while at the same time showing his own preferences for the interplay of characters. It's to the credit of this performance, taken
live from La Scala, that both aspects are thrillingly encompassed by virtue of
Muti's vivid and acute conducting that never allows the score to sag yet allows
for its many and varied moods. Although he plays it at full length, EMI have
nonetheless managed to contain it on three discs. The singers, with one serious
exception, are equal to their roles, none more than Studer as an Elena of positive
character and vocal security. Chris Merritt turns in his best performance on disc
to date as the hero Arrigo. Even better is Zancanaro as the tyrant Montforte,
who yet has an anguished soul. Furlanetto is frankly overparted by the demands
of the role of Procida, leader of the Sicilian rebellion, but that drawback
shouldn't prevent anyone from enjoying the *frisson* of hearing La Scala, on a good
night, performing comparatively rare Verdi with such zest.

Verdi. SIMON BOCCANEGRA. **Piero Cappuccilli** (bar) Simon Boccanegra;
Katia Ricciarelli (sop) Amelia; **Plácido Domingo** (ten) Gabriele; **Ruggero
Raimondi** (bass) Fiesco; **Gian Piero Mastromei** (bar) Paolo; **Maurizio
Mazzieri** (bass) Pietro; **Piero de Palma** (ten) Captain; **Ornella Jachetti**
(sop) Maid; **RCA Chorus and Orchestra/Gianandrea Gavazzeni.** RCA Red
Seal RD70729. Notes, text and translation included. From SER5696 (2/74).

② 2h 5' ADD 9/87

Verdi. SIMON BOCCANEGRA. **Tito Gobbi** (bar) Simon Boccanegra;
Victoria de los Angeles (sop) Amelia; **Giuseppe Campora** (ten) Gabriele;
Boris Christoff (bass) Fiesco; **Walter Monachesi** (bar) Paolo; **Paolo Dari**
(bar) Pietro; **Paolo Caroli** (bar) Captain; **Silvia Bertona** (mez) Maid; **Chorus
and Orchestra of the Rome Opera House/Gabriele Santini.** EMI mono
CMS7 63513-2. Notes, text and translations included. From HMV ALPS1634,
ALP1635/6 (12/58).

② 1h 59' ADD 9/90 ▲

This opera has the most complex of plots, difficult to unravel in the opera house
but more easily understood with the libretto in front of you at home. It mainly
concerns the struggle between the nobility and the populace, represented
respectively by Fiesco and Boccanegra and complicated by the fact that the
seafaring Simon has seduced the noble's daughter Maria, who has borne his
daughter, Amelia. The RCA set is lovingly conducted by Gavazzeni with that easy
yet unassuming command of Verdian structure which is not always achieved by
his successors. His cast is an excellent one headed by the warm, sympathetic
Boccanegra of Cappuccilli and the youthful, attractive Amelia of Ricciarelli. The
recording is spacious and clear in detail.

The EMI issue is an apt alternative to modern versions, a kind of classic
because of the unsurpassed performances of its principals. Gobbi did much to
bring this previously neglected work back into the repertory. He shows a deep
sympathy with the public and private dilemmas of the Doge and expresses them
in plangently accented tones, a true Verdian line, and — in the Council
Chamber scene — supreme authority. As his implacable adversary Fiesco,
Christoff gives one of his most imposing portrayals on disc, inflecting the text

superbly with an exuding authority. Victoria de los Angeles is a pure-voiced, properly intense Amelia, Giuseppe Campora a vibrant Gabriele. Santini's conducting is admirable. With a passing regret at one or two small cuts, this set can be warmly recommended and will show anyone how much can be achieved by acting with the voice. The mono recording is adequate.

Verdi. UN BALLO IN MASCHERA. **Giuseppi di Stefano** (ten) Riccardo; **Tito Gobbi** (bar) Renato; **Maria Callas** (sop) Amelia; **Fedora Barbieri** (mez) Ulrica; **Eugenia Ratti** (sop) Oscar; **Ezio Giordano** (bass) Silvano; **Silvio Maionica** (bass) Samuel; **Nicola Zaccaria** (bass) Tom; **Renato Ercolani** (bar) Judge; **Chorus and Orchestra of La Scala, Milan/Antonino Votto.** EMI mono CDS7 47498-8. Notes, text and translation included. From Columbia 33CX1472/4 (10/57).

② 2h 10' ADD 9/87

Ballo manages to encompass a vein of lighthearted frivolity (represented by the page, Oscar) within the confines of a serious drama of love, infidelity, noble and ignoble sentiments. No more modern recording has quite caught the opera's true spirit so truly as this one under Votto's unerring direction. Callas has not been surpassed in delineating Amelia's conflict of feelings and loyalties, nor has di Stefano been equalled in the sheer ardour of his singing as Riccardo. Add to that no less a singer than Tito Gobbi as Renato, at first eloquent in his friendship to his ruler, then implacable in his revenge when he thinks Riccardo has stolen his wife. Fedora Barbieri is full of character as the soothsayer Ulrica, Eugenia Ratti a sparky Oscar. It is an unbeatable line-up.

Verdi. LA FORZA DEL DESTINO. **Maria Callas** (sop) Leonora; **Richard Tucker** (ten) Don Alvaro; **Carlo Tagliabue** (bar) Don Carlos; **Elena Nicolai** (mez) Preziosilla; **Nicola Rossi-Lemeni** (bass) Il Padre Guardiano; **Renato Capecchi** (bass) Fra Melitone; **Gino del Signore** (ten) Trabuco; **Rina Cavallari** (sop) Curra; **Chorus and Orchestra of La Scala, Milan/Tullio Serafin.** EMI mono CDS7 47581-8. Notes, text and translation included. From Columbia 33CX1258/60 (6/55).

③ 2h 44' ADD 10/87

Maria Callas is more than unusually well-suited to this Verdi heroine. Leonora's ardour, sincerity and, above all, vulnerability are recreated as she threads sadness through a line like "troppo, troppo sventurata", as she exalts in "Tua grazia, O Dio", or gives a heart-rending cry for peace in "Pace, pace". No one, though, should be deceived into thinking that this recording is a mere showcase for Callas, for Richard Tucker's Alvaro is a performance of what one can only call charisma: light and youthful, there is a smile and a sob in the voice as appropriate — and it works. Renato Capecchi offers a sharp vignette of Fra Melitone, Elena Nicolai a thrilling Preziosilla, and Tullio Serafin directs his La Scala forces with a keen ear to both the overt heartbeat and the emotional subtext of Verdi's most potent score.

Verdi. DON CARLOS. **Plácido Domingo** (ten) Don Carlos; **Montserrat Caballé** (sop) Elisabetta; **Shirley Verrett** (mez) Princess Eboli; **Sherrill Milnes** (bar) Rodrigo; **Ruggero Raimondi** (bass) Philip II; **Giovanni Foiani** (bass) Grand Inquisitor; **Delia Wallis** (mez) Thibault; **Ryland Davies** (ten) Count of Lerma; **Simon Estes** (bass) A Monk; **John Noble** (bar) Herald; **Ambrosian Opera Chorus; Royal Opera House Orchestra, Covent**

Garden/Carlo Maria Giulini. EMI CDS7 47701-8. Notes, text and
translation included. From SLS956 (7/71).

⸱⸱ ③ 3h 28' ADD 7/87

In no other Verdi opera, except
perhaps *Aida*, are public and private
matters so closely intermingled, so
searchingly described as in this
large-scale, panoramic work, in
which the political intrigues and
troubles of Philip II's Spain are
counterpointed with his personal
agony and the lives and loves of
those at his court. This vast canvas
inspired Verdi to one of his most
varied and glorious scores. Giulini,
more than any other conductor,
searches out the inner soul of the
piece and his cast is admirable. The
young Plácido Domingo makes a
vivid and exciting Carlos, whilst
Montserrat Caballé spins glorious
tone and phrases in encompassing

Ruggero Raimondi   [photo: EMI/Neuvecelle]

Elisabeth's difficult music. Shirley Verrett is a vital, suitably tense Eboli, Sherrill
Milnes an upright, warm Rodrigo and Ruggero Raimondi a sombre Philip.
Throughout, the Covent Garden forces sing and play with fervour and under-
standing for their distinguished conductor.

Verdi. AIDA. **Maria Callas** (sop) Aida; **Richard Tucker** (ten) Radames;
Fedora Barbieri (mez) Amneris; **Tito Gobbi** (bar) Amonasro; **Giuseppe
Modesti** (bass) Ramfis; **Nicola Zaccaria** (bass) King of Egypt; **Elvira Galassi**
(sop) Priestess; **Franco Ricciardi** (ten) Messenger; **Chorus and Orchestra of
La Scala, Milan/Tullio Serafin.** EMI mono CDS7 49030-8. Notes, text and
translation included. From Columbia 33CX1318/20 (1/56).

⸱⸱ ③ 2h 24' AAD 11/87   ♩ Ⓟ Ⓑ ▲

Aida, the daughter of the Ethiopian king, is a prisoner at the Egyptian court
where she falls in love with Radames, an Egyptian captain of the guard; Amneris,
the Egyptian princess, also loves him. The tensions between these characters are
rivetingly portrayed and explored and the gradual build-up to Aida's and
Radames's union in death is paced with the sureness of a master composer.
Callas's Aida is an assumption of total understanding and conviction; the growth
from a slave-girl torn between love for her homeland and Radames, to a woman
whose feelings transcend life itself represents one of the greatest operatic under-
takings ever committed to disc. Alongside her is Fedora Barbieri, an Amneris
palpable in her agonized mixture of love and jealousy — proud yet human.
Tucker's Radames is powerful and Gobbi's Amonasro quite superb — a portrayal
of comparable understanding to stand alongside Callas's Aida. Tullio Serafin is
quite simply ideal and though the recording may not be perfect by current
standards, nowhere can it dim the brilliance of the creations conjured up by this
classic cast.

Verdi. OTELLO. **Jon Vickers** (ten) Otello; **Leonie Rysanek** (sop)
Desdemona; **Tito Gobbi** (bar) Iago; **Florindo Andreolli** (ten) Cassio; **Mario
Carlin** (ten) Roderigo; **Miriam Pirazzini** (mez) Emilia; **Ferrucio Mazzoli**
(bass) Lodovico; **Franco Calabrese** (bass) Montano; **Robert Kerns** (bar)

Herald; **Rome Opera Chorus and Orchestra/Tullio Serafin.** RCA Victor
GD81969. Text and translation included. From LDS6155 (1/61).

② 2h 24' ADD 11/88 £ Ⓑ ▲

NEW REVIEW

Verdi. OTELLO. **Plácido Domingo** (ten) Otello; **Katia Ricciarelli** (sop)
Desdemona; **Justino Diaz** (bar) Iago; **Ezio di Cesare** (ten) Cassio; **Constantin Zaharia** (ten) Roderigo; **Petra Malakova** (mez) Emilia; **John Macurdy**
(bass) Lodovico; **Edward Toumajian** (bar) Montano; **Giannicola Pigliucci**
(bar) Herald; **Chorus and Orchestra of La Scala, Milan/Lorin Maazel.**
EMI CDS7 47450-8. Notes, text and translation included. From HMV
EX270461-3 (10/86).

② 2h 22' DDD 12/86 ⓆⓅ Ⓑ

NEW REVIEW

Verdi. OTELLO. **Luciano Pavarotti** (ten) Otello; **Dame Kiri Te Kanawa**
(sop) Desdemona; **Leo Nucci** (bar) Iago; **Anthony Rolfe Johnson** (ten)
Cassio; **John Keyes** (ten) Roderigo; **Elzbieta Ardam** (mez) Emilia; **Dimitri
Kavrakos** (bass) Lodovico; **Alan Opie** (bar) Montano; **Richard Cohn** (bar)
Herald; **Metropolitan Opera Children's Chorus; Chicago Symphony
Chorus and Orchestra/Sir Georg Solti.** Decca 433 669-2DH2. Notes, text
and translation included. Recorded at performances in Orchestral Hall, Chicago
and Carnegie Hall, New York in April 1991.

② 2h 9' DDD 11/91 ⓆⓅ Ⓑ

NEW REVIEW

Verdi. OTELLO. **Ramon Vinay** (ten) Otello; **Herva Nelli** (sop) Desdemona;
Giuseppe Valdengo (bar) Iago; **Virginio Assandri** (ten) Cassio; **Leslie
Chasby** (ten) Roderigo; **Nan Merriman** (mez) Emilia; **Nicola Moscona**
(bass) Lodovico; **Arthur Newman** (bar) Montano; **NBC Chorus and
Symphony Orchestra/Arturo Toscanini.** RCA Victor Gold Seal mono
GD60302. From HMV ALP1090/92 (12/53).

② 2h 5' ADD 3/92 £ ⓆⓅ Ⓑ ▲

The role of Otello is notoriously demanding and there are few voices that one
would say were 'made for it'. Jon Vickers's is certainly one of them. Simply as
singing his is a magnificent performance: the voice is at its most beautiful and the
breadth of his tone in the upper notes is astonishing. Stylistically, too, he is quite
remarkably scrupulous, allowing himself no effect that is not authorized in the
score, and always exact in his observations of *piano* markings. Giving this recording a unique distinction is Tito Gobbi as Iago, justly the most famous singer of
the role in post-war years and the Desdemona too is clearly a great artist. Serafin
conducts in a way that allows everything to be clearly heard, forfeiting some
excitement but never cheapening by exaggeration or sentimentality. He secures
clean, spirited playing from the Rome orchestra and keeps a control that is firm
without being inflexible. This is a well-produced set that has scarcely aged over
the years.

Plácido Domingo and Lorin Maazel on EMI give us probably the most exciting
Otello ever recorded. Maazel's is a highly dramatic, theatrical reading, but one
which is equally aware of the need for eloquence and pathos in both the
projection of the central agony of Otello and the pathos of Desdemona's music.
In all this he is thrillingly supported by the Scala forces. The orchestra's string
tone is as sweet and warm as the brass is incisive and the choral singing is
superbly caught by the spacious recording. But it is Domingo who steals the
show. At the time of this recording he had sung almost 100 performances of the
role and it shows. Again and again he makes you feel how Otello's soul is on the
rack, both in forcing ever more jealous-making details from Iago and in berating

Desdemona: he is overwhelmingly moving in the Third Act duet. The death is the more touching for being restrained. The moments of fiery command, before his disputing lieutenants in Act 1 and before the Venetian envoys in Act 3, have all the energetic authority they should have. Has any other Otello, on the other hand, had such a smooth, finely etched legato as Domingo in the love duet? In all these points his central performance conveys tragic stature. Justino Diaz isn't the most convincing Iago on record; he gives a very subtle performance but can't quite match Gobbi or Valdengo, partly because his voice has bass undertones. Katia Ricciarelli's Desdemona is one of her finest ever recordings — tender, vulnerable and totally feminine. Very strongly recommended.

The Decca version, rather hectically conducted by Solti, boasts Pavarotti as an accurately sung, totally Italianate Otello. Without quite possessing the heroic weight for the role, he manages to suggest the tortured Moor's stature and eventual tragedy by virtue of clear, firm tone and unforced diction. Te Kanawa starts a shade anonymously but rises to a deeply moving account of her Act 4 *scena*. Nucci, however, is a disappointingly vulgar Iago.

Luciano Pavarotti   [photo: Decca/Kois]

The signing of that role by Valdengo is what so much distinguishes the classic Toscanini version, a notable bargain at mid-price. His insinuating, plausible, faultlessly sung interpretation owes much to Toscanini's tuition, and the great maestro has yet to be surpassed as a conductor of this supreme opera, in command of every facet of its swift-moving drama. The reading is truly incandescent although the recording itself cannot match the modern sound on the others. Vinay, although slightly thick and baritonal in voice, offers a deeply impassioned and committed Otello, Nelli a straightforward, touching Desdemona. Altogether this is an experience not to be missed.

Verdi. FALSTAFF. **Tito Gobbi** (bar) Falstaff; **Rolando Panerai** (bar) Ford; **Luigi Alva** (ten) Fenton; **Elisabeth Schwarzkopf** (sop) Alice; **Anna Moffo** (sop) Nannetta; **Fedora Barbieri** (mez) Quickly; **Renato Ercolani** (ten) Bardolfo; **Nicola Zaccaria** (bass) Pistola; **Tomaso Spatoro** (ten) Dr Caius; **Nan Merriman** (mez) Meg Page; **Philharmonia Chorus and Orchestra/ Herbert von Karajan.** EMI CDS7 49668-2. Notes, text and translation included. From SAX2254/6 (7/61).

② 2h ADD 9/88   P Ⓑ

Verdi. FALSTAFF. **Giuseppe Valdengo** (bar) Falstaff; **Frank Guarrera** (bar) Ford; **Antonio Madasi** (ten) Fenton; **Herva Nelli** (sop) Alice; **Teresa Stich-Randall** (sop) Nannetta; **Cloe Elmo** (contr) Quickly; **John Carmen Rossi** (ten) Bardolfo; **Norman Scott** (bass) Pistola; **Gabor Carelli** (ten) Dr Caius; **Nan Merriman** (mez) Meg Page; **Robert Shaw Chorale; NBC Symphony Orchestra/Arturo Toscanini.** Notes, text and translation included. Recorded at NBC broadcasts on April 1st and 8th, 1950. From HMV ALP1229/31 (3/55). AIDA. **Herva Nelli** (sop) Aida; **Richard Tucker** (ten) Radames; **Eva Gustavson** (mez) Amneris; **Giuseppe Valdengo** (bar) Amonasro; **Norman Scott** (bass) Ramfis; **Dennis Harbour** (bass) King of Egypt; **Teresa Stich-Randall** (sop) Priestess; **Virginio Assandri** (ten) Messenger; **Robert Shaw Chorale; NBC Symphony Orchestra/Arturo Toscanini.** Notes, text and translation included. Recorded at NBC broadcasts on March 26th and April 2nd, 1949. From RB16021/3 (6/57).

CHORAL WORKS AND OPERA EXCERPTS. **NBC Symphony Orchestra/ Arturo Toscanini.** RCA Gold Seal mono GD60326. Texts and translations included.

Quattro pezzi sacri — Te Deum (with Robert Shaw Chorale. Recorded at an NBC broadcast on March 14th 1954. From HMV ALP1363, 6/56). Requiem (Herva Nelli, sop; Fedora Barbieri, mez; Giuseppe di Stefano, ten; Cesare Siepi, bass; Robert Shaw Chorale. NBC Broadcast, January 27th, 1951. ALP1380/81, 12/56). NABUCCO — Va, pensiero (Westminster Choir. NBC broadcast, January 31st, 1943). LUISA MILLER — Quando le sere al placido (Jan Peerce, ten. NBC broadcast, July 25th, 1943. Both ALP1452, 4/57). Inno delle Nazioni (Peerce; Westminster Choir. NBC broadcasts, December 8th and 20th, 1943. ALP1453, 4/57).

⑦ 6h 13' ADD 5/90

Verdi's *Falstaff* is one of those works that sum up a career with perfection, yet though it was his last opera it was also his first comic opera. The classic EMI recording enshrines one of the finest Falstaffs to have graced the stage in post-war years, Tito Gobbi. His assumption of the role is magnificent, and the completeness with which he embraces the part tends to overshadow his many successors. Assembled around this larger-than-life character is a near ideal cast, sprightly of gait, sparklingly comic and above all, beautifully sung. Karajan's conducting is always deeply cherishable as he leads the Philharmonia Orchestra surefootedly through the score and the recording has come up sounding as fresh as the day it was set down.

In 1990 one of the most enjoyable of all opera recordings became available once again. Nobody knew better than Toscanini how to bring *Falstaff* to life, how to extract from it all the fun and sentiment it contains. Toscanini loved Verdi's great comic masterpiece and he strained every sinew, in matters of tempos, alert detail in the orchestra, control of dynamics, to fulfil his dedicated mission of interpretation. Yet everything seems natural, inevitable, unforced and spontaneous — and the fact that this was a live performance only adds to its feeling of a unique occasion. With this feast laid before it, the audience remained remarkably quiet throughout. The manner in which Toscanini accommodates his singers puts to flight forever his reputation as a martinet, allowing no leeway for personal readings on the part of the singers. The main vocal glory of the set is Giuseppe Valdengo's wonderful reading of the title role, full of subtle inflections, beautifully sung, ripe in characterization, fruit of long hours of preparation with the maestro. Herva Nelli is a delightful Alice Ford, Cloe Elmo a fruity Mistress Quickly, Stich-Randall an ethereal Nannetta, Frank Guarrera an imposing Ford. The remainder of the cast is almost up to this level of achievement. The transfer to CD has been well managed. This is a must for any Verdi lover.

With the *Aida* some caveats have to be entered. In spite of the conductor's contribution, this set suffers both from an indifferent cast and a less successful recording and, in this case, the transfer to digital sound seems to have added an unwanted edge to voices and instruments. Even so, here is further evidence of Toscanini's complete understanding of a composer with whom he had worked and whom he understood better than any of his successors. Although those who must have the Requiem in a modern stereo recording will want to own the Telarc recording, those who are prepared to tolerate mono will have their efforts rewarded by Toscanini's superb interpretation. His has been the classic version by which all its successors have been judged. In its newly-mastered CD version it sounds even more electrifying than in the past. By turns incandescent and beseeching, the interpretation is never self-indulgent, almost at all times faithful to Verdi's ideas about tempo and dynamics, adding up to a spiritual and emotional experience seldom repeated. Also on offer is a selection of choral pieces of which the patriotic *Hymn to the Nations* is an idiosyncratic rarity, ecstatically performed. There is insufficient space to dwell further on the sheer pleasures to be found in these sets. They are representative of the very best in

Verdi conducting, and should be a source of revelation to a new generation of collectors who may have an unclear view of what Toscanini was about.

Tomas Luis de Victoria *Spanish 1548-1611*

Victoria (ed. Turner). Responsories for Tenebrae. **Westminster Cathedral Choir/David Hill.** Hyperion CDA66304. Texts and translations included.

· 1h 15' DDD 7/89

Westminster Cathedral is probably one of the few places where compositions of such noble inspiration may still be heard during the last three days of Holy Week. Such a living link with tradition goes to explain the inner understanding, the tremendous pathos of a superbly tragic and musically satisfying performance. The carefully chosen texts tell of the betrayal and arrest of Jesus, his passion and burial. The music expresses with anguish the suffering and sorrow of those days. Certain passages in the recording are particularly memorable: a gentle treble lead at the opening of "Una hora", the dramatic juxtaposition of the evil vigil of Judas and the naïvety of the disciples' sleep. Variations of tempo, especially that for the plotting of Jeremiah's enemies and the exact dovetailing, as in "Seniores", combine to heighten the dramatic effect. These pieces, of tragic magnificence, are performed with intensity and integrity, so that a great recording will now ensure that an incomparable treasure of Christian music will be safely preserved for future generations.

Victoria. Missa O quam gloriosum. Motet — O quam gloriosum. Missa Ave maris stella. **Westminster Cathedral Choir/David Hill.** Hyperion CDA66114. Texts and translations included. From A66114 (10/84).

· 57' DDD 6/86

The *Missa O quam gloriosum* is not a work of enormous technical complexity but rather seeks for its effect in measure and poise. The long soaring treble lines have a serenity and restrained intensity that have made it Victoria's most often performed Mass. The Westminster Cathedral Choir sing with a fervour and passion that puts their Anglican colleagues in the shade in this repertoire. The *Missa Ave maris stella* is a more elaborate work with a plainchant melody and the highlight of this rarely performed work must be the beautiful second *Agnus dei*, with divided tenors — gloriously performed by the choir. Recording is first rate.

Louis Vierne *French 1870-1937*

NEW REVIEW

Vierne. Triptyque, Op. 58. Pièces en style libre, Op. 31. **Colin Walsh** (org). Priory PRCD319. Played on the organ of Lincoln Minster.

· ② 2h DDD 3/92

Vierne wrote his 24 pieces "in free style" for a specific purpose; to fill the space occupied by the Offertory in the Mass. Of necessity, then, these had to be brief and, as not every church boasted a large pipe organ, they were designed to be played on a harmonium with just a single keyboard. But if this sounds like a menu of aimless miniatures lacking any real interest to the ardent listener, then this two-CD set will come as a bit of a shock. For not only does Vierne respond to these limitations with remarkable creative imagination, but Colin Walsh, always a perceptive and committed interpreter of the French romantic repertoire, brings the full weight of his performing skills to bear, lifting these short pieces way above the level of mere musical fillers and into the realms of true musical poetry. It helps, of course, that he has at his disposal the superb instrument in Lincoln Cathedral which, as the resident organist there, he knows well. He can can find exactly the right sound for each piece, giving a convincing portrayal of its individual character while providing an all-embracing tour around the undeniable charms of this famous Willis organ. Highlights include a sparkling "Carillon", a bustling "Divertissement", a beautifully lyrical "Lied" and, or course, the delightfully innocent "Berceuse" which Vierne dedicated to his young daughter.

NEW REVIEW

Vierne. PIECES DE FANTAISIE — Première Suite, Op. 51; Deuxième Suite, Op. 53; Troisième Suite, Op. 54; Quatrième Suite, Op. 55. **Susan Landale** (org). Adda 581246. Played on the organ of the Abbey Church of Saint Ouen in Rouen.

1h 15' DDD 3/92

Vierne's 24 *pièces de fantaisie* contain some of the most colourful music ever written for the organ. Some, like the atmospheric "Cathédrales", paint vivid musical pictures while others are dazzling showpieces; the best-known being the thrilling "Carillon" based on the Westminster chimes, but there is also an invigorating "Toccata" and a mischievously impish "Impromptu". In a more impressionistic vein there is the haunting "Feux Follets". In all these pieces Vierne takes the organ to new descriptive heights and any successful performance demands a large, resourceful instrument and an organist of exceptional virtuosity. Both have undoubtedly been found here. The Rouen organ is one of the greatest masterpieces of the work of Aristide Cavaillé-Coll while Susan Landale, although Scottish by birth, is now an established figure in Parisian musical life and plays with all the Gallic fervour of a true native. To keep her programme on a single disc (albeit an exceptionally generous 75 minutes long) she plays only 14 of the pieces, but she has chosen with care to provide the perfect balance between pieces of differing moods and character. Adda's atmospheric recording rounds off a most invigorating disc.

Henry Vieuxtemps   *Refer to Index*   *Belgian 1820-1881*

Heitor Villa-Lobos   *Brazilian 1887-1959*

Villa-Lobos. Guitar Concerto[a]. Five Preludes[b]. 12 Etudes[c]. **Julian Bream** (gtr); **London Symphony Orchestra/André Previn.** RCA Red Seal RD89813. Items marked [a] and [b] from SB6852 (2/72), [c] RL12499 (12/78).

1h 9' ADD 2/87

This disc illustrates Villa-Lobos's interest in writing for the guitar. Two sets of solo works flank the concerto, a brief (18 minute) and attractive work of spiky syncopation and fleet-fingered solo writing. The piece retains a 'chamber' feel and Villa-Lobos never unleashes the full might of the orchestra, so one rarely feels the naturalness of the balance to be strenuously or artificially achieved. Bream's warm tone is nicely caught by the recording. The 12 *Etudes* employ a technical range of quite remarkable variety; the *glissandos* are striking and perfectly executed by Julian Bream. The Preludes are bigger works and seek to portray the variety of Brazilian life in a number of moods.

Villa-Lobos. Piano Concertos Nos. 1-5. **Cristina Ortiz** (pf); **Royal Philharmonic Orchestra/Miguel Gómez-Martínez.** Decca 430 628-2DH2.

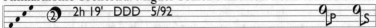

② 2h 19' DDD 5/92

Villa-Lobos's five piano concertos have been unjustly neglected both in the concert-hall and on disc, but these exceptionally committed performance more than make up for any past oversights. The Brazilian pianist Cristina Ortiz makes a most convincing case for these most remarkable and unorthodox concertos, with her colourful and exuberantly rhythmic playing catching every ounce of detail and kaleidoscopic nuance. The best way to approach these sometimes unwieldy concertos is to bear in mind Villa-Lobos's somewhat maverick approach to composition in general and simply go with the flow; melodies are frequently long and spun-out and the orchestral accompaniments are often as dense and as complex as Villa-Lobos's beloved Brazilian forests, but for those of an adventurous spirit there are rich rewards to be had from these highly inventive and uniquely beautiful scores. A critic at the first performance of No. 1 remarked that it "appeared to us too complex to judge and understand at one hearing", but of course the luxury of a recording enables the listener to return at leisure and after only a few hearings memorable landmarks begin to emerge, such as the haunting, almost Rachmaninov-like second subject of the first movement. With the exception of the Fifth, which is shorter and more tightly constructed than the rest, the remaining concertos follow broadly similar lines, with the Fourth and Fifth being perhaps the best places to begin an exploration. Miguel Gómez-Martínez and the Royal Philharmonic Orchestra provide excellent support and make light work of the sometimes horrendously difficult orchestral writing. Stunningly recorded — a must for fans of the exotic.

Villa-Lobos. ORCHESTRAL WORKS. **Czecho-Slovak Radio Symphony Orchestra, Bratislava/Roberto Duarte.** Marco Polo 8 223357.
Gênesis — ballet. Erosão (Origem do rio Amazonas). Amazonas — symphonic poem. Dawn in a tropical forest.

1h 2' DDD 3/92

Do not be deterred by the thought of an Eastern European orchestra playing unfamiliar Villa-Lobos. The Czecho-Slovak Radio Orchestra is clearly a very skilled and flexible body, and the conductor Roberto Duarte, a Brazilian authority on Villa-Lobos, has instilled South American colour and rhythmic vitality into his players quite brilliantly. The best of the four works is probably the earliest, *Amazonas*, which was written in 1917. Here, at the age of 30, Villa-Lobos's imagination was extraordinarily fertile, and this early evocation of Brazilian folklore, with its use of unusual instruments and strange orchestral timbres, is remarkably advanced for its date. The short tone poem *Dawn in a tropical forest* is a late work dating from 1953, and this has a more lyrical, more classical style. The remaining two works also come from the last phase in Villa-Lobos's career, and have similar themes. *Gênesis*, written in 1954, is a large-scale symphonic poem and ballet which depicts its enormous subject with all the extravagant colour and use of complex rhythms which were the composer's trademark. *Erosão*, or *The origin of the Amazon*, composed in 1950, is another ambitiously complex work. All four items are captured in faithful, wide-ranging sound.

Villa-Lobos. CHAMBER WORKS. **William Bennett** (fl); [ae]**Neil Black** (ob); [a]**Janice Knight** (cor ang); [aef]**Thea King** (cl); [acf]**Robin O'Neill** (bn); [d]**Charles Tunnell** (vc); [b]**Simon Weinberg** (gtr). Hyperion CDA66295.
Quinteto em forma de chôros[a]. Modinha[b]. Bachianas brasileiras No. 6[c]. Distribuição de flôres[b]. Assobio a jato[d]. Chôros No. 2[e]. Canção do amor[b]. Trio for oboe, clarinet and bassoon[f].

Ih I' DDD 9/89

If there is one consistent feature in Villa-Lobos's enormous and diverse output, it is his unpredictability. His restless, supercharged mind never tired of experimenting with new sonorities, and he never felt inhibited, in the course of a work, from following unrelated new impulses. This has the effect of making his music at the same time attractive and disconcerting. The multi-sectional Quintet, the most significant item here, is highly complex but extremely entertaining in its quirky way; and it is played with marvellous neatness, finely judged tonal nuances and high spirits. The rarely heard Trio, the earliest work here, is a particularly spiky atonal piece, typical of its period (1921), depending almost entirely on exuberantly thrusting and counter-thrusting rhythm: it calls for virtuosity, and gets it. The sixth of the *Bachianas brasileiras* (easily the best available recorded performance) is most sensitively shaped, and the second *Chôros*, which makes great demands on the two players both individually and in mutual responsiveness, is outstandingly polished. A disc of outstanding artistry.

Villa-Lobos. PIANO WORKS. **Cristina Ortiz.** Decca 417 650-2DH.
Bachianas brasileiras No. 4 (pf version). Guia prático. Poema singélo. Caixinha de música quebrada. Saudades das selvas brasileiras No. 2. As tres Marias. Valsa da dor. Cirandas — No. 4, O cravo brigou com a rosa; No. 14, A canôa virou. Ciclo brasileiro.

Ih 7' DDD 12/87

Cristina Ortiz   [photo: Decca

Cristina Ortiz has chosen a programme which sensitively evokes Brazilian life — children's songs, folk-songs, affectionate pictures in music of favourite places, all add up to a rounded musical portrait. The *Bachianas brasileiras* No. 4 is performed complete and Ortiz reveals her Brazilian nationality in the vivid depiction of the araponga, a bird with a call like a hammer on an anvil. The charming *Caixinha de música quebrada* ("The broken little musical box") has a "Ravelian" flavour, and Ortiz plays it with corresponding attention to detail and delicacy of touch. The recording is very fine indeed and provides an excellent introduction to an all too-rarely heard repertoire.

Villa-Lobos. WORKS FOR STRINGS AND VOICE. [a]**Pleeth Cello Octet;** [b]**Jill Gomez** (sop); [c]**Peter Manning** (vn). Hyperion CDA66257. Texts and translations included where appropriate.
Bachianas brasileiras — No. 1[a]; No. 5[ab]. Suite for voice and violin (1923)[bc].
Bach (trans. Villa-Lobos): The Well-tempered Clavier[a] — Prelude in D minor

(BWV853); Fugue in B flat major (BWV846); Prelude in G minor (BWV867); Fugue in D major (BWV874).

54' DDD 12/87

Sandwiched between two of the composer's best-known works, the First and Fifth of the *Bachianas brasileiras*, are the Suite for voice and violin and four pieces arranged from Bach's *48*. In the Suite Villa-Lobos allows soprano voice and violin to chase, cavort and imitate with great fluidity and freedom. It is just the sort of piece at which Jill Gomez excels, her feeling for mood and rhythm are ideal and Peter Manning is a spirited partner. The other pieces on the disc employ massed cellos and the Pleeth Cello Octet play with uncommon sympathy. The two *Bachianas* capture a real sense of the music's flavour and the Bach arrangements are fascinating studies in the fusion of identities — a fusion developed and perfected in the *Bachianas* where the forms and ideals of Bach are melded with the wholly Brazilian idioms of Villa-Lobos. A well recorded and most intelligently constructed programme.

NEW REVIEW

VILLA-LOBOS CONDUCTS VILLA-LOBOS. [a]**Maria Kareska,** [b]**Victoria de los Angeles** (sops); [c]**Fernand Dufrene** (fl); [d]**Maurice Cliquennois** (cl); [e]**Rene Plessier** (bn); [f]**Henri Bronschwak** (vn); [g]**Fernand Benedetti,** [h]**Jacques Neilz** (vcs); [i]**Manoel Braune,** [j]**Aline von Barentzen,** [k]**Magda Tagliaferro, **[l]**Felicia Blumenthal** (pfs); [m]**Chorale des Jeunesses Musicales de France;** [n]**French Radio National Orchestra/Heiter Villa-Lobos** [o](narr). EMI mono CZS7 67229-2. All items new to UK unless otherwise marked. *Bachianas brasileiras* — No. 1[n]; No. 2[n] (from HMV ALP1603, 9/58); No. 3[in]; No. 4[n] (Columbia 33CX1648, 6/59); No. 5[bgn]; No. 6[ce] (both from ALP1603); No. 7[n] (33CX1648); No. 8[n]; No. 9[n] (ALP1603). Descobrimento do Brasil[an]. Invocacão em defesa da patria[amn]. Chôros — No. 2[cd]; No. 10[mn]; No. 11[jn]. Two Chôros bis[fh]. Momoprecoce[kn]. Piano Concerto No. 5[ln]. Symphony No. 4, "A vitoria"[n]. What is a Chôros?[o]

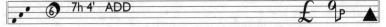

⑥ 7h 4' ADD   £ P ▲

Historical recordings generally attract the more specialized collector but these recordings dating from the late 1950s and conducted by the composer are an exception. For those who have been captivated by Villa-Lobos's more frequently recorded works, the fifth *Bachianas brasileiras* for soprano and eight cellos or the Guitar Concerto for instance, then this generously filled mid-price six-disc set will provide the perfect place for a continued exploration of this fascinating and colourful composer. The set is also made all the more valuable by the inclusion of all nine of the *Bachianas brasileiras* suites: a series of extraordinary works in which Brazilian melorhythms are treated in Bachian counterpoint (Bach was Villa-Lobos's favourite composer) and which are regarded by many to be amongst Villa-Lobos's finest achievements. The suites range in duration from short chamber pieces such as No. 5 and No. 6 for flute and bassoon, to full scale orchestral suites like No. 3 (piano and orchestra) and Nos. 2 (which contains the well-known *Little Train of the Caipira*), 4, 7 and 8. In addition to the complete *Bachianas* EMI have included several of the *Chôros* (of which Villa-Lobos composed 15 altogether) and the four suites that make up the *Descobrimento do Brasil* ("The Discovery of Brazil") that Villa-Lobos composed for Humberto Mauro's film of the same name. The remainder of the set is devoted to some particularly mouth-watering rarities, not least the colourful *Momoprecoce* for piano and orchestra based on popular Brazilian melodies, and the rarely heard *Victory* Symphony which was written to celebrate the allied victory at the end of the First World War. Many of the works are performed by the original dedicatees, and the recordings have been exceptionally well transferred to CD with hardly any noticeable tape hiss. At mid-price this comprehensive survey is a bargain indeed.

Philippe de Vitry

French 1291-1361

NEW REVIEW

Vitry. CHANSONS AND MOTETS. **Sequentia/Benjamin Bagby** (singer, hp) and **Barbara Thornton** (singer). Deutsche Harmonia Mundi RD77095. Notes, texts and translations included.

Ih 8' ADD 1/92

This disc is made up of 14 of the motets which modern scholarship has attributed to Vitry, plus five chansons from the famous *Roman de Fauvel* manuscript and two organ intabulations which may also be by the fourteenth-century theorist. It is a fascinating repertoire, and the academic nature of the motets is offset by the more improvisatory style of the chansons. Sequentia appear undaunted by the rhythmic comlexity of this music; but despite the technical prowess the performances are occasionally a touch too fast: it is good to have a sense of the intricate musical phrases as a whole, but sometimes the dissonant sonorities are passed over too quickly and the words swallowed as a result. Still, in the motets they certainly capture the vehement tone of these profound political arguments. By way of contrast, the chansons all deal with the traditional and more accessible theme of courtly love. These link Vitry and his circle with the troubadours; and Patricia Neely's evocative accompaniments suggest an even earlier, Arab-Andalusian influence. Barbara Thornton's voice is well-suited to the song, although her sense of direction and conviction are not always maintained in the long and elaborate *Talant j'ai*. None the less, it is an intelligent and thoughtful collection, and a welcome contribution to this little-known repertoire.

Antonio Vivaldi

Italian 1678-1741

NEW REVIEW

Vivaldi. CELLO CONCERTOS AND SONATAS. **Christophe Coin** (vc); **Academy of Ancient Music/Christopher Hogwood** (hpd). L'Oiseau-Lyre 433 052-2OH.
Concertos — D minor, RV406; C minor, RV402; G major, RV414. Sonatas — A minor, RV44; E flat major, RV39; G minor, RV42.

Ih 7' DDD 1/92

With this disc Christophe Coin completes his recording of Vivaldi's nine cello sonatas as well as including three of the composer's cello concertos. Vivaldi wrote rewardingly for the cello as the music on this issue demonstrates. Coin's feeling for dance rhythms, his clear articulation and musical phrasing and his sharp ear for detail bring the pieces alive in an infectious way. He is both firmly and imaginatively supported in the sonatas by a fine continuo group, and in the concertos by the strings of the Academy of Ancient Music. In the sonatas Christopher Hogwood varies the colour of the accompaniments by moving between harpsichord and organ while cello and baroque guitar add further variety and support. In the concertos fast movements are characterized by vigorous, idiomatic passagework for the solo instrument punctuated by pulsating Vivaldian rhythms in the tuttis. In the slow movements, richly endowed with lyricism, the expressive intensity of the music is, on occasion, almost startling, revealing Vivaldi as a composer capable of far greater affective gestures than he is often given credit for. This music was intended to move the spirit, to appeal to the senses, and it seldom, if ever, fails to do so.

Vivaldi. FLUTE CONCERTOS. **Lóránt Kovács** (fl); **Franz Liszt Chamber Orchestra/János Rolla.** Hungaroton White Label HRC127.
F major, RV433, "La tempesta di mare"; G minor, RV439, "La notte"; D major, RV428, "Il gardellino"; G major, RV435; F major, RV434; G major, RV437.

• 53' ADD 10/89 £

It was not until the late 1720s that the flute began to gain a foothold in Italy. Vivaldi's six Concertos for Flute and Strings were published in about 1728 though all but one of them were adaptations of earlier concertos in which the treble recorder played a prominent role. These performances are lively and sympathetic and capture much of the impressionist programmatic content implied in the first three concertos of the set. Lóránt Kovács is an accomplished player — he uses a modern flute — and he is sympathetically supported by the strings of the Franz Liszt Chamber Orchestra under their director, János Rolla. Vivaldi requires imagination and at times considerable technical skill from his soloists and Kovács rises to the occasion with panache and stylistic awareness. The performances are not for purists but they will disappoint few who readily respond to Vivaldi's lively rhythmic sense and his feeling for melody. Modestly packaged but effectively recorded and very keenly priced.

Vivaldi. FLUTE CONCERTOS. **Orchestra of the Eighteenth Century/ Frans Brüggen** (fl/rec). RCA Red Seal Seon RD70951. From RL30392 (4/82).
Flute Concertos — G major, RV435; F major, RV442. *Chamber Concertos* — F major, RV98, "La tempesta di mare"; G minor, RV104, "La notte"; D major, RV90, "Il gardellino"; G major, RV101.

• 53' DDD 2/87

Frans Brüggen is well known as a virtuoso recorder player and appears as both soloist and director in these notably imaginative performances of Vivaldi's music. He listens to every nuance of inflexion and unfailingly capitalizes on the rich sonorities provided by Vivaldi's carefully chosen instrumental combinations. What too often sounds routine in the composer's tuttis is here transformed into elegant and bold gestures, with a lively feeling for caricature. Brüggen's own playing reaches a pinnacle in the set of variations which conclude the Sixth Concerto and which he dispatches with dazzling virtuosity. The recording is admirably clear, picking up every detail of baroque bassoon mechanism!

NEW REVIEW

Vivaldi. Violin Concertos, Op. 8 Nos. 1-4, "The Four Seasons" (Manchester version). Concerto for Violin in C major, RV171. Concerto in B flat major for strings, RV163, "Conca". **L'Europa Galante/Fabio Biondi** (vn). Opus 111 OPS56-9120.

• 54' DDD 4/92

Although, understandably, almost all recordings of Vivaldi's *Four Seasons* follow modern editions based on that published in the composer's lifetime, a set of parts preserved in Manchester Central Library provides us with a more faithful account of Vivaldi's intentions. These manuscript parts apparently once belonged to Corelli's influential patron, Cardinal Ottoboni, and probably predate the printed version (1725). This lively performance by L'Europa Galante follows the Manchester version. The soloist/director, Fabio Biondi is an accomplished violinist well able to cope with Vivaldi's supple and athletic writing. He has an intuitive feeling for affective ornamentation and his supportive ensemble complement his engagingly impressionistic view of the music with a highly developed sense of fantasy. Collectors already plentifully supplied with these perennial favourites should be attracted by two further concertos in the programme which are far less often heard. One of them, in C major (RV171), dedicated to the Hapsburg Emperor Charles V, probably appears for the first time on disc. The other (RV163) is intriguingly subtitled *Conca*, a reference it would seem to a primitive instrument made from a conch shell.

Vivaldi. 12 Violin Concertos, Op. 4, "La stravaganza". **Monica Huggett** (vn); **Academy of Ancient Music/Christopher Hogwood.** L'Oiseau-Lyre Florilegium 417 502-2OH2.

> (2) 1h 41' DDD 3/87

In *La stravaganza* Vivaldi makes a further decisive step towards the virtuoso solo violin concerto and though the quality of the music is a little uneven, the set nevertheless contains several movements of outstanding beauty. From among them we might single out the *Grave* of the Concerto No. 4 in A minor whose suspensions, chromaticisms and lyrical solo violin part cast a spell of almost fairy-tale enchantment, and the *Largo* of the Concerto No. 12 in G major with its ostinato bass above which a simple but haunting melody is treated to a series of variations. Monica Huggett gives a lively, inspired account of the music. Her warm tone, well-nigh impeccable intonation, sensitive dynamic shading and sheer virtuosity lead us to the heart of these pieces in a seemingly effortless fashion. There is a rich vein of fantasy coursing through *La stravaganza* and this is vividly realized in her communicative playing. The small string forces provide sympathetic support and Christopher Hogwood generates an enthusiastic atmosphere with well-judged tempos and tautly sustained rhythms.

Vivaldi. 12 Violin Concertos, Op. 9, "La cetra". **Monica Huggett** (vn); **Raglan Baroque Players/Nicholas Kraemer** (hpd). EMI CDS7 47829-8. From EX270557-3 (4/87).

> (2) 1h 56' DDD 11/87

These concertos are not of uniform quality but the best are very fine indeed. The opening *Allegro* of No. 2 has more than a momentary glance at the sparkling bow work of *The Four Seasons*, and the double concerto writing of No. 9 has great finesse. The vigorous *Presto* of No. 5, unusually prefaced by a slow introduction, is a splendid example of virtuoso violin writing. Monica Huggett plays all the concertos with enormous excitement, relishing the *scordatura* (retuning a string) writing and allowing the music to languish when the occasion arises. The Raglan Baroque Players accompany attentively and Nicholas Kraemer provides some inventive harpsichord playing. This is refreshing music, undemanding but full of charm, and the recording is comparably good.

Vivaldi. L'estro Armonico, Op. 3. **Academy of Ancient Music/Christopher Hogwood.** L'Oiseau-Lyre Florilegium 414 554-2OH2. From D245D2 (12/81).

> (2) 1h 36' DDD 1/86

This set of Concertos is arranged as a display of variety, and ordered in a kaleidoscopic way that would maintain interest were it to be played in its entirety. These works are often played with an inflated body of *ripieno* (orchestral) strings, but in this recording they are played as Vivaldi intended them; only four violins are used. The contrast does not come from antiphony or weight of numbers but is provided through the *tutti* versus episodic passages. One could not assemble a more distinguished 'cast' than that of the AAM in this recording, showing clearly just why this music is best played on period instruments, by specialists in baroque style, who are not afraid to add a little embellishment here and there. Neither the enchanting performances nor the quality of their recording could be better; this is required listening.

Vivaldi. CONCERTOS — ALLA RUSTICA. **The English Concert/Trevor Pinnock.** Archiv Produktion 415 674-2AH.
G major, RV151, "Alla rustica"; B flat major for violin and oboe, RV548 (with Simon Standage, vn; David Reichenberg, ob); G major for two violins, RV516 (Standage, Elizabeth Wilcock, vns); A minor for oboe, RV461 (Reichenberg); G major for two mandolins, RV532 (James Tyler, Robin Jeffrey, mndls); C major, RV558 (Standage, Micaela Comberti, vns "in tromba"; Philip Pickett, Rachel Beckett, recs; Colin Lawson, Carlos Reoira, chalumeaux; Tyler, Jeffrey, mndls; Nigel North, Jakob Lindberg, theorbos; Anthony Pleeth, vc).

53' DDD 9/86

The *Concerto con molti stromenti*, RV558, calls for a plethora of exotic instruments and Vivaldi's inventiveness, everywhere apparent, seems to know no bounds. The vigorous melodies have splendid verve whilst the slow movements are no less exciting. The concertos, which employ plucked instruments, are particularly entrancing to the ear — here is virtuosity indeed, with Pinnock sensibly opting for an organ continuo to emphasize the difference between the plucked strings and the bowed. The Double Mandolin Concerto, RV532, is beautifully played with a real build-up of tension in the tuttis. The playing of The English Concert is affectionate and rhythmically precise and the recording is good with the gentler sounding instruments well brought out of the fuller textures.

Vivaldi. MAESTRO DE'CONCERTI. **Taverner Players/Andrew Parrott.** EMI Reflexe CDC7 47700-2.
Multiple Concertos — G minor, RV577, "per l'orchestra di Dresda"; G major, RV575; C major, RV556, "per la Solennita di S Lorenzio". Concerto in C major, RV114. Chamber Concerto in D major, RV95, "La pastorella". Flute Concerto in G minor, RV439, "La notte" (with Janet See, fl).

58' DDD 5/88

This anthology serves to emphasize the great variety of colour and texture that exists in Vivaldi's Concertos and it contains both large- and small-scale orchestral concertos. It is a delightful programme and the playing brings to life Vivaldi's music in an effective manner. There are many fine obbligato contributions and Janet See, the solo flautist in a well-known Concerto from Opus 10, is pleasingly inventive in her embellishments. One of the features which brings additional charm to the performances is the care with which the basso continuo has been 'realized'. As well as the obligatory organ or harpsichord, archlute, theorbo and guitar contribute to the texture, adding a vivid if optional dash of colour. Other instruments which make appearances of varying prominence include treble recorders, oboes, clarinets and bassoons; but it is the smaller-scale works and notably *La pastorella* (RV95) which in the end have the greater appeal. Recorded sound is clear and pleasantly reverberant.

Vivaldi. STRING CONCERTOS. **I Musici.** Philips 422 212-2PH.
D major for two violins and two cellos, RV564; G minor for two cellos, RV531; C major for violin and two cellos, RV561; F major for three violins, RV551; F major for violin and cello, RV544; F major for violin and organ, RV542.

1h 1' DDD 5/89

Many of Vivaldi's concertos deploy two or more string soloists and there are some very attractive examples of them in this recording. To his endlessly resourceful treatment of *ritornello* form in the quicker movements, Vivaldi adds further variety by ringing the changes on his solo forces — the number of violins and/or cellos, which may converse with one another or play in concert. In RV542 the solo honours are shared between violin and organ and some delightful sonorities result, whilst RV531, the only two-cello concerto in Vivaldi's *oeuvre*, contains a lovely *Adagio* in which the soloists speak to one another tenderly. I Musici are renowned for their enthusiasm and love of tonal opulence and this recording is also a fine example of the proper use of modern instruments. Clarity of texture is a *sine qua non* and it is provided by both players and recordists in this very fine issue.

NEW REVIEW

Vivaldi. STRING CONCERTOS. ᵃ**Adrian Chamorro** (vn); ᵇ**Maurizio Naddeo** (vc); **L'Europa Galante/Fabio Biondi** (vn). Opus 3 OPS309004. C minor, RV761; D minor, RV129, "Concerto madrigalesco"; G minor, RV517ᵃ; B flat major, RV547ᵇ; C minor, RV202; E flat major, RV130, "Sonata al santo sepolcro". Sinfonia in B minor, RV169, "Sinfonia al santo sepolcro".

52' DDD 9/91

This invigorating programme contains well-known and less well-known concertos by Vivaldi. The performances sparkle with life and possess an irresistible spontaneity. The Concertos for one and two violins (RV761 and RV202) are comparative rarities and are played with agility and insight by the soloist director Fabio Biondi and his alert and responsive ensemble. Biondi himself is capable of light and articulate bowing and has a natural feeling for graceful turns of phrase. Vivaldi's virtuoso writing occasionally finds chinks in his armour but with enlightened music-making of this order it matters little. Everywhere Vivaldi's infectious rhythms are tautly controlled and the music interpreted with character and conviction. Perhaps the highlight of the disc is the Concerto in B flat for violin and cello. Outer movements are crisply articulated and played with almost start-ling energy while the poignant lyricism of the *Andante* is touchingly captured. A refreshing and illuminating disc whose imaginative and passionate interpretations have few rivals in the catalogue. The recorded sound is clear and ideally resonant.

Vivaldi. CELLO SONATAS. **Anner Bylsma** (vc); **Jacques Ogg** (hpd); **Hideimi Suzuki** (cont). Deutsche Harmonia Mundi RD77909. E flat major, RV39; E minor, RV40; F major, RV41; G minor, RV42; A minor, RV43; A minor, RV44.

1h 2' DDD 6/90

Nine cello sonatas by Vivaldi have survived and in this virtuoso recital Anner Bylsma plays six of them. Vivaldi wrote as expressively for the cello as for his own instrument, the violin, and Bylsma's interpretations are variously endowed with fire and melancholy. He brings gesture to the music, sometimes in the manner of a caricaturist, at others with nobler, grander statements. Tempos are occasionally a little hard driven and technically demanding passages consqently accident prone, but at all times Bylsma sounds passionately involved in the music, giving performances which seem refreshingly far away from the specialized disciplines of the recording studio. Bylsma's choice of sonatas is attractive, though, since none of the nine works are in any sense of the word dull, sacrifices have had to be made. It is regrettable perhaps that neither of the B flat Sonatas is included, but the best known and perhaps finest of all, in E minor, is played with lyricism and a fine sense of poetry. Here and in the G minor Sonata Vivaldi reached considerable expressive heights and if only for these two works Bylsma's performances are to be treasured. Fine recorded sound but the documentation, especially where catalogue numbers are concerned, is slipshod and unhelpful.

Vivaldi. VOCAL AND ORCHESTRAL WORKS. [a]**Emma Kirkby,** [b]**Suzette Leblanc,** [b]**Danièle Forget** (sops); [b]**Richard Cunningham** (alto); [a]**Henry Ingram** (ten); **Tafelmusik** [a]**Chamber Choir and Baroque Orchestra/Jean Lamon** ([c]vn). Hyperion CDA66247. Texts and translations included where appropriate.
In turbato mare irato, RV627[a]. Concertos — D minor, "Concerto madrigalesco", RV129; G minor, RV157; G major, "Concerto alla rustica", RV151. Lungi dal vago volto, RV680[ac]. Magnificat, RV610[a][ab].

·* 57' DDD 12/87

This thoughtfully and effectively chosen programme deserves the attention of all baroque music enthusiasts. The approach of the Tafelmusik Baroque Orchestra, playing period instruments, is both stylish and sympathetic. They are joined by Emma Kirkby who sings two of Vivaldi's little-known chamber cantatas with precision, warmth of sentiment and dazzling virtuosity. These performances are the high spots of the programme but few listeners will be disappointed with the lively account of three of Vivaldi's little concertos for strings; one of them, the *Concerto alla rustica*, is particularly enchanting. The remaining item, the Magnificat, is an effective work scored for divided choir with an orchestra of strings and oboes, although sadly the oboes have been omitted. The choral singing is firm and the disc as a whole is appealing and well recorded.

Vivaldi. SACRED CHORAL WORKS, Volume 1. [abcd]**Margaret Marshall,** [d]**Felicity Lott** (sops); [bc]**Anne Collins** (mez); [b]**Birgit Finnilä** (contr); **John Alldis Choir; English Chamber Orchestra/Vittorio Negri.** Philips 420 648-2PH. Texts and translations included. Items marked [a], [b] and [e] from 6769 032 (12/79), [c] 6768 016 (12/78), [d] 6768 149 (9/80).
Introduzione al Gloria — Ostro picta in D major, RV642[a] (ed. Giegling). Gloria in D major, RV589[b] (ed. Negri). Lauda Jerusalem in E minor, RV609[c]. Laudate pueri Dominum in A major, RV602[d] (ed. Giegling). Laudate Dominum in D minor, RV606[e] (ed. Giegling).

·* 1h 6' ADD 5/88

Vivaldi. SACRED CHORAL WORKS, Volume 2. **Margaret Marshall,** [cd]**Felicity Lott,** [c]**Sally Burgess** (sops); [b]**Ann Murray,** [d]**Susan Daniel** (mezs); [c]**Linda Finnie,** [bc]**Anne Collins** (contrs); [b]**Anthony Rolfe Johnson** (ten); [b]**Robert Holl** (bass); [bcd]**John Alldis Choir; English Chamber Orchestra/ Vittorio Negri.** Philips 420 649-2PM. Texts and translations included. Items marked [a] and [b] from 6768 016 (12/78), [c] and [d] 6769 046 (12/80).
Introduzione al Dixit, RV636. Dixit Dominus, RV594. Magnificat, RV611. Beatus vir, RV598.

·* 1h 7' ADD 2/89

A lively performance of the better-known of Vivaldi's two settings of the *Gloria* as well as several other less familiar items are included in these two volumes. One of the most captivating works is a setting for double choir and soloist of the psalm, *Laudate pueri*, RV602. No lover of Vivaldi's music should overlook this radiant piece which is beautifully sung and vividly recorded. Negri's direction is lively and his evident affection for Vivaldi's music seems to have fired the enthusiasm of

Linda Finnie   *[photo: Chandos/Curzon*

all concerned, prompting firm and responsive support from both choir and
orchestra. Margaret Marshall, who is outstanding in her solos, and Felicity Lott
are well matched in their duets and the timbre of their voices is suited both to
the repertoire and to the style of the performances. Recorded sound is excellent
and full Latin texts with translations are included in the booklet.

NEW REVIEW

Vivaldi. Juditha Triumphans, RV645. **Elly Ameling** (sop); **Birgit Finnilä,
Annelies Burmeister, Ingeborg Springer** (mezs); **Júlia Hamari** (contr);
Berlin Radio Ensemble; Berlin Chamber Orchestra/Vittorio Negri.
Philips 426 955-2PM2. Text and translations included. From 6747 173 (10/75).

② 2h 33' ADD 4/92

This recording of Vivaldi's only surviving oratorio, *Juditha Triumphans,* was made
in 1974 and though various new recordings have appeared since then none have
surpassed it. Vittorio Negri fields an orchestra of modern instruments, and a very
good one it is too. The obbligato playing is first-rate although an over-ornate
harpsichord continuo gives the performance a dated aspect. The soloists are
excellent for the most part with Birgit Finnilä in the title role. Her "Quanto
magis generosa" with viola d'amore, and the memorable "Veni, veni, me sequere
fide" with an obbligato chalumeau are particularly affecting. Júlia Hamari brings a
lively sense of theatre to her portrayal of the warrior, Holofernes, and his servant
Vagaus is agilely sung by the soprano, Elly Ameling. Judith's servant, Abra, is
portrayed with clarity and conviction by Ingeborg Springer. No male voice
soloists here, since Vivaldi wrote the oratorio for the musically gifted girls of the
Pietà orphanage in Venice where he worked on and off for most of his life.
Negri brings as much drama to the piece as music and text will allow and the
results are by-and-large rewarding. Full texts are included and the recorded
sound is excellent.

Kevin Volans

South African 1949-

NEW REVIEW

Volans. White man sleeps (1982[d] and 1986[a] versions). Mbira[b]. She who sleeps
with a small blanket[c]. [bd]**Kevin Volans,** [b]**Deborah James,** [d]**Robert Hill**
(hpds); [d]**Margriet Tindemans** (va da gamba); [bcd]**Robyn Schulkowsky**
(perc); [a]**Smith Quartet** (Steven Smith, Clive Hughes, vns; Nic Pendelebury, va;
Sophie Harris, vc). Landor Barcelona CTLCD111. Item marked [c] recorded at a
performance in Belfast in April 1989.

♪ 1h 12' AAD 10/91 ❓

There's a distinct whiff here of the Third World. Keith Volans is South African
by origin, and his scores pay homage to black musical culture in a manner that is
fresh and wholly unpatronizing. In *Mbira* and the original version of *White man
sleeps,* for example, instruments are tuned to intervals variously wider or
narrower than those of normal Western scales, and their slippery rhythms obliquely
evoke dance and ceremonial ritual. The music has an evasive tunefulness about it:
not tunes that you can actually hum, but rather ones that tread and retread
familiar ground, never quite going anywhere or settling into a final cadence.
Comparisons with American minimalism soon break down. True, Volans's music
relies on harmoniousness and regular rhythmic patter, but there's nothing here of
the endless cellular repetitiveness of a Philip Glass or a Steve Reich. Above all
this is a supremely happy disc, and the performances are wholly in sympathy with
the spirit of the music. Altogether a stunning CD, and warmly recommended.

Richard Wagner

Wagner. ORCHESTRAL WORKS. **Philharmonia Orchestra/Yuri Simonov.** Collins Classics 1207-2.
GOTTERDAMMERUNG — Siegfried's Rhine Journey; Siegfried's Funeral March. PARSIFAL — Prelude, Act 1. SIEGFRIED — Forest Murmurs.
TRISTAN UND ISOLDE — Prelude and Liebestod. DIE WALKURE — Ride of the Valkyries.

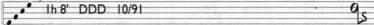

"The old poisoner" Debussy called him. Be it the dragon's blood, a love portion or sacrament from the Holy Grail, for those who prefer it administered in short, concentrated doses, this disc is an obvious choice. If there exists a more forceful paean of brass and timpani as Siegfried and Brünnhilde emerge to greet daybreak before the Rhine journey, it has yet to be heard. Yet this is no mere sonic spectacular: every phrase is lovingly turned and shaded, and the expression in each extract is finely attuned to its dramatic context. The brass intone the "Faith" motive from *Parsifal* with dignity and restraint, and while the playing at the climax of Isolde's Liebestod lacks nothing in passion, Simonov shows respect for Wagner's single *forte* marking. This is also one of the most coherent Wagner sounds on disc, offering separation of textures, a telling projection of the lower orchestral voices, and a real sense of space. You hear the pedal notes that evoke the stillness of the forest, you feel its depths, you rejoice with Siegfried at its natural wonders, and you understand why Debussy (despite his protestations) could never entirely cleanse himself of Wagner's influence.

Wagner. TANNHAUSER — Overture. Siegfried Idyll. TRISTAN UND ISOLDE — Prelude and Liebestod[a]. [a]**Jessye Norman** (sop); **Vienna Philharmonic Orchestra/Herbert von Karajan.** DG 423 613-2GH. Text and translation included. Recorded at a performance in the Grosse Festspielhaus during the 1987 Salzburg Festival.

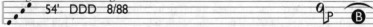

For the Wagner specialist who has a complete *Tannhäuser* and *Tristan* on the shelves, this disc involves some duplication. Even so, it is not hard to make room for such performances as are heard here. For the non-specialist, the programme provides a good opportunity for a meeting halfway, the common ground between Master and general music-lover being the *Siegfried Idyll*. This offers 20 minutes of delight in the play of musical ideas, structured and yet impulsive, within a sustained mood of gentle affection. The orchestration is something of a miracle, and it can rarely have been heard to better advantage than in this recording, where the ever-changing textures are so clearly displayed and where from every section of the orchestra the sound is of such great loveliness. It comes as a welcome contrast to the *Tannhäuser* Overture, with its big tunes and *fortissimos*, the whole orchestra surging in a frank simulation of physical passion. A further contrast is to follow in the *Tristan* Prelude, where again Karajan and his players are at their best in their feeling for texture and their control of pulse. Jessye Norman, singing the *Liebestod* with tenderness and vibrant opulence of tone, brings the recital to an end. There is scarcely a single reminder that it was recorded live.

Wagner. OPERA CHORUSES. **Bayreuth Festival Chorus and Orchestra/ Wilhelm Pitz.** DG Privilege 429 169-2GR. From SLPM136006 (5/59).

Opera Choruses: Der fliegende Holländer; Tannhäuser; Lohengrin; Die Meister-singer von Nürnberg; Götterdämmerung; Parsifal.

53' ADD 4/90 £ ▲

Most of the favourites are here: Spinning Chorus, Wedding Chorus, pilgrims, sailors, vassals, the good folk of Nuremberg, knights of the Grail and boys up in the cupola. There is nothing from *Tristan und Isolde* but one might have expected the hearty Communion chorus from *Parsifal*. As it is, there is much to enjoy as a way of renewing appetite for the operas themselves, and perhaps in some instances serving as an introduction. If the operas are new to any intending purchaser it is as well to note that beyond the German text of the first line no information is supplied. Moreover some of the other printed material is wrong (the mezzo sings in *Der fliegende Holländer* not *Tannhäuser*, and Josef Greindl is in the *Götterdämmerung* excerpt not *Parsifal*). Tracks 5 and 6 (*Tannhäuser*) and 10 and 11 (*Meistersinger*) run without a break, so that the list of items could prove misleading. As to the performances, the choral work is excellent when the men are singing, somewhat tremulous when the sopranos are involved. Recording varies from vivid (as in *Lohengrin* and *Götterdämmerung*) to misty (*Meistersinger*). The bargain price and fond memories of Wilhelm Pitz are the principal incentives here.

NEW REVIEW

Wagner. RIENZI. **René Kollo** (ten) Cola Rienzi; **Siv Wennberg** (sop) Irene; **Janis Martin** (sop) Adriano; **Theo Adam** (bass) Paolo Orsini; **Nikolaus Hillebrand** (bass) Steffano Colonna; **Siegfried Vogel** (bass) Raimondo; **Peter Schreier** (ten) Baroncelli; **Günther Leib** (bass) Cecco del Vecchio; **Ingeborg Springer** (sop) Messenger of Peace; **Leipzig Radio Chorus; Dresden State Opera Chorus; Staatskapelle Dresden/Heinrich Hollreiser.** EMI CMS7 63980-2. Notes, text and translation included. From SLS990 (11/76).

③ 3h 45' ADD 2/92

Rienzi is grand opera with a vengeance. Political imperatives count for more than mere human feelings, and politics means ceremony as well as warfare: marches, ballet music and extended choruses are much in evidence, while even the solo arias often have the rhetorical punch of political harangues. It could all be an enormous bore. Yet the young Wagner, basing his work on Bulwer Lytton's story of the tragic Roman tribune, did manage to move beyond mere tub-thumping into a degree of intensity that — for those with ears to hear — prefigures the mature genius to come. In the end, Rienzi himself is more than just a political animal, and the existential anguish of Tannhäuser, Tristan and even Amfortas glimmers in the distance. It would be idle to pretend that this performance is ideal in every respect, either musically, or as a recording. But its virtues outweigh its weaknesses by a considerable margin. Siv Wennberg was not in best voice at the time, but the other principals, notably René Kollo and Janis Martin, bring commendable stamina and conviction to their demanding roles. Above all the conductor Heinrich Hollreiser prevents the more routine material from sounding merely mechanical, and ensures that the whole work has a truly Wagnerian sweep and fervour. Moreover, it is the only complete recording in the current edition of *The Classical Catalogue*.

Wagner. DER FLIEGENDE HOLLANDER. **Simon Estes** (bass-bar) Holländer; **Lisbeth Balslev** (sop) Senta; **Matti Salminen** (bass) Daland; **Robert Schunk** (ten) Erik; **Anny Schlemm** (mez) Mary; **Graham Clark** (ten) Steersman; **Bayreuth Festival Chorus and Orchestra/Woldemar**

Nelsson. Philips 416 300-2PH2. Notes, text and translation included. Recorded at a performance in the Festspielhaus, Bayreuth in June 1985.

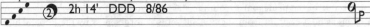

Wagner. DER FLIEGENDE HOLLANDER. **Theo Adam** (bar) Holländer; **Anja Silja** (sop) Senta; **Martti Talvela** (bass) Daland; **Ernst Kozub** (ten) Erik; **Annelies Burmeister** (mez) Mary; **Gerhard Unger** (ten) Steersman; **BBC Chorus; New Philharmonia Orchestra/Otto Klemperer.** EMI Studio CMS7 63344-2. Notes, text and translation included. From SAN207/9 (12/68).

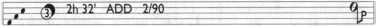

The young Wagner, sailing across the North Sea for the first time to England, went through a violent storm, and the experience left so vivid an impression that it prompted him to go ahead with a project he had already conceived, to turn the legend of the Flying Dutchman, condemned to sail the seas for ever until absolved by love, into an opera. The very opening of the Overture recaptures the violence of that storm at sea, and it leads to a work in which for the first time the full individuality of the would-be revolutionary can be appreciated. The Philips's version, warmly and vigorously conducted by Woldemar Nelsson, vividly captures the excitement and tensions of a stage performance, together — it has to be admitted — with a fair amount of stage noise from the milling choruses of seamen. The cast is a strong one, headed by Simon Estes in the title-role and the nobility and confidence of his performance are most compelling, conveying total involvement. Lisbeth Balslev sings tenderly and movingly and Matti Salminen is outstanding in the role of Senta's father. But it is the chorus which are responsible as much as any soloist in this opera for dramatic excitement, and the finely drilled singers of the Bayreuth chorus crown an electrically intense experience.

Klemperer's magisterial interpretation treats the opera symphonically. As ever he justifies moderate speeds by virtue of the way he sustains line and emphasizes detail. At the same time the reading has a blazing intensity quite surprising from an older conductor. The storm and sea music in the Overture and thereafter has a stunning power and the Dutchman's torture and unrequited passion is graphically evoked in the orchestra. Indeed, the playing of the Philharmonia is a bonus throughout. As well as anyone Klemperer catches the elemental power of the work, its adumbration of surging emotions against a sea-saturated background. Theo Adam conveys all the anguish of the Dutchman's character contained within a secure line. His is a profoundly moving interpretation, most intelligently sung. As Senta, Anja Silja is the very epitome of trust and love unto death, the performance of a great singing-actress, sung in an all-in, occasionally piercing manner. Talvela is a bluff, burly Daland, Ernst Kozub a sympathetic Erik and Unger offers a clearly articulated, ardent Steersman.

Wagner. TANNHAUSER. **Wolfgang Windgassen** (ten) Tannhäuser; **Anja Silja** (sop) Elisabeth; **Eberhard Waechter** (bar) Wolfram; **Grace Bumbry** (mez) Venus; **Josef Greindl** (bass) Hermann; **Gerhard Stolze** (ten) Walther; **Franz Crass** (bass) Biterolf; **Georg Paskuda** (ten) Heinrich; **Gerd Nienstedt** (bass) Reinmar; **Else-Margrete Gardelli** (sop) Shepherd; **Bayreuth Festival Chorus and Orchestra/Wolfgang Sawallisch.** Philips 420 122-2PH3. Notes, text and translation included. Recorded at a performance in the Festspielhaus, Bayreuth in June 1962. From SAL3445/7 (6/64).

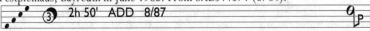

Wagner's opera about the medieval minstrel-knight of the title who wavers between the erotic charms of Venus and the pure love of Elisabeth is hard to bring off in the opera house and in the recording studio. Its structure is diffuse and its demands on the singers, Tannhäuser in particular, inordinate. The opera calls for a dedication and dramatic intensity such as it received in Wieland Wagner's staging at Bayreuth in 1962. Sawallisch directs an account that catches the fervour of the protagonist from the start and goes on to relate the torture in his soul as he is cast out from society and refused forgiveness by the Pope. The title part itself is sung with tense feeling, keen tone and immaculate diction by Wolfgang Windgassen — the famous Rome Narration has seldom sounded so anguished. Anja Silja's clear, evocative voice and youthful eagerness inform all aspects of Elisabeth's role and as Venus, Grace Bumbry caused something of a sensation through her glamorous appearance and rich tones. Eberhard Waechter sings the part of the sympathetic Wolfram with glowing tone and sensitive phrasing. Together, cast and conductor make the inspired Third Act a fitting conclusion to this inspired reading.

Wagner. LOHENGRIN. **Jess Thomas** (ten) Lohengrin; **Elisabeth Grümmer** (sop) Elsa of Brabant; **Christa Ludwig** (mez) Ortrud; **Dietrich Fischer-Dieskau** (bar) Telramund; **Gottlob Frick** (bass) King Henry; **Otto Wiener** (bass) Herald; **Vienna State Opera Chorus; Vienna Philharmonic Orchestra/Rudolf Kempe.** EMI CDS7 49017-8. Notes, text and translation included. From SAN121/5 (2/64).

③ 3h 29' ADD 2/88

This is a *Lohengrin* of considerable historical interest, a finely judged studio recording with a superb cast under a conductor whose ability to shape and control the music's long paragraphs, in the most natural and unobtrusive way, will not be underestimated by listeners who have endured more mannered, less well-integrated performances. To find so much restraint and understatement in Wagner is no mean feat. Among the singers, pride of place must go to Jess Thomas and his persuasive account of the title role. Fischer-Dieskau's Telramund is the perfect adversary; there's a genuine anguish in this interpretation that gives the character rare substance. A comparable contrast exists between Elizabeth Grümmer's Else and Christa Ludwig's Ortrud: Grümmer moving from somanambulistic naïvety to uncomprehending despair, Ludwig from bitterness to malevolent triumph. With Gottlob Frick and Otto Weiner providing strong support, this is a cast with no weak links. Nor should the fine contribution of the Vienna chorus and orchestra be overlooked. Kempe was a musician's conductor, as the uniformly excellent response of all involved in this enterprise amply confirms.

Wagner. DER RING DES NIBELUNGEN.
DAS RHEINGOLD. **Theo Adam** (bass-bar) Wotan; **Annelies Burmeister** (mez) Fricka; **Wolfgang Windgassen** (ten) Loge; **Erwin Wohlfahrt** (ten) Mime; **Gustav Neidlinger** (bass) Alberich; **Anja Silja** (sop) Freia; **Hermin Esser** (ten) Froh; **Gerd Nienstedt** (bass) Donner; **Vera Soukupova** (mez) Erda; **Martti Talvela** (bass) Fasolt; **Kurt Boehme** (bass) Fafner; **Dorothea Siebert** (sop) Woglinde; **Helga Dernesch** (sop) Wellgunde; **Ruth Hesse** (mez) Flosshilde; **Bayreuth Festival Chorus and Orchestra/Karl Böhm.** Philips 412 475-2PH2. Notes, text and translation included. Recorded at a performance in the Festspielhaus, Bayreuth in 1967. From 6747 037 (9/73).

② 2h 17' ADD 7/85 ⓑ

DIE WALKURE. **James King** (ten) Siegmund; **Leonie Rysanek** (sop) Sieglinde; **Birgit Nilsson** (sop) Brünnhilde; **Theo Adam** (bass) Wotan; **Annelies Burmeister** (mez) Fricka, Siegrune; **Gerd Nienstedt** (bass) Hunding; **Danica Mastilovic** (sop) Gerhilde; **Liane Synek** (sop) Helmwige; **Helga Dernesch** (sop) Ortlinde; **Gertraud Hopf** (mez) Waltraute; **Sona Cervená** (mez) Rossweisse; **Elisabeth Schärtel** (contr) Grimgerde; **Sieglinde Wagner** (contr) Schwertleite; **Bayreuth Festival Chorus and Orchestra/**

Karl Böhm. Philips 412 478-2PH4. Notes, text and translation included. Recorded at a performance in the Festspielhaus, Bayreuth in 1967. From 6747 037 (9/73).

| ♪ ④ 3h 30' ADD 2/85 | ℗ Ⓑ |

SIEGFRIED. **Wolfgang Windgassen** (ten) Siegfried; **Theo Adam** (bass) Wanderer; **Birgit Nilsson** (sop) Brünnhilde; **Erwin Wohlfahrt** (ten) Mime; **Gustav Neidlinger** (bass) Alberich; **Vera Soukupova** (mez) Erda; **Kurt Boehme** (bass) Fafner; **Erika Köth** (sop) Woodbird; **Bayreuth Festival Orchestra/Karl Böhm.** Philips 412 483-2PH4. Notes, text and translation included. Recorded at a performance in the Festspielhaus, Bayreuth in 1967. From 6747 037 (9/73).

| ♪ ④ 3h 43' ADD 8/85 | ℗ Ⓑ |

GOTTERDAMMERUNG. **Birgit Nilsson** (sop) Brünnhilde; **Wolfgang Windgassen** (ten) Siegfried; **Josef Greindl** (bass) Hagen; **Gustav Neidlinger** (bass-bar) Alberich; **Thomas Stewart** (bar) Gunther; **Ludmila Dvořáková** (sop) Gutrune; **Martha Mödl** (mez) Waltraute; **Dorothea Siebert** (sop) Woglinde; **Helga Dernesch** (sop) Wellgunde; **Sieglinde Wagner** (contr) Flosshilde; **Marga Höffgen** (contr) First Norn; **Annelies Burmeister** (mez) Second Norn; **Anja Silja** (sop) Third Norn;   **Bayreuth Festival Chorus and Orchestra/Karl Böhm.** Philips 412 488-2PH4. Notes, text and translation included. Recorded at a performance in the Festspielhaus, Bayreuth in 1967. From 6747 037 (9/73).

| ♪ ④ 4h 9' ADD 5/85 | ℗ Ⓑ |

DAS RHEINGOLD[a]. **George London** (bass-bar) Wotan; **Kirsten Flagstad** (sop) Fricka; **Set Svanholm** (ten) Loge; **Paul Kuen** (ten) Mime; **Gustav Neidlinger** (bass) Alberich; **Claire Watson** (sop) Freia; **Waldemar Kmentt** (ten) Froh; **Eberhard Waechter** (bar) Donner; **Jean Madeira** (contr) Erda; **Walter Kreppel** (bass) Fasolt; **Kurt Böhme** (bass) Fafner; **Ode Balsborg** (sop) Woglinde; **Hetty Plümacher** (sop) Wellgunde; **Ira Malaniuk** (mez) Flosshilde.
DIE WALKURE[b]. **James King** (ten) Siegmund; **Régine Crespin** (sop) Sieglinde; **Birgit Nilsson** (sop) Brünnhilde; **Hans Hotter** (bass-bar) Wotan; **Christa Ludwig** (mez) Fricka; **Gottlob Frick** (bass) Hunding; **Vera Schlosser** (sop) Gerhilde; **Berit Lindholm** (sop) Helmwige; **Helga Dernesch** (sop) Ortlinde; **Brigitte Fassbaender** (mez) Waltraute; **Claudia Hellmann** (sop) Rossweisse; **Vera Little** (contr) Siegrune; **Marilyn Tyler** (sop) Grimgerde; **Helen Watts** (contr) Schwertleite.
SIEGFRIED[c]. **Wolfgang Windgassen** (ten) Siegfried; **Hans Hotter** (bass-bar) Wanderer; **Birgit Nilsson** (sop) Brünnhilde; **Gerhard Stolze** (ten) Mime; **Gustav Neidlinger** (bass) Alberich; **Marga Höffgen** (contr) Erda; **Kurt Boehme** (bass) Fafner; **Dame Joan Sutherland** (sop) Woodbird.
GOTTERDAMMERUNG[d]. **Birgit Nilsson** (sop) Brünnhilde; **Wolfgang Windgassen** (ten) Siegfried; **Gottlob Frick** (bass) Hagen; **Gustav Neidlinger** (bass) Alberich; **Dietrich Fischer-Dieskau** (bar) Gunther; **Claire Watson** (sop) Gutrune; **Christa Ludwig** (mez) Waltraute; **Lucia Popp** (sop) Woglinde; **Dame Gwyneth Jones** (sop) Wellgunde; **Maureen Guy** (mez) Flosshilde; **Helen Watts** (contr) First Norn; **Grace Hoffman** (mez) Second Norn; **Anita Välkki** (sop) Third Norn; **Vienna State Opera Chorus; Vienna Philharmonic Orchestra/Sir Georg Solti.** Decca 414 100-2DM15. Notes, texts and translations included. Item marked [a] from SXL2101/3 (3/59), [b] SET312/6 (9/66), [c] SET242/6 (4/63), [d] SET292/7 (5/65).

| ♪ ①⑤ 14h 37' ADD 3/89 | £ ℗ Ⓑ ▲ |

Wagner's *Der Ring des Nibelungen* is the greatest music-drama ever penned. It deals with the eternal questions of power, love, personal responsibility and moral behaviour, and has always been open to numerous interpretations, both dramatic and musical: For every generation, it presents a new challenge, yet certain musical performances have undoubtedly stood the test of time. One would recommend the recording made at Bayreuth in 1967 because, above all others, it represents a true and living account of a huge work as it was performed in the opera house for which it was largely conceived. Every artist who appears at Bayreuth seems to find an extra dedication in their comportment there, and on this occasion many of the singers and the conductor surpassed what they achieved elsewhere. Böhm's reading is notable for its dramatic drive and inner tension. For the most part he also encompasses the metaphysical aspects of the score as well, and he procures playing of warmth and depth from the Bayreuth orchestra. Birgit Nilsson heads the cast as an unsurpassed Brünnhilde, wonderfully vivid in her characterization and enunciation, tireless and gleaming in voice. Wolfgang Windgassen is equally committed and alert as her Siegfried and Theo Adam is an experienced, worldly-wise Wotan. No *Ring* recording is perfect or could possibly tell the whole story but this faithfully recorded, straightforward version conveys the strength and force of the epic's meaning.

So many words have been written about the Decca recordings that to read all of them would undoubtedly take a good deal longer than a complete performance of the *Ring*. What should still be said is that although Solti's interpretation was not captured over a week or so in a single theatrical presentation of the cycle, it remains not only a remarkably consistent but a consistently exciting experience. John Culshaw's production has provoked much comment over the years, usually concerning his use of sound effects, and also debating the vexed question of whether the generally backward placing of the singers makes it difficult or impossible for them to command the full, riveted attention that Wagner's heroes and heroines demand. So it must be emphasized again that for the most part the singers do not sound as if they are drowning in a turbulent orchestral sea; and it is one of the great virtues of these discs that the quality of the singing equals the splendour of the Vienna Philharmonic's playing. Hans Hotter's Wotan is an immensely accomplished, powerful

Dame Joan Sutherland   *[photo: Decca/Barda*

and moving performance and though some collectors may regret that a different singer was used for the *Rheingold* Wotan, George London is excellent in his own right. As Siegfried, Wolfgang Windgassen can seem almost too dignified and decorous in comparison with his more impetuous rivals, but he is always secure and steadfast in face of the role's tremendous challenges, and a worthy partner to Nilsson's mercurial Brünnhilde. One could go on. There really are no weak links, and although at medium price the documentation is not as complete as it might be, Solti's *Ring* is now an irresistible bargain.

Wagner. TRISTAN UND ISOLDE. **Ludwig Suthaus** (ten) Tristan; **Kirsten Flagstad** (sop) Isolde; **Blanche Thebom** (mez) Brangäne; **Dietrich Fischer-Dieskau** (bar) Kurwenal; **Josef Greindl** (bass) King Marke; **Edgar Evans** (ten) Melot; **Rhoderick Davies** (ten) Sailor; **Rudolf Schock** (ten) Shepherd;

Rhoderick Davies (bar) Helmsman; **Chorus of the Royal Opera House, Covent Garden; Philharmonia Orchestra/Wilhelm Furtwängler.** EMI mono CDS7 47322-8. Notes, text and translation included. From ALP1030/5 (3/53).

④ 3h 56' ADD 5/86

Wagner. TRISTAN UND ISOLDE. **Wolfgang Windgassen** (ten) Tristan; **Birgit Nilsson** (sop) Isolde; **Christa Ludwig** (mez) Brangäne; **Eberhard Waechter** (bar) Kurwenal; **Martti Talvela** (bass) King Marke; **Claude Heater** (ten) Melot; **Peter Schreier** (ten) Sailor; **Erwin Wohlfahrt** (ten) Shepherd; **Gerd Nienstedt** (bass) Helmsman; **Bayreuth Festival Chorus and Orchestra/Karl Böhm.** DG 419 889-2GH3. Notes, text and translation included. Recorded during the 1966 Bayreuth Festival. From SKL912/16 (1/67).

③ 3h 39' ADD 7/88

Furtwängler was a supreme interpreter of Wagner and his classic set also features one of the greatest Wagnerian singers of all time, Kirsten Flagstad. Furtwängler's view is spacious, as the relentless crescendo of the opening Prelude makes plain, yet such is the tension and the incandescence of the Philharmonia Orchestra that the whole performance holds together with a compulsion rarely achieved on record. Kirsten Flagstad may be a noble Isolde rather than a sensuously feminine one, but her performance too has never been transcended in its richness, sureness and command, while Ludwig Suthaus sings the role of Tristan with clarity and precision, helped by the finely balanced recording. Notable among the others is the young Fischer-Dieskau as the old retainer, Kurwenal. The balances are almost always undistractingly right and on CD, with intrusive background eliminated, the mono recording is more involving than the modern stereo of more recent versions. One historical oddity is that the top Cs which Isolde has to sing in the opening section of the love duet were taken not by Flagstad but — on her insistence — by the young Elisabeth Schwarzkopf. There was no jiggery-pokery with tape, just a finely placed note or two from Flagstad's chosen deputy, recorded at the same time in the studio. It is a deception one can readily accept for the sake of a supreme recording of a transcendental opera.

Böhm's recording is a live Bayreuth performance of distinction, for on stage are the most admired Tristan and Isolde of their time, and in the pit the 72-year-old conductor directs a performance which is unflagging in its passion and energy. Böhm has a striking way in the Prelude and *Liebestod* of making the swell of passion seem like the movement of a great sea, sometimes with gentle motion, sometimes with the breaking of the mightiest of waves. Nilsson characterizes strongly and her voice with its marvellous cleaving-power can also soften quite beautifully. Windgassen's heroic performance in the Third Act is in some ways the crown of his achievements on record, even though the voice has dried and aged a little. Christa Ludwig is the ideal Brangäene, Waechter a suitably-forthright Kurwenal, and Talvela an expressive, noble-voiced Marke. Orchestra and chorus are at their finest.

Wagner. DIE MEISTERSINGER VON NURNBERG. **Theo Adam** (bass-bar) Hans Sachs; **Helen Donath** (sop) Eva; **René Kollo** (ten) Walther von Stolzing; **Sir Geraint Evans** (bass-bar) Beckmesser; **Peter Schreier** (ten) David; **Karl Ridderbusch** (bass) Veit Pogner; **Eberhard Büchner** (ten) Vogelgesang; **Ruth Hesse** (mez) Magdalene; **Horst Lunow** (bass) Nachtigall; **Zoltán Kélémen** (bass) Kothner; **Hans-Joachim Rotzsch** (ten) Zorn; **Peter Bindszus** (ten) Eisslinger; **Horst Hiestermann** (ten) Moser; **Hermann Christian Polster** (bass) Ortel; **Heinz Reeh** (bass) Schwarz; **Siegfried Vogel** (bass) Foltz; **Kurt Moll** (bass) Nightwatchman; **Leipzig Radio Chorus; Dresden State Opera Chorus; Staatskapelle, Dresden/Herbert von**

Karajan. EMI CDS7 49683-2. Notes, text and translation included. From
SLS957 (10/71).

> ④ 4h 26' ADD 7/88

Joyfully celebrating youth and midsummer, altruism and civic pride, Wagner is
here the unstinting giver. It's a cornucopia of an opera, generous with the tunes,
the colour, the sheer glory of sound as well as the desires and disappointments of
the normal human heart. It is also essentially a company-opera, a vast collabora-
tive enterprise which certainly benefits from the presence of a few great singers
in the leading roles. In this recording, greatness is found not so much in the cast
as in the man at the centre. Karajan directs an inspired, expansive performance,
catching all the splendour and lyrical warmth of the writing. The singers are
excellent in ensemble, and the whole company is alert in the disciplined chaos at
the end of Act 2. Kollo's tone has power and clarity, Helen Donath's Eva is
fresh and pretty and Theo Adam's Sachs is genial and authoritative. But the best
singing comes from the two basses, Karl Ridderbusch (an unusually warm-hearted
Pogner) and Kurt Moll. In a class of its own is Sir Geraint Evans's Beckmesser,
his sly, nervously-calculating absurdity wonderfully preserved in this vivid recording.

Wagner. GOTTERDAMMERUNG. **Hildegard Behrens** (sop) Brünnhilde;
Reiner Goldberg (ten) Siegfried; **Matti Salminen** (bass) Hagen; **Ekkehard
Wlaschiha** (bar) Alberich; **Bernd Weikl** (bar) Gunther; **Cheryl Studer** (sop)
Gutrune; **Hanna Schwarz** (mez) Waltraute; **Hei-Kyung Hong** (sop) Woglinde;
Diane Kesling (mez) Wellgunde; **Meredith Parsons** (contr) Flosshilde; **Helga
Dernesch** (mez) First Norn; **Tatiana Troyanos** (mez) Second Norn; **Andrea
Gruber** (sop) Third Norn; **Metropolitan Opera Chorus and Orchestra/
James Levine.** DG 429 385-2GH4. Notes, text and translation included.

> ④ 4h 30' DDD 8/91

This performance of the climax of the *Ring* cycle is of a stature to match the
inspired nature of the opera. Levine encompasses every aspect, heroic and tragic,
of the vast work, finding the right tempos for each section and welding them
together as imperceptibly as the composer into a consistent and inspired whole.
He is magnificently supported by his own Metropolitan Opera Orchestra who
play and are recorded with remarkable fidelity and virtuosity. Levine's cast, the
one with whom he has performed the work at the Met and on television, is as
about as excellent as could be assembled today, headed by Hildegard Behrens's
all-consuming Brünnhilde, responsive to every aspect of the role's many-faceted
character. Reiner Goldberg isn't quite her equal as an interpreter but, as
Siegfried, he sings with unfailing musicality and with a firm line. Evil is
convincingly represented by Salminen's implacable, black-voiced Hagen. Hanna
Schwarz is a deeply eloquent Waltraute, who makes the very most of her long
narration. Cheryl Studer's lyrical Gutrune and Bernd Weikl's sound Gunther are
further assets, as are the splendid Norns and Rhinemaidens.

Wagner. SIEGFRIED (sung in English). **Alberto Remedios** (ten) Siegfried;
Norman Bailey (bar) Wanderer; **Rita Hunter** (sop) Brünnhilde; **Gregory
Dempsey** (ten) Mime; **Derek Hammond-Stroud** (bar) Alberich; **Anne
Collins** (contr) Erda; **Clifford Grant** (bass) Fafner; **Maurine London** (sop)
Woodbird; **Sadler's Wells Opera Orchestra/Sir Reginald Goodall.** EMI
CMS7 63595-2. Notes and English text included. Recorded at performances in the
Coliseum, London on August 2nd, 8th and 21st, 1973. From HMV SLS875 (4/74).

> ④ 4h 38' ADD 3/91

The Goodall recording of the *Ring* has over the years gained an almost legendary
reputation. Now that the first work that was committed to disc has appeared on

CD, that reputation proves to have been well justified. The breadth and cogency of Goodall's reading, its epic quality, once more stand out as a magnificent achievement. Even more remarkable is Goodall's unerring sense of transition, as important in this opera as it is in any of the cycle's components. For this cycle Goodall had assembled a group of specially prepared singers; every part was carefully cast and sung with a sense of characterization and articulacy of enunciation (in Andrew Porter's excellent translation) that will surely gain the performance new friends. The team is headed by Alberto Remedios's youthful-sounding and forthright Siegfried, a performance that nicely combines lyrical ardour with heroic timbre. Around him in the various colloquia of which this work is largely comprised are Gregory Dempsey's characterful but seldom exaggerated Mime, Norman Bailey's authoritative, worldly-wise Wanderer and eventually, on the mountain-top, Rita Hunter's gleaming Brünnhilde. To these fine performances can be added Derek Hammond-Stroud's menacing Alberich and Anne Collins's grave, imposing Erda. The live recording has stood the test of time. This is a performance worthy to be placed among any in the original language.

Wagner. PARSIFAL. **Jess Thomas** (ten) Parsifal; **George London** (bass-bar) Amfortas; **Hans Hotter** (bass) Gurnemanz; **Irene Dalis** (mez) Kundry; **Gustav Neidlinger** (bass) Klingsor; **Martti Talvela** (bass) Titurel; **Niels Möller** (ten) First Knight; **Gerd Neinstedt** (bass) Second Knight; **Sona Cervená** (mez), **Ursula Boese** (contr), **Gerhard Stolze, Georg Paskuda** (tens) Squires; **Gundula Janowitz, Anja Silja, Else-Margrete Gardelli, Dorothea Siebert, Rita Bartos** (sops), **Sona Cervená** (mez) Flower Maidens; **Bayreuth Festival Chorus and Orchestra/Hans Knappertsbusch.** Philips 416 390-2PH4. Notes, text and translation included. Recorded at the 1962 Bayreuth Festival. From SAL3475 (11/64).

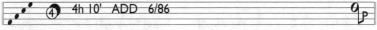

4h 10' ADD 6/86

NEW REVIEW

Wagner. PARSIFAL. **Siegfried Jerusalem** (ten) Parsifal; **José van Dam** (bass-bar) Amfortas; **Matthias Hölle** (bass) Gurnemanz; **Waltraud Meier** (mez) Kundry; **Günter von Kannen** (bass) Klingsor; **John Tomlinson** (bass) Titurel; **Kurt Schreibmayer** (ten) First Knight; **Cornelius Hauptmann** (bass) Second Knight; **Marianne Rørholm, Annette Küttenbaum** (sops), **Helmut Pampuch, Peter Maus** (tens) Squires; **Edith Wiens, Constance Hauman, Daniela Bechly, Hilde Liedland, Pamela Coburn** (sops), **Sally Burgess** (mez) Flower Maidens; **Berlin State Opera Chorus; Berlin Philharmonic Orchestra/Daniel Barenboim.** Teldec 9031-74448-2. Notes, text and translation included.

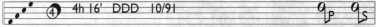

4h 16' DDD 10/91

There have been many fine recordings of this great Eastertide opera, but none have so magnificently captured the power, the spiritual grandeur, the human frailty and the almost unbearable beauty of the work as Hans Knappertsbusch. This live recording has a cast that has few equals. Hotter is superb, fleshing out Gurnemanz with a depth of insight that has never been surpassed. London's Amfortas captures the frightening sense of impotence and anguish with painful directness whilst Thomas's Parsifal grows as the performance progresses and is no mean achievement. Dalis may lack that final degree of sensuousness but gives a fine interpretation. Throughout Knappertsbusch exercises a quite unequalled control over the proceedings; it is a fine testament to a great conductor. The Bayreuth acoustic is well reproduced and all in all it is a profound and moving experience.

While the Knappertsbusch remains, as it always will, a very special performance unlikely to be repeated, Daniel Barenboim's *Parsifal* can be strongly recommended as an alternative for those seeking a more contemporary performance. In the theatre, his Wagner has not met with universal praise. At Bayreuth, his *Tristan* and then his *Ring* have been felt by some to suffer from that 'stop-go' effect which becomes apparent when conductors are not fully in command of the huge structural spans involved. But this studio recording of *Parsifal*, which offers superb sonic engineering, the luminous orchestration more richly projected than ever before on disc, will silence many sceptics. There are occasional passages, especially in the early stages of Act 3, where impetus is lost and the necessary weight is lacking, but these are not extensive enough to be seriously damaging, and — the Knappertsbusch apart — Barenboim's is as involving and as moving a *Parsifal* as has ever been committed to disc. It has the advantage of leading singers at the very peak of their form. Jerusalem and Meier bring a depth of passion to the later stages of Act 2 which is rare in any performance, and van Dam, after a rather too neutral start, grows to convey all the anguish of Amfortas without lapsing into melodrama. The Gurnemanz lacks several degrees of gravitas when compared with the incomparable Hans Hotter, but like all involved he acts well with the voice. It is uncertain whether the exotic haze of overtones created by the electronic bells is a wholly desirable effect, but it does not detract from the majestic choral and orchestral tapestry that Barenboim weaves in the Grail scenes. The final stages of Act 3 have unusual breadth, but the atmosphere of rapt serenity is marvellously sustained by the Berlin Orchestra. Barenboim is indeed fortunate to have recorded his first Wagner opera with such players.

William Walton

British 1902-1983

Walton. Violin Concerto. Viola Concerto. **Nigel Kennedy** (vn, va); **Royal Philharmonic Orchestra/André Previn.** EMI CDC7 49628-2. From EL749628-1 (1/88).

57' DDD 4/88

These Concertos are among the most beautiful written this century. Walton was in his late twenties when he composed the viola work and in it he achieved a depth of emotion, a range of ideas and a technical assurance beyond anything he had so far written. Lacking in the brilliance of the violin, the viola has an inherently contemplative tonal quality and Walton matches this to

perfection in his score, complementing it rather than trying to compensate as other composers have done. There is a larger element of virtuosity in the Violin Concerto, but it is never allowed to dominate the musical argument. Sir Yehudi Menuhin recorded both works and now Nigel Kennedy has equalled, and in some respects surpassed his achievement, giving wonderfully warm and characterful performances which are likely to stand unchallenged as a coupling for a long time. He produces a beautiful tone quality on both of his instruments, which pene-

| *Sir William Walton* [photo: EMI/Allen]

trates to the heart of the aching melancholy of Walton's slow music, and he combines it with an innate, highly developed and spontaneous-sounding sense of rhythmic drive and bounce which propels the quick movements forward with great panache. Previn has long been a persuasive Waltonian and the RPO respond marvellously, with crisp and alert playing throughout. The recordings are very clear and naturally balanced with the solo instrument set in a believable perspective.

Walton. ORCHESTRAL WORKS. **London Philharmonic Orchestra/ Bryden Thomson.** Chandos CHAN8968.
Overtures — Johannesburg Festival; Portsmouth Point; Scapino. Capriccio burlesco. The First Shoot (orch. Palmer). Granada Prelude. Prologo e Fantasia. Music for Children. Galop final (orch. Palmer).

1h 10' DDD 11/91

While enthusiasts for Walton's music may justifiably complain that there is not enough of it, they usually concede that what there is is readily available in good recorded performances. However, thanks to the dedicated and skilful work of Christopher Palmer, still more of it is now coming to light. How many people, one wonders, have ever heard *The First Shoot*, a miniature ballet written for a C.B. Cochran show in 1935, the *Granada Prelude* devised for that television company in the 1960s, or the *Prologo e Fantasia* which was the composer's last work, written for Rostropovich and his National Symphony Orchestra of Washington. Such fresh and welcome goodies as these appear along with familiar material such as the splendidly open-air, nautical overture *Portsmouth Point* that Walton wrote nearly 40 years earlier at the very start of his career. The Cochran piece, as orchestrated by Palmer, has five little sections that are delightfully jazzy in a way that recalls *Façade* and one's only regret is that there's not more of it. All this music is in the excellent hands of the late Bryden Thomson and the LPO, and Palmer's booklet essay is a model of stylish, informative writing. The recording is richly toned in the successful Chandos style, which takes some edge off the composer's characteristically sharp scoring but is still most enjoyable.

Walton. The Quest — ballet (ed. Palmer). The Wise Virgins — ballet suite. **London Philharmonic Orchestra/Bryden Thomson.** Chandos CHAN8871.

1h 2' DDD 4/91

These two strongly-coloured Walton ballets make an especially effective coupling in such brilliantly played, attractively recorded performances. And one, *The Quest*, based on Spenser's *Faerie Queen*, is recorded here in its entirety for the first time. The work was a rushed, wartime enterprise, "written more or less as one writes for the films", as the composer commented in a letter to John Warrack. It was first performed in April 1943 by the Sadler's Wells Ballet company and was not afterwards revived; the score was lost until 1958 and even then only a four-movement suite — arranged by Vilem Tausky, and approved and later recorded by Walton — saw the light of day. In reviving the work, Christopher Palmer has added the extra instruments used in the suite, knowing that Walton had been inhibited by the small size of the band available to him for the work's première. *The Wise Virgins*, based on music by J.S. Bach, is perennially popular and, like *The Quest*, receives a typically full-blooded, totally committed reading from Bryden Thomson, who stirs the London Philharmonic to great heights of power and dexterity. The recording venue's liberal acoustic has not prevented Chandos from letting us hear all that Walton intended.

Walton (arr. Palmer). Henry V — a Shakespeare scenario. **Christopher Plummer** (narr); **Westminster Abbey Choristers; Chorus and Academy of St Martin in the Fields/Sir Neville Marriner.** Chandos CHAN8892. Texts included.

♪ 1h 7' DDD 4/91

A mercurial young actor and a palely reticent young composer, Laurence Olivier and William Walton, met for the first time on a film set in 1935. It was an auspicious day for the British cinema, and long afterwards, in 1982, the great actor paid tribute to his collaborator on three Shakespeare films by saying that Walton's music had a "heart-quickening feeling ... something to do with sex, but a lot more to do with love". *Henry V* (1944) was the first of this celebrated trilogy and Walton's musical score contributed greatly to its scenes of fifteenth-century England, whether in Shakespeare's Globe Theatre, the London inn called The Boar's Head, an army's embarkation at Southampton, at the French court, or — most memorably of all — depicting the Battle of Agincourt in 1415. This disc triumphantly shows us that Walton's music stands up on its own and has beauty as well as tremendous atmosphere. It is thanks to the dedication and skill of Christopher Palmer (whose booklet notes are a model of information and readability) that we now have not just the few extracts from it that were made long ago for concert use, but about 90 per cent of the whole. It is presented in eight sections that follow the order of screen action and make a superb sequence. The performance of all this music under Sir Neville Marriner, which includes the finest of the King's speeches magnificently spoken by Christopher Plummer, is no less than inspired, and Chandos's richly textured recording made in a London church is equally fine. This glorious disc ends with three period pieces that Walton used in his music.

Walton. Symphonies — No. 1 in B flat minor[a]; No. 2[b]. [a]**London Philharmonic Orchestra,** [b]**London Symphony Orchestra/Sir Charles Mackerras.** EMI Eminence CD-EMX2151.

♪ 1h 14' DDD 12/89	£ 9 P

Vaughan Williams. The Wasps — Overture[a].
Walton. Symphony No. 1 in B flat minor[b]. **London Symphony Orchestra/André Previn.** RCA Victor Gold Seal GD87830. Item marked [a] from SB6856 (3/72), [b] SB6691 (1/67).

♪ 52' ADD 2/89	£ 9 P

Walton's First Symphony has yet to receive the ideal recording but Mackerras's version has a weighty vigour that does not give much to any version currently available. Where this issue really scores is in coupling a particularly fine account of the more elusive and rather less popular Second Symphony. This is a much misunderstood and, thereby, underrated work. With its brief span and costly instrumentation it is not its own best advocate for concert programming, yet it provides the ideal complement to the First Symphony. The LPO summon here both brittle incisiveness and luxuriant rapture to capture the quixotic moods of this distracted piece, and Mackerras tailors the balance to the acoustic in order to allow evocative inner lines to emerge. This performance would be very recommendable at full-price: on Eminence, it's essential.

Although Previn's version of the First Symphony is still easily the finest on disc, there were always doubts over the quality of the recording which, even when new, sounded dull-edged and lacking in inner detail. Now, even though the sound is still not first-rate, digital processing has done so much to clean up the textures that the recording quality is no longer an inhibition. From the very opening, Previn maintains enormous tension by keeping the rhythmic vigour at full stretch and, even in the slow third movement, he allows the emotional bite no real relaxation. This singularity of purpose, the great brilliance of orchestral sonority and empathetic balance are the key features in the success of this performance, compounding the intensity as the work progresses. Vaughan Williams's music for Aristophanes's play *The Wasps* was written for a 1909 Cambridge production and its finest features are embodied in the Overture. Previn's dazzling performance has been a long-time favourite, with the LSO at its best and pulling out all the stops. The recording is exemplary, spacious and detailed, marvellously balanced and yet unobtrusive. Coupled, these two performances remain a wonderful reminder of the Previn/LSO partnership at its finest.

Walton. FILM MUSIC, Volume 2. **Academy of St Martin in the Fields/ Sir Neville Marriner.** Chandos CHAN8870.
Spitfire Prelude and Fugue. A Wartime Sketchbook (arr. Palmer). Escape Me Never — suite (arr. Palmer). The Three Sisters (ed. Palmer). The Battle of Britain — suite.

Ih 5' DDD 12/90

Walton's film work reveals a remarkably fluent appreciation of the important role music plays in the medium and his magnificent scores for Olivier's Shakespeare trilogy (*Henry V*, *Hamlet* and *Richard III*) have quite rightly crossed over into the concert repertoire. But it is a little unfortunate that their popularity has somewhat overshadowed Walton's other achievements in this area for, as this collection proves, much more of his film music merits similar recognition. The emphasis here is on the composer's music for the war film and the familiar *Spitfire Prelude and Fugue*, with its stirring and characteristically solid march theme, provides a strong opening. *A Wartime Sketchbook* is an adroit arrangement by Christopher Palmer of contrasting segments from *Went the Day Well?*, *Next of Kin*, *The Foreman went to France* and *Battle of Britain* which lives up to its title most successfully (Walton's own authentic foxtrots, put over with delightful ease by the Academy, are particularly evocative), whilst the 11-minute selection from *Battle of Britain* serves to emphasize once again the idiocy of the nameless studio executive who decreed that the entire score should be scrapped (the stunning "Battle in the air" did remain in the film, however). Away from the battlefield, the programme also includes *Escape Me Never*, a heady and warmly romantic score complete with a strikingly rhythmic ballet, and *The Three Sisters*, Walton's final film score which perhaps overplays its references to the Russian national anthem but compensates with a lovely waltz in the "Dream Sequence". Sir Neville has just the right approach to this music and the orchestra's sturdy performances have been captured in a bright and well-detailed recording.

NEW REVIEW

Walton. String Quartets — No. 1 (1919-22)[a]; A minor (1945-7)[b]. **Gabrieli Quartet** ([a]John Georgiadis, [b]Kenneth Sillito, Brendan O'Reilly, vns; Ian Jewel, va; Keith Harvey, vc). Chandos CHAN8944. Item marked [a] new to UK, [b] from CHAN8474 (10/87).

Ih 5' DDD 10/91

Here is a disc that offers the kind of fascinating musical experience to be encountered only very rarely in the concert-hall. Walton's A minor string quartet is the familiar, late romantic Walton, from a time when the abrasiveness of *Façade* and the swagger of *Belshazzar's Feast* were well in the past, and the relatively relaxed lyricism of the viola and violin concertos was the determining element of his style. The music is nostalgic, neatly crafted and, while undemanding, attractive and distinctive. The early quartet, by contrast, is a product of youthful uncertainty and extravagance which Walton soon discarded but never destroyed. It is the sort of young man's music which leaves you conscious that such a gifted composer could have developed quite differently. Its particular point of reference is the music of Bartók, in the first quartet even more markedly than the second, though whether this was a matter of natural affinity or conscious imitation is difficult to say. While the effect is more that of an instinctive outpouring than a disciplined discourse, the sheer musicality and abundant imagination of the quartet disarm criticism. This is a well-engineered recording of performances in which the Gabrielis demonstrate the range and character of Walton's musical world with a special authority.

NEW REVIEW

Walton. Piano Quartet[a]. Violin Sonata. **Kenneth Sillito** (vn); [a]**Robert Smissen** (va); [a]**Stephen Orton** (vc); **Hamish Milne** (pf). Chandos CHAN8999.

🎵 56' DDD 3/92

Compared with Britten and Tippett, Walton did not leave a large legacy of music, and there is not so much of it that we can afford to neglect the two works here, neither of which is particularly well known. The Piano Quartet was his first major work, started when he was 16 and a very young Oxford undergraduate, though he revised it in later years. It's pretty well the sort of music that one might expect of the young composer who had come to Oxford from unsophisticated Northern England as a chorister and was now quickly absorbing all kinds of new influences: if we want to, we can trace here everything from richly textured Brahms via Vaughan Williams to the brilliant rhythms of Stravinsky's *Petrushka*. But there's also a lyricism that is very much Walton's own, and the writing for the piano and strings is skilful and idiomatic. He also could already write in a fugal style (in the scherzo and finale) that was alive rather than academic. Altogether the work comes over very effectively in this strong yet sensitive performance by four fine British artists, and the slow and romantic third movement, for all its echoes of Vaughan Williams and Ravel, is particularly beautiful, despite what sounds like the accidental plucking of the violin's open A string at 7'18". Walton composed his Violin Sonata soon after the War, partly because he needed the 2,000 Swiss francs which Yehudi Menuhin paid him as a commissioning fee. It is in just two movements, the second being a set of variations, and although it's not the easiest work to hold together in performance (Walton later admitted that it was written sporadically over two years and added, "it's surprising that the piece has any continuity at all!"), it has a bitter-sweet elegance that is attractive. Kenneth Sillito and Hamish Milne bring it off to fine effect, and Chandos's full-toned recording is excellent.

NEW REVIEW

Walton. Belshazzar's Feast[a]. Coronation Te Deum. Gloria[b]. [b]**Ameral Gunson** (contr); [b]**Neil Mackie** (ten); [a]**Gwynne Howell**, [b]**Stephen Roberts** (bars); **Bach Choir; Philharmonia Orchestra/Sir David Willcocks.** Chandos CHAN8760. Texts included.

🎵 1h 2' DDD 1/90

With Sir David Willcocks in charge of the choir which he has directed since 1960, one need have no fears that the composer's many near-impossible demands of the chorus in all three of these masterpieces will be met with elegance and poise. There is as well, in *Belshazzar*, a predictably fine balance of the forces to ensure that as much detail as possible is heard from both chorus and orchestra, even when Walton is bombarding us from all corners of the universe with extra brass bands and all manner of clamorous percussion in praise of pagan gods. Such supremely musical concerns bring their own rewards in a work that can often seem vulgar. The revelation here is the sustained degree of dramatic thrust, exhilaration and what Herbert Howells called "animal joy" in the proceedings. How marvellous, too, to hear the work paced and scaled to avoid the impression of reduced voltage after the big moments. Gwynne Howell is the magnificently steady, firm and dark toned baritone. The *Gloria* and *Coronation Te Deum* are informed with the same concerns: accuracy and professional polish are rarely allowed to hinder these vital contributions to the British choral tradition. The recording's cathedral-like acoustic is as ideal for the *Te Deum*'s ethereal antiphonal effects, as it is for *Belshazzar*'s glorious spectacle; and Chandos match Willcocks's care for balance, bar by bar.

Walton. Façade[a]. Overtures — Portsmouth Point; Scapino[b]. Siesta[b].
Arnold. English Dances, Op. 33[c]. [a]**Dame Edith Sitwell;** [a]**Sir Peter Pears** (spkrs); [a]**English Opera Group Ensemble/Anthony Collins;** [bc]**London Philharmonic Orchestra/Sir Adrian Boult.** Decca London mono 425 661-2LM. Items marked [a] from LXT2977 (11/54), [b] LXT5028 (6/55), [c] LW5166 (6/55).

1h 14' DDD

Walton. Façade — an entertainment[a].
Sitwell. Poems. **Prunella Scales, Timothy West** (spkrs); [a]members of **London Mozart Players/Jane Glover.** ASV CDDCA679. Texts included. Poems: Two Kitchen Songs. Five Songs — Daphne; The Peach Tree; The Strawberry; The Greengage Tree; The Nectarine Tree. On the Vanity of Human Aspirations. Two Poems from "Facade" — The Drum; Clowns' Houses. The Wind's Bastinado. The Dark Song. Colonel Fantock. Most Lovely Shade. Heart and Mind.

1h 4' DDD/ADD 4/90

Both these issues deserve to be considered for a well-stocked collection. The Decca is the classic and authoritative reading of the fully approved selection of *Façade* settings. Dame Edith herself reads two-thirds of the numbers, Sir Peter the remaining third. The poetess herself reads them with such *joie de vivre*, such a natural feeling for her own verses and inflections that nobody could be expected to rival her. Her timing is perfect, her delivery deliciously idiosyncratic, the intonations obviously what she and presumably Walton wanted. Sir Peter isn't far behind her in ability to relish the writing and the instrumental ensemble plays with refinement allied to virtuosity. The 1950s mono recording stands the test of time remarkably well.

Jane Glover   *[photo:ASV/Evans]*

The ASV performance offers something rather different. Scales and West often divide poems between them, which is a modern and not untoward fashion. They also employ accents where the texts suggest them. That gives the famous pieces a different aspect, but one that is in itself quite valid when executed with such flair as here and the speakers are well supported by artists from the London Mozart Players. They also include some rediscovered numbers. Here the fillers are more appropriate than on the Decca/London reissue:

more poems by Sitwell, lambent, florid, wordy verse, read with all the character and feeling one would expect from these actors. The recording is faultlessly managed.

Carl Maria von Weber

German 1786-1826

Weber. Clarinet Concertos — No. 1 in F minor, J114; No. 2 in E flat major, J118. Clarinet Concertino in E flat major, J109. **Orchestra of the Age of Enlightenment/Antony Pay** (cl). Virgin Classics VC7 90720-2.

♪ 52' DDD 10/88

Among the major composers, it was Weber who most of all enriched the solo repertory of the clarinet. He was inspired by his acquaintance with a fine player, in this case Heinrich Bärmann, and for this recording Antony Pay has used a modern copy of a seven-keyed instrument of around 1800, to which two extra keys have been added to come nearer to the ten-keyed instrument that Bärmann played. The orchestra also uses period instruments and in several passages, such as the hymnlike one with horns in the slow movement of the F minor Concerto, one hears this in their subtly different tone. The music itself is consistently fluent and elegant, witty and attractive and is stylishly played, with lovely clarinet tone in all registers.

Weber. ORCHESTRAL WORKS. **Berlin Philharmonic Orchestra/ Herbert von Karajan.** DG Galleria 419 070-2GGA.
Invitation to the Dance. *Overtures* — Der Beherrscher der Geister; Euryanthe; Oberon; Abu Hassan; Der Freischütz; Peter Schmoll.

♪ 56' ADD 6/88

Often rich in atmosphere and melodically inspired, Weber's operas invariably have an overture at which, as this mid-price disc illustrates, he excelled. The distillation of the mood and thematic significance achieved in these brief introductions invariably reached great concentration. A slow prelude, often mystical and veiled in character, leads into a faster *Vivace* section which presents the primary thematic material for the forthcoming opera. The overtures to *Oberon*, *Der Freischütz* and *Peter Schmoll* work in this way, whilst *Abu Hassan*, *Euryanthe* and *Der Beherrscher der Geister* literally burst in with unchecked verve and excitement — the first having a Turkish flavour with its use of percussion, the last having a tremendous timpani call set at its centre. Karajan and the Berlin Philharmonic Orchestra play these skilful works for all they are worth and they sound even better for it.

Weber. DER FREISCHUTZ. **Peter Schreier** (ten) Max (Hans Jörn Weber); **Gundula Janowitz** (sop) Agathe (Regina Jeske); **Edith Mathis** (sop) Aennchen (Ingrid Hille); **Theo Adam** (bass) Caspar (Gerhard Paul); **Bernd Weikl** (bar) Ottokar (Otto Mellies); **Siegfried Vogel** (bass) Cuno (Gerd Biewer); **Franz Crass** (bass) Hermit; **Gerhard Paul** (spkr) Samiel; **Günther Leib** (bar) Kilian (Peter Hölzel); **Leipzig Radio Chorus; Staatskapelle Dresden/Carlos Kleiber.** DG 415 432-2GH2. Notes, text and translation included. From 2720 071 (11/73).

♪ ② 2h 10' ADD 11/86

This opera tells of a forester Max and his pact with the forces of darkness to give him the ability to shoot without missing. Carlos Kleiber's recordings are always fascinating and for this one he went back to the manuscript seeking out details rarely heard in the standard opera house text. His direction is imaginative and where controversial (his tempos do tend to extremes) one feels he presents a strong case. His cast is very fine too: Schreier's Max is more thoughtful than some, though always ready to spring back after his hellish encounters. Janowitz is a lovely Agathe and Mathis a perky Aennchen, whilst Adam's Caspar is suitably diabolic. The use of actors to speak the dialogue does take a little getting used to, but the recording is good and the Dresden orchestra play magnificently.

NEW REVIEW

Weber. OBERON. **Donald Grobe** (ten) Oberon (Martin Benrath); **Birgit Nilsson** (sop) Rezia (Katharina Matz); **Plácido Domingo** (ten) Huon (Gerhard Friedrich); **Hermann Prey** (bar) Scherasmin (Hans Putz); **Júlia Hamari** (contr) Fatime; (Ingrid Andree) **Marga Schiml** (sop) Puck (Doris Masjos); **Arleen Auger** (sop) Mermaid; **Bavarian Radio Chorus and Symphony Orchestra/Rafael Kubelík.** DG 419 038-2GX2. Notes, text and translation included. From 2709 035 (7/72).

② 2h 19' ADD 12/91

Though its characters include Oberon, Titania and Puck, Weber's last opera, to an English libretto and written for Covent Garden, has little to do with Shakespeare's *A Midsummer Night's Dream*. It has been variously called a pantomime and, more rudely, a dramatic shambles, but that is unkind to this story of chivalry and magic telling of the love of Sir Huon of Bordeaux for the daughter of the Sultan Haroun al Rashid and set in varied locations including Tunis and Baghdad. The other characters include Sir Huon's squire Scherasmin and Rezia's attendant Fatime, a pair of mermaids, elves and slaves. Today it is a rarity in the opera house, though the delicately scored overture (beginning with a horn call from fairyland) is well known, as is Rezia's big Act 2 scene, "Ocean, thou mighty monster". This performance uses a German translation and there is a linking narration in that language as well as much spoken dialogue, rather hammily spoken at that — in fact, the roles of Haroun and three other minor characters are not singing ones at all. Furthermore, when Huon and Rezia speak, Domingo and Nilsson are replaced by actors and the two voices of Huon do not resemble each other, while even the Berlin-born baritone Hermann Prey as Scherasmin is not allotted his spoken lines. Still, the speech can be skipped or followed in the translation provided in the booklet which, however, lacks an English synopsis. It's rather for the singers and the music that collectors will enjoy this mid-price set which doesn't show its age of 23 years. The young Plácido Domingo, entering exultantly on track 11 of the first disc, is in turn heroic and gentle, and the celebrated Wagnerian soprano Birgit Nilsson, who is predictably in her element addressing the ocean after the lovers' shipwreck, can also be more intimate as the music demands. The rest of the cast is strong, and the orchestra under Rafael Kubelík play sensitively and, in the storm, excitingly.

Anton Webern

Austrian 1883-1945

Webern. Passacaglia, Op. 1. Five Movements, Op. 5. Six Pieces, Op. 6. Symphony, Op. 21. **Berlin Philharmonic Orchestra/Herbert von Karajan.** DG 20th Century Classics 423 254-2GC. From 2711 014 (3/75).

46' ADD 7/88

This mid-price disc, with good, digitally remastered sound, provides an excellent introduction to one of modern music's most important and influential masters.

All three phases of Webern's development are represented. In the *Passacaglia* the youthful late-romantic is ready to shake off the shackles of Brahms and Strauss, and Karajan brings particular intensity to the work's moments of crisis and upheaval. In Op. 5 and Op. 6 the process of miniaturization is well under way, and together they provide powerful evidence of the fact that concentration and economy brought no loss of emotional power. Even in the less extravagant orchestration of the 1928 version, the funeral march movement from Op. 6 is as stark and volcanic an experience of raw grief and despair as any Mahler Adagio. After this the ten-minute, two-movement Symphony, with its coolly symmetrical serial canons, may sound like a retreat from reality. It is certainly more classical in concept than the earlier works, but that means a more equal balance of restraint and expressiveness, not a rejection of either. As an outstanding exponent of late-romantic symphonies, Karajan is especially sensitive to the lyricism, as well as the refinement, of the music.

Webern. COMPLETE WORKS, Opp. 1-31. **Various artists.** Sony Classical CD45845. Notes, texts and translations included. From 79204 (12/78). Passacaglia, Op. 1 (London Symphony Orchestra/Pierre Boulez). Entflieht auf leichten Kähnen, Op. 2 (John Alldis Choir/Boulez). Five Songs from "Der siebente Ring", Op. 3. Five Songs, Op. 4 (Heather Harper, sop; Charles Rosen, pf). Five Movements, Op. 5 (Juilliard Quartet). Six Pieces, Op. 6 (LSO/Boulez). Four Pieces, Op. 7 (Isaac Stern, vn; Rosen, pf). Two Songs, Op. 8 (Harper, sop; chamber ensemble/Boulez). Six Bagatelles, Op. 9 (Juilliard Qt). Five Pieces, Op. 10 (LSO/Boulez). Three Little Pieces, Op. 11 (Gregor Piatigorsky, vc; Rosen, pf). Four Songs, Op. 12 (Harper, sop; Rosen, pf). Four Songs, Op. 13. Six Songs, Op. 14 (Harper, sop; chbr ens/Boulez). Five Sacred Songs, Op. 15. Five Canons on Latin Texts, Op. 16 (Halina Lukomska, sop; chbr ens/Boulez). Three Songs, Op. 18 (Lukomska, sop; John Williams, gtr; Colin Bradbury, cl/Boulez). Two Songs, Op. 19 (John Alldis Ch, mbrs LSO/Boulez). String Trio, Op. 20 (mbrs Juilliard Qt). Symphony, Op. 21 (LSO/Boulez). Quartet, Op. 22 (Robert Marcellus, cl; Abraham Weinstein, sax; Daniel Majeske, vn; Rosen, pf/Boulez). Three Songs from "Viae inviae", Op. 23 (Lukomska, sop; Rosen, pf). Concerto, Op. 24 (mbrs LSO/Boulez). Three Songs, Op. 25 (Lukomska, sop; Rosen, pf). Das Augenlicht, Op. 26 (John Alldis Ch, LSO/Boulez). Piano Variations, Op. 27 (Rosen, pf). String Quartet, Op. 28 (Juilliard Qt). Cantata No. 1, Op. 29 (Lukomska, sop; John Alldis Ch; LSO/Boulez). Variations, Op. 30 (LSO/Boulez). Cantata No. 2, Op. 31 (Lukomska, sop; Barry McDaniel, bar; John Alldis Ch; LSO/Boulez). Five Movements, Op. 5 — orchestral version (LSO/Boulez). *Bach* (orch. Webern): Musikalischen Opfer, BWV1079 — Fuga (Ricercata) No. 2 (LSO/Boulez). *Schubert* (orch. Webern): Deutsche Tänze, D820 (Frankfurt Radio Orchestra/Anton Webern. Recorded at a performance in the studios of Radio Frankfurt on December 29th, 1932).

③ 3h 43' ADD 6/91 £

Webern is as 'classic' to Pierre Boulez as Mozart or Brahms are to most other conductors, and when he is able to persuade performers to share his view the results can be remarkable — lucid in texture, responsive in expression. Despite his well-nigh exclusive concern with miniature forms, there are many sides to Webern, and although this set is not equally successful in realizing all of them, it leaves the listener in no doubt about the music's sheer variety, as well as its emotional power, whether the piece in question is an ingenious canon-by-inversion or a simple, folk-like *Lied*. From a long list of performers one could single out Heather Harper and the Juilliard Quartet for special commendation; and the smooth confidence of the John Alldis Choir is also notable. The recordings were made over a five-year period (1968-72) and have the typical CBS dryness of that time. Even so, in the finest performances which Boulez himself directs — the *Orchestral Variations*, Op. 30 is perhaps the high point —

that remarkable radiance of spirit so special to Webern is vividly conveyed. It is a fascinating bonus to hear Webern himself conducting his Schubert arrangements — music from another world, yet with an economy and emotional poise that Webern in his own way sought to emulate.

Webern. WORKS FOR STRING TRIO AND QUARTET. **Arditti Quartet** (Irvine Arditti, David Alberman, vns; Levine Andrade, va; Rohan de Saram, vc). Disques Montaigne 789008.
Five Movements, Op. 5. Six Bagatelles, Op. 9. String Quartet, Op. 28. Trio, Op. 20. Movement (1925). String Quartet (1905). Slow Movement (1905). Rondo (*c.* 1906).

1h 6' DDD 12/91

Webern's music, like that of his revered master Schoenberg, is vulnerable in performance. So much of it is so difficult to play at all that its expressive core is easily overlooked, all the more so because of the legend of saintly modernism slapped on it by the post-war avant-garde. The Arditti Quartet are among the select few who can get beyond the surface complexity and play the music like music; they also benefit from exceptional clarity of recording quality. And the works for quartet and trio are in any case particularly encouraging to the non-specialist listener, in that they lead step by step from the warm, Straussian romanticism of Webern's apprentice years, through the highly-charged expressionist masterpieces of his first maturity (Op. 5 and Op. 9) to the apparently forbidding later 12-note works. There's no use pretending that the Trio and the Op. 28 Quartet will ever be easy listening, but at least this disc comes with the guarantee that it's not the players' or the recording's fault if you don't respond.

Kurt Weill
German/American 1900-1950

Weill. Concerto for violin and wind orchestra, Op. 12[a]. Kiddush[b]. Kleine Dreigroschenmusik. [a]**Yuval Waldman** (vn); [b]**Grayson Hirst** (ten); [b]**Ray Pellerin** (org); [b]**Amor Artis Chamber Choir and Orchestra/Johannes Somary.** Newport Classics NCD60098.

55' DDD 12/91

Kurt Weill's posthumous reputation as a composer for the stage, and the universal popularity of his most famous collaboration with Berthold Brecht, *Die Dreigroschenoper* ("The Threepenny Opera"), still tends to divert attention away from his achievements elsewhere, and this disc presents three works which could scarcely offer greater contrasts of style and content. The Concerto for violin and wind orchestra, for example, reveals Weill's close sympathies with the Second Viennese School, and like his two symphonies, this arresting work owes much to the combined influence of Hindemith, Busoni and even Mahler. The idea of setting the solo violin against the pungent background of the wind group is particularly fascinating, and Yuval Waldman's rich tone makes him an ideal exponent of the concerto. He is excellently supported by Johannes Somary and the Amor Artis Orchestra. Weill's setting of the *Kiddush*, in which the incantations of the cantor are set against blues-inspired choral responses underpinned by a discreet organ part, recall the composer's Jewish heritage, and especially his family associations with the synagogue at Dessau. The tenor, Grayson Hirst, sings here with eloquent gravity, and his diction in the Hebrew text is exemplary. Of course, no Weill compilation would be complete without at least some music from *Die Dreigroschenoper* and Johannes Somary's performance of the popular concert suite would be hard to beat. This maudlin assemblage of tawdry dance tunes set in a period idiom includes "Mack the knife" and "Ballad of the easy life", both of which recall Weill's experience of the decadent years, and his admiration for Brecht's acrimonious text, with all the tragicomic, caustic sarcasm of a George Gross cartoon. The performances are first class and the recording could hardly be bettered — strongly recommended.

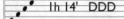

NEW REVIEW

Weill. Symphonies — No. 1; No. 2. Kleine Dreigroschenmusik. **Lisbon Gulbenkian Foundation Orchestra/Michel Swierczewski.** Nimbus NI5283.

· · 1h 14' DDD (?)

The *Kleine Dreigroschenmusik*, a transcription of the jazz-band flavoured numbers from *The Threepenny Opera*, is here given an admirably jaunty performance and serves well as a sweetener to tempt the hesitant to less well-known Weill. The two symphonies couldn't be more different: the First is a student work, never performed in the composer's lifetime. It is full of experimentation, with one eye on Schoenberg, written for large orchestra, and yet with passages of sparse, austere chamber writing; the uninitiated would do well to identify the composer. The Second is a mature composition from the time of Weill's departure from Germany via Paris. Right from the start it is recognizably the Weill of *Mahagonny* or *The Seven Deadly Sins* — a composer speaking with his natural voice. The symphonic Weill, though, has nothing to do with 1920s dance rhythms. These are works in the symphonic line of Mahler, Strauss, Schoenberg, Hindemith and Shostakovich, and it it as such that they should be approached and appreciated. The Second Symphony, especially, is a work crying out for a place in the symphonic repertory — a powerful work with a haunting slow movement. Swierczewski's interpretations are full of assurance, the tempos aptly chosen to bring out all the contrasts of grandeur and introspection in the music.

Weill. SONGS. **Ute Lemper** (sop); **Berlin Radio Ensemble/John Mauceri.** Decca New Line 425 204-2DNL. Texts and translations included. Der Silbersee — Ich bin eine arme Verwandte (Fennimores-Lied); Rom war eine Stadt (Cäsars Tod); Lied des Lotterieagenten. Die Dreigroschenoper — Die Moritat von Mackie Messer; Salomon-Song; Die Ballade von der sexuellen Hörigkeit. Das Berliner Requiem — Zu Potsdam unter den Eichen (arr. Hazell). Nannas-Lied. Aufstieg und Fall der Stadt Mahagonny — Alabama Song; Wie man sich bettet. Je ne t'aime pas. One Touch of Venus — I'm a stranger here myself; Westwind; Speak low.

· · 50' DDD 3/89

The songs in this collection are mostly from the major works Weill composed between 1928 and 1933, but also included are one from his years in France and three items from the 1943 Broadway musical *One Touch of Venus*. The collection introduces a most exciting talent in the person of Ute Lemper. By comparison with the husky, growling delivery often accorded Weill's songs in the manner of his widow Lotte Lenya, we here have a voice of appealing clarity and warmth. What

Ute Lemper [photo: Decca/Rakete]

distinguishes her singing, though, is the way in which these attributes of vocal purity are allied to a quite irresistible dramatic intensity. Her "Song of the Lottery Agent" is an absolute *tour de force*, apt to leave the listener emotionally drained, and her *Je ne t'aime pas* is almost equally overwhelming. Not least in the three numbers from *One Touch of Venus*, sung in perfect English, she displays a commanding musical theatre presence. With John Mauceri on hand to provide authentic musical accompaniments, this is, one feels, how Weill's songs were meant to be heard.

Weill. DIE DREIGROSCHENOPER. **Lotte Lenya,** Jenny; **Erich Schellow,** Macheath; **Willy Trenk-Trebitsch,** Mr Peachum; **Trude Hesterburg,** Mrs Peachum; **Johanna von Kóczián,** Polly Peachum; **Wolfgang Grunert,** Tiger Brown; **Inge Wolffberg,** Lucy; **Wolfgang Neuss,** Streetsinger; **Günther-Arndt Choir;** members of the Dance Orchestra of **Radio Free Berlin/ Wilhelm Brückner-Rüggeberg.** CBS Masterworks CD42637. Notes, text and translation included. From 77268 (12/72).

In *Die Dreigroschenoper* ("The Threepenny Opera") Kurt Weill sought to match the satire of Bertolt Brecht's updating of John Gay's *The Beggar's Opera* with numbers in the dance rhythms and jazz-tinged orchestrations of the time. The number that later became famous as "Mack the Knife" is merely the best known of the many catchy numbers in a score that none the less bears the hallmark of a cultivated musician. This 1958 reading has eclipsed all others. It has the distinction of featuring the composer's widow, Lotte Lenya, in the role of Jenny that she had created back in 1928. The recording carries about it an undeniable feeling of authenticity in the pungency of its satire and the catchiness of its score. Johanna von Kóczian is a charming Polly, Erich Schellow a winning Macheath, and Trude Hesterberg a formidable Frau Peachum, while Wilhelm Brückner-Rüggeberg has just the right feel for Weill's dance rhythms. This is an absolutely complete recording of the score, including the once expurgated "Ballad of Sexual Dependency" and the usually omitted "Jealousy Song". Despite its age, the recorded sound remains good, and the whole is a compelling experience.

NEW REVIEW
Weill. Die sieben Todsünden. Mahagonny Songspiel[a]. **Ute Lemper** (sop); [a]**Susanne Tremper** (sngr); **Helmut Wildhaber, Peter Haage** (tens); **Thomas Mohr** (bar); **Manfred Jungwirth** (bass); **Berlin RIAS Sinfonietta/John Mauceri.** Decca 430 168-2DH. Notes, text and translation included.

In these two works, Brecht and Weill used much the same musical style as in *The Threepenny Opera*. *The Seven Deadly Sins* is a vocal ballet, with sections representing each sin, while the *Mahagonny Songspiel* is a concert piece that summarizes the political thrust and music of the opera *Rise and Fall of the City of Mahagonny*. Superficially it seems a shame that Ute Lemper should adopt an unauthentic downward transposition of *The Seven Deadly Sins* (mostly by a fourth) that was prepared by Wilhelm Brückner-Rüggeberg for the composer's widow Lotte Lenya. Yet there are strong plus points in favour of it as recorded here. In the first place, Weill's original orchestration is fully followed. In the second place, the lower vocal line undoubtedly suits Lemper. And to hear her singing Weill in a register that suits her is joy indeed! She has just the right youthfulness, the musicality and expressiveness, and a control of both music and text that confirm her as a musical theatre singer of rare talent. The intensity that pours forth from singer and orchestra in, say, "Lust", sets this recording apart from earlier versions. In the *Mahagonny Songspiel*, with its irresistible songs, Lemper again seems completely the part.

Weill. DER SILBERSEE. **Wolfgang Schmidt** (ten) Severin; **Hildegard Heichele** (sop) Fennimore; **Hans Korte** (bar) Olim; **Eva Tamassy** (mez) Frau von Luber; **Udo Holdorf** (ten) Baron Laur; **Frederic Mayer** (ten) Lottery Agent; **Cologne Pro Musica; Cologne Radio Symphony Orchestra/Jan Latham-König.** Capriccio 60 011-2. Notes, text and translation included.

♩ ② 1h 47' DDD 8/90

The sub-title of *Der Silbersee*, "A winter's tale", is to be interpreted both literally and metaphorically, for this is a remarkable parable of the dark night of the soul of a Germany about to be plunged into Nazi oppression: the infamous Reichstag fire took place only a matter of days after its première. The symbolism is patent in this tale of poverty, famine, avarice, unscrupulous trickery and turbulent emotions, and a final escape over a bleak lake to an uncharted future: cultured theatre-goers at the time would in any case have remembered that the same sub-title was affixed to Heine's satirical verse epic *Deutschland*. Apart, however, from the punch of Georg Kaiser's social and political message, Weill's music is impressively powerful and moving, both in his 'serious' vein (as in the voices of the policeman Olim's conscience after he has shot Severin, escaping after raiding a food store, or the lovely orchestral passage while snow is falling on the lake) and in his 'popular' (the lottery agent's tango or the foxtrot at a celebratory meal). It should perhaps be emphasized that this is a play with music rather than a 'proper opera'; but the skilful reduction here of the spoken dialogue (very well handled by the actors) throws the music into greater relief. It includes several big set-pieces, such as the girl Fennimore's ballad about Caesar's death (small wonder the Nazis banned the work!), Severin's savage cry for revenge, and the "Fools' paradise" song of the wicked schemers Frau von Lubin and Baron Laub. It is vital however that these should be heard in their rightful context; and the strength of this performance — something of a triumph for Jan Latham-König, his producer and the cast — lies in its tremendous dramatic grip.

NEW REVIEW

Weill. STREET SCENE. **Kristine Ciesinski** (sop) Anna Maurrant; **Richard Van Allan** (bass) Frank Maurrant; **Janis Kelly** (sop) Rose Maurrant; **Bonaventura Bottone** (ten) Sam Kaplan; **Terry Jenkins** (ten) Abraham Kaplan; **Meriel Dickinson** (mez) Emma Jones; **Angela Hickey** (mez) Olga Olsen; **Claire Daniels** (sop) Jennie Hildebrand; **Fiametta Doria** (sop) First Nursemaid; **Judith Douglas** (mez) Second Nursemaid; **English National Opera Chorus and Orchestra/Carl Davis.** TER Classics CDTER21185.

♩ ② 2h 26' DDD 11/91

Street Scene is the most ambitious product of Weill's American years. It's something of a *Porgy and Bess* transferred from Catfish Row to the slum tenements of New York. Where *Porgy and Bess* is through-composed with recitatives, though, *Street Scene* offers a mixture of set musical numbers, straight dialogue, and dialogue over musical underscoring. The musical numbers themselves range from operatic arias and ensembles to rousing 1940s dance numbers. This complete recording is one of two resulting from a joint Scottish Opera/English National Opera production of 1989. This one offers the cast and conductor of the ENO production, with just a couple of relatively minor substitutions. Of the two recordings this is probably the more consistently well sung, particularly where style is concerned. Weill described the work as a "Broadway opera", and it demands a vernacular rather than a classical operatic singing style. This it duly gets from Kristine Ciesinski as Anna Maurrant, while Janis Kelly's beautifully clear but natural enunciation and her sense of emotional involvement make daughter Rose's "What good would the moon be?" a performance of real beauty. Praiseworthy too is Richard Van Allan as the murderous husband, his "Let things be like they always was" creating a suitably sinister effect. Among the subsidiary attractions is the appearance of Catherine Zeta Jones, of ITV's *The Darling Buds of May*, performing the swinging dance number "Moon-faced, starry-eyed".

Jaromir Weinberger   *Refer to Index*   *Czech 1896-1967*

Leo Weiner   *Refer to Index*   *Hungarian 1885-1960*

Samuel Wesley   *British 1766-1837*

NEW REVIEW

S. Wesley. SYMPHONIES. **Milton Keynes Chamber Orchestra/Hilary Davan Wetton.** Unicorn-Kanchana DKPCD9098.
No. 3 in A major; No. 4 in D major; No. 5 in E flat major; No. 6 in B flat major.

1h 4'   DDD   10/91

Son of Charles the hymn-writer and father of Samuel Sebastian, Samuel Wesley was a wunderkind ("an English Mozart" was Boyce's description) who never quite realized his potential, partly, perhaps, because a serious fall in 1787 damaged his skull and left him prone to frequent bouts of irritability and depression. But the four symphonies recorded here — three from 1784 and the fourth from 1802 — are a delightful find, revealing a marvellously fresh and fluent melodic gift allied to a penchant for the quirky turn of phrase. The opening movement of the A major Symphony, for instance, has a grace of demeanour and warmth of sonority characteristic of J.C. Bach (and, for that matter, of Mozart in the same key); but there is an ear-catching individuality both in the themes themselves and in the way the initial idea is augmented and expanded to form the second subject. And the finale, a lusty countrified gavotte, has an unmistakably English flavour. Beguiling as the three teenage symphonies are, the B flat is an altogether more colourful and sophisticated work, and a tantalizing suggestion of what he might have achieved in the form if his health and inclination had allowed. Wesley obviously knew Haydn's "London" symphonies well; but the music has a genial, unfettered quality of melodic invention and an attractive waywardness that are entirely individual. If they lack Haydn's sheer dynamism, both outer movements are purposefully developed, drawing on Wesley's lightly worn contrapuntal skill; and the nonchalant, throw-away ending of the opening *Allegro* is one of many characteristic moments in the work where Wesley slyly foils the listener's expectations. The performances are first-rate: polished, poised, vital of rhythm and fully alive to the warmth of Wesley's lines and textures. The woodwind relish their prominent roles in the B flat symphony, and there's a discreetly balanced harpsichord continuo. The recording is exemplary in its clarity and spaciousness. Highly recommended to any Haydn or Mozart lover with a streak of musical adventure.

Samuel Sebastian Wesley

British 1810-1876

S.S. Wesley. ANTHEMS AND ORGAN WORKS. **New College Choir, Oxford/Edward Higginbottom** (org). CRD CRD3463. Texts included. *Anthems* — Ascribe unto the Lord. Blessed be the God and Father. Cast me not away. Thou wilt keep him in perfect peace. Wash me throughly. The wilderness and the solitary place. *Organ works* — Andante in E minor. Choral song and fugue. Larghetto in F minor.

1h 7'   DDD   10/91

At some time in the last half-century somebody in church-music circles must have compiled a list of anthems comprising what today would be called the "Top Ten". If so, S.S. Wesley would surely be prominent among the composers. *Blessed be the God and Father*, with its famous treble solo, "Love one another", might indeed emerge as the outright favourite. *Thou wilt keep him in perfect peace* is certainly one of the most beautiful, its arching phrases, strong melody and well-judged admixture of polyphony being firmly bound in a well-designed architecture. From the large-scale anthem, *Ascribe unto the Lord*, the final section, "The Lord hath been mindful of us", often serves as an anthem in its own right, and this too has the great merit of tunefulness, with ample opportunity for all voices, including the oft-neglected altos. Then there is *The wilderness and the solitary place*, a cathedral Sunday anthem, 15 minutes long, with one of the supreme challenges to the self-respecting head-choirboy: the clean 'take' of those exposed top As in "and sorrow and sighing". The New College trebles, individually and collectively, are well up to all the demands, and the men's voices (some fine soloists among them too) also sound well. The style of performance, as opposed to the quality of sound, may be more questionable: the slow tempo of the last chorus in *Blessed be the God and Father*, for instance, has a ponderous effect, and the punctuation is frequently too self-conscious. Even so, this is a good disc for representing Wesley in one's collection, especially as it also has two of the finest anthems (*Cast me not away* and *Wash me throughly* that surely come in direct line from Purcell, with the additional pleasure of three organ solos.

Charles Marie Widor
Refer to Index   *French 1844-1937*

Henryk Wieniawski
Refer to Index   *Polish 1835-1880*

Dag Wirén
Refer to Index   *Swedish 1905-1983*

Hugo Wolf
Austrian 1860-1903

Wolf. ORCHESTRAL WORKS. **Orchestre de Paris/Daniel Barenboim.** Erato 2292-45416-2. Items marked [a] recorded at performances in the Salle Pleyel, Paris during February 1988.
Penthesilea[a]. DER CORREGIDOR — Prelude; Intermezzo. Italian Serenade[a]. Scherzo and Finale.

57'   DDD   4/90

Daniel Barenboim has done Wolf's admirers a great service by not only giving *Penthesilea* its first recording for many years, but by adding all of Wolf's other purely orchestral music. We can now speculate about what manner of symphonist he might have become: an assured and masterly one if the so-called scherzo and finale are anything to go by. They date from his teens, and the scherzo in particular is both finely made and ingeniously imagined. The joyously exuberant finale is almost light music, and good company for the two little operatic entr'actes and the already popular *Italian* Serenade. *Penthesilea* prompts similar questions about how Wolf might have developed as an operatic composer if he had followed up the wayward but entrancing *Der Corregidor* with something on a mythic subject and a grander scale. It is gorgeously coloured music, wildly inventive and hugely urgent; a bit undisciplined at times, and occasionally over-scored (Wolf knew that; he was struggling to revise the piece in the last months before his mind broke down) but with unobtrusively firm control from the conductor and superfine playing (both provided here) it becomes possible to suspect that the next stage of Wolf's creativity might have been to rival Strauss as Wagner's operatic successor. The recording, made at a public concert, has a moment or two of congestion but is otherwise both rich and brilliant.

Wolf. Intermezzo. Italian Serenade. String Quartet in D minor. **Artis Quartet** (Peter Schumayer, Johannes Meissl, vns; Herbert Kefer, va; Othmar Muller, vc). Accord 22080-2.

57' DDD 6/90

Wolf's astonishing String Quartet suggests that his early death and the discouragingly contemptuous treatment his larger works received during his lifetime, robbed us of a great composer of chamber music. The Quartet is without the slightest shadow of doubt a masterpiece. For a composer not yet 20 to have had such a mastery of large-scale structure, such skilled command of complex thematic working and such confidence in handling big and dramatic ideas is nothing short of breathtaking. But these profoundly serious qualities are combined with a youthful prodigality of invention and an exuberance of spirit that are winning as well as awesome. Only the work's huge difficulty in performance can have kept it on the furthest fringes of the repertory for so long. How fortunate that for its first recording in many years it should have been taken up by such an urgently communicative as well as such a virtuoso group as the Artis Quartet. The popular *Italian* Serenade, charmingly done, is a welcome supplement; the *Intermezzo*, still more neglected than the String Quartet, shares its qualities and adds to them a measure of enchanting humour. Excellent recorded sound, too: unreservedly recommended.

Wolf. Italienisches Liederbuch. **Elisabeth Schwarzkopf** (sop); **Dietrich Fischer-Dieskau** (bar); **Gerald Moore** (pf). EMI CDM7 63732-2. Text and translation included. From SAN210/1 (2/69).

1h 19' ADD 12/90

Even today the songs of Hugo Wolf are underrated, and do not always draw an audience or sell on disc. If anything can change that situation it ought to be this reissue of a classic account of Wolf's most delightful Songbook, in which the blessings and cares and amusements of love are charmingly retailed. Walter Legge, the century's greatest Wolf advocate after Ernest Newman, was the knowledgeable producer behind this offering, which was joyfully greeted in its LP form some 20 years ago. Its transfer to CD is greatly to be welcomed. Between them Schwarzkopf and Fischer-Dieskau have just about every attribute, vocal and interpretative, to sing these pieces with total devotion and understanding. The many characters portrayed so subtly and unerringly by the composer are all brought to life by the wit and wisdom of their interpreters without whom the songs would lie forgotten on the page. As their partner the veteran Gerald

Moore plays with all his old skill and perception. All one needs to add is that the recording is unforced and natural. This is a 'must' for all lovers of Lieder.

Ermanno Wolf-Ferrari   *Refer to Index*   *Italian 1876-1948*

William Wordsworth   *British 1908-1988*

NEW REVIEW

Wordsworth. Symphonies — No. 2 in D major, Op. 34; No. 3 in D major, Op. 48. **London Philharmonic Orchestra/Nicholas Braithwaite.** Lyrita SRCD207.

 1h 11' DDD 11/90

William Wordsworth   *[photo: Lyrita]*

This composer is a descendant of the poet whose name he shares, and a contemporary of another William W. who did honour to British music. But while Walton won early fame, Wordsworth languished in obscurity, respected by the few who came across his work but unknown to the musical public. The BBC did little to promote his music and actually rejected his Second Symphony of 1948, a scandalously high-handed treatment of a fine creator which may have partly stifled his development. At any rate, this work went on to win an Edinburgh Festival competition two years later and is a forceful, serious statement by a natural symphonist which deserves to be heard and provides some compelling listening. Admittedly, memorable melody and easy charm are in short supply, but there are other rewards, for a strong intellect and imagination are at work. Admirers of the symphonies of Bax and Vaughan Williams (whose Fourth Symphony comes to mind in the brooding slow movement) will find much to satisfy them here, particularly in this committed and well recorded performance. The Third Symphony is shorter but arguably still finer, having just three movements and being lighter in texture and spirit. But once again a powerful imagination is at work, and there is a quirky Shostakovich-like invention, for example in the writing for celesta in the slow movement (the longest of the three). Whatever the case, this disc reminds us of the injustice the British musical establishment did to a composer who died in his eightieth year, two years before its release.

Maurice Wright   *Refer to Index*   *American 1949-*

Robert Wright   *American 1914-*

KISMET (Wright/Forrest, after Borodin). Cast includes **Valerie Masterson, Donald Maxwell, David Rendall, Richard Van Allan, Judy Kaye;**

Ambrosian Chorus; Philharmonia Orchestra / John Owen Edwards.
TER Classics CDTER2 1170. Includes five songs from "Timbuktu".

[② 1h 37' DDD 7/90]

There have been a number of expensively mounted star-led studio recordings of
the big musicals in recent years, most of them flawed somewhere along the line
in their casting of the principal roles. How good then to be able to welcome a
faultlessly performed, superbly played and thrillingly recorded account of Wright
and Forrest's musical extravaganza which was subtitled in the original programme
A Musical Arabian Night. This venerable team would probably be the first to
acknowledge their debt to Borodin whose music, from the opera *Prince Igor* to a
Little Serenade for Piano, they've reworked so convincingly in their tale of a
poet (Donald Maxwell) in ancient Baghdad whose daughter Marsinah (Valerie
Masterson) he plans to marry to a handsome Caliph (David Rendall) after
drowning her husband, the wicked Wazir (Richard Van Allan) in a fountain! The
score reads like a hit parade of the 1950s, "Stranger in Paradise", "Night of My
Nights", "And This is my Beloved" and "Baubles, Bangles and Beads" which has
become a favourite with jazzers over the years. Even those readers who might
shy away from operetta or thumb their noses at the reworking of the classics will
acknowledge the wholehearted conviction with which *Kismet* is executed by this
nearly all British cast, under John Owen Edwards's idiomatic direction. The one
import in this line-up is Broadway's Judy Kaye who delivers a gusty rendition of
"Not Since Ninevah", the score's one homage to syncopation and the glitter of
neon light. Several years after *Kismet*, Wright and Forrest rewrote their old
favourite for Eartha Kitt and an all black cast as *Timbuktu* and it is with several
songs from that score that this pair of CDs is filled out.

Iannis Xenakis

Romanian / French 1922-

NEW REVIEW

Xenakis. Palimpsest. Dikhthas[a]. Epeï. Akanthos[b]. [a]**Irvine Arditti** (vn);
[a]**Claude Helffer** (pf); [b]**Penelope Walmsley-Clark** (sop); **Spectrum / Guy
Protheroe.** Wergo WER6178-2.

[44' DDD ❓]

Contemporary music has often come under attack for being unapproachable,
élitist and intellectual. True, many of the techniques used by contemporary
composers are often heavily indebted to mathematical procedures, but does the
listener need to have a full understanding of these to appreciate the music? After
all, how many music lovers fully understand the working techniques of Mozart or
Beethoven? An over-simplification perhaps, but often the best way to begin
exploring contemporary music is to drop any preconceived ideas and approach
the music on a 'sensational' rather than intellectual level. The music of Iannis
Xenakis, for example, often uses techniques that would seem more at home on
an architect's or mathematician's drawing board, but the resulting music, far
from being arid or intellectual, often has a physical, tactile effect upon the
listener — Xenakis is a true alchemist. In *Palimpsest* a simple idea of non-
repeating scale patterns becomes an exhilarating, roller-coaster ride for the
listener as the instruments jostle for prominence. By contrast, *Epeï* ("since") is
introverted and pensive, a musical ripple emanating from a central musical point
in time. *Dikhthas* (violin and piano) means double or duel, and here Xenakis
explores the two very different qualities of the instruments — sometimes placing
the violin and piano in conflict with each other, sometimes merging them
together as one. *Akanthos* is a marvellous evocation of the twisting, convoluted
patterns produced by the ornamental leaves of the Acanthus plant, with the

miasmatic meanderings of the instruments and solo soprano voice producing some unusual and striking melodic ideas. The performances by the ensemble, Spectrum, under the direction of Guy Protheroe, are of an exceptionally high quality, and the recorded sound is excellent. A tough but very rewarding disc.

Jan Dismas Zelenka *Bohemian 1679-1745*

Zelenka. ORCHESTRAL WORKS. **Berne Camerata/Alexander van Wijnkoop.** Archiv Produktion 423 703-2AX3. From 2710 026 (11/78). Capriccios — No. 1 in D major; No. 2 in G major; No. 3 in F major; No. 4 in A major; No. 5 in G major. Concerto a 8 in G major. Sinfonia a 8 in A minor. Hipocondrie a 7 in A major. Overture a 7 in F major.

③ 2h 44' ADD 1/89 ❓

This three-CD album contains all Zelenka's surviving orchestral music. Most of it is anything but commonplace and some of it has a quirky individuality which baroque enthusiasts will find intriguing. The most readily conspicuous feature of the five *Capriccios* is that of the horn writing whose virtuosity exceeds that of almost all his contemporaries; but he shares with Telemann a predilection for rhythms and melodies deriving from central European folk tradition. Barry Tuckwell and Robert Routch turn in dazzling performances on modern horns and are effectively matched by the crisp and invigorating playing of the Berne Camerata. The remaining pieces are formally varied and though sometimes Zelenka just fails to maintain a high level of interest, for the most part his music is full of charm and, at its best, is quite irresistible. The Berne Camerata present a colourful picture of Zelenka's music in this fascinating anthology and their performances are well recorded and thoroughly documented.

Zelenka. The Lamentations of Jeremiah. **Michael Chance** (alto); **John Mark Ainsley** (ten); **Michael George** (bass); **Chandos Baroque Players.** Hyperion CDA66426. Texts and translations included.

1h 13' DDD 7/91

NEW REVIEW

Zelenka. The Lamentations of Jeremiah. **Ulla Groenwold** (contr); **Hein Meens** (ten); **Max van Egmond** (bass); **Amsterdam Bregynhof Academy/ Roderick Shaw.** Globe GLO5050. Text and translation included.

1h 4' DDD 12/91

Between the incomparable settings by Thomas Tallis and the extremely austere one by Stravinsky (which he called *Threni*) the "Lamentations of Jeremiah" have attracted surprisingly few composers. Perhaps the predominantly sombre tone, without even the dramatic opportunities presented by the *Dies irae* in a Requiem, is off-putting. Be that as it may, Zelenka showed remarkable resourcefulness in his 1722 setting for the electoral chapel at Dresden, where he was Kapellmeister. His musical language is in many ways similar to that of J.S. Bach — they even shared the indignity of being thought old-fashioned for the apparent severity and complexity of their styles — but there are also daring turns of phrase which are entirely personal. The six *Lamentations* feature each singer twice, and the two listed recordings offer complementary virtues. The British performance is more intimate, even mystical, slightly more spacious in tempo and with a resonant acoustic. The Dutch one, directed by an Englishman from the organ, is more immediate, both in expression and in recording quality, with marginally less distinguished voices, but a more upfront, almost operatic delivery, which may appeal to those who tend to be suspicious of the early music manner.

Alexander Zemlinsky

Austrian 1871-1942

Zemlinsky. Lyrische Symphonie, Op. 18. **Julia Varady** (sop); **Dietrich Fischer-Dieskau** (bar); **Berlin Philharmonic Orchestra/Lorin Maazel.** DG 419 261-2GH. Texts and translations included. From 2532 021 (3/82).

> 44' DDD 6/87

Zemlinsky's powerful symphonic song cycle for soprano and baritone employs the vast forces of the late-romantic orchestra at its most opulent. The poems by the composer gradually build up, if not to a narrative, then to a series of symbolist portrayals of the spirit of love. The male singer contributes a more abstract, more idealized yearning after the "dweller in my endless dreams", the soprano a more down-to-earth evocation of emotional longing. Dietrich Fischer-Dieskau and his wife Julia Varady cope well with the tormented legato phrasing and tortured harmonies as the vision of an idealized love shimmers before their eyes just beyond their reach. The Berlin Philharmonic play this unfamiliar score with great virtuosity, strongly conducted by Lorin Maazel and have been recorded in a wonderfully mellow acoustic.

Zemlinsky. EINE FLORENTINISCHE TRAGODIE, Op. 16. **Doris Soffel** (mez) Bianca; **Kenneth Riegel** (ten) Guido Bardi; **Guilermo Sarabia** (bass) Simone. **Berlin Radio Symphony Orchestra/Gerd Albrecht.** Schwann CD11625. From VMS1625 (9/85).

> 53' DDD 12/85

Zemlinsky's *A Florentine Tragedy* is an opulent work entwining adultery, murder and sexual desire in a powerful union. Bianca, the wife of a wealthy Florentine merchant Simone, is having an adulterous liaison with Guido. Simone returns to find the two lovers together; he gradually grasps the situation and after a cat-and-mouse game with Guido challenges him to a duel and kills him. The story is based on a play by Oscar Wilde and, typically, has a verbal lushness powerfully matched by Zemlinsky's potent score. The cast of three is strong with some electric moments as the tension increases. Gerd Albrecht directs sympathetically and the orchestra play this rich score well. Nicely recorded.

NEW REVIEW
Zemlinsky. DER KREIDERKREIS. **Renate Behle** (sop) Tschang-Haitang; **Gabriele Schreckenbach** (mez) Mrs Tschang; **Roland Hermann** (bar) Ma; **Siegfried Lorenz** (bar) Tschao; **Reiner Goldberg** (ten) Emperor Pao; **Uwe Peter** (ten) Tong; **Hans Helm** (bar) Tschang-Ling; **Gertrud Ottenthal** (sop) Mrs Ma; **Kaja Borris** (mez) Midwife; **Gidon Saks** (bar) Soldier; **Celina Lindsley** (sop) A girl; **Berlin Radio Symphony Orchestra/Stefan Soltesz.** Capriccio 60016-2. Notes, text and translation included.

> ② 2h 4' DDD 1/92

This is Zemlinsky's seventh and last opera, composed in 1931-32 and one of the last of its kind to be staged in Germany before the clamp-down of Nazi cultural policy. The story is Klabund's reworking of a Chinese morality play, made more famous in the setting by Brecht, in which a dispute over a child is solved when the true mother refuses to compete for it in a tug-of-war. But where Brecht in 1955 stressed the social message, Klabund in 1923 was equally interested in the exotic and sensual aspects. His version of the story enabled Zemlinsky to blend his late-romantic instincts with a tangy orientalism and elements of the detached matter-of-factness which had come into fashion in the 1920s. It makes for an intriguing mixture, something like Ravel crossed with Weill, and if the drama ultimately lacks a strong centre, the score is still wonderfully seductive in its own right. Strong performances and a warm, realistic recording.

Collections

Orchestral

BALLET GALA. English Concert Orchestra/Richard Bonynge. Decca
421 818-2DH2.
Minkus (arr. March): Paquita. Don Quixote. *Pugni* (arr. March): Pas de
quatre. *Offenbach*: Le papillon. *Drigo* (arr. Lanchbery): Le corsaire — Pas
de deux. *Auber*: Pas classique. Les rendez-vous (arr. Lambert). **Drigo** (arr.
March): Diane et Actéon. *D. Scarlatti* (arr. Tommasini): The good-humoured
Ladies. *Thomas*: Françoise de Rimini.

> ② 2h 6' DDD 11/90

This is a delightful selection of largely unfamiliar ballet music from the nineteenth
century, which makes a pleasant change from the usual collection of oft-recorded
Tchaikovsky favourites. Although many of the excerpts here are heard in
arrangements by more recent hands, the essential flavour of the original works
has been retained. Little of the music is particularly striking but it is all
nonetheless wonderfully tuneful, animated and very easy on the ear. However,
the two sprightly Minkus excerpts, Drigo's exciting *Pas de deux* from *Le corsaire*
and highlights from Offenbach's only full-length ballet *Le papillon* are probably the
pieces most likely to afford prolonged enjoyment. Richard Bonynge is a trusty
interpreter of this sort of repertoire and with the help of equally dedicated
playing from the ECO he makes each work shine to its best advantage. The
excellent recording is a further bonus, bringing out all the colourful orchestral
details with notable clarity. This set is a treat not only for ballet lovers but
anyone who appreciates attractive, well-crafted melodies.

BAROQUE CLASSICS. Taverner Players/Andrew Parrott. EMI Reflexe
CDM7 69853-2.
Handel: Solomon — Arrival of the Queen of Sheba. Harp Concerto in B flat
major, Op. 4 No. 6 (with Andrew Lawrence-King, hp). *Purcell:* Three Parts
upon a Ground. A Suite of Theatre Music: The Indian Queen — Trumpet
Overture, Symphony, Dance. Abdelazer — Rondeau; The Gordion Knot Unty'd
— Chaconne. *Pachelbel:* Canon and Gigue. *Bach:* "Wir danken dir, Gott,
wir danken dir", BWV29 — Sinfonia. "Ich steh mit einem Fuss im Grabe",
BWV156 — Sinfonia. "Der Himmel lacht! die Erde jubiliert", BWV31 —
Sonata. "Ich liebe den Höchsten von ganzem Gemüte", BWV174 — Sinfonia.
Christmas Oratorio, BWV248 — Sinfonia. "Gottes Zeit ist die allerbeste Zeit",
BWV106 — Sonatina. "Herz und Mund und Tat und Leben", BWV147 —
Chorale, "Jesus bleibet meine Freude" ("Jesu, joy of man's desiring") (with
Taverner Consort).

> 1h DDD 12/88

If you have ever felt the desire to hear 'baroque classics' as the composer might
have heard them, but have been deterred by the unfriendly sounds and deadpan
renditions offered by some early-instrument groups, you may do the former
without suffering the latter by adding this disc to your collection. Though the
performances have every benefit of stylistic scholarship and early-instrumental
mastery they are in no way 'dry', nor are there any chalk-on-blackboard sounds
to set the teeth on edge; on the contrary, the late David Reichenberg's oboe
playing is likely to be a delightful revelation. Like other baroque composers, Bach
was wont to rework some of his music for other media: thus you may recognize
the Sinfonias from Cantatas 29, 156 and 31 as being related to the *Preludium* of

the Third Violin Partita (BWV1006), the *Largo* of the F minor Harpsichord
Concerto (BWV1056) and the first movement of the Third Brandenburg
Concerto (BWV1048). This represents a doorway to the appreciation of baroque
music in authentic performance, through which you may enter with as much
enthusiasm as do the Taverner Players.

BAROQUE FAVOURITES. [a]**Academy of St Martin in the Fields/Sir
Neville Marriner;** [b]**Bath Festival (Chamber) Orchestra/Sir Yehudi
Menuhin.** Classics for Pleasure CD-CFP4557.
Pachelbel: Canon in D major[a]. *Purcell:* Chacony in G minor, Z730[a].
Vivaldi: Concerto in B minor, Op. 10 No. 3[b] (with Sir Yehudi Menuhin,
Robert Masters, Eli Goren and Sydney Humphreys, vns). *Corelli:* Concerto
Grosso in F major, Op. 6 No. 2[b] (Menuhin, Masters, vns; Derek Simpson, vc).
Gluck: ORFEO ED EURIDICE — Dance of the Blessed Spirits[a]. *Monteverdi*
(ed. Leppard): Se vittorie si belle. O sia tranquillo (Gerald English, Hugues
Cuenod, tens; Bath Festival Ensemble/Raymond Leppard). *Handel:* Concerto
grosso in A major, Op. 6 No. 11[b].

Ih 6' ADD 11/89

Sir Yehudi Menuhin　　　*[photo: EMI/Snowdon]*

What qualifications are required,
one wonders, for a piece of music
to be eligible for consideration as
a "baroque favourite"? The exclusion of Albinoni's *Adagio* — a
sickly confection with which
Albinoni had nothing whatsoever
to do — merits a strong recommendation for this anthology.
Some of the pieces, such as
Gluck's *Dance of the Blessed Spirits*
and Pachelbel's *Canon* are indeed
standard favourites but others like
the Monteverdi madrigals and the
Corelli Concerto Grosso may
strike listeners as much less familiar. The performances are lively
though somewhat variable in their
degree of finesse. The programme
is somewhat arbitrarily chosen and
the absence of Bach from the
menu a surprising omission. Never mind, the disc offers variety and entertainment and if it leads the curious to explore further the rich legacy of these and
other baroque composers, then its arbitrariness will not have been in vain.

CONCERTANTE CELLO WORKS. Steven Isserlis (vc); **Chamber
Orchestra of Europe/John Eliot Gardiner.** Virgin Classics VC7 91134-2.
Tchaikovsky: Variations on a Rococo Theme, Op. 33. Pezzo capriccioso,
Op. 62. Nocturne, Op. 19 No. 4. Andante cantabile, Op. 11. *Glazunov:* Two
Pieces, Op. 20. Chant du menestrel, Op. 71. *Rimsky-Korsakov:* Serenade,
Op. 37. *Cui:* Deux morceaux, Op. 36 — Scherzando; Cantabile.

Ih 4' DDD 10/90

This delicious collection of Russian concertante works for cello offers the
immediate advantage of a version of Tchaikovsky's *Rococo* Variations that aligns
closely with the composer's original intentions for the work — many other

recordings use heavily edited and reordered versions. Its second advantage is the considered, clean-toned playing of Steven Isserlis, one of a mighty handful of first-rate cello soloists that the UK can now boast. His style is not as demonstrative as that of some, though he is quite capable of opening the emotional floodgates when it is appropriate, and his delicacy and stylish phrasing bring out the best in this programme. Whether the music is lyrical, introspective, or playful, his restraint lends it another level of meaning that illuminates its inner life. Praise must also go to John Eliot Gardiner and the Chamber Orchestra of Europe. Accompanying of this sort is never easy, as expert control is demanded for long periods with few attendant moments in the spotlight. Gardiner and the engineers have attained an ideal balance between soloist and orchestra and the players demonstrate an intuitive feel for the late nineteenth-century idiom of the music.

NEW REVIEW

CONCERTOS FOR TWO FLUTES. Shigenori Kudo (fl); **Salzburg Mozarteum Orchestra/Jean-Pierre Rampal** (fl). Sony Classical CD45930. *Mozart:* Concertone in C major, K190/186E. *Cimarosa:* Concerto in G major. *Vivaldi:* Concerto in C major, RV533. *A. Stamitz:* Concerto in G major.

| ♪ 1h 8' DDD 2/92 |

Two flutes make such amiable companions that it is remarkable to find so few major works — and what is more 'major' than a concerto — for them. Anton Stamitz, the son of Johann of Mannheim fame, wrote one concerto for one flute and one (*Symphonie concertante*) for two, and it is happily strange that Cimarosa, who wrote little instrumental music, gave one of his only two concertos to a pair of flutes. Mozart's two concertos for solo flute, an instrument he claimed not to like, were written in response to a commission, and his generosity did not extend to a double concerto. Two violins are the soloists in the *Concertone*, a precursor of the famous *Sinfonia concertante* for violin and viola but it is no less comfortably playable on two flutes. Vivaldi, another enthusiast of the genre, wrote only one concerto for two flutes. Stamitz, Cimarosa and Mozart all stand under the same stylistic umbrella, and Vivaldi is linked to them by the ritornello form of the first movement of the Mozart concerto — but there is really no need to justify the make-up of such a pleasing programme. Rampal and Kudo, impeccable French-school flautists, make perfectly matched conversation, attentively supported by the Salzburg Mozarteum and vividly recorded.

NEW REVIEW

CONTEMPORARY WORKS FOR ORCHESTRA. [a]**Istvan Matuz** (fl); **Ensemble Intercontemporain/**[b]**Pierre Boulez;** [c]**Peter Eötvös.** Erato 2292-45409-2.
Dufourt. Antiphysis for flute and chamber orchestra[ab]. *Ferneyhough.* Funérailles — versions I and II for strings and harp[b]. *Harvey.* Mortuos Plango, Vivos Voco — concrete sounds processed by computer[c]. *Höller.* Arcus for 17 instruments and tape[c].

| ♪ 1h 12' AAD |

Not easy listening granted, but for those interested in exploring what the outer limits of contemporary music have to offer then the rewards are great indeed. Jonathan Harvey's *Mortuos Plango, Vivos Voco* is arguably one of the most successful pieces of tape montage to have emerged in recent years. The title and text are taken from the inscription on the great tenor bell at Winchester Cathedral: "I count the hours which fly past, I weep for the dead and I call the living to prayer" . From this, and the electronic manipulation of a boy's voice and the great tenor bell itself, Harvey constructs a colourful and chilling atmosphere in which he says: "One must imagine the walls of the concert-hall enclosing the [listener] like the side of the bell around which the soul of the young boy flies freely". The hyper-complexities of Ferneyhough's *Funérailles* I and II for harp and strings are less easily assimilated but no less fascinating, and subsequent hearings yield up more of its inner secrets and labyrinthine workings. Ferneyhough calls them: "Rite[s] taking place behind a curtain, or in the far distance". Dufourt's *Antiphysis* for flute and chamber orchestra, and Höller's *Arcus* for 17 instruments and tape, both date from 1978, and in their own utterly different ways, reflect the extraordinary virtuosity and artistry of the Ensemble Intercontemporain, for whom they were written, and who play with such stunning conviction on this disc. Exceedingly well recorded.

THE ENGLISH CONNECTION. Academy of St Martin in the Fields/Sir Neville Marriner. ASV CDDCA518. From DCA518 (5/83).
Vaughan Williams: The Lark Ascending (Iona Brown, vn). Fantasia on a Theme by Thomas Tallis. *Elgar:* Serenade in E minor, Op. 20. *Tippett:* Fantasia concertante on a Theme of Corelli.

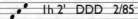 1h 2' DDD 2/85

It is difficult to imagine a more 'English' work than *The Lark Ascending*. Written in the last days of pre-First World War peace, it evokes the tranquillity of a rural England which would never be quite the same again. Iona Brown's solo violin soars effortlessly above the orchestra: she and Marriner contrive a performance which is admirable in every way. This is coupled with the *Tallis* Fantasia, written for the spacious acoustic of Gloucester Cathedral, and Elgar's *Serenade*, an early work but entirely characteristic of the great composer's skill in writing music which pretends no great profundity yet charms and moves the spirit. Tippett's *Fantasia concertante* is a slightly harder piece to assimilate: its busy counterpoint again has a very English quality despite an aura of the Italian *concerto grosso*. There is a slight edge to the string sound on this disc, but it is not enough to affect enjoyment of a very attractive programme.

NEW REVIEW

ENGLISH MINIATURES. Northern Sinfonia/Richard Hickox. EMI CDC7 49933-2.
Gardiner: Overture to a Comedy. *Quilter:* Three English Dances, Op. 11. Where the Rainbow Ends — suite. *Walton:* Siesta. *Goossens:* By the Tarn, Op. 15, No. 1. *Bax:* Mediterranean. *Warlock:* An old song. *German:* Henry VIII — three dances.

 1h 1' DDD 9/91

Here's a collection of lollipops worthy of Sir Thomas Beecham. Richard Hickox and the Northern Sinfonia rise to the occasion with buoyancy and style, revelling in the bright and breezy sounds of Balfour Gardiner's *Overture to a Comedy* and imparting a Purcellian elegance to Quilter's *Three English Dances*. The clear, spacious recording captures the numerous melodic turns and orchestral trimmings which abound in this collection, with wind and strings carefully balanced. More subdued pieces like Walton's curiously chromatic *Siesta* and Warlock's haunting *An old song* are lovingly phrased by the Northern Sinfonia, while Hickox secures a delightful rhythmic lilt in *Where the Rainbow Ends*, a charming suite by Quilter which accompanied the once popular Mills and Owen play. The fine recording assimilates the exotic percussive effects of Bax's *Mediterranean* and the busy orchestral textures of German's *Henry VIII* dances. This disc is a delightful portrait of these lesser-known English masters and captures the gentle benevolence of kinder, simpler times.

ENGLISH MUSIC FOR STRINGS. Guildhall String Ensemble/Robert Salter. RCA Red Seal RD87846.
Britten: Simple Symphony, Op. 4. *Tippett:* Little Music. *Walton:* Sonata. *Oldham/Tippett/L. Berkeley/Britten/Searle/Walton:* Variations on an Elizabethan theme, "Sellinger's Round".

1h 9'   DDD   5/89

ENGLISH MUSIC FOR STRINGS. Guildhall String Ensemble/Robert Salter (vn). RCA Victor Red Seal RD87761.
Holst: St Paul's Suite, H118. *Delius* (orch. Fenby): Two Aquarelles. *Ireland:* A Downland Suite — Minuet. *Finzi:* Prelude, Op. 25. Romance, Op. 11. *Walton:* Henry V — Passacaglia (Death of Falstaff); Touch her soft lips and part. *Elgar* (ed. Young): The Spanish Lady — suite. *Warlock:* Capriol Suite.

1h 1'   DDD   9/88

The Guildhall String Ensemble are a most skilful, professional band and these enterprising collections show them off to great advantage. Britten's early *Simple Symphony*, a slight but accomplished work, is given a suitably playful reading as is Tippett's charming *Little Music*, though here they nicely capture the slightly mysterious quality of the piece. The two substantial works on the disc are also authoritatively despatched. The *Variations on an Elizabethan theme* was composed by five different composers for the 1953 Aldeburgh Festival and these undemanding variations on an old English dance tune make enjoyable listening, especially when performed so well. The Walton Sonata is a 1972 reworking on his 1947 String Quartet. The transformation from solo strings to a more substantial body works well and takes on a new, and for some, more accessible nature. The unusual item in the second collection is the group of five short pieces rescued from a late, unfinished opera by Elgar — not vintage Elgar by any means but attractive nevertheless. Holst's much better-known suite has a simple but robust cheerfulness. Ireland's elegant little *Minuet* began life as a test piece for military band and the two Delius pieces are effective transcriptions by Eric Fenby of two wordless part-songs. Warlock used old French dance tunes in a suite which also conveys his own lively personality; Finzi's two pieces have a typical, wistful nostalgia, and Walton's grave little fragments from his music for Olivier's film are effective in their own right. The recordings are beautifully spacious and capture well the ensemble's fine string tone.

FETE A LA FRANCAISE. Montreal Symphony Orchestra/Charles Dutoit. Decca 421 527-2DH.
Chabrier: Joyeuse marche. España. *Dukas:* L'apprenti sorcier. *Satie* (orch. Debussy): Gymnopédies — Nos. 1 and 3. *Saint-Saëns:* SAMSON ET DALILA — Bacchanale. *Bizet:* Jeux d'enfants. *Thomas:* RAYMOND — Overture. *Ibert:* Divertissement.

1h 10'   DDD   6/89   ⑨ₚ ⑨ₛ Ⓑ

With great style and huge amounts of panache Charles Dutoit presides over a highly enjoyable collection of French 'lollipops'. Moving forward from Chabrier's *Joyeuse marche*, this *fête* includes such favourites as *The sorcerer's apprentice*, deliciously pointed and coloured, Chabrier's tribute to Spain, *España*, and Saint-

Saëns's steamy Bacchanale from *Samson et Dalila*. A cool, limpid interlude is provided by two Satie *Gymnopédies*, here in orchestrations by Debussy. The whole programme is rounded off with tremendous fun by Ibert's outrageous *Divertissement* in a truly winning performance. The Montreal Symphony Orchestra are, without doubt, a first-rate orchestra and their grasp of French repertoire is certainly not equalled by any native band. Add to that a recording of quite breathtaking brilliance and you have a disc to treasure and delight.

FRENCH ORCHESTRAL WORKS. [a]**French Radio National Orchestra;** [b]**Royal Philharmonic Orchestra/Sir Thomas Beecham.** EMI Beecham Edition CDM7 63379-2.
Bizet: Carmen — Suite No. 1 (from HMV HQS1108, 12/67)[a]. *Fauré:* Pavane, Op. 50 (HMV ASD518, 4/63)[a]. *Dolly Suite*, Op. 56 (orch. Rabaud. HQS1136, 5/68)[a]. *Debussy:* Prélude à l'après-midi d'un faune (ASD259, 6/59)[b]. *Saint-Saëns:* Le rouet d'Omphale, Op. 31 (ASD259)[b]. *Delibes:* Le Roi s'amuse — ballet music (HQS1136)[b].

⏺ 1h 8' ADD 7/90   £ ▲

Even to those who never heard him in the flesh there is no mistaking Beecham's relish in, and flair for, the French repertoire. His combination of mischievous high spirits, almost dandyish elegance, cool outer classicism masking passionate emotion, swagger, refined nuance and delicate charm was perhaps unique — not matched even by such committed Francophiles as Constant Lambert. *Elan* is at once in evidence here in the *Carmen* prelude, and subtle dynamic gradations in the entr'actes to Acts 2 and 4; there is lightness, vivacity and tenderness in Fauré's *Dolly* suite and a true Gallic reserve in his *Pavane*; and he enters with prim finesse into Delibes's pastiche dances. Debussy's erotic study, on repeated hearings of this performance, becomes the more Grecian and effective for its conscious understatement; and only the Saint-Saëns symphonic poem, for all the RPO's delicacy, seems to hang fire. But four or five bull's-eyes out of six is a pretty good score, and at medium price not to be missed.

NEW REVIEW

GERMAN CONSORT MUSIC, 1660-1710. The Parley of Instruments/ Roy Goodman, Peter Holman. Hyperion CDA66074. From A66074 (8/83).
Böhm (reconstr. Holman): Ouverture in D major. *Fischer:* Le journal du printems — Suite No. 7. *Rosenmüller:* Sonata da camera No. 2 in D major. *Schmelzer:* Sacro-profanus concentus musicus — Sonata No. 8 in G major. *Telemann:* Ouverture in C major.

⏺ 46' DDD 9/91   🖋

This entertaining and varied programme of German consort music is mainly orientated around composers of the pre-Bach generation. Here we have an early flowering of the mixed influences of France and Italy which were to characterize German music of the late baroque period. As with gardens, architecture and painting so too was music of the French court at Versailles the envy, and thus the model for many an aspiring princely or ducal establishment elsewhere in Europe. Fischer's Suite No. 7 from *Le journal du printems* provides an exemplary instance of the skill with which German composers digested the Lullian overture and dance idioms. In contrast with this piece the Rosenmüller Sonata reveals more strongly Italianate disciplines while the Telemann Ouverture looks further forward though casting a backward glance as well. The playing of the Parley of Instruments is stylish and invigorating but sometimes lacks finesse in ensemble and tuning. The character of period instruments is vividly realized in a recording which furthermore illuminates the rich textures of the music.

NEW REVIEW

HOMMAGE A SIBELIUS. Helsinki Philharmonic Orchestra/Sergiu Comissiona. Ondine ODE767-2.
Sibelius: En saga, Op. 9. *T. Musgrave:* Song of the enchanter. *Englund:* Ciacona. *J. Yuasa:* The midnight sun. *E-S. Tüür:* Searching for roots. *T. Picker:* Séance. *W. Josephs:* In the north. *M. Constant:* Hämeenlinna. *P. Ruders:* Tundra.

Ih 6' DDD 4/92

Apart from *En saga* all the music recorded here was commissioned by the conductor, Sergiu Commissiona, to mark the 125th anniversary of Sibelius's birth. Though they are generously represented, not all are Nordic composers: Marius Constant, Thea Musgrave and the gifted Japanese composer, Joji Yuasa who has as yet made little impact outside specialist circles. Many of the pieces make allusions to Sibelius and the disc is obviously a valuable memento of the Helsinki concert season in which these novelties were presented. Some of the pieces here are more successful than others. The disc starts with a lively — and presumably authentic — account of Sibelius's *En saga*. This music must surely be surging through the veins of all Finnish musicians. The pieces by Musgrave and Constant are quite striking and well worth having on disc. The Helsinki Orchestra play as if they believe in every note and the recordings are well detailed. Although this is a commemorative disc which will be a must for Sibelius admirers, it will also be of interest to those with a taste for the less demanding byways of new music.

ITALIAN BAROQUE MUSIC. English Chamber Orchestra/Raymond Leppard. Classics for Pleasure CD-CFP4371. From HQS1232 (10/70).
Albinoni: Sonatas a cinque, Op. 2 — No. 3 in A major; No. 6 in G minor. *Corelli:* Concerto Grosso in F major, Op. 6 No. 9. *Vivaldi:* Concertos — D major, RV121; E flat major, RV130, "Al Santo Sepolcro"; G minor, RV156.

44' ADD 11/89 £

This well-chosen anthology of late baroque Italian concertos was recorded in 1970. Ideas about how to perform eighteenth-century music have changed considerably since then but in no way does that diminish interpretations as tasteful and animated as these. A disc such as this contains much that was most stylish in baroque performance 20 years ago and many a supposedly 'authentic' approach to the same repertory has subsequently fallen far short of what Raymond Leppard and the English Chamber Orchestra achieve here. The two Albinoni works are, perhaps, especially appealing for their tender slow movements which Leppard treats with affecting warmth; but there is little or nothing here to disappoint listeners. The programme is pleasingly contrasted, well played and well recorded.

NEW REVIEW

ITALIAN FLUTE CONCERTOS. Jean-Pierre Rampal (fl); **I Solisti Veneti/Claudio Scimone.** Sony Classical CD47228.
Romano: Concerto in G major. *Cecere:* Concerto in A major. *Alberti:* Concerto in F major, "Con sordini". *Sammartini:* Concerto in G major.

52' DDD 2/92

Italy was slower than most other countries to favour the transverse flute over its fipple relative, as Vivaldi's well known concertos testify, but there were composers who responded to the flute's siren song, possibly persuaded by approaches from Margrave Carl Friedrich, a player and enthusiast thereof, in whose large collection of music (housed in Karlsruhe) there are numerous flute works. Some of these composers were Italian and four of their flute concertos, unpublished and otherwise unrecorded, form the programme of this recording;

Jean-Pierre Rampal   [photo: Sony Classical]

indeed, only the name of Sammartini was to be found in *The Classical Catalogue* prior to this recording, and of Romano and Cecere it may be said that "little is known of their lives". Alberti's Concerto is high baroque and, time and taste having marched on, Sammartini's is both 'high-transitional' and virtuosic; the others inhabit the middle ground. What they all have in common is clean-cut, melody-rich charm, persuasively displayed by Rampal, the most seductive of flautists, with the spruce support of I Solisti Veneti in a pristine recording. It isn't for instrumental purists but it is certainly for anyone who enjoys happy, uncomplicated and unfamiliar music, played with a smile.

NEW REVIEW

ORCHESTRAL WORKS. ªGuillermo Figueroa (vn); **Orpheus Chamber Orchestra.** DG 431 680-2GH.
Wagner: Siegfried Idyll. *Turina:* La oración del torero. *Wolf:* Italian Serenade. *Puccini:* Crisantemi. *Berlioz:* Rêverie et caprice, Op. 8ª. *Sibelius:* Valse triste, Op. 44. *Dvořák:* Nocturne in B major, B47.

1h 2' DDD 10/91

The Orpheus Chamber Orchestra, of some 25 instrumentalists who play without a conductor, are an American group founded in the 1980s who have achieved success with every one of their discs — and this collection of seven pieces from seven European countries (if we count Wolf's sprightly, single movement *Italian Serenade* as Italian) is another winner. Wagner wrote his *Siegfried Idyll* as a birthday present for his wife, and it was first played in their home to waken her on that day in 1870 (which happened also to be Christmas Day); it is unusually tender music and one of his most immediately attractive works which here receives a loving performance. At 19 minutes this is the longest piece in the programme; the others last under nine, but each of them still comes across strongly. Another example of instrumental music from an opera composer is Puccini's *Crisantemi* ("Chrysanthemums"), an elegiac piece, originally for string quartet, that he wrote in memory of Duke Amadeo of Savoy but which later provided material for his opera *Manon Lescaut*. Like the Puccini, Wolf's *Serenade* was originally for just four players but sounds well when played by larger forces. Guillermo Figueroa is a per-suasive soloist in Berlioz's *Rêverie et caprice*, which is suavely passionate and very Gallic. Indeed, everything in this well chosen programme — a European musical tour — is worth hearing and even the familiar *Valse triste* (Sibelius in waltz time, but mysteriously so) comes up freshly and strongly. The recording is richly atmospheric.

POPULAR ORCHESTRAL MUSIC. Dallas Symphony Orchestra/ Eduardo Mata. RCA VD87727. From RCD14439 (6/83).
Dukas: L'Apprenti Sorcier, *Enescu:* Roumanian Rhapsody No. 1 in A major, Op. 11. *Mussorgsky:* A Night on the Bare Mountain. *Tchaikovsky:* Capriccio Italien, Op. 45.

51' DDD 9/89

This disc is something of a showcase for Eduardo Mata and the Dallas Symphony Orchestra, with a recorded sound that is in the demonstration bracket. All four works receive excellent performances, but the Tchaikovsky and Enescu items are in a class of their own, and can be counted as amongst the finest in the catalogue. The *Capriccio Italien* is a truly riveting performance, with the opening brass fanfares sounding so realistic that you are transported to the best seat in the concert hall. This is a very Italianate reading, which glows with a sumptuous and full-bodied string sound, and the coda has a marvellous feeling of joy and abandonment, whilst still maintaining an air of elegance. Mussorgsky's *A Night on the Bare Mountain* is given a very fine performance technically, with excellent articulation in the strings and powerful playing from the brass section, but somehow misses the terror of the piece. Much the same can be said of their account of Dukas's ever popular *The Sorcerer's Apprentice*, which is a very smooth and polished reading, but lacking perhaps that last ounce of malfeasance required to really make the spine tingle in the climax. Enescu's kaleidoscopic *Roumanian* Rhapsody No. 1 provides the perfect ending to this superb disc (a real encore item if ever there was one). The Dallas Symphony Orchestra play with unflagging energy here, with the woodwind section positively sparkling. At mid-price this disc is an absolute must.

THE ROMANTIC CLARINET. Emma Johnson (cl); **English Chamber Orchestra/Gerard Schwarz.** ASV CDDCA659.
Weber: Clarinet Concerto No. 2 in E flat major, Op. 64. *Spohr:* Clarinet Concerto No. 1 in C minor, Op. 26. *Crusell:* Clarinet Concerto No. 3 in B flat major, Op. 11.

1h 10' DDD

This nicely balanced and beautifully played recital couples three concertos of great charm from around the turn of the last century. All three works were written with specific clarinet virtuosos in mind. Weber's prowess as an operatic composer finds an exciting outlet in his charming Concerto which treats the clarinet very much in the role of soloistic diva. The Spohr Concerto is gentler in texture, searching out the more plangent qualities of the solo instrument. Crusell's three concertos are works of great charm and melodiousness and are rightly enjoying a just revival in recent years — no doubt due to Emma Johnson's characterful advocacy. She plays beautifully and with great taste throughout this disc. The English Chamber Orchestra accompany with great panache and Gerard Schwarz presides sympathetically. The recording is good with a pleasantly immediate presentation of the soloist.

RUSSIAN MUSIC. [a]**London Symphony Chorus; London Symphony Orchestra/Sir Georg Solti.** Decca Weekend Classics 417 689-2DC. From LXT6263 (2/67).
Borodin: Prince Igor — Overture; Polovtsian Dances[a]. *Glinka:* Russlan and Ludmilla — Overture. *Mussorgsky:* Khovanshchina — Prelude. A Night on the Bare Mountain.

1h 16' ADD 1/90 £ 9 P Ⓑ

This excellent collection of Russian orchestral favourites, recorded in 1966, has lost none of its brilliance, warmth or clarity of detail in this CD transfer. The recorded balance is superb and sharply focuses the scintillating playing of the LSO under Solti's baton. This is nowhere more noticeable than in the Overture to *Russlan and Ludmilla*. Solti takes this at breathtaking speed, and one wonders if it is possible to maintain this without coming to grief; doubts, however, are soon dispelled as we are treated to a continuous stream of dazzling virtuosity and meticulous articulation, without losing any warmth of tone. Mussorgsky's gentle, folk-song inspired *Khovanshchina* Prelude provides a perfect foil to the Overture, before we launch once more into the orchestral fireworks with Solti's powerfully evocative account of Mussorgsky's *Night on the Bare Mountain*: a spine-chilling depiction of a witches' sabbath on St John's Eve, whose orgiastic revels are finally exorcized by the tolling of church bells. The two Borodin items that complete the disc come from his opera *Prince Igor* — the twelfth-century Russian warrior hero who was captured by the Polovtsians. The Overture is beautifully played, with a rich and sumptuous tone and equal amounts of élan, and the "Polovtsian Dances" are heard here in the complete version, with its percussion accompanied first dance and chorus (both sometimes omitted), and is the finest available version on disc. An ideal encapsulation of splendid Russian music and a bargain not to be missed.

NEW REVIEW

SAXOPHONE CONCERTOS. John Harle (sax); **Academy of St Martin in the Fields/Sir Neville Marriner.** EMI CDC7 54301-2.
Debussy (ed. Harle): Rapsodie. *Glazunov:* Saxophone Concerto in E flat, Op. 109. *Heath:* Out of the Cool. *Ibert:* Concertino da camera. *R.R. Bennett:* Saxophone Concerto. *Villa-Lobos:* Fantasia.

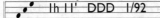 1h 11' DDD 1/92

As the issue of a mixed marriage the saxophone has had problems in gaining general acceptance in 'respectable' (musical) society. Sigurd Rascher did wonders for it in the pre-war years, but overall its image has remained what it has been throughout this century, that of an instrument which rose to fame in houses of ill repute and smoky dens in which jazz developed — and from which came the players with the most fluent techniques. At the same time the saxophone's potential as a solo instrument was recognized by a number of notable composers, among them Glazunov and Ibert in the 1930s, Villa-Lobos in 1958 and, some decades later, by Bennett and Heath — the last a composer with a jazz pedigree. Debussy preceded all these but, writing for a lady of his acquaintance who had breathing problems, didn't really have his heart in it; his *Rapsodie* is here presented with worthier orchestration by John Harle. Harle is the virtuoso for whom the saxophone may have long been waiting; the selected works show his splendid musicianship and spectacular technical command to good advantage. If you have any prejudice against the saxophone that is less than incurable, this outstanding disc could easily change your mind — as well as introducing you to some unfamiliar and attactive music.

NEW REVIEW

SCANDINAVIAN SUITES. Guildhall String Ensemble/Robert Salter. RCA Victor Red Seal RD60439.
Nielsen: Little Suite in A minor, FS6. *Grieg:* Holberg Suite, Op. 40. Two Elegiac Melodies, Op. 34. Two Melodies, Op. 53. *Sibelius:* Romance in C major, Op. 42. *Wirén:* Serenade for strings, Op. 11.

 1h 10' DDD 3/92

All of these, with the possible exception of the Sibelius *Romance*, are popular repertoire pieces, and are eminently well served by the excellent Guildhall String Ensemble and Robert Salter. *The Classical Catalogue* lists few alternatives of the Nielsen and the Wirén that are finer; and although the Grieg pieces are far more generously represented on disc the Guildhall Strings can more than hold their own. Indeed these performances are touched with distinction. Tempos are sensibly judged and their phrasing and blend are admirable. Yet while they are attentive to every detail of dynamic nuance and tonal finesse, there is no trace of self-consciousness. The second of the Grieg *Melodies*, Op. 53, is particularly affecting in their hands. The recording, made at Forde Abbey, Chard in Somerset, is spectacularly good, having altogether excellent range, body and presence.

SYMPHONIC SPECTACULAR. Cincinnati Pops Orchestra / Erich Kunzel. Telarc CD80170.
Shostakovich: Festival Overture, Op. 96. *Wagner:* DIE WALKURE — Ride of the Valkyries. *Falla:* El amor brujo — Ritual fire dance. *Bizet:* L'Arlésienne — Suite No. 2: Farandole. *Järnefelt:* Praeludium. *Chabrier:* España. *Tchaikovsky:* Marche slave, Op. 31. *Halvorsen:* Entry of the Boyars. *Enescu:* Roumanian Rhapsody No. 1 in A major, Op. 11. *Khachaturian:* Gayaneh — Sabre dance.

54' DDD 10/89

From this disc's title you might suppose that it provides a diet of music that is loud, fast, and luridly orchestrated — and you wouldn't be far wrong in that assessment. Yet there must be some leavening to make this palatable and the Cincinnati Pops provide this in those unguarded moments that most of these works contain, when more reposeful ideas allow the players to bring gentle solos and quiet dialogues to the fore. The opening of the first of Enescu's *Roumanian* Rhapsodies, some episodes in Chabrier's *España*, and much of Järnefelt's *Praeludium* are such instances, and the playing here is particularly refined and atmospheric. When the heat is on, the orchestra reveals its familiarity with this music and lets rip with invigorating zest. The recording copes unobtrusively with all this, without complaint or artificial highlighting, and the orchestra is genially set in its moderately resonant acoustic. Tchaikovsky's *Marche slave* is ideally treated by this ambience and Erich Kunzel can maintain a fair pace throughout without the chords producing too lengthy a delay. If a collection of lollipops is what you are looking for, you could do a lot worse than opting for this nicely balanced selection.

TRUMPET CONCERTOS. Håkan Hardenberger (tpt); **Academy of St Martin in the Fields / Sir Neville Marriner.** Philips 420 203-2PH.
Hummel: Trumpet Concerto in E major. *Hertel:* Trumpet Concerto in D major. *J. Stamitz* (realized Boustead): Trumpet Concerto in D major. *Haydn:* Trumpet Concerto in E flat major, HobVIIe/1.

59' 12/87

This recording made such a remarkable impression when it first appeared in 1987 that it created overnight a new star in the firmament of trumpeters. The two finest concertos for the trumpet are undoubtedly those of Haydn and Hummel and Hardenberger plays them here with a combination of sparkling bravura and stylish elegance that are altogether irresistible. Marriner and his Academy accompany with characteristic finesse and warmth, with the lilting dotted rhythms of the first movement of the Hummel, seductively jaunty. The lovely *Andante* of the Haydn is no less beguiling and both finales display a high spirited exuberance and an easy bravura which make the listener smile with pleasure. He is no less distinctive in the lesser concerto of Johann Hertel and the other D major work attributed to Johann Stamitz but probably written by someone with the unlikely name of J.B. Holzbogen. This takes the soloist up into the stratosphere of his range and provides him also with some awkward leaps. The Hertel work also taxes the soloist's technique to the extremities but Hardenberger essays all these difficulties with an enviably easy aplomb and remains fluently entertaining throughout. The recording gives him the most vivid realism and presence but it is a pity that the orchestral backcloth is so reverberant; otherwise the sound is very natural.

NEW REVIEW
TRUMPET CONCERTOS. [a]**Hannes Läubin,** [b]**Wolfgang Läubin,** [c]**Bernhard Läubin** (tpts); **English Chamber Orchestra / Simon Preston** (hpd, org). DG 431 817-2GH.

Telemann: Concerto in D major for three trumpets, timpani, two oboes, strings and continuo[abc]. Concerto in D major for three trumpets, timpani, strings and continuo[abc]. **Rathgeber:** Concerto in E flat major for two trumpets, two violins and continuo, Op. 6 No. 15[ac]. **Franceschini:** Sonata in D major for two trumpets, strings and continuo[ab]. **Albinoni:** Concerto in B flat major for trumpet and orchestra[a]. **Vivaldi:** Concerto in C major for two trumpets, strings and continuo, RV537[ab].

46' DDD 12/91

This is a disc of trumpet concertos with a difference. All the works included here except one (the Albinoni B flat major Concerto, originally written for oboe) involve two or more of the very gifted Laubin family of virtuosos. The first piece by Telemann calls not only for three trumpets, but a pair of oboes, too, and the wind and brass instruments sing along together with the most colourful interplay of ideas. There are five movements and the composer's invention is inexhaustibly diverse. The Double Concerto by Rathgeber is hardly less winning, with glittering bravura in the two outer movements while the relaxed central *Adagio* makes a captivating contrast of expressive repose. The Double Concerto by Vivaldi is better known and does not disappoint here while the Franceschini Sonata has four sections, none of which outstay their welcome. Telemann's second Triple Concerto is perhaps less memorable than the work with oboes, but still enjoyable when presented with such assurance. The vital solo playing is matched throughout by spiritedly polished accompaniments from the ECO and Simon Preston, who also provides the organ continuo. What a good case this beautifully recorded concerto makes for playing these baroque works on modern instruments!

TWENTIETH-CENTURY FLUTE CONCERTOS. Jennifer Stinton (fl); [a]**Geoffrey Browne** (cor ang); **Scottish Chamber Orchestra/Steuart Bedford.** Collins Classics 1210-2.
Honegger: Concerto da camera[a]. **Ibert:** Flute Concerto (1934). **Nielsen:** Flute Concerto, FS119. **Poulenc** (orch. L. Berkeley): Flute Sonata.

1h 6' DDD 8/91

This is basically a vehicle for the artistry of the flautist Jennifer Stinton who presents two flute concertos (by Nielsen and Ibert) plus a transcription of the Poulenc Flute Sonata and a duo concertante by Honegger for flute, cor anglais and strings dating from the period of the Fourth Symphony. The Honegger in which Jennifer Stinton is joined by Geoffrey Browne will come as a surprise to those music-lovers who have not encountered it before; it is pastoral in character and has enormous charm and these artists play with great sympathy for the idiom. Gallic charm is a feature of the Ibert Concerto which also comes off very well. Stinton gives thoroughly expert performances both of this lollipop and Sir Lennox Berkeley's arrangement of the no-less delightful Poulenc. The note reminds us that Honegger was present at the first performance of the Nielsen Concerto (which took place

Jennifer Stinton   [photo: Collins Classics

in Paris in 1926), which as the only Scandinavian piece is the 'odd-man-out' here. Though it is less brilliant than the Gallois performance, it is well played and the recording is very good in respect to balance, naturalness and presence.

NEW REVIEW

TWENTIETH CENTURY PLUS. [f]**Andrew Marriner** (cl); [ace]**BBC Symphony Orchestra**/[a]**Peter Eötvös,** [c]**Matthias Bamert,** [e]**Lothar Zagrosek;** [b]**BBC Philharmonic Orchestra/Sir Peter Maxwell Davies;** [f]**London Symphony Orchestra/Michael Tilson Thomas;** [d]**English Chamber Orchestra/ Steuart Bedford.** Collins Classics 2001/5-2. Items marked [a] recorded at a performance in the Royal Albert Hall, London on August 30th, 1990, [b] Cheltenham Town Hall, July 12th, 1990, [c], [d] and [e] recorded in association with the Arts Council.
2001-2: **Birtwistle:** Earth Dances[a]. *2002-2:* **Maxwell Davies:** Caroline Mathilde — Concert Suite from Act One[b]. *2003-2:* **Saxton:** In the beginning[c]. Music to celebrate the resurrection of Christ[d]. *2004-2:* **Mason:** Lighthouses of England and Wales[e]. *2005-2:* **Tavener:** The Repentant Thief[f].

⑤ 37', 25', 30', 16', 20' DDD 3/92 ⓟ ❓

No, not a five-CD set, but five separately available CD singles, each featuring the music of a contemporary British composer. At first sight the overall title "Twentieth Century Plus" may seem a contradiction in terms (the longest CD has a duration of only 37 minute) but when one considers that the price of each CD is considerably less than that of a full-price issue and that both performances and recordings are of exceptionally high quality then these are bargains indeed. The most important (and long awaited) issue here is perhaps Birtwistle's large and impressive orchestral work — *Earth Dances*. Though massively complex in its construction and organization of material, *Earth Dances* can be a richly rewarding experience for the listener. Its title relates both to the 'geological' strata-like layers of the music, and often violent surface energy that almost makes the earth dance. Tavener's *The Repentant Thief* for clarinet and orchestra is built around a rondo-like structure made up of 10 segments — five "Refrains", three "Dances" and two "Laments", and its title refers to the thief who was crucified with Jesus on Golgotha. It was composed shortly after Tavener had finished work on two large scale works (*Resurrection* and the opera *Mary of Egypt*) and is described by the composer as "a shorter, simple and rather primitive piece". Its simplicity, clear-cut formal scheme and tunefulness make it an immediately accessible and absorbing experience, and this is all the more enhanced by a magical performance of the solo clarinet part by Andrew Marriner. Like the *Eight Songs for a Mad King* before it, the Concert Suite from Act 1 of the ballet *Caroline Mathilde* by Maxwell Davies explores the subject of madness — Caroline Mathilde was the wife of the unbalanced King Christian VII of Denmark. The ballet traces the King's gradual mental deterioration, and his wife's subsequent love affair with the King's physician (Dr Struensee) through a series of short tableaux that mix Maxwell Davies's musical parody style with his more acerbic and intricate methods of composing. The remaining discs feature music by the younger composers Benedict Mason and Robert Saxton. The highly original, if somewhat unusual *Lighthouses of England and Wales* reveals Mason to be a composer of a striking individuality, not to mention an extremely gifted orchestrator, and Saxton's richly colourful pieces — *In the beginning* and *Music to celebrate the resurrection of Christ* — continue the composer's interest in the religious theme of darkness into light.

NEW REVIEW

VICTORIAN CONCERT OVERTURES. English Northern Philharmonia/ David Lloyd-Jones. Hyperion CDA66515.
Macfarren: Chevy Chace. *Pierson:* Romeo and Juliet. *Sullivan:* Macbeth.

Corder: Prospero. *Elgar:* Froissart, Op. 19. *Parry:* Overture to an Unwritten Tragedy. *Mackenzie:* Britannia, Op. 52.

Ih 7' DDD 1/92 ❓

With the exception of Elgar's *Froissart*, none of the concert overtures featured on this valuable Hyperion disc have remained in the repertory, and indeed, this release stands as a fitting tribute to the unwarranted neglect of some splendid music. Through no particular fault of their own, the works of many composers prominent in British musical life a century or so ago have fallen into virtual, if not total oblivion, and David Lloyd-Jones and the English Northern Philharmonia make the best possible case for a timely revival of interest in this unique area. The lively rhythmic energy and genuine melodic worth of George Macfarren's *Chevy Chace* Overture makes it an ideal curtain-raiser for any orchestral concert, and the work found willing advocates in Wagner and Mendelssohn, both of whom included it in public concerts. Even though Macfarren, a blind stalwart of the mid-Victorian musical establishment, does not hide his admiration for Beethoven's Seventh Symphony, this engaging work will be a revelation to many listeners, as will Sullivan's superbly dramatic *Macbeth* Overture, intended for Sir Henry Irving's 1888 Lyceum season. The influence of the new German school looms large in Frederick Corder's idiomatic *Prospero*, and the sonorous Wagnerian gestures are convincing, even if any Shakespearian connections are rather vague, as is the case with Hugo Pierson's competent *Romeo and Juliet* overture, a work in which the enmity of bitter family rivalry is subordinate to expressive piquancy and grace. Elgar scored his first real orchestral triumph with *Froissart*, a depiction of knightly renown of noble utterance; the Parry work which follows it is the least memorable work here, whilst Mackenzie makes good use of Dr Arne's famous tune, in his nautical overture, *Britannia*. The performances are consistently alert and spontaneous and much of the music, although unfamiliar, will fascinate adventurous devotees of British music.

NEW REVIEW

WALTON CONDUCTS WALTON. [a]**Dennis Noble** (bar); [a]**Huddersfield Choral Society;** [a]**Liverpool Philharmonic Orchestra,** [b]**Philharmonia Orchestra,** [c]**London Philharmonic Orchestra,** [d]**Hallé Orchestra/Sir William Walton.** EMI Great Recordings of the Century mono CDH7 63381-2. Text included.
Belshazzar's Feast[a] (from HMV C3330/34, 3/43). Henry V[b] — Death of Falstaff; Touch her soft lips and part (both from C3480, 1/46). Scapino — comedy overture[b] (HMV DB21499, 8/52). Façade[c] — Suites Nos. 1 and 2 (C2836/7, 5/36 and C3042, 1/39). Spitfire Prelude and Fugue[d] (C3359, 8/43). Siesta[c] (C3042).

Ih 19' ADD 4/92

In his younger days Walton was an exciting conductor of his own music, far more so than in his comfortable middle and old age. So although EMI re-recorded the composer in most of the items listed above during the LP era, they have been right to go back to the original versions. The major work here, *Belshazzar's Feast*, was recorded under the auspices of the British Council, and was an amazing venture in time of war. There is certainly the atmosphere of a special occasion in the performance, with everybody singing and playing their hearts out, and Walton driving his forces with enormous energy. Dennis Noble was the soloist at the work's first performance: he sings in a highly dramatic fashion, and with perfect diction. The recording sounds dated of course, but the transfer has been well-made. Ensemble is not always perfect in the *Façade* Suites, but the LPO play with tremendous zest and high spirits. Here the recording does sound a little confined. *Scapino* was recorded some years later, in rather better sound, and Walton gets magnificently vital playing from the superb Philharmonia Orchestra.

The four remaining shorter pieces all receive excellent performances, and the sound is never less than acceptable. This is a desirable reissue and a must for all who enjoy Walton's music.

WIEN MODERN. [a]**Vienna Jeunesse Choir; Vienna Philharmonic Orchestra/Claudio Abbado.** DG 429 260-2GH. Texts and translations included. Recorded at performances in the Musikverein, Vienna in October 1988. *Boulez:* Notations I-IV (1945/78). *Ligeti:* Atmosphères (1961). Lontano (1967). *Nono:* Liebeslied (1954)[a]. *Rihm:* Départ (1988)[a].

46' DDD 4/90

Live recordings of contemporary music concerts are, understandably, rare. Too much can go wrong: in particular, the playing, however well-rehearsed, can develop the rough edges of anxiety and even hostility which make for dispiriting listening, especially when repeated. All the more reason, then, to celebrate the fact that *Wien Modern* is something of a triumph. Even without the crowning glory heard at the actual event, Berg's great set of *Three Orchestral Pieces*, Op. 6, the programme has the strong central focus of two of Ligeti's hypnotic orchestral soundscapes, played with brilliant precision under Abbado's strong yet never over-bearing control. The Boulez miniatures — reworkings of early piano pieces — are no less riveting. The rarity, Nono's early exercise in 12-note lyricism, and the novelty, Wolfgang Rihm's specially-composed Rimbaud setting, are not on the same high level of inspiration, but in these secure, confident performances, with an electric, live concert atmosphere conveyed in a first-class recording, they contribute substantially to what was, unmistakably, a very special musical occasion.

NEW REVIEW

WORKS FOR CHAMBER ORCHESTRA. Polish Chamber Orchestra/Jan Stanienda ([a]vn). Linn Records CKD001. Recorded at a performance in the City Halls, Glasgow on May 24th, 1990.
Bach: Violin Concerto in A minor, BWV1041[a]. *Bartók:* Divertimento, Sz113. *Elgar:* Introduction and Allegro, Op. 47. *Mozart:* Divertimento in F major, K138/125c. *Vivaldi:* 12 Concertos, Op. 3, "L'estro armonico" — No. 10 in B minor.

1h 10' DDD 12/91

Under its long-standing conductor, Jerzy Maksymiuk, the Polish Chamber Orchestra developed a world-wide reputation during the early 1980s for its polished virtuosity and clarity of articulation. Maksymiuk now has close links with the BBC Scottish Symphony Orchestra, and it seems fitting that this association enabled his Polish colleagues to take part in the Glasgow 1990 Mayfest when this attractive programme, directed by the Polish Chamber Orchestra's concert-master, Jan Stanienda, was recorded live. The orchestral and solo playing is masterly, and the recording superb, resulting in a wholly credible and enjoyable listening experience. The effervescent Mozart Divertimento reveals the stylish and refined orchestra to be as fine as ever, with some impressively clear violin articulation in rapid passagework. Stanienda is joined by soloists from the orchestra in Vivaldi's Concerto for four violins from the *L'estro armonico* set, and this performance, like his own reading of the A minor Bach Concerto, is dramatic and large-scale in concept. Meanwhile, the convulsive energy and latent remorse of Bartók's *Divertimento* receives a highly charged reading, characterized by an added sense of immediacy only really attainable in the concert-hall. The supremely disciplined Polish players revel in Bartók's taxing score, making this the highlight of their programme. They also offer a noble and committed version of Elgar's masterpiece for strings, the *Introduction and Allegro*, played with great breadth and appropriate gravity, especially in the response of the solo quartet.

This enjoyable disc recreates all the excitement and sense of occasion of a public event, while the recorded sound is vivid and spacious.

WORKS FOR OBOE AND ORCHESTRA. John de Lancie (ob); [a]**London Symphony Orchestra/André Previn;** [b]**chamber orchestra/Max Wilcox.**
RCA Victor Gold Seal GD87989. Items marked [a] from SB6721, 11/67,
[b] Recorded in 1987 and new to UK.
Français. L'horloge de flore[a]. *Ibert.* Symphonie concertante[a]. *Satie* (orch.
Debussy). Gymnopédie No. 1[a]. *R. Strauss.* Oboe Concerto[b].

1h 12' [a]ADD/[b]DDD 12/91

This delightful collection focuses on the career and talent of the American oboist John de Lancie. De Lancie was the American soldier who in 1945 asked Strauss to write him a few bars of music for the oboe — the result, no less, was the delightfully sunny Oboe Concerto. De Lancie's return to the United States prevented him from attending the première, but a few years later Strauss granted him permission to give the work its American première. Bureaucracy and protocol intervened however, and in the event the solo part was entrusted to Mitchell Miller. This 1987 recording (and a very fine one it is too) therefore closes the circle that began over 45 years ago in the Bavarian Alps. It was de Lancie too, who commissioned Françaix's gorgeous suite for oboe and orchestra, *L'horloge de flore* ("The flower clock"). Each of its seven movements represent a flower (and the time of day that the bloom opens), in the Flower Clock developed by the Swedish botanist Carl von Linne. Quite why this charming and melodious work should not be more well known and indeed performed is a complete mystery — it would certainly be a winner with any audience. Inexplicable, too, is the apparent neglect in the catalogue at present of Ibert's *Symphonie concertante* for oboe and strings. This substantial work is a fine example of Ibert's natural gift for seamless melodic invention and exquisite string writing; if you know and love the Flute Concerto then this work should be next on your list of acquisitions. The Françaix and Ibert items were recorded in 1966 but are remarkably fresh and clear, with Previn and the LSO providing most sympathetic accompaniments.

WORKS FOR TWO AND FOUR HORNS AND ORCHESTRA. Israel Philharmonic Orchestra/Meir Rimon (hn). Pickwick IMP Masters MCD31.
Handel (arr. Rimon): Double Concerto in F major. *Barsanti:* Concerto Grosso for two horns in D major, Op. 3 No. 4. *Haensel:* Double Concerto in F major, Op. 80. *O. Franz:* Concert Piece for two horns in F major, Op. 4. *Hübler:* Concerto for four horns in F major. *Schumann:* Konzertstück for two horns in F major, Op. 86.

1h 7' DDD 2/92 £

Meir Rimon was born in 1946 and, sadly, died just after completing this recording. It demonstrates that he was not only a skilful horn player but also a versatile and positively hyperactive one, for he plays all the solo parts himself — 16 in six works — conducts the orchestra, and arranged some of the music. The playing and conducting obviously involved multitracking, and you may feel that a double concerto goes better with two different artists and instruments, just as a quadruple one is better with four. But the result here is satisfying, and at least Rimon gives us a unified view of each piece. Handel's Concerto exists as two quick outer movements and Rimon has placed another Handel piece between them as a slow one to make up the usual three. The cheerful finale is familiar, being identical to a hornpipe in the *Water Music*; Francesco Barsanti, A. Haensel,

Oscar Franz and Heinrich Hübler are little known figures (we don't even know Haensel's first name), and the musical quality here is more patchy. But the Barsanti *Concerto grosso* has a richly Italianate slow movement and Franz's *Concert Piece* conveys the "happy mood" that the composer asks for. Hübler's Concerto for four horns is a pleasingly warm romantic work, written in 1854 and owing something to the example set shortly before by Schumann with his strikingly vigorous and telling *Concert Piece* (in three movements and a concerto in all but name) for the same combination. While there's a lot of F major in this programme, it is attractive and well recorded and features this golden-toned instrument in the hands of a master performer.

WORKS FOR VIOLIN. Cho-Liang Lin (vn); [a]**Sandra Rivers** (pf); [b]**Philharmonia Orchestra/Michael Tilson Thomas;** [c]**Chicago Symphony Orchestra/Leonard Slatkin.** CBS Masterworks CD44902. Items marked [a] from IM39133 (2/85); [b] 39007 (6/84), [c] 42315 (3/87).
Mendelssohn: Violin Concerto in E minor, Op. 64[b]. *Bruch:* Violin Concerto No. 1 in G minor, Op. 26[c]. *Sarasate:* Introduction et Tarantelle, Op. 43. *Kreisler:* Liebesfreud[a].

• 1h 1' DDD 3/91   £

The current catalogue is not short of good recordings of the Mendelssohn Violin Concerto and Bruch's First Concerto, and the two certainly make a good pair on a CD, particularly when the 50 odd minutes that they take are complemented, as here, with two short pieces (though only with piano) by virtuoso violinists who not surprisingly wrote superbly for their instrument. At medium price, this is a desirable disc, for Cho-Liang Lin plays with passion and tenderness, bringing out the various, but always romantic, moods of the two main works and the graceful *salon* charm of the others. He has an unfailingly expressive tone quality, and can shape an individual phrase with elegance while keeping in perspective the longer term issues of paragraphs and indeed whole movements. Maybe some other players have found a more sensuous beauty in the melody of the slow movement in the Mendelssohn, and let themselves go more as regards tempo in the finale, but Lin's slight restraint pays dividends with its own kind of aristocratic eloquence and his refinement is also a positive feature in the Bruch. The recordings are not especially new and come from different locations, which in three cases are American ones: the oldest is that of the Mendelssohn, which was recorded in London and dates from 1982. But the sound is well enough matched and fully digital as well as offering both clarity and atmosphere.

NEW REVIEW
WORKS FOR VIOLIN AND ORCHESTRA. Joshua Bell (vn); **Royal Philharmonic Orchestra/Andrew Litton.** Decca 433 519-2DH.
Saint-Saëns: Introduction and Rondo capriccioso, Op. 28. *Massenet:* THAIS — Méditation. *Sarasate:* Zigeunerweisen, Op. 20. *Chausson:* Poème, Op. 25. *Ysaÿe:* Caprice d'après l'etude en forme de valse de Saint-Saëns. *Ravel:* Tzigane.

• 1h DDD 1/92

The Spaniard, Pablo de Sarasate, and the great Belgian virtuoso, Eugene Ysaÿe, both travelled to study in Paris during the second half of the last century, and although both were celebrated as distinguished exponents of violin technique, their collective influence upon the composers active in France at much the same time proved to be far more significant, as this brilliant selection of virtuoso showpieces will readily confirm. The young American violinist, Joshua Bell, himself a grand-pupil of Ysaÿe via his teacher, Joseph Gingold, is heard to superb advantage here in commanding performances of music which will captivate as

Joshua Bell   [photo: Decca/Mouison]

much as it will astonish. Bell captures the heady bravura of Saint-Saëns *Introduction and Rondo capriccioso* with breathtaking ease, and his spiccato playing in the coda is little short of phenomenal. Sarasate's perennial favourite *Zigeunerweisen* will also astound, with Bell's mastery of the whole panoply of technical effects, including multiple-stopping and left hand pizzicato, contributing to an authentic gypsy-style performance. No recording of this kind would be complete without the celebrated "Méditation" from Massenet's *Thaïs*, made especially compelling here, in Bell's affectionately rich-toned account. The same tonal refinement and sensitivity characterize his elegiac reading of the *Poème* by Chausson, ably supported by the Royal Philharmonic Orchestra under Andrew Litton. Ysaÿe's *Caprice d'après l'etude* is another, although rather less familiar *tour de force*, affording every possibility for virtuosic display, although it does not challenge Ravel's devilish *Tzigane* in terms of pure technical difficulty. This truly hair-raising rendition of the *Tzigane* would bring any concert audience to its feet, and Bell is wholly at ease with its Bartókian gypsy style. This thrilling playing crowns a hugely enjoyable collection from this dazzling young virtuoso. The clear and incisive Decca sound ensures that the forces are balanced effectively, and the natural ambience of Watford Town Hall lends a realistic dramatic weight to full orchestral climaxes, without undue spotlighting of the soloist. An admirable and meticulous release, then, whose appeal will gain Joshua Bell many new admirers.

NEW REVIEW
WORKS FOR VIOLIN AND ORCHESTRA. Hideko Udagawa (vn); London Philharmonic Orchestra/Kenneth Klein. Pickwick IMP Classics PCD966.
Glazunov: Violin Concerto in A minor, Op. 82. *Tchaikovsky* (arr. Glazunov): Souvenir d'un lieu cher, Op. 42. *Chausson:* Poème, Op. 25. *Sarasate:* Danzas españolas, Op. 22 No. 1 (Romanze andaluza). *Saint-Saëns* (trans. Ysaÿe): Caprice en forme de valse, Op. 52.

1h 4'   DDD   3/92

Although it begins with a full-scale concerto, this disc is essentially a collection of what Sir Thomas Beecham used to call lollipops, in other words romantic works intended to fall sweetly on the ear, which in this case are for violin and orchestra. The Glazunov Concerto was written in the early twentieth century but is a romantic Russian work in the tradition of Tchaikovsky although certainly none the worse for that. Indeed, for people who wish there were more such concertos in the repertory this one may confidently be recommended, particularly as Hideko Udagawa plays it with full-blooded, passionate commitment. Thereafter the programme is of shorter pieces, each one a fine example of its kind, with the Tchaikovsky triptych, *Souvenir d'un lieu cher* (which was actually orchestrated by Glazunov) being particularly winning, with the final "Mélodie" as the most glowing gem of all. However, Chausson's eloquent and ardent *Poème* for violin and orchestra is also a masterpiece and, like the Saint-Saëns *Caprice en forme de valse*, which was orchestrated by the violinist Eugène Ysaÿe, reminds us how lovingly and idiomatically French composers, too, wrote for the violin. The solo instrument is placed fairly close in this richly-toned recording, but few will mind that in this repertory and the orchestral playing of the LPO under Kenneth Klein matches Udagawa's own warmly expressive and strongly projected style.

Chamber

CONTEMPORARY WORKS FOR STRING QUARTET. Kronos Quartet (David Harringon, John Sherba, vns; Hank Dutt, va; Joan Jeanrenaud, vc). Elektra-Nonesuch 7559-79111-2. From 979 111-1 (7/87).
P. Sculthorpe: String Quartet No. 8. **Sallinen:** String Quartet No. 3. **Glass:** Company. **C. Nancarrow:** String Quartet. **J. Hendrix** (arr. Rifkin): Purple Haze.

 49' DDD 2/89

Of all string quartets currently active none has done more than the Kronos to change the image of the medium. Snappy dressing and theatrical presentation are part of it, so are rock arrangements like the Jimi Hendrix *Purple Haze* on this CD. But there is nothing trendy about their choice of repertoire and the technical finish of their playing can stand the closest scrutiny — it's just that they have an added rhythmic bounce and colouristic flair which are the envy of many another ensemble. The stylistic and geographical spread of this programme is impressive. There is Sculthorpe, an Australian responding to the music of Bali, Sallinen, a Finn responding hauntingly to his own country's folk-music and Nancarrow, an American now resident in Mexico and best known for his zany series of Studies for pianola. This selection should win over any listener wary of anything more modern than Bartók. And you could not wish for more full-blooded advocacy or more vivid recording quality.

FRENCH CHAMBER MUSIC. [a]**Catherine Cantin** (fl); [b]**Maurice Bourgue** (ob); [c]**Michel Portal** (cl); [d]**Amaury Wallez** (bn); [e]**André Cazalet** (hn); **Pascal Rogé** (pf). Decca 425 861-2DH.
Saint-Saëns: Caprice sur des airs danois et russes, Op. 79[abc]. **d'Indy:** Sarabande et menuet, Op. 72[abcde]. **Roussel:** Divertissement, Op. 6[abcde]. **Tansman:** Le Jardin du Paradis — Danse de la sorcière[abcde]. **Françaix:** L'heure du berger[abce]. **Poulenc:** Elégie[e]. **Milhaud:** Sonata for flute, oboe, clarinet and piano, Op. 47[abc].

1h 7' DDD 5/91

French composers are noted for their special fondness for writing for wind instruments, but their wide diversity of styles is illustrated by this attractive disc, which is notable for superbly clean and sensitive playing by musicians in complete accord with each other and in instinctive sympathy with the music. Of the three works here for wind quintet and piano, the Roussel *Divertissement* is a particular delight, in turn sprightly and seductive; the d'Indy movements (transcribed from an earlier suite for the curious combination of trumpet, two flutes and string quartet) are an expressively contrapuntal sarabande and an oddly chirpy minuet; and the pungent Tansman dance is from an unfinished ballet. Jean Françaix's habitual spirit of *gaminerie* reigns in his three portraits for wind quartet and piano, written with his usual consummate craftsmanship. The works for wind trio and piano could scarcely be more unlike: Saint-Saëns's suave confection on (reputedly bogus) Danish and Russian airs, with a brilliant piano part, and Milhaud's often abrasive sonata (despite a pastoral opening), which ends with a dirge for victims of a Spanish influenza epidemic. And there's Poulenc's elegy for Dennis Brain, its broad lament tinged with just a touch of the humour that Dennis himself would have enjoyed.

GERMAN CHAMBER MUSIC. Barthold Kuijken (fl); **Sigiswald Kuijken** (vn, va da gamba); **Wieland Kuijken** (vc, va da gamba); **Robert Kohnen** (hpd). Accent ACC58019D. From ACC8019 (8/81).
J.S. Bach: Trio Sonata in E flat major, BWV525 (trans. for flute, violin and continuo in G major). *C. P. E. Bach:* Trio Sonata in A major for flute, violin and continuo, Wq146. *Telemann:* Sonata in G major for flute, two violas da gamba and harpsichord. Suite in D minor for flute, violin and continuo.

• 57' DDD 3/86

A recital of carefully chosen pieces, sensitively played and extremely well recorded, makes this baroque anthology very appealing. The interpretative skills of these musicians are impressive, both on account of their thoughtfulness and for their unerring sense of an appropriate style. The repertoire consists mainly of rarely performed pieces of more than passing interest. The J.S. Bach 'Sonata in G major' is an arrangement for transverse flute, violin and continuo of the E flat Sonata for two manuals and pedal, whilst the two Telemann pieces show off the composer's chamber style at its most original and engaging. The C.P.E. Bach Trio Sonata, though marginally less interesting, perhaps, is a long way from being either dull or routine. Documentation is sketchy but is hardly required when the music speaks for itself as eloquently as this.

IN NOMINE. Fretwork (Richard Campbell, treb viols; Julia Hodgson, Richard Boothby, ten and bass viols; Elizabeth Liddle, treb and ten viols; William Hunt, treb, ten and great bass viols) with [a]**Christopher Wilson** (lte). Amon Ra CDSAR29.
Tallis: In Nomines — à 4 Nos. 1 and 2. *Tallis* (attrib.): Solfaing Song à 5[a]. Fantasia à 5 (reconstr. Milsom). Libera nos, salva nos à 5. *Tye:* In Nomines — à 5, "Crye"; "Trust". *Cornyshe:* Fa la sol à 3. *Baldwin:* In Nomine à 4. *Bull:* In Nomine à 5[a]. *Byrd:* In Nomine à 4 No. 2. Fantasia à 3 No. 3[a]. *Taverner:* In Nomines — for lute[a]; à 4. *Preston:* O lux beata Trinitas à 3[a]. *R. Johnson*: In Nomine à 4. *Parsons:* In Nomine à 5. Ut re mi fa sol la à 4. *Ferrabosco I:* In Nomine à 5[a]. Lute Fantasia No. 5[a]. Fantasia à 4[a].

• 1h DDD 3/88

For the wary, *In Nomines* are instrumental chamber works popular in England during the sixteenth and seventeenth centuries, in which counterpoints are woven around a pre-existing tune from the Sarum antiphon *Gloria tibi Trinitas*. Fretwork is an ensemble of young viol players who are rapidly revitalizing the English repertory. Many of the composers will be familiar; others — such as Tye, Cornyshe, Baldwin, Preston, Johnson and Parsons — will be known only to the initiated. Nevertheless, together they represent the core of a rich tradition of music for accomplished amateurs, music which kings and commoners alike enjoyed playing up until the Restoration. This is a very attractive and well recorded programme of undemanding music.

NEW REVIEW

ITALIAN RECORDER MUSIC. Amsterdam Loeki Stardust Quartet (Daniel Brüggen, Bertho Driever, Paul Leenhouts, Karel van Steenhoven, recs). L'Oiseau-Lyre 430 246-2OH.
Battiferri: Ricercare secundo. *Cima:* Canzon la Capriccio. *Conforti:*

Ricercar del quarto tono. *Frescobaldi:* Capriccio sopra la Spagnoletta. Canzon decima detta la Paulini. Ricercare terzo. Capriccio V sopra la Bassa Fiamenga. *Guami:* Canzons — La Bastina; La Brillantina; La Gentile. *Merula:* Canzons — La Ghirardella; La Merula. Dum Illuscescente Beati. Iste est Joannes. O Glorioso Domina. *Palestrina:* Lamentationes Hieremiae. *Trabaci:* Canto fermo primo del primo Tono. Canzona franzesa quinta sopra dunque credete ch'io. Canzona franzesa terza.

| 1h 2' DDD 2/92 |

None of the music in this programme was written for recorders but this is not important: it dates from a time when the boundaries between instrumental and vocal music were far less clear than they later became, and in which the music was very often more important than the identity of the instruments on which it was played. What mattered most was that the interwoven lines should be heard clearly and in proper balance. Italy was the Alma Mater of such music and it was also the country in which the recorder resisted the onslaught of the transverse flute for the longest. Few sounds are more depressing than that of an ensemble of mediocre recorder players, but few are more suited to presenting music of the above kind with the clarity and (thanks to the recording engineers) precise balance, and without a variety of tone-colours to seduce the ear in the direction of one line or another, than a recorder consort of the impeccable quality of the Amsterdam Loeki Stardust Quartet. For those who delight in hearing contrapuntal lines, mellifluously and ingeniously spun, this disc is custom-made.

JACQUELINE DU PRE — HER EARLY BBC RECORDINGS. Jacqueline du Pré, [f]William Pleeth (vcs); [deg]**Ernest Lush,** [c]**Stephen Kovacevich** (pfs). EMI Studio mono CDM7 63165/6-2. Recorded at broadcast performances on [a]January 7th, 1962, [b]January 26th, 1962, [c]February 25th, 1965, [dg]March 22nd, 1961, [e]September 3rd, 1962, [f]March 17th, 1963.
CDM7 63165-2 — Bach: Solo Cello Suites — No. 1 in G major, BWV1007[a]; No. 2 in D minor, BWV1008[b]. *Britten:* Cello Sonata in C major, Op. 65 — Scherzo and March[c]. *Falla* (arr. Maréchal): Suite populaire espagnole[d]. *CDM7 63166-2 — Brahms:* Cello Sonata No. 2 in F major, Op. 99[e]. *F. Couperin:* Nouveaux Concerts — Treizième Concert[f]. *Handel* (arr. Slatter): Oboe Concerto in G minor, HWV287[g].

| ② 1h 52' ADD 9/89 £ 9 P ▲ |

We owe the BBC and EMI a debt of gratitude for making these valuable recordings available on disc. The performances date from her mid- to late- teens, and reveal a maturity and passion that is rare in so young a performer. This,

together with her wonderful gift of communication, make these performances very special indeed. The two Bach Cello Suites have a magical, intimate poetry that transfixes the attention from the very first note and her beautifully phrased and lyrical readings more than compensate for any slight imperfections of articulation. Sadly we have only the Scherzo and March movements from the Britten Cello Sonata, and judging by the quality of these, a complete performance would surely have been a recording to treasure. These are sparkling performances, full of wit and good humour, reflecting the obvious rapport between the two young artists. The recording of Falla's *Suite populaire espagnole* dates from 1961 when du Pré was only 16 but is no less assured or technically accomplished. The performance is full of life and rhythmic vitality, with some very tender and expressive playing, as in the cantabile melodies of the "Nana" and "Cancion" movements. The mono recordings are not of the highest quality (the Bach Suites are taken from transcription discs, so there are traces of surface noise and clicks) but this is of little relevance when we are presented with playing as beautiful and captivating as this.

MUSIC FOR WIND ENSEMBLE. Aulos Quintet ([a]Peter Rijkx, fl; [a]Diethelm Jonas, ob; [a]Karl-Theo Adler, cl; [a]Ralph Sabow, bn; Dietmar Ullrich, hn). Schwann Musica Mundi 310087.
Briccialdi: Wind Quintet, Op. 124. *Lefébure:* Suite, Op. 57. *Rossini:* Wind Quartet No. 6[a]. *Taffanel:* Wind Quintet.

| 59' DDD 10/91 |

The image of wind music for some people is of something faintly comic, even perhaps of piping, burping and blasting, according to whether the instruments are high or low and playing softly or loudly — certainly not music offering the expressive sophistication that we associate with piano or strings. Nevertheless, in the hands of first-class players these instruments are as refined and subtle as any others. It's a pity that some of the great composers — Mozart is a notable exception — gave us little music for wind alone, though they often wrote splendidly for these instruments in orchestral music. Still, Rossini is a great figure, and even if the others represented in this nineteenth-century programme are not, they make up for lack of depth by writing superbly for the players. The members of the Aulos Wind Quintet are totally equal to this music and the performances are a delight — but then, so is the music itself, mainly on the lighter side and presented here with tremendous panache as well as affection. Each work here has its own kind of charm, and each player brings both skill and refinement to a satisfyingly well-blended whole; the second movement of Rossini's Quartet is particularly good at showing them off individually in a series of variations. The recording is clear, atmospheric and well balanced. This is a disc to give much delight.

ROMANTIC MUSIC FOR VIOLIN AND PIANO. Vera Vaidman (vn); **Emanuel Krasovsky** (pf). CDI/Pickwick PWK1137.
Tchaikovsky: Méditation, Op. 42 No. 1. Valse-Scherzo, Op. 34. Mélodie, Op. 42 No. 3. *Dvořák:* Violin Sonatina in G major, B183. *Schubert:* Violin Sonatina in A minor, D385. *Kreisler:* Schön Rosmarin. Liebeslied. Liebesfreud.

| 1h 11' DDD 6/90 |

Here is a splendid collection of inspired music for violin and piano, marvellously played and given a digital recording of great realism and immediacy. The Dvořák *Sonatina* was written in New York at around the same time that the great Czech composer created his most popular work, the *New World* Symphony, and it deserves to be equally well known. All four movements are brimming over with the same kind of memorable melody that makes the symphony such a favourite with the public. The first movement makes an impression of great vigour and impulse, the *Larghetto* sings beguilingly, the *Scherzo* dances vivaciously and the finale sparkles and introduces another quite lovely lyrical folksy melody which is instantly memorable and stays in the mind long after the work has concluded. Vera Vaidman's performance has great sympathy and spontaneity and her partner, Emanuel Krasovsky gives all the support she could ask for, though it is she who

dominates — for that is the way the music is written. The programme opens
with an engaging Tchaikovsky triptych, each miniature strikingly characterful and
the third, *Mélodie*, having that bittersweet Russian melancholy for which the
composer is famous. The Schubert *Sonatina* which follows the Dvořák has a
disarming, simple lyricism. Like the Dvořák it is in four movements: the *andante*
is gently eloquent, and the finale flows with captivating innocence. The
programme ends with three Kreisler lollipops, dashingly played, to end the
recital exuberantly. This disc is in the bargain price range and the recording is in
the demonstration class: on a minor label, with an Israeli source, it could be so
easily passed by, but it should be sought out, for its rewards are very
considerable.

**SCHERZOS FROM SEVENTEENTH CENTURY GERMANY. Cologne
Musica Antiqua/Reinhard Goebel.** Archiv Produktion 429 230-2AH.
J.H. Schmelzer: Balletto in G major, "Fechtschule". Polonische Sackpfeiffen in
G major. *Biber:* Sonata in B flat major, "Die Bauern-Kirchfartt genandt".
Battalia in D major. Serenade in C major, "Nightwatchman's Call". Sonata in
A major, "La Pastorella". Sonata jucunda in D major (attrib). Sonata in G major,
"Campanarum" (attrib). *J.J. Walther:* Sonata in G major, "Imitatione del
Cuccu".

 1h 6' DDD 1/91

This entertaining disc is not without its zany moments; do not, for instance, be
unduly deterred at the outset by hearing the band cross a spacious hallway or
saloon before tuning up, for what follows is a highly imaginative sequence of
largely unfamiliar pieces of a mildly programmatic character. Most of the music
hails from the Austrian south of Germany and contains that rewarding blend of
fantasy and virtuosity which Reinhard Goebel and his Musica Antiqua Köln
understand so well. They play with rhythmic clarity and a feeling for gesture and
Goebel, furthermore, overlooks neither the humour nor the charming eccentricities present in some of these fascinating pieces. His own solo violin playing in
Sonatas by Biber (*La Pastorella*) and Walther (*Imitatione del Cuccu*) is detailed,
incisive and passionate and he demands both these and other estimable qualities
from his ensemble. Unusual sonorities and startling harmonies are inherent in this
music and Goebel savours every one of them. Biber's *Battalia* is vividly interpreted, at times with ferocious but entirely appropriate zeal and the delightful
Nightwatchman's Call is played with warmth and sensibility. Goebel's accompanying essay and Arcimboldo's illustration provide a pleasing complement to an
entertaining programme.

NEW REVIEW

TRANSCRIPTIONS FOR GUITAR AND HARPSICHORD. Norbert Kraft
(gtr); **Bonnie Silver** (hpd). Chandos CHAN8937. All works transcribed by
Kraft and Silver.
Vivaldi: Lute Concerto, RV93. *Haydn:* Divertimenti a quattro, Op. 2 —
No. 2 in D major. *Boccherini:* Guitar Quintet No. 4 in D major, G448.
Rodrigo: Fantasia para un gentilhombre.

 54' DDD 11/91

The guitar and harpsichord are both plucked-string instruments and thus are
natural bedfellows, so too were the lute and harpsichord or virginal, yet there is
very little original repertory for either combination. The guitar in its present
form sprang to life in the early 1800s, when the harpsichord had fallen on hard
times, but in this century it has revived and the advent of numerous playing
partnerships has stimulated composers to write for them. This said, all the music
in this recording has been arranged by the performers from other sources, the

harpsichord gracefully wearing an 'orchestral' or 'chamber-strings' mantle and, in the Vivaldi and Haydn, with the guitar reading the lute's lines. The husband-and-wife duo of Kraft and Silver represents the marriage of two fine musicians and outstandingly capable performers, and is here responsible for the variety of beguiling sounds in which the light but good-quality music is dressed — and which are faithfully preserved in the recording. As a pleasingly new musical experience this would be hard to beat.

TWENTIETH-CENTURY CHAMBER WORKS. Jascha Heifetz (vn); [a]**Gregor Piatigorsky** (vc); [b]**Emanuel Bay**, [c]**Artur Rubinstein** (pfs). RCA Victor Gold Seal GD87871.
Debussy[b]: Violin Sonata in G minor. Préludes — Book 1, No. 8, La fille aux cheveux de lin (arr. Hartmann. Both mono and new to UK). *Respighi:* Violin Sonata in B minor[b] (new to UK). *Ravel* (arr. Roques): Sonatine in F sharp minor — Menuet[b] (from RB16243, 6/61). Piano Trio in A minor[ac] (HMV mono DB9620/22, 6/51). *Martinů:* Duo[a] (SB6661, 7/66).

 1h 13' ADD 9/90

Though the twentieth century has produced many fine violinists, the name of Jascha Heifetz still inspires a special awe, not least among fellow musicians, for his playing had exceptional eloquence and personality alongside a technical command that he displayed not only in dexterity but more often than not by imparting a subtle, inimitable colour to his tone when shaping a phrase. The works here are of the violinist's own time, for he had already made his début aged five a decade before Debussy wrote his Violin Sonata towards the end of the First World War. He recorded that Sonata with Emanuel Bay in 1950, but we would not know it when hearing the sound as successfully remastered here, and this is playing of real distinction, even if the elusive middle movement is arguably over-forceful. Heifetz and his celebrated colleagues are also impressive in the Ravel Trio recorded in the same year, also a wartime work but of a different kind, having great power and feeling, though the gentle little Minuet from the piano Sonatine is taken too briskly. The Respighi and Martinů pieces are perhaps less striking at first, but here too we are fully held by the authority of the playing. As already suggested, little apology need be made for the sound in the major works despite the age of the recordings, though there is 78-type needle hiss in *La fille aux cheveux de lin* and one misses really quiet tone in the Ravel Trio. This disc is for everyone, not just for connoisseurs of fine violin playing.

TWENTIETH CENTURY OBOE MUSIC. Robin Williams (ob); [a]**Julian Kelly** (pf). Factory Classical FACD236.
Poulenc: Oboe Sonata[a]. *Britten:* Six Metamorphoses after Ovid, Op. 49. *Hindemith:* Oboe Sonata[a]. *Lalliet:* Prelude and Variations[a].

49' DDD 1/90

A very enjoyable recital of twentieth-century oboe music. The Poulenc Sonata was written in 1962, and was one of his last compositions. It is largely elegiac in character and this is finely captured in this elegant and sensitive performance. The gently flowing tempo in the opening Elegie is just right, and Williams's carefully shaped phrasing has much beauty and symmetry. The spirit of Prokofiev (whose memory the work is dedicated to) seems to hover over the energetic Scherzo with its spiky rhythms and angular melodic line, and the sadness of the "Deploration" has great plangency. The highlight of the disc is Williams's performance of Britten's *Six Metamorphoses after Ovid*; this highly inventive piece for solo oboe is a set of six character studies after Greek mythological beings: Pan, Bacchus, Phaeton et al. Williams's musicality really shines through, coupling subtle dynamic shading (Pan and Niobe) with great dexterity (Arethusa).

Rhythmic vitality is strongly projected by both players in the jaunty opening movement of Hindemith's two movement Sonata (1938), and this is well contrasted with the more introspective *Sehr langsam* movement. A first-rate performance of Lalliet's *Prelude and Variations* rounds off the disc nicely. The recorded sound is fine, if a little close.

WORKS FOR VIOLA AND PIANO. Yuri Bashmet (va); **Mikhail Muntian** (pf). RCA Victor Red Seal RD60112.
Schubert: Sonata in A minor, D821, "Arpeggione". *Schumann:* Märchenbilder, Op. 113. Adagio and Allegro, Op. 70. *Bruch:* Kol nidrei, Op. 47.
Enescu: Konzertstück.

| | 1h 13' DDD 12/90 | |

The booklet tells us that Yuri Bashmet, aged 38 at the time of this recording, had already 30 new works for the viola dedicated to him. And on the strength of this recital, excellently recorded in 1989 in a Bristol church, one is tempted to predict that the number will very soon be doubled — not least because of this Russian artist's glorious tone. Perhaps first thanks should go to him and his closely attuned pianist, Mikhail Muntian, for enriching the CD catalogue with Georges Enescu's rarely heard *Konzertstück*, written in Paris in the composer's impressionable early twenties, and played here with intuitive understanding of its fantasy and lyrical rapture. Like that work, the four miniatures of Schumann's *Märchenbilder* of 1851 were also inspired by the viola itself, whereas Schumann's *Adagio and Allegro*, Bruch's *Kol nidrei* (based on one of the oldest and best-known synagogue melodies) and Schubert's A minor Sonata were originally written for valve-horn, cello and the now obsolete arpeggione respectively. But with his wide range of colour and his "speaking" phrasing Bashmet makes them all entirely his own, only causing the occasional raised eyebrow with slower tempo for slow numbers (such as Schumann's lullaby-like Op. 113, No. 4 and the *Adagio* of Schubert's Sonata) than could be enjoyed from players without his own fine-spun, intimately nuanced line. Strongly recommended.

Instrumental

THE ALDEBURGH RECITAL. Murray Perahia (pf). Sony Classical CD46437.
Beethoven: 32 Variations in C minor on an Original Theme, WoO80.
Schumann: Faschingsschwank aus Wien, Op. 26. *Liszt:* Hungarian Rhapsody No. 12, S244. Consolation No. 3 in D flat major, S172. *Rachmaninov:*
Etudes-tableaux, Op. 33 — No. 2 in C major. Etudes-tableaux, Op. 39 — No. 5 in E flat minor; No. 6 in A minor; No. 9 in D major.

| | 59' DDD 4/91 | | |

Murray Perahia's attachment to Beethoven and Schubert has always been close. What may surprise some of his followers is to find the second half of this recital given over to such overtly demonstrative romantics as Liszt and Rachmaninov. It was a programme he had recently played at London's Festival Hall before recording it in 1989 at the Maltings in Snape — though not as part of that year's Aldeburgh Festival, as the title might suggest. Collectors can rest assured that no extraneous audience noise disturbs these 59 minutes. The piano is faithfully and sympathetically reproduced, with only an occasional touch of edginess in some of Rachmaninov's bigger climaxes. The playing itself is a joy. Potent contrasts of character allied with an inevitable-sounding continuity give Beethoven's C minor Variations (allegedly disowned by their composer) a maturity commensurate with his 36 years of age. Schumann's *Faschingsschwank aus Wien* in its turn gains a new youthful spontaneity and sparkle from his delectable lightness of touch and rhythmic *élan*. Even if rubato could have been more teasing in Liszt's twelfth *Rhapsody*, its virtuoso demands are brilliantly met, and surely not even Liszt himself could have floated the melody of the D flat *Consolation* with more assuaging beauty of tone and line. In the concluding Rachmaninov group Perahia throws his cap to the winds with the best of them while at the same time preserving his own unmistakably crystalline sound-world.

AMERICAN PIANO SONATAS, Volume 1. **Peter Lawson.** Virgin Classics VC7 91163-2.
Copland: Piano Sonata. *Ives* (ed. Cowell): Three-page Sonata. *Carter:* Piano Sonata. *Barber:* Piano Sonata, Op. 26.

Ih 16' DDD 5/91

This disc offers four relatively unfamiliar but highly characterful American piano works in authoritative performances by a British-born pianist who clearly has their idiom at his fingertips — as well as their pretty challenging notes. As played here, the Copland Piano Sonata of 1941 has softness as well as strength, and for all its powerful utterance there is a strangely compelling lyricism at work too; one can see why the young Leonard Bernstein adored the work and played it. The recording matches the music, being on the close side but extremely lifelike as piano sound. Ives's *Three-page Sonata*, which at over seven minutes is longer than the miniature that its title suggests, is a gnomic utterance, but as always with this composer we feel that he has something to say that could be said in no other way. Carter's Piano Sonata is an early work of 1946, which the composer revised much later in 1982; its debt to Copland is evident, but there is also a personal voice and the scope and sweep of the music is deeply impressive. Barber's Sonata (1949), which was written for Horowitz, is less radical in idiom than the other works played and thus more immediately approachable if by no means conventional, being a work of considerable power and eloquence, very well written for the piano.

NEW REVIEW
SIMON BARERE. THE COMPLETE HMV RECORDINGS, 1934-6. **Simon Barere** (pf). APR mono CDAPR7001.
Liszt: Etudes de concert, S144 — La leggierezza (from HMV DB2166, 7/34). Années de pèlerinage, Deuxième année, S161, "Italie" — Sonetto 104 del Petrarca. Etudes de concert, S145 — Gnomenreigen (both from DB2167, 9/34). Réminiscences de Don Juan, S418 (two versions. DB2749/50. Recorded 1934 and 1936). Valse oubliée, S215 No. 1. Rhapsodie espagnole, S254 (DB2375/6, 6/35). *Chopin:* Scherzo No. 3 in C sharp minor, Op. 39 (APR7001, 12/85. 1935). Mazurka in F sharp minor, Op. 59 No. 3 (two versions — DB2674, 1/37; second previously unpublished. 1935-6). Waltz in A flat major, Op. 42 (DB2166). *Balakirev:* Islamey — Oriental Fantasy (two versions. DB2675, 4/36). *Blumenfeld:* Etude for the left hand. *Glazunov:* Etude in C major, Op. 31 No. 1 (DB2645, 12/35). *Scriabin:* Etudes — C sharp minor, Op. 2 No. 1 (1934); D sharp minor, Op. 8 No. 12 (two versions. 1934-5). *Lully* (arr. Godowsky): Gigue in E major. *Rameau* (arr. Godowsky): Tambourin in E minor (both 1934. All from APR7001). *Schumann:* Toccata in C major, Op. 7 (three versions — two on DB2674, 1/37; third previously unpublished. 1935-6).

② 2h 6' ADD 5/91

For many years following his death in 1951 Simon Barere was simply a legendary name to conjure with, whose phenomenal pianism appeared to have been lost to

future generations of music lovers. Then in the late 1980s a small specialist
company, Appian Recordings, began to reissue his recordings — all extremely
rare — in a series of three volumes. This, the first, contains all of the
recordings (including rejected takes) which Barere made for HMV between 1934
and 1936, following his emigration from Russia and then Germany to the USA
where his reputation was firmly, if briefly, established. Barere was part of the
generation of super-pianists, including Horowitz, who succeeded the first wave of
Russian virtuosos such as Rachmaninov and Lhévinne. For musicians such as these
the normal peaks of the piano literature became mere starting points for
complete and thorough investigations of the musical and technical capabilities of
the instrument itself. The HMV sessions included such monumental tests of
virtuosity as Balakirev's fantasy *Islamey*, Liszt's *Réminiscences de Don Juan*, and
"Gnomenreigen", together with a whole range of shorter but equally testing
pieces by Schumann, Chopin, Scriabin, Godowsky and Barere's final teacher,
Blumenfield. To all of this music Barere brought a technique which knew no
difficulties and a sense of musical taste which kept vulgar display firmly at bay.
The results are frankly benchmarks of performance by which all aspiring virtuosos
must be tested and which few will ever equal. Simon Barere's playing is simply
breathtaking in its unrestrained vigour and superb technical control, both laid at
the feet of a unique and powerful musical insight. This two-CD set is an essential
memorial to one of the greatest, if unsung, heroes of the piano this century. The
production by Bryan Crimp is faultless, with full and highly faithful transfers
from the original 78s, and completely comprehensive accompanying documentation. No lover of truly great piano playing can afford to be without this issue.

BAROQUE ORGAN MUSIC. Peter Hurford (org). Argo 414 496-2ZH.
Played on the Blank organ of the Bethlehemkerk, Papendrecht, The Netherlands.
G. Böhm: Prelude and Fugue in C major. Vater unser im Himmelreich. Auf
meinen lieben Gott. Von Himmel hoch da komm'ich her. ***L. Couperin:*** Branle
de basque. Fantaisie in G minor. ***J. K. Kerll:*** Capriccio sopra il cucu.
Buxtehude: Mensch, willt du leben seliglich. Wir danken dir, Herr Jesu
Christ. Vater, unser im Himmelreich. ***Walond:*** Voluntary No. 5 in G major.
G. B. Pescetti: Sonata in C minor. ***Pachelbel:*** Ciaccona in D minor.
Sweelinck: Unter der Linden grüne. ***Stanley:*** Voluntary in C major, Op. 5
No. 1.

Ih II' DDD 10/87

At first glance we may be a little dismayed to find an anthology called "Baroque
Organ Music" which omits a single note of Bach. More careful scrutiny of the
contents, however, may well persuade us that it is for our own good since Peter
Hurford has chosen a programme of all too seldom-heard music by composers
who were also noted organists of their day. The outstanding figures here are Jan
Pieterszoon Sweelinck, Georg Böhm, Dietrich Buxtehude, Johann Pachelbel and
Louis Couperin and although these works form the main body of the recital,
listeners are unlikely to be disappointed by the several smaller, lighter-textured
pieces with which Hurford makes discerning contrast, as well as showing off the
appealing character of the organ.

NEW REVIEW

BEST LOVED PIANO CLASSICS, Volume 1. **Moura Lympany** (pf). EMI
Laser CDZ7 62523-2.
Chopin: Fantaisie-Impromptu in C sharp minor, Op. 66. Etudes, Op. 10 — C
sharp minor, No. 4; G flat major, No. 5, "Black Keys". ***Brahms:*** Waltz in A
flat major, Op. 39 No. 15. ***Mozart:*** Piano Sonata in A major, K331 — Rondo
alla turca. ***Beethoven:*** Minuet in G major. Bagatelle No. 25, "Für Elise".
Schumann: Kinderszenen, Op. 15 No. 7, Träumerei. ***Liszt:*** Concert Studies,

S144 — Un sospiro. **Dvořák:** Humoresque, Op. 101 No. 7. **MacDowell:** Woodland Sketches, Op. 51 No. 1, "To a Wild Rose". **Chaminade:** Automne, Op. 35 No. 2. **Debussy:** Suite Bergamasque No. 3, "Claire de lune". Children's Corner — Suite No. 6, "Golliwog's Cakewalk". **Rachmaninov:** Prelude in C sharp minor, Op. 3. No. 2. **Rubinstein:** Melody in F major, Op. 3 No. 1. **Granados:** Goyescas — No. 4, "The Maiden and the Nightingale". **Falla:** El amor brujo: Ritual Fire Dance. **Albéniz / Godowsky:** España, Op. 165 — Tango.

Ih 11'   DDD   1/89

This is not a reissue but a new recital digitally recorded in January 1988, and the consistently excellent Moura Lympany shows no sign of her 71 years. Indeed her technique is as sure as ever, as she demonstrates at the start in the tricky *Fantasie-Impromptu*, while she shows her musical sensitivity no less emphatically in the celebrated central section of the same piece, the melody of which was once made into a popular song called "I'm always chasing rainbows". Lympany mixes virtuoso pieces with more intimate, gentler ones, so that elaborate numbers like Liszt's concert study, *Un sospiro* ("A sigh") and Granados's "The Maiden and the Nightingale" contrast beautifully with Brahms's Waltz in A flat major and Schumann's *Träumerei* ("Dreaming"), from *Kinderszenen* ("Scenes of childhood"). Altogether, this is an admirably chosen sequence of piano classics from Mozart to Godowsky, and Lympany shows sympathy with every piece that she performs. Not only is it finely played, it is excellently recorded and the disc is a remarkable bargain and a quite splendid example of the art of a pianist whose skills seem only enhanced by the passing years. It would make a perfect present for someone new to classical piano music, yet will have no less appeal for a sophisticated and discriminating connoisseur.

BLACK ANGELS. Kronos Quartet (David Harrington, John Sherba, vns; Hank Dutt, va; Joan Jeanrenaud, vc). Elektra-Nonesuch 7559-79242-2. **Crumb:** Black Angels. **Tallis** (arr. Kronos Qt): Spem in alium. **Marta:** Doom. A sigh. **Ives** (arr. Kronos Qt/Geist): They are there! **Shostakovich:** String Quartet No. 8 in C minor, Op. 110.

Ih 2'   DDD   4/91

This is very much the sort of imaginative programming we've come to expect from this talented young American quartet. With an overall theme of war and persecution the disc opens with George Crumb's *Black Angels*, for electric string quartet. This work was inspired by the Vietnam War and bears two inscriptions to that effect — *in tempore belli* (in time of war) and "Finished on Friday the Thirteenth of March, 1970", and it's described by Crumb as "a kind of parable on our troubled contemporary world". The work is divided into three sections which represent the three stages of the voyage of the soul — fall from grace, spiritual annihilation and redemption. As with most of his works he calls on his

instrumentalists to perform on a variety of instruments other than their own — here that ranges from gongs, maracas and crystal glasses to vocal sounds such as whistling, chanting and whispering. *Doom. A sigh* is the young Hungarian composer István Marta's disturbing portrait of a Roumanian village as they desperately fight to retain their sense of iden-

Kronos Quartet   *[photo: Elektra Nonesuch/Lavine*

tity in the face of dictatorship and persecution. Marta's atmospheric blend of electronic sound, string quartet and recorded folk-songs leave one with a powerful and moving impression. At first sight Tallis's *Spem in alium* may seem oddly out of place considering the overall theme of this disc, but as the sleeve-notes point out the text was probably taken from the story of Judith, in which King Nebuchadnezzar's general Holofernes besieged the Jewish fortress of Bethulia. Kronos's own arrangement of this 40-part motet (involving some multi-tracking) certainly makes a fascinating alternative to the original. A particularly fine account of Shostakovich's Eighth String Quartet (dedicated to the victims of fascism and war) brings this thought-provoking and imaginative recital to a close. Performances throughout are outstanding, and the recording first class.

NEW REVIEW

THE BRITTEN CONNECTION. Anthony Goldstone (pf). Gamut Classics GAMCD526.
Bridge: Dramatic Fantasia, H66. Gargoyle, H177. *Ireland:* Ballade of London Nights. *Britten:* Five Waltzes. Night Piece. *L. Berkeley:* Six Preludes, Op. 23. *R. Stevenson:* Sonatina Serenissima. *C. Matthews:* Five Studies.

1h 9' DDD 3/92

Britten never taught composition, but his contacts with other composers extended from his own years as a pupil (of Frank Bridge and John Ireland) to the final period of ill-health when he needed assistants like the young Colin Matthews. Otherwise, 'the Britten connection' was through friendship (Lennox Berkeley) or homage (Ronald Stevenson). As is well known, Britten was a fine pianist who wrote little solo music for the instrument. Yet one cannot imagine slight compositions like the *Waltzes* and *Night Piece* being better done than they are here by Anthony Goldstone. The whole programme, even though the music is of variable quality, is performed with the kind of poise and unobtrusive technical skill which stands out even in an era of wall-to-wall virtuosity. The weakest pieces are the Ireland and the early *Dramatic Fantasia* by Bridge. Bridge's *Gargoyle* is a different matter, written in 1928, and with precisely the kind of tough-minded features that the young Britten was to seize on as the basis for his own style. The Berkeley Preludes and the Matthews Studies are attractive, economical display pieces, while Stevenson's *Sonatina Serenissima*, deriving from Britten's *Death in Venice*, complements the opera by moving into a quite different musical world. A fascinating compilation, then, with admirably natural recorded sound.

NEW REVIEW

SHURA CHERKASSKY LIVE. PIANO RECITAL. **Shura Cherkassky.** Decca 433 653-2DH. Items marked [a] from L'Oiseau-Lyre DSL015 (11/76), [b] DSL024 (6/78).
Albéniz (arr. Godowsky): España, Op. 165 — Tango[a]. *Chopin:* Ballade No. 3 in A flat major, Op. 47[a]. Etudes[a] — C sharp minor, Op. 10 No. 4; C sharp minor, Op. 25 No. 7; B minor, Op. 25 No. 10. Preludes, Op. 28[b] — No. 4 in E minor; No. 6 in D minor; No. 7 in A major; No. 10 in C sharp minor; No. 13 in F sharp minor; No. 17 in A flat major; No. 20 in C minor; No. 23 in F major. Nocturne in F minor, Op. 55 No. 1[b]. *Rachmaninov:* Polka de V.R.[b]. *Rubinstein:* Melody in F, Op. 3 No. 1[b]. *Schubert:* Piano Sonata in A major, D664[b]. Moment musical in F minor, D780 No. 3[a] (arr. Godowsky). *Scriabin:* Prelude in D major, Op. 11 No. 5[b].

1h 12' ADD 10/91

Shura Cherkassky has always been one of the most mercurial pianists of the day, a throwback — if you like — to the great virtuosos of bygone days — brilliant, unpredictable, wholly spontaneous. This disc is as fair a representation of his extraordinary abilities as any. You can hear here his delightful if idiosyncratic Chopin, wilful maybe but surely in the spirit of the composer's genius. Schubert's A major Sonata has long been a favourite of his, featuring in many of his recitals; he seems to warm to its slightly elusive, elegiac nature, and in the *Moment musical* (in Godowsky's arrangement), Cherkassky is at his most tellingly teasing. The pieces by Albéniz, Rachmaninov and Rubinstein have always been favourite encores of this pianist, and here they receive performances of amazing lightness and dexterity.

NEW REVIEW

COLSTON HALL ORGAN CLASSICS. Malcolm Archer (org). Priory PRCD305. Played on the organ of The Colston Hall, Bristol.
W. Faulkes: Grand Choeur. *Mascagni* (arr. Lloyd Webber): Cavalleria rusticana — Intermezzo. *Wagner* (arr. Archer): Parsifal — Fanfares from Good Friday Music. *Saint-Saëns* (arr. Guilmant): The Carnival of the Animals — The Swan. *Salomé:* Grand Choeur. *Pierné:* Trois Pièces — Prelude; Cantilene; Scherzando. *H. Smart:* Festive March. *F. Rickman:* Mélodie Lyrique. *W.T. Best:* Concert Fantasia on an Old Welsh March. *J. Strauss II:* Tritsch, Tratsch Polka (arr. Lowry); Radetsky March (arr. Archer). *Holzmann:* Blaze Away.

· 1h 9' DDD 8/91

Malcolm Archer's career has taken him through cathedral organ lofts at Norwich and Bristol but in addition to these impeccable credentials in the British organ establishment he is also well known and admired by aficionados of the theatre organ and its music. The reason is not hard to discern from these ebullient performances which simply erupt with sparkling wit and infectious fun. Underlying it all, though, is the security of technique and musical sensitivity which can only come from a thorough grounding in the more serious side of musical performance. The programme harks back to the days when organ recitals could fill provincial town halls and civic theatres with audiences thirsty for spectacular displays of virtuosity from organist and organ alike. Transcriptions of orchestral and operatic items were a popular feature. These not only proved the technical virility of the recitalist but gave plenty of opportunity to display the lavish pseudo-orchestral effects which no self-respecting concert or theatre organ would be without. This marvellous recording of a splendid virtuoso player on a magnificent concert instrument recreates vividly the flavour of those spectacular organ concerts. Transcriptions of Saint-Saëns, Mascagni, Wagner and Johann Strauss sit happily alongside original organ pieces (including W.T. Best's scintillating *Fantasia on "Men of Harlech"*) and this immensely enjoyable disc ends with that all-time theatre organ favourite, *Blaze Away.*

THE ESSENTIAL HARPSICHORD. Virginia Black. Collins Classics 5024-2.
Arne: Keyboard Sonata No. 3 in G major. *D. Scarlatti:* Keyboard Sonatas — C major, Kk159; G major, Kk337; E major, Kk380. *J.S. Bach:* Italian Concerto, BWV971. *Balbastre:* Pièces de clavecin I — La Suzanne. *Daquin:* Pièces de clavecin I — Le coucou. *Duphly:* Pièces de clavecin III — Le Forqueray. *F. Couperin:* Livre de clavecin II — Les baricades mistérieuses; Le dodo; Le tic-toc-choc. *Handel:* Keyboard Suites — No. 5 in E major, "Harmonious Blacksmith"; No. 7 in G minor — Passacaille. *Mozart:* Piano Sonata in A major, K331/300*i* — Rondo alla turca. *Paradies:* Toccata in A major. *Rameau:* Les cyclopes. *W.F. Bach:* Polonaise in E minor.

· 1h 14' DDD 5/91

Virginia Black has assembled a delightful programme of music which should conquer all ears not yet won over by the sound of a harpsichord. She is a communicative player, spontaneous in transferring her thoughts to the keyboard and with a lively sense of poetry. These qualities and others too may be sensed in her interpretation of Bach's *Italian Concerto*. This is the most substantial piece in her recital and it comes over well with clearly articulated phrases, rhythmic elasticity and well-chosen tempos. There are occasions when Miss Black pushes the music along just a little harder than is good for it — listeners may sense that in the concluding Variations of Handel's famous so-called *Harmonious Blacksmith* theme — but her liveliness of temperament ensures her performances against any accusations of stuffy convention or dullness. Only the W.F. Bach Polonaise seems perhaps not to speak from the heart. A recital, in short, which deserves to win friends. Few are likely to be disappointed either by her choice of music or her colourfully imaginative treatment of it.

A EUROPEAN ORGAN TOUR. Priory PRCD903.
Reger: Symphonic Fantasia and Fugue, Op. 57, "Inferno" (Graham Barber/St Mary Magdalene, Bonn). *Bowen:* Fantasia, Op. 136 (Marc Rochester/St David's Hall, Cardiff). *Dupré:* Variations sur un Nöel, Op. 20 (Kimberly Marshall/St Sernin, Toulouse). *Karg-Elert:* Cathedral Windows (John Scott Whiteley/York Minster). *Bach:* Fantasia in C major, BWV573 (Scott Whiteley/St Bavo, Haarlem).

1h 10' DDD

From the comfort of your armchair, you can enjoy a real taste of Europe. Here on a single, generously-filled disc are the authentic voices of some of the finest organ builders (Muller, Cavaillé-Coll, Klais, Walker and Peter Collins) from Europe's leading organ building nations (Holland, France, Germany and Britain). There is also an interesting programme of music, with only one of the pieces available elsewhere. That is Dupré's Op. 20 Variations. He wrote it with a Cavaillé-Coll organ in mind, and the example in St Sernin, Toulouse is certainly one of the best-preserved. Not only that, in Kimberly Marshall this music finds a most sensitive and eloquent advocate. It is good to hear Bach played on an instrument built in his lifetime too. But this Fantasia in C is unusual: only the first page exists in Bach's manuscript and the version played here was completed this century by Wolfgang Stockmeier. John Scott Whiteley gives it a compelling performance as he does Karg-Elert's beautifully evocative and richly colourful suite. York Bowen's only published organ work is the Fantasia written for the Festival of Britain in 1951. That was a time of radical thinking and fundamental changes in British organ design and it is entirely appropriate that it should be played on the brand new Peter Collins instrument in Cardiff's magnificent concert hall.

NEW REVIEW

EVGENI KISSIN CARNEGIE HALL DEBUT CONCERT. Evgeni Kissin (pf). RCA Victor Red Seal RD60443. Recorded at a performance in Carnegie Hall on September 30th, 1990.
Chopin: Waltz in C sharp minor, Op. 64 No. 2. *Liszt:* Etude d'exécution transcendante in F minor, S139 No. 10, "Appassionata". Liebestraum No. 3, S541. Rhapsodie espagnole, S254. *Prokofiev:* Etude in C minor, Op. 2 No. 3. Piano Sonata No. 6 in A major, Op. 82. *Schumann:* Etudes symphoniques, Op. 13. Theme and Variations on the name "Abegg", Op. 1. *Schumann/ Liszt:* Widmung, S566.

② 1h 43' DDD 3/91

A Carnegie Hall début is a rite of passage for any pianist on the way to international stardom. To make that début ten days before your nineteenth birthday and with top recording engineers present is really something. Evgeni Kissin's reputation preceded him, as anyone will realize who has heard his phenomenal Tokyo recital (reviewed below) and recorded three years earlier; he did not disappoint. Starting with a beguiling account of Schumann's Op. 13 and finishing with a mind-boggling display of dexterity in Prokofiev's Etude, this is one recital which lived up to all its hype. In between, Kissin occasionally seems determined to prove his worth rather than just revelling in the music — the Prokofiev Sonata, for example, is more finished, but less electrifying than in Tokyo. But as a rule his youthful virtuosity and almost preternatural maturity of temperament have you on the edge of your seat. The recording is bright and close, with some loss of atmosphere but with the bonus of minimal audience noise; and playing like this sounds marvellous in close-up.

EVGENI KISSIN IN TOKYO. Evgeni Kissin (pf). Sony Classical CD45931. Recorded at a performance in Suntory Hall, Tokyo on May 12th, 1987.
Rachmaninov: Lilacs, Op. 21 No. 5. Etudes tableaux, Op. 39 — No. 1 in C minor; No. 5 in E flat minor. **Prokofiev:** Piano Sonata No. 6 in A major, Op. 82. **Liszt:** Concert Studies, S144 — La leggierezza; Waldestauschen. **Chopin:** Nocturne in A flat major, Op. 32 No. 2. Polonaise in F sharp minor, Op. 44. **Scriabin:** Mazurka in E minor, Op. 25 No. 3. Etude in C sharp minor, Op. 42 No. 5. **Anonymous** (arr. Saegusa): Natu — Wa Kinu. Todai — Mori. Usagi.

‡ 1h 13' DDD 11/90   9 p

One reason for buying this CD is that it contains dazzling piano playing by a 15-year-old Russian set fair for a career of the highest distinction. A better reason is that the recital contains as full a revelation of the genius of Prokofiev as any recording ever made in any medium. The Sixth Sonata is the first of a trilogy which sums up the appalling sufferings of Russia under Stalin in a way only otherwise found in Shostakovich's 'middle' symphonies. Kissin plays it with all the colour and force of a full orchestra and all the drama and structural integrity of a symphony, plus a kind of daredevilry that even he may find difficult to recapture. As for the rest of the recital only the Rachmaninov pieces are as memorable as the Prokofiev, though everything else is immensely impressive (the Japanese encore-pieces are trivial in the extreme, however). Microphone placing is very close, presumably in order to minimize audience noise; but the playing can take it, indeed it may even be said to benefit from it.

FRENCH ORGAN WORKS. Jennifer Bate (org). Unicorn-Kanchana DKPCD9041. From DKP9041 (1/86). Played on the organ of St Peter's Cathedral, Beauvais, France.
Boëllman: Suite gothique, Op. 25. **Guilmant:** Cantilène pastorale. March on Handel's "Lift up your heads", Op. 15. **Saint-Saëns:** Sept Improvisations, Op. 150 — No. 7 in A minor. **Gigout:** Dix pièces d'orgue — Scherzo; Toccata in B minor. Grand choeur dialogué.

‡ 44' DDD 10/87

Jennifer Bate reminds us in this recital that the French tradition of organ music was already strong in the nineteenth and early twentieth centuries. Boëllman's *Suite gothique* is richly written and culminates in the brilliant Toccata which is often played on its own in recitals, whilst Guilmant's *Pastoral Cantilena* is a gently flowing piece. Saint-Saëns's *Seven Improvisations* were composed when he was 82, but the durability of his craftsmanship is evident in the brisk and elegant scherzo of the Seventh. The Gigout Toccata is appropriately fiery, while the Scherzo which follows is gentler and the *Grand choeur dialogué* provides a vivid dialogue between two manuals with contrasting registration. Bate plays all this music with both affection and panache, and the quality of the recording is first rate, the reverberant acoustic never blurring textures.

NEW REVIEW

FROM STANLEY TO WESLEY, Volume 6. **Jennifer Bate** (org). Unicorn-Kanchana DKPCD9106. Played on the organs of Adlington Hall, Cheshire; The Dolmetsch Collection, Haslemere, Surrey; The Chapel of St Michael's Mount, Cornwall; The Iveagh Bequeast, Kenwood, London; Killerton House, Broadclyst, Exeter, Devon and The Chapel of Our Lady and St Everilda, Everingham, Yorkshire.
Boyce: Voluntary in D major. *Handel:* Fugue in G major. Voluntary in C major. *Heron:* Voluntary in G major. *Hook:* Voluntary in C minor. *Russell:* Voluntary in F major. *Stanley:* Voluntaries — A minor, Op. 6 No. 2; D minor, Op. 7 No. 4; G major, Op. 7 No. 9. *Stubley:* Voluntary in C major. *S. Wesley:* Voluntaries — E flat major, Op. 6 No. 7; B flat major.

1h 5' DDD 11/91

Whilst most people would regard Bach and his North German contemporaries as synonymous with all that is best in eighteenth-century organ music there was also a significant school of organist-composers thriving in England. Chief amongst these was John Stanley whose music was greatly admired at the time, in particular by a recent immigrant from Germany, one George Frederic Handel (two fine examples of his own organ music are to be found on this CD). But while the German composers were writing for their great, majestic organs, their English counterparts were faced with something far humbler in scope and more delicate and intimate in character. To hear this music played on such an instrument is to have its true beauty revealed: here it is played not just on one authentic contemporaneous instrument, but the Unicorn-Kanchana team have scoured the length and breadth of England, from Cornwall to Yorkshire, to unearth six classic, and virtually unaltered examples. Jennifer Bate's immense musical and technical powers and her innate, native sense of style, imbues this disc with compelling musical authority which, added to the captivating sound of these six delightful organs, makes it an intriguing historical document — real 'living history', if you like. This CD is the sixth in a series and while each is a valuable addition to the recorded legacy of English music, this one in particular gives the less specialist collector a representative and varied selection of this wonderful, yet woefully overlooked area of our musical heritage.

GUITAR RECITAL. Eleftheria Kotzia (gt). Pearl SHECD9609.
Tippett: The blue guitar. *Pujol:* Tristango en vos. Preludio tristón. Candombe en mi. *Villa-Lobos:* Five Preludes. *Delerue:* Mosaïque. *Giorginakis:* Four Greek images. *Fampas:* Greek Dances Nos. 1 and 3.

1h 7' DAD 6/89

Many guitar recitals have a familiar appearance, but Ms Kotzia is not given to stale cloning in her choice of repertory. Here she assembles a nicely varied programme of music by six composers, none of whom is Spanish. The Five Preludes of Villa-Lobos, vignettes of Brazil and its life, have been recorded many times but this clear and firm account is, if not the best, good enough to live with. The most substantial is Tippett's only solo-guitar work, *The blue guitar*. Georges Delerue is briefer but no less purposeful in putting together his 'mosaic' of textures. The rest speak with distinctly regional accents: Pujol's Preludes celebrate Argentinian folk idioms in present-day popular terms, whilst Giorgi-nakis's *Images* and Fampas's arrange-ments of traditional dances are as Greek as Ms Kotzia herself. Her freshness, spontaneity and positiveness are mirrored in this squeaky-clean and admirable recording. She clearly enjoys herself and transmits her pleasure to the listener.

THE HARP OF LUDOVICO. Andrew Lawrence-King (hpd). Hyperion CDA66518.

A. Mudarra: Fantasia que contrahaze la harpa en la maniera de Ludovico. Divisions on Spagnoletta. *L. Milan:* El Maestro — Fantasia de consonancias y redobles. Divisions on the Spanish Pavan. *D. Ortiz:* Trattado de glosas — Fantasia; Divisions on Paradetas. Tutte le vecchie. *G. de Macque:* Prima stravaganza. Gagliarda prima. Toccata a modo di trombetta. *O. Michi:* Arie Spirituali — Su duro tronco; I diletti di mundo; Quel signor. *Frescobaldi:* Il primo libro di Toccate — Toccata quinta; Toccata Nona; Toccata Decima; Ciacona. Il secondo libro di Toccate — Arie detta Balletto; Arie detta la Frescobalda. *Monteverdi:* Vespro della Beata Vergine — Nigra sum.

Ih II' DDD 6/92

The earliest harps had a single row of strings, tuned only to the notes of the prevailing key; today's harp also has one row of strings but their pitches can be varied chromatically by means of pedals. Before this happy state of affairs was reached the harp was made 'chromatic' during baroque times by having two (or even three) rows of strings, one for the white notes and the other for the black. The two rows of the Spanish *arpa doblada* crossed one another, whilst those of the Italian *arpa doppia* were parallel — which made life a lot easier for the player; in his recording Lawrence-King uses both types. Though the music he plays was not specifically written for it, the harp was a common and valid optional instrument — the 'wrong-note' Fantasia by Mudarra was written for the vihuela but in the style of Ludovico, a popular harpist of the time. It was also usual for players to improvise their own variations on grounds and dance-form pieces, and Lawrence-King exercises this licence with the greatest of skill and enthusiasm. Much of this music has no other recording — and none of it on the harp, and Lawrence-King plays it with rare sensitivity and conviction. In every respect this is a marvellous disc, with none of the barbiturate effect that some harp music can have. If you doze off before this one ends you should consult your doctor. Vivid, stimulating and highly recommended — you should treat yourself to it, even if it means pawning something you can live without.

HARP RECITAL. Maria Graf. Philips 432 103-2PH.

Caplet: Divertissements. *Debussy:* Deux arabesques. *Fauré:* Une châtelaine en sa tour, Op. 110. Impromptu, Op. 86. *Ravel:* Pavane pour une infante défunte. *Roussel:* Impromptu, Op. 21. *Tailleferre:* Harp Sonata. *Tournier:* Au matin.

54' DDD 11/91

The harp is a very idiosyncratic instrument and the composers who have made the most skilful use of its resources have been those who, like Tournier, played it. Prominent amongst those who were/are not harpists have been those of French birth, as were all the others represented in Maria Graf's recording — and as the modern harp itself was. The works by Caplet, Fauré, Roussel and Tailleferre were written specifically for the harp; those of Debussy and Ravel were originally for the piano, though both used the harp in their chamber music. However, all five composers has as instinctive an understanding of the harp's essence as Spanish composers have had of that of the guitar; even the items by Debussy and Ravel sound like original harp music. Performer/composers have often relied overly on the seductive effects the harp can produce, and much harp music by others is little more than pleasantly soporific; the music in this recording is neither 'tricksy', trivial nor anodyne. Maria Graf, one of the very best harpists to have emerged during the last few years, is a fine player, with a touch that is responsive to every nuance and, irrespective of instrument, a first-class musician. The recording is vivid enough to have picked up any extraneous mechanical noise such as harpists are wont to produce, but there is none.

NEW REVIEW

VLADIMIR HOROWITZ. PIANO WORKS. RCA Gold Seal mono/[a]stereo. GD60377.
Prokofiev: Piano Sonata No. 7 in B flat major, Op. 83 (from RB6555, 12/63. Recorded 1945). Toccata, Op. 11. **Poulenc:** Presto in B flat major (both from HMV DB6971, 1947). **Barber:** Piano Sonata, Op. 26 (RB6555. 1950). **Kabalevsky:** Piano Sonata No. 3, Op. 46 (new to UK. 1947). **Fauré:** Nocturne No. 13 in B minor, Op. 119[a] (RL12548, 2/78. Recorded at a performance in May 1977).

1h 5'   ADD   6/92   £ 9 P   ▲

Even today, when there is a six-deep queue of virtuosos that, laid end to end, would stretch halfway round the world, Vladimir Horowitz's playing is something to make the listener gasp and sit up. He has been called, with justification, "the greatest pianist alive or dead". Horowitz was associated with all three of these sonatas from their very beginnings. Prokofiev wrote his Seventh Sonata in 1942, and Horowitz gave the first American performance less than two years later. He sent a copy of this 1945 recording to the composer, and Prokofiev sent him an autographed copy of the score in return, inscribed "to the miraculous pianist from the composer". The performance is indeed superlative, with playing of extraordinary virtuosity, and Horowitz responds with equal flair to the sonata's 'barbaric' and lyrical elements. Kabalevsky's Third Sonata dates from 1946, and Horowitz gave the American première in February 1948, two months after he made this recording. The work is of lesser stature than the Prokofiev, but its three well-contrasted movements make up an effective enough sonata. Again, Horowitz plays brilliantly and very sympathetically throughout the work. The world première of Barber's Piano Sonata was given by Horowitz in 1949. This piece is brilliantly written and technically very difficult to play — a perfect vehicle, in fact, for Horowitz the virtuoso. The great pianist brings great flair to the shorter Poulenc and Prokofiev items: the Fauré was recorded at a later stage of his career, and is played in a more deliberate, though perfectly idiomatic fashion. Four of the items have been transferred from 78s in good sound. The Barber and Fauré come from tape sources and sound well — the latter is even in stereo. This is a disc all pianists and piano enthusiasts should have — and it's mid-price too!

NEW REVIEW

LATE ROMANTIC MASTERWORKS. Andrew Fletcher (org). Mirabilis MRCD903. Played on the organ of St Mary's Collegiate Church, Warwick.
Andriessen: Thema met variaties. **Bridge:** Three Organ Pieces, H63 — Adagio in E major. **Dupré:** Cortège et litanie, Op. 19 No. 2. **Howells:** Siciliano for a High Ceremony. **Pach:** Introduction and Fugue. **Peeters:** Aria, Op. 51. Variations on an Original Theme, Op. 58. **Reger:** Benedictus, Op. 59 No. 9. **Schmidt:** Prelude and Fugue in D major, "Hallelujah". **Willan:** Introduction, Passacaglia and Fugue.

1h 21'   DDD   11/91   9 S   ❓

St Mary's Church, Warwick, boasts an extraordinary organ. In fact it is two quite separate organs housed at opposite ends of the church but playable from just one console. Listening to this disc using an UHJ Ambisonic decoder the spatial effect is most vividly recreated: Mirabilis's 'surround-sound' recording places the West End organ through the front pair of speakers while the Transept organ speaks from the rear speakers. The effect is aurally astonishing, but it could be a recipe for musical disaster. As it is, Andrew Fletcher knows better than almost anyone what its strengths and weaknesses are — what works and what doesn't; he was responsible for its present design and in this thoroughly enjoyable recital guides us expertly through its manifest glories. Fletcher not only shows the organ off to best effect, he also plays this entire programme with impressive fluency. Most of these pieces are old favourites to church organists but neither the music nor, in many cases, the names of the composers will be familiar to those outside the intimate world of organ aficionados. But don't be put off, everything here from Flor Peeter's appealing *Aria* to Healey Willan's dramatic *Introduction, Passacaglia and Fugue* is well worth exploring, and you can rest assured that Fletcher's stirring playing, the organ's wonderful wealth of sounds and Mirabilis's top-notch recording provides an exceptionally generous programme of real delights.

NEW REVIEW

LIGHT IN DARKNESS. PERCUSSION WORKS. **Evelyn Glennie.** RCA Victor Red Seal RD60557.
Rosauro: Eldorado. ***Abe:*** Dream of the cherry blossoms. ***McLeod:*** The Song of Dionysius (with Philip Smith, pf). ***Edwards:*** Marimba Dances. ***Miki:*** Marimba Spiritual (with Steve Henderson, Gregory Knowles, Gary Kettel, perc). ***Glennie:*** Light in darkness. ***Tanaka:*** Two Movements for Marimba.

59' DDD 1/92

Evelyn Glennie   *[photo: BMG/Haughton]*

Evelyn Glennie has transformed her chosen instrument (in this case a whole kitchen cabinet of percussion) into a real solo one and has opened up fresh vistas not only to the musical public but also to the composers who have written for her. One is John McLeod, with his Percussion Concerto as well as the longish piece played here, *The Song of Dionysius*. This was inspired by the ancient world, for Dionysius I was a ruler of Syracuse (*c.*430-367 BC) who, suspicious of all around him, devised a listening chamber so as to hear every whisper in his palace. Hence the mysterious, hollowly echoing murmurs and tappings on which the piece is based. It uses a wide variety of instruments, including the marimba which has tuned wooden bars and produces notes of definite pitch, and there's also a piano part played by Philip Smith which seems rather a modern intruder. Glennie also plays the marimba with three percussionist colleagues in Miki's vivid *Marimba Spiritual* (which has shouting as well!), and then solo in her teacher Keiko Abe's gentler but no less oriental-sounding *Dream of the cherry blossoms* and other pieces including her own *Light in darkness*, which she says expresses religious feeling and relaxation. Relaxation is the keynote of much of this music, which is inspired by Brazilian, Australian and Japanese styles among others and is atmospheric though not always substantial. The sound is immediate and spacious, with a large dynamic range, but one would have welcomed pictures and perhaps descriptions of the instruments used, which include "stones" and "small bits".

ORGAN FIREWORKS, Volume 3. **Christopher Herrick.** Hyperion CDA66457. Played on the organ of St Eustache, Paris.
Batiste: Offertoire in D minor. *Bossi:* Pièce héroïque in D minor, Op. 128. Scherzo in D minor, Op. 49 No. 2. *Dubois:* Grand choeur in B flat major. *Dupré:* Cortège et Litanie, Op. 19 No. 2. *Jolivet:* Hymne à l'Univers. *Lefébure-Wély:* Marche in F major, Op. 122 No. 4. *Lemare:* Concert fantasy on "Hanover", Op. 4. Marche héroïque in D major, Op. 74. *Saint-Saëns:* Allegro giocoso in A minor, Op. 150 No. 7.

Ih II' DDD 9/91

Here is something truly spectacular. The brand new organ in St Eustache's Church, Paris was designed by the organist Jean Guillou who made sure it was an instrument fit for the finest of players and the greatest of music. In addition to a large array of stops, manuals and pipes it also boasts such extravagances as two consoles and a playback facility which enables the organ to play unattended. For this disc Christopher Herrick took advantage of this latter facility so that performances made during the day could be recorded in the small hours when extraneous noise was at a minimum. But the organ itself makes such a tremendously powerful, not to say, awesome noise, that one would have thought such a precaution unnecessary. Hyperion's vivid recording of this magnificent instrument stands out as one of the best recordings of an organ currently available on CD. Herrick's programme shows both the instrument and his own amazing virtuosity off to brilliant effect. There is great fun to be had from these pieces, none of which can really be said to be well-known. This is a disc of pure, unadulterated pleasure.

PIANO RECITAL. Sviatoslav Richter. DG Dokumente 423 573-2GDO.
Scriabin: Piano Sonata No. 5 in F sharp major, Op. 53. *Debussy:* Estampes (both from SLPM138849, 4/63. Recorded at performances in Italy during November 1963). Préludes, Book 1 — Voiles; Le vent dans la plaine; Les collines d'Anacapri. *Prokofiev:* Piano Sonata No. 7 in B flat major, Op. 84. Visions fugitives, Op. 22 — Nos. 3, 6 and 9 (all from SLPM138950, 8/65).

Ih 7' ADD 9/88

Richter has long been acclaimed as one of the most dedicated champions of Prokofiev's keyboard music, with the Eighth Sonata always particularly close to his heart. It would certainly be hard to imagine a more profoundly and intensely experienced performance than the one we get here, or one of greater keyboard mastery. After the yearning introspection of the temperamental opening movement and the *Andante*'s evocation of a more gracious past, the rhythmic tension and sheer might of sonority he conjures in the finale make it easy to understand why the composer's biographer, I.V. Nestyev, suspected some underlying programme culminating in "heroic troops resolutely marching ahead, ready to crush anything in their path". In the uniquely Prokofievian fantasy of the three brief *Visions fugitives* he is wholly bewitching. As for the Fifth Sonata of Scriabin, his impetuous start at once reveals his understanding of its manic extremities of mood. For just these Russian performances alone, this excellently refurbished disc can be hailed as a collector's piece. And as a bonus there is Debussy too, with infinite subtleties of tonal shading to heighten atmospheric evocation.

PIANO TRANSCRIPTIONS. Louis Lortie. Chandos CHAN8733. Items marked ᵃ from CHAN8620 (5/89), remainder new to UK.
Stravinsky: Three movements from "Petrushka"ᵃ. *Prokofiev:* Ten pieces from "Romeo and Juliet", Op. 75 — Juliet as a young girl; Montagues and Capulets;

Romeo and Juliet before parting. **Ravel:** La valse[a]. **Gershwin:** Rhapsody in Blue.

In Liszt's day the piano transcription could be a valuable means for the wider dissemination of orchestral music, as well as a vehicle for dazzling individual virtuosity. Since the advent of the recording the educational function has ceased to apply, but the potential for audience-dazzlement remains. With all four composers in Louis Lortie's recital it is also true to say that orchestral inventiveness draws an important part of its inspiration from pianistic idioms and *vice versa*. The three *Petrushka* movements are notorious for their pyrotechnic demands — none of which floor Lortie, whose playing is quite breathtaking in its finesse. His Prokofiev and Ravel are no less outstanding, with an almost uncanny ear for atmospheric texture (beautifully captured by Chandos in as fine a piano recording as you are likely to hear). The Gershwin *Rhapsody* is less happy — its individual touches seem more forced than idiomatic. But that's a minor blemish on an otherwise magnificent recital.

PIANO WORKS. Maurizio Pollini. DG 419 202-2GH. Items marked [a] from 2530 225 (6/72), [b] 2530 893 (7/78).
Stravinsky: Three movements from "Petrushka"[a]. **Prokofiev:** Piano Sonata No. 7 in B flat major[a]. **Webern:** Variations for piano, Op. 27[b]. **Boulez:** Piano Sonata No. 2 (1948)[b].

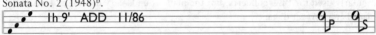

The capacity to stupefy is not the only measure of greatness in a performer; but it is an important factor, and in very few piano recordings is it embodied to the extent of this one. It is there from the very first bar of the first *Petrushka* movement — few pianists have ever attempted the tempo Pollini takes. Similarly, the Boulez Second Sonata has never been recorded with anything approaching this accuracy, glinting articulation and incandescent vigour. The bitterness at the heart of Prokofiev's slow movement with its remorseless tolling of bells is starkly revealed, and Pollini responds no less acutely to the distilled poetry behind the apparently arid surface of Webern's *Variations*. Clearly the Russian works are the more likely to grab the first-time listener; the Webern and Boulez may leave you utterly cold, or else touch regions of your psyche you did not know you had. With Pollini as exponent and with exemplary DG recording, the second possibility should not be ruled out. Intellectually, dramatically, lyrically, virtuosically, whichever way you look at it, this is a superlative disc.

NEW REVIEW

RAGS AND TANGOS. Joshua Rifkin (pf). Decca 425 225-2DH.
Nazareth: Apanhei-tecavaquinho. Cavaquinho. Vitorioso. Odeon. Nove de Julho. Labirinto. Guerreiro. Plangente. Cubanos. Fon-Fon! **Scott:** Evergreen Rag. Modesty Rag. Peace and Plenty Rag. Troubadour Rag. **Lamb:** Ragtime Nightingale. American Beauty Rag. Bohemia Rag. Topliner Rag.

Though he made his name as a scholar of renaissance and baroque music, Joshua Rifkin is also a pianist who has popularized the piano rags of Scott Joplin. Here, however, he turns his attention to three other composers from the same continent and period. Of these, James Scott from Missouri seems the nearest to Joplin and his *Evergreen Rag* only differs from him in having less memorable tunes than Joplin at his best. Still, he is well worth hearing, and Joseph F. Lamb even more so because his music has a different feel to it, more introspective as if a pianist is playing not to entertain but just for himself. Lamb spent nearly all his

Joshua Rifkin   [photo: Decca / Roosevelt

life in New York, but there's nothing urban about his style unless its intimacy suggests the loneliness that can affect those who live in a huge city. Ernesto Nazareth was also a lifelong city-dweller, but in Rio de Janeiro, where he became the 'demo pianist' of a music publisher; later he became insane and escaped from an asylum into a forest where he was found dead "with his arms outstretched, as if he was playing an invisible piano". His music, too, has an inward-looking quality and also a dreamy delicacy that shows his love of Chopin: try *Nove de Julho* or *Plangente* to hear this. But there is also a Latin quality here and most of the nine pieces by him which Rifkin plays are tangos (sometimes labelled as Argentine or Brazilian) rather than rags, although the one called *Apanhei-tecavaquinho*, is neither and makes unusual play with the top register of the keyboard. Villa-Lobos and Milhaud admired Nazareth and the latter said that hearing him play the piano gave him a "deeper insight into the Brazilian soul". Improbably, this sensitively and affectionately played recital was recorded in the UK in a Bristol church (St George's, Brandon Hill) that is regularly used for BBC concerts; but the piano sounds very natural and is rightly placed at a correct distance.

SPANISH GUITAR WORKS. Eduardo Fernández (gtr). Decca 417 618-2DH. *Albéniz:* Suite española — Sevilla (arr. Llobet); Asturias (arr. Segovia). España — Tango (arr. Segovia). *Llobet:* Six Catalan folk-songs. *Granados* (arr. Fernández): Danzas españolas — Andaluza; Danza triste. *Alard* (arr. Tárrega): Estudio brillante. *Tárrega:* Five Preludes. Minuetto. Five Mazurkas. Recuerdos de la Alhambra. *Segovia:* Estudio sin luz. Estudio. *Turina:* Fandanguillo. Ráfaga.

1h 4'   DDD   2/88

When the classic guitar came to life around the turn of this century it was carried on a wave of Spanish romanticism and this area of the repertory remains central to an understanding of it. The virtuoso/composer Francisco Tárrega was the 'father of the modern guitar', Miguel Llobet was his student, and it was Andrés Segovia who carried their 'gospel' around the world; they thus represent a kind of 'dynasty'. This programme, including both arrangements and original guitar works, is a document of the guitar's renaissance and it is cleanly played by the Uruguayan virtuoso Eduardo Fernández, with clear tone and with an expressiveness that never overflows into sentimentality. The recording is utterly lifelike.

SPIRIT OF THE GUITAR. MUSIC OF THE AMERICAS. **John Williams** (gtr). CBS Masterworks CD44898. *York:* Sunburst. Lullaby. *Mangoré:* Aconquija. La ultima canción. *Piazzolla:* Verano porteño. Cueca. *Ponce:* Scherzino mexicano. *Lauro:* Natalia. El niño. Maria Luisa. *Brouwer:* Berceuse. Danza caratelistica. *C. Byrd:* Three blues (for classic guitar). *Villa-Lobos:* Chôros No. 1. *Sagreras:* El colibri. *Crespo:* Norteña.

54'   ADD   8/89

Early forms of the classic guitar were among the instruments introduced into South America by the Spanish *conquistadores* in the sixteenth century; there they survived and prospered. Together with various other related plucked-string instruments, the present-day 'classic' guitar now flourishes in the multi-racial climate of that continent and its music has acquired a concomitant diversity of styles, characterized by tunefulness and rhythmic vitality. John Williams has assembled an immediately attractive programme of pieces by composers (some of whom play or played the guitar) from Paraguay, Argentina, Mexico, Venezuela, Brazil and Cuba. In time, the guitar spread through North America and, in this century, learned to speak jazz; items in Williams's programme by two guitarist-composers from the USA mark this further spread, those by Charlie Byrd are benignly jazz-based. The disc as a whole, played with Williams's precision-engineered perfection and finely recorded, celebrates the guitar's transatlantic transposition of a wholly light-musical level.

TWENTIETH CENTURY PIANO WORKS. Rolf Hind. Factory Classical FACD256.
Ligeti: Six Etudes, Book 1. *Martland:* Kgakala. *Messiaen:* Catalogue d'oiseaux — Le courlis cendré. *Carter:* Piano Sonata.

| 1h 6' DDD 1/90 |

Even if you would need a lot of persuading to attend an all-twentieth century piano recital in the concert hall, you might well find Rolf Hind's programme well-chosen and well-balanced enough to listen to as if it were a short, continuous concert. Hind is a powerful player who needs good reason (that is, unambiguous instructions in the score) before he takes refuge in restraint. This means that his reading of Ligeti's second study is less gentle that it might be, but this is a rare miscalculation, and he crowns the set with an overwhelming realization of the complex textures of the sixth study, which seems to express a very direct and intense anguish. Martland's *Kgakala* — an African word meaning 'distance' — is the shortest item, but earns its place alongside Carter and Messiaen at their grandest. Carter's Sonata, from the days before he set tonality aside, and Messiaen's hypnotic evocation of the curlew's piercing melancholy are both, in their utterly different ways, major works, as well as intensely personal statements. Rolf Hind penetrates to the personalities behind the structures, and a close but undistorted recording helps to make sure that the listener is involved from first note to last.

VARIATIONS ON AMERICA. Simon Preston (org). Argo 421 731-2ZH. Recorded on the organ of the Methuen Memorial Music Hall, Massachusetts, USA.
Sousa (arr. anon): Stars and Stripes Forever! *Saint-Saëns* (arr. Lemare): Danse macabre, Op. 40. *Ives:* Variations on "America". *Buck:* Variations on "The Last Rose of Summer", Op. 59. *Bossi:* Etudes symphonique, Op. 78. *Lemare:* Andantino in D flat major. *Guilmant:* Sonata No. 1 in D minor, Op. 42.

| 1h 6' DDD 11/90 |

There is more outrageous fun and brilliant showmanship on this CD than anyone has a right to expect. Argo have certainly made their comeback to the catalogue with a bang! The large organ in the Methuen Memorial Music Hall, Massachusetts actually began life in the Boston Music Hall, but was moved to its new home in 1899 in order to give more platform space to the newly-created Boston Symphony Orchestra. Boston's loss (albeit generously compensated by the new orchestra) was certainly Massachusetts's gain for here is an instrument capable of providing thrills and excitement in ample measure. It does demand, though, a player of exceptional virtuosity and music of suitable flamboyance. Both these criteria are more than met with Simon Preston and his programme of American or American-inspired music. All of these pieces would have been used at some time to entertain the huge audience which would flock to recitals in the days of the great travelling virtuosos such as France's Alexandre Guilmant and England's Edwin Lemare, whose *Andantino* in D flat became so popular that it was turned into an immensely successful 'pop' song — *Moonlight and Roses*. The home-grown composers, Messrs Sousa, Buck and Ives (the 'America' of the *Variations* actually being the same tune as the English National Anthem), vie with the Europeans in providing truly outrageous pieces. Here is organ music of the most extrovert kind. While Simon Preston's playing of these pieces is undeniably brilliant, for sheer technical audacity nothing outdoes his spectacular performance of Bossi's *Etudes symphonique* — a piece requiring from the player footwork which would be the envy of the most accomplished breakdancer on the Manhattan sidewalks.

VIHUELA MUSIC OF THE SPANISH RENAISSANCE. Christopher Wilson. Virgin Classics Veritas VC7 91136-2.
Milán: Libro de musica de vihuela de mano, "El Maestro", Book 1 — Fantasias I, VIII, XI and XII; Pavanas IV and VI. *Narváez:* Los seys libros del Delfin — Guardame las vacas (two versions); Milles regres; Fantasia; Baxa de contrapunto. *Mudarra:* Tres libros de música en cifra para vihuela — Romanesca: O guardame las vacas; Pavana de Alexandre; Gallarda; conde claros; Fantasia que contrahaze la harpa en la manera de Ludovico. *Valderrábano:* Silva de Sirenas — Fantasia; Soneto lombardo a manera de dança; Soneto. *Fuenllana:* Orphenica Lyra — Duo de Fuenllana; Tant que vivray; Fantasia de redobles; De Antequera sale el moro. *López:* Fantasia. *Pisador:* Libro de Musica de Vihuela — Dezilde al cavallero que; Madona mala vostra; Pavana muy llana para tañer. *Mendoza:* Diferencias de folías. *Daza:* El Parnasso — Quien te hizo Juan pastor; Fantasia. *Anonymous sixteenth century:* La morda.

· 59' DDD 4/91

This generously filled disc reflects virtually the entire vihuela repertory from Luis Milán (1536) to the much less familiar Esteban Daza (1572). The vihuela is a member of the viol family but whose strings, typically arranged in six or seven courses, each paired in unison, are plucked rather than bowed. Christopher Wilson, better known to us as a lutenist, has chosen his programme well though the quality of the music is, almost inevitably, uneven. The most impressive pieces belong to the earliest of the composers represented here — Milán, Mudarra and Narváez. Between them they produced music rich in fantasy and varied both in colour and form. Wilson brings their compositions to life imaginatively, rhythmically and with a fluent technique that should win many friends. The recording itself is admirable, capturing the wide range of colours of which both instrument and performer are capable.

VLADIMIR HOROWITZ. THE LAST RECORDING. **Vladimir Horowitz** (pf). Sony Classical CD45818.
Haydn: Keyboard Sonata in E flat major, HobXVI/49. *Chopin:* Mazurka in C minor, Op. 56 No. 3. Nocturnes — E flat, Op. 55 No. 2; B major, Op. 62 No. 1. Fantaisie-impromptu in C sharp minor, Op. 66. Etudes — A flat major, Op. 25 No. 1; E minor, Op. 25 No. 5. *Liszt:* "Weinen, Klagen, Sorgen, Zagen", Präludium, S179. *Wagner/Liszt:* Paraphrase on Isolden's Liebestod from "Tristan und Isolde", S447.

· 58' DDD 8/90

More than any other pianist of his generation, Vladimir Horowitz was a legend in his lifetime, not only for his staggering technique but also for the personality and authority of his playing. Other pianists such as Rubinstein and Arrau may have been finer all-rounders (there were gaps in his repertory even in the classical and romantic field), but none has left so many performances distinguished by a special individuality that is covered, though hardly explained, by the word magic. As Murray Perahia has written, from the point of view of a pianist over 40 years his junior, "he was a man who gave himself completely through his music and who confided his deepest emotions through his playing". The performances in this last of his recordings, made in New York in 1989 and with superlative piano sound, are wonderfully crystalline and beautifully articulated, yet there is warmth too in the Haydn sonata that begins his programme and nothing whatever to suggest that octogenarian fingers were feeling their age or that his fine ear had lost its judgement. The rest of the disc is devoted to Chopin and Liszt, two great romantic composers with whom he was always associated, the last piece being Liszt's mighty transcription of Wagner's *Liebestod*, in which the piano becomes a whole operatic orchestra topped by a soprano voice singing out her love for the last time. Apparently this was the last music Horowitz ever played, and no more suitable ending can be imagined for a great pianistic career informed by a consuming love of music that was expressed in playing of genius. A uniquely valuable record.

Choral and Song

NEW REVIEW

AWAKE, SWEET LOVE ... [a]**James Bowman** (alto); [b]**David Miller** (lte); [c]**King's Consort of Viols** ([d]Wendy Gillespie, Richard Boothby, William Hunt, [e]Mark Caudle). Hyperion CDA66447. Notes and texts included.
Dowland: Can she excuse my wrongs[abc]. Flow my teares[abe]. A fancy, P5[b]. Sorrow stay[abe]. Queene Elizabeth, her Galliard[b]. Goe nightly cares[abde]. Now, O now I needs must part[ab]. Preludium[b]. A Fantasie, P1[b]. Say love if ever thou didst finde[ab]. Frogg Galliard[b]. Awake sweet love, thou art returned[ab]. Tell me, true Love[abc]. *Campion:* Author of light[abe]. Oft have I sigh'd[abe]. *Ford:* Since first I saw your face[ab]. *Johnson:* Eliza is the fairest queen[ac]. *Ferrabosco:* Pavin[b]. *Danyel:* Eyes, look no more[abe]. Thou pretty bird how do I see[abe]. I doe whenas I do not see[ab]. *Hunnis:* In terrors trapp'd[ac]. *Anonymous:* Come, tread the paths[ac].

1h 12' DDD 10/91

Domestic music-making flourished in the times of Good Queen Bess, when many households boasted the odd lute, maybe a chest of viols, and citizens whose singing voices could be heard (not only at bathtime); many were those who rewarded the publishers of music for their use and delight. This situation is mirrored in the programme of songs (with lute or consort) and lute solos, by James Bowman and the King's Consort. The music of Dowland lies naturally at the heart of the matter and here it frames that of some of his distinguished contemporaries. The inclusion of the viol part specified in some of the lute songs restores a dimension of beauty that is often sacrificed in present-day performances. In keeping with the album title, many of the songs deal with aspects of love — even the lute-solo *Frogg Galliard* pokes fun at the unrequited love of Mounsier le Duc d'Alençon for the Queen herself. James Bowman brings more than two decades of experience and devotion to bear in these memorable performances, and he is most sympathetically supported by the King's Consort, amongst whom David Miller should be singled out for special mention for his clear and intelligent playing of the lute solos. Happy the family that spent its leisure hours with this music, and happy the owner of this disc.

AMERICAN CONCERT SONGS. Thomas Hampson (bar); **Armen Guzelimian** (pf). EMI CDC7 54051-2.

Griffes: An Old Song Re-sung. *Giannini:* Tell me, oh blue sky! *Sacco:* Brother Will, Brother John. *Hanby:* Darling Nelly Gray. *Foster* (trans. Riegger): Ah! May the red rose live always (with Kenneth Sillito, vn). *Romberg:* MAYTIME — Will you remember? *Damrosch:* Danny Deever, Op. 2 No. 7. *Harrison:* In the Gloaming. *Speaks:* On the Road to Mandalay. *Hageman:* Do not go, my love. *J. Duke:* Luke Havergal. *Charles:* When I have sung my songs. *Cadman:* At Dawning, Op. 29 No. 1 (Sillito, vn). *Korngold:* Tomorrow. *Haydn Wood:* Roses of Picardy. *Messager:* MIRETTE — Long ago in Alcala. *Traditional:* Shenandoah. The Erie Canal (both arr. Ames). The nightingale (arr. C. Shaw). The lass from the Low Countree (arr. Niles).

· 1h 6' DDD 3/91

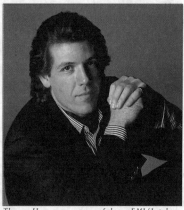

Thomas Hampson   *[photo: EMI/Leighton*

"Why should the beautiful die?" asks Thomas Hampson in Stephen Foster's song *Ah! May the red rose live always* and, by applying this notion to neglected songs, he and Armen Guzelimian (with Kenneth Sillito riding violin obbligato in a couple of the numbers) take a journey down Memory Lane. "American Concert Songs" refers here to those popular numbers that might have been included in a typical American concert of the earlier years of this century, rather than ones specifically written by American composers — in fact, a few on this disc are of British origin. Hampson has a rare feel for the idiom and a powerful, solid-toned voice that he can turn to delicate and touching effect in the more sentimental items. However, his musicality and good taste never let sentimentality take hold of these performances, and in this, and every other aspect, he is admirably supported by the subtle accompaniment of Guzelimian. The recording engineers have reflected and enhanced the variety of timbre the performers bring to the different songs so that the recital retains interest throughout and each item attains maximum individual impact. Altogether a delight.

NEW REVIEW

LE BANQUET DU VOEU 1454. Gilles Binchois Ensemble/Dominique Vellard. Virgin Classics Veritas VC7 91441-2. Notes, text and translations included.

First entertainment — *Vide:* Et c'est asses. *Anonymous:* Adieu ma tres belle maistress. Une foys avant que morir. *Legrant:* Wilhelmus Legrant. *Dufay:* Ave regina celorum. *Second entertainment: Anonymous:* Au chant de l'alowette. *Binchois:* Je ne vis oncques le pareille. Vostre tres doulx regart plaisant. Gloria, laus et honour. *Frye:* Ave regina celorum. *Third entertainment* — *Grenon:* Je ne requier de ma dame. *Dufay:* Je me complains pitieusement. *Anonymous:* Ellend du hast. *Binchois:* Chanson. *Fontaine:* Pur vous tenir. *Fourth entertainment: Anonymous:* Du cuer je suopire. Venise. Preambulum super re. *Binchois:* Seule esgarée. Deo gracias. *Vide:* Il m'est si grief.

· 1h DDD 3/92/

When Philip the Good of Burgundy was invited by the Pope to lead a new crusade against the Turks, who had taken Constantinople in May 1453, it was public confirmation of his power and influence. Philip acknowledged this, and kicked off his campaign for support with an extravagant, and now famous, banquet, known in English as the Feast of the Pheasant. A pie with 28 minstrels inside, and a model church — complete with bells and organ, and containing four singers — provided the musical entertainment, along with 'loud' minstrels in the hall. Jousting, dancing, mimes telling the story of Jason, speeches, and the taking of vows also contributed to the festivities. Although the crusade itself never came to anything, the structure of four groups of entertainments to be performed between the courses of the feast has survived, and pieces that might have been performed have been put together for this disc. These are subtle, elegant readings which, though they may lack the boisterous *bonhomie* that was probably in attendance at the original feast, are particularly suited to repeated listening on disc. The performances of the a cappella pieces clearly maintain the independence of the voices, rather than aiming for a smooth meld, and the instrumentation of the other works has been sensitively chosen. Playing is well articulated and not without virtuosity. The spacious acoustic lends an agreeably authentic ambience to the whole.

CABARET CLASSICS. Jill Gomez (sop); **John Constable** (pf). Unicorn-Kanchana DKPCD9055. Texts and translations included.
Weill: Marie Galante — Les filles de Bordeaux; Le grand Lustucru; Le Roi d'Aquitaine; J'attends un navire. Lady in the Dark — My ship. Street Scene — Lonely house. Knickerbocker Holiday — It never was you. *Zemlinsky:* Songs, Op. 27 — Harlem Tänzerin; Elend; Afrikanischer Tanz. *Schoenberg:* Arie aus dem Spiegel von Arcadien. Gigerlette. Der genügsame Liebhaber. Mahnung. *Satie:* La diva de l'Empire. Allons-y, Chochotte. Je te veux.

57' DDD 6/88

Schoenberg writing cabaret songs with a popular touch? Yes, and quite catchy ones too, as can be heard particularly in *Gigerlette* — prompting the intriguing speculation of what might have been had he not concentrated on *Gurrelieder*. On the other hand, his *Der genügsame Liebhaber* and Zemlinsky's three songs would have been most unlikely to go down with cabaret audiences, however intellectual. At the other end of the spectrum are Satie's café-concert songs (the sentimental waltz *Je te veux* is languidly attractive) and the Weill items, which were not written for cabaret but are drawn from a 1934 Paris play and post-war Broadway musicals. That all these songs do not require a gin-sodden voice or raucous delivery is demonstrated with the utmost artistry by Jill Gomez, in turn seductive, pathetic, sly, sweet, swaggering, passionate, salacious — or simply singing beautifully. Her performance of Weill's *Lonely house* (one of his best) remains hauntingly in the mind.

NEW REVIEW
CANTICLES FROM ELY. Ely Cathedral Choir/Paul Trepte with **Jeremy Filsell** (org). Gamut GAMCD527.
Bairstow: The Lamentation. *F. Jackson:* Benedicite in G major. *Noble:* Magnificat in A minor. *Stanford:* Morning Services — A major, Op. 12; C major, Op. 115. Evening Service in B flat major.

52' DDD 2/92

For Matins the *Te Deum*, with *Benedicite* or *Jubilate* for a somewhat rare change, for Evensong *Magnificat* and *Nunc Dimittis*: these were the canticles sung or recited at Church of England services throughout the centuries, and in most cathedrals they are so still. Setting them to music has also been a preoccupation of British composers through the ages. In late Victorian times and the early part of the twentieth century it was almost a national industry, with Sir Charles Villiers Stanford as its High Master. He wrote ten services altogether, the one in

B flat being the most popular, that in C probably the most admired among musicians. A notable feature in their time was the independence of the organ parts, but to modern listeners it is the richness of sound, the unfailing tunefulness and the sure professionalism of craftsmanship that are likely to be most striking. The Morning Service in A, written in 1880, is also remarkable for boldness of invention with some fine modulations and a particularly inspired breadth at the end of the *Jubilate*. In between the three Stanford services heard here come others by three organists of York Minster: Tertius Noble (represented by a less well-known and on the whole less successful setting than his B minor service), Sir Edward Bairstow, and Francis Jackson (a colourful, and in this company distinctly modern, setting of the *Benedicite*). The *Lamentations* of Jeremiah are designed for alternative use in Lent but, while Bairstow's music is resourceful, it is probably not sufficiently so to justify the length of the piece on musical grounds alone. The Choir of Ely Cathedral sing with fine tone and precision, the organ accompaniments are distinguished by imaginative registration and a strong rhythmic sense, and the disc is well produced.

NEW REVIEW

CHORAL WORKS. [a]**Michael Pearce,** [c]**Leo Hussain** (trebs); [a]**Peter Winn** (alto); [b]**Ameral Gunson** (mez); [a]**John Bowley,** [c]**Simon Williams** (tens); [a]**Daniel Sladden** (bass) [a]**Rachel Masters** (hp); [ac]**David Corkhill;** [c]**Michael Skinner,** [c]**Stephen Whittaker,** [c]**Nigel Bates** (perc); **Choir of King's College, Cambridge/Stephen Cleobury** with [ac]**Peter Barley** (org). EMI CDC7 54188-2. Texts and translation included.
Bernstein: Chichester Psalms[a]. *Copland:* In the Beginning[b]. *Ives:* Psalm 90[c]. *Larsen:* How it thrills us. *Schuman:* Carols of Death.

> 1h DDD 10/91

Bernstein's familiar *Chichester Psalms* were composed to a commission from our own Southern Cathedrals Festival in 1965 and this unusual programme gives us a chance to place them in the context of the English choral tradition. There are some problems of co-ordination in the resonant cavern of King's College Chapel, but it is fascinating to hear again the reduced scoring for organ, harp and percussion. In his cruelly exposed solo, young Michael Pearce has nothing to fear from his rivals. The rest of this accessible all-American collection is no less appealing. Copland's *In the Beginning* is one of his best pieces, and William Schuman's Holstian *Carols* suit the King's acoustic and performance style particularly well. Libby Larsen wrote *How it thrills us* specifically for King's. Only in Ives's extraordinary *Psalm 90* is there perhaps some lack of transcendental magic — that English reserve again? EMI provide unusual, provocative notes from David Nichols and full texts.

NEW REVIEW

CHRISTMAS MUSIC. [bd]**Gavin Williams** (org); [a]**Pro Arte Orchestra,** [b]**Guildford Cathedral Choir/Barry Rose;** [c]**Light Music Orchestra/Sir Vivian Dunn.** EMI Classics CDM7 64131-2. From CSD3580.
Hely-Hutchinson: Carol Symphony[a]. *Vaughan Williams:* Fantasia on Christmas Carols[bd] (John Barrow, bar). *Warlock:* Bethlehem Down[b] (words Blunt); Adam lay y-bounden[bd] (Robert Hammersley, ten). *Quilter:* Children's Overture, Op. 17[c]. *E. Tomlinson:* Suite of English Folk Dances[c]. And all in the morning[bd] (trad. Derbyshire arr. Vaughan Williams). Wassail Song[bd] (trad. Yorkshire arr. Vaughan Williams with Clifford Mould, ten).

> 1h 12' ADD 12/91

Few people in the musical world can point to such success as Barry Rose who, appointed as Guildford Cathedral's first choirmaster, built up (literally from nothing) a choir which was generally considered the best of its day. It is a testament to the quality of his choir that many of the records it made in the 1960s have now been reissued on CD. The sensitivity of Rose's direction and the musical commitment he inspires from his choristers is most obvious in four unusual Christmas carols. Peter Warlock's have a depth and sincerity one doesn't usually associate with this genre while the innocent beauty of two traditional carols is perfectly captured in a recording which doesn't begin to show its age. Vaughan Williams's *Fantasia* is altogether better known, but here again this performance is imbued with a rare feeling for the essential spirit of the music and the poetry of the words. The real gem on this disc, though, is the remarkably vivid account of Hely-Hutchinson's ingenious *Carol Symphony*, an orchestral suite based on several well-known carols. Again Rose directs an outstanding performance which underlines magnificently the inventiveness and near-genius of Hely-Hutchinson's music. The disc is rounded off with two justly popular examples of British light orchestral music at its best.

DRAW ON SWEET NIGHT. Hilliard Ensemble/Paul Hillier. EMI Reflexe CDC7 49197-2. Texts included.
Morley: O greefe even on the bud. When loe, by breake of morning. Aprill is in my mistris face. Sweet nimphe, come to thy lover. Miraculous love's wounding. Fyer and lightning. In nets of golden wyers. *Weelkes:* Thule, the period of cosmographie. O care thou wilt dispatch mee. Since Robin Hood. Strike it up tabor. *Wilbye:* Sweet hony sucking bees. Adew, sweet Amarillis. Draw on sweet night. *J. Bennet:* Weepe O mine eyes. *Gibbons:* The silver swanne. *Tomkins:* See, see, the shepheard's Queene. *Ward:* Come sable night. *Vautor:* Sweet Suffolke owle.

55' DDD 2/89

This refreshingly attractive and well-presented anthology of English madrigals promises to be a delight for the specialist and non-specialist alike. The programme is nicely balanced: the more richly textured, *Sweet hony sucking bees*, are interspersed with a number of the little two- and three-part Morley canzonets, either charmingly phrased and dovetailed by two well-matched sopranos (*Sweet nimphe, come to thy lover*), or sung with boundless energy by two tenors, or two tenors and a bass (the tautly drummed *Strike it up tabor*). The order in which the pieces occur is planned to reflect the changing moods of a single day and variety of mood and emotion is perhaps the chief characteristic of this choice collection. Another unusual feature is the adoption of what is claimed to have been Elizabethan pronunciation of English. This gives the sound of the music a rather special flavour, with the style, the tuning, the lively diction and the wit all contributing to the general excellence and immediacy of this performance.

FRENCH SONGS. Rachel Yakar (sop); **Claude Lavoix** (pf). Virgin Classics VC7 91089-2. Texts and translations included.
Hahn: Quand je fus pris au pavillon. Je me metz en vostre mercy. Le rossignol des lilas. Si mes vers avaient des ailes. L'Air. La Nuit. L'Enamourée. Seule. Les Fontaines. Le souvenir d'avoir chanté. L'Incrédule. D'une prison. Chansons grises. *Bizet:* Sonnet. Rose d'amour. Pastorale. *Chabrier:* Chanson pour Jeanne. Lied. L'Ile heureuse.

1h 2' DDD 3/90

Reynaldo Hahn was too much of a conductor to be rated very highly as a composer, too much of a pianist and singer to be thought of primarily as a conductor, and too witty a writer and talker to be taken quite seriously in any capacity. His talent was prodigious, and it was as a child prodigy that he wrote his best-known song, *Si mes vers avaient des ailes*. It was composed when he was

13, its melody a little more obvious, its accompaniment more simple than in the songs of his later years, yet having qualities of grace and lightness that were to remain typical. He never wrote with weighty pretensions, and when sadness tinges a song, as in *D'une prison*, it is never taken to justify harshness in the music. Other feelings enter, just as a nostalgia for the courtly graces of time past, and this is found in *Quand je fus pris au pavillon* and *Je me metz en vostre mercy*. There is also the more impressionistic style of the *Chansons grises*, the title suggesting their delicacy of colouring and emotion. All of these find suitable companions in the songs of Bizet and Chabrier, and sensitive interpreters in Rachel Yakar and Claude Lavoix, the singer keenly attentive to the word-setting, the pianist subtle in his appreciation of the underlying mood of each song.

FRENCH SONGS AND DUETS. [a]**Ann Murray** (mez); [b]**Philip Langridge** (ten); **Roger Vignoles** (pf). Virgin Classics VC7 91179-2. Texts and translations included.
Chausson: La caravane, Op. 14[b]. Sept mélodies, Op. 2 — No. 3, Les papillons[a]; No. 5, Sérénade italienne[b]; No. 7, Le colibri[a]. Two duos, Op. 11 — No. 2, Le réveil. *Fauré:* Arpège, Op. 76 No. 2[b]. Pleurs d'or, Op. 72. Puisqu'ici bas, Op. 10 No. 1. Soir, Op. 83 No. 2[a]. *Gounod:* Barcarola. Boire à l'ombre[b]. Ce que je suis sans toi[a]. Le premier jour de mai[a]. Sérénade[b]. *Messiaen:* La mort du nombre (with Andrew Watkinson, vn). *Saint-Saëns:* Aimons-nous[b]. L'attente[a]. La cloche[a]. Danse macabre. Viens!

1h 7' DDD 6/91

This enterprising collection includes some little-known works, thanks for their rescue being due to this intelligent husband-and-wife team, backed by an excellent and sympathetic pianist. Chausson's sombre *La caravane*, for example (admirably sung by Langridge), can fairly be called an unjustly neglected masterpiece. The most substantial work here, of particular interest in view of the composer's later development, is the 22-year-old Messiaen's *La mort du nombre*, a dialogue between a soul in purgatory and his beloved who has attained spiritual peace: it calls forth feelings of intense torment by Langridge and rapt serenity from Murray, with a first-class contribution from Vignoles (plus a small but significant violin obbligato). Fauré's warmly sensuous *Pleurs d'or* is perhaps the most outstanding other duet here, but there is charm, also, in Gounod's *Barcarola* (sung in the French translation of the Italian original) and satiric humour in Saint-Saëns's *Danse macabre* (later expanded into the popular symphonic poem). In the solos, *La cloche* (with Murray at her best) belies its composer's reputation for only superficial facility, and Langridge shows a striking range from the easy lyricism of Gounod's *Sérénade* to the passion of Saint-Saëns's *Aimons-nous*.

THE GARDEN OF ZEPHIRUS. FIFTEENTH-CENTURY COURTLY SONGS. **Gothic Voices/Christopher Page** with **Imogen Barford** (medieval hp). Hyperion CDA66144. Texts and translations included. From A66144.
Dufay: J'attendray tant qu'il vous playra. Adieu ces bons vins de Lannoys. Mon cuer me fait tous dis penser. *Briquet:* Ma seul amour et ma belle maistresse. *Anthonello de Caserta:* Amour m'a le cuer mis. *Landini:* Neesun ponga speranza. Giunta vaga biltà. *Reyneau:* Va t'en, mon cuer, avent mes yeux. *Matheus de Sancto Johanne:* Fortune, faulce, parverse. *Francus de Insula:* Amours n'ont cure de tristesse. *Brollo:* Qui le sien vuelt bien maintenir. *Anonymous:* N'a pas long temps que trouvay Zephirus. Je la remire, la belle.

50' DAD 12/86

Springtime, as Chaucer and almost all medieval poets remind us, stirs the gentle heart from sleep. But it was Zephyr, the West Wind, who inspired the humble lover to seek his lady. As often as not she was unattainable but it was an ennobling aspiration, nonetheless. This aspect of refined or courtly society is engagingly captured by Gothic Voices under Christopher Page in a selection of French and Italian chansons, ballades and rondeaux dating from the early to mid fifteenth century. The wealth of vivid images, warm sentiments and formal variety contained in the poems is highlighted both by the musical settings themselves and by polished, communicative performances. The rondeaux of Dufay are perhaps especially affecting — ardent lovers of France and followers of Bacchus will be refreshed by a fragrant tribute to the wines of the Laon district in his *Adieu ces bons vins de Lannoys* — but Landini's ballate, sounding a more objective note, are hardly less so. Full texts with translations are provided and the recorded sound is excellent.

GERMAN CHURCH MUSIC. Exon Singers/Christopher Tolley. Priory PRCD243.
H.L. Hassler: Motets — Deus noster refugium; Verbum caro factum est; O admirabile commercium; Cantate Domino Jubilate Deo; O Domine Jesu Christe; O sacrum convivium. **Bruckner:** Tantum ergo in A flat major. **Liszt:** O salutaris hostia, S43. **Cornelius:** Three Choral Songs, Op. 18.

53' DDD 7/89

The Exon Singers began as a group of students from Exeter University who gathered during vacations to sing the services in various cathedrals. Here they explore an unjustifiably neglected area of the repertoire. Hassler studied with Gabrieli in Venice and became a master of the Venetian Polyphonic style. The motet, "O admirabile commercium", is one of his best examples, bearing comparison with anything by Palestrina. Bruckner was a devout Catholic and composed some of his most personal and deeply-felt music for liturgical use. This is one of no less than eight settings he made of the *Tantum ergo* and its simple, direct style will come as a surprise to those who know Bruckner only through the symphonies. Peter Cornelius's songs for unaccompanied eight part choir are richly colourful and the Exon Singers produce some sumptuous singing here. Christopher Tolley is a thorough and sympathetic musician who inspires his singers to some magnificent performances. Their beautifully blended and perfectly balanced tone, caught in a splendidly warm and full-bodied recording, is a model of unaccompanied choral singing. This is a disc to treasure.

NEW REVIEW

GERMAN SONGS BY AMERICAN COMPOSERS. Thomas Hampson (bar); **Armen Guzelimian** (pf). Teldec 9031-72168-2. Notes, texts and translations included.
Griffes: Am Kreuzweg wird begraben. An den Wind. Auf geheimem Waldespfade. Auf ihrem Grab. Das ist ein Brausen und Heulen. Das sterbende Kind. Elfe. Meeres Stille. Mein Herz ist wie die dunkle Nacht. Mit schwarzen Segeln. Des Müden Abendlied. Nachtlied. So halt' ich endlich dich umfangen. Der träumende See. Wo ich bin, mich rings umdunkelt. Wohl lag ich einst in Gram und Schmerz. Zwei Könige sassen auf Orkadal. **Ives:** Du bist wie eine Blume. Feldeinsamkeit. Frühlingslied. Gruss. Ich grolle nicht. Ilmenau. Marie. Minnelied. Rosamunde. Rosenzweige. Ton. Weil' auf mir. Widmung. Wiegenlied. **MacDowell:** Drei Lieder, Op. 11. Zwei Leider, Op. 12.

1h 12' DDD 4/92

This is a most rewarding American collection which will appeal to lovers of Lieder who can trace some of the same poems, mostly by Heine, set by German composers. Followers of American music will also be intrigued by the early works of Ives, MacDowell and Griffes which, in performances like these, come close to the impact of their German models. It is particularly fascinating to see what Ives does with these romantic poems made famous by the great Lieder composers. He originally set them in German, when he was a student at Yale, and then adapted them to various English texts of a quite different purport. Familiar Ives songs such as *The World's Wanderers* (Shelley) and *I travelled among unknown Men* (Wordsworth) started life as settings of Heine. Ives's ravishing *Wiegenlied* started life in partnership with a poem from *Des Knaben Wunderhorn*. Then, compare his *Ich grolle nicht* with Schumann and no apologies need to be made. These unexpected and little-known connections between the old and the new worlds provide endless richness and the same goes for the MacDowell and the Griffes, if not to quite the same extent. MacDowell, with his gift for miniatures, is adept both at near-salon melody and eloquent piano parts. These may not be the best songs of Griffes, or even the other two composers, but since they were all under 30 at the time and the songs get such revelatory performances from the distinguished team of Thomas Hampson and Armen Guzelimian, it hardly matters. Well recorded too.

NEW REVIEW

HAIL, GLADDENING LIGHT. Cambridge Singers/John Rutter.
Collegium COLCD113. Texts and translations included.
Anonymous: Rejoice in the Lord. *Purcell:* Remember not, Lord, our offences, Z50. *J. Amner:* Come, let's rejoice. *Tomkins:* When David heard. *Bairstow:* I sat down under his shadow. *J. Goss:* These are they that follow the lamb. *Taverner:* Christe Jesu, pastor bone. *Philips:* O beatum et sacrosanctum diem. *Howells:* Nunc dimittis. *Vaughan Williams:* O vos omnes. *Dering:* Factum est silentium. *Stanford:* Justorum animae, Op. 38 No. 1. *C. Wood:* Hail, gladdening light. *Tavener:* A hymn to the mother of God. Hymn for the dormition of the mother of God. *Elgar:* They are at rest. *Walton:* A litany. *Morley:* Nolo mortem peccatoris. *Tallis* O nata lux. *Rutter:* Loving shepherd of Thy sheep. *R. Stone:* The Lord's Prayer. *J. Sheppard:* In manus tuas. *W.H. Harris:* Bring us, O Lord God.

Ih 12' DDD 4/92

This has the subtitle "Music of the English Church" and it is arranged under four main headings: anthems and introits (these count as one), Latin motets, settings of hymns and other poetry, and prayer-settings. Each of them is well represented in a programme that varies delightfully in period and style, and in performances which are remarkably consistent in quality. Some of the items will come as discoveries to most listeners: for example, the anthem *Come, let's rejoice*, a splendid, madrigal-like piece written by John Amner, organist from 1610 to 1641 at Ely Cathedral where these recordings were made. Others are equally impressive in their present performance: a deep quietness attends the opening of Richard Dering's *Factum est silentium*, which ends with rhythmic Alleluias set dancing with subdued excitement. Among the hymn-settings is one by a 16-year-old called William Walton. Included in the prayers is the choirmaster's own setting, characteristically made for pleasure, of *Loving shepherd of Thy sheep*. All are unaccompanied, and thus very exactly test the choir's blend of voices, its precision, articulation and feeling for rhythm. In all respects they do exceptionally well; the tone is fresh, the attack unanimous, the expression clear and sensitive, the rhythm on its toes. These are young and gifted singers, formed with disciplined enthusiasm into a choir with a distinctive style — and, incidentally, recorded with admirable results by a family firm which operates from a studio built at the bottom of the garden.

NEW REVIEW

HEAR MY PRAYER. [a]Jeremy Budd (treb); St Paul's Cathedral Choir/John Scott with [b]Andrew Lucas (org). Hyperion CDA66439. Texts and
translations included.

Allegri: Miserere (with Nicholas Thompson, treb; Wilfred Swansborough, alto; Timothy Jones, bass)[a]. *B. Rose:* Feast Song for St Cecilia (Simon Hill, alto; Alan Green, ten)[a]. *Brahms:* Ein deutsches Requiem — Ich hab nun Traurigkeit (sung in English)[ab]. *Britten:* Festival Te Deum, Op. 32[ab]. *Harvey:* Come, Holy Ghost (Andrew Burden, ten; Nigel Beaven, bass)[a]. *Mendelssohn:* Hear my prayer[ab]. *Stanford:* Evening Canticles in G major (Jones)[ab]. *Tavener:* I will lift up mine eyes. *Wise:* The ways of Zion do mourn (Charles Gibbs, bass)[ab].

Ih 16' DDD 10/91

The special distinction of this disc is the work of the treble soloist, Jeremy Budd. He sings in a programme which is very much the choirboy's equivalent of an operatic soprano's "Casta diva" and more of that sort (come to think of it, Master Budd could probably have sung a splendid "Casta diva" into the bargain). As it is, he crowns the Allegri *Miserere* with its five top Cs, spot-on, each of them (rather like Melba singing "Amor" at the end of Act 1 in *La bohème* five times over). He commands the breath, the long line and the purity of tone needful for the solo in Brahms's Requiem. He follows in the Ernest Lough tradition in Mendelssohn (who, with his 78rpm recording of *Hear my prayer*, now transferred to CD — EMI CDH7 63827-2 — became one of the most famous singers in the world) and copes with the difficult modern idiom of Jonathan Harvey's *Come, Holy Ghost* with an apparent ease that to an older generation may well seem uncanny. Other modern works are included. John Tavener's *I will lift up mine eyes*, written for St Paul's in 1990, has its characteristic compound of richness and austerity; and in

this, the words penetrate the mist of echoes more successfully than do those of the *Feast Song for St Cecilia*, written by Gregory Rose and set to some very beautiful music by his father Bernard. It is good, as ever, to hear Stanford's Evening Service in G, with its almost Fauré-like accompaniment finely played by the excellent Andrew Lucas; and for a morning canticle there is Britten's *Te Deum* with its effective build-up to "Lord God of Sabaoth" and its faint pre-echo of *The Turn of the Screw* at "O Lord, save Thy people". There is also a melancholy anthem by Michael Wise, whose fate it was to be knocked on the head and killed by the watchman to whom he was cheeky one night in 1687.

Jeremy Budd *[photo: Hyperion*

NEW REVIEW

INTERMEDIOS DEL BARROCO HISPANICO. [a]**Montserrat Figueras** (sop); **Hespèrion XX/Jordi Savall** (va da gamba). Auvidis Astrée E8729. *M. Romero:* Caiase de un espino[a.] *Aguilera de Héredia:* Tiento de Batalla. Ensalada. *Lope de Vega/Anonymous:* De pechos sobre una torre[a]. Como retumban los remos[a]. *F. Guerrero:* Si tus penas[a]. *J. Cabanilles:* Pasacalles V. Tiento Ileno. Corrente italiana. *J.K. Kerll:* Batalla Imperial. *M. Machado:* Afuera, afuera que sale[a]. *Correa de Arauxo:* Batalla des Morales. *J. Blas de Castro:* Desde las torres del alma[a]. Entre dos Alamos verdes[a]. *J. Marin:* Ojos, que me desdenais[a]. *Anonymous:* No hay que decirle el primor[a].

Ih II' DDD 2/92

A heady Hispanic baroque cocktail. All the vocal numbers here are settings of texts by the colourful and astonishingly prolific Spanish poet and dramatist Lope de Vega (1562-1635), described by Cervantes as "a monster of nature". They range from blithe, folkish pieces through the powerful *De pechos sobre una torre*, in whch a woman laments her lover who has sailed for England with the Armada, to Guerrero's haunting prayer to Jesus, declaimed over a bare string bass and culminating in an extraordinary spoken climax. The instrumental items interspersed with the vocal settings include several rousing battle pieces — a popular seventeenth-century genre — and, for contrast, three beautiful polyphonic numbers by one of the greatest figures of the Spanish Baroque, Joan Cabanilles. If Jordi Savall has touched up the scoring of some of the pieces, no matter: the performances are exciting, sensual, dramatic, with kaleidoscopically varied instrumental colouring, from the entertaining percussion effects of Machado's *Afuera, afuera que sale* to the grave viol consort of Cabanilles's *Pasacalles V* (strong Purcellian associations here). And Savall's wife, Montserrat Figueras, with her distinctive, plangent tone, makes a subtle, stylish, richly imaginative soloist. An irresistible disc, and an ideal introduction to the largely unexplored treasures of the Spanish Baroque.

LAMENTO D'ARIANNA. VARIOUS SETTINGS. **The Consort of Musicke/ Anthony Rooley.** Deutsche Harmonia Mundi Editio Classica GD77115. Texts and translations included. From 1C 165 169504-3 (2/85).
Monteverdi: Lamento d'Arianna a voce sola. Lamento d'Arianna a 5. Pianto della Madonna voce sola. *Bonini:* Lamento d'Arianna in stile recitavo. *Pari:* Il lamento d'Arianna. *Costa:* Pianto d'Arianna a voce sola. *Il Verso:* Lasciatemi morire a 5. *Roscarini:* Reciproco amore a 3.

> ② 1h 48' ADD 12/90 £ ✎

This is an historic recording and it recalls a moment of particular significance in the history of music. Monteverdi's *Arianna* first saw the light of day in Mantua in 1608. None of it survives except for Arianna's great dramatic lament after she has been abandoned by Teseo. The lament, which had apparently moved the Mantuan audience to tears, was central to the whole opera and it became extremely popular in its own right. Other composers imitated it and a new style of dramatic composition for solo voice was born as a result. In 1984 Anthony Rooley had the splendid idea of searching out some of these other seventeenth-century compositions and bringing them all together in a single programme. The two resulting LPs are now reissued as CDs and we can enjoy, first and foremost, Monteverdi's own original version, ably sung with profound understanding by Emma Kirkby, with accompaniment for chitarrone; and also the composer's well-known five-part madrigal using the same material (1614), as well as his much later (1640) reworking of this music, transformed into a somewhat sentimental meditation, for solo voice and organ, a religious lament placed in the mouth of the Madonna at the foot of the Cross. The five lesser-known compositions have each something new to offer: Bonini's dramatic setting may well come closest to the action of the original opera; Pari's contribution is a series of 12 madrigals analysing the successive emotions of the heroine. Costa's solo lament (Emma Kirkby again) is totally restrained and dignified. Antonio il Verso's madrigalian version, for all its extravagance, is clearly derived from Monteverdi's model. Roscarini, the latest of the six (1695), pushes extravagance to its limits. All of this is delightfully performed. This is a recording that throws much fascinating light on the way music changed course during the seventeenth century, but it is no less enjoyable for fulfilling such a useful purpose.

NEW REVIEW

LANCASTER AND VALOIS. Gothic Voices (Margaret Philpot, contr. Rogers Covey-Crump, Andrew Tusa, Charles Daniels, Leigh Nixon, tens; Stephen Charlesworth, Donald Grieg, bars; Andrew Lawrence-King, hp)/**Christopher**

Page (lte). Hyperion CDA66588. Texts and translations included.

Machaut: Donnez, signeurs. Quand je ne voy ma dame. Riches d'amour et mendians. Pas de tor en thies pais. *Solage:* Tres gentil cuer. *Cesaris:* Se vous scaviez, ma tres douce maistresse. Mon seul voloir/Certes m'amour. *Cordier:* Ce jur de l'an. *Pycard:* Credo. *Sturgeon:* Salve mater domini/Salve templum domini. *Fonteyns:* Regali ex progenie. *Anonymous:* Puis qu'autrement ne puis avoir. Soit tart, tempre, main ou soir. Le ior. Avrai je ja de ma dame confort? Sanctus. Je vueil vivre au plaisir d'amours.

| 59' DDD 9/92 | |

This is the tenth recording to come from Christopher Page's Gothic Voices and, the considerable success of their previous recordings notwithstanding, this is perhaps their best yet. In the space of 11 years, Page and his group have reinvented performance practice in medieval and fifteenth century music, as powerful and popularizing an influence as David Munrow and his Early Music Consort of London in the 1970s. "Lancaster and Valois" takes its name from the chosen repertoire: French secular songs of the late fourteenth and early fifteenth centuries juxtaposed with sacred English pieces from around 1400. Much thought has been given to the ordering of the pieces and the grouping of the voices, resulting in the greatest possible diversity. In *Tres gentil cuer* by Solage, Page sets an ideally lilting tempo, with the text finely enunciated by Margaret Philpot, the tenors (in this instance Charles Daniels and Leigh Nixon) adding definition but never threatening to engulf. This is followed by a *Credo* by the English composer Pycard, the longest and most stately piece on the disc, exploiting the richer timbres of tenors and baritones. With excellent sound and entertaining and scholarly notes by Christopher Page, this is an irresistible disc.

LIEDER RECITAL. Dame Janet Baker (mez); **Martin Isepp** (pf). Saga Classics SCD9001. Texts and translation included. From STXID5277 (4/66).

Schumann: Frauenliebe und -leben, Op. 42. *Brahms:* Die Mainacht, Op. 43 No. 2. Das Mädchen spricht, Op. 107 No. 3. Nachtigall, Op. 97 No. 1. Von ewiger Liebe, Op. 43 No. 1. *Schubert:* Heimliches Lieben, D922. Minnelied, D429. Die abgeblühte Linde, D514. Der Musensohn, D764.

| 47' AAD 3/92 | £ |

AN ANTHOLOGY OF ENGLISH SONG. Dame Janet Baker (mez) **Martin Isepp** (pf). Saga Classics SCD9012. From STXID5213 (8/66).

Vaughan Williams: Five mystical songs — The call. Songs of travel — Youth and love. *Ireland:* A Thanksgiving. Her song. *Head:* A piper. *Armstrong-Gibbs:* This is a sacred city. Love is a sickness. *Dunhill:* The cloths of heaven. To the Queen of heaven. *Warlock:* Balulalow. Youth. *Howells:* King David. Come, sing and dance. *Gurney:* Sleep. I will go with my father a-ploughing. *Finzi:* Let us garlands bring, Op. 18 — Come away, death; It was a lover and his lass.

| 45' AAD 3/92 | £ |

These recordings were rapturously reviewed in *Gramophone* when they first appeared, and there was no doubt that a singer of great achievement and still greater promise had arrived in our midst. Over the next many years, the name of Janet Baker (Dame-to-be) graced the monthly lists of new recordings and unfailingly brought distinction with it. Her interpretative powers were to mature, and she was certainly to be better recorded, but it is quite likely that nothing brought greater pleasure in the sheer sound of the voice than these early recitals, one of English song, one of Lieder. Her *Frauenliebe und -leben* here has the mark of a great interpreter upon it particularly in the song of happy motherhood, "An meinem Herzen"; but earlier, the conviction of her singing irradiates the performance, and in the last song the fine dark tone and change of expression on the 'face' of the voice are both eloquent and moving. In the Schubert group, her *Musensohn* has a joyous unselfconsciousness, and in the Brahms her *Von ewiger Liebe* still ranks among the finest of all. The selection of English songs is a joy in itself, with Howells's *King David* and *Come, sing and dance* as perhaps the most memorable of all. And nothing could be lovelier than Finzi's setting of *Come away, death* or this performance of it. Some listeners may be deterred by the level of tape-hiss; regrettable too are the short playing times of both discs and the failure of the presenters to give the dates of the original recordings. These are small matters, however, and there is nothing small about such singing.

LIEDER AND SONG RECITAL. Peter Schreier (ten); **Wolfgang Sawallisch** (pf). Philips 426 237-2PH. Texts and translations included. Recorded at a performance in Munich on 6th February 1984.
Brahms: Deutsche Volkslieder — No. 1, Sagt mire, o schönste Schäf'rin; No. 4, Guten Abend, mein tausiger Schatz; No. 15, Schwesterlein, Schwester-lein; No. 34, Wie komm'ich denn zur Tür herein? Wiegenlied, Op. 49 No. 4.
Prokofiev: Three Children's Songs, Op. 68. The Ugly Duckling, Op. 18 (all sung in German). *Schumann:* Dichterliebe, Op. 48. Der Nussbaum, Op. 25 No. 3.

· 1h 12' DDD 4/90

This live recital caught Schreier and his pianist, Sawallisch, at the top of their form as a partnership. Their account of *Dichterliebe* encompasses every facet of the cycle, holding the attention from start to finish through the intensity of its utterance and flights of imagination. The grief, so poetically and movingly expressed by Heine and Schumann, is here delineated with raw immediacy yet no sense of exaggeration. The troubled, abandoned lover sings, in Schreier's plangent tones, with a poignant, tearful feeling that goes to the heart of things and Sawallisch's playing is fully supportive of the tenor's reading. As compared with Bär (refer to the Index to Reviews), Schreier sings in the original keys throughout: his is a more overtly emotional reading, but both deserve recommendation. In the Brahms, Schreier and Sawallisch rightly adopt a lighter, yet equally pointed style. The Prokofiev group shows Schreier equally adept in a very different idiom. Here, instead of attempting phonetic Russian, he very sensibly uses his own German translations and thus makes the most of the text. The audience noises, applause apart, are minimal and the recording conveys the sense of a real occasion.

NEW REVIEW

MASTERS OF TWENTIETH CENTURY A CAPPELLA. [a]**Susse Lillesoe** (sop); [b]**Karl-Gustav Andersson** (ten); **Danish National Radio Chamber Choir/Stefan Parkman.** Chandos CHAN8963. Texts and translations included.
I. Lidholm: … a riveder le stelle (1971-73)[a]. *Henze:* Orpheus behind the wire (1981-83)[b]. *Schoenberg:* Friede auf Erden, Op. 13. *Nørgård:* Wie ein Kind (1979-80). *Poulenc:* Figure humaine (1943).

· 1h 17' DDD 12/91

This is one of the most impressive displays of unaccompanied choral singing you are likely to hear for a very long time. The Danish National Radio Chamber Choir have mastered the fiendish technical demands of these pieces with breathtaking success. Schoenberg's *Friede auf Erden* was considered so difficult that in 1911 the composer was obliged to add an accompaniment for it, but here it is sung in its original version with total authority, while the awesome technical obstacles thrown up by the other composers (sliding tonality from Ingvar Lidholm, distorted vocalizations from Per Nørgård, dense chromatic harmonies from Henze) are overcome with an ease which seems almost condescending. It is the emphasis placed on the musical and emotional aspects of the pieces that is the most impressive quality in Stefan Parkman's direction. It would be easy to leave the listener aghast at the sheer virtuosity of it all, but Parkman has gone beyond that and shows, by means of meticulously prepared performances just what truly beautiful music there is to be found in these uncompromising twentieth-century scores. For the uninitiated, 77 minutes of modern unaccompanied choral music might seem rather an over-indulgence, but few could fail to be captivated by Per Nørgård's delightful setting of nonsense verses, while the emotional power of Poulenc's *Figure humaine* (written during the Nazi occupation of France this became something of an unofficial anthem for the Resistance organization) culminating in the wonderfully hypnotic *Liberté* is beyond adequate description especially given such a powerfully committed performance as this one.

MELODIES FRANCAISES. José van Dam (bar); **Jean-Philippe Collard** (pf). EMI CDC7 49288-2. Texts and translations included.
Berlioz: Les nuits d'été, Op. 7. *Ibert:* Chansons de Don Quichotte. *Fauré:* Claire de lune, Op. 46 No. 2. Les berceaux, Op. 23 No. 1. En prière. *Poulenc:* Chansons gaillardes. *Ropartz:* Quatre poèmes d'après l'intermezzo.

1h 17' DDD 1/90

Berlioz's cycle *Les nuits d'été* dates from 1841 and though these six songs are more often heard in their later orchestral version this original one with piano is more intimate and helps us to appreciate Theophile Gautier's texts. Fauré is represented by three characteristically gentle songs; but otherwise the recital invites us to explore less familiar territory. The songs that Ibert wrote for a 1932 film about Don Quixote are less well known than Ravel's on the same subject, but they offer both tenderness and wit, and although Guy Ropartz's *Four Poems* have less obvious charm they too are beautifully imagined. For many people, though, a special delight in this collection will be Poulenc's *Chansons gaillardes*, whose title might perhaps be translated as "Saucy Songs"; these are vivid settings of eight anonymous and uninhibited seventeenth-century texts about such pleasures as love and drinking. José van Dam has a vocal maturity and keen intelligence that together allow him to do justice to all this music, and his deft and sensitive piano partner Jean-Philippe Collard could not be bettered. The recording is clear and atmospheric.

MELODIES SUR DES POEMES DE BAUDELAIRE. Felicity Lott (sop); **Graham Johnson** (pf). Harmonia Mundi Musique d'abord HMA90 1219. Texts included.
Duparc: L'invitation au voyage. La vie antérieure. *Fauré:* Chant d'automne. La rançon. Hymne. *Bréville:* Harmonie du soir. *Sauguet:* Le chat. *Capdevielle:* Je n'ai pas oublié, voisine de la ville. *Chabrier:* L'invitation au voyage. *Debussy:* La balcon. Harmonie du soir. Le jet d'eau. Recueillement. La mort des amants. *Séverac:* Les hiboux.

1h 5' DDD 4/88

This is an outstandingly creative and ingenious piece of programme-planning. The recital begins with Duparc's two masterly Baudelaire songs, demonstrating that with the right temperament and approach the writer is by no means unsettable. The Fauré, Chabrier and Debussy settings are in a sense uncharacteristic. In another sense, though, how very characteristic of Fauré that the most successful of his three songs (the charming *Hymne*) should set a poem that is hardly characteristic of Baudelaire, and how thoroughly typical that Chabrier should have lavished on *L'invitation au voyage* a virtual prospectus of his later musical style, and that he should then have withdrawn the song in modest acknowledgement of Duparc's supremacy. It is a striking piece, sung here with all the panache that its bold gestures need. The Debussy here is the enraptured young Wagnerite, matching Baudelaire's imagery with his own rich, saturated colours and brocaded textures: heady, sumptuous and impulsive. The four 'minor' composers each contribute a more than minor song that makes one eager to hear more of their work: a finely spun line rising to genuine passion from de Bréville, a delicately pretty miniature from de Séverac, Capdevielle's amply curving melody and, best of all, Sauguet's haunting evocation of a cat. Felicity Lott has the subtlety and the intelligence for these pieces and her pianist is no less resourceful. The recording is good and though texts are provided, translations are not.

MUSIC OF THE GOTHIC ERA. Early Music Consort of London/ David Munrow. Archiv Produktion 415 292-2AH. From 2723 045 (11/76). *Léonin:* Viderunt omnes. *Pérotin:* Viderunt omnes. ***Anonymous thir- teenth century French*** (Montpelier Codex): Alle, psallite cum luya. Amor potes. S'on me regarde. In mari miserie. O mitissima. ***Petrus de Cruce:*** Aucun ont trouvé. ***Adam de la Halle:*** De ma dame vient. J'os bien a m'amie parler. ***Anonymous fourteenth century French*** (Roman de Fauvel): La mesnie fauveline. ***Philippe de Vitry:*** Impudentur circumivi. Cum statua. ***Anonymous thirteenth/fourteenth centuries French*** (Ivrea Codex): Clap, clap, par un matin. Febus mundo oriens. ***Machaut:*** Qui es promesses. Lasse! comment oublieray. Hoquetus David. ***Anonymous four- teenth century French*** (Chantilly Codex): Inter densas deserti meditans.

1h 1' ADD 8/85

There is still no better all-round introduction to the marvels of medieval music than this exquisite anthology, a selection from the last and arguably the most enduring project undertaken by the late David Munrow. Much of this music had never been performed in modern times before and the singing and playing exude unusual freshness and vitality, inspired no doubt by the sheer excitement of discovery. The most indispensable performances here are without question those of music by Léonin and Pérotin, the earliest named European composers of polyphony. Their audacious and ambitious settings of *Viderunt omnes*, written for the newly-built Cathedral of Notre Dame in Paris during the second half of the twelfth century, rank among the most thrilling and taxing music ever devised for the human voice, and Munrow's interpretations remain unsurpassed. Following them comes a survey of the early history of the motet which in its chronological layout and comprehensiveness is no less an education than an entertainment. The only real regret is that the contents of the original three-LP boxed set have been pared down to an hour's worth of highlights.

MUSIC FOR THE LION-HEARTED KING. Gothic Voices/Christopher Page. Hyperion CDA66336. Texts and translations included. ***Anonymous Twelfth Century:*** Mundus vergens. Novus miles sequitur. Sol sub nube latuit. Hac in anni ianua. Anglia, planctus itera. Etras auri reditur. Vetus abit littera. In occasu sideris. Purgator criminum. Pange melos lacrimosum. Ver pacis apperit. Latex silice. ***Gace Brulé:*** A la doucour de la bele seson. ***Blondel de Nesle:*** L'amours dont sui espris. Ma joie me semont. ***Gui IV, "Li chastelain de Couci":*** Li nouviaz tanz.

1h DDD 10/89

Christopher Page has a remarkable gift for creating enthralling programmes of early music bound together by a brilliantly-chosen central theme, or appellation. This new collection is no less distinguished and every bit as fascinating, musically and historically. Whether or not Richard himself ever actually listened to any of these pieces is beside the question: they are all representative of the period of his lifetime and are gathered together here in his name for the 800th anniversary of his coronation (1189). Two types of twelfth-century vocal music are represented: the *conductus* — which can be written for one, two, three or even four voices and the *chanson*, or noble, courtly love song. The singers cannot be applauded too highly for performances marked by an extraordinary insight into how this music should be tackled, that is, with a fair degree of restraint as well as know-how, given the sort of audience it might have had in Richard's day: the royal court or the household of some high-ranking ecclesiastic.

NEW REVIEW

ORPHEUS I AM. Tragicomedia/Stephen Stubbs. EMI Reflexe CDC7 54311-2. Texts and translations included.
Anonymous: Cock Lorel. The ape's dance at the Temple. **Dowland:** Doulands Rounde Battell Galyard. **W. Lawes:** The catts. Come, my Daphne, come away. Gather ye rosebuds while ye may (two versions). Haste you, nimphs. He that will not love. A masque. Royall Consorts — Sett No. 1 in D minor: Fantazy, Aire, Almain, Corranto I and II, Saraband and Ecco; Sett No. 2 in D minor: Aire. To the dews. To pansies. To the sycamore. White though yee be. Wise nature that the dew of sleep prepares. Ye feinds and furies. **R. Johnson:** Arm, arm!. As I walked forth. Baboon's Dance. Care-charming sleep. Charon, oh Charon. Dear, do not your fair beauty wrong. The first of the Temple. Full fathom five. Have you seen the bright lily grow?. Mascarada. The noble man's masque tune. Orpheus I am. Satyr's Dance. The third of the Temple. Tis late and cold. Where the bee sucks.

 1h 19' DDD 2/92

The Jacobean masque was an extremely popular form of entertainment at the Stuart court, one in which all the arts, visual and aural, were brought to the service of fantasy, fun and, sometimes, the making of political points. It was staged at the end of a spoken play, preceded by the antimasque in which various kinds of professional entertainer appeared, and ending in general revelry with audience participation. Despite all this only one masque (by William Lawes) and fragments of a few others have survived in detail. Tragicomedia have used surviving fragments of masques and theatre music of the time to reconstruct a notional masque, together with a musical synopsis of the preceding — equally notional play. The result is an adroit juxtaposition of vocal and instrumental music, and a kaleidoscope of changing moods that is punctuated at appropriate moments by the appearance of various grotesques and an early version of *Cats* — Lawes got there long before Lloyd Webber. In its conception, execution (both vocal and instrumental) and quality of recording and balance, this disc is a touchstone by which others might be measured. It is also first-class entertainment.

NEW REVIEW

THE ROSE AND THE OSTRICH FEATHER. Music from the Eton Choirbook, Volume 1. **The Sixteen/Harry Christophers.** Collins Classics 1314-2. Notes and texts included.
Fayrfax: Magnificat ("Regale"). *Hygons:* Salve regina. **Turges:** From stormy wyndis. **Browne:** Stabat iuxta Christi crucem. **Anonymous:** This day day dawes. **Cornysh:** Salve regina.

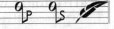 1h 3' DDD 4/92

The sacred music of early Tudor England (the end of the fifteenth century) has been unjustly neglected on CD and the welcome extended to this Collins release is further enhanced by the fact that Harry Christophers and his ensemble have since added two further volumes to this series dedicated to music from the Eton Choirbook. The destruction of great swathes of manuscript in the sixteenth century has left us with only isolated jewels such as this to remind us in sound what the eye can behold in the Perpendicular style of the architecture of the cathedrals of Canterbury, Worcester, Winchester and the Minster at York. Both

architecture and music present soaring vaulted vistas and an attention to florid and ornate tracery. The Rose and the Ostrich Feather? These were both potent symbolic emblems of members of the royal house of Tudor and the words are incorporated into the two secular songs with English texts. The white rose was also an image closely associated with the Virgin Mary and most of the scores

Harry Christophers and The Sixteen [photo: Collins Classics/White

in the Choirbook are dedicated to her. Sadly, the disc is without translations of the Latin works but there is a fascinating essay by John Milsom. This music finds The Sixteen at their best, especially attentive to the severe tuning demands placed on the singers, for whom there is no instrumental accompaniment. Particularly notable is the control that Christophers exerts over the sound of his singers in this very taxing music (four of the performances on the disc last for over ten minutes). The recorded sound expertly captures and balances the expressive singing. Whether used as an aural accompaniment to a great architectural style or enjoyed purely for its sharply-defined reflection of one of the greatest periods of English music (existing within the choral traditions which continues to this day), this disc is altogether outstanding and should not be missed.

SACRED CHORAL WORKS. Westminster Abbey Choir/Simon Preston.
Archiv Produktion 415 517-2AH. Texts and translations included.
Palestrina: Missa Papae Marcelli. Tu es Petrus. *Allegri:* Miserere.
Anerio: Venite ad me omnes. *Nanino:* Haec dies. *Giovannelli:* Jubilate Deo.

59' DDD 5/86

To listen to this disc is to enjoy a feast of sacred choral music composed by members of the well-known school of eminent Roman musicians of the sixteenth and early seventeenth centuries. Palestrina heads the list with his *Missa Papae Marcelli*, but no less famous is the Allegri Miserere, which is performed here with a musical understanding and penetration that is comparatively rare. The alternating *falsobordone* verses excel in richness, and those of the semi-chorus, admirably distanced from the main choir, float across and upwards with an ethereal quality of amazing beauty and magic. The Choir of Westminster Abbey find plenty of scope to display their varied musical skills in the Mass itself, the psalm, and the four motets, and particularly enjoyable is the precision and crispness of the rhythm in Giovannelli's *Jubilate*, and also the careful balance and fullness of the sound in Anerio's *Venite ad me*. The unlikely venue of All Saints, Tooting has proved to be a particularly rewarding one.

SACRED CHORAL WORKS. Various artists. Classics for Pleasure CD-CFP4532. From EMI recordings made between 1957-81.
Arias from Sacred Choral Works by: **Bach, Handel, Mozart, Haydn, Rossini, Mendelssohn, Fauré** and **Verdi.**

1h 5' ADD 8/89

Here is a good collection of popular arias, which includes some interesting contributions from singers of the recent past. Elsie Morison's clear soprano tone and unfussy musicianship can be admired in "I know that my Redeemer liveth" from Handel's *Messiah*, from which oratorio Richard Lewis also sings "Comfort

ye" and "Ev'ry valley" in fine style. Lewis's acount of "Sound an alarm" from
Handel's *Judas Maccabeus* is also very accomplished, as is the young Kiri Te
Kanawa's rendering of "Laudamus te" from Mozart's Mass in C minor, K427.
Janet Baker's "O rest in the Lord" from Mendelssohn's *Elijah* was also recorded
at a fairly early stage in her career, when her gorgeous voice still had a contralto
characteristic and Lucia Popp's singing of the "Alleluja" from Mozart's *Exsultate,
jubilate*, K165, also has an appealing freshness. Victoria de los Angeles is not
quite at her best in the "Pie Jesu" from Fauré's Requiem and Robert Gambill's
comparatively recent recording of "Cujus animan" from Rossini's *Stabat mater* is
fairly ordinary, but items from Joan Sutherland, John Shirley-Quirk, Dietrich
Fischer-Dieskau and Nicolai Gedda all have some distinction. The recordings are
mostly over 20 years old, but all bear their years lightly.

NEW REVIEW

**SACRED AND SECULAR MUSIC FROM SIX CENTURIES. Hilliard
Ensemble.** Hyperion CDA66370. Texts and translations included.
Anonymous: Dezi, flor resplandeciente. Nuevas, nuevas Por tu fe!. *Byrd:* Ne
irascaris Domine. *Dufay:* Gloria ad modem tubae. Vergene bella. *Fayrfax:*
Most clere of colour. *Flecha:* El jubilate. *Hermannus Contractus:* Salve
regina. *Godefroy de St Victoire:* Planctus ante nescia. *Goudimel:* Bonjour
mon coeur. *Isaac:* Tota pulchra es. *Janequin:* Le chant des oiseaux. *Machaut:*
Quant je sui mis au retour. *Peñalosa:* Sancta mater. *Tallis:* O nata lux.

| 1h 2' DDD 6/91 |

The title of this disc might lead you to expect a selection of pieces progressing
gently from the renaissance to the present day. But in fact the *latest* item recorded
here dates from the sixteenth century; the earliest is by a Benedictine monk born
in 1013 — a reminder of the way in which, these days, the boundaries of vocal
repertoire are being pushed further and further back into the mists of musical
history. As always with the Hilliards, though, this is far from being just a dry,
academic survey: the primary consideration is the music — and on this recording
they have included many of their own favourite pieces. Not surprisingly, then, it
is a selection that shows the group at its best — from the restrained devotion of
the eleventh-century antiphon to the Virgin which begins the programme, through
the extrovert hocketing of Dufay's *Gloria ad modem tubae* (which ends in a blaze
of what can only be described as vocal ping-pong), through to the concluding item:
Janequin's famous musical representation of French bird-life. En route, there are
many other delights, both familiar and unusual — and although some faintly
audible traffic noise provides an occasional reminder of the twentieth century it
doesn't detract from these highly polished — and highly enjoyable performances.

THE SERVICE OF VENUS AND MARS. [a]**Andrew Lawrence-King**
(medieval hp); **Gothic Voices/Christopher Page.** Hyperion CDA66238.
Texts and translations included where appropriate.
Philippe de Vitry: Gratissima virginis/Vos qui admiramini/Gaude gloriosa/
Contratenor. *P. des Molins:* De ce que fol pense. *Pycard:* Gloria. *L.
Power:* Sanctus. *F. Lebertoul:* Las, que me demanderoye. *J. Pyamour:*
Quam pulchra es. *Dunstable:* Speciosa facta es. *Soursby:* Sanctus. *R.
Loqueville:* Je vous pri que j'aye un baysier[a]. *Anonymous fourteenth
century:* Singularis laudis digna. De ce fol pense (after des Molins)[a]. Lullay,
lullay. *Anonymous fourteenth or fifteenth centuries:* There is no rose
of swych virtu. Le gay playsir[a]. Le grant pleyser[a]. The Agincourt Carol.

| 50' DDD 11/87 |

This collection is of music loosely associated with the Order of the Garter,
founded by Edward III in the middle years of the fourteenth century. It includes

some wonderful English works from the years 1340-1440, including the motet *Singularis laudis digna*, a wonderful canonic Gloria by Pycard, works by composers of the school of Dunstable (who influenced continental composers as no English composer has done since), and finally the famous carol celebrating Henry V's victory at Agincourt. Gothic Voices have in the last few years set new standards in the performance of this kind of music and their attention to inner detail produces some beautiful results. Hyperion's characteristically informative and persuasive notes are also considerably helpful in bringing this music to life.

SIXTEENTH- AND SEVENTEENTH-CENTURY CHORAL WORKS. King's College Choir, Cambridge / Stephen Cleobury with [a]**David Briggs** (org). EMI CDC7 47065-2. From EL270095-1 (12/84).
Allegri: Miserere mei, Deus (with Timothy Beasley-Murray, treb). *Nanino:* Adoramus te Christe a 5. *Marenzio:* Magnificat a 8[a]. *Frescobaldi:* Messa sopra l'aria della Monica. *Ugolini:* Beata es Virgo Maria a 12[a].

> 45' DDD 5/85

The central work on this disc, Allegri's setting of the penitential Psalm 51, *Have mercy upon me, O God*, is by far the simplest in construction, alternating a single strand of plainsong with straightforward harmonic passages for five-part choir and verses for a quartet of solo voices. Yet it speaks to the heart nowadays as clearly as it did in the early seventeenth century when it was written. There is a special frisson each time the treble soloist soars effortlessly to his top C. All the composers represented here worked in Rome, and this anthology seeks to illustrate the variety of musical styles current in Roman church music at this time. The choir sing all this ageless music with that understated confidence for which they are famous. Their voices are as cool as the spreading fan vault high above their heads. The recording embraces the stillness of this great space but with a balance which loses no detail.

NEW REVIEW

SONG RECITAL. Anne-Lise Berntsen (sop); **Einar Henning Smebye** (pf). Victoria VCD19012. Texts and translations included.
Mussorgsky: Songs and Dances of Death. *Sibelius:* The dream, Op. 13 No. 5. And I questioned them no further, Op. 17 No. 1. Black roses, Op. 36 No. 1. But my bird, Op. 36 No. 2. *Wagner:* Wesendonk Lieder.

> 56' DDD 11/91

SONG RECITAL. Anne-Lise Berntsen (sop); [a]**Terje Tønnesen** (vn); [a]**Aage Kvalbein** (vc); **Einar Henning Smebye** (pf). Victoria VCD19017. Texts and translations included.
Berg: Four Songs, Op. 2. *Kvandal:* Norwegian folk-songs, Op. 40. *Shostakovich:* Seven Romances, Op. 127[a].

> 57' DDD 11/91

Here is an interesting singer with interesting programmes. In the first disc the *Songs and Dances of Death* live an intensely imaginative life, the voice ranging widely with at first a hollow, other-worldly tone in the "Lullaby", then a silvery quality to set the starlit scene in the "Serenade", with a ringing power in Death's rapacious call at the end. In the third song, the famous "Trepak", the story-telling has a ghostly eeriness, and there is apt command in the voice of the "Commander-in-Chief". These are grimly compassionate songs, contrasting with the warmer romanticism of Sibelius (even when a folk-idiom is present), and still more with Wagner's five songs dedicated to his beloved Mathilde Wesendonk who herself wrote the poems. Anne-Marie Berntsen is less well-suited in these, yet here too (and particularly in "Im Treibhaus") her mastery of mood is very evident. This remains impressive throughout the second recital. Berg's *Four Songs* again have an element of ghostliness about them, mirrored in the singer's tone. The folk-songs of John Kvandal, published in 1970, bring the voice out into the happier world of nature, and it is good to find a smile in the singing. There are 12 songs, all attractive in words and melody, arranged in a well-disciplined style that has individuality and some sophistication but does not impose. Shostakovich's songs of 1967 add violin and cello to the voice and piano, though only the last, "Music", brings all of them together. Emotions here may be fierce one moment, tender another, and all are beautifully caught by the string players as they are by the singer and her excellent accompanist.

NEW REVIEW

SONGS BY FINZI AND HIS FRIENDS. [a]**Ian Partridge** (ten); [b]**Stephen Roberts** (bar); **Clifford Benson** (pf). Hyperion CDA66015. Texts included. *Finzi:* To a Poet, Op. 13a[b]. Oh fair to see, Op. 13b[a]. *Milford*[a]: If it's ever spring again. The colour. So sweet love seemed. *Farrar:* O mistress mine![a]. *Gurney*[b]: Sleep. Down by the salley gardens. Hawk and Buckle. *Gill:* In Memoriam[b].

> 51' ADD 9/91

This is a record that drew from its original reviewer, Trevor Harvey, high and unstinting praise when it appeared in 1981 as part of the commemoration of Finzi 25 years after his death. Finzi was never an avant-garde composer and during his lifetime received quiet and grateful acknowledgement from kindred spirits rather than anything more spectacular. In the last 20 years or so, appreciation has deepened and become more widespread. His songs, particularly, have a depth of feeling that is not always apparent at first hearing, and their idiom is that of a writer to whom overstatement or any other kind of cheapening would have been abhorrent. In this selection most of the chosen poems are affectionate and gentle, but F.L. Lucas's *June on Castle Hill* contains "whispers of wars to come", and George Barker's "Ode on the Rejection of St Cecilia" is a strong and sombre utterance that evokes an uncommonly hard-hitting style in the composer. His friend, Robin Milford, sets Hardy and Bridges with comparable sensitivity, and Ernest Farrar (killed in 1918) is remembered by his charmingly nonchalant "O mistress mine!". Stephen Roberts is an admirable singer of the songs by Ivor Gurney, and Ian Partridge gives a lovely account of Finzi's Op. 13b songs. Clifford Benson is the excellent accompanist throughout and recording and presentation are first-rate.

SONGS OF LOVE AND WAR. Julianne Baird (sop); **Myron Lutzke** (vc); **Colin Tilney** (hpd). Dorian DOR90104. Texts and translations included. *Caccini:* Amor, ch'attendi, amor, che fait. Amarilli mia bella (two versions). Caduca fiamma. *Sances:* Usurpator tiranno — cantata a voce sopra la Passacaglia. Accenti queruli — cantata a voce sopra la Ciaconna. *Monteverdi:* Lasciatemi morire — Lamento d'Arianna a 1. *Handel:* O numi eterni, "La Lucrezia", HWV145. *Frescobaldi:* Il secondo libro di Toccate ... — Toccata VIII (harpsichord solo). *Hasse:* Pastorelle che piangete.

> 1h 4' DDD 1/91

The time has passed when early music performance was governed by the Rule Book without benefit of emotional response, an approach that did more harm to vocal than to instrumental music. Julianne Baird is prominent amongst those devoted to restoring common humanity to early music, aware and mindful of what the 'bible' says but reacting to her texts in ways she feels to be comfortable and natural. The songs and cantatas in this recording centre on the more sombre aspects of love — longed-for, one-sided or lost, and the war *per se* which features in the album title appears only peripherally in part of the programme. Another unifying feature is that the style of all the music is Italian, even when the composers are not. Two juxtapositions are particularly interesting: the two 'ground-based' cantatas by Sances, and the two versions of *Amarilli*, the second a floridly decorated one, despatched with consummate ease. Ms Baird's voice is clear (but warm) and flexible, and her portrayals of emotion never step out of proper stylistic line. Colin Tilney's solo contribution allows Baird (and us) to breathe in mid-programme. The admirable quality of the recording and of the annotation (texts given in four languages) helps to make this an irresistible disc.

NEW REVIEW

SPANISH AND MEXICAN RENAISSANCE VOCAL MUSIC. **Hilliard Ensemble** (David James, Ashley Stafford, altos; John Potter, Rogers Covey-Crump, tens; Gordon Jones, bass). EMI Reflexe CDS7 54341-2. Texts and translations included.
Including works by *Alonso de Mondejar, Francisco de Peñalosa, Juan del Encina, Cristobal de Morales* and *Pedro de Escobar*.

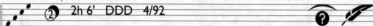

② 2h 6' DDD 4/92

It seems that golf is not the only activity in which one can concentrate on only one thing at a time: in 1492 the Spaniards were so focused on celebrating their expulsion of the Moors that their composers seem not to have noticed the discovery of the New World in the same year. However, the Spaniards exported their religion and its associated music, and both flourished on Mexican soil; the indigenous natives were surprisingly adept pupils. Catholicism remains entrenched there, but as Spanish polyphony passed its apogee its transatlantic reflection also faded. The backbone of this programme is the religious music — Spanish from the time of Ferdinand and Isabella, and the Mexican that followed in its wake, and it is lightened with some of the secular (and often humorous) Spanish music of the period. The renaissance polyphony of many European countries has been explored but only recently has attention been given to that of Spain and Mexico — and in 1992 it is not hard to guess why! The beauty of this music, and its unfamiliarity, and the quality of these performances and their recording are compelling reasons to add this disc to your collection.

SWEET POWER OF SONG. **Felicity Lott** (sop); **Ann Murray** (mez); **Graham Johnson** (pf) with [a]**Galina Solodchin** (vn) and [a]**Jonathan Williams** (va). EMI CDC7 49930-2. Texts and translations included.
Beethoven[a]: 25 Irish Songs, WoO152 — Sweet power of song; English Bulls. 12 Irish Songs, WoO154 — The Elfin Fairies; Oh! would I were but that sweet linnet. *Berlioz:* Pleure, pauvre Colette. Le trébuchet, Op. 13 No. 3. *Brahms:* Vier Duette, Op. 61. *Chausson:* Two duos, Op. 11. *Fauré:* Pleurs d'or, Op. 72. Tarantelle, Op. 10 No. 2. *Gounod:* D'un coeur qui t'aime. L'Arithmétique. *Saint-Saëns:* Pastorale. El desdichado. *Schumann:* Liederalbum für die Jugend, Op. 79 — No. 15, Das Glück; No. 19, Frühlings Ankunft; No. 23, Er ist's; No. 26, Schneeglöckchen.

Ih 2' DDD 11/90

This is a delightful presentation of an entertaining programme. The singers' careers have run concurrently with growing success on the international scene yet faithful to Graham Johnson as founding members of the Songmakers' Almanac. Here they recall many evenings of happy duetting at that group's recitals. They sing together with an instinctive rapport that is most gratifying. Johnson has devised a programme for them that provides an ingenious variety of mood and style. Beethoven's Irish Songs may not be great music but they are given vivid advocacy here. So are the more attractive and deeper duets by Schumann and Brahms. The Berlioz pieces, nicely contrasted, are well done; so are the Gounod, Fauré and Chausson items, even if a shade more accenting of words would have been welcome here. The real winner among the French items — surely a collector's item of the future — is Gounod's *L'Arithmétique*, an amusing lesson in Victorian thrift delivered in both French and English. Johnson supplies appropriate accompaniments and interesting notes. The recording naturally balances voices and piano.

A VENETIAN CORONATION, 1595. Gabrieli [a]Consort and Players/Paul McCreesh. Virgin Classics Veritas VC7 97110-2. Texts and translations included.

G. Gabrieli: Intonazioni — ottavo tono; terzo e quarto toni; quinto tono alla quarta bassa (James O'Donnell, org solo). Canzonas — XIII a 12; XVI a 15; IX a 10. Sonata VI a 8 pian e forte. Deus qui beatum Marcum a 10[a]. Omnes gentes a 16[a]. **A. Gabrieli:** Intonazioni — primo tono (O'Donnell); settimo tono (Timothy Roberts, org). Mass Movements[a] — Kyrie a 5-12; Gloria a 16; Sanctus a 12; Benedictus a 12. O sacrum convivium a 5[a]. Benedictus Dominus Deus sabbaoth (arr. Roberts. O'Donnell, Roberts). **Bendinelli:** Sonata CCC-XXXIII. Sarasinetta. **M. Thomsen:** Toccata I.

1h 11' DDD 5/90

The coronation of a new Doge of Venice was always a special occasion, and never more than when Marino Grimani (1532-1605) was elected to that office. We do not know what music was played then, but the whole ceremony is notionally and credibly reconstructed in this recording by Paul McCreesh and his cohorts. The recording was made in Brinkburn Priory, a church whose acoustic (aided by some deft manipulation of the recording controls) is spacious enough to evoke that of the Basilica of St Mark, the site of the original event. Space *per se* is vital to the music of the Gabrielis, who excelled in using it by placing instrumen-

tal and vocal groups in different parts of the building — which thereby became an integral part of the music. A fine selection of music that *could* have been played then is enhanced by the opening tolling of a bell, a crescendo marking the leisurely approach of the ducal procession, and the impression of architectural space created by changing stereo focus. It would be difficult to speak too highly of the performances, supplemented by first-class annotation, in this memorable recording. A trip to Venice would cost a lot more than this disc but, though you could visit the real St Mark's, it would not buy you this superb musical experience.

Paul McCreesh   *[photo: Virgin Classics/Chlala]*

NEW REVIEW

VENICE PRESERV'D. [a]Emma Kirkby, [b]Judith Nelson (sops); **[c]Nigel Rogers** (ten); **[d]Academy of Ancient Music/Christopher Hogwood** ([e]org). L'Oiseau-Lyre 425 891-2OH. Texts and translations included. From FS1007/08 (6/81).

A. Gabrieli: Intonatione del primo tono[e]. *Cavalli:* Canzon a 3[d]. *Cima:* Canzona, La Novella[d]. *G. Gabrieli:* Fuga del nono tono[e]. Intonatione del primo tono[e]. Sonata con tre violini[d]. *Grandi:* O intemerata (1621)[cd]. *Legrenzi:* Trio Sonata, Op. 4 No. 6, "La pezzoli"[d]. *Marini:* Sonata a tre, Op. 22[d]. *Monteverdi:* Exulta, filia Sion[abd]. Laudate Dominum[cd]. Salve, O regina[cd]. Salve regina (1640)[cd]. Sancta Maria, succurre miseris[abd]. *Spiridion:* Toccatina I[e].

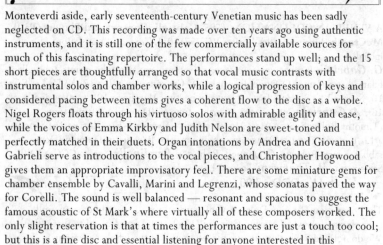

52' ADD 8/91

Monteverdi aside, early seventeenth-century Venetian music has been sadly neglected on CD. This recording was made over ten years ago using authentic instruments, and it is still one of the few commercially available sources for much of this fascinating repertoire. The performances stand up well; and the 15 short pieces are thoughtfully arranged so that vocal music contrasts with instrumental solos and chamber works, while a logical progression of keys and considered pacing between items gives a coherent flow to the disc as a whole. Nigel Rogers floats through his virtuoso solos with admirable agility and ease, while the voices of Emma Kirkby and Judith Nelson are sweet-toned and perfectly matched in their duets. Organ intonations by Andrea and Giovanni Gabrieli serve as introductions to the vocal pieces, and Christopher Hogwood gives them an appropriate improvisatory feel. There are some miniature gems for chamber ensemble by Cavalli, Marini and Legrenzi, whose sonatas paved the way for Corelli. The sound is well balanced — resonant and spacious to suggest the famous acoustic of St Mark's where virtually all of these composers worked. The only slight reservation is that at times the performances are just a touch too cool; but this is a fine disc and essential listening for anyone interested in this rewarding repertoire.

VIRTUOSO ITALIAN VOCAL MUSIC. Catherine Bott (sop); **New London Consort/Philip Pickett.** L'Oiseau-Lyre Florilegium 417 260-2OH. Texts and translations included.

Rore/Casa: Beato me direi. *Cavalieri:* Godi turba mortal. *Cavalieri/Archilei* (attrib.): Dalle più alte sfere. *Luzzaschi:* O primavera. *G. Caccini:* Sfogava con le stelle. Filli, Mirando il cielo. Al fonte, al prato. *F. Caccini:* O che nuovo stupor. *Rasi:* Ahi, fuggitivo, ben. *Gagliano:* Pastor levate sù. *Marini:* Con le stelle in ciel che mai. Ite hormai, "Invito all'allegrezza". *Frescobaldi:* Dunque dovrò — Aria di Romanesca. A piè della gran croce — Sonnetto spirituale, "Maddalena alla Croce". Se l'aura spira. *Monteverdi:* Exulta, filia Sion. Laudate Dominum in sanctis eius. *Bernardi:* O dulcissima dilecta mea. *Rossi:* La gelosia. *Carissimi:* Ferma, lascia ch'io parli — Il lamento in morte di Maria Stuarda.

1h 9' DDD 11/88

To perform Italian early baroque virtuoso pieces convincingly requires not only technical mastery and a certain elegance of vocal delivery, but also an intimate understanding of that bond between words and music that lies at the heart of the style. On this recording Catherine Bott displays a rich emotional range which projects the music to great dramatic effect. Part of her success is to do with the power and tonal flexibility of her voice, clear and bright at the upper end of the range and warm and evocative in its lower register. As to the ornamentation itself, this is negotiated almost effortlessly and to literally breathtaking effect in a piece such as Monteverdi's *Exulta, filia Sion*. The New London Consort accompany with great sensitivity, exploring in the process extremes of timbre and effect ranging from a simple organ accompaniment in Luzzaschi's *O primavera* to the excitingly full and percussive qualities of *Dalle più alte sfere*. This is a remarkable disc, not least for its brave exploration of unfamiliar repertory; no one with an interest in Italian music of the early baroque can afford to miss it.

VOCAL RECITAL. Régine Crespin (sop); [b]**John Wustman** (pf); [a]**Suisse Romande Orchestra/Ernest Ansermet.** Decca 417 813-2DH. Texts and translations included. Items marked [a] from SXL6081 (3/64), [b]SXL6333 (6/68). *Berlioz:* Les nuits d'été. *Ravel:* Shéhérazade[a]. *Debussy:* Trois chansons de Bilitis[b]. *Poulenc:* Banalities[b] — Chansons d'Orkenise; Hôtel. La courte paille[b] — Le carafon; La reine de coeur. Chansons villageoises[b] — Les gars qui vont à la fête. Deux poèmes de Louis Aragon[b].

1h 8'   ADD   11/88

Some recordings withstand the test of time and become acknowledged classics. This is one of them. Crespin's voluptuous tone, her naturally accented French and her feeling for the inner meaning of the songs in both these cycles are everywhere evident. Better than most single interpreters of the Berlioz, she manages to fulfil the demands of the very different songs, always alive to verbal nuances. In the Ravel, she is gorgeously sensuous, not to say sensual, with the right timbre for Ravel's enigmatic writing. The other songs on this CD enhance its worth. Crespin offers a highly evocative, perfumed account of the Debussy pieces and is ideally suited to her choice of Poulenc, of which her interpretation of "Hôtel" is a classic. Ansermet and his orchestra, though not quite note perfect, are — like the singer — right in timbre and colour for both these rewarding cycles. The sound is reasonable given the age of the recording. This is a most desirable acquisition.

NEW REVIEW

WATKINS ALE. MUSIC OF THE ENGLISH RENAISSANCE. **Baltimore Consort.** Dorian DOR90142. Texts included. *J. d'Estrée:* The Buffens. *J. Johnson:* Green garters. Greensleeves. *Ravenscroft:* There were three ravens. *R. Alison:* Goe from my window. The Quadro Pavin. De la tromba pavin. *Morley:* La sampogna. Joyne hands. *Byrd:* The carmans whistle, BK36. *Dowland:* Can she excuse, P42. Lachrimae, P15. *R. Nicolson:* Jewes daunce. *Anonymous:* Nuttmigs and ginger. Howells delight. Unto the prophet Jonas I read. Singers Jig. Grimstock. Pavane Quadro and Galliard. Watkins ale.

1h 8'   DDD   4/92

In early times the boundary between popular and art music was less clearly marked than it is now; they spoke recognizable variants of the same musical languages and composers based sets of variations on popular tunes with no air of patronization. The "garde" was not so "avant". In England a more or less standardized band of instruments evolved — the 'mixed' or 'broken' consort, since it included instruments of different types — wind and strings, both plucked and bowed; to this The Baltimore Consort add a singer and a keyboard instrument (a virginal). There is splendid vitality in both the selected music and the way it is played in this recording, a happy view of the English musical scene of those times, consort and solo instrumental items and songs, one of which, *Watkins ale*, is robustly salacious. Song texts and helpful notes are provided. The pleasures enjoyed by our ancestors (and here by our transatlantic 'cousins') may and should be shared through this splendid disc.

NEW REVIEW

MARY WIEGOLD'S SONGBOOK. Mary Wiegold (sop); [a]**Composers Ensemble/Dominic Muldowney.** NMC NMCD003. Texts included. *Dowland* (arr. J. Woolrich)[a]: Complaint, P63. Galliard to Lachrimae, P46. Lachrimae, P15. *J. Weir:* The Romance of Count Arnaldos. *C. Matthews:* Cantata on the death of Antony. Strugnell's Haiku. *S. Bainbridge:* A song from Michelangelo. *H. Skempton:* How slow the wind. *Birtwistle:* White and Light. *P. Wilby:* Easter Wings. *K. Tippett:* Sun — The Living Son. *J. Woolrich:* The Turkish Mouse. *Muldowney:* On Suicide. *S. Beamish:* Tuscan Lullaby. *B. Northcott:* "The maidens came …". *D. Bedford:* Even Now. *Nyman:* Polish Song.

55' DDD 4/92 ❓

If this disc serves one particularly useful purpose, it is as a sampler for a wide range of living British composers. It reflects current fashions in playing down the more complex, modernist manner (no Ferneyhough, no Maxwell Davies) in favour of compositions which display varying degrees of closeness to the 'romantic' past. Yet there is nothing predictable or uniform about the selection of songs, which takes in the sweet simplicity of Howard Skempton and the folk-like vigour of Michael Nyman as well as the terse expressionism of Colin Matthews and the chilly eloquence of Sir Harrison Birtwistle. The enterprise is all the more valuable for introducing relatively unfamiliar composers — Sally Beamish, Bayan Northcott, John Woolrich — and for providing the further perspective and contrast of Woolrich's three Dowland arrangements for the instrumental ensemble (two clarinets with saxophone, viola, cello and double bass). Mary Wiegold is a leading advocate of contemporary music, and the Songbook is a tribute to her dedication and technical skill. One or two of the pieces strain her resources to the limit, but everything is musical, the words clearly articulated, the melodies sensitively phrased in a warm but never over-bright recording. Further instalments of "Mary Wiegold's Songbook" are to be anticipated with pleasure.

Operatic highlights

THE ART OF THE PRIMA DONNA. Dame Joan Sutherland (sop); Chorus and Orchestra of the Royal Opera House, Covent Garden/ Francesco Molinari-Pradelli. Decca 425 493-2DM2. Texts and translations included. From SXL2556/7 (12/60).
Arne: ARTAXERXES — The soldier tir'd. *Bellini:* LA SONNAMBULA — Care compagne … Come per me sereno … Sopra il sen. NORMA — Sediziose voci … Casta diva … Ah! bello a me ritorna. I PURITANI — Son vergin vezzosa; O rendetemi la speme … Qui la voce … Vien, diletto. *Delibes:* LAKME — Ah! Où va la jeune Indoue. *Gounod:* FAUST — O Dieu! que de bijoux … Ah! je ris. ROMEO ET JULIETTE — Je veux vivre. *Handel:* SAMSON — Let the bright Seraphim. *Meyerbeer:* LES HUGUENOTS — O beau pays de la Touraine! *Mozart:* DIE ENTFUHRUNG AUS DEM SERAIL — Martern aller Arten. *Rossini:* SEMIRAMIDE — Bel raggio lusinghier.
Thomas: HAMLET — A vos jeux, mes amis. *Verdi:* OTELLO — Mia madre aveva una povera ancella … Piangea cantando. LA TRAVIATA — E strano … Ah fors' è lui … Sempre libera. RIGOLETTO — Gualtier Maldè … Caro nome.

② 1h 49' ADD 1/90

Those who have not heard Dame Joan until recent times can only speculate on the full beauty of her voice in its prime. This album, from 1960, preserves the real Sutherland quality as well as any of her records have done and it is a delight from start to finish. Sutherland and her husband, Richard Bonynge, have long been interested in the history of opera and particularly of its singers, so *The Art of the Prima Donna* was arranged to relate each of the solos to a famous soprano of the past. Arne's *Artaxerxes* recalls Mrs Billington, and the final items are associated with more recent artists such as Tetrazzini and Galli-Curci. It presents a brilliant conspectus, with Sutherland mastering the most fearsome of technical demands and showing a wonderfully complete command of the required skills. She was then fresh from the triumph at Covent Garden in *Lucia di*

Lammermoor which brought her international fame in 1959. Her voice was at its purest, and her style had not developed the characteristics which later partly limited the pleasure of her singing. What the record may not quite convey is the sheer house-filling volume of her voice. Even so, nobody who hears these recordings can be in any doubt about her mastery or about the aptness of the title, bestowed on her by the Italians, of "la stupenda".

OPERA CHORUSES. Chorus and Orchestra of the Royal Opera House, Covent Garden/Bernard Haitink. EMI CDC7 49849-2. Texts and translations included.
Beethoven: FIDELIO — O welche Lust (with John Mark Ainsley, ten; Alistair Miles, bar). ***Berlioz:*** LES TROYENS — Royal Hunt and Storm. ***Bizet:*** CARMEN — Les voici! voici la quadrille! (Haberdashers' Aske's School Boys' Choir). ***Donizetti:*** LUCIA DI LAMMERMOOR — Per te d'immenso giubilo; D'immenso giubilo. ***Giordano:*** ANDREA CHENIER — O pastorelle, addio. ***Mascagni:*** CAVALLERIA RUSTICANA — Easter Hymn (Helen Field, sop). ***Verdi:*** AIDA — Gloria all'Egitto. NABUCCO — Va, pensiero. OTELLO — Fuoco di gioia. IL TROVATORE — Vedi! le fosche notturne spoglie. ***Wagner:*** LOHENGRIN — Treulich geführt. ***Weber:*** DER FREISCHUTZ — Was gleicht wohl auf Erden dem Jägervergnügen.

Ih I' DDD 12/89

After an evening at the opera it is usually the arias and soloists that come in for remark and discussion, but quite often what actually brings the greatest enjoyment and remains in the memory as most vivid and colourful is a chorus or a passage of ensemble. Composers tend to reserve their broadest tunes for the chorus, and in this selection we have the Easter Hymn, Anvil Chorus, Wedding March and Chorus of Hebrews, all among the world's best. Less obvious, and a delight in context (both here and in the opera), is the Pastoral from *Andrea Chenier*. Altogether deeper in feeling, and most moving of all, is the Prisoners' Chorus from *Fidelio*. In each of the excerpts, the Covent Garden Chorus (so often overlooked in reviews) show themselves fully worthy of the attention bestowed on them. Haitink, never insensitive, sometimes misses the full effect of a climax, but the Orchestra are in fine form and give a particularly good account of the "Royal Hunt and Storm" from *The Trojans*. For the general listener it is a disc that will give pleasure in itself and in stirring up a determination to go and see the operas again; for the Covent Garden *habitué* it will bring back memories, almost as if one were turning the pages of a picture-book, as the scenes and evenings return vividly to mind.

OPERA FINALES. Josephine Barstow (sop); **Scottish Opera ᵃChorus and Orchestra/John Mauceri.** Decca 430 203-2DH. Texts and translations included.
R. Strauss: SALOME — Es ist kein Laut zu vernehmen ... Ah! Du wolltest mich nicht deinen Mund küssen lasses, Jokanaan! (with Claire Livingston, mez; Graham Clark, ten). ***Cherubini:*** MEDEE — Eh quoi je suis Médée!ᵃ (Clare Shearer, mez; John Treleaven, ten). ***Janáček:*** THE MAKROPULOS AFFAIR — She's on the whisky! (Anne Williams-King, mez; Graham Clark, Alasdair Elliott, tens; Jason Howard, Steven Page, bars). ***Puccini*** (comp. Alfano): TURANDOT — Principessa di morte!ᵃ (Lando Bartolini, ten).

Ih 17' DDD 9/90

At the world première of *Turandot* in 1926 Toscanini turned to the audience and said "This is where the master laid down his pen." In fact Puccini had written sketches for the last scene, and Franco Alfano had worked on them very ably, producing a version which was played on the second night and has been adopted

Josephine Barstow   [photo: Avid Images/Scheinmann]

ever since. What was not generally known until as late as 1982 is that Alfano's reconstruction had been reduced by about a third. This is the first recording of the complete score, and after hearing it the listener is very unlikely to be satisfied with the finale as usually given, for this has far more colour, imagination and splendour. The disc is a valuable addition to the catalogue if on this account only. But its appeal does not end there. The closing scene in *Salome* has rarely leapt out from the disc to make as vivid a dramatic effect as here, and the ending of *The Makropulos Affair* loses surprisingly little of its inspired effectiveness by being heard as an excerpt. It is here that Josephine Barstow is at her best: elsewhere one feels a need for firmer production and more opulent tone, but this is her music, and she sings with touching beauty as well as the intelligence and spirit that so regularly distinguish her work. It is a pity that the printed notes do not put the scenes into dramatic context, but all else is fine, including the orchestral playing and contributions of the other singers.

NEW REVIEW

OPERA RECITAL. Ezio Pinza (bass) with various artists. Pearl mono GEMMCD9306. *Verdi:* AIDA — Mortal diletto ai Numi (Metropolitan Opera Orchestra, New York/Giulio Setti); Nume custode vindici (Giovanni Martinelli, ten; Metropolitan Opera Chorus and Orchestra. Both from Victor 8111). ERNANI — Che mai vegg'io ... Infelice! (orchestra/Rosario Bourdon. HMV DB1750). DON CARLOS — Dormiro sol nel manto mio regal (orchestra/Bourdon. DB1087, 3/28). I VESPRI SICILIANI — O patria ... O tu Palermo (orchestra/Bourdon. DB1087). Messa da Requiem — Confutatis maledictis (orchestra/Bourdon. HMV AGSB103). SIMON BOCCANEGRA — A te l'estremo addio ... Il lacerato spirito (chorus and orchestra/Carlo Sabajno. DB699, 6/24). IL TROVATORE — Di due figli ... Abbietta zingara (chorus and orchestra/Sabajno. DB828). *Mozart:* DON GIOVANNI — Finch'han dal vino; Deh vieni alla finestra (orchestra/Bourdon. HMV DA1134, 10/31). DIE ZAUBERFLOTE — O Isis und Osiris (sung in Italian. Orchestra/Bourdon. DB1088, 3/28). *Meyerbeer:* ROBERT LE DIABLE — Nonnes, qui reposez (sung in Italian. Orchestra/Bourdon. DB1088). *Thomas:* LE CAID — Enfant chéri ... Le tambour-major (orchestra/Bourdon. DB1086, 3/28). *Gounod:* FAUST — Le veau d'or (Metropolitan Opera Chorus and Orchestra/Setti. DA1108, 9/38). *Bellini:* NORMA — Ah del tebro (Chorus and orchestra/Sabajno. DA566, 5/25). *Bellini:* I PURITANI — Cinta de fiori (Orchestra/Sabajno. HMV VB70, 6/52). *Donizetti:* LA FAVORITA — Splendon più belle (orchestra. DA708). LUCIA DI LAMMERMOOR — Dalle stanze (chorus and orchestra/Sabajno. VB70). *Boito:* MEFISTOFELE — Ave Signor (orchestra. DB829); Son lo spirito (orchestra/Sabajno. DA567). *Halévy:* LA JUIVE — Si la rigeur (sung in Italian. Orchestra/Sabajno. DB698, 11/24); Vous qui du Dieu vivant (sung in Italian. Orchestra. DB829).

Ih 16' AAD 2/89   9 P ▲

The first half of the century brought forth three fine Italian basses: Nazzareno de Angelis, Tancredi Pasero and Ezio Pinza. Of these it was Pinza who gained the greatest international fame, partly through the beauty of his voice and partly through the strength and vividness of his personality. Eventually it was the musical *South Pacific* that made him a household name, but his success here owed much in turn to the fact that he came to the Broadway show from the Metropolitan Opera House where he was leading bass from his house début in 1926 until 1948. Before coming to America he had sung at La Scala under Toscanini, his repertoire then ranging from the role of Pimen in *Boris Godunov* (he was later to sing Boris himself) to King Mark in *Tristan und Isolde*. At the Metropolitan he sang mostly in the Italian and French operas, with an increasing interest in Mozart, whose Don Giovanni became his most famous role, which he sung also at Salzburg and Covent Garden. This is represented in the present selection (called "The Golden Years") by two short solos, which may well be found to be the least satisfying of the performances. Sarastro's "O Isis und Osiris", on the other hand, sung in Italian as "Possenti numi" is magnificent in the sonority of tone and dignity of style. There is also some superb Verdi, above all the aria from *Ernani*, sung with deep feeling and subtlety of shading, and the "Confutatis" from the *Requiem*, ideally smooth, resonant and authoritative. In these and the earlier pre-electrical recordings Pinza shows clearly why he is so widely regarded as having been the supreme *basso cantate* of the century.

RICHARD TAUBER. OPERA ARIAS AND DUETS. Richard Tauber (ten) with various artists. EMI Références mono CDH7 64029-2. All items sung in German except that marked [a].

Mozart: DON GIOVANNI — Dalla sua pace (from Odeon O-8227. Recorded 1922); Il mo tesoro[a] (Parlophone R20444, 7/39). DIE ZAUBERFLOTE — Dies Bildnis ist bezaubernd schön (O-8226. 1922). *Méhul:* JOSEPH — Champs paternels (R20543, 12/45). *Offenbach:* LES CONTES D'HOFFMANN — Il était une fois; O Dieu! de quelle ivresse (R20089, 10/29). *Thomas:* MIGNON — Adieu, Mignon; Elle ne croyait pas (both from O-8229). *Tchaikovsky:* EUGENE ONEGIN — Faint echo of my youth (O-8224. All 1923). *Smetana:* THE BARTERED BRIDE — Faithful love cannot be marred (with Elisabeth Rethberg, sop); How could they believe (O-8027. 1919). *Wagner:* DIE MEISTERSINGER VON NURNBERG — Am stillen Herd; Morgenlich leuchtend (Odeon 123506. 1927). *Puccini:* MADAMA BUTTERFLY — Quest'obi pomposa di scioglier mi tarda (Rethberg. O-8055. 1922). TURANDOT — Non piangere, Liù; Nessun dorma (O-8401. 1926). *Korngold:* DIE TOTE STADT — Glück das mir verblieb (Lotte Lehmann, sop); O Freund, ich werde sie nicht wiedersehen (O-9507. 1924).

1h 12'   ADD   3/92

This is a must for anyone interested in the history of singing on disc. Richard Tauber had a voice of irresistible charm and individuality that was instantly recognizable. This issue includes some of his most desirable recordings, if not necessarily his most popular. From Mozart to Wagner he shows a sovereign style and tone allied to that uniquely ardent manner of his: a heady combination. Everything is sung from the heart and goes to it. The disc also demonstrates the breadth of his repertory when he was in his prime and before he became the star of operetta. In a couple of duets he is joined by his soprano colleagues of his time — the lovely Elisabeth Rethberg and the impulsive Lotte Lehmann. Tauber's voice rings out full and true on these transfers, though a few are troubled by extraneous noises. A treasure of glorious singing.

VIVA ROSSINI. OPERA AND ORATORIO ARIAS. Various artists. Testament mono SBT1008.

IL BARBIERE DI SIVIGLIA — Largo al factotum (Titta Ruffo, bar. From HMV 2-052184. Recorded 1920); Se il mio nome (Dino Borgioli, ten. Columbia

L2054, 5/28); O meglio mi scordavo … Numero quindici (John McCormack, ten; Mario Sammarco, bar. 2-054021); Una voce poco fa (Luisa Tetrazzini, sop. 2-053046. Both 1911); La calunnia (Adam Didur, bass. Fonotipia 74119. 1908); Dunque io son (Maria Barrientos, sop; Riccardo Stracciari, bar. Columbia 71003D. 1919); Ah! qual colpo (Giuseppina Huguet, sop; Fernando De Lucia, ten; Antonio Pini-Corsi, bar. G&T 054083. 1906). LA CENERENTOLA — Miei rampoli (Arcangelo Rossi, bass. Victor 4406. 1905); Nacqui all'affanno … Non più mesta (Conchita Supervia, mez. Parlophone R20140, 5/31). GUILLAUME TELL — Sombre forêt (Lina Pagliughi, sop. R30004, 3/50); Ses jours qu'ils ont osé proscrire (Giovanni Martinelli, ten; Giuseppe de Luca, bar; José Mardones, bass. 2-054130. 1923); A sa voix … Sois immobile (Alexander Sved, bar. All sung in Italian. HMV DB5366. 1940); Asile héréditaire (André d'Arkor, ten. French Columbia RFX22. 1930); Amis, amis, secondez ma vengeance (Francesco Tamagno, ten. Italian. G&T 52683. 1903). MOSE IN EGITTO — Dal tuo stellato soglio (Anna Turchetti, sop; Ezio Pinza, bass; chorus. DB698, 11/24). SEMIRAMIDE — Ah! quel giorno (Ebe Stignani, mez. R30023, 10/50); Bel raggio lusinghier (Celestina Boninsegna, sop. Columbia 30539. 1910). Stabat mater — Cuius animam (Enrico Caruso, ten. 2-052086. 1913); Inflammatus (Florence Austral, sop; Chorus of the Royal Opera House, Covent Garden. HMV D1506, 1/29).

1h 16' ADD

This disc came out in 1992 to mark the bicentenary of Rossini's birth. It demonstrates the skills of Rossini singers from the dawn of recording through to the end of the 78rpm era. It offers a vocal panorama of changing styles in the execution of Rossini's music, and includes such famous pieces as Tetrazzini's coruscating "Una voce poco fa", Titta Ruffo's unsurpassed "Largo al factotum", Martinelli's sovereign "O muto asil" from *William Tell*, Austral's glorious singing of the "Inflammatus" from the *Stabat mater*, Supervia's irresistible "Non più mesta" from *La cenerentola* and other items not so well-known but equally interesting. Technically today's singers may be superior; in terms of character their predecessors carry off the honours. Excellent transfers.

Information

Compact Disc Outlets-UK

AVON
†BATH COMPACT DISCS, 11 Broad Street, Bath BA1 5LJ
CLASSICAL WORLD, 80 Whiteladies Road, Bristol BS8 2NT
HMV SHOP, 13-15 Stall Street, Bath BA1 1QE
THE GRAMOPHONE RECORD, 65 Westbury Hill, Westbury-on-Trym, Bristol BS9 3AD
MILSOM & SON LTD, Northgate, Bath BA1 5AS
†PASTORAL MUSIC, 11 Christmas Steps, Bristol BS1 5BS
RAYNER'S RECORD CENTRE, 84 Park Street, Bristol BS1 5LA
PAUL ROBERTS HI-FI & VIDEO, 203 Milton Road, Weston-Super-Mare, BS22 8EF (branches elsewhere)

BEDFORDSHIRE
BEDFORD AUDIO-COMM, 29 Bedford Road, Kempston MK43 0EU
CLASSIC MUSIC, 7 Lime Street, Bedford MK40 1LD

BERKSHIRE
HICKIE & HICKIE, 153 Friar Street, Reading RG1 lHG

BUCKINGHAMSHIRE
CHAPPELL'S OF BOND STREET, 21 Silbury Arcade, Central Milton Keynes MK9 3AG
RECORD HOUSE, 36 High Street, Aylesbury HP20 lSF

CAMBRIDGESHIRE
CMS RECORDS, la All Saint's Passage, Cambridge CB2 3LT
HEFFER'S BOOKSELLERS, 20 Trinity Street, Cambridge CB2 3ET
MILLER'S MUSIC CENTRE, 12 Sussex Street, Cambridge CB1 lPW

CHESHIRE
ASTON AUDIO, 4 West Street, Alderley Edge, Cheshire SK9 7EF
CHESTER CD CENTRE, 14 Godstall Lane, Chester CH1 lLN
CIRCLE RECORDS, 33-35 Victoria Street, Liverpool L1 6BG
CONCERT CORNER, 9 Union Street, Southport, PR9 0QF
RUSHWORTH'S MUSIC HOUSE, Rushworth's Corner, 42-6 Whitechapel, Liverpool L1 6EE (branches elsewhere)

CLEVELAND
PLAYBACK, 122 Linthorne Road, Middlesborough TS1 2JR

CORNWALL
MUSIC MASTERS, 28 Fore Street, Lostwithiel PL22 0BL

DERBYSHIRE
COLLECTOR'S RECORD CENTRE, 6 Duckworth Square, Derby DEl lJZ
MDT CLASSICS, 6 Old Blacksmith's Yard, Sadler Gate, Derby DE1 3PD
OASIS RECORDS, 314 Strand Arcade, Sadler Gate, Derby DE1 1BQ

DEVON
ACORN MUSIC (inc. PETER RUSSELL'S HOT RECORD STORE), Grove Hill, Victoria Road, Barnstable, EX32 8DS
AMADEUS CLASSICS, 7 Frankfort Gate, Plymouth PL1 lQA
THE MUSIC DISC, 3 Cross Street, Barnstaple EX31 1BA
OPUS RECORDS, 14a Guildhall Centre, Exeter EX4 3HW

DORSET
BEALES, RECORD DEPT, 36 Old Christchurch Road, Bournemouth BH1 1LJ
COMPACT CLASSICS, 17 Quadrant Centre, St Peter's Road, Bournemouth BH1 2AB
COMPACT SOUNDS, 238 Ashley Road, Parkstone, Poole BH14 9BZ
THE MUSIC HOUSE, The Green, Sherborne DT9 3HX
MUSIC FORUM, 47c East Street, Blandford Forum, Dorset DT11 7DX

DURHAM
CLASSICAL CHOICE, 71 North Road, Durham DH1 4SQ

ESSEX
BILLERICAY RECORD SUPPLIES, 7 Radford Way, Billericay CM1Z 0AA
BRENTWOOD MUSIC CENTRE, 2 Ingrave Road, Brentwood CM15 8AT
CHEW & OSBORNE LTD, 148 High Street, Epping, CM16 4AG
THE COMPACT DISCOUNT CENTRE, 5 Headgate Buildings, Sir Isaacs Walk, Colchester CO1 lJJ
JAMES DACE & SON LTD, 33 Moulsham Street, Chelmsford CM2 0HX
HOWARD LEACH CLASSICAL, 49 Crouch Street, Colchester CO3 3EN

FALKIRK
SLEEVES, 4 Cow Wynd, Falkirk FK1 1PL

GLOUCESTERSHIRE
†AUDIOSONIC (GLOUCESTER) LTD 6 The Promenade, Eastgate Shopping Centre, Gloucester GL1 lXJ
GOODMUSIC, 16 Cheltenham Trade Park, Arle Road, Cheltenham GL51 8LX
OTTAKAR'S, 15 Eastgate Street, Gloucester GL1 1NS
SOUNDS GOOD, 26 Winchcombe Street, Cheltenham GL52 2LX

HAMPSHIRE
CARUSOS, Unit 4, Bargate Centre, Southampton
COUNTY MUSIC, 14 St George's Street, Winchester SO23 8BG
ORPHEUS RECORDS, 27 Marmion Road, Southsea PO5 2AT
VENUS, 8 Downing Street, Farnham GU9 7PB
WHITWAMS, 70 High Street, Winchester SO23 9DE

HEREFORDSHIRE
KING'S RADIO (HEREFORD) LTD, 35 Widemarsh Street, Hereford HR4 9EA

KENT

†CAMDEN CLASSICS, 16 Camden Road, Tunbridge Wells TN4 0DS

THE CLASSICAL LONGPLAYER, 6 St Peters Street, Canterbury CT1 2AT

THE CLASSICAL LONGPLAYER, 99 High Street, Maidstone, ME14 1SA

†EDEN COMPACT DISCS, PO Box 29, Edenbridge, TN8 5AW

THE MUSIC CENTRE, Grove Hill Road, Tunbridge Wells, TN1 1R2

LANCASHIRE

†CLASSICAL CDs, Repeat House, Bright Road, Eccles, Manchester M30 0WR

FORSYTHS, 126-8 Deansgate, Manchester M3 2GR

GIBBS BOOKSHOP, 10 Charlotte Street, Manchester M1 4FL

HMV SHOP, 90-100 Market Street, Manchester M1 1PD

REIDY'S, 11-13 Penny Street, Blackburn BB1 6HJ

SMITH'S, 41 Mesnes Street, Wigan WN1 1QY

†SQUIRES GATE MUSIC CENTRE, Squires Gate Station Approach, Blackpool FY8 2SP

LEICESTERSHIRE

CLASSIC TRACKS, 21 East Bond Street, Leicester LE1 4SX

ST MARTIN'S RECORDS, 23 Hotel Street, Leicester LE1 5EW

HMV SHOP, 9-17 High Street, Leicester LE1 4FP

LONDON

LES ALDRICH MUSIC SALON, 98 Fortis Green Road, Muswell Hill, London N10 3HN

BARBICAN MUSIC SHOP, Cromwell Tower, Whitecross Street, Barbican, London EC2Y 8DD

BARGAIN RECORDS, 9 The Arcade, High Street Eltham, London SE9 1BE

BUSH RECORDS, 113 Shepherd's Bush Centre, London W12 8PP

CHIMES MUSIC SHOP, 44 Marylebone High Street, London W1M 4AD

COLISEUM SHOP, St Martin's Lane, London WC2N 4ES

COVENT GARDEN RECORDS, 84 Charing Cross Road, London WC2H 0JA

DILLON'S UNIVERSITY BOOKSHOPS, 3 Malet Street, London WC1E 7JN (branches elsewhere)

†FARRINGDON RECORDS, 52-54 High Holborn, London WC1V 6RL (branches elsewhere in London)

HARRODS LTD, Knightsbridge, London SW1X 7XL

THOMAS HEINITZ LTD, 35 Moscow Road, London W2 4AH

HMV RECORD SHOPS, 363 Oxford Street, London W1R 1FD (branches elsewhere)

HAROLD MOORES RECORDS, 2 Great Marlborough Street, London W1V 1DE

†MUSIC DISCOUNT CENTRE, 437 The Strand, London WC2R 0QU (branches elsewhere in London)

MUSIC & VIDEO EXCHANGE, 38 & 56 Notting Hill Gate, London W11 3JS

ORCHESOGRAPHY, 15 Cecil Court, St Martin's Lane, London WC2N 4EZ

SOUND EXCHANGE, 50 Spencer Court, Spencer Road, London SW20 0QW

†TEMPLAR RECORDS, 9a Irving Street, London WC2H 7AT

TOWER RECORDS, 1 Piccadilly, London W1V 9LA (branches elsewhere in London)

TURNTABLE, 40 Station Road, Chingford, London E4 7BQ

VIRGIN MEGASTORE, 14-16 Oxford Street, London W1N 9FL (branches elsewhere)

MIDDLESEX

THE CD SHOP, 206 Field End Road, Eastcote, Pinner HA5 1RD

MUSIQUE, 1 Market House, High Street, Uxbridge UB8 1AQ

NORFOLK

†CD SEND, 105b Dereham Road, Norwich NR2 4HT

JARROLD & SONS LTD, 1-7 London Street, Norwich NR2 1JF

PRELUDE RECORDS, 25b St Giles Street, Norwich NR1 2SL

NORTHAMPTONSHIRE

POLYHYMNIA, 3 Derngate, Northampton NN1 1TU

SPINADISC RECORDS, 75a Abington Street, Northampton NN1 2BH (branches elsewhere)

NOTTINGHAMSHIRE

CLASSICAL CDs, 27 Heathcote Street, Nottingham NG1 3AA

†WINGS MAIL ORDER, 52 Laverick Road, Jacksdale NG16 5LQ

OXFORDSHIRE

BLACKWELL'S MUSIC SHOP, 38 Holywell Street, Oxford OX1 3SW

RMR RECORDS, 3 Wilcote View, North Leigh, Witney OX8 6SF

SHROPSHIRE

CROTCHET & Co, Church Stretton SY6 6DR

DURRANT RECORDS, 84 Wyle Cop, Shrewsbury, SY1 1UT

STAFFORDHIRE

FIRST CLASS CDs, 2 St Mary's Mews, Stafford ST16 2AR

SUFFOLK

†MAILDISC & Co, Linstead Road, Huntingfield, Halesworth IP19 0QP

GALLEON MUSIC, High Street, Aldeburgh, IP15 5AX

SURREY

H & R CLOAKE LTD, 29 High Street, Croydon CR0 1QB

COMPACT DISC INTERNATIONAL, 24 Tunsgate, Guildford GU1 3QS

MINIM, 916 London Road, Thornton Heath CR4 7PE

RECORD CORNER, Pound Lane, Godalming GU7 1BX

†RICHMOND RECORDS, 19 Paradise Road, Richmond TW9 1SA

TRANSITIONS, 19 The Centre, Walton-on-Thames KT12 1QJ

SUSSEX

BASTOW CLASSICS, 50 North Street, Chichester PO19 1NQ

THE CLASSICAL LONGPLAYER, 31 Duke Street, Brighton BN1 1AG

THE COMPACT DISC CLUB, The Woods,
14 The Arcade, Bognor Regis PO21 lLH
FINE RECORDS, 32 George Street, Hove
BN3 3YB
GRAMMAR SCHOOL RECORDS, The Old
Grammar School, High Street, Rye
TN31 7TF
MICHAEL'S CLASSICAL RECORD SHOP,
183 Montague Street, Worthing BN11 3DA
OTTAKERS PLC, 34 Duke Street, Brighton
BN1 lAG (branches elesewhere)
†CG ROBSON IMPORTS LTD, 39
Winchcombe Road, Eastbourne BN22 8DE
SEAFORD MUSIC, 24 Pevensey Road,
Eastbourne BN21 3HP
SOUNDS, 2 New Road, Brighton BN1 1UF

TYNE & WEAR
†JG WINDOWS LTD, 1-7 Central Arcade,
Newcastle-upon-Tyne NE1 5BP

WARWICKSHIRE
SOUNDS EXPENSIVE, 12 Regent Street,
Rugby CV21 2QF

WEST MIDLANDS
EASY LISTENING, 1135 Warwick Road,
Acocks Green, Birmingham B27 6RA
FIVE WAYS HIGH FIDELITY, 12 Islington
Row, Edgbaston, Birmingham B15 lLD
HMV, 38 High Street, Birmingham B4 7SL
HUDSONS BOOKSHOP, 116 New Street,
Birmingham B2 4JJ (branches elsewhere)
†SPINADISC RECORDS, 83-87 Lower
Precinct, Coventry CV1 1DS
†TANDY'S RECORDS LTD, 24 Islington Row,
Edgbaston, Birmingham B15 lLJ

WILTSHIRE
MITCHELL MUSIC, 15 Cross Keys Chequer,
Salisbury SP1 1EL
THE COLLECTOR'S ROOM AT SUTTON'S,
3 Endless Street, Salisbury SP1 lDH

YORKSHIRE
ADAGIO CLASSICAL RECORDS,
6 Westminster Arcade, Parliament Street,
Harrogate HG1 2RN
BANKS & SON (MUSIC) LTD, 18 Lendal,
York YO1 2AY
CALM & CLASSICAL, 144 West Street,
Sheffield S1 4ES
CLASSICAL RECORD SHOP, 2 The Merrion
Centre, Leeds LS2 8NG
FORSYTHS, 40 Great George Street, Leeds
LS1 3DL
GOUGH & DAVY, 13-16 Savile Street, Hull
HU1 3EH
†MAXJON RECORDS, 32 Elmfield Road,
Huddersfield HD2 2XH
METRO MUSIC, 12 Victoria Road,
Scarborough, YO11 1SD
RIVERSIDE RECORDS, 2 Low Ousegate, York
YO1 1QU
TIME & TUNE, 14-16 Otley Street, Skipton,
BD23 1D2
J WOOD & SONS, 11 Market Street,
Huddersfield HD1 2EH (branches elsewhere)
WILSON PECK, 13 Rockingham Gate, Sheffield
S1 4JD

CHANNEL ISLANDS
BASE HI-FI, 35 Hilgrove Street, St Helier,
Jersey
COMPACT DISC CENTRE, 25 Halkett Street,
St Helier, Jersey
DISC CENTRE, 13 Don Street, St Helier,
Jersey
LES RICHES STORES LTD, St Brelade's Bay,
St Brelade's, Jersey
NO. 19 RECORDS & TAPES, 19 Le Pollet,
Guernsey
SOUNDTRACK, Church Square, St Peter Port,
Guernsey
TELESKILL LTD, 3-4 Market Street, St Peter
Port, Guernsey

ISLE OF MAN
ISLAND COMPACT DISC CENTRE,
Parliament Square, Ramsey

N IRELAND
CLASSICAL TRACKS, 15 Castle Arcade, Belfast
BT1 5DG
KOINONIA, 6 Pottinger's Entry, High Street,
Belfast BT1 2JZ

SCOTLAND
BAUERMEISTER BOOKSELLERS,
15-16 George IV Bridge, Edinburgh EH1 lEH
DEVOY, 1099 Argyle Street, Glasgow G3 8ND
FOPP, 58 Byres Road, Glasgow G12 4EQ
JAMES KERR & Co, 98-110 Woodlands Road,
Glasgow G3 6HB
RAE MACINTOSH (MUSIC) LTD,
6-8 Queensferry Street, Edinburgh EH2 4PA
McALISTER MATHESON MUSIC LTD, 1
Grindlay Street, Edinburgh EH3 9AT
†SILVER SERVICE CD, 24 Touch Wards,
Dunfirmline, Fife KY12 7TG
SLEEVES, Whytescauseway, Kirkcaldy, Fife
KY1 1XS
JOHN SMITH & SON, 69 Kent Road, Glasgow
G3 7EG
JAMES THIN LTD, 53-59 South Bridge,
Edinburgh EH1 lYS
RECORD RENDEZVOUS, 14a Church Street,
Inverness IV1 1EE

WALES
ABERGAVENNY MUSIC, 23 Cross Street,
Abergavenny WP7 5EW
†CITY RADIO, 24 Charles Street, Newport,
Gwent NP9 lJT (branches elsewhere)
PALACE BOOKS LTD, 78 High Street,
Porthmadog, Gwynedd LL49 9NW (branches
elsewhere)

MULTIPLES
The following outlets have branches throughout
the country:

ALTO	BOOTS
DILLONS	HMV
OUR PRICE	WH SMITH
VIRGIN	TOWER

Many shops listed offer a mail order service. At
the time this list was compiled those marked †
were known to be specialists.

Record Company Names and Addresses

Unless otherwise indicated all the companies below are based in the UK; addresses for record companies from outside the UK are given, where available.

ABBEY RECORDING CO—1 Abbey Street, Eynsham, Oxford OX8 1HS (0865 880240)

ACCENT RECORDS—Eikstraat 31, 1673 Beert, *BELGIUM* (322 356 1878)

ACCORD—3-5 Rue Albert de Vatimsnil, 92300 Levallois, *FRANCE* (4758 1290)

ADDA—8 Rue Jules Verne, 93400 Saint-Ouen, *FRANCE* (1 4012 6030)

ADES—54, Rue Saint Lazare, 75009 Paris, *FRANCE* (1 4874 8530)

ALBANY RECORDS: UK—PO Box 12, Carnforth, Lancashire LA5 9PD (0524 735873); USA—Box 5011, Albany NY12205, *USA* (518 453 2203)

ALTARUS RECORDS—17 Knole Road, Sevenoaks, Kent TN13 3XH (0732 455972)

APPIAN PUBLICATIONS AND RECORDINGS (APR)—PO Box 1, Wark, Hexham, Northumberland NE48 3EW (0434 220627)

ARABESQUE RECORDINGS—60 East 42nd Street, New York NY10165, *USA* (212 983 1414)

ARCHIV PRODUKTION—1 Sussex Place, Hammersmith, London W6 9XS (081-846 8515)

ARGO—1 Sussex Place, Hammersmith, London W6 9XS (081-846 8515)

ARION—36, Avenue Hoche, 75008 Paris, *FRANCE* (1 4563 7670)

ASV—Martin House, 179-181 North End Road, London W14 9NL (071-381 8747)

AUVIDIS—12 Avenue Maurice Thorey, 94200 Ivry-sur-Seine, *FRANCE* (1 4672 3939)

SIR THOMAS BEECHAM TRUST—Denton House, Denton, Harleston, Norfolk IP20 0AA (098686 780)

GRAMMOFON AB BIS—Bragevägen 2, 18264 Djursholm, *SWEDEN* (8 755 4100)

BMG CLASSICS—Bedford House, 69-79 Fulham High Street, London SW6 3JW (071-973 0011)

BMG UK—Lyng Lane, West Bromwich, West Midlands B70 7ST (061-525 3000)

BNL PRODUCTIONS—901 Chemin du Puits du Plan, 06370 Mouans Sartoux, *FRANCE* (9292 2584)

BRIDGE RECORDS—GPO Box 1864, New York, NY10116, *USA* (516 487 1662)

SCOTT BUTLER DISC AND TAPE FACTORS—Unit 2, Lansdowne Mews, Charlton Lane, London SE7 8AZ (081-858 9190)

CALLIOPE—14 Rue de la Justice, Boðóite Postale 166, 60204 Comprègne Cedex, *FRANCE* (4423 2765)

CAPRICCIO—5020 Frechen 4 (Königsdorf), *GERMANY* (02234 60060)

CBC RECORDS—PO Box 500, Station A, Toronto, Ontario M5W 1E6, *CANADA* (416 975 3501)

CBS RECORDS—*see* SONY MUSIC ENTERTAINMENT

CHANDOS RECORDS—Chandos House, Commerce Way, Colchester, Essex CO2 8HQ (0206 794000)

CHANNEL CLASSICS RECORDS—Jacob van Lennepkade 334 e, 1053 NJ Amsterdam, *THE NETHERLANDS* (20 6161775)

CHESKY RECORDS—311 West 43rd Street, Suite 702, New York, NY10036, *USA* (212 586 7799)

CHORD RECORDS AND DISTRIBUTION— PO Box 1, South Street, Axminster, Devon EX13 7UQ (0404 45693)

CLASSICS FOR PLEASURE—1-3 Uxbridge Road, Hayes, Middlesex UB4 0SY (081-561 8722)

CLAVES RECORDS—Trüelweg 14, 3600 Thun, *SWITZERLAND* (0 3323 1649)

COLLEGIUM RECORDS—PO Box 172, Whittlesford, Cambridge CB2 4QZ (0223 832474)

COLLINS CLASSICS—Electron House, Cray Avenue, St Mary Cray, Orpington, Kent BR5 3PN (06898 98711)

THE COMPLETE RECORD CO—2 Hepburn Mews, 63a Webbs Road, London SW11 6SE (071-924 3174)

CONIFER RECORDS—Horton Road, West Drayton, Middlesex UB7 8JL (0895 447707)

CONTINUUM CDs—Flat 3, 65 Cromwell Avenue, London N6 5HS (081-348 0466)

CPO—Ackerstrasse 59, 4500 Osnabruck, *GERMANY* (54157 1087)

CRD—PO Box 26, Stanmore, Middlesex HA7 4XB (081-958 7695)

DECCA CLASSICS—1 Sussex Place, Hammersmith, London W6 9XS (081-846 8515)

DELOS INTERNATIONAL—Hollywood and Vine Plaza, 1645 North Vine Street, Suite 340, Hollywood, California CA90028, *USA* (213 962 2626)

DENON/NIPPON COLUMBIA—14-14, Akasaka 4-Chome, Minatu-Ku, Tokyo 107-11, *JAPAN* (03 3584 8271)

DEUTSCHE GRAMMOPHON CLASSICS—1 Sussex Place, Hammersmith, London W6 9XS (081-846 8515)

DISCOVERY RECORDS—The Old Church Mission Room, King's Corner, Pewsey, Wilts SN9 5BS (0672 63931)

DISQUES MONTAIGNE—15 Avenue Montaigne, 75008 Paris, *FRANCE* (1 4234 6540)

DORIAN RECORDINGS—17 State Street, Suite 2E, Troy, NY12180, *USA* (518 274 5475)

ECM—Gleichmanstrasse 10, 8000 München 60, *GERMANY* (08985 1048)

ELEKTRA-NONESUCH: USA—75 Rockefeller Plaza, New York NY10019, *USA* (212 484 7200); UK—46 Kensington Court, London W8 5DP (071-938 5542)

EMI RECORDS—Customer Services Dept, 20 Manchester Square, London W1A 1ES (071-487 4442)

EMI CLASSICS—30 Gloucester Place, London W1A 1ES (071-486 6022)

EMI—Sales & Distribution Centre, Hermes Close, Tachbrook Park, Leamington Spa, Warwickshire CV34 6RP (0926 888888)

ERATO: FRANCE—50 Rue des Tournelles, 75003 Paris, *FRANCE* (1 4827 7000); UK—46 Kensington Court, London W8 5DP (071-938 5542)

ETCETERA—Keizersgracht 518, 107 EK Amsterdam, *THE NETHERLANDS* (020 23 48 05)

FACTORY CLASSICAL—322 Uxbridge Road, London W3 9QP

FINLANDIA RECORDS—PO Box 169, 02101 Espoo, *FINLAND* (358 0 435011)

GAMUT DISTRIBUTION—Gamut House, Lancaster Way, Ely, Cambridgeshire CB6 3NP (0353 662366)

GIMELL RECORDS—4 Newtec Place, Magdalen Road, Oxford OX4 1RE (0865 244557)

GLOBE—Klaas Posthuma Productions, Tapuit 4, 1902 KP Castricuum, *THE NETHERLANDS* (2518 55584)

BRIAN GRIFFIN DISTRIBUTION—Storey House, White Cross, South Road, Lancaster LA1 4XQ (0524 846446)

HANSSLER CLASSIC—PO Box 1220, 7303 Neuhausen, Stuttgart, *GERMANY*

HARMONIA MUNDI: UK—19-21 Nile Street, London N1 7LR (071-253 0863); FRANCE—Mas de Vert, 13200 Arles, *FRANCE* (9049 9049); USA—3364 S. Robertson Boulevard, Los Angeles, California CA90034 *USA* (310 559 0802)

HARMONIC RECORDS—Parc de Montigny, Maxilly-sur-Léman, 74500 Evian-les-Bains, *FRANCE* (5075 6900)

HERALD AUDIOVISUAL PUBLICATIONS— The Studio, Alfred Road, Farnham, Surrey GU9 8ND (0252 725349)

HUNGAROTON—Vörösmarty tér 1, 1051 Budapest, *HUNGARY* (361 1187 193)

HYPERION RECORDS—PO Box 25, Eltham, London SE9 1AX (081-294 1166)

JECKLIN & CO—Rämistrasse 42, 8024 Zürich, *SWITZERLAND* (01 261 7774)

KEYBOARD RECORDS—418 Brockley Road, London, SE4 2DH (081-699 2549)

KINGDOM RECORDS—61 Collier Street, London N1 9BE (071-713 7788)

KOCH INTERNATIONAL: UK—23 Warple Way, London W3 0RX (081-749 7177); USA—177, Cantiague Rock Road, Westbury, NY11590 *USA* (516 938 8080)

KOCH SCHWANN—PO Box 7640, AM Wehrahn 1000, 4000 Düsseldorf 1, *GERMANY*

LARGO RECORDS—Mommsenstrasse 61, 5000 Köln 41, *GERMANY* (0221 431313)

LINN RECORDS—Floors Road, Waterfoot, Eaglesham, Glasgow G76 0EP (041-634 5111)

L'OISEAU-LYRE—1 Sussex Place, Hammersmith, London W6 9XS (081-846 8515)

LYRITA—99 Green Lane, Burnham, Slough, Bucks SL1 8EG (0628 604208)

MARCO POLO—58 Pak Tai Street, 8th Floor, Kai It Bldg, Tokwawan, Kowloon, *HONG KONG* (852 760 7818)

MERCURY—1 Sussex Place, Hammersmith, London W6 9XS (081-846 8515)

MERIDIAN RECORDS—PO Box 317, Eltham, London SE9 4SF (081-857 3213)

MIRABILIS RECORDS—5 King's Croft Gardens, Leeds LS17 6PB (0532 685123)

MUSIC AND ARTS PROGRAMS OF AMERICA—PO Box 771, Berkeley, California CA94701, *USA* (415 525 4583)

MUSIC FOR PLEASURE—1-3 Uxbridge Road, Hayes, Middlesex UB4 0SY (081-561 8722)

MUSICA SVECIAE—Knugl, Musikalaiska Akadamien, Blasieholmstorg 8, 111 Stockholm, *SWEDEN* (468 611 1870)

MUSIDISC (UK)—32 Queensdale Road, London W11 4SB (071-602 1124)

NAXOS—58 Pak Tai Street, 8th Floor, Kai It Bldg, Tokwawan, Kowloon, *HONG KONG* (852 760 7818)

NEW ALBION RECORDS—584 Castro Street, Suite 515, San Francisco, CA94114, *USA* (415 621 5757)

NEW NOTE—Unit 2, Orpington Trading Estate, Sevenoaks Way, St Mary Cray, Orpington, Kent BR5 3SR (06898 77884)

NEW WORLD RECORDS—701 Seventh Avenue, 7th Floor, New York, NY10036, *USA* (212 302 0460)

NEWPORT CLASSIC—106, Putnam Street, Providence, Rhode Island RI02909, *USA* (401 421 8143)

NIMBUS RECORDS—Wyastone Leys, Monmouth, Gwent NP5 3SR (0600 890682)

NMC—West Heath Studios, 174 Mill Lane, London NW6 1TB (071-431 3752)

NUOVA ERA RECORDS—Via Vincenzo Monti 38, 22060 Carugo (Como), *ITALY* (031 763 838)

OLYMPIA COMPACT DISCS—4th Floor North, Glenthorne House, Hammersmith Grove, London W6 0LG (081-741 8729)

ONDINE—Frederilinkatus 77 A 2, 00100 Helsinki, *FINLAND* (358 0493 913)

ORFEO INTERNATIONAL MUSIC— Augustenstrasse 79, 8000 München 2, *GERMANY* (089 522031)

OTTAVO RECORDINGS—Nassau Dillenburgstraat 1, 2596 AB The Hague, *THE NETHERLANDS* (7032 47557)

PAVANE RECORDS—17 Rue Ravenstein, 1000 Bruxelles, *BELGIUM* (02 513 0965)

PAVILION RECORDS—Sparrows Green, Wadhurst, East Sussex TN5 6SJ (0892 783591)

PHILIPS CLASSICS—1 Sussex Place, Hammersmith, London W6 9XS (081-846 8515)

PICKWICK GROUP—The Waterfront, Elstree Road, Elstree, Hertfordshire WD6 3BE (081-207 6207)

PINNACLE—Electron House, Cray Avenue, St Mary Cray, Orpington, Kent BR5 3PN (06898 70622)

POLYGRAM CLASSICS AND JAZZ—1 Sussex Place, Hammersmith, London W6 9XS (081-846 8515)

POLYGRAM RECORD OPERATIONS—PO Box 36, Clyde Works, Grove Road, Romford, Essex RM6 4QR (081-590 6044)

POLSKIE NAGRANIA—6, Goleszowska Street, 01249 Warsaw, *POLAND* (373794)

PRIORY RECORDS—Unit 9b, Upper Wingbury Courtyard, Wingrave, Nr. Aylesbury, Bucks HP22 4LW (0296 82255)

QUANTUM AUDIO—PO Box 26, Kilmarnock, Ayrshire KA1 1BA (0563 71122)

RARE RECORDS—13 Bank Square, Wilmslow, Cheshire SK9 1AN (0625 522017)

RCA—Bedford House, 69-79 Fulham High Street, London SW6 3JW (071-973 0011)

REFERENCE RECORDINGS—Box 7725X, San Francisco, California CA94107, *USA* (415 355 1892)

REM EDITIONS—4 Rue Sainte Marie des Terreaux, 69001 Lyon, *FRANCE* (7830 0571)

RICERCAR—Burnaumont 73, G912 Anloy, Liban, *BELGIUM*

ROYAL OPERA HOUSE RECORDS—*see* Conifer

SAYDISC—Chipping Manor, The Chipping, Wotton-under-Edge, Glos GL12 7AD (0453 845036)

SELECT MUSIC AND VIDEO DISTRIBUTORS—34a Holmethorpe Avenue, Holmethorpe Estate, Redhill, Surrey (0737 760020)

SIMAX—Sandakerveien 76, PO Box 4379, Torshov, 0402 Oslo 4, *NORWAY* (271 0140)

SONY MUSIC ENTERTAINMENT—1 Red Place, London W1Y 3RE (071-629 5555)

SONY MUSIC OPERATIONS—Rabans Lane, Aylesbury, Buckinghamshire HP19 3RT (0296 395151)

SUPRAPHON—Palackéhol, Praha 1, 11299, *CZECHOSLOVAKIA* (268141)

TACTUS—Via S. Allende 26, 40065 Pianoro Bologna, *ITALY* (051 775799)

TARGET RECORDS—26 Gardner Industrial Estate, Kent House Lane, Beckenham, Kent BR3 1QZ (081-778 4040)

TELARC INTERNATIONAL—23307 Commerce Park Road, Cleveland, Ohio 44122, *USA* (216 464 2313)

TELDEC CLASSICS—46 Kensington Court, London W8 5DP (071-938 5542)

TER CLASSICS—107 Kentish Town Road, London NW1 8PB (071-485 9593)

TESTAMENT—14 Tootswood Road, Bromley, Kent BR2 0PD (081-464 5947)

TRIM RECORDS—10 Dane Lane, Wilstead, Bedford MK45 3HT (0234 741152)

TUXEDO MUSIC—Avenue des Baumettes 15, 1020 Renens, *SWITZERLAND* (021 635 9091)

UNICORN-KANCHANA RECORDS—PO Box 339, London W8 7TJ (071-727 3881)

VANGUARD CLASSICS—27, West 72nd Street, New York, NY10023, *USA* (212 769 0360)

VICTORIA—Sandakerveien 76, PO Box 4379, Torshov, 0402 Oslo 4, *NORWAY* (271 0140)

VIRGIN CLASSICS—*see* EMI

WARNER CLASSICS (UK)—46 Kensington Court, London W8 5DP (071-938 5542)

WERGO—Weihergarten 5, Postfach 3640, 6500 Mainz 1, *GERMANY* (06131 246801)

Manufacturers and Distributors

Entries are listed thus: MANUFACTURER or LABEL. UK Distributor *(Series)*

ABBEY. Gamut

ACCENT. Gamut

ACCORD (Musidisc). Brian Griffin

ADDA. Gamut

ADES. Brian Griffin

ALTARUS. New Note

AMON RA (Saydisc). Gamut/Harmonia Mundi

APR. Harmonia Mundi

ARABESQUE. Albany

ARCHIV PRODUKTION. PolyGram Record Operations *(Archiv Produktion, Archiv Produktion Galleria)*

ARGO. PolyGram Record Operations

ARION. Discovery Records

ASV. ASV/Koch International *(ASV, Gaudeamus).*

AUVIDIS. Koch International *(Astrée, Valois)*

BEECHAM TRUST. Sir Thomas Beecham Trust

BIS. Conifer

BNL. Koch International

BRIDGE. Albany

CALLIOPE. Harmonia Mundi

CAPRICCIO. Target

CBC RECORDS. Albany

CBS. Sony Music Entertainment *(Masterworks, Masterworks Portrait, Digital Masters)*

CHANDOS. Chandos *(Chandos, Chaconne, Collect)*

CHANNEL CLASSICS. Complete Record Co.

CHESKY. New Note

CLASSICS FOR PLEASURE. Music for Pleasure

CLAVES. Albany

COLLEGIUM. Gamut/Koch International

COLLINS CLASSICS. New Note *(Collins Classics, Quest)*

CONIFER. Conifer

CONTINUUM. Complete Record Co.

CPO. Priory

CRD. Chandos

DECCA. PolyGram Record Operations *(Decca, New Line, London, Ovation, Enterprise, Grand Opera, Headline, Historic, Serenata, Weekend)*

DELOS. New Note

DENON. Conifer *(Denon, Allare)*

DEUTSCHE HARMONIA MUNDI. BMG UK *(Deutsche Harmonia Mundi, Editio Classica)*

DG. PolyGram Record Operations *(DG, DG Galleria, 3-D Classics, 20th Century Classics, Compact Classics, Dokumente, Karajan Symphony Edition, Privilege)*

DISQUES MONTAIGNE. New Note

DORIAN. Conifer

ECM NEW SERIES. New Note

ELEKTRA-NONESUCH. Warner Classics

EMI EMINENCE. Music for Pleasure

EMI LASER. Music for Pleasure

EMI. EMI *(EMI, Reflexe, Studio, Beecham Edition, British Composers, Great Recordings of the Century, Melodiya, Phoenixa, Références, Rossini Edition, Rouge et Noir)*

ERATO. Warner Classics *(Erato, MusiFrance, Libretto, Emerald)*

ETCETERA. Scott Butler

EURODISC. BMG UK

EUROPA MUSIC. Koch International

FACTORY CLASSICAL. New Note

FINLANDIA. Conifer

GAMUT CLASSICS. Gamut

GIMELL. Gamut/Pickwick

GLOBE. New Note

HANSSLER. Koch International

HARMONIA MUNDI. Harmonia Mundi *(Harmonia Mundi, Musique d'abord)*

HARMONIC. Complete Record Co.

HERALD. Gamut

HUNGAROTON. Conifer *(Hungaroton, Antiqua, White Label)*

HYPERION. Complete Record Co./Gamut *(Hyperion, Helios)*

JECKLIN DISCO. Pinnacle

KEYBOARD RECORDS. Scott Butler

KINGDOM RECORDS. Kingdom

KOCH INTERNATIONAL CLASSICS. Koch International

KOCH SCHWANN. Koch International

LANDOR BARCELONA. New Note

LARGO. New Note

LASERLIGHT (Capriccio). Target

LINN RECORDS. New Note

LYRITA. Conifer

L'OISEAU-LYRE. PolyGram Record Operations

MARCO POLO. Select

MERCURY. PolyGram Record Operations

MERIDIAN. Gamut

MIRABILIS. Priory

MUSIC AND ARTS. Harmonia Mundi

MUSICA SVECIAE. Gamut

NAXOS. Select

NEW ALBION. Harmonia Mundi

NEW WORLD. Harmonia Mundi

NEWPORT CLASSICS. Rare Records
(Newport Classics, Premier)

NIMBUS. Nimbus

NMC. New Note

NOVALIS. Complete Record Co.

NUOVA ERA. Complete Record Co.

OLYMPIA. Complete Record Co. *(Olympia, Explorer)*

OMEGA (Vanguard Classics). Complete Record Co.

ONDINE. Koch International

OPUS 3. Quantum Audio

OPUS III. Conifer

ORFEO. Koch International

OTTAVO. Priory

PAVANE. Kingdom

PEARL (Pavilion). Harmonia Mundi

PHILIPS. PolyGram Record Operations
(Philips, Silver Line, Legendary Classics, Mozart Edition, Musica da Camara, Concert Classics)

PICKWICK. Pickwick/Gamut *(IMP Masters, IMP Classics, IMP Red Label)*

POLSKIE NAGRANIA. Complete Record Co.

PRELUDIO. Scott Butler

PRIORY. Priory

RCA. BMG UK *(RCA Victor, Red Seal, Gold Seal, Papillon, Seon, Victrola)*

REFERENCE RECORDINGS. Quantum Audio/Trim Records

REM EDITIONS. Priory

RICERCAR. Gamut

ROYAL OPERA HOUSE RECORDS. Conifer

SAGA CLASSICS. Complete Record Co.

SALABERT ACTUELS. Harmonia Mundi

SIGNUM. Chord

SIMAX. Gamut

SONY CLASSICAL. Sony Music Entertainment *(Sony Classical, Vivarte, Essential Classics)*

SUPRAPHON. Koch International

TELARC. Conifer

TELDEC. Warner Classics *(Teldec Classics, British Line, Das Alte Werk, Das Alte Werk Reference)*

TER CLASSICS. Conifer

TESTAMENT. Gamut

TUXEDO. Complete Record Co.

UNICORN-KANCHANA. Harmonia Mundi
(Unicorn-Kanchana, Souvenir)

VANGUARD CLASSICS. Complete Record Co.

VICTORIA. Gamut

VIRGIN CLASSICS. EMI *(Virgin Classics, Veritas, Virgo, Venture)*

WERGO. Harmonia Mundi

Indexes

Index to Names and Nicknames

A

A wandering minstrel (Sullivan): (The) Mikado — operetta

Abegg Variations (Schumann): Theme and Variations on the name "Abegg" — piano, Op. 1

Abraham and Isaac (Stravinsky): Abraham and Isaac

Academic Festival Overture (Brahms): Academic Festival Overture, Op. 80

Accademico (Vaughan Williams): Concerto for Violin and Strings in D minor

Accursed Huntsman (Franck): (Le) Chasseur maudit — symphonic poem

Adelaide (Beethoven): Adelaide — Lied, Op. 46

Adelaide Concerto (Mozart [attrib]): Concerto for Violin and Orchestra in D, K294a

Adieu (Mendelssohn): Songs without Words in A minor, Op. 85/2

Adieu a Varsovie (Chopin): Rondo in C minor, Op. 1

Aeolian Harp (Chopin): Etudes, Op. 25 — No. 13 in A flat

Africa (Saint-Saëns): Fantasie for piano and orchestra in G minor, Op. 89

Age of Anxiety Symphony (Bernstein): Symphony No. 2

Age of Gold (Shostakovich): (The) Age of Gold — suite from the ballet, Op. 21a

Agon (Stravinsky): Agon — ballet

Air de ballet (Gretry): Zemire et Azor — Air de ballet

Air on a G string (Bach): Suite No. 3 in D, BWV1068 — Air

Alassio (Elgar): In the South, Op. 50

Alexander Nevsky (Prokofiev): Alexander Nevsky — cantata

Alla francesca (Vivaldi): RV117 — Concerto for Violin and Strings in A minor

Alla Rustica (Vivaldi): RV151 — Concerto for Strings in G

Alleluja (Haydn): Symphony No. 30 in C

All'Inglese (Vivaldi): RV546 — Concerto for Violin and Strings in A

Alpine Symphony (Strauss, R): (Eine) Alpensinfonie, Op. 64

Also sprach Zarathustra (Strauss, R): Also sprach Zarathustra — tone poem after Nietzsche

American Quartet (Dvořák): String Quartet in F, Op. 96

Amico Fritz (Mascagni): (L')Amico Fritz — opera

Amoroso (Vivaldi): RV271 — Concerto for Violin and Strings in E

Ancient Airs and Dances (Respighi): Antiche arie e danze per liuto — orchestra

Andante cantabile (Tchaikovsky): String Quartet No. 1 in D, Op. 11 — movement 2

Antar (Rimsky-Korsakov): Symphony No. 2, Op. 9

Antartica (Vaughan Williams): Symphony No. 7

Anvil Chorus (Verdi): (Il) Trovatore — No. 4a

Appassionata (Mendelssohn): Songs without Words — A minor, Op. 38/5

Appassionata Sonata (Beethoven): Piano Sonata No. 23 in F minor, Op. 57

Aranjuez (Rodrigo): Concierto de Aranjuez — guitar and orchestra

Archduke Trio (Beethoven): Piano Trios — No. 7 in B flat, Op. 97

Arioso (Bach): Cantata No. 156 — Ich steht mit einem Fuss im Grabe — Sinfonia

Arrival of the Queen of Sheba (Handel): Solomon — No. 8c

Art of Fugue (Bach): Art of Fugue, BWV1080

Art thou troubled (Handel): Rodelinda — Dove sei

Arte del Violino (Locatelli): Concerti and Caprices, Op. 3

As Vesta was from Latmos Hill (Weelkes): As Vesta was, from Latmos Hill descending — madrigal

Au fond du temple saint (Bizet): (Les) Pêcheurs de perles — No. 2b

Autumn
(Chaminade): Automne — piano, Op. 35
(Vivaldi): (12) Concerti, Op. 8 — No. 3 in F, RV293

Awake, thou wintry earth (Bach): Cantata No. 129 — Gelobet sei der (Herr, mein Gott)

B

Babar the Elephant (Poulenc): Babar the Elephant — narrator and piano

Babiy Yar Symphony (Shostakovich): Symphony No. 13 in B flat minor

Bach goes to Town (Templeton): Topsy-Turvy Suite — harpsichord

Bachianas brasileiras No. 5: (Villa-Lobos): Bachianas brasileiras No. 5 — voice and cellos

Ballet of the Sylphes: (Berlioz): (La) damnation de Faust — No. 12a

Balm Study (Chopin): Etudes, Op. 25 — No. 14 in F minor

Barber of Bagdad (Cornelius): (Der) Barbier von Bagdad — opera

Barcarolle
(Mendelssohn): Songs without Words — in B flat, Op. 85/6
(Offenbach): (Les) Contes d'Hoffmann — No. 16

Battle of Kerzhents (Rimsky-Korsakov): (The) Legend of the Invisible City of Kitezh — No. 3

Battle of Prague (Kotzwara): (The) Battle of Prague

Battle of the Huns (Liszt): Hunnenschlacht — symphonic poem

Battle of Vittoria / Battle Symphony (Beethoven): Wellingtons Sieg (Die Schlacht bei Vittoria), Op. 91

Baïlèro (Canteloube): Chants d'Auvergne — No. 2

Bear Symphony (Haydn): Symphony No. 82 in C

Beau Brummel Minuet (Elgar): Beau Brummel — incidental music

Bee's Wedding (Mendelssohn): Songs without Words — in C, Op. 67/4

Beggar Student (Millocker): (Der) Bettelstudent — operetta

Beggar's Opera (Gay): (The) Beggar's Opera

Bell (Khachaturian): Symphony No. 2, Op. 25

Bell Anthem (Purcell): Rejoice in the Lord Alway

Bell Chorus (Leoncavallo): Pagliacci — No. 5b

Bells, The (Rachmaninov): (The) Bells — choral symphony, Op. 35

Bells of Zlonice (Dvořák): Symphony No. 1 in C minor

Belshazzar's Feast
(Handel): Belshazzar — oratorio
(Sibelius): Belshazzar's Feast — incidental music, Op. 51
(Walton): Belshazzar's Feast — cantata

Berceuse (Mendelssohn): Songs without Words — in F, Op. 53/4

Bird Catcher (Zeller): (Der) Vogelhändler

Bird Quartet (Haydn): String Quartets, Op. 33 — No. 3 in G

Black Domino (Auber): (Le) Noir Domino — opera

Black Key Study (Chopin): Etudes, Op. 10 — No. 5 in G flat

Black Mass (Scriabin): Piano Sonata No. 9 in F, Op. 68

Black roses (Sibelius): (6) Songs, Op. 36 — No. 1

Blue Danube (Strauss II, J): An die schönen, blauen Donau — waltz, Op. 314

Bluebird (Stanford): (The) Bluebird — part-song, Op. 119/3

Boléro (Ravel): Boléro

Botticelli Pictures (Respighi): (3) Botticelli Pictures — orchestra

Bridal chorus (Wagner): Lohengrin — No. 18

Brindisi
(Donizetti): Lucrezia Borgia — Brindisi
(Mascagni): Cavalleria Rusticana — No. 15a
(Verdi): Otello — No. 4b Verdi (La) Traviata — No. 3

Bunte Blätter (Schumann): Bunte Blätter — piano, Op. 99

Butterfly's wings (Chopin): Etudes, Op. 25 — No. 21 in G flat

C

Caccia (Vivaldi): (12) Concerti, Op. 8 — No. 10 in B flat, RV362

Caliph of Bagdad (Boieldieu): (Le) Caliph de Bagdad — opera

Camp Meeting (Ives): Symphony No. 3

Campanella
(Liszt): Etudes d'exécution transcendente d'après Paganini — No. 3
(Paganini): Concerto for Violin and Orchestra No. 2 in B minor, Op. 7 — Rondo

Canary Cantata (Telemann): Trauser-music eines kunsterfahrenen canarien-vogels — cantata

Canon (Pachelbel): Canon and Gigue in D

Can-Can (Offenbach): Orfée aux enfers — Overture

Capriccio espagnol (Rimsky-Korsakov): Capriccio espagnol, Op. 34

Capriccio italien (Tchaikovsky): Capriccio Italien, Op. 45

Capriccio Sonata (Scarlatti, D): Keyboard Sonatas — E, Kk20

Caprice in A minor (Paganini): Caprices, Op. 1 — No. 24 in A minor

Capricieuse
(Berwald): Symphony No. 3 in D
(Elgar): (La) Capricieuse — violin and piano, Op. 17

Capriol Suite (Warlock): Capriol Suite

Card Scene (Bizet): Carmen — No. 18a

Care selve (Handel): Atalanta — Care selve

Carillon de Westminster (Vierne): Pièces de fantaisie, Suite No. 3 — organ, Op. 54/6 —

Carmina Burana (Orff): Carmina Burana — oratorio

Carnival in Paris (Svendsen): Carnival in Paris — orchestra, Op. 9

Cat Duet (Rossini): Duetto dei due gatti — 2vv and piano

Catalogue Song (Mozart): Don Giovanni — No. 4

Cathédrale engloutie (Debussy): Préludes — No. 1

Cat's Fugue (Scarlatti, D): Keyboard Sonatas — G minor, Kk30

Celeste Aida (Verdi): Aida — No. 3

Celtic (MacDowell): Piano Sonata No. 4

Cendrillon (Massenet): Cendrillon — opera

Cenerentola (Rossini): (La) Cenerentola — opera

Cetra, La (Vivaldi): (12) Concerti, Op. 9

Champagne Aria (Mozart): Don Giovanni — No. 11

Champêtre (Poulenc): Concert châmpetre for harpsichord and orchestra in D minor

Chanson de Matin (Elgar): Chanson de Matin, Op. 15/2

Chanson de Nuit (Elgar): Chanson de Matin, Op. 15/1

Chasse
(Haydn): Symphony No. 73 in D
(Mozart, L.): Sinfonia da caccia in G

Chasseur maudit (Franck): (Le) Chasseur maudit — symphonic poem

Checkmate (Bliss): Checkmate — ballet

Child of Our Time (Tippett): (A) Child of Our Time — oratorio

869

Children's games (Bizet): Jeux d'enfants — petite suite

Children's Overture (Quilter): (A) Children's Overture, Op. 17

Choral Symphony (Beethoven): Symphony No. 9 in D minor, Op. 125

Chorus of the Hebrew Slaves (Verdi): Nabucco — No. 18

Chromatic Fantasia and Fugue (Bach): Chromatic Fantasia and Fugue in D minor, BWV 903

Cimento dell'Armonia e dell'Inventione (Vivaldi): (12) Concerti, Op. 8

Cinderella
(Massenet): Cendrillon — opera
(Rossini): (La) Cenerentola — opera

Clair de lune (Debussy): Suite bergamasque — No. 3

Classical Symphony (Prokofiev): Symphony No. 1 in D, Op. 25

Clock Symphony (Haydn): Symphony No. 101 in D

Clog Dance (Herold): (La) Fille mal gardée

Cockaigne Overture (Elgar): Cockaigne (In London Town) — Overture, Op. 40

Coffee Cantata (Bach): Cantata No. 211 — Schweigt stille, plaudert nicht

Colas Breugnon (Kabalevsky): Colas Breugnon — opera

Colloredo (Mozart): Serenade in D, K203

Colour Symphony (Bliss): (A) Colour Symphony

Come beloved (Handel): Atalanta — Care selve

Come to me, soothing sleep (Handel): Ottone — Vieni, o figlio caro

Comedians (Kabalevsky): (The) Comedians — suite for small orchestra, Op. 26

Concerto accademica (Vaughan Williams): Concerto for Violin and Strings in D minor

Concerto pathétique (Liszt): Concerto pathétique — two pianos, S258

Concierto de Aranjuez (Rodrigo): Concierto de Aranjuez — guitar and orchestra

Consolation (Mendelssohn): Songs without Words — in E, Op. 30/3

Coronation Concerto (Mozart): Piano Concerto No. 26 in D, K537

Coronation Mass (Mozart): Mass No. 16 in C, K317

Coucou (Daquin): Premier livre de pièces — Le coucou

Countess Maritza (Kálmán): Gräfin Mariza — operetta

Country Gardens (Grainger): Country Gardens

Creation (Haydn): (Die) Schöpfung — oratorio

Creation Mass (Haydn): Mass No. 13 in B flat

Creatures of Prometheus (Beethoven): Geschöpfe des Prometheus — incidental music

Creed, The (Grechaninov): (The) Russian Creed

Crimond (Roberton): Psalm 23

Crisantemi (Puccini): Cristantemi for string quartet

Cuban Overture (Gershwin): Cuban Overture

Cuckoo and the Nightingale (Handel): Concerti for Organ and Strings III — No. 13 in F, HWV295

Cuckoo Concerto (Vivaldi): RV335 — Concerto for Violin and Strings in A minor

Czardas (Strauss II, J): (Die) Fledermaus — operetta

D

Daisies (Rachmaninov): Daisies — song, Op. 38/3

Dance of the Blessed Spirits (Gluck): Orfeo ed Euridice — No. 30

Dance of the Little Swans (Tchaikovsky): Swan Lake — No. 14

Dance of the Seven Veils (Strauss, R): Salome — No. 1

Dance of the Sugar-Plum Fairy (Tchaikovsky): (The) Nutcracker — No. 14c

Dance of the Tumblers (Rimsky-Korsakov): Snow Maiden — No. 4

Dance Symphony (Copland): (A) Dance Symphony

Dank sei Dir, Herr (Ochs): Dank sei dir, Herr — song

Danse de Puck (Debussy): Préludes — Book 1 — No. 11

Dante Sonata (Liszt): Années de pèlerinage — année deuxième — No. 6

Dante Symphony (Liszt): (A) Dante Symphony

Daughter of the regiment (Donizetti): (La) Fille du régiment — opera

Dawn over the Moscow River (Mussorgsky): Khovanshchina — No. 1

Death and the Maiden Quartet (Schubert): String Quartet No. 14 in D minor, D810

Death and transfiguration (Strauss, R): Tod und Verklärung — tone poem, Op. 24

Death in Venice theme (Mahler): Symphony No. 5 — Adagietto

Death of Cleopatra (Berlioz): (La) Mort de Cléopâtre

Decoration Day (Ives): Holidays — Symphony — No. 2

Dein ist mein ganzes herz (Lehár): (Das) Land des Lachélns — operetta — No. 11

Deliciae Basiliensis (Honegger): Symphony No. 4

Depuis le jour (Charpentier, G): Louise — Depuis le jour

Destiny Waltz (Baynes): Destiny Waltz

Desérts (Varèse): Desérts

Devil and Kate (Dvořák): (The) Devil and Kate — opera

Devil's Trill Sonata (Tartini): (12) Sonatas — violin and continuo, Op. 2 — No. 12

Di Ballo (Sullivan): Overture di Ballo — overture

Di tre re (Honegger): Symphony No. 5

Diabelli Variations (Beethoven): 33 Variations on a waltz by Diabelli, Op. 120

Didione Abbandonata (Tartini): Sonatas for Violin and Continuo, Op. 6 — No. 10 in G minor

Dido's Lament (Purcell): Dido and Aeneas — No. 2

Dissonance Quartet (Mozart): String Quartet No. 19 in C, K465

Distratto (Haydn): Symphony No. 60 in C

Divine Poem (Scriabin): Symphony No. 3 in C, Op. 43

Doctor Gradus ad Parnassum (Debussy): Children's Corner — No. 1

Doctor Miracle (Bizet): (Le) Docteur Miracle

Doktor Faust (Busoni): Doktor Faust — poem for music

Domestica (Strauss, R): Sinfonia domestica, Op. 53

Don Quichotte (Telemann): Overture-Suite for Strings in G (Burlesque de Don Quichotte)

Don Quixote
  (Minkus): Don Quixote — ballet
  (Strauss, R): Don Quixote — fantastic variations for cello and orchestra

Donnerwetter (Mozart): (6) German Dances, K605 — No. 3

Don't be cross (Zeller): (Der) Obersteiger Sei nicht bös

Dorian Fugue (Bach): Toccata and Fugue in D minor, BWV538

Dove sei (Handel): Rodelinda — Dove sei

Dream of Gerontius (Elgar): (The) Dream of Gerontius — oratorio

Dream Quartet (Haydn): String Quartets, Op. 50 — No. 5 in F

Drum Mass (Haydn): Mass No. 10 in C

Drum-roll Symphony (Haydn): Symphony No. 103 in E flat

Duetto (Mendelssohn): Songs without Words — in A flat, Op. 38/6

Dumbarton Oaks (Stravinsky): Concerto in E flat

Dumky (Dvořák): Piano Trio in E minor, Op. 90

Dusk (Armstrong Gibbs): Fancy Dress — Dance Suite, Op. 82/1 — No. 3

E

E lucevan le stelle (Puccini): Tosca — No. 16

Easter Hymn (Mascagni): Cavalleria rusticana — No. 6a

Easter Symphony (Foerster): Symphony No. 4 in C minor

Ebony Concerto (Stravinsky): Ebony Concerto — clarinet and jazz ensemble

Eco in Lontano (Vivaldi): RV552 — Concerto for two Violins and Strings in A

Edward (Brahms): (4) Ballades — No. 1 in D minor

EC Anthem (Beethoven): Symphony No. 9 in D minor, Op. 125 — movement 4 (finale)

Egdon Heath (Holst): Egdon Heath (Homage to Hardy) — orchestra, H127

Egyptian Concerto (Saint-Saëns): Concerto for Piano and Orchestra No. 5 in F, Op. 103

Eine kleine Nachtmusik (Mozart): Serenade in G, K525

Eine kleine Trauermusik (Schubert): Nonet in E flat, D79

Elegiac Symphony (Stanford): Symphony No. 2 in D minor

Elegy (Bax): Trio for flute, viola and harp

Elevamini (Williamson): Symphony No. 1

Elizabeth of Glamis (Coates): (The) Three Elizabeths — Suite

Elvira Madigan (Mozart): Piano Concerto No. 21 in C, K467 — movement 2

Emerald Isle (Sullivan): (The) Emerald Isle — operetta

Emperor Concerto (Beethoven): Piano Concerto No. 5 in E flat, Op. 73

Emperor Quartet (Haydn): String Quartets, Op. 76 — No. 3in C — Theme and Variations

En bateau (Debussy): Petite Suite — No. 1

En blanc et noir (Debussy): En blanc et noir — two pianos

English Folk Song Suite (Vaughan Williams): English Folk Song Suite — wind band

Enimga Variations (Elgar): Variations on an Original Theme, Op. 36

Entry of the Gladiators (Fučík): Entry of the Gladiators — triumph march, Op. 68

Eroica Symphony (Beethoven): Symphony No. 3 in E flat, Op. 55

Eroica Variations (Beethoven): (15) Variations and Fugue in F flat, Op. 35

España (Chabrier): España — Rapsodie

España Waltz (Waldteufel): España — waltz

Espansiva (Nielsen): Symphony No. 3

Estro armonico (Vivaldi): (12) Concerti, Op. 3

Eyeglass Duet (Beethoven): Duo in E flat for viola and cello

F

FAE Sonata (Brahms): Scherzo in C minor (FAE Sonata), Op. 5

Fair Maid of Perth (Bizet): (La) Jolie fille de Perth — opera

Fairest Isle (Purcell): King Arthur — Fairest Isle

Fairy Queen (Purcell): (The) Fairy Queen — semi-opera

Fairy's kiss (Stravinsky): (La) Baiser de le fée — ballet

Fall of Warsaw (Chopin): Etudes, Op. 10 — No 12 in C minor (Revolutionary)

Fancy (Stanley): (10) Voluntaries, Op. 7 — No. 6 in F

Fantasia Quartet (Haydn): String Quartets, Op. 76 — No. 6 in E flat

Fantasy Sonata (Tippett): Piano Sonata No. 1

Fantasía para un gentilhombre (Rodrigo): Fantasía para un gentilhombre — guitar and orchestra

Farewell Symphony (Haydn): Symphony No. 45 in F sharp minor

Faust Symphony (Liszt): (A) Faust Symphony — tenor, chorus and orchestra, S108

Favorito (Vivaldi): RV277 — Concerto for Violin and Strings in E minor

Façade (Walton): Façade — reciter(s) and chamber ensemble

Feast of Saint Lawrence (Vivaldi): RV556 — Concerto in C

Feste Romane (Respighi): Roman Festivals — symphonic poem

Festin de l'araignée (Roussel): (Le) Festin de l'Araignée

Festive (Smetana): Triumph Symphony in E, Op. 6

Fifths Quartet (Haydn): String Quartets, Op. 76 — No. 2, D minor

Fileuse (Raff): Pieces, Op. 157 — No. 2

Fille aux cheveux (Debussy): Préludes — Book 1 — No. 8

Fille de Madame Angot (Lecocq): (La) Fille de Madame Angot

Fingal's Cave (Mendelssohn): (The) Hebrides Overture, Op. 26

Finlandia (Sibelius): Finlandia, Op. 26

Fire Symphony (Haydn): Symphony No. 59 in A

Fireworks (Stravinsky): Fireworks — fantasy for orchestra, Op. 4

Fireworks Music (Handel): Music for the Royal Fireworks

First cuckoo (Delius): On hearing the first cuckoo in Spring

Flight of the Bumble Bee (Rimsky-Korsakov): (The) Tale of Tsar Saltan — No. 3

Flocks in pastures green abiding (Bach): Cantata No. 208 — Schlafe können sicher weiden

Flower Duet (Delibes): Lakmé — No. 4b

Flower Song
  (Bizet): Carmen — No. 15c
  (Puccini): Madama Butterfly — No. 13c

Foggy Dew (Britten): The Foggy, Foggy Dew — folk-song arrangement

Forelle (Trout) (Schubert): (Die) Forelle — Lied, D550

Forest Murmurs (Wagner): Siegfried — No. 25

Fountains of Rome (Respighi): Fountains of Rome — symphonic poem

Four Ages (Alkan): Grande Sonate, Op. 33

Four Last Songs (Strauss, R): Vier Letze Lieder

Four Saints in Three Acts (Thomson): Four Saints in Three Acts — opera

Four Sea Interludes (Britten): Peter Grimes — Nos. 2, 11, 16 and 25

Four Seasons (Vivaldi): (12) Concerti, Op. 8 — Nos. 1-4

Four Serious Songs (Brahms): (4) Erste Gesänge — song collection, Op. 121

Four Temperaments
  (Hindemith): (The) Four Temperaments
  (Nielsen) Symphony No. 2

Fourth of July (Ives): Holidays — Symphony — No. 3

Frank Bridge Variations (Britten): Variations on a theme of Frank Bridge, Op. 10

Frauenliebe und -leben (Schumann): Frauenliebe und -leben — song cycle, Op. 42

Frei aber Einsam (Brahms): Scherzo in C minor (FAE Sonata), Op. 5

Frog Quartet (Haydn): String Quartets, Op. 50 — No. 6, D

From Bohemia's woods and fields (Smetana): Má Vlast — No. 4

From My Life (Smetana): String Quartet No. 1 in E minor

From Old Note Books (Prokofiev): Piano Sonata No. 4 in C minor, Op. 29

From the Home Country (Smetana): Duos for violin and piano

From the New World (Dvořák): Symphony No. 9 in E minor, Op. 95

Funeral March
  (Beethoven): Piano Sonata No. 12 in A flat, Op. 26
  (Beethoven): Symphony No. 3 in E flat, Op. 55 — movement 2
  (Chopin): Piano Sonata No. 2 in B flat minor, Op. 35 — movement 2

Funeral Ode (Bach): Cantata No. 198 — Lass Furstin, lass noch einen Strahl

Funeral Symphony (Haydn): Symphony No. 44 in E minor

Fur Elise (Beethoven): (25) Bagatelles — No. 25 in A minor

Fêtes (Debussy): Nocturnes — No. 2

G

Gardellino (Vivaldi): RV90 — Concerto in D

Garden of Fand (Bax): Garden of Fand — tone poem

Gaîté Parisienne (Offenbach): Gaîté Parisienne — ballet

Geist Trio (Beethoven): Piano Trios — No. 5 in D, Op. 70/1

Gesängszene (Spohr): Concerto for Violin and Orchestra No. 8 in A minor, Op. 47

Ghost Trio (Beethoven): Piano Trios — No. 5 in D, Op. 70/1

Gianni Schicchi (Puccini): Gianni Schicchi — opera

Gipsy and the Nightingale (Benedict): Gipsy and the Nightingale — Song

Gipsy Princess (Kálmán): Zirkusprinzessin — operetta

Gipsy Songs (Dvořák): Gypsy Melodies

Girl with the flaxen hair (Debussy): Préludes — Book 1 — No. 8

Glagolitic Mass (Janáček): Glagolitic Mass

Goin' home (Dvořák): Symphony No. 9 in E minor, Op. 95

Golden Age (Shostakovich): (The) Age of Gold — suite from the ballet, Op. 21a

Golden Cockerel (Rimsky-Korsakov): (Le) Coq d'Or — opera

Golden Legend (Sullivan): (The) Golden Legend — cantata

Golden Sonata (Purcell): Sonatas in four parts — No. 9 in F

Goldfinch Concerto (Vivaldi): (12) Concerto, Op. 10 — No. 3 in G, RV248

Goldfish (Debussy): Images — No. 6

Golliwog's cakewalk (Debussy): Children's Corner — No. 6

Good Friday Music (Wagner): Parsifal — No. 32

Gothic Symphony (Brian, H): Symphony No. 1 in D minor

Il'ya Muromets (Glière): Symphony No. 3

Im chambre separée (Heuberger): (Der) Opernball — operetta

Im Walde (Raff): Symphony No. 3, Op. 153

Imperial Mass (Haydn): Mass No. 11 in D minor

Imperial Symphony (Haydn): Symphony No. 53 in D

In a Monastery Garden (Ketèlbey): In a Monastery Garden — characteristic intermezzo

In a Persian Market (Ketèlbey): In a Persian Market — intermezzo music

In a Summer Garden (Delius): In a Summer Garden

In an Eighteenth-century drawing room (Mozart): Piano Sonata No. 15 in C, K545

In an English country garden (Grainger): Country Gardens

In London Town (Elgar): Cockaigne Overture, Op. 40

In the steppes of Central Asia (Borodin): In the steppes of Central Asia

Incantation (Martinů): Piano Concerto No. 4

Indian Queen (Purcell): (The) Indian Queen — semi-opera

Indian Suite (MacDowell): Suite No. 2, Op. 48

Inextinguishable (Nielsen): Symphony No. 4

Intimate letters (Janáček): String Quartet No. 2

Invitation to the Dance (Weber): Invitation to the Dance — Rondo brillant in D flat, J260 (orch Berlioz)

Irene (Holbrooke): Nonet for woodwind and strings

Irish Symphony
(Stanford): Symphony No. 3 in F minor, Op. 28
(Sullivan): Symphony in E

Isle of the Dead (Rachmaninov): Isle of the Dead — symphonic poem

It was a lover and his lass (Morley): It was a lover and his lass — ayre

Italian caprice (Tchaikovsky): Capriccio italien, Op. 45

Italian Concerto (Bach): Concerto in the Italian style (Italian Concerto), BWV971

Italian impressions (Charpentier, G): Impressions d'Italie

Italian Serenade (Wolf): Italian Serenade — string quartet

Italian Symphony (Mendelssohn): Symphony No. 4 in A, Op. 90

Ivan IV (Bizet): Ivan IV — opera

Ivanhoe (Sullivan): Ivanhoe — opera

J

Jardins sous la Pluie (Debussy): Estampes — No. 3

Jena Symphony (Witt): Symphony in C

Jeremiah Symphony (Bernstein): Symphony No. 1

Jesu, joy of man's desiring (Bach): Cantata No. 147 — Herz und Mund und Tat und Leben — No. 10

Jeunehomme Concerto (Mozart): Piano Concerto No. 9 in E flat, K271

Jeux d'enfants (Bizet): Jeux d'enfants — petite suite

Jewel Song (Gounod): Faust — No. 13

Jewels of the Madonna (Wolf-Ferrari): (I) Gioielli della Madonna — opera

Jig Fugue (Bach): Fugue in G, BWV577

Job (Vaughan Williams): Job — masque for dancing

Joke Quartet (Haydn): String Quartets, Op. 33 — No. 2 in E flat

Josephslegende (Strauss, R): Josephslegende — ballet

Jota Aragonesa (Glinka): Jota aragonesa — Spanish Overture No. 1

Joyeuse marche (Chabrier): Joyeuse marche — marche française

Jupiter Symphony
(Haydn): Symphony No. 13 in D
(Mozart): Symphony No. 41 in C, K551

K

Kaddisch Symphony (Bernstein): Symphony No. 3

Kaiser Quartet (Haydn): String Quartets, Op. 76 — No. 3 in C — Theme and Variations

Katharinentanze (Haydn): (12) Minuetti da ballo, HobIX/4

Kegelstadt Trio (Mozart): Trio in E flat, K498

Kindertotenlieder (Mahler): Kindertotenlieder — song cycle

King Arthur
(Elgar): King Arthur — incidental music
(Purcell): King Arthur — semi-opera

King of the stars (Stravinsky): (Le) Roi des étoiles — cantata

King's Hunt (Byrd): (The) Hunt's up — keyboard

Kreutzer Sonata
(Beethoven): Sonata for Violin and Piano No. 9 in A, Op. 47
(Janáček): String Quartet No. 1

Kullervo (Sibelius): Kullervo Symphony, Op. 7

L

L'Allegro ed il peneroso (Stanford): Symphony No. 5 in D

La donna è mobile (Verdi): Rigoletto — No. 17

Lady and the Fool (Verdi): (The) Lady and the Fool — ballet

Lamentatione Symphony (Haydn): Symphony No. 26 in D minor

Lamentations of Jeremiah
(Lassus): Lamentations of Jeremiah
(Tallis): Lamentations of Jeremiah — 5vv

Land of Hope and Glory (Elgar): Pomp and Circumstance Marches, Op. 39 — No. 1 in D

Land of my Fathers (James, J): Land of my Fathers — song

Land of Smiles (Lehár): (Das) Land des Lächelns — operetta

Largo al factotum (Rossini): (Il) Barbiere di Siviglia — No. 4

Largo (Handel's) (Handel): Serse — No. 1b

Lark ascending (Vaughan Williams): (The) Lark ascending — romance for violin and orchestra

Lark Quartet (Haydn): String Quartets, Op. 64 — No. 5 in D

Lascia ch'io pianga (Handel): Rinaldo — No. 21b

Laudon Symphony (Haydn): Symphony No. 69 in C

Left-hand Concerto (Ravel): Concerto for the Left-Hand and Orchestra in D

Legend of the Invisible City of Kitezh (Rimsky-Korsakov): (The) Legend of the Invisible City of Kitezh — opera

Leierman (Mozart): German Dances, K602 — No. 3

Lelio (Berlioz): Lélio, ou La retour à la vie — monologue lyrique, Op. 14b

Leningrad Symphony (Shostakovich): Symphony No. 7 in C

Lenore (Raff): Symphony No. 5 in E, Op. 60

Les Adieux Sonata (Beethoven): Piano Sonata No. 26 in E flat, Op. 81a

Let the bright Seraphim (Handel): Samson — No. 95

Let us wander not unseen (Purcell): (The) Indian Queen — semi-opera

Letter V Symphony (Haydn): Symphony No. 88 in C

Leçons de Ténèbres
(Charpentier, M-A): Leçons de Ténèbres (five sets)
(Couperin): (3) Leçons de Ténèbres

Liebestod (Wagner): Tristan und Isolde — No. 18

Liebestraum (Liszt): Liebestraum — piano, S541 — No. 3

Light Cavalry (Suppé): (Die) Leichte Kavallerie — operetta

Lilacs (Rachmaninov): Lilacs — song, Op. 21/5

Lincoln Portrait (Copland): Lincoln Portrait — narrator and orchestra

Lindaraja (Debussy): Lindaraja

Linden lea (Vaughan Williams): Lindea Lea — song

Linz Symphony (Mozart): Symphony No. 36 in C, K425

Little C major (Schubert): Symphony No. 6 in C, D589

Little Organ Mass (Haydn): Mass No. 7 in B flat

Little Russian Symphony (Tchaikovsky): Symphony No. 2 in C minor, Op. 17

Liturgique Symphony (Honegger): Symphony No. 3

Lo, here the gentle lark (Bishop): Lo, here the gentle lark — song

London Overture (Ireland): (A) London Overture

London Symphonies (Haydn): Symphonies Nos. 93-104

London Symphony
(Haydn): Symphony No. 104 in D
(Vaughan Williams): Symphony No. 2

Long Day closes, The (Sullivan): (The) Long day closes — partsong

Lost chord (Sullivan): (The) Lost chord — song

Lost Happiness (Mendelssohn): Songs without Words — C minor, Op. 38/2

Love and music (Puccini): Tosca — No. 12

Love for Three Oranges (Prokofiev): (The) Love for Three Oranges — opera

Lovely maid in the moonlight (Puccini): (La) Bohème — No. 4

Lover and the Nightingale (Granados): Goyescas — No. 4

Lucy Long (Godfrey): Variations on "Lucy Long"

Lulu (Berg): Lulu — opera

M

Mad Scene (Donizetti): Lucia di Lammermoor — No. 13

Madrigelsco (Vivaldi): RV129 — Concerto for Violin and Strings in D minor

Magic Fire Music (Wagner): Die Walküre — No. 31

Mahagonny (Weill): Aufstieg and Fall der Stadt Mahagonny — opera

Malédiction (Liszt): Malédiction — piano and orchestra, S121

Manfred (Schumann): Manfred — incidental music, Op. 115

Manfred Symphony (Tchaikovsky): Manfred Symphony, Op. 58

March of the Little Fauns (Pierné): Cydalise et le chevre-pied — ballet suite

Marche Slave (Tchaikovsky): Marche slave, Op. 31

Maria Theresia Symphony (Haydn): Symphony No. 48 in C

Mariazellermesse (Haydn): Mass No. 8 in C

Marseillaise, La (Berlioz): La Marseillaise (Rouget de Lisle): Hymne à la liberté

Maskarade (Nielsen): Maskarade — opera

Masquerade (Khachaturian): Masquerade — incidental music

Mass in the Time of War (Haydn): Mass No. 10 in C

Mastersingers (Wagner): (Die) Meistersinger von Nürnberg — opera

Mathis der Maler (Hindemith): Mathis der Maler — symphony

Matin Symphony (Haydn): Symphony No. 6 in D

Mattinata (Leoncavallo): Mattinata — song

May Breezes (Mendelssohn): Songs without Words — in G, Op. 62/1

May Day Symphony (Shostakovich): Symphony No. 3 in E flat

Méditation (Massenet): Thaïs — No. 5

Mediterranean (Bax): Mediterranean

Mefistofele (Boito): Mefistofele — opera

Melody in F (Rubinstein): (2) Pieces — No. 2

Menuets des follets (Berlioz): (La) Damnation de Faust — No. 18

Mercury Symphony (Haydn): Symphony No. 43 in E flat

Merry Widow (Lehár): (Die) Lustige Witwe

Midi, Le (Field): Nocturnes — No. 18 in E, H13K

Midi Symphony (Haydn): Symphony No. 7 in C

Midsummer Vigil (Alfvén): Swedish Rhapsody No. 1, Op. 19

Mikrokosmos (Bartók): Mikrokosmos

Military Polonaise (Chopin): Polonaises — No. 3 in A, Op. 40/1

Military Symphony (Haydn): Symphony No. 100 in G

Mimi's farewell (Puccini): (La) Bohème — No. 11

Minute Waltz (Chopin): Waltz in D flat, Op. 64/1

Miracle Symphony (Haydn): Symphony No. 96 in D

Missa Papae Marcelli (Palestrina): Missa Papae Marcelli — 6vv

Missa Solemnis (Beethoven): Mass in D minor, Op. 123

Mládi (Janáček): Mládi (Youth) — septet for wind ensemble

Moldau (Smetana): Má Vlast — No. 2

Moonlight Sonata (Beethoven): Piano Sonata No. 14 in C sharp minor, Op. 27/2

Morning, Noon and Night (Suppé): (Ein) Morgen, ein Mittag, ein Abend in Wien — local play with songs

Morning papers (Strauss II, J): Morgenblätter — waltz, Op. 279

Morning song (Mendelssohn): Songs without words — in G, Op. 62/4

Mortify us by Thy goodness (Bach): Cantata No. 22 — Jesus nahm zu sich die Zwölfe

Moses and Aaron (Schoenberg): Moses und Aron — opera

Mozartiana (Tchaikovsky): Suite No. 4 in G, Op. 61

Musetta's Waltz Song (Puccini): (La) Bohème — No. 7b

Musica Notturna della strade di Madrid (Boccherini): String Quartet in C, G324

Musical Joke (Mozart): (Ein) Musikalischer Spass, K522

My heart ever faithful (Bach): Cantata No. 68 — Ach Gott, wie manches Herzlied — No. 2

N

Naïla (Delibes): Naïla — waltz (Pas de fleurs)

Nelson Mass (Haydn): Mass No. 11 in D minor

Nessun dorma (Puccini): Turandot — No. 17

New Lambach Symphony (Mozart): Symphony in G

New World Symphony (Dvořák): Symphony No. 9 in E minor, Op. 95

Night in Venice (Strauss II, J): (Ein) Nacht in Venedig — operetta

Night music in the streets of Madrid (Boccherini): String Quartet in C, G324

Night on a bare mountain (Mussorgsky): (A) Night on a bare mountain

Nightingale Song (Zeller): (Der) Vogelhändler — No. 12b

Nights in the gardens of Spain (Falla): Noches en los jardines de España — symphonic impressions

Nightwatchman (Biber): Serenade in C

Nimrod (Elgar): Variations on an Original theme, Op. 36, 'Enigma'

None but the weary heart (Tchaikovsky): Songs, Op. 6 — No. 6

None shall sleep (Puccini): Turandot — No. 17, Nessun dorma

Noonday Witch (Dvořák): (The) Noonday Witch — symphonic poem

Norse (MacDowell): Piano Sonata No. 3 in D minor

Norwegian Moods (Stravinsky): (4) Norwegian Moods — orchestra

Norwegian rhapsody (Lalo): Rapsodie norvégienne

Notte
  (Vivaldi): RV439 — Concerto for Flute, Bassoon and Strings in F
  (Vivaldi): RV501 — Concerto for Bassoon and Strings in B flat

Novelletten (Schumann): (8) Novelletten — piano, Op. 21

November steps (Takemitsu): November Steps — orchestra

Nuages (Debussy): Nocturnes — No. 1

Nuits d'été (Berlioz): Nuits d'été — solo voices and orchestra

Nullte Symphony (Bruckner): Symphony No. 0 in D minor

Nuns' Chorus (Strauss II, J): Casanova — Nuns' Chorus and Laura's Song

Nursery Suite (Elgar): Nursery Suite — orchestra

O

O my beloved father (Puccini): Gianni Schicchi — O mio babbino caro

O praise the Lord (Greene): Praise the Lord, o my Soul — anthem

O Star of Eve (Wagner): Tannhäuser — No. 25b

Ocean Symphony (Rubinstein): Symphony No. 2 in C, Op. 42

Oceanides (Sibelius): (The) Oceanides — tone poem

October (Shostakovich): Symphony No. 2 in C

Ode for St Cecilia (Handel): Ode for St Cecilia's Day

Ode to Joy (Beethoven): Symphony No. 9 in D minor, Op. 125 — movement 4

Ode to Queen Mary (Purcell): Welcome to all the pleasures

Oedipus Rex (Stravinsky): Oedipus Rex — opera

Offrandes (Varèse): Offrandes — soprano and chamber ensemble

Oh! my beloved father (Puccini): Gianni Schicchi — O mio babbino caro

Ombra cara (Handel): Radamisto — opera — Ombra cara

Ombra mai fù (Handel): Serse — No. 1

On hearing the first cuckoo in Spring (Delius): On hearing the first cuckoo in Spring

On Wenlock Edge (Vaughan Williams): On Wenlock Edge — tenor, string quartet and piano

On wings of Song (Mendelssohn): Lieder, Op. 34 — No. 2

Prussian Quartets
(Haydn): (6) String Quartets, Op. 50
(Mozart): String Quartets, K575; K589; K590

Prussian Sonatas (Bach, C P E): Keyboard Sonatas, Wq48

Prélude à l'après-midi d'un faune (Debussy): Prélude à l'après-midi d'un faune

Purcell's Trumpet Voluntary (Clarke, J): Suite for Trumpet and Strings in D — No. 4

Q

Quartet for the end of time (Messaien): Quatuor pour le fin de temp

R

Rage over a lost penny (Beethoven): Rondo a Capriccioso in G, Op. 129

Ragtime (Stravinsky): Rag-time — chamber ensemble

Raindrop Prelude (Chopin): Preludes, Op. 28 — No. 15 in D flat

Razor Quartet (Haydn): (3) String Quartets, Op. 55 — No. 2 in F minor

Razumovsky Quartets (Beethoven): String Quartets Nos. 7-9, Op. 59

Recondita armonia (Puccini): Tosca — No. 2

Red Pony (Copland): (The) Red Pony — orchestral suite from the film score

Red Poppy (Glière): (The) Red Poppy — ballet

Rediffusion March (Coates): Music Everywhere — march

Reflets dans l'eau (Debussy): Images — No. 1

Reformation Symphony (Mendelssohn): Symphony No. 5 in D

Reine de France Symphony (Haydn): Symphony No. 85 in B flat

Relique Sonata (Schubert): Piano Sonata No. 15 in C, D840

Renard (Stravinsky): Renard — burlesque in song and dance

Resurrection Symphony (Mahler): Symphony No. 2

Revolutionary Study (Chopin): Etudes, Op. 10 — No. 12 in C minor

Rhenish Symphony (Schumann): Symphony No. 3 in E flat, Op. 97

Ride of the Valkyries (Wagner): (Die) Walküre — No. 31

Rider Quartet (Haydn): (3) String Quartets, Op. 74 — No. 3 in G minor

Rio Grande (Lambert): (The) Rio Grande — alto, chorus and orchestra

Riposo (Vivaldi): RV270 — Concerto for Violin and Orchestra in E

Ritorna vincitor! (Verdi): Aida — No. 6a

Ritual Fire Dance (Falla): El amor brujo — No. 8

Rococo Variations (Tchaikovsky): Variations on a Rococo Theme — cello and orchestra

Roi des étoiles (Stravinsky): (Le) Roi des étoiles — cantata

Roman Festival (Respighi): Roman Festival — symphonic poem

Roman Symphony (Widor): (Organ) Symphony No. 10, Op. 73

Romantic Symphony
(Bruckner): Symphony No. 4 in E flat
(Prokofiev): Romeo and Juliet — ballet

Romeo and Juliet (Tchaikovsky): Romeo and Juliet — Fantasy Overture

Roméo et Juliette
(Berlioz): Roméo et Juliette — dramatic symphony
(Gounod): Roméo et Juliette — opera

Rondo alla turca (Mozart): Piano Sonata in A, K331 — movement 3

Rosary Sonatas (Biber): (16) Sonatas for Violin and Continuo

Rouet d'Omphale (Saint-Saëns): (Le) Rouet d'Omphale in A — orchestra

Roxelane Symphony (Haydn): Symphony No. 63 in C

Rugby (Honegger): (3) Symphonic Movements — No. 2

Rule, Britannia (Arne): Rule Britannia

Russian Quartets (Haydn): (6) String Quartets, Op. 33

Rustic Scenes (Brian): English Suite No. 5

Rustic Wedding Symphony (Goldmark): Symphony, Op. 26

Rustle of Spring (Sinding): Rustle of Spring — piano, Op. 32/3

S

Sabre Dance (Khachaturian): Gayaneh — ballet — No. 1

Sailors' Chorus (Wagner): (Der) Fliegende Holländer — No. 20

Salomon Symphonies (Haydn): Symphonies Nos. 93-104

Salut d'amour (Elgar): Salut d'amour (Liebesgrüss), Op. 12

Salzburg Symphonies (Mozart): Divertimenti, K136-8

Santa Lucia (Cottrau): Santa Lucia — song

Sardana (Casals): (La) Sardana — cello ensemble

Scapino (Walton): Scapino — Comedy Overture

Schelomo (Bloch): Schelomo — cello and orchestra

Schoolmaster Symphony (Haydn): Symphony No. 55 in E flat

Schubert's Serenade (Schubert): Schwanengesang, D957 — song collection — No. 4, Ständchen

Schulmeister Symphony (Haydn): Symphony No. 55 in E flat

Scottish Symphony (Mendelssohn): Symphony No. 3 in A minor

Sea Drift (Delius): Sea Drift — baritone, chorus and orchestra

Sea fever (Ireland): Sea Fever — song

Sea Pictures (Elgar): Sea Pictures — contralto and orchestra, Op. 37

Sea Symphony (Vaughan Williams): Symphony No. 1

Seasons
(Glazunov): (The) Seasons — ballet
(Haydn): (Die) Jahreszeiten — oratorio
(Spohr): Symphony No. 9 in B flat, Op. 143
(Tchaikovsky): (The) Seasons — piano, Op. 37b

Seguidille (Bizet): Carmen — No. 10a

Sei nicht bös (Zeller): (Der) Obersteiger — Sei
nicht bös

Semplice Symphony (Nielsen): Symphony No. 6

Senta's Ballad (Wagner): (Der) Fliegende
Holländer — No. 13

Serenade for the doll (Debussy): Children's
Corner — Suite — No. 3

Serenata notturna (Mozart): Serenade in D,
D239

Serieuse Symphony (Berwald): Symphony No. 1
in G minor

Seven Deadly Sins (Weill): (Die) Seiben
Todsünden — spectacle

Seven Last Words of Christ (Haydn): Seven
Last Words — orchestral and string quartet
versions

Seven Stars Symphony (Koechlin): Seven Stars
Symphony

Sheep may safely graze (Bach): Cantata No.
208 — Was mir behagt, ist die muntre Jagd

Shepherds' Farewell (Berlioz): (L')Enfance du
Christ — trilogie sacrée

Shepherds' Thanksgiving (Beethoven): Symphony No. 6 in F, Op. 68 (Pastoral)

Show Boat (Kern): Show Boat — musical comedy

Shropshire Lad
(Butterworth): (A) Shropshire Lad — Rhap-
sody (orchestra)
Butterworth): (A) Shropshire Lad — song cycle

Si tra i ceppi (Handel): Berenice — opera — Si
tra i ceppi

Siegfried Idyll (Wagner): Siegfried Idyll

Siegfried's Journey to the Rhine (Wagner):
Götterdämmerung — No. 5

Siegfried's Funeral March (Wagner):
Götterdämmerung — No. 37

Silver swan (Gibbons): (The) Silver swan —
madrigal (5vv)

Simple Symphony (Britten): Simple Symphony,
Op. 4

Sinfonia Antartica (Vaughan Williams):
Symphony No. 7

Sinfonia da Requiem (Britten): Sinfonia da
Requiem, Op. 20

Sinfonia tragica (Brian): Symphony No. 6

Singuliere Symphony (Berwald): Symphony No.
3 in C

Sirènes (Debussy): Nocturnes — No. 3

Skaters' Waltz (Waldteufel): (Les) Patineurs —
Waltz

Skazka (Rimsky-Korsakov): Skazka — orchestra,
Op. 29

Slavonic March (Tchaikovsky): Marche slave,
Op. 31

Sleepers, awake (Bach): Cantata No. 140 —
Wachet auf, ruft uns die Stimme

Snow is dancing (Debussy): Children's Corner
— Suite — No. 4

Softly awakes my heart (Saint-Saëns): Samson
et Dalila — No. 13b

Soir Symphony (Haydn): Symphony No. 8 in G

Soirée dans Grenade (Debussy): Estampes —
No. 2

Soldiers' Chorus (Gounod): Faust — No. 18a

Song of the birds (Casals): (El) Cant dels ocells
— cello and piano

Song of the Earth (Mahler): (Das) Lied von der
Erde — symphony for contralto, tenor and
orchestra

Song of the Flea (Mussorgsky): Mephistopheles'
song of the flea

Song of the Night
(Mahler): Symphony No. 7
(Szymanowski): Symphony No. 3, Op. 27

Song of the Volga Boatmen (Traditional): (The)
Song of the Volga Boatmen — Russian
folksong

Sorcerer's Apprentice (Dukas): (L')Apprenti
sorcier — Scherzo on a ballad by Goethe

Sortie in E flat (Léfebure-Wély): Sortie in E
flat — organ

Sospetto (Vivaldi): RV199 — Concerto for
Violin and Strings in C minor

Sound the trumpet (Purcell): Come ye sons of
art away

Source, La (Delibes): (La) Source — ballet

Souvenir de Florence (Tchaikovsky): Souvenir
de Florence — string sextet, Op. 70

Spanish caprice (Rimsky-Korsakov): Capriccio
espagnol, Op. 34

Spanish Lady (Elgar): (The) Spanish Lady —
opera

Sparrows Mass (Mozart): Mass No. 6 in F, K192

Spartacus (Khachaturian): Spartacus — ballet

Spem in alium (Tallis): Spem in alium — motet
(40vv)

Spider's web (Roussel): (Le) Festin de l'araignée
— symphonic fragments

Spinning Chorus (Wagner): (Der) Fliegende
Holländer — No. 11

Spinning Song (Mendelssohn): Songs without
Words — in C, Op. 67/4

Spring (Vivaldi): (12) Concerti, Op. 8 — No. 1
in E, RV269

Spring is coming (Handel): Ottone — La
speranza è giunta

Spring Sonata (Beethoven): Sonata for Violin
and Piano No. 5 in F, Op. 24

Spring Song (Mendelssohn): Songs without
Words — Op. 62 No. 6

Spring Symphony
(Britten): Spring Symphony — soloists, chorus
and orchestra, Op. 44
(Schumann): Symphony No. 1 in B flat, Op. 38

St Anne's Fugue (Bach): Prelude and Fugue in E
flat, BWV552

St Anthony (Haydn (attrib): Divertimento in B
flat

St Anthony Chorale (Brahms): Variations on a
theme by Haydn, Op. 56a

St Paul's Suite (Holst): St Paul's Suite, H118

Starlight Express (Elgar): (The) Starlight Express — incidental music

Stenka Razin (Glazunov): Stenka Razin — symphonic poem in B minor, Op. 13

Storm at sea (Vivaldi): RV253 — Concerto for Violin and Strings in E flat

Strange contrasts of harmony (Puccini): Tosca — No. 2

Study Symphony (Bruckner): Symphony No. 00 in F minor

Submerged Cathedral (Debussy): Préludes — No. 13

Suite Gothique (Boëllmann): Suite Gothique — organ, Op. 25

Summer (Vivaldi): (12) Concerti, Op. 8 — No. 2 in G minor (RV315)

Sun Quartets (Haydn): (6) String Quartets, Op. 20

Sunrise Quartet (Haydn): (6) String Quartets, Op. 76 — No. 4 in B flat

Surprise Symphony (Haydn): Symphony No. 94 in G

Survivor from Warsaw (Schoenberg): (A) Survivor from Warsaw

Susanna's Secret (Wolf-Ferrari): (Il) Segreto di Susanna — opera

Swan, The (Saint-Saëns): (Le) Carnaval des Animaux — zoological fantasy — No. 13

Swan of Tuonela (Sibelius): Legends (Lemminkaïnen Suite), Op. 22 — No. 2

Swan White (Sibelius): Swan White — incidental music

Swedish Rhapsody (Alfven): Swedish Rhapsody No. 1, Op. 19 (Midsummer Vigil)

Sweet honey-sucking bees (Wilbye): Sweet honey-sucking bees — madrigal (5vv)

Symphonia brevis (Brian): Symphony No. 22

Symphonie espagnole (Lalo): Symphonie espagnole — violin and orchestra

Symphonie fantastique (Berlioz): Symphonie fantastique, Op. 14

Symphonie funèbre et triomphale (Berlioz): Symphonie funèbre et triomphale, Op. 15

Symphony 5 1/2 (Gillis): Symphony No. 5 1/2, "Symphony for Fun"

Symphony of a Thousand (Mahler): Symphony No. 8

Symphony of Psalms (Stravinsky): Symphony of Psalms — chorus and orchestra

Syrinx (Debussy): Syrinx for solo flute

T

Tahiti Trot (Shostakovich): Tahiti Trot — orchestra, Op. 16 (trans of Youman's 'Tea for Two')

Tales of Hoffmann (Offenbach): (Les) Contes d'Hoffmann — opera

Tango
(Albéniz): España — piano, Op 165 — No. 2
(Stravinsky): Tango — 19 instruments

Tapiola (Sibelius): Tapiola — tone poem

Tea for two (Youmans): No, no Nanette — Tea for two

Tempest Sonata (Beethoven): Piano Sonata No. 17 in G, Op 31/2

Thanksgiving Day (Ives): Holidays — Symphony — No. 4

Theresia Mass (Haydn): Mass No. 12 in B flat

They call me Mimi (Puccini): (La) Bohème — No. 3

Three Elizabeths (Coates): (The) Three Elizabeths — Suite

Three Places in New England (Ives): Orchestra Set No. 1

Till Eulenspiegel's merry pranks (Strauss, R): Till Eulenspiegls lustige streiche — symphonic poem

Titan Symphony (Mahler): Symphony No. 1

To a Wild Rose (MacDowell): Woodland Sketches, Op 51 — No. 1

Toccata (Widor): Symphony No. 5 in F minor, Op 42/1 — Toccata

Toccata and Fugue in D minor (Bach): Toccata and Fugue in D minor, BWV565

Tonadillas (Granados): (10) Tonadillas al estilo antiguo

Toreador's Song (Bizet): Carmen — No. 12b

Tost Quartets (Haydn): String Quartets, Opp. 54-56

Toy Symphony (Mozart, L): Cassation in G

Tragic Overture (Brahms): Tragic Overture, Op. 81

Tragic Symphony
(Mahler): Symphony No. 6
(Schubert): Symphony No. 4 in C minor, D417

Transfigured night (Schoenberg): Verklärte Nacht — string orchestra/string sextet

Trauer Symphony (Haydn): Symphony No. 44 in E minor

Tremolo Study (Tárrega): Recuerdos de la Alhambra — guitar

Trial of Harmany and Invention (Vivaldi): (12) Concerti, Op. 8

Tristesse Study (Chopin): Etudes, Op. 10 — No. 3 in E

Trout Quintet (Schubert): Piano Quintet in A, D667

Trumpet shall sound (Handel): Messiah — No. 51

Träumerei (Schumann): Kinderszenen — piano, Op. 15 — No. 7

Turkish Concerto (Mozart): Concerto for Violin and Orchestra No. 5 in A, K219

Two Pigeons (Messager): (Les) Deux pigeons — ballet

U

Una voce poco fa (Rossini): (Il) Barbiere di Siviglia — No. 7

Under the greenwood tree (Arne): As You Like It — songs from Shakespeare's play

Unfinished Symphony
(Borodin): Symphony No. 3 in A minor
(Bruckner): Symphony No. 9 in D minor
(Schubert): Symphony No. 8 in B minor, D759

V

Venetian Gondola Song
(Mendelssohn): Songs without Words — G minor, Op. 19b/6
(Mendelssohn): Songs without Words — F sharp minor, Op. 30/6
(Mendelssohn): Songs without Words — A minor, Op. 62/5

Verklärte Nacht (Schoenberg): Verklärte Nacht — string orchestra/string quartet

Vesti la guibba (Leoncavallo): Pagliacci — No. 9b

Vie Parisienne (Offenbach): (La) Vie Parisienne — operetta

Vilja (Lehár): (Die) Lustige Witwe — No. 7b

Violet, The (Mozart): (Das) Veilchen — Lied, K476

Visse d'arte (Puccini): Tosca — No. 12

Vltava (Smetana): Mà Vlast — No. 2

Voces intimae (Sibelius): String Quartet in D minor, Op. 56

Volkslied (Mendelssohn): Songs without Words — A minor, Op. 53/5

W

Wagner Symphony (Bruckner): Symphony No. 3 in D minor

Waldstein Sonata (Beethoven): Piano Sonata No. 21 in C, Op. 53

Waldweben (Wagner): Siegfried — No. 25b

Waltz Dream (Straus, O): (Ein) Waltztraum — operetta

Wand of Youth (Elgar): Wand of Youth Suites Nos. 1 and 2

Wanderer Sonata (Schubert): Fantasia in C, D760

War and Peace (Prokofiev): War and Peace — opera

War Requiem (Britten): War Requiem — soloists, choirs, chamber orchestra and orchestra, Op. 66

Washington's Birthday (Ives): Holidays — Symphony — No. 1

Wasps (Vaughan Williams): (The) Wasps — Aristophanic Suite (from incidental music)

Water Goblin (Dvořák): (The) Water Goblin — symphonic poem

Water Music (Handel): (The) Water Music

Wayside rose (Schubert): Heidenröslein, D257

Weber's Last Waltz (Reissiger): Danses brillantes, Op. 26 — No. 5

Wedding Cake Caprice (Saint-Saëns): Wedding Cake — caprice for piano and orchestra

Wedding Cantata (Bach): Cantata No. 202 — Weichet nur, betrubte schatten

Wedding Day at Troldhaugen (Grieg): Lyric Pieces, Op. 65 — No. 6

Wedding March
(Mendelssohn): (A) Midsummer Night's Dream — incidental music — No. 6
(Wagner): Lohengrin — No. 18

Wedge Fugue (Bach): Fugue in E minor, BWV548

Wellington's Victory (Beethoven): Wellingtons Sieg (Die Schlacht bei Vittoris), Op. 91

Well-Tempered Clavier (Bach): Wohltemperirte Klavier, BWV846-893

When I am laid in Earth (Purcell): Dido and Aeneas — No. 2

When other lips (Balfe): (The) Bohemian Girl — When other lips

When the stars are shining bright (Puccini): Tosca — No. 16

Where the bee sucks (Arne): Where the bee sucks — song for Shakespeare's "Tempest"

White Horse Inn (Stolz): In weissen Rössl — operetta

White Lady (Auber): (La) Dame Blanche — opera

White Mass (Scriabin): Piano Sonata No. 7 in F, Op. 64

Will o' the Wisps (Berlioz): (La) Damnation de Faust — No. 18

Wine, woman and song (Strauss II, J): Wein, Weib und Gesang — waltz, Op. 333

Wine of Summer (Brian): Symphony No. 5

Winter (Vivaldi): (12) Concerti, Op. 8 — No. 4 in F minor, RV297

Winter Daydreams (Tchaikovsky): Symphony No. 1 in G minor, Op. 13

Y

You are my heart's delight (Lehár): (Das) Land des Lächelns — No. 11

Young Person's Guide to the Orchestra (Britten): (The) Young Person's Guide to the Orchestra, Op. 34

Your tiny hand is frozen (Puccini): (La) Bohème — No. 2

Z

Zadok the priest (Handel): Coronation Anthems — No. 1

1812 (Tchaikovsky): 1812 Overture, Op. 49

1905 (Shostakovich): Symphony No. 11 in G minor

1912 (Shostakovich): Symphony No. 12 in D minor

Index to Reviews